FROMMER'S

SWITZERLAND
AND
LIECHTENSTEIN

DARWIN PORTER

Assisted by
Danforth Prince
and Margaret Foresman

1990–1991

Published by Prentice Hall Trade Division
A Division of Simon & Schuster Inc.
15 Columbus Circle
New York, NY 10023

ISBN 0-13-217324-7
ISSN 1044-2294

Manufactured in the United States of America

*Although every effort was made to ensure the accuracy
of price information appearing in this book,
it should be kept in mind that prices
can and do fluctuate in the course of time.*

CONTENTS

MAPS

INFLATION ALERT: In researching this book I have made every effort to obtain up-to-the-minute prices, but even the most conscientious researcher cannot keep up with the inevitable price changes. As we go to press, I believe we have obtained the most reliable data possible. Nonetheless, in the lifetime of this edition—particularly its second year (1991)—the wise traveler will need to allow for a certain increase in prices, although Switzerland, compared to the rest of the world, keeps its prices relatively stable.

A DISCLAIMER: Although every effort was made to ensure the accuracy of the prices and travel information appearing in this book, it should be kept in mind that prices do fluctuate in the course of time, and that information does change under the impact of the varied and volatile factors that affect the travel industry.

FROMMER'S SWITZERLAND AND LIECHTENSTEIN

□ □ □

Switzerland . . . the name conjures up a kaleidoscopic range of sensory perception—snowy Alps, happy yodelers, lakes whose quiet is broken only by the sound of chugging steamers, skiers schussing down mountains, watches and clocks, flavorful cheeses, the tinkle of cowbells in still mountain pastures, the scent and rustle of money on the way to numbered bank accounts. All these images and more are connected with the small but strong federal republic of Switzerland.

Neutral since the 19th century, avoiding embroilment in the wars that have devastated its neighbors, Switzerland nevertheless has a fascinating history of external and internal conflicts since prehistoric tribesmen struggled to hold tiny settlements along the great Rhône and Rhine rivers. The Swiss of today, at peace from the highest village in the Grisons to the biggest cities in the lowlands since the middle of the last century, are a happy, thriving, hospitable people.

In this introduction, I will give you a brief look at the country, with further exploration to follow. This may seem like a fat book to deal with a small country (15,830 square miles with nearly 6½ million inhabitants), but I've only skimmed the surface of establishments and attractions available. What I'm sharing with you are my favorites. Perhaps, using the book as a basic guide, you'll find dozens more on your own.

Readers of this book will also be introduced to the tiny **Principality of Liechtenstein,** which nestles into a niche formed by the river Rhine on the west with Switzerland just across the water, Austria on the east, and Switzerland on the south. With a total area of 62 square miles and a population of 20,000 souls, Liechtenstein, like its western neighbor, is a neutral country. Also like Switzerland, it has lowlands and highlands, mountains and rich pastureland. Most of its people are descended from the early Alemanni or Germanic tribes who settled there, but some are of Swiss immigrant stock. Switzerland is the representative of Liechtenstein in diplomatic affairs, and the close ties of the neighbor countries are reflected in many other areas.

The Principality of Liechtenstein will be discussed and its attractions described in the final chapter of this book.

THE COUNTRY: Switzerland occupies a position on the rooftop of the continent of Europe, with the drainage of its mammoth alpine glaciers becoming the source of such powerful rivers as the Rhine and the Rhône. The appellation "the crossroads of Europe" is fitting, as all rail lines, road passes, and tunnels through the mountains seem to lead to it. From the time the Romans crossed the Alps, going through Helvetia (the old name for part of today's Switzerland) on their way north, the major route connecting northern and southern Europe has been through Switzerland. The old roads and paths were just developed into modern highways and railroads.

The main European route for east-west travel also passes through Switzerland between Lake Constance and Geneva, and intercontinental airports connect the country with cities all over the world. London and Paris, for instance, are less than two hours away by air.

The tourist industry as we know it started in Switzerland, and the tradition of welcoming visitors is firmly entrenched in Swiss life. The first modern tourists, the British, began to come here "on holiday" in the 19th century, and other Europeans and some North Americans followed suit. The "nation of hotel-keepers" now hosts some 20 million visitors from abroad annually. Swiss catering, based on years of experience, has gained a worldwide reputation, and the entire country is known for its cleanliness and efficiency.

Switzerland has many great museums and a rich cultural life, but that's not why most people visit the country. They come mainly for the scenery, which is virtually unrivaled in the world, from alpine peaks to mountain lakes, from the palm trees of Ticino to the "Ice Palace" of Jungfrau.

Restaurant and hotel prices remained stable in the 1980s. The Swiss rate of inflation has been modest compared to many of the other countries of Europe, making it increasingly attractive to tourists who might in earlier years have made France or Germany their primary vacation goals.

Your reasons for coming here may be many, ranging from mountain climbing to opening a numbered bank account to learning to yodel, from skiing in winter to hiking through alpine meadows and along country roads. Although the country has four recognized national languages, many of its people, at least in the major tourist regions, speak English, so you'll find help in pursuing your goals.

THE BEST OF BOTH: I have set for myself the formidable task of seeking Switzerland and Liechtenstein at their finest. The best towns, villages, cities, and sightseeing attractions are documented, as well as the best hotels, restaurants, bars, cafés, shops, and nightspots.

But the best need not be the most expensive. My ultimate aim—beyond that of familiarizing you with the offerings of Switzerland and Liechtenstein—is to stretch your dollar power . . . to reveal to you that you need not pay scalper's prices for charm, top-grade comfort, and gourmet-level food.

In this guide I'll devote a lot of attention to those old tourist meccas—Geneva, Zurich, St. Moritz, Zermatt—focusing on both their obvious and hidden treasures. But important as they are, they simply do not reflect fully the widely diverse and complicated countryside of Switzerland. To discover that, you must venture deep into the "William Tell country" in the heart of Switzerland, or perhaps to a chalet in the Engadine with its mountain-bordered valley and chain of lakes.

Using This Guide: In brief, this is a guidebook giving specific details—including prices—about Swiss hotels, restaurants, bars, cafés, sightseeing attractions, nightlife, tours, and activities. Establishments in many price ranges have been documented and described, although I am constantly searching for bargains. Along with the deluxe citadels and large hotels, I am interested in the family-run *gasthof*-type places where you can often bask in gemütlich warmth, but at moderate prices.

Deluxe or budget, each establishment was measured by a strict yardstick of value. If they measured up—if they were the best in their category—they were included.

Now more than ever an accurate guidebook, including tips for saving money, is needed for independent travelers as well as those who visit Switzerland on a package tour. If you're one of the latter, and already have your flight ticket and hotel, you'll still need a guide to direct you to restaurants, nightlife, and sightseeing attractions rarely covered on a package tour. If you're given a car, then you'll be in the market for suggestions on where to go in the country, once you leave either Zurich or Geneva, whichever is your "gateway" city.

SOME WORDS OF EXPLANATION: No restaurant, inn, hotel, nightclub, shop, or café paid to be mentioned in this book. What you read are entirely personal recommendations; in many cases the proprietors never knew their establishments were being visited or investigated for inclusion in a travel guide.

Unfortunately, although I have made every effort to be accurate, prices change, and they rarely go downward. Always, when checking into a hotel, inquire about the rate and agree on it. That policy can save much embarrassment and disappointment when it comes time to settle the tab.

This guide is revised cover to cover every other year. But even in a book that appears with such frequency, it may happen that that cozy little wine tavern of a year ago has changed its stripes, or some of the people or settings I've described are no longer there or have changed.

THE ORGANIZATION OF THIS BOOK: Here's how *Frommer's Switzerland and Liechtenstein* sets forth its information:

Chapter I deals with how to get to Switzerland, followed by a section on transportation within the country, including trains, car rentals, and lake steamers. Special bargain passes, such as the "Holiday Card," will be described. A concluding section deals with alternative and special-interest travel.

Chapter II is a survey of Switzerland in general, its people, customs, four languages, and cuisine, plus a brief historical outline. A section is devoted to sports, focusing on winter skiing at alpine resorts, but also on activities for the non-skier. Summer skiing (or glacier skiing) is described, along with such other sports possibilities as curling (rapidly gaining in popularity), ice skating, tennis, swimming, hang-gliding, horseback riding, golf, hiking, mountaineering, and cycling. The chapter concludes with the ABCs of Switzerland, all the details from electric current to legal holidays.

Chapter III introduces our "touchdown" city for Switzerland—Zurich, the gateway for the entire country. Accommodations here will range from two of the greatest hotels in the world to hillside-perching boardinghouses that are both immaculate and charming. Zurich's elegant restaurants as well as less expensive places, such as bierhalles and wine cellars, are surveyed. A discussion of Zurich transport is followed by practical ABC-type hints. A preview of shopping, including a walk along the Bahnhofstrasse, one of the world's great shopping streets, precedes an exploration of the city's cafés and nightspots. The chapter concludes with the most interesting excursions around Zurich, ranging from mountainside to lakeside.

Chapter IV takes us into the countryside of Switzerland, beginning in the northeast sector, which is the least known to North Americans. Our major stopover here is St. Gallen, from which it is easy to reach the attractions of Lake Constance. A trip through the Appenzell countryside, the heart of the cheese country, is included. Medieval Schaffhausen, built on terraces on the right bank of the Rhine, is explored, followed by an excursion to the Rheinfall (Rhine Falls).

Chapter V visits the "second city" of Switzerland, prosperous Basel (Swiss spelling, *Basle*) with its port, which is rich in sights (its art museum is ranked among the top ten in the world). It's also the center for exploring Switzerland's Rhineland. A full range of hotels and restaurants is previewed, including Drei Könige (Three Kings), the country's oldest hotel, founded in A.D. 1026. Following Basel, we'll go through the Jura mountains, a land of lakes, vineyards, and such charming old towns as Fribourg and Neuchâtel, once a haven for Dumas and Gide, among others. The cheese town of Gruyères gets the attention it deserves, for it's here that the Middle Ages live on. You'll get to see a model dairy where you can watch cheese being made, and, naturally, the restaurants will feature fondues and raclette.

Chapter VI highlights historic Bern (or Berne), capital of the Confederation, a cosmopolitan city that still retains a medieval flavor. All of its major sights, including its famous bear pits, are described, along with hotels that go from the historic and inexpensive Zum Goldenen Schlüssel in the heart of Old Town to the deluxe Bellevue Palace. Since the cookery is exceptional, special attention is devoted to restaurants, followed by a range of cultural activities and nightlife. Shopping in nearly four miles of medieval arcades is included.

In this same chapter, we'll blaze a trail through the Bernese Oberland, one of the most popular tourist districts of Europe, with its glacial valleys, high alpine peaks, and lakes. Interlaken, the best known of the sports centers and health spas, will be our gateway city to this area. Schilthorn, at 9,750 feet, and Mürrenbach, Europe's highest waterfall, are described. Interlaken can also be used as a center for exploring Jungfrau with its glacial slopes. Since the Bernese Oberland is one of the best equipped sports centers in the world, a full range of winter activities is presented. All the major centers are spotlighted, especially Gstaad, at the point where five alpine valleys and part-time resident Elizabeth Taylor meet.

Chapter VII goes to the Valais, one of the great tourist attractions of the world, starting at Lake Geneva and following the river valley up into the mountains. Along the way, visitors pass the Rhine Glacier heading for Zermatt (reached by cogwheel train), and the towering 14,780-foot Matterhorn. Another excursion can be taken to the Great St. Bernard Pass, with its famous monastery and kennels. We'll go through Sion, with its old ruins and vineyards. The trip ends at Brig, the start of Simplon, Europe's longest railway tunnel, the gateway to Italy. Its winter sports facilities are among the best equipped in the world, rivaling the Grisons and Bernese Oberland.

Chapter VIII, in the footsteps of Shelley and Byron, explores Lake Geneva (Lac Léman), in the southwest corner of Switzerland. Excursions by lake steamer, motorcoach, car, and train are detailed, plus a tour to the Mount Blanc tunnel. Lausanne, the cultural center of French-speaking Switzerland, is previewed, with its hotels that range from the Beau-Rivage (once a favorite of visiting royalty) to such inexpensive retreats as the family-run Beau Site. Entertainment, museums, shopping, and nightlife are all surveyed, plus excursions to such towns as Vevey, a small holiday resort known to Victor Hugo and Thackeray, and in later years to Charlie Chaplin. Montreux, once on the "Grand Tour" of Europe at the turn of the century, is the chief tourist center. Other descriptions will take in the vineyards of La Côte.

Chapter IX delivers us to Geneva, where a full range of accommodations is surveyed, beginning with the grand old Richemond, run by the great hotel family of Armleder, all the way down to that same family's little bargain oasis, the Grand-Pré. The food of Geneva is exceptional, and you'll discover where to find it, ranging from candlelit deluxe citadels with a view of the lake to inexpensive little bistros. The shopping section gives hints on what to buy (Geneva invented the wristwatch) and where to buy it, and the nightlife section previews the cafés, brasseries, and bars where the local people gather for apéritifs, followed by nightclubs, discos, opera, and movies. Following that, we'll explore the most immediate excursions possible on the doorstep of Geneva. The chapter concludes with a description of local transportation, along with practical ABCs of life in this French-speaking city.

Lucerne and Central Switzerland come up in Chapter X. A storybook Swiss city that is most favored by visiting Americans, Lucerne is also a center for winter and summer sports. Lake Lucerne itself will be traversed on colorful little paddlesteamers. In Lucerne there is a full range of hotels, restaurants, museums, shopping, and entertainment possibilities. The ski resorts and facilities of central Switzerland conclude the chapter.

Chapter XI, the Grisons and the Engadine, covers the winter playground of the world. From historic Chur excursions are possible to the legendary resorts of St. Moritz, Davos, Klosters, and Pontresina, and to the Swiss National Park. The Engadine is a valley bordered by mountains of the River Inn and its string of lakes, lying across the southern sector of the more frequented Grisons. A full survey of the Grisons, with its many hotels, restaurants, nightspots, and winter sports facilities, is included.

Chapter XII provides our final look at Switzerland, as we head south to Lugano, Locarno, and the Ticino. Lugano and Locarno share the lakes of Lugano and Maggiore with Italy and, as such, are among the most attractive sightseeing attractions in the country. Ascona is another one of its important tourist centers. The Ticino is the Italian-speaking section of Switzerland, and is completely different from the rest of the country.

Chapter XIII journeys to the postage-stamp principality of Liechtenstein to visit the world's oldest living democracy. Methods of transportation are detailed, along with formalities, hotels, restaurants (both Swiss and Austrian cuisines), entertainment, shopping, museums, sports, and some useful addresses.

A WORD ABOUT COSTS: Quite frankly Switzerland is not the travel bargain of Europe. If economy is a major factor in your travel plans, Portugal or Yugoslavia, are far cheaper. The tariffs you'll face are very similar to those you'll find in the United States. Sometimes you'll pay more for certain items than you would Stateside.

Even the three most famous products of Switzerland, watches, chocolate, and cheese (not necessarily in that order), might—just might—cost you more than they would back in Kansas. Of course staggering prices reflect a standard of living that is among the very highest in the world. The efficient government does not believe in poverty, and it offers many social welfare programs to its citizenry, with the subsequent higher taxes.

There are many bargains, but don't expect to find them in the high-priced cities of Zurich and Geneva or in such resorts as St. Moritz and Arosa.

Since virtually everything in Switzerland can be driven to in a short time, try to stay at small villages, such as Klosters, on the periphery of celebrated resorts if you're keeping costs bone-trimmed. Get up, have breakfast, then drive into the heartbeat of the chic action, and avoid paying 400F ($272) a night for a double room.

TIME OUT FOR A COMMERCIAL: The very fact that you have purchased a guide to a small country of Europe, plus a tiny principality, puts you into a special, sophisticated category of traveler—that is, those who want to explore and get to know a single country or two, as opposed to the "Grand Tour" individual who wants to do not only Belgium on Tuesday, but Rome on Wednesday, and the North Cape by Friday.

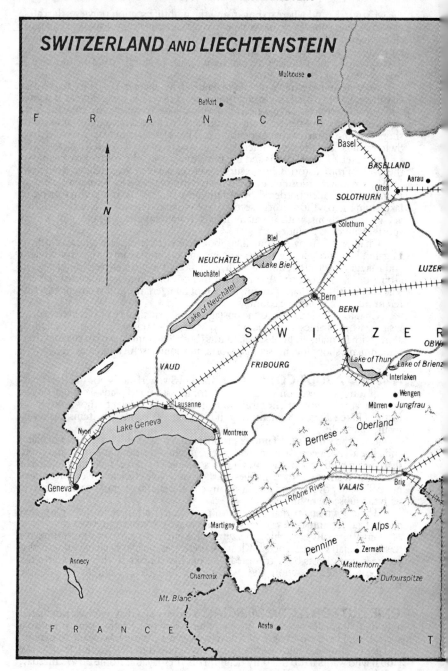

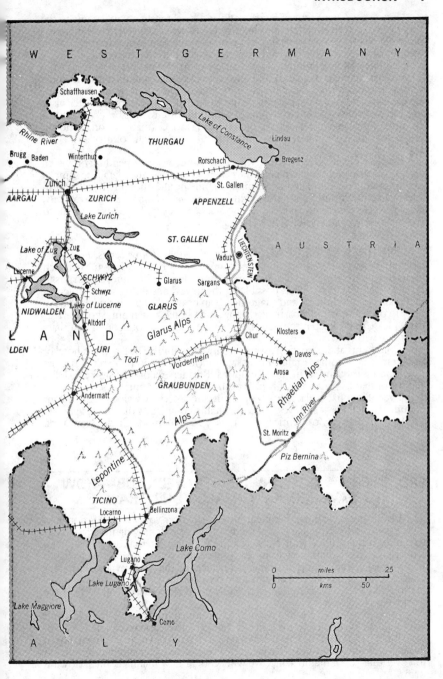

Even so, on your tour of Switzerland and Liechtenstein you'll come to the very doorstep of major attractions in other countries which you may want to explore. Since I had to set some limitation on the number of pages in this book, it was impossible to devote separate chapters to neighboring attractions.

I'll cite only an example or two to prove my point. When you visit the Ticino district of Switzerland, its Italian-speaking part, you'll be on the doorway of the beautiful Lake District of Italy and will surely want to cross it. At Geneva, the spectacular French Alps will be at your doorstep. After visiting Liechtenstein, you might be interested in driving to Innsbruck in Austria for an exploration of the Tyrolean country. And since Germany lies on the northern border of Switzerland, the manifold attractions of that country also await you.

Because of the geography of Switzerland, and, again, depending on which sections of that country you plan to travel in, you may want to take along some of our sister guides as traveling companions. Four specific ones on "border countries" that might appeal to you include: *Frommer's France, Frommer's Italy, Frommer's Germany,* and *Frommer's Austria and Hungary.* Ski buffs will want to pick up a copy of *Frommer's Skiing Europe.*

AN INVITATION TO READERS: Like all books in this series, *Frommer's Switzerland and Liechtenstein* hopes to maintain a continuing dialogue between its author and its readers. All of us share a common aim, I'm sure, and that is to travel as widely and as well as possible, at the lowest possible cost. In achieving that goal, your comments and suggestions can be of aid to other readers. Therefore if you come across a particularly appealing hotel, restaurant, shop, or bargain, please don't keep it to yourself. It will be good for your soul if you share your gem with others.

Comments about existing listings are always helpful. The fact that a hotel or restaurant (or any other establishment) appears in this edition doesn't mean that it will necessarily appear in future editions if readers report that its service has slipped or that its prices not only have risen drastically but unfairly.

Even if you like a place, your comments are especially welcome. Send your comments or finds—and, yes, those inevitable complaints that always arise—to Darwin Porter, c/o Prentice Hall Travel, 15 Columbus Circle, New York, NY 10023.

FROMMER'S™ DOLLARWISE® TRAVEL CLUB—HOW TO SAVE MONEY ON ALL YOUR TRAVELS

In this book we'll be looking at how to discover your value-for-money in Switzerland and Liechtenstein, but there is a "device" for saving money and determining value on *all* your trips. It's the popular, international Frommer's Dollarwise Travel Club, now in its 28th successful year of operation. The club was formed at the urging of numerous readers of the $-A-Day and Frommer Guides, who felt that such an organization could provide continuing travel information and a sense of community to value-minded travelers in all parts of the world. And so it does!

In keeping with the budget concept, the annual membership fee is low and is immediately exceeded by the value of your benefits. Upon receipt of $18 (U.S. residents), or $20 U.S. by check drawn on a U.S. bank or via international postal money order in U.S. funds (Canadian, Mexican, and other foreign residents) to cover one year's membership, we will send all new members the following items.

(1) Any *two* of the following books

Please designate in your letter which two you wish to receive:

Frommer™ $-A-Day Guides

Europe on $40 a Day
Australia on $30 a Day
Eastern Europe on $25 a Day
England on $50 a Day
Greece (including Istanbul and Turkey's Aegean Coast) on $30 a Day
Hawaii on $60 a Day
India on $25 a Day
Ireland on $35 a Day
Israel on $30 & $35 a Day
Mexico (plus Belize and Guatemala) on $25 a Day
New York on $50 a Day
New Zealand on $40 a Day
Scandinavia on $60 a Day
Scotland and Wales on $40 a Day
South America on $35 a Day
Spain and Morocco (plus the Canary Is.) on $40 a Day
Turkey on $30 a Day
Washington, D.C., & Historic Virginia on $40 a Day

($-A-Day Guides document hundreds of budget accommodations and facilities, helping you get the most for your travel dollars.)

Frommer™ Guides

Australia
Austria and Hungary
Belgium, Holland, & Luxembourg
Bermuda and The Bahamas
Brazil
Canada
Caribbean
Egypt
England and Scotland
France
Germany
Italy
Japan and Hong Kong
Portugal, Madeira, and the Azores
South Pacific
Switzerland and Liechtenstein
Alaska
California and Las Vegas
Florida
Mid-Atlantic States
New England
New York State
Northwest
Skiing USA—East
Skiing USA—West
Southeast and New Orleans
Southeast Asia
Southwest
Texas
USA

(Dollarwise Guides discuss accommodations and facilities in all price ranges, with emphasis on the medium-priced.)

Frommer's™ Touring Guides
Australia
Egypt
Florence
London
Paris
Scotland
Thailand
Venice

(These new, color illustrated guides include walking tours, cultural and historic sites, and other vital travel information.)

Gault Millau
Chicago
France
Italy
Los Angeles
New England
New York
San Francisco
Washington, D.C.

(Irreverent, savvy, and comprehensive, each of these renowned guides candidly reviews over 1,000 restaurants, hotels, shops, nightspots, museums, and sights.)

Serious Shopper's Guides
Italy
London
Los Angeles
Paris

(Practical and comprehensive, each of these handsomely illustrated guides lists hundreds of stores, selling everything from antiques to wine, conveniently organized alphabetically by category.)

A Shopper's Guide to the Caribbean
(Two experienced Caribbean hands guide you through this shopper's paradise, offering witty insights and helpful tips on the wares and emporia of more than 25 islands.)

Beat the High Cost of Travel
(This practical guide details how to save money on absolutely all travel items—accommodations, transportation, dining, sightseeing, shopping, taxes, and more. Includes special budget information for seniors, students, singles, and families.)

Bed & Breakfast—North America
(This guide contains a directory of over 150 organizations that offer bed & breakfast referrals and reservations throughout North America. The scenic attractions, and major schools and universities near the homes of each are also listed.)

Frommer's Cruises
(This complete guide covers all the basics of cruising—ports of call, costs, fly-

cruise package bargains, cabin selection booking, embarkation and debarkation and describes in detail over 60 or so ships cruising the waters of Alaska, the Caribbean, Mexico, Hawaii, Panama, Canada, and the United States.)

Frommer's Skiing Europe
(Describes top ski resorts in Austria, France, Italy, and Switzerland. Illustrated with maps of each resort area. Includes supplement on Argentinian resorts.)

Guide to Honeymoon Destinations
(A special guide for that most romantic trip of your life, with full details on planning and choosing the destination that will be just right in the U.S. [California, New England, Hawaii, Florida, New York, South Carolina, etc.], Canada, Mexico, and the Caribbean.)

Marilyn Wood's Wonderful Weekends
(This very selective guide covers the best mini-vacation destinations within a 200-mile radius of New York City. It describes special country inns and other accommodations, restaurants, picnic spots, sights, and activities—all the information needed for a two- or three-day stay.)

Manhattan's Outdoor Sculpture
(A total guide, fully illustrated with black-and-white photos, to more than 300 sculptures and monuments that grace Manhattan's plazas, parks, and other public spaces.)

Motorist's Phrase Book
(A practical phrase book in French, German, and Spanish designed specifically for the English-speaking motorist touring abroad.)

Paris Rendez-Vous
(An amusing and *au courant* guide to the best meeting places in Paris, organized for hour-to-hour use: from power breakfasts and fun brunches, through tea at four or cocktails at five, to romantic dinners and dancing 'til dawn.)

Swap and Go—Home Exchanging Made Easy
(Two veteran home exchangers explain in detail all the money-saving benefits of a home exchange, and then describe precisely how to do it. Also includes information on home rentals and many tips on low-cost travel.)

The Candy Apple: New York for Kids
(A spirited guide to the wonders of the Big Apple by a savvy New York grandmother with a kid's-eye view to fun. Indispensable for visitors and residents alike.)

The New World of Travel
(From America's #1 travel expert, Arthur Frommer, an annual sourcebook with the hottest news and latest trends that's guaranteed to change the way you travel —and save you hundreds of dollars. Jam-packed with alternative new modes of travel that will lead you to vacations that cater to the mind, the spirit, and a sense of thrift.)

Travel Diary and Record Book
(A 96-page diary for personal travel notes plus a section for such vital data as passport and traveler's check numbers, itinerary, postcard list, special people and places to visit, and a reference section with temperature and conversion charts, and world maps with distance zones.)

Where to Stay USA
(By the Council on International Educational Exchange, this extraordinary guide is the first to list accommodations in all 50 states that cost anywhere from $3 to $30 per night.)

(2) Any one of Frommer's™ City Guides

Amsterdam
Athens
Atlantic City and Cape May
Belgium
Boston
Cancún, Cozumel, and the Yucatán
Chicago
Dublin and Ireland
Hawaii
Las Vegas
Lisbon, Madrid, and Costa del Sol
London
Los Angeles
Mexico City and Acapulco
Minneapolis and St. Paul
Montréal and Québec City
New Orleans
New York
Orlando, Disney World, and EPCOT
Paris
Philadelphia
Rio
Rome
San Francisco
Santa Fe and Taos
Sydney
Washington, D.C.

(Pocket-size guides to hotels, restaurants, nightspots, and sightseeing attractions covering all price ranges.)

(3) A one-year subscription to *The Dollarwise® Traveler*

This quarterly eight-page tabloid newspaper keeps you up to date on fastbreaking developments in low-cost travel in all parts of the world bringing you the latest money-saving information—the kind of information you'd have to pay $35 a year to obtain elsewhere. This consumer-conscious publication also features columns of special interest to readers: **Hospitality Exchange** (members all over the world who are willing to provide hospitality to other members as they pass through their home cities); **Share-a-Trip** (offers and requests from members for travel companions who can share costs and help avoid the burdensome single supplement); and **Readers Ask . . . Readers Reply** (travel questions from members to which other members reply with authentic firsthand information).

(4) Your personal membership card

Membership entitles you to purchase through the club all Frommer publications for a third to a half off their regular retail prices during the term of your membership.

So why not join this hardy band of international budgeteers and participate in its exchange of travel information and hospitality? Simply send your name and address, together with your annual membership fee of $18 (U.S. residents) or $20 U.S. (Canadian, Mexican, and other foreign residents), by check drawn on a

U.S. bank or via international postal money order in U.S. funds to: Frommer's Dollarwise Travel Club, Inc., 15 Columbus Circle, New York, NY 10023. And please remember to specify which *two* of the books in section (1) and which *one* in section (2) you wish to receive in your initial package of members' benefits. Or, if you prefer, use the order form at the end of the book and enclose $18 or $20 in U.S. currency.

Once you are a member, there is no obligation to buy additional books. No books will be mailed to you without your specific order.

CHAPTER I

GETTING TO AND AROUND SWITZERLAND

□ □ □

1. PLANE ECONOMICS
2. TRAVELING WITHIN SWITZERLAND
3. ALTERNATIVE AND SPECIAL-INTEREST TRAVEL

In the geographic center of Europe, Switzerland is a focal point for international air traffic. The busy intercontinental airports of Zurich and Geneva can be reached in about eight jet hours from the East Coast of North America. Scheduled services to Switzerland are maintained by American Airlines, Pan Am, Swissair, and TWA, with information on air fares available from both travel agents and the airlines themselves.

1. PLANE ECONOMICS

Several U.S.-based airlines compete intensely for the popular transatlantic run between North America and the cities of Zurich and Geneva. One of the best-recommended newcomers to the scene is **American Airlines,** which began making major inroads into the European market in 1982 and now services a number of the busiest capitals of Europe. Today, the airline makes daily nonstop flights to both Zurich and Geneva from New York and Chicago.

Most of American's flights to Europe are on wide-bodied Boeing 767s, which transport passengers to Switzerland with first-rate style, efficiency, and comfort. For reservations and information, call toll free 800/433-7300 throughout North America.

Pan American flies to Zurich from New York twice daily. One of the flights continues to Geneva. **TWA** flies to Zurich from New York daily in summer and five times a week in winter. Finally, **Swissair** flies to Zurich every day from Chicago, Boston, Atlanta, and New York, usually with connecting service on to Geneva.

TYPES OF TICKETS: Most airlines operate on similar fare plans. American Airlines, for example, divides its year into low, shoulder, and high season. The least-expensive (low season) fares usually apply between November and mid-

December, between Christmas and late March, and during most of April. Slightly more expensive, shoulder season fills most of May and October.

Regardless of which ticket you select, it is best to make your reservation as far in advance as possible.

American's least expensive fare requires that passengers reserve and pay for a round-trip ticket at least 30 days in advance. Lowest fares are for those who fly Monday through Thursday. You must plan to stay a minimum of 7 days, and return within 21 days. Called an Advance Purchase Excursion (APEX) fare, this reduced ticket currently costs from $488 to $734 per person, depending on the season (and subject to change), round-trip from New York to Zurich.

An unrestricted economy class ticket from New York to Zurich is currently priced at $1,625 all year round. Prices for economy tickets with booking or staying time restrictions vary throughout the year. However, if you cannot qualify for the APEX fare, you may be able to buy a less expensive economy class ticket—a number of economy-class seats are always held at less expensive prices to be sold as promotional fares. These tickets may be released at any time when there is a large inventory of unsold seats, so it might pay you to call daily to find out if any of these less expensive promotional tickets are available.

Many passengers opt for the wider seats, increased leg room, and greater comfort of **Business Class** travel, which offers many (but not all) of the comfort of **First Class** travel. American Airline's First Class is, of course, the most expensive. It offers the selection of food and wine that you might find at an outstanding on-the-ground restaurant, plus an array of extra services designed to make your transit as comfortable as possible.

2. TRAVELING WITHIN SWITZERLAND

BY TRAIN: The comfort and cleanliness of Swiss trains, all of them electric, are widely known, and no less renowned are the numerous mountain railways which convey visitors to mountain resorts and summits, reaching the remote sections of the country with frequent, efficient service. Most trains carry two classes: first class for more comfortable travel and second class for economy. International through trains link many Swiss cities with other European centers. From your European gateway, many comfortable express trains carry you straight into the heart of Switzerland. Other intercity trains, those coming from Holland, Scandinavia, and Germany, require a change at Basel SBB station, where a connection is usually offered on the same platform. Most intercity trains offer the fastest connections, and as trains leave the Basel station hourly, you don't have to wait there very long.

It is advisable to purchase transportation tickets for Europe before leaving home, especially to made-to-order tickets issued for specific and complicated itineraries. Some advance notice is required for such tickets. All tickets are available from your travel agent or the Swiss National Tourist Office (SNTO) in New York, which acts as the official agency of the Swiss Federal Railways. From other offices of the SNTO you can secure tickets as follows: Chicago—Swiss Pass; San Francisco—Eurailpass, Eurail Youthpass, Swiss Pass, Half-Fare Travel Card, and Senior Card; Toronto—Swiss Pass, Half-Fare Card for 15 days and one month, Senior Half-Fare Travel Card, and one-month Junior Travel Card.

Addresses and phone numbers for these offices will be found under "Information" in "The ABCs of Switzerland," in Chapter II.

It is not possible to reserve seats on Swiss trains, except for groups of ten or more persons traveling together. Unlimited stopovers en route are permitted without formality.

Swiss Pass

This is the most practical and convenient ticket for your Swiss trip. It entitles the holder to unlimited travel on the entire network of the **Swiss Federal Railways,** including most private and mountain railroads, on lake steamers, and on most postal motor coaches, linking Swiss cities and resorts. This pass also permits the holder to purchase in Switzerland an unlimited number of transportation tickets at a reduction of up to 50% for excursions to mountaintops. The Swiss Pass is issued at half price to children over 6 years old and under 16.

With a Pass, you don't need to plan in advance. Just get on a train, a boat, or a postal bus, show your card to the ticket collector, and enjoy your trip. You'll never have to wait long for your next travel link.

A first-class Swiss Pass for four days costs 235F ($159.80); for eight days, 280F ($190.40); for 15 days, 335F ($227.80); and for one month, 465F ($316.20). A pass for second-class travel is 160F ($108.80) for four days, 195F ($132.60) for eight days, 235F ($159.80) for 15 days, and 325F ($221) for one month.

For information, telephone 01/211-50-10 in Switzerland.

Half-Fare Travel Card

The half-fare card, called the "Swiss Card," entitles the holder to purchase in Switzerland an unlimited number of regular transportation tickets, both round trip and one way, at half the fare on all scheduled services by rail (including mountain railroads), postal buses, and lake steamers. One month of second-class travel costs 100F ($68) for adults and 50F ($34) for children. First-class travel is 125F ($85) for adults and 75F ($51) for children 6 to 16. You must know the first day the half-fare is to be valid. Also, in order to purchase a one-month card, you must give your passport number when you apply. For information, telephone 01/211-50-10 in Switzerland.

Eurailpass

This ticket entitles bona fide residents of North America to unlimited first-class travel over the 100,000-mile national railroad networks of Western European countries, except Great Britain, and including Hungary in Eastern Europe. It is also valid on some lake steamers and private railroads. For many years travelers to Europe have been taking advantage of the Eurailpass, one of the continent's great travel bargains. Passes may be purchased for as short a period as 15 days or as long as three months.

Here's how it works: The pass cannot be purchased in Europe. Vacationers planning a trip can secure the pass at $320 for 15 days, $398 for 21 days, $498 for one month, $698 for two months, or $860 for three months. Children under 4 years of age travel free if they don't occupy a seat (otherwise, they pay half fare). Children under 12 pay half fare. If you're under 26, you can obtain unlimited second-class travel, wherever Eurailpass is honored, on a **Eurail Youthpass,** which costs $360 for one month, $470 for two months.

The advantages are tempting. No tickets, no supplements—simply show the pass to the ticket collector, then settle back to enjoy the scenery. Seat reservations are required on some trains. Many of the trains have couchettes (sleeping cars) for which an additional fee is charged. Obviously, the two- or three-month traveler gets the greatest economic advantages; the Eurailpass is ideal for extensive trips.

Fifteen-day or one-month tourists have to estimate rail distance before determining if such a pass is to their benefit. To obtain full advantage of the ticket for 15 days or a month, you'd have to spend a great deal of time on the train.

Eurail Saverpass is a money-saving ticket providing discounted 15-day travel for groups of three people traveling constantly and continuously together between April and September, or two people so traveling between October and March. The price of a Saverpass, valid all over Europe and good for first-class travel only, is $230 per person for the 15 days.

Eurail Flexipass is a time-flexible Eurailpass giving travelers nine days of rail travel that can be used either consecutively or otherwise in 16 countries within any one 21-day period. It costs $340 and ensures nine days of travel of your choice without the feeling you're losing travel days after you have validated your pass if you elect to stay in one place a little longer. Travel agents in all towns and railway agents in major cities such as New York, Montréal, Los Angeles, and Chicago sell the tickets. The Eurailpass is also available at the offices of CIT Travel Service, the Swiss Federal Railways, the German Federal Railroads, and the French National Railroads.

Glacier Express

Perhaps the most famous part of Switzerland's clean and efficient electrical railway system is the *Glacier Express,* connecting the highest peaks and glaciers of the eastern Alps around St. Moritz with those of the western Alps around Zermatt. This train has been running since 1928, crossing the Furka mountain, but because of the dangers from blizzards and avalanches, the mountain railroad bridges had to be removed in October and reinstalled in May, necessitating a long detour to Zurich in order to go from Zermatt to St. Moritz. Now, since the opening of the eight-mile-long Furka Tunnel in 1982, the *Glacier Express* runs one train each way between the two major resorts daily.

The 7½-hour, 150-mile trip between Zermatt and St. Moritz on the narrow-gauge railroad takes you through 91 viaducts and tunnels and over 291 bridges in comfortable coaches with restaurant cars. Advance seat reservations for the *Glacier Express* are obligatory. From May 23 to September 25, a second train, which requires a change in Reichenau, leaves each station daily. The one-way fare is $72 per person in first class, $48 in second class.

For more information, get in touch with the Swiss National Tourist Office at the addresses listed under "Information" in "The ABCs of Switzerland," Chapter II. The Swiss Center in New York is at 608 Fifth Ave., New York, NY 10020 (tel. 212/757-5944).

BY BUS: The yellow alpine postal buses are popular and provide an unrivaled service over numerous and beautiful Swiss passes. Experienced drivers with special training operate these coaches, which have three independent brake systems. Most travelers who choose this type of ticket are Swiss residents of remote regions that aren't reached by train and those who travel the same route frequently. Most foreign visitors prefer the Swiss Pass (see above), which allows greater flexibility in routings. Nonetheless the postal buses travel all around the country and will carry you from your railroad station to remote valleys and across the great alpine passes. A **Postal Coach Holiday Season Ticket,** available at offices of the Swiss Postal Passenger Service, provides half-fare travel for one year on all scheduled Swiss postal bus lines. The price is 100F ($68) per person. **Postal Coach Weekly Passes,** for unlimited travel in the regions of Sion, Sierre, Upper Valais, Ilanz, Thusis, Appenzell, Toggenburg, and the Principality of Liechtenstein, are available at the post offices of the regions in question. Hand baggage up to 110 pounds can be taken on a postal bus free.

For information, call 01/463-8666.

The extremely dense network covered by the Swiss postal buses is useful for trips into the mountains and is a much safer and more comfortable way of seeing the Alps than trying to do your own driving in those regions.

BY BOAT: Passenger boats sail on all the major Swiss lakes and many of the country's rivers, ideal waterways for voyages to scenic spots, and most of the boats have excellent restaurants aboard. In summer more than 100 ships with accommodations for 60,000 passengers operate on many of the Swiss lakes and certain stretches of the Rhine and the Aare. Evening trips with music and dancing are popular. Pleasure boats and lake steamers are ideal means of transportation for the unhurried traveler. The old paddle-steamers on the lakes of Brienz, Geneva, Lucerne, and Zurich, all of which date from before World War I, are particularly attractive and provide a touch of unspoiled romanticism.

Your Swiss Pass or half-fare travel card entitles you to travel on lake steamers and on most postal motor coaches, as well as on trains.

The complete official **timetable** covering trains, buses, and lake steamers is available from the Swiss National Tourist Offices in New York and San Francisco at $8 per copy, or in Toronto for $10 Canadian. Addresses and phone numbers for the offices are listed under "Information" in "The ABCs of Switzerland," Chapter II.

BY CAR: Switzerland provides a system of well-constructed roads and super-highways. Everywhere, at every turn of the road, the Swiss landscape has something new to offer. Travel is made easy by good signposts and clear road signs. Alpine passes are not difficult to cross, except in snowstorms, when they may shut down suddenly. Special rail facilities are provided for motorists wishing to transport their cars through the alpine tunnels of the Albula, Furka, Lötschberg, and Simplon. A timetable with rates is available from the Swiss National Tourist Offices.

Apart from these facilities and the Great St. Bernard Tunnel, there is only a single superhighway toll of 30F ($20.40) per vehicle per year in Switzerland.

Permits are available at the border crossings and are valid for multiple re-entries into Switzerland within the licensed period. An additional fee of 30F ($20.40) applies to trailers and motor homes. Rental cars in Switzerland come with the permit. Vehicles rented in other countries may lack it, and motorists caught without one face a fine of more than twice the cost of the permit. To avoid waiting in a long line at border crossings to purchase your permit, you can buy the sticker in advance at Swiss National Tourist Offices in Italy, Austria, and Germany. It is not sold in France. If you drive into Switzerland on a secondary road, a sticker is not required, but you can't drive on a Swiss superhighway without one. It takes the place of road tolls.

If you are 18 years old, you can drive in Switzerland on your valid home driver's license. However, car-rental companies set their own driving age, which is usually higher than 18.

You drive to the right in Switzerland, and with the exception of superhighways where the speed limit is about 75 miles per hour, the national speed limit for passenger vehicles is 50 mph. In built-up areas, such as cities, towns, and villages, the speed limit is usually 31 mph, unless otherwise posted.

Headlights must be on and dimmed while driving through road tunnels. Passing on the right is strictly prohibited (even on superhighways), and seatbelts must be worn while driving. You cannot allow children under 12 to ride in the front seat. And *don't* take a chance and drive when you've been drinking.

The Swiss Automobile Clubs, **Automobil-Club der Schweiz,** 39 Wasser-werkgasse, CH-3000 Bern 13 (tel. 031/22-47-22), and **Touring Club Suisse,** 9 rue Pierre-Fatio, CH-1211 Genève 3 (tel. 022/37-12-12), and their branch offices will assist motorists at all times. If you have a breakdown, dial 140 for help. To learn of road conditions, call 163. On mountain roads, emergency call boxes will allow you to call for help.

Car Rentals

Many American companies cooperate with European affiliates to guarantee prompt delivery of a car upon your arrival in Switzerland.

One of the most reliable firms is **Budget Rent-a-Car,** whose prices are competitive with those of the other major firms, Avis and Hertz.

Budget offers one-way rentals between any of its more than 60 Swiss offices at no additional charge. That means you can rent a car in Geneva, for example, and return it in Zurich before flying home. A wide range of vehicles is offered, from dependably conservative cars to sporty ones, including four-wheel drive "fun machines." All cars are equipped with snow tires on all four wheels in winter, and snow chains and ski racks are available upon request. There are even cars equipped for handicapped drivers.

At press time, the best deal, which may still be available for your visit, is Budget Plan Europe. The only restrictions are that you need to reserve the car by calling Budget's toll-free number at least two days in advance and that you must keep the car at least a week. An Opel Corsa, suitable for four passengers, rents for 309F ($210.10) weekly, with unlimited mileage. The next category, an automatic-transmission Opel Vestra, shoots up to 540F ($367.20) per week.

There is no tax on car rentals in Switzerland, but most car rental companies will offer you an optional insurance policy that will eliminate any financial responsibility for collision damages in the event of an accident. This costs around 12.25F ($8.35) per day. Without it, you'll pay up to the first 1,800F ($1,224) worth of damage to your car. The amount charged by Avis, for example, for accidents involving renters who decline the policy is almost twice as much, while the cost of the Avis policy is almost 60% more expensive than that of Budget. As many rueful renters know, it's better to accept the optional insurance. I always do. For more information, call Budget's toll-free number: 800/527-0700.

Since the European car-rental market is highly competitive and subject to change, you might also check with the international departments of **Hertz** (tel. toll free 800/654-3001) or **Avis** (tel. toll free 800/331-2112), in case of any last-minute changes in their price structures.

Gasoline

The cost varies throughout the country. Gas stations are usually open from 8 a.m. to 10 p.m. U.S. gasoline credit cards are generally not accepted.

ITINERARIES: Only ten days for Switzerland? In these modern times, when one no longer has eight months for "The Grand Tour," so popular with Victorians, the reality must be dealt with.

A Ten-Day "Quickie"

For the visitor who has a foot on the gas pedal and an eye on the time clock, the Classic Tour of Switzerland is to drive from Zurich to Geneva or vice versa. As you look at a map, Geneva will appear to be in France. At the end of this tour, you won't know Switzerland but you will have sampled a wide diversity of its landscape and its people, as you go from the German-speaking sector to a lakefront land where French is spoken. Along the way you'll see an alpine landscape of snow-covered mountains, ice-blue lakes, and lush valleys. You also will have visited five of the most interesting cities of Switzerland: Zurich, Lucerne, Bern, Lausanne, and Geneva.

Figure on losing the first day just flying into Zurich and settling into a hotel and coping with jet lag. The second day can be spent touring the attractions of Zurich as outlined in Chapter III. On the third day you can check out of your hotel and head south from Zurich along the N3, staying on the west side of Lake Zurich. Near Wädenswil (the signs to Lucerne are clearly marked) you'll head west, and will have gone a distance of only 35 miles when you reach Lucerne.

You'll need an absolute minimum of two nights in Lucerne, which seems to be the one city of Switzerland most favored by Americans. Lucerne deserves plenty of time all on its own, but after a night's rest, I suggest that you spend the following day touring Lake Lucerne by paddle-steamer and taking cable cars or funiculars to towering mountain peaks, such as Rigi and Pilatus. This is the heartland of Switzerland—William Tell country. Frankly, you could spend two weeks and not even skim the highlights of Central Switzerland. To select specific points of interest, refer to Chapter X.

After two nights, you can leave Lucerne and head south and west to Interlaken (take the N8), the centuries-old tourist capital of the Bernese Oberland. You will go via the Brünig Pass, a distance of only 35 miles (but it will seem much longer). Interlaken is mainly a summer retreat, lying between two lakes, Thun and Brienz. One of the main reasons people come here is to take excursions to the frozen Jungfrau, which at 11,333 feet is the highlight of many a visitor's trip to Switzerland. After settling into Interlaken, you'll be ready for an early departure to Jungfrau the following morning, returning late that afternoon. That means two nights in Interlaken.

Following that, it's an easy and scenic drive west and north to Bern, the capital of Switzerland, a distance of 34 miles via Thun along the N6. A citadel of diplomats, and one of the great medieval cities still standing in Europe, Bern deserves at least a night's stopover. For its attractions, refer to Chapter VI.

After a night, you can head west and then south to Lausanne, the fifth-largest city in Switzerland, rising in tiers from Lac Léman (Lake Geneva). Get on the N12 for a drive of 56 miles. One of the most fascinating cities of Switzerland, Lausanne deserves at least a day and night of your time.

The next day you can begin your approach to Geneva, which lies only 38 miles from Lausanne. I recommend that you take the western route along the northern arc of Lac Léman. You can make the trip in two hours, but you'll enjoy it more if you allow at least half a day. A good luncheon stopover along the way is at Nyon. If you take your time and sample the beauty of the towns and villages along the lake, you'll arrive in Geneva in the late afternoon.

After a night's rest, that will leave only one full day for Geneva, the third-largest city of Switzerland. It deserves far more, of course. At some point, I suggest that you break your concentration on this lively, cosmopolitan city for at least a short boat trip on the lake itself. (Those who have an extra day can take an all-day trip to Mont Blanc, including a cable-car ride to the summit of Aiguille du Midi at 12,610 feet, one of the all-time greatest alpine panoramas.) A border crossing into France will be part of the experience, but a visa is required.

And that's it—Switzerland in ten days.

As one of the crossroads of Europe, Geneva is an easy place to make plane connections to the rest of the world.

For a Deeper Look

Those with an extra week or so to spend in Switzerland might want to consider another major tour through the country.

This second excursion will take us from Zurich all the way to Lugano, which is the capital of Ticino, the Italian-speaking part of Switzerland. We'll detour via one of the most charming valleys of Europe, the Engadine whose touristic capital is St. Moritz. In all, it will be a distance of some 200 miles just to get there, but it will seem far shorter, of course, because every kilometer will be rich in some scenic treasure.

Unlike some routes in Switzerland, the roads to the Grisons and the Engadine are open year round, and are usually filled with skiers heading for such popular resorts as Davos, Arosa, and Klosters. If you're motoring in winter, make sure your car has the proper equipment.

Take the freeway south from Zurich, the N3, running along the southern shores of Lake Zurich and Lake Walen, until you come to Chur, a distance of 76 miles. (The attractions of the Grisons and the Engadine are outlined in Chapter XI.)

A ROAD MILEAGE CHART
Distance in Miles

	Zurich	Zermatt	St. Moritz	St. Gallen	Rome	Paris	Montreux	Lugano	Lucerne	Lausanne	Interlaken	Innsbruck	Geneva	Frankfurt	Davos	Chur	Buchs	Brig	Biel/Bienne	BERNE	Basle
Basle	53	161	179	97	586	302	121	188	59	118	96	231	155	227	145	128	117	146	50	62	—
BERNE	80	127	197	122	562	341	58	168	57	56	34	258	93	289	168	146	136	107	18	—	62
Biel/Bienne	73	134	204	130	580	345	65	188	66	65	52	240	103	277	161	139	125	120	—	18	50
Brig	119	27	153	143	466	424	79	102	87	95	73	354	119	373	144	108	137	—	120	107	146
Buchs	63	164	76	28	524	419	203	125	79	194	126	115	232	344	46	29	—	137	125	136	117
Chur	76	135	48	60	495	446	122	99	89	202	117	144	222	356	37	—	29	108	139	146	128
Davos	92	171	41	113	520	483	221	122	105	224	135	183	262	390	—	37	46	144	161	168	145
Frankfurt	280	419	406	328	—	390	348	415	286	345	323	352	382	—	390	356	344	373	277	289	227
Geneva	174	136	273	217	547	325	53	222	151	37	127	352	—	382	262	222	232	119	103	93	155
Innsbruck	178	381	182	143	—	—	316	237	192	312	237	—	352	352	183	144	115	354	240	258	231
Interlaken	81	90	164	126	525	378	75	127	45	83	—	237	127	323	135	117	126	73	52	34	96
Lausanne	134	112	249	179	548	325	16	197	114	—	83	312	37	345	224	202	194	95	65	56	118
Lucerne	35	107	140	73	527	361	116	129	—	114	45	192	151	286	105	89	79	87	66	57	59
Lugano	143	129	79	158	399	490	180	—	129	197	127	237	222	415	122	99	125	102	188	168	188
Montreux	138	96	233	187	532	345	—	180	116	16	75	316	53	348	221	122	203	79	65	58	121
Paris	355	451	481	403	—	—	345	490	361	325	378	—	325	390	483	446	419	424	345	341	302
Rome	540	496	456	555	—	—	532	399	527	548	525	—	547	—	520	495	524	466	580	562	586
Salzburg	278	406	228	243	—	—	412	304	295	407	340	—	445	—	—	—	215	379	360	350	330
St. Gallen	48	160	108	—	555	403	187	158	73	179	126	143	217	328	113	60	28	143	130	122	97
St. Moritz	126	180	—	108	456	481	233	79	140	249	164	182	273	406	41	48	76	153	204	197	179
Venice	357	310	236	349	—	—	348	216	343	365	341	—	363	—	315	289	318	283	388	370	402
Vienna	465	679	469	430	—	—	604	608	479	599	524	—	639	419	460	341	402	652	550	545	518
Zermatt	145	—	180	160	496	451	96	129	107	112	90	381	136	419	171	135	164	27	134	127	161
Zurich	—	145	126	48	540	355	138	143	35	81	134	178	174	280	92	76	63	119	73	80	53

A short drive south from Chur will take you to Valbella/Lenzerheide on Lake Heid at 4,757 feet. After perhaps a luncheon stopover, continue along the same route to Savognin at the mouth of the Val Nandro.

At the famed Julier Pass at some 7,500 feet, you'll be at the main entrance to the Engadine, one of the most spectacular valleys in Europe. The first village you'll come to in the Engadine is Silvaplana. You can either spend the night there or press on to the more glamorous (and more expensive) St. Moritz, a short drive to the east.

On this first day of motoring, by the time you reach St. Moritz you will have covered a distance of 126 miles since leaving Zurich. If you drive straight through without stopping, it will take four hours from Zurich to St. Moritz.

I suggest the very minimum of a two-night stopover in St. Moritz. The following day you can continue your drive up the Engadine Valley, which stretches for 60 miles from the Maloja Plateau at 5,955 feet to Finstermünz.

After leaving St. Moritz, you might head south to Lugano, some 79 miles away. Surprisingly, because of the mountainous roads it takes four hours. The route takes visitors into Italy, and it's a beautiful trip, in spite of the fact you'll have to cross the frontier twice (border formalities, however, are generally relaxed). A postal coach makes this run twice a day, leaving from the rail stations and in front of the main post offices of both cities.

You should get an early start from St. Moritz, heading in a southwesterly direction toward the Maloja Pass, traveling through Vicosoprano. Continue along Route 37 to Chiavenna, crossing into Italy at Castasegna. You'll be in the sunny south in a land of fruit trees and vineyards. Once you reach Chiavenna, you can travel along a narrow main highway, following the westerly side of Lake Como, heading toward Lugano. Your turnoff will come at Menaggio. Once there, head right along Route 340 in the direction of Lake Lugano, passing through such charming little villages as Cima along the northern shoreline.

You'll need a two-night stopover in Lugano. After your first night, you can explore this cultural center of Ticino. Its attractions are outlined in Chapter XII.

Leaving Lugano, you can head north along the N2, taking the western exit to the second major resort of Ticino, Locarno. I suggest another night's stopover there. Or else you can drive slightly west along Route 13 to Ascona, which many visitors find even more inviting.

To return to Zurich, you can take the E9 toward the St. Gotthard Pass, one of the most historic and most frequented routes in Switzerland. The pass provides a link between the Grisons and the Valais Alps. The road tunnel, which was inaugurated in 1980, is open year round.

Before returning to Zurich, you should stay overnight in one of the following resorts: Andermatt (at the crossroads of the Alps), or along the N2 to Amsteg or Altdorf. For suggested stopovers along this route, refer to Chapter X.

From wherever you spend the night, northern routes to Zurich are clearly marked. In general count on about 3 to 3½ hours of driving time between the St. Gotthard Pass and Zurich.

Don't dare show these itinerary suggestions to a native-born Swiss citizen. They would surely be shocked to see their country treated so cursorily, although they themselves often move with the feet of Mercury when visiting the United States.

What about lonely, isolated Zermatt, within view of the towering Matterhorn? Isn't the Valais and the Great St. Bernard Pass (as outlined in Chapter VII) one of the major attractions of Europe? What about Basel and the Juras (in Chapter V)? And let's not forget tiny Liechtenstein (in Chapter XIII).

These itinerary suggestions are only to get you going. Switzerland is one of the greatest tourist countries of the world, and you're not expected to explore it and know it in just one short trip. My suggestion is to plan a second visit, even a third, and most definitely a fourth trip.

TOURS: Many questions arise for persons planning their first European trip, whether to Switzerland or elsewhere. Sometimes a prospective traveler isn't really sure where he or she wants to visit. There can also be other troublesome thoughts: How will I get around in a country with a different language? How do I plan my trip to be sure of seeing the most outstanding sights of the country? How much of a problem will I have in trying to get from place to place, complete with luggage? Am I too old to embark on such a journey? Will I meet people who speak my language with whom to compare notes?

My answer to all these questions—indeed, my advice to many people going to Europe for the first time—is simply: Go on a good tour. By this I don't mean simply a tour of one city or of one building. I refer to a vacation tour where you and your needs are looked after from your arrival at a European airport to your departure en route back to the United States. Choose a tour suited to the time you have for your trip, the money you can spend, and the places you want to go.

Finally, booking a tour is almost invariably cheaper than the cost of exploring a country on your own. You save on both transportation and meals.

One of the best tour operators in the business, of course, is **American Express.** If you've been considering going to Switzerland, for instance, with perhaps questions about other countries and whether you would like to spend time there, American Express offers a choice of trips that include Germany and Austria. For example, you can take a Rhineland 12-day trip costing from $1,155 to $1,255 plus airfare. You stay at first-class hotels for seven nights in rooms with private bath or shower. You're also given outside cabins on the cruise ship with private facilities. The plan also includes 19 meals, counting 10 continental breakfasts, and guided sight-seeing. Such German cities as Rothenburg and Munich are taken in; the Swiss part takes in Davos and Lucerne, among other destinations.

Switzerland is also included in the American Express tour of "Romantic Europe," with destinations in Switzerland, Italy, Austria, West Germany, and Liechtenstein. The cost for 14 days ranges from $929 to $999, plus airfare. The Swiss part begins after Innsbruck when passengers are taken to chic St. Moritz and then later to Lucerne via Liechtenstein. This plan includes seven hotel dinners.

By choosing either tour, you will get a good look at a number of countries. For your next trip, you should have a pretty firm idea of your exact destination. You'll already know a lot about it. It will help you enjoy your tour if you take along a copy of this and other Frommer guides about the countries you visit, giving the background of the areas you'll see, where to shop, and other practical information.

The great advantage of such tours, particularly for persons who are hesitant about setting out alone or as a couple to foreign shores, is that everything is arranged for you—transportation in Europe, hotels, services, sight-seeing trips, excursions, luggage, tips and taxes, and many of your meals (as mentioned). But you're not led around like a little lamb. Plenty of time is provided on every trip for shopping, recreation, or little side trips, perhaps to see the little town where your grandmother was born.

Whether you have a week or a month or so, don't put off your European experience just because you are afraid to go. For a pleasant, rewarding, and safe trip, book one of these tours that include Switzerland. Any travel agent can arrange it for you.

3. ALTERNATIVE AND SPECIAL-INTEREST TRAVEL

Mass tourism of the kind that has transported vast numbers of North Americans to the most obscure corners of the map has been a by-product of the affluence, technology, and democratization which only the last half of the 20th century was able to produce.

With the advent of the 1990s, and the changes this decade promises to bring, some of America's most respected travel visionaries have perceived a change in the needs of many of the world's most experienced (and sometimes jaded) travelers. There has emerged a demand for specialized travel experiences whose goals and objectives are clearly defined well in advance of an actual departure. There is also an increased demand for organizations that can provide likeminded companions to share and participate in increasingly esoteric travel plans.

Caveat: Under no circumstances is the inclusion of an organization in this section to be interpreted as a guarantee either of its credit-worthiness or its competency. Information about the organizations coming up is presented only as a preview, to be followed by your own investigation should you be interested.

MEET THE SWISS: I'd like to endorse a life-seeing program called **"Meet the Swiss."** Sponsored by the Zurich Tourist Office, 15 Bahnhofplatz (tel. 01/211-40-00), it's a unique program that connects foreign visitors, such as Canadians and Americans, with personal contacts in Zurich. As much as possible, families of similar backgrounds and interests are matched (after all, you have to have something to talk about). After the red tape is out of the way, you're given an invitation to a Swiss home. I recently tested this program and was invited into the home of a Swiss writer and his family, his beautiful wife and two daughters. He was working on a biography of Carl Jung. An enjoyable evening was climaxed by coffee, Kirschwasser, and a dessert that one of the daughters had baked. He gave me some white chocolate to take back to my hotel. The next day, to reciprocate, I sent flowers. Obviously this is a noncommercial arrangement, and you should never go expecting a meal or an accommodation. Incidentally, you'll be matched with an English-speaking family. The tourist office will work out the details, but give them a little time to set up your visit (at least three days).

SPAS: The spa treatment, a form of therapy many thousands of years old, is still in vogue despite the progress achieved in medical science. The natural curative springs of Switzerland are said not only to help restore the sick to health but also to ward off disease. Proponents of spa therapy point to the quiet and relaxation found in the health resorts as remedies for psychological stress and the pressures of everyday life.

Most resorts with the marked seal of approval by the Association of Swiss Health Spas and the Swiss Society of Balneology and Bioclimatology include a medical examination in their package plans for visitors, together with thermal baths and excursions.

There are 22 recognized in spas in Switzerland, many of them open all year.

The following will provide you with information about spa vacations: Health and Fitness Vacations, 100 N. Biscayne Blvd., Miami, FL 33132 (tel. 305/379-8451); Health and Pleasure Tours, Inc., 165 W. 46th St., New York, NY 10036 (tel. 212/586-1175); Odyssey Travel Ltd., 2050 Chestnut St., San Francisco, CA 94123 (tel. 415/567-9164); Ring International, P.O. Box 118, Novato, CA 94947 (tel. 415/892-3966); Selective Tours of Switzerland, 301 E. 48th St., New York, NY 10017 (tel. 212/758-4275 or toll free 800/223-6764); or Swissair, Tours Dept., 608 Fifth Ave., New York, NY 10020 (tel. 212/995-4400 or toll free 800/221-6644; in New York State, 800/522-9606).

MOUNTAINEERING: Mountain-climbing schools, where you can learn all about this exciting sport, are found in Andermatt, Champéry, Crans, Davos, Les Diablerets, Fiesch, La Fouly, Glarus, Grindelwald, Kandersteg, Klosters, Meiringen, Pontresina, Riederalp, Saas-Fee, Saas-Grund, Schwende, Täsch, Zermatt, and Zinai, and guides are available at many other resorts. The peaks of the Swiss Alps offer challenges in both summer and winter.

Access to these peaks has been facilitated by the **Swiss Alpine Club,** which has built mountain huts at strategic spots throughout the country. Also, there are comfortable hotels and inns at favorable altitudes for alpine treks, many on high peaks and passes. The huts of the Swiss Alpine Club are modest, with bunkrooms sleeping 10 to 20, and are open to every alpinist. The average rate for a night's lodging (without food) is 25F ($17) daily for nonmembers of the club, 13F ($8.85) for members. The Swiss Alpine Club, founded in 1863, promotes mountaineering and ski tours in the high mountains and also organizes rescue service in the Swiss Alps. You can get a membership in the SAC for a three-year period. The fees are 100F ($68) for the first year and 65F ($44.20) for each succeeding year. The fees include postage and admission. You cannot get the membership for just one year merely to get reduced rates in the SAC huts. The SAC is not an organization for hiking or trailing. The main task is organizing the alpine rescue service. Application forms can be requested from Edmund F. Krieger, secretary-treasurer, Swiss Alpine Club (SAC), Section Zermatt, P.O. Box 1, CH-3920 Zermatt, Switzerland.

INTERNATIONAL UNDERSTANDING: About the only thing the following organizations have in common is reflected in that heading. They not only promote trips to increase international understanding, but they also often encourage and advocate what might be called "intelligent travel."

Servas, 11 John St., New York, NY 10038 (tel. 212/267-0252). Servas ("to serve" in Esperanto) is a non-profit, non-government, international, interfaith network of travelers and hosts whose goal is to help build world peace, good will, and understanding by providing opportunities for deeper, more personal contacts among people of diverse cultural and political backgrounds. Servas travelers are invited to share living space in a privately owned home within a community, normally without charge, for visits lasting a maximum of two days. Visitors pay a $45 annual membership fee, fill out an application, and are interviewed for suitability by one of more than 200 Servas interviewers throughout the country. They then receive a Servas directory listing the names and addresses of Servas hosts who will allow visitors in their homes.

International Visitors Information Service, 733 15th St. NW, Suite 300, Washington, DC 20005 (tel. 212/783-6540). For $4.95, this organization will mail anyone a booklet listing opportunities for contact with local residents in foreign countries. Switzerland is featured. Checks should be made out to Meridian House IVIS.

TRAVEL AND LEARNING: An international series of programs for persons over 50 years of age who are interested in combining travel and learning is offered by **Interhostel,** developed by the University of New Hampshire. Each program lasts two weeks and is escorted by a university faculty or staff member, arranged in conjunction with a host college, university, or cultural institution. Participants can extend a stay beyond two weeks if they wish. Interhostel offers programs that consist of cultural and intellectual activities, with field trips to museums and other centers of interest. For information, get in touch with the University of New Hampshire, Division of Continuing Education, 6 Garrison Ave., Durham, NH 03824 (tel. 603/862-1147). It's best to phone between 1:30 and 4 p.m. EST.

In Switzerland, Interhostel has a program in Leysin, lasting for two weeks and hosted by the American College of Switzerland. Guests remain on campus, staying at what had been a former grand hotel and sanitorium. The program consists of assorted lectures on the French-speaking sections of Switzerland, taking in such topics as the economy, the cultural life, the political life, and the history, including folk customs and a discussion of Swiss neutrality. The cost is in the range of $1,100 to $1,300 per person, which covers room and board and tuition.

Another program, which operates in conjunction with Franklin College, is in Lugano. Participants stay at the college. This is very similar to the program offered by Leysin, except the focus is on the Italian section of Switzerland. A field trip goes to Milan for two days. Land prices are from $1,295 per person per week.

SENIOR CITIZEN VACATIONS: One of the most dynamic organizations of post-retirement studies for senior citizens is **Elderhostel,** 80 Boyleston St., Boston, MA 02116 (tel. 617/426-7788), established in 1975. Elderhostel maintains an array of programs throughout Europe, including Switzerland. Most courses last for around three weeks, representing good value, considering that air fare, hotel accommodations in student dormitories or modest inns (perhaps with a private family), all meals, and tuition are included. Courses involve no homework, are ungraded, and are especially concerned with liberal arts. In no way is this to be considered a luxury vacation, but rather an academic fulfillment of a type never possible for senior citizens until a few years ago. Participants must be more than 60 years of age. However, if a pair of members goes as a couple, only one member needs to be over 60. Anyone interested in participating in one of Elderhostel's programs should write for a free newsletter and list of upcoming courses and destinations.

GOLDEN COMPANIONS: If you're between the ages of 50 and 86, and need a travel companion, **Golden Companions,** P.O. Box 754, Pullman, WA 99163 (tel. 208/883-5052), might provide the answer. A research economist and writer, Joanne R. Buteau, founded this helpful service, and is quick to point out it's not a dating game. The service provides the means whereby travelers can seek introductions to possible travel companions through a confidential mail network service. Members, once they have "connected," make their own travel arrangements. Created in 1988, this organization draws members from many walks of life, including professional types and retirees as well as the single, divorced, widowed, or married. Members also receive a bimonthly travel newsletter, *The Golden Traveler,* which outlines travel discounts for senior citizens, vacation home exchanges, or other data. Membership for a full year costs $60 per person.

CHAPTER II

SETTLING INTO SWITZERLAND

□ □ □

1. THE SWISS
2. FOOD AND DRINK
3. SPORTS, WINTER AND SUMMER
4. THE ABCs OF SWITZERLAND

A peace-loving people, the Swiss are polite but reserved, much more so than Americans. But I've found them helpful to visitors, especially if you're struggling with a map. The Swiss love maps, and they understand those showing the dense network of well-constructed roads of their country.

For a motoring holiday in Switzerland, I suggest June as the ideal month, followed by either September or October, when the mountain passes are still open. In summer the country is often overrun with visitors. The Swiss are a law-abiding people, and they expect tourists to obey their laws, not the least of which involves drunk driving. Don't drink and drive in Switzerland, not only because it's against the law but because you'll need to be not only sober but a skilled motorist to navigate some of those hairpin curves in the mountains.

The country may be peace-loving, having followed a course of neutrality during all wars since 1815, but it has compulsory military service. Its army is devoted solely to the defense of the homeland. Unlike his counterpart in many countries, the Swiss soldier is ever ready. He keeps his military gear at home, including a gas mask, rifle, and plenty of ammunition, and attends obligatory shooting practice annually. In other words, he's ready to fight at any moment, as most Swiss feared would be necessary during World War II, when the country was encircled by Axis powers. Many people believe that the Swiss "sat out the war." Actually, they helped hundreds of men of the Allied air forces find safety and eventual freedom. They also aided prisoners who escaped from the Nazis to find a haven behind Swiss lines.

However, their record in women's rights has not been the best. It wasn't until 1971 that Swiss women were granted the right to vote.

1. THE SWISS

HISTORY: The history of Switzerland has not been all marked by happy yodeling and edelweiss, since such a strategically situated area was certainly an irresistible lure to empire builders since Roman times. The presence of mankind in the region has been traced from the Ice Age through the Bronze Age and the Early Iron Age. The first identifiable occupants were the Celts, who entered the alpine regions from the west. The Helvetii, a Celtic tribe defeated by Julius Caesar when they tried to move into southern France in 58 B.C., gave their name to a portion of the country which was known as Helvetia to the Romans, who defeated the resident tribes of barbarians in 15 B.C. Peaceful colonization under Roman rule was ended about A.D. 455, when frequent incursions of barbarians and later of Christian forces began. Taken over by Charlemagne, the sector now known as Switzerland (then a hodgepodge of cantons with no centralized definition as a country) became a part of the Holy Roman Empire, and through various land grabs and battles came eventually under Habsburg domination.

The Swiss may be peace-loving people now, but they have always jealously guarded what they considered theirs. In 1291 an association of three small states (now cantons), the Perpetual Alliance, was formed and was the germ of the Swiss Confederation of today. To be rid of the greedy Habsburgs, the Confederation broke free of the Holy Roman Empire in 1439; however, this did not bring freedom from attack by Austria, sometimes supported by France. It was as a result of a treaty with France during one of these allied attacks that Switzerland, now with a growing Confederation, began providing mercenary troops to a foreign power, a practice which at the beginning of the 16th century led to Swiss fighting Swiss. The agreement was ended in about 1515, and in 1516 the Confederates gave up their role as an important military force and declared their complete neutrality.

In 1814–1815 at the Congress of Vienna, with Switzerland consisting of 22 of its present 26 cantons (23, with three politically subdivided), the present-day national boundaries of the country were fixed and the perpetual neutrality of the country guaranteed. Free-trade zones were set up on the borders of Geneva, and in 1848, by national referendum, a federal constitution was adopted.

This achievement and maintenance of peace and neutrality in time of wars involving even its closest neighbors has helped the country toward becoming one of the world's greatest tourist centers—small in area but with an extraordinary variety of natural beauty.

LANGUAGES: The Swiss are vastly diverse as a people, comprising four separate linguistic and ethnic groups—German, Italian, French, and Romansh—with four different overlapping cultural influences. Most of the people of the country—some 70%—speak Swiss-German, or Schwyzerdütsch. French is the second language at 20%, with about 9% speaking Italian (in the Ticino district). One percent speaks the language called Romansh, which contains a pre-Roman vocabulary of words and a substratum of Latin elements. It is believed to be the language of old Helvetia and is spoken mainly by people in the Grisons.

For some incredible reason Switzerland has formed a national identity despite this variation, and it is rare to find a Swiss who speaks only one of the four languages. In addition, many of the country's people speak English, so you might accurately say that Switzerland has five languages.

As well as the four national languages, each district, and in certain parts of the country even each village, has its own dialect. My visits there have begun to enable me to distinguish (slightly) between the idiomatic vocabulary of a native of Bern, Basel, and other major cities, but I never expect to learn the patois of, say, the villagers in German-speaking Switzerland.

THE PEOPLE: The linguistic situation has brought about an abundance and variety of Swiss folklore, and since every Swiss belongs to a minority of some sort, I find that the people have an inherent tolerance of different lifestyles, recognizing the right of each person to live as he or she chooses. The Swiss are opposed to any form of compulsion or subordination. They definitely do not like bureaucracy and autocracy.

Industry, crafts, and tourism contribute the major portion of the national income, giving employment to more than a million persons. Only about 7% of the Swiss are engaged in agriculture and forestry, and the country produces about half of its food supply, its reputation as an agrarian state being gained through its dairy products, especially cheese. The engineering, chemical, and pharmaceutical industries, as well as makers of clocks and watches, spread Swiss products worldwide.

Three-quarters of the 6,365,960 Swiss people reside in the central lowlands between the Alps and the Jura, more than two-fifths of them in cities and towns of more than 10,000 population, so that in this small country there are some 400 inhabitants per square mile.

RELIGION: As in other European countries, the Reformation, led in Switzerland by Ulrich Zwingli in 1519, brought about internal conflicts between Roman Catholic and Protestant cantons, spurred on by the arrival in 1536 of John Calvin, fleeing France. The spread of Calvinism led to the coining of the French term *Huguenot,* a corruption of the Swiss word *Eidgnosse* ("confederate"). After Zwingli's defeat and death in a religious war in 1531, a peace treaty gave each territory the right to choose its own faith. Thus today, living peaceably together, 55% of the Swiss are Protestant, 43% Catholic, and 2% of other faiths.

GOVERNMENT: Swiss motor vehicles carry the international sign "CH," which stands for *Confoederatio Helvetica* and means "Swiss Confederation."

The Federal Parliament of Switzerland consists of a National Council of 200 members, elected by the people, and the Council of States (cantons) in which each canton has two representatives, making 46 State Councilors in all. The two chambers constitute Switzerland's legislative authority. The executive body, the Federal Council, is made up of seven members who make decisions jointly, although each councilor is responsible for a different department. The presidency of the Federal Council changes annually and the *primus inter pares* ("first among equals") has the responsibility of acting as president of the Confederation. While not particularly flexible, this system of government does guarantee a measure of continuity and stability.

There are 3,029 communes in Switzerland, each largely responsible for the independent administration of its public affairs, including the school system, taxation, road construction, water supply, and town planning, among other activities. The cantons were formed by communes joining together over the centuries for mutual advantages. Each canton has its own constitution, its own laws, and its own government. They have surrendered only certain aspects of their authority to the Federal Parliament, including foreign policy, national defense, and the general economic policy, as well as such matters as finance and civil and penal legislation.

All Swiss citizens, in general, are eligible to vote on federal matters at the age of 20. However, in the subdivided cantons of Appenzell and in a few small communes the vote is restricted to men, who vote only in cantonal and communal matters, not in the federal referendums or elections.

ART AND CULTURAL LIFE: The Public Art Collection in Basel, the Oskar Reinhart Foundation and Collection in Winterthur, and some private collections with limited public access are known throughout the world. The art museums of Zurich, Bern (including the Klee Foundation), and Geneva, as well as the Avegg Foundation in Bern (Riggisberg) and the Foundation Martin Bodmer (Geneva-Cologny), are also important. The Swiss National Museum in Zurich, the historical museums of Basel, Bern, and Geneva, and numerous local museums contain many valuable exhibits on history, archaeology, and the history of art. There are museums of church treasures as well as ethnological displays at cities throughout the country, and an International Museum of Horology at La Chaux-de-Fonds.

Roman ruins are open to visitors at several sites, and churches vie with the thousands of ruined castles as tourist attractions. The architecture of cities and monasteries has been preserved, and examples of superb mastery of the building crafts of earlier days can be seen.

Every town of any size has a resident symphony orchestra and a municipal theater. The theater and concert season begins in September and continues until the end of May. In summer, music lovers from all over the world come to the many music festivals as well as the film and folklore festivals. In some alpine valleys I've enjoyed joining the Swiss as they mark special holidays, dressed in old local costumes.

Switzerland's association with the cultural circles of its neighbors, Germany, France, and Italy, and the multilingual character of the country have been favorable to the development of Swiss culture.

Eminent Switzerland-born personalities include:

Paul Klee, painter, who used fantasy forms in line and light color, combining abstract elements with recognizable images.

Alberto Giacometti, sculptor, whose work was characterized by surrealistically elongated forms. He worked first in painting, then sculpture, then painting again, with pictures of sculptural quality.

Le Corbusier (Charles Edouard Jeanneret-Gris), architect and abstract painter, who designed, among other work, the Visual Arts Center at Harvard University.

Friedrich Durrenmatt, playwright, known for a grotesque farce, *The Visit,* and a mordant satire, *The Physicists.*

Carl Gustav Jung, psychologist and psychiatrist, an early associate of Freud.

Revered as the national poet and novelist of Switzerland is **Gottfried Keller** (1819–1890).

2. FOOD AND DRINK

Switzerland's cuisine, like its languages, is varied, borrowing heavily from the kitchens of Germany, France, and Italy, but with its own unique specialties that can only be called Swiss cookery. Overall, the cuisine is definitely international, but you'll want to try the repertoire of local foods.

CHEESE AND CHEESE DISHES: Cheesemaking is part of the Swiss heritage. Cattle breeding and dairy farming, concentrated in the alpine areas of the country, were pursuits of the inhabitants of the region some 2,000 years ago, when the Romans ate *caseus Helveticus* ("cheese from Helvetia"). The St. Gotthard Pass was a well-known cattle route to the south as far back as the 13th century, and the Swiss have exported not only cheese but cattle and know-how to the world, and were important in the development of the dairy industry in the United States.

More than 100 different varieties of cheese are produced today in Switzerland, some of only local use. The cheeses are not mass produced but are made in hundreds of small, strictly controlled dairies, each under the direction of a master cheesemaker with a federal degree, to ensure that the product is made by strict manufacturing standards and properly cured to produce its own natural, protective rind.

The cheese with the holes, known as Switzerland Swiss or Emmentaler, has been widely copied, since nobody ever thought to protect the name for use only on cheeses produced in the Emme Valley until it was too late. Other cheeses of Switzerland, many of which have also had their names plagiarized, are Gruyère, Appenzeller, raclette, royalp, sap sago, and several mountain cheeses including sbrinz and spalen, which are probably most closely related to the *caseus Helveticus* of Roman times.

Cheese fondue is the national dish of Switzerland: cheese (Emmentaler and natural Gruyère used separately, together, or with special local cheeses) melted in white wine flavored with a soupçon of garlic and lemon juice. Seasonings used are traditionally freshly ground pepper, nutmeg, paprika, and Swiss kirsch. Guests surround a bubbling *caquelon* (an earthenware pipkin or small pot) and use long forks to dunk cubes of bread into the hot mixture, stirring them on the bottom of the pot. Other dunkables besides bread cubes are chunks of apples and pears, grapes, cocktail wieners, cubes of boiled ham, shrimp, pitted olives, and tiny boiled potatoes. These morsels are usually secured to the fork by spearing a bread cube after them.

Fondue tradition says that if a woman loses her bread cube in the pot, she owes the man on her right a kiss. If a man loses his morsel when dining in a restaurant, he has to buy the next round of drinks. If the feast is being enjoyed at home, a man owes his hostess a kiss if he loses his cube.

Raclette, another cheese specialty, is almost as famous as fondue. Popular for many centuries, its origin is lost in antiquity, but the word "raclette" comes from the French word *racler,* meaning "to scrape off." In Switzerland, raclette's home is the Valais, source of the Rhône River and one of the most picturesque of the Swiss cantons. Although originally raclette was used only for the dish made from the special mountain cheese of the Valais, today it not only describes the dish itself but also the cheese varieties suitable for melting at an open fire or in an oven. A piece of cheese (traditionally a half to a quarter of a wheel of raclette) is held in front of an open fire. As it starts to soften, it is scraped off onto your plate with a special knife. Diners do not wait until everyone is served, as the unique flavor of the cheese is more delicious when the cheese is hottest. Fresh, crusty, homemade dark bread, potatoes boiled in their skins, pickled onions, cucumbers, or small corncobs are the classic accompaniments. You usually eat raclette with a fork, but if you need your knife, use it too.

Besides sampling the cheese fondue and raclette in Swiss restaurants (or homes, if you're lucky enough to get an invitation), you may want to discover favorite cheeses among the many more varieties.

OTHER FOOD SPECIALTIES: The most ubiquitous vegetable dish of the country is **röchti** or **Rösti** (hash brown potatoes). I find this excellent when it's been popped into the oven coated with cheese, which melts and turns a golden brown. **Spätzli** (Swiss dumplings) often appear on the menu.

Lake fish is a specialty in Switzerland, with ombre (a grayling) and ombre chevalier (char) heading the list, the latter being a tasty but expensive treat. From alpine lakes, among other varieties of fish you can enjoy trout or fried filets of tiny lake perch.

Country-cured **sausages** are another good food product in Switzerland, being offered for sale in many of the open markets you'll see as you travel around the country. The best known, air-dried beef, is called **bündnerfleisch,** a specialty in the Grisons. This meat isn't cured; it's dried in the clear, crisp, dry alpine air. Before modern refrigeration this was the Swiss way of preparing meat for winter consumption. Now bündnerfleisch is most often offered as an appetizer. My favorite place to order it is at one of those belvedere restaurants at the top of a chair lift on some alpine perch.

The **Bernerplatte** is the classic provincial dish of Bern. For gargantuan appetites, it's a version of the choucroûte garnie known to French citizens of Alsace.

If you order this typical farmer's plate, you'll be confronted by a mammoth pile of sauerkraut or french beans, topped with pigs feet, sausages, ham, bacon, pork chops—whatever.

In addition to cheese fondue, you may enjoy **fondue bourguignonne,** a dish that has become popular around the world. It consists of chunks of meat spitted on wooden sticks and broiled in oil or butter, seasoned as you choose. Also, many establishments offer **fondue Chinoise,** made with thin slices of beef and Oriental sauces. At the finish, you sip the broth in which the meat was cooked.

In Zurich and the northeast you'll get a German cuisine; in Geneva, French cookery; and in Ticino, Italian foods, which always taste slightly different from what you're served south of the border. Typical Ticino specialties include **risotto** with mushrooms and a mixed grill known as **fritto misto. Polenta,** made with cornmeal, is popular as a side dish. Ticino also has lake and river fish such as trout and pike. **Pizza** and **pasta** have spread to all provinces of Switzerland. If you're watching your centimes, either one is often the most economical dish on the menu.

Salads often combine both fresh lettuce and cooked vegetables such as beets. For a dining oddity, ask for a zwiebeln salat (cooked onion salad). In spring, the Swiss adore fresh asparagus. In fact, police have been forced to increase their night patrols in parts of the country to keep thieves out of the asparagus fields.

The glory of Swiss cuisine is its **pâtisseries,** little cakes and confections served all over the country in tea rooms and cafés. The most common delicacy is **gugelhopf,** a big cake shaped like a bun which is traditionally filled with whipped cream.

WHERE TO FIND FOOD: Breakfast, usually included in the price of your hotel room, will probably be continental style and is often served as a buffet meal. You'll get rolls, butter, preserves, coffee or tea, and some fruit juices. If you order such extras as orange juice, bacon, ham, or eggs, you may be stuck with a stiff tab.

When in doubt about where to eat in Switzerland, try a railroad station buffet. They're generally excellent and medium in price. If you want a fast-food meal, head for an *imbiss,* or snackbar, where the food is tasty, especially the open-face sandwiches. Prices are modest, as working people frequent these establishments.

HAVE A DRINK: Never order water, beer, or coffee with fondue. Your Swiss waiter will be horrified and will privately consider you a barbarian. White wine is the invariable choice of beverage with such a dish. If you don't like white wine, however, you might get by with substituting kirsch or tea.

There are almost no restrictions on the sale of alcohol in Switzerland, but prices of drinks such as bourbon, gin, and scotch are usually much higher than in the States, and bartenders are not noted for their generosity in pouring.

Swiss **wines** are superb, especially if you're in the region where the grapes are grown. Many I've tasted along, say, Lake Geneva are not even exported but are consumed entirely by the local populace. If possible, always try to ask for a local wine when ordering a meal. Unlike French wines, Swiss wines are best when "new." Wine in French-speaking Switzerland is as popular as beer to a Münchner. Instead of a martini before a meal, a Swiss business person is likely to order white wine as an apéritif. As you are unlikely to be familiar with the local Swiss wines of a particular canton, you should ask the headwaiter for advice. You'll usually be sure of a good selection.

In this relatively small country, vineyards, stretching along the lakes, nestling in the hills, or tucked away on mountainsides, produce a variety of excellent wines. Most are white, but there are also good rosés and fragrant red wines. Most wines that are produced in sufficient quantity for export are from four wine-making areas: Valais (the valley of the Rhône), Lake Geneva, Ticino, and Seeland. However, more than 300 small wine-growing areas are spread over the rest of the country, especially where German dialects are spoken. You'll have to try these on their home ground, as quantities are so limited that the wines are easily consumed by the commune that produces them.

For information on where to look for wines, plus advice on taking some home with you, get in touch with the **Swiss Wine Growers Association,** P.O. Box 1346, 4 Ave. Avant-Poste, CH-1001 Lausanne, Switzerland (tel. 021/20-32-31), or in the United States, from **Swissmart, Inc.,** 444 Madison Ave., New York, NY 10022 (tel. 212/751-3768).

Swiss **beer** is an excellent brew, and is of course the preferred drink in the German-speaking part of the country. It varies in quality. If you want to face a mug of *Hell*, you'll be served a light beer. *Dunkel* is dark beer.

Swiss **liqueurs** are tasty and highly potent. The most popular are kirsch, the national hard drink of Switzerland (made of the juice of cherry pits), Marc, pflümli, and Williamine, my personal favorite, made of pears.

3. SPORTS, WINTER AND SUMMER

When you think of sports in Switzerland, it's a safe bet that the first thing that springs to mind is skiing, which is available in both winter and summer, although, of course, winter is the prime time. In fact in some resorts of the country winter is the "high season" and tariffs are higher than in summer, unlike most of the rest of Europe. However, Switzerland seems to have been designed with the sports person in mind. The country has everything from Swiss-style wrestling to "alpine baseball."

The abundance of magnificent mountain slopes guarantees every possible skiing thrill plus facilities for other snow- and ice-related sports. These include cross-country skiing, skating, ice hockey, curling, tobogganing, and ski-bobbing in winter.

SKIING: Ski schools, ski instructors, and the best ski equipment in the world are available all over, and Switzerland constantly improves on its skiing facilities. Nearly all resorts are blessed with ski-rental shops. *Warning:* Always carry plenty of sun screen, even in winter. I've seen experienced alpine visitors get badly sunburned because of the intense reflection of sunlight off the snow.

The best-known areas for skiing are the Bernese Oberland, the Grisons, and the Valais, but there are many, many others. Skiing facilities will be previewed under these individual chapter headings. Skiing is big business in Switzerland — an estimated 40% of the tourist dollar is spent in pursuit of it. There are more than 1,700 mountain railways and ski lifts to take you effortlessly to the starting point of downhill runs.

Summer skiing is most often called **glacier skiing.** This sport takes place on glaciers that still keep their snow even in July and August. Glacier skiing is best before lunchtime, especially in the early-morning hours. After that the snow might become a little mushy. The best glacier ski resorts are Zermatt, St. Moritz, Engelberg, Saas-Fee, Gstaad, and Pontresina. Ski schools and ski lifts are open in summer.

Experienced skiers may wish to take a popular spring ski tour, the **Haute Route,** which crosses the French Alps into Switzerland via various routes; it is a week's tour that can usually be made from March to May. Led by a professional guide, skiers stop overnight and for noon rests at cabins maintained by the Swiss Alpine Club.

Cross-country skiing (called *Langlaufing*) is the fastest-growing sport in Europe. St. Moritz, Pontresina, and Montana are among the leaders in this field. A ski instructor told me that "it's hardly possible to break a bone" in this sport! You go at your own speed, and you never have to stay in your hotel if high slopes are closed when you ski cross-country. This sport allows many visitors who can't do downhill skiing to "be a part of things." There are no age limits and no charges for use of the cross-country trails, which are well marked.

From December 16 to March 31 you can get information on conditions in major ski areas in Switzerland before you leave home by calling the Swiss National Tourist Office snow report (tel. 212/757-6336), 24 hours a day.

For the Non-skier

Believe it or not, the so-called non-skier is a major factor at all ski resorts. It's estimated that at such fashionable resorts as Gstaad, Pontresina, Arosa, and Davos, one out of two guests is a non-skier. That trend is growing rapidly too. If you don't ski, there are a host of other activities—not just après ski. With sunbathing on mountain terraces, walks through forests, nightclubs, sleigh rides, and sightseeing excursions, the non-skier manages to fill up his or her day.

CURLING AND SKATING: Curling is another "boom" sport in Switzerland. Professional skiers dismiss it as a "sport for the elderly," but this "ain't necessarily so." Curling requires team effort, and is particularly popular at Davos, Villars, Gstaad, and Zermatt.

Ice skating is one of the leading winter sports of Switzerland, and nearly all major resorts have natural ice rinks. Also, there are dozens more artificial ones, of which Davos has the best.

GOLF: There are 30 golf courses in Switzerland at strategic spots throughout the country, so you can almost always find one in easy reach. The altitude at which they lie ranges from 700 feet above the sea level to the one at St. Moritz, 6,100 feet up. You can enjoy your game while viewing beautiful scenery and breathing the bracing Swiss air. Visitors are welcome at local clubs, particularly on weekdays. Golf clubs can be rented at the course's pro shop, and you can get instruction to improve your game if you wish. There are also many miniature golf courses to be found.

TENNIS: Tennis is popular, and there are many courts all over the country, both outdoor and indoor, including those at Saas-Fee and Flims. Most resorts have tennis courts, but if your hotel does not, you can probably use a local club for a nominal fee.

WATER SPORTS: You'll find opportunities for swimming at all altitudes in Switzerland, both at beaches along lakes and rivers and in pools. Most beaches are open from June to September or even longer in warmer regions, although if you grew up in hotter climes the water may be too cold for you in any season. Beaches are equipped for all manner of water sports. More and more of the big hotels provide indoor swimming pools, heated for use all year if you can't take the cold lakes. Sailing, waterskiing, windsurfing, and canoeing are all available.

HORSEBACK RIDING: St. Moritz and Arosa are both good centers for this recreational activity. Horse racing on the snow, in my opinion, is best left for connoisseurs. There are horses for rent at some 230 riding centers.

HANG-GLIDING: This dangerous and expensive sport is one of Switzerland's newest. The mountains and passes are subject to wind currents that may be exciting but are certainly scary, sometimes even for the most experienced gliders.

FISHING: The dedicated angler will find plenty of excitement in fishing some of Switzerland's abundant rivers, lakes, and streams. Trout are found in most waters up to altitudes of 6,000 feet. Lake trout have been known to weigh in at 22 pounds. You need a license to fish, but municipal authorities can get you one easily. Regulations vary from place to place, so to be sure you're legal, inquire at a hotel or local tourist office.

CYCLING: Riding a bicycle is both a sport and an economical way of touring the country. You can rent one for a small fee at many railroad stations and turn it in at another station. A bicycle can be transported on a passenger train for a nominal fee. You should reserve a bicycle at the station from which you plan to start a day or so ahead if possible.

The Swiss Touring Club maintains ten cycling centers throughout the country where you can rent bicycles and get brochures and maps of cycling circuits in the vicinity of the center. The touring club directs you along routes where there isn't much motor traffic, taking you through villages and past castles and manor houses you might not otherwise discover. Even in remote areas you can usually find someone with good enough English to help you if you have a problem or if you're lost.

HIKING: With 30,000 miles of well-marked and well-maintained walking paths, Switzerland is ideal for hikers. The paths lead through alpine valleys, over lowlands, up hills to meadows, or into the heart of the Alps. Whether you choose a gentle walk or a rigorous trek to the high areas, you will see unspoiled beauty such as alpine meadows luxuriant with blooming wildflowers, which make your hike worthwhile. Many hotels offer walking or hiking excursions.

4. THE ABCs OF SWITZERLAND

Before you check into your hotel, immediately upon your arrival in Switzerland, you'll need to know some "facts of life" to ease your adjustment into the country.

There are various customs, such as tipping, you'll need to know about. And a number of situations, such as a medical emergency, might arise during your vacation.

The concierge of your hotel, is a usually reliable dispenser of information, offering advice about everything. If he or she fails you, the following summary of pertinent survival data may prove helpful.

Note: Much of this ABC-type data, such as how to get from the Zurich airport into town, will be listed under the individual cities.

BANKS: Banks are usually open Monday through Friday from 8:30 a.m. to 4:30 p.m.; they are closed Saturday, Sunday, and legal holidays. Foreign currency may be exchanged at larger railroad stations and airports until 10 p.m. daily.

BUSINESS HOURS (OFFICES): Most offices are open on weekdays from 8 a.m. to noon and from 2 to 6 p.m.; closed Saturday.

CIGARETTES: Most popular U.S. brands can be found. However, there are many British- and Swiss-made brands you may want to try, especially if you like a mild cigarette. Cigars and pipe tobacco are available almost everywhere as well.

CLIMATE: The temperature range is about the same as in the northern United States but without extremes of hot or cold. Summer temperatures seldom rise above 80° F in the cities, and the humidity is low. Because of clear air and lack of wind in the high alpine regions, sunbathing is possible even in winter. In the southern part of Switzerland the temperature is mild year round, allowing sub-tropical vegetation to grow.

CURRENCY: The basic unit of Swiss currency is the **franc (F),** with banknotes issued for 10- to 1,000-franc denominations, and coins being minted in 5-, 10-, 20-, and 50-centime values as well as for 1, 2, and 5 francs. One franc is worth 100 centimes. As a general guideline, the price conversions in this book have been computed at the rate of 1.47 Swiss francs to $1 U.S. (1 F equals 68¢). Bear in mind, however, that international exchange rates are far from stable, and this ratio might be hopelessly outdated by the time you arrive in Switzerland. As a guide only, I'll include the following equivalents at the exchange rate given above, which may be invalid at the time of your trip.

Francs	U.S.$	Francs	U.S.$
1	.68	100	68.00
2	1.36	125	85.00
3	2.04	150	102.00
4	2.72	175	119.00
5	3.40	200	136.00
10	6.80	225	153.00
20	13.60	250	170.00
30	20.40	275	187.00
40	27.20	300	204.00
50	34.00	400	272.00
75	51.00	500	340.00

CUSTOMS: U.S. residents returning from abroad are allowed to bring back $400 in duty-free items for personal use only. To qualify, you must have been outside the United States at least 48 hours and not have claimed an exemption in the past 30 days. Articles valued in excess of $400 will be assessed at a flat duty rate of 10%. Antiques and original works of art produced 100 years prior to your date of re-entry to the United States may be brought home duty free, but you must be able to prove their authenticity. Gifts for your personal use, but not for business purposes, may be included in the $400 exemption. Gifts sent home from abroad may be valued at $50. Liquor is limited to one 32-ounce bottle; tobacco, to 200 cigarettes and 100 cigars. Keep all your receipts for purchases made in Switzerland or elsewhere on your trip abroad as you may be asked for proof of the prices you paid.

ELECTRIC CURRENT: The current used in Switzerland is 220 volts, alternating current (AC), 50 cycles. Some international hotels are specially wired to allow North Americans to plug in their appliances, but you'll usually need a transformer for your electric razor, hairdryer, or soft-contact-lens sterilizer. Ask at the electrical department of a large hardware store for the size converter you'll need. You'll also need an adapter to channel the electricity from the Swiss system to the flat-pronged American system. Don't plug anything into the house current in Switzerland without being certain the systems are compatible.

GAMBLING: A number of Swiss towns and resorts have casinos that, while perhaps not enjoying the affluence of casinos in other countries because of certain restrictions, still offer a wide choice of entertainment, including folklore displays. Gambling in Switzerland is restricted to *boule* games, and the maximum bet that can be placed is 5F ($3.40). The minimum age for gambling in Switzerland is 20.

HOTELS: The legend is that there's no such thing as a bad Swiss hotel. That's an old claim, and unfortunately it isn't as true as it once was. In most cases hotels in Switzerland are clean, comfortable, and efficiently run. On the deluxe level they are among the finest in the world (two in Zurich are, in fact, the very best in all of Europe). César Ritz, incidentally, who went on to other places, came from Switzerland. The hotel situation in general, however, isn't quite the same as it was in the good old days. Many Swiss citizens are lured to more attractive jobs (such as making Swiss watches) rather than scrubbing toilets. Foreign workers—many not as well trained as the Swiss—have been imported, and as a result many hotels report what is politely called "problems of staff." Even if standards aren't up to the legend, however, Swiss hotels are still among the finest in the world, taken as a whole. In one hostelry, when irate maids walked off the job, the manager rushed to scrub the bathtubs himself.

INFORMATION: Before you go, you can get the latest in tourist information from the **Swiss National Tourist Office,** 608 Fifth Ave., New York, NY 10020 (tel. 212/757-5944); 150 North Michigan Ave., Chicago, Ill. 60601, (312/630-5840); 250 Stockton St., San Francisco, CA (tel. 415/362-2260); and in Canada, P.O. Box 215, Commerce Court West, Toronto, Ont. M5L 1E8 (tel. 416/868-0584).

LEGAL HOLIDAYS: In Switzerland, January 1 and 2 (New Year), Good Friday, Easter Monday, Ascension Day, Whit Monday, Bundesfeier (August 1, the Swiss "Fourth of July"), and December 25 and 26 for Christmas are celebrated as legal holidays.

METRIC CONVERSION CHART: In Switzerland, you face a whole new way of measuring. Even the temperature (all-important in this country) will be expressed in Celsius. This chart will show you how to convert kilometers into miles, grams into pounds, meters into yards, and liters into ounces. Once you get the hang of it, it isn't as hard as it first appears.

Length
1 millimeter = 0.04 inches (*or* less than 1/16 in)
1 centimeter = 0.39 inches (*or* just under 1/2 in)
1 meter = 1.09 yards (*or* about 39 inches)
1 kilometer = 0.62 mile (*or* about 2/3 mile)

To convert kilometers to miles, take the number of kilometers and multiply by .62 (for example, 25 km × .62 = 15.5 mi).

To convert miles to kilometers, take the number of miles and multiply by 1.61 (for example, 50 mi × 1.61 = 80.5 km).

Capacity
1 liter = 33.92 ounces
= 1.06 quarts
= 0.26 gallons

To convert liters to gallons, take the number of liters and multiply by .26 (for example, 50 l × .26 = 13 gallons).

To convert gallons to liters, take the number of gallons and multiply by 3.79 (for example, 10 gal × 3.79 = 37.9 l).

Weight

    1 gram   = 0.04 ounces (*or* about a paperclip's weight)
    1 kilogram = 2.2 pounds

To convert kilograms to pounds, take the number of kilos and multiply by 2.2 (for example, 75 kg × 2.2 = 165 pounds).

To convert pounds to kilograms, take the number of pounds and multiply by .45 (for example, 90 lb × .45 = 40.5 kg).

Area

    1 hectare (100m²) = 2.47 acres

To convert hectares to acres, take the number of hectares and multiply by 2.47 (for example, 20 ha × 2.47 = 49.4 acres).

To convert acres to hectares, take the number of acres and multiply by .41 (for example, 40 acres × .41 = 16.4 hectares).

Temperature

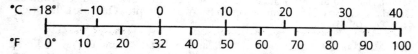

To convert degrees C to degrees F, multiply degrees C by 9, divide by 5, then add 32 (for example 9/5 × 20°C + 32 = 68°F).

To convert degrees F to degrees C, subtract 32 from degrees F, then multiply by 5, and divide by 9 (for example, 85°F − 32 × 5/9 = 29°C).

PASSPORTS AND VISAS: Every traveler entering Switzerland must have a valid passport, although it is not necessary for North Americans to have a visa if they do not stay longer than three continuous months. For information on permanent residence in Switzerland, as well as on work permits, get in touch with the nearest Swiss Consulate.

PETS: Dogs and cats brought into Switzerland from abroad will require a veterinary certificate stating that the animal has been vaccinated against rabies not less than 30 days and not more than one year prior to entry into the country. This regulation also applies to dogs and cats returning after a temporary absence from Switzerland but is not applicable to animals transported through the country by rail or air traffic.

POST OFFICES: Post offices in large cities are open from 7:30 a.m. to noon and 1:45 to 6:30 p.m. Monday to Friday, from 7:30 to 11 a.m. on Saturday. If you have letters forwarded to a post office to be collected after you arrive, you'll need a passport for identification. The words "Poste Restante" must be clearly written on the envelope. Letters not collected within 30 days are returned to the sender. It costs 1.10F (75¢) to send an airmail postcard to Canada and the United States. Airmail letters weighing up to 10 grams to Canada and the United States cost 1.40F (95¢), rising to 1.70F ($1.16) if the letter weighs from 10 to 20 grams. Both letters and postcards weighing up to 250 grams can be mailed for 50 centimes (34¢) to points within Switzerland.

SHOPPING: Switzerland's superb products make it a shopper's paradise, although it is an expensive indulgence. English is spoken in most shops and department stores. Fine watches come in a wide variety and are likely to sell at about half the price you'd pay back home. Excellent buys are textiles, embroideries, fine handkerchiefs, wool sportswear, and linen. Those luscious Swiss chocolates are to be found in many sizes, shapes, and flavors. The craftsmanship for which the country has long been noted is to be found in precision instruments, drafting sets, multiblade pocketknives, typewriters, music boxes, woodcarvings, ceramics, and other handmade items. Antiques and art books, ski clothes and equipment, and shoes are just a few of the fine articles you can buy in Switzerland.

SHOPPING HOURS: Shops are usually open Monday to Friday from 8 a.m. to 12:15 p.m. and 1:30 to 6:30 p.m., from 1:30 to 4 p.m. on Saturday. In large cities most shops do not close during the lunch hour, although many do so on Monday morning.

TAXES AND SERVICE CHARGES: No taxes are added to purchases in Switzerland. Swiss merchants pay tax to the government, but the percentage is included in the price marked on any object. Likewise, service charges are included in restaurant bills. If a service charge is not indicated, ask the waiter or waitress. The only unclear area is in taxicabs. Signs will be posted in the cab, and usually the tip is included, but sometimes it isn't.

In addition, motorists entering Switzerland are required by law to purchase a windshield sticker for 30F ($20.40), good for travel on Swiss roads for one year. Swiss drivers too have to pay the same tax, so at least it's democratic. Without a sticker on your shield, you can be subject to a $40 fine. Stickers are sold at all Customs posts upon entering Switzerland.

TELEPHONES: Always enter the phone booth with enough change, since your call will be cut off once your Swiss francs run out. The telephone system is well organized, reaching everywhere in the country, and it's entirely automatic. Helpful numbers to know are: 111 for directory assistance; 120 for tourist information or in winter for snow reports; 140 for help on the road; 162 for weather forecasts; and 163 for up-to-the-minute information on road conditions. It's possible to call your home collect. As in many European countries, it's considerably less expensive to make calls from a public phone booth, as substantial service charges are added for calls made at hotels.

To use a coin-operated telephone in Switzerland, you must lift the receiver and then insert 40 centimes (27¢) to get the dial tone. If you happen to insert more coins than necessary, the excess amount will be returned if the machine is working properly. Then proceed to make your call just as you do in the United States. Have additional coins on hand, as you are required to insert more for each message unit over your initial deposit. A pay phone will accept up to 5F ($3.40). To call a number in the area where you are, dial directly after you hear the dial tone (no area code needed). For other places in Switzerland, dial the area code and then the number, and to call a foreign country, dial first the code of the country, then the area code, and then the number. In this book, I have given the area code for each city and town visited.

TIME: Switzerland's clocks (and there are plenty of them) are always six hours ahead of Eastern Standard Time in the United States, and only one hour ahead of Greenwich Mean Time.

TIPPING: The tip—usually a 15% service charge—is automatically included on all hotel and restaurant bills. It's neither necessary nor expected for you to leave anything extra, although some people do if the service has been satisfactory.

TOILETS: Most Swiss public rest rooms are clean and modernized. Except, in this multilingual country, you'll have to know what you're looking for—be it WC, Toiletten, Toilettes, or Cabinetti. Women might be Damen or Frauen, Signore or Donne, Femmes or Dames, and men might be Herren or Männer, Signori or Uomini, Hommes or Messieurs. Most public rest rooms are at bus stations, railway termini, cable-car platforms, or wherever. There are never enough when you need one. You may have to rely on cafés, as many Swiss do. Most of the public lavatories are free; if not, have a 20-centime or 50-centime piece ready.

CHAPTER III

ZURICH

□ □ □

Deep in the heart of Helvetia, Zurich is the largest city in Switzerland. At an elevation of 1,332 feet, it sprawls across 36 square miles, with a population of 380,000, a decline since its 1960 high. The city is big enough to offer all the amenities a visitor would need, but it's also small enough to discover easily on your own.

At the northern end of Lake Zurich in northern Switzerland, Zurich is one of the most beautiful cities on the continent. Since it suffered no war damage, it still has very much a 19th-century appearance. Unlike French-speaking Geneva (which we'll visit later), Zurich is firmly German speaking (or rather, Zurichers speak "Schwyzerdütsch"). A *rue* becomes a *Strasse* in Zurich.

Zurich is the capital of a canton of the same name, having joined the Swiss Confederation in 1351. However, contrary to what many visitors erroneously think, it is not the capital of Switzerland, or at least it hasn't been since 1848. That distinction belongs to Bern.

Zurich is the leading tourist attraction of the country, and that's probably because it has the tiny nation's biggest airport and therefore becomes the natural gateway to Switzerland. The city is also heavily industrialized, but it isn't the Manchester of Switzerland. The factories run on electricity, which keeps the skies over Zurich from being polluted. It earns a fifth of the national income.

But it's far from being a dreary city of commerce. Zurich was a great center of liberal thought, having attracted Lenin, Carl Jung, James Joyce, and Thomas Mann. The Dadaist school was founded here in 1916.

Yet when Zurich makes the headlines today, it's usually in reference to being a center of international finance. The city's bankers have earned the unflattering name of the "gnomes of Zurich." The headquarters of five major banks lie on the Bahnhofstrasse alone. Virtual mountains of gold lie buried in vaults underneath these banks. To say the least, Zurich is a very wealthy city, and has been for centuries, since it first prospered as a textile center. Its gold trading and stock exchange are part of the legend of the city, which has come a long way since it was a Roman settlement known as Turicum.

1. AN ORIENTATION

Called the city by the lake, Zurich lies on both banks of the Limmat River and its tributary, the Sihl. Quays line the riverbanks and the lake. Overall, it's like a capital Y formed by the corner of the lake and the river. It spreads across a ravine in the eastern hills between the wooded slopes of the Zürichberg and the Käferberg hills and into the Glatt River valley.

In the heart of Europe, Zurich doesn't enjoy Riviera-type summers. Often in July and August it's possible to swim in the lake (which is never warm enough for Miami-reared me). Many days are likely to be chilly and cloudy, obscuring the view of the Alps in the distance. Spring and fall can be quite nippy, but when a sunny, bright clear day dawns, Zurich is one of the most enjoyable cities of Europe. It gets cold here in the winter, but not as severely as it does farther north. The temperature rarely goes below zero. The average temperature in January is 30°F, rising to an average of only 61°F in July.

A former seat of the Reformation, Zurich is staunchly Protestant (some say Puritan). It's known for its hard-working people, who are honest, industrious, and to many critics, too stiff and formal. But in spite of this reputation, it doesn't fold up at ten o'clock. Perhaps it would like to if it followed its own heart, but in the past two decades it has received too many foreign visitors who need entertainment, and being canny merchants, the Zurichers try to oblige.

Zurich might be said to have begun at the Lindenhof, and so might you in your orientation to the city. This square is the architectural heart and soul of historical Zurich. From here, you can survey the city as it rises on both banks of the Limmat from Bahnhofbrücke (*brücke* means "bridge") to Quaibrücke. Between these two bridges are four other spans over the river: Mühle-Steg, Rudbrunbrücke, Rathausbrücke, and Münsterbrücke.

Below this square runs the Bahnhofstrasse, one of the most elegant and expensive streets in the world. It begins in the west at the Hauptbahnhof, the railway station opening onto Bahnhofplatz, and runs east, crossing Paradeplatz, a converging point for trams and virtually the modern center of the city. This street of exclusive shops continues east to the lake.

Back at Paradeplatz, you can continue east, passing Fraumünster church and going across Münsterbrücke until you reach the right-hand side of the river, the Limmatquai, which with its many little narrow streets and alleyways is the second most significant shopping area of town. Running parallel to Limmatquai is the Niederdorfstrasse, the so-called red-light district of Zurich.

The old town, or Altstadt, in early medieval days had as its main centers the already mentioned Lindenhof as well as Fraumünster, Grossmünster, and St. Peter's. In time, it expanded to the Weinplatz, the oldest market square, and the Strehlgasse. By the 11th century, streets and centers such as Kirchgasse and Neumarkt had spilled over onto the right bank.

GETTING AROUND: Zurich is an easy city to get around in, after you make the fairly long trip in from the airport. The streetcars (trams) and buses of the city system are reliable and can take you to most areas you wish to visit. As mentioned in Chapter I, train service in Switzerland is excellent, and can be counted on to transport you to outlying points of interest not served by the Zurich transport system.

Flying In

Kloten Airport, the international airport of Zurich, is considered one of the ten most active in Europe—some 50 scheduled airlines use it (not to mention all the charter connections). It lies a long way from the center of Zurich, some seven miles in fact, and if you go by taxi you can count on paying a fare that may total 40F ($27.20) to 50F ($34) or more. A much cheaper way of going is by train, a feeder service operated by Swiss Federal Railways. For a fare of 4.60F ($3.15), you'll be delivered in less than ten minutes to the Zurich Hauptbahnhof, the main railway station. The train runs every 20 to 30 minutes, usually between the hours of 5:30 a.m. and 11 p.m. You can also go by bus (no. 68, Zurich Airport-Seebach), but this is more awkward, as you'll have to change to tram service (no. 14) for the center of town.

Public Transport

The public transport system of Zurich is operated by VBZ Züri–Linie, which has a modern and extensive network. Trams and buses run daily from 5:30 a.m. to midnight, every seven minutes at rush hours. There is no subway or underground, but rather a network of streetcars and buses, which for the most part originate at the Zurich Hauptbahnhof in the heart of the city, branching out to the suburbs.

Tickets are purchased on a self-service system from automatic vending machines that do not make change and are located at every stop. Tickets must be purchased before you get on a vehicle; and if you're caught without a valid ticket, you'll pay a fine of 30F ($20.40).

For a journey of up to five stops the fare is 1.50F ($1.02), for anywhere from six stops to the edge of town. Best bet for visitors is to order a "one-day ticket," costing 5F ($3.40) within the city network, and allowing you to travel on all buses and trams for 24 hours. For information about public transport in Zurich, call 01/211-50-10.

Car Rentals

All the major car-rental firms are represented at Kloten Airport. That includes **Avis** at 17 Gartenhofstrasse (tel. 01/242-20-40), and **Budget** at 9 Tödistrasse (tel. 01/44-43-34).

Before driving around Zurich, you should be armed with a street plan. Most such maps indicate multistory car parks within the city limits by a "P" sign for parking. The police of Zurich also publish a leaflet indicating all such parking garages.

Taxis

They are lethal in price—among the most expensive in Europe. Ride them only as a last resort. The only good thing about them is that the service charge is included in the fare. Taxis can be phoned. **Taxi-Zentrale Zürich,** for example, can be called at 01/44-44-41.

Bicycles

If you're energetic, bicycling is a good way to get around Zurich, especially in the outlying areas. Bicycles can be rented at the railway station for 12F ($8.15) per day.

PRACTICAL FACTS: To make your stay in Zurich more pleasurable, here are a few points of information you may find helpful.

Banks: In general, banks are open Monday to Friday from 8:15 a.m. to 4:30 p.m. (to 6 p.m. on Thursday). Two well-known banks are the **Union Bank of Switzerland,** at Shopville (tel. 01/234-11-11) and the **Swiss Bank Corporation,** 70 Bahnhofstrasse (tel. 01/211-31-71).

Children: During regular business hours, parents on a shopping expedition can park their children at either the Globus or Jelmoli Department Store.

Otherwise, call **Kady** (tel. 01/211-37-86), which has English-speaking babysitters.

Consulate: If you lose your passport or have some other such emergency, go to the U.S. Consulate, 141 Zollikerstrasse (tel. 01/55-25-66).

Currency exchange: Most banks and travel agencies will exchange money for you. There's also an exchange office at the Zurich Hauptbahnhof, the main railway station, open from 6:30 a.m. to 11:30 p.m., including Sunday.

Drugstore: An all-night drugstore is the **Bellevue Apotheke,** 14 Theaterstrasse (tel. 01/252-44-11).

Information: Visitors can find assistance at the **Zurich Tourist Office,** 15 Bahnhofplatz (tel. 01/211-40-00), the main railway station. From March to October, it's open Monday to Friday from 8 a.m. to 10 p.m. and on weekends from 8 a.m. to 8:30 p.m. November to February, it's open Monday to Thursday from 8 a.m. to 8 p.m., on Friday to 10 p.m., and on weekends from 9 a.m. to 6 p.m. There's a branch office at the airport (tel. 01/816-40-81), which is open daily year-round from 8 a.m. to 8 p.m.

Laundry: One of the best laundromats is **MM Speed-Wash,** 55 Mullerstrasse (tel. 01/242-99-14), in the vicinity of Stauffacher Strasse and Helvetia Platz. It is open from 7 a.m. to 10 p.m. Monday to Saturday, from 10:30 a.m. to 10 p.m. Sunday.

Lost property: There is a lost property office at 10 Werdmühlestrasse (tel. 01/216-25-50), open from 7:30 a.m. to 5:30 p.m. Monday to Friday.

Medical care: For first aid, illness, and accident cases, phone 01/47-47-00 or the **City Ambulance Service** at 01/361-61-61. There is an accident department at the **Cantonal University Hospital,** 8 Schmelzbergstrasse (tel. 01/255-11-11).

Police: In urgent emergency cases, call the **police** at 117.

Post office: The main post office is the Sihlpost, 95-99 Kasernenstrasse (tel. 01/245-41-11), just across the Sihl River from Löwenstrasse, which has an emergency service window always open. Most post offices—listed under "Post" in the phone directory—are open during regular business hours, from 7:30 a.m. to 6:30 p.m. However, they close at 11 a.m. on Saturday.

Religion: There are some 100 churches and other places of worship in Zurich, which has a strong religious tradition. Three synagogues are here. Of course, the list is too numerous for this limited space. However, the times of worship and address of various church services are given in a leaflet, *Zürcher Kirchen laden ein,* available at the tourist office.

Telecommunications: The telephone area code for Zurich is 01. A telephone and Telex office is open at the Zurich Hauptbahnhof, the main railway station, from 7 a.m. to 10:30 p.m. seven days a week.

2. ACCOMMODATIONS

Zurich is one of the most rewarding sightseeing targets in the country (and a few pages from now we'll see why). However, in Zurich we face what can indeed be a problem—finding an accommodation. Members of the international community of commerce, finance, and business fill up the top hotels of Zurich, and in addition, the city has frequent conventions and fairs. You can have trouble finding an accommodation even in February. If possible, then, you should arrive with a reservation. And be prepared to pay handsomely for your stay in Zurich, although I'll survey an array of moderately priced lodgings for the economizer.

These warnings aside, Zurich is an ideal place to get acquainted with Swiss hospitality. You're faced with at least 120 hotels and some 11,000 beds. They range from the most deluxe and sumptuously furnished suites in Europe (rivaled only by a few deluxe hotels in Asia) to a lowly pension that isn't so lowly (likely to be perched on a hillside and run by a kindly frau who keeps everything immaculate).

It's hard to find a dirty hotel in Zurich. Some of the cheaper accommodations may be a little rawbone in decor, but, chances are, they'll be well kept. You'll often end up in an *alkoholfrei* hotel, which means simply that they don't have a liquor license.

I'll start with a survey of the most expensive offerings, then descend the price scale. In other words, if you want the least expensive, read from the bottom of the list.

THE DELUXE CITADELS: A prestigious place to stay is the **Dolder Grand Hotel,** 65 Kurhausstrasse, CH-8023 Zurich, Switzerland (tel. 01/251-62-31), which still basks in the belle-époque era. The cogwheel funicular which connects this hotel to the center of Zurich is only one of the unusual features of an establishment noted around the world as the epitome of class, style, and comfort. I consider this the greatest hotel in all of Europe, as do many of the well-heeled clients from all over the world who frequent it. In days of yore, those clients included Einstein, Toscanini, Churchill, and even Henry Kissinger. Today you are likely to run into someone like movie actor and singer Yves Montand. Built on top of a wooded promontory of 50 acres in a conservative residential section of Zurich, the hotel is made up of two balconied wings with half-timbered replicas of watchtowers on the far ends that seem to pivot around an enormous dungeon capped with a soaring copper spire. Were it not for the carefully maintained flowerbeds, the modern annex extending off the back, and the conservatively dressed clients getting into or out of their limousines, you could almost imagine yourself gazing up at a building that, depending on your mood, is a medieval fortress, a Renaissance château, or a 19th-century pleasure palace.

You can enjoy the renovated ambience of the public rooms, including the Gobelin salon with its huge tapestry worth several small fortunes. The superb restaurant, La Rotonde, is staffed by a small army of Swiss technicians to serve your every culinary need. A continental breakfast is included in the room rates, which range from 220F ($149.60) to 300F ($204) daily in a single and from 340F ($231.20) to 450F ($306) for a double. The Dolder has 200 rooms, with 140 in the main building, which is about 90 years old. Its architecture has been called turn-of-the-century alpine spa style. A 60-room annex was added in 1964.

A private hotel limousine takes up to six persons to or from the railroad station or to or from the airport. The funicular and the sports facilities may be used free by guests on presentation of a pass available at the reception desk. Only six minutes from the center of Zurich, the hotel is surrounded by six tennis courts, an immaculately maintained nine-hole golf course, a swimming pool that can only be described as vast (with its own waves), and about the best-tended gardens to be found in a country full of well-kept landscapes, with beeches, birches, pines, and oaks. In winter, a skating rink is an attraction.

Baur au Lac, 1 Talstrasse, CH-8022, Zurich, Switzerland (tel. 01/221-16-50), is one of the great hotels of the world. It has been owned by the same family since it opened in 1844, next to the swan-dappled Schanzengraben Canal. The son of an Austrian baker, Johannes Baur wanted the hotel to have a view of Zürichsee (Lake Zurich) and the Alps. He got his wish. Quietly elegant, superbly located, and forever stylish, this Zurich landmark is cosmopolitan, grand, and luxurious. In the late 1800s members of the Prussian, Russian, and English royal families stayed here. In more modern times, it might have been Marc Chagall and, later, John Lennon. Today, it is likely to be Margaret Thatcher or Plácido Domingo. Sitting like a grand lady on the shore of the lake, the hotel has a unique location at the end of the fashionable Bahnhofstrasse. The façade of this stone building rises three stories above an idyllic private park that blossoms with red geraniums in summer.

Inside, guests are treated to some of the grandest hotel service in Europe. In rooms where Wagner and Franz Liszt entertained at the piano, they are today treated to Jugendstil glass, tapestries, antiques, marble floors, and floral carpet-

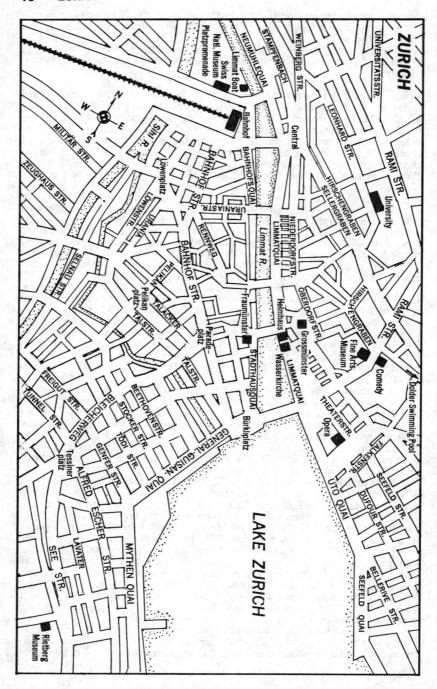

ing. All bedrooms and suites are luxuriously furnished in individual styles. Suites get the best antiques, of course, but regular rooms might be Empire or from one of the Louis periods, or even modern. These rooms are the ideal choice for those who appreciate the traditional amenities of a luxury class hotel of the highest standing—and can afford the cost. Singles range from 250F ($170) to 280F ($190.40) daily, with doubles costing from 430F ($292.40). Prices include tax, service, and a continental breakfast.

The dining facilities are among the finest in Zurich. The year-round Grill Room, decorated in an elegant rustic style, is a Zurich institution. It is especially popular with members of the Swiss business world at noon. Open in winter, the Restaurant Français, decorated in soft salmon tones, offers a French cuisine and vintages from the hotel's own wine cellar. The summertime Pavillon, open from May to October, enjoys a garden setting and evokes the 19th century.

Savoy Baur en Ville, 12 Poststrasse, CH-Zurich, Switzerland (tel. 01/211-53-60), is a conservative and refined hotel conscious of its role as one of the premier hotels of Zurich, conspicuously located on the Paradeplatz and rising grandly six floors above the exclusive stores around. The Baur en Ville has always been a Zurich landmark, and after recent renovations it's better than ever. Owned by bankers, the hotel has rooms that are quietly dignified, decorated in a wide range of styles. The public rooms are high-ceilinged, decorated either in a somber forest green with lots of wood detailing or, in the case of the main salon, in a vivid scarlet with white and gilt rococo adornment. All rooms are air-conditioned, although you'll be able to open the windows of those units with balconies if you want to catch a few minutes of sunbathing or choose to take breakfast on your terrace. Singles cost from 300F ($204) and doubles from 450F ($306), breakfast included.

The sidewalk café is one of the most frequented daytime establishments of the city, while the Restaurant Français is a top-notch restaurant.

Hotel Zurich, 42 Neumühlequai, CH-8001 Zurich, Switzerland (tel. 01/363-63-63), is one of the most preferred among all the high-rise modern hostelries of Zurich. Rising high above the banks of the Limmat, a short walk across the river from the railroad station, the hotel looks from the outside like a tasteful black-and-white tower of modern architecture. The views from the top are spectacular, showing to maximum advantage the spires and green parks of downtown Zurich.

The bedrooms are often sunny, well decorated, and well appointed with all the modern conveniences you'd expect in a deluxe hotel, including attractive bathrooms, many dramatically tiled in black or midnight blue. When you tire of the view from your room, the public bars, salons, and restaurants cater to a sophisticated, well-to-do crowd from around the world. Singles here rent for 180F ($122.40) to 220F ($149.60) daily, while doubles cost 220F ($149.60) to 320F ($217.60). Large by Zurich standards, with 221 rooms to select from, you won't lack for choice accommodations. Breakfast and use of the swimming pool are included in the tariffs.

Hilton International Zurich, CH-8058 Zurich, Switzerland (tel. 01/810-31-31), sprawling across several hundred yards of forested hillside near Kloten Airport, has curving wings that look like a well-ordered expanse of international railroad cars joined at the center by the panoramic windows of the restaurant and sun terrace. Many visitors in Zurich prefer the pastoral setting, which, despite the adjacent meadows, lies only 15 minutes by taxi or city bus from Zurich's downtown rail station. Since the airport closes every evening and the rooms are all soundproofed, sleepers aren't bothered by the noise of departing jets. Those who like to keep fit make use of the nearly two-mile outdoor exercise and jogging track, with 20 exercise or rest stations scattered along its length, plus an invigorating fitness program.

Many guests precede dinner with a drink at the Bonanza Bar, with live piano music. The hotel coffeeshop is suitable for light meals. Many guests prefer the open grill, copper sheathing, and meticulous service of Sutter's Grill. In the Taverne, the setting is a red-and-white-striped decor reminiscent of a mountain chalet, where accordion music accents the aromas from the raclettes and fondues. A branch of the Swiss Bank Corporation, a car-rental service, and a souvenir shop are on the premises. The bedrooms are sunny, well appointed with conservatively modern furniture, and filled with all the conveniences you'd expect from an international Hilton. Each is air-conditioned and contains a TV, radio, mini-bar, phone, and private bath. Doubles cost 210F ($142.80), with singles priced from 170F ($115.60) to 250F ($170), depending on the room assignment.

To get here from the main autobahn running between downtown Zurich and Kloten Airport, follow the signs to the Flughaven (the airport), getting off at the Glattbrugg/Opfikon/Kloten exit, which is the last one before the airport exit. From there, dark-yellow and black signs will point you to the nearby hill on which the hotel sits.

Hotel International Zurich, Am Marktplatz, CH-8001 Zurich, Switzerland (tel. 01/311-43-41), owned by the Swissôtel chain, offers excellent service and a modern streamlined format to clients. That the rooms are not just meant for sleeping is denoted by their practical and comfortable appointments: bathroom with hair dryer, writing table, mini-bar, direct-dial phone, radio, and color TV with in-house video. Facilities include a swimming pool, a sauna, and a fitness corner with a solarium on the 32nd floor, and the Panorama Grill and "Club" disco on the 31st, as well as a Chinese restaurant and a steakhouse. Elsewhere in the 700-bed complex are a coffeeshop, Brasserie restaurant, a Swiss bank, news kiosk, hairdresser, jewelry store, deluxe leather and gift shop, and, adjacent to the hotel, a shopping center with more than 30 boutiques and shops. Single rooms rent for 180F ($122.40) daily, while doubles cost 220F ($149.60).

The hotel has good tram service, with four separate lines extending to all parts of the city. There is also a train station adjacent to the hotel, with the downtown city center only a six-minute train ride away. A courtesy airport shuttlebus service has vehicles departing every half hour from the hotel from 6 a.m. to midnight. In addition to all these transportation possibilities, the Hotel International has an underground parking garage, with 450 spaces for the vehicles of guests.

Atlantis Sheraton Hotel, 234 Döltschwieg, CH-8055 Zurich, Switzerland (tel. 01/463-00-00), lies in a forested parkland at the foot of the Uetliberg. Bus service provided takes guests on frequent runs to the Hauptbahnhof, a 15-minute ride. With 224 rooms, the hotel has enough amenities to satisfy all your needs. The lobby area is tastefully decorated in steel grays and reds, with a burnished metal chimney tube descending from the ceiling to funnel smoke from the open fireplace safely upward. The staff is efficient and often includes local musicians who play Swiss band music.

The rooms are attractively decorated in shades of gray with wood detailing. Singles pay 240F ($163.20) to 280F ($190.40) daily for rooms, 360F ($244.80) to 420F ($285.60) for junior suites. Double rooms cost 320F ($217.60) to 360F ($244.80), with double occupancy junior suites going for 400F ($272) to 460F ($312.80). The cheapest accommodations lie at the far end of an underground tunnel in the "Guesthouse" annex, where singles rent for 155F ($105.40) and doubles for 175F ($119). In both areas of the hotel, breakfast, service, and taxes are included in the tariffs. However, no room service is available in the guesthouse. A pool and a fitness center can be used free by guests, who are also given free entrance at Le Club, an in-house disco.

Hotel Eden au Lac, 45 Utoquai, CH-8023 Zurich, Switzerland (tel. 01/47-94-04), is a grand hotel with an ornamented façade. From certain vantage points you could almost imagine yourself sleeping in the Paris Opera, because of the hotel's neoclassical columns, pediments, corner urns, and wrought-iron garlands of fruits and flowers. The walk from the hotel to downtown Zurich is like an old-fashioned promenade (be sure to allow plenty of time). You can bask in a little bit of nostalgia here, thanks to the efforts of the manager, R. A. Bärtschi, who was once described as the kind of administrator who has made Swiss hôteliers famous throughout the world. The hotel's French restaurant is one of the finest in Zurich. The service is among the best I encountered in this city, where the competition is keen for such a compliment.

Many bedrooms have a rose theme. Singles cost from 190F ($129.20) to 270F ($183.60), and doubles go for 330F ($224.40) to 420F ($285.60), breakfast included. All rooms have baths or showers, air conditioning, radios, TV, and private phones. The units in the rear are less expensive because they don't have views of the lake. The hotel is privately owned.

Hotel Ascot, 9 Tessinerplatz, CH-8002 Zurich, Switzerland (tel. 01/201-18-00), is one of the most stylish four-star hotels in Zurich, the beneficiary of expensive renovations that transformed its bedrooms into citadels of Italian style. Originally built in 1954, its six floors were overhauled in 1987. Today, even the façade (pink and maroon, with lots of both etched and unetched glass) looks new. Even if you don't stay here, the jazzed-up bar and restaurant (the Jockey Club) deserve serious attention (see "Where to Dine"). You register in a lobby filled with black-and-white checkerboard floors and mahogany paneling. The more expensive of the 73 bedrooms have patios, baths sheathed in Italian marble, intricately crafted paneling made from tropical woods, air conditioning, TV, phones, mini-bars, radios, and extra amenities. With breakfast, service, and taxes included, singles range from 130F ($88.40) to 190F ($129.20) daily, twins or doubles costing 190F ($129.20) to 290F ($197.20). The hotel sits in a residential/commercial neighborhood within a ten-minute walk from both the lake and the Bahnhofstrasse.

THE UPPER BRACKET: Long a favorite with the Swiss themselves is **Hotel St. Gotthard,** 87 Bahnhofstrasse, CH-8023 Zurich, Switzerland (tel. 01/211-55-00). On one of the main shopping streets, the St. Gotthard is only one block from the railroad station. The Hummer Bar specializes in lobster flown in from Canada and attracts a well-heeled clientele from all over the city. This and three other cosmopolitan restaurants—the Café St. Gotthard for snacks and pastries, the Steakhouse for the red meats you miss from back home, and La Bouillabaisse, a French restaurant known for seafood—make the St. Gotthard one of the premier rendezvous points on the Bahnhofstrasse. Throughout all of the bedrooms there is a rather plush decor, although if you can get an accommodation on the upper floors it will be far superior. Singles cost from 180F ($122.40) to 210F ($142.80) daily, while doubles rent for 250F ($170) to 320F ($217.60).

Hotel Zum Storchen, 2 Am Weinplatz, CH-8022 Zurich, Switzerland (tel. 01/211-55-10). Important visitors to Zurich have enjoyed the hospitality of this hotel for about 635 years. Paracelsus, Burgomaster Pfyffer, envoys of the Swedish king Gustavus Adolphus, Richard Wagner, and Gottfried Keller have all been among the illustrious guests partaking of the old Storchen's cuisine, cellar, and accommodations. It sits on a bank of the Limmat looking across the river to the floodlit Rathaus and is undeniably romantic. Dedicated to the stork, it supposedly took its name from nonpaying guests who nested on its roof. My favorite part of this beflowered hotel is the café terrace cantilevered above the sidewalk on granite columns hundreds of years old. From the terrace you'll be able to see a sweeping panorama of old Zurich without ever having to leave your *kaffeeklatsch.* A large statue of an enraged stork decorates the façade of Zum Storchen, wrapping itself around a corner of the building and advertising the place to the river traffic passing below. The Rôtisserie restaurant inside offers first-class facilities, complete with river views and ornate stucco ceilings. In the cocktail bar, lots of pewter tankards, warm colors, and stained glass welcome you to converse with local entrepreneurs and bankers.

Singles rent for 150F ($102) to 240F ($163.20) daily, while doubles cost from 240F ($163.20) to 360F ($244.80), breakfast included. Many in-the-know Swiss consider this place to be finer than any of the deluxe accommodations of Zurich. Since rooms are hard to get in summer, it's best to reserve ahead.

Hotel Schweizerhof, 7 Bahnhofplatz, CH-8001 Zurich, Switzerland (tel. 01/211-86-40), is a gabled and turreted structure whose façade is covered with flags and ornate columns in high relief against the stonework. In one of the city's busiest areas, the Schweizerhof, through the tram system, is convenient to everything in town. The public rooms are pleasing and unpretentious, painted in clear colors with subdued furniture clustered into appealing conversational groupings. This is a grand old station hotel in the tradition so beloved at the turn of the century. People no longer arrive with trunks and maidservants (the doorman confided that some of today's guests bring a "change of underwear" and little else), but the Schweizerhof goes on. Recent major renovations have been highly successful, keeping the hotel in step with the times. The ideal rooms are the semi-circular corner units. The 115 units cost from 160F ($108.80) to 240F ($163.20) daily for a single and from 240F ($163.20) to 360F ($244.80) for a double, each with breakfast, a modern bath, air conditioning, radio, TV, mini-bar, and direct-dial phone. A French restaurant and well-appointed bar area are to be found on the premises, as well as a coffeeshop, Le Gourmet.

Hotel Simplon, 16 Schützengasse, CH-8023 Zurich, Switzerland (tel. 01/211-61-11), is opposite the Hotel St. Gotthard in a sought-after location, although a quick review of the prices will reveal that this is one of the special hotel bargains on this side of the river. The Simplon offers 115 beds priced at 115F ($78.20) daily for a single with bath, 60F ($40.80) for a bathless single. Doubles cost 90F ($61.20) to 170F ($115.60), depending on the plumbing. Rooms are spacious, filled with modern furniture, and have sunny views from most windows. The façade is one of those fine, solid pieces of masonry breathing reliability, as so many of the buildings in Zurich do. A disco, Birdwatchers, is a popular and rather exclusive dancing spot for nightlife lovers.

Hotel Opera, 5 Dufourstrasse, CH-8008 Zurich, Switzerland (tel. 01/251-90-90), offers 100 beds in a clean, well-maintained, and cozy atmosphere of Swiss efficiency. Next to the Opera House, the hotel has a large, attractive lobby area with an assortment of comfortable armchairs spread over a warmly patterned carpet. You should try for a room on the top floor here because they're the best, although the rooms on the lower floors are perfectly satisfactory. All rooms are soundproof and fully air-conditioned, with radios, color TVs, and mini-bars. Singles with modern bathrooms rent for 115F ($78.20) to 150F ($102) daily, doubles cost from 200F ($136) to 240F ($163.20), and triples go for 220F ($149.60) to 270F ($183.60). Rates include a buffet breakfast. The hotel maintains a bus departing for Kloten Airport every 1½ hours during the day.

The largest hotel in Switzerland, **Hotel Nova-Park,** 420 Badenerstrasse, CH-8040 Zurich, Switzerland (tel. 01/491-22-22), is a modern complex whose lobby, restaurants, and rooms are adorned with sculpture, paintings, and a dramatic color scheme. Only ten minutes from the center of town, the hotel is connected by a good network of bus and tram lines. Some 365 rooms are equipped with radios, TVs, mini-bars, and phones. The units, recently renovated, rent for 140F ($95.20) to 220F ($149.60) daily for a single, 185F ($125.80) to 265F ($180.20) in a double. All rooms have audio-visual hookups, which can receive films in seven languages, including English. This was the first hotel in Europe possessing a comprehensive audio-visual installation, with in-house cable TV allowing programs to be transmitted simultaneously throughout the hotel and onto a wide screen in the Nova Business Center. The availability of fitness facilities, six restaurants, and a disco make this property a popular gathering spot for locals and tourists alike. The Nova-Park also boasts the largest fitness center with a therapy center in Switzerland and the first indoor golf course in Zurich.

Seiler Hotel Neues Schloss, 17 Stockerstrasse, CH-8022 Zurich, Switzerland (tel. 01/201-65-50), lies conveniently close to some of the most prestigious (and far more expensive) hotels of Zurich, a few steps from the Kongresshalle, the lake, and tram lines 7, 8, 10, and 13 at tramhalt Stockerstrasse. The hotel is an unobtrusive gray building, art deco detailing modestly covering its exteriors and balconies curving around its corners. The comfortable and conservative interior is warmly decorated in autumnal colors, and big windows let in the bright sun. Each of the 59 rooms has a color TV, mini-bar, radio, phone, and private bathroom. Prices range from 165F ($112.20) to 190F ($129.20) daily for a single, from 240F ($163.20) to 290F ($197.20) for a double. Breakfast, taxes, and service are included in the price. A member of the family-owned Seiler Hotel chain, the establishment contains a comfortable restaurant, Le Jardin, favored by lunching bankers and business people on the ground floor. Joggers and nature lovers will find a handful of lakeside parks nearby.

Hotel Waldhaus Dolder, 20 Kurhausstrasse, CH-8030 Zurich, Switzerland (tel. 01/251-93-60), is surrounded by forests in the Dolder residential section of Zurich. A nine-hole golf course and 19 tennis courts, along with mini-golf and a swimming pool, make this an experience in country living. The hotel rises high above the surrounding trees, with balconies, some with awnings, on every floor. The spacious bedrooms are decorated in comfortably upholstered sofas and armchairs, with big windows to let in the forest light. Manager Hans Jorg Tobler rents singles with modern baths, balconies, and views of the lake and the mountains for 150F ($102) to 220F ($149.60) daily, with doubles (which actually comprise what is almost a two-room private apartment) going for 220F ($149.60) to 320F ($217.60), with breakfast included. The rustic restaurant has a collection of 19th-century saws and woodworking tools hanging on the walls.

Seehotel Meierhof, Bahnhofstrasse, CH-8810 Zurich-Horgen Switzerland (tel. 01/725-29-61), a modern steel-and-concrete hotel, lies ten miles from the center of Zurich on the south shore of the lake. The restaurant offers a panoramic view of the lake, but the decor is angular, metallic, and somewhat stark. Guests have a covered swimming pool at their disposal, and several discos and shopping areas are nearby. Rooms inside tend to be small, and although a rail line separates the hotel from the lake, the units facing in that direction are the more desirable ones. Singles rent for 120F ($81.60) to 160F ($108.80) daily, and doubles cost 160F ($108.80) to 220F ($149.60). Accommodations contain private baths, phones, radios, TVs and mini-bars and include a generous breakfast in the price. Guests can take a public ferryboat to the piers of Zurich from a pier near the hotel, or they can go by train.

Novotel Zurich Airport, CH-8152 Zurich-Glattbrugg, Switzerland (tel. 01/810-31-11). If your schedule requires that you spend the night near Kloten Airport, this might be an ideal choice. Don't worry about being awakened in the night by the scream of jet engines: Zurich city ordinances prohibit airline departures or arrivals after 11 p.m. The airport is only five minutes away, and you can be in downtown Zurich in just 20 minutes. Known for its streamlined rooms and check-in, the Novotel offers 256 comfortable bedrooms, each with private bath and TV set. Singles go for 120F ($81.60) to 150F ($102) daily, and doubles for 140F ($95.20) to 170F ($115.60). There is also garage parking. In the evening, a piano bar in the lobby is popular, attracting a host of the international business crowd. After that, guests patronize Le Grill, a good restaurant offering food service until midnight daily. Specialties include a smoked fish plate, dried meat and cheese, and chipped veal in a well-flavored cream sauce served with Rösti. There is also a special children's menu (Novotel, in fact, caters to children, who find games waiting for them in the lobby). Check-in is expedited with the use of carts on wheels (it also avoids expensive tipping). The hotel opened in the autumn of 1986.

Hotel Glockenhof, 31 Sihlstrasse, CH-8023 Zurich, Switzerland (tel. 01/

211-56-50), is a modern hotel halfway between the train station and the lake. A sunny courtyard contains a café-terrace with parasols, while the spacious lobby offers leather-upholstered chairs ideal for reading the local newspapers. Bedrooms are comfortable and invitingly decorated with dark carpeting and an occasional Oriental rug. They all contain full baths, cosmetic bars, mini-bars, phones, and color TV. The Glogge-Egge restaurant is warmly surrounded with wooden planks, hanging lights, and lots of brickwork. Singles rent for 135F ($91.80) daily, and doubles cost 210F ($142.80), with a buffet breakfast included.

Hotel Glarnischlof, 30 Claridenstrasse, CH-8022 Zurich, Switzerland (tel. 01/202-47-47), looks from the outside like one of those forbiddingly anonymous Swiss banks that seem to dot the street corners in downtown Zurich. The interior, however, is warmly paneled in light-colored woods, with patterned rugs and elegant armchairs. Each of the 70 rooms has its own bath and spacious, high-ceilinged dimensions. Three deluxe junior suites have whirlpool baths. Single rooms rent for 140F ($95.20) to 180F ($122.40) daily, while doubles cost 190F ($129.20) to 260F ($176.80), with a buffet breakfast included. The establishment contains a grill room, a snack restaurant, and a bar. Since you're in the midst of the financial district here, you'll be close to everything in town. Urs Mathys, the manager, runs his hotel as part of the Best Western hotel chain.

THE MEDIUM BRACKET: Dating from the 16th century, **Hotel Kindli**, 1 Pfalzgasse, CH-8001 Zurich, Switzerland (tel. 01/211-59-17), stands at the end of a steep little street in the old town, Rennweg. It mixes the antique with the contemporary in a blend that makes it one of my favorite little hotels in the city. Painted a pastel gray, the exterior shelters cozy and well-planned bedrooms furnished in an eclectic mix. Each contains a bathroom, color TV, a radio, and an icebox. Singles cost 120F ($81.60) daily, with doubles going for 140F ($95.20) to 190F ($129.20). The view from the windows reveals perspectives of the old town that can't be had from the street below. A favorite aspect of this place is the folk singing of Willi Schmid, owner of the establishment, who, with his orchestra and international singing stars, plays to a full house practically every night of the week. (For more information, see the nightlife section.)

Hotel Ambassador, 6 Falkenstrasse, CH-8008 Zurich, Switzerland (tel. 01/261-76-00). Staying here is about the most practical way to get a view of the lake but avoid paying the monstrous "lakeside view" prices so popular in Zurich hostelries. You'll be near the opera and the Bellevueplatz and within one block of the lake. The staff does everything it can to treat you "like royalty." All rooms are soundproof and contain baths or showers, radios, mini-bars, and phones, as well as color TV. The rooms tend to be irregularly shaped, which lends character, and if you ever tire of the view from your window, you can descend to street level to sample the specialties of the popular sidewalk café below. Singles rent for 120F ($81.60) to 150F ($102) daily, and doubles cost 180F ($122.40) to 240F ($163.20). A crib can be set up in any room. Rates include a buffet breakfast.

Hotel Helmhaus, 30 Schifflandeplatz (corner of Limmatquai), CH-8001 Zurich, Switzerland (tel. 01/251-88-10), originally built in 1356, is a simple hotel rising six unadorned stories above the boatlanding square, a block from the river. Shops fill the space on the ground floor, and in its category it's one of the best hotels in Zurich. The establishment, under the direction of Anni Guler, is extremely well run and presents good value. Singles cost from 115F ($74.80) to 118F ($80.25) daily, and doubles run from 150F ($102) to 185F ($125.80). All units have at least a toilet and shower, and many of them have a bathtub too, along with color TV, radios, mini-bars, and direct-dial phones. Since the hotel was renovated in 1984, many of the rooms contain mod geometrically patterned curtains and contoured chairs, and all are comfortable and impeccable. A generous buffet breakfast is included in the price. Light meals are available in the evening between 6:30 and 8:30. A little shuttle bus takes two persons between the airport and the city.

Hôtel du Théâtre, 69 Seilergraben, CH-8023 Zurich, Switzerland (tel. 01/252-60-62). The first thing you'll notice when approaching this modern hotel is the emphasis that the management places on art. A life-size statue of a nude woman struggling to escape the captivity of the stone from which she's carved greets you near the entrance, while a dramatically colored abstract collage of intricately worked metal hangs over a 20-foot expanse of the façade. The rooms are comfortable and not without their own unusual prints and artwork. The hotel is attractively located near the central zone of the Zurich tram system, with direct lines to practically everything in town. Singles go for 86F ($58.50) to 100F ($68) daily, while doubles cost from 110F ($74.80) to 140F ($95.20), breakfast included, all with private bath and soundproof windows.

Hotel Chesa Rustica, 70 Limmatquai, CH-8001 Zurich, Switzerland (tel. 01/251-92-91), lies five minutes from the train station, about two blocks from the Rathaus. Some visitors have said that it's so cozy it could easily be an inn instead of a big-city hotel, a feeling enhanced by the fact that it contains only 23 rooms. The counter in the lobby is fashioned from an antique piece of Swiss cabinetry whose naïve designs reflect another era of craftsmanship. Throughout the hotel are placed items of genuine beauty, such as antique clocks and hanging cupboards containing hand-painted china. Rooms, comfortably furnished and spacious, cost from 105F ($71.40) to 145F ($98.60) daily, in a single, from 150F ($102) to 220F ($149.60) in a double, breakfast included. All units have baths, phones, private bars, radios, TVs, soundproof windows, and a rustic ambience that helps you to imagine yourself far away in the Alps.

Hotel Ermitage am See, 80 Seestrasse, CH-8700 Küsnacht-Zurich, Switzerland (tel. 01/910-52-22). Zurich is surrounded by several small suburbs, and Küsnacht is only seven minutes by car from the center of town. This hotel offers 46 beds in a lakeside ambience of panoramic windows, large trees, and all the character of a large country house. Many of the units open onto balconies, which welcome in large doses of fresh air and sunshine, and all of them have bathrooms and modern conveniences. The public rooms are painted a clear white and contain vivid carpeting and scattered Oriental rugs, fine furniture, and an airy, spacious feeling of well-being. A private lakefront beach and well-maintained grounds are for the use of guests, along with a warmly decorated bar area. The French restaurant offers candlelight dinners in an elegant setting every night. Single rooms cost 120F ($81.60) to 130F ($88.40) daily, and doubles rent from 170F ($115.60) to 210F ($142.80). Rooms facing the lake are of course more expensive.

Hotel Montana, 39 Konradstrasse, CH-8005 Zurich, Switzerland (tel. 01/271-69-00), is three minutes north of the Hauptbahnhof in a six-story building with two bluish-white neon signs illuminating both the façade and the portico over the sidewalk. An underground garage in the basement makes arrival easy for motorists. The public rooms are streamlined and comfortable, bedrooms are impeccably clean and warmly appointed with monochromatic themes. Singles cost 95F ($64.60) daily, and twins go for 145F ($98.60). All units have bathrooms and color TV and come with breakfast.

Arc Royal Comfort Inn, 6 Leonhardstrasse, CH-8001 Zurich, Switzerland (tel. 01/261-67-10), is one of the most modern bed-and-breakfast hotels in downtown Zurich. It's operated by Peter and Mervé Vogel. Greeted at the front door by a rounded awning advertising the name of the hotel, you'll be served by a staff that tries to give personalized attention to the inhabitants of the hotel's 58 rooms. All rooms have modern bathrooms, phones, radios, color TV, and minibars. There's an airport bus service, a round-the-clock Telex service for business clients, and an underground garage for easy parking. Singles here cost 120F

($81.60) to 130F ($88.40) daily, doubles go for 160F ($108.80) to 170F ($115.60), and triples are priced at 170F ($115.60) to 180F ($122.40).

Spirgarten Hotel and Restaurant, 5 Am Lindenplatz, CH-8048 Zurich, Switzerland (tel. 01/62-24-00), offers clean and well-maintained rooms with the kind of oversize windows that are soundproof when closed and pivot on a horizontal pin to let in lots of sunshine and fresh air. The hotel is set up to accommodate groups of people either for large conferences or small reunions in a wide assortment of modern rooms. Whenever you walk through the lobby, you'll see lots of dark-suited businessmen, here either as hotel guests or to attend meetings. Singles rent for 65F ($44.20) daily bathless, 100F ($68) for a single with bath. Doubles, all with bath, cost 140F ($95.20) to 160F ($108.80). All units have phones and radios. Most guests go into the city center by train.

Hotel Seegarten, 14 Seegartenstrasse, CH-8008 Zurich, Switzerland (tel. 01/252-37-37), lies just off the eastern shore of the lake in a pleasant residential section of Zurich built in the 19th century. The hotel is a renovated older building, and all units have mini-fridges and TV on request. An awning identifies the restaurant section of the hotel, which serves well-prepared Italian food in a mellow atmosphere of brown and beige walls with wood trim and hanging brass lamps. Singles cost from 95F ($64.60) to 110F ($74.80) daily, and doubles go from 120F ($81.60) to 170F ($115.60). Each room is equipped with phone, radio, and in all but the cheapest units, private bath and toilet. Breakfast is included.

Hotel Franziskaner, 1 Niederdorfstrasse, CH-8001 Zurich, Switzerland (tel. 01/252-01-20), is a small, 20-room hotel of long standing in the historic part of Zurich. The building is on a cobblestone square where a helmeted warrior stands above a Renaissance fountain. The interior is a classy combination of fine woodwork, warm colors, brass candelabra, and wrought iron. The bedrooms are clean and comfortable, and rent for 95F ($64.60) to 130F ($88.40) daily in a single, 125F ($85) to 180F ($122.40) in a double, with a buffet breakfast included. All units have private baths. A bistro-style restaurant, a busy meeting place for the "in" crowd of Zurich, serves everything from snacks to full meals from 7 a.m. to midnight daily year round.

Hotel Olympia, 324 Badenerstrasse, CH-8040 Zurich, Switzerland (tel. 01/491-77-66). The façade of this family-run hotel curves gracefully around a street corner in the northern part of Zurich. Easily accessible to the rest of the city (if you don't mind taking tramline 2, 3, or 10), the hotel is comfortably furnished and decorated with wall-size murals of classical ruins. The bar and kitchen are directed with first-class flair. Single rooms cost from 80F ($54.40) to 105F ($71.40) daily, while doubles rent for anywhere from 90F ($61.20) to 115F ($78.20), which gives you a wide choice of plumbing options as well as a free breakfast.

Hotel Stoller, 357 Badenerstrasse, CH-8040 Zurich, Switzerland (tel. 01/492-65-00), conveniently located next to several major tram lines, is an old-fashioned hotel offering 118 beds to travelers who are immediately placed at ease by the helpful staff, ably directed by W. Stoller. The salons are decorated in grained heavy furniture that seems to symbolize at a glance the aesthetic taste of the *haute bourgeoisie* 100 years ago. Some of the Oriental carpets are boldly patterned in muted colors, while the dining room is tastefully lit and decorated with wood paneling. Comfortably furnished singles rent for 140F ($95.20) to 150F ($102) daily, and doubles go for 190F ($129.20) to 210F ($142.80). Triples are available in limited numbers, costing 250F ($170).

Hotel Rigihof, 101 Universitätstrasse, CH-8033 Zurich, Switzerland (tel. 01/361-16-85), is on a busy street in the university section. It is modern, functional, and efficient, with an angular lobby area and a dining room crowned by an intricate geometrical ceiling. This is not the kind of hotel where the decorator went in for soft curves, but everything is clean and well run. The outdoor terrace can be lovely on a hot day. Rooms are priced depending on whether they're on the street side or the quiet, rear courtyard, costing from 110F ($74.80) to 125F ($85) daily for a single, from 140F ($95.20) to 170F ($115.60) in a double, with breakfast included, in rooms with private baths, TV with video, radios, minibars, and phones.

Hotel Limmathaus, 118 Limmatstrasse, CH-8031 Zurich, Switzerland (tel. 01/271-52-40), is easily reached by tram 13 or 4 to the Limmatplatz (it's only three stops). The 120-bed hotel has recently been renovated, and now more units have shower, toilet, and even new windows. The furnishings are modern. A single without shower costs 60F ($40.80) daily, a double without shower, 76F ($51.68). These are the bargain rooms. A double with shower or bath, along with a toilet, ranges in price from 125F ($85) to 135F ($91.80), whereas triples with the same plumbing go for 145F ($98.60) to 155F ($105.40). These tariffs include breakfast, service, and taxes.

Hotel Florhof, 4 Florhofgasse, CH-8001 Zurich, Switzerland (tel. 01/47-44-70), quickly gives a sense of being indeed a glamorous hotel. You'll arrive at a paved walkway leading to the double staircase of a large, patrician house, which was formerly, I was told, a private residence. The blue of the façade is repeated in the blue-and-white Swiss tile oven that heats the dining room inside. Some of the bedrooms still have their high molded-plaster ceilings, and all of them contain private baths. Singles cost 105F ($71.40) to 145F ($98.60) daily, while doubles range from 150F ($102) to 210F ($142.80), including breakfast.

Hotel Sternen, 335 Schaffhauserstrasse, Oerlikon, CH-8050 Zurich, Switzerland (tel. 01/311-77-77), sits quietly in a Zurich suburb between the city center and the airport. Many of the tram lines pass through Oerlikon, so getting there is not a problem. The hotel, like many of the buildings around it, is constructed in a kind of internationally modern style, with a façade broken into various planes of angles and colors. Rooms inside are predictably comfortable, while many of the public rooms are dramatically decorated in dark colors with lots of Oriental rugs. Singles cost from 60F ($40.80) to 90F ($61.20) daily, doubles from 110F ($74.80) to 150F ($102), and triples from 150F ($102) to 180F ($122.40), breakfast included. Not all units have private baths.

Hotel Trümpy, 9 Sihlquai, CH-8005 Zurich, Switzerland (tel. 01/271-54-00). The octagonal spires of the National Museum rise only a block away from this grand old building near the railroad station. Its buff-colored façade usually flies a Swiss flag over its roofline, with a canopy sheltering the sidewalk café from the direct rays of the sun. The lobby has a large stone fountain spewing water from a human head in bas-relief against one wall, and there's a muted collection of Oriental rugs. Bedrooms are comfortably appointed and sometimes come in a vivid choice of colors. All rooms have modern baths with accessories, TVs, soundproof windows, radios, and phones. The dining room serves good meals. With breakfast included, singles cost from 120F ($81.60) to 145F ($98.60) daily, and doubles range from 140F ($95.20) to 180F ($122.40).

THE BUDGET CATEGORY: For many years, **Hotel Bristol,** 34 Stampfenbachstrasse, CH-8035 Zurich, Switzerland (tel. 01/47-07-00), has been one of the best known and most successful budget hotels of Zurich. It lies on a small hill near the main train station, in back of the major road to the airport, with a ramp at street level that leads you to the main entrance of the hotel. Bedrooms are well maintained, frequently renovated, and simply furnished. No alcoholic beverages are allowed. The hotel has an elevator and a large TV room with a wide screen for the use of its guests in one of the public rooms. The Bristol offers 100 beds in singles that, breakfast included, cost from 55F ($37.40) to 80F ($54.40) daily and in doubles priced at 75F ($51) to 120F ($81.60). The higher prices are for rooms with private bath. All units have radios, direct-dial phones, and color TV.

Hotel Leonhard, 136 Limmatquai, CH-8001 Zurich, Switzerland (tel. 01/251-30-80), is in the old city, two minutes on foot from the main railroad station. The establishment is owned by the Leonhard family, who charge 115F ($78.20) daily for a single, 130F ($88.40) for a double, with breakfast included. All the rooms have twin beds, private baths, color TVs, radios, wake-up alarms, safes, and direct-dial phones. A typical Swiss restaurant is on the premises.

Pension St. Josef, 64/68 Hirschengraben, CH-8001 Zurich, Switzerland (tel. 01/251-27-57), is a Catholic hotel run by Sister Michelle, who welcomes visitors from around the world. Only six minutes on foot from the central station, the establishment is clean, strictly run, and represents good value for the money. Singles are priced at 45F ($30.40) to 50F ($34) daily, doubles at 65F ($44.20) to 70F ($47.60), and triples at 85F ($57.80). Units are clean, comfortable, and safe, especially for women traveling alone.

Hotel Vorderer Sternen, 22 Theaterstrasse, CH-8001 Zurich, Switzerland (tel. 01/251-49-49), stands on the shore of the lake on the famous Bellevueplatz, which has excellent tram connections to every part of the city. The hotel looks like a small rectangular building with a gabled roof, the kind you'd find in dozens of typical Swiss towns, but it has the Boulevard Restaurant at street level and a garden restaurant with a terrace one flight up. The ten bedrooms, none with private bath, are simple, but everything is clean, scrubbed every day. There is hot and cold running water in the units, and shared showers are off the hallways. Including breakfast, prices are 50F ($34) to 60F ($40.80) daily in singles, 70F ($47.60) to 80F ($54.40) in doubles. The management here is cooperative.

Jolie Ville Motor Inn, 105 Zürichstrasse, CH-8134 Adliswil, Switzerland (tel. 01/710-85-85), constructed in 1966 as part of the Mövenpick chain, is in the suburb of Adliswil, south of Zurich on the southwest edge of the lake. You can get there by taking tram 7 and bus 84 from downtown Zurich. Many visitors tend to be motorists who don't want to negotiate city traffic. Most of the rooms are rustically paneled, and all are clean and comfortably furnished. From the outside the place looks like a low-lying modern building with bright red awnings. All rooms have twin beds that can be pushed together to form a double. Singles are charged 78F ($53.05) to 96F ($65.30) daily, and doubles pay 103F ($70.05) to 121F ($82.30). A rustically decorated restaurant (also managed by Mövenpick) lies in a half-timbered grangelike building 500 yards away.

Hotel Krone, 88 Limmatquai, CH-8001 Zurich, Switzerland (tel. 01/251-42-22). The original building on this spot dates back to the beginning of the 17th century, although the hotel you'll see today has had many facelifts. The location is only 500 yards from the railroad station and a few steps from Bahnhofstrasse, and you'll have a view of the Limmat if your windows happen to face that way. The interior is decorated in a series of pleasing beiges and creams, with warmly patterned Oriental rugs reflecting the sepia tones of the woodwork's detailing. The hotel offers only 25 rooms. Singles, all bathless, rent for 48F ($32.65) to 58F ($39.45) daily. Bathless doubles cost 78F ($53.05) to 90F ($61.20), and doubles with bath go for 95F ($64.60) to 115F ($78.20). Breakfast is included in the prices.

Hotel Bahnpost, 6 Reitergasse, CH-8004 Zurich, Switzerland (tel. 01/241-32-11), has the double benefit of being smack in the center of Zurich without being too noisy. With 44 beds, this place is among the best in its price range. Don't expect much in the way of a lobby or a lounge, but the rooms here are a good choice for people who like to spend most of their day out exploring, retiring to the hotel only for sleep—or whatever. Some of the rooms are covered with painted paneling, and all of them have color TV and hot and cold running water. Singles cost from 56F ($38.10) daily, doubles from 86F ($58.50), triples from 112F ($76.15), and quads from 125F ($85), with breakfast included. An Italian restaurant on the premises, the Balestra, serves good meals.

Hotel Martahaus, 36 Zähringerstrasse, CH-8001 Zurich, Switzerland (tel. 01/251-45-50). Because of its popularity with budget travelers, it's often very hard to get a room here during summer. The hotel offers 85 beds in rooms sleeping one, two, three, or six persons, none of which contains a private bathroom, although a sink is in each of the units. The establishment is ideally located, within walking distance of the main station. Rooms are not luxurious, but at these prices, who expects art? Singles go for 46F ($31.30) daily, doubles for 70F ($47.60), and triples for 84F ($57.10). In the upstairs dormitories holding six beds, each bed costs 23F ($15.65) per person. Showers are on each floor, and breakfast is included in the price.

3. WHERE TO DINE

More than 1,200 restaurants, with a widely diversified cuisine ranging from Swiss to foreign, are at your culinary disposal in Zurich. Obviously I've had to do some powerful trimming to come up with my own preferred list, which, although modest in size, still covers a diverse gastronomic range that should also appeal to a wide range of tastes and purses.

As for Zuricher specialties, Rösti (potatoes grated and fried) is one of my all-time favorite Swiss dishes. You might also try Züri-Gschnätzlets (shredded veal cooked with mushrooms in a cream sauce laced with white wine) and kutteln nach Zürcherart (tripe with mushrooms, white wine, and caraway seed). Another classic dish is leberspiesschen (liver cubes skewered with bacon and sage and served with potatoes and beans). Zouftschriibertopf is a potpourri of bacon, grilled meat, and mushrooms.

Among local wines, the white Riesling Sylvaner is outstanding (the vines were first cultivated along Lake Zurich). For a typical fish platter, a Zuricher often prefers a white räuschling. The light Clevner wines, always chilled, are made from blue Burgundy grapes growing around the lake. Even in first-class restaurants you can order wine by the glass.

THE UPPER BRACKET: One of the brightest luminaries of European gastronomy is **Agnès Amberg,** 5 Hottingerstrasse (tel. 01/251-26-26). The haute cuisine dispensed here is inspired by a woman author who has devoted most of her life to turning out epicurean delights and writing about them in her many books on cuisine. At her table in Zurich, you'll be served one of your most elegant and sumptuous repasts in Switzerland, pleasing to both the palate and the eye. A fine way to begin your meal is to order the fresh foie gras fashioned into a delectable terrine or a pâté of duckling. One salad, available seasonally, is made with sweetbreads. Or perhaps you might like to select mussel soup with curry. Among the more recommendable main courses (if they're available on the night of your visit) are St. Pierre farci (stuffed John Dory) de poireaux (leeks) au beurre blanc (white butter), lobster in Sauterne, guinea fowl with honey, and sea bass in a saffron sauce. The restaurant is closed at lunch Monday and Saturday and all day Sunday. Dinners, depending on your selection, can range widely in price, but count on spending in the neighborhood of 100F ($68) to 175F ($119). A four-course lunch is featured for 39F ($26.50). The wine selection, incidentally, is notable. If you can't arrive by Rolls-Royce, you can take the tram to Pfauen.

Chez Max, Seestrasse (tel. 01/391-88-77), lies in the suburb of Zollikon, 2½ miles from Zurich. In an attractive house by the lake, about a 12-minute ride from the center, Max Kehl lures the world to his door. And with good reason. You don't come here by chance, and you definitely need a reservation. All the backdrop, including the decoration and the attention to china and table settings, has been planned by Herr Kehl himself. Gleaming silver blends with modern art. Regular customers, including the top business leaders of Zurich, treat themselves to some delicate and uncommon dishes. But Chez Max also knows the beauty and palate-pleasing allure of simplicity, particularly when the produce is very,

very fresh, as his invariably is. Two of his cuisine moderne concoctions—each one different, each one brilliant—included a purée of white eggplant and an equally memorable plate of truffles with Vacherin cheese. You might follow with crayfish in a cream and champagne sauce, duck with black truffle sauce, or veal filets with a homemade mustard sauce. To finish, a soufflé from the chef's repertoire is a celestial experience.

Luncheon menus are offered for 65F ($44.20). Set meals in the evening cost from 120F ($81.60) to 185F ($125.80). If you order à la carte, expect to spend from 175F ($119) to 225F ($153). The wine selections, both Swiss and French, are among the best in Zurich. Chez Max is closed all day Sunday and Monday, and it also shuts down in mid-July, reopening in August. Hours are noon to 2 p.m. and 6:30 to 11:30 p.m.

Haus zum Rüden, 42 Limmatquai (tel. 01/47-59-90), is one of the historic Gothic guild houses of Zurich, dating from 1295. Renovated in 1936, its Gothic room houses one of the best restaurants in the city, especially popular with foreign visitors, who ask for a table with a view of the Limmat. You'll enter under an arcade as you preview the posted menu on the sidewalk. You then climb an elegant stairwell. Medieval halberds decorate the walls, and other touches of decor include stag horns, polished balustrades, and Oriental rugs. The restaurant has a curved roof of elaborately crafted hardwood and exposed stone walls between the huge, many-paned windows. The restaurant is spacious, yet somehow produces an intimate feeling of well-being.

The owner is respectful of the tradition of the house, but has hired a chef who keeps abreast of changing culinary taste. The house specializes in a cuisine du marché, which means "market-fresh cookery." Therefore, since all the foodstuff is likely to change by the time of your visit, I won't recommend any specialty. However, on my recent dinner visit with companions, several dishes were outstanding, including a salad of roebuck and sweetbreads, a soup of saffron-flavored mussels, snails in truffle sauce, and lamb cooked with green peppercorns. Service is from noon to 1:30 p.m. and 6 to 10 p.m. A five-course menu costs 95F ($64.60), with a menu dégustation (eight courses) going for 130F ($88.40). However, at lunch, you can order meals for either 35F ($23.80) or 55F ($37.40).

Jacky's Stapferstube, 45 Culmannstrasee (tel. 01/361-37-48), enjoys considerable renown, especially among the chic and fashionable. The owner, Jacky Schläpfer, a local celebrity, serves some of the best beef and veal steaks in town (priced according to weight). The veal cutlets, incidentally, are among the best I've ever sampled in Switzerland. You might also consider the veal shank, which is treated with consideration and delectably flavored. Daily specials are offered, and frequently these meats are braised. Assorted fresh mushrooms are presented, much to the delight of gourmet clients. The goose liver is superb, as is the fresh lobster salad. The wine list is most distinguished, with both Swiss and French vintages featured in a wide price range. Count on spending about 85F ($57.80) and up for dinner. Hours are 11 a.m. to 2 p.m. and 6 to 11 p.m. The restaurant is closed all day Sunday and Monday, and shuts down from mid-July to mid-August.

Kronenhalle, 4 Rämistrasse (tel. 01/201-02-56), basks in the limelight generated by good food courteously served, former and present celebrity customers, and the warm legend created by its originator, the late Hulda Zumsteg, and carried on by her son, Gustav. Patrons of other days include such luminaries as Thomas Mann, Balenciaga (who created dresses for Mother Zumsteg), Miró, Braque, Picasso, Richard Strauss, Igor Stravinsky, and James Joyce. Today, you may join Plácido Domingo, Roman Polanski, Catherine Deneuve, playwright Friedrich Durrenmatt, or Yves Saint Laurent dining amid a crowd of Zurichers and foreigners from many walks of life.

In a gray Biedermeier building with gold crowns above the six windows of the first of its five floors, the restaurant dispenses traditional Swiss and international dishes. There are three dining rooms—the brasserie, the adjacent Chagall room, and the upstairs room—plus the Kronenhalle Bar. Throughout the place, original paintings by Klee, Chagall, Matisse, Miró, Kandinsky, Cézanne, Braque, Bonnard, Monet, and Picasso from the art collection of Gustav Zumsteg hang on the walls. Regional specialties, served on a trolley at lunch and dinner, may include smoked pork with lentils, glazed calf breast, or bollito misto (boiled beef, chicken, sausage, and tongue). Dinner, served both à la carte and from a plats du jour menu, might begin with such offerings as blinis with smoked salmon and caviar, veal sausage salad, and bouillon with pancake and marrow, then perhaps shredded calves' liver with Rösti, or young chicken with rosemary, risotto, and bolets, topped off with fresh fruit salad, chocolate mousse, or a sorbet. The dining rooms are open daily from noon to midnight. Expect to pay from 125F ($85) for a complete meal. In the bar, open daily from 11:30 a.m. to midnight, in addition to your drinks (try the Ladykiller, the bartender's specialty) you might enjoy bündnerfleisch, the thinly sliced, smoked, dried beef the Swiss prepare so well.

Nouvelle, 46 Erlachstrasse (tel. 01/462-63-63), is one of the most talked-about restaurants in Zurich. In a brown-walled, high-ceilinged room, its visual focus includes a row of paintings celebrating the Maxim's of Paris a century ago, hung below rows of surreal paintings by the well-known Zurich artist, H. R. Giger. A cross section of Zurich society patronizes Nouvelle, ranging from successful artists to conservatively solid Swiss merchants, all in obvious harmony, all united by a love of good food.

Meals are served daily except Sunday from noon to 3 p.m. and 7 p.m. to midnight. The owner, Ueli Steinle, is ably assisted by his skilled chef, Marc Zimmermann. À la carte meals cost from 50F ($34) at lunch, rising to 75F ($51) at dinner. Fixed price meals go for 40F ($27.20) at lunch and 80F ($54.40) at dinner. A "romantic menu" at 75F ($51) per person includes portions of everything that must be prepared for two, including duck with orange sauce, turbot in puff pastry, and beef Wellington. À la carte selections are likely to include mussels and crayfish with lobster butter and other dishes. Menu items, however, change with the season and the inspiration of the chef. The presentation of the food may remind you of intricately arranged collages, made of creatively sliced vegetables and herbs. Reservations are necessary.

Veltliner Keller, 8 Schlüsselgasse (tel. 01/221-32-28), in the old town of Zurich, has been a restaurant since 1551. Next to St. Peter's Church, it's expensive but worth every centime, and it literally reeks with atmosphere, a virtual museum of carved wood. The restaurant was once a wine cellar, and is paneled in a mountain pine called *arve* (grown only in Switzerland). The chef prepares many familiar Swiss specialties, including the classic chopped veal dish of Zurich, but he is also versatile, embracing many Italian dishes as well. The macaroni comes with a mixed grill of sausage, liver, veal, kidney, and beef. Based on seasonal availability, several Swiss dishes are likely to be featured, including game, wild mushrooms, and fresh berries from the mountains. Count on spending from 60F ($40.80) for a meal, served from 11:30 a.m. to 2 p.m. and 6:30 to 10 p.m. daily except on Sunday, for two weeks in July, and the first week in August. On Saturday the restaurant opens at 6 p.m.

Restaurant Piccoli (Accademia), 48 Rotwandstrasse (tel. 01/241-42-02), is one of the most elegant and finest Italian restaurants in Zurich. Service is skilled and efficient, and its many classic Italian dishes range from Venice to Naples. Chef's specialties include agnolotti alla piemontese and different types of spaghetti, as well as risotto with mushrooms. You might prefer the filetto alla napoletana among the meat courses, or veal liver alla veneziana. Furthermore, look for the daily specialties, which in season are likely to include pheasant and partridge. The restaurant is closed on Saturday and Sunday and also takes a summer vacation in July. Otherwise, it is open from noon to 2 p.m. and 6 to 10 p.m.

daily. The average price for a very good lunch or dinner begins at 95F ($64.60), with wine included. Mr. Panardo-Piccoli runs an outstanding operation in every way, and always sees that only the finest meals and produce are used.

The Jockey Club, Hotel Ascot, 9 Tessinerplatz (tel. 01/201-18-00), in the previously recommended hotel, emulates in its decor the same English style that influenced its name. Opulent, elegant, and warmly masculine, the place is a fantasy of silver chafing dishes, burnished mahogany paneling, brass rails, and supple leather upholstery. Meals and the impeccable service that comes with them are offered every day from 11:45 a.m. to 2 p.m. and 6:30 to 11 p.m. A fixed-price lunch or dinner costs 50F ($34), while à la carte meals begin at 75F ($51). Specialties include sirloin beef from the trolley (both large and small portions), trout, sole, salmon marinated in anise, chicken breast in gelatin, a brouillade of chicken livers, foie gras, florentine-style monkfish, and filet of beef Stroganoff, plus an elaborate array of desserts from the trolley. Reservations are suggested.

Many diners wouldn't miss a drink in the adjacent Turf Bar, where the mirrored tables reflect a fascinating mural on the ceiling. Even the plush bar is shaped like a horseshoe. At lunch, the place becomes a less-expensive version of The Jockey Club restaurant, a few steps away. Snacks and platters of food are served daily from 11:30 a.m. to 3 p.m. The rest of the day sandwiches are available along with the beer and single-malt scotches, which are served until midnight. Live piano music is heard every day from 5:30 to 11 p.m.

Restaurant Tübli, 8 Schneggengasse (tel. 01/251-24-71), is small, intimate, cozy, and chic, with fewer than ten tables. Therefore, reservations are very important. Everything seems to enhance the "cuisine as theater" approach of the kitchen. The dishes are fresh from the market that day, very much of a cuisine du marché. The chefs use subtlety in their flavorings, and the presentation of the platters, as well as the service, are top-notch. You face a changing array of dishes, perhaps duckling with figs or veal cutlet with mushrooms, baked turbot with herb rice, and their own special version of Rösti, the famed Swiss potato dish. The house ravioli, if featured on the menu, also is uniquely prepared. A selection of wines to accompany your meal is sold by the glass. A fixed price meal is served at lunch for 30F ($20.40), the cost rising to 105F ($71.40) at dinner.

THE MIDDLE RANGE: The building housing **Zumfthaus zur Saffran,** 54 Limmatquai (tel. 01/47-67-22), was constructed on the banks of the Limmat in 1740 as a headquarters for the spice merchants and apothecaries of Zurich. Renovated in 1971, it is one of the most interesting examples of updated 18th-century architecture in Zurich. You enter the front door under an arcade, and follow the passageway past an abstract wall hanging to the elegantly curved stone stairs that lead you to one of those perfectly proportioned delights that millionaires have tried for centuries to re-create in their private homes. Opulent woodwork decorates the ceiling in voluptuous curves. The far wall is pierced from floor to ceiling with glass overlooking the Limmat, half columns with gilded capitals separating the many panes from one another. The tables and chairs are of the most elegant sort, and you can sit in the attractively grouped series of Voltaire chairs for an apéritif before your meal if you choose.

A specialty of the house is zunfttopf served in old bronze pots with saffron rice; that is, filet mignon of beef with tomatoes and veal medallions with mushrooms. Or you might prefer sautéed minced veal with kidney in a mushroom cream sauce served with Rösti, or minced calves' liver with butter and fresh herbs. A set menu, offering only fish, costs 55F ($37.40) per person, the same price as most à la carte meals. Food is served daily from noon to 2 p.m. and 6 to 11:30 p.m.

Zunfthaus zur Zimmerleuten, 40 Limmatquai (tel. 01/252-08-34). Set beneath the sheltering arcades that line the river, this is one of the most charming restaurants in its neighborhood. Its foundations date from 1336, but the rows of leaded glass, intricately carved paneling, and high ceilings of today date from 1790. You climb a flight of baroque stairs to reach the elegant dining room. Amid an ambience of hunting trophies, you can enjoy full meals every day of the week from 11 a.m. to 2 p.m. and from 6 to 10 p.m. Annual vacation is from mid-July to mid-August, presumably when all the well-heeled regular clients are vacationing in the mountains. Full meals cost from 50F ($34) and include air-dried slices of ham and beef, veal liver with bacon and beans, minced veal with a mushroom and cream sauce, beefsteak tartare, and sirloin steak, followed by an iced soufflé with Grand Marnier. Reservations are a good idea.

Fischstube Zürichhorn, 160 Bellerivestrasse (tel. 01/55-25-20), is ideal on a summer evening. A fish specialty restaurant, it is built on piles over the lake with al fresco dining in fair weather. The scenery is hard to beat, but the cuisine measures up admirably. Among the dishes I can recommend are the lake trout or turbot poached, the filet of Dover sole Champs-Élysées, the grilled lobster, or the sirloin steak Café de Paris. À la carte prices begin at 50F ($34), and daily changing menus are featured from 28F ($19.05) to 36F ($24.50). The food and the service are top-notch. The restaurant is closed during the winter months. When it's open, lunch is served daily from noon to 2 p.m. and dinner from 6 to 10 p.m. Reservations are important.

Casino Zürich Horn, 170 Bellerivestrasse (tel. 01/55-20-20), has both an indoor restaurant and an outdoor dining terrace right on the lake. The place is large and popular, with excellently prepared food and courteous service. Of course, I prefer the outdoor dining spot in fair weather. From one of its tables you'll have a view of the night sightseeing boats with their strings of white lights. Count on spending from 50F ($34) and up for a meal here. Food is served from 11:30 a.m. to 2 p.m. and 6 to 10 p.m. Closed Tuesday.

Zur Oepfelchammer, 12 Rindermarkt (tel. 01/251-23-36), is for food, wine, and song, often to a guitar accompaniment. The house is from 1357, and over the years it's been frequented by students, who have made it a virtual drinking fraternity. You raise your glass of wine in a toast at one of the carved wooden tables. The owner also has a winery, and naturally some of the bottles come from his vineyards. The place is smoke-stained and loaded with atmosphere—many famous professors and academicians have frequented the restaurant. The restaurant was once patronized by Gottfried Keller, known as Switzerland's national poet and novelist. He lived at 9 Rindermarkt and made the house famous in his novel, *Der Grüne Heinrich (Green Henry).*

The menu is in English, including such specialties as French onion soup, air-cured smoked beef, a pot of lentils with a choice of sausages, shredded calves' liver in butter with Rösti, and shredded veal Zuricher style. Desserts include a vodka sherbet and apple fritters with a hot vanilla sauce. Prices begin at 45F ($30.60). Remember to nail down a reservation before heading here. The restaurant is closed on Sunday, but open otherwise from 11 a.m. to midnight.

Restaurants Bahnhofbuffet Zürich, 15 Bahnhofplatz (tel. 01/211-15-10), are nine railway station restaurants under one roof, lying at the end of your stroll down Bahnhofstrasse in the heart of Zurich. With so many restaurants and such different specialties and prices, this coterie of dining establishments caters to most tastes and pocketbooks. Its cuisine reaches its zenith at its prestigious French restaurant, au Premier, which has an elegant belle-époque atmosphere, with meals ranging in price from 25F ($17) to 65F ($44.20). A specialty is les médallions de filet de veau au citron vert (with lemon sauce).

If you want something less elaborate, try traditional Swiss country cuisine at the wine restaurant, Trotte, in a rustic setting, with prices starting at 15F ($10.20). Other restaurants include Da Capo (Italian specialties), Alfred Escherstube (try the grilled sole or salmon), Le Bistro de le Gare (entrecôte maître d'hôtel), the Cafeteria (roast veal sausage with french fries), the Brasserie (ten hash-brown potato dishes with garnishes ranging from cubes of vegetables to thinly sliced veal with mushrooms in a cream sauce) to the Winterthurer Stübli (sample pork Casimir in curry sauce) to the Chüechli-Wirtschaft (apple fritters with vanilla sauce). They're open seven days a week from 6 a.m. to 11:30 p.m. year round.

Hotel Florhof Restaurant, 4 Florhofgasse (tel. 01/47-44-70), is a small, cozy, and elegant restaurant run by the Schilter family in an old patrician house renovated in 1973. The menu is limited, but carefully chosen. The soups are especially good, as are the appetizers, which might include risotto with mushrooms or air-dried prosciutto. Among the fish dishes, you can order filets of fera (a kind of trout) or shrimp Indian style with rice and curry. Among the special dishes, try calves' brains in butter or kidneys in mustard sauce. There is also a good selection of beef and veal dishes. A good meal costs 50F ($34). The restaurant is open from 11:30 a.m. to 2 p.m. and 5:30 to 9:30 p.m. daily.

Restaurant Conti, 1 Dufourstrasse (tel. 01/251-06-66), is the personal statement of Richard Rizzi, a well-known Swiss restaurateur. Next to the Opera House, it attracts devotees who often interrupt their dinner for a particular performance, returning for dessert and coffee. The decor is in the opulent belle-époque style. The carefully chosen menu is based on seasonal specialties such as venison, which might appear in cream soup or meatballs. Two persons can order Le Menu Gourmet "Saint-Pierre," at a cost of 82F ($55.75) per person. This is a showcase treat, where the chefs display their skills. This menu includes both meat and fish selections: both fresh and ocean fish, followed by, perhaps, pheasant. À la carte meals, costing from 45F ($30.60), allow you to choose from such specialties as oysters, salmon, turbot, dourade, and sea bass. Hours are from noon to 2 p.m. and 6 to 11:30 p.m. daily except Sunday.

Restaurant Taverne, 9 Zugerstrasse (tel. 01/752-52-52), lies at Horgen on the left shoreline of Lake Zurich (Zürichsee), and makes a pleasant outing from the center of the city. The name of the restaurant suggests hearty, basic cookery, but this little citadel actually is a sophisticated restaurant with a sure sense of cuisine moderne combined with subtle flavors. Located in the Hotel Schwan, the inner one of its pair of dining rooms is nearly always booked. Full meals are served daily except Sunday from 11:30 a.m. to 2:30 p.m. and 6:30 to 9:30 p.m. Fixed price meals cost only 18F ($12.25) at lunch, rising to 65F ($44.20) at dinner. À la carte meals range from 30F ($20.40) at lunch to 80F ($54.40) at dinner.

Gabriele Keusch is the empress in the kitchen. Peter Döscher rules supreme in the dining room and is the man to ask about the little restaurant's superb wine list. Amid rustic accessories, and lots of Middle Europe comforts, you can select from such well-rehearsed specialties as fresh Scottish salmon with an herb-flavored cream sauce, fresh goose liver marinated in armagnac, roast guinea fowl with a walnut-flavored vinaigrette, medallions of venison with a browned cream sauce with white truffles and homemade noodles, and, for dessert, a soufflé of mandarin oranges. The menu changes daily, based on the availability of only the freshest of ingredients. Annual closing is for a week at both Christmas and Easter.

Le Dézaley, 7-9 Römergasse (tel. 01/251-61-29), is a landmark house that is practically a private club of French-speaking Zurichois. With a typical French-Swiss ambience, it lies in the center of town and has a long history, these two adjoining buildings dating from 1274. The city of Zurich acquired the house in 1916. Pascal Ruhlé, the manager, offers a carefully assembled repertoire of specialties from the Vaudoise region, including cheese fondue, fondue chinoise, and fondue bourguignonne. A favorite of mine is a plate of sausages made with leeks, the minced liver and kidney with Rösti. I also like the sliced veal Zurich style. Forty different wines from the canton of Vaud are offered. The menu is in English, and for dessert you can order a fruitcake, based on the fresh fruit of the season. You'll most likely spend from 45F ($30.60), and you can do so from 9 a.m. to 2:30 p.m. and 5 p.m. to midnight daily except Sunday.

Ribó, 43 Luisenstrasse (tel. 01/44-48-64), is the best Spanish restaurant in Zurich, lying just off the Limmatplatz. It makes for marvelous change-of-pace dining, which is made even more inviting by the warm welcome accorded by the English-speaking host, Rodolfo Ribó, along with his wife, Rosita. I suggest you begin your repast by ordering a glass of sherry such as Tío Pepe. You might then select the garlic soup or the Catalán salad with ham, eggs, sardines, olives, tuna, and asparagus tips. For a main course you might order the paella (made with chicken, mussels, squid, scampi, and shrimp), or a zarzuela (boiled seafood fisherman's style). The restaurant is fairly small, decorated in a regional tavern decor, and is known for its cozy atmosphere and well-prepared specialties. A complete meal costs from 50F ($34) up. The restaurant is open daily except Sunday from 11:30 a.m. to 2:30 p.m. and 6 to 11 p.m. It closes annually from mid-July to mid-August.

Bodega Española, 15 Münstergasse (tel. 01/251-23-10), has been a well-known Spanish restaurant for some 30 years now. It's open throughout the year except Christmas from 10:30 a.m. to midnight daily. The ground-floor restaurant has what the owner aptly calls a "special bohemian ambience," where patrons order tapas (Spanish hors d'oeuvres) and drink the vino. The upstairs restaurant is more impressive, with original woodcarvings that must have been made more than 150 years ago. Both establishments, in fact, are in much the same style they were a century ago. This may be the only restaurant in Zurich and its environs still using coal for cooking. A traditional Spanish cuisine is served here, including tortillas, calamares romana, and paella of the house with chicken and shrimp. Hot meals are served daily only from noon to 1:30 p.m. and 6 to 10 p.m. The price of a repast is from 30F ($20.40) up, especially if you order the paella.

BUDGET DINING: In one of the oldest burgher houses in Zurich, **Bierhalle Kropf,** 16 In Gassen (tel. 01/221-18-05), or "Der Kropf" (as it's affectionately called), is where everyone in town eventually goes, from the most conservative to the most liberal factions in the city. The food is generously served in an old-fashioned setting, and the waitresses are of the kind and motherly type. The overflow from the main dining room sometimes spills into the entrance area, where some people specifically request to sit, and there's always a convivial hubbub. The decor is high-ceilinged and elaborate, with stag horns and painted hunting scenes, well-polished paneling, hanging chandeliers, and columns which could be made either of marble or of skillfully painted plaster. The restaurant is attractively located in a building with lots of stained glass in front, a few steps from the Paradeplatz.

In this venerated establishment, you face a choice of Swiss and Bavarian specialties, including chopped veal with Rösti, stewed meats, pork shank, and pot-au-feu Zurich style, followed by palatschinken or apfelstrudel for dessert. Simple meals range in price from 18F ($12.25) to 25F ($17), but you could spend as much as 45F ($30.60) on the à la carte menu should you decide to go the whole hog. Lunch is served from 11:30 a.m. to 1:45 p.m. and dinner from 5:45 to 9:45 p.m. daily except Sunday, Christmas Day, and Easter.

Zeughauskeller, Am Paradeplatz (tel. 01/211-26-90). The proportions of this room, dating from 1487, are nothing short of vast, with a high ceiling covered with black and yellow rococo stencils between hewn timbers, all of it supported by massive round stone columns. The simple tables are made of wood, and even the chandeliers are crafted in massive wood with cast-iron chains, while the walls are decorated with medieval halberds and illustrations of Zurich noblemen of another era. The portions of typically Swiss dishes are more than generous, and are usually accompanied by steins of local beer. In fact many patrons come here just to drink.

In what was the former arsenal of Zurich, Kurt Andreae and Willy Hammer manage to keep 200 beer drinkers at a time happy and well fed. They serve Hürlimann draft beer from 1,000-liter barrels, which are something new for Switzerland, being ten times as big as the barrels previously used. It's estimated that the cooks make some 25 tons of potato salad a year. Many specialties of the Zurich kitchen are featured, including calves' liver. The kitchen also specializes in sausages of the various regions of Switzerland, including the original saucisson of Neuchâtel. Talk about foot-long hot dogs—for 55F ($37.40), my party of four recently had a dinner out of one huge sausage—it was more than a yard long. Set meals cost from 18F ($12.25) to 35F ($23.80). Daily specials are offered, and service is quick, efficient, and friendly. The beer hall serves Monday to Saturday from 11:30 a.m. to 10:30 p.m., Sunday from 11:30 a.m. to 11 p.m. The kitchen is open from 11:30 a.m. to 10:15 p.m.

California, 125 Asylstrasse (tel. 01/53-56-80), has an unusual name for a restaurant in this city, but then, who wouldn't want to be in California during a cold Zurich winter? At least, that seems to be the mentality of the commercial and fashion photographers who come here for lunch, with or without their models of that day. Super-hip, this is one of those low-key, hi-tech establishments that could be in Milan, New York, or Los Angeles. Everyone seems to speak English. The food will certainly be familiar to you—hamburgers, cheesecake, corn on the cob, T-bone steak, and fresh mushroom salad. This is a fun address, with meals going for 35F ($23.80) and up. It's open daily from 11:45 a.m. to 1:45 p.m. and 6:30 p.m. to midnight. You can reach it by tram 3, 8, or 15, getting off at Hölderlinstrasse. No lunch is served on Saturday and Sunday.

Hiltl Vegi, 28 Sihlstrasse (tel. 01/221-38-70). The interior of this vegetarian restaurant is similar to Swiss establishments in that it's clean, orderly, appealing, and very neat. You can choose from two floors of dining areas here, the lower one has a floor of roughly polished granite blocks set on end in semicircular patterns, a green-and-wood ceiling, and an elaborate array of vegetarian salads laid out American style on a stainless-steel rack. Upstairs is sunnier, decorated in maroon with one wall completely covered with oversize windows.

Ever had a raclette vegi-burger? You can here, along with the well-prepared and nutritious salads, hearty soups, and rich desserts. One of the least expensive items on the menu is spaghetti, which is served in five different ways. Many curry dishes are also featured. You can dine for 18F ($12.25) to 28F ($19.05) and up. For your drink, you have a selection of more than two dozen different blends of tea. Hours are daily from 6:30 a.m. to 11 a.m. for breakfast and 11 a.m. to 9 p.m. for lunch or dinner. The full menu is served from 11 a.m. This restaurant was established in 1887.

"vis-à-vis," 40 Talstrasse (tel. 01/211-73-10), is the house that king salmon built. Inaugurated in 1982, it became an immediate favorite, especially at lunch when it is crowded with office workers in the district. This popular restaurant stands close to a small city park near a cluster of banks in the center of town. You can select from one of two dining and drinking areas, the Salmon Bar or the Saumonerie, the latter being the more spacious of the two. In the Salmon Bar, you might settle for an open-faced smoked salmon sandwich with a glass of champagne, costing 12.50F ($8.50), ideal for either before or after attending the theater. Should you stay for a full meal, you'll find salmon (raised in hatcheries in Norway) prepared in many different ways, including salmon with a dill-flavored mustard sauce or a poached filet in a bell pepper sauce. The kitchen also turns out more rib-sticking fare; the array of daily specials might include Russian salad, roast beef with potatoes, or medallions of pork with Chinese cabbage. Full meals are reasonably priced at 25F ($17). The restaurant is open Monday to Friday from 7 a.m. to 11 p.m. and on Saturday from 10 a.m. to 3 p.m. (closed Sunday).

Mère Catherine, Am Rüdenplatz (tel. 01/69-22-50). You'll have to negotiate some complicated back streets to reach this courtyard, which is anything but prominent on a city map, since it measures only about 35 feet on any side. In the daytime you'll find sunlight, ivy, and lots of quiet café tables, while at night a lot of attractive young people fill the bar area with quiet conversation, all of them casually dressed in leather or jeans. The bar area is marble topped with brass trim, filled with rock music and lots of Jean-Paul Belmondo look-alikes. Through a corridor to the back of the bar you'll see a high-ceilinged restaurant with stone floors, timbers, and a dimly lit ambience suitable for people-watching and drinking. A balcony area with a stenciled ceiling is connected to the ground floor by a gently rising staircase, and is usually filled shoulder to shoulder with young diners. The French food, even the hand-scrawled menu, is bistro style. Salade paysanne is the most popular opener, and the chef also does good terrines. Specials change daily, but include such familiar fare as stuffed eggplant, fish soup, fried squid, and lamb cutlets in the Provençal style. Expect to spend from 35F ($23.80) up for a meal. The place is open from 11 a.m. to 10:45 p.m.

Ravi's Indian Cuisine, 29 Rütschistrasse (tel. 01/361-66-56), is often viewed as a welcome relief to anyone seeking respite from a constant continental cuisine. Lying on the northern edge of Zurich, this restaurant is the domain of a pair of India-born entrepreneurs hailing from Bombay and Delhi. Amid the sounds of recorded Indian music, in a room ringed with mogul-styled arched windows and hanging musical instruments, you can order full meals whose origins lie in northern India. Full dinners cost from 40F ($27.20) per person and are served only at night from 6 to 11; closed Monday. The staff also takes an annual vacation of three weeks in August. Your waiter will advise you of what he thinks you might like, but several sure bets include long-marinated shrimp grilled over charcoal, grilled lamb with Indian herbs, or an array of dishes where prime ingredients are laced with pungent herbs, and sometimes fiery spices, and cooked in a clay pot until juicy and tender.

Blockhus, 4 Schifflände (tel. 01/252-14-53), is a good typical old Swiss restaurant. The staff gives guests a warm welcome. Cheese fondue is the specialty of the house, but other dishes are prepared equally well. These include beefsteak tartar and the ubiquitous minced veal with Rösti, Zurich's classic dish. The location is near Bellevueplatz. Lunch sees a choice of five menus. The chef serves some costly items, but the majority of his meals are reasonable in price, the quality high. Hot meals are served from 11 a.m. to 11:30 p.m. seven days a week. Lunch specials, including soup, main course, and salad, cost as little as 11.50F ($7.80). However, expect to spend from around 25F ($17) up in the evening. The restaurant lies off Bellevueplatz and Limmatquai.

Augustiner, 25 Augustinergasse (tel. 01/211-72-10). Who would believe that such an old-fashioned dining room, with such reasonably priced meals, would lie just right off the chic and super-expensive, merchandise-loaded Bahnhofstrasse? Such is the wonder of the Augustiner, which is regarded as a secret address by many locals who go on shopping expeditions during the day. Lunches cost from 20F ($13.60) and dinners from 30F ($20.40), which is the price of appetizers in some of the places in the neighborhood. Warm food is available Monday to Friday from 11 a.m. to 10 p.m., Saturday from 11 a.m. to 9 p.m.; closed Sunday. You get rib-sticking fare here, most often served by motherly waitresses who bring heaping platters of food from the kitchen. That fare might include lamb cutlets with bacon and green beans, the house steak, pot-au-feu, veal piccata, sauerbraten, or a mixed grill. The Nerlich-Polli family keep alive this tradition of fine dining at prices that most visitors can afford.

4. WHAT TO SEE

Rich in history as well as in material possessions, Zurich has many reminders of its development, ranging from museum displays of the remains of prehistoric lake-dwellers and of the mighty Charlemagne, through religious monuments, governmental structures, quays, and well-preserved homes of rich burghers, as well as lovely parks and gardens. I'll begin by previewing the most outstanding buildings and museums, and then take you on walks throughout the city so that you can spot other sights of particular interest.

THE GREAT CHURCHES: The Romanesque and Gothic cathedral of Zurich, **Grossmünster,** was, according to legend, founded by Charlemagne, whose horse bowed down on the spot marking the graves of three early Christian martyrs. Rising on a terrace above the Limmatquai, the cathedral has twin three-story towers, a city landmark. On the right bank of the Limmat, the present structure dates principally from 1090–1180 and from 1225 to the dawn of the 14th century.

The cathedral is dedicated to those early martyrs, the patron saints of Zurich: Felix, Regula, and Exuperantius. Back in the third century they had a rough time converting the denizens of Turicum (the original name for Zurich) to Christianity. According to the legend, the governor of that day had them plunged into boiling oil and then made them drink molten lead. The indefatigable trio refused to renounce their faith and were beheaded. Miraculously, they still had enough energy to pick up their heads and climb to the top of a hill (the present site of the cathedral) and dig their own graves to inter themselves. The seal of Zurich honors these saints, depicting them carrying their heads under their arms. The remains of the saints are said to rest in one of the chapels of the Münster.

The cathedral was once the parish church of Zwingli, one of the great leaders of the Reformation. He urged priests to take wives (he himself had married) and attacked the "worship of images" and the Roman sacrament of mass. Needless to say, he stirred up some Catholic ire. This led to his death at Kappel in a religious war in 1531. The public hangman quartered his body, and soldiers burnt the pieces with dung. That spot at Kappel today is marked with an inscription: "They may kill the body but not the soul." Almost to assert the truth of that, Zurich's Grossmünster, long stripped of the excessive ornamentation you find in the cathedrals of Italy, is austere, the way Zwingli would have wanted it.

However, if you visit the choir you'll come upon stained-glass windows Giacometti completed in 1933. In the crypt is the original (but weather-beaten) 15th-century statue of Charlemagne. A copy of that same statue crowns the south tower.

Visiting hours are from 9 a.m. to 4 p.m. Monday to Friday from April 1 until the end of September (until 5 p.m. on Saturday). For the remainder of the year the cathedral is open daily from 10 a.m. to 4 p.m. If the weather's good, you'll be admitted to a tower from May 1 until the end of October for an impressive view, costing only 1F (68¢). If you want to know if the tower is open before heading there, phone 01/47-52-32.

On the left bank, **Fraumunster,** with its slender blue spire, was founded as an abbey in 853, but dates mainly from the 13th and 14th centuries in its present form. The church overlooks the Münsterhof, the former pig market of Zurich. In the undercroft are the remains of the crypt of the old abbey church. The Emperor Ludwig (Louis the German) was the founder. He was the grandson of Charlemagne, and along with the Benedictines, he installed his daughter as abbess in 853. The chief attractions of Fraumünster are five stained-glass windows—each with its own color theme—by Marc Chagall dating from 1970. Obviously they are best seen in bright morning light. The Münster is also celebrated for its elaborate organ. The Gothic nave is from the 13th to the 15th centuries, and the basilica has three aisles. In the Romanesque and Gothic cloisters are 1920s paintings depicting old Zurich legends about the founding of the abbey. Visiting hours are Monday to Saturday from 9 a.m. to 6 p.m. May to September (on Sunday, from noon to 6 p.m.). For the remainder of the year, Fraumünster is open daily from 10 a.m. to 5 p.m. (closes at dusk or around 4 p.m. in winter).

After leaving the church, you might want to walk across **Münsterbrücke**, an 1838 bridge that leads to the already-previewed Grossmünster. On the bridge is a pre–World War II statue of Burgomaster Waldmann, who was beheaded in 1489. Under him, the city became a ruler of considerable lands.

The Münsterhof itself is one of the historic old squares of Zurich, well worth a visit. On the square stands the Zunfthaus zur Meisen, which we'll visit later. Buildings on the square are painted in pastels, lilacs and sky blues, with contrasting shutters. The rooftops for the most part are gabled and pointed, really Hansel-and-Gretel-type roofs that look as if a pencil sharpener has been at work on them.

On the left bank, **St. Peter's Church** (Peterskirche), from the 13th century, is the oldest in Zurich. The church is visited mainly by those wishing to view its mammoth timepiece, the largest clockface in Europe, measuring 28½ feet in diameter. The minute hands alone are four yards long. The clock is gold faced, and is installed in the massive tower of the church. You'll easily spot the church to the south of the Lindenhof. Under the tower, its choir is in the late Romanesque style, but the three-aisle nave is baroque.

THE BEST OF THE MUSEUMS: If your time is limited, the three most outstanding museums of Zurich are the Swiss National Museum, the Fine Arts Museum, and the Rietberg Museum.

The **Landesmuseum** (Swiss National Museum) is an epic survey of the Swiss people, covering their culture, art, and history. The saga of artifacts begins in dim unrecorded time and carries you up to the present day. The location, in a big, sprawling gray stone Victorian building, is in back of the Zurich Hauptbahnhof. It's like a storybook of all the cantons, and you turn it page by page as you go from gallery to gallery. You enter at 2 Museumstrasse, and you can do so admission free daily except Monday from 10 a.m. to 5 p.m. For information, call 01/221-10-10.

Religious art sounds a dominant theme, represented by stained glass from the 1550s, removed from Tänikon Convent. Some of the Carolingian art dates back to the ninth century. See especially the frescoes from the church of Müstair. Altarpieces—carved, painted, and gilded—bring back the glory of the Swiss medieval artisan. The prehistoric section is exceptional, dipping back to the fourth millennium B.C. when Switzerland was a Roman outpost.

Several rooms from Fraumünster Abbey are on view. The displays of utensils and furnishings of Swiss life over the centuries are staggering: Roman clothing, medieval silverware, 14th-century drinking bowls, 17th-century china, tiled 18th-century stoves, painted furniture, costumes, even dollhouses. Naturally, arms and armor revive Switzerland's military legacy, from 800 to 1800, although some weapons date from the late Iron Age.

In the basement are several workshops, showing the everyday life of 19th-century craftsmen. Naturally there's an exhibition tracing Swiss clockmaking from the 16th to the 18th centuries.

Zurich Kunsthaus or fine arts museum is devoted to works mainly from the 19th and 20th centuries, although many of its paintings and sculpture dip back to antiquity. Begun in Victorian times, the collection has grown and grown until today it is one of the most important in Europe.

The location is at 1 Heimplatz (tel. 01/251-67-65). Following its 1976 overhaul, the museum is now one of the most modern and sophisticated anywhere, both in its superb lighting and in its arrangement of art. Visiting hours are Tuesday to Friday from 10 a.m. to 9 p.m. and Saturday and Sunday from 10 a.m. to 5 p.m. Monday hours are from 2 to 5 p.m. The regular admission is only 3F

($2.05), rising to 5F ($3.40) to 10F ($6.80) for special exhibitions, which are usually stunning and well worth the investment.

As you enter, note Rodin's *Gate of Hell*. Later on you can explore one of my favorite sections, the Giacometti wing, showing the artistic development of this amazing Swiss-born artist (1901–1966), whose works are characterized by surrealistically elongated forms and hallucinatory moods.

All the legendary names of modern art parade through the galleries: Picasso, Cézanne, Monet, Lipschitz, Marini, Mondrian, Bonnard, Braque, and Chagall (more than a dozen works). The gallery contains the largest collection of the works of the Norwegian artist Edvard Munch to be seen outside of Oslo. Old masters such as Rubens and Rembrandt are suitably honored, and one salon contains 17 Rouaults. Among national artists, Ferdinand Hodler is an outstanding candidate, having "made waves" in the early 20th century. Pictures by Degas, Toulouse-Lautrec, and Utrillo are likely to brighten a gray day.

Rietberg Museum, 15 Gablerstrasse (tel. 01/202-45-28), is installed in the former Wesendonck Villa in the center of a garden, opening onto a view of Lake Zurich. The villa, enclosed by Rieter Park, is in the neoclassical style, having been modeled after Villa Albani in Rome. It was constructed in 1857 by a German industrialist, Otto Wesendonck, and in time it was visited by Richard Wagner who fell in love with the hostess, who inspired his *Tristan and Isolde.* The museum today, acquired by the city of Zurich in 1952, contains the collection of Baron von der Heydt, a vast assemblage of non-European art, one of the most stunning collections in Europe.

The collection is eclectic, roaming the South Sea islands, going to the Near East, dipping into mysterious Tibet, journeying by way of Africa and Java to pre-Columbian America. The Chinese and Japanese are represented, and of all the treasures, my favorite is the *Dancing Shiva,* a celebrated Indian bronze. In addition to that, seek out the votive stelae of the Wei dynasty (dating from the archaic Buddhist period). Of course not all these treasures were collected by the baron; many have been donated by others, as the collection has grown considerably over the years.

Admission to the gallery is 3F ($2.05). It's open Tuesday to Sunday from 10 a.m. to 5 p.m. (also Wednesday from 5 to 9 p.m.). The museum is reached after a 12-minute ride from the center of town (take tram 7).

Zunfthaus zur Meisen (tel. 01/221-28-07), opening onto the Münsterhof, across the bridge from the Wasserkirche, is one of the famous old guildhouses of the city. This one was owned by the wine merchants of Zurich, and it's a beautifully maintained structure with a wrought-iron gatehouse. The late baroque guildhouse dates from 1752, and has today been turned into a branch museum of the overstuffed Swiss National Museum. Along with some antiques, it's devoted mainly to Swiss 18th-century ceramics and the porcelain of Zurich. Frankly, the stuccoed rooms are so splendid that they compete with the exhibits. No admission is charged, and hours are daily, except holidays, from 10 a.m. to noon and 2 to 5 p.m. It's closed Monday.

OTHER INTERESTING SIGHTS: Of special interest to stargazers is the **Urania Observatory,** 9 Uraniastrasse (tel. 01/211-65-23), where you can see displays and take a peek through the telescope if the weather is right. It's open on clear weekdays from April to September from 8:30 to 11 p.m. and October to March from 8 to 10 p.m. Admission is 3F ($2.05) for adults, 1F (68¢) for children. The observatory is about halfway between Bahnhofstrasse and the Limmat River on Uraniastrasse.

Zurich University's **Botanic Garden,** 107 Zollikerstrasse, contains 15,000 living species. Some rare specimens from New Caledonia and Southwest Africa are growing here. The park is open March to September from 7 a.m. to 6 p.m.

Monday to Friday, from 8 a.m. to 6 p.m. Saturday and Sunday. October to February, hours are 8 a.m. to 6 p.m. Monday to Friday and 8 a.m. to 5 p.m. Saturday and Sunday. The glasshouses are open daily from 9:30 to 11:30 a.m. and 1 to 4 p.m. Admission is free. Take bus 31 or tram 11 to Hegibachplatz, or tram 2 or 4 to Höschgasse.

Devotees of Thomas Mann, who won the Nobel Prize for literature in 1929, will be richly rewarded in Zurich. Mann, who opposed the Nazi regime and lived in the United States from 1938 to 1953, also lived in Zurich. The **Thomas Mann Archives of the Swiss Federal Institute of Technology,** 15 Schönberggasse, next to the university, contain manuscripts and mementos of the celebrated author of such works as *Death in Venice* and *The Magic Mountain.* Visiting hours are Wednesday and Saturday from 2 to 4 p.m. If you're a true admirer, you might also want to journey to **Kilchberg,** four miles from Zurich, along the southwest shore of the lake. This town is more famously associated with the Swiss author Conrad Ferdinand Meyer, a 19th-century figure. However, Thomas Mann spent the last years of his life here, and was buried on the south side of the small church in the village in 1955. His grave is marked, as is his wife's, who died in 1980.

The **Bührle Collection,** 172 Zollikerstrasse, is a jewel of a collection, an art aficionado's dream. However, it can only be visited on Tuesday and Friday from 2 to 5 p.m. The admission is 6.60F ($4.50) for adults and 3F ($2.05) for students. There is a limited but very special section devoted to medieval sculpture, but most visitors seem to be more interested in the French impressionists, including works by Monet, Degas, Renoir, and Manet. The collection also includes paintings by Rubens, Rembrandt, and Fragonard. The collection is private, but the owners have chosen to share it with the public.

TOURS: The easiest, quickest, and most convenient way to get acquainted with Zurich is to take a two-hour **motorcoach tour** with an English-speaking guide, costing 19F ($12.90). Departures are daily at 10 a.m. and 2 p.m. all year. From May 1 until the end of September there's also a noon departure, plus a 4 p.m. departure from May until the end of October. The tour takes in both the commercial and shopping center and the old town, and goes along the lake for a visit to see the Chagall windows at Fraumünster. It also stops at the Institute of Technology.

Another exciting tour is by both coach and aerial cableway, lasting 2½ hours and costing 25F ($17). This tour swings through the Reppischtal-Albispass-Adliswil recreational sector. The highlight is a ride on an aerial cableway, climbing to the **Felsenegg** at 2,650 feet. From here, there's a panoramic view of the lake and the Alps beyond. The tour also takes in an animal farm and an indoor cactus garden. It leaves daily at 9:30 a.m. from May 1 until the end of October.

Tours leave from the tourist office at the main station, and tickets can be purchased from the Zurich Tourist office.

At some point in your stay you'll want to take a **lake steamer** for a tour of Lake Zurich. You can do this on your own if you wish, and a short trip costs 8F ($5.45). Walk to the end of Bahnhofstrasse and buy your own ticket there at the pier. In peak season ferries depart about every 30 minutes. A regular round-trip tour of the lake to Rapperswil will cost 20F ($13.60) in second class, or 30F ($20.40) in first class.

You might also want to take a **boat trip** along the Limmat, looking close up at the historic buildings of Zurich. Departures are from the Landesmuseum at the Hauptbahnhof. After traversing the Limmat, the boat heads out into the lake for further views. In the far distance you'll see the snow-capped Alps. The boat lands at the Zürichhorn. Departures are every half hour in April and October daily from 1 to 6 p.m.; in May, June, and September, from 1 to 9 p.m., and in July and August, 10 a.m. to 9 p.m. The fare is only 6.30F ($4.30).

One of my favorite tours in Zurich is a **stroll through the old town** with a guide. The tour lasts two hours, and the meeting point is at 9:30 a.m. and again at 3 p.m. in front of the tourist office at 15 Bahnhofplatz. The price is 10F ($6.80) for adults and 5F ($3.40) for children 6 to 12. Departures are June 1 through September 30 every Tuesday, Thursday, and Saturday.

ZURICH ON FOOT: If you do nothing else in Zurich, walk along the world-famed **Bahnhofstrasse,** which has been called one of the most beautiful shopping streets on earth. Planted with linden trees, the street was built on the site of what used to be a "frogs' moat." The street is relatively free from traffic, except for trams. Beginning at the **Bahnhofplatz,** the street extends for nearly 4,000 feet until it reaches the lake. The drab Bahnhofplatz, the hub of Zurich's transportation network, is the railway station square. The Hauptbahnhof central railway station was built in 1871 on this square. Escalators will take you from the central station to Bahnhofstrasse, allowing you to go through an underground shopping mall, ShopVille.

With your back to the railway terminus, you can head up Bahnhofstrasse, filled with shops selling such luxury merchandise as Swiss watches, and banks, those "gnomeries" referred to earlier. You can select a favorite café and people-watch when you get tired of shopping. Incidentally, if you do shop, take along plenty of cash or else a gold-plated credit card. The merchandise is exquisite, but it's also some of the most expensive in the world. Only a couple of blocks along Bahnhofstrasse, on the left between Schweizergasse and Usterigasse, lies a little park, with benches to rest on or to reconnoiter. The park is dominated by a statue of Johann Heinrich Pestalozzi (1746–1827), an educator and reformer who had an impact on the education standards of the United States. Farther along, in the vicinity of Augustinergasse and Pelikan Strasse, take the pedestrian walk and admire the sculpture in the area.

After you pass St. Peter Strasse and then Barengasse on the left, you'll come to **Paradeplatz,** called the hub of the city, today the tram interchange center. It was the market for cattle in the 18th century. If you're not loaded down with packages from a shopping spree, stroll on to the end of the Bahnhofstrasse where the Limmat River empties under Quai Brücke into the lake. On the right is Bürkli Platz, opening onto the shore of the lake. A pint-size vegetable and fruit market flourishes here, and in summer an active flea market is in business on Tuesday and Friday morning. If you turn left across the bridge, you'll find Bellevueplatz, where you can enjoy the view while you rest on a bench.

To walk the **"Quays of Zurich"** is, in the view of many, an attraction rivaled in the city only by the Swiss National Museum. These promenades have been built along the Zürichsee (Lake Zurich) and the Limmat River. The most famous is Limmat Quai, in the virtual heart of Zurich, beginning at the Bahnhof Bridge and extending east to the Rathaus (town hall) and beyond. These quays for the most part have lovely gardens with beautiful trees. The Swiss are known for their love of flowers, which is much in evidence as you join Zurichers in their promenade, especially invigorating when spring comes to the city. Uto Quai is the major lakeside promenade, running from Badeanstalt Uto Quai, a swimming pool, to Bellevueplatz and Quai Brücke. Incidentally, you can swim at this pool from 8 a.m. to 7 p.m. daily. The beautiful swans you see in the lake aren't just a scenic attraction. Zurichers have found that they're an efficient garbage disposal system, keeping the lake from being polluted as it laps up on their shores. If you stroll as far as Mythen Quai, you'll be following the lake along its western shore and out into the countryside where vistas open onto the Alps and, on the far horizon, the Oberland massifs.

Whenever I'm in Zurich, I always head for the **Altstadt** (old town), which is known for its romantic squares, narrow cobblestone streets, winding alleyways that aren't as sinister as they look, fountain-decorated corners, medieval houses, art galleries, boutiques, quaint restaurants, shops, a scattering of hotels (often budget), and antique stores. The old town lies on both sides of the Limmat River, and you might begin your exploration at the Münsterhof, or former swine market. Excavations have turned up houses here that date from the 1100s. Once it was the tarrying place of Charlemagne, and to walk its old streets is to follow in the footsteps of everybody from Goethe to James Joyce, from Carl Jung to Einstein, from Mozart to Lenin.

Shaded by trees, the belvedere square of **Lindenhof** is one of the most scenic spots in Zurich, especially favored at twilight time by those who believe in "young love." It can be reached by climbing medieval alleyways from the Fraumünster. Once the site of a Celtic and Roman fort, Lindenhof is a good point to watch the crossing of the Limmat River. The lookout point is graced with a fountain, of course. There's also a good view of the medieval Old Quarter, which rises in layers on the right bank. Many excellent restaurants are located in this vicinity.

Weinplatz is another landmark square you'll invariably reach in your exploration of Zurich. It lies right off the 1878 Rathausbrücke (town hall bridge) spanning the Limmat. Once this was the only river crossing in Zurich (not the present structure, however). The Weinplatz is named for its 1909 Weinbauer fountain depicting a "little ole Swiss wine-grower," basket of grapes in hand. Many visitors like to stop here to take a picture of the old burghers' houses with Flemish-style roofs on the opposite bank.

At this point you may want to cross the bridge for a visit to the **Rathaus,** the late Renaissance town hall of Zurich, erected in the closing years of the 17th century, and opening onto Limmatquai. Its rooms are darkly paneled, and it has those antique porcelain stoves so beloved in Switzerland and Austria. In a setting of rich sculptural adornment, cantonal councils still meet here. It's open Tuesday, Thursday, and Friday from 10 to 11:30 a.m. No admission is charged, but you should tip the guide who shows you around.

Directly south of Münsterbrücke is a Gothic church, rather austere, called the **Wasserkirche** or "water church." When it was built in 1479 it was surrounded by the river—hence its name. Here you'll see a statue of Zwingli, the famous Swiss reformer.

On the north side of the church is the **Helmhaus,** a 1794 building with a fountain hall, where the city shows changing exhibitions, showing mainly Swiss art. The address is 31 Limmatquai, and the gallery is on the second and third floors. It's open daily except Monday from 10 a.m. to 6 p.m. (also on Thursday evening from 8 to 10 p.m.).

5. SHOPPING AND SPORTS

Daytime activities in Zurich include, besides sightseeing, at least taking a look at the marvelous shops with their breathtaking merchandise—and often even more breathtaking prices. Zurich has been called a shopper's Valhalla, if that's not too pagan a term for such a Protestant city. There are also facilities for sports and games, for those who are committed to physical pursuits apart from just walking through the city.

SHOPPING: Within the heart of Zurich is a square kilometer (or 25 acres) of shopping, including the exclusive stores along the **Bahnhofstrasse,** already previewed in the sightseeing section. Along this gold-plated street you can walk with oil-rich sheiks and their families in your search for furs, watches, jewelry, leather goods, silks, and embroidery. If your own oil well didn't come in, you can still shop for souvenirs.

Most shops are open from 8 a.m. to 6:30 p.m. Monday to Friday and from

8 a.m. to 4 p.m. on Saturday. Some of the larger stores stay open until 9 p.m. on Thursday, and other shops are closed on Monday morning.

Your shopping adventure might begin more modestly at the top of the street, the **Bahnhofplatz.** Underneath this vast transportation hub is a complex of shops known as **Shop Ville.**

Grieder les Boutiques, 30 Bahnhofstrasse (tel. 01/211-33-60), is one of the choicest department stores in Switzerland, and includes both ready-to-wear and couture facilities of such designers as Ungaro, Scherrer, Dior, and many others. The facility fills two floors of a stone building on Zurich's most fashionable commercial street, where the saleswomen tend to be bilingual and formidably well dressed. The accessories are well selected, including a wide range of purses, scarves, and leather goods.

Schuhhaus Bally Capital, 66 Bahnhofstrasse (tel. 01/211-35-15), is the largest official outlet of this famous Swiss chain in the world, occupying a prominent place in a big-windowed store on this shopping artery. For lovers of Bally shoes, this is the place to buy them. The store carries the most complete line of Bally shoes in the world, along with accessories and clothing for men, women, and children.

Jelmoli Department Store, 69 Bahnhofstrasse (tel. 01/220-44-11), is a Zurich institution, having everything a large department store should, from cookware to clothing. Founded more than 150 years ago by the Ticino-born entrepreneur Johann Peter Jelmoli, the store and the success of its many branches is a legend among the Zurich business community.

Meister Silber, 28a Bahnhofstrasse (tel. 01/221-27-30). The location of this elite shop couldn't be more prestigious, directly on the Paradeplatz in the center of Zurich. It's the kind of shop where many people stop to browse through the well-dusted showrooms, and where many of them return to buy that art object in silver or porcelain they never really needed but just had to have anyway. The prices are high but reasonable considering that every article is either exquisitely handcrafted in their own ateliers or comes from producers internationally known for quality and fine design. For this reason, the store does a brisk business, particularly since they have one of the widest selections of flatware and gift items in Switzerland.

Beyer, 31 Bahnhofstrasse (tel. 01/221-10-80). If your heart is set on buying a timepiece in Zurich, try this well-established store midway between the train station and the lake. Besides carrying just about every famous brand of watch made in Switzerland, such as Rolex and Patek Philippe, they also have a museum in the basement, containing timepieces from as early as 1400 B.C. Exhibitions include all kinds of water clocks, sundials, and hour glasses.

Bucherer, 50 Bahnhofstrasse (tel. 01/211-26-35). A longtime name in the Swiss watch industry, this store carries an impressive collection of jewelry as well.

Sturzenegger, 48 Bahnhofstrasse (tel. 01/211-28-20), is a good place to buy all kinds of delicate hand-embroidered items. A back room contains tall shelves of tablecloths, placemats, doilies, and napkins in all prices and sizes. Many of them are intricately patterned, while the room in front sells blouses, handkerchiefs, shawls, scarves, and children's frocks. Upstairs is a large assortment of nightgowns, pajamas, women's underwear, blouses, and embroidered curtains. The store is old-fashioned and wood-paneled, and much of the merchandise is partially concealed in drawers or high on shelves, so it's the kind of place where you'll need a salesperson.

Mädler, 26 Bahnhofstrasse (tel. 01/211-75-70), specializes in leather bags and suitcases at this most famous emporium of Swiss leather goods. If you don't see what you like, be sure to take the elevator to the massively stocked second floor. Stephanie Mädler and her family have owned this shop (which has since become a famous chain) since 1951.

Musik Hug, 28 Limmatquai (tel. 01/47-16-00), is the kind of shop that musicians will love, particularly if they need sheet music for anything from flügelhorn concertos to yodeling duets. It might be the largest repository of alpine musical tradition anywhere, as well as a commercial music shop stocking recorders of all sizes and pitches (I saw one in the window at least four feet tall) along with flügelhorns and French horns. There are several other branches of this store around Zurich, although this one near the lake is the most interesting.

The **Travel Book Shop,** 20 Rindermarkt (tel. 01/252-38-83), sells what could be called a very complete set of travel books, for anyone interested in going into great depth of research about an upcoming trip. Many of the books are in German, but about half the stock is in English. Maps for trekking and mountaineering from all over the world are sold. In fact, the collection of maps is said to be one of the best in Europe. Munich-born Gisela Treichler is the owner and creative force behind this bookstore. Formerly a German-language guidebook writer, she still keeps a finger on the pulse of the travel community by organizing and leading yearly tours to such destinations as the silk road of China and the northern provinces of Pakistan.

Buchhandlung Friedrich Daeniker, 11 In Gassen (tel. 01/211-27-04). If being in Zurich inspires you to reread excerpts from Carl Jung, this is the place to find them, along with the works of many other authors whose books have been translated into English. In addition to scholarly works, the helpful staff sells novels, periodicals, old-fashioned spellbinders, all of them in German. It's between the Paradeplatz and the river, in an area where many of the shops are worth looking at.

Teuscher, 9 Storchengasse (tel. 01/211-51-53). If you have a sweet tooth and have ever noticed an epicurean chocolate shop in New York or Los Angeles selling the most divine chocolates in the world, then you'll be interested in seeing the original shop that began the empire years ago. It lies on a narrow cobblestone street in the old town of Zurich and is surprisingly small. You can tell you're in the area by the smell of chocolate truffles, which comes in such flavors as champagne, orange, and cocoa. They sell for 6.60F ($4.50) per 100 grams. There's usually a seasonal theme in this store, where a decorator creates a fantasy.

Romana Boutique, 5 Stadthausquai (tel. 01/211-42-22), carries a wide variety of fashionable, discounted European designer clothes for women of all ages. In addition, they offer an assortment of sweaters hand-knitted by local women. The quality of merchandise here is outstanding, and the prices are lower than on the nearby Bahnhofstrasse. The obliging staff speaks English.

To Buy Traditional Swiss Souvenirs

The folk art and fine craftsmanship of Switzerland has not been lost in today's world of plastics and assembly lines. In 1930, in an effort to give a hand to the people of remote areas who were economically distressed, the Swiss government encouraged the organization of a nonprofit society, **Schweizer Heimatwerk,** whose aim is to keep alive the creative crafts of all the cantons. Today, the Heimatwerk shops sell only items designed and made in Switzerland, most of them handcrafted. The society also has courses for training and perfecting the skills of crafts workers in underdeveloped areas of the country.

Among the items offered in the Heimatwerk shops (ten throughout the country), are copperware, ceramics, wood carvings, ironwork, jewelry, toys, naïve paintings, crystal, tinware, baskets, music boxes, and paper cutout pictures. Puzzles, games, puppets and marionettes, Swiss Army knives, even a Noah's ark with its carved wooden animals two by two, are among the offerings—all bearing the legend, "Made in Switzerland."

The headquarters shop and four other outlets of Schweizer Heimatwerk are in Zurich. The largest assortment of products can be browsed through at the main store, **Heimathuus,** on Rudolf Brunbrücke (tel. 01/211-57-80). Other shops are at 2 Bahnhofstrasse (tel. 01/221-08-37); 14 Rennweg, a modern crafts gallery (tel. 01/221-35-73); the shop at the National Museum; and at the Zurich Airport, Transit Halls A and B. The articles offered are not cheap, but the prices do range from reasonable to expensive.

SPORTS: Many of the larger hotels have added swimming pools and tennis courts or handball and racquetball facilities to their attractions. Some have fitness centers, making staying fit while staying in Zurich an inviting possibility. Zurich also has seven "Vita-Parcours," or keep-fit trails. The nearest woodland jogging route is on the Allmend Fluntern, although joggers are seen frequently along the quays and elsewhere in the city.

Besides the hotel swimming pools, there are city indoor and open-air **pools.** The one at 71 Sihlstrasse also has a sauna with its indoor swimming facilities. You can go swimming in the lake of Zurich, which has an average summer temperature of 68° F. The finest beach here is the **Tiefenbrunnen,** and is enjoyed by topless bathers.

The two golf courses nearest the heart of town are the **Golf and Country Club Zurich** at Zumikon (tel. 01/919-00-51), which has an 18-hole, par-72 course, and **Dolder Golfclub** (tel. 01/47-50-45), with a 9-hole, par-60 course.

The closest ski region to Zurich is **Hoch-Ybrig,** about an hour's journey from the Hauptbahnhof. Take the train to Einsiedeln, where a connection can be made by bus to Weglosen and the aerial cableway that will take you to Hoch-Ybrig, which has five ski lifts and two chair lifts.

ZURICH FOR CHILDREN

The Swiss people are fond of children, and even in a large metropolis like Zurich there are many things to interest young people from tots to adolescents. There are some 80 playground and recreation areas, suitable for children. The most central are **Lindenhof, Platzspitz,** and **Hohe Promenade.** Boat excursions are always attractive to children, and Zurich has a number of interesting trips that can be found at many of the marinas, with a concentration at the end of Bahnhofstrasse on the right. Most youngsters also enjoy train rides, and rail excursions from Zurich abound.

Zurich takes good care of tots. For example, all the major department stores have **babysitting** services. You leave your child at a crêche, then proceed on your carefree way to shop. For information about this service, telephone 01/271-37-86.

In the women's room at Shop Ville, and at the Paradeplatz and Oerlikon railway stations, you can change diapers free; you'll also find milk-warming facilities.

Restaurants, for the most part, are also aware of children's needs, providing special dishes for them or else half portions.

THE ZOO: Zoos are not just for children, of course, but observation tells me that the young, both in body and in heart, experience the greatest pleasure at seeing the many species of animals, some endangered in their native habitats, as they are cared for and have adapted to the world's great zoos. Zurich's **Zoological Garden,** 221 Zürichbergstrasse (tel. 01/251-54-11), is one of the best known in Europe, containing some 2,400 animals belonging to around 350 species. It also has an aquarium and an open-air aviary. You can visit the Africa house, the ape house, and the terrariums, along with the elephant house and the giant land turtle house. There are special enclosures for pandas, seals, otters, and snow leopards, and a house for clouded leopards, tigers, Amur-leopards, and Indian lions. Hours in summer are from 8 a.m. to 6 p.m. and in winter from 8 a.m. to 5 p.m. Adults are charged 7.70F ($5.25) and children 3.30F ($2.25). The zoo lies in the eastern sector of the city, called Zürichberg, on a wooded hill. From the Hauptbahnhof in Zurich, take tram 6.

TOYS: At the **Zurich Toy Museum** (Zürcher Spielzeugmuseum), 15 Fortunagasse (tel. 01/211-93-05), in one of the oldest parts of the city, is the collection of Franz Carl Weber. More than 1,200 toys from previous centuries and from all over Europe can be admired. The museum is open Monday to Friday from 2 to 5 p.m., Saturday from 1 to 4 p.m. There is no charge for admission.

The largest toy shop in Europe is the **Franz Carl Weber,** 62 Bahnhofstrasse (tel. 01/211-29-61), named for the famous toy collector mentioned above.

There is also a specialist toy shop, **Pastorini,** 7 Weinplatz (tel. 01/211-74-26).

CHILDREN'S BOOKS: The most complete children's bookstore in Switzerland is called **Kinderbuchladen Zürich,** 9 Grossmünsterplatz (tel. 01/47-53-30). The staff here sells many books in English, both hardcover and paperback, which are printed for children aged 1 to 15.

OTHER ACTIVITIES: If you're in Zurich in off-season, there's a children's workshop at the **Kunsthaus** from October until June, every Wednesday from 2 to 4 p.m. It's suitable for children ages 6 to 12.

There are regularly changing programs for children at select theaters in Zurich. Ask at the tourist office or get a copy of *Zurich Weekly Official,* available at most newsstands.

7. AFTER DARK IN ZURICH

The city's nightlife is much more liberated than it was when I first checked it out as a college student. But, on the other hand, don't expect anything to rival Hamburg's Reeperbahn.

Since most of Zurich closes down fairly early, your nightlife might also begin early.

TEA ROOMS, BARS, AND CAFES: Founded in 1836, **Confiserie Sprüngli,** Am Paradeplatz (tel. 01/211-57-77), is the Zurich equivalent of the legendary Demel in Vienna. Many Zurichers remember episodes from their childhoods that took place at this quintessentially old-fashioned pastry shop on the Bahnhofstrasse. It's been said that listening to the chatter of the clients in the late afternoon is a good insight into the sociology of the city. It's open Monday to Friday from 7 a.m. to 6:30 p.m. and on Saturday from 7:30 a.m. to 5:30 p.m. An area on the ground floor sells a staggering array of pastries (to go) and chocolates (the justly famed Lindt chocolates and the specialties of the house are about the best you'll ever devour). You can also order light meals here costing from 18F ($12.25), but most guests order tea from 2.60F ($1.75). Desserts begin at 2.50F ($1.70).

If you like your tea rooms more modern, try **Nô das Köstliche Teehaus,** 7 Kuttelgasse (tel. 01/211-75-50). Even the matchbooks this tea house distributes are tasteful and understated, as is the Japanese decor. On a small street in the old town, it stands in an area filled with boutiques and well-dressed women. The shop is sensitively decorated with potted bamboos, live trees, and well-constructed furniture in light woods. The tea house seems to have been warmly received by the community around it. All drinks are alcohol-free, although the choice of tea is very complete. Simple menus range from 12F ($8.15) to 18F ($12.25). Hours are Monday to Friday from 7:30 a.m. to 8 p.m. (Thursday to 10 p.m.), and Saturday to 5 p.m. Closed Sunday.

Conditorei Café Schober, 4 Napfgasse (tel. 01/251-80-60), is one of the most select cafés in Zurich. The building it occupies, *zum grossen Erker* (the great alcove), was first mentioned in the archives of the cathedral in 1314. It first began to cater to the collective sweet tooth of Zurich when it was turned into a confectionery and coffeeshop by Theodor Schober after 1875. It soon became a well-known Zurich meeting place, and there was a sigh of relief city-wide when, after the retirement of the last Schober, it was taken over and renovated by Teuscher, the epicurean name in chocolates. In fact the café lies a few steps away from the original store (see "Where to Shop"). The old-fashioned café, with its beautiful lighting fixtures and molded ceilings, is known for its hot chocolate. With your refreshing drink, you can make a selection from an array of pastries and cakes, all homemade. Even the ice cream is homemade. At this confectionery shop, prices begin at 3F ($2.05), going up. Hours are Monday to Friday from 8 a.m. to 6:30 p.m., Saturday from 8 a.m. to 5 p.m., and Sunday from 10 a.m. to 5:30 p.m.

Cafeteria zur Munst, 3 Munzplatz (tel. 01/221-30-27). Considered one of the most unusual and alluring coffeehouses in Zurich, it sits behind an uncompromisingly severe concrete façade on a quiet street that runs into the Bahnhofstrasse. Aside from the gossiping clientele and the delectable pastries, the most interesting thing about the interior is the chandeliers. Designed and executed by Swiss artist Jean Tinguely, they evoke living (and very funny) creatures, half-human, half-robot that spin, wave feathers, and pivot at one another. The establishment is open Monday to Friday from 7:30 a.m. to 7 p.m. On Thursday, the place closes late, at 9 p.m. Saturday, it's open from 7:30 a.m. to 5 p.m. It's closed on Sunday, when even robots deserve a rest. One of the elaborate ice-cream confections goes for 6F ($4.10), while light meals are priced from 15F ($10.20).

Café/Bar Odeon, 2 Limmatquai (tel. 01/251-47-60), is one of the most legendary turn-of-the-century Bohemian landmarks of Zurich, and it might be fun to stop in for a coffee and check out the action, especially in the evening when it gets much singles action. Lenin discovered it in World War I and sat there late into the evening, uttering such pronouncements as "The neutrality of Switzerland is a bourgeois fraud and means submission to the imperialist war." The café is decorated in art nouveau, with an intimate format of banquettes and cubbyholes, plus a prominently curved bar and lots of tables on the sidewalk outside. It's open from 7 a.m. to 2 a.m. Monday to Saturday and 11 a.m. to 2 a.m. on Sunday. You can also order light meals costing from 15F ($10.20). However, the price of coffee depends on what hour you show up: Before 11 a.m., it costs 1.80F ($1.25), rising to 2.30F ($1.55) thereafter and peaking at 5F ($3.40) after dark.

Café Select, 16 Limmatquai (tel. 01/252-43-72), a gathering place of the so-called literati, is Zurich's closest rival to the Odeon. The restaurant has 350 seats on an outdoor terrace that is partially protected from noise and traffic because of its location in an open area surrounded by buildings. It's open daily from 7 a.m. to 11:30 p.m. It doesn't serve alcohol, but offers other drinks such as coffee beginning at 2.50F ($1.70). Café-style snacks and light meals cost from 12F ($8.15) to 18F ($12.25), with cakes and sandwiches averaging around 6F ($4.10).

Oliver Twist Pub, 6 Rindermarkt (tel. 01/252-47-10). The bartenders here speak with an Irish accent and are quick to give tips on life in Zurich. You can have intimate talks with your companion beneath portraits of QEII and the Duke of Edinburgh. In the back room, the dartboard is much in use with lots of visiting English or among the Anglophilic Swiss. An outer courtyard adds a charming Middle European touch, with marble pavement and a modern statue of a crouching laborer. The place offers plenty of food and drink items. Daily specials, such as schnitzel, salad, and polenta, cost from 15F ($10.20). Sometimes for the same price you get spare ribs, and in season, "original curry." Two large beers cost 9F ($6.10). It's open 11:30 a.m. to midnight Monday to Saturday, 6 p.m. to midnight Sunday.

James Joyce Pub, 8 Pelikanstrasse (tel. 01/221-18-28). Architectural purists might note that the interior of this pub would look more at home in Ireland than on the continent. In the early 1970s the Union Bank of Switzerland acquired the interior decor of the bar area of an 18th-century hotel in Dublin (Jury's), which was being demolished for urban renovation. Because the UBS wanted a suitable place near the Bahnhofstrasse to entertain business clients, they assembled the bar on a street near their main offices and named it after the quintessential Dubliner himself. Joyce had described Jury's Bar (when it was still in Dublin) in passages of *Ulysses*. Today the banquettes are slightly more comfortable than they were before, and the entire establishment is impeccably clean, oiled, and polished with Swiss efficiency that even the Union Bank can be proud of. The blackboard menu contains daily specials (you can order complete meals here), and there's always a good assortment of soups, such as potato with shrimp, salads, cheese, and cold snacks. You can also order such pub specials as Irish stew and fish and chips, along with hamburgers and fried chicken legs. The menu is in English, and meals begin at 15F ($10.20), going up. Open Monday to Friday 11 a.m. to midnight, Saturday 11 a.m. to 7 p.m.; closed Sunday.

CULTURAL NOTES: Concerts, theater, opera, and ballet flourish in Zurich, reaching their peak of activity at the International Festival in June. The cultural tradition of Zurich is strong: it not only has 20 museums, of which we have visited only the most important, but nearly 100 galleries and some two dozen archives and galleries, including one devoted to Thomas Mann.

In June these cultural activities are spotlighted at the fine performances given at the **Zurich Opera House,** 1 Falkenstrasse (tel. 01/251-69-22). The Opernhaus, built in 1891, has recently been renovated and offers better sight and acoustics. The ticket office is open daily from 10 a.m. to 6 p.m.; Sunday from 10 a.m. to noon. Prices vary according to the performance.

Zurich has many well-respected theaters, but unless your German is good you won't understand the classic productions of *Hamlet* or Goethe's *Stella* presented at the **Schauspielhaus,** 34 Rämistrasse (tel. 01/251-11-11). The ticket office is open from 10 a.m. daily except Sunday, when hours are 10 a.m. to noon. The actors take a vacation from late June until the beginning of September.

Big, splashy musicals are often presented at the **Volkshaus,** on Stauffacherstrasse. For tickets and information, visit BiZZ on Werdmühleplatz (tel. 01/221-22-83).

For more experimental works—again, only if your German is good—catch a production at **Theater am Hechtplatz,** Theaterkasse (tel. 01/252-32-34).

FOLKLORIC: For a night on the town, you might go to **Kindli Swiss Chalet,** 1 Pfalzgasse, Rennweg (tel. 01/211-41-82). Although yodeling is said to be the specialty of the bands that play here, their repertoires sometimes include everything from Dixieland jazz to Mozart, complete with flügelhorns and regional costumes. The owners, the Schmid family, take to the platform to perform their own kind of alpine music. Dinner is served from 7:30 p.m., and the music begins at 8:30. An average meal usually costs 60F ($40.80) per person, although clients can visit just for drinks after 9:30 p.m., paying a cover charge of 10F ($6.80), plus another 10F for the first alcoholic drink. The decor is pine paneled and rustic, with lots of timbers and hewn beams, while the food is gutburgerlich.

A much cheaper way to hear alpine music is to join the often rowdy patrons at the **Bierhalle Wolf,** 132 Limmatquai (tel. 01/251-01-30). Folkloric music from an oompah band in regional garb greets you as you enter this large rectangular beer hall, decorated with triangular pendants, many hanging from the ceiling, plus flags from the different cantons. To the sound of a guitarist, trumpeter, accordionist, and tuba player, waiters bring beer in tankards. Live music is presented from 4 to 6 p.m. and again from 8 p.m. to midnight. In between rounds the management shows slides on the wall of, say, happily laughing couples chugging beer in alpine meadows. The place is centrally located and one of the most gemütlich establishments in Zurich. Some of the beer halls in this section of Zurich can be dangerous, but the Wolf attracts a friendly, nonhostile crowd. Daily set menus are offered for 9F ($6.10) to 12F ($8.15). If you don't have dinner, the cover charge is 3.50F ($2.40) Monday to Friday, 4.50F ($3.05) Saturday and Sunday. A large mug of beer costs about 4F ($3.05).

DISCO: Besides being a restaurant, **La Ferme,** 13 Stadthausquai (tel. 01/211-57-50), is a popular dance hall and disco. On one of the quays on the Bahnhofstrasse side of the river, this lively establishment has a decor of rustic pine beams arranged to look like a barnyard fence. During the day this dark-hued place is a lunch restaurant and café, with sidewalk tables overlooking the Limmat and the Grossmünster across the river. At night, disco action takes place in front of a DJ's platform covered with rustic planks. On some nights, they present folkloric amusement. Top bands perform here in a high-spirited atmosphere. Dancing is from around 8:30 p.m. to 2 a.m. seven days a week. Depending on the night of the week, the cover charge ranges from 5.50F ($3.75) to 11F ($7.50). Beer costs about 11F ($7.50).

If you're a motorist, you may want to join a lot of attractive young Swiss and patronize the **Swing-Swing,** at the Mövenpick Hotel in Regensdorf (tel. 01/840-25-20), a few miles from the heart of town. In this rustically decorated pub, the DJ is proud of his tape collection. It's open daily except Sunday and Monday from 9 p.m. to 2 a.m. There's a cover charge of 7F ($4.75) on Thursday, Friday, and Saturday. A bottle of beer costs 8F ($5.75), a mixed drink about 14F ($9.50).

Mascotte Action 1, 10 Theaterstrasse (tel. 01/252-44-81), has long been one of the leading discos in the city. It's known for its good bands, which appear only on Thursday. Otherwise, you get recorded music. Open from 9 p.m. to 2 a.m., it charges entrance fees likely to range from 5F ($3.40) to 12F ($8.15). Drinks start at 10F ($8.60).

Joker, 5 Gothardstrasse (Kongresshaus) (tel. 01/202-22-62), isn't necessarily wild—rather, it is self-styled as an "unconservative but respectable" nightclub. Some fine international bands often perform here. It is open nightly from 9 p.m. to 2 a.m. A beer costs 12F ($8.15), with a scotch and soda beginning at 19F ($12.90). The management doesn't allow patrons to enter with dirty jeans or dirty tennis shoes, and they feel strongly about this.

Xenox, 43 Dufourstrasse at Kreuzstrasse (tel. 01/01-251-94-22), is hip and unusual, a place that defines itself more as a bar and club where, although music is played to dance to, "no one has to dance." The place is open at 8 p.m. on Thursday, Friday, and Saturday, and at 9 p.m. on other days of the week. Closing time is 2 a.m. A 10F ($6.80) cover charge is levied only after 9 p.m. on Thursday, Friday, and Saturday. Once inside, a scotch and soda costs 15F ($10.20) with a beer going for 13F ($8.85). Amid a decor of neon, white marble flooring, and beige walls, you can party the night away in youth-conscious abandon.

JAZZ: Switzerland's most famous and Zurich's oldest jazz club is **Casa Bar,** 30 Münstergasse (tel. 01/47-20-02). It features Dixieland and New Orleans–style bands seven nights a week. It is open nightly from 8 p.m. to 2 a.m., with a live band playing till midnight. There's no cover charge, but "everyone must drink something." A large beer costs 8.50F ($5.80). The jazz is good, and everybody has a fine time.

EROTICA: A little erotic theater, Las Vegas style, is sponsored by **The Red House,** 17 Marktgasse (tel. 01/252-15-30), with what the management claims are "the nicest girls in town." It is a real nightclub, with strip acts, a floor show, and vaudeville attractions. There are continuous shows from 6 to 8 p.m., with performances continuing nonstop from 9 p.m. to 2 a.m. There is no action on Sunday, however. No cover charge is imposed, but each drink, no matter what, costs 22F ($14.95).

8. EXPLORING THE ENVIRONS

Zurich is encircled by some of the most interesting sightseeing areas in Switzerland. Many are close at hand. Out of a maze of possibilities I have picked a few of exceptional interest. When feasible, suggestions for food and lodging have been included as well. However, all of these attractions can be easily reached on a short day trip while you are still based in Zurich. A few interesting tours—all of which you can do on your own—make use of funiculars and trains.

The **Polybahn** funicular leaves every three minutes from Central, the square near the Main Station Bridge (Bahnhofbrücke) on the Limmatquai. The funicular, operating since 1889 and used daily by students attending the Federal Institute of Technology and the University of Zurich, takes you to the Poly terrace, from which you can view the city and the Alps. Outdoor performances are held on the terrace, and it's a stopping place for official tours of the city. The Mensa restaurant of the technology institute and its coffeeshop are open to the public.

An interesting jaunt, summer or winter, takes you aboard the **Dolderbahn** for a short aerial cable ride to the Dolder Recreational Area, 1,988 feet up above the city. Trains leave every ten minutes from Römerhofplatz, which you can reach by taking tram 3, 8, or 15. The recreational area has restaurants, nature trails, old rustic taverns, a path to the zoo, a miniature golf course, and from October to March, a huge ice-skating rink. Also in the area is a delightful place to swim, the Dolder Schwimmbad, which is carved into a hillside with a view over Zurich. To reach it, you have about a five-minute trek along a forest trail from the end of the cable-car line. Just follow the signs to Dolder Wellenbad. Even if you don't want to swim, the view makes this excursion worthwhile. Swimmers who wish to try the pool with its artificial waves will be admitted for a charge of 5F ($3.40). The Dolderbahn ride costs 1.20F (85¢). You buy your tickets from a machine.

If you're looking for rest and recreation close to Zurich, I recommend a trip on the **Forchbahn**, which leaves from the Stadelhofen station. The train takes you up to the city limits and out into the green country, where you find a strolling and rambling area with fine views and wooded paths leading down to one of the two lakes, Greifensee or Zürichsee (Lake Zurich). From the latter, you can take a boat back to Zurich if you wish. Swiss woodlands, as decreed by law, are open to the public even if they are privately owned. Of course you must respect the rights of the individual property owners and not be a litterbug. Forchbahn trains run without conductors so you must buy your tickets from a machine at the stops. A round-trip ticket to Forch and back costs 6.40F ($4.35); to Esslingen, 8.80F ($6). For information, telephone 01/918-01-08.

Another place you may wish to visit is the **Alpamare**, reached by Pfäffikon SZ on the lake of Zurich. Its attractions include a heated indoor swimming pool with artificial waves and a slide; an open-air thermal pool with underwater music, massage jets, and bubbling water "couches"; other outdoor thermal baths containing iodine and brine to relieve rheumatism; a well-equipped playground; free deck chairs; a snack restaurant; grills; saunas; and a large solarium. The Alpamare is open daily from 10 a.m. to 10 p.m. Admission for three hours for adults is 18F ($12.25), 12F ($8.15) for children 6 to 16. For information, call 055/48-32-22.

UETLIBERG: Southwest of Zurich, Uetliberg, the most northern peak in the Albis ridge, is one of the most popular excursions from the city. A mountain railway, called the Uetlibergbahn, travels from the Selnau station in Zurich to the site, a round-trip fare costing about 10F ($6.80). The station is on the Sihl River, and the trip to a height of about 2,800 feet should take about half an hour.

When the train lets you off, it's about a ten-minute hike up to the summit where there's a café and restaurant (many bring a picnic lunch with them). The tower is a climb of about 170 steps. From the lookout post, you can see as far away as the Black Forest on a clear day, as well as to the Bernese Alps and the Valais.

WINTERTHUR: An industrial town, only 25 minutes from Zurich, Winterthur is also a music and cultural center, with an art collection that makes it a worthy detour from Zurich. In the Töss Valley, Winterthur was once a Roman settlement and in time became the seat of the Counts of Kyburg. It later became one of the strongholds of the Habsburgs until falling to Zurich, to which it was literally sold.

The ideal time to visit is on Tuesday or Friday, when the narrow streets of the old town are busy with fruit, flower, and vegetable peddlers. Another exciting time to explore is on the last Saturday of every month, when a flea market brings in people from the countryside who have merchandise to hawk.

The skyline of Winterthur is dominated by the twin towers of its parish church, the **Stadtkirche,** which was built from 1264 to 1515, although the towers date from a later period.

The **Oskar Reinhart Foundation,** 6 Stadthausstrasse (tel. 052/84-51-72), displays part of the art that this famous patron and collector assembled before his death in 1965. It is considered one of the most distinguished private collections given to the public. He willed his fabulous collection to the city of Winterthur, providing that they would let it remain in Winterthur, to which the government agreed. It is open from 10 a.m. to noon and 2 to 5 p.m. daily (except Monday morning), charging an admission of 3F ($2.05) for adults, 1.50F ($1.02) for children. The gallery is devoted mainly to works of Austrian, German, and Swiss artists, with a fine show provided by the romantic painters, including Blechen, Friedrich, Kersting, and Richter. Canvases by Hodler, in particular, are plentiful. In all, the collection comprises about 600 works by Middle Europe artists of the 18th, 19th, and 20th centuries.

The other part of the collection is shown at **Am Römerholz,** 95 Haldenstrasse (tel. 052/23-41-21), which was the private home of Oskar Reinhart. The mansion, standing on its own grounds, is open daily except Monday (by now, you're learning that nearly everything in the area is closed on Monday). Hours are 10 a.m. to 4 p.m., and the admission is 3F ($2.05). The rooms of the house are not as large as to deny the visitor a feeling of intimacy when viewing the art. The collection of paintings and related art here spans a period of 500 years, ranging from Cranach the Elder to Breughel. There are some fine drawings by Rembrandt and a painting by El Greco, *Portrait of the Cardinal Inquisitor Don Fernando Niño de Guevara,* circa 1600. Herr Reinhart was especially fond of French painters, and he collected quite a few, many of the biggest names such as Watteau, Fragonard, and Poussin. Daumier appears with some excellent drawings. A host of other more outstanding artists are also represented, with works by Delacroix, Manet, Cézanne, Van Gogh, and Corot, and dare I leave out Renoir? Some drawings from Picasso's "blue period," my favorite, are also shown. Winterthur is proud that the world now comes to its doorstep. There is a small café near the reception desk, where you can have refreshments either before or after you embark on your tour to view the splendid collection.

Herr Reinhart wasn't the only collector of art in the town. The **Kunstmuseum,** the fine arts museum of the city, is in the Kunsthaus at 52 Museumstrasse, north of the Stadthaus. The impressive collection of European art and sculpture is mostly from the end of the 19th century to the present time. Works by Swiss-born Giacometti are shown, and the French artists such as Bonnard and Vuillard are well represented. Highlights of the collection are works by Miró, Van Gogh, Magritte, Mondrian, Kokoschka, Calder, and Klee, among others. Some sculpture by Rodin is displayed, along with works by Marini and Maillol. Hours are daily except Monday morning from 10 a.m. to noon and 2 to 5 p.m. The collection can be seen only from June to August. The rest of the year, temporary exhibitions are presented.

If you can spare the time, I'd recommend a drive four miles from Winterthur to **Schloss Kyburg,** the biggest stronghold in eastern Switzerland left over from the Middle Ages. If you don't have a car, it can be reached on foot from the Kemptthal rail station, the Zurich-Winterthur line, or the Sennhof-Kyburg, which is the Winterthur-Bauma railway line. This castle was the ancestral home of the previously mentioned Counts of Kyburg, who faded into history in 1264. It then became a stronghold of the Habsburgs, until it was ceded to Zurich in the 15th century. It's now a museum, displaying antiques and armor. There's a good view from the keep, which is still standing, as is the residence hall of the knights. You can explore the parapet walk and visit a chapel as well. The admission is only 2F ($1.35), and it's open March 1 until the end of October daily from 9 a.m. to noon and 1 to 5 p.m. It's closed on Monday. In winter it's open daily except Monday from 9 a.m. to noon and 1 to 4 p.m.

The **Technorama of Switzerland,** 1 Technoramastrasse (tel. 052/87-55-55), is roughly equivalent to an American museum of science and industry, with 6,000 square meters of displays, many with tape-recorded explanations of what they are. These exhibits reveal current technological breakthroughs in metallurgy, electronics, physics, and textile technology. A youth lab, the Jugendlaber, with 120 experiments helps young people discover the wonderful world of science. Set into a natural green area, the museum offers pleasant walkways near its main building. A restaurant is on the premises.

Children ages 5 to 13 can be left in care of a supervised Mini-Technorama, with exhibits designed especially for them. By car, take autobahn N1 north of Zurich in the direction of St. Gallen, exiting at Ober-Winterthur. From there, go about a mile in the direction of Winterthur. By train, you can go from Zurich to Winterthur, from which you can take a double-decker bus from the station, which leaves a quarter to and a quarter past the hour (except at noon). Visiting hours are 10 a.m. to 5 p.m. daily. It is closed on Christmas Day. The entrance fee is 6.40F ($4.35) for adults and 3.50F ($2.40) for children.

Food and Lodging

Garten-Hotel, 4 Stadthausstrasse, CH-8402 Winterthur, Switzerland (tel. 052/84-71-71), is situated in the city park, an oasis of tranquility right in the center of Winterthur. All rooms have private bath and toilet, and are comfortably equipped with modern furnishings. Most of them overlook the beautiful green park. The rates, including breakfast and taxes, are 110F ($74.80) to 124F ($84.30) daily in a single and 146F ($99.30) to 188F ($127.85) in a double. When you stay here, you can also enjoy the cuisine in the hotel's restaurant, La Jardinière. The hotel bar, Belle Époque, is a meeting place for both young and old.

Zur Hotel/Restaurant Krone, 49 Marktgasse, CH-8401 Winterthur, Switzerland (tel. 052/23-25-21), can be identified by its elaborate gilt and wrought-iron bracket hanging over an embellished stone façade. The bracket is voluptuously curved, with a host of gilt ribbons and acanthus whorls, the hotel's trademark, an emperor's crown, hanging at its tip. The hotel offers doubles with bath or shower for 115F ($78.20) to 120F ($81.60) daily, and singles with bath or shower for 70F ($47.60) to 85F ($57.80). A breakfast buffet is included in all prices. In the heart of the old town, the simple and comfortable rooms are cheaper than the better known Garten-Hotel, and consequently are heavily booked in advance. The restaurant, where meals cost 38F ($25.85), has polite service and several French and Swiss specialties, including the classic sliced veal dish in a cream sauce, Zuricher style, and a filet of beef in a peppercorn cream sauce.

Schloss Wülflingen, Winterthur-Wülflingen (tel. 052/25-18-67), on the outskirts, is the best and most romantic place to dine. It was built in 1644 in a rustic stone, stucco, and slate style, and reeks with solidity and permanence. In summer, owner Rolf Aberli and his family place garlands of greenery between the intricate shutters of the step-gabled house. Ivy grows over the door and café tables are set up in front. Aside from an extensive wine list, the restaurant offers a gastronomic menu costing from 64F ($43.52) to 95F ($64.60) per person, a good value since it consists of six courses. However, it's possible to order an à la carte meal for 29F ($19.70) to 45F ($30.60). Specialties include beef in red and green pepper sauce with gratin potatoes, sole, turbot, catfish, salmon, giant shrimp, and other seafood. A simpler menu is offered at lunch, slightly less elaborate, but with excellent meat dishes such as veal stuffed with country ham and a mousse of foie gras, served with tiny homemade noodles, as well as fish dishes. It costs 39F ($26.50) for two persons. You dine in an elegantly paneled ambience, where many of the rooms have their original ceramic stoves. It's best to go from noon to 2 p.m. and 6:30 to 9:30 p.m. any day except Monday.

REGENSBERG: About ten miles northwest of Zurich, the village of Regensberg is a nugget from medieval days. It looks as if it has slumbered through the past centuries. Because of that, it's a national trust village of Switzerland, and nothing can be altered—not that anybody would want to anyway. It's best reached by car, about a 20-minute drive from Zurich, depending on traffic (take the road out of Zurich in the direction of Dielsdorf). If you don't have a car, you must go by postal bus from Dielsdorf, itself reached on the Zurich-Oberglatt-Niederweningen railway line. If you drive, you must park your car outside the town hall and walk into the walled town on its cobblestone streets.

Regensberg is a village of wine makers and vineyards, with some remarkably well-preserved half-timbered houses clustered around the main square, which is most colorful. The most famous of these old burghers' homes is the **Rote Rose house,** dating from 1540 and containing a little museum of the painter Lotte Günthard. The village church is from the early 16th century, but it was built on the site of a structure dating from the early 13th century.

Dominating the hamlet is a **castle** once owned by the Habsburgs. This was once the headquarters of the Barons of Regensberg, who ruled the town. The watchtower affords a view of the local vineyards and the Lägern hills. On a clear day you can see all the way to Zurich. The castle is from the 16th century, and today contains a children's home. You can climb the tower, the highest point in Regensberg, during most of the year. If it's closed, inquire at the castle.

Where to Dine

The biggest half-timbered house in the village contains the **Gasthaus Krone,** Oberburg (tel. 01/853-11-35), which serves both lunch and dinner, and wines from local vineyards. These wines are excellent, almost worth the pilgrimage from Zurich. You face a choice of dining rooms; my favorite is the Biedermeier salon, whose casement windows overlook the valley. But you don't come here for the view. The food is exceptional, with an emphasis on local and seasonal produce. It's also expensive; a menu costs from 80F ($54.40).

The menu is in French, and the chef knows how to prepare all the classical dishes, along with some innovative cuisine moderne touches. The food and its preparation are excellent in every way, and the service is attentive and meticulous. The Krone is a gourmet citadel although located in a tiny hamlet. In summer you may want to enjoy the terrace. The restaurant is open from 11 a.m. to 11 p.m., but it doesn't serve hot food during all those hours. It's closed Sunday night and Monday, and shuts down from December 20 to January 20.

RAPPERSWIL: A lake steamer from Zurich will take you to the "town of roses," lying on the northern part of the lake, 19 miles away. If you're based in

Zurich for just a short time and have no other chance to visit the rest of the country, then spend a day going to Rapperswil to see a typical Swiss town.

Many streets remain from the Middle Ages, and the town is dominated by a castle built about the year 1200 by the young Count of Rapperswil, who had just returned from the First Crusade.

Rapperswil Castle (tel. 055/27-44-95) is today the principal attraction of the town. Built on a rocky hill, it was an imposing medieval stronghold, with its towers, parapet walks, and inner ward. In 1870, it became the Polish National Museum, serving as a repository of national relics of that beleaguered country. One part is still devoted to Polish art, folklore, and mementos, including those of Copernicus, Chopin, Kościuszko, and Solidarność (Solidarity). It's open daily from 10 a.m. to noon and 2 to 5 p.m., charging an admission of 3F ($2.05). In winter, it's open only on Sunday and holidays or on special request.

On the north side of the hill is the **Hirschgarten** (or deer park) in the Linderhof. There's also a **Children's Zoo** (tel. 055/27-52-22), which is run by the Knie National Circus. The zoo is on the Strandweg, a road which runs along the lake, south of the railway station. Trained dolphins and other acts perform here. It's open daily from 9 a.m. to 6 p.m. Admission is 6.50F ($4.40) for adults, 3F ($2.05) for children 4 to 14, and free to children under 4. It is closed in winter.

On the Herrenberg, the **Heimat-museum** (tel. 055/27-71-64) is a museum of local history, east of the parish church. It contains Roman artifacts and a collection of weaponry, along with paintings and antiques. It's open only in high season, between Easter Monday and November 1. Hours are from 2 to 5 p.m. daily except Friday. Admission is 2.50F ($1.70) for adults, 1F (86¢) for children 6 to 13, and free for children under 6.

In the main square is the **Rathaus** (town hall), from 1471, with a richly embellished Gothic portal.

If you wish, you can go from Zurich to Rapperswil by lake steamer. A round-trip ticket costs 30F ($20.40) in first class, 20F ($13.60) in second class.

Where to Dine

If you're down just for the day, you may want to patronize the **Hotel Eden** (tel. 055/27-12-21) for either lunch or dinner. If so, you'll be following in the footsteps of many food connoisseurs from Zurich. The ample local vineyards produce a wine that, along with dozens of other vintages, is stocked in the cellars. The Ganahl family owns the six-story house and maintains it in a condition compatible with all the gourmet delicacies served inside. Specialties include fresh goose liver pâté, rack of lamb Eden, baby veal, lobster salad with artichoke hearts, and saltwater fish, along with fresh vegetables, always selected according to the season and market. Desserts are consistently excellent. The average meal costs 40F ($27.20) to 50F ($34). The Eden restaurant is closed Sunday night and all day Monday, but open otherwise from noon to 2:30 p.m. and for dinner after 5 p.m. It's in the old town.

Where to Stay

Should you be fortunate enough to spend the night in Rapperswil, I have the following suggestions.

Hotel Schwanen, 12 Seequai, CH-8640 Rapperswil, Switzerland (tel. 055/21-91-81), is a beautifully ornate building with white walls and buff-colored shutters. The columns holding up the balconied portico have seen generations of vacationing Swiss pass between them, a function it continues to perform for the grandchildren of the original visitors. The interior has been tastefully modernized for a warm-textured comfort. The host charges 160F ($108.80) daily in a well-furnished double room with bath, from 90F ($61.20) to 100F ($68) in singles with bath.

Hotel Freihof, Hauptplatz, CH-8640 Rapperswil, Switzerland (tel. 055/ 27-12-79), near the castle, is a 33-bed hotel with an antique façade and a modernized interior. All of the units contain private baths. Singles rent for 60F ($40.80) to 80F ($54.40) daily, with doubles going for 100F ($68) to 110F ($74.80). Breakfast is included in all the tariffs.

Hotel Bellevue, 21 Marktgasse, CH-8640 Rapperswil, Switzerland (tel. 055/27-66-30), is in the oldest part of town at the edge of the lake, making touring the historic district quite convenient. This small, intimate, and cozy hotel has a modernized interior behind a 17th-century façade that fits harmoniously in the old section around it. There are only 19 beds, each of the rooms having a private bathroom. With breakfast included, singles cost 70F ($47.60) to 80F ($54.40) daily, while doubles rent for 108F ($73.45) to 120F ($81.60).

Hotel Speer, 5 Bahnhofplatz, CH-8640 Rapperswil, Switzerland (tel. 055/27-31-31), lies in a position to receive much of the resort traffic from Zurich. Its presence is announced by illuminated letters over the streetside terrace, which opens into a cozy modern bar with accents in green tile. The paneled dining area is carpeted. The bedrooms at their best are furnished with upholstered rococo beds and Jacobean chairs, and in the less expensive ones, in functional pieces. Singles with bath cost from 68F ($46.25) daily, while singles without bath go for 45F ($30.60). Doubles with bath cost 100F ($68) to 115F ($78.20), and bathless chambers go for only 75F ($51), including breakfast.

NORTHEASTERN SWITZERLAND

□ □ □

If numbers mean anything, northeastern Switzerland is the most neglected part of the country from the standpoint of the North American tourist. What a shame! It's one of the most unspoiled regions of Switzerland, perhaps because of that oversight.

Old customs and traditions live on steadfastly here, as much of the green and rolling countryside is still deeply rooted in the past. The region is separated from southern Germany and Austria by the Rhine and Lake Constance. (The Principality of Liechtenstein is also part of the region, but because it's a separate country I've chosen to treat it individually in its own section—refer to Chapter XIII.)

In this part of Switzerland lie the cantons of Appenzell, Glarus, St. Gallen, Schaffhausen, and Thurgau. Many striking beauty spots abound, including St. Gallen Rhine Valley and the Rhine Falls near Neuhausen. St. Gallen is the cultural and economic center. There are many holiday resorts in the Toggenburg Valley, and some of the most splendid orchards in the country dot the shores of Lake Constance.

As for mountain peaks, the Säntis reaches a height of 8,200 feet and Mt. Tödi in Glarus tops it at 11,880 feet.

If economy is a factor in your travel, then you should definitely consider exploring the region, as the prices for food and lodging in its Old World inns are among the lowest in the country.

1. ST. GALLEN

This is an ancient town, tracing its history back to when an Irish monk, Gallus, built himself a hermitage here in 612. In time a cloister grew from his "humble cell," and by the 13th century it was an important cultural outpost for the Western world. St. Gallen became a free imperial city in 1212, and in 1454 it joined the Swiss Confederation. Today it's the capital of a canton that bears its name, lying 53 miles east of Zurich. It is the highest city of its size in Europe, with 75,000 inhabitants living 2,200 feet up in the foothills just north of the Alps, tucked into a charming valley.

St. Gallen is one of the primary sightseeing targets in northeastern Switzerland, mainly because of its old city with its restored half-timbered houses with their characteristic turrets and oriels. Many lanes and alleys, left over from the Middle Ages (some closed to traffic) await the explorer. St. Gallen also makes a good center for exploring Lake Constance, the Säntis mountains, and the Appenzell countryside.

THE SIGHTS: The Protestant Reformation was victorious in St. Gallen, but the Benedictine monastery remained, with Catholics and Protestants living together in amicable separation of town politics (Protestant) and church pursuits. The walls of the abbey were razed, and the monastery today contains the Catholic bishop's residence, the abbey library, the canton's government offices, and various other offices and schools.

Pause in the **Klosterhof** (the abbey yard) to take in the splendor of the former Benedictine abbey. The present structures date mainly from the 17th and 18th centuries. Here are the major sights of the town, including the twin-towered Domkirche (the cathedral) and the world-famous Stiftsbibliothek, or abbey library.

The **Domkirche,** Switzerland's best example of baroque architecture, dates in its present form from 1756. It grew up on the site of the more celebrated Gothic abbey from the 14th century. The interior is also in the rich baroque style, reaching the zenith of its decorative beauty in its chancel.

From an inner courtyard you can enter the **Stiftsbibliothek,** 6c Klosterhof (tel. 071/22-57-19). This abbey library survived the secularization of the abbey, and it has a collection of some 130,000 volumes. Some of its manuscripts are from the 8th to the 12th centuries. It also displays around 500 books printed in the 15th century. Several Renaissance manuscripts are stunningly illustrated. The library hall is a delight, built in a charming rococo style, with stucco art and ceiling paintings. The plan of St. Gallen abbey in 820 is exhibited under glass.

The library, charging 2F ($1.36) for admission, may be visited from May to October daily except Sunday afternoon from 9 a.m. to noon and 2 to 5 p.m. (it opens at 10:30 a.m. on Sunday). In winter, it's open daily except Sunday and Monday from 9 a.m. to noon and 2 to 4 p.m.

St. Gallen is known as the embroidery capital of Europe. Much of the work is done in factories using computer-driven machines, but St. Gallen women or those in the country nearby still do embroidery by hand. This is also the lace center of Switzerland, and it was here that three dozen seamstresses worked for a year and a half to make a lace gown for Empress Eugénie, the consort of Napoleon III. Buyers from the world's fashion houses come to St. Gallen for the embroidered clothing and handsome lace produced. Textile plants in the area sometimes have clearance sales, usually in January and July, when visitors can find real bargains.

The gown of Empress Eugénie and other priceless objects, such as Coptic textiles from Egyptian tombs, dating from the early Middle Ages, as well as Renaissance Italian lace, 17th-century French silk embroidered vests, and church robes richly embellished with needlework can be seen at the **Museum of Arts** and Trades (Textilmuseum), 2 Vadianstrasse (tel. 071/22-17-44). Many of the rich displays in the museum come from Iklé and Jacoby collections. Antique sewing machines are also here, together with a vast library on the textile industry. Charging 4F ($2.72) admission, it's open from 10 a.m. to noon and 2 to 5 p.m. except on Sunday in summer and on Saturday and Sunday in winter.

The **Historical Museum** (Historisches Museum), 50 Museumstrasse, has among its exhibits reconstructions of the Benedictine Abbey as it appeared in the Middle Ages. Hours are from 10 a.m. to noon and 2 to 5 p.m. daily except Monday. Admission is free.

If you head south of St. Gallen for two miles you reach **Freudenberg**, at nearly 3,000 feet. Once here, a panoramic view unfolds of the Säntis mountains, St. Gallen itself, and Lake Constance, which they call the Bodensee in this part of the country.

After you've seen the sights, you may be ready for some outdoor exercise. The town's 18-hole golf course is one of the most scenic in Switzerland. Tennis, riding, or swimming in one of three public outdoor pools are also offered.

WHERE TO STAY: The most desirable hotel in town is the **Einstein Hotel,** 2 Berneggstrasse, CH-9001 St. Gallen, Switzerland (tel. 071/20-00-33), with its gray-and-white neoclassical façade. Near the center of the historic district, it was originally built 150 years ago as a factory for Swiss embroidery. It was renovated in 1983 into a stylish provincial hotel, owned and operated by one of Europe's largest chains, Mövenpick. You register within a marble-sheathed lobby, usually within earshot of the live piano music reverberating from the pub/cocktail bar. Each of the 65 rooms contains a private bathroom, phone, radio, TV, mini-bar, and conservatively tasteful furnishings. Single rooms rent for 140F ($95.20) daily to 170F ($115.60), doubles 220F ($149.60) to 230F ($156.40).

Hotel Metropol, 3 Bahnhofplatz, CH-9001 St. Gallen, Switzerland (tel. 071/20-61-61). Set within a commercial neighborhood a few steps from both the railway station and the bus depot, this comfortable four-star hotel has a modern façade of grid-shaped concrete. One floor above street level, a well-recommended restaurant, Au Premier, offers views of the Bahnhofplatz and well-prepared food. Upstairs, the conservatively decorated bedrooms each contain phone, color TV, radio, mini-bar, and private bath. Singles cost 95F ($64.60) to 130F ($88.40) daily, and doubles go for 158F ($107.45) to 180F ($122.40).

Hotel Walhalla, Bahnhofplatz, CH-9001 St. Gallen, Switzerland (tel. 071/22-29-22), is a modernized Best Western first-class hotel in the shopping district. It stands opposite the main rail station and parking garage, about a three-minute stroll from the Old Town. Many visitors find it a suitable center for making excursions for the day to Appenzellerland and the Lake Constance area. You'll receive a warm welcome in one of the hotel's two restaurants and a convivial bar. All 54 bedrooms are well furnished and contain a bath or shower, as well as a toilet, multilingual TV programs, a radio alarm, and a mini-bar. Prices go from 98F ($66.65) to 105F ($71.40) daily in a single, rising to 170F ($115.60) to 180F ($122.40) in a double, including a buffet breakfast. Roland and Dany Studer are your concerned hosts.

Garni-Hotel Gallo, 62 St. Jakobstrasse, CH-9000 St. Gallen, Switzerland (tel. 071/25-27-27). Some of the detailing of its art nouveau façade is still visible, although the two dozen rooms of this hotel were radically renovated in 1984. It stands within a ten-minute walk of the center of town, alongside a busy traffic artery. Each of the rooms has a private bath/shower, color TV, radio, mini-bar, and tall, sun-flooded windows. With breakfast included, singles rent for 80F ($54.40) daily and doubles for 140F ($95.20) to 160F ($108.80). An attractive restaurant next door, Galletto, is recommended separately.

Hotel Continental, 95 Teufenerstrasse, CH-9000 St. Gallen, Switzerland (tel. 071/27-88-11). Two minutes away from the train station by car, this hotel is warm and comfortable inside in spite of its relatively unadorned exterior. A garage is beneath the hotel, and many of the rooms have recessed balconies covered with awnings. Accommodations are simply but adequately furnished, and the beds are comfortable. All units contain phone, radio, color TV, mini-bar, and private bath. Doubles rent for 125F ($85) to 150F ($102) per day, while singles cost 78F ($53.05) to 120F ($81.60), with breakfast included.

Hotel Dom, 22 Webergasse, CH-9000 St. Gallen, Switzerland (tel. 071/23-20-44), is an inviting hotel run by Lendi Silvia. It's near the cathedral of St. Gallen, as its name suggests. On a pedestrian street in the center of town, it is reached by taking an elevator to one floor above street level. Its 42 rooms are simply but comfortably furnished, and the staff is cooperative. Rooms contain private showers and rent for 75F ($51) in a single, 115F ($78.20) in a double, all rates including breakfast.

Hotel Ekkehard, 50 Rorschacher Strasse, CH-9000 St. Gallen, Switzerland (tel. 071/22-47-14), is a typical, three-star Swiss hotel that is clean and neat and well located in the center of town. The hotel contains 34 accommodations, each pleasantly outfitted with simple, functional furniture. Rooms are compact but well maintained. The more expensive rooms contain private baths. Singles range from 60F ($40.80) to 85F ($57.80) daily, with doubles costing from 95F ($64.60) to 140F ($95.20). Also on the premises is a wood-trimmed restaurant with a modern decor, serving Swiss and continental dishes, all reasonably priced.

WHERE TO DINE: In the restaurants recommended below, as well as in the area's tea rooms and inns, you should try the famous local sausage, the bratwurst, and St. Gallen's rich regional pastries.

One of the finest restaurants in the city is in a four-star hotel: **Hotel Einstein Restaurant,** 2 Berneggstrasse (tel. 071/20-00-33). Nestled under the eaves of the top (fifth) floor, this cozy restaurant combines elements of half-timbered rusticity with stylish marble-trimmed formality. Full à la carte meals cost from 39F ($26.52) each and are served every day from noon to 2 p.m. and 6 to 10 p.m. Specialties include calves' liver with coriander and cider sauce, cream of spinach soup with salmon strips, filet of sole with artichokes and sherry-flavored butter, and veal steak with herb-flavored butter. Reservations are suggested.

Restaurant "Au Premier," Hotel Metropol, 3 Bahnhofplatz (tel. 071/20-61-61). Sheathed with modern paneling and illuminated with cut-glass sconces, this popular restaurant sits one floor above the reception area of the previously recommended Hotel Metropol. Fixed price meals begin at 60F ($40.80), while à la carte dinners cost from 70F ($47.60) each. Meals are served every day from 11:45 a.m. to 2 p.m. and 7 to 10 p.m. The menu changes frequently, but usually features an array of seafood and the finest cuts of meat. Representative dishes include fresh salmon with tarragon cream sauce, terrine of duckling, lamb pré-salé, fricassée of chicken with morels, and sole normand. The polite and uniformed staff prefers reservations.

Stadtkeller/Bistro à l'Escargot, Spisermarkt, 17 Spisergasse (tel. 071/22-00-88). Despite the old-fashioned implications that seem to be associated with every restaurant named "Stadtkeller," this particular version might be the most fashionable in town. It lies within a busy collection of cafés, bars, and boutiques in the center of the oldest part of the city. A curved flight of stone steps descends to its windowless depths, and beneath a vaulted ceiling, by flickering candles, you can order full meals priced from 55F ($37.40). The elegant fare includes such dishes as fish soup with saffron, sweetbread salad with a morel-flavored vinaigrette, snails in a red wine and butter sauce, sole filets in a tarragon sauce, and smoked salmon. Reservations are strongly advised.

If you're looking for a less formal, and less expensive, ambience, you can rub elbows with your chattering fellow diners in the vastly popular Bistro à l'Escargot, a few steps away. There, in brightly illuminated sociability, you can order full meals at 25F ($17) and up. These might include three different preparations of snails, snail soup, tripe with calvados, boiled beef with mustard and onions, and three different varieties of pasta, including spaghetti in a gorgonzola sauce. Lamb chops provençale are featured, as is veal scallopini with marsala, pork provençale, and steaks. Full meals are served in both restaurants every day except Sunday from 11:30 a.m. to 2 p.m. and 6 to 11:30 p.m. Incidentally, the Schnecken Bar, behind the bistro, is invariably packed with university-age students virtually every night of the week.

Am Gallusplatz, 24 Gallusstrasse (tel. 071/23-33-30). Reaching its historic location, opposite the cathedral, is part of the fun of dining here. The restaurant lies behind a pink façade and a low wall that identifies one of the most famous dining houses of the old town. The sienna-walled dining room is the long-standing domain of the Hans J. Sistek family. Three-course meals on the menu gourmet cost 47.50F ($32.30), rising to 92F ($62.55) for seven-course repasts on the menu gastronomique. They are served daily from noon to 2 p.m. and 6 to 11 p.m. except all day Monday and at lunch on Saturday. Priding itself on freshness and seasonality, the restaurant changes its menu often. I have enjoyed bouillabaisse "chef," entrecôte Madagaskar, grilled sole and salmon Florentine style, and lamb medallions provençale. For lighter appetites, the wine bar (Weinstube) offers a selection of smaller dishes. Because of its intimate size, reservations are suggested.

Restaurant Galletto, 62 St. Jakobstrasse (tel. 071/25-03-03), modern, and very, very Italian, has a black coffered ceiling, bouquets of flowers, pastries set on moveable tables like sculptures, and lots of greenery. It lies on a busy traffic artery, about a ten-minute walk from the historic center of town. Meals are served from 11 a.m. to 2 p.m. and from 6 to 11 p.m. every day except Monday at lunchtime and all day Sunday. Both fixed-price and à la carte dinners begin at 50F ($34). The menu includes a tempting array of antipasti, plus a wide pasta selection, all homemade, including lasagne verde, taglierini with salmon, ravioli, and many excellent veal dishes, including one with porcini mushrooms. Other choices include eggplant parmigiana, veal liver Venice-style, and a limited selection of fish, including a mixed fry from the Adriatic. The big wine list contains excellent vintages from all parts of Italy as well as Swiss and French wines. Reservations are suggested.

Schwartzer Bären, 151 Speicherstrasse (tel. 071/35-30-55), can be found after a ten-minute drive from the center of town, in a locale that is a rustic blend of wrought iron, antiques, and textile wall hangings. The food items would tempt even the most traditional tastes, a conservative yet well-prepared array of meats, fish, and vegetables, which are always fresh. The filet of sole with capers and the cutlet of beef with homemade cabbage butter are savory. Many specialties are Italian. The restaurant serves fixed-price meals for 55F ($37.40) to 75F ($51) and à la carte meals costing from 50F ($34) up. The place is closed Wednesday and Thursday. Hours otherwise are from 11 a.m. to 11 p.m.

Schnäggehösli, 31 Hagenbuchstrasse (tel. 071/25-65-25). Because of the intimate size of this unusual restaurant, it's best to phone ahead for a reservation. Even then, you're likely to find some of the best-heeled residents of St. Gallen climbing with you to the top of this hillock above the old town. The century-old building, which houses the restaurant, is clean and attractively decorated, the perfect setting for a combination of traditional and modern cuisine that has made this place so famous locally. Fixed-price menus run a wide range, from 40F ($27.20) to 85F ($57.80), the latter the gastronomic delight of the town. À la carte meals cost 30F ($20.40) to 55F ($37.40), and might include such dishes as poached salmon in dill sauce, filet of sole in champagne sauce with crayfish sections, and an excellent cut of filet of beef with nouvelle cuisine cration: baby veal in raspberry vinegar sauce. Schnäggehösli is open from 11:30 a.m. to 2 p.m. and 6:30 to 10 p.m. daily.

SHOPPING: The importance of St. Gallen for textiles and embroidery has already been stressed. Many Zurichers go here just to shop, looking for scarves, handkerchiefs, and table linen among other items.

The best place is **Sturzenegger,** 12 St. Leonhardstrasse (tel. 071/22-78-97), part of a nationwide chain. You might also check the wares at the **Bambola Boutique,** 11 Teufenenstrasse (tel. 071/20-11-40).

2. APPENZELL

Known for its baked goods and chocolates, Appenzell is one part of Switzerland where folk tradition lives on. Don't be surprised to encounter men with earrings but no shoes! Its folk costumes are distinctive, and I hope you'll get to see a woman in her ceremonial garb, wearing a coif with large tulle wings. The district has long been known for its Grandma Moses–type painters, and is also said to produce the best yodelers in the country.

As for the landscape, someone once compared the setting to a combination "of the rolling green hills of Vermont with a Yosemite-like limestone upthrust at its center." In the environs are several mirror lakes, and trusty cable cars haul visitors and locals alike over an otherwise inaccessible terrain. For centuries the district was relatively isolated from the rest of the world.

Set in the foothills of the Alpstein, the Appenzell district sweeps southward from Lake Constance. As you drive from hamlet to hamlet, you'll note artistically painted houses, inhabited by people who believe in keeping alive firmly rooted traditions.

The town of Appenzell is a good base for excursions. From the town you can journey to **Ebenalp,** a distance of only four miles. Take the Weissbad-Wasserauen road until it ends. At the terminus, you can go by cable car, about an 11-minute ride to the summit at some 5,400 feet. The cable car leaves about every 30 minutes in season, a round-trip fare costing 14F ($9.50). For information, call 071/88-12-12.

The mountaintop promontory of Ebenalp, with its cliffs jutting out, affords a spectacular view of the Appenzell district with its contented cows. If you've wisely worn good, strong, and sturdy walking shoes, you can walk down to **Wildkirchli,** a chapel in a cave or grotto. It was once inhabited by hermits, from the mid-17th to the mid-19th century. Around the turn-of-the-century Paleolithic artifacts were discovered there, making it the oldest prehistoric settlement so far found in Switzerland.

The major attraction in the area is the climb up **Mt. Säntis,** the highest peak (8,200 feet) in the Alpstein massif. It's the principal viewing platform for those wanting a panoramic sweep of eastern Switzerland. Spread before you will be the Grisons, the Bernese Alps, the Vorarlberg mountains, Lake Constance, even Lake Zurich. On the clearest of days you can see as far as Swabia in southern Germany. However, many readers are likely to be disappointed, as there are many hazy days, even in July, when the panoramic view is obscured.

To reach the cable car, which will take you to the Säntis belvedere, drive first to Schwägalp. The cable car leaves about every 30 minutes year round. A round trip costs 19F ($12.90).

APPENZELL: The few Americans who visit this district reportedly are always in a rush, but perhaps you'll have time to stop over in the town of Appenzell. Try to visit the main street, the **Hauptgasse.** Here are shops selling the famous embroidery of the area. It's not cheap, but most women will want to make off with at least one souvenir of this exquisite craft.

The town has many traditional old painted houses that have been well preserved. At the square, the **Landsgemeindeplatz,** the men of the community, wearing swords, hold an annual meeting where you see democracy in action.

WHERE TO STAY: On the town's main square, **Hotel Appenzell,** CH-9050 Appenzell, Switzerland (tel. 071/87-42-11), painted an enticing combination of whimsically folkloric colors, is a recently built hotel occupying a desirable position on the town's main square. Only part of its space is devoted to the 16 comfortable bedrooms, since it also contains a restaurant, a café, and a pastry shop. Each of the rooms offers a travertine-sheathed bathroom, a TV, mini-bar, radio, and phone, and conservatively modern walnut furniture. With breakfast included, singles cost 85F ($57.80), and doubles go for 140F ($95.20), an extra bed in any double room tabbed at 25F ($17). The hotel is closed every Tuesday from 7:30 a.m. to 2 p.m., so guests should plan to go out during those hours.

The street-level café, with its warm-weather outdoor terrace, is open daily except Tuesday morning from 7:30 to 11:30 a.m. If you're looking for a full meal, pass through the café and enter an elaborately paneled dining room, whose walls were removed intact from a much older house. (The older house, which was enlarged to make room for the new hotel, belonged to a local doctor, hence this lovely dining room bears his name, the Dr. Hildebrand-Stube.) Today the Sutter family, Leo and Margrit, serve hot meals every day except Tuesday at lunch, from 11 a.m. to 2 p.m. and from 5:30 to 10 p.m. Full dinners cost from 10.50F ($7.15) to 30F ($20.40) and might include curried pork, sautéed veal, and a house specialty of pork steak with smoked ham, tomatoes, Appenzeller cheese, vegetables, and croquettes. Lunches tend to be less elaborate, and could include a vegetarian risotto, an array of toasts, salads, and one of the establishment's famous pastries.

Hotel Hecht, CH-9050 Appenzell, Switzerland (tel. 071/87-10-25), is a clean, attractive, conservative alpine hostelry, a 300-year-old accommodating place. It's the biggest inn in Appenzell, and the Knechtle family, who have been here for 50 years, often host family celebrations, even marriages. The overall effect is gemütlich. Doubles without bath cost 85F ($57.80) daily, the price rising to 140F ($95.20) for a double with private bath. Singles rent for 50F ($34) to 80F ($54.40), depending on the plumbing. Half board is available for 25F ($17) per person extra daily.

Romantik Hotel Säntis, CH-9050 Appenzell, Switzerland (tel. 071/87-87-22) has a façade that is stenciled and painted with dozens of symmetrical regional designs and a series of small-paned windows in long horizontal rows. In summer the Heeb family sets out a few café tables so guests can take in the alpine sunshine before retiring to the cozy bedrooms, many of which are filled with regional antiques. On the premises is a snug dining room in Appenzell style with a wood ceiling and colorful tablecloths. All units contain private bath or shower. A single ranges in price from 75F ($51) to 90F ($61.20) daily, with doubles going for 120F ($81.60) to 160F ($108.80). Full board is another 45F ($30.60) per person daily. The hotel stands on a small square in the heart of town, and the reception is cordial.

WHERE TO DINE: With a view over the elaborately detailed houses of the main square, **Restaurant Säntis** (tel. 071/87-87-22) is on the first floor of the popular Romantik Hotel Säntis. The menu changes frequently, but usually has two or three specialties of the day, many of them regional. An appetizer might be a nourishing bouillon or a plate of alpine dried beef garnished with pickles and onions, followed by loin of lamb provençale or roast filet of pork. Even the noodles are homemade with eggs, carrots, and spinach, and beautifully served al dente as an accompaniment to some of the meat and fish dishes. Bottled wines are available, but the house wine, served in carafes, is also good. Fixed-price meals are offered for 28F ($19.05) to 55F ($37.40), while à la carte dinners begin at 20F ($13.60) and climb steeply from there. Food is served daily from 11:30 a.m. to 2 p.m. and 6:30 to 10 p.m. (to 9 p.m. in winter). The chef, Joseph Heeb, is also the owner, and he has an annual closing from January 10 to February 25.

Hotel Hecht Restaurant (tel. 071/87-10-25) is the oldest in town. Long known for its excellent cuisine and wine cellar, the hotel specializes in local fresh-water fish, especially trout (served au bleu or meunière) in its rustic restaurant. Appenzell food, along with continental dishes, are featured. A sausage platter is called Vesper-Plättli. A cherry paneling and paintings by local artists add a homey touch. Specialties of the chef include rice Casimir, veal with mushrooms in a cream sauce, and filet Gulyas Stroganoff. Meals cost from 35F ($23.80) up, and are served daily from 11 a.m. to 2 p.m. and 7 to 10 p.m. Count yourself fortunate if you get to hear typical Appenzell string-instrument music and see the unique Talerschwingen (rotating coins in a pot).

TROGEN: If you'd like to absorb the spirit of the Appenzell district, I suggest at least a night in Trogen, with its little historic hotel. The hamlet is the terminus of the St. Gallen–Speicher and Trogen tramway. The village has many frescoed 18th-century houses, and the people still cling to time-honored traditions.

Hotel Krone, CH-9043 Trogen, Switzerland (tel. 071/94-13-04), lies about five minutes away from the railway station by foot, in an elaborately painted gem of a building, with five floors and a hexagonally capped tower. The façade is pure country rococo from the 18th century. In summer you'll see a few tables in front, which will give you a chance to sit down and observe the building more closely. The owner is responsible for the food coming from the kitchen, which is well spoken of in the region. The hotel charges 35F ($23.80) per person daily in a bathless single or double, and 40F ($27.20) to 45F ($30.60) per person in a single or double with bath. Breakfast is included in these rates, although full and half board are available for an additional 32F ($21.75) or 18F ($12.25), respectively, per person daily. English is spoken.

3. LAKE CONSTANCE

Even though three nations—Austria, Germany, and Switzerland—share the 162-mile shoreline of this large inland sea, the area around Lake Constance is united in a common cultural and historical heritage. The hillsides sloping down to the water's edge are covered with vineyards and orchards, and are dotted with hamlets and tourist centers. The mild climate and plentiful sunshine make Lake Constance a vacation spot for lovers of sun and sand, as well as for sightseers and spa-hoppers. A well-organized network of cruise ships and ferries links every major center around the lake.

Lake Constance is divided into three parts, although the name is frequently applied to the largest of these, the Bodensee. The western end of the Bodensee separates into two distinct branches, including the Überlingersee, a long fjord. On the other hand the Untersee is more irregular, jutting in and out of the marshlands and low-lying woodlands. It's connected to the larger lake by only a narrow channel of water—actually, the young Rhine, whose current flows right through the Bodensee. Tip: The blue felchen, a pike-like fish found only in Lake Constance, furnishes the district with a tasty and renowned specialty.

Favorite targets along the Swiss side of the lake follow.

ROMANSHORN: This town is one of the best centers on the Swiss side, and it's even convenient should you wish to explore the attractions on the German side. It has its own resort facilities, including a swimming pool, sailing school, waterskiing school, and tennis courts, but it's also a big excursion center.

A ferry runs all year from Romanshorn to Friedrichshafen, in Germany, with its castle, a summer residence of the Württemberg kings and its Zeppelin mementos. In summer, boat trips are organized to the island of Mainau, a German island (the former home of the Grand Duke of Baden) that lies about four miles north of Constance. Boats also visit Meersburg and Lindau.

Romanshorn has a beautiful park with stunning summer flora, plus a zoo. But mainly visitors come here because, as the largest port on Lake Constance, it's the base of the Swiss lake steamers.

Food and Lodging

Park-Hotel Inseli, Inselistrasse, CH-8590 Romanshorn, Switzerland (tel. 071/63-53-53), under the management of Anton Stäger and his family, is a modern hotel with red-trimmed extensions and big windows, secluded in a grove of trees in sight of a soaring stone church. Views from the comfortable rooms are over an expanse of lawn, some with a glimpse of the lake. Many of the public rooms are appealingly decorated with wood, chrome, and lots of plush carpeting, and the kind of informal ambience that lets you feel at home. All rooms have private baths/showers, toilets, color TV, radios, phones, mini-bars, and mini-safes. Singles cost 73F ($49.65) to 117F ($79.55) daily. Doubles go for 123F ($83.65) to 147F ($99.95). Half board is available for another 33F ($22.45) per person daily. You can hear birds singing as you dine in the indoor/outdoor café and the more formal rôtisserie, both of which have large windows through which the sunlight streams in.

Hotel Bodan, Bahnhofstrasse, CH-8590 Romanshorn, Switzerland (tel. 071/63-15-02), is a large, old-fashioned two-star hotel with buff-colored exterior walls and simple, sanitary bedrooms. This establishment sits across the street from the lake, near the railway station. The registration rituals might best be described as casual, although you might eventually find a receptionist if you ring the appropriate buzzer enough times. Bedrooms rent for 43F ($29.25) to 50F ($34) daily in a single, 72F ($48.95) to 85F ($57.80) in a double. The more expensive rates are for units with private baths. On the premises are an array of attractive eating areas.

ARBON: One of the best spots on the lake is Arbon, whose lakefront promenade offers a view over Constance, the German shore opposite and both the Swiss and Austrian Alps. Arbon is well equipped with facilities, including a large boat harbor, swimming pools, and a school for sailing and surfing. It's the starting point for many interesting excursions.

Arbon Castle was a medieval stronghold that has been turned into a local museum. Its keep is from the 13th century, and the residential wings date from the beginning of the 16th century. Arbon occupies the site of an ancient Celtic community. It was known to the Romans as Arbor Felix.

Food and Lodging

Hotel Metropole, CH-9320 Arbon, Switzerland (tel. 071/46-35-35). Considered an interesting example of creative urban planning, this concrete-sided Best Western hotel lies within a lakeside complex that includes a department store, a grocery store, and a busy cafeteria popular with shoppers. You register within a functional, Nordic modern lobby before heading up to your comfortable but unfrilly bedroom. Each unit has its own loggia, bath, radio, phone, and color TV. Depending on the season, singles rent for 85F ($57.80) to 105F ($71.40) daily, doubles for 135F ($91.80) to 195F ($125.80), with breakfast included. On the premises is a hot whirlpool, plus a sauna, an aboveground swimming pool sunk into the roof of one of the public rooms, a warmly inviting dark-toned bar, and a restaurant and café whose lakeside tables do a thriving business in warm weather.

Hotel Rotes Kreuz, 3 Hafenstrasse, CH-9320 Arbon, Switzerland (tel. 071/46-19-14), sits at the edge of a lawn bordering the lake, behind a low wall and a clipped barrier of sycamores. A stucco-sided house with red shutters and an ample outdoor terrace, it was originally built in 1760. Today, it contains a rambling duet of indoor dining rooms and a handful of simple but well-scrubbed bedrooms. Per person rates, single or double occupancy, for units with baths and phones are 45F ($30.60) to 50F ($34) per day. Half board can be arranged for an additional 16F ($10.90) per person per day.

If you want to stop in just for a meal, you can select a seat outdoors, within a glassed-in solarium or a cozy pine-paneled stube. Meals are served daily from 11:30 a.m. to 2 p.m., and from 5 to 9 p.m. You can snack for 10F ($6.80), although full meals cost from 20F ($13.60) each. Specialties include all kinds of lake fish, such as felchen filet with fennel and white wine sauce, or veal strips with a mushroom and cream sauce, calves' liver, peppersteak, and sausage salad, well known locally.

HORN: This ancient fishing village lies five minutes by car from Arbon. The hamlet belongs to the canton of Thurgau, and it's an idyllic little spot in which to base during your exploration of Lake Constance. The large port of Rorschach lies farther east.

Food and Lodging

Try the **Hotel Bad Horn,** 36 Seestrasse, CH-9326 Horn, Switzerland (tel. 071/41-55-11), which stands in an idyllic position at the end of a small peninsula extending into the lake. The building is painted a vivid ochre, with big windows, a gabled tile roof, rooftop terraces, and an expanse of grassy lawn extending almost to the water. From the street side of the hotel you'll get an idea of how large it really is, encompassing conference rooms, two restaurants, and the Bounty Bar in addition to its 37 bedrooms, all with bath. Singles rent for 65F ($44.20) to 75F ($51) daily, and doubles go for 140F ($95.20) to 170F ($115.60).

The establishment's more interesting restaurant is the Captain's Grill, with an elegant nautical decor. In an ambience of sun-dappled windows, a ceiling frieze of acanthus leaves, and intricately detailed models of clipper ships, you can enjoy full meals costing from 50F ($34). Such specialties are offered as aiguillettes of pink duck, two preparations of trout, quenelles of a local fish, scampi with calvados, filet of beef with Armagnac, and many dishes flambéed at your table, including giant shrimp with sherry or filet of pork with gin. Meals are served from 11:30 a.m. to 2 p.m. and 6:30 to 9 p.m. daily.

RORSCHACH: If you're planning to tour Lake Constance and visit the German side as well, Rorschach is a harbor town on the Swiss side of the lake. The thousand-year-old port lies at the foot of the Rorschacher Berg at the most southerly part of the lake. If based here, you can virtually decide which country you want to visit on any given day, as the Principality of Liechtenstein, Germany, and Austria are at the doorstep.

Rorschach has had an illustrious past, as many of its buildings testify to this day. These include the Kornhaus, a granary built in 1746, the painted 18th-century houses along Hauptgasse with oriel windows, and the former Mariaberg cloister.

Of these, the **Kornhaus** is now a museum, which has a collection of prehistoric artifacts and examples of local weaving and embroidery as well as a section on the Castle of Wartegg. It's open from 9:30 to 11:30 a.m. and 2 to 5 p.m. (on Sunday, from 10 a.m. to noon and 2 to 5 p.m.), charging an admission of 2.50F ($1.70). Closed from November to April.

The town also has lakeside gardens, modern passenger ships that go for trips on the lake, an extensive promenade, plus facilities for sailing, rowing, swimming, fishing, and windsurfing.

Food and Lodging

Parkhotel Waldau, CH-9400 Rorschach, Switzerland (tel. 071/43-01-80). Designed to look like a sprawling manor house, this country hotel was originally built just after World War II as a private school for boys. When it proved to be unsuccessful, it was transformed into a substantial and modern five-star hotel. It lies about four miles southwest of the commercial center of town on a knoll which overlooks the lake, surrounded by grassy lawns, tennis courts, stately trees, and an elegant indoor/outdoor restaurant. The warm and comfortable interior is accented with stone blocks, paneling, and tufted leather banquettes. Each of the rooms contains a safe, a TV, a radio, a phone, and a mini-bar. Depending on the plumbing and the accommodation, singles cost 118F ($80.25) to 132F ($89.75) daily, and doubles go for 230F ($156.40) to 250F ($170), with breakfast, service, and taxes included. On the premises are both an indoor and an outdoor pool, a fitness center, and an array of hydrotherapy services.

The hotel's elegant restaurant is known throughout the region as a glamorous stopover for local business people entertaining their clients. Depending on the weather, meals are served either in the rear garden or one floor above the reception area. If you're inside, you'll be surrounded with heavy ceiling beams, a scattering of tapestries and heavy antiques, and a battalion of polite, formal employees. The candlelit dinners usually include a pianist who moves to the bar after 11 p.m. Lunch is served from noon to 2 p.m., dinner from 7 to 11 p.m. every day. Fixed-price lunches cost from 40F ($27.40). Full à la carte dinners cost from 65F ($44.20). Menu specialties include veal kidneys with truffles, elegant pasta dishes, different preparations of perch and trout, goose liver terrine, U.S. beefsteak, and a mixed grill with a choice of sauces. Reservations are suggested.

If you like boats, you'll love the **Hotel Anker,** CH-9400 Rorschach, Switzerland (tel. 071/41-42-43), across the street from a marina where many of the town's boats are anchored. Covered with flowers in summer, the hotel is a substantial looking building with a light-gray façade, a gabled red-tile roof, and scattered balconies that overlook the busiest commercial street in town and the lakefront beyond. To register, you climb a flight of stairs. With breakfast and a private bathroom included, year-round prices are 55F ($37.40) to 80F ($54.40) daily for a single, 100F ($68) to 150F ($102) for a double. The 33 bedrooms were originally built in 1720, but have been modernized frequently.

Don't overlook the possibility of a meal in the quintet of dining areas near the reception desk. My preferred spot is a glassed-in terrace overlooking the lake. Hot meals are served daily from 11 a.m. to 2 p.m. and from 5 to 10 p.m. Full meals here are a good value, beginning at 35F ($23.80) each. You can start with baked Camembert with cranberries and orange sauce, follow with squid in a remoulade sauce, at least two varieties of trout, salmon with Madeira sauce, several kinds of grilled fresh fish, veal, steaks, pastas, and a rijsttafel for two persons.

Hotel Mozart, Hafenzentrum, CH-9400 Rorschach, Switzerland (tel. 071/41-06-32). Opened in 1986, this comfortable hotel is attractively set between the main street of town and the lake, behind a façade of polished granite and modern windows. Each of the 30 charmingly decorated bedrooms has a private bath, TV, phone, radio, and mini-bar. Seven of the units offer views of the nearby lake. Depending on the season, singles cost 80F ($54.40) to 90F ($61.20) daily, and doubles go for 130F ($88.40) to 150F ($102), with breakfast, service, and taxes included. Because of the lack of easy parking in the town center, motorists appreciate the hotel's free parking garage.

The hotel's Café Mozart, with its Old World ambience, is known for its variety of tempting pastries, costing from 3F ($2.05). Another specialty is tea—19 varieties including essence of kiwi, linden blossom, and tea leaves grown on the foothills of Mount Everest or the coast of Morocco. The café also offers simple meals and daily plates at prices starting at 8F ($5.45).

HEIDEN: High above Lake Constance on a sunlit ridge in the canton of Appenzell, the little health resort of Heiden lies about four miles south of Rorschach. Virtually undiscovered by Americans, it's reached by cog railway in about 20 minutes. There's a 1960s monument to Henri Dunant, founder of the Red Cross, who lived here until his death in 1910 and gave the resort much publicity.

Even if you can't stay at one of Heiden's hotels (recommended below), you may want to take the cog railway just for the view of the valleys set against a mountain backdrop. You pass through an orchard setting, with an occasional castle in the background, and go across several viaducts to reach the little spa.

Food and Lodging

Hotel Krone, CH-9410 Heiden, Switzerland (tel. 071/91-11-27), is housed in an elegantly ornate building, painted white, with a red tile roof capped by ornate gables and a modified onion-shaped dome. The grounds around the hotel are well maintained with lots of flowers, and the public rooms have well-polished collections of Victorian and Biedermeier chairs and beautifully aged cupboards and chests. The bedrooms have good views of the surrounding countryside, all the modern comforts, and enough personal touches to make you feel at home. It's been owned by the same family, the Kühnes, for 60-plus years. A bathless single costs 75F ($51) daily, the rate going up to 90F ($61.20) with private bath. The tariff rises to 140F ($95.20) to 180F ($128.40) in a double with private bath or shower. Lunch or dinner costs from 35F ($23.80). A heated swimming pool is available for guests.

Hotel Linde, CH-9410 Heiden, Switzerland (tel. 071/91-14-14), is housed in an attractive four-story building with lots of shutters and a sunny terrace extending out of sight off to the side of the house. A Swiss flag usually flies in front, hoisted every morning by the Ruppanner family, who charge 75F ($51) to 95F ($64.60) daily in a single, 116F ($78.90) to 160F ($108.80) in a double. The comfortable bedrooms have phones, radios, and showers or baths. Meals in the dining room are varied from day to day, lunches costing from 22F ($14.95) and dinners going for 35F ($23.80).

4. STEIN-AM-RHEIN

Only 12 miles from Schaffhausen, on the right bank of the Rhine, Stein-am-Rhein is celebrated as one of the most authentic medieval towns of Switzerland. It lies at the western edge of the Untersee, an arm of Lake Constance from which the Rhine leaves the lake.

Nearby was the first Roman bridge ever built over the Rhine. Records of the town go back to 1094.

Its principal sights are the **Rathausplatz** (the Town Hall square) and **Hauptstrasse** (the main street). Here the houses evoke that much-overused word "quaint," with their oriel windows, richly embellished frescoes, studded timberwork, and flower-bedecked fountains. They often have themes such as the house of the red ox or the white eagle. The townspeople love flowers so much that in summer the place virtually bursts into bloom.

The **Historische Sammlung** (Historical Museum) is in the Town Hall (tel. 071/41-42-31). It has the usual collection of a small Swiss town: weaponry, banners, and stained glass. Charging 1F (68¢), the museum is open from 10 to 11:30 a.m. and 2 to 5 p.m. Monday to Friday. It's closed on Saturday, Sunday, and holidays.

A Benedictine abbey was erected in the town at the beginning of the 11th century but was dissolved in 1524. The **Klostermuseum St. Georgen** (St. George's Abbey Museum) is housed there (tel. 054/41-21-42). Devoted to local history and art, the rooms are often more fascinating than the exhibits, with their rich ceilings and panelings and their 16th-century murals by Thomas

Schmid and Ambrosius Holbein. The convent church of St. George, a 12th-century Romanesque basilica, has been renovated. It's now a Protestant parish church. The museum is open daily from 10 a.m. to noon and 1:30 to 5 p.m., charging 3F ($2.05) for adults, 1.50F ($1) for children.

If you're driving, perhaps you'd like to journey for two miles to visit **Hohenklingen Castle**, a medieval hilltop stronghold constructed in the mid-16th century. It's open from the first of March until mid-December daily except Monday. A tavern opened here in the 19th century, and at present a castle restaurant, popular with summer visitors, has been installed.

FOOD AND LODGING: The finest hotel in town, the **Hotel Chlosterhof,** CH-8260 Stein am Rhein, Switzerland (tel. 054/42-42-42), was dramatically created out of an abandoned shoe factory. It's been turned into one of the most elegant and comfortable hotels in the area, occupying a choice position right on the river. The hotel has an architectural harmony, with rich colors, an open fireplace, a lobby with a sweeping cruciform vault, and fields of Italian marble. Often used in off-season for conferences, summer it is likely to be filled with foreign visitors enjoying one of the stylized 68 bedrooms. Four-posters are used in ten of the rooms, which, management says, were designed for romantics. A single rents for 120F ($81.60) to 160F ($108.80) daily, two persons paying from 160F ($108.80) to 210F ($142.80), with suites costing more. Fine dining is available in the nautically decorated Le Bateau.

Hotel Rheinfels, Rathausplatz, CH-8260 Stein am Rhein, Switzerland (tel. 054/41-21-44). The very large building that contains it was built in 1448 beside the rapidly flowing source of the Rhine. The hotel is as well known for its waterside terrace as it is for its 16 pleasantly decorated bedrooms. You can dine on the terrace within sight of a border of flowers, a few feet from a modern concrete bridge that spans the water and leads to the heart of the old city. Upstairs, one flight above the restaurant, is an antique room with wide, creaking floorboards, massive chandeliers, old portraits, and a collection of medieval armor. All but four of the rooms have private baths. Throughout the year, singles cost 90F ($61.20) daily, and doubles go for 120F ($81.60), with breakfast included.

Hotel-Restaurant Adler, Rathausplatz, CH-8260 Stein am Rhein, Switzerland (tel. 054/42-61-61). Simple, honest, and comfortable, this 25-room hotel sits behind one of the old city's most flamboyant façades. Covered with painted characters from Rhenish legends, it depicts such medieval references as a tree of life, martyrs at the stake, and audiences groveling before Oriental potentates. You register at the bar of the street-level restaurant, where few of the staff will speak English. No one will mind if you delay your ascent to your room by ordering a drink, snack, or meal. On all sides of you, card-playing groups of cronies and scatterings of families create what might be the most quietly gregarious gatherings in town.

The two sections of the hotel date from 1461 and 1957, respectively. Each of the rooms has been recently renovated into a streamlined Nordic design containing a private bath, radio, phone, and TV. Prices range from 50F ($34) to 60F ($40.80) daily per person, single or double occupancy, with breakfast included. The in-house garage charges 10F ($6.80) per night for parking.

For fine dining, try **Restaurant Sonne,** 127 Rathausplatz (tel. 054/41-21-28), in the center of town. It's one of the most famous establishments in this historic town, benefiting from its location on the well-preserved marketplace. In the intimate dining room inside, head chef and owner Philippe Combe practices a form of cuisine moderne that is likely to include fresh river crabs in a vinaigrette sauce, wild game in a beaujolais sauce (served with wild mushrooms sautéed in butter), or roast hare with mustard sauce. Other dishes include ravioli stuffed with lobster, sea bass with fresh asparagus, pigeon with truffles, and filet of beef with citrus or herbs. Good wines complement a fine repast, all of it capped by a smooth dessert such as chocolate mousse. Fixed-price meals cost 99F ($67.30), while à la carte dinners cost from 65F ($44.20). The restaurant is open from noon to 2 p.m. and 6 to 9:30 p.m. except on Thursday.

Hotel Rheinfels (tel. 054/41-21-44). Contained within the previously recommended hotel, this pleasant restaurant offers a trio of dining rooms and a riverside terrace. Even if it's too cold (or too crowded) for you to dine beside the rapidly flowing Rhine, the big windows of the other rooms offer watery views anyway. Open daily except Monday, the restaurant serves hot meals from 11 a.m. to 2 p.m. and from 5:30 to 9:30 p.m. Full dinners cost from 40F ($27.20), and might include filets of fera (a lake fish) with lemon and capers, fricassée of Rhenish fish with baby vegetables, hot bauernschinken (farmer's ham), grilled veal steak, a "fitness lunch" of salad and grilled meats, and a "potpourri of Rheinfels desserts." Throughout the afternoon, the establishment serves drinks and snacks. The annual closing is in January and February.

5. SCHAFFHAUSEN AND RHEINFALL

An atmosphere from the Middle Ages still hangs over this old town constructed on terraces on the Rhine's right bank. The whole effect makes it one of the most charming little cities in the country. If that weren't reason enough to visit, it's also a center for visiting the Rhine Falls (Rheinfall), one of the most popular sights in this part of the country.

The city is modern and industrial, but it has integrated its industry into its physical setting in such a way that the ancient charm has still been preserved. The town has many romantic fountains, and its brown-roofed houses are decorated with statues and paintings, and often contain oriel windows.

The capital of a Swiss canton of the same name, Schaffhausen lies about 31 "rail miles" to the west of Constance. Once an imperial free city, it was before that ruled by the Habsburgs. Many troops have marched through here, notably the Swedish and Bavarian armies. Today Schaffhausen is enclosed on three sides by Germany.

THE SIGHTS: You can spend a morning touring the old town at your leisure. Crowning the town is the **Munot,** dating from 1564. Along the battlements, you'll have a good view of the old town. It's reached by stairs and a covered footbridge across the moat. This round fortress has a tower, platform, and parapet walks. Built in 1564, it was the only fortress to be based on the ideas of Albrecht Dürer, which were published in a book in Nürnberg in 1527. It's open May to September from 8 a.m. to 8 p.m. daily and October to April from 9 a.m. to 5 p.m.

Back in the old town, visitors always like to photograph the frescoed **Haus zum Ritter** from 1485. Find your way to Vordergasse, the most charming street in the old town. The outstanding fountain is the Fronwagplatz, actually two fountains, both from the 1520s. The Rathaus (town hall) was built in 1632, but the crowning glory of Schaffhausen is All Saints' Church (or the **Münster** as the locals call it). Now Protestant, it was formerly a Benedictine monastery, consecrated in 1052. Its Romanesque architecture represents the sternest and plainest style. In a small courtyard nearby is the 15th-century bell that inspired Schiller's "Song of the Bell" and the opening of Longfellow's "Golden Legend."

The **Museum zu Allerheiligen,** or All Saints' Museum (tel. 053/5-43-77), housed in a former abbey, today is one of the most important national museums in Switzerland. Its exhibits range from the prehistoric to the present day. Look for the "Treasury" in the former abbots' salon. You'll see everything from the traditional regional garb of the province to old weaponry and period furnishings. It's open from 10 a.m. to noon and 2 to 5 p.m. except Monday.

Leaving the town, you can take the trail of beauty-lover John Ruskin to the **Rheinfall** (Rhine Falls), the most celebrated waterfall in central Europe, certainly the most powerful, as 700 cubic meters of water per second rush over a width of 150 yards.

At this point the Rhine falls 70 feet, a sight that inspired Goethe to liken it to the "source of the ocean." The fall is most spectacular in the peak months of early summer when it's fed by mountain snows.

Most American visitors are based in Zurich when they decide to visit this falls. From the Hauptbahnhof in Zurich, they can travel by train to Neuhausen and the Rheinfall stop. The train reaches Neuhausen in less than an hour. From the train depot at Neuhausen you can walk to the waterfall in about 15 minutes. You can take a 10F ($6.80) boat trip to the rock in the center of the Rheinfall, a most dramatic experience.

Others prefer to view the falls from a belvedere provided for that purpose. On the left bank, this is best done at **Laufen Castle,** which has been converted into, naturally, a restaurant with a view of the falls. To stand on a belvedere, go inside the forecourt of the castle and down a staircase until you are on the same level as the falls (better carry a raincoat).

You can also take a ferry across the river to the little **Wörth Castle,** which was a customs post at the falls, probably built in the 12th century. It too has been turned into a restaurant, and is open from the first of March until mid-November.

FOOD AND LODGING: Next to a riverside promenade on which you can see activity on the Rhine, **Rheinhotel Fischerzunft,** 8 Rheinquai, CH-8200 Schaffhausen, Switzerland (tel. 053/25-32-81), is an inviting inn. Once occupied by the Fishermen's Guild, in 1898 it became the property of the Jaeger family, who made it into an inn. The modernized accommodations today consist of nine rooms and three suites, all with baths or showers, toilets, phones, color TV, radio alarm clocks, and mini-bars. The charges, with breakfast, service, and taxes included, are 120F ($81.60) to 180F ($122.40) daily in a single, depending on the standard of the room and the view. Doubles rent for 160F ($108.80) to 240F ($163.20). Suites are higher, of course.

In charge are André Jaeger and his Chinese wife, Doreen Jaeger-Soong, both highly trained and charming hoteliers and restaurateurs. After their meeting in Hong Kong and subsequent move to Schaffhausen to be married, the young couple, both of whom speak good English, took over operation of the family inn from André's father and began what has proved to be a happy alliance of East and West, especially in the culinary department of the Fischerzunft. Chinoiserie in the main public room initiated the changes in the traditional Swiss hotel, soon followed by André's experimentation with Chinese ingredients and recipes.

Oriental flower arrangements are placed throughout the Fischerzunft and its restaurant. The pleasure to the eye is present also in the dishes served. Classic European and Chinese-Asian combinations include curried chicken consommé with Chinese ravioli, filet of venison with five Chinese spices and sautéed mustard cabbage, and lobster salad with coriander, Chinese noodles, and creamy sesame sauce. In his repertory of dishes rich in taste, texture, and design, André Jaeger offers filet of salmon trout in cream of lobster with wild rice and a special treat for those who love fish, a potpourri made up of many kinds of fresh- and saltwater denizens. Desserts, too, are things of beauty to behold and to eat: mango with raspberry sauce and mango sherbet or a fan of figs and pineapple with iced vanilla mousse being my favorite selections. Expect to pay 120F ($81.60) for a fixed-price gourmet menu, or 50F ($34) to 85F ($57.80) for an à la carte meal. The restaurant is open from noon to 2 p.m. and 7 to 9:30 p.m. daily.

In a building set among massive trees, **Hotel Park Villa,** 18 Parkstrasse, CH-8200 Schaffhausen, Switzerland (tel. 053/25-27-37), stands on a green area close to the train station. The towers, steep roofs, and gables are covered with terracotta tiles, and the façade is crafted of chiseled gray rocks, giving a pleasingly uneven texture to the surfaces. The interior is as elegantly graceful as the exterior is rough. There are crystal chandeliers, a bar area with wooden backdrops that are more like furniture than paneling, and a series of public rooms dotted with fresh flowers, comfortable chairs, and oil paintings. A few of the bedrooms are regally decorated with antiques. The manager, Max Schlumpf, charges from 120F ($81.60) to 160F ($108.80) daily in a double with bath and from 80F ($54.40) to 95F ($64.60) in a single with bath. Bathless rooms rent for 50F ($34) to 60F ($40.80) in a single and from 100F ($68) in a double. A two-room apartment with bath, suitable for three persons, rents for 180F ($122.40). For a game of tennis, there's a well-maintained court only a few feet away from the back of the building.

Hotel Bellevue, Bahnhofstrasse, CH-8212 Neuhausen am Rheinfall, Switzerland (tel. 053/22-21-21), has the advantage of having a terrace where you can sip drinks and watch the waterfall without being drenched. With the green countryside stretched out beyond the water, you can imagine yourself in an area more primitive than industrialized Europe. The interior of the hotel is simple and modern. Singles rent for 45F ($30.60) to 55F ($37.40) daily without bath, 80F ($54.40) to 98F ($66.65) with large tile baths. Doubles go for 140F ($95.20) to 170F ($115.60), all with bath. Breakfast is included in the rates. The owner, Thomas Nohava, does everything he can to make his guests comfortable. The restaurant, with a view of the falls, serves fixed-price meals costing from 25F ($17).

Other good dining choices include the following.

Restaurant Gerberstube, 8 Bachstrasse (tel. 053/25-21-55). The Guidi family runs the finest Italian dining room in Schaffhausen. Occupying a 17th-century guildhall, the restaurant is attractively decorated, enhanced by a changing exhibition of modern painters. The chef is known mostly for his veal and pasta dishes. You might begin with the famous egg and consommé soup of Rome, stracciatella, following with either spaghetti or cannelloni, perhaps a veal schnitzel pizzaiola. Many dishes are from a classic repertoire, including chateaubriand with béarnaise sauce. À la carte meals cost from 35F ($23.80) up, and are served daily except Monday from noon to 2 p.m. and from 6:30 to 10 p.m.

6. TOGGENBURG

Once this part of Switzerland was independent, but it's now part of the cantonal district of St. Gallen. The valley of Toggenburg has some of the most varied scenery in eastern Switzerland. Lying south of Thurgau, it takes in the Upper Thur Valley and several little offshoot valleys, all rich in scenic attractions (but little else). The valley follows a curvy line between the Walensee and Mt. Säntis. A series of three resorts, Alt St. Johann, Unterwasser, and Wildhaus, are here, each one attracting a summer market, mainly German or the Swiss themselves, who know of the charm of the place and the moderate prices.

WILDHAUS: This resort is built on a plateau over the Toggenburg. It was the birthplace of Zwingli, the great Swiss reformer. The modest cottage in which he was born in 1484 still lies in the hamlet of Lisighaus.

Wildhaus, standing at a height of about 4,000 feet, is both a summer and a winter resort. The gateway airport is usually Zurich. However, many motorists cross the Rhine from Vaduz, the capital of Liechtenstein, going through the town of Buchs. The scenery along the road from Buchs is magnificent, and in about 18 miles you reach Wildhaus. Zurich is some 40 miles away.

Wildhaus has an indoor swimming pool, a curling rink, and an ice rink, and is a cross-country skiing center. It occupies a splendid setting on the south side of the Wildhauser Schafberg. A chair lift transports skiers to Gamplüt, at a height of about 4,412 feet. Another chair lift goes to Oberdorf at 4,165 feet, from which another lift takes passengers to Gamsalp and from there to Gamserugg. Children are especially catered to at Wildhaus. You'll find a kindergarten, even a ski school for them.

The Resort Hotels

Hotel Acker, CH-9658 Wildhaus, Switzerland (tel. 074/5-91-11), is in two separate buildings, one older than the other, and connected by a passageway containing an all-season swimming pool that, in winter, looks out through big windows onto the rolling hills in the distance. All of the bedrooms are modern, streamlined, and comfortable, with competent management by Werner J. Beck. There are enough mountain trails in the vicinity to make anyone a sports enthusiast. Rates, which are slightly higher in the newer section, range from 160F ($108.80) to 280F ($190.40) daily in a double, depending on the exposure and the season, and from 95F ($64.60) to 165F ($112.20) in a single. Half-board is included.

Hotel Hirschen, CH-9658 Wildhaus, Switzerland (tel. 074/5-22-52). The rooms are unpretentiously but comfortably furnished, with rustic paneling on some of the walls. The setting is alpine, with good views in many directions. A sauna and a large swimming pool are provided. The hotel is a small-scale resort, with facilities such as a hairdresser, disco or folklore dancing, a restaurant, and a snackbar. The Walt family offers rooms with bath or shower on the European plan for 88F ($59.85) to 98F ($66.65) daily for singles, 154F ($104.72) to 198F ($134.65) for doubles. Reductions are granted for children. The hotel also offers special arrangements for weekends, ski weeks, or hiking weeks. It is only a drive of about 1¼ hours from Zurich's Kloten Airport.

Hotel Toggenburg, CH-9658 Wildhaus, Switzerland (tel. 074/5-23-23). The designer of this hotel understood the technique of adding rustic touches to bring the outdoors inside. The bedrooms usually have areas covered with amber-tinted planks, on sloped ceilings or in partially tiled baths. The big windows make the rooms bright and sunny, and the restaurant provides nourishing, well-prepared meals in a timbered room with a view over the countryside. Depending on the season, singles with private bath rent for 85F ($57.80) to 105F ($71.40). Doubles, also with private bath, cost 150F ($102) to 190F ($129.20). These prices include half board. Peter Arn and his family are your congenial hosts.

UNTERWASSER: Two miles from Wildhaus, Unterwasser is another small resort in a tranquil setting, lying between the Mt. Säntis chain and the Churfirsten. Two streams merge here to create the Thur River. From Unterwasser you can take a mountain railway to Iltios at 4,430 feet, which has a big restaurant with a sunning platform where skiers soak up alpine sun in winter. From Iltios, the cableway continues to Chäserugg at 7,415 feet, from which there is a view over the Walensee to Flumserberg (see below). It offers suitable skiing for all grades.

Hotel Säntis, CH-9657 Unterwasser, Switzerland (tel. 074/5-28-11), is comfortable, and it's in the center of this fast-rising summer and winter playground. Designed for maximum balcony space, the hotel attracts many families who enjoy the sunny spacious rooms for their vacations, as well as local business people who use it for their conferences. Children receive special discount rates when they stay in a room with their parents. The rate structure is complicated, too much so to detail here, but prices are roughly from 110F ($74.80) to 125F ($85) daily in a single, from 180F ($122.40) to 210F ($142.80) in a double, depending on the season. All units have private baths, and breakfast is included in the prices.

7. WALENSEE

This nine-mile-long lake, one of the most beautiful in Switzerland, is nestled between the Glarus Alps and the Churfirsten, a relatively undiscovered area for Americans. Immortalized by Liszt, the lake is often glimpsed by tourists sailing from Zurich when they pass through the gap at Weesen-Sargans, heading for the Grisons, a much more popular destination. The lake is studded with some sleepy little resorts and in the mountains are some ski centers.

FLUMSERBERG: This alpine district of grazing meadows and little mountain chalets is reached from Flums. Two small, winding roads lead up to it. It's both a winter and a summer resort, overlooking Lake Walen. It offers good snow conditions throughout the winter, and in summer attracts mountain hikers. Ski courses are available. A vast network of marked hiking trails lead across wide alpine pastures, and the tiny resort also has an indoor swimming pool, tennis courts, cable cars, and, always, that view of Lake Walen.

Flumserberg can be reached by way of the Zurich-Chur expressway or railway by using the cable car leaving from Unterterzen. It can also be reached by postal bus on a mountain road from Flums. The trip from Zurich is about an hour and a half.

The resort is connected with the fast-rising ski areas in the villages of Tannenheim at 4,000 feet and Tannenbodenalp at 4,595 feet.

The Resort Hotels

Hotel Gauenpark, CH-8897 Flumserberg, Switzerland (tel. 085/3-31-31), is beautiful in any season, but is particularly dramatic in winter, when the snow on the alpine ridge behind the four-star hotel makes the mountains look even closer. That's when the lights from the weatherproof windows of this place look especially inviting, and when you're likely to meet visitors from all over Europe. The interior makes use of every natural material, from the naturally finished vertical pine slats on the walls to the rough stone blocks of the floors in the snackbar. There's also lots of high-gloss wood in the intimately lit disco. Prices for bed and breakfast are on a per-person basis in a double room. All units have private baths and toilets. From December to April, rooms for double occupancy rent for 68F ($46.25) to 76F ($51.70) per person daily. The charge from May to October, also double occupancy, is 62F ($42.15) to 68F ($46.25) per person. Half board costs 80F ($54.40) to 96F ($65.30) per person daily, double occupancy, from December to April, and 78F ($53.05) to 84F ($57.10) per person for double occupancy from May to October. A supplement is charged for single occupancy. Facilities include a whirlpool bath, a sauna, and a solarium. The Restaurant Gauenstube is known for its fine service and à la carte dishes.

Hotel Alpina, CH-8894 Flumserberg, Switzerland (tel. 085/3-12-32), has exquisite views of the nearby alpine ridge from its many balconies, some of which are set at oblique angles to the main building for maximum advantage. The outside looks surprisingly urban for a village landscape (lots of concrete), but the interior is pierced with enough windows to allow views in many directions. The public rooms are warmly appointed with natural wood and well-chosen textiles. The Güller family is your host. Comfortably furnished singles rent for 70F ($47.60) to 100F ($68) daily, while doubles range from 140F ($95.20) to 170F ($115.60), depending on the season and the plumbing. Rates include half board. Closed in May, October, and November.

8. BAD RAGAZ

This alpine Rhine Valley spa—one of the best known in Switzerland—has been famous for its mineral waters since the 11th century. Guests suffering from rheumatism and circulatory disorders are attracted to Bad Ragaz, but even if you're in perfect health you may want to make this a holiday center. The setting for the resort is a park-like landscape in the foothills of the Alps at about 1,673 feet, and from a comfortable base here you can branch out on many a hiker's trail, especially through "the wild and romantic" Tamina Gorge.

The spa is well equipped with hotels, and chances are, your bedroom window will open onto a view of the rugged crests of the Falknis. The spa is also a departure point with cable cars and ski lifts to the Bad Ragaz–Pardiel-Pizol mountain railways, with connections to ski districts of the same name.

In summer you can enjoy the town's beautiful 18-hole golf course, along with tennis, riding, fishing, hiking (as mentioned), and mountain climbing, plus an open-air swimming pool. In winter, nature-lovers fill their days with ski runs, natural skating rinks, indoor tennis, riding, and footpaths, later soothed by a special concert. In other words, this is one resort that's in business!

The **Bad Ragaz Tourist Office** in town (tel. 085/9-10-61) will give you a map and outline excursions in the area, especially to spots such as Bad Pfäfers (see below).

Golfers can try the facilities of the Bad Ragaz Golf Club (tel. 085/9-15-56). A day's card to play the 18-hole course costs 50F ($35) to 60F ($40.80).

WHERE TO STAY: A five-star spa and golf hotel at the foot of the Alps, **Quellenhof,** Bernhard Simon Strasse, CH-7310 Bad Ragaz, Switzerland (tel. 085/9-01-11), is set in its own landscaped park and gardens. It has a somber design of symmetrical wings and elaborate cast-iron balustrades, very much a product of 19th-century grandeur. Inside, clusters of Victorian armchairs alternate with velvet-covered barrel-shape chairs in a modernized format of much comfort. A glass-fronted sun terrace, overlooking a manicured park, is in back. Many persons suffering from rheumatic or circulatory disorders come here for the mineral-water cures that are so famous throughout Switzerland. In former days the hotel attracted that once-reigning king and queen of Hollywood, Douglas Fairbanks and Mary Pickford. And over the years much real royalty has stayed here as well, including the crown prince of the Netherlands. Since those golden days, the bedrooms, which are spacious and tasteful, have been modernized, and each unit has a phone, frigobar (mini-bar), TV, and radio. Attractively furnished and generally spacious rooms, either single or double, cost 150F ($102) to 225F ($153) per person daily. The hotel is open all year, offering reduced rates from November 1 to mid-April. The finest food at the spa is served here at what is one of the most distinguished restaurants in the east of Switzerland. It offers a sophisticated continental menu, with dinners costing from 48F ($36.65) to 80F ($54.40).

Grand-Hotel Hof Ragaz, Bernhard Simon Strasse, CH-7310 Bad Ragaz, Switzerland (tel. 085/9-01-31), adjoining the Quellenhof, offers its own medical department, with a host of physical-therapy treatments. The location of this first-class hotel is calm and scenic. The Hof Ragaz is actually part of a complex of therapy-related buildings, connected by covered passageways, including at least 34 separate hotel, cure, and sports facilities stretched over a landscaped garden. Charges in rooms with private bath or shower, including breakfast, range from 125F ($85) to 160F ($108.80) per person daily. On the premises are one thermal and one plain-water swimming pool reserved exclusively for hotel guests. The Hof Ragaz has much 19th-century comfort and has been successfully modernized. Like the Quellenhof, it is also noted for its food. Guests have a choice of dining in a rather grand and immense dining room or else in the more intimate grill room, the Aebtestube.

Hotel Cristal, 36 Bahnhofstrasse, CH-7310 Bad Ragaz, Switzerland (tel. 085/9-28-77), is an imaginatively designed construction built of concrete with lots of glass and with plants hanging from its prominent balconies and terraces. Easily reached from the train station, the hotel has well-appointed rooms, all with private baths, radios, phones, and refrigerators. Singles cost 81F ($55.10) to 96F ($65.30) daily, and doubles go for 67F ($45.55) to 75F ($51) per person. The hotel has a heated swimming pool open all year. The Gourmet-Cristal is the specialty restaurant, and the Adler, in a separate building just behind the hotel, offers a good, plain cuisine. Owned by the Reber family, the Cristal is open year round.

Garni Hotel Poltéra, CH-7310 Bad Ragaz, Switzerland (tel. 085/ 9-25-01), is a three-story modern building on the main street, operated by the Casanova family. The spacious rooms have showers, toilets, radios, phones, and TV on request. Yours might have a balcony or else open onto the sun terrace or the lawn. Open all year, the hotel charges 100F ($68) daily for a double. As an added touch, the owners present guests with small complimentary boxes of chocolates. An excellent buffet breakfast is part of the room cost.

WHERE TO DINE: One of the best seafood restaurants in East Switzerland, **Restaurant Paradies** (tel. 085/9-14-41) lies on Bidemsstrasse, in a private villa outside town, near the golf course. It's well signposted, so you should have no trouble finding it. Run by Rolf and Marianne Koskamp-Akermann, the chefs de cuisine, it offers a greenhouse setting with a fireplace burning in chilly weather. When the weather's fair, guests dine on a sunny terrace. There is also an inside dining room. The food is in the best tradition of moderne cuisine: even the boiled potatoes are al dente. Among the more fanciful creations are pot-au-feu with fruits of the sea, langoustines with red butter, bouillabaisse Marseillaise for two, and seabass suprême. You might also enjoy a red tuna with tomatoes and olives or else grilled Norwegian salmon in a dill cream sauce. For a beginning, I'd suggest a carpaccio with seafood. If you order à la carte, expect to spend from 75F ($51). A menu du pêcheur is featured for 75F also. The restaurant is closed Tuesday and in January and February, but open otherwise from noon to 2 p.m. and 6 to 9 p.m.

Schlössli Büel (tel. 085/9-12-65) could serve as your destination if you need an excursion from Bad Ragaz. It lies less than two miles away. You'll drive between the rolling hills above the town before arriving at this spot, which is woodsy enough to be idyllic, yet where the cuisine is good enough to be called intensely civilized. You could order a well-prepared plate of food if your appetite is small, although most diners prefer a complete meal, attractively priced at 30F ($20.40), with à la carte meals costing about 25F ($17) to 55F ($37.40). One of my favorite appetizers is melon with ham, followed by a good veal pie and vegetables fresh from the market. The place is open from noon to 2 p.m. and 6 to either 9 or 10 p.m. daily except Thursday. You might be interested in ordering the local wine (Büel), or any of the other vintages listed on the wine card.

BAD PFÄFERS: The ancient baths of Pfäfers were discovered in the Tamina Gorge in the Middle Ages, on property belonging to the Benedictine monastic order. An abbey was founded here in 740 and continued until its dissolution in 1838, serving as the spiritual and cultural center of the area as well as owning the spa. The famous naturalist, physician, and philosopher Paracelsus (Theophrastus of Hohenheim) lived and worked here in the 16th century. The baths became a meeting place for the humanists, and the baroque buildings were constructed in the 18th century.

The spa is mainly known for its two huge indoor swimming pools, where you can enjoy the hot mineral waters whether you have rheumatism or not. The Abbey Museum and a restaurant (tel. 085/9-12-60) complete the facilities.

Bad Pfäfers is only accessible on foot or by means of public transport; a special bus runs from Bad Ragaz. It takes about an hour and a half to walk there on an unpaved road. Pfäfers is 2,231 feet above sea level. Admission to the Bad Pfäfers museum and to the spa costs 3F ($2.05) for adults, 2F ($1.35) for children. A round-trip bus ride from Bad Ragaz is 8F ($5.45) for adults, 4F ($2.70) for children. A swim in the thermal pools goes for 11F ($7.50) to 13F ($8.85).

9. GLARUS

In the foothills of the Vorder Glärnisch cliffs, Glarus lies to the south of the Walensee in a deep ravine, surrounded on three sides by mountains, near a nature reserve and close to many of Switzerland's large winter sports resorts. It's also a center for excursions, including an eight-mile run to Lake Klöntal. An illuminated ski lift as well as a ski school, a skating rink, and a toboggan run operate in winter.

The town has a historic hotel, the **Glarnerhof**, CH-8750 Glarus, Switzerland (tel. 058/63-11-91), a recently renovated family-run establishment in a good location in a city park with a view of the mountains. The hotel looks like a generously proportioned private villa, with a red tile roof and shutters. A jet of water spews foam into the air not far from the front door. The renovated bedrooms are clean and comfortable. They all have either baths or showers. The rate for a single room is 58F ($39.45) and 106F ($72.10) for a double. Breakfast is included in the prices.

10. BRAUNWALD

For the relatively few Americans who venture into the canton of Glarus, Braunwald is a lovely little resort. It's rapidly developing as a Swiss ski center. Mt. Tödi, at 11,900 feet, lies on its southern border. The canton itself, south of St. Gallen, has several industrial towns, but is mainly characterized by mountain lakes, alpine meadows, and tiny hamlets, all set off against a backdrop of snow-peaked mountains.

Braunwald is an appealing alternative to Glarus, the cantonal capital, an industrial town that will hold little interest for the tourist.

Go first to Linthal, which is enveloped by high mountains. There you can park your car in a garage and ascend in ten minutes on a mountain railway to Braunwald, the only traffic-free holiday resort in eastern Switzerland, which should make it attractive for parents with small children.

From Zurich, Braunwald is reached in about two hours, along the southern shores of Lake Zurich. The setting of the resort is most attractive, especially its pine trees and, in summer, when the sycamores are at their peak. In winter it attracts mainly beginner and intermediate skiers.

The resort has a ski school. You and one other passenger can take a little two-seater gondola that rises over those pines and sycamores to Grotzenbühl at 5,250 feet, which on my last visit was filled with British skiers. After some refreshment at the restaurant there, you can go on a chair lift to the ridge of Seblengrat at 5,905 feet. It hooks up with the Bächital chair lift.

From another part of Braunwald you can take a chair lift north to Gumen at 6,250 feet, which has a mountain chalet inn.

THE RESORT HOTELS: A good choice is **Hotel Bellevue,** CH-8784 Braunwald, Switzerland (tel. 058/84-38-43), a pastel-yellow symmetrical hotel with green shutters and a glass-walled series of modern extensions that include a restaurant and a swimming pool. The hotel opens onto a view of the mountains, with large terraces covered with plants and café tables in summer. The bedrooms are comfortable with bright accents and big windows. The Bellevue offers a range of sports facilities and grants reductions for children who share their parents' room. Singles rent for 70F ($47.60) to 110F ($74.80) daily without bath, for 90F ($61.20) to 137F ($93.15) with bath, depending on the season. Doubles cost 180F ($122.40) to 274F ($186.30) with bath, dropping to 140F ($95.20) to 220F ($149.60) without, again depending on the season. Breakfast and dinner are included in the tariffs. The hotel is ideal for families, with a children's storyteller, kindergarten, an indoor swimming pool, tennis courts, and skiing areas. The hotel is closed in May and November.

Idealhotel Alpina, CH-8784 Braunwald, Switzerland (tel. 058/84-32-84), offers a spectacular view from a series of terraces of a range of mountains that look almost close enough to touch. The interior has been constructed with comfort and panoramic views in mind, so that some alpine features can be seen from practically anywhere inside. The hotel is owned by the Schweizer family. Bathless singles cost from 65F ($44.20) to 84F ($57.12) daily, going up to 97F ($65.95) for singles with shower or bath. A bathless double costs 124F ($84.30) to 168F ($114.25), climbing to 148F ($100.65) to 196F ($133.30) with private bath. These tariffs include half board. The hotel is closed in November.

Hotel Tödiblick, CH-8784 Braunwald, Switzerland (tel. 058/84-12-36), is built on a foundation of local stone sunk deep into the hillside. The masonry looks solid enough to allow you an untroubled sleep, and the views from the verandas are nothing short of spectacular. The Stuber family always keeps a Swiss flag flying. The interior is a gemütlich collection of Oriental rugs, comfortable armchairs, and alpine knickknacks, while the restaurant serves well-prepared meals in a panoramic setting. The bedrooms are usually wood paneled, and contain simple modern pieces. Bathless singles cost from 73F ($49.65) to 85F ($57.80) daily; with bath, 89F ($60.50) to 98F ($66.65). Doubles cost 146F ($99.30) to 170F ($115.60) without bath, 178F ($121.05) to 196F ($133.30) with. Rates include half board.

CHAPTER V

BASEL AND THE JURA

□ □ □

Northwest Switzerland is one of the most rewarding targets in the country. Your center is likely to be the old university and trading center of Basel (also spelled Basle) that straddles the Rhine, lying between Alsace in France and the Jura canton in Switzerland.

Most visitors from North America get to see only Basel, but if time is on your side you can motor into these hills, so rich in culture and tradition. You'll be zigzagging between two cultures, and the names will often confuse you. If you ask a French person for directions, it's Morat (but Murten to a German).

Everybody has heard of Gruyères, known for its cheese, but the old walled university town of Fribourg and historic Neuchâtel are just two of the other rewarding targets. Numerous castles in the area recall the Middle Ages.

The Jura, a range of folded mountains between two great rivers, the Rhine and the Rhône, forms the frontier of Switzerland and France and extends from Geneva to Schaffhausen. Very different in height and character from the Alps, the Jura mountains do belong to the alpine system geologically, and the same forces that built up the Alps produced the folds and faults found in the Jura.

Few peaks in the Jura range exceed 5,500 feet, and the region is made up of lush pastures, pine forests, and deep valleys. Until the coming of railroads and vehicular roads, farmers of the Jura lived in relative isolation, and beef and dairy cattle raising, as then, are still a major economic resource.

Motorists or railroad passengers will find a trip through the region worthwhile for its panorama of scenic delight. The highways have belvederes from which the Alps can be seen to the southeast, as well as broad views of the surrounding land.

The center of the Swiss watchmaking industry is here, with little pockets of industry located particularly in the part of the mountains to the south as you travel from Basel toward Geneva.

Thriving winter sports resorts can also be found throughout the mountains, although most of them draw a local rather than an international clientele. Despite its beauty and its obvious attractions, the Jura does not as yet have a heavy tourist industry.

The canton of Jura was established in January 1979, becoming the 23rd member of the Confederation. A total of 82 communes make up the canton, with Delémont as its capital. This is a strongly Roman Catholic section of Switzerland (nearly 88% of the population) and the language is mainly French, as is to be expected from its location along the French-Swiss border.

A region of beautiful valleys, waterfalls, Old-World villages and churches, lakes, rivers, and mountain crags make the Jura a part of Switzerland travelers should make a special effort to visit.

1. BASEL (BASLE)

Basel, the second-largest city of Switzerland, stands on the Rhine at the point where the borders of France, Germany, and Switzerland meet. Grossbasel (or greater Basel) lies on the steep left bank and Kleinbasel (or lesser Basel) on the right bank. The old imperial city stood at Grossbasel on the left bank.

The city is linked by half a dozen bridges, plus three ferries which cross on power supplied by the current of the river. The first bridge (no longer standing) was erected in 1225. Replaced by the present Mittlere Rheinbrücke (Middle Rhine Bridge), it was for centuries the only one spanning the Rhine.

The town was a Roman fort in A.D. 374, ruled by prince-bishops for some 1,000 years. The Great Council met within the walls of Basel between 1431 and 1448, and a pope was crowned here. After it joined the Swiss Confederation in 1501, Basel became Protestant. At the advent of the Reformation in 1529 it became a refuge for victims of religious persecution. They flooded in here from Holland, Italy, and France, bringing renewed vitality to the city and laying the foundation for its great "golden age" in the 18th century.

Today Basel is an important banking and industrial city. It is said that half the millionaires of Switzerland live here. Its chemical and pharmaceutical industry is one of the most important in the world. Basel is also the headquarters of the Bank for International Settlement, the BIS tower stands near the railway station, and is irreverently nicknamed "the cotton reel" by the people of the town.

Basel is also one of the most important cultural centers of Switzerland. A humanistic city, it saw the rise of the printing press and the book trade within its borders. Among outstanding early residents was Erasmus, who came here from Holland and published the first edition of the New Testament in the original Greek in 1516. The great humanist, writer, and savant is buried in the cathedral. Among other thinkers and scholars born in Basel or making their homes here over the centuries have been Nietzsche, who taught at Basel University for ten years and did some of his philosophical writing here; Theodor Herzl, who spoke to the first Zionist Congress in 1897; and Jacob Burckhardt, a Basel native who gained fame for his history of the Italian Renaissance. Hans Holbein the Younger journeyed here to paint portraits of Erasmus.

Cultural traditions live on in Basel, with many museums, art galleries, and schools. The city has become known as an international art and antiquities marketplace. To illustrate Basel's love of art, in 1967 its citizens voted by referendum to purchase two well-known works by Picasso: *L'Arlequin Assis* and *Les Deux*

Frères. Picasso was so moved that he donated four other paintings to the town. Basel is rich in museums with a total of 27.

Basel has three railway stations—Swiss, French, and German—making it one of the largest railway junctions in Europe. It's also an international motorway junction. Because the Jura canton is so tiny, the Basel-Mulhouse international airport is actually on French soil.

Except at carnival, the citizens of Basel are considered rather self-restrained, hard-working, and industrious. Of the Baslers, Rolf Hochkuth once wrote: "English understatement looks like megalomania when compared to the people of Basel." However, Basel goes wild during its three days of carnival, when no one in town—seemingly—goes to bed. Festivities begin in late February or early March when three mythological figures appear to chase away winter.

AN ORIENTATION: At the entrance to the Swiss Rhineland, Basel is the capital of the Swiss half-canton of Basel-Stadt. On its borders lie the French Vosges, the German Black Forest, and the Swiss Jura mountains. As mentioned, the city is divided into two parts by the Rhine: Kleinbasel to the north, which is the Rhine port and industrial center, and Grossbasel, south of the Rhine, the cultural and commercial center (your hotel is likely to be here).

On a terrace high above the south bank of the river, the Münster (or cathedral) dominates the city skyline. You may want to confine your entire time to getting to know Grossbasel or the old town, occasionally enjoying one of the city's six bridges. The most historic is the Mittlere Rheinbrücke. If you walk onto this bridge, you'll have a panoramic view of the river, and you can also see many medieval buildings.

The historic heart of Basel is the Münsterplatz, dominated by the Rathaus or town hall, an early Renaissance building. Branching off from this square are two of the city's principal shopping arteries, the Gerbergasse and the Freiestrasse.

Basel is fortunate in having three remaining medieval gates: the St. Alban gate to the east of the city, and Spalen or St. Paul's Gate (considered one of the finest of its period in Europe), and St. Johann's Gate to the west.

GETTING THERE AND GETTING AROUND: To fly to Basel from the United States requires going to Zurich or Paris, for a connecting flight. Switzerland and France share the **Basel-Mulhouse Airport** (Bâle-Mulhouse in French), five miles northwest of Basel, under a special treaty. Buses leave the airport for the Swissair city terminal adjoining the Swiss Federal Railroads Hauptbahnhof. At 20- to 30-minute intervals, you can make the 15-minute bus trip for 5F ($3.40) one way. You will rarely be hassled by Swiss Customs during this frontier crossing, unless you look mighty suspicious.

Basel has a good, relatively cheap system of public transportation, using both bus and tram. You purchase your tickets in advance at any station before boarding. Clear, concise maps will help you pinpoint your target. For 5F ($3.40), you can buy a ticket allowing you unlimited travel for a 24-hour period if you plan to stay within two geographical zones during that time. For unlimited travel within four geographical zones, which includes most of greater Basel, the ticket costs 8F ($5.45). A single, once-only tram ride costs .80F (54¢) for travel beyond more than two stops, 1.30F (88¢) for travel beyond more than four different tram stops.

PRACTICAL FACTS: Of course, the ABCs of Switzerland in Chapter II pertain to life in Basel too. However, a couple of specific facts for this city should be listed.

American Express: The office in Basel is at 10 Aeschengraben (tel. 061/23-66-90), open from 8:15 a.m. to 6 p.m. Monday to Friday and from 9 a.m. to noon Saturday. Closed Sunday.

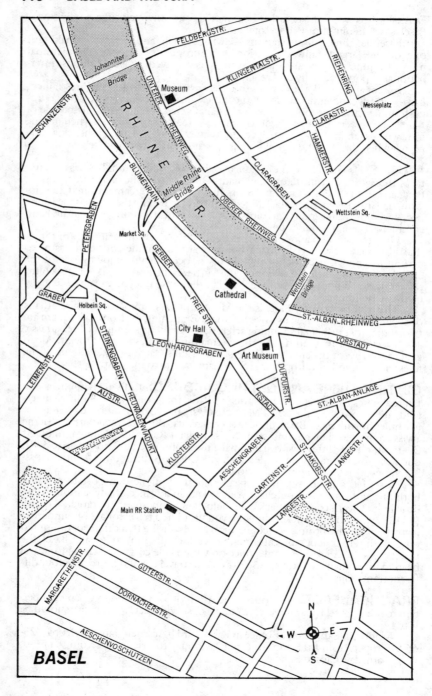

BASEL

Drugstore: Whether you're looking for a drugstore, a pharmacy, or an apothecary, you need seek no further than **City Apotheke,** 4 Aeschenvorstadt (tel. 061/23-10-44). Dr. W. Meier and his staff stock just about every medication made in health-conscious Switzerland and will give helpful advice about over-the-counter Swiss remedies for common traveler's ailments. The drugstore is open Monday to Friday from 7:30 a.m. to 6:30 p.m. and on Saturday from 8 a.m. to 5 p.m., and is centrally located to points of interest in the center of the banking and old town area. On weekends and at night, call the emergency number in Basel for medical, dental, and pharmacological emergencies: 061/25-25-15.

Information: To help visitors, the Basel Tourist Office, 2 Blumenrain (tel. 061/25-50-50), is open from 8:30 a.m. to 6 p.m. Monday to Friday and 8:30 a.m. to 1 p.m. Saturday, closing Sunday. This is a year-round schedule.

ACCOMMODATIONS: Hotel reservations are tight, almost impossible, at the time of the Swiss Industries Fair that attracts about a million visitors every spring. Rooms are also impossible to find at carnival time. Otherwise, you shouldn't have a problem, but reservations are always advised. Hotels often raise their prices from 25% to 40% during the fair and the carnival.

The Deluxe Citadels

Hotel Drei Könige, 8 Blumenrain, CH-4001 Basel, Switzerland (tel. 061/25-52-52). The white, generously proportioned hotel sits with great dignity directly on the Rhine at a point where the river flows swiftly past its stone banks. A tapestry that looks suspiciously like a Gobelin hangs in the wood-paneled lobby, while the bar area might quickly become a favorite place for your rendezvous with Swiss locals, paneled and accented the way it is with pin lights and brass detail. The hotel is officially recognized as the oldest hostelry in Switzerland, established in 1026 under the name Zur Blume ("at the sign of the flower"). History records that soon after the establishment of the inn, three kings (Conrad II, emperor of the Holy Roman Empire; his son, later Henry III; and Rudolf III, the last king of Burgundy) drew up a treaty that divided western Switzerland and southern France. Since that time the political and literary figures who have signed the guest book (now a museum piece) include Voltaire, Napoleon, Princess (later queen) Victoria, and Kaiser Wilhelm II.

You'll find this an impeccably run and updated hotel. Some of the rooms have their original ornamentation on the ceilings and irreplaceable furniture, while others have been renovated with attractively modern decor. One of the salons has a lifelike mural covering the entire expanse of one wall. A canopy covers the riverfront café, which has dozens of miniature Swiss flags fluttering at its borders.

Roman Steiner, the director, charges from 150F ($102) to 210F ($142.80) daily in a single, from 275F ($187) to 405F ($275.40) in a double. All units have baths, air conditioning, radios, mini-bars, TV, and phones.

Basel Hilton International, CH-4002 Basel, Switzerland (tel. 061/22-66-22). Visitors are treated to Hilton style and service from the moment they disembark from their vehicles under the massive steel portico that extends unsupported from the glass-and-steel cube of this dramatically modern building. Constructed in an elegantly streamlined format of matte black and glass, the Hilton is considered a chic and appealing place for Baslers to visit late in the evening, particularly for its lower-level piano bar and its Polynesian-style disco. All this is maintained and directed by one of the city's most charming hoteliers, general manager Urs Hitz. Directly in the center of the city, the Hilton offers 226 rooms, each tastefully furnished in shades of brown, beige, and wheat, often with interesting views of the city skyline. Each accommodation contains a color TV, radio, air conditioning, direct-dial phone, and a refrigerated bar. Year-round rates for the comfortably appointed rooms range from 140F ($95.20) to 200F ($136) daily in a single and from 190F ($129.20) to 250F ($170) in a double.

Many members of the business community of Basel enjoy a rendezvous under the lighting of the Wettstein Grill, where uniformed waiters prepare delectable specialties right at tableside. There is an indoor swimming pool, plus a sauna, massage facilities, conference rooms, and a coffeeshop serving light meals and snacks. Room service is 24 hours a day, and the multilingual staff is eager to help with any business or touring problem. If you're a motorist, you'll welcome the underground parking garage below the hotel. The Hilton is connected via an underground shopping arcade to the main railway station, so you're within easy reach of everything in the center.

Hotel Euler, 14 Centralbahnplatz, CH-4051 Basel, Switzerland (tel. 061/ 23-45-00), is everything you'd expect a grand hotel in this city to be. The outside is a symmetrical rectangle, elegantly detailed in white with gray stone half-columns and window frames, set off by an awning on the ground floor. The chandeliered dining room serves first-class dinners, while a less expensive snackbar offers less formal meals. The warm-hued bar is richly ornamented with leather and lots of wood, while a garden terrace is a relaxing place for coffee. The main salon is supported by red marble columns, the kind you have to touch to see if the stone is really just painted wood, with a ceiling painstakingly crafted into geometrical patterns.

The bedrooms are luxuriously paneled; all of them impeccably up to Swiss standards of good hotelkeeping. The Euler was built in 1865 near the railroad station. Today it's directed by J. Pernet-Monkewitz who, for his 65 rooms, charges a maximum of 155F ($105.40) to 225F ($153) daily in a single and 235F ($159.30) to 350F ($238) in a double.

The Upper Bracket

Hotel International, 25 Steinentorstrasse, CH-4001 Basel, Switzerland (tel. 061/22-18-70), is a first-class hotel with 200 spotlessly clean rooms, all of which have been improved in the last several years. The well-trained management does everything it can to keep the hotel well groomed, which means replacing furniture when it becomes worn out and maintaining the many fitness facilities, such as the gym, sauna, and indoor swimming pool, whose use is included in the rates. All rooms are air-conditioned, many with a view, renting for 195F ($132.60) to 280F ($190.40) daily in a double, 145F ($98.60) to 199F ($135.30) in a single; all rates including a copious breakfast. However, bargain seekers will check in on Friday, Saturday, or Sunday night when singles rent for only 90F ($61.20) daily, with doubles costing 160F ($108.80). An appealing rôtisserie, Charolaise, is on the premises. This and the timbered and rustically appointed dining room, Steinenpick, are particularly popular with the Basel business community. A less-expensive tavern on the premises, Kaffi-Mühli, draws a less formal crowd.

Hotel Europe, 43 Clarastrasse, CH-4058 Basel, Switzerland (tel. 061/690-80-80). Besides the obligatory Swiss flag, you'll find an enormous half-rounded canopy sheltering this establishment's entrance from the busy sidewalk. A modern, informal hotel, it is owned by the ETAP chain. The 190 rooms, fully air-conditioned, include baths tiled in dark colors, radios, and mini-bars, plus TVs upon request. Gathering places include the "oldtimer bar," a sidewalk café, and a restaurant, the Bajazzo, furnished with wooden banquettes and decorated with unusual murals, which are brilliantly lit while the rest of the room is left in semi-darkness. Accommodations, both in the main building and in the annex, are usually compact units of bed and bathroom, priced at 112F ($96.15) to 146F ($99.30) daily in a single and 170F ($115.60) to 210F ($142.80) in a double. A generous buffet breakfast is included in the price.

Hotel Alexander, 85 Riehenring, CH-4058 Basel, Switzerland (tel. 061/ 26-70-00). Aside from the hotel, which is directly across from the Swiss Trade Fair and the Basel Congress Center, you'll find a popular dancehall with live music and occasional disco. The appointments at the Alexander are modern, with a curved bar area and warm hospitable colors. A big-windowed restaurant with rustic half-timbering and a six-lane bowling alley complete the facilities. Singles rent for 90F ($61.20) to 125F ($85), while doubles range from 130F ($88.40) to 190F ($129.20), breakfast included. You'll be only ten minutes from the train station. Peter Schumacher is the director.

Hotel Basel, 12 Münzgasse, CH-4058 Basel, Switzerland (tel. 061/25-24-23), is ideally situated in a modern building that has been designed to blend tastefully with its surroundings in the old town, a street of buildings roughly the same height. Many of its 72 bedrooms are wood paneled, even on the sloping parts under the eaves of the gabled roof, and all are comfortably carpeted and decorated in clean, simple designs. The public rooms are high-ceilinged, with crystal chandeliers. A café with bright parasols serves drinks and coffee in front of the hotel, while a rough-walled weinkeller and a brasserie offer light snacks or full meals. Otti Bäriswyl, the manager, directs the eating, lodging, and sports facilities with professional panache. He charges 102F ($69.35) to 149F ($101.30) daily in a single, from 160F ($108.80) to 230F ($156.40) in a double. Breakfast is included. Prices are increased to the upper levels of the scale during trade fairs.

Hotel Merian am Rhein, 2 Rheingasse at Greifengasse, CH-4058 Basel, Switzerland (tel. 061/681-00-00). The history of this establishment is intimately wrapped up in the history of Basel. The hotel is in a spot just off the quay where a bishop in the 13th century commissioned the construction of the only bridge across the Rhine between Lake Constance and the sea. Today the Merian is a hotel in the oldest part of the city, with atmosphere, charm, and updated conveniences such as comfortable beds. The more expensive double rooms are on the Rhine side of this 60-room hotel. All rooms have baths or showers and TV. A single costs 108F ($73.45) daily, a double going for 140F ($95.20) to 180F ($122.40). The Café Spitz, recommended separately, is on the ground floor of the hotel.

Hotel Schweizerhof, 1 Centralbahnplatz, CH-4002 Basel, Switzerland (tel. 061/22-28-33), has been in the same hotelkeeping family for the past three generations. Near the train station, not far from the old town, the hotel contains a bar, a restaurant, a sun terrace, and several conference rooms that are used sometimes for wedding receptions and business meetings. The building, across the street from a landscaped park with a fountain, rises six ornamented stories and has a few wrought-iron balconies and the obligatory Swiss flag flying on top. The salons are decorated with Oriental rugs and some 19th-century antiques, while the bedrooms are clean and pleasingly appointed in a simple modern format of understated good taste. The host Goetzinger family charges from 115F ($78.20) to 170F ($115.60) daily in a single and 180F ($122.40) to 230F ($156.40) in a double, all with bath or shower and breakfast.

The Medium Price Range

Hotel Bernina, 14 Margarethenstrasse, CH-4051 Basel, Switzerland (tel. 061/23-73-00), a modern hotel in downtown Basel next to the railroad station, is closer to the zoo than any other hostelry. All the up-to-date rooms have baths and comfortable beds. Jo Scheuerer, the director, is ably assisted by a well-picked staff. They maintain the six-story façade in impeccable condition, frequently changing the collection of international flags hanging over the sidewalk in front. Singles rent for 98F ($66.65) and doubles for 160F ($108.80), with breakfast included.

Hotel Münchnerhof, 75 Riehenring, CH-4058 Basel, Switzerland (tel.

061/691-77-80), lies close to the Bahnhof in a brownish-ochre–colored building with white trim around the well-designed modern windows, some of which are arched over small balconies. The interior is attractively decorated in a streamlined sort of way, keeping the ambience attractively traditional although everything looks recently updated. The owners are the Früh family, who also operate the two restaurants attached to the hotel, one with live music. The hotel is known for its French and Italian cuisine. Depending on the plumbing, singles range from 40F ($27.20) to 70F ($47.60) bathless, 70F ($47.60) to 150F ($102) with complete bath. Doubles go for 65F ($44.20) to 120F ($81.60) without bath, for 90F ($61.20) to 230F ($156.40) with private bath. The location is in front of the Swiss Trade Fair.

City Hotel, 12 Henric-Petri-Strasse, CH-4010 Basel, Switzerland (tel. 061/23-78-11), lies near St. Elisabeth's Church, not far from the railroad station. It's informal and modern, with lots of oversize windows looking either over the street or onto a tree-filled central garden. In summer a ring of flowers circles the hotel in a continuous planter approximately 12 feet above the ground. The lobby has a gray marble floor, a vividly patterned Oriental rug, and an attentively polite receptionist who does everything possible to make your stay pleasant. Bedrooms are up-to-date and well equipped, with two-tone white and natural-grain furniture and baths. Singles cost 80F ($54.40) to 120F ($81.60) per day, while doubles rent for 140F ($95.20) to 210F ($142.80), breakfast included.

Hotel Krafft am Rhein, 12 Rheingasse, CH-4058 Basel, Switzerland (tel. 061/961-88-77), is easily reached from the railroad station by taking tram 8 to the Rheingasse, where you'll be across the river from the old town's Rathaus and Münster, in a quiet ambience caused partly by the riverfront location. An attractive café/sun terrace gives you an opportunity to watch summer sunbathers on the stepped banks of the river, while the tastefully modern rooms offer comfortable lodgings, often with a view. The public rooms are spacious, tasteful, and decorated with 19th-century antiques, oversize gilt mirrors, and Oriental rugs. The Waldmeyer-Schneiter family, the owners, spend much of their time maintaining the hotel, seeing to the needs of their guests and directing the service in the well-known attached restaurant, Zem Schnooggeloch. Rooms without bath rent for 47F ($31.95) to 69F ($46.90) daily in a single, 89F ($60.50) to 114F ($77.50) in a double. Rooms with shower cost from 74F ($50.30) to 102F ($69.35) daily in a single, 110F ($74.80) to 156F ($106.10) in a double.

Hotel Drachen, 24 Aeschenvorstadt, CH-4010 Basel, Switzerland (tel. 061/23-90-90), is artfully maintained by Joe and Pia Dietlin, who offer pleasant, rather small but comfortably furnished rooms. Many repeat visitors have come to know this well-established hotel. The 40 rooms have modern and spacious baths tiled in dark colors with checkerboard floors. All units also have radios, TV, safes, mini-bars, and phones. Some apartments are offered to guests who plan to stay a long time. Two restaurants are connected to the hotel (see my dining recommendations). The hotel lies on a commercial street close to the Kunsthaus and the old city. Singles rent for 100F ($68) to 130F ($88.40) daily, with doubles ranging from 165F ($112.20) to 200F ($136), prices depending on the plumbing you choose. Breakfast is included.

Hotel Admiral, 5 Rosentalstrasse, CH-4021 Basel, Switzerland (tel. 061/691-77-77). If you're athletic, you'll be happy to discover the heated open-air swimming pool on the eighth floor of this commercial hotel, next door to the massive bulk of the Swiss Trade Fair. On clear days the view from here covers much of the surrounding area. The hotel is a balconied rectangle, and the roof section not covered by the pool is capped by a modified mansard roof of brown tiles. The 130 rooms are sunny and decorated in pleasing, coordinated colors, usually browns and soft oranges. The hotel also has a bar and a pleasant restaurant. Single rooms cost from 47F ($31.95) to 115F ($78.20) daily (the lack of private bathrooms accounts for the low rate of the less expensive ones), while doubles range from 130F ($88.40) to 195F ($132.60), with breakfast. All units contain toilets, phones, and radios and allow free access to the pool.

Hotel Spalenbrunnen, 2 Schützenmattstrasse, CH-4051 Basel, Switzerland (tel. 061/25-82-33), is an old-fashioned shuttered and gabled house sitting on a public square a few buildings from the green checkerboard roof of the Spalentor. The red stone fountain you'll see from many of the windows has the octagonal basin and the central statue on an ornate column you've seen often in Switzerland, but the setting is nevertheless charming and especially convenient, thanks to its location near a tram line. The house dates from the Middle Ages. Today the bedrooms are comfortably carpeted, each with modern appointments, tile bath, phone, TV, radio, and mini-bar. Singles rent for 80F ($54.40) to 120F ($81.60) daily, and doubles cost 130F ($88.40) to 195F ($132.60), breakfast included. The attached restaurant has lots of area and looks like an up-to-date urban nightclub. Peter Allemann is the owner-manager.

Economy Oases

Hotel Steinenschanze, 69 Steinengraben, CH-4051 Basel, Switzerland (tel. 061/23-53-53), offers clean, safe, comfortable lodgings in a modern five-story building with lots of big windows, only ten minutes by foot away from the train station. Rooms are simply furnished, quiet, and sunny. The hotel sits on its own grounds, with a slightly overgrown garden behind the building. Singles rent for 50F ($34) daily with hot and cold running water, 80F ($54.40) with shower and toilet. Doubles cost 75F ($51) with running water, 100F ($68) with shower and toilet. A continental breakfast is included in all rates.

Hotel St. Gotthard—Terminus, 13 Centralbahnstrasse, CH-4051 Basel, Switzerland (tel. 061/22-52-50), is perfect for late night train arrivals in Basel. Opposite the station, the hotel is identified by five arched canopies stretching above the two doors and three picture windows on the façade. The bedrooms are clean, comfortable, and safe, and some in the main building contain tile baths, although others have only hot and cold running water (always less expensive, of course). Actually, you may prefer to ask for a room in the completely modern annex, which is equipped with the latest comforts. Accommodations in this section have complete facilities along with direct-dial phones. The Geyer-Arel family, now in their third generation of running the hotel, charges reasonable rates. Depending on the plumbing, singles rent for 50F ($34) to 100F ($68) daily or 80F ($54.40) to 210F ($142.80) in a double. An American restaurant chain operates the dining room and restaurant of the hotel. The hotel's bar, the Gotthard Club, has a cozy atmosphere.

Hotel Bristol, 15 Centralbahnstrasse, CH-4051 Basel, Switzerland (tel. 061/22-38-22), facing the train station, rises like a baroque town house, with an embellished step pediment capping the façade's roofline, an ornately carved stone loggia between the windows of the third and fourth floors, and heavy stone detailing around the arches on the ground floor. The restaurant inside looks like a woodworker's dream because of its meticulously covered ceiling, walls, and floor, in polished paneling with dozens of architectural motifs worked into the designs. Comfortable singles rent for 60F ($40.80) daily without bath, 95F ($64.40) with bath. Bathless doubles cost 95F ($64.40), and doubles with bath go for 120F ($81.60). Bathless triples go for 90F ($61.20). Rates include a continental breakfast, service, and taxes. The staff is accommodating and helpful.

Hotel Cavalier, 1 Reiterstrasse, CH-4054 Basel, Switzerland (tel. 061/39-22-62), is a small hotel (27 rooms) in a residential area west of the train station in a less congested part of town. The hotel sits at the end of a grassy plot of land, on a tree-lined street. It can be identified by its white façade and boxy shape. Each room has bath or shower, phone, and radio. A ground-floor restaurant is a little bare, but serves satisfying meals to local residents. Walter Gehrig, the owner-manager, charges 65F ($44.20) to 95F ($64.60) daily in a single, 95F ($64.60) to 140F ($95.20) in a double, breakfast included.

WHERE TO DINE: Nearly 500 years ago Basel had an illustrious visitor, the humanist Enea Silvio de' Piccolimini, who later became pope. About Baslers, he wrote: "Most of them are devotees of good living. They live at home in style and spend most of their time at the table." Not much has changed.

The Upper Bracket

Restaurant Stuckl Bruderholz, 42 Bruderholzallee (tel. 061/35-82-22). The gardens that surround the house serve as a backdrop for those diners who prefer to eat on the backyard terrace, but even the most elegant of gardens might not be an adequate format for the delicious cuisine cooked by Hans and Susi Stuckl in their gourmet restaurant right outside the city limits. The house was formerly a private residence, which is today decorated with a gemütlich and patrician collection of antiques, oil paintings, and carefully crafted details. My favorite room is the salon vert, with its green napery, Empire chairs, and light-patterned Oriental rug, whose colors are reflected in the cream-colored wooden walls. There are two other well-appointed rooms at your disposal.

The restaurant enjoys renown all over Switzerland, and is considered the Basel citadel of haute cuisine with each dish prepared with artistry. Specialties are likely to include a filet of saltwater red mullet with coriander, a terrine of foie gras, a tomato stuffed with frogs' legs and served in a thyme cream sauce, or a lobster ragoût with truffles and baby leeks. The selle d'agneau (lamb) is cooked with a gratin of green beans, and the sweetbreads are masterful. For dessert I'd suggest a compote of pears or a soufflé made with the fresh fruits of the season. A fixed-price lunch costs 40F ($27.20) to 70F ($47.60), with set dinners beginning at 90F ($61.20) and ranging up to 150F ($102) for a ten-course "menu surprise." Lunch is served from noon to 1:30 p.m. and dinner from 6:30 to 9:30 p.m. The restaurant is closed on Sunday and Monday and from mid-July to mid-August.

Schloss Binningen, 5 Schlossgasse at Binningen (tel. 061/47-20-55), is owned by the township and run by Gusti and Julia Beerli, who lavish attention on this 16th-century château. The entrance hall is appropriately baronial, with a high ceiling and a carefully crafted loggia looking down onto the tile floor. The dining rooms are grand enough for a retinue of courtiers, packed with real antiques, and with an attractively understated service area of the most modern sort of stainless steel for efficient and excellent service. The grounds look almost like those of a private park; with a glass of wine, from the terrace you could almost transport yourself back to another century.

The wine cellar is among the best in the region. There are at least 50 vintages not listed in the carte (the wine steward will make appropriate suggestions depending on what you order). The menu changes at least three times a year, so I hesitate to make specific suggestions. The fare, however, is likely to include such delectable dishes as a timbale de langoustines with caviar, a selle de chevreuil rôti (roebuck), or fresh lobster, followed by a cold soufflé—truly a celestial cuisine. A set lunch costs from 20F ($13.60), set dinners from 70F ($47.60) to 100F ($68), and à la carte meals from 50F ($34). Hours are from noon to 2 p.m. and 6:30 to 10 p.m. except Sunday and Monday.

Wettstein Grill, Basel Hilton International, 31 Aeschengraben (tel. 061/22-66-22). Known as one of the greatest restaurants in Basel, this warmly decorated enclave of chic is near the hotel's bar, one flight below street level of this previously recommended hotel. Amid a scattering of antique portraits of Swiss heroes, your meal will be enhanced with unobtrusively formal service and some of the greatest culinary creations of the region. À la carte meals cost from 75F

($51), while a fixed-price gourmet menu goes for around 95F ($64.60) per person. Specialties change with the season. Menu listings might include smoked giant shrimp with horseradish, carpaccio with a mustard-flavored cream sauce, filet of turbot with shrimp and a chive-flavored wine sauce, saffron-laced seafood soup, sliced veal in an apple cream sauce with calvados, mignon of beef with foie gras, and veal with morels, followed by an elaborate dessert choice from a trolley. Lunch is served daily from noon to 3 p.m. and dinner from 7 to 11 p.m.

La Rôtisserie des Rois, Hotel Drei Könige, 8 Blumenrain (tel. 061/25-52-52). Contained within what's reputed to be the oldest hotel in Europe (see "Accommodations"), this formal and elegant restaurant is famous for its riverside terrace. During cold weather, the party moves inside, to a high-ceilinged room with immaculate napery and an alert battalion of uniformed employees. Lunch is served daily from noon to 2:30 p.m. Dinner is presented every night from 6:30 to 10 p.m. "No trouble is too great" according to the chef, who prepares, within earshot of the piano music in the adjacent bar, a sophisticated cuisine du marché. You can order a gourmet set menu for 88F ($59.85) or a full à la carte meal for 80F ($54.40) and up. Specialties change with the seasons, but you might be tempted by warm goose liver with light port wine sauce, guinea fowl with chanterelles, breast of chicken with a leek-flavored cream sauce, mussel soup flavored with saffron, or chateaubriand in a confit of shallots. Reservations are suggested.

Golden Gate, 42 Steinengraben (tel. 061/22-04-13), is a rendezvous for gastronomes in Basel. In summer you can dine in its attractive garden, retreating when the wind blows cold into its rustic interior, where you can order good-tasting and attractively served French specialties. It's open from 9 a.m. to midnight daily except Sunday. The interior, especially in winter, is very cozy, and the staff is most accommodating. The Markus Hauenstein family, the owners, are proud of their many specialties, beginning with feuilletée de saumon, followed by those wide-flap mushrooms in the provençale style. It's on to escargots Bercy, coquilles St. Jacques, filet of beef calvados, sole meunière, veal kidney with mustard sauce, or other dishes. An excellent meal will cost from 60F ($40.80). There's a direct entrance from the second floor of the Steinenparking (elevator).

The Middle Bracket

Zum Goldenen Sternen, 70 St. Albanrheinweg (tel. 061/23-16-66), is the oldest pub in Switzerland, with a continuous history stretching back to 1421. It stands on the banks of the Rhine, sharing a common entrance with the apartment house next door. Wide planks are on the floor and wood beams and stenciled flowers cover some of the walls, while in some sections of the ceiling you'll notice lots of small panels with a star (*stern*) carved into the center of each. Oriental rugs are scattered across the floor, and the front windows are covered with leaded strips of rounded glass. These details, plus the green tile ceramic stove against one wall, make up the decor of a historic locale that every Basler knows about.

The dishes are not outrageously complicated, but they're classic and good. The appetizers are especially tempting, particularly the smoked eel and smoked trout. I've visited this establishment on several occasions over the years, and have also been fond of the terrine maison and the lobster soup. For the main course I'd recommend one of the following: carré d'agneau (lamb), filet of veal with citron, vol-au-vent, or Hungarian goulash with spätzli. Lunch is served from noon to 2:30 p.m. daily and dinner from 6 to 10 p.m. Fixed-price luncheon menus cost from 18F ($12.25). À la carte meals at lunch or dinner cost 40F ($27.20) and up. During the afternoon, snacks and drinks are served.

Fischstube zum Pfauen, 13 St. Johanns–Vorstadt (tel. 061/25-32-67), is known for its fish specialties, both freshwater and seafood. Günter Blum and his charming wife, Hortensia, welcome guests to their tables in a building whose façade is similar to that of a narrow townhouse in a large city, with a view into the restaurant from the partially curtained windows on the ground floor. The half-paneled, up-to-date interior has simple chairs and hanging lamps. Diners can select meals centering on such fish as perch, fera, zander, salmon, angler, salmon-trout, and shrimp, prepared in the French style. A fixed-price menu is available at both lunch and dinner for around 55F ($37.40). A la carte meals cost from 50F ($34) to 60F ($40.80). Lunch is served from 11:30 a.m. to 2 p.m. and dinner from 6 to 10 p.m. daily except Sunday and Monday in June, July, and August. Otherwise, they close only on Monday. The annual closing is from mid-July to mid-August.

Kunsthalle Restaurant, 7 Steinenberg (tel. 061/23-42-33), is one of my favorite places to eat in Basel. In the same building at the Kunsthalle art gallery, the restaurant is under different management, but a link is maintained, with pictures from the gallery hanging on the restaurant walls. Peter Wyss and Romano Villa, restaurant managers, have renovated the place since they took it over. Guests enter a long, narrow room, one wall of which is made up of long windows giving a view of the garden where meals are served in warm weather. The parquet floors, handsome rugs, and chandeliers allow elegant dining in the main restaurant. Along the wall opposite the windows, stone arches lead into the bar area, with murals on the walls. There is also a bar upstairs.

In the main dining room, cold specialties are spread on a flower-bedecked buffet. White-jacketed waiters will take your order for hot dishes prepared by a French chef. The same menus are offered for both lunch and dinner, with selections ranging from such appetizers as sherry consommé to main dishes that might include steak or sole with risotto. In the bar through the archways, you can enjoy some of the specials offered in the dining room, as well as omelets and salads. After-theater supper is also available. Expect to pay from 40F ($27.20) to 65F ($44.20) for a complete meal. Coffee is offered beginning at 8 a.m. in the downstairs bar area, although food is not available until 11 a.m., ending at midnight. Hours in the main dining room are daily from noon for lunch, from 6 to 10 p.m. for dinner. Reservations are recommended, except on Monday when the Kunsthalle gallery is closed so there isn't such a demand on the restaurant. The restaurant is closed Sunday.

Café Spitz, 2 Rheingasse (tel. 061/681-00-00), on the ground floor of Hotel Merian am Rhein, recommended above, is one of Basel's more prominent restaurants, located near one end of a busy cross-river bridge (which has a Madonna's shrine midway across it). The building is designed to permit maximum views of the river traffic a few dozen feet away. The outside is elegantly airy, with big graceful windows, pleasing proportions, and a 19th-century construction of cream and light-mauve stonework in a style that is vaguely Moorish. The outdoor terrace is palatial, covered with many plants and flowers, with a canopy over part of it. I always come here to sample one of the chef's six specialties of Basel, which range from salmon to beef goulash. For an appetizing beginning, try either the smoked river trout or the smoked morels. Among the tasty freshwater fish dishes, the pike with tarragon sauce is excellent, as is the sliced veal Zurich style (prepared in a cream sauce). Count on spending around 50F ($34) for a big, filling meal here, although one of the daily specials, a platter of good food, costs only 15F ($10.20). The place opens for coffee and pastries at 6:30 a.m. and remains open until midnight for snacks and drinks. Formal hot meals are served only from noon to 2 p.m. and 6 to 9 p.m. The restaurant is open seven days a week.

Restaurant Safran-Zunft, 11 Gerbergasse, (tel. 061/25-19-59). While admiring the medieval façade of this building, be careful not to step back into the narrow street—you might get run over by a tram. The entire structure is elegantly proportioned, with four to five floors (depending on how you count the stairwells) of carved stone. On either side of the main entrance you'll see replicas of scholars or students crouched slightly above head level, while a fleur-de-lis graces the top of the archway. A wrought-iron sign hangs over the street with the logo of the restaurant, showing a gluttonous monk inhaling the aroma from a goblet of wine. Inside, the restaurant is set up in a tavern style of red-checked tablecloths, paneling, and oversize Gothic windows with a stained-glass medallion set into the middle of each of them. Most guests seem to visit this place to order the fondue Bacchus, done with veal with all the condiments. The soups are usually good, most often clear broths. Irma and Jakob Stähli supervise a kitchen that turns out many other more elaborate specialty meals, which might begin with such elegant appetizers as caviar or smoked salmon. You'll regularly find veal steak and Chateaubriand on the menu. A la carte meals cost from 45F ($30.60) for lunch or dinner. Two fixed-price lunches are offered, costing 12F ($8.15) and 17F ($11.55). Lunch is from noon to 2 p.m. and dinner from 6 to 10 p.m. daily except Sunday, with no service between meals.

Hotel Drachen, 24 Aeschenvorstadt (tel. 061/23-90-90), serves some of the finest meals in the city. There's a snack bar downstairs, with menus costing from 15F ($10.20), in a decor of stippled stucco and hanging lamps. The snack bar hours are from 7 a.m. to midnight Monday to Saturday for hot food, snacks, and drinks (from 11 a.m. to 9 p.m. on Sunday). Upstairs, in the finer restaurant, lunch is served from noon to at least 2 p.m. and dinner from 6 p.m. to midnight. It's open daily, although Sunday hours are only from 6 to 9 p.m. A four-course, fixed-price meal costs around 36F ($24.50), 31F ($21.10) if you leave off dessert. À la carte meals go for about 50F ($34). Many French dishes appear on the menu, which is international in scope. Favorite orders include filet goulash Stroganoff, selle d'agneau (lamb), and veal piccata along with truite (trout) au bleu. The decor is appealing, with a personalized blend of modern tables and chairs in pleasingly ordered rows. There are wheeled trays with cognacs and after-dinner drinks, warm colors, and a long wall of big windows with views onto the elegant buildings on the far side of the street. The cellar boasts more than 150 wines.

Walliser Kanne, 50 Gerbergasse (tel. 061/25-70-17), a restaurant built in the typical old Swiss style, attracts a loyal crowd rich in government and business leaders, soccer stars, and local show-business types. The co-owner, Kurt Walter, directs this popular eatery with his charming wife, Peggy. All dishes are impeccably fresh and well prepared. The food is traditional, *gutburgerlich*, and the portions are generous. At lunch, prices begin as low as 18F ($12.25) for a simple meal. One of the specialties is a Swiss fondue. A typical meal might start with an hors d'oeuvre of air-dried alpine meat, followed by a veal steak with a savory hollandaise sauce. Swiss Rösti accompanies most platters. For dessert, try the öpfelchüechlis (apple fritters) or an excellent chocolate mousse (or else one made with fresh fruits). Dinners begin at 50F ($34), going up. The place is open daily except Sunday from 10 a.m. to midnight. It's wise to call for a reservation.

Escargot, 14 Centralbahnstrasse (tel. 061/22-52-33), is reached by going down a set of green terrazzo steps, marked by a potted andromeda, leading into the cellars of the SBB (where the trains to the rest of Switzerland leave from). Don't be put off by the fact that this restaurant is in a train station. Inside it's warm and cozy, thanks to the blue-and-white ceramic pots with ornate lids and handles, which hang on heavy chains and are illuminated from within. These, along with some discreetly placed spotlights, serve as lighting fixtures over the elegant bar area, whose walls are decorated with provincial illustrations of castles and trees, all very folkloric. The waitresses wear white blouses, blue aprons, and vivid red skirts.

This is one of the best restaurants in Basel for la cuisine bourgeoise. A special part of the menu is devoted to French regional cookery, including tripe à la mode de Caen and other dishes. In honor of the restaurant's namesake the kitchen prepares snails in three different ways. My favorite European vegetable, endive, is braised and served with butter here instead of just appearing in a salad. In season you might order roebuck, and all year round unusual dishes appear, perhaps eggplant gratinée in the Egyptian style. I've always found the apfelstrudel the most reliable dessert. Expect to spend from 35F ($23.80) to 50F ($34) for a complete meal. Hours are from 11:15 a.m. to 2:30 p.m. and 6:15 to 11:45 p.m. daily except Sunday.

Schlüsselzunft, 25 Freie Strasse (tel. 061/25-20-46). After a quick glance around the dining room you'll believe the claims that this is one of the oldest guildhouses in Basel. Against one wall of the main room you'll see a very ornate ceramic tile stove, embellished and painted over most of its intricate surface. The wooden ceiling is supported by a centrally placed wooden beam, worn smooth by the thousands of polishings. Look for a special menu that lists seasonal specialties such as various types of fish or, in the autumn, venison. The menu has explanations in English. Strasbourg in Alsace moves a little closer to Basel when you order the foie gras from that area. Soups include all the familiar ones, but each one is well prepared. A fine selection of pasta is also featured, including cannelloni au gratin. The standard grills can always be ordered, but the chef has any number of other meat specialties, including shredded calf kidney in a Madeira sauce. Specialties include veal curry, tenderloin steak with goose liver and morels, and shredded veal and kidney in a cream sauce with spätzli. If you're dining with a partner you can order a double sirloin steak. Full à la carte meals cost around 50F ($34). Three-course, fixed-price meals at both lunch and dinner cost 27F ($18.35) and 33F ($22.45). Hours are from noon to 2 p.m. and 6 to 11 p.m. daily except Sunday.

Chez Donati, 48 St. Johanns–Vorstadt (tel. 061/57-09-19), is a rendezvous point for Baslers, who come to savor the Italian specialties known throughout the region and who seek the intimacy of the brasserie tables and chairs interspersed with statuary and elegant columns. The food here is among the best in the city. The chef's favorite specialties are homemade lasagne verdi and ravioli ricotta, followed by scallopini in purgatorio and fegato (liver) alla veneziana. From October to December the chef is able to obtain white truffles, which he uses with style and flourish. He also makes a spicy scampi maison. The price for an average meal ranges from 45F ($30.60) to 75F ($51), and hot meals are served daily except Monday from noon to 2 p.m. and 6 to 10 p.m. The restaurant is closed in July.

The Budget Range

St. Alban Eck, 60 St. Albanvorstadt (tel. 061/22-03-20). Some of the original stonework can still be seen at the corner of this half-timbered house with the symmetrical glass windows. From the street you'll open a beautifully refinished oak door to reveal a small intimate restaurant with many graceful touches. The wooden tables with turned legs have without a doubt witnessed more than a few generations of Baslers sipping Warteck beer, the local brew of the region. The sign in front is in Victorian gilt lettering, and the place is set in a district with lots of architectural charm. This restaurant could be both a budget choice or an expensive place, depending on what you order. For example, if you go here for lunch you can select a soup and main course beginning at 30F ($20.40). However, should you elect to order from the à la carte specialty menu it takes no talent to spend 60F ($40.80) and up. For that, you're likely to be tempted with such superb dishes as filet of perch with almonds, mignons de veau in calvados, or grilled sole with a remoulade sauce. The restaurant is open from 11:30 a.m. to 2:30 p.m. and 6:30 to 11:30 p.m. Closed Saturday, Sunday, and holidays.

Da Roberto, 3 Kuchengasse (tel. 061/23-46-80), is housed in a series of rooms where you'll immediately feel at home, especially since you'll have a choice of three separate seating areas. Decor includes checked tablecloths, rustically paneled walls, and several kinds of hanging lamps shaped like persimmons or 1890s mid-Victorian fantasies. The casual staff will make you feel like one of Basel's younger crowd, particularly if you just prefer to sit at the mahogany bar with the comfortably padded leather chairs. The restaurant is only one block from the SBB train station, on a narrow side street with lots of activity. At night much of young Basel often drops in here for the tasty pizzas, costing from 12F ($8.15). You can also order a daily special, which is likely to range from gnocchi with gorgonzola all the way to filet of beef with fresh mushrooms and homemade fettuccine. Soups are a good buy, as are the spaghetti dishes. Depending on what you order, you can dine here relatively inexpensively, enjoying the good food, lively atmosphere, and polite service. An average meal ranges from 25F ($17) to 50F ($34). It's open daily from 11:30 a.m. to 2 p.m. and 5 p.m. to midnight.

Mövenpick, 30 Marktplatz (tel. 061/25-31-00). In this restaurant, try to get a chair with a view of the buildings around the historic square where its located. The room is an extended series of brick walls, rustic beams, dark paneling, and above the bar, an enormous inverted copper dish looking like a brewery kettle. The restaurant caters with efficient Swiss service to a middle-class crowd of locals. Chefs turn out the typical Mövenpick menu, which is international in scope, ranging from curry dishes from India to chili con carne from Texas to lasagne verdi from Italy. You can always get a rumpsteak or a mixed grill. Expect to spend from 18F ($12.25) to 35F ($23.80) for an average meal. It's open daily 11 a.m. to midnight.

Restaurant Markthalle, 8 Viaduktstrasse (tel. 061/23-64-64), stands near the central railway station (SBB) in the heart of Basel in a long building whose façade curves around the bend in a busy city street, with four rows of massive windows edged in smooth-cut stone. Clients can sit on a raised dais, semi-separated from the main room, but many prefer a table in the large room near the windows. You can dine here reasonably, paying 25F ($17) to 35F ($23.80). Watch for the daily specials. In season the wild game dishes might include wild stag peppersteak prepared hunter's style with homemade spätzli. The restaurant is open from 6 a.m. to midnight daily except Sunday in summer. Hot formal meals are served from 11 a.m. to 2 p.m. and 5 to 10 p.m. Sunday hours are from 10 a.m. to 10 p.m.

Restaurant Elisabethenstübli, 34 Elisabethenstrasse (tel. 061/23-11-05). Rita and Ruedi Forster are the congenial owners who themselves prepare the well-seasoned budget-oriented fare served on the checkered tablecloths in this charming restaurant. The intimate lighting, beamed ceiling, and the green trim make the whole place cozy and gemütlich. The restaurant is a local eatery, and if you're here at closing, you'll see the staff diligently polishing every chair, table, and lighting fixture for the upcoming day's business. Meals from 18F ($12.25) to 30F ($20.40) include the range of standard Swiss dishes with such specialties as fondue. The place is open from 8 a.m. to 11 p.m. for continuous serving of drinks and snacks, although hot meals are offered only from 11:30 a.m. to 2 p.m. and 6:30 to 10 p.m. They're closed Sunday. Little English is spoken here, but the polite staff endeavors to please foreign customers.

WHAT TO SEE: The citizens of Basel have worked hard to preserve their old sector, which is one of the finest in Europe. Towering over this old town is the **Münster** (cathedral). This red Vosges sandstone building was consecrated as far back as 1019, but after an earthquake destroyed it in 1356, it was rebuilt along Romanesque and Gothic lines with a tile roof in green and yellow. The cathedral (actually an abbey church since 1528) was founded by the Emperor Henry II.

The view of the cathedral from the right bank of the Rhine is renowned, as is the view from the Pfalz (palace), a 65-foot terrace in back of the building. From that terrace, you'll have a splendid panorama of the Rhine and can see into Germany's Black Forest.

The Münsterplatz, on which the cathedral sits, was built on the site of an old Roman fort. This 18th-century square is celebrated as being one of the most perfectly proportioned in Europe. There's an excellent view from the twin Gothic towers of the cathedral for those who pay the 2F ($1.35) admission to go up. The façade of the cathedral is richly decorated, with figures depicting everybody from prophets to foolish virgins. Inside, the church has five aisles. One of its many treasures, seen at the end of the south aisle, is an 11th-century bas-relief. Its 1486 pulpit was carved from a single block of stone. There's a monumental slab on one of the pillars honoring Erasmus of Rotterdam, who died in Basel in 1536. The church also contains the tomb of Anna von Hohenberg, wife of Rudolf of Habsburg.

The double cloister is entered on Rittergasse, and was erected in the 15th century on the foundations of the much earlier Romanesque structure.

Visiting hours are Easter to mid-October from 10 a.m. to 6 p.m. Monday to Friday, from 10 a.m. to noon and 2 to 5 p.m. on Saturday, and from 1 to 5 p.m. on Sunday. Otherwise, hours are 10 a.m. to noon (not on Sunday) and 2 to 4 p.m.

Kunstmuseum (fine arts museum), 16 St. Alban–Graben (tel. 061/22-08-28), contains one of the most remarkable collections of paintings in Europe, certainly the greatest in Switzerland. It has everybody from the old masters to 20th-century artists, and became a repository of many paintings labeled "decadent" by the government of Nazi Germany. Visiting hours are daily except Monday from 10 a.m. to 5 p.m. Entrance is 3F ($2.05), free on Sunday.

You approach the massive building housing the museum through a courtyard graced by sculptures by Rodin, Calder, and Hans Arp. The collections represent the development of art of the Upper Rhine Valley from the 14th to the 17th century, as well as work by outstanding artists from many countries all the way to the present century.

In addition to works by Hans Holbein the Elder, the gallery has an outstanding collection of the works of Holbein the Younger, who lived in Basel between 1515 and 1538, and came to the city when he was only 18 years old. For centuries the people of Basel have been able to view superb works of art by German and Swiss artists from the 15th and 16th centuries. Among these, Konrad Witz is a worthy candidate. But there is also a stunning collection of impressionist and of modern art, including Picasso, Braque, Chagall, and Dali. The largest collection of Légers in the world is here, plus works by Klee and Van Gogh (see his *Le Jardin de Daubigny 1890*).

Just a block away from the Kunstmuseum is the **Kunsthalle,** a gallery in the same building at 7 Steinenberg as the Kunsthalle Restaurant, recommended above under "Where to Dine." You go left from the Kunstmuseum on St. Alban–Graben, cross Bankenplatz, and follow Theaterstrasse. Hours and admission are the same as those for the Kunstmuseum, except that the Kunsthalle is not free on Sunday. Experimental works by contemporary artists are frequently changed.

Zoologischer Garden (zoological garden) adjoining the Hauptbahnhof (tel. 061/54-00-00), is known for its success in breeding in captivity wild animals on the endangered species list. It has some 2,000 animals and 600 different species in a park right in the middle of the city. The zoo is one of the greatest in the world, enjoying wide acclaim. You can get *very* close to the animals. Trained elephants and sea lions perform tricks. The Vivarium is filled with everything from penguins to reptiles, and the monkey house has an array of orangutans and gorillas. Visiting hours daily are 8 a.m. to 6:30 p.m. (closes an hour earlier in winter). Admission is 8F ($5.45) for adults and 3F ($2.05) for children.

Spalentor (Spalen Gate) is one of the great monuments of Basel, dating from 1400 but much restored in the 19th century, and is considered one of the most beautiful in the country. It has two battlemented towers and is crowned with a pointed roof. The location is to the west of the university, marking the end of the medieval sector.

At some point in your sightseeing you'll want to take a ferry boat, one of a trio crossing to the right bank of the Rhine. The most colorful of these is the *Münsterfähre*, operating during the daylight hours only (usually from 7 a.m. to 7 p.m.) throughout the year. In summer, the time might be extended by an hour or so depending on business. A one-way passage for a pedestrian costs 70 centimes (50¢). Once you get off, you can stroll along the **Oberer Rheinweg,** a river esplanade filled with wood-frame houses pressed tightly against each other.

Historisches Museum (History Museum), Barfüsserplatz (tel. 061/22-05-05), is installed in a former 14th-century Franciscan church, containing many relics of medieval Basel among other exhibits. In this "church of the barefoot friars" on "barefoot square" are magnificent 15th-century tapestries and ecclesiastical art, including some removed from the cathedral. One of the best known sculptures is in the late Gothic style, depicting a *Babbling King*. Many treasures from the old Basel guildhouses rest here, as do upper-Rhenish Gothic sculptures. Its greatest exhibit is a reliquary bust of St. Ursula, in silver and gold, commissioned by the people of Basel to contain the saint's relics. The museum also displays mementos of Erasmus. It's open from 10 a.m. to 5 p.m. daily except Tuesday. It charges 3F ($2.05) for admission, but is free on Sunday.

Haus zum Kirschgarten, 27 Elisabethenstrasse (tel. 061/22-13-33), is an 18th-century mansion turned into the "cherry orchard" museum, which may be visited from 10 a.m. to noon and 2 to 5 p.m., daily except Monday, for a 3F ($2.05) admission. It has an antique watch collection, plus some stunning porcelain, along with many old toys and period furnishings, including a kitchen. Look for the Aubusson tapestries.

The **Rathaus** (town hall), on Marktplatz, dominates the market square of Basel. It was built in the late Burgundian style in 1504, and is decorated with shields of the ancient city guildhouses. The sandstone building is adorned with frescoes, and has seen several later additions.

Mention should be made of the **University of Basel,** which lies on the south side of Petersplatz. Built during World War II, it was actually founded in 1460, making it one of the oldest citadels of learning in Switzerland. Its library, with one million volumes, has a rare collection of manuscripts, including works by Martin Luther, Erasmus, and the reformer Zwingli. The charter was signed by Pope Pius II, who participated in the Great Council that first met in Basel in 1431. The university has had some distinguished associates, including the cultural and art historian Jakob Burckhardt, the philosopher Friedrich Nietzsche, the physician Paracelsus, the mathematicians Jakob and Johann Bernoulli, and, of course, Erasmus.

Jüdische Museum (Jewish Museum of Switzerland), 8 Kornhausgasse (tel. 061/25-95-14), displays valuable items connected with Jewish worship, religion, folklore, and history. It has mementos of the first Zionist Congress presided over by Theodor Herzl in Basel in 1897. The museum is open from 2 to 5 p.m. Monday and Wednesday, from 10 a.m. to noon and 2 to 5 p.m. Sunday.

Museum für Gegenwartskunst (museum for contemporary art), 60 St. Alban–Rheinweg (tel. 061/23-81-83), is one of Europe's leading museums of modern art of the '60s, '70s, and '80s, including the works of such artists as Bruce Nauman, Richard Long, Jonathan Borofsky, Frank Stella, and Donald Judd. It's open from 10 a.m. to 5 p.m. May to October, 10 a.m. to noon and 2 to 5 p.m. November to April. Closed Tuesday. Admission is 3F ($2.05).

North of the center, the **Port of Basel** is the terminus for navigation on the Rhine. The "Hafen," as it's called, is home to barge people from many European countries. From the silo terrace atop a Swiss Navigation Company tower, reached by an elevator ride, there's a panoramic view of the Alsace plain, the Vosges, the Black Forest in Germany, and the Jura mountains. Unless it's iced over (and dangerously slippery), the tower is open daily from 10 a.m. to noon and 2 to 5 p.m., charging an admission of 1F (68¢). The port, which was opened in 1924, paved the way for Basel to become a great city of commerce.

Visitors to the tower can combine it with a stop at the adjacent museum, **Unser Weg zu Meer** (Our Way to the Sea), with exhibits on Swiss navigation. Small but interesting artifacts trace the history of navigation through the centuries on the inland waterways of Mitteleuropa. Hours are the same as for the tower. Admission is 2F ($1.35) for adults, 1F (68¢) for children under 16. A slide presentation of special interest to children is shown.

A promontory called **Dreiländereck** (three countries' corner) juts out into the Rhine. If you walk around a pylon marking the spot, you can in just a few steps cross from Switzerland into Germany and then into France—and you don't need a passport.

TOURS: You can take sightseeing tours of Basel at 15F ($10.20) for adults, 7.50F ($5.10) for children. Departures are at 10 a.m. daily in front of the Hotel Victoria at the railroad station. Tickets can be purchased in advance at the hotel reception desk. The tour lasts 1¾ hours.

From the end of May until the beginning of October it's also possible to take a guided stroll through the old town. Tickets, purchased from the guide, cost 6F ($4.10) for adults and 3F ($2.05) for children. Tours are conducted on Sunday and Monday, departing at 3 p.m. in front of the cathedral.

As the gateway to Switzerland's Rhineland, Basel is a popular embarkation point for cruises on the river. The Rhine is navigable to Rheinfelden, and in summer **Basler Personenschiffahrt**, 2 Blumerain (tel. 061/25-24-00), conducts cruises to Rheinfelden, which cost 17.80F ($12.10) for adults, 8.90F ($6.05) for children. Also **City Panorama Tours** offers trips on the Rhine costing 7.20F ($4.90) for adults for a one-hour cruise, 3.60F ($2.45) for children.

WHERE TO SHOP: The fashionable shopping street of Basel is the **Freie Strasse,** leading to the market square and the town hall.

Bally Capitol zum Pflug, 38 Freie Strasse (tel. 061/25-18-97), sells shoes and leather goods from the most important shoe manufacturer in Switzerland. The staff makes every effort to keep well stocked with the most recent models. Their elegant store has big display windows set into a five-story building that is whimsically decorated with three-quarter columns and carved bas-reliefs. There is also an exclusive clothes boutique.

Kurz, 39 Freie Strasse (tel. 061/25-26-20), sells an impressive display of watches, jewelry, and mantel clocks.

For selections of the best in European china, glass, and gifts, go to Fügli. That's what Baslers call the **Füglistaller,** 23 Freie Strasse (tel. 061/25-78-78), a store whose architecture is as handsome as its stock, with an elegant chandelier and a famous staircase. You can purchase choice gift items at reasonable prices here.

Leder-Droeser, 11 Eisengasse (tel. 061/25-42-53), offers a variety of fine leather goods, including clothing, umbrellas, and foulards, plus a whole department of leather luggage. The shop, long a landmark in Basel, is between the Markplatz and the Mittlere Brücke.

Wehrli, 49 Clarastrasse (tel. 061/33-77-77), stocks a large range of photo and film material, as well as video and audiovisual material. A color laboratory can process film within six hours. A well-trained staff assists customers.

Antiquités M. & G. Ségal, 14 Aeschengraben (tel. 061/23-39-08), founded in 1862, is one of Switzerland's oldest and most respected antique shops. Furniture, gold and silver articles, faïence, porcelain, paintings, are among the impressive collection of antiques from the 16th to the 19th centuries. Dr. Georges B. Ségal, representing the fourth generation of the founding family, is a renowned expert in selection of antiques, presiding over the shop as well as over an exhibit at the annual Swiss Art and Antique Fair held every fall.

Münzen und Medaillen A.G., 25 Malzgasse (tel. 061/23-75-44), offers a wide selection of ancient and medieval coins and other European coins up to about the middle of the 19th century. You can receive expert professional help from the staff members here, whether you are in the market to buy or to sell coins or medals.

Ernest Beyeler Gallery, 9 Bäunleingasse (tel. 061/23-54-12). Collectors from all over the world frequent this internationally famous gallery, which sells a rotating series of paintings and sculpture.

Davidoff, 4 Aeschenvorstadt (tel. 061/23-47-50), stocks a collection of an item that every pipesmoker knows about—briarwood and meerschaum pipes—along with cigarettes and cigars from around the world, including Havana.

Galerie Gisele Linder, 54 Elisabethenstrasse (tel. 061/23-83-77). The average visitor to Basel won't be in the market for an avant-garde painting, although many might be interested in a glimpse at the newest waves on the European art scene. The creative force behind the gallery is Swiss-born Gisele Linder, who keeps in touch with art patterns as far away as Berlin, Paris, and Los Angeles. As part of your browsing patterns, you might want to drop in. The gallery lies at the edge of an inner-city park across from the Basel Hilton, not far from the railway station. The gallery is open from 2 to 6:30 p.m. Tuesday, Wednesday, and Friday; from 2 to 8 p.m. Thursday, and from 10 a.m. to 4 p.m. Saturday. Closed Sunday and Monday.

BASEL AFTER DARK: Musical acts offered at **Stadt-Casino,** Barfüssenplatz (tel. 061/22-23-23), in the Hans-Hüber Saal, are frequently televised. Drinks cost from 16F ($10.90). It also has a disco inside, which you enter through the massive concrete entranceway of this 1930s-modern downtown building.

Café des Arts (Kunsthalle-Garden), 7 Steinenberg (tel. 061/22-36-19), lies in front of the famous Tingueley fountain in the garden of the Kunsthalle. This is one of the finest places in the city for drinks. In summer you might choose one of the café tables set up among ivy-covered trellises and modern and classical sculpture in the forecourt. The walls are full of risqué art, such as nudes in many manifestations, including that of artfully blindfolded maidens holding lampshades above their heads. There's a lot of attractively stylized buttock photography below ornate brass chandeliers. As in many places in Basel, you'll hear a lighthearted blend of American pop/rock music playing while you drink wine at 3.20F ($2.20) per glass. The café is open seven days a week, from 9 a.m. to midnight Sunday to Thursday, to 1 a.m. Friday and Saturday.

Hazyclub, Heuwaage (tel. 061/23-99-82), is a pop-oriented nightclub attracting a music-loving crowd generally under 35. A rotating group of live musicians is engaged to play here. The club is open seven nights a week from 9 p.m. to 2 a.m. Drinks start at 14F ($9.50), and there's a restaurant inside.

Kronen Bar, Hotel Drei Könige, 8 Blumenrain (tel. 061/25-52-52). What's said to be the oldest hotel in Europe is also the host to some of the most avant-garde music in town. Presenting a changing array of pianists, many of them American, the bar does a thriving after-dark business as a place where the tuned-in and turned-on citizens of Basel meet and mingle. Large, airy, and darkly comfortable, the bar sports paneling and a collection of silk-screened prints. Live music plays nightly except Sunday from 6 to 8 p.m. and then from 8:30 to midnight. Hard liquor costs from 14F ($9.50).

Hotel Euler, 14 Centralbahnplatz (tel. 061/23-45-00), has an elegantly appointed bar area covered with crimson fabric, with tables that look like teak and contain little brass lamps. It's known internationally as a chic watering hole for many members of the world business community. The ceiling is one of those elaborately coffered renditions. Even when it's crowded you'll rarely hear more than a polite murmur throughout its appealing, square floor area. The chairs and banquettes are in dark leather. Hours are daily from 11 a.m. to midnight. Drinks cost from 12F ($8.15).

Café Atlantis, 13 Klosterberg (tel. 061/23-34-00). Through the amber-tinted glass of the street level's panoramic windows you'll be able to judge if the ambience of this up-to-date hangout is for you. The cover charge varies according to the popularity of whatever musical act is appearing. Usually it's 6F ($4.10). The interior has beams, columns, and is open even for coffee in the morning. While you're there, be sure to walk up to the second floor for a view of the cathedral in an ambience of psychedelic mirrors, two bars, and a red-painted coffee room. It's open seven days a week from 8 a.m. Monday to Friday, from 10 a.m. Saturday and Sunday. It closes at 1 a.m. on Friday, midnight on Saturday.

Old City Bar, Basel Hilton, 31 Aeschengraben (tel. 061/22-66-22), is one of the most elegantly and consistently attractive places for a late-night drink or a before-dinner cocktail. The decor is plush, intimate, and low-key, with a pianist thumping out music that ranges from sophisticated sambas to understated show tunes. The location is one floor beneath the Hilton's main lobby, which you'll reach via a curved illuminated staircase. Drinks start at 6F ($4.10) to 8F ($5.45). It's open from 11 a.m. to midnight daily (to 1 a.m. on Friday).

Bora-Bora Disco, Basel Hilton International, 31 Aeschengraben (tel. 061/22-66-22), is a relatively small room with a Polynesian theme, plus a DJ who plays everything from regional music to disco to Elvis Presley to an occasional piece by Mozart if he feels the audience would appreciate it. Lying two floors below the lobby of the Hilton, the club has a plush ambience. The cost is from 9F ($6.10) for a drink. The place is open from 8:30 p.m. to 2 a.m. Sunday to Thursday, to 3 a.m. Friday and Saturday.

2. TARGETS IN THE ENVIRONS

Everything in this chapter can be safely visited on a day trip while based in Basel. You're not only on the northeastern end of the Swiss Jura, but also in quick driving distance of Germany's Black Forest and the Vosges mountains of France. If you'd like to drive east, you can travel along Switzerland's Rhineland, heading in the direction of Lake Constance.

Instead of staying in Basel, you might want to locate at one of the smaller towns or villages nearby. I have a few suggestions, and they'll be followed by the major sightseeing targets of northwestern Switzerland, including Fribourg.

LANGENBRUCK: Lying about 19 miles from Basel, 5 miles from the Autobahn, Langenbruck is a small holiday resort set in the midst of meadows and woods. The mountain ranges, which rise to 3,610 feet, shelter it from the east and north winds. The village lies on top of the Upper Hauenstein Pass, a meeting point of several mountain valleys. The tourist office estimates that there are 125 miles of walks. With its ski lifts and ski jumping, it is also becoming a modest winter resort.

For food and lodging, the logical choice is the **Landgasthof Bären,** CH-4438 Langenbruck, Switzerland (tel. 062/60-14-14), a comfortably proportioned, very old inn, with a hipped tile roof, green-and-buff shutters, and a faithful clientele. It was built in 1577 and reportedly sheltered Napoleon during one of his junkets in this part of Switzerland. Owned by the Grieder family since 1898, the hotel celebrates its status with a wrought-iron bracket holding an ornate depiction of a bear hanging over the pavement. The interior is predictably rustic, and includes a restaurant with three distinct rooms and a piano bar with a little restaurant for snacks. A single with bath costs 50F ($34) to 70F ($47.60) daily, depending on the size of the bed. A double with bath rents for 90F ($61.20) to 105F ($71.40).

OLTEN: This important railway junction and industrial town lies on the banks of the Aare River at the foot of the Hauenstein. Because of its ideal location, the Swiss use it for many conventions and conferences. Frankly, for the tourist it merits only a passing stopover.

Take the covered wooden bridge (for pedestrians only) to the Altstadt or old town, which has many interesting old buildings. The **Kunstmuseum** (fine arts) is open to the public from 10 a.m. to noon and 2 to 5 p.m. except Monday and from mid-July to mid-August, charging an admission of 2F ($1.35). It contains mostly 19th- and 20th-century paintings and sculpture. However, the work of the 19th-century artist Martin Disteli makes the museum notable. He was a famed artist, painter, and political caricaturist of his day.

Food and Lodging

Hotel Europe, CH-4600 Olten, Switzerland (tel. 062/32-33-55), welcomes visitors with a warm display of neon signs advertising the restaurant, pub, and café, as well as the Tropicana dancing bar. The interior is tastefully appointed in floral prints, autumnal colors, and wicker furniture, with lots of big windows. Comfortably furnished doubles with bath cost 125F ($85) daily, while singles rent for 85F ($57.80), including breakfast. The hotel lies right in the geographical heart of town.

For dining, **Zunfthaus zum Löwen,** 6 Hauptstrasse, CH-4600 Olten, Switzerland (tel. 062/32-21-17), is Olten's most colorful restaurant, housed in the former meeting place of a medieval guild. Modernized with a panache that brings it very much into the 20th century, the establishment serves a cuisine moderne selection of such delicacies as terrine of crab, cabbage soup with rosemary and herbs from southern France, filet of sole, navarin of veal with crayfish (offered with a delectable spinach soufflé), and a pot-au-feu made with seafood and shellfish. Fixed-price meals range from 28F ($19.05) to 100F ($68), the latter an epicurean delight, while à la carte choices range from 35F ($23.80) to 55F ($37.40). It's open daily from noon to 2:30 p.m. and about 6:30 to 10 p.m. This is also a small hotel, with bathless singles renting for 45F ($30.60) daily, singles with bath going for 65F ($44.20). Doubles cost from 90F ($61.20) to 130F ($88.40) daily, depending on the plumbing. The establishment is in the very center of the old town.

Restaurant Felsenburg, 157 Aaraustrasse (tel. 062/26-22-77), run by Salsi Adriano, is decorated with lots of pieces of original art on its wood-paneled walls. Everything here is efficient and professional, so much so that many residents of Olten make this their preferred restaurant, especially for those who like elegant Italian food. Specialties include homemade pastas of all sorts, grilled meats, and an Italian delicacy known as cappelleti à la crème. You might also try escalope of veal with marsala, and as a main course, an entrecôte scheck. Fixed-price meals cost from a modest 18F ($12.25) to 25F ($17), with à la carte prices ranging from a low of 18F ($12.25) to a high that rarely goes beyond 55F ($37.40). Hours are noon to 2:30 p.m. and 6:30 to 10 p.m. The restaurant is closed Tuesday and for four weeks at some point every summer.

RHEINFELDEN: Called "Royal Rheinfelden," this is Switzerland's lowest altitude health spa. It faces the southern slopes of the Black Forest. Its salt springs, the Rheinfelden natural brine, are considered one of the major salt springs in Europe. Chances are, however, you won't be coming here to take "the cure," but to enjoy the Altstadt (old town), one of the most colorful in Europe. Old towers and ancient walls rise above the turbulent river, and at sunset, if caught in the right light, this is one of the most dramatic town views in Switzerland. The town has open-air swimming pools and modern therapeutic equipment. Just outside the city are the famous breweries of Feldschlösschen and Cardinal.

Food and Lodging

Hotel Eden Solbad, CH-4310 Rheinfelden, Switzerland (tel. 061/87-54-06). From the front this family-run hotel looks like an old-fashioned resort. Partially hidden by towering trees and painted white, it's capped with a complicated red-tile roof. From the rear you'll quickly see that the Wiki-Rupprecht family has added a modern extension flanked by a landscaped swimming pool. This forms an attractive combination of old architecture, as exemplified by the high-ceilinged dining room with its vaulted arches, with expanses of panoramic glass, as seen in the main lobby and reception area. With half board included, the price is 130F ($88.40) to 150F ($102) per person daily, either single or double occupancy of a room with a shower. Rooms with bath cost 160F ($108.80) to 180F ($122.40) per person for either double or single occupancy. The hotel is within walking distance of the railway station.

Schützen Solbad, 19 Bahnhofstrasse, CH-4310 Rheinfelden, Switzerland (tel. 061/87-50-04), has 22 rooms, some of which are delightfully old-fashioned, decorated with parquet floors, high ceilings, and antiques. You'll reach them via a sloping staircase, which is adorned with curlicues of wrought iron climbing up its balustrade, or by taking one of two elevators. All of this is housed in a restrained yellow-painted building with a roofline that looks like something from Paris in the 19th century. The hotel can arrange a collection of water and massage therapies, any of which will be explained by Mrs. Offerbach, the manager. Singles with private bath cost 99F ($67.30) to 108F ($71.45) daily, and doubles rent for 182F ($123.75) to 195F ($132.60), the latter price for rooms with private baths. Breakfast, which can be delivered to your room, is included, as is dinner. The kitchen serves some of the best food at the spa, traditional Swiss cookery such as veal Zuricher style and pork steak. Lunches cost from 18F ($12.25) and dinners from 35F ($23.80). There is an indoor, warm, natural saltwater swimming pool.

Schwanen Solbad, CH-4310 Rheinfelden, Switzerland (tel. 061/87-53-44), is an elegantly constructed 65-room building, originally a villa from 1835. In renovating, maximum attention has been paid to the inclusion of large panoramic windows overlooking a flagstone terrace and manicured garden. The well-planned public room has a gemütlich feeling. The framework is of early 1970s construction, but many of the accessories, such as the chandeliers, are traditional. The combination of new and old is attractive. The hotel, in the center of town, has a swimming pool and a sauna to help you unwind before dinner in the comfortable restaurant. A full range of massage and mineral springs facilities is available, with special prices offered for stays of more than one week. However, for tourists in transit, singles cost from 86F ($58.50) to 134F ($91.10) daily and doubles from 188F ($127.85) to 260F ($176.80), depending on the plumbing. All tariffs, both single and double, include half-board.

Among the restaurants, **Zum Goldenen Adler** (tel. 061/87-53-32), specializes in cheese dishes from all over the country. Amid a rustic decor, beneath beamed ceilings, you can order raclette at 12.50F ($8.50) per person and a limited array of meat dishes. Six different kinds of fondue are offered: a plain one for simpler tastes, hunter's style fondue with mushrooms, fondue valaisanne with tomatoes, even a champagne fondue. Full meals cost from 20F ($13.60) per person, with an array of wines to accompany all dishes. To enhance the ambience, alpine evergreen music is presented from 7:30 to 11 p.m. Friday, Saturday, and Sunday evening. Warm meals are served from 11 a.m. to 11 p.m. every day except Monday.

ZURZACH: This popular spa, with three open-air swimming pools, grew up on the site of a Roman fort. Once it was a big river port with lots of Rhineland traffic. It lies across from Rheinheim, a German village reached by bridge. In fact, Zurzach is a good base for exploring many of Germany's Rhineland attractions, including the city of Koblenz. The town today contains many old burghers' houses and a church whose origins go back to the 10th century.

For food and lodging, my preferred choice is the **Hotel Zurzacherhof,** CH-8437 Zurzach, Switzerland (tel. 056/49-01-21). In summertime its bright awnings and concrete balconies can be seen from a distance. The interior of the hotel is a winning mixture of contemporary with traditional. The most expensive rooms are decorated in a plush combination of padded French armchairs, ruffled vanity tables, and gold and scarlet brocades. The dining room has a beautifully grained wood-beamed ceiling and an intricately patterned Oriental rug set against the far wall. A fitness room, a sauna, and a covered swimming pool are on the premises. Each of the units has a private bath, and with half board, the prices are from 80F ($54.40) to 120F ($81.60) daily in a single and from 140F ($95.20) to 210F ($142.80) in a double.

The dining room, one of the best in town, specializes in such dishes as filet of sole, scampi, veal steak, regional dishes, and a gratinée of seafood chef's style. For diners not staying at the hotel, reservations are suggested. Fixed-price meals cost 26F ($17.70) to 50F ($34). The restaurant serves from 11:30 a.m. to 2 p.m. and 6:30 to 11 p.m. daily.

3. BADEN

The Romans, who called it Aquae Helvetiae, came here to bathe in its hot curative sulfur springs, hoping for relief from their rheumatism. By the close of the medieval period Baden's fame had grown until it had become one of the most important spas in the country, attracting the aristocrats of Zurich. The Roman baths were rebuilt in all their splendor, and the Habsburgs chose this as their seat of residence and garrison location, endowing it with the rights of a town around 1290. The baths, boasting of the highest mineral content in Switzerland, became a cultural center, and handsome mansions and ecclesiastical buildings were constructed here, constituting what is now the old town, architecturally independent of the rest of Baden until the end of the 19th century.

Baden springs today attract many guests, and claims beneficial results in the relief and healing of rheumatic ailments. Medical doctors are in attendance, and modern therapeutic equipment is available in the spa hotels and the medical center, as well as in one of Switzerland's most up-to-date hospitals.

In the early 20th century, trade and commerce became an important part of Baden's economic base, and today it's known as the center of the Swiss electrical industry. That doesn't mean to suggest that it's a dreary industrial town. Far from that, it's a tourist attraction even if you aren't interested in "taking the baths." The town is well endowed with hotels, tranquil parks, and a gambling casino.

The first railway line in Switzerland started at this spa, and the old town where those passengers got off is still there. From the modern road bridge you'll have a good view of this medieval sector, with its colorful roofs split by dormers, and its narrow streets and squares. Later you can explore it, discovering many boutiques, shops, and art galleries.

The spa enjoys a panoramic site in the foothills of the Jura, built on both banks of the Limmat River (the same river we discovered in Zurich). Although included in this section on Basel for touring purposes, Baden is much closer to Zurich, which can be reached in less than half an hour.

THE SIGHTS: The old covered wooden bridge across the Limmat has been preserved. If you walk across it, you'll end at the **Landvogteischloss** (tel. 056/22-75-74), or governor's mansion. The bailiffs lived here from 1415 to 1798, and the schloss has been turned into a historical and admission-free museum that is open from 10 a.m. to noon and 2 to 5 p.m. except Monday. It has displays of pottery from the area, antiques, armor, excavated coins, and folk clothing from the Canton of Aargau, in which Baden is situated.

You can also climb to the ruins of the **Castle of Stein,** a much-photographed site where a Swiss flag flies. That wasn't always so: it was once a seat of the Habsburgs, and was attacked and destroyed more than once. The spa's skyline will unfold for you, characterized by the parish church, **Stadtkirche,** originally constructed from 1457, and by the **Tower of Baden,** a city landmark.

From Baden you can take at least two excursions, the first to visit **Habsburg Castle** (tel. 056/41-16-73), ancestral seat of the Counts of Habsburg. About ten miles from Baden, it lies near Brugg and Bad Schinznach. Built on the summit of the Wülpelsberg, the castle today—or what remains—hardly suggests the power and sweep of a family that was to play such a central role in European affairs. There is a good view from the 11th-century keep, and a restaurant with a terrace has been installed. The place seems to be open all the time, at least from 9 a.m. to midnight any day except Tuesday off-season.

If you're motoring and it's a good day, you might also want to visit the old Cistercian **Abbey of Wettingen** (tel. 056/26-76-20), which has been turned into a school for teachers. It lies only two miles south of Baden. Founded in the 13th century, it receives visitors daily from 2 to 5 p.m., March to October, charging 3F ($2.05) admission. The cloisters are Gothic, and the stained glass is from the 13th to the 17th centuries, some of the most remarkable I've ever viewed in Switzerland. The original abbey church was destroyed, but the present building, in the baroque style, contains some finely carved choir stalls that are exceptional in their artistry and detail.

THE SPA RESORTS: A 73-room, modern red-brick hostelry, **Hotel/ Restaurant Du Park,** 24 Römerstrasse, CH-5400 Baden, Switzerland (tel. 056/ 20-13-11), enjoys an attractive location between the city park and the thermal baths. It benefits from the most up-to-date architectural principles and partially encloses a massive copper beech. The rooms are tasteful, filled with warm colors and lots of light. The bar, the informal bistro, the restaurant, and the grill room are engagingly decorated with natural materials such as wood, stone, and unglazed tile. Archaeologists will be interested in the statuette of Silenus, companion god of Bacchus, discovered by workmen during excavations for the hotel. The bronze depiction of the wizened deity is displayed along with other ancient objects and has become the logo of the hotel. Du Park is affiliated with the Best Western chain, charging from 140F ($95.20) daily in a single and from 190F ($129.20) in a double. Each unit contains private bath, radio, mini-bar, color TV, and phone, and tariffs include breakfast.

Verenahof Hotels, CH-5401 Baden, Switzerland (same telephone for all three—056/22-52-51), are actually a well-planned complex of three hotels, all of them connected by a covered passageway to a thermally heated swimming pool and a well-equipped medical therapy center. The entire complex is surrounded by landscaped gardens, lawns, and terraces. The hotels making up this group include the following: **Hotel Verenahof** dominates the Kurplatz with its imposing façade of 19th-century, gray carved stone. Its interior is filled with tall Doric columns, geometrically patterned carpeting, paneling, and elegant bedrooms with antiques and big windows. Bedrooms, either single or double, with full board cost from 180F ($122.40) to 200F ($136) per person with private bath.

Hotel Ochsen looks more like a homey country inn than the others in the group. It has a red-tile sloped roof and flowers on the ledges of the second floor. The hotel lies on both sides of Badstrasse, with a covered passageway connecting the second floors of both sections. The bedrooms have been completely renovated. Including full board, rates range from 90F ($61.20) to 105F ($71.40) per person daily in a single or double without private bath, and from 115F ($78.20) to 135F ($91.80) with private bath.

Finally, the **Hotel Staadhof** is the most recently constructed of the three, and the most imaginatively designed. The exterior almost resembles a cascade of gray stalactites clustered into symmetrical rows, with tall narrow windows piercing the façade. The entire edifice is capped with garlands of greenery that grow in pots hanging from the upper terraces. The interior is spacious, with good color choices and ample use of natural materials. The most expensive of the three hotels, it charges from 170F ($115.60) to 180F ($122.40) per person daily in a room with a shower for single or double occupancy with full board included. Rooms with full bath range from 190F ($129.20) to 240F ($163.20) per person daily, with the most expensive room being an opulent suite. These latter rates also include full board.

Hotel Linde, 22 Mellingerstrasse, CH-5400 Baden, Switzerland (tel. 056/ 22-53-85), rises in a multitiered collection of angles and jutting balconies. The street-level floor and the two floors above it house restaurants, summer terraces, and attractively decorated public rooms (one of which is surprisingly rustic for such a modern skyscraper). The bedrooms are decorated in functional furniture and fiesta colors. The Wanner family are your hosts, charging 78F ($53.05) to 110F ($74.80) daily in a single with bath and 145F ($98.60) to 175F ($119) in a double with bath, breakfast included. The same family runs a popular cafeteria and a pastry shop and bakery on the ground floor as well.

Badhotel Limmathof, CH-5400 Baden, Switzerland (tel. 056/20-14-11). Sections of this hotel still retain their 19th-century opulence and have plenty of romantic touches, from the wrought-iron on the riverside terrace to the tapestries, antique carpets, and settees of the public rooms. The building is a well-constructed remnant of another era, with a beautiful two-tone façade complete with corner mullions and restrained detailing around the windows. The hotel also has a swimming pool and a formidable array of massage and hydrotherapy programs, which complement the good cuisine and attentive service. Singles with private toilet and running water cost 95F ($64.60) to 130F ($88.40) daily, rising to 130F ($88.40) to 180F ($122.40) with full bath. Doubles with running water and private toilets cost 200F ($136) to 250F ($170), peaking at 290F ($197.20) with full bath. Rates include half board.

Atrium Hotel zur Blume, 4 Am Kurplatz, CH-5400 Baden, Switzerland (tel. 056/22-55-69). Resting on a foundation dating from 1421, the rooms of this hotel are ringed in a series of ascending balconies around a glass-covered courtyard. The hotel was formed when a medieval stable was joined to a newer building that was completed in 1873. About half of the 35 bedrooms contain private baths, and each is large enough to really move around in. Each has a phone and an eclectic collection of old-fashioned furniture. Depending on the plumbing and the accommodation, singles rent for 65F ($44.20) to 130F ($88.40) daily, doubles for 130F ($88.40) to 250F ($170), with half board included. As the hotel's name implies, in summer the shuttered façade is wreathed with flowers. In cold weather, the greenhouse effect of the skylight turns the iron columns and wraparound balconies of the atrium into a winter garden.

WHERE TO DINE: My preferred dining choice at the resort is the **Goldener Schlussel,** in the Limmathof Hotel (tel. 056/20-14-11). A mellow atmosphere mixes happily with a real concern for cookery. The building dates back some 500 years, and is rich with Oriental carpets and wood details, most elegant and intimate. Fine service and traditional cookery will bring you such dishes as veal steak with morels, veal liver sautéed with herbs, beef Stroganoff, and trout meunière. The chef also specializes in grills. Food is served daily except Monday from noon to 2 p.m. and from 5 to 11:30 p.m. Meals cost around 40F ($27.20).

For a change of pace fare, try **La Trattoria,** 2 Theaterplatz (tel. 056/22-64-64), which is, as its name suggests, the place for Italian fare. It's served daily from 11 a.m. to 2 p.m. and 6 p.m. to midnight. Incongruously, you'd expect an English pub behind the half-timbered decor with herringbone brick. Inside, humorous versions of Fassnacht (carnival) masks decorate the place, along with a beamed ceiling and ceramic tile floors. The daily menu offers such items as ravioli, beefsteak Café de Paris, veal scallopini with lemon butter or marsala, and veal liver Venetian style. The pizzas are superb, and the chef also does any number of pasta and grilled meat dishes. Meals cost from 20F ($13.60) to 40F ($27.20).

A SIDE TRIP TO BRUGG: Six miles northwest of Baden, Brugg was founded by the Habsburgs in 1232. It lies near the point where three rivers converge, the Reuss, the Aare, and the Limmat (the latter flowing through Zurich). It's a minor tourist center and also a headquarters of industry. But mainly it's known for its bridge, as its name suggests. Near the bridge stands the Schwarzer Turm (black tower), dating from the 11th century. At no. 39 on the main street is the house in which Heinrich Pestalozzi, the educator, died in 1827. A local museum, the Vindonissa, contains artifacts excavated from a Roman fort.

4. SOLOTHURN

The capital of a same-name Swiss canton, Solothurn, at the foot of the Jura mountains, is ancient. On the banks of the Aare, it is, according to a 16th-century rhyme, "the oldest place in Celtis save Trier." Roman inscriptions calling it Salodurum have been found, as have the remains of a Roman castrum. In its long history it has been fortified many times—and with good reason.

THE SIGHTS: Like most Swiss towns of vintage charm, it has an old town, lying on the left bank of the river and still partially enclosed by 17th-century walls. Inside are numerous Renaissance and baroque buildings. The town enjoyed its greatest prestige when it was the residence of the French ambassadors to the Swiss Confederation from the 16th to the 18th centuries. Solothurn became part of the Confederation as early as 1481.

The old town is entered through the Biel Gate or the Basel Gate. The heart of the old sector is the Marktplatz with its clock tower, a pulsating place with a wide variety of fruits and vegetables. The **Rathaus** (town hall) is 15th century, with a notable Renaissance doorway. The two most colorful streets are Hauptgasse and Schaalgasse, where you'll see many wrought-iron signs and brightly painted shutters.

The **Cathedral of St. Ursus,** in the grand baroque style, dates from the 18th century. It is said to have been erected on the spot where its namesake was martyred. The cathedral lies just inside the 16th-century Basel Gate and was constructed by builders from Ticino, hence its Italian appearance. Try to visit the gardens on the east side of the church. Since 1828 this has been the seat of the bishop of Basel.

Nearby, slightly to the northwest of the cathedral, stands the **Museum Altes Zeughaus** (old arsenal), 1 Zeughausplatz (tel. 065/23-35-28), said to house the second-largest collection of weapons in Europe. The most fascinating exhibits are the medieval weaponry and flags. Many military uniforms of the Swiss are also shown. Admission free, it is open March to October, Thursday to Sunday from 10 a.m. to noon and 2 to 5 p.m. From November to February, it is open Tuesday to Friday from 2 to 5 p.m. and Saturday and Sunday from 10 a.m. to noon and 2 to 5 p.m. It stays open until 9 p.m. Thursday. It is closed Monday.

You should visit the **Kunstmuseum Solothurn** (municipal museum), 30 Werkhofstrasse (tel. 065/22-23-07), if for no other reason than to see the *Madonna of Solothurn* by Holbein the Younger, a notable painting. Also outstanding is a 15th-century painting on wood from the Rhenish school, the *Madonna with the Strawberries.* The museum emphasizes Swiss art from the mid-19th century up to the present. A collection of excellent works represents the artistry of Buchser, Frölicher, Hodler, Vallotton, Trachsel, Amiet, Berger, and Gubler, among others. Contemporary Swiss art appears in a choice of prominent objects. The museum is open from 10 a.m. to noon and 2 to 5 p.m. except Monday, and the entrance fee is discretionary.

The **Jesuitenkirche,** or Jesuits' church, on Hauptgasse between the cathedral and the marketplace, dates from 1680. It should be visited for a look at its three-bay nave, which is richly frescoed.

The Solothurn tourist office, the **Verkehrsbüro,** 69 Hauptgasse (Kronenplatz) (tel. 065/22-19-24), will provide you with a map and pinpoint several interesting day excursions, such as a trip by boat on the Aare River to Biel, with a stopover at the Altreu, the first stork colony in Switzerland. If you've got two hours to spare, take the six-mile run to one of the major attractions of the country, the **Weissenstein.** The panoramic view of the Jura from here is about as impressive as you'll see anywhere. Getting there by car will be difficult, even dangerous, on narrow roads with hairpin curves, so it's best to take the chair lift from the Oberdorf station, which will deliver you to Kurhaus Weissenstein.

In fair weather the lift runs from 8 a.m. to noon and 1:30 to 6 p.m. (on Sunday, from 8 a.m. to 6 p.m.). In winter service is curtailed to 9 a.m. to noon and 1:30 to 5 p.m. (open Sunday, from 8 a.m. to 5 p.m.). The round-trip fare is about 12F ($8.15). On a clear day you can't see forever, but you can view Mont Blanc, Berne, and Neuchâtel Lake, among other horizon-spanning geography.

WHERE TO STAY: The medieval logo of **Hotel/Restaurant Roter Turm,** CH-4500 Solothurn, Switzerland (tel. 065/22-96-21), hangs from a wrought-iron bracket depicts red enameled tower, and the illuminated sign below it spells out the name of the hotel in French. And so you'll be sure to find it, remember that it's next door to the gargoyled clock tower of St. Ursus's Cathedral. The Lorenz family rents out 23 bedrooms, the largest ones overlooking the front square. The units are modern, with comfortable beds, all with phones, TVs, mini-bars, radios, and complete baths. Doubles cost 105F ($71.40) to 115F ($78.20) daily, with singles going for 70F ($47.60) to 85F ($57.80), with breakfast included.

On the lobby level of the hotel (with a separate entrance opening onto the street) there's an informal brasserie open throughout the day for drinks, snacks, and platters of food. Most cognoscenti of the city's restaurant scene, however, take the hotel's elevator up to the fifth floor Rôtisserie. This is by far the more elegant and sophisticated of the establishment's two restaurants. Ringed with big windows, it serves lunch from 11:30 a.m. to 2:30 p.m. and dinner from 6:30 to midnight seven days a week. The menu is seasonal, changing with whatever ingredients are available that week. A three-course fixed-price meal goes for 30F ($20.40), a full à la carte dinner for 50F ($34). Specialties include fresh filet of sole in butter, Italian-style scampi, filets of perch meunière, smoked trout, veal steak with morels, lamb, and steak au poivre. Reservations are a good idea.

Hotel Krone, CH-4500 Solothurn, Switzerland (tel. 065/22-44-12), is one of the oldest inns in the country and still basks in its reputation as the hotel where Napoleon's wife, Josephine, chose to stay for several days in 1811. That was a long time ago, and a lot of things have changed since then. Nevertheless, this inn attracts nostalgia buffs. Because of the links Solothurn has traditionally maintained with France, the gilt lettering on the pink façade spells out the name in French (Hôtel de la Couronne). Each of the old-fashioned bedrooms has a private bath. Singles rent from 95F ($64.60) to 125F ($85) daily, with doubles costing from 130F ($88.40) to 180F ($122.40). These tariffs include an abundant breakfast buffet, services, and taxes. The Küng family are the directors of the hotel, a member of Ambassador Swiss Hotels. The restaurant satisfies most clients (see below).

WHERE TO DINE: Among the city's many fine restaurants, the **Hotel Krone Restaurant,** 64 Hauptgasse (tel. 065/22-44-12), has long been known for its cuisine and its cellar of wines. During the summer, a garden restaurant is a good change. Otherwise, diners enjoy an elegant beerhall format of modern crystal chandeliers, plasterwork ceilings, and a traditional Swiss decor, with wood tables. A four-course fixed-price menu goes for 75F ($51), or else guests can order à la carte, paying from 35F ($23.80) for the privilege. The chef has a varied cuisine, including such fare as scampi with crabmeat, filet of sole with riesling, suprême of salmon with champagne, cream of snail soup, and carpaccio. There is also a special children's menu. Service is daily from 11 a.m. to 2 p.m. and 6 to 9 p.m.

Weinstube Misteli-Gasche, 14 Friedhofplatz (tel. 065/22-32-81), is simple, unpretentious, honest, and devotedly regional in both its cuisine and its outlook. It lies on one of the loveliest squares of town, surrounded by old Teutonic buildings dripping with seasonal flowers. Inside, within a tavern filled with wooden tables and hard-bottomed chairs, you can enjoy full lunches costing from 20F ($13.60) or à la carte dinners from 50F ($34). These are served from noon to 2 p.m. and from 6 to 10 p.m. every day except Tuesday. The bill of fare includes fish, veal, and beef dishes, fondue, sole, scampi, filet goulash, and an incongruous scattering of Oriental dishes.

Restaurant Tiger, 35 Stalden (tel. 065/22-24-12), is easy to find in a historic building in the center of town near the cobblestone Friedhofplatz. The chef prepares such specialties as fresh- and saltwater fish, veal steak with aromatic herbs, filet of pork Portuguese style, and calves' liver with the preferred potato dish of Switzerland, Rösti. You might try some of the Swiss cheese selections you've heard about, since the cheese platter here contains some local varieties never exported. A set menu costs from 25F ($17), while à la carte meals range from 35F ($23.80) to 50F ($34). In summer, you might prefer to dine on the terrace of this restaurant, which is open from 5:30 to 10 p.m. except Wednesday and for two weeks in February.

5. FRIBOURG

One of the great medieval towns of Switzerland, Fribourg, a stronghold of Catholicism in the country for centuries, is decidedly bilingual. Its German name is Freiburg. Places on the left bank of the Sarine River possess French names and those on the right bank go by German titles.

Fribourg has been called a "flower of the Gothic age," and as that appellation would suggest, there is much to see and explore here. Allow at least a day for it, and know then that you will only have skimmed the surface. Once a sovereign republic, Fribourg today has a population of some 40,000 people, including many university students. It has not only a Catholic university but also a famous boys' college, and many other educational establishments that enrich its cultural life.

It's easily reached by rail or road, and is served by the Federal Railways express trains, lying less than two hours from the international airports of Geneva, Basel, and Zurich. It's at the hub of a network of motorways, the position so strategic that it's been called a veritable crossroads of Europe.

In a setting between lakes and mountains, Fribourg was founded in 1157. In medieval days it became known throughout Europe for its dyers, weavers, and tanners. Once it was ruled by the House of Savoy, but in 1481 it became a member of the Swiss Confederation and is today the capital of a canton of the same name.

The oldest part of town, called "the Bourg," lies just above the Sarine riverbank and is flanked by the Auge and Neuveville sectors. These, along with the Planche sector on the right bank, form what is known as the Ville Basse.

THE SIGHTS: Other than the wide panoramic view of the site of Fribourg, its single major attraction is **St. Nicholas's Cathedral,** whose lofty Gothic 15th-century belltower dominates the rooftops of the medieval quarter. The nave dates from the 13th and 14th centuries, although the choir was reconstructed in the

17th century. The choir stalls are exceptional, some carved as early as the 15th century, and the Chapel of the Holy Sepulchre, also 15th century, has some remarkable stained glass, and a celebrated organ. Much about this cathedral impresses me, but especially the tympanum of its major "porch," which is surmounted by a stunning rose window devoted to the Last Judgment.

After leaving the cathedral, you'll be in a particularly fascinating architectural zone of Fribourg, with many old patrician houses. You can walk and explore at your leisure, taking in the high-ranging rows of houses from the Gothic era, the small steep streets, and the squares adorned with fountains.

Whether it's called the Rathaus in German or the Hôtel de Ville in French, the **Town Hall** of Fribourg is a notable building from the 16th century, with an octagonal clock tower where mechanical figures strike the hours. Outside the Town Hall, the seat of the State Parliament of Fribourg, farmers' wives sell their produce fresh from the fields nearby. Many are in traditional garb, and market days are Wednesday and Saturday, which I find the most colorful time to visit the city.

Église des Cordeliers, or Franciscan Church, is the second ecclesiastical building of note, lying north of the place Notre-Dame with its 12th-century church, the oldest in the city. The choir at the Franciscan church is from the 13th century, the nave from the 18th century. The church has an outstanding triptych, gilded and carved in wood, which dates from 1513, but its pièce de résistance is the splendid altarpiece rising over the main altar. This was the work of the "Masters of the Carnation," 15th-century artists who signed their works with a white and a red carnation. Before leaving the church, try to find the carved oak stalls from the late 13th century in the chancel.

The city also has an outstanding **Art and History Museum** (Musée d'art et d'histoire or Museum für Kunst und Geschichte), 12 rue de Morat (tel. 037/22-85-71), housed in an imposing historic 16th-century building, the Hotel Ratze, and a transformed old slaughterhouse. Its treasures include archaeological collections of prehistoric, Roman, and High Middle Ages objects. There's a remarkable series of Burgundian belt buckles. The epic sweep of Fribourg's history comes alive, especially in the sculpture and painting from the 10th to the 20th century, along with the largest collection in Switzerland of wood sculpture from the first half of the 16th century. There are also displays on the political, military, and economic life of the canton, numerous 15th- to 18th-century stained-glass windows, stone sculptures, and monumental pieces. The museum is open daily except Monday from 10 a.m. to 5 p.m. (also from 8 to 10 p.m. on Thursday). Admission is 5F ($3.40).

If your schedule can possibly accommodate it, the ideal time of the year to visit Fribourg is for the international folkloric meeting, usually at the beginning of September or perhaps earlier. Yodeling, wrestling, and a game called *hornussen* dominate the festivities, and hotel bookings are difficult to get.

To reach the **upper town** of Fribourg, you can take a funicular, and at some point in your discovery you'll want to seek out the covered wooden bridge, the **Ponte de Berne,** constructed in 1580.

Fribourg is also the center for some important tours, although the Freiburger will tell you, "One has everything here, one doesn't have to go anywhere." Nevertheless, an 18-mile, hour-and-ten-minute ride will take you to **Schwarzee,** or black lake, at about 3,500 feet. This is both a summer and a winter resort (a very minor one), and is known for its beautiful mountain setting with wooded hills.

Another excursion will take you to **Hauterive Abbey** (tel. 037/24-17-83), some 4½ miles southwest of Fribourg. This is a Cistercian abbey built on a bend of the Sarine River. Its church, dating from the 12th century, has some beautiful 14th-century stained glass and some elaborately carved 15th-century stalls. Visits are possible Easter until mid-September from 2:30 to 5 p.m. Monday to Saturday and from 10:45 to 11:30 a.m. and 2:45 to 4:45 p.m. Sunday. Otherwise, hours are 2 to 4:30 p.m. Monday to Saturday, from 10:45 to 11:30 a.m. and 2 to 4 p.m. Sunday.

If you get back in Fribourg by sunset, you can cross the **Zähringen Bridge,** from which you can enjoy a great view of this famous old city that has loomed so large in Swiss history books.

The **Office du Tourisme** is at 30 Grand-Places (tel. 037/22-11-56).

WHERE TO STAY: Set high on a cliff, the **Eurotel Fribourg,** 14 Grand'Places, CH-1700 Fribourg, Switzerland (tel. 037/81-31-31), only a few blocks from the main railway station, provides a view of the historic city in the valley below. With easy parking and convenience to Fribourg's modern sector, this hotel is preferred by many business people to lodgings in the old town. Rooms are cheerfully decorated, with lots of space and good value. Like other Eurotels, many of the rooms here are designed with Murphy beds, enabling occupants to create a sitting room from their bedrooms just by folding the bed into the wall. Singles cost from 85F ($57.80) to 123F ($83.65) daily, and doubles go for 138F ($93.85) to 185F ($125.80). All accommodations contain private baths. The brasserie restaurant serves American-style beef in a nautical setting. Fixed-price meals cost around 60F ($40.80), with à la carte dinners beginning at 45F ($30.60). The hotel has a swimming pool, plus a bar, a nightclub for dancing, and several sun-drenched terraces with waiter service.

Hotel de la Rose, place Nôtre-Dame, CH-1700 Fribourg, Switzerland (tel. 037/22-46-07), occupies a very grand, restrained sandstone building near the cathedral. The painted panels of the lobby's ceiling, in a flamboyant flowering design, are the hotel's most dramatic feature. The 40 bedrooms are outfitted in a modern style, each with a phone, TV, radio, and mini-bar. Depending on the accommodation and the plumbing, singles rent for 65F ($44.20) to 85F ($57.80) daily, doubles 105F ($71.40) to 130F ($88.40), with breakfast, service, and taxes included. On the premises is a pizzeria, plus a café terrace raised about 15 feet above the whizzing traffic outside, and a bar (the Four Roses) set within the cavelike 17th-century vaults of the hotel's foundation. Popular with the under-25 crowd, it has a tiny dance floor, a bar, and a nightly opening at 10 (except Sunday).

Hotel Duc Berthold, 112 rue des Bouchers, CH-1700 Fribourg, Switzerland (tel. 037/81-11-21). Set close to one of the city's major bridges, beside a busy traffic artery which parallels the side of the cathedral, this hotel has a grand façade of gray stone and a roof of terracotta. About half of the 40 rooms inside have been modernized into a streamlined format of efficient furniture. Each contains a private bath, radio, TV, and phone. With breakfast, service, and taxes included, singles cost 75F ($51) to 95F ($64.40) daily, and doubles go for 120F ($81.60) to 180F ($122.40). A handful of bathless singles rent for 50F ($34) per night. On the premises is a popular café and brasserie, and an attractive restaurant (La Marmite), which is recommended separately.

Hotel Alpha, 13 rue du Simplon, CH-1700 Fribourg, Switzerland (tel. 037/22-72-72), is one of the best bargains in town, lying about 300 yards from the train station (CFF), behind a modern façade. Its reception area is two floors above the ground. Each of the accommodations is simple, but adequately equipped, including a color TV, radio, phone, mini-bar, big windows, and a bath. In all, 27 bedrooms are rented, costing 56F ($38.10) to 62F ($42.15) daily, in a single, 84F ($57.10) to 125F ($85) in a double. There's a restaurant and bar on the first landing, but it's independent of the hotel.

WHERE TO DINE: It is worth the effort of a gastronomic stop if you decide to dine at **Buffet de la Gare,** place de la Gare (tel. 037/22-28-16). It contains several different dining areas. At street level is a café and snack bar, with a straightforward brasserie a few steps away. In an environment of polished brass and old-fashioned paneling, you can enjoy a fixed-price meal for 22F ($14.95) and à la carte menus for 40F ($27.20). Tripe Milanese, blue trout in butter sauce, escargots bourguignonne, and a number of veal and pork dishes are featured, but the specialty is lake fish. At the brasserie, meals are served all year and daily from 11 a.m. to 11 p.m. The menu changes with the hours. Therefore, you get a wider choice if you visit from 11 a.m. to 2 p.m. and 6:15 to 9:30 p.m.

A more expensive dining enclave, **Restaurant Français,** 1 place de la Gare (tel. 037/22-28-16), lies one floor above street level (take the tiny elevator). Here you can order a five-course, fixed-price meal for 70F ($47.60) and à la carte meals beginning at 80F ($54.40). Specialties include pot-au-feu, filets of pike-perch provençale, fricassée of chicken with cider, veal kidneys with mustard sauce, pig's feet with morels in puff pastry, and a terrine of veal with pistachio and truffles. However, main dishes change, based on the season. A business lunch costs 35F ($23.80), usually served from 11:45 a.m. to 3 p.m. Dinner can be ordered from 7 to 9:30 p.m., although a limited menu is available until midnight. The restaurant is closed Sunday year round and Saturday from May to September. It takes a holiday from July 20 to August 20, but that varies slightly from year to year.

L'Aigle Noir, 58 rue des Alpes (tel. 037/22-49-77), tends to attract a wealthy and conservative crowd of seasoned diners who appreciate the 17th-century ambience of the former aristrocratic residence that houses it. The owners are a gifted and dynamic couple named Raemy, who have established a brasserie on the ground floor and a more formal, small, and intimate French restaurant to the right of the brasserie as you enter. In both rooms, modern paintings by a number of Fribourg artists, done between 1950 and 1985, are displayed.

In the French restaurant, fixed-price meals cost from 66F ($44.90) to 78F ($53.05), à la carte menus from 60F ($40.80). At lunch, a fixed-price meal is offered for 45F ($30.60). Specialties vary with the season and include fresh asparagus, morels, baby lamb, zander from Lac de la Gruyère, rack of rabbit, and pike-perch, plus a ragoût of fresh mushrooms in a Gruyère cream sauce, wild trout with caviar, and game cock sautéed with fresh mushrooms. Meals in the brasserie are more reasonably priced. A light, fixed-price menu goes for 40F ($27.20) at night, a three-course, fixed-price lunch for 25F ($17). In the brasserie, drinks, light meals, and platters of food are available during the afternoon.

Full meals in both the brasserie and the restaurant are served from 11:30 to 3 p.m. and 6:30 to 9:30 p.m. Reservations are required only in the French restaurants because of the limited number of tables. Both establishments close Sunday at 5 p.m. and remain closed all day Monday.

Chalet Suisse, place Georges-Python (tel. 037/22-83-06). Pass by the popular snackbar in front, heading for the rustic wood-lined Swiss tavern in the rear. As you listen to recorded "evergreen" (mountain) music, you can soak up the atmosphere of local artifacts and red-check tablecloths. This is one of the finer restaurants in the city, serving meals for 40F ($27.20) and up. The kitchen specializes in American beef, and you can also order a fondue of beef. Many international dishes are presented, including filet of sole in a white wine sauce. Service is daily from noon to 2:30 p.m. and from 6 to 9:30 p.m.

Restaurant la Marmite, Hotel Duc Bertold, 112 rue des Bouchers (tel. 037/81-11-21). Don't confuse this hideaway restaurant with the larger, less expensive, and more popular café/brasserie (the Escargot) that precedes it. Go into the inner room for impeccable cuisine and a lovely antique ambience, but only if you've made a reservation. It has a painted ceiling—one of the loveliest in town—a ceramic stove, antique tables, paintings, and intimate lighting. Full à la carte meals cost from 50F ($34), with a comprehensive fixed-price meal going for 70F ($47.60). Meals are served every day from noon to 2 p.m. and 6 to 11:30 p.m. The specialties prepared by the likeable chef, Rolf Baumann, include magret of duckling with raspberry vinegar, exotic mushrooms (steinpilz) in puff pastry, gratinée of salmon, darne of seabass, mignons of veal with port, and desserts from a trolley.

6. GRUYÈRES

This small town, which once belonged to the Counts of Gruyères, is known for its castle, its history, its houses from the Middle Ages, but mainly for its cheese. It is a highlight for anyone taking the "cheese route" through Switzerland. It's also a good base for exploring the district of Gruyère (the region is spelled without an *s*, the town itself with an *s*).

In the canton of Fribourg, the little town of Gruyères still seems to slumber somewhere back in the Middle Ages. Enclosed by ramparts from the 12th century, it is dominated by its castle where the Counts of Gruyères held sway, mainly from the 12th to the 16th centuries. Their crest bears a crane, a symbol much used even today in Gruyères.

Because the town would be overrun by vehicular traffic, cars are forbidden to enter between Easter and the first of November (and on Sunday all year round). You park your car outside the gates and walk into this formerly fortified town.

THE SIGHTS: The Renaissance houses along the main street are in excellent condition. However, some of their charm is obscured in summer by all the tour buses that descend on the area. If you're here when the tour buses aren't, you'll discover all on your own one of the most charming villages on the continent, lying on a rocky crag with a single main street that leads to the much photographed town fountain.

At the entrance to the town, the Swiss Cheese Union operates a **Model Dairy** (tel. 029/6-14-10) for demonstration purposes. Here you can see workers produce the famed Gruyère cheese, which is a more piquant version of the equally famous Emmenthaler. A cheese wheel weighs about 75 pounds. An audiovisual show reveals how the cheese is made. The dairy is open from 8 a.m. to 6 p.m. daily, but it's best to go between 10 and 11 a.m. or 2 and 3 p.m. when the cheese is actually made. The dairy lies at the foot of a hill near the railway station.

The traditional lunch in all the restaurants is raclette, which is prepared and served in Gruyères with a certain fanaticism. A machine is usually placed on your table and you melt and scrape the cheese at your own speed and your stomach's capacity. You can eat right down to the rind, which is crunchy (many Swiss gourmets consider this the best part of the raclette). In the right season, you can finish with a large bowl of fresh raspberries in thick cream.

Just as Switzerland is associated with cheese, it is also famous for its chocolates. At neighboring Broc, Peter Cailler-Kohler founded his chocolate factory (tel. 029/6-10-36) in 1898, and conducted tours are possible (but consult first with the tourist office about changing opening hours before heading there).

You can walk to the **Castle of Gruyères** (tel. 029/6-21-02) on foot on cobblestones, along the way passing the former house of the famed court jester, Chalamala. Some parts of the castle, with its keep, bastion, chapel, and outer walls, date from the 13th century, but mainly from the 15th century. Today it's the property of the canton of Fribourg, and has been since 1938. However, when the Bovy family of Geneva acquired it in 1848, they were responsible for saving it from demolition and also for many of its present embellishments. Many famous artists, including Corot, have lived here. The château contains many rich objets d'art, the most outstanding of which are three mourning copes from the Order of the Golden Fleece, part of the bounty grabbed up in the Burgundian wars. The castle is open to the public daily from June until the first of October from 9 a.m.

to 6 p.m. In winter it's open only from 9 a.m. to noon and 1:30 to 4:30 p.m., charging an admission of 3F ($2.05).

A popular excursion outside Gruyères is to **Moléson-Village,** at about 6,565 feet, a four-mile journey, plus an additional half hour by cable car, which swings up from the village from 8:30 a.m. to noon and 1:30 to 5:30 p.m. at a cost of 20F ($13) round trip (there's no service from November to mid-December). Once at the peak, from the observatory you can see from Titlis to Mont Blanc, and the whole Gruyère countryside unfolds before you. In winter the slopes become ski runs, as Moléson-Village is emerging as a fledgling ski resort.

You can not only visit Gruyères from Basel, but it also makes an easy day trip from Bern, about a 40-mile drive, going via Fribourg and Bulle.

FOOD AND LODGING: The only *Relais & Château* in the region, **Hostellerie des Chevaliers,** CH-1663 Gruyères, Switzerland (tel. 029/6-19-33), is set at the end of a private driveway a short distance from the main town square. The restaurant section is contained within what was originally built as a discreetly detailed private villa in the 1950s. The 34 very comfortable bedrooms are contained within a more recent addition a few steps away. Each of the rooms has a color TV, bath, phone, radio, and a well-insulated kind of conservative style. The best rooms afford sweeping views of the valley. Singles cost 100F ($68) to 120F ($81.60) daily, and doubles go for 120F ($81.60) to 200F ($136), with breakfast, taxes, and service included.

Even if you're not a guest at the hotel, the owner-chef will welcome you for an elegant meal in one of the trio of dining rooms. The one with the best view is covered floor to ceiling in an imitation of garden lattices. The others have a scattering of antiques, a view of an open grill, Delft tiles, and lots of softly gleaming paneling. Lunch is from noon to 2 p.m., dinner from 7 to 9 p.m., daily except Wednesday and from mid-January till mid-February. The menu changes with the seasons, with à la carte meals averaging 75F ($51) each. Typical menu items include filet of turbot with baby onions, veal with an artichoke ragoût, fricassée of pigeon, a duet of quail cooked in cinders, escalope of goose liver with lentils, fourrée of trout, and selections from a dessert trolley. Reservations are suggested.

Hostellerie de St-Georges, CH-1663 Gruyères, Switzerland (tel. 029/6-22-46), in a building dating from the 1500s, is a peaceful hideaway owned by Héribert Miedler and acclaimed by repeat visitors as one of the best places to stay in the region. Centrally located, it offers 14 bedrooms, each with a private bath, TV, a phone, and a radio. In a single with bath, the rate ranges from 90F ($61.20) to 100F ($68) daily. For a double with private bath or shower, the charge goes from 120F ($81.60) to 180F ($122.40). There's a cozy, heavily beamed café suitable for drinks, snacks, and light lunches, but many guests head for the elegantly formal dining room in back, where big windows and courteous employees imbue a meal with Old World charm. Specialties in the restaurant include filet of beef served on a slate platter, breast of duckling with green peppercorns, local hens cooked with tarragon, pheasant suprème, and a quiche made with, of course, Gruyère cheese. You might also like a platter of cured alpine meats, thinly sliced and served with pearl onions and pickles. Meals generally cost from 32F ($21.75) to 45F ($30.60). The restaurant is open from 11:30 a.m. to 10 p.m. daily. It's closed on Monday in spring and autumn, and the hotel closes completely in December, January, and February.

Hôtel de la Fleur-de-Lys, CH-1663 Gruyères, Switzerland (tel. 029/6-21-08), is set at a point where the longest street in town widens into a carefully maintained main square. It was created when two neighboring houses, one of which was completed in 1653, were combined into a 10-room hotel. Each of the rooms is sheathed in pinewood paneling; many have additional Murphy beds. Each contains a private bath and phone, and a handful offer TV and radio. Madame Janine Doutaz is the French- and German-speaking owner of this place, charging 60F

($40.80) daily in a single, 120F ($81.60) in a double, 145F ($98.60) for a triple, with breakfast included. The hotel is an excellent and relatively reasonable choice.

If you're interested in having only a meal, the street-level dining room offers well-prepared alpine specialties, in an appealing milieu of stone and wood planking. A simple platter of food, perhaps with a salad, costs 18F ($12.25), while more elaborate full meals go for 45F ($30.60). Lunch is served from 11:30 a.m. to 2:30 p.m., dinner from 6 to 9:30 p.m. The restaurant (but not the hotel) is closed every Tuesday from November to Easter. On Sunday, the restaurant is open continuously until the 9:30 closing.

Hôtel de Ville, CH-1663 Gruyères, Switzerland (tel. 029/6-24-24), is housed in a historic building in the center of the old town, with a café terrace in front. Owned and directed by Michel Murith, it offers nine comfortable, pleasantly furnished rooms with showers or baths for 50F ($34) to 70F ($47.60) daily in a single, 80F ($54.40) to 100F ($68) in a double. An attractive restaurant, which takes up most of the ground floor, serves regional specialties such as ham and trout, the latter kept in an aquarium on the premises.

You can dine—often very well—in any of the above inns, but for an independent restaurant that doesn't also rent rooms, consider the following.

Restaurant Le Chalet de Gruyères (tel. 029/6-21-54) was originally built as a wood-sided chalet around 1900. Flowers still adorn the front balconies in summer, but inside, much of the ornamentation has been stripped to reveal beautifully aged timbers and honey-colored planks. Set in the geographical center of town, a few minutes' walk below the château, it has a café on the lowest floor, plus an upstairs dining room. (This you reach by entering the only door on the chalet's uphill side.) There you'll meet the same waitresses and see the same polished farm implements that greeted former President Carter. The establishment serves the same menu every day from 11 a.m. to 10 p.m. Full meals cost from 40F ($27.20) each, including traditional Swiss dishes such as fondue, raclette, hot Gruyère cheese on toast with ham, and a "Gruyère platter" piled high with ham, cheese, sausage, and air-dried beef.

On the Outskirts

Hostellerie le Castel (tel. 029/2-72-31). Making an excursion to this restaurant high in an alpine meadow above the town gives a view of the Alps near Fribourg, the town of Gruyères, and the famous castles that surround it. Many of the guests prefer the terrace precisely because of that view, yet many guests make special efforts to dine in the French provincial dining room where elegant table service and a large stone fireplace-grill provide a welcome warmth. Specialties include gratinée of asparagus, tender calves' liver with onions, plump Bresse hen, ragoût of fish, tournedos, and mussel soup with thyme. The list is added to according to what head chef and owner Christian Roth found that day in the market. Many guests prefer the fixed-price menus, costing 50F ($34) to 78F ($53.05). One corner of the dining room is reserved as a café section, for people who do not wish to order a full meal. If you sit there you can have a plat du jour for 16F ($10.90). Madame Canisia Roth welcomes guests in the dining room at lunchtime, noon to 2 p.m., and for dinner, 7 to 9 p.m., daily except Sunday evening and all day Monday. The establishment closes for two weeks in February. It lies a short distance from Gruyères in a suburb called Le Paquier.

In Bulle

In the district of Gruyère, Bulle lies some 17 miles south of Fribourg, on the banks of the Trême River. It stands in the midst of what is called "green Gruyère." The bishops of Lausanne, who used to hold sway over the town, built a large castle here in the 13th century, which is not open to the public.

However, in this market town you can visit the well-known **Gruérien Mu-**

seum, Place du Cabalet (tel. 029/2-72-60), which is open to the public from 10 a.m. to noon and 2 to 5 p.m., except Sunday morning and Monday, charging an admission of 3.50F ($2.40). A regional author, Victor Tissot, established the museum, which is devoted to popular art: rustic furniture, naïve paintings of herds' ascents to alpine pastures, cream spoons and butter molds carved in wood, and reconstructions of typical rooms in a rural dwelling. There are also works by Corot, Courbet, Crotti, and Vallotton. An audiovisual presentation further helps you understand life in the district.

For food and lodging, try the following:

Hôtel des Alpes & Terminus, CH-1630 Bulle, Switzerland (tel. 029/2-92-92). This family-run hotel appears somewhat anonymous from the outside, yet opens into a more imaginative decor in its interior with appealing modern hanging lamps, comfortable banquettes, and warm colors. The walls of the dining room have interesting art and an 11-foot flügelhorn. Bedrooms are carpeted and decorated in attractive shades. Across the train station, the location is most convenient. Doubles with private bath cost 82F ($55.75) to 95F ($64.60) daily, while singles with bath go for 42F ($28.56) to 57F ($38.76), including breakfast.

7. MURTEN (MORAT)

This small medieval town carries a double name because it's bilingual, the denizens speaking either French or German, and often both. In Switzerland it's called "the language demarcation line." Murten forms a gateway into French-speaking Switzerland, lying on the southern side of Murtensee, or Lac de Morat.

Of all the old towns in Switzerland I've sought out, I found this one most idyllic and beautifully preserved. Many of its houses date from the 15th to the 18th centuries. Not only that, but the town is surrounded by ramparts with a wall-walk. In the Middle Ages these were defensive walls of course, but you can stroll along them today, taking in a view of the roofs of the Altstadt, with the castle, lake, and Jura mountains as a backdrop.

Peter of Savoy, a duke, built the **castle** in the 13th century. It's bleak and foreboding, but impressive nevertheless, and from its inner courtyard (which you enter free) there's a vista of the lake and the Jura foothills.

The main street, **Hauptgasse,** is the major attraction of Murten, running through the center of the old quarter and taking you to the **Bernegate,** a baroque structure with one of the oldest clock towers in the country, dating from 1712.

Outside Murten on June 22, 1476, a fierce battle was fought between the Confederates and Charles the Bold of Burgundy.

The lake has a maximum depth of 150 feet, taking in an area of nearly ten square miles. Between May and September you can take lake trips on motor vessels and circular tours on the three lakes from Neuchâtel to Bienne to Murten, with trips through the canals in the Great Marshes.

Musée Historique, adjacent to the château (tel. 037/71-30-00), contains everything from archaeological excavations of the city's earliest history to a diorama of the 15th-century Battle of Morat. It is housed within an old mill a few steps from the walls of the château. In summer, it's open daily from 10 a.m. to noon and from 1:30 to 5 p.m.; winter, from Tuesday to Saturday, 2 to 5 p.m. The museum is closed every Monday regardless of the season. Entrance is 2F ($1.35).

FOOD AND LODGING: At the edge of the lake near the harbor is **Hotel Schiff,** CH-3280 Murten, Switzerland (tel. 037/71-27-01). Well-maintained parks surround much of the hotel, leading to the water, where you'll be tempted to stop for a drink at the lakeside café. The building is a complicated collection of 19th-century gables and porches, with a hipped roof, a few arched windows, and a modern extension containing some of the well-decorated public rooms. The bedrooms are fairly plush, with frequent use of nostalgically patterned wallpaper. All the rooms contain private baths and cost from 55F ($37.40) to 90F ($61.20) daily in a single and 110F ($74.80) to 160F ($108.80) in a double, including breakfast. Half board is another 35F ($23.80) per person. The hotel's restaurant is considered one of the best in town, its big windows opening onto clipped lawns with chestnut trees leading down to the lake. Set menus cost 49F ($33.30), 62F ($42.15), and 80F ($54.40). The 49F meal is a menu du pecheur, featuring bouillabaisse, poached trout with scallops, and perhaps a passion-fruit mousse. Other fare includes crème parmentier with snails, noisettes of rabbit with morels, seabass with pernod, and a three-meat platter of medallions.

Hotel Krone (Hotel de la Couronne), CH-3280 Murten, Switzerland (tel. 037/71-52-52), is a good and reasonably priced hotel, sitting on a cobblestone street in the center of town, behind a gabled, red-shuttered façade with plenty of character. It was originally built in the 15th century as an inn, but most of what you'll see today was added in the 1930s and early 1970s. Each of the 35 accommodations has a bath or shower; a few share a common toilet in the hallway. Set on hallways laden with antique armoires, each is very clean, albeit slightly old-fashioned. Any inconvenience is offset by the outgoing young owner, Werner Nyffeler, his wife, Christine, and his mother, Louise. Depending on the accommodation and its plumbing, singles cost 42F ($28.55) to 75F ($51) daily, and doubles go for 84F ($57.10) to 125F ($85), with a continental breakfast, service, and taxes included.

This place has no less than five different eating areas. You can opt for a seat within the street-level pizzeria or the adjacent café/brasserie, or a large, sun-flooded restaurant one floor above the lobby. A beautifully paneled, almost square room, with a sweeping view over the lake, has a massive salad bar every day with as many as two dozen different varieties of lettuce and cold vegetables. A fixed-price meal costs 29F ($19.70). Menu items include filet of beef Stroganoff, filet of trout, scampi, veal, and pork dishes. The upstairs restaurant serves meals, costing 9F ($6.10) to 41F ($27.90) from 11 a.m. to 10 p.m. daily except for periods when the hotel is closed (from mid-November to mid-December.)

Hotel Weisses Kreuz (Hotel de la Croix Blanche), 31 Rathausgasse, CH-3280 Murten, Switzerland (tel. 037/71-26-41), is, quite simply, a superb hotel. Clean and attractive, it has both a sense of history and a sense of humor, plus a gracious staff whose manners and happy demeanor are inspired by the co-owner, Mrs. Alice Bischoff. The hotel occupies a pair of historic buildings that lie behind a screen of climbing roses on either side of a cobblestone street in the center of the old town. Bedrooms are antique or modern in style, always with private baths. One of the buildings was originally built as stables. There is a scattering of antiques along with cozy conversational corners and a large baronial dining room where Daniel Bischoff, co-owner and chef, hosts a concert series every spring of his particular passion, baroque music.

The hotel is closed every year from mid-December to early March. The rest of the year, a series of frequently returning clients fill the bedrooms and the dining room. With breakfast included, singles cost 65F ($44.20) to 85F ($57.80) daily, and doubles rent for 112F ($76.15) to 150F ($102). Meals are served in the dining room—where a sweeping view of the town shows through big windows—every day from noon to 2 p.m. and 6 to 9:30 p.m. Full à la carte meals cost from 40F ($27.20) each, and might include medallions of pork, fricassée of veal with wild mushrooms, an array of local fish dishes, of English-style roast beef.

Le Vieux Manoir au Lac, CH-3208 Murten-Meyriez, Switzerland (tel. 037/71-12-83), 1½ miles from the town center, is constructed of one of those elaborately Swiss conglomerations of stucco, weathered planking, slate, and fieldstone, with half-timbered gables, covered chimneys, and a gurgling hitching post with a fountain splashing into a basin. The scene is idyllic, and the service impeccable in both the hotel and the restaurant. Balconies and windows open onto the grassy banks of Lake Morat. A parasol-dotted sundeck allows guests the chance to relax in the summer sun, while the restaurant inside collects reservations for local wedding receptions and business conventions with gratifying regularity. The comfortable rooms rent for 95F ($64.60) to 120F ($81.60) daily in a single, 160F ($108.80) to 200F ($136) in a double. Breakfast is included in all the tariffs. The hotel is closed from mid-December to mid-February.

The restaurant attached to the establishment is excellent, with fish specialties printed on a separate menu. You'll appreciate the decor of the regional antiques while waiting for your meal. A fixed-price menu ranges from 50F ($34) to 110F ($74.80), 35F ($23.80) to 75F ($51) if you order à la carte. Reservations are suggested.

8. NEUCHÂTEL

One of the most charming and elegant towns of Switzerland, Neuchâtel was a haven for such notables as Mirabeau, Alexandre Dumas, and André Gide. It stands at the border of a lake of the same name—the largest lake entirely within Switzerland—and at the foot of the green slopes of Chaumont (3,871 feet). The majority of its population are French-speaking and Protestant. Once a Prussian principality, Neuchâtel became a member of the Swiss Confederation in 1815, and is today the capital of a Swiss canton of the same name. By the end of the 18th century watchmaking had earned Neuchâtel fame throughout Europe.

At the foot of the Jura mountains, Neuchâtel enjoys an idyllic setting in the midst of vineyards. Many of its limestone houses have a distinctive yellow or ochre color, conjuring up for Dumas an image of the town as having been carved out of a "block of butter."

Neuchâtel is a seat of culture and learning (its citizens are said to speak the finest French in Switzerland), and you'll see many university students on the streets and in the cafés. Its university was founded in 1838.

The historic old sector is traffic-free in the center. The French influence is very evident in architectural styles. Many houses in the old town date back to the 16th century, and some were built with defensive towers. The spirit of old Neuchâtel is best seen at the Maison des Halles, the market square where you may want to buy some well-known local cheese, de Jura, to eat later at a picnic around the lake.

THE SIGHTS: The medieval section is dominated by the **Château of Neuchâtel** and the **Collégiale** (university church), which along with the **Tour des Prisons** (prison tower) form an architectural complex of great interest. The castle has been much changed and altered over the years. The earliest part, the west wing, goes back to the 12th century, but most of the building is from the 15th to the 17th centuries. From the castle, a panoramic view of the old town unfolds.

The university church goes back to the 12th and 13th centuries, although parts of it, the west towers, are from the latter 19th century when the church underwent (some say suffered) a major overhaul. The church is characterized by glazed tiles in many hues. The highlight of the church is found in the Romanesque choir, a monument to the Counts of Neuchâtel, created in the 14th century. With more than a dozen painted effigies, this is considered the most spectacular Gothic memorial in the country. These counts—actually there are 15—are in austere and dignified poses.

The Collégiale is open every day from 8 a.m. to 8 p.m. (to 6 p.m. in winter). To visit the interior of the castle, apply to the concierge (you will find him at the gate to the castle under an arch). Accompanied visits, for a minimum of two to three persons, are at 9, 10, and 11 a.m. and at 2, 3, and 4 p.m.

The prison tower also offers a magnificent view and is open from April 1 to the last Sunday in September daily from 8 a.m. to 8 p.m. Admission is 1F (68¢).

For more information, write or call Service des Monuments et Sites, 23 rue du Château, CH-2001 Neuchâtel (tel. 038/22-36-10).

The **Griffin Fountain** from 1664 lies nearby on the rue du Château. It's one of the most famous in the country, owing to the generosity of Henri II of Orléans who in 1657 had it filled with 1,300 gallons of red wine to honor his entry into Neuchâtel.

The **Musée d'Art et d'Histoire** (museum of art and history tel. 038/25-17-40), near the end of quai Léopold-Robert, northeast of the harbor, is open from 10 a.m. to noon and 2 to 5 p.m. except on Monday, charging 5F ($3.40) for admission. The museum has an excellent collection of paintings, many by local artists, who worked mainly in the late 19th and early 20th centuries. You can see works by Léopold Robert, for whom the quay was named. Many works are also displayed by artists painting in Neuchâtel today. But for the three-star attraction of the museum you have to go back to the 15th century for a painting on wood, called *The Coronation of the Madonna*. It has been attributed to one of the "Masters of the Carnation," who signed their works with a red or a white carnation. Neuchâtel's role as a watchmaking city is honored by the museum's clocks and watches. There is also a collection of automata (mechanical figures), of which a trio from the 18th century, the work of Jaquet-Droz, shows great talent and imagination.

You spend a lot of time in Neuchâtel walking the **quays,** and well you should: there are three miles of them. The finest view of the Lake of Neuchâtel, with the Alps as a backdrop, is from Osterwald Quay.

The little city also has an exceptional **Museum of Ethnography,** 4 rue Saint-Nicholas (tel. 038/24-41-20), which can be reached easily from the castle by heading up rue Saint-Nicholas. It's open from 10 a.m. to 5 p.m. except on Monday, charging 5F ($3.40) admission. A knowing museum designer arranged the exhibits for easy viewing. You're taken on a journey from the mysterious kingdom of Bhutan at the top of the world, to Egypt at the time of the pharaohs. On the outer side of the annex a mammoth fresco, *Conquest of Man,* is by the artist **Hans Erni.**

Near the faubourg de l'Hôpital, in the patrician part of the city, **Musée Cantonal d'Archéologie** (museum of archaeology), 7 avenue Du Peyrou (tel. 038/25-03-36), displays artifacts discovered at La Tene, a late Iron Age site excavated in 1858 at the northern end of the Lake of Neuchâtel (incidentally, this site, near St. Blaise, can be visited). Other revealing objects of the long archaeological period of the canton of Neuchâtel (50 millennia) are also presented. The museum is open daily except Monday from 2 to 5 p.m.

Nearby you can stroll into the garden of the **Hôtel Du Peyrou,** dating from 1764. This excellent patrician house was constructed for Du Peyrou, who was a friend of Rousseau and published some of his works. *The Bather,* a statue in the pool, is by Ramseyer.

For a final look at Neuchâtel, you can take a funicular (approached from the rue de l'Écluse, on the border of the medieval sector, heading up for the **Crêt du Plan**) to a height of 1,962 feet. Before you will be a great view of the Lake of Neuchâtel and the distant Alps.

Sights in the Environs

If you base in Neuchâtel, you can explore many sights in the environs, especially along Lac de Neuchâtel, the lake that inspired Gide. If you drive northeast of town, you'll reach **La Coudre,** a distance of 2½ miles. From there you can take a funicular to the top of **Chaumont** at 3,862 feet. The round-trip fare is 12F ($8.15), and the ride takes about 15 minutes. From the summit you'll have a view of Mont Blanc and the Bernese Alps.

Back in Neuchâtel, you can strike out to the west this time, going along the lake to discover a number of stopovers. You'll come to **Auvernier** after about three miles. It's a fishing village (the lake is filled with fish), but mainly it's known for its vineyards. You can make purchases from wine makers and consume your drink later at a picnic along the lake. The town is also noted for its beautiful Renaissance houses.

Leaving it, continue west to **Colombier,** a small village with a large castle, which produces an outstanding white wine. The late-Gothic Castle of Colombier, from the 15th century, has two museums, and guided tours are conducted Monday to Friday from the first of March until the end of October at 2 and 3:30 p.m. free. The castle was built on the ruins of a Roman villa, and Rousseau stayed here. One museum is devoted to military artifacts, another to "chintz."

Boudry, very medieval looking, is our next stop. The Castle of Boudry, from the 16th century, has a museum of viticulture, which is open from 9 a.m. to noon and 2 to 6 p.m. (on Sunday, from 10 a.m. to noon and 2 to 5 p.m.). It's closed on Monday and in August. Boudry is known mainly, however, as the birthplace of Marat, the French revolutionist.

WHERE TO STAY: Almost on top of the lake, **Hotel Beaulac,** 2 quai Leopold-Robert, CH-2000 Neuchâtel, Switzerland (tel. 038/25-88-22), is at the junction of the quay of its address and the quai du Port. Guests can watch ducks and marina activity as they relax on the waterside terrace below the four floors of the hotel. The façade is modern in appearance, particularly when compared to the grand 18th-century sandstone buildings surrounding it. The bedrooms are modern, clean, and comfortable, all with private baths. Singles cost from 105F ($71.40) to 145F ($98.60) daily, and doubles range from 150F ($102) to 190F ($129.20), with breakfast included. The establishment has three restaurants, one of them, Le Colvert, specializing in fish dishes.

Hotel/Restaurant City, 12 place A.M. Piaget, CH-2000 Neuchâtel, Switzerland (tel. 038/25-54-12). When this comfortable and dignified building was erected in the early 1800s, the edge of the lake came to within a few feet of its entrance. Today, after thousands of cubic meters of rock and earth were dumped into the lake many years ago as a landfill, the hotel sits in the commercial center of town, across from the massive art nouveau post office whose graceful sculptures appear when viewed from the hotel's well-insulated windows.

The hotel and its 35 comfortably decorated bedrooms are the domain of two of the most charming hoteliers in Neuchâtel, Thony and Madeleine Blaettner. Each of the carefully scrubbed rooms contains a private bath, color TV, radio, phone, and Swiss-made copies of hand-carved Louis XIV furniture. Known for its good value and comfortably updated accommodations, the hotel —thanks to its hosts—welcomes a varied clientele, including members of the Chinese delegation to Neuchâtel, visiting bankers from Zurich, and dozens of franc-wise Swiss who appreciate its welcome and its central location. Singles range from 70F ($47.60) to 90F ($61.20) daily and doubles from 100F ($68) to 150F ($102), all units with private baths. On the premises is one of the city's few Chinese restaurants, and a well-recommended brasserie.

Novôtel Neuchâtel-Est, autoroute Neuchâtel-Bienne, CH-2075 Neuchâtel-Thielle, Switzerland (tel. 038/33-57-57), is in a very modern building in a tranquil setting only six minutes by car from the heart of Neuchâtel (get off at the Thielle exit). The hotel is built on a large scale in an aluminum, glass, and concrete format familiar to Americans. The entire structure angles itself around an outdoor swimming pool, and contains two restaurants and a bar. All the well-equipped accommodations have private bath, and cost 68F ($46.24) to 95F ($64.60) daily in a single and 90F ($61.20) to 135F ($91.80) in a double.

Hôtel des Beaux-Arts, 5-7 rue Pourtelès, CH-2000 Neuchâtel, Switzerland (tel. 038/24-01-51). Modern, unpretentious, and simple, this hotel offers 26 well-scrubbed bedrooms, only 15 of which contain a private bath or shower. Built in the early 1970s, behind a concrete façade with a scattering of recessed balconies, the hotel has a pair of congenial restaurants near its street-level reception area. Maria Mutti, the owner, charges 50F ($34) to 68F ($46.25) daily in singles, 95F ($64.40) to 125F ($85) in doubles. The more expensive units contain private baths. Breakfast, service, and taxes are included in the price. Half board can be arranged for a supplement of 17F ($11.55) per person per day. The hotel lies not far from the lake, beside a relatively quiet street near the center of town.

WHERE TO DINE: A floating restaurant moored beside one of the docks of Neuchâtel, **Le Vieux Vapeur,** Port de Neuchâtel (tel. 038/24-34-00), overlooks colonies of ducks that paddle contentedly searching for table scraps from its kitchens. Inside its gleaming hull, a bar ("Le Britchon") has a television set and lots of gleaming brass, plus a disco with a dance floor the size of medium-sized dinghy, and a nautically decorated restaurant lined with teak and low-slung banquettes.

If you're looking for a bargain, head below deck for the bar, where grills and various kinds of spaghetti are served as part of full meals costing from 32F ($21.75). Meals are served at the bar and at its adjoining tables from noon to 2 p.m. and from 7 p.m. to 1:30 a.m. every day except Sunday. More formal meals, costing from 50F ($34), are served in the restaurant on the upper deck. These might include veal kidneys with juniper berries and mint, mignon of veal stuffed with foie gras and truffles, salad of fresh mussels, lake trout with champagne sauce, and grilled John Dory flavored with tarragon. Hours in the restaurant are the same as those for the bar, except that the last dinner order in the restaurant is accepted at 10 p.m. Because of the cold and damp on the lakefront, the restaurant is closed every year between December 20 and the end of January.

Restaurant City, Hotel City, 12 place A.M. Piaget (tel. 038/25-54-12), contains the best elements of both a formal restaurant and a lighthearted brasserie, with a well-trained and polite staff who usually caters to a diner's every whim. Set within curving walls studded with big windows, the restaurant stands in a location which, until 1958, was one of the city's private walled gardens. Today, amid a warmly decorated ambience of exposed pinewood paneling, you can enjoy well-prepared meals priced at 40F ($27.20) at dinner, and from 25F ($17) at lunch. Served every day from 11 a.m. to 3 p.m. and 6 and 10:30 p.m., meals are inspired by French traditions, but laced with healthy doses of regional flair. Perhaps the most unusual dish, entrecôte Gerle, is a juicy slab of beef laced with a deliciously mysterious layer of creamy sauce whose recipe is known only to the proprietor himself. With his elegant wife, Madeleine, Thony Blaettner draws on century-old family recipes for a dish whose ingredients you won't quite be able to decipher, but whose delicacy you won't soon forget. Other specialties include coq au vin with gratin dauphinoise, chicken with whiskey sauce, stuffed snails, filets of palee (a lake fish), and succulent desserts.

Buffet de la Gare, 1 place de la Gare (tel. 038/25-48-53), is about the closest thing to a food factory there is in Neuchâtel. It has a standup eatery in the train station, a catering service, and a less expensive brasserie. At the top of the list, however, you'll find a high-quality restaurant with excellent service, a functionally elegant decor, and a chef, Lucien Gétaz, who takes his cookery seriously. Specialties include such rarified dishes as baby crayfish in saffron, quail mousse, trout garnished with smoked salmon and served with a horseradish mousse, filet of sole with three kinds of mushrooms, pike flan, sea trout with grapefruit, and young hare with cabbage leaves. À la carte dinners range from 60F ($40.80) to 75F ($51). The buffet is open every day of the week from 6 a.m. to midnight.

9. LA CHAUX-DE-FONDS

The birthplace of Le Corbusier, La Chaux-de-Fonds is a clean industrial town, where streets cross each other at right angles, the result of planning when the town was rebuilt in the 19th century after it was destroyed by fire in 1794. A residential sector has grown up on the western side of town, with high-rise apartment blocks.

It isn't much of a tourist town, but because it's the capital of the Neuchâtel mountains, lying in a valley of the Jura, many visitors base here while exploring the encircling district. The location is about 1¼ hours from Bern, and just 15 minutes from the French border.

A center of Swiss watchmaking, it seems to employ everybody in town in the industry. The town has a **Musée International d'Horlogerie** (international watch and clock museum), 29 rue des Musées (tel. 039/23-62-63), which is open from 10 a.m. to noon and 2 to 5 p.m. except Monday, charging an admission of 6F ($4.10). In this museum you'll see a cavalcade of timepieces dating back to the Egyptians. Some of the clocks, especially the enamel ones, are works of art. The museum also displays a collection of clocks with automata (mechanical figures). There is a documentation center with a library on horology. Expert appraisals are made and private clients accepted by the center for the restoration of antique clocks and watches.

Nearby stands the **Musée des Beaux-Arts** (fine arts museum), 33 rue des Musées (tel. 039/23-04-44), open from 10 a.m. to noon and 2 to 5 p.m. daily except Monday (until 8 p.m. on Wednesday). Admission is free. It has a good collection of the great romantic painter Leopold Robert, who was born in the town in 1794, and a few works by Le Corbusier, born here in 1887. Painting and sculpture of the 19th and 20th centuries are on display. The Swiss school is represented by A. Anker, Ed. Kaiser, F. Vallotton, R. Auberjenois, and C. L'Éplattenier, while international contemporary artists are Penalba, Kemeny, Pomodoro, Magnelli, Mortensen, and Mosset, among others.

WHERE TO STAY: Built in the mid-1970s, **Hotel Club,** 71 rue du Parc, CH-2300 La Chaux-de-Fonds, Switzerland (tel. 039/23-53-00), stands on a quiet street near the center of town. This comfortable concrete-sided hotel contains a bar and a breakfast room, but no restaurant. One of its best features is the seventh-floor solarium, where streams of sunlight from the three walls of glass create a greenhouse effect even in midwinter. Each of the 40 tastefully streamlined bedrooms contains wall-to-wall carpeting, a TV, phone, radio, frigo-bar, and private bathroom. Throughout the year, with breakfast included, singles rent for 90F ($61.20) to 105F ($71.40) daily and doubles for 140F ($95.20) to 165F ($112.20), depending on its facilities.

Hotel Moreau, 45 avenue Leopold Robert, CH-2302 Chaux-de-Fonds, Switzerland (tel. 039/23-22-22). Stone-sided, substantial, and traditional, this hotel curves around a corner of a busy street in a commercial section of the city. Neon signs identify the hotel. Guests register in an old-fashioned lobby dotted with a scattering of antiques. Each of the 46 bedrooms contains TV, radio, and mini-bar. Of the two in-house restaurants, I prefer the street-level grillroom, whose lovely decor includes a coffered ceiling, Louis XIII–style furniture, and heavy mantelpieces. Depending on the plumbing and the accommodation, rooms with one bed rent for 50F ($34) to 140F ($95.20) daily, units with two beds for 90F ($61.20) to 210F ($142.80), with breakfast service, and taxes included.

WHERE TO DINE: One of the best restaurants is **Le Provençal,** place de la Gare (tel. 039/23-19-22). Don't confuse the informal café, near this establishment's entrance, with the more formal restaurant in back. Both are inside a very grand Italiante building to the side of the railway station. Within a stylishly modern decor you can enjoy well-prepared meals every day except Sunday from 11:45 a.m. to 1:30 p.m. and from 6:45 to 9:30 p.m. Fixed-price meals cost from 52F ($35.35). The specialty is fish, many of which are kept fresh within holding tanks until the last minute. Menu items include crayfish in puff pastry, terrine of trout, lobster salad with truffle juice, turbot in champagne sauce or with raspberry vinegar, Nordic filet of sea perch, sole grilled with pine nuts, bouillabaisse (in season) for two persons, and a well-flavored version of marmite dieppoise. Several meat dishes are offered for guests not in the mood for fish. Reservations are suggested.

Club 44, 64 rue de la Serre (tel. 039/23-11-44), is probably the most unusual, and certainly the most visually stimulating, restaurant in town. It combines within one slickly modern space a privately managed restaurant and a publicly funded art gallery. The array of European paintings changes almost as frequently as the menu items that are prepared with skill by Daniel Collon. Meals are served daily except Sunday from 11:30 a.m. to 2 p.m. and from 6 to 10 p.m. A contemporary bar area serves drinks to an iconoclastic crowd of artists and art lovers every day except Sunday from 6 p.m. to midnight. In addition to the paintings and pieces of sculpture, you might catch an art-related lecture before or after your meal, depending on the monthly schedule.

Fixed-price meals are appropriately inexpensive, accounting for the students who have been known to show up, beginning at around 20F ($13.60) for a three-course fixed-price meal. À la carte meals cost from 45F ($30.60). They change with the seasons, but the food might include escargots en cassoulet, filet of monkfish in green pepper sauce, filet of perch with white wine and grapes, and beef "cordon rouge," with a stuffing of foie gras. Because the kitchens seem to alter their schedule according to the business they anticipate that day, it's usually a good idea to call ahead before setting out for a meal here. Club 44 is sheltered behind one of the loveliest art nouveau façades in town, in a building on a quiet residential street a short walk from the center.

10. BIENNE (BIEL)

This is one of the bilingual cities of Switzerland. Citizens often address you in French, and before they've finished a thought they've switched to German. The street names are in both French and German. An industrial town noted for its watchmaking, Biel lies at the northeastern end of Lake Biel (Bielersee in German), from which many excursions can be taken. It stands in the foothills of the Jura.

The town has grown rapidly in recent years, and is now said to contain 300 watchmaking workshops or factories, employing thousands of people. Omega was launched here in 1879.

THE SIGHTS: Ignoring the industrial suburbs, the sightseer will want to head directly for the Upper Town, especially the attractive old square, the landmark of Biel, which is known as **"The Ring."** The square is surrounded by step-gabled houses, the most outstanding of which is the **Zunfthaus der Waldleute,** a former guildhouse with its tower crowned by an onion-shaped dome. When the town was ruled by the Prince-Abbots of Basel, they seated themselves in a half-moon position, condemning the guilty and freeing the innocent. In time the square became known as "The Ring." The Banneret fountain in the center is from 1546.

Nearby, the **Rathaus** (town hall) was built in 1530, but is much restored. It is step-gabled, like many buildings in this part of town, and in front stands the Fountain of Justice from 1714.

Other than the arcades and Burgundian homes along the High Street, the single most important attraction of Biel is its **Schwab Museum** (tel. 032/22-

76-03), open daily from 10 a.m. to noon and 2 to 5 p.m. except Monday. It is named for a colonel who pioneered excavations to discover prehistoric Switzerland. On display are artifacts relating to the prehistoric period when the country was inhabited by lake-dwellers. The rooms also contain relics of the Gallo-Roman period and some cases showing tools of the Iron Age. Entrance is free.

OUTSIDE BIENNE: If you want to follow in the footsteps of Goethe, who stayed at the former inn Zur Krone, and make Biel your base, you can take a number of interesting excursions. The most recommendable one is to **St. Petersinsel** (St. Peter's Island) in Lake Biel. You can reach it by boat from Biel, a round-trip fare costing 12F ($8.15). For details, inquire at the Biel tourist office, the **Verkehrsbüro,** Bahnhofplatz (tel. 032/22-75-75). The boat ride and exploration will take most of your day.

Noteworthy is the Three-Lake cruise, which takes visitors through the Lake of Bienne and navigable waterways to the lakes of Neuchâtel and Morat in the heart of the Swiss wine country. There is no change of ship, and your ticket is good for the full-day excursion. A round-trip costs 28F ($19.05).

Jean-Jacques Rousseau in 1765 chose this island as a place of refuge, which he recalled in his *Confessions*. He lived at the 12th-century Cluniac priory, which when it was dissolved in 1530 was turned into an inn.

You can take many strolls around the island, which is really a peninsula, as the water level of the lake has been lowered. The little island you'll see off the coast is Rabbit's Island, which might more accurately be called "Bird Island." Some deer roam through this natural sanctuary.

If you wish, you can also take a cruise around **Lake Biel,** which is of glacial origin. It's 7½ miles long, and was the site of many lake dwellings. The little villages, such as **La Neuveville,** which dot the lake are known for their wines and gastronomy. That village, rather grandly, is known as the "Montreux of the Jura." Its church is 1,000 years old.

On the north side of the lake the villages of **Twann** and **Ligerz** can be visited. Twann has many venerated old vintner houses, and the upper part of the village touches the vineyards. The adjacent village, Ligerz, in a setting right in the midst of vineyards, has a church dating from 1482. It also has a Wine Museum, and from there you can take a funicular to Prêles for a magnificent view.

Armed with a good map, you can seek out **Aarberg,** another interesting town. It's positively medieval, with a fortress towering over the town and old bourgeois houses. Its wooden bridge is more than four centuries old.

FOOD AND LODGING: With an imposing ochre-colored façade, **Hôtel Elite,** 14 rue de la Gare, CH-2500 Bienne, Switzerland (tel. 032/22-54-41), curves, art deco style, around a bend in the street. The rooms are modern and conservative, with patterned wallpaper and comfortably overstuffed armchairs. The public rooms include a masculine bar area, a restaurant serving French food, and a plushly upholstered nightclub, which usually has a pianist. All accommodations have private bath, costing 100F ($68) to 120F ($81.60) daily in a single and 170F ($115.60) to 300F ($204) in a double. Half board costs another 32F ($21.76) per person daily.

The hotel's formal dining room offers a decor that includes a high coffered ceiling, big windows, and a full staff of uniformed service personnel. The menu changes with the season, but typical dishes are a ragoût of mussels en croûte, carpaccio of salmon with a mousse of caviar, oyster cream soup with broccoli, escalope of poached turbot, sweetbreads with chanterelles, and fresh salmon. Full meals cost from 60F ($40.80) and are served daily from 11:30 a.m. to 12:30 a.m. Reservations are suggested, although there is usually a table available anyway.

Hotel Continental, 29 Aarbergstrasse, CH-2501 Bienne, Switzerland (tel.

032/22-32-55), is a modern hostelry with a balcony outside many of the bedrooms, plus a warm color choice in the lobby and bar area. Rooms are soundproof, containing TV, radios, refrigerators, and private baths. Singles range from 90F ($61.20) to 132F ($89.75) daily, with doubles costing 125F ($85) to 180F ($122.40), breakfast included. The location is halfway between the city center and the lake.

Poissonnière (Buffet de la Gare), 4 place de la Gare (tel. 032/22-33-11). On the top floor of this busy rail station is an ambience far more elegant than you might have expected. As its name implies, the restaurant specializes in fish. Specialties include dorade en papillote, oysters florentine (or fresh oysters), several versions of lobster, fera (a lakefish) with almonds, and bouillabaisse. The menu also offers some Indonesian specialties, all under the direction of Esther Hoppeler, who is one of the outstanding food experts in the area. À la carte meals range from 25F ($17) to 35F ($23.80). Hours are from 11 a.m. to 2 p.m. and 6 to 11:30 p.m. daily.

Restaurant Bielstube, 18 Rosius (tel. 032/22-65-88). Set within one of the most charming old Teutonic buildings of the historic center of town, this well-known restaurant serves honest but innovative meals that usually begin at 25F ($17) each. Amid a typical Swiss decor of ceiling beams, lace curtains, and tavern accessories, you can enjoy such daily specials as beef carbonnade, ragoût of rabbit, saltimbocca, gratinée of mussels, escargot en brioche, several kinds of spaghetti, and Chinese noodles. The restaurant is open from 11:30 a.m. to 2 p.m. and 6:15 to 10 p.m. every day except Sunday.

Goya, 11 rue Hôpital (tel. 032/22-61-61), is the place to go for good Spanish cookery. The aura is enhanced by several reproductions of the works of the 19th-century artist himself. The Spanish wine, coupled with the personality of the owner, Joaquin Guanter, helps everyone have a good time. Specialties include two kinds of paella, both Catalán and marinara. Other dishes include a zarzuela of shellfish, rabbit Valencian style, and spaghetti Catalán style. À la carte dinners cost from 40F ($27.20). Hours are daily from 11:30 a.m. to 1:30 p.m. and 6:30 to 9 p.m. The restaurant is closed on Sunday. The owner also rents out 16 comfortable rooms, charging 76F ($51.68) to 84F ($57.12) daily for singles, 105F ($71.40) to 115F ($78.20) for doubles. All units have showers or baths, color TV, phones, mini-bars, and radios.

CHAPTER VI

BERN AND THE BERNESE OBERLAND

□ □ □

The best known holiday region of Switzerland, the Bernese Oberland is one of the great tourist attractions of the world, and one of the best equipped for winter sports. The beauty of the area has long been extolled by writers, including Jean-Jacques Rousseau and Goethe. Interlaken—the best center for exploring the Bernese Oberland—became famous and fashionable in the 19th century. Over the years the district attracted such distinguished company as Madame de Staël, La Rochefoucauld, and others. The English were not far behind. Byron visited in 1816, and he was followed by Ruskin, Shelley, and Thackeray. Longfellow and Mark Twain came from America.

This famed winter sports area is not only the center of Europe, but the heart of Switzerland. More than 150 installations transport skiers to all grades of well-prepared and maintained downhill runs. The Bernese Oberland sprawls between the Reuss River and Lake Geneva, the Rhône forming its southern border.

The canton of Bern, in which most of it falls, is the second largest in Switzerland and has some 100 square miles of glaciers. The River Aare forms the lakes of Thun and Brienz, two rewarding sightseeing targets in summer. But the Oberland also takes in the Alps, culminating in the Jungfrau at 13,642 feet and the Finsteraarhorn at 14,022 feet.

The most acclaimed summer resort is Interlaken, but Meiringen and Thun also merit listing. Others, such as Gstaad, Grindelwald, Kandersteg, and Mürren, are both summer and winter playgrounds. The fame of Lenk and Adelboden dates from the early 19th century at the beginning of modern tourism. The district also takes in the cheese-making land of Emmental (see a description in the environs of Bern).

The Bernese Oberland is ideal country for both the sports enthusiast and the nature lover. You can ski in the mountains or, in summer, sail, surf, and waterski on Lake Thun. Yodelers, alpine horn blowers, and folklore musicians keep alive ancient traditions. Mountain forests and alpine pastures invite the rambler, and trout fishing is possible in mountain streams after you've completed a climb over a glacier the previous day. You're likely to see the mountain chamois, the ibex, or marmot, and certainly some alpine toadstools, crocuses, and rhododendrons.

Getting there is often half the fun, whether you arrive at your destination by steam railway, cog-wheel railway, aerial cableway, or a steamboat across Lake Brienz. Once you've arrived at your hotel, you can enjoy mountain cheese and the wine of Spiez.

A Regional Holiday Season Ticket for the Bernese Oberland is available at 102F ($69.35) for adults, 51F ($34.70) for children from 6 to 16 years old. The ticket is valid on nearly all railroads including mountain trains, cable cars, chair lifts, steamers on Lake Thun and Brienz, and most postal bus lines in the Bernese Oberland. There's also a 25% reduction on the Kleine Scheidegg–Eigergletscher–Jungfraujoch railway and the Mürren-Schilthorn aerial cable line, and on the bus to Grosse Scheidegg and Bussalp. The ticket, valid for 15 days, allows you to use it as a general season ticket for unlimited travel on five days of your choice and as a season ticket entitling you to any number of tickets at half fare. You must book your Regional Holiday Season Ticket not less than one week before your arrival. Get in touch with your nearest Swiss tourist office for more information

1. BERN (BERNE)

In the heart of Switzerland, Bern, the capital of the Confederation, is a city of diplomats and one of the loveliest of Europe. The city is ancient, built between the 12th and 18th centuries. It is, in fact, one of the great medieval cities still left in Europe that hasn't been destroyed—either torn down or bombed in wars. The United Nations in 1983 declared it a "World Landmark."

In spite of the fact that it's host to many international organizations, and is a beehive of activity, it still has many touches of a big country town, as reflected in the bright splashes of red geraniums on many windowsills.

Bern is a city of arcades, nearly four miles of them running along the streets of the old sector, and they're weatherproof and traffic-free. Underneath these arcades are shop windows, everything from exclusive boutiques to department stores, from antique dealers to jewelers. It's a city of fountains and oriel windows, and its old sandstone steps have been trodden for centuries. The buildings, for the most part, are built of a yellowish-green sandstone.

But don't get the idea that all of Bern is dripping in antiquity. Modern-day residents have discreetly imposed contemporary living over their centuries-old environment, showing a healthy respect for the past. Beginning with your arrival at the Hauptbahnhof (railway station), you'll encounter "New Bern" right away. It has many modern houses, bridges and streets.

A university town, Bern is one of the centers of Swiss culture and education.

Its research workers have been pioneers in many scientific fields. Among their achievements was a device used to measure solar winds on the moon.

Bern stands on a thumb of land, surrounded on three sides by the River Aare, to which it is linked symbolically, much as Paris is to its Seine. Many bridges, often sightseeing attractions in themselves, connect Bern to its newer sections.

Bern joined the Swiss Confederation in 1353, becoming the seat of the federal government in 1848, replacing Zurich. It is easily reached, either by motorway or rail. The city publishes a map that puts Bern at the virtual crossroads of Europe. You can also arrive at the international airports at Zurich or Geneva, both within easy commuting distance, or at Bern's own airport at Belpmoos.

Bern is also the center for many excursions, especially to the lakes and peaks of the Bernese Oberland (this vast playland is reached in only minutes from the capital).

On Tuesday and Saturday Bern holds its market days when the country people come to town, ideal days to visit to see the city in full bloom. But a time of revelry is the fourth Monday of November when Bern stages the centuries-old Zibelmärkt, or onion market. At that time Bernese housewives stock up on onions for the winter, and it's turned into a popular festival, as the city's one last big fling before the onset of winter.

To familiarize yourself with the geography of Bern, refer to "What to See," following the restaurant section below.

GETTING AROUND IN BERN: For reliable service, try the **Public Transport System (SVB)** with a self-service ticket-purchasing system on all routes. You must obtain your ticket at an automat (there's one at each stop on the bus and tram network) *before* you board the vehicle, as there are no conductors or ticket dispensers aboard. If you're caught traveling without a ticket, it'll cost you 30F ($20.40) in addition to the fare for the ride. To save yourself time, trouble, and possibly money, you can purchase a one-day ticket for 4F ($2.70), which entitles you to unlimited travel on the 38-miles SVB network during any 24-hour period of your choice. Just get the ticket stamped at the automat before you begin your first trip. One-day tickets are available at the ticket offices at 5 Bubenbergplatz (tel. 031/22-14-44) and in the underpass of the main railroad station (tel. 031/22-62-04), as well as at some other sales outlets in the city, including newsstands.

Taxis are found at the public cab ranks, or you can phone for one: Casinoplatz (tel. 031/22-18-18); railway station (tel. 031/22-18-18); Weisenhausplatz (tel. 031/23-53-53); or Bundesplatz (tel. 031/23-53-53).

For information as to timetables and tickets on the **Swiss Federal Railways,** phone 031/22-24-04 daily from 7:30 a.m. to 8:30 p.m.

PRACTICAL FACTS: Besides the information given in Chapter II in "The ABCs of Switzerland," there are some items pertaining particularly to Bern.

American Express: From Monday to Friday, the American Express office, 11 Bubenbergplatz (tel. 031/22-94-01) is open from 8:30 a.m. to 6 p.m.; closed Saturday and Sunday.

Banks: Hours are from 8 a.m. to 4:30 p.m. Monday to Wednesday, 8 a.m. to 6 p.m. Thursday, and 8 a.m. to 4:30 p.m. Friday. Closed Saturday and Sunday.

Children: You can check the children into kindergarten while you shop. The Loeb department store, 47-51 Spitalgasse (tel. 031/22-73-21), will accept responsibility for children, including serving them a meal, from 2 to 6 p.m. on Monday, 9 a.m. to 6 p.m. Tuesday to Friday, and 9 a.m. to 3:30 p.m. on Saturday. The fee is 4F ($2.70) for two hours, 4F for each additional hour per child. For babysitting services at other times, your hotel or the tourist office can probably accommodate you.

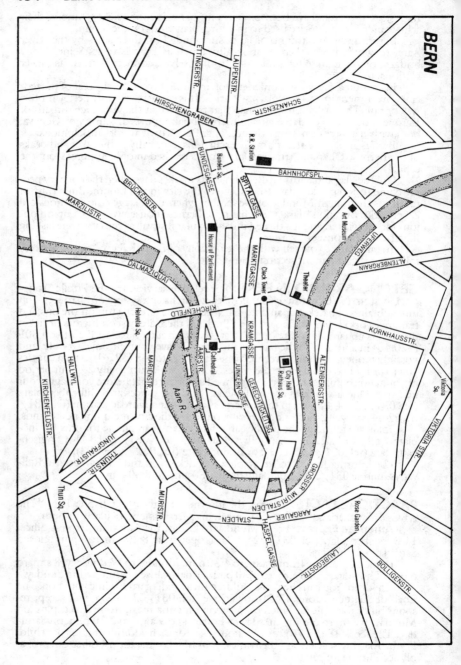

Drugstore: If you need a pharmacy, try Central-Apotheke Volz and Co., 2 Zeitglockenlaube (tel. 031/22-10-94), which has served Bern's residents since 1885. Near the clock tower in the old city, it employs English-speaking staff members who are happy to suggest over-the-counter substitutes for American drugs that may not be obtainable in Europe. It's open Tuesday to Friday from 7:45 a.m. to 6:30 p.m., on Saturday to 4 p.m., and on Monday from 1:45 to 6:30 p.m.; closed Sunday.

Embassy: If you lose your passport, go to the **U.S. Embassy, 93** Jubiläumsstrasse (tel. 031/43-70-11).

Emergencies: Numbers to call in Bern in case of an emergency are **police, 117; ambulance, 144; fire, 118; doctor** or **dentist,** 031/22-92-11; and **road patrol,** 140.

Information: To help visitors, the **Bern Tourist Office** in the Bern Hauptbahnhof (tel. 031/22-76-76) is open from 8 a.m. to 8:30 p.m. Monday to Saturday and 9 a.m. to 8:30 p.m. on Sunday from May to October. From November to April, hours are 8 a.m. to 6:30 p.m. Monday to Saturday, 10 a.m. to 5 p.m. on Sunday. If you need help finding a hotel room, they'll make a reservation for you in a price range you select.

Lost property: A lost property office is maintained at 18 Zeughausgasse (tel. 031/64-67-72). Hours are from 7:30 to 11:30 a.m. and 1:45 to 5 p.m. Monday to Friday.

Swimming: Of several swimming pools, I especially recommend **Hallenbad,** which has the best indoor pool, along with a Turkish bath and sauna. It's at 14 Maulbeerstrasse (tel. 031/25-36-56). Hours vary daily. Admission is 3F ($2.05) to swim, with another 7F ($4.75) charged to use either the sauna or the Turkish bath.

Telecommunications: Telephone and telegraph service is available at the main railway station from 6:30 a.m. to 10:30 p.m., to 5 p.m. Saturday; closed Sunday.

ACCOMMODATIONS: The range of accommodations is vast—everything from a park bench to a Louis XV four-poster. As the federal capital, Bern is the center of many conventions and international meetings, and at times its hotels are fully booked. Try to arrive with a reservation.

The Deluxe Choices

Hotel Schweizerhof, 11 Schweizerhoflaube, CH-3001 Bern, Switzerland (tel. 031/22-45-01), is directed by the Gauer family (some people even call this the Gauer Hotel), whose personal antique collection is probably better than anything else a visitor might see in the way of decorative arts in Bern. In all the public rooms and in many of the better suites, you'll see many pieces ranging from naïve provincial to formal drawing room articles of the 18th century, wall-size tapestries, and crystal chandeliers. Even some of the upper-floor hallways are laid out like a museum of the folk arts, with polychromed statues of saints hanging next to weathered wooden chests from the 17th century.

Because of its location in the heart of the Swiss capital, a lot of diplomatic guests stay here. You're likely to meet them in one of the formal restaurants or in the 16th-century Simmentalerstube, whose walls, ceilings, and furnishings came almost intact from a much older building. The Schultheissenstube is my personal favorite, offering a rustic elegance and an attentive service that rates high even by competitive Swiss standards. Each of the bedrooms and suites is differently decorated, but almost all of them offer a lighthearted combination of comfortably upholstered chairs and sofas with a fairly good chest, desk, or table. All bedrooms have modern baths and all the accessories. Singles rent for 190F ($129.20) to 240F ($163.20) daily, while doubles range from 250F ($170) to 350F ($238). Breakfast is included in the price, and an extra bed can be set up in any unit for an additional 60F ($40.80). Jaylin's nightclub provides live music and an elegant, intimate ambience for one of your nights out.

Bellevue Palace, 3-5 Kochergasse, CH-3001 Bern, Switzerland (tel. 031/ 22-45-81), is what would have been called—even when it was built in 1913— majestic. Next door to the Bundeshaus, the seat of the Swiss government, the five-star hotel could easily be mistaken for part of the governmental complex, especially since, with its carved Corinthian columns, its ornate detailing, and its gray stone façade, it looks solid enough to support an Alp. Parts of the inside literally make the first-time visitor gasp—especially the stained-glass ceiling that arches over the wide expanse of one of the salons.

The hotel offers 30 single rooms at 180F ($122.40) to 210F ($142.80) daily, 112 double-room units at 250F ($170) to 350F ($238), and eight suites for two persons at 380F ($258.40) to 700F ($476), all of them with bath and luxuriously appointed, each opulently proportioned with lots of space. The views to the southeast, weather permitting, are of the Jungfrau and her surrounding forests. The setting is undeniably Old World, and the service is impeccable. You'll find a beautifully monochromatic dining room with high arched windows, a sun terrace with laughing couples and green-and-white parasols, and a bar.

The Upper Bracket

Hotel Metropole, 28 Zeughausgasse, CH-3011 Bern, Switzerland (tel. 031/22-50-21), is conveniently situated in the heart of Bern within the loop of the River Aare that contains the medieval city. The hotel offers a series of public rooms, decorated with such artifacts as an antique water mill hanging over the full expanse of a wall in the Old Mill Restaurant and old photographs of political leaders in the President Club (you'll have to ask the bartender to identify many of them). Bedrooms contain modern baths, and the rooms are carpeted and, except for their cramped size, very comfortable. Breakfast is included in the prices of 105F ($71.40) to 130F ($88.40) in a single and 145F ($98.60) to 180F ($122.40) for a double.

Hotel City, 7 Bubenbergplatz, CH-3011 Bern, Switzerland (tel. 031/22-53-77), sits behind its gray stone façade near the railroad station. The front is accented with colorful awnings above a bustling sidewalk café. You'll find an elevator in the lobby. The hotel usually fills all six floors to capacity. The 47 rooms rent for 105F ($71.40) to 140F ($95.20) daily in a single, for 145F ($98.60) to 170F ($115.60) in a double. Children under 16 share their parents' room free. Breakfast is included in the price. Each of the predictably modern units comes equipped with radio, color TV, phone, and mini-bar.

Hotel Ambassador, 97 Seftigenstrasse, CH-3007 Bern, Switzerland (tel. 031/45-41-11), rises nine stories into the Bernese sky, in a well-proportioned format of modern windows and streamlined decorations. You'll notice that it's the tallest building around, its neighbors being older houses with red-tile roofs. You'll be able to see the Bundeshaus (seat of government) from the windows of many of the rooms. You can savor the food in the French restaurant and the snack bar or enjoy drinks in the liquor bar. Singles cost from 100F ($68) to 120F ($81.60) daily, with doubles renting for 130F ($88.40) to 160F ($108.80). A generous buffet breakfast is included. All rooms have baths, toilets, phones, refrigerators, and TV. Guests can use the sauna and fitness rooms, as well as the swimming pool in the basement, open 24 hours a day. The pool and the sauna are swimsuit optional for both sexes.

Hotel Alfa, 15 Laupenstrasse, CH-3008 Bern, Switzerland (tel. 031/25-38-66), is housed in a concrete-and-glass building just to the west of the train station. A restaurant occupies a big-windowed annex that is raised above the street level on stilts. A Swiss flag usually flies high above this 40-unit establishment. Bedrooms are attractively decorated, with modern baths and lots of light. Most of them contain a radio, TV connection, alarm clock, phone, and mini-bar.

A parking lot and an elevator are on the premises. Singles rent for 90F ($61.20) to 110F ($74.80) daily, and doubles cost 120F ($81.60) to 150F ($102), breakfast included.

Hotel Bern, 9 Zeughausgasse, CH-3011 Bern, Switzerland (tel. 031/21-10-21). If you like art deco, you'll love the façade of this city hotel. The gray front is a massive testament to the art form that was so chic in the 1920s and so valued today. It consists of a massively arched roof with smaller arches and half-columns repeated throughout the rest of the construction. Several iconoclastic sculptures flank the entranceway that leads to the reception desk and a series of seven attractive rooms for dining and drinking, each different in character. The 100 well-furnished rooms, often attracting a diplomatic crowd, all have private bath, mini-bar, phone, radio, and TV connection, costing from 105F ($71.40) to 140F ($95.20) daily in a single and from 145F ($98.60) to 190F ($129.20) in a double, including breakfast.

The Middle Range

Hotel Wächter-Mövenpick, 4 Genfergasse, CH-3011 Bern, Switzerland (tel. 031/22-08-66), is a Bern hotel efficiently managed by the Mövenpick chain. The Wächter is fairly small, offering 44 rooms on four floors of a corner building near the railroad station. A sidewalk café occupies most of the pavement in front of the building, whose windows are protected in summer with awnings. Each of the modern rooms has a bath, radio, color TV, mini-bar, and special outlets for American electric razors. A bathless single costs 56F ($38.10) to 83F ($56.45) daily, rising to 100F ($68) to 125F ($85) with either a private bath or shower. Doubles, all with private bath or shower, cost from 135F ($91.80) to 170F ($115.60).

Hotel Krebs, 8 Genferstrasse, CH-3011 Bern, Switzerland (tel. 031/22-49-42), lies close to the train station in a recently remodeled building with a storefront sharing part of the three-star hotel's ground floor. The management is helpful, charging from 55F ($37.40) to 90F ($61.20) daily in a single, from 100F ($68) to 130F ($88.40) in a double. Breakfast is included in the price. Most of the rooms have private baths of showers. Accommodations are often sunfilled, some partially paneled with vertical slats of light-grained wood, and decorated with attractive utilitarian furniture.

Hotel Continental, 27 Zeughausgasse, CH-3011 Bern, Switzerland (tel. 031/22-26-26). This two-star hotel is close to the railroad station in front of a square with a fountain. The building has simple windows and flower boxes filled with blossoms almost constantly throughout the summer. The public rooms are functional and unpretentious, while the bedrooms are clean and spacious. A restaurant is attached to the hotel. All rooms have been renovated and modernized, and each now contains a private bath or shower as well as a toilet. Singles cost from 75F ($51) to 100F ($68) daily, and doubles go for 104F ($70.70) to 140F ($95.20). Breakfast is included in all the rates.

Hotel Bristol, 10 Schauplatzgasse, CH-3011 Bern, Switzerland (tel. 031/22-01-01). Set behind a somber neoclassical façade, next door to its sister hotel, the Bären, this hotel benefits from a convenient location and 90 comfortably furnished accommodations. Few attempts were made to dress up the lobby, and there is neither a bar or a restaurant on the premises. Guests, therefore, tend to gravitate toward the dining and drinking facilities of the hotel next door. There is, however, a sauna on one of the upper floors. Rooms have high ceilings, Nordic-inspired furniture, TV, mini-bar, phone, video movies, private bathrooms, and minor accessories. With breakfast included, singles range from 115F ($78.20) to 120F ($81.60) daily, and doubles cost 165F ($112.20) to 185F ($125.80).

Hotel Bären, 4 Schauplatzgasse, CH-3011 Bern, Switzerland (tel. 031/22-33-67). Conveniently close to the Swiss Parliament, near the oldest section of the city, this clean and straightforward hotel offers 57 cozily modern accommodations. Each contains a TV, a mini-bar, radio, phone, private bath, and a small but stylish floor space filled with contemporary furnishings in warm shades of beige and brown. With a breakfast buffet included, singles cost 115F ($78.20) to 120F ($81.60) daily, and doubles go for 165F ($112.20) to 185F ($125.80). An extra bed can be set up in any double room for 35F ($23.80) per day. You register in a lobby filled with replicas of bears in one form or another. A member of Switzerland's Best Western/Ambassador Hotel reservation system, the establishment contains an excellent tavern, the Bärenstube, recommended separately.

Hotel Astor-Touring, 66 Zieglerstrasse (tel. 031/45-86-66), is a few minutes by foot from the train station, next to the Eigerplatz. Everything here is modern, in working order, and well maintained. The bedrooms are clean, fairly spacious, and occasionally sun-filled. Many of the rooms have balconies and wood-paneled ceilings, and all of them have tile baths, some of them impressively well-proportioned. Each of the refurbished bedrooms contains a radio, phone, and TV. Singles rent for 70F ($47.60) to 80F ($54.40) daily, doubles for 55F ($37.40) to 65F ($44.20) per person, and triples for 50F ($34) to 53F ($36.04) per person, breakfast included. The hotel gives reductions of 50% for children under 6 and 30% for children under 12 if they sleep in the same room as their parents. The attached restaurant serves attractive meals at attractive prices.

Hotel Regina Arabelle, 6 Mittelstrasse, CH-3012 Bern, Switzerland (tel. 031/23-03-05), is a tranquil choice set pleasantly on its own grounds. The easygoing management tries to be helpful in every way. A grassy lawn with roses and a fountain lies just to the side of the backyard sun terrace. Some of the bedrooms have Oriental rugs placed over the parquet floor. All the units are conservatively and functionally comfortable. The cheapest accommodations are in the older building, which lies on the side of the small garden. These rooms share corridor toilets, although most have showers. In the newer building, all rooms have showers and toilets. Singles without bath cost 55F ($37.40) daily, rising to 64F ($43.50) to 80F ($54.40) with private bath. Doubles, all with private baths, cost from 89F ($60.50) to 110F ($74.80). The hotel lies about ten minutes by foot from the old town and the Bahnhof. To reach it by bus, take number 3 from the Bahnhof and get off at Mittelstrasse, the third stop.

Gasthof zum Löwen, 3 Enggisteinstrasse, CH-3076 Worb, Switzerland (tel. 031/83-23-03), in Worb, is the kind of romantic country inn that devotees of nostalgia seek out. Set in the residential suburb of Worb, which lies 15 to 20 minutes from the center of Bern, the hotel is easily reached by superhighway. The inn is an ivy-covered, hip-roofed, elegantly furnished establishment that is 600 years old. It's been in the same family for 11 generations and is now owned by Hans-Peter Bernhard. It's also bigger than it looks. You'll see mementos of a bygone era throughout the hotel, fine examples of handcraftsmanship, including the gently sloping stairway leading to the reception area from the lobby of the ground-floor restaurant. Antiques are scattered throughout. The 14 rooms cost 75F ($51) daily in a single with shower and toilet. A double with a shower is priced at 80F ($54.40), going up to 125F ($85) with complete shower and toilet. Tariffs include a buffet breakfast served in a wood-paneled room.

The ambience of the restaurant is elegant and rustic, with a large bar filled with locals who drop in to drink. It's closed all day Wednesday and Thursday. Specialties include sauerbraten, mignon de boeuf, entrecôte Café de Paris, and in season, wild game. Lunch is usually served daily from noon to 2 p.m. and dinner from 6:30 to 9:30 p.m. Fixed-price meals range from 30F ($20.40) to 40F ($27.20). The restaurant is closed from mid-July to mid-August.

Economy Choices

Hospiz zur Heimat, 50 Gerechtigkeitsgasse, CH-3011 Bern, Switzerland (tel. 031/22-04-36), is, from the point of view of both charm and price, perhaps the outstanding economy choice in Bern. You couldn't possibly be more favorably situated than here, in the very heart of the old city, almost in the center of the peninsula on which Bern was originally built. The arches on the street level face a painted and gilded fountain whose waters splash into an octagonal basin below an ornate column holding a statue of a regal figure. The windows are big and, weather permitting, contain boxes laden with heavy masses of flowers. The bedrooms are clean and well maintained, with functional furniture. A restaurant serves nourishing meals in a cozy ambience of wood paneling, hanging lamps, and a wall-size blowup of a Renaissance map of Bern. No alcohol is served in the restaurant.

Prices for rooms without private baths (although you'll find a sink with hot and cold running water in each of them) are 48F ($32.65) daily in a single, 74F ($50.30) in a double, 96F ($65.30), and 128F ($87.05) in a room for four people. With a private shower and toilet, the charges are 66F ($44.90) daily for a single, 94F ($63.90) for a double, and 114F ($77.50) for a triple. Breakfast is included. For easy access to the hotel from the train station, you can take trolleybus no. 12 for a ten-minute ride, getting off near the Rathaus and Münster.

Hotel zum Goldenen Adler, 7 Gerechtigkeitsgasse, CH-3011 Bern, Switzerland (tel. 031/22-17-25), lies a few buildings away from its neighbor, listed above, the Hospiz Zur Heimat, sharing the same fine site from which to tour the old city, especially since the Rathaus, the cathedral, and the Bearpit are all within a few blocks. The façade of this efficiently managed (by the Peter Balz family) hotel hints at its former glory as a private residence. The lobby has an elevator leading to the redecorated rooms containing the hotel's 40 beds. The decor is a bit threadbare but clean, usually sunny and cozy. Children are especially welcome here. Rooms are priced at 55F ($37.40) to 90F ($61.20) daily in a single, 85F ($57.80) to 120F ($81.60) in a double, breakfast included. The cheaper rooms contain no private baths.

Hotel Goldener Schlüssel, 72 Rathausgasse, CH-3011 Bern, Switzerland (tel. 031/22-02-16), looks from the outside like a beautifully maintained patrician house with barn-red shutters. Swiss flags, and a wrought-iron oval sign containing the hotel's symbol, a golden key. The building dates from the 13th century, when it was used as a stable with a handful of rooms for riders. A sidewalk café does a thriving business in summer, and the restaurant, recommended separately, offers reasonably priced meals. The 29 bedrooms in this hotel are carpeted, some having a wall covered with mellow wooden planking and some with baths. Marianne and Jost Troxler are the owners of this establishment, and they charge from 52F ($35.35) to 68F ($46.25) daily for a single and from 88F ($59.85) to 104F ($70.70) in a double, depending on the plumbing.

WHERE TO DINE: The cuisine of Bern is international. The famous Swiss potato dish, Rösti, is served everywhere, and there are dozens of specialty restaurants offering every dish from paella to porterhouse. Or best of all, you might head for one of the charming country inns on the outskirts.

The Leading Restaurants

Grill Schultheissenstube, Hotel Schweitzerhof, 11 Schweizerhoflaube (tel. 031/22-45-01). A curved horseshoe bar occupies the center of this elegantly rustic secondfloor restaurant, which some food critics hail as one of the 20 best in the country. Brown walls, polished paneling, and lots of elegant accessories contribute to the feeling of an elite sophistication. The menu was designed by Jean Cocteau. A menu gastronomique, which changes daily, costs 120F ($81.60) per person. In addition there's a daily carte of *les suggestions du chef,* which is likely to include a terrine of foie de canard (duckling) naturelle to lobster soup flavored with tarragon to a blanc de turbot bordelaise. The regular menu is also superb in every way, featuring among other dishes my favorite, sea bass with fennel, or perhaps mignonnettes of lamb flavored with basil. Meals are served from noon to 2 p.m. and 6:30 p.m. to midnight. The restaurant is closed on Sunday.

Three fine restaurants are at **Bellevue Palace Hotel,** 3 Kochergasse (tel. 031/22-45-81), allowing a choice of prices and cuisine, for either lunch or dinner. Bellevue Grill, an exclusive gourmet restaurant, is considered one of the best of the hotel's dining rooms. You can arrive here through the lobby of the hotel, or you might instead use the street-level entrance to the right of the hotel as you face its main portal. French specialties are created and served with panache by Maître Aeberhard and his staff. Try, for example, pheasant suprême with foie gras or a grilled American steak with an herb-flavored sabayon. Meals cost 90F ($61.20) and up. The grill is open from 5:30 to 11 p.m. daily October to April. Restaurant la Terrasse offers an elegant ambience combined with the delights of its "cuisine d'aujour d'hui" to provide a unique gastronomic experience. In summer, you can enjoy the spectacular panorama of the majestic Alps—Eiger, Mönch, and Jungfrau—while you're seated in comfort on the lovely flowered terrace high above the Aare River. Meals cost from 85F ($57.80) and might include such dishes as turbot in white butter and breast of duckling à l'orange. The terrace dining room is open daily from 11:30 a.m. to 3 p.m. and 6:30 to 11:30 p.m. The bistro-style restaurant at the Bellevue is Stadtrestaurant zur Münz, whose refined interior is the ideal setting for early morning coffee, a business lunch, afternoon tea, a gastronomic dinner, or an after-theater supper. The menu includes fried breast of guinea fowl with mustard and sesame, and young rabbit ragoût with mushrooms and Savoy cabbage. Expect to pay from 55F ($37.40) for a complete meal. Hours are daily from 8 a.m. to 11 p.m.

Restaurant Bärenstube, Hotel Bären, 4 Schauplatzgasse (tel. 031/22-33-67). Near the Parliament house, in the oldest part of the city, this is a favorite rendezvous for government ministers. Known for its particularly elegant version of a traditional Swiss tavern, it's a few steps from the reception desk of the previously recommended Hotel Bären. Original murals of bears in the roles of socialites and winebibbers cover those walls now sheathed in polished paneling. The restaurant is in an attractively proportioned room with some interesting frescoes of typical Swiss farming scenes. The cuisine is light and up-to-date. The chef cooks many savory dishes with sophisticated touches. His *cuisine créative* features such dishes as fera, a freshwater fish from the Vaudoise. Fixed-price menus cost 25F ($17) and à la carte meals from 30F ($20.40). However, you can order just a platter of food, costing from 20F ($13.60), each usually big enough for a full meal. The restaurant is open for service daily from 11:30 a.m. to 1:45 p.m. and 6:30 to 9:30 p.m.

Café-Restaurant du Théâtre, 7 Theaterplatz (tel. 031/22-71-77), is housed in a grand baroque building near the famous clock tower in the old city. The high ceilings of its interior are partially covered with lighthearted murals of courtly scenes from the 18th century, as well as a discreet placement of a few hunting trophies. The chef serves such dishes as a tégamino of turbot with a mousseline of salmon, quenelles on a skewer with spinach, salmon steak with baby leeks, and sweetbreads with shrimp. Open every day but Sunday evening and all day Monday from 9:30 a.m. to midnight, the restaurant charges from 35F ($23.80) to 45F ($30.60) for a four-course fixed-price meal, and around 100F ($68) for a seven-course gourmet repast. An à la carte meal averages from 40F ($27.20) to 55F ($37.40). The annual closing is from the last three weeks of July until early August. Reservations are suggested.

Restaurant Della Casa, 16 Schauplatzgasse (tel. 031/22-21-42). Entering from under an arcade, you'll go into a low-ceilinged paneled room painted a mellow off-white. The room is usually crowded with tables, chattering diners, and hausfraus serving large platters of food. An inner room contains daily newspapers, which are quietly perused by an older generation of politically conscious retired persons. It's an attractive place, perhaps the only one like it in Bern. A quiet upstairs dining room, lies one floor above ground level. The menu is continental, with an emphasis on Italian dishes such as bollito misto, a mixed potpourri of boiled meats. Two of my favorite dishes are the ravioli maison and the fried zucchini. The featured meat specialty is a filet mignon à la bordelaise with créole rice. Lunch costs from 18F ($12.25) to 40F ($27.20) and dinner from 40F ($27.20) up. Hours are from 11 a.m. to 2 p.m. and 6 to 9:30 p.m. daily except Sunday. The ground level restaurant is closed in July, but the upstairs dining room remains open. Reservations are important because of the popularity of this place.

Restaurant Commerce, 74 Gerechtigkeitsgasse (tel. 031/22-11-61), is a small Spanish tavern near the Fountain of Justice where the waiters seem to know many of the satisfied regular patrons. The restaurant attracts many expatriate Spaniards, especially those connected to the Spanish Embassy. The decor is appropriately Iberian and the paella is very good. Scampi, prepared in several different ways, is the specialty. You might also want to sample their zarzuela, a Spanish-style bouillabaisse. Everything is backed up by good rice dishes and salads. À la carte meals cost 38F ($25.85) to 55F ($37.40) on the average. The restaurant, which is closed in July, serves Tuesday to Saturday from 9 a.m. to midnight.

Le Mistral, 42 Kramgasse (tel. 031/22-82-77), named after the cold, violent winds that blow through Provence, is made up of an easily visible street-level pizzeria and brasserie, and a more difficult to find restaurant in the basement. Upstairs, the Italian specialties include salade niçoise, spaghetti, bolognese, and an array of pizzas, beginning at 9.60F ($6.55). Tortellini is always a favorite. If you order à la carte, expect to spend from 25F ($34) for a meal. In summer, there's a sidewalk café separated from the light traffic outside with a row of potted geraniums.

It's in the basement, however, that the establishment's real glamor unfolds. Decorated to give the place a feeling of a chic stable, it evokes an informally formal Mediterranean retreat. Full meals begin at 45F ($30.60) but could go much higher. Specialties include well-seasoned lamb, veal or steak with morels and cream, several fish dishes, and grilled U.S. beefsteaks, including a filet of beef with a special sauce, Le Filet Mistral. Crêpes suzettes or sabayon au Marsala makes an appropriate dessert. Mealtimes upstairs are from 11 a.m. to 2 p.m. and 6 to 11 p.m. and from 6:30 p.m. to 1 a.m. in the downstairs. The place is open daily except Sunday.

Frohsinn, 54 Münstergasse (tel. 031/22-37-68), is a small dining room in which Leonello Rubli, the owner, manager, and chef serves traditional and innovative cooking. With only a dozen tables, the little eating place almost in the shadow of the Tour de l'Horloge (clock tower), has a beamed ceiling and an inviting ambience. The cuisine du marché (based on the freshest available ingredients in the market place) might include goose liver mousse, liver with rösti, or filet of beef in a whiskey sauce. Such seasonal specialties are served as sabayon with strawberries. Meals cost from 45F ($30.60). Hours are from 8 a.m. to 2 p.m. and 6 to 10 p.m. The place is closed Sunday and Monday. Customers include business people and journalists, as well as politicians.

Räblus, 3 Zeughausgasse (tel. 031/22-59-08), is the premier French restaurant of Bern, serving extravagant specialties. On the first floor of a central building, near the famous old clock tower, the restaurant suggests that guests have an apéritif at the ground-floor bar, which the piano players make a popular rendezvous place. You climb upstairs for dinner. Specialties include a gratinée of seafood, mignons of veal with morels, Indian chicken curry, Chinese fondue, coq au vin with noodles, and veal kidney flambé. For dessert, try the crêpes suzette. Peter Pulver, owner and chef de cuisine, offers fixed-price meals for 38F ($25.85) to 48F ($32.65), with à la carte dinners averaging 40F ($27.20) to 70F ($47.60). The restaurant is open daily except Sunday from 11 a.m. to 2 p.m. and 5 p.m. to midnight. Räblus is popular with the business world at lunchtime.

Ratskeller, 81 Gerechtigkeitsgasse (tel. 031/22-17-71), is an attractive combination of old masonry with a conservative modern update. Tables and chairs are made of patterned wood surrounded by lots of mirrors and an airy, well-lit ambience. Friendly waitresses serve savory food typical of the Bernese region. The wine cellar is worth a visit as well. For your meal, you might choose a carré d'agneau (lamb) à la diable for two persons. Other specialties include an omelet soufflée aux fruits, also for two persons. Main-course dishes are likely to feature veal kidneys Robert or côte de veau in butter. Fixed-price lunches and dinners begin at 18F ($12.25), with full à la carte meals costing from 35F ($23.80). You can get light meals, snacks, and drinks from 9 a.m. to 11 p.m., but hot meals are served only from noon to 2 p.m. and 6 to 10 p.m. daily.

Budget to Moderate Dining

Churrasco, 60 Aarbergergasse (tel. 031/22-82-88). You can imagine yourself in Argentina here, as many of the Bernese seem to when they come to enjoy "something different." The decor is ranchero, with hanging lamps fashioned from pierced tin drums and cowhide covering the banquettes. Rustic pine branches (supposedly) support the ceiling, and at the far end of the room a chef dressed like an Argentinian cowboy grills deliciously flavored meat over a wood fire. Dishes include rumpsteak and entrecôte specialties (medium and "grande"), along with gazpacho, sangría, fried potatoes, and a special coffee. A daily lunch menu is offered for 18F ($12.25). Otherwise, meals begin at 35F ($23.80). The restaurant is open from 11:30 a.m., closing at 11:30 p.m. Sunday to Thursday and at midnight on Friday and Saturday.

Restaurant Goldener Schlüssel, 72 Rathausgasse (tel. 031/22-02-16), is a typical downtown restaurant where you can relish the traditional Swiss surroundings, food, and atmosphere. From the tables, you can look at the massive wood vaulting and stonework of this restored 13th-century building. The restaurant, run by Marianne and Jost Troxler, is part of a budget-priced hotel, previously recommended. Specialties are inexpensive to moderately priced. Try mignon d'agneau poivre vert (tenderloin of lamb with green pepper sauce and corn croquettes) or schweinbratwurst with zwiebelsauce (butter-fried sausage with onion sauce) and Rösti. At lunch, two fixed-price meals are served, costing 11F ($7.50) for two courses and 14.50F ($9.85) for three courses. A la carte meal prices range from 13F ($8.85) to 30F ($20.40). The restaurant is open daily from 7 a.m. to 11:30 p.m. (until 12:30 a.m. on Friday and Saturday). However, full hot meals are served only from 11:30 a.m. to 2 p.m. and 6 to 10:30 p.m.

Arlequin, 51 Gerechtigkeitsgasse (tel. 031/22-39-46), in the heart of the city, offers both local and Italian cuisine. The establishment has a rustic interior highlighted by art and bronze pieces. Trudi Wild, the owner and manager, offers such dishes as chicken pâté with morel mushrooms in puff pastry, farmhouse ham and potato salad, and goulash soup among the Swiss dishes. Meals cost from 35F ($23.80) in this haunt of Bern socialites, literati, musicians, and artists. Hours are 3 p.m. to 12:30 a.m. daily except Sunday. A pergola-shaded terrace is an inviting place to dine in summer.

Restaurant Harmonie, 3 Hotelgasse (tel. 031/22-38-40), lies at the corner of Münstergasse, a few blocks from the Houses of Parliament. This art nouveau charmer is directed by Fritz and Marlise Gyger. It evokes Paris in the 1890s, with wooden paneling, blue trim, and earth colors. The new generation has operated this gathering place since 1981 and has tried to maintain it in the style of their grandparents, who took it over in 1915. The establishment encourages an efficient service to its many tables, which are set far enough apart to give one a feeling of intimacy. There are two separate entrances, two separate rooms, and a few sidewalk tables protected by ivy-clad trellises. Evening meals begin at 35F ($23.80), and might include such good hearty food as tripe in tomato sauce with rösti, fresh homemade egg noodles bolognese or spinach ravioli. Other dishes, which might also be served at noon, include rösti with ham and eggs, cheese fondue, curried rice, and ratatouille. A simple fixed-price meal costs from 18F ($12.25), with à la carte meals ranging all the way up to 40F ($27.20) and on. The establishment is open on Monday from 3 to 11:30 p.m., Tuesday through Friday from 8 a.m. to 11:30 p.m., and Saturday from 8 a.m. to 3 p.m. It's closed Sunday.

Piazza Lorenzini, 3 Marktgass-Passage (tel. 031/22-78-50), serves Tuscan food in a typical, colorful, rustic restaurant operated by Thomas Allemann. Specialties include beefsteak florentine beautifully flavored with garlic, coniglio alle erbe con legumi (Tuscan rabbit), tiramisu, and zuppa inglese (trifle). Meals cost from 25F ($17). The restaurant is open daily except Sunday from 11:30 a.m. to 2:30 p.m. and 7 p.m. to 12:30 a.m. Hot meals are served until 11:45 p.m.

Gfeller am Bärenplatz, 21 Bärenplatz (tel. 031/22-69-44), serves wholesome meals in several different ambiences to a loyal crowd of Bernese who pack into almost every seat, especially at lunchtime. The ground floor is divided into three seating areas, all with waitress service. Upstairs is a self-service cafeteria, American style, with panoramic windows opening onto the Bärenplatz. Lunches begin at 18F ($12.25). On the premises is a Swiss-style tea room with a patisserie buffet with pastries costing from 3.50F ($2.40). The sidewalk tables are crowded in summer, almost spilling over into the nearby flower market. The food comes in large, filling portions. Specializing in lunch, midafternoon snacks, and early dinners, the establishment is open daily except Christmas from 10:30 a.m. to 8 p.m. Hot food is always available.

Confiserie Feller, 31 Marktgasse (tel. 031/22-35-56), is a café/bar/restaurant/tea room that attracts mainly a female patronage. It's set under the busy arcades of the Marktgasse, and there's usually a flower vendor just outside the front door, along with other street merchants. It's a long way from the front to the rear of the restaurant. A bar with leatherette stools flanks the corridor-like section leading to the back, and some clients prefer to take their meals here. Set lunches are offered for 12F ($8.15), with a supplement should you wish dessert. Breakfast is 6F ($4.10) and rich pastries begin at 2.50F ($1.70). If you like, you can have at lunch or dinner a green card on which you check the kinds of salads preferred, to be brought to the table assembled on a plate. Meals begin at 12F ($7.80). The main hours for serving are daily from 11 a.m. to 2 p.m. (on Thursday from 5 to 9 p.m., but closed other evenings).

Café Tschiren, 73 Kramgasse (tel. 031/22-18-64), under the arcades near the clock tower, is in a renovated room with a lot of natural wood and a vaguely nostalgic ambience. There is a tea room on the first floor, where you can enjoy light lunches, probably topped off with one of the luscious chocolate cakes made here. The place fosters the Swiss coffee house tradition. A light meal costs from 15F ($10.20). It's open daily from 7:30 a.m. to 6:30 p.m., although it doesn't open until 11:30 a.m. Monday; closed Sunday. To reach the tea room, you climb a twisting flight of stairs.

WHAT TO SEE: The principal artery of the old town, **Marktgasse,** is lined with luxurious shops and boutiques. The number of florists reveals the Bernese love of flowers. In this traffic-free sector you can stroll at your leisure, shopping and admiring the 17th and 18th-century houses. Eventually you come to **Junkerngasse,** the most prestigious street in Bern, lined with patrician houses.

Marktgasse rolls on until it becomes **Kramgasse,** the first street to the right of the clock tower. It has many antique shops and art galleries. You'll also see many turrets and oriel windows, and the Zähringen fountain, showing a bear, the city's mascot, in armor. The **Käfigturm** (prison tower) on Marktgasse in the 13th century marked the boundary line of Bern. Restored in the 18th century, it stands at the top of the Marktgasse.

To the east stands the **Zeitglocken,** or clock tower, which was built in the 12th century and restored in the 16th century. Until 1250 it was the west gate of Bern. Four minutes before every hour, crowds gather for what has been called "the world's oldest and biggest horological puppet show." Mechanical bears (the little bear cubs are everybody's favorite), jesters, and emperors put on an animated show—one of the longest running acts in show business, staged since 1530.

The **Cathedral of St. Vincent** (Münster), on Münsterplatz (tel. 031/22-05-72), was begun in 1421, although its tower wasn't completed until 1893. Its belfry, dominating Bern, is 300 feet high, and at the top a panoramic sweep of the Bernese Alps unfolds. You can climb a staircase, some 270 steps, to the platform tower from 10:30 a.m. to 4 p.m., costing 2F ($1.35) for adults, 1F (68¢) for children. You'll have a great vista over the old town and its bridges and a view of the Aare River.

The Münster is one of the newer of the Gothic churches of Switzerland. Its most exceptional feature is the tympanum over the main portal, with more than 200 figures (I lost count!). Some of them are painted, and the vanquished ones in this Last Judgment setting are singled out for particularly harsh treatment. The mammoth stained-glass windows in the chancel were created in the 15th century. The choir stalls from 1523 brought the Renaissance to Bern, and in the Matter Chapel is a curious stained-glass window, the *Dance of Death,* constructed in the closing year of World War I but based on a much older design.

Once you leave the three-aisle, pillared basilica, you come upon the 1545 Moses Fountain on the Münsterplatz. The cathedral is open from 10 a.m. to noon and 2 to 4 p.m., except on Sunday afternoon and Monday from November to Easter Sunday.

The **Rathaus** (town hall) on Rathausplatz is ancient, but still a center of political life. Erected in 1406 in the late Burgundy Gothic style, with a double staircase and a covered porch, it was restored during World War II, when there wasn't much overhauling of old monuments going on elsewhere in Europe.

The **Kunstmuseum** (the city's art museum), 12 Hodlerstrasse (tel. 031/22-09-44), was built in 1879, and is the proud possessor of the world's largest collection of the works of Paul Klee. A German painter, born in Switzerland in 1879, Klee had a style characterized by fantasy forms in line and light colors. He combined abstract elements with recognizable images. The works by Klee are the museum's star attraction. There are at least 40 oils and 2,000 drawings, gouaches, and watercolors. The museum has both Swiss and foreign works, with emphasis on the 19th and 20th centuries. There is a collection of Italian 14th-century primitives, such as Fra Angelico's *Virgin and Child.* Swiss primitives include some from the "Masters of the Carnation" who signed their work with either a red or white carnation.

Hodler, the romantic painter, is represented by allegorical frescoes, depicting *Day* and *Night.* Impressionists include Monet, Manet, Sisley, and Cézanne, along with Delacroix and Bonnard. There are the inevitable scenes of Montmartre by Utrillo. Surrealistic painters include Dali, Seligman, Oppenheim, and Tschumi. You'll see works by Kandinsky, Modigliani, Soutine, Marc, and Picasso. Representing constructivist painters are Taueber-Arp, Graeser, Lohse, Bill, Gorin, and Glarner, and the museum has a collection of "Zero"-art and works by Swiss artists of the 1970s. The museum is open from 10 a.m. to 5 p.m. Wednesday to Sunday, to 9 p.m. on Tuesday. It's closed on Monday. Admission is 3F ($2.05) to see the museum collection, although 5F ($3.40) to 10F ($6.80) additional is charged for special exhibitions.

The **Bundeshaus** (federal palace) (tel. 031/61-85-22) rises on the Bundesplatz, containing two chambers of the Swiss Parliament. A flower market takes place in front on Tuesday and Saturday mornings. The dignified domed building was constructed in Renaissance style. Guided tours are conducted through the building except when Parliament is in session. They depart every hour from 9 to 11 a.m. and then at 2, 3, and 4 p.m. (none at 4 p.m. Sunday). The building is closed on public holidays.

The famous **Bärengraben** (bear pits) is a deep, moon-shaped den where the bears, those mascots of Bern, have been kept since 1480. Beloved by the Bernese, the bears are pampered and fed. Everybody seemingly drops by there, throwing these hungry beasts a carrot. The bears have long been adopted as the heraldic symbol of Bern. Legend has it that when the Duke of Zähringen established the town in 1191, he sent his hunters out into the encircling woods, which were full of wild game. The first animal slain would be honored by having the city named after it. A *Bär*, or bear, was the first animal killed, and since then the town was known as *Bärn* or Bern. Many scholars discount this legend, but it makes for a good story nonetheless.

The pits are reached by going across Nydegg Bridge, which has a great view of the city. It was built over a gorge of the river and its major stone arch has a span of 180 feet. Right below the bear pits you can visit the stunningly beautiful **Rosengarten** (rose gardens). From these gardens you'll have a splendid vista onto the medieval sector and the river.

Try to fit in a visit to the **Schweizerisches Alpines Museum** (Swiss Alpine Museum), 4 Helvetiaplatz (tel. 031/43-04-34), which is normally open from May 15 to October 15 on Monday from 2 to 5 p.m. and Tuesday to Sunday from 10 a.m. to 5 p.m.; October 15 to May 15 the hours are the same on Monday and 10 a.m. to noon and 2 to 5 p.m. Tuesday to Sunday. Admission is 1F (68¢). You find, among other things, exhibits on the scenery and cultural life in the Swiss Alps, their research and exploration, mountaineering and skiing equipment, the history of mountaineering, and a collection of relief maps and other cartography. This museum is likely to be closed for most of the lifetime of this edition, so check locally.

Swiss PTT Museum (post, telegraph, and telephone museum), 4 Helvetiaplatz (tel. 031/44-92-88), which is open in summer from 2 to 5 p.m. on Monday and from 10 a.m. to 5 p.m. Tuesday to Sunday. In winter, the hours are the same on Monday and from 10 a.m. to noon and 2 to 5 p.m. Tuesday to Sunday. The museum depicts the development of the country's postal and telecommunication systems, and contains one of the largest stamp collections in the world. Check locally on the status of this museum, as it was moving into new headquarters at presstime.

Bernisches Historisches Museum (Bernese historical museum), 5 Helvetiaplatz (tel. 031/43-18-11), is housed in a neo-Gothic structure, built in the style of a 16th-century schloss. It's open from 10 a.m. to 5 p.m. (closed on Monday). It has many tapestries and much splendid antique furniture, but is visited mainly by those desiring to see the loot captured from the Burgundians in 1476 at Grandson. These treasures are stunning, including standards and tapestries that once belonged to Charles the Bold. Admission is 3F ($2.05).

The **Naturhistorisches Museum** (natural history museum), 15 Bernastrasse (tel. 031/43-18-39), is one of the great museums of Bern, often overlooked, regrettably, by the hurried visitor to the capital. You can view stuffed African beasts in a simulated natural habitat, along with everything from Arctic mammals to local fauna. There's an excellent exhibit of the endangered whale, although the reptile collection seems to hold the most fascination. The museum is open from 9 a.m. to noon and 2 to 5 p.m., except on Sunday when it opens at 10 a.m. It's free on Wednesday, Saturday, and Sunday afternoon; otherwise it charges a 1F (68¢) admission.

Nobel Prize–winning and world-renowned physicist Albert Einstein's Bern residence, **Albert Einstein Gesellschaft,** 49 Kramgasse, can be visited from 10 a.m. to 5 p.m. Monday to Saturday. It was here that the great man spent some of the happiest years of his life, 1902 to 1909, with his family and his work on the theory of relativity. Admission is free.

If you like your animals alive, head for the **Dählhölzli Tierpark,** 149 Dalmaziquai (tel. 031/43-06-16), one of the most interesting zoos in Europe. You will find the complete range of European fauna, from the tiny harvest mouse up to the elk and musk oxen. You can admire more than 2,000 animals, including exotic birds, reptiles, and fish. In summer, it is open daily from 8 a.m. to 6:30 p.m., and winter hours are from 9 a.m. to 5 p.m. The charge is 1.50F ($1) for adults, .05F (3¢) for children. Take bus 18.

In the immediate vicinity of Bern, you can visit one of the most spectacular attractions, **Mt. Gurten,** with a panoramic belvedere, a distance of only 1½ miles from the city. Depart Bern on the Monbijoustrasse, the road to Thun, heading for the suburb of Wabern. At Wabern, take a right turn (the road is marked) toward the funicular platform. In about ten minutes you'll arrive at the summit of Mt. Gurten at 2,815 feet. There are a children's fairyland and a walking area as well as the lookout point. Round-trip fare on tramway 9 and the fastest cable railway in Europe is 5F ($3.40) to and from any stop on the municipal transport system. If you drive to the bottom station, where you can park, round-trip passage to and from the summit costs 4F ($2.70).

TOURING BERN: For a good look at Bern, conducted sightseeing tours are offered from 10 a.m. and 2 p.m. seven days a week from May to the end of October, at 2 p.m. Monday to Saturday during the month of April, and at 2 p.m. only on Saturday from November to March. The charge is 15F ($10.20), and the tour leaves from in front of the tourist office at the main railroad station. An English-speaking guide will escort you on the trip to the rose garden for a view over the old city, through the city's residential quarters, past museums, and down to the River Aare which flows below the Houses of Parliament. You'll see the late-Gothic cathedral and have a stroll under the arcades to the clock tower. The tour takes you to the bearpits for a view of Bern's heraldic animals, through the medieval streets of the city, and back to the railroad station. This half-day look at Bern is highly recommended.

SOME SHOPPING NOTES: Stores in the city center are usually open from 2 to 6:30 p.m. on Monday; 8:15 a.m. to 6:30 p.m. Tuesday to Friday; and 8:15 a.m. to 4 p.m. on Saturday. They're open until 9 p.m. on Thursday and closed Sunday. Some specialty shops have different hours.

Heimatwerk, 61 Kramgasse (tel. 031/22-30-00), is a tourist store deluxe, selling souvenirs and handcrafts from all of Switzerland, particularly from the Bernese Oberland. Typical objects include woodcarvings from Brienz, scissor cuts (originals and prints), brass coffeepots, copper gelatin molds, and textiles of all kinds, as well as music boxes, and silver, gold, wood, and ceramic jewelry. Ceramic and wooden objects are to be found in the basement. If you're a dressmaker, be sure to look at the bolts of yard goods brightly patterned in regional designs. The shop can be found under the arcades of a gray stone building on a historic street near the clock tower.

Alstadt Galerie, 7 Kramgasse (tel. 031/22-23-81), is an antique shop. The store is loaded with two floors of Swiss chests and tables, many of them made from pine and many originating in the Bernese Oberland. If you like antiques and aren't familiar with this type, come in and look. Prices are clearly marked. Mrs. R. Christen, owner of the gallery, also regularly exhibits works by Swiss painters.

Stamp collectors will want to go to the philatelic agency, **PTT,** 19 Zeughausgasse (tel. 031/62-36-96), open from 8:30 a.m. to 5:30 p.m. Monday to Friday, from 8:30 a.m. to noon on Saturday, and closed Sunday.

Jemoli, 10 Marktgasse (tel. 031/22-61-22), a branch of the famous department store, claims you can find "everything you want." It offers 100 special departments on seven floors.

Loeb AG Bern, 47 Spitalgasse (tel. 031/22-44-55), is an important emporium "for everything." It's a good bet if you forgot to pack some essential item, perhaps underwear.

Ciolina Modehaus, 51 Marktgasse (tel. 031/22-11-91), is a high-fashion boutique for women.

One of the finest jewelry stores in Bern is **Gübelin,** 11 Bahnhofplatz (tel. 031/22-54-33), the longest-established jewelry and watch manufacturer in central Switzerland. The family-owned business has seven branches throughout Switzerland.

For books of many types, including many in English, try **Scherz Buchhandlung,** 25 Marktgasse (tel. 031/22-68-37).

Capitol Bally, 9 Spitalgasse (tel. 031/22-54-81). Naturally, this famous Swiss shoe manufacturer couldn't overlook the Bern market.

Gygax Mode in Leder, 4 Spitalgasse (tel. 031/22-25-61), is the leading name in leather.

Globus, 17 Spitalgasse (tel. 031/22-12-55), has been called the Bloomingdales of Berne.

Fein-Kaller + Co., 55 Marktgasse (tel. 031/22-12-20), is one of the leading stores for men's fashions.

NIGHTLIFE: Most of the Bernese are good, hard-working people who have to get up early for work. That means they have an early "last drink" in one of the city's historic cellars, such as Kornhauskeller of the Klötzlikeller, then stroll home under the lamplights through the lanes and byways of the old town. However, for the international crowd, there are several clubs offering dancing and entertainment, perhaps cabaret, which remain open until the wee hours.

If you speak German, you can see some very good theater in Bern. The leading theater is the **Stadttheater** (municipal theater) at 20 Kornhausplatz (tel. 031/22-07-77). Even if you don't speak German you might want to attend, as it has a program of operas and ballets where the artistic language is universal.

Ballet, cabaret, and many other types of performances are presented at the **Theater am Käfigturm,** 4 Spitalgasse (tel. 031/22-61-00). Contemporary plays in German are presented at the **Kleintheater,** 6 Kramgasse (tel. 031/22-42-42). *This Week in Bern,* distributed free by the tourist office, has a list of current cultural events.

Arcady Bar, Hotel Schweitzerhof, 11 Schweizerhoflaube (tel. 031/22-45-01), might be the best place to begin your evening with an apéritif. You can also drop in later for an after-dinner nightcap. Here you're likely to see ambassadors drinking champagne and eating oysters. The decor is centered below an elliptical wood-covered ceiling, where butler's tables and Chinese lamps are accessories to the elegantly restrained decor. The clientele is well dressed, so you should be too. Snacks are available, including omelets at 16F ($10.90) and an assiette grisonnaise at 23F ($15.65), the latter consisting of plates of air-dried meats from the Grisons. It's open daily from 11 a.m. to midnight.

The **Bellevue Bar,** 3 Kochergasse (tel. 031/22-45-81), at the Bellevue Palace Hotel, is the favorite meeting place of both the international and the Bernese business world. Here you meet leading politicians and interesting people to talk to. In the evening, a pianist provides background entertainment for social gatherings. The bar opens at 10 a.m., with seating on the terrace in summer, closing according to the interest of the customers.

Kursaal, 71-77 Schanzlistrasse (tel. 031/42-54-66), is the only place in Bern for gamblers. The Kursaal maintains betting limits of 1F (68¢) to 5F ($3.40) as required by Swiss law. The gaming tables are open from 9 p.m. to midnight daily. This is a good place for novices to learn gambling, in a place where serious money rarely changes hands. Also on the premises are restaurants, dance halls, and bars. The Kursaal lies across the river from the oldest section of Bern.

Jaylin's Club, Hotel Schweizerhof, 11 Bahnhofplatz (tel. 031/22-45-01), is the most elegant club in town, sheltered in this prestigious hotel in a plush and glittering ambience, where the clientele seems to come from many parts of Europe. Entrance is free to hotel guests, but others pay an admission fee of 14F ($9.50). Musical acts are likely to include a host of American and English jazz groups. Live entertainment is supplemented by disco music with dancing. The club sponsors a Saturday apéritif concert from 4 to 7 p.m., which draws an active crowd, especially toward the end. At the next table might be a visiting head of state. Drinks cost from 19F ($12.90). Hours are 9 p.m. to 4 a.m. Closed Sunday.

Kornhaus Keller, 18 Kornhausplatz (tel. 031/22-11-33), was once a grain warehouse but is today the best known historic wine cellar in Bern. It's in the old city in a stone building with symmetrical proportions and an arcade on the ground floor. It's a huge cellar, seating hundreds of diners in a getmütlich baronial kind of ambience. Musical acts perform here frequently. Often there is a Sunday brunch concert from 10 to 11:45 a.m., as well as a changing schedule of evening entertainment, including, on one occasion, the "Red Hot Peppers." Of course the repertoire always consists of alpine melodies produced by a brass band and accordions. This is Bern's answer to the Hofbräuhaus in Munich. Dinners cost about 30F ($20.40), a simple meal going for 15F ($10.20). A Berner plate of smoked meats and sauerkraut is the classic dish to order. Hot food is served from 11:30 a.m. to 1:45 p.m. and 6:30 to 8:45 p.m. daily.

Klötzlikeller, 62 Gerechtigkeitsgasse (tel. 031/22-74-56). Everybody in Bern knows about this place near the Gerechtigkeitsbrunnen (Fountain of Justice), the first fountain you see on your walk from the Bärengraben to the Zeitglockenturm. Watch for the lantern outside an angled cellar door, which brings you down to the oldest wine tavern in Bern, dating from 1635. Technically the site is owned by the city, which has leased it to the sophisticated and attractive Isabella Gschwind, who fulfills a long-established tradition: a long time ago the town fathers decreed that only an unwed woman with children should get the lease. Everybody congregates here, from students to members of Parliament. The menu is limited, wisely so, and includes traditional rösti and bratwurst with salad and rösti with ham. Simple meals cost from 25F ($17). Also, you can order traditional Swiss cheese dishes (raclette, cheese toast, and sliced cheese). Try the wine from the city's own vineyard—red or white—costing from 30F ($20.40) per bottle. Whatever you wish, ask Isabella. The place is open from 4 p.m. to 12:30 a.m.; closed on Sunday.

Charley's Beef and **Cadillac Disco,** 10 Laupenstrasse (tel. 031/25-34-34), are a few blocks west of the train station, in a corner building with big windows and an attractive and informal ambience. Charley's is known for the best steaks and grills in town, costing from 45F ($30.60) for a meal that might include onion soup, a sirloin, a good salad, and such side dishes as baked potato with chives and bacon. Many of the dessert specialties are flambé extravaganzas, made with bananas or peaches. Food is served from 11:30 a.m. to 2 a.m. except on Friday, Saturday, and Sunday when hours are 6 p.m. to 3:30 a.m. In the same building downstairs is the Cadillac Disco, probably the most fun nightspot in town. It opens Sunday through Thursday at 9 p.m., closing at 3:30 a.m. On Friday and Saturday, the opening time is 11 p.m., with closing at 3:30 a.m. The cover charge is 12F ($8.15).

Mocambo, 10 Genfergasse (tel. 031/22-50-41), is a night club combining striptease with disco. Its decor evokes the skyline of New York, and the disc jockey operates out of a pink Cadillac. On Friday and Saturday night, the cover charge of 19.50F ($13.25) includes one soft drink. There are four bars on the premises. It is open daily from 9 p.m. to 3 a.m.

Swiss Chalet Restaurant, 75 Rathausgasse (tel. 031/22-37-71), is the setting for a popular folkloric show, where yodelers call to one another and a brass band goes oom-pah-pah in a setting of brick walls, beamed ceilings, and red-checkered tablecloths. The walls are hung with oversize cow bells and alpine farm implements. The singers sit or stand on a recessed area which, during lunch, is concealed by a curtain. At night the place is brilliantly lit and a lot of fun. The music begins at 8:30 p.m. on a quiet note as patrons finish their dinner. From 9:30 to 10:30 p.m. there's a full-blown concert, with dancing after 10:30. The kitchen stays open to 12:45 a.m. for after-theater visits. Dinner averages anywhere from 40F ($27.20) up, but no one will mind if you drop in for just a beer, costing from 5.50F ($3.75). There's no cover charge. The establishment lies in the Hotel Glocke.

A SIDE TRIP THROUGH EMMENTAL: The district of Emmental, in the canton of Bern, is famous for its cheese. Just ten miles or so from the capital, you'll be plunged into a pastoral world that is the home of the famous "hole-filled" Swiss cheese. Some of these wheels of cheese weigh 180 pounds. Set against a backdrop of snowy Alps, it's a world of verdant fields and plump Swiss cows. Some of the farms set on rolling hillsides have been in the same family for generations. Even the smallest hamlet has its little ole local cheesemaker.

Emmentaler (sometimes spelled Emmenthaler), the most famous cheese of Switzerland, is commonly called "Swiss cheese."

Much of the architecture is similar: large Bernese farmhouse complexes, embracing both a main house, the bauernhaus, and an adjoining stöckli, where the grandparents retire when they get too old to run the farm. Government officials from Bern often take special guests outside the city for a country dinner in one of the local inns, usually named after a lion or a bear (the symbol of Bern), and which are known for their good, hearty food and abundant hospitality.

If you're planning to visit Lake Lucerne after Bern, the quickest way is through the Emmental, and you'll have a sightseeing adventure along the way.

The gateway to the district is:

Burgdorf

Northeast of Bern, this small town is known for its castle, characterized by a trio of towers that have been turned into a historical museum of passing interest. The view of the Bernese Alps is memorable. This large stronghold stands on an isolated crag, dating from the 12th century when it was founded by the dukes of Zähringen, who turned it into one of the country's most formidable bastions of defense. It's open April 1 until the end of October from 2 to 5 p.m. and on Sunday from 9:30 to 11:30 a.m. and 2 to 5 p.m. Admission is 2F ($1.35). Burgdorf also has a late Gothic church from the end of the 15th century, and many attractive and well-maintained guildhouses.

If you're in need of food and lodging, consider the following suggestion:

Hotel Touring Bernerhof, am Bahnhofplatz, CH-3400 Burgdorf, Switzerland (tel. 034/22-16-52), was constructed in 1954 in front of the train station, but is considerably quieter than you'd expect for such a location. The bedrooms have been renovated in a cozy style, sometimes with Oriental rugs, and always with comfortable beds. A staff of cooks prepare food for the brickwalled pizzeria, rustic restaurant, and steakhouse. Each of the 34 rooms has its own bath, radio, phone, and TV hookup. Alice Portmann, the owner-manager, charges 55F ($37.40) daily in a single and 100F ($68) in a double, including breakfast.

2. LAKE THUN

Occupying an ancient terminal basin of a glacier, Lake Thun (Thunersee) was connected to Lake Brienz (Brienzersee) until they were divided into two at Interlaken. Over the years the Lütschine River deposited so much debris at Interlaken that the one body of water eventually became two.

Beloved by Brahms, the lake is not as well known as others and is a discovery to many North Americans. The Swiss are rightly proud of it, keeping it as a "secret address" for a lakeside holiday. It's about 13 miles long and two miles wide.

The area has a mild climate, earning for it the title of the "Riviera of the Bernese Oberland." The lake is a playground for waterskiers, the yachting set, and windsurfers. It also has excellent swimming pools (both indoor and outdoor), as well as windsurfing schools. There's plenty of activity along its shores too, including golf, mountain railways, underground caves, tennis, and horseback riding.

Two major centers are Thun and Spiez (see below), although there are many other towns and villages off the beaten track that are worthy of your attention. Because of space limitations, I'll document only the more interesting ones.

THUN: At the gateway to the Bernese mountains, the little city of Thun began on an island at the point where the Aare River flows into Lake Thun. Lying 19 rail miles southeast of Bern, Thun is the capital of the Bernese Oberland. It long ago outgrew its island origins and overflowed onto both banks of the river.

The most interesting sector is on the Aare's right bank. The curiosity there is the busy main street, **Hauptgasse,** where walkways, flower-decorated in summer, have been built across the arcaded shops below.

At the Rathausplatz, with its 17th-century town hall, you can take a covered staircase up to the formidable **Schloss Thun** (also called Castle Kyburg) (tel. 033/23-20-01). Built by the dukes of Zähringen at the close of the 12th century, it was later possessed by the Counts of Kyburg, and became in time the residence of the Bernese bailiffs. Today it's a historical museum, open daily from the first of June until the end of September from 9 a.m. to 6 p.m.; otherwise, April, May, and October, from 10 a.m. to 5 p.m.; and charging 2.50F ($1.70) for admission. Inside its massive residential tower is one of the largest baronial halls in Switzerland, the Knights' Hall, with an ancient chimneypiece, two altar frontal tapestries, a Gobelin tapestry from the time of Charles the Bold, and a fine collection of halberds and other weapons. In other rooms are collections of furniture, agricultural implements, period toys, ceramics including old Heimberg pottery, and some important archaeological finds, as well as an exhibit of military uniforms. From the turrets, there's a magnificent view over the surrounding district.

If you'd like to take an excursion, head for **Schloss Schandau** (tel. 033/22-25-00), a 19th-century manor house on Lake Thun. Grandiose and baronial in style, it was built by a French architect in 1848. It's been called, if you can imagine such, "English Tudor Gothic" and "French Early Renaissance." On the ground floor is a restaurant, and on the second floor changing art exhibitions are shown. It's open in July and August daily from 10 a.m. to noon and 2 to 6 p.m. except Monday, charging an admission of 2.50F ($1.70). It can be reached on foot if you're athletic, as it lies only a mile south of Thun in the village of Scherzlingen.

East of Thun on the road to Interlaken, **Schloss Hünegg** (tel. 033/43-19-82) at Hilterfingen is a museum of historicism and the Germanic form of art nouveau called Jugendstil, from the late 19th and early 20th centuries. The furnishings have been unchanged since the castle was the property of a manufacturer around 1900. It lies in a park with many old trees, on the shore of Lake Thun. It is open from the end of May until October Monday to Saturday from 2 to 5 p.m.

and on Sunday from 10 a.m. to noon and 2 to 5 p.m. Admission is 2F ($1.35) for adults, 1F (68¢) for children.

Where to Stay

Hotel Beau Rivage, Aare Quai, CH-3600 Thun, Switzerland (tel. 033/22-22-36), rises from the shores of the lake with everything that a 19th-century resort hotel should have. Its heavily detailed façade is painted alpine white, with accents of natural stone. The configurations of the red-tile roof probably couldn't be duplicated today. Guests enjoy the sun terrace, the indoor swimming pool, and the antique-filled public rooms. A garage maintained by the hotel will park your car, although if you arrive by train you'll be only five minutes by foot from the Beau Rivage. The hotel usually closes between mid-October and the end of April. The bedrooms most often face south, with a view of lake and mountains. Bathless singles cost 40F ($27.20) to 60F ($40.80) daily, going up to 70F ($47.60) to 100F ($68) with bath. Bathless doubles range from 70F ($47.60) to 100F ($68), the charges rising to 105F ($71.40) to 160F ($108.80) with bath, depending on the season and the situation of the room. Breakfast is included.

Elite Hotel Thun, 1 Bernstrasse, CH-3600 Thun, Switzerland (tel. 033/23-28-23), is a modern and comfortable hotel in the center of the city. It's soundproof and equipped with an attractive restaurant, a dimly lit bar, and a sun terrace with meal service. The bedrooms, for the most part, are flamboyantly decorated with vividly patterned geometric wallpaper. In the basement are some automated bowling alleys. The Riesen family, the English-speaking owners, do what they can to make guests feel at ease. All rooms contain private baths and cost 65F ($44.20) to 80F ($54.40) daily in a single in low season, 80F ($54.40) to 110F ($74.20) in high. Doubles go for 110F ($74.20) to 140F ($95.20) in low season, 130F ($88.40) to 170F ($115.60) in high. The daily platter in the snack restaurant costs 14F ($9.50), and a good Chinese restaurant is also on the premises.

Schlosshotel Freienhof, 3 Freienhofgasse, CH-3600 Thun, Switzerland (tel. 033/21-55-11), is quietly situated on the Aare close to the center of town. The hotel consists of an older four-story symmetrical core with a modern addition extending to the side. There, balconied rooms give views of the river on one side and a landscaped park on the other. The public rooms are richly but unpretentiously outfitted with natural grained woods and tastefully modern furniture. The comfortable accommodations, all with private baths, TV, radios, direct-dial phones, and mini-bars, cost 110F ($74.80) to 180F ($122.40) daily in a double, 65F ($44.20) to 105F ($71.40) in a single. Half board goes for 30F ($20.40) additional per person.

Hotel Krone, Rathausplatz, CH-3600 Thun, Switzerland (tel. 033/22-82-82), is a historic building with a prominently turreted extension projecting into the front yard. Owned and operated by the Lamprian family, the hotel has well-decorated rooms, each with private bath, plus a swimming pool. Singles cost 75F ($51) to 100F ($68) daily, while doubles range from 130F ($88.40) to 160F ($108.80). The Krone is very popular and fills up early in peak season.

Where to Eat

Restaurant Turm, Schwäbisgasse (tel. 033/22-84-85), is in a very old tower. The ground floor attracts shoppers with its rich and varied salad buffet, with meals costing from 15F ($10.20). On the second floor, you can order à la carte in more formal surroundings. The food is well prepared, with many excellent veal and fish dishes. Meals cost from 40F ($27.20). Hours are daily except Sunday and Monday from 8:30 a.m. to 11:30 p.m. It is closed during part of July as well.

Casa Barba, Rathausplatz (tel. 033/22-22-27), is the most popular place in town for Spanish food, such as paella and Spanish filet of sole. The grilled meats are especially good, as are the Iberian wines. This congenial spot is centrally located and open every day except Monday from 11:30 a.m. to 2 p.m. and 6:30 to 9 p.m. À la carte meals cost from 25F ($17) to 40F ($27.20). A quiet terrace is available should you wish to dine outdoors.

BEATENBERG: A modest high-altitude health resort, Beatenberg lies about six miles from Interlaken, reached by climbing a steep, narrow road (or you can take the funicular from Beatenbucht). Beatenberg is the end of the line, as there is no through traffic. On the north side of Lake Thun, Beatenberg, at 4,265 feet, lies on the southern slopes of the Niederhorn, which can be reached by chair lift, taking you to a height of 6,400 feet.

The winter season, lasting from December to April, appeals to both beginning and experienced skiers. The chair lift to Neiderhorn and four ski tows take skiers to various runs. The Swiss Ski School also operates in the resort, and a cross-country and ski touring track is permanently marked. All access roads are open throughout the year. In the heart of the village is an ice rink for skating, hockey, and curling devotees. There's also a heated swimming pool.

Once at Beatenberg, you'll have splendid views of the highest peaks in the Jungfrau region, along with views of Lake Thun, the Eiger, and the Mönch.

Beatenberg also enjoys a brilliant summer season from May to October, with alpine flowers and mild autumn-like days. The area has 20 miles of signposted paths.

Food and Lodging

Hotel Kurhaus Silberhorn, CH-3803 Beatenberg, Switzerland (tel. 036/41-12-12), is sheltered inside a five-story clapboard building with lots of windows and four floors of covered loggias strewn with geraniums and begonias in summer. The sunny terrace is an inviting spot for coffee and snacks, especially since it allows for views of the Eiger, the Jungfrau, the Mönch, and Lake Thun. The inside is pleasantly furnished. A heavily beamed bar and a glass-walled restaurant might be restful places for stopovers. The Jansen family charges from 40F ($27.20) to 50F ($34) daily in a bathless single and from 55F ($37.40) to 65F ($44.20) in a single with bath. For doubles, they charge from 80F ($54.40) to 100F ($68) without bath and 110F ($74.80) to 130F ($88.40) with. Diet meals are offered. There's an elevator on the premises.

MERLIGEN: The major reason for staying here is the elegant resort hotel described below. Tiny Merligen (not to be confused with Meiringen) lies on Lake Thun, about six miles from Interlaken, at an altitude of 1,863 feet. This lakeside resort is perched at the gateway to the Justis Valley, enjoying a sheltered situation, and is the center of many summer sports.

For food and lodging, try the **Hotel Beatus Merligen,** CH-3658 Merligen am Thunersee, Switzerland (tel. 033/51-21-21). The best view of this hotel might be from a boat in the middle of a Lake Thun (the hotel will rent you one, along with equipment for most other water sports). The Beatus stands in a large park. It's sports oriented, with its own private lido and an indoor swimming pool, along with a sauna, underwater jet massage, table tennis, boccia, a private jetty with rowboats, motorboats, tennis courts, and facilities for waterskiing, windsurfing, and fishing. There's even a yachting school.

The architect of this establishment designed it in long horizontal lines that, when coupled with its bright awnings, give it a pleasantly restful impression of well-maintained calm. The spacious bedrooms usually offer balconies, which you can enjoy at breakfast. All the accommodations at this 140-bed hotel contain a private bath or shower, toilet, phone, radio, and if desired, TV. A single room ranges from 95F ($64.60) to 180F ($122.40) daily, and a double goes for 160F ($108.80) to 340F ($231.20). The interior includes an array of well-staffed public rooms, many of them with panoramic views of the lake. They include Karl-

Seegers Stube, along with a French restaurant and bar. Music is also played for dancing.

3. SPIEZ

SPIEZ: Dominated by its castle and vineyards, Spiez is an easily reached resort on the left bank or southern shore of the lake. Pleasantly situated at the foot of the Niesen, Spiez is mainly a summer resort, offering fishing, windsurfing, tennis, horseback riding, open-air theater performances, folklore evenings, and many hiking paths. It also has a sailing school.

The **Castle of Spiez** (tel. 033/54-15-06), near the landing stage, has a museum open April to October daily from 9:30 a.m. to noon and 2 to 6 p.m. (closed on Monday morning). The museum charges 3F ($2.05) for admission. The best attraction of the castle is its panoramic vista over the lake and the Niesen. Once the home of the Minnesinger of Stretlingen and of the Bernese Bubenberg and Erlach families, the structure was changed from a medieval fortress on the lake to a rich man's castle in the 17th and 18th centuries. Relics of the former owners can be seen in the living rooms and halls, with features ranging from the Romanesque to the baroque.

The town also has an 11th-century Romanesque church with frescoes, known simply as **Alte Kirche** or old church.

The major attraction, however, lies outside the resort. Near the end of town, take a road leading to Simmental, heading via Mülenen for about five miles to the funicular station. There you can board the funicular, paying 26F ($17.70) for a round-trip ticket that will take you to the summit of pyramid-shaped Mount Niesen at 7,615 feet. From here, the panoramic vista covers the area from the Jura to the Vosges massif in eastern France and from the central Swiss peaks over the summits of the Bernese Oberland to the Vaud Alps. The view takes in a colorful panoply, including Lakes Thun and Brienz plus villages, towns, valleys, forests, and rivers. The ride to the summit takes about half an hour, so you should allow at least two hours in order to take in the splendor of the scene. Departures are fairly often from 8 a.m. to 5 p.m. daily from May to the end of October. For information, call 033/76-11-12 or 033/76-11-13.

Food and Lodging

Belvédère Silence Hotel, CH-3700 Spiez, Switzerland (tel. 033/54-33-33). Only a large open meadow separates this elegant hotel from the lake. Since much of it is planted with flowers and old trees, it's a pleasure just walking around. The hotel has been added onto several times, so that it resembles a 19th-century gabled house with a panoramic series of public rooms extending toward the lake and several sunny terraces. A modern and comfortable annex is set nearby to accommodate overflow guests from the main building. In a single with bath, rates range from 90F ($61.20) to 100F ($68) daily, with doubles going for anywhere from 160F ($108.80) to 200F ($136), depending on the season. On the premises is a tennis court, plus facilities for waterskiing, windsurfing, and sailing, along with instructions. There's also a heated outdoor swimming pool.

Hotel Bahnhof Terminus, CH-3700 Spiez, Switzerland (tel. 033/54-31-21) is a curious mixture of a steep-roofed 19th-century core with a steel-and-glass annex extending toward the lake to the rear. The public rooms in the old section are cozy, while those in the modern part are streamlined, functional, and panoramic. The simply furnished bedrooms cost from 80F ($54.40) to 96F ($65.30) daily in a bathless double and from 42F ($28.55) to 52F ($35.35) in a bathless single. Rooms with bath range from 110F ($74.80) to 130F ($88.40) in a double, 60F ($40.80) to 70F ($47.60) in a single. Half board is another 22F ($14.95) per person daily.

Hotel Bellevue, 36 Seestrasse, CH-3700 Spiez, Switzerland (tel. 033/54-

23-14), is a tall building, higher than it is wide, giving it an unmistakably Victorian aura. Its façade is accented with brown shutters and a few centrally placed wrought-iron balconies. It's been owned since 1944 by the Maurer family, who have redecorated the interior in an updated rusticity, including the obligatory heavy-beamed ceilings. You're only five minutes on foot from the train station, yet the sunny terrace gives good views of the town with an almost unobstructed view of the lake beyond. With private bath, the charge ranges from 94F ($63.90) to 106F ($72.10) daily in a double. Singles, each with private shower or bath, range from 48F ($32.65) to 52F ($35.35). Half board is available for another 20F ($13.60) per person daily.

OBERHOFEN: This town, on the eastern shore, is dominated by the most romantic-looking castle on the lake. The **Castle of Oberhofen** (tel. 033/43-12-35) dates back to the 12th century, and was once owned by one of the Habsburgs. In private hands since 1798, its last owner was an American attorney, William Maul Measey of Pennsylvania, who turned it over to the Oberhofen Castle Foundation in 1940. Over the past centuries the castle has been reconstructed in a rather self-conscious historical style. Its museum has a wide collection of furniture and artifacts, ranging from the Gothic to the baroque. It can be visited from mid-May to mid-October daily from 10 a.m. to noon and 2 to 5 p.m., charging 3F ($2.05) for admission. It is closed on Monday morning.

AESCHI: A fast-rising winter sports resort in the Bernese Oberland, Aeschi stands on a sunny terrace overlooking Lake Thun. Easily within commuting distance of Spiez, it is reached by a good road or by the post bus from the rail station at Spiez, the end of the autobahn, about four miles from Aeschi. It's also a summer playground, with many walks (some are conducted, allowing you to visit an alpine cheese dairy).

Swimming and other water sports are possible in the indoor swimming pool at Aeschi or at nearby Lake Thun. The resort is unspoiled and has two ski lifts and two training lifts, offering skiing for beginners and those more advanced on mechanically prepared runs. Tobogganing is also possible, and there's a ski school as well as bus service to nearby skiing grounds.

Hotel Restaurant Baumgarten, CH-3703 Aeschi, Switzerland (tel. 033/54-41-21). Usually the flag of the canton flies above the hotel, which is painted a pastel yellow with black shutters. The interior is outfitted with a few well-placed Oriental rugs and comfortable, serviceable furniture. You're likely to meet some of the locals in the heavily timbered bar area. The owner-manager, Hansjürg Bürki, charges from 32F ($21.75) to 36F ($24.50) daily in a bathless single with a private toilet, the rates going to 45F ($30.60) to 50F ($34) in a single with bath. Doubles cost from 59F ($40.10) to 65F ($44.20) without bath, 80F ($54.40) to 96F ($65.30) with bath. The hotel is open year round.

4. INTERLAKEN

A holiday resort for some 300 years, Interlaken is the tourist capital of the Bernese Oberland. The "town between the lakes" (Thun and Brienz), lies below the north side of the Jungfrau. The excursion possibilities from Interlaken, including one to the Jungfrau, are numerous, as cableways and mountain rails bring most of the dazzling sights of the Bernese Oberland within fairly convenient reach.

For years Interlaken was known mainly as a summer resort, but it has gained considerable winter business as well. Skiers use the resort in winter, even though it's a long haul from Grindelwalk, Mürren, and Wengen. Money, however, is a factor: Interlaken charges low season prices in winter, when those resorts impose their highest tariffs. Interlaken assesses its highest tariffs in summer, when the ski resorts are charging their lowest rates.

An Augustinian monastery was founded here in 1130 and lasted until it was closed by the Reformation (the ruins can still be seen in the grounds of the castle and the Protestant church). Tourism to the area could be said to have begun in 1690 when Margrave Frederic Albert of Brandenburg undertook a journey into the snowy alpine world of the mountains and glaciers of the Jungfrau massif. However, real tourism dawned at the beginning of the 19th century. The festivals of alpine shepherds drew many artists and writers to the area who did much to publicize the resort. Steamer services on the lakes and the railway brought a steady stream of visitors, who over the years have included royalty, along with such eminent names as Goethe, Mark Twain, and Mendelssohn.

The view of the Jungfrau from the Höhenpromenade in Interlaken is justly famed. The Höheweg goes between the west and east train stations of Interlaken. About 35 acres in the middle of town, once the property of the Augustinian monks, was acquired in the mid-19th century by the hotelkeepers of Interlaken, who turned it into a park.

As you stroll along the promenade, you'll pass the Kursaal (casino), where everybody stops to gaze at the flower clock. The clip-clop of the fiacres adds a nostalgic touch, as they were so beloved by the visiting Edwardians. The promenade is lined with hotels, cafés, and gardens.

At some point in your exploration you'll want to cross over the Aare River to Unterseen, built in 1280 by Berthold von Eschenbach and standing opposite Interlaken. There you can visit the parish church with its late Gothic tower dating from 1471. This is one of the most photographed sights in the Bernese Oberland. The Mönch appears on the left of the tower, the Jungfrau on the right.

Each summer, while seated in a covered grandstand, visitors watch the saga of William Tell, according to Friedrich Schiller's version of the formation of the Swiss Confederation.

Interlaken is well equipped for tourists, with its indoor swimming pools, cafés with calorie-loaded pastries, and animal parks. As a throwback to Victoria's day, afternoon concerts are still presented.

In addition to mountain trekking, many local sports are available, including sailing, windsurfing, rowing, fishing, golf, tennis, even glider flying. You can also go on many lake steamers across Brienz and Thun.

While sightseeing in town, consider a visit to **Touristik-Museum der Jungfrau-Region,** Am Stadthausplatz, 26 Obere Gasse (tel. 036/22-98-30), which is the first regional museum of tourism in the country. Through specially arranged exhibitions, visitors are shown the rich and colorful growth of tourism in the region in the past two centuries. The museum is open only from May to mid-October, Tuesday through Sunday, from 10 a.m. to 12:30 p.m. and 2 to 5 p.m. The cost is 3F ($2.05), but with a visitor's card you are admitted for just 2F ($1.35).

PRACTICAL FACTS: A few specifics relating to Interlaken may make your stay here more enjoyable.

Children: Need a babysitter? The tourist office (tel. 036/22-21-21) will help you find one.

Drugstore: I recommend **Apotheke Dr. Portmann,** 4 Höheweg (tel. 036/22-34-26).

Information: Of assistance to visitors is the **Tourist Office,** 37 Höheweg (tel. 036/22-21-21), in the Hotel Metropole Building. The office is open from 8 a.m. to noon and 2 to 6 p.m. Monday to Friday year round. In summer, it is also open on Saturday from 8 a.m. to noon and 2 to 5 p.m. and on Sunday from 4 to 6 p.m. In winter, it is open from 8 a.m. to noon on Saturday.

Sightseeing: Take a horse-drawn cab (fiacre), that form of transport so beloved by the Victorians, for a round trip through Interlaken, Matten, and Unterseen, about a half-hour's ride. The cost is 20F ($13.60) for one person, 25F

($17) for two, and 30F ($20.40) for three riders. These cabs leave from the Westbahnhof.

WHERE TO STAY: Interlaken has a wide range of accommodations suitable to most tastes and pocketbooks. Some of the leading hostelries were around long *before* grandmother's day, but others are new and modern and have kept abreast of the times.

The Leading Hotels

Hotel Metropole, CH-3800 Interlaken (tel. 036/21-21-51), offers luxury at a good price. Its sleek modern lines and big-city format are often preferred by Americans, who shun the aging dowager palaces of Interlaken. Owned by the Kantonal Bank of Bern, this is the most up-to-date and best managed hotel in town. At 18 stories, it is also the tallest. Originally constructed in 1976, it was stylishly renovated and enlarged in the late 1980s. As you sip your drink in the pale blue and birchwood piano bar, you might suspect you've been transported into a chic and stylish hotel in Munich or Hamburg. On the premises is one of the city's finest restaurants, Le Charolais (see "Where to Dine"); a spacious and glistening indoor pool and sauna with its own convivial early evening bar; and a duet of medium-priced restaurants where lunchtime salads, platters, and fondues are always in demand. Its panoramic café is one of the meeting places of Interlaken.

Each of its 100 bedrooms affords a spectacular view south over Interlaken and the towering mountains around it. Accommodations contain thick carpeting, color TV with at least 16 channels, mini-bars, radios, tile-covered baths, and comfortable modern furniture. Rooms have balconies and a calm-inducing color scheme of beige, blue, bordeaux, or pale green. Charles Zimmermann, the manager, charges from 160F ($108.80) daily for a single and 280F ($190.40) for a double in high (midsummer) season, or 120F ($81.60) for a single to 200F ($136) for a double in low season, with breakfast, taxes, and service included. For reservations and information, call 212/593-2988 in New York City; toll free 800/882-4777 in New York State, or toll free nationwide at 800/223-5652, which is the Steigenberger Reservation Service.

Grand Hotel Victoria-Jungfrau, CH-3800 Interlaken, Switzerland (tel. 036/21-21-71), has been considered for generations one of the most important hotels in Switzerland. Catering to a resort-seeking customer, it appeals to Swiss and foreigners alike. This is one of the *grande-dame* hotels of the region, designed around a central tower capped by a curved roof below a slender needle-shaped spire. The rest of the façade extends in a series of recessed planes to either side of the main tower. In summer, colorful awnings stretch above the balconied windows toward the rigid symmetry of the well-kept gardens. Everywhere your attention is drawn to the mountains around you, whose savagery seems to dwarf the cultivated plants near the hotel. A swimming pool is within view of the colonnade of one of the porches, while indoor-outdoor tennis courts support a sports facility.

The interior is gracefully high-ceilinged, with ornate plasterwork and lots of antiques from several different periods. The bar area has comfortable settees, space, and good service, and might afford a pleasant diversion. Depending on the season, singles with full bath and all the amenities rent for 180F ($122.40) to 255F ($173.40) daily, while doubles cost from 280F ($190.40) to 395F ($268.60), including a buffet breakfast, taxes, and service charges. You'll find enough wining, dining, and musical facilities here to keep anyone entertained for many days. On the premises are two elegant restaurants, three bars (some of which serve snacks), and a disco with live music.

Grand Hotel Beau-Rivage, CH-3800 Interlaken, Switzerland (tel. 036/21-62-72), is a five-star hotel, long a leader among the grand hotels of Interlaken.

The hotel is built in a vaguely Italian Renaissance style, with a central tower capped by a triangular pediment below a modified mansard roof. The rest of the central tower has an ascending series of covered loggias, bedecked with flowers and ornamented with restrained carving. Two wings radiate to either side of the loggias, with wrought-iron balconies and gabled rooflines. The ceiling of the reception area is covered with elaborate designs in the plaster and supported by four garlanded columns in the center of the room.

Despite the promise of old-fashioned decor hinted at by the façade, the bedrooms have been renovated in a conservative style, with modern pieces used against the backdrop of prominently displayed curtains. Rates include access to the indoor pool and the fitness club. The hotel offers a wide choice of rooms, ranging from 230F ($156.40) to 310F ($210.80) daily in a double, 140F ($95.20) to 194F ($132.60) in a single, breakfast included. High season is from July till September, during which half-board costs another 45F ($30.60) per person.

Bellevue-Garden Hotel, CH-3800 Interlaken, Switzerland (tel. 036/22-44-31), looks a lot like an updated version of a fortified castle with windows, shutters, and a glass-fronted restaurant and cozy bar. The hotel sits directly on the banks of the Aare River in a grass-covered setting with flowering trees, landscaped walkways, and roses. The garden style is definitely English, of great appeal to plant lovers. The Fink-Uetz family, the nature-conscious owners of this place, prefer not to do business between mid-October and the first week of April each year. The rest of the time they are gracious hosts to guests who fill the single rooms at 55F ($37.40) to 102F ($69.35) per night or doubles at 94F ($63.90) to 178F ($122.40), including breakfast. Half board is another 25F ($17) per person daily. Public rooms are furnished with comfortable late-19th-century chairs and couches, creating a cozy, old-fashioned ambience where your great-grandmother would feel very much at home. On the shores of the river a rustic gazebo stands next to a wrought-iron fence.

Hotel Royal St. Georges, CH-3800 Interlaken, Switzerland (tel. 036/22-75-75), is adorned over most of the outside and inside with a confectionery type of elaborate decoration that the 19th century produced. The roofline is capped with dozens of small, hand-turned spires placed above each of the gables on the red-tile roof. The lower floors have balconies, loggias, and lengths of wrought iron. In the public rooms, the architectural details have been pampered, painted, preserved, and protected in their original rococo splendor of French Second Empire and art nouveau. Some of the more expensive rooms have been restored to their original high-ceilinged condition, while others have been updated to a conservatively modern format of utilitarian furniture and panoramic windows. Public rooms include a bar area in a well-proportioned salon-type room, and two restaurants. Hermann Kurzen and his family are the proprietors here. In a single with bath, the rate ranges from 92F ($62.55) to 118F ($80.25) daily, doubles with bath going for 150F ($102) to 196F ($133.30). The hotel is open from April to October.

Stella Hotel, CH-3800 Interlaken, Switzerland (tel. 036/22-88-71). From the balconies of this resort hotel you'll get a good view of the mountains in any season. The bright awnings are removed in winter, when the hotel's white concrete superstructure seems to blend in with the snowy field around it. Inside you'll find a tile swimming pool, protected by a roof but with a glass wall to the outside that can be opened or shut according to the weather. The lounge/bar area is rustically decorated with a planked ceiling, heavy timbers, and a piano, while the unpretentious restaurant serves nourishing meals. Werner and Christine Hofmann-Frei, the couple who direct this place, are themselves interested in winter sports. They'll prove helpful in every way, perhaps even accepting an offer to play Ping-Pong on the table set up outside on the grassy lawn in summer.

Single rooms rent for 85F ($57.80) to 118F ($80.25) daily, while doubles range from 141F ($95.90) to 195F ($132.60), including breakfast. The wide range of prices stems from the management's policy of increasing prices by about 25% in high season (summer and the Christmas and New Year's holidays), and charging much less during any season for rooms facing north with an inferior view. Full- and half-board plans are available, as are apartments. Reductions are offered for children.

Hotel Interlaken, 74 Höheweg, CH-3800 Interlaken, Switzerland (tel. 036/21-22-11). Since Byron and Mendelssohn stayed here in 1816 and 1832, respectively, the hotel has been gutted and rebuilt along pleasing lines. The most expensive rooms contain a scattering of 19th-century antiques, although all of the others have conservative modern pieces. Each of the 60 bedrooms has a bath, phone, radio, TV, and mini-bar. With breakfast included, singles cost 75F ($51) to 110F ($74.80) daily, and doubles go for 120F ($81.60) to 200F ($136). The hotel has a salmon-colored façade, with certain baroque touches, lying within a 12-minute walk from the most congested part of town. There's a rustic bar and a Swiss-style tavern inside, and one of the city's only Chinese restaurants, the latter recommended separately.

Hotel Krebs, 4 Bahnhofstrasse, CH-3800 Interlaken, Switzerland (tel. 036/22-71-61), owned by a family with the same name, looks over the shopping district of Interlaken. Set into its own gardens in front of a sidewalk with a fairly active commerce, it is very much a downtown hotel, although the mansard roof and the green shutters could almost make you think it's a private home. The interior benefits from the carpenters who, years ago, built beautifully finished wooden ceilings and walls, along with a skillfully crafted wooden staircase leading to the upper floors. Bedrooms are pleasant, often with timbered ceilings and enough space to feel comfortable in. From the terrace there's a good view of the Jungfrau. Singles rent for 85F ($57.80) to 118F ($80.25) daily, while doubles cost 145F ($98.60) to 196F ($133.30). Breakfast is included in the tariffs. Half- and full-board plans are available, costing from 28F ($19.05) to 46F ($31.30) per person extra.

The Middle Bracket

Hôtel du Nord, 70 Höheweg, CH-3800 Interlaken, Switzerland (tel. 036/22-26-31), was built at the turn of the century and, as was the fashion at the time, given a French name. Today, much of its allure is thanks to the sophisticated warmth of its hardworking owner, Reinhard Engel. The hotel sits at the edge of a wide city park, behind a yellow façade and a modified mansard roof. Its public rooms, and especially its restaurant (Im Gade) contain enough homey touches to make anyone feel cozy and sheltered. A special spot is the warm confines of the street-level bar, where local residents seem more than willing to strike up conversations. (Look for the rack of neckties which are said to have been removed from guests to help them relax.)

Of course, the staff is what makes or breaks a hotel stopover, and the staff here seems especially cooperative. Each of the 59 pleasant, well-scrubbed rooms contains a bath, TV, radio, phone, mini-bar, and a collection of modern furniture. With breakfast included, singles cost 65F ($44.20) to 110F ($74.80) daily, and doubles are priced at 100F ($68) to 180F ($122.40). A satisfying half board can be arranged for an additional 25F ($17) per person.

Hôtel de la Paix, 24 Bernastrasse, CH-3800 Interlaken, Switzerland (tel. 036/22-70-44). This family-run hotel is a pleasant surprise, especially since it's only a block away from the Bahnhof (Interlaken West). The roofline is fairly ornate, gabled and tiled like a legend from Grimms' fairy tales. The relaxed atmosphere is partly the result of the efforts of owners Gillian and Georges Etterli, who do everything they can to help the guests quickly adjust to the slower place of Interlaken. An elevator will carry you to one of the 45 beds upstairs. All rooms have showers or baths. A double costs 85F ($57.80) to 130F ($88.40) daily, while a single rents for 50F ($34) to 65F ($44.20). Breakfast, service, and taxes are included.

Park-Hotel Mattenhof, CH-3800 Interlaken, Switzerland (tel. 036/21-61-21), is a large, old-fashioned hotel in a secluded spot at the edge of a forest. The management guarantees a quiet and calm sojourn to its many guests who marvel at the manicured lawns and panoramic views of the Alps. The outside looks like a private castle, because of its high, pointed roof, its tower, and its many loggias and balconies. Attached to the hotel are a swimming pool, a tennis court, facilities for amusing children away from their parents, terraces, bars, and restaurants. Many of the salons are sunny and airy, warmly decorated in a way that makes you want to sit down and enjoy the ambience. The proprietors are Peter Bühler and his family, who charge from 97F ($35.95) to 136F ($92.50) daily in a single and from 79F ($53.70) to 118F ($80.25) per person in a double, including full board. The rooms facing north fall into the cheaper range of the prices.

Hotel Weisses Kreuz, am Höheweg, CH-3800 Interlaken, Switzerland (tel. 036/22-59-51), is in the center of Interlaken, under the direction of the Bieri family. The hotel is built inconspicuously on a street corner at the end of a row of buildings. The interior is pleasantly decorated with white walls and half-paneling, with a few Oriental rugs for extra color. Open all year, the hotel rents singles for 65F ($44.20) to 100F ($68) daily, and doubles go for 100F ($68) to 160F ($108.80), depending on the season. All rooms have baths or showers, and breakfast is included in the prices. Half board is available for an additional 24F ($16.30) per person per day.

Hotel Bernerhof, CH-3800 Interlaken, Switzerland (tel. 036/22-31-31) can be found close to the Interlaken West train station in the center of town. Open year round, the hotel presents an interesting angled façade to the street. Each room has its own recessed balcony. The main salon is vividly decorated with scarlet wall-to-wall carpeting and modish chairs with delta-shaped supports. An open fireplace in the center sends smoke through a tubular chimney. The Hanspeter-Anderegg family are the owners. Depending on the season, doubles cost from 60F ($40.80) to 95F ($64.60) per person, with a supplement of 25F ($17) for a single. A buffet breakfast is included.

Hotel Beau-Site, 16 Seestrasse, CH-3800 Interlaken, Switzerland (tel. 036/22-81-81), can be found after a short walk from the Interlaken West train station. Surrounded by its own spacious gardens, dotted in summer with parasol-shaded card tables and chaise longues, the hotel proves to be a pleasant and relaxing oasis in the middle of town. The owners are the Ritter family. From June to September, two persons pay 180F ($122.40) daily, with a buffet breakfast included. During the rest of the year, prices are reduced to 160F ($108.80) daily for two. A few rooms with hot and cold running water are rented year round for 80F ($54.40) daily in a double. Singles with shower and toilet range from 70F ($47.60) to 107F ($72.75) daily. The hotel has two fine restaurants, the budget-price Stübli and the more elegant and pricier Veranda.

The Budget Range

Hotel Lötschberg, CH-3800 Interlaken, Switzerland (tel. 036/22-25-45), is one of the best bargains of the centrally located hotels. Enjoying a lot of repeat business, the 25-bed establishment is open all year. It was built in a baroque style, and, in summer, tables are placed outside so guests can soak up the sunshine. The Hutmacher family are your considerate hosts. The location is only two blocks from Interlaken West train station. The staff maintains the premises well, and each of their bedrooms is comfortably furnished. Singles range in price from 50F ($34) to 85F ($57.80) daily, depending on the plumbing and the season. Doubles cost from 76F ($51.70) to 140F ($95.20). The Lötschberg also offers a reasonably priced restaurant.

Gasthof Hirschen, CH-3800 Matten/Interlaken, Switzerland (tel. 036/ 22-15-45), is a family-run inn slightly outside of town on the road to Grindelwald. The place looks like a rustic chalet, set directly on the road but with gardens behind. The inside offers 32 beds to guests, who frequently choose to dine in the paneled and timbered dining room or in the less formal bar area. The Graf Sterchi family, the owners, charge from 80F ($54.40) to 140F ($95.20) daily for a double room, 45F ($30.60) to 85F ($57.80) in a single, depending on the plumbing. Breakfast is included in the prices. The establishment is open all year.

Swiss Inn, 23 General Guisan Strasse, CH-3800 Interlaken, Switzerland (tel. 036/22-36-26), is a small inn, offering 25 beds to tourists for 45F ($30.60) to 80F ($54.40) daily in a single, 80F ($54.40) to 160F ($108.80) in a double or suite, all with bath or shower, depending on the season and the length of stay. Prices include breakfast. A series of five apartments, containing one, two, or three rooms, can also be rented, ranging in price from 80F ($54.40) to 240F ($163.20) per night. Units are equipped with kitchenettes, along with baths or showers, mini-bars, living rooms, balconies, phones, radios, and TV. The smallest unit can accommodate two persons, and the largest houses seven guests. All rooms are tastefully decorated and comfortable.

Jazz plays softly in the breakfast room, and the inn has a lounge and sitting area with fireplace as well as a grill for barbecues in the garden. Mrs. Vreny Müller-Lohner is the charming and attractive hostess, who will direct guests to her garden or allow them to use a refrigerator or laundromat. The hotel is a five-minute walk from the Interlaken West train station. The building is Edwardian, with elaborate detailing and gables.

Hotel Alfa Garni, 7 Bernastrasse, CH-3800 Interlaken (tel. 036/22-69-22), stands within a few blocks of the Interlaken West train station. This gabled and turreted villa was originally built as the residence and office of a local doctor. It appears far older, but it was actually constructed in the 1950s in the peak-roofed style so associated with the 19th century. Containing about a dozen accommodations, the hotel is the domain of Swiss-born hoteliers Rolf Schertz and Margaret Weibel. All but two of the smallest singles contains a private bath, and rates include breakfast. Doubles rent for 85F ($57.80) per night. The hotel is closed for three weeks in January.

WHERE TO DINE: Most guests dine at their hotels, which partially explains why such a world-famed resort as Interlaken has so few very good independent restaurants. But there are some, should you be staying in a hotel "garni" or else want a change of fare.

The Schuh, 56 Höheweg (tel. 036/22-94-41), has long been known for its pastries. It's an attractive restaurant, confiserie, and tea room in the center of town. It's housed in an alpine building with a thick roof extending in an arch over the fourth-floor windows like a woman's bonnet. In the rear is a sunny terrace with globe lights and a well-kept lawn. Inside is a large restaurant with over-size windows and a live pianist. The ambience is almost Viennese, with heavy silver on the well-set tables, as well as candles in antique brass holders and lights with pink silk lampshades. The establishment is owned by the Beutler-Kropf family, who charge 18F ($12.25) and up for set meals, although you could spend as much as 50F ($34) ordering á la carte. Hot food is served from 11 a.m. to 2 p.m. and 6 to 9 p.m. daily except Monday. The restaurant is near the Hotel Victoria.

Chez Pierre, Hotel Bristol, 39 Bahnhofplatz (tel. 036/23-12-22), stands in Interlaken West, across from the rail station. Sometimes known as "Le Bistro," it's one of the most sophisticated dining rooms at the resort, certainly the most authentic French bistro in Interlaken. It's best to go for dinner from 7 to 9:30 p.m., when you are offered a menu gastronomique at 65F ($44.20). If fresh fish from the tank doesn't tempt you, then you might happily settle for such superb dishes as filet of beef with tarragon sauce or roast saddle of lamb provençale. Oysters are served au gratin, and lobsters, one of the chef's specialties, appears in many different incarnations. You might begin, for example, with a goose liver terrine, following with a double sirloin steak with mushrooms. The restaurant is closed on Wednesday and in January.

Le Charolais, Hotel Metropole, 37 Höheweg (tel. 036/21-21-51), is one of the most elegant of the hotel specialty restaurants. It offers a refined cuisine and superb service. Reached by heading up a flight of stairs, it is open for dinner nightly from 6:30 to 9:30. You are likely to spend from 70F ($47.60) by ordering à la carte. You might begin with a terrine of quail, then move on to such excellent main courses as filet of sole with morels, sliced veal with three kinds of mushrooms, grilled lobster with armagnac butter, or medallions of pork flavored with Roquefort. If you want a lavish bash, then ask for the chef's gastronomic menu at 95F ($64.60) in which he takes understandable pride. An excellent wine list backs up this cuisine which turns to France for its inspiration. You can also visit for lunch daily, enjoying one of the finest table d'hôte menus at the resort at a cost of 38F ($25.85). Service is daily from 11:30 a.m. to 2 p.m.

For change-of-pace fare, try **Restaurant Lotus,** Hotel Interlaken, 74 Höheweg (tel. 036/21-22-11), which is incongruously located in this conservative, very Swiss hotel. The restaurant is the only Chinese dining room in town, open nightly except Wednesday from 6 to 9:30. Three set menus are offered, ranging in price from 28F ($19.05) to 55F ($37.40), the latter a four-courser. Otherwise, you can peruse the à la carte menu, beginning with such standard fare as spring roll, fried wonton, or Peking ravioli. The menu is evenly balanced among fish, poultry, and meat dishes, including fish Peking style (or else with black beans), duck with Chinese mushrooms, beef in oyster sauce, and pork Szechuan. A limited selection of wine is also offered.

Pizpaz, 1 Bahnhofstrasse (tel. 036/22-25-33), is a pizzeria in the center of town. Its many outdoor tables make it a busy, bustling place, serving primarily Italian specialties. Charges are from 35F ($23.80) for an average meal, which might include any of the standard Italian specialties such as calves' liver in marsala, or osso buco, plus at least 20 different types of pizza. Gelato misto, a mixed selection of ice cream, is the most popular dessert. The establishment is very popular with families. It's closed Monday but open every other day from 10:30 a.m. to 1 a.m.

Gasthof Hirschen, Matten/Interlaken (tel. 036/22-15-45), previously recommended for its lodgings, also offers some of the best and most reasonably priced meals in town. Outside the center, the restaurant is richly decorated in an alpine style with paneled walls and local artifacts. It serves daily from 11:30 a.m. to 2 p.m. and 6 to 9 p.m. However, it is closed on Tuesday and for lunch on Wednesday. It's a small guesthouse but the menu is large and sophisticated. You might begin with the potato and mushroom soup, probably the finest you'll ever taste. Another appetizer might be the ravioli filled with crab or else a homemade terrine. For your main course, you might order sautéed calves liver, filet of beef Bordelaise, beef goulash, broiled trout, or perhaps Chateaubriand if you're feeling really elegant. Meals average 40F ($27.20) but lunches tend to be much cheaper.

Restaurant Burestube and **Ryter-Bar,** 57 Höheweg (tel. 036/22-65-12), is a rustically bierstube, with lots of polished wood. This place draws a wide range of clients, and everybody is very democratic, often sharing tables. The hubbub of conversation competes with the rock music. You might have a drink at the crowded bar, where a gregarious bartender entertains a retinue of customers while keeping up a brisk service. You'll see wrought-iron cages for wine, lots of timbered beams, and an occasional painted alpine chest The kitchen prepares good salads, some on giant plates. Children's plates are also offered. You can choose your favorite meat (priced by the gram) at a buffet. Here you'll find the finest quality veal steak, tenderloin, sirloin, or pork cutlet. There are at least eight chef's specialties, including the Bernese plate with smoked pork products, sausage, sauerkraut, and boiled potatoes. Hot meals cost from 25F ($17). The restaurant is open from 10 a.m. to 1 a.m. daily. However, the full array of hot dishes is offered only from 11:30 a.m. to 2 p.m. and 6 to 9:45 p.m. It is closed Monday and takes an annual vacation from early January to mid-February.

NIGHTLIFE: In the heart of Interlaken stands **Casino Kursaal** (tel. 036/22-25-21) with its well-tended gardens, world-famous flower clock, and magnificent view of the Jungfrau. The Kursaal is one of the largest convention centers of Switzerland. It is also the center of Swiss folklore in the Bernese highlands. At the Folklore Spycher, which is open daily except Sunday from 7 p.m. to 2:30 a.m., a Swiss folklore show is presented every evening from May to September. In winter, the show is offered only on Thursday. You can also order Swiss food specialties. The gaming room is open daily from 9 p.m. to 2:30 a.m., but remember in Switzerland you can bet only 5F ($3.40) as your largest wager. The Restaurant, Le Petit Casino, offers two terraces. It is open daily from 10 a.m. to midnight. The kitchen specializes in cheese fondue as well as a large variety of international dishes. The ice creams are exceptional. Count on spending from 35F ($23.80) and beyond.

Highlife, 2 Rugenparkstrasse (tel. 036/22-15-50), is about as far from a wood-paneled gemütlich stube as you are likely to find in Interlaken. Sheathed with glistening chrome and mirrors, it offers a high-tech disco format of focused spotlights, popular music, and gaiety. It opens at 9 p.m., remaining so until 2 a.m. nightly. Drinks cost from 12F ($8.15) on Friday and Saturday and from 8F ($5.45) to 10F ($6.80) on other nights.

Barbarella, Grand Hotel Victoria-Jungfrau, am Höheweg (tel. 036/22-12-38), is a popular disco, with klieg lights, a nightly live act with local and international bands, and lots of comfortable seating. Drinks cost from 14F ($9.52) on Friday and Saturday, from 9F ($6.10) to 12F ($8.15) other weekdays. It's open daily from 9 p.m. to 3 a.m.

Western Saloon, Grand Hotel Victoria-Jungfrau, am Höheweg (tel. 036/22-12-38), is incongruously located in this belle-époque hotel. If, after touring the Jungfrau, you get nostalgic for the Old West, then come here to dine on U.S. beef and fresh salads while listening to country-and-western acts from the United States and Britain. The place doubles as a sort of bar-steakhouse and concert hall. It opens nightly at 8:30 p.m., remaining so until 2 a.m. This place is not cheap, and you can easily spend more than you bargained for on an evening here, at least from 50F ($34).

SPORTS: If you need some exercise to rejuvenate yourself after a lot of sightseeing and fondue dipping, I suggest the following:

Swimming: There's a public indoor swimming pool (tel. 036/22-24-16) behind the casino, with a solarium and a fitness room. It's open Tuesday to Friday from 9 a.m. to 9:30 p.m. and on Saturday and Sunday from 9 a.m. to 6 p.m. year round. Adults are charged 5.50F ($3.75), 4F ($2.70) with a visitor's card. Children under 6 are admitted free. From 6 to 16, they pay 3F ($2.05).

Interlaken also has an open-air pool with a 33-foot diving board, operating May to September daily from 8:30 a.m. to 6 p.m. Charges are 3F ($2.05) for adults, 2.50F ($1.70) for holders of a visitor's card. Children are charged 2F ($1.35).

Golf: You can play at the Interlaken-Unterseen course from April 1 to October 31. The cost is 42F ($28.55) Monday to Friday but 45F ($30.60) on Saturday and Sunday. With a tourist card, the cost is reduced to 37F ($25.15) Monday to Friday, to 40F ($27.20) Saturday and Sunday. For more information, phone the clubhouse (tel. 036/22-60-22).

Tennis: Use of an outdoor court at the Höhematte will cost 15F ($10.20) per hour, 12.50F ($8.50) with a visitor's card. If you're alone and willing to take your chances on being matched up with another loner, it will cost you half the court fee. For reservations, phone 036/22-14-72 from 8 a.m. to noon and 2 to 5 p.m. Monday to Friday. The courts are open from mid-April to mid-October from 8 a.m. to 5 p.m. Monday to Friday.

Horseback riding: A number of bridle paths lead between Lake Thun and Lake Brienz. The Voegeli Riding School, 66 Scheidgasse in Unterseen (tel. 036/22-74-16), and Häsler Riding Stables, 21B Alpenstrasse, Bönigen (tel. 036/22-52-70), offer accompanied rides, costing 25F ($17) for one hour, 40F ($27.20) for two hours.

Information on all sports is available at the **Tourist Office** (see Practical Facts).

EXCURSIONS FROM INTERLAKEN: Swiss engineering genius reaches its apex in the Bernese Oberland, as the mountains are filled with cogwheel trains, cables, chair lifts, and aerial cabins. A network of roads and mountain railways— many of which were once thought impossible to erect—serves the Jungfrau district.

Jungfraujoch

For many, the highlight of every Swiss tour is the trip to Jungfraujoch at 11,333 feet, the highest railway station in Europe for more than half a century. It's also one of the most expensive: a second-class, round-trip tour ticket costs adults 113.40F ($77.10). However, families can fill out the forms for a family card, available at the railway station, with which children up to age 16 ride free. Departures are usually daily at 8 a.m. (this could vary) from the east station in Interlaken, the return scheduled for about 4 p.m. For information apply at the sales office of Jungfrau Railways, 37 Höheweg, CH-3800 Interlaken, Switzerland (tel. 036/22-52-52).

The excursion is comfortable and safe, and packed with adventure. You first take the Wengernalp railway (nicknamed WAB), a rack railway that opened in 1893. It takes you to Lauterbrunnen at 2,612 feet. At Lauterbrunnen you change trains, heading for the Kleine Scheidegg station at 6,762 feet. This is avalanche country, as a view unfolds of the Jungfrau (named for the white-clad Augustinian nuns of Interlaken), the Mönch, and the Eiger Wall.

At Kleine Scheidegg you change to the highest-situated rack railway in Europe, the Jungfraubahn. You have six miles to go, and four of those miles will be spent in a tunnel ambitiously carved into the mountain between 1896 and 1912 under the direction of Adolf Guyer-Zeller. You stop twice, for about five minutes each, at Eigerwand and Eismeer, where you can view the sea of ice from windows built into the rock. The Eigerwand is at 9,400 feet and Eismeer is at 10,368 feet. Leaving the tunnel, you are likely to be blinded by the contrast if you forgot to bring along a pair of sunglasses. The Eigernordwand (north wall) is so steep it's been called "notorious."

Once at the Jungfraujoch terminus you may feel a little giddy until you get used to the air. There's much to do here, as Jungfraujoch forms its own little eerie world.

You can take a free elevator behind the post office to a corridor that will lead to the famed Eispolast (Ice Palace). Here you'll be walking on what is called "eternal ice" in caverns hewn out of a glacier by a Swiss guide in 1934. These caverns were cut 65 feet below the surface of the glacier. Everything—walls, floors, whatever—has been made of ice, and in various niches you can see ice sculptures, including one of a vintage automobile.

Once you return to the station, you can take another corridor, called the Sphinx Tunnel, to yet another free elevator. This one takes you up 356 feet to an observation station called the Sphinx Terraces, overlooking the saddle between the Mönch and Jungfrau peaks. You can also take in the expanse of the Aletsch Glacier, at 14 miles the longest river of ice in Europe. The snow melts into Lake Geneva and is eventually carried to the Mediterranean.

A scientific station here conducts astronomical and meteorological research, and has a research exhibition that explains weather conditions and offers a video presentation. You have a choice of dining places here, either in the Jungfraujoch Glacier Restaurant, the traditional choice, or in a self-service cafeteria, or Top of Europe, opened in 1987 with a choice of five different restaurants. As a further adventure, you can take a sleigh ride, pulled by stout huskies.

On your way back down, you return to Kleine Scheidegg station but can vary your route by going through Grindelwald (see the description coming up), from which you'll have panoramic views of the "north wall" that has claimed so many lives.

Let us hope the weather and the visibility will be ideal. You should always ask at the tourist office in Interlaken before making the trip. Remember, once again, that your body metabolism will be affected, and you may find the slightest body movement tiring.

Harder Kulm

From Interlaken east, you can strike out on a much less ambitious excursion, this time to Harder Kulm at 4,337 feet. This belvedere gives you not only a view of Interlaken and the Bernese Alps, but of both lakes, Thun and Brienz. A funicular will take you up to Harder Kulm, the trip taking about 15 minutes and costing 13.60F ($9.25) for a round-trip ticket. Departures are about every half hour, and service is daily from May to mid-October. You can have drinks or a meal at the Harder Kulm mountain restaurant, with its observation terraces.

For information about Harder Kulm, phone 036/22-12-56. If there's no answer, try 036/22-52-52.

Heimwehfluh

You can also take a funicular up to Heimwehfluh, at 2,215 feet, where you'll be rewarded with views of both of the lakes, Brienz and Thun. The funicular station is about a six-minute walk from the west rail station in Interlaken, at the southern end of Rugenparkstrasse. From the belvedere at the top you'll also have views of Jungfrau, Mönch, and Eiger, the classic trio. There's a lookout tower at the top along with a café and restaurant. The funicular ride takes about five minutes, costing 6.40F ($4.35) for a round-trip ticket for adults, 4.40F ($3) for children. Departures are May until the middle of October from 9:30 a.m. to 5:30 p.m.

Lake Tours

A fleet of motor ships with a total capacity of 6,720 passengers operates on **Lake Thun** from April to October. Trips cover the 11½-mile length of the lake, as well as its width, 2½ miles at the maximum. A four-hour voyage from Interlaken West to Beatenbucht, Spiez, Overhofen, Thun, and return costs about 20F ($13.60); free to holders of a Swiss holiday card. A shorter trip, Interlaken West to Beatenbucht to Spiez and back, taking two hours, costs about 15F ($10.20).

Boat trips on **Lake Brienz,** also from April to October, are made by five motor ships and one steamship, total capacity 3,160 passengers. On the nearly 9-mile-long lake (1½ miles wide), the journeys, costing 15F ($10.20), free with a holiday card, last 2½ hours on a jaunt from Interlaken East to Iseltwald, Giessbach, Brienz, and return. A voyage of 1¼ hours, costing 8F ($5.45), also starts at Interlaken East and goes to Iseltwald and back. For information, call 033/36-02-58.

The St. Beatus Caves

According to an old legend, Beatus, a sixth-century Irish missionary, lived at the entrance to the caves, called Grottes de St-Béat in French and St.-Beatus-Höhlen in German. The story goes that he got rid of a dangerous dragon who lived in the cave, set up his own missionary headquarters there, and preached Christianity to the pagan population of the area. The caves were the home of cave dwellers thousands of years ago. The caves can be reached by boat, by bus or car along the cliff-bottom road, or on foot along the historic pilgrim's way. The caves are in the cliffs above Lake Thun, between Beatenbucht and Sundlauenen, to the west of Interlaken.

The caves can be explored to a depth of some 3,300 feet, along a path lit by electricity. After passing through the reproduction of the cave-dwellers' prehistoric settlement and the cell of St. Beatus, which form the museum section, tours take visitors through huge caverns and grottoes with striking stalactites and stalagmites. The caves are open from Palm Sunday to October from 9:30 a.m. to 5:30 p.m. daily, with guided tours about every 30 minutes. The cost is 6F ($4.10) for adults, 2.50F ($1.70) for children. For more information, telephone 036/41-16-43).

Just inside the cave entrance, there's a well-managed restaurant. You can have a meal or a snack inside the cozy dining area or outside on the cave terrace.

Wilderswil/Schynige Platte

Lying less than two miles to the south of Interlaken, Wilderswil stands on a plain between Lakes Brienz and Thun at the foot of the Jungfrau mountains. It is both a summer and a winter resort, and the starting point for many excursions. The resort has 16 different levels of accommodations, ranging from hotels to guesthouses, but most visitors stay in Interlaken, visiting Wilderswil to take the excursion to Schynige Platte.

Ruskin came this way, finding that the view of the Jungfrau from here was one of a trio of great sights in all of Europe. Take the train from Interlaken East station, arriving in Wilderswil in about six minutes, maybe a little more. Here you can switch to a cogwheel train for the harrowingly steep, nearly hour-long ascent to the Schynige Platte at 6,454 feet. The rack railway, which opened in 1893, travels a distance of 4½ miles, with gradients up to 25%. More than a dozen trips a day leave in season from late May to mid-October, costing 37.20F ($25.30) for a round-trip ticket.

Once you arrive at Schynige Platte, you'll find an alpine garden, charging an admission of 2F ($1.35), with some 500 species of plants. At the belvedere, you'll have a splendid view of the Eiger, Mönch, and Jungfrau. Food and drink are offered at the Hotel Restaurant Schynige Platte. For information on Schynige Platte, phone 036/22-28-35.

If you'd care to stay in Wilderswil instead of Interlaken, I have some recommendations.

Hotel Jungfrau, CH-3812 Wilderswil, Interlaken, Switzerland (tel. 036/22-35-31). The best part of this hotel is its location, surrounded by trees and meadows with an alpine backdrop that inspires you to begin a sports regime. The hotel is a boxy modern interpretation of a mountain chalet, with lots of rustically wooden balconies over a cement superstructure. The interior is attractively decorated with heavy beams, lots of wrought-iron detailing, and a sympathetic bar area near the restaurant. Three minutes from the train station, it has nearby bus and train connections not only to Interlaken, but to Grindelwald, Mürren, and Wengen. The comfortable and well-furnished rooms cost from 35F ($23.80) to

50F ($34) daily in a bathless single, from 50F ($34) to 85F ($57.80) with bath. Bathless doubles range from 65F ($44.20) to 90F ($61.20). Doubles with bath include a wide range of accommodations, from a single room to a penthouse or apartment, and these cost from 90F ($61.20) to 140F ($95.20) daily. The price of any room goes up or down the above-mentioned scales according to the season. Half board is offered for 20F ($13.60).

Hotel Bären, CH-3812 Wilderswil, Switzerland (tel. 036/22-35-21, stands in the village square. An old inn with a license dating back to 1706, it's been fully renovated, and each bedroom has a bath, phone, radio, and mini-bar. Singles range in price from 60F ($40.80) to 78F ($53.05), with doubles going for 95F ($64.60) to 125F ($85), all tariffs including a buffet breakfast. There is an excellent restaurant downstairs with a public bar and a good local atmosphere. Service is daily from 11 a.m. to 11 p.m. Adjoining is an attractively decorated pizzeria and a French restaurant. On the first floor is a sitting room for guests, leading out onto a large terrace with views over the surrounding mountains. Next door is the guests' dining room, a large, sunny facility seating up to 130 people, where the breakfast buffet is offered, with a large choice of dishes. The Bären is under the ownership of the fifth generation of the same family, Mädi and Fritz Zurschmiede. The hotel lies only a five-minute walk from the railway leading to the famous Jungfrau.

5. MÜRREN

This village, one of the most stunningly situated in the Bernese Oberland, is cut off from traffic. If you're driving, you can go as far as Stechelberg, which lies at the terminus of the Lauterbrunnen Valley road. From there you must take a cable car to Mürren, costing 20F ($13.60) for a round-trip fare. The ride, which is part of the fun, takes about ten minutes, and departures are about every half hour.

Long enjoyed by the British, Mürren was discovered by the Romantics some 150 years ago. It has been famous as a skiing center since 1910. In fact, downhill skiing was developed at the slalom invented here in the 1920s, and Mürren is the birthplace of modern alpine racing.

Mürren occupies a sheltered and sunny balcony high above the Lauterbrunnen Valley, and once there you'll breathe pure mountain air, as you take in a trio of wonders, the peaks of the Jungfrau, the Eiger, and the Mönch. At 5,414 feet, Mürren is the highest permanently inhabited village in the Bernese Oberland. It's an exciting excursion from Interlaken in summer and a major ski resort in winter. There are 30 miles of prepared runs, consisting of 16 downhills. The longest run measures 7½-miles. For cross-country skiers there's a 7½-mile track in the Lauterbrunnen Valley, ten rail minutes from Mürren.

If you're not driving, you can reach Mürren in one hour by mountain railway from the east rail station in Interlaken going via Lauterbrunnen and Grütschalp, and in half an hour from Lauterbrunnen via Grütschalp. The Lauterbrunnen-Mürren railway opened in 1891 and is made up of two sections: the cog railway from Lauterbrunnen to Grütschalp and the narrow-gauge railway from Grütschalp to Mürren.

A famous cable car, which visitors take from a point on the northwestern periphery of Mürren, is called the **Mürren-Allmendhubel Cableway.** It departs daily throughout the year from 8 a.m. to 6 p.m., costing 7.40F ($5.05) per person for a round-trip fare. From the top, you will have a panoramic view of the Lauterbrunnen Valley as far as Wengen and Kleine Scheidegg. Between mid-June and late August, you can use the rail for the access it gives to alpine meadows rife with wildflowers. A hill walk in this region might be one of the memorable events of a trip to Switzerland.

The most popular excursion from Mürren is to the famous **Schilthorn,** which is reached after a 40-minute cable-car ride, a round-trip ticket costing 42F ($25.55). In summer, departures are about every 30 minutes. The Schilthorn,

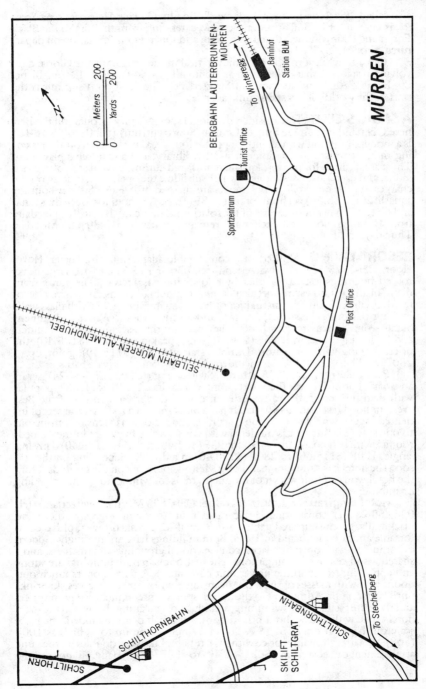

MÜRREN

also called "Piz Gloria," after the James Bond film *On Her Majesty's Secret Service,* is known for its 360° panoramic view, extending from the Jura to the Black Forest and taking in the Mönch, Jungfrau, and Eiger. For information on departures, phone 036/23-14-44.

Once at Schilthorn you can enjoy a meal in the restaurant Piz Gloria, a revolving restaurant that in less than an hour will give you a view of Mont Blanc, the Bernese Alps, and the heart of Switzerland. The Schilthorn summit is the start of the world's longest downhill ski race.

A SPORTS CENTER: Considered a model sports facility throughout the Bernese Oberland, the alpine **Sports Center** (Sportzentrum) (tel. 036/55-16-16) is a modern building with an indoor pool, a lounge, a snackbar, an outdoor skating rink, a tourist information office, a toy library, and a children's playroom. There are facilities for playing squash, tennis, and curling, as well as a solarium, a sauna, and exercise classes. Hotel owners subsidize the operation, tacking on the charges to your hotel bill. Supplements are charged of 10F ($6.80) per hour for squash, 20F ($13.60) per hour for tennis, 8F ($5.45) per hour for use of the sauna, and 5F ($3.40) per hour for use of the solarium. The facility is usually open daily from 10 a.m. to noon and 2 to 6 p.m., remaining open until 9:30 p.m. Monday, Thursday, and Friday.

RESORT LIVING: Housed in a comfortable adaptation of a chalet, **Hotel Eiger,** CH-3825 Mürren, Switzerland (tel. 036/55-13-31), is two large peak-roofed buildings joined together by a low-lying passageway. The views from many of the windows are spectacular, and the public rooms are warmly decorated. Facilities include a bar, an indoor heated swimming pool (with glass walls looking out onto the snow), a sauna, and a fitness room. Walter and Annelis Stähli–von Allmen are your hosts. They have set three seasons: low, shoulder, and high. Singles begin at 95F ($64.60) daily, peaking at 155F ($105.40), the prices varying with the season. Doubles start at 170F ($115.40), going up to 280F ($190.40). Halfboard is included. All units contain private baths.

Hotel Mürren, CH-3825 Mürren, Switzerland (tel. 036/55-24-24), set in an isolated position near the Sports Center, was once the Palace Hotel, popular with British skiers in the early 20th century. Today, it's a member of the Best Western hotel reservations service. It has a black mansard roof, several sets of indented loggias with wrought-iron balconies, and a modern extension jutting out to one side. The interior is modern, with conservative furniture in the 46 bedrooms. With half board, units rent for 95F ($64.60) to 155F ($105.40) daily in a single, 170F ($115.60) to 280F ($190.40) in a double, depending on the season. The hotel has a restaurant and a bar. Tennis courts are on the grounds. From the hotel, you can follow a set of mountain trails for winter cross-country skiing or summer treks.

Hotel Jungfrau and **Jungfrau Lodge,** CH-3825 Mürren, Switzerland (tel. 036/55-28-24), consist of a 19th-century four-story building with stucco and brick walls, green-shuttered gables, and a small-scale peaked tower, plus a comfortable annex constructed in 1965. Both buildings have an invitingly modern decor inside, with open fireplaces, conversational groupings of armchairs, and a shared wood-ceilinged dining room. The bedrooms in both buildings are sunny and appealing (those in the newer unit cost more). A terrace offers lunch outdoors even with masses of snow on the ground, and a bar serves après-ski drinks until late at night. Admission to the hotels' sports center is included in the price, and there are facilities for swimming, squash, and ice skating. Rooms in the main hotel come with and without private bath. With half board included, the price scale can begin at only 65F ($44.20) in a single going up to as high as 100F ($68), the latter the winter price with private bath. Likewise, doubles on the same arrangement can cost from 130F ($88.40) to 200F ($136) daily. All units in the lodge, which has larger accommodations, contain a private bath. With half board included, the single rate ranges from 90F ($61.20) in summer to a high of 120F ($81.60) per day in winter. Two persons, also paying for half board, are charged from 180F ($122.40) to 240F ($163.20), depending on the season.

Hotel Alpenruh, CH-3825 Mürren, Switzerland (tel. 036/55-10-55). Its interior is more plush and elegant than its chalet façade implies. Owned and operated by the same company that operates the aerial cable cars to the top of the Schilthorn's Piz Gloria, this is very much a company hotel run along modern corporate lines. Part of the establishment's appeal lies in the fact that it was an older building that was meticulously upgraded in 1986 into the premier hotel of town without sacrificing any of its small-scale charm. Therefore, you get a combination of antique furniture and contemporary. Each of the 26 bedrooms has pine paneling, modern baths, plush carpeting, TV, phone, radio, and mini-bar. Facing south, most have balconies with views over the steep gorge of the valley. The highest prices are charged in winter when half board costs 210F ($142.80) to 240F ($163.20) daily in a double and 105F ($71.40) to 120F ($81.60) in a single. Otherwise, the single half-board rate ranges from 75F ($51) to 120F ($81.60) daily, the double tariff going from 150F ($102) to 210F ($142.80). The hotel is conveniently close to the cable-car terminus, near the most congested (and charming) section of the village.

Hotel Blumental, CH-3825 Mürren, Switzerland (tel. 036/55-18-26), is a gracefully decorated family-run hotel with an exterior crafted of a masonry base and a weathered clapboard upper section. The interior has lots of timbers and various areas of exposed stonework and paneling that combine into a pleasing and unpretentious whole. The von Allmen family, who have innkeeper relatives all over the region, are the owners. The wooden walls of the bedrooms contrast tastefully with the bedcovers. All units have private baths, showers, radios, and mini-bars. There is a wide scale of prices depending on the season, ranging from 65F ($44.20) to 110F ($74.80) daily in a single, from 130F ($88.40) to 200F ($136) in a double, including half board. Guests have free use of the squash court, tennis court, swimming pool, and, in winter, the skating and curling facilities.

Sporthotel Edelweiss, CH-3825 Mürren, Switzerland (tel. 036/55-26-12), is boxy and flat-roofed, with red shutters and several Swiss flags fluttering against the white balconies. The architecture may not be inspiring, but the view is. The sun terrace is built over an extremely steep dropoff. Except for Swiss engineering, there might not be a hotel here at all. When you're not overcoming your vertigo on the terrace, you can drink in a modern attractive bar or eat in an alpine dining room. Mrs. Affentranger, who obviously isn't bothered by heights, is your hostess. The place has a folksy, slightly kitschy decor, dating from 1927. All 26 simple rooms have radios, mini-bars, and phones. Most also have private baths. The highest half-board tariffs are in effect in winter and from July 8 to August 25, when singles pay 80F ($54.40) to 100F ($68) daily, depending on the plumbing, and two persons are charged from 160F ($108.80) to 200F ($136). Otherwise, half-board rates, again depending on the plumbing, range from 55F ($37.40) to 75 ($51) daily in a single, 110F ($74.80) to 180F ($122.40) in a double.

RESORT DINING: The best food at the resort is said to be offered at the already recommended **Hotel Eiger Restaurant** (tel. 036/55-13-31). In an inviting ambience with spectacular views of the mountains, guests can enjoy hot food served daily from 11:30 a.m. to 9:30 p.m. During the day your best bet is to order a "quick menu" costing only 15F ($10.20) and served from 11:30 a.m. to 6:30 p.m. At night, in a more festive atmosphere, you can enjoy delectable dishes and fondues along with an international range of specialties. All main dishes, if you wish, are served with Rösti. Many skiers at night want a fondue, and both the classic chinoise or bourguignonne versions are served here. There is also a children's menu. A set dinner costs from 30F ($20.40), and you are more likely to spend 45F ($30.60) ordering à la carte. For dessert try if featured either the vodka sherbet or else an iced soufflé Grand Marnier.

Restaurant Im Gruebi, Hotel Jungfrau (tel. 036/55-28-24). Popular, attractive, and graced with a sun-flooded outdoor terrace, this restaurant is on the lobby level of the Hotel Jungfrau. Most of the tables are within a large hexagonal room with views of both the mountains and the terminus of many of the village's ski slopes. Food is served from noon to 2 p.m. and from 7 to 9 p.m. daily. A special lunch is offered for 28F ($19.05), a set dinner going for 28F also. You can also order from the à la carte menu at an average price of 45F ($30.60). The chef specializes in flambé dishes, including a peppersteak. His other specialties are prepared only for two persons, including a Chateaubriand, a New York steak, a rack of lamb flavored with herbs, and veal filets with fruits in a cognac sauce, and, of course, the classic fondue bourguignonne. A wide choice of appetizers, including hors d'oeuvres, both hot and cold, as well as soups and salads are offered.

Restaurant Schilthorn, Piz Gloria (tel. 036/55-21-41). Its setting is so dramatic, and its architecture so futuristic, that it's been used as a movie location of a James Bond film. It was built at a staggering expense atop one of the region's most dizzying heights, the Schilthorn. Not open during blizzards, it has a 360-degree view and an outdoor sun terrace where untanned newcomers can develop a serious sunburn if they expose their face to the unfiltered sunlight for too long. The restaurant opens every day in time for the arrival of the morning's first cable car. This leaves the valley of Stechelberg at 7:25 a.m. The last cable car comes down the mountain, back to Stechelberg, at 5 p.m., so any meals not yet consumed are hurriedly finished by that time. Round-trip passage from Stechelberg to the top costs 35F ($23.80) per person.

The menu is simple, but this far up in the sky you're glad for the offerings. You might begin with one of the rib-sticking soups such as Hungarian goulash, or else a cold plate, perhaps air-dried meat from the Grisons. Hot meals are also featured, including a daily special, but you can also order more elaborate fare, including sirloin steak Café de Paris and veal steak in a mushroom cream sauce with noodles. Meals cost from 18F ($12.25). There's also a special plate for children.

Hotel Alpenruh (tel. 036/55-10-55) is one of the finest hotel dining rooms in Mürren, welcoming outsiders. It has an attractive alpine theme, serving hot meals daily from 12:30 a.m. to 2 p.m. and from 6:30 to 9:30 p.m. In season, reservations are important. The room opens onto wide panoramic terraces with views of the surrounding mountains. The menu, for such a small hotel, is large and continental, costing from 45F ($30.60) and up for a meal. You might begin with half a dozen snails in herb butter or else agnolotti flavored with basil. Main courses are likely to range from chicken breast Maryland to lamb cutlet Marie-Louise. The steaks, especially the tenderloin with morels, are delectable. Fish courses often include sole Colbert and salmon steak in a tarragon cream sauce. Desserts include fresh pineapple with a caramel mousse or a gratin of kiwi and oranges. There is also a very respectable wine carte.

As you arrive at the cable-car station, you'll see the **Taverne** (tel. 036/55-10-55), which is under the auspices of the neighboring Hotel Alpenruh. Behind a pinewood alpine façade, it serves food from 11 a.m. to 11 p.m. daily, while diners take in a view overlooking the village and mountains. Fondues are served to two persons, and you can also order three different kinds of pizzas. If you want more substantial fare, try either the grilled pork or the rumpsteak. Dinner costs from 12F ($8.15).

APRÈS SKI: This activity is very informal in Mürren, taking place for the most part in the hotels previously recommended. One of the most popular is the **Hotel**

Eiger (tel. 036/55-13-31), which has the rustic, dark, a bit rowdy, and almost invariably overcrowded **Tächi-Bar,** one of the resort's best-known après-ski bars. Children are never allowed inside after 9 p.m. Open daily from 5 p.m. to 2:30 a.m., it has a small stage upon which a visiting band usually performs. Entrance is free. Champagne by the glass or flambéed alpine coffee cost from 11F ($7.50) each.

One of the popular nightspots in town is the **Inferno-Bar** at the previously recommended Hotel Mürren (tel. 036/55-24-24). Its musical choices range from mild punk to rock 'n' roll to 1960s pop classics, which the young Europeans somewhat myopically refer to as "retro." It's open every night except Monday from 8:30 p.m. to 2:30 a.m. There's no cover charge. Long drinks inside cost from 11F ($7.50) each. If you're hungry, you can order cheese platters and steaming bowls of goulash soup.

Bliemlichaller, Hotel Blumental (tel. 036/55-18-26), within the cellar of a previously recommended hotel, is carefully insulated so that the disco music doesn't rise to the upper floors. This is a rustic disco/bar and lots of noise. There's no cover charge, but you can quickly run up a bill at the rambling bar if you're a drinker. It's open in winter only from 9 p.m. to 2 a.m. daily. If you're hungry, a limited menu features entrecôtes and cutlets for 12F ($8.15) to 17F ($11.55) per platter.

Finally, several mountain chalet restaurants have fondue and raclette parties at the height of the winter ski season.

6. WENGEN

A resort village at the foot of that monstrous trio, the Mönch, the Jungfrau, and the Eiger, Wengen (pronounced *Ven*-ghen) lies on a sheltered sunny terrace high above the Lauterbrunnen Valley, at about 4,160 feet above sea level. One of the most chic and best-equipped ski and mountain resorts in the Bernese Oberland, it has 30 hotels in all price categories as well as 500 apartments and chalets to rent.

The ski area around Wengen is highly developed, including Männlichen, Kleine Scheidegg, Lauberhorn, and Eigergletscher, with three mountain railways, two aerial cableways, one gondola, five chair lifts, nine ski lifts, and three practice lifts. In the center of the village is a beginner's slope, along with a Swiss ski school. Other facilities and sports include an open-air and an artificial ice rink, a curling hall with two rinks, cross-country skiing (a 7¼-mile track at the bottom of the valley), sledging, an indoor swimming pool, glacier skiing, and a day nursery.

Drawn to its location not far from the Matterhorn, the English were the first to popularize the resort after World War I, although its history as a resort goes back to the 1830s, when the International Lauberhorn Ski Race was established. Some parts of it still look like the farm community it was back in the 19th century; however, the main artery of town is filled with cafés, shops, and restaurants, most of which are geared to tourists, the most celebrated of whom is Robert Redford, a frequent visitor.

No cars are allowed in Wengen, but even so there's a lot of activity from service vehicles and those electric carts that carry luggage from the train station to the hotels. If you're driving, you can go as far as Lauterbrunnen, where there's a large covered garage. From there, you board a cog railway for the 15-minute ride to Wengen, a ticket costing 8F ($5.45).

Skiers in winter take the cableway to **Männlichen** at 7,335 feet, which opens onto a panoramic vista of the treacherous Eiger. From here, there is no direct run back to Wengen; however, skiers can avail themselves of a 4½-mile run to Grindelwald (see below).

Before heading back to Wengen by rail, many visitors linger long enough in the Lauterbrunnen Valley to take some excursions. One is to **Trümmelbach**

Falls, plunging in five powerful cascades through a gorge. You can take an elevator (bring a raincoat) through the rock to a series of galleries. At the end of the line you come to the bottom of a wall into which the upper fall descends. These falls can be visited from the first of April until the end of October daily from 8 a.m. to 6 p.m. for an admission of 6F ($4.10) for adults, 3F ($2.05) for children 10 to 16. It takes about 45 minutes to reach them on foot. For information, call 036/55-32-32.

You might also want to seek out the **Staubbach Waterfall.** An early visitor, Lord Byron, compared this fall to the "tail of the pale horse ridden by Death in the Apocalypse." Above Lauterbrunnen, these falls plunge nearly 1,000 feet, a sheer drop.

WHERE TO STAY: The only five-star hotel in Wengen, **Parkhotel Beausite,** CH-3823 Wengen, Switzerland (tel. 036/56-51-61), sits like a crown on the top of a hill overseeing the action going on down below. The celebrity favorite, the hotel has hosted thousands upon thousands of visitors. In 1893, it consisted of a main structure painted a buttercup yellow with a vaguely Georgian architectural styling. Its continuing popularity has led to the creation of another two additions, plus a heated indoor swimming pool with a Finnish sauna. It was renovated and modernized in 1983.

Rooms come in a wide range of styles here, but for the most part they are spacious and certainly comfortable. The accommodations have balconies opening onto views of the village and the surrounding alpine vista. The highest tariffs are in effect in winter, when half-board arrangements cost from 180F ($122.80) to 230F ($156.40) daily in a single and from 350F ($238) to 450F ($306) per day in a double. In summer, half board costs 135F ($91.80) to 200F ($136) daily in a single, 260F ($176.80) to 370F ($251.60) in a double. The dining room becomes a social center in season (dozens of the guests are repeat visitors who always demand their favorite table). With continental chic, the tuxedo-clad waiters will cook your eggs at breakfast the way you like them right at your table. In the evening, the five-course table d'hôte dinners are the finest served in Wengen. The Rondo serves fondues and snacks.

Sunstar Hotel, CH-3823 Wengen, Switzerland (tel. 036/56-51-11), is a four-star hostelry right in the center of Wengen. Margrit and Erich Leemann are the congenial hosts of this many-balconied hotel, consisting of a new and an old wing. Each of the wooden balustrades around the weatherproof windows has a medallion carved in an alpine design, repeated in the ceiling of one of the salons. The salon is filled with leather-and-metal chairs and rustic timbers outlined against the white stucco walls, plus a wood-burning fireplace. An oval bar area is a relaxing place for a few drinks, while an indoor swimming pool with panoramic views of the snow-covered mountains allows year-round use. The hotel has a sauna, a solarium, and a high-quality dining room. The well-furnished and comfortable bedrooms, which vary widely in style, all with private baths, cost from 109F ($74.10) to 168F ($114.25) daily in a single and from 194F ($131.90) to 320F ($217.60) in a double, including half board.

Hotel Regina, CH-3823 Wengen, Switzerland (tel. 036/55-15-12), might be called the dowager empress of all the hotels at the resort. It stands near the cog railway station in an embellished Victorian elephant of a building, with great amounts of charm and dozens of balconies facing the valley and the alpine sunshine. Guido Meyer, the owner, has been known to arrange unusual concerts for his guests. Once when I was there a group of high school students from Oklahoma was giving a concert on the front lawn. One of the public rooms has a baronial carved stone fireplace usually blazing in winter. There's also a disco with live bands and an attractive bar. Meals are varied and interesting, with fixed-price menus providing a choice from a large buffet of hot and cold appetizers, soups from a sideboard, and a dessert buffet, as well as several different main dishes. A

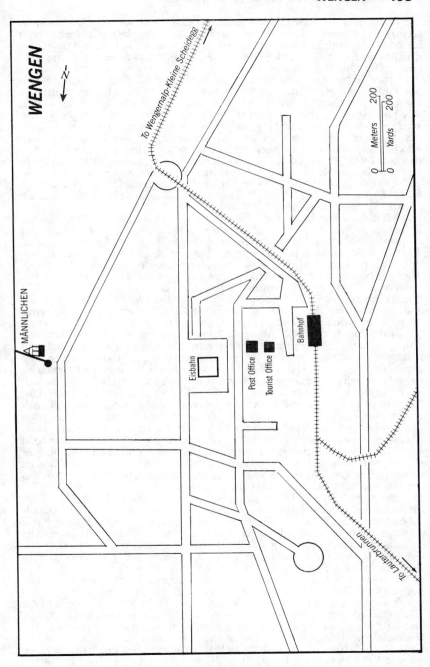

la carte meals are also offered. This hotel, like all the others, is mobbed in winter, so make reservations during the season. There's a wide range of prices: in high season singles with bath cost from 106F ($72.10) to 135F ($91.80) daily, and doubles go for 208F ($141.45) to 266F ($180.90), doubles, including half board. The hotel closes in May.

Hotel Silberhorn, CH-3823 Wengen, Switzerland (tel. 036/56-51-31). Some of its accommodations are privately owned by absentee investors, and most of its two lowest floors are devoted to dining and drinking facilities. In fact, this hotel contains the single most concentrated collection of nightspots in Wengen. Despite the fact that it's vastly better known for its entertainment facilities, the hotel offers about 75 comfortably modern accommodations, 20 of which contain kitchenettes. The hotel is composed of a simple Victorian-era core (built in 1893) with major additions completed by the early 1980s. It's easy to recognize because of its position close to the train station and because of its dozens of wood-sided balconies. Depending on the season, single rooms range from 83F ($56.45) to 142F ($96.55) daily and doubles from 150F ($102) to 268F ($182.25), doubles, with half board included.

Victoria-Lauberhorn, CH-3823 Wengen, Switzerland (tel. 036/56-51-51). Many-gabled, venerable, and centrally located in the center of Wengen, this frequently modernized hotel contains an array of dining and drinking facilities. These include a pizzeria pub, a crêperie, a popular bar (the Parasol), and an outdoor café that seems to do business in any season, whenever the sun is shining. The cozy bedrooms are decorated in a bewildering array of styles, ranging from modern to "evergreen" (mountain style). Each contains a private bath, TV, phone, and a radio. With half board included, singles cost 142F ($96.55) daily, and doubles go for 150F ($102) to 268F ($182.25). The actual price within this range depends on the exposure of your room and the season when you arrive.

Hotel Eiger, CH-3823 Wengen, Switzerland (tel. 036/55-11-31). The walls and ceilings of this attractive hotel back of the train station are covered with rustic timbers or planking, giving a warmly decorated gemütlich ambience. The overall impression is one of well-padded comfort in an environment conducive to outdoor sports. The entire facility was constructed and renovated by the Karl Fuchs family in the center of town in 1981. The bedrooms are spacious and for the most part attractively decorated in beiges and browns with private baths, balconies, phones, radios, TV, and double glazing on the windows. Rates are from 70F ($47.60) to 130F ($88.40) per person daily, depending on the season and the exposure of the room. Some family apartments are also available. The hotel has a regular modern dining room with large picture windows offering views of the Jungrau massif and the Lauterbrunnen Valley. However, more inviting is La Cabana grill room, which is recommended separately. Its Arvenstube also merits a separate recommendation on the après-ski rounds.

Falken Hotel, CH-8323 Wengen, Switzerland (tel. 036/56-51-21). Its gabled roof and cream-colored façade were built as part of the resort's second-oldest hotel in 1895. Dozens of others followed quickly afterward, although this might be the only one which consciously retains the old-fashioned charm of its original interiors. Very much a family hotel, it's owned and managed by the Cova family. You register at a desk within a rambling sitting room filled with Beidermeier sofas, Oriental rugs, and dated furniture. Don't overlook the companionable bar in one corner, which has remained intact for so long that it now boasts a well-oiled patina and lots of turn-of-the-century charm.

Take the elevator (installed in 1908, the first one in Wengen) to one of the 50 simple bedrooms. Most have private baths, phones, mini-bars, and balconies. You'll often find dado paneling, old tiny sinks, and a kind of never-renovated Victorian-era rusticity. In the adjacent chalet annex are ten additional rooms, none of which has a private bath. With half board included, single rooms range from 58F ($39.44) to 134F ($91.10) daily, and doubles cost 116F ($78.90) to

260F ($176.80), depending on the accommodation and the season. The hotel lies a brisk five-minute uphill walk from the railway station. It is closed in November.

Hotel Eden, CH-3823 Wengen, Switzerland (tel. 036/55-16-34), is the economy oasis of Wengen. What it lacks in facilities it makes up for in homelike comfort. It stands amid a nest of guesthouses and private chalets, above the commercial center of town. A symmetrical villa with red shutters, it's run by Kerstin Bucher and a cooperative and businesslike staff. This is one of the few hotels that remains open all year. Most guests opt for half board, which is served in a simple modern room with few frivolous touches. There's a small TV lounge, plus a tiny Jägerstübli favored by kibbitzing groups of local residents and chalet guests for Swiss wine and specialties. The hotel contains only 30 beds; only six of the rooms have private baths or showers. Depending on the season, rooms without bath rent for 48F ($32.65) to 58F ($39.45) per person daily, those with bath costing 60F ($40.80) to 75F ($51) per person, with half board included.

Hotel Hirschen, CH-3823 Wengen, Switzerland (tel. 036/55-15-44). Simple, very pleasant, and inexpensive, this family-run hotel lies above the town, with ski slopes passing a few steps from the front door. You can't be shy about registering here—just approach the bar inside the restaurant and ask one of the personnel if there's an available room. These rent for 40F ($27.20) to 75F ($51) daily, single or double occupancy, depending on the season and the plumbing, with breakfast included. You'll recognize the hotel by its sheathing of ornate cedar shingles.

WHERE TO DINE: It would be difficult to grow bored with the restaurants offered by the Hotel Eiger, led by **Restaurant Arvenstube/Restaurant La Cabana** (tel. 036/55-11-31). Among them, my favorite is the Arvenstube. Sheathed in glowing pinewood panels, and staffed by a polite crew of vested or dirndl-clad employees, it remains open every day from 7 a.m. to midnight, with lunch served from 11:30 a.m. to 2 p.m., dinner from 6:30 to 9 p.m. A three-course fixed-price dinner costs 35F ($23.80), and à la carte meals go for 40F ($27.20). The bill of fare might include smoked trout with horseradish, air-dried alpine beef, smoked breast of goose, Bernese-style beef with mushrooms, filet of fera (a lake fish), veal steak Alfredo with morels, fondues, and a Valais-style braserade of beef cooked on a skewer by means of a small flame brought directly to your table.

La Cabane Restaurant is a more formal option. Sheathed in pine and filled with glamorously rustic accessories, it's the most prestigious restaurant within the hotel. Your meal might begin with a tempting selection of hors d'oeuvres, including some unusual selections such as cold game pie in a cumberland sauce or smoked goose breast. There is also a big choice of salads. Specialties of the chef include a mixed grill Eiger, which is your choice of the finest cuts for grilling. Some dishes are flambéed at your table. A rib roast of lamb is prepared after an old recipe of Provence and dedicated to Cézanne, and Texas or T-bone steak is served with a choice of sauces, including pepper or barbecue. Meals cost from 55F ($37.40). At lunch you can dine considerably lighter and less expensively, from 25F ($17). They serve Swiss meals with Rösti, various Swiss sausages, clear and cream soups, omelets, and sandwiches, along with plates for children. Food is served daily from 11 a.m. to 2 p.m. and 6 to 9 p.m.

Falsenkeller (tel. 036/56-51-31) is the most elegant restaurant at the Hotel Silberhorn. This establishment has many dining and drinking facilities (see "Après Ski"), but its Falsenkeller offers the finest food. The winter menu tends to be very sophisticated. I like their policy of featuring the cuisine of a different nation on various nights of the week (of course, that means the chefs have to be mighty versatile). For example, on my latest visit, the Grand Menu Russe at 40F ($27.20) per person evoked a cold Siberian night with its good, hearty food.

Against a medieval decor with stone walls, you can order elegant continental fare, including many grills and fish dishes. You might begin with a cream-of-snail soup, then follow with perhaps strips of beef filet in a beetroot sauce, veal kidneys simmered in chablis, or medallions of beef with vodka (back to Russia again). A Saturday night gourmet menu goes for 85F ($57.80) per person, and a Délices de Neptune buffet on Friday night is 45F ($30.60) per person. Most à la carte dinners cost from 45F ($30.60) but could go much higher. Save room for dessert, perhaps crêpes suzette, parfait Grand Marnier, or the prune sherbet with prune liqueur. Service is nightly from 7 to 10 in winter only.

Hotel Bernerhof Restaurant (tel. 036/55-27-21) is an old family favorite, and is, in fact, run by a family, the Schweizers. There's a bar with a rustic alpine theme near the entrance for snacks and drinks. It fills up in the early evening with beer drinkers returning from the slopes. In back is a better appointed dining room where the business of eating is approached with dedicated seriousness. Hearty alpine grub is served from 11 a.m. to 10 p.m. daily. Pause at the door of this old-fashioned family hotel built of wood with wine-red shutters and check out the action in the trout tank. Raclette, as you can tell by the smell, is served nightly, as is fondue. Several Italian dishes are featured, including spaghetti. If you didn't go for trout (the chef prepares it in five different ways), try the perch with almonds. Pork and veal dishes, most often served with a mushroom cream sauce, are invariably featured. Meals begin at 30F ($20.40).

Hotel Hirschen Restaurant (tel. 036/55-15-44) is ideal if you're looking for a quiet retreat at lunch or dinner. At the foot of the slopes, this place is vaguely reminiscent of a secret mountain lodge I once discovered in the wilds of Canada. Its dining room in the rear is decorated with hunting trophies, pewter, wine racks, and imbued with an alpine flavor. Full meals, costing from 25F ($17), are served daily from 11:30 a.m. to 2 p.m. and 6 to 8:45 p.m. At night they feature the house special, a galgenspiess, which is filet of beef, veal, and pork flambéed at your table. You might prefer instead filet of breaded pork, rumpsteak Café de Paris, or fondue Bacchus, bourguignonne, or chinoise. A good and hearty lunch is winzerrösti, which is homemade Rösti, a platter covered with country ham, cheese, and a fried egg. You're welcomed by Johannes Abplanalp et famille.

APRÈS SKI: Nightlife, such as it is, begins early here—at sunset. Everybody seemingly turns out to watch the sun set over Wengen. Regardless of where you've seen the sunset before, check out this one. It's spectacular.

Sometimes there's night skiing, torchlit of course, following a raclette party at the Wengenalp, an untamed perch at 6,140 feet at the foot of the glacial slopes of the Jungfrau.

Most of the nighttime diversions take place in the hotels, although little discos come and go, some hardly lasting through a season.

Hotel Silberhorn (tel. 036/56-51-31), offers enough nightlife options to keep a night owl amused for a week. The best known of these is the Tiffany Disco, which stays open every night from 9 p.m. to 2 a.m. Unlike many other late-night spots in Wengen, this one remains open throughout the summer. Entrance is free, but beer costs 11F ($7.50).

A popular pizzeria, where no one minds if you order just a pizza or a full Italian meal, is La Strada. Set into a long and narrow hallway (a miniature thoroughfare between two crowded sections of the ground floor), it serves pizzas and Italian specialties on red-and-white-checked tablecloths. Meals range from 8F ($5.45) to 35F ($23.80) each. Hot food is served every day from 11 a.m. to 11 p.m.

Perhaps the most alluring drinking area is within the Silberhorenhitta, on the street level of the hotel, almost directly in back of the reception area. This is possibly the most rustic bar in town, dimly illuminated, and a favorite of anyone who is appreciative of alpine decor. Open from 11 a.m. to 11 p.m. daily, it might be the most popular après ski place in town, every winter's day just before sundown.

The Silberhornstube serves fondues that cost 16F ($10.90) each, in an appropriately rustic decor. The hotel and all of these nightlife recommendations are closed every year between late April to the end of May and from October 20 to early December.

One haven that is almost certain to draw an action-oriented crowd is the **Carrousel,** in the Hotel Regina (tel. 036/55-15-12). Part of its allure is the unusual groups of musicians that owner Guido Meyer imports from everywhere—from Hungary to Holland to Britain. You'll have to negotiate a maze of hallways and stairs, passing through the large lobby of the hotel to reach it. Once you're there (open hours are from 9 p.m. to 2:30 a.m. in winter only, every night except Sunday), you'll find one of the hottest scenes in Wengen, probably the only one which offers live music. If you're looking for the unusual, this is probably it. Long drinks cost from 11F ($7.50) each. The winter garden, with windows overlooking the village, has been completely rebuilt.

Skiers are reputed for their taste in artfully rustic, consciously simple drinking spots. A good example of this is the almost aggressively plain **Pickel Bar,** within the previously recommended Hotel Eiger (tel. 036/55-11-31). The stand-up bar corresponds to the contours of the trapezoidal-shaped walls, which are covered in a blend of thick unfinished planks and stout timbers. Illuminated by candlelight, the place is open from 4 p.m. to 2 a.m. daily except Monday, in winter only. A medium-size beer costs 3F ($2.05).

KLEINE SCHEIDEGG: A skiing center in the Jungfrau region, Scheidegg lies close to Wengen. A mountain resort, popular in both summer and winter, it stands on a balcony connecting the Grindelwald valley with that of Lauterbrunnen. As mentioned, it's the starting point for the excursion to Jungfraujoch at 11,333 feet. The highest cogwheel railway in the world leaves from here, taking you to "the top of the world." If you board the train in Scheidegg at 8 a.m., you'll get a fare reduction of 25%. Many guests spend the night at one of the Scheidegg hotels to get an early start on this trip. A round trip between Interlaken East and Kleine Scheidegg costs 40.60F ($27.60) per person.

If you're coming from Interlaken, you'll face a difference in altitude of some 10,000 feet. There's a difference of only 4,500 feet between Scheidegg and Jungfraujoch.

In winter there's skiing from door to door, with thousands of yards of downhill skiing. Snow is virtually certain from mid-November until well into May.

In summer, visitors can go hiking, climbing, and rambling. There are no motor cars. The Wengernalp and Jungfrau railways, the Wengen-Männlichen aerial cableway, and the Scheidegg-Lauberhorn chair lift makes hiking routes accessible, and you see not only alpine flora, but most likely ibex, chamois, marmots, or eagles. From your hotel room here you can watch high-altitude ascents and climbing parties.

Food and Lodging

Scheidegg Hotels, CH-3801 Kleine Scheidegg, Switzerland (tel. 036/55-12-12). Since Kleine Scheidegg is little more than a railroad terminus and a handful of Swiss buildings, these hotels stand out, lying at a very high altitude between the massive rocks and the surrounding alps. Skiers love to stay here because of the proximity to the surrounding slopes, but even in summer it's the ultimate in isolated comfort. There are plenty of well-marked paths with spectacular views. This is one of my favorite spots for hill-climbing in summer, especially since the paths are well maintained and follow the safest possible routes. *Warning:* There is little to do here after dark, so expect to retire early after a day of exercise in the Alps. Of course, you can always stop in for a drink at the hotel bar where music is sometimes provided. The director, Heidi von Almen, will answer your questions and be helpful in many ways. Singles cost 85F ($57.80) to 145F ($98.60) daily, while doubles rent for 150F ($102) to 260F ($176.80), depending on the plumbing, the accommodation, and the season. Half board is included in the price. The interior is beautifully decorated with Oriental rugs, comfortable leather chairs, and often blazing fireplaces. The hotel is open June to September and December to April.

7. GRINDELWALD

Set against a backdrop of the Wetterhorn and the towering north face of the Eiger, Grindelwald is both a winter and a summer resort. The altitude of the highest "skiable mountain" is 12,000 feet, a vertical drop of 5,010 feet. There's a total of 22 lifts, gondolas, and mountain railroads. For "intermediate" training before making the long descent, Oberjoch at 8,226 feet is a good point.

Grindelwald is often called the "glacier village." Unlike Wengen and Mürren, which we've already visited, it's the only major resort in the Jungfrau region that can be reached in your automobile. Because of that accessibility, Grindelwald is often overrun with visitors, many of whom come just for the day. The streets can get very crowded.

It's also easy to visit Kleine Scheidegg from here, which is the departure point for the final ascent to the Jungfraujoch by train. From Grindelwald-Grund, where there's parking, you can also take Europe's longest gondola cableway to Männlichen. Along the way you'll have a panoramic view of all the peaks of the Jungfrau. The second-class round-trip fare from Grindelwald-Grund to Männlichen is 36.60F ($24.90).

If you don't drive to Grindelwald, you can take a train from the east station in Interlaken, the Bernese Oberland Railway (BOB), which will take you there in 40 minutes. Grindelwald lies 14 miles from Interlaken.

The **Grindelwald Tourist Office** is at Sportszentrum, Hauptstrasse, CH-3818 Grindelwald (tel. 036/53-12-12). It can be particularly helpful in answering questions about excursions possible in the area (more about this later).

WHERE TO STAY: A good place to stay is **Grand Hotel Regina,** CH-3818 Grindelwald, Switzerland (tel. 036/54-54-55), with an architectural format attractively balanced between the country-style rustic and urban-modern slick. One of the salons is filled with Victorian chairs pulled up around bridge tables, with pieces of sculpture placed in wall niches. The art collection of hotel owner Krebs graces many of the walls with etchings, gouaches, and oil paintings. The hotel is open every year from December to October, offering 120 rooms and several deluxe suites in the chalet-style buildings next door. The bedrooms are comfortable, running the range from rustically masculine to a more subdued format of pink quilts and flowery wallpaper. In low season, rates are 160F ($108.80) daily in a single, 300F ($204) in a double. In high season, singles pay 180F ($122.40) daily, and doubles cost 340F ($231.20). Half board is available for an extra 35F ($23.80) per person per day. The façade of the oldest part of the hotel is designed with an imposing set of turrets capped with red tile. A steel-and-glass low-lying extension houses the large swimming pool and sauna. Another outdoor pool is near the tennis courts. The hotel's disco attracts live bands and groups of happy drinkers.

Hotel Belvedere, CH-3818 Grindelwald (tel. 036/54-54-34), is a special place, offering what is considered *the* most spectacular view in Grindelwald. In addition to other mountains, you'll have a panoramic view of the north face of the Eiger, that famous mountain wall. Some views for a Clint Eastwood film were taken from the terrace of the Belvedere. The hotel rating is four stars, but it could just as well be five—A four-star hotel in Switzerland needs to score 96 points

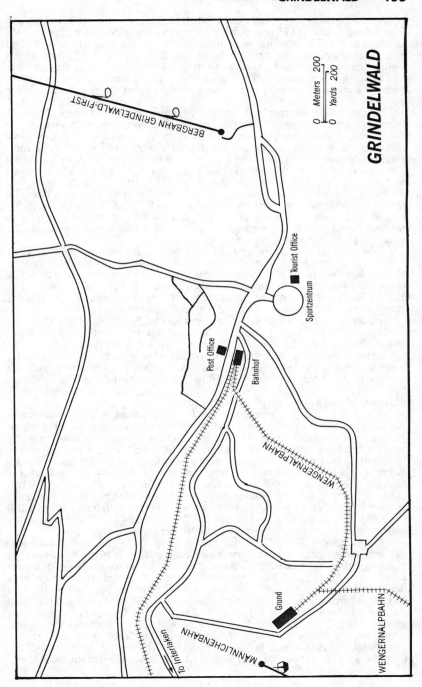

GRINDELWALD

on a government questionnaire and a five-star hotel must tally up to 105 points. The Belvedere scored 115 points, but preferred to keep its four-star status to hold its prices in line. The hotel has extensive public rooms which have been renovated and made cozy and luxurious. Facilities include an indoor pool, along with a Finnish sauna, a bio-health sauna, a sun studio, a massage parlor, a fitness room, and a children's game room. The main lobby is graced with a fireplace and comfortable armchairs, at which guests, tired from a day on the slopes, relax in the evening.

Guests have a choice of standard rooms, junior suites, and suites. The well-furnished, attractive, and comfortable accommodations have such amenities as radios, mini-bars, phones, private baths, TV, room safes, bathrobes, and balconies opening onto that view already mentioned. For most of January and in summer, singles range from 80F ($54.40) to 110F ($74.80) daily, with doubles costing 146F ($99.30) to 190F ($129.20). In winter prices rise to 95F ($64.60) to 120F ($81.60) daily in a single and 176F ($119.70) to 230F ($156.40) in a double. Junior suites are priced at about 50F ($34) per room extra per day. The most lavish suites in the house cost from 400F ($272) to 500F ($340) daily for two to six persons. A well-conceived breakfast buffet is included. Guests who take half board get not only the buffet but a six-course dinner that evening, all for only 25F ($17) per person extra per day.

The hotel offers free parking and has a lovely garden in front of the house. It is only a five-minute walk from the center of the resort, and in winter has one of the best locations because of its easy access to the mountain railway systems. The owner, Urs Hauser, is most hospitable and often goes skiing with his guests. The Hauser family has been running the hotel for three generations, and their clients always mention their very helpful and personal attention.

Hotel Sunstar & Adler, CH-3818 Grindelwald, Switzerland (tel. 036/54-54-17), occupies a tranquil setting with a magnificent view of the surrounding mountains, the First and the Kleine Scheidegg. In 1983, the Adler Hotel joined the well-known Sunstar Hotel in Grindelwald and now has better-furnished and more spacious accommodations, often with balconies. The addition is built in a chalet style and harmoniously nestled into its rural surroundings. The buildings have a connecting passage on the ground level and make a happy union of modern comfort and a lively, easygoing atmosphere.

The decor inside is ornamented with Oriental carpets, wood furniture, and low-slung sofas with views of the stone fireplace or the mountains, all of which give an inviting warm reception to summer and winter visitors alike. In chilly weather, log-burning fires make for a cozy atmosphere. The bar area is popular in the evening, as is a tavern restaurant with rustic decor. The hotel has an indoor swimming pool, a sauna, and a solarium. In summer, rooms with breakfast cost 86F ($58.50) to 118F ($80.25) daily in a single, 115F ($78.20) to 216F ($146.90) in a double. All units contain private baths. Half board is available for another 25F ($17) per person daily. In winter, rates are 110F ($66.70) to 138F ($93.85) daily in a single are 182F ($123.75) to 256F ($174.10) in a double, and half board goes for another 30F ($20.40) per person daily.

Hotel Spinne, CH-3818 Grindelwald, Switzerland (tel. 036/53-23-41). Modern and angular, this well-insulated four-star hotel is better known for its many nightlife and restaurant facilities than it is for its rooms (see "Where to Dine" and "Après Ski"). The hotel is a five-story flat-roofed construction with dark bands encircling it both horizontally and vertically. Each of the 48 units contains a private bath, and singles rent for 80F ($54.40) to 120F ($81.60) daily and doubles for 130F ($88.40) to 200F ($136), depending on the season, plus another 25F ($17) per person daily for half board. On the premises are a sauna, whirlpool, and at least three different restaurants. It is closed in November.

Hotel Weisses Kreuz & Post, CH-3818 Grindelwald, Switzerland (tel. 036/54-54-92), occupies an ideal position, directly on the main square of town, across from the sports center. The Konzett family takes advantage of this by setting up an outdoor café on the sidewalk in front. The façade of the hotel is angular, modern, and layered with balconies, but the interior is far more inviting and pleasant. There's a separately recommended restaurant (see "Where to Dine"), a rooftop sun terrace with a magnificent view of the mountains, and a covered indoor pool. Its disco, the Challi-Bar (see "Après Ski"), is popular after dark. Each of the pleasantly conservative bedrooms has a private bath, radio, and phone. The single rate, depending on the season, ranges from 80F ($54.40) to 110F ($74.80) daily, the double rate going from 140F ($95.20) to 190F ($129.20), including half board.

Parkhotel Schoenegg, CH-3818 Grindelwald, Switzerland (tel. 036/53-18-53). One of my favorite building materials is hewn stone, and this comfortable hotel uses it in some of the public rooms in abundance, along with thick slabs of native wood. The exterior is grandly expansive, with several tiers of balconies with wooden dividers between the sections pertaining to each room. It was established by the Stettler family in 1890, and is still under their wing. Many of the local ski runs terminate at the hotel, while a ski lift to the ski school is close to the front door. In winter the hotel gives fondue parties for its guests in the basement bar area, the Gydis-Bar, the oldest in Grindelwald, dating from the 1940s. A swimming pool, fitness room, sauna, and massage are offered. Singles cost 75F ($51) to 105F ($71.40) daily, and doubles go for 130F ($88.40) to 190F ($129.20), depending on the season and the plumbing. Half board costs an additional 25F ($17) per person daily.

If you stay here, ask managing owner Tom Stettler or his beautiful wife, Christine, to show you their kennels behind the swimming pool and service buildings. Their passion is the breeding of award-winning Siberian huskies. A visit to the kennels, if you like dogs, is an enjoyable albeit muddy experience.

Hostellerie Eiger, CH-3818 Grindelwald, Switzerland (tel. 036/53-21-21), appears as a collection of balconies, each of them on a different plane usually facing the alpine sunshine, in contrasting shades of white stucco and natural wood. The interior is attractive, unpretentious, and simple, with lots of warmly tinted wood, hanging lamps, and strong areas of light and cozy shadow. There are lots of places for drinking and a rendezvous. The Gepsi-Bar often has live music or recently released songs and also "evergreen" (mountain) tunes. Sports facilities include a sauna and a whirlpool, along with two bars and two restaurants, one a steak house. Owned and operated by the Heller family, the establishment charges from 95F ($64.60) to 120F ($81.60) per person daily in a double and from 110F ($74.80) to 135F ($91.80) in a single, depending on the season, plumbing, and exposure. The above prices are per person, with half board included.

Derby Hotel, CH-3818 Grindelwald, Switzerland (tel. 036/54-54-61), run by Peter and Christiane Märkle, is a large adaptation of a mountain chalet, although many modern twists have been given to its traditional architectural forms. This centrally located, three-star hotel has a century of family tradition behind it. The Hotel de la Gare stood here in 1892, but it was torn down and rebuilt several times in its long history. Its latest incarnation stems from 1973. The hotel has two distinct roof areas, both of them peaked at the same angle. Several floors of sliding glass doors give access to the irregularly shaped balconies attached to most of the 70 brightly furnished and pine-paneled bedrooms. All units have their own private baths and showers, with singles costing from 65F ($44.20) to 98F ($66.65) daily and doubles ranging from 110F ($74.80) to 178F ($121.05). Prices depend on the season. For half board, guests are charged another 24F ($16.30) per person extra per day. The interior of the hotel is filled with wood paneling and warmly tinted fabrics. Its drinking and dining facilities are among the best in town. The best is the Föhrenstube (Pine Room), an à la carte restaurant which is elegantly decorated, opening onto the Eiger side. The

Grosses Restaurant is big enough for a banquet, but the Gaststube is more intimate, a place to drink draught beer. The rustic cellar bar, Cava Bar, is one of the preferred rendezvous points on the après-ski circuit.

Hotel Hirschen, CH-3818 Grindelwald, Switzerland (tel. 036/53-27-77). It's a relatively modern building, but its façade is handsome, decorated with richly grained balconies, a row of wrought iron, and boxes of seasonal flowers. This is a three-star, comfortable, budget oasis, attracting people who really like to ski instead of those on the see-and-be-seen circuit. For what it is, and for the price, this is one of the best hotels at the resort. The Bleuer family maintains a popular bowling alley in the cellar, and a respectable dining room as well. Rooms come in a wide array of styles and accessories. With breakfast included, singles cost 60F ($40.80) to 85F ($57.80) daily, doubles going for 100F ($68) to 144F ($97.90). Half board is another 22F ($14.95) per person per day. All rooms have toilets, phones, and radios, but several lack private baths or showers.

Sport Jungfrau, CH-3818 Grindelwald, Switzerland (tel. 036/53-13-41) is an attractive chalet-style hotel at the entrance to the village, three minutes from the train station. The hotel has been modernized over the years and has a new wing built alongside. There's a bar next to the à la carte dining room and a lounge where you can relax with a drink and gaze out at the north face of the magnificent Eiger. The café/terrace at the front of the hotel has the same views of the mountain. You'll find the shops and entertainment facilities of the resort, as well as the public swimming pool, all within easy reach of the hotel. The 55-bed hotel is open all year, charging from 60F ($40.80) to 85F ($57.90) in a single, depending on the season and the plumbing. Doubles cost 96F ($65.30) to 130F ($88.40). Half board costs another 20F ($13.60) per person in any season.

Central Hotel Wolter, CH-3818 Grindelwald, Switzerland (tel. 036/53-22-33). It's more modern and boxy than many other hotels in town, but its central location just a few steps from several much more expensive hotels makes it attractive. There's a popular outdoor café terrace a few steps from the traffic, near the hotel's front entrance, a substantial restaurant on the ground floor, and a well-furnished salon one floor above the street level. This is furnished like something in a private home with armchairs, a few antiques, and tuckaway bar. You'll have to climb a flight of stairs to reach the reception area. Unlike many other hotels in Grindelwald, this one remains open all year. The simply decorated modern bedrooms are very clean and, at their best, cozy. With breakfast included, depending on the season, singles cost 65F ($44.20) to 98F ($66.65) daily, and doubles go for 110F ($74.80) to 178F ($121.05). Half board can be arranged for an additional 24F ($16.30) per person per day.

WHERE TO DINE: What's probably the best restaurant in Grindelwald, the **Grill Room** at the previously recommended Grand Hotel Regina (tel. 036/54-54-55) lies one floor below lobby level. This is a formal and elegant version of a hunter's stube, with immaculate napery, scattered hunting trophies, and formally correct service. A maître d' will offer you separate meat and fish menus, each of which is surprisingly detailed. Full meals cost from 60F ($40.80) but could go much higher. Representative menu items include poached eel with crayfish tails, French snails, two different preparations of salmon, turbot, Russian caviar, steak tartare, Long Island sirloin steak, scampi flambéed with Chivas Regal, and aiguillettes of veal in a saffron sauce. The place is open only in winter and only for dinner from 7 to 11 p.m. daily. Reservations are a good idea, especially since from time to time the entire dining room is given over to conferences.

Rôtisserie, Hotel Spinne (tel. 036/53-23-41). Its elegant alpine decor focuses mainly on a big-windowed view of the mountains and lots of wooden trim. During warm weather, doors open onto a wide flower-dotted terrace, set up with tables and chairs. At this gourmet restaurant, which adjoins an Italian dining room, the Mercato (also recommended), you don't have to make decisions, as the chef nightly prepares two different set menus. One is called a menu dégustation, costing 65F ($44.50), the other is "le menu surprise," for those who want to be really daring and don't mind spending 85F ($57.80) per person. If you like to make your own decisions, you can order from the à la carte, costing from 60F ($40.80). You might begin with snails en cocotte, a terrine of foie gras with cognac, or else one of the good-tasting soups (my favorite is a soup made with morels). The fish and meat dishes are usually delectable, including filets of sea bass, lobster in the style of the chef, and salmon stuffed with leeks and tarragon. Desserts tend to be elaborate and include a sabayon with marsala or a "black and white" chocolate mousse. The sorbet du jour is the choice of many diners, who can enjoy all this fine food only at night from 6:30 to 10:30 daily. On the other hand, summer visitors can patronize the Garden Restaurant, with its elaborate salad buffets and specialties from the charcoal grill.

Ristorante Mercato, Hotel Spinne (tel. 036/53-23-41). Its decor—much like that of an Italian pizzeria—gives no hint at the really fine Italian food whose seasonings have nothing less than panache. The wooden ceiling and the alpine views seem an unusual foil but the Italian food is good, at times evoking memories of some of the finer dishes you may have had if you've visited Italy. Naturally, the chef does a classic minestrone, but you may want to select antipasto instead, perhaps Parma ham, which is always magnificent, or else a classic Italian salad, frutti di mare, or fruits of the sea. On my latest rounds, the chef offered eight kinds of pasta, everything from agnolotti alla panna to the more common spaghetti with clam sauce. Main dishes include saltimbocca or osso buco. In addition you can order a wide variety of pizzas. A set menu is offered for 35F ($23.80) or else you can select from the à la carte, with meals beginning at 30F ($20.40). It's open daily from 11 a.m. to 11:30 p.m.

Steakhouse, Hostellerie Eiger (tel. 036/53-21-21). There's a darkly rustic rectangular bar (the Gepsi) set near its entrance; the rambling restaurant stretches out behind it. To reach it, climb a flight of stairs to the hotel's second floor. The restaurant is open only from 5 p.m. to midnight Sunday to Thursday, until 1 a.m. on Friday and Saturday. In summer, it's closed on Monday. Within a milieu of stone walls, half-timbering, and barnyard accessories whose origin lies somewhere between the Alps and the Rocky Mountains, you can enjoy what might be the best beefsteaks in town. Most dishes come in "midi" and "maxi" portions, suitable for most appetites. Many cuts are of U.S. beef as well as the other countries featured. Specialties include steak au poivre, filet, veal steak, Chateaubriand, rack of lamb, pork steak with calvados, julienne of veal with mushroom cream sauce, cheese crêpes, and a limited fish menu. Full meals cost from 40F ($27.20). Live music is presented in a wide array of musical styles from 8 p.m. to midnight.

Restaurant Weisses Kreuz, Hotel Weisses Kreuz (tel. 036/54-54-92), is filled with such alpine accents as pine paneling. The matronly looking waitresses will probably be wearing dirndls. Don't be afraid to explore this restaurant before you select a seat. Concealed in a hideaway corner is the most impressive and attractive room, the Challi-Stube. There, the ceiling and paneling are especially well crafted and intricate. During the day, you might order a simple menu with soup for 18F ($12.25), served daily from 11:30 a.m. to 1:30 p.m., but at dinner from 6:30 to 9:30 p.m. the fare tends to be more elaborate and more expensive. You are likely to spend from 40F ($27.20) then. The menu's in English, and you can peruse it at leisure, selecting perhaps smoked salmon followed by oxtail soup. Then it's on to the steak and pork selections or else one of the main course fish dishes, including blue trout sautéed in butter. Traditional Swiss dishes are offered, including sliced veal Zuricher style with Rösti. Specialties are the two classic fondues, chinoise and bourguignonne, either served only for two persons.

Restaurant Alte Post (tel. 036/53-11-43). Reeking of Swiss tradition, and conveniently located on the sloping main road above the commercial center of the resort, this pleasant restaurant is appropriately sheathed in pinewood paneling. It opens at 8 a.m. for coffee, and remains open until after dinner for drinks and snacks. Hot meals are served from 11:30 a.m. to 2 p.m., dinner from 6:30 to 9 p.m. every day except Wednesday, when it's closed. Full meals cost from 40F ($27.20), and might include a terrine of morels, smoked filet of trout, asparagus with air-dried ham, filet steak with green peppers, scallop of veal Cordon Bleu, and lamb or pork cutlets.

Restaurant Sportzentrun (tel. 036/53-33-66). Except for its rows of big windows, which look down on both the indoor swimming pool and an enormous ice hockey rink, this restaurant looks like many other rustically timbered Swiss establishments. It's contained within the modern Sports Center in the middle of the resort. Many diners prefer it because of the almost guaranteed visual distraction of some kind of athletic event going on within your immediate view. The establishment opens early in the morning, remaining open throughout the day for snacks and drinks. Hot meals are served noon to 2 p.m. and 6 until a relatively early closing at 7 p.m. Throughout the day, you can have a main dish with salad for 12F ($8.15), then follow it with an elaborate dessert. During mealtime, you can order full meals from 35F ($23.80). The fare may include a wide range of Swiss specialties, including cheese fondue, pork, veal, and beef dishes. It is open daily.

DAYTIME ACTIVITIES: For a close look at a glacier ravine, you'll find a gallery at the base of the Lower Grindelwald glacier that takes you on a trip for more than half a mile past glacier mills, striation, and marble to the glacier tongue. The ravine gallery is easy to reach on foot or by car up to the entrance. Bus service is available, and there's a car park and restaurant.

A visit to the **Blue Ice Grotto** may give you an uneasy feeling, as it requires entering the Upper Grindelwald glacier that is currently experiencing a great deal of movement. However, I was assured that it's perfectly safe, and I found the grotto, which gives the visitor a direct encounter with the glacier world, to be worth the visit. The blue ice walls of the grotto, almost 150 feet deep, are unforgettable. The grotto is open from the middle of June till the middle of September.

Other glacier tours are offered, on which you will spend two days traveling from Jungfraujoch on the Aletsch glacier to Lake Marielen to Kuhboden (Valais), with an overnight lodging at the Konkordia cabin. These tours are made from July to the end of September.

An exhibition of Grindelwald history is found in the **Museum of Local Arts and Crafts,** where an alpine cheesery may be visited, as well as a retrospective of mountain climbing and winter sports. The museum is open daily from June until the middle of September and February to April.

The tourist office has two **guided tours** a week from the end of June to the middle of September, free for those who hold a visitor's card, except for the cost of transport. A gamekeeper shows you mountain flora and fauna and an alpine cheesery. For one of these tours, register at the tourist office (tel. 036/53-12-12).

For a further look at the local plant life, I suggest you take a journey along the Grütli forest path, called the **Burglauenen/Grindelwald Nature Trail.** More information on this pleasant and educational tour is available from a brochure you can purchase at the tourist office or at the Burglauenen train station for 2F ($1.35).

For an active holiday to suit your taste and benefit your health, you may want to try **hiking** along with the many diverse Grindelwald paths and mountain trails which are well marked and well maintained. From a walk on the valley floor to a challenging mountain trek along the north face of Mt. Eiger or to the Gleckstein cabin, you can take your choice. A map showing the Grindelwald region's paths and trails is available at the tourist office for 9.50F ($6.45).

If you're courageous and adventurous enough to be tempted by peaks 13,000 feet high or higher, or if you'd like to learn the proper way to climb rocks and ice, get in touch with the **Bergsteigerzentrum,** CH-3818 Grindelwald (tel. 036/53-20-21).

Faulhorn, 8,796 feet high, has a historic vantage point from which you can view a panorama of untouched alpine beauty. There's also a mountain hotel that has been here for more than 150 years. It can be reached only by going on foot from Bussalp (2¾ hours), from First (2½ hours), or from Schynige Platte (4 hours). The hotel is **Hotel Faulhorn,** CH-3818 Grindelwald (tel. 036/53-21-13), containing 80 beds. This hotel is very remote and is patronized only in summer by hill climbers. It charges 25F ($17) per person for its very simple mountain accommodations. No one has a private bath here, of course. A restaurant open throughout the day offers sustaining food and drink.

A 30-minute ride on Europe's longest chair lift, via Oberhaus, will take you to **First,** 7,113 feet up. You can stop at Bort and Egg intermediate stations as you cross the lovely alpine meadows to the First mountain terminal and sun terrace. You'll have many hiking possibilities into either the neighboring Bussalp or Grosse Scheidegg areas, returning by bus. An hour's brisk hike will take you to idyllic Lake Bachalp. Besides the 2½-hour trek to Faulhorn, cited above, you can also make a trek by foot to the Schynige Platte in six hours. A round-trip chair-lift ride between Grindelwald and First costs 22F ($14.95). At First is a 450-seat restaurant, offering one of the most panoramic views in Europe.

Grosse Scheidegg, at 6,434 feet, is a famous pass which since recorded history allowed transit between the Grindelwald and the Rosenlaui valleys. You can climb there in three hours from Grindelwald, or you can take a 40-minute bus ride from Grindelwald. This is a favorite climbing destination from the village of Wengen as well. My preference is usually to take a bus to Grosse Scheidegg, and then begin my hillwalking away from the congestion of village traffic and crowds. Round-trip bus passage from Grindelwald to Grosse Scheidegg costs 19F ($12.90) per person. If you want to climb in the upper regions of the Oberland with a destination in mind, you might consider this itinerary: Travel from Grindelwald to Grosse Scheidegg by bus. Walk for 2½ hours from Grosse Scheidegg to Schwartzwaldup. On either side of you will soar the twin peaks of First and Wetterhorn. After a panoramic respite in Schwartzwaldup, you can catch a bus which will retrace your steps, first to Grosse Scheidegg, then to Grindelwald. The total bus fare for this summer only excursion is 25F ($17) per person.

A short aerial cable-car ride will take you to **Pfingstegg,** at 4,564 feet, from which point you can make memorable hikes to the Lower and Upper Grindelwald glaciers. A hike to Bäregg-Stieregg (one hour) is highly recommended as a one-day journey, as is the trek to Bänisegg (two hours). You'll get a view of the Eismeer and the Fiescherwand, both worth the hike. A popular half-day journey on foot is to Milchbach. In about an hour, you find yourself at the base of the Upper Grindelwald glacier, with the Blue Ice Grotto nearby. You don't have to hike all the way back, as a bus trip is available. The round-trip fare between Grindelwald and Pfinstegg is 10F ($6.80) or 8F ($5.45) if you have a visitor's card of Grindelwald.

Want to learn how to skate from Swiss experts? A **Swisskate Skating School** for beginners to advanced skaters is run by Karl-Heinz Zitterbart. For information on times and tariffs, get in touch with Mr. Zitterbart at the Sportzentrum or by phone at the Hotel Schweizerhof (tel. 036/53-22-02).

Summer ice skating: The big ice hall at the Sports Center is open from July until the following Easter. The charge for skating is 4.50F ($3.05) for adults staying in Grindelwald, 6F ($4.10) otherwise. Children pay 3F ($2.05) or 4F ($2.70).

Tennis: Six sand courts are available through the tourist office at a rental of

17F ($11.56) per hour per court. The Regina, Spinne, and Sunstar Hotels all have courts, and you can play indoors on one of the four hard courts in the Sportzentrum (Sports Center) from the end of April until mid-June. Other indoor tennis facilities are available at Wilderswil and at Interlaken all year.

Swimming: A heated open-air swimming pool is open in Grindelwald from June to August. The Sports Center has an indoor pool and sauna open daily. Adults staying in Grindelwald pay 6F ($4.10) to swim, 8F ($5.45) if they come from elsewhere. Prices for children are 4.50F ($3.05) and 6F ($4.10).

Fishing: With a permit from the tourist office, you can try your angling skill in the Lütschine and the Bachalpsee.

APRÈS SKI: After dark, Grindelwald is one of the liveliest towns in the Bernese Oberland.

Spinet, Hotel Spinne (tel. 036/53-23-41). Sometimes a day in the mountains elicits a craving for pastries. When that urge hits you, an establishment which is eager to provide the necessary calories is this well-known pastry shop and coffeehouse. Proudly displayed behind glass cases, you'll find an elaborate array of very fresh confections, priced from 3.50F ($2.40) each. There are also sandwiches and snacks. The place is open daily from 10 a.m. to 10 p.m.

Cava Bar, Derby Hotel (tel. 036/54-54-61). Open only in winter, this popular bar offers danceable live music, a rustic decor, and a long bar area for drinking. There's no cover charge. It opens daily at 9 p.m., closing at 1:30 a.m. On Saturday, it closes at 2:30 a.m. It lies within the cellars of the previously recommended Derby Hotel, near the railway station.

Chez Marianne/Gepsi-Bar, Hostellerie Eiger (tel. 036/53-21-21). Two of the resort's most popular après-ski and nightlife bars are within the previously recommended Hostellerie Eiger. The Gepsi-Bar is the place for live music. For a description, refer to the Steakhouse in the "Where to Dine" section. Chez Marianne lies behind a thick wooden door, carefully concealed from the adjacent lobby. Old movie posters of the greatest days of Hollywood mingle with alpine rusticity. Open from 4 p.m. to 1 a.m. nightly, the place has stout, almost indestructible walls and furniture, dim lighting, and beer which sells from 3.50F ($2.40) a glass.

Fondue-Stübli, Hotel Spinne (tel. 036/53-23-41), is contained within the labyrinth of drinking and dining facilities of the previously recommended Hotel Spinne. This rustic alpine restaurant is the least pretentious of any of its neighbors. The place has music, along with intimate lighting, big mugs of beer, and savory portions of raclette priced at 12F ($8.15) per person. If fondue bourguignonne is more to your liking, it costs from 35F ($23.80) for two persons. In winter only, the place is open daily except Tuesday from 5 p.m. until very, very late.

Spider Disco, Hotel Spinne (tel. 036/53-23-41). Somehow, electronic rhythms seem to reverberate more eerily when a disco is covered with simulated stalactites. Such is the case with this popular disco, where even the entrance is accented with a painted spider's web. There's a cover charge only on Friday and Saturday of 5F ($3.40). The place is open nightly from 8:30 p.m. to at least 1:30 a.m.

Herby's Bar, Grand Hotel Regina (tel. 036/54-54-55), is probably the most interesting feature on the entire lobby level of this previously recommended hotel. Filled with Oriental carpets, comfortable sofas, and interesting paintings, the space is leased by one of the resort's most charming and sophisticated barmen, Herbert Kuhn. A rectangular bar seems to invite intimacy, while a piano provides danceable music. The bar remains open every night to 2 a.m., often welcoming diners from the hotel's Grill Room (see "Where to Dine") in for a nightcap. Long drinks cost from 11F ($7.50).

Challi-Bar, Hotel Weisses Kreuz & Post (tel. 036/54-54-92). Decorated like a romanticized version of an alpine barnyard, this popular bar and disco has a thick-timbered ceiling, solidly reinforced plank siding, and a dance floor. A prominent neon sign announces its presence near the front of the previously recommended Hotel Weisses Kreuz & Post. It opens every night from 9 p.m. to closing. There's no cover charge, but once inside, beer costs from 5F ($3.40).

Espresso Bar, Hotel Spinne (tel. 036/53-23-41). Despite its name, the most popular drink at this bar probably isn't espresso. Cramped, hot, and crowded, it's little more than a hole in the wall. Nonetheless, it fills to capacity almost every evening with skiers midway between their days on the slopes and their nights on the town. Beer costs from 3.50F ($2.40). This place lies behind a log-cabin façade, a few steps from the main entrance of the Hotel Spinne. It's open daily from 11 a.m. to 1 a.m.

Le Plaza Club, Hotel Sunstar & Adler (tel. 036/53-42-40). You'll have to negotiate a labyrinth of hallways and staircases to find this popular disco and nightclub. It opens at 8 every night, closing at 3 a.m. or later. Entrance is free, but each guest is requested to order at least one drink. Beer costs from 7F ($4.75), hard liquor from 10.50F ($7.15).

There are also "get-together" parties once a week on the open-air ice rink.

8. LAKE BRIENZ

Once this lake was connected to Lake Thun, but that was long ago. It measures about nine miles long and from one to two miles wide. It's the smaller of the two blue Oberland lakes (Thun, which we've already visited, is larger). Around its shores are many holiday areas and resorts little visited by North Americans, who seem to popularize the more traditional sightseeing target, Lake Thun.

However, Lake Brienz has much charm, and there are many vacationers, especially Europeans, who prefer it. You might make your center in the town of Brienz or, and I prefer this, the little resort of Bönigen.

BRIENZ: On the upper end of the lake, the town of Brienz is the center for many an excursion. The town faces Giessbach Falls on the opposite side of the lake (you can hear the roar). Among the excursions, one of the most popular is to take a cogwheel railway for the climb to **Brienzer Rothorn,** where you'll be rewarded with a magnificent vista of the Bernese Alps and Lake Brienz. The tour takes about two hours, and you reach an elevation of some 7,105 feet. Service is from the first of June until the end of October, and there are usually about nine trips a day, a round-trip ticket going for 44F ($29.90) per person.

To visit the already mentioned **Giessbach Falls,** you can go by funicular. The loading platform, across the lake from Brienz, can be reached by car or boat. The funicular costs 4.20F ($2.85) for adults and 2F ($1.35) for children 6 to 16. Allow two hours for the entire excursion. The boat to the funicular departs from the lake shore wharf in the center of Brienz, and is marked *Giessbach.* If you want, you can drive all the way to the falls, but most visitors prefer the fun of the funicular.

Brienz is famous for its Bernese Oberland woodcarvers, as you will quickly testify if you've been to a souvenir shop in Switzerland. It's also known for its violin makers (the school is open to the public).

For food and lodging, seek out the following.

Hotel Bären, CH-3855 Brienz, Switzerland (tel. 036/51-24-12), is an ideal spot for a lakeside holiday or one of the best dining choices if you're only passing through. On the shores of the lake, in a balconied building, it offers comfortable, modern rooms at attractive prices: 32F ($21.75) to 45F ($30.60) daily in a single and from 64F ($43.50) to 120F ($81.60) in a double. All accommodations have hot and cold running water, but not all contain private baths. The owners of "Hotel Bear" are concerned and thoughtful hosts. Their special feature is a private lake swimming pool with a small garden. They are also known for their good food, and in summer will serve you grilled meats from their garden grill. Many different fish dishes are offered. Food is served daily from 11 a.m. to 10 p.m., but the hotel is closed from December 15 to March 15.

The Most Popular Excursion

A visit to the **Swiss Open-Air Museum of Rural Dwellings and Lifestyle** at Ballenberg, near Brienz in the Bernese Oberland, is like a trip back into Switzerland's rural history. Visitors are afforded the opportunity to see typical buildings from farms and tiny settlements in groups surrounded by gardens and farm fields cultivated in the old ways peculiar to the area represented. Seven scenic areas are open to visitors taking the good roads found in the recreation area encompassing nearly 2,000 acres, which includes a nature park and Lake Wyssen, between the villages of Hofstetten and Brienzwiler.

The museum was developed after realization that changes in the old ways of farm and village life and methods have imperiled historic buildings all over the country. Many scenic areas are already open to the public, and others are in preparation or projected. You can see how life was lived in eight different cantons at different periods in their history. Mittelland units include Central, Bernese, Eastern, and Western, allowing you to learn about rural trades, farm products, forest life, folk customs, and other phases of country life from the Jura to Zurich to Bern and elsewhere.

A round trip through the museum will take about three hours, and I recommend that you wear comfortable walking shoes to allow you to go through the houses and farm buildings, gardens and artisans' quarters, with ease. The museum is open daily in April, May, and October from 10 a.m. to 5 p.m. and June through September from 9:30 a.m. to 5:30 p.m. Adults are charged 10F ($6.80) and children pay 5F ($3.40) for admission. On request, a guided tour can be arranged, but reservations are necessary. There is a minimum charge of 60F ($40.80) for a guide to lead you on a tour. In busy seasons, groups of 15 can be created from a community of strangers, each participant paying only 4F ($2.70). Otherwise, if you want a tour and there are fewer than 15 interested parties, you will pay 60F ($40.80) regardless of how many participants go along with you.

Car parks will be found at the Hofstetten and Brienzwiler entrances. To come here by train, take the Interlaken-Meiringen-Lucerne line to the Brienz railroad station, where you can make a bus connection to the museum, or to the Brienzwiler station, from which a forest path will lead you to the museum route.

For information, get in touch with the Ballenberg Swiss Open-Air Museum Foundation, Direction CH-3855 Brienz, Switzerland (tel. 036/51-11-23).

BÖNIGEN: On the south shore of Lake Brienz, the lakeside resort of Bönigen has many old timbered houses, some of which go back to the 16th century. The location is only five minutes from Interlaken. Opening onto Lake Brienz, Bönigen is ideal for many walks, excursions, and trips by lake steamer. Go here for peace and tranquility—and don't expect a lot of excitement.

Food and Lodging

Hotel Seiler au Lac, CH-3806 Bönigen, Switzerland (tel. 036/22-30-21). This well-established hotel with a good reputation was almost completely rebuilt by the Zingg-Dinkel family in 1983. Consequently, guests here will receive the best of a new facility and experienced hosts as well. The hotel sprawls over two interconnected sections at the edge of the lake. Each room contains big windows, and those overlooking the lake have balconies. Rooms in the new addition also have separate sitting areas. The public rooms look out over well-maintained gardens, where fruit trees blossom throughout the springtime. On the premises is a mountain-style bar with hanging Victorian lanterns and a heavily beamed ceiling. The dining room serves well-prepared meals in a modern setting. On the premises is a pizzeria, along with a bar called La Bohème. With half board included, singles range from 110F ($74.80) to 140F ($95.20) daily, and doubles cost 230F ($156.40) to 280F ($190.40). The hotel is closed in November.

Park Hotel, CH-3806 Bönigen, Switzerland (tel. 036/22-71-06), is a renovated, 19th-century family hotel in the center of a large, quiet parkland on the shore of Lake Brienz. Centrally located, it lies two minutes from the bus stop and boat station. Rooms are pleasant and peaceful, opening onto views of the lake or mountains. Each accommodation has a bath or shower, along with a toilet, and most of them come with a balcony. There is an elevator on the premises, and toys and a swing set are provided for children on the lawn. For half board, two persons in a double pay from 140F ($95.20) to 160F ($108.80) daily. A single on the same arrangement costs from 80F ($54.40) to 88F ($59.85). Closed in November.

9. MEIRINGEN

If you plan to center in the eastern part of the Bernese Oberland, which contains the upper reaches of the River Aare, an ideal center in the Haslital district is the old resort of Meiringen, famous throughout the world for the dessert concoction *meringue.* The district attracts mountaineers, rock climbers, and just plain ramblers.

Above Lake Brienz, Meiringen is the major town in the Haslital district, lying about eight miles from the town of Brienz, which we have previously visited. The resort is centered among the Grimsel, Brünig, and Susten passes. Among its attractions are excursions to the Aare gorge, the Rosenlaui glacier, and the Reichenbach Falls, as well as a folklore museum, a crystal grotto, a water mill, and a glacier path. There are some 185 miles of marked paths for hiking and walks in unspoiled nature, and a large network of lifts to reach panoramic vantage points.

Everybody seemingly visits the parish church in the upper part of the village, which dates from 1864, although there has been a church on this spot since the 11th century (the remains of a crypt from that era can still be seen).

If you're staying in the town, you can ask your hotel to prepare a meringue dessert for you. However, if you're passing through, you can buy one or two at one of the local bakeries, perhaps enjoying it at teatime. As the story goes, the dessert was created when Napoleon visited the town and the local chef had a lot of leftover egg whites. Inspired, he created these puffy mounds and served them in a saucer brimming with sweet mountain cream, much to the general's delight. Most historians, however, dismiss this tale as apocryphal.

After you've found a room in Meiringen, you can strike out the next day on any number of interesting excursions. One is to the **Aare Gorge,** a wonder of nature. It's reached by road from Meiringen or from the Grimsel-Susten road by the so-called Kirchet. The gorge, charging an admission of 4F ($2.70) for adults, 2.50F ($1.70) for children, is open every day from 8 a.m. to 6 p.m. May to October. You'll enter a world of grotesque nooks and recesses, grottoes, precipices, galleries, inlets, and arches—all fashioned by the waters of the Aare in the course of thousands of years. The 1,500-yard-long and 650-foot-deep cleft carved in the Kirchet, a craggy barrier left over from the ice age, is a unique natural wonder of the Swiss Alps. The towering rock walls of the gorge are so close together at the narrowest points that only a few rays of sunshine manage to penetrate briefly to the depths just before noon.

Another excursion, which fans of Sherlock Holmes will want to take, is to the **Reichenbachfall.** The watercourses of the Rosenlaui Valley meet in the Reichenbach Falls. The beauty and impressive nature of the falls have lured many visitors, beginning with the British in the 19th century. One visitor, Conan Doyle, was so impressed with the falls that he used it in *The Final Problem,* in which the villain, Dr. Moriarty, struggles with the detective to toss him in the falls. A Sherlock Holmes commemorative plaque can be seen today near the upper station of the funicular. The falls can be visited from mid-May to mid-September at a cost of 5F ($3.40). Departures are every ten minutes daily from 8 a.m. to noon and 1:15 to 6 p.m. To go from Meiringen to the base of the funicular requires a ten-minute walk. If you're driving, leave Meiringen on the road to Grimsel, then take a right turn in the direction pointing to Reichenbach Falls and Mervenklinik.

After you admire the cascade of the Reichenbach Falls, you can set out on foot through the valley of the river that feeds the falls. This is known as **Rosenlaui Valley.** After a 90-minute walk on marked footpaths through the valley, you'll arrive at the entrance to Rosenlaui Gorge. It is open only from May to October daily from 8 a.m. to 4:30 p.m., charging 4F ($2.70) for adults and 2.50F ($1.70) for children. The surfaces of the sheer rock faces echo and reverberate in bizarre ways the sound of the many small waterfalls within it. You can walk from one end to the other end of this gorge in about 30 minutes, and the footpath is well marked. There's a small hotel and a small seasonal restaurant near the entrance to the gorge. Most visitors turn around at the uppermost reaches of the gorge, walking the two-hour trek back to Reichenbach Falls and the funicular going back to Meiringen.

WHERE TO STAY AND EAT: A longtime favorite, the old-fashioned **Park Hotel Sauvage,** CH-3860 Meiringen, Switzerland (tel. 036/71-41-41) is the traditional choice. This is the kind of hotel that makes special efforts to make guests feel at home. Clients are usually greeted with a welcoming drink shortly after their arrival, just before being ushered into their high-ceilinged bedroom, which, although renovated, still has much of the 19th-century charm of its original building. The structure dates from 1880. The breakfast buffet is served in a big art-nouveau dining room, while a French à la carte restaurant, La Meringue, serves a well-prepared cuisine. On the premises are lots of outdoor walkways with enough café tables to ensure a relaxing afternoon in the sun. The service is likely to be very good, since the establishment serves as the staff-training grounds of the Swiss Hotel Association. The hotel has weekly specialty evenings, such as fondue or raclette parties, which are usually followed by dancing in the bar with live entertainment. The accommodations all have private baths, with singles costing from 75F ($51) to 110F ($74.80) daily and doubles going for 120F ($81.60) to 180F ($122.40). Half board is available for another 24F ($16.30) per person. The hotel's indoor swimming pool is 300 yards from the hotel, while tennis courts are out back. The owner manager is J. Musfeld.

Sporthotel Sherlock Holmes, CH-3860 Meiringen, Switzerland (tel. 036/71-42-42). A silhouette of the profile of the detective himself adorns the wall above one of the entrances. The hotel is buff-colored, with balconies that look reddish by contrast. A swimming pool and sauna are on the premises, and there are lots of sun terraces. The bedrooms, comfortably furnished, are decorated with modern pieces. Rents are 66F ($44.90) to 79F ($53.70) daily per person, based on double occupancy and 78F ($53.05) to 94F ($63.90) in a single, breakfast included. Half board is another 22F ($14.95) per person daily.

Hotel Tourist, CH-3860 Meiringen, Switzerland (tel. 036/71-10-44), is a small hotel with room for only 25 guests, which ensures a maximum amount of attention for each of them from the owners, the Wyss family. The building is a brown-and-white four-story structure with a gently sloping peaked roof and an extension on the back. The family is happy to serve food and drink to hotel guests and to passing motorists on the parasol-covered terrace in front. Otherwise, the hotel is attractively outfitted with large windows and rustic beams in the public rooms and small-scale furniture in the bedrooms. Many of the clean and well-kept accommodations have their own bath. For a room with breakfast, the cost is from 30F ($20.40) per person daily, rising to 46F ($31.30) per person if half board is taken.

10. KANDERSTEG

Between Grindelwald and Gstaad, Kandersteg is at a southerly point in the Bernese Oberland. It's a tranquil and lovely mountain village—spread over 2½ miles so nothing is crowded—and characterized by its rust- and orange-colored rooftops and its green, green Swiss meadows, where wildflowers bloom in spring. It's framed by mountain passes in almost every direction. From the village, about six alpine huts are not-so-easily reached.

The resort, which is active in both summer and winter, lies at the northern terminus of the Lötschberg Tunnel, which stretches for nine miles, making it the third longest in the Alps. Ever since the beginning of World War I it has linked Bern with the Rhône Valley. Cars can be transported on the railway going through the tunnel. Trains leave every 30 minutes, and no reservations are necessary. From Brig, it's possible to take the car through another tunnel into Italy.

Once, however, Kandersteg was known all over Switzerland for another reason. It was a stage on the road to the Gemmi Pass, which long ago linked the Valais with the Bernese Oberland.

The village still has many old farm homes and a tiny church from the 16th century. It is proud of its traditions.

In summer, horses can be rented at the local riding school, but only qualified riders are accepted, and "proper" clothes are preferred. The environs of Kandersteg are riddled with an extensive network of level footpaths and strategically located benches. These paths are also open in the winter.

As for skiing in winter, top-speed skiers avoid the place, but it attracts both beginners and cross-country devotees. Facilities include an open-air ice rink and an indoor artificial ice rink. For the downhill skier, there are a cable car, two chair lifts, and four ski tows. Kandersteg is also the site of the National Nordic Ski Center, with its ski-jumping station. In winter it has a floodlit cross-country track of about 1½ miles, which is open in the evening.

At the foot of the Blümlisalp chain (12,000 feet), Kandersteg is served by the Berne-Lötschberg-Simplon railway. Perhaps it no longer attracts the celebrities it used to (Gstaad has taken over that position), but it's very popular nevertheless.

The **Oeschinensee** (or Lake Oeschinen) is high above Kandersteg, towered over snow-covered peaks, dropping 6,000 feet to the rim of the lake. This, of course, is the most popular excursion from Kandersteg. You can walk to it from the Victoria Hotel or take a chair lift, costing 10F ($6.80), to the Oeschinen station and walk down from that point. The lake, at the foot of the Blümlisalp, has extremely clear water.

Another popular excursion is to **Klus,** a journey of some two miles (park your vehicle at the cable station's lower platform at Stock). You climb the rest of the way on foot, going through a tunnel over this untamed gorge, filled with the rushing falls of the Kander River. The wildly flowing Kander creates a romantic setting. However, you must watch your step, as the path gets very slippery in places, the spray coating the stones and pebbles.

FOOD AND LODGING: Built in 1912, **Royal Hotel Bellevue,** CH-3718 Kandersteg, Switzerland (tel. 033/75-12-12), is graced with a free-form swimming pool in the back garden from which you can see a magnificent mountain vista in all directions. The hotel is a four-story brown-and-white chalet whose stone and stucco walls don't really give a preview of the luxury to be found inside. This is one of the finest hotels in the region—or in Switzerland, for that matter. The interior is elegant, with flagstone floors covered with dozens of Oriental rugs, Louis XIII–style armchairs, and rococo lighting fixtures. Fireplaces crackle during most of the winter, with carved armchairs covered with gray brocades clustered into conversational groups around them. Other rooms include barrel chairs in supple leather in an ambience of live piano music and mellow antiques.

Sports and leisure occupy the day, with elegant and often festive dining and drinking taking up the evening. The Rôtisserie is undeniably glamorous, with French armchairs, crystal chandeliers, paneling, and handcrafted tapestries from the 16th century, set beautifully against oak paneling. It offers a fine light French cuisine without excess. The Grill-Stubli is a gemütlich lunchtime restaurant. Guests are requested to wear dinner jackets and formal or semiformal dresses for dinner. Nonresidents of this luxurious hotel are not admitted to the restaurants or bar unless invited by a hotel guest. On the premises are an indoor and outdoor swimming pool, a sauna, a riding stable with a host of well-seasoned horses (bring riding clothes, including boots, if you have them), a well-maintained tennis court, and more than 7,000 square feet of gardens and lawns dotted with evergreens. Bicycles and mountain bikes are provided free, and hiking excursions are arranged. The hotel has a putting green. Winter sports available are easy alpine skiing, cross-country skiing, ice skating, and riding in the hotel's horse-drawn sleigh. On the lake, 20 minutes away, the hotel owns a 33-foot yacht suitable for six passengers and a motorboat for waterskiing. In a nearby park, the hotel owns three separate chalets, each with apartment facilities and suites.

In brief, this is one of the most elegant hotels in the region. Rooms range from 150F ($102) to 250F ($170) per person daily with half board included. This includes a variety of accommodations during a full range of seasons. The hotel, a member of *Relais & Châteaux* and The Leading Hotels of the World, has been owned by the Rikli family for three generations. The hotel is closed in November.

Hotel Victoria & Ritter, CH-3718 Kandersteg, Switzerland (tel. 033/75-14-44), was created in 1789 when a chalet, the Ritter, was merged with an Edwardian-era monument to the architecture of the gilded age, the Victorian. Most of the 84 modernized accommodations are contained within the rambling white-walled headquarters of the establishment, which was completed in 1912. A kindergarten is on the premises, as is a glassed-in covered pool and tennis courts, and a row of jagged cliffs rises practically behind the rear garden. Each of the comfortably furnished accommodations contains a private bath, phone, and radio. Depending on the season, singles cost 95F ($64.60) to 105F ($71.40) daily, and doubles go for 180F ($122.40) to 220F ($149.60), with half board included. The gemütlich and comfortable restaurant is on the street level of what used to be the Hotel Ritter. It serves good food in a series of rustic paneled rooms.

Hotel Alfa-Soleil, CH-3718 Kandersteg, Switzerland (tel. 033/75-17-18). Built in several stages throughout the 1960s and 1970s, this comfortable hotel is the first hotel many visitors see as they approach the periphery of the resort. Solid, substantial, and popular, the hotel is owned by a local ski enthusiast, Peter Seiler, and his wife Agnes. The hotel contains 37 rooms, each of which has a private bath, a phone, TV, and (in about 60% of them), a private balcony. Depending on the season, singles rent for 75F ($51) to 80F ($54.40) daily, with doubles costing from 130F ($88.40) to 140F ($95.20), plus another 20F ($13.60) per person daily if clients want half board.

Many nonresidents of the hotel make the trek to the hotel's Stella Restaurant, because its array of fanciful accessories make it seem perfect as an après-ski haven. Its dining room ceiling is crafted from mature saplings spaced between rows of century-old doors removed from a much older hotel. A collection of antique sleighs and wrought-iron implements sit on upper galleries. Lunch is served daily from 11:30 a.m. to 2 p.m., dinner 6:30 to 9:30 p.m. The menu is wide and varied enough to suit most palates and pocketbooks. Pizzas and steaming bowls of pasta begin at 10F ($6.80), while a seven-course menu dégustation costs 50F ($34) to 60F ($40.80), depending on the price of the ingredients in the local market. Many guests order a four-course meal for 25F ($17). Dishes include large shrimp, filet of turbot, fresh cream of avocado soup, risotto with five mushrooms and gorgonzola, spaghetti carbonara, filet of pork with Roquefort, and an array of grilled meats. Both the hotel and its restaurant are closed October to mid-December.

Hotel Adler, CH-3718 Kandersteg, Switzerland (tel. 033/75-11-22). An open fire crackling in the foyer sets the tone of this warm, cozy inn. This woodsided chalet is set alongside the main street of the resort near the center. Operated by its fourth-generation owner, Andreas Fetzer, and his Finnish-born wife Eija, it was built in 1906 with thick walls and solid construction. Most of the ground floor is devoted to the Adler-Bar, one of the most popular après-ski hangouts in town, a brasserie (the Adlerstübe), and a relatively formal à la carte restaurant where full meals cost from 40F ($27.20). In both restaurants, lunch is served from noon to 2:30 p.m. daily and dinner from 5:30 to 9:30 p.m., with a limited menu in the brasserie being offered throughout the afternoon. Candlelight dinner, buffets, and fondue and raclette parties add to the fun of staying here. Later, guests recover in a Finnish sauna. Each of the 20 wood-paneled accommodations contains a TV hookup, a private bath (a few with Jacuzzis), phone, and radio. Depending on the season, rates with half board included are 75F ($51) to 100F ($68) per person daily.

Hotel Alpenblich, CH-3718 Kandersteg, Switzerland (tel. 033/75-11-29), small, with only a dozen well-maintained rooms, is a chalet in the center of town, about a five-minute walk from the train station. You enter and register near the bar of a popular and pine-paneled bar/brasserie (the Oberlanderstübe) lined with hunting trophies. Many of these date from 1902, when the hotel was originally built. The restaurant is open from 8 a.m. to midnight every day of the year except in October and for four weeks between March and April. Full meals cost from 20F ($13.60). Depending on the plumbing (not all the units have private showers), rooms rent for 30F ($20.40) to 40F ($27.20) per person daily, with breakfast included. In season, live music is provided by the owner's alpine band (he plays the clarinet) every Friday night.

APRÈS SKI: Although it's on the periphery of the resort, a healthy hike from the center, many visitors head late at night for the **High Moon Disco** at the previously recommended Hotel Alfa-Soleil (tel. 033/75-17-18). It's open nightly except Monday from 9 p.m. to 2 a.m. Once inside, beer costs from 5F ($3.40), scotch from 10F ($6.80). There's an octagonal dance floor, plus a light show and danceable electronic music.

In the center of town, on the ground floor of an early 20th-century chalet, is the **Adler-Bar,** Hotel Adler (tel. 033/75-11-22). Sheathed with timbers and pinewood paneling, it attracts a crowd of skiers every afternoon between sundown and the dinner hour, and again, later in the evening. It's open from 4 p.m. to at least 1:30 a.m. daily. Depending on the hour of the evening you show up, beer costs from 3.50F ($2.40) to 5F ($3.40). Live piano music is presented daily in winter. The bar and the hotel that contains it is closed in November.

11. LENK

Tucked snugly into the western sector of the Bernese Oberland, Lenk lies at the head of the picture-postcard Simmental, the grazing range of some of those famous Swiss cows. In the background is the snow-capped Wildstrubel, but the mountains around Lenk are less formidable. In the area are several mirror-like lakes and some stunning waterfalls. In all, it's an idyllic setting, with glaciers as a backdrop.

Since the 19th century Lenk has been a popular health spa, owing to its pleasant situation, mild climate, and the strongest alpine sulfur springs in Europe. These springs have been known for centuries, and today attract a thriving health-spa clientele to a center dating from 1977, standing in a large woodland park.

In summer Lenk attracts those interested in mountain climbing, hiking, and playing tennis, or those "taking the cure." In winter it's a sports area, and its major ski centers are at Betelberg, Metsch, Bühlberg, and Hahnenmoos. For the cross-country skier there's a choice of circuits at 3,600 and 6,500 feet. For the less adventurous, there are 20 miles of well-tended walks.

WHERE TO STAY: A rambling Victorian-era hotel, **Hotel Lenkerhof,** CH-3775 Lenk, Switzerland (tel. 030/6-31-31), stands in isolated grandeur in the upper reaches of the village. General manager Ursula Rüfenacht has run the hotel and the connected spa center for some ten years. Many of the customers have been regular guests for around three decades, occupying the same rooms with an almost religious fervor. The hotel has undergone so many renovations that now it has a modernized ground floor, with comfortable restaurants and coffee-drinking facilities. The best of the bedrooms are comfortably furnished with a mixture of 19th-century antiques and modern pieces and have a sanitary kind of decor. The least expensive units are quite small. Throughout the year, singles cost 75F ($51) to 135F ($91.80) daily, and doubles go for 80F ($54.40) to 150F ($102) per person, prices including a Swiss buffet breakfast and a four-course dinner. Because of the charges, guests feel that staying in an inexpensive room at this four-star hotel is one of the best bargains in town.

The Taverne restaurant is an attractive place to dine, with live music throughout the year. The summer garden grill terrace is an ideal stop for lunch or dinner. The hotel's gastronomically sophisticated Le Beaujolais restaurant is recommended separately. The Spa Center that is directly connected to the Lenkerhof offers various hydrotherapies. Dr. Peter Gross, head resident doctor, gives clients the chance for classic cures, supervised by professional physiotherapists. The hotel and Spa Center are closed from late October to mid-December.

Parkhotel Bellevue, CH-3775 Lenk, Switzerland (tel. 030/3-17-61), is a white rectangular building that looks somewhat like a Mediterranean villa when the snow doesn't cover the red-tile roof. It's a family hotel, with a large outdoor swimming pool set into the grassy lawns behind the hotel, out of earshot of the comfortable bedrooms. Many of the accommodations have private loggias or balconies, which permit views of the surrounding rocky hills. The location somewhat outside the center of town is one that many clients find restful. Since the hotel was built in 1905 without private plumbing in any of the bedrooms, the Victorian lines of each accommodation are interrupted by the walls of added-on bathrooms. Accommodations are conservatively decorated and well scrubbed. The Nussbaum-Perrollaz family, your hosts, charge 75F ($51) to 120F ($81.60) daily in a single, depending on the season. Doubles cost 150F ($102) to 240F ($163.20). For half board, another 25F ($17) per person is added. The excellent French cuisine is one of the reasons guests return to the Bellevue. Meals are taken in a spacious dining room or else a cozy restaurant. There is also a warmly inviting bar with piano music.

Hostellerie Kreuz, CH-3775 Lenk, Switzerland (tel. 036/3-13-87), is a more than usually attractive modern chalet in the center, built in 1979 and directed by the Trittens. The swimming pool is covered with pine slats and brick facing, while the sunlight streaming into the dining room is mellowed by the surrounding areas of polished pine. The sun terraces allow guests a chance to get a tan. The wood theme is repeated in many of the bedrooms, which are crafted with weatherproof windows. The sloping roofline makes some units irregularly shaped. Most of the accommodations have private baths. Rates, depending on the season, exposure of the room, and plumbing, range from 52F ($35.35) to 95F ($64.60) daily in a single and from 100F ($68) to 160F ($108.80) in a double.

The hotel is also a popular choice for dining. An informal restaurant in front serves lunch from 11:30 a.m. to 2 p.m. daily, charging from 16F ($10.90) to 28F ($19.05). The Le Tonneau grill room, the more formal restaurant in the rear, has a modern alpine decor. It is open only for dinner from 6:30 to 9 p.m., with meals costing from 45F ($30.60). You might begin with smoked trout, following with one of the grilled specialties, perhaps veal steak or a Chateaubriand. The chef also prepares fondue bourguignonne and chinoise.

Hotel Wildstrubel, CH-3775 Lenk, Switzerland (tel. 030/6-31-11). Designed like a soaring chalet in the center of town, this attractive and substantial hotel was one of the first inns in town. Constructed in 1895, it contains 52 rooms, each of which has a private bath, phone, and TV. Depending on the season and the room assignment, single rates range from 67F ($45.55) to 95F ($64.60) daily, with doubles costing 122F ($82.95) to 182F ($123.75). For half board, the charge is another 24F ($16.30) per person daily. Rooms are clean and acceptable in their price level, but the real reputation of this hotel is because of its in-house disco. Designed like an alpine barn with lighting hanging from the metallic gridwork of the ceiling, it's open from 8:30 p.m. to either 1 or 2 a.m., depending on the night of the week. Closing day is Sunday. Entrance is free, but drinks are expensive. A small beer costs from 10F ($6.80). The hotel is closed in November.

WHERE TO DINE: For consistently good dining, I recommend **Le Beaujolais,** Hotel Lenkerhof (tel. 030/6-31-31), which produces a sophisticated cuisine for much less than you'd pay in better-decorated enclaves of haute gastronomy. The establishment lies in the nether regions of the previously recommended Lenkerhof, within a room whose only noticeable decor is a row of windows and the layers of immaculate napery. Meals are served only at dinner, every night except Monday and Tuesday from 7:30 to 10:30 p.m.

The featured offering is the seven- or eight-course "menu dégustation," which changes with the week. Priced at 70F ($47.60), it's prepared by Austrian-born chef Werner Strauss. A la carte meals cost from 50F ($34). Typical menu items include noodles with clams and artichokes belle forestière, one of the more delectable cold hors d'oeuvres. For your main course you might sample sole suprêmes either grilled or meunière, perhaps a ragoût of "fruits of the sea." The meat dishes are especially savory, including chicken fricassée with zucchini, veal marsala, or grilled beef filet. Desserts are reason enough to go. Try, if featured, the plum cake glacé. The restaurant, like the hotel which contains it, is closed from late October to December 19. Reservations are important.

12. ADELBODEN

Adelboden has a real alpine atmosphere with lots of charming farmhouses. It lies in the western part of the Engstligen valley, and is known for its scenery. It's both a summer resort and a winter ski center. This town of about 3,500 permanent inhabitants has at least 26 hotels and guest houses, plus some 1,500 chalets and holiday apartments. Its major ski areas are those at Geils, Boden, Birg, and Tschentenegg.

Its mountain transportation includes the Engstligenalp aerial cableway (2,162 yards), Schwandfeldspitz chair lift (2,131 yards), the Hahnenmoos cabin cableway (2,152 yards), and the Elsigenalp aerial cableway (1,980 yards). In winter, downhill and cross-country skiing, ski tours, winter walks, ice-skating, curling, skibob, swimming, riding, and sledging are offered, while in summer, the holiday schedule can include hiking, swimming, ice-skating, climbing, glacier tours, fishing, riding, tennis, and hang gliding. A walk along the Grutli forest trail is a good alpine experience.

The village church, built in 1433, has some interesting frescoes. Near the center of the village is a children's playground.

WHERE TO STAY: One of the leading hotels at the resort, **Nevada Palace,** CH-3715 Adelboden, Switzerland (tel. 033/73-21-31), was built in 1911–1913 by three French brothers who, when thwarted in their plans to move to America's Sierra Nevada, named their Swiss property after their lost dream. At the time, Adelboden was very much a summer-only resort, but over the years this hotel has kept abreast of changing times. The Palace is commodious, rambling, and thoroughly Edwardian in its decor and design. Many rooms on the top (fourth) floor have beamed ceilings and regional furniture. Others are invariably large and comfortable, offering well-insulated shelter from the cold winds outside. Most units contain balconies and baths, and some have well-used Oriental carpets. Winter rates are the highest, with singles on half board paying from 125F ($85) to 175F ($119) daily and doubles costing from 250F ($170) to 340F ($231.20). At other periods, singles, also on half board, cost from 85F ($57.80) to 120F ($81.60) daily, doubles paying from 170F ($115.60) to 240F ($163.20). Even more expensive suites are available. When you're in the high-ceilinged dining room, look for the intricately embroidered silk bedcover (said to be English and so old that even experts can't exactly date it), which hangs in an enormous frame. In one of the outbuildings lies the Alte Taverne, separately recommended in the "Après Ski" section. The hotel is open from June to September and December to April.

Hotel Beau-Site, CH-3715 Adelboden, Switzerland (tel. 033/73-22-22). Designed like a wood-sided chalet, this hotel was built in 1982 between the main street of town and the sheer drop-off of the mountainside. The warm and inviting lobby is filled with Oriental carpets and knickknacks that the Stirnimann family brought from their much older hotel, which was demolished to make room for the new building. On the premises is a pleasant lobby-level restaurant (see "Where to Dine"), and a rustically alpine-style stübli. Each of the 40 rooms contains a private bath, a phone, TV, and a view over the mists of the valley far below. Half-board rates in a single range from 100F ($68) to 150F ($102) daily, depending on the season, and doubles cost from 190F ($129.20) to 260F ($176.80). The hotel has a sauna, plus a children's playroom, and a particularly beautiful Turkish carpet in the lobby, which the aging owners, Mr. and Mrs. Stirnimann, brought back from a trip on the Orient Express from Istanbul many years ago.

Parkhotel Bellevue, CH-3715 Adelboden, Switzerland (tel. 033/73-16-21), is an attractive, updated establishment with many balconies, a flat roof, and several low-lying extensions spreading out from the main building. It is set on a steep slope above the resort. The Bellevue is landscaped into the hillside, with flagstone terraces, lots of flowers in summer, and a small reflecting pool. The decor is pleasingly understated, with a bar area and a warm-hued brick- and wood-walled restaurant. The Richard family, your hosts, charge from 100F ($68) to 150F ($102) daily, in a single and from 150F ($102) to 260F ($176.80) in a double, all tariffs including half board. The prices depend on the plumbing, season, and room exposure. The hotel is open June to October and December to April.

Hotel Huldi and **Waldhaus,** CH-3715 Adelboden, Switzerland (tel. 033/73-15-31), occupies two chalets, one old, one new, facing each other across the main street. My favorite part of this 50-room hostelry is its terrace, the chiseled flagstones of which look down on the large swimming pool and an alpine valley dotted with trees. The hotel has big windows, lots of balconies, and a secure niche dug into the side of the hill. The interior is cozily rustic, with masonry detailing, warm colors, and hewn beams and timbers. The restaurant prides itself on its cuisine and merits a separate recommendation. In high season, singles without bath cost 100F ($68) daily, rising to 105F ($71.40) to 120F ($81.60) with shower or bath. The rates based on double occupancy are 90F ($61.20) to 95F ($64.60) per person daily without bath, rising to 100F ($68) to 110F ($74.80) with bath. A buffet breakfast and dinner are included. In other seasons, doubles range from 65F ($44.20) to 90F ($61.20) per person, singles costing from 75F ($51) to 95F ($64.60), also including half board. Open June to September and December to April.

Hotel Kreuz, CH-3715 Adelboden, Switzerland (tel. 033/73-21-21), is a chalet right in the center. Well maintained, this well-known family hotel offers café tables set into a narrow embankment in summer, plus a popular pizzeria. A rustic restaurant serves meals to guests on the board plan, while the pizzeria prepares Italian specialties for the general public. The bedrooms are immaculate, with wood ceilings, big windows, private showers or baths, radios, and mini-bars. Depending on the season, the rate for half board ranges from 60F ($40.80) to 80F ($54.40) per person per day. Guests have free access to the nearby swimming pool and ice-skating rink.

WHERE TO DINE: A good place to eat, **Restaurant Panorama,** Hotel Beau-Site (tel. 033/73-22-22), is warmly decorated with lots of exposed wood, but the thing that most diners remember is the sweeping panorama of its views over the valley. Full meals are well prepared and generously portioned, so much so that occasionally, residents of other hotels will make it a special point to dine here. Fixed-price menus range from 35F ($23.80) to 40F ($27.20), but you can spend from 50F ($34) and more ordering à la carte. The chef prepares many grilled specialties, include Chateaubriand, served for two persons, and also fondue chinoise or bourguignonne. You might begin with one of the smoked-fish dishes, salmon or eel, or a plate of air-dried beef from the Grisons. Filets of fera, a lake fish, is served with herbs, or you can enjoy one of the tasty veal dishes. A tempting array of desserts are offered, but many skiers prefer the Irish coffee. Meals are served daily from noon to 2 p.m. and 6 to 9:30 p.m.

Rôtisserie Le Tartare (tel. 033/73-15-31) is the specialty restaurant of the previously recommended Hotel Huldi and Waldhaus. The maître rôtisseur, K. P. Gygax, who is also the owner, has earned a distinguished reputation locally for his superb food, which is served only at dinner seven days a week from 6 to 11 p.m. in winter (closed in summer). Against a backdrop of a regional tavern decor, you can peruse the menu. You might select one of the hors d'oeuvres, both hot and cold, including snails in brioche. Many choice cuts of meat are grilled on the open fire, including lamb cutlets or entrecôte. The specialties of the chef, however, are steak tartare, contrefilet Carmen, beef Stroganoff, tournedos maître queux, and fondue bourguignonne. Expect to spend 50F ($34) and up, perhaps finishing off with a kirsch sorbet.

APRÈS SKI: There are several small nightclubs and bars, and the place isn't as sleepy as it first appears to be. **Alte Taverne,** Hotel Nevada Palace (tel. 033/73-21-31), lying within an outbuilding of the previously recommended Nevada Palace, is the premier nightlife facility of Adelboden. Although it could easily pass for a building at least 200 years old, it was constructed when the weathered timbers collected from six of the region's old barns were used to expand a very old chalet. Beginning every evening at 5 p.m., and lasting until at least 1 a.m., some corner of the rustic building comes alive with an influx of customers.

À la carte meals are served by flickering candles inside the Grill Room. Meals are offered from 11 a.m. to 2 p.m. and from 6 to 11 p.m. As you'd expect from the decor, the specialties are each Swiss-inspired, and include an array of veal and beef dishes, raclette, small grills, fish dishes, fondues, veal kidneys, flambé and crêpes Suzette. Meals cost from 35F ($23.80).

An even more rustic dining spot is the Chasstuben (Cheese Stube), where a cheese fondue with coffee costs 15F ($10.20) per person. Also in the basement is yet another dining room, still heavily beamed and very, very alpine, the Spaghetti Room, where a half-dozen kinds of pasta sell for 10F ($6.80) per platter.

Naturally, there's a barnlike disco with a high ceiling and an adjacent bar festooned with antique farm implements. A cover charge is imposed only when there's a particularly popular musical group imported from the urban part of Europe. A large beer costs 7F ($4.75).

My best advice is to wander through this building's labyrinth of dark hallways until you find the restaurant, drinking spot, or dancing corner you feel most at home in. The entire complex is open in winter only, between mid-December and Easter.

Many après-skiers gather in the Tiefen Keller of the **Hotel Huldi** (tel. 033/73-15-31) for a tangy fondue, good company, or else, much later in the evening, a nightcap. It is open only in winter from 5 p.m. to midnight nightly. Happy hour is from 5 to 7 p.m., after which food is served.

The Pizzeria da Alberto at the **Hotel Kreuz** (tel. 033/73-21-21) also draws a lively après-ski crowd. The oven is exposed to the customers and some of the world's tallest peppermills await your request. Pizzas cost from 8.50F ($5.80) and are served daily from 5 to 11 p.m. in summer, from 11:30 a.m. to 11 p.m. in winter. Closed Wednesday.

13. GSTAAD

Against a backdrop of glaciers and mountain lakes, Gstaad is a haven of movie stars and the wealthy, including Elizabeth Taylor, Prince Karim Aga Khan, King Juan Carlos of Spain, and Baroness Hubert de Rothschild. Princess Grace formerly paid an annual visit. Director Blake Edwards and his wife Julie Andrews, have set up a chalet in Gstaad. However, celebrities in Gstaad are usually treated simply as ordinary persons, except by first-time tourists.

Gstaad, at a junction of a quartet of sleeping valleys and practically at the southern tip of the Bernese Oberland, was once only a depot at which to change horses. Some travelers put up here if they were journeying between Lausanne and Montreux by a brass-and-redwood steam engine. And thus it began to grow as a resort, beginning with the opening of the deluxe Alpina Grand.

In those days summer was the peak season, and a string of White Russian and Hungarian families, all wealthy, arrived with vast entourages that included everybody from valets to nannies. By 1912, two years before the outbreak of World War I, the Palace opened, promising "the ultimate" in luxury.

In the middle of World War I (1916), Le Rosey school opened in the satellite town of Tolle. The *Guinness Book of World Records* considers it "the most expensive prep school in the world." The school helped fan the reputation of Gstaad because it brought a string of visitors to see their children, including King Leopold of Belgium (who is said to have been the first crowned head of Europe to pay a visit). In time he was followed by such celebrated, and sometimes infamous, personages as the Shah of Iran, King Farouk of Egypt, and even Winston Churchill.

With its chalet hotels it somehow retains an Old World atmosphere. Many of these chalets are privately owned, and some of the bistros and cafés in town (which are only open in peak season) operate like private clubs. In chic, Gstaad is equaled in winter only by St. Moritz, Arosa, and Davos. Certainly there is nothing to equal it for fashion in the Bernese Oberland.

Gstaad has many winding narrow streets and fashionable boutiques that open and close with frightening irregularity. The hamlet also has many detractors. Lured by extensive media coverage, many unsuspecting visitors have arrived, especially at the "wrong" time of the year, and found Gstaad a "bloody bore," to quote one irate British reader. "Unless you're a house guest of Roger Moore, or are staying in a suite at the Gstaad Palace, you'll miss out on what's going on."

That, perhaps, is an overstatement. Actually, life flourishes on many levels in Gstaad, and although the resort is expensive, there are many moderately priced hotels, taverns, and guest houses as well.

Gstaad is at 3,445 feet, and the altitude of its highest skiable mountain is 6,550 feet, with a vertical drop of 3,555 feet. In all, it has access to 70 lifts, mountain railroads, and gondolas. East of the village is Eggli, a ski area reached by cable car. Here, with its sunny, southern exposure, are the most beginner and intermediate runs. Wispellan-Sanetch is favored for afternoon skiing, with lots of runs down to the village. At the summit is the Glacier des Diablarets at a height of 9,900 feet. Wasserngrat, reached from the south side of the resort, is another area favored for skiing. More advanced skiers prize Wasserngrat for its powder skiing on steep slopes. Even though Gstaad's own skiing is limited, it lies near half a dozen major ski resorts of Switzerland. Many prefer to stay in Gstaad, visiting the ski areas farther afield during the day. Saanen to the east lies at 3,450 feet above sea level and can be easily reached by car or via the Montreux-Oberland railway from north or south. There's also a small airfield for guests who fly in.

To reach Gstaad, many fly to Geneva, only a 2½-hour drive away. Others fly into Zurich.

The resort is rich in entertainment and sports facilities, including the world-class Gstaad International Tennis Tournament, the most important tennis event in the country, with prize money sufficient to attract such tennis greats as Lewis Hoad, Budge Patty, Rod Laver, John Newcombe, Ilie Nastase, and many others. In addition it offers a 200-mile network of hiking paths, cable cars (to altitudes of 5,250, 6,560, and 10,000 feet—the last offering skiing even in summer), 20 open-air and covered tennis courts, and both heated indoor and outdoor swimming pools.

The **Swiss Ski School** at Gstaad (tel. 030/4-18-65) has first-class teachers and qualified mountain and touring guides. Special classes for children are offered. Some 100 private instructors are available.

A full day ski pass is sold costing 37F ($25.15) per person which is good for the use of all lifts in the Gstaad area. It includes passage on a bus departing from Gstaad for the base of the gondola platform at Reusch, which is the point where all the ski lifts begin.

You don't have to stay only in Gstaad—in fact, many guests prefer one of the satellite resorts of **Saanen** or **Schönried,** both of which are summer resorts as well as winter sports centers and have excellent accommodations. Saanen, is, in many ways, the more important town. In August the occasion of the Menuhin Festival draws an international music-loving crowd there. Some of its wood built chalets with their handsomely carved façades and projecting gables date from the 1500s. Whichever resort you chose—Gstaad, Saanen, or Schönried—you'll be surrounded by a countryside of dramatic glaciers and peaceful alpine pastures. This part of the country, called Saanenland, is considered the most beautiful part of the Bernese Oberland, which itself is considered one of the most beautiful parts of Switzerland.

ACCOMMODATIONS: Don't come here if economy is a major factor in your holiday. The prices, as you'll soon see, are lethal, especially in high season. When business is slow, many of the hostelries shut down.

In a Class by Itself

Palace Hotel Gstaad, CH-3780 Gstaad, Switzerland (tel. 030/8-31-31). In a world of declining standards, this hotel remains one of the most sought-after luxury hideaways in the world, where the heads of industry, cinema stars, and the fashionable artistocracy come to romp and play. Both the hotel and the guests, seem to revolve in an almost frighteningly chic lifestyle with a kind of very expensive complicity. The hotel was opened in 1913 on a forested knoll high above the center of Gstaad. Its mock-fortified corner towers and neo-medieval façade are often the first structures in Gstaad to be recognized by new arrivals.

The nerve center of this citadel lies near the baronial stone fireplace of the elegantly paneled main salon. (Kept constantly burning, the fireplace with its baroque columns is in a way the symbol of the hotel.) From various hallways radiate a cluster of restaurants, bars, discos, sports, and physical/psychological maintenance services that, by even the most demanding standards, are simply superb. More information about the restaurants and nightlife facilities are coming up. Contained within the hotel is the most avant-garde swimming pool in Gstaad, one that boasts an underwater sound system. It is transformed into an extension of the adjacent disco late at night when a platform is lowered over the top of its waters.

Each of the 150 accommodations is as plush, tasteful, large, and distinguished as you'd expect. Many are suites. Even the medieval tower, mentioned above, contains a vertical row of what might be the most luxurious bathrooms in Switzerland. None of this tasting of the grand life comes cheaply. In winter with half board included, singles range from 340F ($231.20) to 490F ($333.20) daily, and doubles go for 590F ($401.20) to 820F ($557.60). In summer, with half board, singles are charged 250F ($170) to 350F ($238) daily, with doubles costing 380F ($258.40) to 600F ($408). The hotel is open from June 10 to September 20 and from mid-December to late March. Always in attendance at his court is the hotel's distinguished owner, Ernst Scherz, whose motto "Every king is a client, and every client is a king" seems appropriate, and if you can afford it, true.

The Upper Bracket

Standing against a backdrop of an evergreen-studded mountain, **Steigenberger Hotel,** CH-3792 Saanen, Switzerland (tel. 030/8-33-88), is one of the most inviting in the Bernese Oberland. It is a cluster of Saanen chalets (all linked together), designed by an architect who wanted the wooden buildings to blend harmoniously into the landscape. From any vantage point on the property, guests enjoy one of the most panoramic vistas over the Saane Valley and neighboring Gstaad. The chalets have wide overhanging eaves and balconies and peaked roofs; a view of the inside reveals careful craftsmanship and a sense of design. Many of the ceilings are of polished pine. On a winter's night, guests gather around a crackling fire in the lobby lounge, while enjoying a pre-dinner drink. The hotel is equally inviting in summer, when balcony geraniums make for a cascade of floral splendor.

Guests register under massive beams and are shown to one of the 145 handsomely equipped bedrooms. The cozy rooms are fitted with spruce and mountain pine paneling and traditional furniture, and even the windows and balcony doors contain wooden crossbars. Modern amenities include direct-dial phone, radio, mini-bar, and baths with large mirrors. Including half board, singles range from 130F ($88.40) to 290F ($197.20) daily, with doubles costing from 110F ($74.80) to 270F ($183.60) per person, depending on the season.

Steigenberger is proud that its heated pool inside is "always in season." Guests can swim in warm water while enjoying a view of snow-capped mountain peaks. Facilities also include a solarium and a sauna. The hotel is also an active center for night life (more about that later), and it offers two restaurants, one elegant and one rustic. The kitchen prepares both hearty regional dishes and cuisine moderne specialties (see "Where to Dine"). The hotel, like everything else in Saanen, lies 1¼ miles from Gstaad.

To reserve a room, call the Steigenberger Reservation System (in New York

City, 212/593-2988; toll free in New York State at 800/882-4777; and toll free nationwide at 800/223-5652.

Other Leading Hotels

Grand Hotel Alpina, CH-3780 Gstaad, Switzerland (tel. 030/4-57-25), was the first deluxe hotel to be built in Gstaad. It sits in an isolated position on a pine-covered hill slightly above the resort. The hotel is a half-timbered building with a well-maintained tile roof that curves slightly at the outer ends of its many gables and ridges. A square-based turret caps the entire structure with a happily Victorian symbol of another era. The interior has been renovated into a modern style, with patterned carpeting and deep armchairs. Very little of the original embellishments remain inside, but the place is still warm, inviting, and restful. The Burri family are your hosts, charging from 120F ($81.60) to 210F ($142.80) per person with half board in accommodations with private bath. The hotel has an outstanding restaurant and it's known for its superb service. Open June to September and December to March.

Bellevue Grand Hotel, CH-3780 Gstaad, Switzerland (tel. 030/8-31-71). Superb hospitality, good food, excellent housekeeping, and lavish comfort have made this hotel a favorite for longer than anyone cares to remember. A leading four-star hotel (the top of the first-class charts), it stands in a serene park with tall old trees. The bedrooms are a strong point, as many of them are spacious with light, restful colors. The price depends on the season and the room assignment. Most guests book in here on the half-board plan, paying from 105F ($71.40) to 180F ($122.40) daily in a single, 85F ($57.80) to 165F ($112.20) per person in a double. Guests are accepted from June through September and from December through March. All units contain bath or shower, a mini-bar, a self-dial phone, radio, and TV. Many open onto balconies. The long-standing motto, "Every guest is a king and every king only a guest," may never have been literally true, but it's a charming thought, nonetheless.

Guests dine in the regular dining room, the Grill Room, or the Curling Restaurant. Many regional specialties are served, along with international favorites, including veal steaks in raspberry vinegar, fondues (either cheese, bourguignonne, or chinoise). Favorite dishes from the Grisons are also served. Menus cost from 38F ($25.85) to 85F ($57.80). The piano bar is a focal point in the evening. Everyone's favorite spot is in front of the fireplace in the elegant public salon.

Hostellerie Alpenrose, CH-3778 Schönried-Gstaad, Switzerland (tel. 030/4-12-38), is justifiably famous as one of the best restaurants in the Bernese Oberland, but many visitors overlook it as a charming and secluded place to spend the night. It lies beside the main highway about 2½ miles northwest of Gstaad. Schönried is said to offer better skiing longer into the season than even that found in nearby Gstaad. The only *Relais & Chateaux* within 30 miles, the establishment is loaded with regional charm, an aesthetically satisfying collection of local antiques, and dozens of charming extras. Many of these adopt an added luster because of the well-bred charm of the establishment's owner, Monika von Siebenthal. Soft-spoken friend to rich and famous guests, who have stayed or dined here for many years, she is probably the most memorable and gracious hotelière in the valley.

The solidly constructed chalet that contains this hotel was built in 1907. There are only five exquisitely decorated rooms, each of which has a sheathing of carefully crafted pine, a private bath, TV, phone, and a gracefully rustic collection of old pinewood furniture. Because of the elegant nature of the in-house restaurant (see "Where to Dine"), it would be regrettable to stay here on anything less than half board. On that plan, the rate for two persons ranges from 270F ($183.60) to 320F ($217.60) per day. Children under 12 receive a reduction of 30% to 50%, depending on their age.

Residence Cabana, CH-3792 Gstaad-Saanen, Switzerland (tel. 030/4-48-55). By the looks of the modern façade, which nonetheless retains a chalet ambience about it, you'll guess that something unusual waits for you inside—a series of rooms with massive polished beams supporting the ceiling, a complete exercise room, and an imaginative selection of textiles, which include boldly patterned pieces from underdeveloped countries. The indoor swimming pool has lounge chairs and coffee tables placed around it, Caribbean style, while the heated outdoor swimming pool welcomes swimmers with clouds of steam, even during snowstorms. This hotel is part of a Swiss chain, so although you might miss the sense of being part of a family-run establishment, you make up for it in the quality of the accommodations. Each of the comfortable bedrooms has a private bath. In low season, the half-board rate for two persons ranges from 230F ($156.40) to 270F ($183.60) daily, rising in winter to 260F ($176.80) to 320F ($217.60).

Hotel Bernerhof, CH-3780 Gstaad, Switzerland (tel. 030/8-33-66), a leading four-star hotel, has uninterrupted wood balconies stretching across the façade. These and the many additional touches make a stay here enjoyable, especially with the restaurant (see "Where to Dine"). Your host is Leonz Brunschi, who charges from 109F ($74.10) to 125F ($85) daily in a single in low season, the rate rising to 157F ($106.75) in high season. Doubles in off-season cost 194F ($131.90) to 226F ($153.70), jumping to 270F ($183.60) to 290F ($197.20) in high season. All tariffs quoted are half board, and each well-furnished unit contains a private bath or a shower. Use of the sauna, indoor swimming pool, and whirlpool is included in the rates.

Hotel Ermitage-Golf, CH-3778 Schönried-Gstaad, Switzerland (tel. 030/4-27-27), is a hotel for all seasons, and it's one of the largest in the area. In spite of its name, it is not near a golf course, although there is a nine-hole course in the area. This is a warm, cozy retreat on a cold winter's night and a summertime pleasure chalet, when its balconies burst into bloom with boxes of red geraniums. The pool is also good in both seasons: There is a heated and protected indoor version as well as one outside. In fair weather, parasols and chaise longues are placed on the grounds while guests soak up the alpine sunshine. The bedrooms are individually furnished, with an accent on maximum comfort. Well-upholstered pieces and wood paneling, with an occasional Oriental rug, give the accommodations atmosphere. Per person rates for half board (a stay of three days is required) cost from 95F ($64.60) to 260F ($176.80), depending on the season and the room assignment. The most expensive accommodations are junior suites with balconies facing south. Innkeepers Heiner Lutz and Laurenz Schmid receive guests all year from December to April and from mid-May until the end of October.

Other facilities on the premises include a Finnish sauna, a bio-sauna, a Turkish bath, a Jacuzzi, a solarium, a bodybuilding room, a panoramic resting lounge, massage treatments, and a tennis court. If you're not staying here you might want to consider the hotel's drinking and dining facilities, among the best in the area. They also cover a wide price range, from the elegantly decorated and expensive Le Gourmet to the more democratic Stübli. Other restaurants on the premises include Table d'Hotes and Spycher. Most evenings end in the disco-bar, Happy Night, which often is.

Hotel Christiana, CH-3780 Gstaad, Switzerland (tel. 030/4-51-21), is beautifully outfitted inside with a satisfying combination of white walls and glowing paneling, Oriental rugs, and tasteful furniture. The bedrooms are comfortable, but some of the suites are spectacular, especially one with white carpets and white upholstery. This is the smallest first-class hotel in Gstaad, which presumably means the service will be more individualized. From the outside the establishment looks like a chalet, with particularly elaborate gingerbread under the eaves. Singles rent for 210F ($142.80) to 260F ($176.80) daily, while doubles cost 350F ($238) to 430F ($292.40), depending on the plumbing, the exposure, and the season. Half board is included. In summer guests have free entrance to the heated swimming pool near the Palace Hotel.

Hotel Olden, CH-3780 Gstaad, Switzerland (tel. 030/4-34-44), is one of the most charming hotels in Gstaad, its façade painted over with regional floral designs, pithy bits of folk wisdom, and the date of the initial construction (1899). The interior has all the architectural delights you'd expect in a building like this, ranging from the embellishments carved or painted into the stone lintels around many of the doors to the elegant woodworking over the ceilings and walls. A summer terrace in front serves meals and drinks. If you want to stay in both the geographic and spiritual heart of Gstaad, you've come to the right place. The owner, Hedi Donizetti, is the hearty ruling "empress of Gstaad." Even though many of her celebrity guests prefer to stay elsewhere, such as at the Palace, they still frequent her restaurant, lodge, and bar (see both "Where to Dine" and "Aprés Ski"). Rooms are pleasantly and attractively furnished in a typical style. In off-season, half-board rates range from 110F ($74.80) to 128F ($87.05) daily in a single, depending on the plumbing. Doubles, on the same arrangement, pay from 220F ($149.60) to 256F ($174.10). In the peak season, which is during certain parts of the winter and from July 6 until the end of August, singles pay from 130F ($88.40) to 170F ($115.60) daily, while doubles are charged 260F ($176.80) to 340F ($231.20), including half board.

Hotel Hornberg, CH-3770 Saanenmöser, Switzerland (tel. 030/4-44-40), is a pleasant family-style chalet hotel about six miles outside Gstaad. The hotel is outfitted in a well-maintained format that is half-rustic, half-modern. The dining room has one wall of hewn native stone and a wooden ceiling, with white napery covering the sunlit tables. Outdoor and indoor pools on the premises offer a chance to use up the excess energy you didn't already burn off on your winter or summer sports regimes. Children are welcomed here as well. Peter and Elisabeth von Siebenthal, the owners, have set up a children's playroom. Fireplaces take off much of the winter chill. The meal plan here is called the "brunch-pension" arrangement, because the breakfast served is actually a very ample meal offered buffet style every day from 8 to 11 a.m. It's so generous that many clients prefer to skip lunch altogether and wait for the traditional meal in the evening. Rooms come with and without private baths. From December through April and in July and August, guests are charged from 78F ($53.05) to 150F ($102) per person daily on half-board terms. At other times, the half-board rate ranges from 70F ($47.60) to 140F ($95.20) per person. Rates depend on the season and the plumbing, and the hotel receives from June to October and December to April.

Hôtel Arc-en-Ciel, CH-3780 Gstaad, Switzerland (tel. 030/8-31-91), is an attractively decorated alpine chalet ten minutes from the center of Gstaad, which many lovers of calm will appreciate in peak season. The bedrooms are tasteful, combining lots of horizontal wood planking with white plaster walls for a cozy, well-lit ambience of great comfort. All accommodations have private bath. Singles cost 65F ($44.90) to 150F ($102) daily, depending on the season, and doubles go for 140F ($95.20) to 300F ($204), all tariffs including breakfast. The hotel has a pizzeria, two tennis courts, and a heated swimming pool on the premises. Open May to October and December to April.

Less Expensive Choices

Posthotel Rössli, CH-3780 Gstaad, Switzerland (tel. 030/4-34-12), is rustically authentic according to the Bernese Oberland style, but it's also well heated and furnished with modern conveniences. Huge acres of the interior are covered with paneling, including the bedrooms, which are cozy behind the weatherproof windows. The establishment lies in the center of the village, in a chalet with green shutters and a flag of the Bernese canton flying over the front door. The restaurant and bierstube inside welcome almost as many local residents as they do international guests. All units contain private baths or showers. Depending on the season, singles go from 80F ($54.40) to 130F ($88.40) daily, and doubles from 160F ($108.80) to 260F ($176.80), all with half board included. Reudi Widmer and his family, your hosts, also maintain the restaurant, where fixed-price meals cost from 28F ($19), with à la carte meals beginning at 25F ($17). The Rössli is open June to October and December to April.

Hotel Alphorn, CH-3780 Gstaad, Switzerland (tel. 030/4-45-45), was opened in 1970 at the base of the Wispile cable car. The chalet is owned by the Mösching family. The intimate hotel offers 21 cozy rooms to guests. Singles, which come with and without private bath, range in price from 65F ($44.20) to 110F ($74.80) daily, depending on the season. Doubles, all with private bath, go from 140F ($95.20) to 240F ($163.20) daily. Half board is included in all tariffs. The difference in rates depends on the season. The hotel has an indoor pool, plus a ski shop. Specialties of the restaurant include trout and cheese dishes as well as a "dish of the house" made with fresh mushrooms. Open June to October and December to April.

Sporthotel Victoria, CH-3780 Gstaad, Switzerland (tel. 030/4-14-31), is the personal statement of the Oehrli family, who prove to be congenial hosts. Their three-story hotel is in the center of town, two minutes from the train station. The accommodations are tastefully furnished with simple furniture, some of it alpine, and the bedrooms usually have lots of paneling and every comfort. A musical group performs in the rustic restaurant and dancing bar. Singles cost 100F ($68) to 130F ($88.40) daily, while doubles range from 200F ($136) to 260F ($176.80), including half board. Rates depend on the season. An à la carte pizzeria is also on the premises.

Hotel Boo, CH-3792 Saanen (tel. 030/4-14-41), was originally built in 1891 but was tastefully upgraded in 1962. This cozy chalet boasts row upon row of German language verses stencilled onto its wooden façade. It is most visited for its rustic and convivial pub (which we'll go to later), but Boo also contains a handful of cozy and comfortable bedrooms, each with a private bath and plenty of frilly and floral accents. Other amenities include a phone, radio, and, in only the most expensive ones, a kitchenette with private balcony. Open year round, the hotel charges from 80F ($54.40) to 110F ($74.80) daily in a single, the cost going up to 140F ($95.20) to 180F ($122.40) in a double, including breakfast (the only meal served). One of its most memorable features is its location in this antique town on the main street. The unusual name of the hotel comes from Thomas Boo, its owner.

WHERE TO DINE: Most guests take either half or full board at their hotel, which is often required in the very peak seasons. There are few independent eateries in Gstaad that are noteworthy, perhaps owing to that very reason. Some notable exceptions follow.

Hostellerie Alpenrose, Schönried-Gstaad (tel. 030/4-12-38). Within a series of carefully paneled and charming dining rooms, it combines superb gastronomy with a feeling of personal, even intimate, warmth and well-being. Considered one of the very finest restaurants in the Bernese Oberland, this is the domain of the gracious and charming Monika von Siebenthal. Her father built the first ski lift in the region in 1935, setting off a craze which today continues unabated. She has elevated a modest pension into a culinary citadel known throughout Switzerland for its superb cuisine. Her five capable and attractive children aid in the administration of this landmark restaurant.

In high season, residents of the surrounding chalets seem to descend en masse on the elegantly decorated dining rooms. Menu items are as sophisticated and ultrafresh as the demanding clientele requires. Specialties include a traditional family recipe for slices of marinated saltwater salmon, various types of smoked fish with fresh baby vegetables, ravioli of Canadian lobster with spring vegetables, and a three-filet extravaganza "Michel" (named after Mrs. von Siebenthal's talented young son, who was trained as a chef in France). Other treats include medallions of hare with basil on a bed of eggplant and fresh peas, and Scottish lamb with lentils and pink peppercorn sauce. Don't overlook desserts—they're sumptuous. Examples include an apple sorbet with a champagne sabayon, or a pineapple crêpe with a ragoût of oranges.

The establishment, the only *Relais & Châteaux* within many miles, charges around 120F ($81.60) for a seven-course menu gastronomique. Full à la carte meals begin at 75F ($51). Meals are served every day in winter, with orders accepted from noon to 2 p.m. and from 7 to 10 p.m. In summer, meal hours are the same as in winter, although no lunch is ever served on Monday or Tuesday. Reservations are a very good idea. Don't overlook the possibility of an after-dinner drink in the nightclub Sammy's (see the "Après Ski" section that follows). This hotel, its restaurant, and nightclub lie about 2½ miles northwest of Gstaad.

Restaurant Chesery (tel. 030/4-24-51) is considered one of the ten best restaurants in Switzerland. It was originally built in 1962 by Karim Aga Khan and later occupied by German playboy Gunther Sachs. It's behind a carefully crafted chalet façade in the geographical heart of town. Its interior, sheathed as it is with a combination of pink marble floors and polished pine, is alluring. Meals are served from 11:30 a.m. to 11:30 p.m. every day, while a piano bar entertains from 9 p.m. to 3 a.m. Franz Rosskogler, the director of this place, calls upon the suppliers of Europe for the freshest seasonal ingredients. A nine-course menu dégustation sells for 108F ($73.45), while full à la carte meals cost from 90F ($61.20). Menu choices change almost every day, depending on the ingredients of the season. Representative offerings include a warm salad of red snapper, terrine of goose liver with a sherry-flavored gelatin, a cassolette of flap mushrooms with a suprême of quail, filet of beef poached with grated horseradish, and a soufflé of white cheese resting on the essence of fresh seasonal fruits. Reservations are suggested.

Grill Room, Palace Hotel (tel. 030/8-31-31). The never-ending parade of the rich and the chic, make a meal here more than totally entertaining. Depending on the number of guests in residence, the hotel opens up to three different dining rooms, each outfitted with elegant paneling, and accompanied with the impeccable service you'd expect from such a prestigious hotel. Even though the Palace is open only seasonally, it manages to snare some of the finest chefs in the Bernese Oberland. They are needed to please an exceptionally demanding clientele. The grill is open nightly from 7:30 to 11 p.m. Many guests prefer to let these fine chefs make their decisions for them by ordering the 80F ($54.40) set dinner. These meals are carefully balanced, contain an array of tempting and delectable dishes, and are beautifully served by a well-trained staff.

Naturally you can also order from the à la carte menu, a typical meal averaging 100F ($68) and beyond—way beyond. The modern-day version of Onassis always makes for the caviar or the foie gras, but you might happily settle for one of the superb hors d'oeuvres (which include beefsteak tartare) or one of the delicate soups or consommés. Main courses are broken down on the menu into five major divisions: fish or shellfish, poultry, beef, veal, and lamb. This wide repertoire includes imaginative interpretations of old favorites. Desserts tend to be elaborate, but you could settle for a sorbet made with fresh fruits of the season. Be forewarned that the maître d' at this restaurant has absolutely no sense of humor about clients who aren't dressed in appropriately formal garb. If you or your companion happens to be a male without a necktie, he'll be requested to dine in the Sans-Cravatte (see below).

Sans-Cravatte, Palace Hotel (tel. 030/8-31-31). Don't assume that this is a budget restaurant just because the very formal staff doesn't require men to wear neckties. It's on a raised and rustically elegant platform a few steps above the elegant main dining room of the intensely prestigious Palace Hotel. There's a separate entrance so that the latest visiting movie star or whatever reclusive billionaire happening to be in residence can come and go in a sweater and not feel out of place by mingling with the formally dressed clients of the other public rooms. Only dinner is served, every night from 7:30 to 11:30. The menu is the same as that served within the Palace Hotel's Grill Room (see above), a fixed-price meal costing 80F ($54.40), while an à la carte repast goes for 100F ($68) and up.

La Grande Terrasse, Palace Hotel (tel. 030/8-31-31), accepts the honor of being the largest covered terrace in Switzerland, with an almost alarmingly large floor space which is either sheltered from the cold or exposed to the sun at the flick of an electric switch. The floor of the place is covered in white tiles in a classical Greek or Roman pattern. In winter, the terrace is open for lunch only when the sun is shining and then from noon to 3 p.m. daily. In summer, service is daily from noon to 3 p.m. and 7 to 11 p.m. However, evening service depends entirely on the whim of management and the weather, of course. Amid flourishing pine trees and masses of flowers, the restaurant offers elegant meals brought out by a battalion of white-jacketed employees. Full meals begin at 35F ($23.80) but could cost far more, of course, depending on what you order. The food is the same as that offered in the main dining room of the hotel (not the more elaborate Grill).

Fromagerie, Palace Hotel (tel. 030/8-31-31), might be the way even a budgeteer can catch a glimpse of the most famous and prestigious hotel in the Bernese Oberland. It's actually a dignified and elegant version of an alpine raclette stube, with a deceptively simple menu and walls paneled in the same light-grained pine you've seen in hundreds of other Swiss restaurants. Only dinner is served, every night from 7 to 10:30. Most of the dishes are concocted in one way or another with cheese, although a salad buffet and a pasta menu are also available. A full meal will cost from 50F ($34). Jackets and ties are not required, but reservations are a good idea. The Fromagerie is below the lobby level.

D'Halte Beiz, Steigenberger Hotel, Auf der Halten, Saanen (tel. 030/8-33-88), is the regional restaurant of this previously recommended hotel. It is open all year except from November 1 to December 15 until 11:30 a.m. to 11 p.m. daily. Under rustic beams, while seated at a colorfully laid table, diners can partake of Swiss specialties. At lunch in winter, when most skiers are on the slopes, a magnificent salad table with many types of fresh, crisp lettuce, is spread before you. Your meal is served as you take in a view of the Rüblihorn. You might order a local herb schnapps, a Bätzi, and finish with Swiss cherry cake. In between you can select such dishes as filet of fera, a fish from Lake Thun, or one of the grill dishes including Chateaubriand or carré d'agneau (lamb). Lunches cost from 25F ($17), while dinners range from 40F ($27.20).

The more formal restaurant, the **Sonnenhalte,** sets a sumptuous breakfast buffet every morning from 7 to 10:30 daily. That is patronized mainly by hotel guests. But nonresidents can come here, too, especially in the evening from 7 to 9:30 when both a set menu (which changes daily) and an à la carte menu are offered. The chefs prepare several cuisine moderne dishes as well as a wide array of regional and continental dishes. Only the freshest of ingredients are used. The best time to visit is on Wednesday for the buffet with live folkloric music, costing from 55F ($37.40) per person. The daily set menu costs 45F ($30.60) and is a well-prepared, multi-course affair, one of the best food values at the resort. From the hotel's cellars comes a wide selection of Swiss wines from such cantons as Vaud and the Tessin, as well as a selection of continental wines, such as those from France and Italy, with some vintages from faraway California.

Hotel Olden (tel. 030/4-34-44). Within the street level of the previously recommended hotel, you'll have the choice of a duet of eating areas. La Pinte, closest to the front entrance, has floral patterns painted onto its paneling, which make the cozy room appear a lot like an enormous piece of alpine furniture. Open continuously as a bar and restaurant from 11 a.m. to 11 p.m. daily, it offers platters of food from 14F ($9.50). These include straightforward dishes such as brochettes, grilled meats, bündnerfleisch (air-dried beef), and a kirsch-laden tart. This is very much of an all-purpose room that, depending on the time of day, doubles as an après-ski bar for the chic, the prestigious, and the merely beautiful, who mingle with a rustic crew of locals, often oldtime ski instructors.

In terms of gastronomy, the more sophisticated (and more expensive) dining area is toward the rear of the street level. There, the Olden Restaurant serves full meals from noon to 2 p.m. and from 7:30 to 10 p.m. daily. Surrounded with pine paneling while given formal service, you can order full à la carte meals for 55F ($37.40) and up. Fixed-price menus range from 35F ($23.80) to a many-faceted menu gastronomique at 90F ($61.20). Dishes are likely to include smoked salmon, fresh goose liver terrine, shrimp bisque with green peppercorns, house-style tagliatelle, raclette, medallions of veal with a confit of lemon, and Scottish lamb. Reservations are suggested for the more formal restaurant.

Restaurant Chlösterli, at Grund-Gstaad (tel. 030/5-10-45), requires a three-mile trek south of Gstaad, to the farming hamlet of Grund. Originally built as a heavily timbered barn in the 1600s, it now contains an interesting disco (see "Après-Ski") and a trio of cozily decorated dining rooms. Except during its annual closings, meals are served only in the evening, 7 to 10:30 p.m. daily. (Of course, thanks to the adjacent disco, the place stays open much, much later.) Full meals cost from 40F ($27.20), and might include an array of soups, selections from a salad board, medallions of veal with morels, grilled veal or beef steaks, house-style smoked trout, and flambéed mocha ice cream. Reservations are suggested, especially in the height of the midwinter season. The establishment is closed from Easter to June and during all of November.

Ristorante Rialto (tel. 030/4-34-74), in the heart of Gstaad, is one of the finest Italian restaurants in the Bernese Oberland. Rome-born Francesco Naredi is the chef de restaurant, and he uses only the freshest ingredients. Like all good Italian cookery, his menu changes with the seasons. Hours are daily from 11:30 a.m. to 10 p.m. However, it shuts down on Monday during the slow seasons in Gstaad, from April to June and October and November. You can order meals costing from 40F ($27.20). You might begin with a selection of antipasti, followed by the salmon carpaccio with a truffle cream sauce, or one of the pasta dishes, including pappardella. The risotto, served with fresh asparagus, is also excellent, and I'm fond of the chef's sole Caruso. You can drop in from 2:30 to 6:30 p.m., ordering from La Piccola Carta, a limited menu with such dishes as soups, pastas, salads, and one or two veal dishes.

Restaurant Bernerhof, in the Hotel Bernerhof (tel. 030/8-33-66), is a tavern-style restaurant serving many Italian specialties, such as risotto with "fruits of the sea," excellent soups, sometimes with mussels and scampi, veal liver Venetian style, ravioli in a basil-flavored sauce, filet of beef in a mustard sauce, and some good pork dishes. A meal costs from 35F ($23.80), a menu gastronomique going for 50F ($34). Hours are from 7:30 a.m. to 11:30 p.m. daily except Tuesday and in May, October, and November. On the premises is the popular Stöckli Bar.

APRÈS SKI: Gstaad has the most fashionable après-ski scene in the Bernese Oberland. Many nightclubs come and go, but **La Pinte** (also known as the Café Olden) at the Hotel Olden (tel. 030/4-34-44), is one of the most popular places in town. (Even guests from the Gstaad Palace go here for a lark.) If you're here just to mingle with the skiers, a large mug of beer costs 3F ($2.05).

The Olden Hotel also has a disco, **La Cave.** In the basement level of the famous hotel, it's open nightly only in winter, from December 20 until mid-

March. During that period, it opens at 8 p.m., closing at 2 or 3 a.m., depending on the crowd. Entrance is free, the decor is barnyard-rustic, and it offers both live bands and the option of ordering light meals.

The owner of the hotel, Hedi Donizetti, along with her husband, Fausto, purchased the Olden in the 1920s, and ever since then the world has come to their door, including King Juan Carlos of Spain. Hedi, who is likely to be found at the rear of the bar, has glass bar mugs, painted with larkspur and edelweiss, for her favorite clients. One such client is Liza Minnelli, who one night took the microphone to sing her version of "New York, New York."

Green Go Disco, Palace Hotel (tel. 030/8-31-31), is the most expensive disco in town, but a visit to its futuristic interior affords an opportunity to see the rich and famous at play. Filled with a shadowy decor of orange, green, and black, it's illuminated with pinpricks of light that manage to make everything twice as mysterious. When it's crowded, a platform descends over the waters of the adjacent indoor swimming pool so that an additional dance floor is created. The winter entrance fee is 40F ($27.20), which includes the first drink. The second drink costs from 15F ($10.20), however. In summer, no entrance fee is charged.

Sammy's Bar / Bistro, Hostellerie Alpenrose, Schönried (tel. 030/4-12-38). Humorous, lighthearted, and charming, this basement nightclub seems a consciously exuberant foil for the very grand restaurant upstairs (see the "Where to Dine" section). Named after a sometimes friendly canine belonging to the proprietors, the place features a charming staff, a cozy bar, and a changing array of fine paintings (the place doubles as an art gallery), plus live musical entertainment. You can dine here on such fare as fondues, raclette, or veal in a mushroom/cream sauce from around 25F ($17) per person. Many people, however, come to mingle, to flirt, to laugh, to relax, and to drink. There's no cover charge, and long drinks cost from 12F ($8.15) each. The establishment is rollicking fun every day in winter only from 7 p.m. to 3 a.m. The location is about 2½ miles northwest of Gstaad, in the alpine hamlet of Schönried.

The Pub ("Of Course"), Hotel Boo, Saanen (tel. 030/4-14-41). The only reason many residents of Gstaad ever venture into the neighboring hamlet of Saanen is for the animated action at this rustically elegant pub owned by Thomas Boo. Guests enjoy drinks and their companions in a wood-trimmed Swiss milieu, with a blazing fireplace and a wood-topped curved bar. You can order simple meals such as soups, salads, grilled fish, and steaks, costing from 30F ($20.40), but most visitors come just for the drinks. The pub is open every day in winter from 11 a.m. to 1 a.m.

Isolated amid fields and meadows about three miles south of Gstaad, the **Restaurant Chlösterli** (tel. 030/5-10-45) is a favorite watering hole of an array of celebrities that includes Tina Turner, England's Prince Charles, and Roger Moore, who maintains a more-or-less permanent table in one of the semi-secluded dining rooms. About half of its floor space is devoted to its restaurant facilities (see "Where to Dine"), but many people come here to disco beneath the soaring timbered ceiling of what was originally a barn, with foundations dating from at least the 17th century. Dancing begins every night at 9:30, lasting to at least 2 a.m. except during annual closings. These are from Easter to June and during all of November. Ruedy Mullener is the owner.

Rialto Bar (tel. 030/4-34-74), in the heart of Gstaad, is elegant and chic. This beautifully decorated bar, attached to the Ristorante Rialto, is one of the most popular places to visit after dark. The bar is actually open from noon to 1 a.m., but occasionally it has live music from 6 to 7:30 p.m. and from 9 p.m. to closing (on my latest rounds, it was a country western singer from Nashville). You can also order light meals here, costing from 30F ($20.40) and likely to include such dishes as smoked salmon, the pasta of the day, or a mixed Italian salad. Champagne by the glass costs 11F ($7.50) and seems to be the thing to order. In summer more limited hours are kept: from 5 p.m. to 1 a.m. daily.

Dancing Der Stollen, Steigenberger Hotel, Auf der Halten, Saanen (tel. 030/8-33-88), translates as "the gallery." A steep flight of stairs leads down into a dimly lit room which, for some disco lovers, evokes the feeling of a mine. The Swiss metal sculptor, Freddy Madörin, created Der Stollen, making original sculptures and mechanical models with parts from mining locomotives and trucks. Top bands and singers often appear here. It is open nightly in season from 9:30 p.m. to either 2 or 3 a.m. in the morning. No admission is charged, and drinks begin at 9F ($6.10).

An attractive young crowd goes dancing at the **Hostellerie Chesery** (tel. 030/4-24-51), which has a good restaurant and a piano bar open daily from 9 p.m. to 3 a.m. See the "Where to Dine" section above for details.

Wednesday is fondue party night in Gstaad, with the events taking place in turn at mountain restaurants such as the **Berghaus Eggli** (tel. 030/4-30-69) or the **Berghaus Wispile** (tel. 030/4-33-98). Departure is between 7 and 8 p.m. using the ski lifts, returning around 10 p.m., skiing down in a torchlight tattoo.

Visitors are sure to discover some newly opened piano bars and hot spots on their own. Some may last only six weeks, but in their heyday they can be lots of fun. During the whole winter season, there are many gala evenings, ski balls, concerts, and cabarets at different hotels and bars.

CHAPTER VII

THE VALAIS

□ □ □

The Matterhorn . . . the Great St. Bernard Pass . . . Zermatt . . . all these legendary names in tourism are part of the canton of Valais, called by Goethe "that wondrous beautiful valley." Its name, derived from the one given to it by the Romans about 2,000 years ago, described what the region was: the valley of the upper Rhône, a great river that springs from a huge glacier near the Furka Pass and flows westward and northward to Lake Geneva and beyond, into France, and then southward to empty into the Mediterranean. The Latin name for that upper Rhône Valley was Vallis Poenina, and the Germans still call it Wallis.

The boundaries of the Valais are obviously the result of its topographical features. Carved out through the millennia by the Rhône, the river valley was the natural recipient of the waters from many tributaries making their way from the lofty glacial Alps surrounding it. More than 50 major mountain peaks tower around the Valais, with the Matterhorn (14,701 feet) as the reigning queen. The most considerable stretch of glaciers in Switzerland is here, as well as some five square miles of lakes. The Dufourspitze summit of Monte Rosa (15,200 feet) is the loftiest point, but the Dom (14,942) is the tallest mountain lying completely within the canton.

The Rhône corridor, protected from storms by the mountains, with lots of sunshine, and a stable climate, was a choice place of habitation from prehistoric times, many tribes having happened onto it during migrations when they found their way through alpine passes. It has for centuries been a major route over the Alps. The Great St. Bernard and Simplon Passes saw the passage of Celts before the Christian era, and it was held by the Gauls for some 500 years. Some historians say that Hannibal's elephants came this way long before Napoleon made the Simplon passable for his huge cannons. Pilgrim and merchant, beggar and emperor—all have traveled the alpine passes of the Valais. Today wide highways, many with tunnels going through the most forbidding mountains, provide motorists with the shortest route to and from Italy by way of the valley of the Rhône, many still going over the Great St. Bernard Pass (8,094 feet) and the Simplon Pass (6,591 feet).

Two languages are spoken in the Valais, with the two-thirds of the population living in the west—Lake Geneva to Sierre—speaking French and those on eastward to the Simplon Pass speaking a German dialect. Many of the inhabitants, however, speak both tongues fluently, as well as some English. The Valais people are strong adherents of the Roman Catholic faith, as indicated by their many churches with lofty spires, their abbeys, and their monasteries.

The vineyards of the Valais are second only to those of the Vaud, and the fruity bouquet and delicate flavor of the upper Rhône Valley wines are known to all connoisseurs. The canton is rich in *mazots* or *raccards,* small barns standing on piles and used for the storage of grain, as dairy farming is carried on here. The favorite cheeses for raclette, the Swiss dish described in Chapter II under "Food and Drink," are made of rich, unskimmed milk from the Bagnes Valley, near the Great St. Bernard Pass.

With a climate that has been likened to that of Spain and Provence, the Valais attracts skiers and followers of other winter sports. Zermatt and its neighbors are known for having good snow conditions even when other parts of Switzerland do not. The increasing popularity of this canton in both summer and winter has brought an increase in accommodations ranging from resort facilities to modest boardinghouses. Tourism forms a major part of the Valais economy, and almost every tributary glen and alpine meadow seemingly has a hotel or at least a small inn. But I've observed that, through careful and realistic planning, the region has managed to keep its countryside intact, by and large. Many little valleys with their Rhône tributaries are tranquil havens even today, the silence broken only by the tinkle of cowbells from mountain pastures, the buzz of bees over alpine flowers, and the song of birds. The sounds of passing human beings are muted by the surrounding mountains.

International flights leave daily from New York to Geneva, and from there you can go by car or train to towns in the Valais.

Now, if you're ready for a journey through this "wondrous valley," we'll begin our trek from Lake Geneva, which is the major tourist routing.

1. LEYSIN

Our first stopover will be at Leysin, which is reached by turning left at Aigle after you've left Lake Geneva, and journeying up into the mountains for about ten miles. It's also possible to reach it by cogwheel railway from Aigle.

A year-round resort, Leysin overlooks a vast alpine panorama, with 112 miles of marked paths for walks. Views extend from the Bernese Alps to Mont Blanc.

At some 4,760 feet, the resort is one of the largest winter sports playgrounds in Switzerland. It has two centers, each on different levels. There's also a snow nursery for children.

FOOD AND LODGING: In a modern building, **Hôtel Central-Résidence,** CH-1854 Leysin, Switzerland (tel. 025/34-12-11), stands out in the alpine panorama around it. The six-story flat-roofed building has two floors of upholstered public rooms capped with four levels of comfortably low-key bedrooms, all of which contain kitchenettes and southern balconies. The downstairs bar and sitting rooms have a cheerful ambience that is improved with fires blazing in the round fireplace, the smoke from which is funneled through a metallic chimney in the middle of the room. Sports facilities include a covered swimming pool and outdoor tennis courts, as well as sauna and massage facilities. Guests dance in the Casanova Club, the most popular après-ski spot. Each of the accommodations has a private bath. Singles range in price from 80F ($54.40) to 95F ($64.60) daily, with doubles costing 120F ($81.60) to 150F ($102). Half board is available for another 22F ($14.95) per person daily. The hotel is open from June to September and December to April.

Hôtel le Relais-Regency, CH-1854 Leysin, Switzerland (tel. 025/34-24-24), in the center of the village, is a boxy building with different series of wood-grained panels offset against the irregular lines of the modern windows. Inside, a comfortable snackbar and restaurant looks vaguely English, with its half-timbering and Windsor chairs, while another dining room is more formal. The decor of the bedrooms is comfortable and unpretentious. Open all year, the hotel has 100 beds and charges 75F ($51) to 130F ($88.40) daily for a single and 110F ($74.80) to 180F ($122.40) in a double, including breakfast. Rates depend on the season. Half board is offered for an additional 20F ($13.60) per person daily. Upon your arrival the management will present you with a booklet that allows free entrance to some of the village's sports facilities.

Hôtel Mont-Riant, CH-1854 Leysin-Feydey, Switzerland (tel. 025/34-12-35), is a 36-bed hotel operated by the Ryhen family. Their hostelry is six minutes from the railway station Leysin-Feydey in a quiet part of what residents call "the upper part of town." This affords views as far away as the Rhône Valley. The hotel is close to the chair lift of Solacyre. Guests receive passes in winter admitting them at a reduced price to a covered skating rink, a nearby indoor swimming pool, and all cable cars and ski lifts. In summer, the same reductions are granted as well as to the outdoor swimming pool, miniature golf, and the tennis courts. All of the accommodations facing south have private balconies. Depending on the season, singles range from 33F ($22.45) to 62F ($42.15) daily, while doubles cost from 61F ($41.50) to 112F ($76.15), with half board available for another 19F ($12.90) per person daily. It is open from June to September and December to April.

Hôtel Restaurant les Orchidées, CH-1854 Leysin, Switzerland (tel. 025/34-14-21), is a small hotel landscaped into the hill on which it was placed. Many of its bedrooms face an alpine vista across a private balcony. The public rooms are trimmed in wood. The Haupt-Glinickes, the multilingual proprietors, prepare attractive meals and offer free mini-golf, use of a swimming pool, and ice skating to their guests. Depending on the season, singles range from 36F ($24.50) bathless to 70F ($47.60) daily with bath, while doubles cost 66F ($44.90) to 130F ($88.40), with half board going for an additional 18F ($12.25) per person per day. It's open from December to October.

2. CHAMPÉRY

Near the French border, about a 1½-hour drive from Geneva, Champéry lies in the center of the so-called Portes du Soleil, a complex of 13 French and Swiss ski resorts, including the famed Avoriaz on the French side. In fact, Champéry is linked to Avoriaz by a lift system.

Champéry stands at the beginning of the Illiez Valley (the Val d'Illiez), at an altitude of 3,450 feet. It's overshadowed by the Dents du Midi range. You find yourself in a setting of forests and impressive peaks. The resort enjoys international acclaim, yet it's very small, and all the local inhabitants know each other. It's very much a family-type place, and there are ski classes for children as well as adults.

You can go by cable car to Planachaux, another kilometer higher up. From there you can climb to the Cross at 6,440 feet for a splendid view of the Alps. This is a very popular ski area, where there are several lifts opening onto some magnificent runs.

FOOD AND LODGING: A beautifully rustic chalet, **Hôtel Beau Séjour,** CH-1874 Champéry, Switzerland (tel. 025/79-17-01), has lots of handcrafted detailing. It's five minutes away from the Planachaux cableway terminus and is very popular, especially in winter with skiers. Owned and managed by the Avanthey family, the hotel offers different levels of accommodation, some contemporary, some oldtimey in style. Even if you're not staying here you may want to patronize its Vieux Chalet. In season a musical group often provides entertainment, and it's one of the liveliest stops on the après-ski circuit. All units contain baths, costing 72F ($48.95) to 90F ($61.20) daily in a single and 120F ($81.60) to 140F ($95.20) in a double, depending on the season. Half board is offered for another 25F ($17) per person daily.

Pension de la Gare, CH-1874 Champéry, Switzerland (tel. 025/79-13-29), is a well-run pension/café/restaurant. Set in an alpine house with masonry detailing and a half-timbered upper floor, the establishment offers bed and breakfast in bathless rooms for 32F ($21.75) to 38F ($25.85) per person daily, with half board in the pleasant restaurant costing an additional 15F ($10.20) per person daily.

Pension Rose des Alpes, CH-1874 Champéry, Switzerland (tel. 025/79-12-18), is an attractive double chalet. One section is newer than the other but crafted nonetheless in the traditional style. The interior has all the wood detailing and alpine furniture you've come to expect, along with a modern lounge with leatherette chairs. Managed and owned by the Delalay family, the hotel charges 42F ($28.55) daily per person for bed and breakfast in a room with hot and cold running water, 48F ($32.65) per person for a room with shower, also including breakfast. With half board, the charges per person are 56F ($38.10) and 60F ($40.80) depending on the plumbing, while with full board, rates are 68F ($46.25) and 72F ($48.95) per person. All taxes and service are included in the rates. None of the rooms contains a private toilet, but there are three on each floor per five bedrooms.

APRÈS SKI: If popularity contests were held, **Le Levant,** rue Principale (tel. 79-12-72), would get the nod as one of the liveliest places to go after you've finished your day on the ski runs. The villagers themselves patronize the establishment as well, for it is known for its raclette. You'll see a sign posted, *"Ici Raclette."* The patron of this Valais tavern cuts wheels of cheese as large as pumpkins. In this wainscotted room you can also drink Fendant, the white wine famous throughout the Valais. In fact it's most preferred with raclette (never order beer!). Besides raclette, you can order fondue with tomatoes, fondue bourguignonne, fondue chinoise, steak, croûtes, or assiette valaisanne (air-dried) meats. The establishment is open daily from 9 a.m. to 3 a.m. Hot meals—that is, the full menu—are served from noon to 2 p.m. and 7 to 10 p.m. daily. There is no fixed-price meal, but fondue costs 16F ($10.90), with raclette going for 22F ($14.95). A disco on the premises is open nightly from 10 p.m. to 3 a.m. Entrance is free, and a beer costs from 8F ($5.45). The annual vacation is for two weeks in April and again for two weeks in October.

Among hotels, the most action is at the Beau Séjour. See above for details, or, better yet, call (tel. 025/79-17-01) to see what, if anything, is happening.

MORGINS: There has been a collection of chalet farms on the steep hillsides of this region since time immemorial. However, a more formal classification of the village as an alpine station occurred in 1820, when the region became better known. Since then a steadily increasing flow of tourism has contributed to the prosperity of this place. Today the village is dotted with intricately crafted chalets and a few buildings of more modern design, all of which made Morgins both a summer mountain resort and a winter ski center. In winter, residents have the extraordinary choice of more than 150 ski lifts in the entire area. The motto of the town is "unbordered skiing" (that is, without frontiers), since you could for a long time ski to France without a passport. However, Americans and other visitors must now have a visa to cross into France.

Nightlife is not Las Vegas in dimension, but there are several bars, restaurants, and discos. If you want to base here, try the following hotel.

Hostellerie Bellevue, CH-1875 Morgins, Switzerland (tel. 025/77-27-71), is a pleasingly proportioned chalet with balconies covering the front and back. It contains 70 comfortably carpeted and upholstered bedrooms, each of which has its own bath and balcony, with a view of the green hills around the hotel. On the premises you'll find a disco/nightclub, a pool, a sauna, four different eateries, and a piano bar. All this is in addition to the electronically up-to-date conference rooms. Singles cost 57F ($45.55) to 78F ($53.05) daily in summer, 83F ($56.45) to 113F ($76.85). In summer, doubles are priced at 103F ($70.05) to 124F ($84.30) daily, going for 134F ($91.10) to 194F ($131.90) in winter. The hostelry is open from June to September and December to April.

3. MARTIGNY

Everybody has marched through here, including Roman legions and, much later, the armies of Napoleon heading across the Great St. Bernard Pass. In time it attracted Goethe, Byron, and Rousseau. The Gallo-Roman settlement was called Octodurus. Today counting some 13,000 inhabitants, Martigny is more than 2,000 years old, making it the oldest town in the Valais.

In the Rhône Valley, the town lies in a setting of vineyards, orchards, and forests, with mountain ranges in the background. It's completely different from the towns in the north of Switzerland, taking on a more southern aura, as reflected by its Place Centrale, with its café terraces shaded by large plane trees.

For centuries Martigny has been an international road junction. Dominating the town is the 13th-century castle—now in ruins—of La Bâtiaz, which was the property of the powerful bishops of Sion. The tower, most visible today, was restored at the end of the 19th century. As a memory of its Roman occupation, an amphitheater lies to the southeast of the town. Chances are you'll be just like most motorists and pass through Martigny for the day. However, it merits a stopover, if only to see a number of sights in the general vicinity.

The cultural life of Martigny has been enriched by **La Fondation Pierre Gianadda** (tel. 026/2-39-78), inspired by the wish of landowner Léonard Gianadda to honor his dead brother through establishment of an archaeological preservation and a place where artists and musicians could exhibit their skills. The remains of a Gallo-Roman temple, the oldest discovered so far in Switzerland, were unearthed during construction of a modern building. In order to assure its preservation, Gianadda had his foundation structure built around and in the midst of the temple remains. An archaeological exhibition is on the upper gallery level, and the lower gallery houses temporary art exhibits, which include works of such major art figures as Klee, Picasso, Goya, Rodin, Giacometti, and Toulouse-Lautrec. In music presentations, well-known performing artists appear as well as local and regional musicians.

The most recent addition to the foundation's complex is the **Automobile Museum,** with a collection of some 50 vintage cars, most of them in running condition, made between 1897 and 1939. Car aficionados can admire vehicles by Hispano-Suiza, Rolls-Royce, Benz, Bugatti, Alfa Romeo, De Dion-Bouton, and

Mercedes, as well as Swiss makes—Pic-Pic, Turicum, and Sigma. The museum and other parts of the foundation are open from 10 a.m. to 7 p.m. daily in summer, from 10 a.m. to noon and 1:30 to 6 p.m. daily in winter. Admission fees are 9F ($6.10) for adults, 4F ($2.70) for children 10 to 18 years old.

From Martigny, there are excursions to the **Trient Gorges,** which are open from May 1 until the end of September from 8 a.m. to 6 p.m., charging an admission of 4F ($2.70) for adults, 2F ($1.36) for children. You can drive your car to Vernayaz where there's a car park. At this site you can see where the Trient pours into the Rhône Valley.

Also in the vicinity is the **Pissevache waterfall,** which plunges earthward from a large rock near Vernayaz. This waterfall gave Goethe much pleasure, as he later recorded, although we are told by guides that it was much more powerful in that writer's day.

WHERE TO STAY: As an alternative to staying in Martigny, you might want to consider one of the little satellite resorts in its environs, which immediately follow.

In medieval times, the name for Martigny was La Porte d'Octodure. That memory lives on in a modern hotel, **La Porte d'Octodure,** route du Grand-St-Bernard, CH-1920 Martigny, Switzerland (tel. 026/2-71-21). The hotel sits near the junction of two very important roads on a sunny plain at the edge of town. Designed around an eight-sided core, this is a stylishly modern building with lots of marble and 55 comfortable bedrooms. Depending on the season, singles rent for 66F ($44.90) to 113F ($76.85) daily and doubles for 112F ($76.15) to 192F ($130.55), with breakfast included. On the premises is a sauna, plus a Jacuzzi, a Swiss tavern and an Italian trattoria where full meals cost from 25F ($17). The most glamorous, the Rôtisserie le Grognard, is reviewed separately.

Hôtel du Rhône, 11 avenue Grand-St-Bernard, CH-1920 Martigny, Switzerland (tel. 026/21-17-17), is a modern white-faced building that looks very much like an urban hotel. It has big windows, plus one section with covered loggias outside each of the bedrooms. The ground floors are covered with curtained glass, which reveal comfortable public rooms filled with '60s-style furniture. The sunny bedrooms are carpeted, sometimes in an attractive forest green, with clean sheets and soundproof windows. This hotel accommodates 100 visitors in rooms, all with bath, priced at 75F ($51) to 85F ($57.80) daily in a single, 110F ($74.80) to 140F ($95.20) in a double, depending on the season. Breakfast is included in the tariffs. The hotel is affiliated with Best Western.

Hôtel de la Poste, 8 rue de la Poste, CH-1920 Martigny, Switzerland (tel. 026/2-14-44), does everything it can to maintain the service of the 19th century in a modern format of a rectangular concrete building with big windows and a flat roof. The bedrooms are tastefully filled with striped bedcovers, an occasional Oriental rug, and modest furniture. The restaurant is a popular local eatery that serves food brasserie style. Marcel Claivaz and his family charge 89F ($60.50) to 118F ($80.25) in a double, depending on the season.

WHERE TO DINE: The best food in town is found at **Le Gourmet,** 74 avenue du Grand-St-Bernard (tel. 026/22-18-41). It is one of the most beautiful restaurants in the area, decorated in a style using both Empire and Louis Philippe. Each chair is swan-headed. In such a fine setting, only the best of an international cuisine will do. Many of the dishes are in the school of cuisine moderne. For example, you get gazpacho made with crayfish. Carpaccio is not raw meat, but raw fish. Filet of lamb, served in the special mode of the chef, is one of the featured main dishes, as is saffron-flavored lobster. For dessert, you might enjoy a spectacular soufflé glacé or a sabayon with caramelized pears. Set menus cost 65F ($44.20),

82F ($55.75), and 95F ($64.60). Hours are from noon to 2 p.m. and from 7 to 9:30 p.m. except Sunday night and all day Monday.

Rôtisserie le Grognard, Hotel la Porte d'Octodure, route du Grand-St.-Bernard (tel. 026/2-71-21). Named after the Napoleonic soldiers whose illustrations are scattered throughout the hotel, this very modern restaurant is outfitted in pleasing shades of pink and lavender. The most glamorous (and expensive) of the three restaurants in this hotel, it serves a four-course fixed-price menu for 44F ($29.90) and full à la carte meals for 70F ($47.60). Food is served daily except all day Monday and Sunday night from noon to 1:30 p.m. and from 7 to 9:30 p.m. Specialties include carpaccio with cider vinegar, homemade terrine of goose liver, Valaisian-style wine soup, medallions of monkfish with green peppercorns, magret of duckling with blackberries, and a darne of salmon. For dessert, you might want a terrine of apricots with an apricot compote.

Restaurant du Léman, 19 avenue du Léman (tel. 026/2-30-75), is owned and operated by a man with a lot of relatives in the district, Michel Claivaz. Near the exit to Martigny from the autoroute, the restaurant specializes in seafood, serving whatever looked freshest in the market that day, along with regional specialties familiar in the Alps. International dishes include beef with chanterelles, rack of lamb provençale, and rognons de veau (veal kidneys) if you have a taste for them. In summer you might prefer to eat on the garden terrace. The restaurant is closed on Sunday and Monday, for two weeks in June, and from December 25 to January. Hours are 7 a.m. to midnight. Fixed-price meals range from 25F ($17) to 55F ($37.40), with an à la carte dinner costing about the same.

CHAMPEX: This tiny resort, reached by taking a road south from Martigny, is popular in both summer and winter. It lies in the Mont Blanc massif, and opens onto what is called the most beautiful alpine lake in the Valais, Lake Champex. The setting is in a mountain valley at a height of 4,800 feet, about 19 miles from Martigny (head in the direction of the St. Bernard road tunnel).

Summer sports include riding, hiking, and fishing, certainly walking. Boat trips are possible on the lake, although motorboats are forbidden. Windsurfing is popular, and you can also hire pedal boats, or swim in the resort's heated swimming pool, later visiting an alpine botanical garden. One of the most thrilling adventures here is to go for a walk up to the glaciers.

In winter Champex naturally attracts skiers. There is rarely any waiting for the resort's two chair lifts or its ski lift.

Hotel Glacier Sporting, CH-1938 Champex, Switzerland (tel. 026/4-14-02), was originally built in the chalet style in the 1950s. Today, this family-run hotel sits conveniently in the center of the resort, near the lake and the terminus for the chair lifts. It also stands near the beginning of the summertime footpaths. Completely renovated in the 1980s, it contains 60 comfortable beds, a handful of dining and drinking areas, a modernized and comfortable interior, and it also has a capable management directed by the Biselx family. It closes from mid-November to mid-December and again from early April until mid-June. In winter, per person rates, either single or double occupancy, costs 82F ($55.75) daily, with half board included. In low season, the per person rate, either single or double occupancy, is 70F ($47.60) daily, with half board included. Each room contains a phone, private bath, and plenty of exposed wood trim.

LES MARÉCOTTES: One mile southwest of Salvan, you reach the mini-resort of Les Marécottes, which draws both a summer and a winter crowd. Known mostly to Europeans, it's a little undiscovered nugget of the Valais. At 3,600 feet, it has both a natural swimming pool and a zoo of alpine animals. A chair lift takes you up to Creusaz at 5,840 feet. When you reach Les Marécottes, you will have come to the end of the road, but a railway will take you to the famous ski resort of Chamonix in France.

Food and Lodging

Hôtel aux Mille Étoiles, CH-1923 Les Marécottes, Switzerland (tel. 026/ 16-16-66), is a member of the Silence Hotels and the Swiss Happy Family Hotels. Jan and Elly Mol are the directors of this chalet hotel whose interior and exterior are covered with textured pine siding. From the sunny patio in front, guests can admire the surrounding landscape as well as the evenly spaced wooden slats of the upper balconies. Guests register under a re-creation of an alpine hut's flagstone-covered roof. The public rooms include an open fireplace, plenty of tartan upholstery in autumnal colors, and knotty paneling rising in vertical strips above the cushioned chairs. Accommodations are pleasantly proportioned and warmly decorated, often with big windows and plenty of space for children. Each contains a private bath or shower, phone, and radio. Only double occupancy is accepted in high season. Singles can stay for 73F ($49.65) daily in low season, and doubles rent for 116F ($78.90) daily in low season, rising to 178F ($121.05) in high. Breakfast is included. Half board is another 30F ($20.40) per person year round.

On the premises are a children's playroom, a Ping-Pong room, and a wading pool. Adults are welcome to use the hotel's indoor pool, fitness room, and sauna. Since the hotel is centrally located, a short walk from the ski lifts, it's a favorite with winter holiday-makers. When the snow is heavy outside, a disco/bar often provides live entertainment. The hotel is open May to the end of October and December to mid-April.

Hôtel Joliment, CH-1923 Les Marécottes, Switzerland (tel. 026/61-14-70), is a centrally located composite of an old-fashioned balconied hotel with plenty of charm. A nearby flat-roofed annex is built with a connecting passage. The roof of the annex is set with pink tiles and serves as a sundeck. The establishment is only a few steps from the village church, yet you'll still feel you're in the countryside because of the sloping garden leading off toward a view of the mountains. Many of the accommodations have balconies, and even the new annex is comfortably outfitted with rustic beams and pleasing colors. Depending on the season and the plumbing, doubles rent for 60F ($40.80) to 120F ($81.60) daily, while singles cost 45F ($30.60) to 70F ($47.60) daily. Half board is offered for an additional 26F ($17.70) per person daily. The hotel is open June to September and December to April. The Délez family are your hosts.

4. VERBIER

Lying on a sunny plateau in Switzerland's southernmost Alps, Verbier looks toward the Combin and Mont Blanc mountains, snow-covered even when the town is burgeoning with green grass, leafy trees, and flowers in their summer glory. The vast plateau in the Bagnes Valley of Valais, at an elevation of about 5,000 feet, was once mainly pastureland largely protected from the wind, and you can still hear the sound of cowbells in the hills around Verbier in summer.

Since 1950, however, this area has come to be an outstanding sports center both in summer and winter, with skiing being at the top of the list of its attractions. It was in that year that a group of merchants, hoteliers, and artisans began the creation of a system to provide conveyances that now, through **Téléverbier SA,** the mechanical lift company they founded, forms one of the biggest conveyance systems in all of Switzerland. A recent addition, a heavy-duty cable car between La Chaux region and the Col des Gentianes, is the largest lift in the country. Today there are in the Verbier area alone 47 ski lifts, shuttlebuses, an ELP search system, avalanche dogs, and patrols, serving more than 190 miles of ski runs.

In cooperation with neighboring regions, visitors can use their Téléverbier passes on more than 85 different lifts in the area known as Les 4 Vallées (the four valleys) and l'Entremont. This means that a single lift ticket can take skiers as high as 11,000 feet, as well as allowing cross-country skiing. Skiers can, for example, make such circuits as Verbier to Mont-Gelé to Mont-Fort to La Chaux and back to Verbier. Other circuits go to Tortin, Mont-Fort, and La Chaux and back to Verbier or from Verbier's Médran lift to Col des Mines and back. For information on skiing in the Téléverbier SA network, phone 026/31-60-00 or write to the company at CP 326, CH-1936 Verbier, Switzerland.

Ski tours on the slopes of Mont-Gelé, Col de Chassoure, Vallon d'Arbi, and Col des Mines, plus other unmarked slopes, are not ski runs but high-mountain tours, and skiers, even in summer, should be accompanied by an experienced mountaineer.

The **Swiss Ski School** (tel. 026/31-68-25), with 140 instructors, offers group lessons from 9:30 to 11:45 a.m. daily, as well as private lessons. A ski nursery is operated in the daytime. Lessons for adults cost 19F ($12.90) for half a day, 90F ($61.20) for six half days. For children 3 years old and up, lessons cost 18F ($12.25) for a half day, 75F ($51) for six half days.

Construction of the **Verbier Polysports Centre** (tel. 026/31-76-01) has greatly expanded the activities possible here in all seasons. It boasts a covered swimming pool, ten indoor curling lanes, an indoor ice rink, ten tennis courts, squash courts, saunas, whirlpools, a solarium, and a games area, plus a restaurant. There's also an 18-hole golf course. The sports center is open daily from 9 a.m. to 9 p.m. The prices of its facilities are lowered by around 25% for those who stay in hotels that are members of the resort's sports association. Most hotels are members, so the prices here are those most clients will pay. Tennis costs 22F ($14.95) per hour, and ice skating goes for 5.50F ($3.75) for adults and 3.50F ($2.40) for children. Curling costs 13.50F ($9.20) for adults and 10F ($6.80) for children. Use of the indoor pool with its adjacent sauna is 13.50F ($9.20) for adults and 10F ($6.80) for children.

Many visitors come not for the sports facilities but for the beauty of the mountains in summer, which they view on walks, on horseback, or from cable cars. The **Haut Val de Bagnes Nature Reserve,** a protected alpine expanse of a rich variety of flora and fauna, provides an opportunity to see some rare species of plants, including the alpine aquilegia, white gentian, yellow pond lily, edelweiss, and several kinds of orchids. In Verbier, botanical walks are organized in summer. A particularly stunning sight is afforded by looking down into the Bagnes Valley from the Combe des Violettes. Farther on, Mont-Pleureur can be seen, with Italy in the blue mist on the horizon.

Verbier lies 80 miles from the Geneva Airport and 25 miles from the Great St. Bernard Tunnel. You can reach it by the N 9 and N 12 motorways as far as Martigny on the Great St. Bernard route. Turn left for Verbier at Sembrancher. A train from Martigny takes you to Le Châble. Then you go by postbus or Le Châble-Verbier aerial cableway. In winter, there's a direct bus service from Martigny to Verbier.

The **Verbier Tourist Office** (tel. 026/31-62-22) is happy to supply information about the area.

ACCOMMODATIONS:
The first hotels and chalets were built in Verbier in the 1930s. It was a modest beginning, but at the latest count there were 38 hotels with 2,200 beds, plus 20,000 extra beds in chalets and apartments. I'll try to pick the nuggets out of this vast field.

The Upper Bracket

Hotel Rosalp, CH-1936 Verbier, Switzerland (tel. 026/31-63-23), a *Relais & Châteaux* offers 24 first-class rooms with some excellent suites. Later I'll rave about its two restaurants and its chic bar—but first the lodgings. This place is more than a *restaurant avec chambres,* although considering the quality of the cuisine by master chef Roland Pierroz, that would be reason enough to check in.

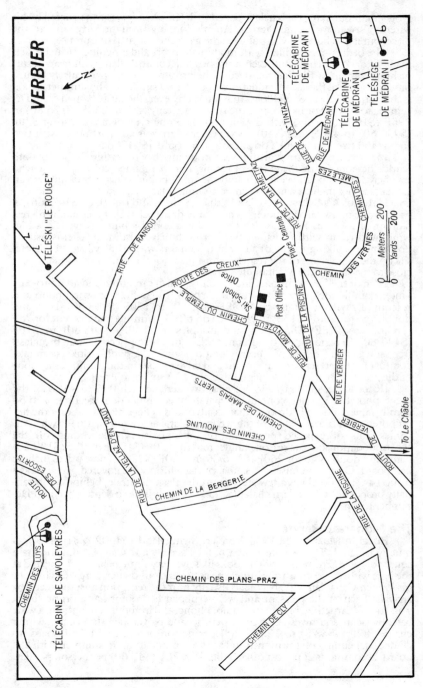

Now rated four stars, this chalet opened in 1945 when it was constructed by his parents, Roger and Anita Pierroz. Anita's cooking brought early fame to the place, but it was her son who put it on the gastronomic map of Europe.

The bedrooms are filled with modern comfort and amenities. Much use is made of dark paneling, and each unit shows decorator's flair, with tasteful furnishings and an individualized decor. The private baths are particularly luxurious, and some of the accommodations open onto a sundeck. The summer season is short, from July to September. In winter, however, the relais is open from December to April. For half board, the single rate ranges from 260F ($176.80) to 290F ($197.20) daily, with doubles on the same arrangement costing 370F ($251.60) to 430F ($292.40). Two persons can rent an apartment, with two rooms and two baths, plus a private salon, for 650F ($442) daily.

Many visitors return year after year, knowing they're getting the best of both worlds here, not only the excellent rooms, but that refined cuisine. Those who stay here long enough eventually find the small public salon, a tranquil retreat. Other facilities include a fitness center, a sauna, a Jacuzzi, and a garage.

Hôtel les 4 Vallées, CH-1936 Verbier, Switzerland (tel. 026/31-60-66), is frankly one of my favorite hotels, whose only drawback is that it contains no restaurant of its own. Breakfast, to be sure, is a copious buffet served in a big-windowed room with paneling, but during lunch and dinner, clients usually don't mind walking to any of a dozen restaurants within the village. The hotel sits on the main street of the resort, a short distance above the main square, very close to the start of the Médran life station.

Each of the 22 rooms has pine paneling, plush carpeting, and an up-to-date kind of sun-flooded style. Each contains a bath, TV, radio, mini-bar, phone, and balcony. In winter, singles cost 135F ($91.80) to 170F ($115.60) daily, and doubles go for 200F ($136) to 245F ($166.60). In summer, singles rent for 98F ($66.65) to 125F ($85) daily and doubles for 160F ($108.80) to 210F ($142.80), depending on the accommodation. These prices include breakfast, free saunas, and free use of a nearby indoor swimming pool. Drinkers can take comfort in the presence of an elegant and civilized bar in the comfortable lobby of the hotel. It's open July to September and November to April.

Hôtel Vanessa, CH-1936 Verbier, Switzerland (tel. 026/31-61-41), the biggest hotel in Verbier, contains a separately recommended restaurant and 56 comfortable modern bedrooms that its advocates believe place it among the finest hotels of the resort. Most of the accommodations are suites, usually with balconies, lots of exposed pine, and bright upholstery. Depending on the accommodation and the season, singles rent for 150F ($102) to 190F ($129.20) daily, and doubles go for 260F ($176.80) to 350F ($238). These prices include half board. On the premises is a sauna, plus a whirlpool, a covered garage, and a piano bar. The hotel lies a few steps from the Place Centrale, behind a substantially proportioned modern chalet façade. It's open June to September, and December to April.

The Moderate Range
Hôtel le Mazot, CH-1936 Verbier, Switzerland (tel. 026/31-64-04), is quietly isolated. This well-managed hotel sits only a few steps from the main square of town. From the front, it looks like two very similar chalets connected at the base with a reception area. Either the conscientious owner, Serge Tacchini, or his French-Canadian wife, Nicole, is usually near the reception area to greet new arrivals. Each of the pleasant and well-scrubbed bedrooms has a private bath, wall-to-wall carpeting, big closets, radio, phone, and in about half of them, a wide balcony facing southwest. Closed in October and November, the hotel in winter charges 82F ($55.75) to 125F ($85) per person per day, with half board included, depending on the month and the accommodation. In summer, with half board, accommodations cost 60F ($40.80) to 70F ($47.60) per person per day,

depending on the accommodation. The hotel, built in the early 1970s, contains a pleasant alpine dining room and bar. It's open July to September and December to April.

Hôtel Grand Combin + Golf, CH-1936 Verbier, Switzerland (tel. 026/ 31-65-15), sits in isolated grandeur, a soaring chalet, a short walk downhill from the main square of town. Officially rated three stars, its accommodations are probably the equivalent of four-star hotels in other towns. Many of the rooms contain an Oriental carpet, pine paneling, and a tasteful arrangement of conservative furniture. Each is different from its neighbor and usually offers phone, radio, at least one original painting, and (in all but six) a private balcony. Originally opened in 1953, the hotel charges 130F ($88.40) to 150F ($102) daily in a single, 160F ($108.80) to 300F ($204) in a double, with half board. The hotel contains an attractive lobby with antique nuances, and a sophisticated bar (Jacky's, recommended separately). There's also a sauna and a steam bath. Jacques Bessard, the owner, ran in the New York City marathon several years ago. It's open June to September and December to April.

Hôtel de la Poste, CH-1936 Verbier, Switzerland (tel. 026/31-66-81), is a red-shuttered chalet set on the main street of town, a few paces above the principal square. Its special feature is a covered swimming pool. Its 36 simple but clean accommodations do not all contain private baths, a fact which leads many discerning repeat clients to request one of the 28 bedrooms in the hotel's chalet annex across the street, above the recommended restaurant, à la Bonne Franquette. In the annex, each room has a private bath and a comfortable but utilitarian decor. The dining and drinking facilities for both establishments are in the main building, in rooms ringed with pine paneling and filled with old-fashioned alpine accessories. With half board included, singles are from 63F ($42.85) to 126F ($88.70) daily, doubles 126F ($88.70) to 235F ($159.80). Rates depend on the season and the plumbing. It's open from June to September and December to April.

Hôtel les Chamois, CH-1936 Verbier, Switzerland (tel. 026/31-64-02). Clean, predictable, and cozy, this alpine chalet lies just above the center of town. It has a big-windowed restaurant/dining room filled with roughly textured beams and alpine accessories, plus 21 accommodations. Each of these contains a private bath. Depending on the season, singles range from 70F ($47.60) to 120F ($81.60) daily, with doubles costing 134F ($91.10) to 228F ($155.05), including half board. The hotel is closed between late April and late June and from mid-October to early December.

Hôtel Farinet, CH-1936 Verbier, Switzerland (tel. 026/31-66-26), is a comfortable and elaborate chalet hotel, set in the most visible section of the main square of town. Its sun-flooded terrace is probably the most popular in town, ideal for watching the pedestrian activities of the resort. The place is slightly more formal, and perhaps somewhat better furnished, than many other hotels in its price category. It has a warmly attractive bar and restaurant on its street level, filled with exposed wood and alpine accessories. If you arrive here, even in high season, in the middle of the day, you might discover that the entire administration is away skiing. All rooms are comfortably furnished, containing private baths. Singles range from 50F ($34) to 100F ($68) daily, and doubles cost 90F ($61.20) to 170F ($115.60), depending on the season. The Farinet is a garni hotel, serving breakfast only. It's open from June to September, December to April.

Hôtel Catogne, CH-1936 Verbier, Switzerland (tel. 026/31-65-05). The upper half looks like a chalet; the lower half is masonry and stucco, with big windows and a modern extension containing the restaurant. The inside is as rustically paneled as you'd expect, with bright tablecloths near the well-stocked bar. Jean-Marc Corthay, the owner, bases his rates on the season. All units have private baths. With half board included, singles rent for 70F ($47.60) to 120F ($81.60) daily, and doubles cost 153F ($104.05) to 228F ($155.05). The hotel is closed in October and November.

WHERE TO DINE: Verbier has a number of excellent restaurants, serving variously traditional Swiss dishes and continental cuisine, plus other good food. I'll recommend some of my favorites, but you're sure to discover places you particularly like in this resort town. Most of the best restaurants are connected with hotels, but there are a few others worth visiting.

Rosalp, route de la Tintaz (tel. 026/31-63-23), is a previously recommended *Relais & Châteaux,* offering the finest food in the Valais. Gourmets drive across national borders to sample the cuisine of master chef Roland Pierroz. He is one of the great chefs of Switzerland, ranked among the top four or five. He prepares regional specialties for those who order them, but his light cuisine moderne is what is really the occasion. Seasonally adjusted specialties include oysters with caviar in puff pastry, turbot with crab, quail eggs, chicken with chervil, a host of game dishes, and imaginative renderings of lobster and salmon. On my latest rounds, I enjoyed my finest meal in Switzerland here (apologies to Frédy Girardet, who incidentally has been a visitor at "Chez Pierroz"—chefs like to know what the competition is doing).

My repast began with a fourrée of quail eggs and scallops tartare with caviar and bits of endive, followed with a langoustine couscous. Next appeared a delectable tortelloni gorgonzola, reinforced with a plate of sea bass and sea urchins. But the pièce de résistance was a pigeon with truffles. The cheese trolley emerged with at least 35 selections, and it was followed with a crisp and tasty apple tart with ice cream that was celestial. All this fine food was backed up with one of the finest wine cellars in the Valais, which I was allowed to tour. Fixed-price menus range from 115F ($78.20) to 165F ($112.20), with à la carte meals costing from 105F ($71.40) to 135F ($91.80). The restaurant serves dinner only in winter and summer from 7 to 11 p.m. daily. Reservations are imperative. The establishment is closed in May, June, October, and November. It lies about 200 yards from the center of town.

La Pinte, Hotel Rosalp (tel. 026/31-63-23), is the second restaurant run by the master cuisiner, Roland Pierroz. It's on the ground floor of his previously recommended hotel, a *Relais & Châteaux.* Prices here are much more reasonable than the gourmet restaurant upstairs, but you still get superb cookery. You can order from the menu provided, with meals costing from 40F ($27.20), and you can also avail yourself of the gastronomic treats of the main restaurant if that is your desire.

Service is daily from noon to 2 p.m. and 7 to 10 p.m. At lunch you might begin with a tempting tart, made perhaps with leeks or Gruyère cheese. Perhaps you'll sample a gratin of escargots flavored with basil or a terrine of roebuck with foie gras. Meats, ranging from a brochette of lamb to tournedos, are grilled over an open fire. Several regional dishes are offered, including sausage with lentils, and you might also find what you're looking for under *les spécialités du jour.* The decor is of antique paneling whose 19th-century designs of painted flowers have faded gloriously. A small room decorated with hunting trophies is in back, and it's a snug retreat on a winter's night.

Hotel Vanessa Restaurant (tel. 026/31-61-41) was installed at the lobby level. It's possibly disturbing location a few steps from the reception desk lets passersby see whatever's happening at the tables. In a modern room, you can order lunch daily from noon to 2 p.m. and dinner 7 to 10 p.m. À la carte meals cost from 85F ($57.80), while a six-course menu gastronomique goes for 95F ($64.60). Representative menu items include fresh oysters, salmon tartare, terrine of fish with two types of mint, salmon and turbot in puff pastry, essence of crayfish with crayfish quenelles, pigeon with truffles, and rack of lamb. If you're looking for something hearty and not as esoteric, try the fondue chinoise. Reservations are strongly suggested, especially for nonresidents.

Au Vieux Verbier (tel. 026/31-16-68) is one of the rare independent restaurants of the resort—it's not connected with a hotel. It's filled with a collection of brightly polished brassware, exposed beams, and stone. Near a high point of the village, it stands a few steps from the ski lifts and the Médran cable-car depot. The staff serves excellent meals costing from 35F ($23.80) at lunch, 11:30 a.m. to 3 p.m. Dinner from 45F ($30.60) is served from 6:30 to 10:30 p.m. Closing day is Monday, but only in summer and autumn. A house specialty is pigs' trotters in Madeira with Rösti. Other choices include a heaping platter of sauerkraut garnished with local sausages and boiled ham, salmon steak with lime, filet of sole in Pinot Noir, suprême of duckling with red currants, hot foie gras with apples, and leek flan. The restaurant is closed sometime in May and June.

Grill/Bar La Luge, rue de la Piscine (tel. 026/31-31-43). Many first-time visitors get so caught up in the bar scene on this establishment's street level, that they never descend the wooden stairs going down to the restaurant. The true allure of the place, however, lies within its plank-and-stucco-sided basement. There, with an atmosphere reeking of alpine coziness, is a grill-restaurant that is one of the most popular and gregarious places in town. Only dinner is served here, and that only in winter, from 7 to 11 p.m. daily. Uniformed employees attend the flames of the open grill, out of which come most of the house specialties, usually grills that are particularly juicy and flavorful. You can order veal steak, brochette of filter, Chateaubriand, entrecôte, julienne of filet La Luge, and a high-calorie choice from a short list of desserts. Full meals cost from 40F ($27.20) to 60F ($40.80). Reservations are suggested, especially in the midwinter crush of high season. Wine or two-hand mugs of beer can accompany your simple but hearty meal. The bar upstairs is open every day in winter from 10 a.m. to midnight.

Restaurant Au Robinson, Place Centrale (tel. 026/31-32-13). Housed in a stucco building, neatly camouflaged at the side of the town's main square, this place is larger, more active, and more animated than you'd imagine by looking at its façade. No one will mind if you show up just to drink, but if you want a meal, hot lunches are served from noon to 2 p.m. and 7 to 10 p.m. every day. Its long wooden bar is especially popular after 9:30 p.m., when recorded rock 'n' roll reverberates between the paneled walls. Full meals cost 30F ($20.40) to 45F ($30.60) and might include one of three kinds of spaghetti, scallops of pork, roast chicken, three varieties of fondue, filet Stroganoff, and a heaping platter (an assiette Valaisanne) of air-dried alpine beef with pickles and onions.

Restaurant à la Bonne Franquette, Hotel Auberge rue de Médran (rue Principale tel. 026/31-62-74). Devotedly regional, both in its decor and in its menu, this brightly decorated tavern is on the street level of the annex of the previously recommended Hôtel de la Poste. It's open every day except during the annual May vacation, from 11:30 a.m. to 2 p.m. and 6:30 to 10 p.m. A two-course evening meal costs only 25F ($17), while full à la carte meals cost 35F ($23.80) each. The menu lists raclette, four different types of fondue, four different preparations of spaghetti, and julienne of veal braised with cream or with exotic mushrooms (bolets). Wine is usually sold by the carafe. You won't be alone if you select this simple but respectable restaurant. It seems to be an early-evening favorite of vacationing families with small children and diners looking for an inexpensive alternative to higher-priced restaurants.

Pizzeria Fer à Cheval, rue de Médran (rue Principale tel. 026/31-26-69). Set behind a plank-covered façade, just uphill from the main square of town, this rustic pizzeria has an outdoor terrace for warm summer and winter days, plus a big-windowed, slightly cramped interior sheathed with pine and big windows. It's open from 8 a.m. to midnight every day between December and early May, and then during July and August. Food is offered throughout the day except between the hours of 3 to 6 p.m., when only drinks are served. You can order nine varieties of pizza, priced from 11F ($7.50) each, along with lasagne, spaghetti, steaks, and a choice from an array of ice creams. There's even a mini-menu for children. It's reasonable to assume that you can dine here for 22F ($14.95) and up.

APRÈS SKI: The après-ski life begins early in Verbier. In the late afternoon, skiers returning from the slopes fortify themselves with a glass of Dôle, a red wine native to the region.

The most conservative, the most elegant, and the most comfortable bar in town is **Bar l'Arlequin,** Hotel Rosalp (tel. 026/31-63-23). It's also known informally as "Chez Corinne." From 5 p.m. to 3 a.m. daily it serves the most elegant drinks in town. The fireplace gives a warm glow. The visiting celebrity is likely to be the king of Sweden, Roman Polanski, or Diana Ross.

Farm Club, rue Principale (tel. 026/31-61-21). Some of the staff of many of the resort's restaurants claim that this is the most fun disco, with the best dancing, in all of Verbier. The decor is modern, but a scattering of weathered beams lends an alpine ambience to the dance floor. There's usually a fire burning on one of the hearths, and so many people that your high stepping might not be in the style to which you're accustomed. The place is open only in winter, every day from 10 p.m. to 3 a.m. In the height of the ski season, you'd better arrive as close to the opening as possible, because arrivals after 11 p.m. on weekends require an advance reservation. You'll pay 20F ($13.60) at the door, which entitles you to one free drink.

Tara Club, rue des Creux (tel. 026/31-35-15). Popular as one of the leading discos of the resort, it's filled with alpine detailing, rustically textured plank-covered walls, wooden bar stools, and a dance floor. It's open in mid-winter nightly from 10 p.m. to 3 a.m. You'll pay a cover charge of 15F ($10.20), after which a beer costs from 10F ($6.80).

Bar New Club, rue de la Piscine (tel. 026/31-52-67). There's something about the proportions of the room and the lack of a dance floor that make for the best conversations in town. This is a comfortable and glossy version of a private living room, where rows of comfortable couches are pulled into discreet groupings. No food is served except for steak sandwiches and croque monsieurs. Purely and simply, this is a bar for adults who want to congregate in a warm, well-lit place. A large beer costs 7F ($4.75), scotch and soda 11F ($7.50). The establishment remains open every day from 4 p.m. to 1 a.m. in winter. In summer, it is open only on Friday and Saturday from 4 p.m. to 1 a.m.

Nelson Pub, Hotel Eden, Place Centrale (tel. 026/31-52-02). Its rows of small-paned bay windows are hard to miss as you come up the hill toward the main square of town. Inside, it's larger, better built, and more elaborate than you might have expected. François Frohbosi is the German-born entrepreneur who maintains the place in its neo-Victorian style. Such snacks as cheeseburgers, croque monsieurs, pizzas, and platters of air-dried alpine beef are offered in winter only, and cost from 8F ($5.45) per item. The specialty, however, is beer, with more than 40 varieties in bottles and at least three on tap. A foaming mug costs from 3.50F ($2.40). The place is open daily from 4 p.m. to 1 a.m. but closed from May 1 to June 15 and during the first two weeks in November.

Jacky's Bar (Chez Walter), Hotel Grand Combin (tel. 026/31-65-15). Most of the habitués of this comfortable bar are residents of neighboring hotels who come for the adult ambience and the low energy level. You can sit at the wooden bar on a high stool or sink into one of the comfortable couches scattered through the large wood-paneled room to its side. The bar is open from 5 p.m. to 2 a.m. every day.

Le Milk Bar, Place Centrale (tel. 026/31-25-30). If your weakness is pastries, you'll find them in abundance between the alpine panels of this family-run coffeehouse. The place is not licensed to sell alcohol, so your beverage will be coffee, tea, mineral water, or hot chocolate. Chocolate chaumière, one of the specialties, comes in a two-handled ceramic bowl frothy with whipped cream. The best cakes in town are displayed in the center of the room on an open table. These include a Black Forest tart, banana cake, and a "sinful" chocolate cake loaded with sugar and calories. Cake costs from 3F ($2.05) per slice, chocolate 3.50F ($2.40) per bowl. The place is open daily from 8 a.m. to 7 p.m. but only from December to April and during July and August. Quiches and platters of air-dried alpine beef are also available.

5. GREAT ST. BERNARD PASS

The St. Bernards are beloved in Switzerland, even though they aren't as in demand as they once were. In winter motorists in general take the four-mile-long Great St. Bernard Tunnel between Italy's Aosta Valley and the Valais instead of the road over the Great St. Bernard Pass. Alas, the dogs no longer carry brandy in their casks. But they're still bred by monks at the Great St. Bernard Hospice. If you wish to visit the hospice, you should make inquiries prior to your arrival: **Hospice du Grand-St-Bernard,** Le Grand-St-Bernard, CH-1931 Bourg-St-Pierre, Switzerland (tel. 026/4-92-36).

This famed hospice was established in the mid-11th century to aid stranded travelers trying to make it across the pass. At the hospice you can visit the dogs in their kennels. Allow about an hour's drive from Martigny. You can also visit a small museum illustrating the history of the pass.

Many visitors in summer make the pilgrimage over this pass, following in the footsteps of Napoleon in 1800 when his army used it to cross into Italy. The road is usually open from mid-June (perhaps a little later) until October.

BOURG-ST-PIERRE: For those wishing to stop over, a good accommodation may be found in a small, 30-bed roadside inn, **Auberge du Vieux-Moulin,** CH-1946 Bourg-St-Pierre, Switzerland (tel. 026/87-11-69). Built by blasting away part of a rocky hillside beside the highway, its rooms are clean, streamlined, and comfortable, usually with a private bath. A pleasant restaurant with big windows and wood paneling is on the premises, with a gas station and a currency-exchange office on the same grounds. This inn lies in a hamlet that you might not even notice if you blink, so you might consider this as a practical way station en route to somewhere else. Singles range from 30F ($20.40) to 40F ($27.20) daily, while doubles cost from 55F ($37.40) to 80F ($54.40). Half board is offered for an additional 18F ($12.25).

6. SION

The capital of the Valais, Sion is known for its glorious springs and falls (summer is considered divine all over Switzerland). Easily reached from either France or Italy, Sion dates from Roman times. Most of its population speaks French. The silhouettes of the castles of Valère and Tourbillon dominate this small capital.

THE SIGHTS: Crowning the north hillock is the **Castle of Tourbillon,** perched on a steep rock above the town. It's the ruin of a medieval stronghold built at the end of the 13th century by a bishop wanting to defend Sion against the House of Savoy. It was mainly destroyed by a fire in 1788 and has never been rebuilt, although you'll see the remains of a keep, watchtower, and chapel, among other sights. It makes an ideal place to go for a stroll. At a height of 2,149 feet, there's a view of the Rhône Valley.

On the other hill, the **Collegiale de Valère** at 2,038 feet is more interesting, because this fortified Gothic church is in much better shape. In Roman times it was believed to have been a citadel. The church in its present structure is mainly from the 12th and 13th centuries. A three-aisle basilica, the church contains some splendid stalls from the 17th century, and what has been called "the oldest playable organ in the world," dating from the 14th century.

In the former residence of the cathedral chapter is the **Valere Museum** (tel. 027/21-69-22), with fine works of religious art dating from the Middle Ages, ancient arms and armor, uniforms, Roman and Gothic chests, and interesting ethnological collections. Hours are 9 a.m. to noon and 2 to 6 p.m. from April 1 to October 31, to 5 p.m. from November 1 to March 31. It is closed on Monday except in July and August. Admission is 2F ($1.35) for adults, 1F (68¢) for children. You must make a steep climb up to the church and museum (you can park down below).

After you've made this exhausting climb, you can descend to the town to check it out. The **Hôtel de Ville** (town hall) has beautiful doors and columns from the 17th century. On the main street of Sion, the rue du Grand-Pont, it has an astronomical clock you may want to photograph. The Roman stones on the ground floor date from A.D. 377, and are reputedly the earliest known evidence of the spread of Christianity in the country.

Northeast of the Hôtel de Ville is the **Cathédrale de Notre-Dame-du-Glarier,** reconstructed by 15th-century builders, although the Romanesque belfry remains, dating from the 11th and 13th centuries. Inside, look for the triptych in gilded wood, called *The Tree of Jesse.*

The **Supersaxo House** dates from 1505 and is sumptuously impressive. Built by a provincial governor of the same name, it stands at 7 rue de Conthey and is open to the public from 8 a.m. to noon and 2 to 6 p.m. except on Sunday and holidays. The house is richly decorated, including one room with a decorated rose ceiling that's stunning.

The **Cantonal Art Museum,** 15 Place de la Majorie (tel. 027/21-69-11), is also open to the public from 10 a.m. to noon and 2 to 6 p.m. (to 5 p.m. in winter) daily except Monday, charging an admission of 3F ($2.05). Once a residence of the "Major," an episcopal authority, it today houses a fine arts museum. To reach it, head up the rue des Châteaux in the direction of the hilltop castles (the museum will be on your left). Special attention is devoted to Valais-born artists and to artists who chose to work in the Valais.

Sion can also become an important excursion center for you, as you explore such places as Crans-Montana, covered separately in this guide, and Zermatt, which is a drive of only 1½ hours. The Office du Tourisme, Place de la Planta (tel. 027/22-85-86), in Sion will assist you in planning day trips.

WHERE TO STAY: Many visitors prefer to avoid the impossible traffic and narrow medieval streets of the old city in favor of the **Hôtel du Rhône,** 10 rue du Scex, CH-1950 Sion, Switzerland (tel. 027/22-82-91). This is a bustling modern hotel whose public rooms seem filled with all the carefully orchestrated activity of a busy provincial city. The street-level café-restaurant is almost always overcrowded at lunch with the employees of nearby offices and shops. Take the stairs or the smallish elevator to a floor above street level to check in. Each of the 45 bedrooms has a private bath, TV, phone, radio, mini-bar, and an angular nononsense collection of contemporary furniture. Depending on the season, single rooms rent for 80F ($54.40) to 90F ($61.20) daily, doubles for 120F ($81.60) to 145F ($98.60), with breakfast included.

Hôtel du Castel, 38 rue du Scex, CH-1950 Sion, Switzerland (tel. 027/22-91-71). Modern and boxy, this simple hotel is set at the edge of the busy autoroute that curves around one edge of town. From many of the rooms, you can admire the forbidding cliffs that soar upward to support the base of the medieval château. The accommodations are unfrilly, filled with slightly dated modern furniture, and clean. Singles rent for 63F ($42.85) daily, doubles go for 93F

($63.25) to 95F ($64.60), and triples cost 120F ($81.60), with breakfast, service, and taxes included. Each contains a private shower, radio, phone, TV, minibar, and soundproof windows.

WHERE TO DINE: Not far from the chateau, **Enclos de Valère**, rue des Châteaux (tel. 027/23-32-30), is a small and intimate restaurant. You can just barely drive a car up the steep cobblestones leading to this restaurant, but if another vehicle happens to be coming down the hill, you might be in for trouble. The most popular warm-weather seating area is within the labyrinth of the multileveled garden, where terraces and banks of flowers create dozens of seating niches. In inclement weather, you'll sit within a regionally decorated room with flagstone floors, a beamed ceiling, and a country-inn kind of allure. Open only from May to September, it offers lunch from 11:30 a.m. to 2 p.m. and dinner from 6 to 10:30 p.m. daily. The menu changes with the month, although you'll usually spend from 55F ($37.40) for a fixed-price meal and from 70F ($47.60) for à la carte dishes. Representative menu specialties include foie gras, cassolette of exotic mushrooms, lamb with garlic and thyme, sea bass with mustard and red cabbage, veal kidneys with saffron, and lobster with olives. Reservations are recommended.

Chez **Tchetchett** (les Mayennets), 36 avenue de Tourbillon (tel. 027/22-18-98), about two minutes from the train station, is a good restaurant decorated with wood panels. Fish is one of the specialties, including young turbot with vegetables and bouillabaisse. The chef also does an excellent sole in tarragon butter and, in season, mussels marinara. Some dishes are Italian inspired, including the lasagne and the triples milanese. Try, if available, the fresh frogs' legs. Fixed-price meals begin at 35F ($23.80), while à la carte dinners range from 50F ($34). The restaurant, which has sidewalk tables, is open from 7 a.m. to midnight every night but Sunday. It's closed for about a month in summer.

Caves de Touts-Vents, 22 rue des Châteaux (tel. 027/22-46-84), stands right next to Enclos de Valère in the 13th-century cellar of a pink stucco building. You descend a steep flight of stone-capped stairs to reach the first (and most interesting) room of this deep cellar. Claustrophobes might elect to go no further, although a dimly lit vaulted dining room lies a few steps away. After the sun goes down, the lack of windows and the flickering candles makes the room strangely cozy. The place opens as a café at 5:30 every night. Meal service begins at 6:30 p.m. and continues until 11 p.m. Full meals cost from 45F ($30.60), but you can eat less expensively by ordering raclette at 21F ($14.28) per portion or fondue at 14F ($9.50) per person. Specialties include warm noodles with chanterelles, tagliatelle with salmon, mushrooms in puff pastry, calves' liver with shallots, lamb and steaks.

HAUTE-NENDAZ: Above Sion, facing the Bernese Alps, Haute-Nendaz at 4,116 feet is gaining steadily in popularity. And when (or if) you get bored there, you can always go on to Super-Nendaz, an even more recent tourist center at 5,525 feet. Haute-Nendaz is both a winter and a summer resort. In fair weather, skiing is still possible, along with tennis, swimming, running, walking, and angling. But Haute-Nendaz's reputation is primarily as a ski resort.

It's rapidly emerging as a competitor to Verbier. There are more than 124 miles of walks taking you along *bisses* (irrigation channels), which are sometimes several miles long, and leading you to the edge of glaciers. Among other excursions, you can take a cableway to Tracouet, at 7,220 feet, for skiing.

Food and Lodging

Hôtel Mont Calme, CH-1961 Haute-Nendaz, Switzerland (tel. 027/88-11-56) is a modern adaptation of a chalet, with a sunny restaurant, grill room, pizzeria, and disco bar. The hotel really is calm, as its name suggests, even though the tongue-in-cheek logo is an illustration of a small child raucously raising hell for everyone to hear. Most of the comfortable bedrooms are fairly large and have some wood paneling. Doubles cost from 90F ($61.20) to 110F ($74.80) daily, depending on the season, with breakfast included. Open June to October and December to April.

Hôtel Sourire, CH-1961 Haute-Nendaz, Switzerland (tel. 027/88-26-16), was built in 1970 in the center of the village and is now run by the Mottier-Constantin family, generous and responsible hosts. The public rooms have well-polished wooden ceilings and comfortable modern furniture, while the bedrooms contain private baths, radios, and phones, and there is a good view from your balcony across the Alps as far as the Rhône Valley. Depending on the season, doubles go from 109F ($74.10) daily, and singles cost 64F ($43.50). All tariffs include breakfast. Half board is available for an additional 19F ($12.90). The Sourire is open from December to October.

ANZÈRE: Overlooking the valley of the Rhône, Anzère gets quite a bit of sunshine. The views from this pint-size resort are spectacular, opening onto the Alpes Vaudoises all the way to Mont Blanc. It draws visitors in both summer and winter. Summer activities include numerous walks in the forest, swimming in alpine pools, tennis, and fishing in the cold waters. Lying to the north of Sion, Anzère is just beginning to emerge as a ski resort. It seems to have a bright future. The center has been carefully conceived, with the modern tourist in mind.

The resort lies at 4,920 feet. A cableway will take you to the Pas de Maimbré at 7,752 feet, where there's not only a panoramic vista, but ski runs as well.

In Anzère, traffic is forbidden in the main square.

Food and Lodging

Résidence et Hôtel Grand-Roc, CH-1972 Anzère, Switzerland (tel. 027/38-35-35), has beautiful views from the balconies of its well-furnished rooms, as well as a well-designed series of inviting public rooms. The bar area is my favorite, and the flagstone-covered tavern is attractive also. The hotel has set up a fitness course nearly two miles long in the nearby woods which, if you're not out promenading through the hills, might make a healthy diversion. Depending on the season, singles cost from 60F ($40.80) to 90F ($61.20) daily, with doubles renting for 90F ($61.20) to 140F ($95.20). Half board is offered for another 20F ($13.60) per person daily.

Restaurant les Premiers Pas, Place du Village (tel. 027/38-29-20), on the central square of town, is a gemütlich restaurant open every day of the week in high season from 9 a.m. to midnight. In low season the place closes on Monday and also shuts down from the first of November until mid-December. Specialties are the best raclette in town, tournedos on a slate with morels, cheese fondue, and different items that are either flambéed or grilled over an open fire, as well as regional dishes. A noontime menu offers fixed-price meals beginning at 18F ($12.25), while evening dinners cost from 35F ($23.80).

EVOLÈNE: From Sion, another road heads south through the beautiful Val d'Hérens, a historic district, leading to Evolène at 4,525 feet. The village contains dark-brown larch-wood-fronted houses that, in summer, blossom with brightly colored flowers in the windowsills. Women still wear their national costume at work (and not just on holidays or to awe the tourists).

As you drive through the valley you'll see a crown of mountain peaks: the Dent Blanche, Pigne, Mont-Collon, Veisivi, and several others. Other villages have melodious names like Les Haudères, La Sage, Villa, La Forclaz, and Ferpècle. Higher up, at 6,670 feet, you reach Arolla, only a stone's throw from the glaciers.

Winter sports were introduced a few years ago. At Arolla there are ski tows,

10

R671	67082			BIO	2		11249	6
PUB	STOCK NO.		LOC.	CAT	LEVEL		INIT. DATE	QTY.

DE CORDOVA	7085		6			
	STORE	N. RO	TOT. SAL	T	SEC. REC.	QTY.

	4.95							
	PRICE						LAST DATE	QTY.

JOHNNY CAME LATELY

B 97 98 99 100 101 102 103 104 105 106 107 108 109 110 111 112 113 114 115 116 117 118 119 120 121 122 123 124 125 126 127 128 B

A A

and cross-country skiers like it a lot. The region is also rich in alpine flora and fauna.

Food and Lodging

Hôtel Hermitage, CH-1968 Evolène, Switzerland (tel. 027/83-12-32), is a family-run, white-walled house with balconies set in a park area filled with pines. The inside is rustically paneled with light-grained wood. The floors are flagstone or parquet, while the bedrooms are freshly painted and cheerful. The Chevrier and the Gaspoz families, the owners, know everybody in town. Depending on the season, they charge 35F ($23.80) to 50F ($34) daily in a single and 70F ($47.60) to 100F ($68) in a double, including breakfast. Half board is an additional 20F ($13.60) per person daily. Open June to September and December to April.

7. CRANS-MONTANA

Crans and Montana-Vermala, at 4,985 feet, are twin resorts accessible by good roads from Sion or the market town of Sierre (also by funicular from Sierre). They are modern and fashionable ski areas, and they lie on a handsome plateau with air that's been called "lighter than champagne." Skiers can not only ski, but enjoy views of the valley of the Rhône. Connected to the Crans-Montana area is Aminona, at 4,920 feet, still an infant resort, but rising rapidly.

Crans is made up for the most part of colonies of apartments and hotels, often in the half-timbered mountain style. Montana, the older part, is built around a lake.

Montana was born as a resort in 1892, with Crans getting into the picture with construction of hotels in 1912. Besides the fine winter sports here, the two places have gained in year-round interest. Montana became a health resort, and Crans is now a golf center, with the 18-hole Plan-Bramois course and the 9-hole Xires golfing lure. The Swiss Open held at Crans draws top golfers from all over the world. Tennis is the main sport in summer at Montana, with international tournaments held in July.

The plateau is also attractive for horseback riding, hiking, fishing, and summer skiing in warm weather, and many winter activities take place here—skating, ski-bobbing, ice hockey matches, what have you.

One of the most spectacular ascents is to Point Plaine-Morte at nearly 10,000 feet, which, even at so great a height, still has runs suitable for the neophyte. To reach it, take the gondola at Montana-Barzettes, to the east of Montana, stopping at Les Violettes first. There's a restaurant at Plaine-Morte.

Holiday-makers also like to head for the Cry d'Err at 7,430 feet for its big dining room (the terrace is popular for sunbathing). A gondola—again from Montana—goes to Cry d'Err, and there's another gondola departing from Crans as well.

The Piste Nationale is known for its steep, narrow runs, which attract many skiers. Mount Tubang, with its more challenging runs, is another slope only for the more skilled skier.

WHERE TO STAY: There are accommodations in all of these tiny resorts, but the following are my recommendations:

Hotels at Crans

Hôtel du Golf et des Sports, CH-3963 Crans-sur-Sierre, Switzerland (tel. 027/41-42-42), is an attractively designed, five-star establishment with lots of windows and a flat roof that sprawls across a green area near a lake, a five-minute walk from the commercial center of the resort. There is, as you'd expect, a golf course and an elegant series of salons and bars, many of them with fireplaces. The decor is warmly upholstered, with deep-seated reproductions of antique chairs clustered into attractive groupings. The bedrooms come in both older and renovated decor, depending on the particular wing of the hotel in which they're found. Each contain a balcony, mini-bar, radio, phone, and TV, and costing from 85F ($57.80) to 210F ($142.80) daily in a single, from 200F ($136) to 480F ($326.40) in a double, depending on the season. Half board is available for an additional 40F ($27.20) per person per day. This is one of the only large hotels in town that remains open all year. It has a number of spa and dieting facilities on the premises.

Hotel Alpina & Savoy, CH-3963 Crans-sur-Sierre, Switzerland (tel. 027/41-21-42), originally built in 1912, is the oldest and most historic hotel in Crans. It has always been under the ownership of the Mudrey family, now in its third generation, and has been frequently modernized and expanded since its original construction. By far the most contemporary section is the pine-ringed pool area, with its adjacent saunas. A big-windowed restaurant, a pleasant bar area, and a wide outdoor sun terrace add to this consciously unfashionable but venerable hotel's charm. This is the kind of place where guests usually check in and consume most of their meals on the premises, an act encouraged by management. Singles rent for a low of 73F ($49.65) to a high of 200F ($126) daily, depending on the season and room assignment. Doubles cost from 131F ($89.10) to 290F ($197.20). Half board is another 35F ($23.80) per person daily. Each of the 75 rooms contains a private bath and is slightly old-fashioned but most comfortable.

Hôtel de l'Etrier, CH-3963 Crans-sur-Sierre, Switzerland (tel. 027/40-11-81), is composed of two steeply roofed modern buildings, with prominent balconies and big windows. They're connected to one another and set at slightly different angles for an unusual effect that is particularly dramatic at night when the light filters through the colored curtains, giving the windows the impression of stained glass. The swimming pool is well heated and partially covered for year-round bathing, and has a fully staffed bar operating out of one corner. The rest of the hotel is comfortable, modern, and attractive, with pleasing abstract murals color coordinated to the plants and shaggy area rugs. A 7½-acre park in front of the hotel is dotted with lawn chairs in summer. Well-furnished singles range from 73F ($49.65) to 210F ($142.80) daily, while doubles go from 138F ($93.85) to 290F ($197.20). Half board is another 35F ($23.80) per person per day.

Hôtel des Mélèzes, CH-3963 Crans-sur-Sierre, Switzerland (tel. 027/43-18-12), lies about a half-mile from the congestion of the town's most commercial districts, in a forest of deciduous pines that the French call *mélèzes.* Many guests prefer it for its relative isolation. It has one of the most appealing sun terraces and greenhouse-style dining rooms in town. Its windows lie a few feet from the end point of one of the resort's ski runs, so you can watch the end of the trail while sipping coffee and chatting with the gregarious owners, Henri and Marie-Louise Lamon. The hotel has a pleasant and high-ceilinged bar area, where you'll never want for company after dinner. Each of the 21 bedrooms contains its own bath, phone, balcony, and radio. If you stay here in summer, you'll enjoy your breakfast outdoors, near the seventh hole of the resort's 18-hole golf course. Singles cost from 56F ($38.10) to 115F ($78.20) daily, and doubles go for 95F ($64.60) to 196F ($133.30), plus another 29F ($19.70) per person daily for half board. The hotel is open June to September and December to April.

Hotel Pension Centrale, CH-3963 Crans-sur-Sierre, Switzerland (tel. 027/41-37-67), is a comfortable family-run boarding house in the center of town. The exterior is a solid-looking stone building with shutters and has a restaurant on the ground floor. The renovated rooms have phones and radios, and the hotel offers personalized service. Miss Hurlimann and Mr. Funkenberg, your hosts, maintain this 36-bed establishment, charging 35F ($23.80) to 50F ($34) per person daily, single or double, with breakfast included. Half board costs an additional 20F ($13.60) per person daily.

Hotels at Montana-Vermala

Hotel Crans Ambassador, CH-3962 Montana, Switzerland (tel. 027/41-52-22), set high above the town in a pocket of isolated chic, is a stylish and dramatic hotel with a steeply inclined roof that resembles a triple alpine peak. The lobby is one of those exceptional rooms where you can sit in modern, well-upholstered comfort while gazing over the rugged mountains and the snow. There's a bar in one corner, and philodendron trails over the exposed wooden beams. In warm weather, guests take advantage of a flower-ringed outdoor terrace and a swimming pool. Each of the conservatively modern bedrooms contains a private bath, phone, radio, a balcony or terrace, and color TV. In addition to the 70 rooms, there are 20 large apartments, each with two to five rooms. Depending on the season and the accommodation, singles range from 170F ($115.60) to 225F ($153) and doubles from 270F ($183.60) to 510F ($346.80). Junior suites begin at 470F ($319.60) in low season, and at 610F ($414.80) in high season. These prices include half board service and taxes. It's open June to September, December to April.

Hotel-Residence Super Crans, CH-3962 Montana, Switzerland (tel. 027/41-29-15). Stylishly iconoclastic, this soaring hotel breaks the sometimes stifling monotony of chalet Swiss hotels. It rises in an angular design that might be at home on the streets of a large North American city. It's surrounded by alpine meadow and evergreens high above the town, in the hamlet called Vermala. Despite its modernity and the stark beauty of its slate floors, the hotel contains a pleasing collection of Oriental carpets, antique chests, and unusual paintings. It also has a magnificent indoor swimming pool flooded with sunlight from its angled window. On the premises are a restaurant, a bar, a sauna, two tennis courts, and access to dozens of ski or hiking paths. Rates, depending on the season and the accommodation, range from 140F ($95.20) to 205F ($139.40) daily for a single, from 160F ($108.80) to 330F ($224.40) for a double. Each of the rooms has a south-facing balcony, a bath, a phone, and conservatively modern furniture. It is open June 15 to September 30 and December to April 15.

Les Hauts de Crans, CH-3962 Montana, Switzerland (tel. 027/41-55-53), is the most dramatic and probably the most isolated hotel in town. To reach it, you'll have to negotiate a winding forest-lined road that will eventually funnel you into the submerged concrete bunker of the hotel's underground garage. The hotel is part of a multi-chalet complex. Each of the 36 accommodations has a private balcony, a bath, and many of the luxuries you'd expect from a four-star hotel. Depending on the season and the accommodation, singles rent for 123F ($83.65) to 210F ($142.80) daily, and doubles for 208F ($141.45) to 385F ($261.80), with breakfast, service, and taxes included. A few steps from the hotel is the meeting point of several forested walkways, ideal for cross-country skiing or summer hiking. There's also an indoor pool capped with a thick-beamed ceiling, plus a sauna, a restaurant and bar, a grill room, and outdoor tennis courts. It's open June to September and December to April.

Hôtel Curling, CH-3962 Montana, Switzerland (tel. 027/41-12-42). You'll have a pleasant time here even if you don't like to curl. But if you do, there's ample opportunity on the ice-skating rink near the hotel. The interior is warmly and rustically decorated with leather chairs, paneling, and flagstone floors, plus centrally placed hearths that funnel their smoke up through metallic stovepipes. All rooms contain private baths. Rates depend on the season and the placement. Singles range from 54F ($36.70) to 116F ($78.90) daily, with doubles costing 92F ($62.55) to 196F ($133.30). Half board is another 29F ($19.72) per person daily. The hotel is closed in May and November.

Hôtel de la Forêt, CH-3962 Montana, Switzerland (tel. 027/40-21-31), lies only 200 yards from the cable car of Les Violettes–Plaine-Morte. Recently renovated, it is set below the center of the village behind a repetitive modern balconied façade. Alain and Serge Morard set a lighthearted ambience, which is most successful during the weekly raclette parties. The view through the huge windows of the swimming pool is spectacular, and guests have a choice of three terraces for summer or midwinter sunbathing. A large dining room serves well-prepared meals, while the pianist in the bar often encourages people to dance. The establishment is laid out in three buildings—the main hotel, an annex, and the pool with apartments nearby. Hotel rates range from 92F ($62.55) to 141F ($95.90) daily in a double in low season, rising to 150F ($102) to 187F ($127.15) in a double in high season, with breakfast included. Half board is available for an additional 26F ($17.68) per person.

Hôtel St-Georges, CH-3962 Montana, Switzerland (tel. 027/41-24-14). On a sunny summer's day, with the rock garden and swimming pool in front and the blinding white balconies stretching overhead, you'd imagine you were in the Caribbean. The interior has enough intimate corners, conversational groupings, and coziness to make any recluse happy, along with well-decorated bedrooms with conservatively traditional furniture. Roland Grunder-Fischer is the capable owner, charging 59F ($40.10) to 126F ($85.70) daily in a single and 100F ($68) to 214F ($145.50) in a double, depending on the season and the plumbing. Half board is an additional 32F ($21.75) per person daily. The hotel is closed in November.

Hôtel Cisalpin, CH-3962 Montana, Switzerland (tel. 027/41-25-69), is a multiroofed hotel with white walls and dark wood trim at the top of a steep hill. It has its own mountaineering and ski school, and is close to the cable car leading to Les Violettes–Plaine-Morte. The interior is filled with the kind of nooks and crannies where you can relax with a drink (or a friend). One of the dining rooms has an attractive format of local flagstones built into two sides of the room, with a fireplace burning against one corner. Bedrooms are clean, modern, and functional, and they're also comfortable. Mr. and Mrs. J.P. Clivaz, the owners, charge 65F ($44.20) to 105F ($71.40) daily for a double, with breakfast included, depending on the season. Half board is available for another 22F ($14.95) per person daily. The hotel is open June to October and December to April.

RESTAURANTS IN THE AREA: The grand restaurant of the region is **Restaurant de la Côte,** Corin-sur-Sierre (tel. 027/55-13-51), the domain of Monsieur and Madame Georges Burguet-Vieusart. They are indisputably the gastronomic stars of the region, in spite of their location almost 2 miles from Sierre and 7½ miles from Montana. And don't judge the quality of their fare by the unprepossessing façade. It improves considerably when you go inside, where you're rewarded with a panoramic vista and most comfortable appointments. Hours are daily except Monday and Tuesday from 11 a.m. to 2 p.m. and from 7 to 9:15 p.m. (they are closed annually from May 20 to June 20).

Perched high above the vineyards and the valley below, you can peruse the menu with its sumptuous selections. If you want your decisions made for you, you can order the fixed-price lunch at 50F ($34), one of the finest values in the area, considering the quality of the food presented. A set dinner is offered for 90F ($61.20), or else you can order à la carte, with meals costing from 60F ($40.80). Mr. Burguet is a master chef in the kitchen, presenting such elegant fare as sea bass grilled with fennel, red mullet grilled with thyme, oysters gratinée with champagne, and an array of delectable desserts. Their fine establishment clearly should be on any gastronomic tour of Switzerland.

Rôtisserie de la Channe Valaisanne, rue Centrale (tel. 027/41-12-58), in Crans-sur-Sierre, is the place to go for what is probably the best meat in the region. The bar area is so pleasantly gemütlich that many guests ask to wait awhile before going to their table. You might begin your meal with a homemade pâté in puff pastry or a plate of air-dried alpine beef. For a follow-up, try the côte de Charolais or Chateaubriand, or two kinds of fondue, even a spit-roasted lamb or chicken. Fish might appeal to you when you learn it's blue trout. You'll also be interested in the wine list, which understandably places the local Fendant as the first category. The restaurant is open daily except Monday from 8:30 a.m. to midnight, but closes yearly from mid-May to mid-June and for the month of November. Fixed-price meals range from 30F ($20.40) to 45F ($30.60), while à la carte dinners cost from 60F ($40.80) per person.

Rôtisserie de la Reine (tel. 027/41-18-85) is the domain of Bernard Léonard. Meals are served from noon to 2 p.m. and 7 to 10 p.m. every day of the year, except during most of May and November. The restaurant specializes in sole, oysters, and bouillabaisse. Salmon is often cooked en papillote; a "regal" sauerkraut is offered, as are medallions of chicken liver with truffles. Set menus are featured at 52F ($35.35) to 98F ($66.65), or you can order à la carte, paying around 70F ($47.60).

Auberge de la Diligence, at Montana (tel. 027/41-13-28), is an alpine tavern below the village beside the highway. It remains an enduring favorite for its tasty specialties of both the Valais and Italy. Offering parking and a seasonal terrace, it is open daily except Monday and Tuesday from 8 a.m. to midnight. Careful cookery and efficient service make for a winning combination. At night you can order raclette along with fondues and grilled fish. Other specialties include ravioli maison and piccata marsala. You can also order a risotto flavored with mushrooms and sautéed beef with Rösti. You're welcomed by Oreste Casarotti, the chef de cuisine, who doesn't serve lunch in May, June, and November. Menus cost from 35F ($23.80) up.

La Trappe, at the already-recommended Hôtel Cisalpin (tel. 027/41-24-25), is away from the center of the action but still considered the place to go for those desiring typical specialties of the Valais in an Old World–tavern setting. It's decorated with heavy beams, brass, copper pots, and antique accessories, everything enhanced in cold weather by a blazing fireplace. It is closed from late April until the first week of June, but serves lunches from 11 a.m. to 3 p.m. and dinner from 5 to 10 p.m. daily. For such a small hotel, the menu is large. Grilled meats over the open fire are featured, but you can also indulge in such favorites as frogs' legs, crêpes Valaisanne, escargots bourguignonne, filet perch meunière, and lamb provençal. Fondue Bacchus (with white wine) and raclette are regular features. Meals cost from 45F ($30.60).

Le Pavillon (also known as Cheza Micha), in Montana (tel. 027/41-24-69), has a desirable lakeside frontage that makes it a favorite in all seasons. Its outdoor terrace is often packed. In summer it's open daily from 9:30 a.m. to 1 p.m. (opens at 10:30 a.m. in winter). You can drop in for snacks and drinks any time, but hot food is served only from noon to 2 p.m. and from 7 to 9:15 p.m. The chef presents a cuisine du marché, based on whatever was good and fresh at the market place, and he also offers what is termed a grande carte de poissons. From that menu, you can select oysters Rockefeller, and many other delectable "fruits of the sea." Other platters are likely to include carpaccio, tagliatelle with a truffle cream sauce, and filet goulash. Meals cost from 75F ($51) unless you order simply, perhaps having an assiette du jour at 20F ($13.60). The restaurant is closed in May and November.

Restaurant du Cervin, in Vermala (tel. 027/41-21-80), is worth the trek. It is red-shuttered and barnlike, set in an alpine meadow high above the resort. Every night raclette is featured, along with succulent grilled meats over charcoal fires. The location is near the previously recommended Hôtel-Residence Super-Crans. It's also ideal as a luncheon stopover for cross-country skiers. Sometimes, if the sun is out, guests enjoy the terrace even in winter. In summer, of course, it's ideal. An array of specialties is presented, including salmon salad with fresh mushrooms, tournedos with onions, and a gourmet's delight—a salad with romaine, quail, and foie gras. A good selection of fresh fish is always presented for your pleasure. Meals cost from 40F ($27.20). You can partake of this fare daily from 10 a.m. to 1 p.m. except from May to June 15.

APRÈS SKI: Most of the hotels have bars that are lively at night. Often skiers and nonskiers spend their entire evening in one of the local restaurants, enjoying pizza, fondue, or raclette, along with beer or wine. One of the most pleasant bars, drawing an attractive crowd, is the one in the **Hôtel Mirabeau** (tel. 027/41-39-12). Valasian specialties are served here.

At the **Hôtel de la Forêt** (tel. 027/41-36-08), raclette evenings are sometimes offered, along with music and a pleasant bar where a pianist entertains.

Hotel Rodania (tel. 027/40-11-41), a five-star hotel, is an important après-ski hangout. Its disco is decorated in a 1925-era art deco, and is appropriately stylish. It is open from 9 p.m. to 2 a.m. nightly in winter only, with drinks costing from 12F ($8.15).

Jack and Lucy (tel. 027/41-12-61), is a warmly decorated disco, oozing with "sport-chic." It rolls merrily along every night in winter from 9 p.m. to 2 a.m., with drinks costing from 12F ($8.15).

The most interesting piano bar in Crans is **Le Memphis** (tel. 027/41-24-30). The bar attracts an attractive après-ski crowd throughout the day. As dusk descends, piano music provides melodies which filter out onto a terrace. Inside, the style is art deco, with drinks costing from 10F ($6.80). Hours are daily from 11 a.m. to midnight. The location is in the center of Crans.

The **Crans-Ambassador,** at Montana (tel. 027/41-52-22), draws a generally chic crowd to its Binocle, with handsome decoration and good music. It also has a rôtisserie and a grand buffet.

The Lobby Bar at the **Hôtel du Golf et des Sports** (tel. 027/41-42-42) is elegant. Even when there's practically no afternoon business, a uniformed barman stands stoically behind the bar in this hotel's dignified lobby. A musical group plays amid the Louis Philippe–style furniture every evening in season from 6:30 till very late at night. The ambience is sophisticated, adult, and if you're with the right people, a lot of fun.

Club Gypsy (tel. 027/41-23-73), under the already recommended Rôtisserie de la Reine, often draws an energetic young crowd on cold alpine nights. Entrance is free, but most hard drinks begin at 16F ($10.90). It's open in summer and winter except in May and November. To reach it, descend a flight of stairs adjacent to the bar of the Rôtisserie.

8. LEUKERBAD

At 4,630 feet, this centuries-old spa is connected with Sierre and Leuk-Susten by road. Its water cure has drawn spa devotees from all over Europe, and it now complements taking the waters by offering good skiing on the slopes of the Torrent area and on the Gemmi Pass, accessible by cable cars. It had a great heyday of fashion in the 19th century, and has spent millions of dollars adjusting to the needs of modern tourists. It has a total of ten indoor and seven outdoor thermal baths, and a host of sports activities.

Called in French, Loèche-les-Bains, Leukerbad enjoys a particularly romantic site, surrounded by alpine meadows on the northern part of the upper Rhône Valley, lying on the route to the Gemmi Pass.

FOOD AND LODGING: Occupying two almost identical balconied buildings sharing a common swimming pool, the **Badehotel Bristol,** CH-3954

Leukerbad, Switzerland (tel. 027/61-18-33), is a modern hotel facility. The buildings are connected by a heated underground tunnel, which makes sharing the solarium and hairdressing facilities easier. Clients who stay in Bristol I usually select full board, while guests in Bristol II have kitchenettes and usually take one of the half-board plans. The entire complex is set off by a background of rocky alpine cliffs, and the management occasionally holds summer buffet picnics on the lawns in front. Bedrooms are elegantly modern, with grained trim from exotic wood. The pine-paneled public rooms are, at their best, gemütlich. The Erwin Lorétan family, the owners and conscientious hosts, charge from 162F ($110.15) to 256F ($174.10) daily in a single and from 265F ($180.20) to 346F ($235.30) in a double, with half board included.

Hotel Les Sources des Alpes, CH-3954 Leukerbad, Switzerland (tel. 027/62-11-51), completely renovated and reopened since 1988, stands on the southern slopes of the northern alps. It is well situated, lying amid rolling mountain meadows and health-giving springs. Françoise and René Isler welcome guests from all over the world, and are eager to point out their spa facilities, including thermal therapy. They have a fitness and training center, along with a sauna, Turkish bath, and open-air swimming pool. Modern amenities include a beauty parlor. Guests can wander in the garden before heading for the hotel's restaurant, Malvoisie, which offers a refined continental cuisine along with low calorie but quality produce for those watching the waistline. The bedrooms are well furnished and comfortable. Including half board, singles pay 282F ($191.75) per day, with doubles costing from 434F ($295.10) to 484F ($329.10). Some suites are even more expensive.

Hotel Zayetta, CH-3954 Leukerbad, Switzerland (tel. 027/61-16-46), is a modern hotel with four tiers of balconies angled toward the sun for maximum illumination of the attractive bedrooms. A sauna is on the premises, along with a host of therapy and massage facilities, which include even the more exotic mudpacking techniques. The dining areas and the bar are intimately lit in a way that makes virtually anybody look good, and the salons are finished in a kind of understated elegance that usually centers on a blazing fire. All the accommodations contain private bath, costing 80F ($54.40) to 109F ($72.10) daily in a single and 135F ($91.80) to 175F ($119) in a double, with half board included.

Hotel Dala, CH-3954 Leukerbad, Switzerland (tel. 027/61-12-13), is an angular modern building with a restaurant on the ground floor and four tiers of balconied bedrooms on top. Each of the colorful units has its own bath. The Lorétan-Grichting family, your hosts, charge 155F ($105.40) to 195F ($132.60) daily for a double room, 69F ($45.90) to 95F ($64.60) for a single. Half board is included. On the premises is a marble-floored dancing bar, plus a warmly decorated dining room with stone detailing and a large staff.

9. GRIMENTZ

At 5,150 feet, Grimentz has much traditional allure, and is known for its alpine hospitality. Many visitors drive here just to look at its old chalets mellowed by the sun. The town has known many hard times, but has survived them nobly, and today maintains many of its old customs and traditions.

It's the starting point for several well-known walks—the lake and hut at Moity, pas de Lona, and Cold de Torrent, with its rich alpine flora and fauna—and offers mechanical ski lifts up to the Becs de Bosson. It also has a heated closed swimming pool, two tennis courts, and an outdoor skating rink, and many cross-country trails.

FOOD AND LODGING: A three-star hostelry, **Hôtel Marenda,** CH-3961 Grimentz, Switzerland (tel. 027/65-11-71), is a white stucco house with blue-gray shutters and a modified mansard roof. It has a pleasant garden, a wood-trimmed extension, and cozy sitting rooms with pine paneling and prominent fireplaces. A flagstone and gravel terrace offers drink service in a spacious area surrounded by trees. Rooms are comfortably, not lavishly, furnished, and the least-expensive accommodations do not have private baths. Rates depend on the season and room assignment. Singles cost from 35F ($23.80) to 65F ($44.20) daily, with doubles going for 58F ($39.45) to 109F ($74.10). Half board goes for another 21F ($14.30) per person daily.

Hôtel la Cordée, CH-3961 Grimentz, Switzerland (tel. 027/65-12-46), has many elegant touches and a thick-beamed construction that reminds you you're in the Alps. The bedrooms are outfitted with comfortable beds that neatly tuck into armoires every morning for a maximum of living space during the day. Each of the accommodations has a private balcony and bath, plus an individualized decor in warm colors. Doubles cost from 84F ($57.10) daily in low season to 90F ($61.20) in high season. Half board goes for an additional 23F ($15.65). The good food is served in a well-appointed dining room.

Hôtel de Moiry, CH-3961 Grimentz, Switzerland (tel. 027/65-11-44), is an attractively simple establishment owned by local ski instructor and mountain guide Vital Salamin. His son, Aurel, manages this friendly, pleasantly pine-paneled hotel. A nearby annex provided additional bedrooms under a low-lying roof covered with thick cedar shingles, surrounded by a summer garden. Doubles cost from 74F ($50.30) to 88F ($59.85) daily, depending on the plumbing and the season. Half board is offered for another 20F ($13.60) per person daily. English is spoken.

10. ZERMATT AND THE MATTERHORN

Zermatt (5,315 feet above sea level), a small village in the shadow of the great Matterhorn mountain (14,690 feet), made its debut as a ski resort more than 100 years ago when it was "discovered" by the British, the first major tourists of Switzerland. The spotlight of world interest was turned on the **Matterhorn** when Edward Whymper, British explorer and mountaineer, began a series of determined efforts to climb it. He made the attempt half a dozen times between 1861 and 1865, trying it from the Italian side of the Pennine Alps. By a freak accident Whymper saw the Swiss side of the great mountain, which appeared to him less formidable than he had heard it described. On July 14, 1865, he became the first man to climb the Matterhorn, reaching the summit from the Swiss side, although in the process four of the climbers of his team fell to their deaths. Whymper and two guides made it to safety and into history. Three days later an Italian guide, Jean-Antoine Carrel, successfully made the climb from the Italian side.

The Matterhorn, called Mont Cervin by the French-speaking Swiss, still lures mountain climbers, with the two most outstanding "hikes" being the climb up to the **Mettelhorn** (11,000 feet) and the hike up to the **Matterhorn Hut,** lying at the base of the peak.

Since Whymper's time, Zermatt has become a world-renowned international resort, with deluxe and first-class amenities. However, in many of its little satellite hamlets you'll still find much of the original charm that put Zermatt on the tourist map long ago. From Zermatt you can look onto some of the highest peaks in Switzerland.

You can walk from one end of Zermatt to the other in about 15 minutes. Along the way from the railroad station to the parish church you'll see little except shops, hotels, and masses of tourists. Only horse-drawn carriage taxis and small battery-run vehicles are permitted in the town, but still, with carts, carriages, and milling throngs of people, there are such things as traffic jams in "traffic-free" Zermatt in peak season.

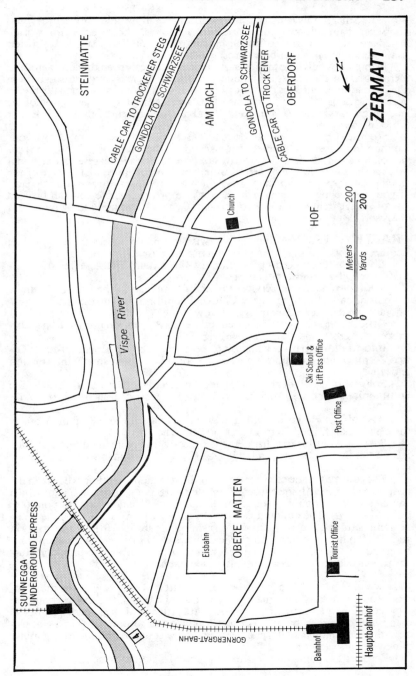

ZERMATT

STEINMATTE

CABLE CAR TO TROCKENER STEG

GONDOLA TO SCHWARZSEE

AM BACH

GONDOLA TO SCHWARZSEE

CABLE CAR TO TROCKENER

OBERDORF

Church

HOF

Meters
Yards
200
200
0
0

Vispe River

Ski School &
Lift Pass Office

Post Office

SUNNEGGA
UNDERGROUND EXPRESS

OBERE MATTEN

Eisbahn

Tourist Office

GORNERGRAT-BAHN

Bahnhof

Hauptbahnhof

The Seiler family launched the resort concept in the mid-19th century, and the Seiler chain still owns many fine Zermatt hotels. The style the family originated is used for a number of establishments today. You'll see many Valais chalets as well as some *mazots,* or little barns, which are characteristic of the region.

More snow falls here than at most other winter resorts on the continent, and Zermatt boasts the best spring skiing in the Alps. There is a high season both in the peak summer months and in winter when skiers pour in, but actually the resort is fairly busy all year. Skiing lasts until late spring since the inception of the high-altitude ski tours *(Haute Route),* and it goes right through the summer at Théodul Pass.

To reach Zermatt, you can drive to **Täsch,** three miles away, and park your car there in an open lot. A rail shuttle takes you to the resort for 9.60F ($6.55) per person for a round trip. Always arrive at Zermatt with a hotel reservation, and if you let the staff know your arrival time, you'll probably be met by one of the hotel's battery-powered pickup carts, which will transport you and your luggage. If you're traveling by train, take one to Visp or Brig, where you can board a narrow-gauge train for the ride to Zermatt. Geneva is about 3½ to 4 hours from the resort.

PRACTICAL FACTS: To make your visit to this alpine area more enjoyable, here are a few points of information you may find useful.

Children: If you need a babysitter, try **Kinderheim Theresia** (tel. 028/67-20-96) or **Seiler's Kindergarten** (tel. 028/66-11-21).

Churches: Religious services in Zermatt are held in the Roman Catholic church and at the English St. Peter Church. For information on times of worship, phone Tourist Office Zermatt, listed below.

Drugstore: For your pharmaceutical needs, **Pharmacie International Zermatt** (tel. 028/67-34-84) is your answer.

Information: To make your visit to Zermatt a happy experience, **Tourist Office Zermatt,** am Bahnhofplatz (tel. 028/66-11-81), will supply information and advice.

Police: To get in touch with the local protectors of law and order, call the **community police** (tel. 028/67-38-22) or the **district police** (tel. 028/67-21-97).

Post office: Hours are 7:30 a.m. to noon and 1:45 to 6:30 p.m. Monday through Friday, from 7:30 to 11 a.m. on Saturday.

Rescue: Available to help skiers and others who explore the alpine landscape is **Swissair Rescue Service** (tel. 028/47-47-47), operating on a 24-hour emergency basis.

Telecommunications: The telegraph and telephone building is between the post office and the Alpine Museum. Inside are 18 phone booths, one of which contains a Telex for public use and one fitted for use of handicapped persons (tel. 028/67-41-94). The building is open December 1 to April 15 and June 15 to September from 8 a.m. to 9 p.m. Monday through Saturday, from 9 a.m. to noon and 5 to 9 p.m. on Sunday and public holidays. In the off-season it's open from 8 a.m. to noon and 1:45 to 7 p.m. Monday through Friday, to 5 p.m. on Saturday. It's closed on Sunday and holidays in low season.

WHERE TO STAY: The innkeepers of Zermatt have seen tourists by the thousands come and go. Many a manager started as a 12-year-old bellboy carrying the luggage of foreign tourists. They have grown a little world-weary perhaps, after so many years of service, but nevertheless, following an autumnal lull in their business, they polish their smiles and get ready to welcome an ever-increasing influx of new visitors each year.

Zermatt has something for most purses. Its hotels come in all sizes and shapes, both large and small. In all, the resort has about 100 hotels and guest houses—your first impression might be that every chalet in town is a hotel. These hotel beds are backed by a wide range of holiday apartments and private rooms.

The Upper Bracket

Seiler Mont Cervin, CH-3920 Zermatt, Switzerland (tel. 028/66-11-22), has been considered one of Zermatt's leading hotels since it was established more than 130 years ago. The interior includes many of the sunny, spacious, and well-appointed rooms you'd expect from a first-class hotel, with all of the fine craftsmanship and service for which the Seiler chain is known. The well-dressed guests dine, drink, and dance to a live band in the top-notch bar, among the best known in Zermatt. In the center of town, it has one of the most luxurious pools in Zermatt, along with the usual sauna and massage facilities. A kindergarten cares for children under the supervision of a nursery school teacher. With half board included, singles peak in the winter season at 170F ($115.60) to 230F ($156.40) daily and doubles at 290F ($197.20) to 460F ($312.80). In summer, half-board tariffs are 135F ($91.80) to 180F ($122.40) daily in a single, 230F ($156.40) to 360F ($244.80) in a double. For 10F ($6.80) additional, someone will pick you and your bags up at the hotel in a horse-drawn sleigh in winter, in an old-fashioned, horse-drawn carriage in summer. The hotel is closed in November and May.

Grand Hotel Zermatterhof, CH-3920 Zermatt, Switzerland (tel. 028/66-11-01), seems to be one of the few hotels in town not designed to look like a chalet. Its symmetrical white façade looks vaguely Régence-style. The interior is attractive in an understated kind of well-upholstered way, with bronze-colored detailing in the intimate bar area, cane-backed French provincial chairs in the dining room, a carpeted exercise unit, and a beautifully illuminated swimming pool. The floors usually have at least one handmade rug, while the bedrooms are accented with wood paneling and vivid colors. Prices, with half board included, range from 125F ($85) to 260F ($176.80) per person daily, depending on the season and the accommodation. Closed in November.

Hotel Alex, CH-3920 Zermatt, Switzerland (tel. 028/67-17-26), run by Alex and Gisela Perren, is filled with lots of rarely seen architectural details, such as a free-form swimming pool beneath a half-timbered ceiling with a round lunette window on top. The flagstoned public rooms are outfitted with elegant paneling and amusingly grotesque statues of demigods, one of whom stirs a cauldron with his trident (he happens to be standing on top of an open fireplace). Everywhere you look you'll see original and creative statements in natural materials. These features have not been lost upon the Zermatt community, who flock to the dancing bar virtually every evening. The bar stools are carved into replicas of ibex torsos, with cowhide covering the padded seats. The bedrooms usually have good views of the mountains, are beautifully appointed, and have private baths in each of them. Singles cost from 101F ($68.70) to 210F ($142.80) daily, depending on the season, while doubles range from 202F ($137.35) to 420F ($285.60), with half board included. In the hotel are fitness rooms, squash courts, summertime tennis courts (plus a covered one), community saunas, and a private sauna. The hotel is closed in November.

Hotel Monte Rosa, CH-3920 Zermatt, Switzerland (tel. 028/66-11-31), is the hotel that Edward Whymper, the English alpinist who first conquered the Matterhorn, recommended in the 1860s as the best hotel in Zermatt. Still renowned, the hotel is a tall, old-fashioned structure on the main street of Zermatt, with stone posts and lintels around the red-shuttered windows. The lounges inside are cozy, thanks to their parquet floors, thick rugs, and crackling fireplaces. The antique armchairs are beautifully upholstered in conservative stripes or more daring patterns of red and blue. The pleasant bedrooms are among the most comfortable in Zermatt, with occasional floral designs covering the walls and immaculately pressed bedcovers. Since the hotel is part of the Seiler chain, guests have free use of the swimming pool a short distance away at the Mont Cervin Hotel. Singles rent for 89F ($60.50) to 178F ($120.05) daily, with doubles costing 180F ($122.40) to 356F ($242.10), half board included. Prices, of course, depend on the season, with midwinter being by far the most expensive. Open June to October and December to April.

Alex Schlosshotel Tenne, CH-3920 Zermatt, Switzerland (tel. 028/67-18-01). To find it, you'll have to follow the painted signs that begin behind the Gornergrat ski lift, just across the square from the main railway station. With its chiseled stonework, palatial proportions, and baroque-style step roofs, it's easy to imagine this place as having been originally built as a private castle. Upon entering, the first thing you'll see is the Bar Tenne (see the "Après Ski" section) whose mixture of medieval with turn-of-the-century styling make it one of my favorite nightlife hangouts in Zermatt. The owner, Alex Perren, also runs the previously recommended Hotel Alex (both are four-star).

The bedrooms, however, are unique. While not particularly large, richly textured fabric woven into art nouveau designs imparts a welcome feeling of cozy comfort, especially on a cold and windswept day, a decor that might be a welcome change from the pine-covered chalet rooms you might by now be used to. Eight of the accommodations are suites, each of which has a separate sitting room with a fireplace. Regardless of the price category of the rooms, each contains a whirlpool bath and TV. On the half-board arrangement, singles cost from 100F ($68) to 180F ($122.40) daily, depending on the season. Doubles range from a low of 150F ($102) to a high of 320F ($217.60). Duplex suites are more expensive, of course.

Hotel Schweizerhof, CH-3920 Zermatt, Switzerland (tel. 028/66-11-55), opened in 1982, is part of a nationwide Seiler chain of tastefully appointed hotels, with a conscientious management. Centrally located on the main street of town, the chalet building has shops on its ground floor and a spacious lobby area covered with carpeting, designed around comfortable modern armchairs and a blazing central fireplace. Most of the sunny bedrooms are monochromatically outfitted with carved blond-wood furniture and the grays and buffs that go best with it, although some of them are done in fresh mountain springtime colors. Elegant dining, everything from Italian specialties to raclette and fondue, a popular bar, and a disco complete the hotel's allure. Each of the 104 accommodations has its own bath and costs 101F ($68.70) to 210F ($142.80) in a single, 202F ($137.35) to 420F ($285.60) in a double, depending on the season, with half board included. The hotel is closed every year for roughly the first three weeks of May and from October 15 till December.

Hotel Mirabeau, CH-3920 Zermatt, Switzerland (tel. 028/67-17-72), is a modern piece of architecture, shaped vaguely like a chalet, with lots of balconies. Owned by the Julen family, the hotel has many traditional touches inside, including an effective use of stone and beams, along with a fireplace. Rooms are attractively furnished, and each contains a private bath. Singles begin at 89F ($60.50) in low season, rising to 155F ($105.40) in high season. With doubles costing from 178F ($121.05) in low season to 320F ($217.60) in high season. All these tariffs include half board. You can enjoy drinks on the terrace, while taking in a view of the Matterhorn. The menu in the hotel's dining facilities is excellent, with both Swiss and continental specialties, and there is a good wine list. In the basement is a fitness room, along with a sauna and a heated swimming pool. The management caters especially to children, offering them cots for use in their parents' room and early dinners.

Hotel Pollux, CH-3920 Zermatt, Switzerland (tel. 028/67-19-46), lies in a brown-and-white balconied structure on the main street of Zermatt, with several discreet signs announcing the disco and the inviting restaurant. The interior has beautiful ceilings, lots of exposed stone, and comfortable leather chairs and sofas that will probably tempt you to have a drink in front of one of the cheerful fireplaces. The bedrooms are sunny, well upholstered, and well carpeted, with private baths and your choice of views over the busy street or toward the back of the hotel (the ones behind are slightly more expensive). Depending on the season, singles range from 82F ($55.75) to 154F ($104.70) daily, while doubles cost from 206F ($140.10) to 310F ($210.80), including half board. Children who stay in a room connected to their parents' quarters receive a 60% reduction. The restaurant is a very good choice for an evening meal (see the dining recommendations).

Hotel Walliserhof, CH-3920 Zermatt, Switzerland (tel. 028/67-11-74), lies in the center of town in a building that was an old Valaisian farmhouse. It has red shutters, balconies, and window boxes. A streetside café serves drinks and food. The interior has attractive groupings of stone fireplaces, masonry columns, thick walls, and flagstone floors. The carpeted bedrooms are filled with modern comfort and pleasantly furnished with many wooden pieces. In winter, half-board costs from 110F ($74.80) to 160F ($108.80) daily in a single, 220F ($149.60) to 280F ($190.40) in a double. In summer, the single half-board rate ranges from 100F ($68) to 130F ($88.40) daily, with doubles costing 190F ($129.20) to 240F ($163.20). The hotel also has a popular restaurant for dining and drinking (I'll have comments on it later on).

Hotel Garni Simi, CH-3920 Zermatt, Switzerland (tel. 028/67-46-56), set about a block from the main street of town, is a four-star hotel offering a stylish lobby and 23 comfortably furnished bedrooms. There are no restaurant facilities other than those used at breakfast, although the Dancing Bar (Dancing Delphine) is a very interesting disco bar. The hotel charges winter rates of 75F ($51) to 110F ($74.80) daily for a single, 70F ($47.60) to 100F ($68) per person in a double, depending on the month, with breakfast included. In summer, singles or doubles cost 55F ($37.40) to 80F ($54.40) per person daily, with breakfast included. Each of the rooms has a bath, a balcony, TV, phone, and a modernized collection of alpine furniture. The hotel's name, is a derivative of the name of its owner, Simon Biner.

Seiler Hotel Nicoletta, CH-3920 Zermatt, Switzerland (tel. 028/66-11-51). Skiers entering the lobby of this modern hotel are greeted by a fireplace set beneath an exposed chimney, a cozy sight. You'll recognize the façade of the hotel by the 18 panels set between the windows, designed in op-art patterns of two shades of brown. Near the edge of the resort, but still within a short walk of everything, the hotel should prove pleasant in every way, especially with its small swimming pool, plus two nearby saunas. The Seiler hotels took · er the management of this four-star hotel in late 1988. It was constructed in 1970 but has been newly decorated. Each of its well-furnished bedrooms, 60 in all, is complete with bath, phone, radio, TV, video, mini-bar, and hairdryer. Daily rates for two persons range from 250F ($170) to 420F ($285.60), including half board. The charge for one person (occupying a twin room) is 150F ($102) to 260F ($176.80), also including half board. The hotel also has a notable restaurant and dining room, as well as a piano bar. In winter guests can use the solarium and can also obtain massages.

The Medium-Priced Range

Hotel Excelsior, CH-3920 Zermatt, Switzerland (tel. 028/67-30-17), was built from concrete, but it has enough weathered wooden trim to appear like a modernized chalet. On the opposite bank of the river from the most commercial section of town, it contains only 32 beds in rooms that each have radio, TV, balcony, and often a view of the Matterhorn. Closed for three weeks in May, the hotel charges 71F ($48.30) to 141F ($95.90) daily for a single, 142F ($96.55) to 282F ($191.75) for a double. The hotel's lobby level contains two bars (see "Après Ski") and an attractive restaurant, La Ferme, recommended separately.

Hotel Butterfly, CH-3920 Zermatt, Switzerland (tel. 028/67-37-21), is a modern Best Western hotel with a peaked roof and an airy façade, thanks to its large expanses of glass. The balconies have garlands of flowers in boxes during the summer. In winter the snowy expanse of the Alps serves as a backdrop. The inside is warmly rustic, with arched windows, Oriental rugs, knotty-pine furniture, and lots of exposed wood and stone. A well-stocked bar serves as an intimate rendezvous point for hotel guests and their friends. Each unit contains a private bath or shower, toilet, balcony with a southern exposure, radio, and phone, plus TV on request. In winter, two persons pay $160F ($108.80) to 240F ($163.20) daily, with singles going for 90F ($61.20) to 130F ($88.40). In summer, doubles are priced at 160F ($108.80) to 200F ($136) daily, and singles rent for 90F ($61.20) to 110F ($74.80). The tariffs include half board, which features a buffet breakfast. On the premises is a sauna, plus whirlpool, solarium, and fitness center. Mrs. Gunda Woischnig is the manager. It is closed in November.

Hotel Romantica, CH-3920 Zermatt, Switzerland (tel. 028/67-15-05). If you should look onto the roof from one of the windows of the fourth floor, you'd notice that it's made of flagstones over a structure built in 1962. That and other well-planned details make this a fortunate choice of hotels, particularly since the rooms, although small, are clean and efficient, and the establishment is thoughtfully staffed with capable French and Swiss employees. In summer one of the loveliest gardens in Zermatt blooms on either side of the flagstone path leading up to the hotel. You'll have somewhat of a walk up the main street of town before arriving here, although the owner, Mrs. Yvonne Cremonini, will have some young man come to fetch you and your bags in an electric cart if you phone ahead. Rooms rent for 38F ($25.85) to 45F ($30.60) per person daily without private bath, 49F ($33.30) to 70F ($47.60) per person with private plumbing facilities. Rates include breakfast. The hotel has converted two small log cabins, formerly used for grain storage, into guest cottages a few paces from the front door of the main building. These might be perfect for clients with a taste for the rustic.

Hotel Darioli, CH-3920 Zermatt, Switzerland (tel. 028/67-27-48), is housed in a balconied five-story building on the main street of Zermatt not far from the train station. You'll need to climb a flight of stairs (or take the elevator) to get to the sunny reception area, where you'll probably get a greeting from a member of the Darioli family. The interior is large and sunny, with a blue-and-white ceramic stove, Oriental rugs, and an attractive wood-grained bar curving around one of the corners. Each of the comfortable bedrooms is furnished with regional furniture, usually painted in vivid colors with floral patterns stenciled at the corners. Depending on the season, doubles cost 72F ($48.95) to 176F ($119.70) daily, while singles range from 36F ($24.50) to 88F ($59.85), all tariffs including breakfast. The least-expensive rooms don't have private baths.

Hotel Carina, CH-3920 Zermatt, Switzerland (tel. 028/67-17-67), lying a few minutes away from the most congested part of town, has an interior plushly covered with wood paneling and stenciled plaster, for a gemütlich ambience that is heightened by the blazing fireplace. The outside is similar to dozens of other chalet buildings in Zermatt. The Fritz Biner family, the owners, charge 50F ($34) to 100F ($68) per person daily, with breakfast included, in rooms with private baths or showers. Half board costs an additional 28F ($19.05) per person. Guests have free use of the swimming pool at another nearby hotel.

Hotel Post, CH-3920 Zermatt, Switzerland (tel. 028/67-19-33), was built in 1903, although it's gone through an overhaul since Karl Iversson took over some 30 years ago. Its most important function in Zermatt is as a nightlife center (see "Après Ski"), but it maintains 40 beds in unusual rooms that have much of the hotel's original furniture along with modern plumbing in arrangements that sometimes put the bath into the living quarters in a somewhat risqué way. These rooms are often reserved months in advance for the winter season by regular clients whom the hotel refers to as "almost family." Singles rent for 36F ($24.50) to 60F ($40.80) daily in summer, for 68F ($46.25) to 88F ($59.85) in winter. Doubles are charged 94F ($63.92) to 120F ($81.60) in summer, 135F ($91.80) to 176F ($119.70) in winter. Breakfast is included in the tariffs. A minimum stay of ten days is required in high season.

Hotel Restaurant Orion, CH-3920 Zermatt, Switzerland (tel. 028/67-16-67). The traditional façade of this cozy hotel has one continuously sloping roofline and is circled with bands of weathered shingles and white stucco. The interior is warmly decorated in a modernized rusticity, which includes all the heavy timbers you'd expect, along with several skylights that illuminate the colorful tablecloths of the pleasant dining room. All the comfortably furnished units have private baths and rent for 66F ($44.90) to 126F ($85.70) daily in a single, 132F ($89.70) to 252F ($171.35) in a double, including half board. Rates depend on the season. Closed in November.

Hotel Alfa, CH-3920 Zermatt, Switzerland (tel. 028/67-27-84), is an attractive chalet with the inevitable balconies and big windows letting light into the simply furnished public rooms. The hotel lies a few steps away from the main street of Zermatt, so you can avoid the congestion of high season. It has a sauna and fitness room on the premises. There's no meal service, although cold platters are available on request. Rents are 33F ($22.45) to 65F ($44.20) daily in a single in summer, 66F ($44.90) to 130F ($88.40) in a double. Winter prices are 48F ($32.65) to 80F ($54.40) daily in a single, 96F ($65.30) to 160F ($108.80) in a double. The lower-priced rooms don't have private baths.

Romantik Hotel Julen, CH-3920 Zermatt, Switzerland (tel. 028/67-24-81), is an attractively weathered balconied hotel across the inner-town river from the historic cemetery. You'll get a clear view of the Matterhorn from the windows of this place, as well as a good meal in the main dining room with its elaborately crafted wooden ceiling and beautifully paneled walls. An indoor swimming pool is about 50 yards away. The Julen family, the owners, charge from 71F ($48.30) to 141F ($95.90) for a single and 142F ($96.55) to 282F ($191.75) for a double. Rates include half board and depend on the season. Its Schäferstube is recommended separately.

Hotel Europe, CH-3920 Zermatt, Switzerland (tel. 028/67-10-66), would be the kind of place where a skier could spend a happy winter holiday. The hotel is in a tall white structure with the kind of well-built furniture that won't break if you sit down too hard. The Europe is also well heated and weatherproof, with a sauna on the premises. With a view of the Matterhorn next to the Hotel Julen and under the same management, the hotel charges 36F ($24.50) to 72F ($48.95) daily for a single and 72F ($48.96) to 144F ($97.90) for a double in summer. Winter rates in a single are 51F ($34.70) to 88F ($59.85) daily, rising to 102F ($69.35) to 176F ($119.70) in a double. The cheaper units are bathless.

Hotel Antika, CH-3920 Zermatt, Switzerland (tel. 028/67-21-51). Parts of this hotel are dramatically designed, including an attractive façade where each room has a covered loggia with flower boxes and wood trim. The interior is paneled with weathered slats and decorated with Oriental rugs. Facilities include a Jacuzzi whirlpool with a covering of smooth river rocks. A large garden behind offers accommodations for quiet contemplation of the Matterhorn. While the hotel doesn't serve meals, the nearby Stockhorn restaurant, under the same management, offers good food in a rustic, mellow setting (see the dining recommendations). Rooms rent in summer for 52F ($34.70) to 67F ($45.55) daily in a single, 104F ($70.70) to 134F ($91.10) in a double. In winter, prices go up to 64F ($43.50) to 130F ($88.40) daily in a single, 128F ($87.05) to 166F ($112.90) in a double.

The Budget Choices

Seilerhaus, CH-3920 Zermatt, Switzerland (tel. 028/67-35-20), is linked with the prestigious Seiler Mont Cervin, previously recommended, but is an establishment in its own right. This little 22-bed, two-star guest house is one of the most reasonably priced in town, and is often eagerly sought out in winter by frugal skiers.

It is open all year except in December. Rooms are simply but comfortably furnished. With breakfast included, winter peak season rates range from 62F ($42.15) to 80F ($54.40) per person. Prices are lowered in summer to 42F ($28.55) to 65F ($44.20) per person. These are daily charges, but guests tend to linger much longer. Actually the Seilerhaus is better known for its dining facilities than for its rooms. It offers a bustling Brasserie, serving a variety of tasty dishes, both Swiss and continental, and a cozy Valais tavern. Raclette is just one of the typical mountain dishes offered nightly. Both of these facilities will be recommended separately.

Hotel Alphubel, CH-3920 Zermatt, Switzerland (tel. 028/67-30-03), is three minutes from the train station in a large chalet with a well-constructed stone foundation. The entrance leads up a short flight of curved stone stairs into the lobby area. The Julen family, the owners, took the name from a local mountaintop. The management encourages guests to take at least half board, which costs from 65F ($44.20) to 95F ($64.60) per person daily, depending on the season.

Hotel Riffelberg, CH-3920 Zermatt-Umgebung, Switzerland (tel. 028/67-22-16), was built in 1853 by a local clergyman who placed it in a dramatically desolate area at a high altitude just below the Matterhorn. It was purchased by the city of Zermatt in 1862, serving ever since as a hotel and restaurant with the kind of view, summer or winter, which people come from miles around to see. The director says that an ibex colony lives close to the nearby Riffelsee and that this location, which is farther south than Lugano, gets eight full hours of sunshine in December and even more than that in summer. The interior was recently renovated, but retains its rustic ambience of alpine decor. With half board (which you'd better take, since there's no place else around to eat, rooms rent for 79F ($53.70) to 99F ($67.30) daily in a single, 136F ($92.50) to 178F ($102.05) in a double. Skiers find this hotel attractive as it lies at the foot of the Gornergrat cableway.

Kulmhotel Gornergrat, CH-3920 Zermatt, Switzerland (tel. 028/67-22-19). The only way to get here is to take the cable car from Riffelberg or a mountain railway from Zermatt. Because the spot is so gloriously isolated, you'd better call ahead or make reservations long in advance. The two sun terraces adjoining the hotel offer vistas of the Matterhorn's glacier with high-altitude views in almost every direction. The building is a fortress-like structure crafted from local stone, with what looks like an observatory in one of its towers. This is perfect in summer for guests who want to get away from urban bustle to use as a base for exploratory walks through the region. In winter it's usually a popular way station for energetic skiers, with lots of activity in the downstairs restaurant. The hotel was recently renovated and extended to include more of the simple, well-heated, weather-proof rooms, all with running water. In winter, prices are 70F ($47.60) daily in a single, 65F ($44.20) per person in a double or triple, and 50F ($34) per person in a dormitory room. Summer rates are 80F ($54.40) daily in a single, 75F ($51) per person in a double or triple, and 60F ($40.80) per person in a dormitory accommodation. Tariffs include breakfast, dinner, and taxes.

Hotel Malva, CH-3920 Zermatt, Switzerland (tel. 028/67-30-33), is a pretty chalet built in 1936 and added onto sometime later. The property of the Julen family for the past 30 years, the hotel charges from 29F ($19.70) to 67F ($45.55) daily in a single and from 58F ($39.45) to 134F ($91.10) in a double, including breakfast. Rates depend on the season and the plumbing, as the cheaper accommodations don't have baths. Closed in November.

Hotel Touring, CH-3920 Zermatt, Switzerland (tel. 028/67-11-77), is a pleasant hotel with green shutters, wooden walls, and a chalet format with wintertime ski racks set up outside the front door. Many of the rooms have private balconies and a view of the Matterhorn. Depending on the season, singles range from 43F ($29.25) to 96F ($65.30) daily, with doubles costing from 86F ($58.50) to 192F ($130.55). The least expensive accommodations don't have private baths. Wendelin Julen and his family are the owners. Closed in November.

Hotel Gabelhorn, CH-3920 Zermatt, Switzerland (tel. 028/67-22-35), is an attractive chalet with a flagstone roof and four stories of simple and unpretentious comfort. Mrs. Zumtaugwald, your hostess, is helpful in practically every way, particularly in giving advice on the attractions of Zermatt. She charges from 35F ($23.80) to 55F ($37.40) per person daily, breakfast included, in rooms with or without bath. Prices depend on the season.

DINING AROUND: Most clients are booked into a hotel in Zermatt on the half-board plan. This is the best arrangement, as it leaves you free to shop around for either lunch or dinner, while still taking advantage of the food reduction that often comes with the plan. By having at least one main meal outside every day, you also don't feel "hotel bound." If you don't like to take any of your meals at your hotel, other than breakfast, then book into one of the "garni" hotels, which serve only breakfast. Zermatt is filled with many local eateries, and the discriminating visitor will want to sample the fondue and raclette at various places, not to mention rack of lamb grilled over larchwood fire. A random sampling of the leading dining choices follows.

Le Mazot (tel. 028/67-27-77) is considered the best restaurant in Zermatt. It sits behind a chalet whose red shutters overlook the river flowing through the center of town. It's owned and operated by Hermann Perren and his English-born wife Chantal. He is a noted ski instructor and mountain guide, and has made a staggering 75 ascents of the Matterhorn. On some evenings, when the service has slowed down and everybody is in a convivial mood, he has been known to take his guitar and launch a sing-along.

The restaurant serves hearty yet sophisticated meals to a group of clients who search it out for its sizzling grill, whose flames provide partial illumination for the wood-sheathed interior, and its delectable lamb dishes, many of which are done over the open fire. The building which contains the restaurant is only 30 years old, but its style makes it look much older. The place opens daily at 4 p.m., closing at midnight. Food orders are accepted from 6:30 to 11 p.m. Full meals cost around 75F ($51) per person, but many diners do it for less. You get several preparations of lamb raised on a sheep farm directed by Hermann himself. Other specialties include a hot and cold salad with filet of rabbit, mushrooms, and garlic, and scampi flavored with ginger sauce. The establishment is closed from mid-May to late June and from mid-October to early December.

Alex Schlosshotel Tenne (tel. 028/67-18-01). On the lobby level of the hotel, this restaurant is designed in a duplex that includes an upper wraparound gallery and a ceiling fresco covered with a representation of the zodiac. The ambience is a bit like a chic interpretation of a stable, with alpine accessories scattered judiciously between the tables. Lunch is served only in high season, every day from noon to 2 p.m. Dinner is every day from 7 to 10:30 p.m. Reservations are important in winter. Menu items include lobster cream soup, chipped pike with saffron sauce and vegetables, an array of fresh shellfish kept fresh in aquariums, sweetbreads and veal kidneys, woodcock braised in tarragon, and duckling breast in an Armagnac-flavored sauce. For dessert, you might be tempted with a soufflé of white cheese covered with essence of apricots. Full meals begin at 70F ($47.60), but could go as high as 100F ($68) per person.

Alex Grill, Hotel Alex (tel. 028/67-17-26). Although this basement restaurant is the same as that used by half-board residents of the hotel, it's so stylish that many outsiders call ahead for a reservation to dine here à la carte. It contains an alpine decor of carved paneling, leaded windows, flagstone floors, sky-blue upholstery, and rich accessories. You can begin with a platter containing three varieties of smoked fish or fresh Atlantic oysters, then try lobster grilled over a wood fire, grilled salmon scallop, or giant shrimp with a chive-flavored cream sauce. Meat dishes include veal kidneys in a mustard sauce, an array of seasonal game dishes, grilled rack of lamb, and filet of beef with bordelaise sauce. Full meals cost 70F ($47.60) and are served at dinner nightly from 7 to 10.

Restaurant Seilerhaus (tel. 028/66-11-21). The hanging lamps are made of densely leaded glass, tinted red, which vibrate musically if you touch them. You'd never expect such an unpretentious decor to house such a fine restaurant. Upstairs is an elongated, paneled stone-walled room with a timbered ceiling, an open fireplace, and a large expanse of glass overlooking a terrace popular in summer. The table d'hôte menu changes weekly, costing 80F ($54.40) to 90F ($61.20). À la carte meals average around 75F ($51). You might begin with a dandelion salad with poached egg or (in season only) fresh asparagus with a mousseline sauce. For a main course, salmon trout with braised chicory and stewed onions is a tempter, as is a braised leg of duck with new vegetables. There's a nostalgic array of regional dishes, including leek-and-potato stew with smoked sausages. Lunch is served daily from 11:45 a.m. to 2 p.m., dinner from 7 to 10 p.m.

In the same building is the **Otto Furrer Stube** (tel. 028/63-35-20), named after the famous skier and mountain guide of the 1930s. It is open only for dinner from 6 to 11 nightly, with meals costing from 35F ($23.80). There's an annual closing from April 25 to June. It features a country grand mère cuisine, and that means hearty fare, such as a cassoulet from Toulouse, a gigot d'agneau (lamb) with garlic, and other dishes. Of course, skiers have for many years been fond of the regular staples, which means cheese or meat fondues and raclettes. You descend a flight of stairs to reach this underground cellar, lined with 19th-century engravings of the Matterhorn and other alpine memorabilia. Waitresses appear in regional garb.

La Ferme, Hotel Excelsior (tel. 028/67-30-17), below the reception area of the previously recommended hotel, is a large-scale restaurant pleasantly sheathed with knotty pine and filled with plants and racks of wine. An elegant fixed-priced "menu du patron" costs 45F ($30.60) and might include cream of zucchini soup, a salad with quail breasts, and filet goulash Stroganoff. A more elaborate fixed-price menu is offered for 80F ($54.40). Many of the featured specialties are prepared only for two persons, and include a veal steak with morels and flambéed filet Medici. À la carte meals cost from 65F ($44.20) each. Lunch is almost never served here—only when blizzards have closed the resort's ski lifts. Dinner every night is from 6:30 to 11, except when the hotel is closed. Those dates are from early October to mid-November and from early May to mid-June.

Ristorante da Mario, Hotel Schweizerhof (tel. 028/66-11-55). This trattoria attracts a strong following with its style, flair, and imaginative cookery. You get many of the familiar dishes, but you can receive creative cookery as well. The antipasti are invariably tempting, including the chicken-stuffed ravioli or the risotto with porcini. Personally, I like to begin with pasta e fagioli, moving on to one of the homemade pastas. The fish dishes are limited, but choice, including scallops with small vegetables. The meat dishes have a wider range, everything from saltimbocca to veal liver Venetian style. If you're splurging, try the tenderloin steak with goose liver and a red wine sauce. Desserts (if there's any room left) are classic, including a cassata with pistachio sauce. But have you ever had an apricot-iced mousse? Meals cost from 45F ($30.60) up. Hours are daily from 6:30 to 10:30 p.m. The trattoria is decorated stylishly, with modern burgundy and wood. It has brass accents and a wood ceiling, and you're soothed with piano music as you dine.

Grillroom Stockhorn (tel. 028/67-17-47) is elegantly outfitted with travertine floors, heavy beams, smoky stucco walls, an alpine wedding chest, and best of all, a blazing fire extending into the room. The establishment is directed by Emil Julen, who years ago set up this restaurant in a chalet, with wooden tables and regional chairs. You'll enjoy a drink at the ski-hütte bar, followed by one of the specialties, which include raclette. Or you may prefer piccata with spaghetti, fondue bourguignonne, or a wide range of meats grilled over an open fire. An average meal might cost from 45F ($30.60) at dinner, 30F ($20.40) at lunch. Lunch is from noon to 1:30 p.m., dinner from 6:30 to 11 p.m. daily.

Restaurant Walliserhof (tel. 028/67-11-74), at the hotel of the same name, has a particularly elegant selection of hors d'oeuvres, including goose liver and caviar. Specialties include fondue bourguignonne or chinoise, along with ribs of lamb with herbs, a double veal cutlet with noodles Alfredo, and brook trout. An average à la carte meal will cost from 65F ($44.20) for two persons. A table d'hôte is priced at 35F ($23.80). Hot food is served from noon to 2 p.m. and 7 to 9:30 p.m. daily.

Le Gitan (tel. 028/67-10-98) is the grill room and bar area of the Hotel Darioli. On the ground floor of a building on the busy main street of town, it serves grilled meats daily from noon to 1:45 p.m. and 6:30 to 10 p.m. The specialty here is beef fondue, along with beef filet or shrimp. If it appeals to you, you might begin your meal with a savory tomato soup spiked with gin. This cozily rustic restaurant with an antique fireplace has candlelit tables, good service, and meals from 40F ($27.20).

Arvenstube, in the Hotel Pollux (tel. 028/67-19-46), is divided from a less formal restaurant on the floor above by a stairwell and an open wrought-iron gate. The L-shaped room is beautifully paneled in a light-grained pine, with a bar curving invitingly around one corner. The staff is helpful, serving a tempting variety of international dishes. These might begin with assiette valaisanne, a plate of air-dried meats from the Grisons. Specialties include riz Casimir (a curry dish), tournedos in a savory mustard sauce, or sliced veal in a mushroom cream sauce. These dishes are often served with Rösti. Trout with almonds is another favorite. Meals cost 40F ($27.20) and up. Upstairs you can order the same menu in the more informal tavern, Pinte Valaisanne. Hours are daily from noon to 2 p.m. and 6 to 9:30 p.m.

Spaghetti Factory, Hotel Post (tel. 028/67-19-32), is, believe it or not, the most popular restaurant in Zermatt in the peak of the winter season. Reservations for a table are needed three or four days in advance. The hotel is mostly noted for its après-ski activities (more about this later). But earlier in the evening, many skiers come here just to eat, ordering several types of spaghetti costing from 16F ($10.90). You might begin with a tomato and mozzarella salad, then follow with either carpaccio or Parma ham. The pasta dishes include not only spaghetti but linguini, fettuccine and lasagne verdi. You can also order a risotto with three mushrooms, grilled scampi, or beefsteak pizzaiola. Full meals cost from 35F ($23.80) up. It's best from 8:30 p.m. to midnight daily. This Italian tavern is on a balcony overlooking the dance floor, and you dine to disco music. The entire construction was at one time an alpine barn, which an engineer with a lot of imagination transformed into a gemütlich hangout.

Schäferstube, Romantik Hotel Julen (tel. 028/67-24-81), is a respectable, moderately priced enclave for atmospheric dining. No lunch is ever served, but it opens for drinks every day at 4 p.m. Dinner is nightly from 6 to 9. Amid plank-covered walls, heavy beams, flickering candles, and leaded-glass window, you'll enjoy cheese fondues priced at 16F ($10.90) per person, portions of raclette at 6F ($4.10) each, and full à la carte meals costing from 35F ($23.80) each. The house specialty is lamb, served in a wide array of styles. You can also order grilled veal and beef dishes, prepared in traditional Swiss recipes. A four-course fixed-price meal costs 28F ($19.05). The restaurant has its own entrance, at street level within the previously recommended Romantik Hotel Julen. Reservations are needed.

A Mountain Restaurant

Zermatt is said to possess the most mountain restaurants—and the best—in the Alps. The recommendation below is reputed to be the finest mountain restaurant in Switzerland.

It's **Enzo's Hitta** (tel. 028/67-25-88). Part of its allure lies in the difficulty you'll experience getting there; regardless of your mode of transport, the effort you'll expend will contribute to a healthier, heartier appetite, well suited to the beauty of the alpine landscape around you. Located in the small hamlet of Findeln, it sits on the side of a steep mountain and requires an ascent via the Sunnegga chairlift to the first stop, then a hike across the fields. Leave your skis in the snow and head down a steep, winding pathway, passing palm trees (true, they are plastic).

If you ski or sledge here, you won't be alone, and that's part of the trouble. The place is likely to be packed, especially between noon and 3 p.m., so always call for a reservation. It is open only for lunch, snacks, and drinks from 10 a.m. to 5 p.m. daily. Reminiscent of a wooden mountaineer's hut, the Hitta has a sun terrace and also a roof terrace facing south, opening onto spectacular views of the Matterhorn. The chef and owner is Enzo himself, a Swiss Italian. Full meals cost from 50F ($34), but you might settle for a light lunch at 25F ($17). Specialties include carpaccio, spinach salad, several kinds of grilled meats, and excellent pasta dishes. Don't overlook "Eskimo spaghetti"—it's made with smoked salmon. For dessert, spring visitors are rewarded with homemade ice cream.

EXCURSIONS: Zermatt has a total of 36 mountain railroads, lifts, and gondolas, 21 of which operate in summer. You can go to the Tourist Office, am Bahnhofplatz (tel. 028/66-11-81), for the latest information about any of these jaunts outlined below. There are dozens of excursion possibilities, the one with the highest popularity rating being a visit by rack railway to **Gornergrat** (10,170 feet). This is the highest open-air railroad in Europe. At **Riffelberg** you'll have a spectacular view of the Matterhorn. If you elect to go only this far, a round-trip ticket will cost you 29F ($19.70). For the entire journey to Gornergrat you'll pay 42F ($28.55) for a round-trip ticket. Once at Gornergrat, you can take a two-stage cableway to Stockhorn (11,180 feet), for another 16F ($10.90) round trip. There's an observatory at Gornergrat that looks out onto the Gorner glacier. The view takes in the **Dom,** part of the Mischabel massif, which at 14,912 feet is the highest mountain entirely within Switzerland.

A second popular visit is to the **Schwarzsee** (8,480 feet), the "black lake." Magnificent vistas can be seen from the Schwarzseehotel. This much-photographed lake lies at the foot of the Matterhorn. Allow an hour to reach it. The round-trip fare on the cable car is 20.60F ($14). **Klein Matterhorn** (12,533 feet) is reached by the highest aerial cableway in Europe, with departures every day from Zermatt at 8 a.m. Following this dramatic itinerary requires three different cable cars. If you begin at Zermatt, you'll change cable cars first in Furi, then in Trockenersteg. Near the top of the Klein Matterhorn, an elevator will take you to the bottom of a flight of stairs, which you'll ascend on foot to reach the panoramic terrace (12,747 feet). From there, you can see both Mont Blanc and the Italian Alps, if the day is clear. A round-trip ticket to Klein Matterhorn costs 40F ($27.20). If you go the longer way, via Schwarzee, it costs 58F ($39.45) per round trip. There is also an underground funicular "Alpine Métro" to Sunegga (7,546 feet) as well as the cable car to the Rothorn (10,181 feet).

Helicopter rides around the Matterhorn are possible, but I advise you to go only on a clear day. You'll be flown to a nearby glacier if the weather is good long enough for you to snap pictures. The whirlybird then takes you around the Matterhorn pyramid before making its descent. This is a pretty frightening trip for some visitors, but it's relatively safe and certainly thrilling. The cost is 140F ($95.20) per person, and the flight lasts about 20 minutes. A minimum of four passengers is required. The rides are operated by **Air-Zermatt** from the heliport (tel. 028/67-34-87) outside the village.

Zermatt has varied skiing, from wide, gentle slopes to difficult runs. At the official **ski school** (tel. 028/67-24-51), instruction is provided in the various classes by certified ski instructors and mountain guides. The three principal ski areas are the already-mentioned **Gornergrat-Stockhorn** site; the **Blauherd–Unter Rothorn** area, reached by underground mountain rail from the village to Sunegga and then by gondola; and the **Schwarzsee-Théodul** sector, reached on its first stage by cableways to Furi. You can even ski across Théodul Pass to Cervinia in Italy for lunch. For the cross-country skier and the touring skier, a variety of courses is offered. There's a cross-country pavilion in Furi-Schweigmatten.

Zermatt is also a popular curling center, with eight rinks all equipped with precision curling stones. There are also two natural ice-skating rinks as well as sunny, sign-posted paths for walking.

In such a setting, with mountains to climb and snowy peaks to view, you may not fancy museums, but there is one, the **Alpine Museum** (tel. 028/67-41-00), charging 3F ($2.05). It's open daily from July 1 to the beginning of October from 10 a.m. to noon and 4 to 6 p.m.; from December to the end of June, from 4:30 to 6:30 p.m. On display are relics of Edward Whymper, detailing the conquest of the Matterhorn; relief models of the great mountain; and artifacts from the prehistoric and Roman eras.

APRÈS SKI: Zermatt is known for its après-ski activities, which include tea dances, restaurants, bars, nightclubs, and discos. It has more nighttime diversions than any other resort in the Valais.

Elsie's Place (tel. 028/67-24-31) lies on the main street of Zermatt, close to the Zermatterhof Hotel. In a house dating from 1879, it's not a place that overwhelms by its size, but it usually manages to pack in a big crowd, everybody seemingly showing up here for a 6 p.m. hot chocolate or Elsie's famous Irish coffee. You can also drop in during the day to order ham and eggs and hot dogs (but how did those incongruous escargots get on the menu?). Light plates of food cost from 18F ($12.25), but many people come here just to drink. It's open daily in winter from 3 p.m. to midnight and in summer from 10 a.m. to midnight. If you're really flush, you can order such gourmet fare as caviar and (a luxury in these parts) oysters.

The **Hotel Post** (tel. 028/67-19-32), where everybody shows up after they've recovered from Elsie's Irish coffee, has a virtual monopoly on nightlife in Zermatt. After staggering out of the Hotel Post at 2 a.m. most skiers hit the sack, while the entrepreneurs of other nightspots and bars in town often want for customers.

At the long-famous Hotel Post, below the plate glass of the lobby's reception desk, you'll see photographs of the smiling athletes, models, and good-hearted people who fall into the unusual ambience of this unusual hotel. The founder is Karl Ivarsson, an American, who for more than 30 years has ruled over one of the oldest hotels in Zermatt, built in 1903. He has gradually expanded it into the most complete entertainment complex in Zermatt, sheltering many nightspots and restaurants under one roof.

The **Brown Cow,** on the street level, is a rustic room with a 19th-century earth rake hanging from the ceiling (it's almost a work of art). The "Cow," as it's called, serves drinks and snacks to jukebox music. Featured are hamburgers, BLTs, goulash soup, Beach Bun sandwiches, and salads in general. Light meals cost from 18F ($12.25). The place is open from 7:30 a.m. to midnight daily.

A walk past the reception desk will lead you to the **Pink Elephant,** which in all its art nouveau glory is one of the most exclusive bars in Zermatt. It has Edwardian palms, leather couches, candles, and bentwood chairs. It's a favorite with David Bowie and John Lord (Deep Purple), both of whom have entertained here. A stainless-steel dance floor is surrounded by marble tables where attractive barmaids serve drinks costing from 9F ($6.10) during happy hour from 7 to 10 p.m. and 16F ($10.90) after 10 p.m. The dress code is informal, yet many clients still manage an aura of casual chic.

When you tire of the potted palms and worldly conversations here, you can move on to **Le Village,** which is the most interesting disco in Zermatt. Opening at 9 p.m., it shows sports movies (most often skiing) from 9:30 to 10:30 nightly, which sets the pace for the sports enthusiasts attracted to this place. The action takes place in a high-ceilinged and rustic room. The price of entrance and one drink is 12F ($8.15). The place is fun and very crowded, but don't be afraid to move on. Another ambience (and another restaurant) can be found in the basement. To get there, you'll pass yards of amusing original murals telling the story of the lonely tourist who looked for love in Zermatt.

Finally, for the rowdiest dive of them all, the **Broken Bar,** in another section of the cellar, attracts the most hardened ski bums, who listen to hard rock at very loud volumes, drink heavily, and generally raise hell. The sound amplifier on this one is below an oval wine keg in the middle of the floor. It's said that any one of a dozen dancers usually tries to cave it in. Prices here are the same as for Le Village, a 12F ($8.15) cover charge, which includes the coat check and the price of the first drink. After that, beer costs from 9F ($6.10). In winter the entire complex will sometimes rock with anywhere from 700 to 800 people. Open 5 p.m. to 2 a.m. nightly.

My advice is to enter once and to keep walking and exploring. You'll never know what (or who) you'll find.

In the unlikely event that the action at the Hotel Post is not for you, you might try one of the following recommendations.

Hotel Pollux Disco (tel. 028/67-19-46) gets very crowded in winter with everyone from local service personnel to ski instructors to visitors from Europe and America. It's open every evening in winter from 9 p.m. to 2 a.m. The disco has a glossily modern decor with a central dance floor surrounded by little tables seating from two to four persons. There's no cover charge, and drinks average from 7F ($4.75) to 10F ($6.80).

Grill Restaurant Spycher and Scotch Corner Bar (tel. 028/67-11-41) is connected to the Hotel Aristella, and under the direction of Elsbeth and Manfred Perren-Lehner. Alpine carved facial masks leer above the doorway of this half-timbered restaurant, with a large weathered bar set against one wall. It usually opens November 15 when it immediately becomes popular with skiers and visitors "from everywhere." This is the perfect place for après-ski drinks. Swiss coffee, Café Normand, and French coffee all cost from 9F ($6.10) each. Full meals, and very good ones at that, are also served from the excellent kitchen. There is a carefully selected wine list from the restaurant's superb cellar. Hours for the grill restaurant are daily from 11:30 a.m. to 1:30 p.m. and 6:30 to 9:30 p.m.

Whymperstube, Hotel Monte Rosa (tel. 028/67-19-22), on the cellar level of this previously recommended hotel, is accessible from the street via its own separate entrance. It contains a warmly intimate alpine decor, filled with antique planking and a busy and popular bar. There are handfuls of battered wooden tables to drink at, and a brisk business distributing such mountain snacks as raclette, hot sausages with potato salad, platters of air-dried alpine beef, and Wiener schnitzel. There's no incentive to order full meals here, but they're available for 25F ($17) if you want them. The place is open from 6 p.m. to midnight every day.

Dancing Delphine, Hotel Simi (tel. 028/67-46-56), is open only in the height of the winter and summer seasons, and it's known and frequented by full-time residents of Zermatt as well as visitors. There's no cover charge to enter during open hours, which last from 9 p.m. to 2 a.m. daily. A large, almost square alpine room has lots of exposed paneling, a comfortable bar, and a dance floor. Beer costs from 7F ($4.75).

Matterhornstube, Hotel Mont Cervin (tel. 028/66-11-22). In one of the village's most glamorous hotels, this large alpine room has two different stand-up bars, a wooden ceiling, many wooden tables, and an over-30 crowd of well-heeled patrons. Entrance is free. It's open every night from 9 p.m. to 2 a.m. Long drinks cost from 11F ($7.50) each.

Bar Tenne, Alex Schlosshotel Tenne (tel. 028/67-18-01), is one of the very few art nouveau rooms in Zermatt, a change from the traditional chalet form. It has turn-of-the-century silver sconces set into the roughly textured stone walls, quadruplicate stone columns that support an impressively beamed truss above the circular dance floor, and a bar that looks a lot like a miniature version of a medieval monastery's ambulatory. Even the disk jockey operates from a booth that might once have been a church pulpit, high above the comfortable clusters of sofas and chairs. Drinks are served, and the music begins every night at 8 p.m. and continues to either midnight or 2 a.m., depending on the season. There's no cover charge, but scotch and soda costs from 12F ($8.15).

Ex-Bar/Luna Bar, Hotel Excelsior (tel. 028/67-30-17). These twin bars are a few steps from the lobby of the previously recommended Hotel Excelsior. The more raucous (and somewhat less expensive) is the Ex-Bar, which serves such snacks as cheeseburgers and steaks to accompany the drinks. Recorded pop music plays amid rustically beamed walls. The Luna Bar, more quiet, lies behind thick doors and is perhaps more sedate. Both bars are open every night when the hotel is open from 9 to midnight.

The Bar/The Kegelstube, Hotel Bristol (tel. 028/67-24-98). A few people come to this place's smallish tables for a full meal, but the majority usually stand by the long wood-topped bar to listen to the live music. There's a dance floor, and a series of stucco-sided arches separate the various sections of the bar and restaurant. A fire flickers brightly against one wall. The bar is open daily from noon to 2 a.m., but it doesn't get interesting until after sundown. Long drinks cost from 9F ($6.10), and dancing begins around 9 p.m. Full meals at one of the tables cost from 45F ($30.60) each.

If you're looking for a change of pace, head for the basement of this hotel's Kegelstube (Bowling Alley Bar). There are a pair of bowling lanes in one corner (for which a by-the-hour reservation is usually needed at least one day in advance). Unusual for Zermatt, this is the only bowling alley in town. I like this place for its blue-collar lack of pretension, and sometimes drop in for a beer and a wurst salad at one of the establishment's badly lit and battered tables. You might have fun, and it's certainly an unusual alternative to Zermatt's sometimes cloying picture-postcard image. It costs 12F ($8.15) per hour to bowl. The place is open between 4:30 p.m. to midnight. It is closed Sunday.

Castle Club (tel. 028/67-22-98). Rustic and designed on two different levels, this place seems ideal for maximum people-watching—that is, if you like all your people under 25. If you want to dance, your movements will be visible from the low-slung couches on the gallery upstairs. The place is open from 9 p.m. to 2 a.m. nightly in winter only. There's no cover charge.

Papparla Pub (tel. 028/67-40-40), is fronted with rows of many-paned windows and graced with a wide sun terrace in front of its neo-Victorian façade. This is one of the town's most popular pubs. Within a wood-paneled room that curves a bit like the hull of a boat, you can order beer from Japan, China, Finland, Australia, and most of the countries of Europe. (If you're hankering for a Budweiser, they have that, too.) Open daily from 11 a.m. to midnight, the place is also the site of dart and pool tournaments and recorded rock music from a jukebox. Beer begins at 3F ($2.05), long drinks at 11.50F ($7.80). To accompany your beer, you can order cheeseburgers, pork chop platters, fish and chips, and steaks. Snacks cost from 8F ($5.45).

11. SAAS-FEE AND GRÄCHEN

SAAS-FEE: In the 13th-century village of Saas-Fee (pronounced "sauce-fay") you'll often hear the terms "glacier village" and "pearl of the Alps." As in Zermatt, cars are forbidden. The village is perched on a grassy plateau, and from its citadel you can enjoy unparalleled vistas of the mammoth and encircling glaciers. The resort is surrounded by a total of 13 mountains, each towering more than 13,000 feet high. These include a view of the Dom.

Trail blazers have spread the fame of the "highwire" mountain trails along the western and eastern escarpments of the Saas Valley. Here you'll meet all those Swiss cows you've heard so much about. Occasionally you'll come across locals in traditional garb, and stumble upon places seemingly little changed since the turn of the century.

The terminus of the famous "High Route" from Verbier through the Alps, Saas-Fee lies in a valley east of Zermatt. From Saas-Fee, unlike Zermatt, you can't view the tilted pyramid of the Matterhorn, but you'll have a lot of other peaks to look at. These include the mammoth **Feegletscher** (Fee Glacier).

Saas-Fee is reached from the Rhône Valley by a steep and narrow road or by postal bus from Brig, Visp, or Stalden. Cars can be parked in large garages or parking lots outside the village. If road conditions are bad in winter, a policeman will turn cars back on the approach to Saas-Fee if they don't have chains.

Its many facilities include two aerial cableways, three multicabin cableways, two chair lifts, 15 ski lifts, and 32 miles of well-laid-out ski runs, plus 11 tennis courts and two ice rinks. The mountaineering school offers you several skiing tours, climbing and excursion weeks from April to October. It also has a widely spread network of 175 miles of footpaths, including the Gemsweg ("chamois track") from Hannig to Plattjen and the geological mountain high-level trail from Felskinn to the Britannia Hut.

At the entrance to the village is a large indoor swimming pool.

Of course, visitors to Saas-Fee want to get as close to the mountains as they can. The townspeople happily oblige. You can take a gondola cable lift to **Plattjen,** enjoying a panoramic view of the Saas Valley and the artificial lake of Mattmark. Along the way you'll see many alpine flowers in spring, and if you're lucky, a chamois.

The **Felskinn** aerial cableway heaves you up to the summer skiing area of Egginer-Felskinn. Two or three ski lifts are open the whole year, but in summer only from 8:30 a.m. to 1:30 p.m. daily (the snow is likely to get mushy in the afternoon).

The Spielboden gondola ski lift and the Längfluh aerial cableway bring you to **Längfluh,** an oasis in the middle of the Fee Glacier. This is the starting point for the classic mountain tour and the grand glacier tour to the Britannia Hut and to Mattmark.

Another gondola cableway explores **Hannig.** You arrive at the balcony of the Saas Valley, with a scenic alpine view for 360 degrees. Here you can go on many walking tours in a virgin area. It's the starting point to the Mischabel Hut and many alpine tours in the Mischabel massif. A special attraction of the sloping area are the chamois and ibex.

Food and Lodging

Apart Hotel Saaser Hof, CH-3906 Saas-Fee, Switzerland (tel. 028/57-15-51), is constructed almost entirely of weathered beams of thick wood, with an occasional flower box set at irregular intervals along the three tiers of balconies. The decor inside is that of a well-heeled old Valais house. The windows are criss-crossed with strips of geometrically patterned lead, and the wood paneling of the ceilings is appropriately complicated. In one of the sitting rooms a central fireplace funnels its smoke through an elaborately crafted tube of hexagonal copper. On the premises is a sauna to warm you after a winter day outside. The apartments are decorated in contrasting patterns of geometric lines, along with modern upholstered furniture, sometimes with wood trim. Some of the accommodations are traditional hotel rooms, while others are apartments with kitchenettes, accommodating as many as eight guests. Prices range from 72F ($48.95) to 139F ($94.50) daily in a single, from 144F ($97.90) to 278F ($189.05) in a double. The difference in the rates depends on the season. However, half board is included, and all units contain private baths. Open June to October and December to April.

Hôtel Beau-Site, CH-3906 Saas-Fee, Switzerland (tel. 028/57-11-22), is a very large brown-and-white building with lots of balconies and a prominent position in the center of the village. The original hotel was built during the heyday of the British tourist in 1893. In 1957 the hotel was greatly expanded and modernized, so that today a decor of masonry walls, timbers, and lots of paneling covers the inside of this family-run (third-generation) house. A swimming pool with a ceiling low enough to keep it well heated is on the premises. Each of the comfortable bedrooms has a private bath. Depending on the season, singles cost from 98F ($66.65) to 137F ($93.15) daily, and doubles range from 156F ($106.10) to 254F ($172.70) daily, with half board included. The breakfast buffet is copious, and the evening meal includes five courses.

Grand Hotel Saas-Fee, CH-3906 Saas-Fee, Switzerland (tel. 028/57-10-01), in the center of the village, is an elegant establishment with lots of renovated touches, which include a sauna, whirlpool, richly beamed ceilings, and a scattering of 19th-century antiques. The comfortable bedrooms are usually trimmed with pine paneling and are decorated in monochromatic earth tones. The exterior of the hotel resembles three streamlined chalets set next to one another, with balconies extending from the southern side. Ursula and Hans Hess-Zurbriggen are the English-speaking hosts. For one of their comfortably furnished rooms, all of which contain private bath, they charge 90F ($61.20) to 140F ($95.20) daily for singles, while doubles cost 180F ($122.40) to 280F ($190.40), with half board included. Rates depend on the season. Guests from the outside are welcome to patronize their restaurant, which has both an à la carte selection and a table d'hôte of four to five courses. The hotel bar is a popular rendezvous, as is its disco, Sans Souci. The hotel is open June to September and December to April.

Hotel Burgener, CH-3906 Saas-Fee, Switzerland (tel. 028/57-15-22), near the ski lifts, has only 30 beds. The format is chalet style, this time with a yellow trim. A low-lying building next door, called the Ski-Hütte, does a thriving business as a terrace restaurant, especially during high season. The decor of this hotel is rustic, even by alpine standards, but comfortably appropriate after a day outdoors. The Burgener family maintains the place, charging from 65F ($44.20) to 90F ($61.20) daily in a single and from 134F ($91.10) to 186F ($126.50) in a double. Rates depend on the season. All accommodations have private bath, and tariffs include half board. Closed in November.

Hotel Britannia, CH-3906 Saas-Fee, Switzerland (tel. 028/57-16-16) is in the center of the village on a raised site that gives especially good views of the mountains around it. Most of the rooms have balconies with eastern or southern exposure, which illuminate the comfortable bedrooms. These units are filled with brightly colored furniture that makes everything functional yet comfortable. The exterior is a wood-covered six-story chalet with a concrete extension on the back. Singles range from 60F ($40.80) to 97F ($65.95) daily, while doubles cost from 120F ($81.60) to 194F ($131.90), with half board included. Rates depend on the season.

Hotel Allalin, CH-3906 Saas-Fee, Switzerland (tel. 028/57-18-15), is a modern three-star hotel with a warm ambience. Contributing to this atmosphere are old timber, hand-carved furniture, a varied cuisine, and excellent service. All units contain bath, sitting area, a balcony, and open views onto the surrounding mountains and glaciers. Among other amenities are a Jacuzzi, sauna, bar, two restaurants, and an elevator. Singles are charged 115F ($78.20) per day, the cost being 105F ($71.40) per person in a double. The Allalin is open June to September and December to April.

Hotel Sonnehof, CH-3906 Saas-Fee, Switzerland (tel. 028/57-26-93), is an intimately small, 35-bed hotel with a personalized management. The views from the bedrooms are good. Prices for this centrally located hotel, where each of the rooms has a private bath, are 60F ($40.80) to 97F ($65.95) daily in a single and 120F ($81.60) to 194F ($131.90) in a double, with half board included. Rates vary according to the season. The hotel is open June to October and December to April.

Hôtel des Alpes, CH-3906 Saas-Fee, Switzerland (tel. 028/57-15-55), is a rambling chalet hotel with one of its wings in traditional weathered wood and another wing crafted from white stucco. Alpine balconies surround the entire construction on several tiers to give practically every bedroom a balcony. The decor inside is cozily informal with the kind of furniture that children don't easily demolish. The hotel is neither glossily elegant nor stylish but provides relaxed comfort with a conscientious management by the Zurbriggen family. Singles range from 30F ($20.40) to 57F ($38.75) daily, and doubles go from 56F ($38.10) to 110F ($74.80), including breakfast. Tariffs depend on the season. The cheaper units don't have baths. Open June to September and December to April.

For dining outside the hotels, consider the following.

Waldhotel Fletschorn (tel. 028/57-21-31) serves some of the best food at the resort, and even nonguests may want to stop in here for at least one meal. This establishment lies in a handsome chalet beside a footpath a 20-minute walk north from the center of Saas-Fee. Practically every diner who comes here to eat arrives on foot, a traditional way of working up an appetite. The restaurant lies on the road to Wildi. Irma Dütsch-Grandjean and her husband, Jorge, are said by many to be among the finest chefs in the region. Their menu is extremely varied, and someone will be happy to guide you through a satisfying selection if you want assistance. Your meal might include cream of snail soup or frogs' legs in puff pastry, perhaps fresh duck liver with endive in the cuisine moderne style. Among the recommendable courses are filet of red snapper grilled with walnuts and rack of lamb that has been marinated, perhaps escalope of salmon à la crème de ciboulette, or flambéed beef. At certain times of the season a consommé of quail is served. Among their regional dishes, you may want to sample their veal. Fixed-price meals cost from 85F ($57.80) to 110F ($74.80) in the evening but are cheaper at noon. A la carte meals range from 50F ($34) to 85F ($57.80). Food is served from 7 a.m. to midnight daily. The restaurant closes from late April to mid-June and mid-October to mid-December.

Après Ski

My favorite place after dark is the rustic tavern, Sans-Souci, of the four-star **Grand Hotel** (tel. 028/57-10-01), which often has live groups who play for dancing. It can pack in 300 on a big night. Call the hotel to see what, if anything, is happening.

If you like a cozy bar on a cold winter's night, check out the rustic one at the four-star **Beau Site** (tel. 028/57-11-22).

Action at Saas-Fee is very casual at night, nothing very formal unless a group of visitors spontaneously decide to "dress up," which is known to happen.

Try also the Yeti Bar at the **Dom Hotel** (tel. 028/59-11-01), where you will be welcomed by Urs Bucher.

GRÄCHEN: This was just a tiny farming village that has lately realized its potential as a ski resort for those looking for lower prices than traditionally found at its more famous neighbors, Saas-Fee and Zermatt. Its popularity as a ski resort has been very recent, and it attracts a lively family trade of mostly European visitors. (All the Americans, seemingly, are headed for Zermatt and the Matterhorn.)

Grächen is built on a wind-sheltered sun terrace, set against a panoramic alpine backdrop of mountain peaks. It has several ski runs, cableway, ski lifts, and trails.

At the east of the village you can take a gondola to **Hannigalp,** which has a restaurant that can seat hundreds. From this vantage point you face a total of four drag lifts. The loftiest point is **Wannihorn,** at 7,530 feet.

Food and Lodging

Hotel Elite, CH-3925 Grächen, Switzerland (tel. 028/56-16-17), is a wood-balconied chalet that is landscaped into the hillside. The interior is rustic with white stucco between the overhead ceiling beams. Spacious public rooms are there if you need them, although most guests will probably stay on their balconies in summer and ski outdoors in winter. The Reynard family, your hosts, charge from 78F ($53.05) to 84F ($57.10) daily in a single and from 144F ($97.90) to 168F ($114.25) in a double, including half board. Tariffs depend on the season. Open June to September and December to April.

Hotel Restaurant Hannigalp & Valaisia, CH-3925 Grächen, Switzerland (tel. 028/56-25-55), looks like a mix between a chalet and a Mediterranean villa, with a rustic upper section and two lower floors of big-windowed terraces that extend far out on either side. The entire complex overlooks the hotel's tennis courts. The interior is pleasantly decorated with a checker-board parquet floor in the dining room and lots of paneling and patterned carpets in the bedrooms. A nearby chalet, the Christiania, accommodates the overflow from the main hotel, for a total sleeping capacity of 50. A rustically beamed bar area serves food and drink. Singles cost 56F ($38.10) to 80F ($54.40) daily, while doubles are priced at 110F ($74.80) to 150F ($102), with half board included. The less expensive accommodations don't have private baths. Rates depend on the season. Open June to October and December to April.

Hotel Walliserhof, CH-3925 Grächen, Switzerland (tel. 028/56-11-22), offers 50 beds in a six-story chalet with red shutters and lots of balconies. A dancing bar in the basement usually has live musical groups for listeners of all ages. The Walter family, your hosts, charge from 60F ($40.80) daily to 80F ($54.40) in a single and from 108F ($73.45) to 150F ($102) in a double, depending on the season. Half board is included in these prices.

Après Ski

The action, such as there is, is very subdued. The rowdy crowd heads for Zermatt or Saas-Fee, and many people turn in early in Grächen. However, not everything shuts down at night.

To get myself started, I always drop in at the **Hotel Hannigalp & Valaisia** (tel. 028/56-25-55) for one of its Hannigalp cocktails for fortification. After that, the best place in the village for entertainment is the **Hotel Walliserhof** (tel. 028/56-11-12), which often has dancing to a live band. If the action seems dull there, you might go over to the **Hotel Bellevue & Romantica** (tel. 028/56-24-44), which has a bar with music and a good kitchen.

Hotel Grächerhof and Schönegg (tel. 028/56-25-15) also provides dancing and a choice of bars, along with a rôtisserie. Alex Fux is your obliging host.

12. BRIG AND THE SIMPLON PASS

Lying south of the Rhône River, Brig is a historic stopover for international travelers, both today and centuries ago. It's also the capital of the Upper Valais region, and a major railway stopover. Famed as the starting point for the great road over the **Simplon Pass**, it lies at the north end of the **Simplon tunnel**, at 12 miles the longest in the world. Work began on the first of these twin tunnels at the turn of the century. You board the train at Brig, a one-way passage costing 22F ($14.95). Trains leave every hour. The last departure is at 8 p.m. Conversely, you can also take your car to Kandersteg, a mountain resort in the Bernese Oberland.

Napoleon ordered the road over the Simplon Pass, and construction was launched in the early years of the 19th century, making it the shortest road between the Valais and Ticino. The Swiss try to keep the pass open all year, but sometimes don't succeed. If the pass is not open, cars can be carried by rail through the tunnel. The road, if the weather's right, is one of the most stunning views in Europe, and should be taken for sightseeing alone. Like a slide show, the views change constantly, and there are many tricky turns—so drive carefully.

Back in Brig is a sightseeing attraction all on its own, **Stockalperschloss** or Stockalper's Castle, through which guided tours are conducted May to October from 9 to 11 a.m. and 2 to 5 p.m., daily except Monday, for a 3F ($2.05) admission. It's Switzerland's largest manor house, built by Kasper vön Stockalper between 1658 and 1678. He grew rich and prosperous by recognizing the benefits of trade with Italy and by exploiting trade along the Simplon Pass. However, he was chased out of his beloved home by irate citizens of the Valais, although he returned from exile in time to die there, perhaps with memories of when he'd been welcomed into some of the royal courts of Europe. The manor consists of a mammoth building with four floors and a large gateway. The three towers with their bulbous domes symbolize the Wise Men. Ever since 1948 Brig has owned the manor, and today uses it as a museum and for administrative purposes. In its heyday it was the biggest privately owned residence in all of Switzerland.

FOOD AND LODGING: The best hotel of a lackluster lot is the **Schlosshotel Garni**, CH-3900 Brig, Switzerland (tel. 028/23-64-55). It is not, as its name implies, a castle hotel, but a modern, clean-cut, and functional establishment. It often attracts overnighters who wait till morning to try to cross the Simplon Pass. At the foot of the château, the hotel in some respects resembles a modernized version of a medieval fortress. It opens onto a playground and a good view of the castle. Rooms are well kept and comfortable, costing 55F ($37.40) to 95F ($64.60) daily in a single, 95F ($64.60) to 150F ($102) in a twin. Breakfast is the only meal served.

Hotel Restaurant Victoria, 2 Bahnhofstrasse, CH-3900 Brig, Switzerland (tel. 028/23-15-03), facing the railway station, has been the traditional favorite.

It is a convenient stopping point if you've missed the last train to either Kandersteg or Italy. The hotel was inaugurated in the 19th century, and many of its bedrooms reflect the spaciousness of that era. However, it has a modern extension. A three-star choice, it offers singles for 75F ($51) to 90F ($61.20) daily, depending on the plumbing. Doubles cost from 130F ($88.40) to 150F ($102). All doubles contain showers or baths, and some of the rooms have TV and mini-bars.

Schlosskeller, 26 Alte Simplonstrasse (tel. 028/23-33-52), is in a historic building in the center of town, serving filling meals in a rustic setting. The food includes a plate of air-dried alpine beef, followed by, perhaps, filets of fera with wild rice or filet of pork madeleine. Fixed-price meals cost from 25F ($17) to 35F ($23.80), and à la carte dinners are priced from 30F ($20.40) to 45F ($30.60). It's open from 8 a.m. to 11 p.m. daily except Monday and for three weeks in January.

Restaurant Channa, 5 Furkastrasse (tel. 028/23-65-56), is the sympathetic restaurant managed by Peter Walch, who often invites his clients to dine on the flowery terrace in warm weather. Specialties include green pepper filet steak Madagascar, frogs' legs in the style of Provence, and veal kidneys flambé. Fixed-price meals range from 28F ($19.05) to 45F ($30.60). Hours are noon to 2 p.m. and 6 to 9 p.m. daily.

13. THE GRIMSEL PASS

Another one of the great scenic roads of Switzerland, the Grimsel Pass lies on the boundary between the canton of Bern and the canton of Valais, which we are now leaving. Take it if you want to go back to the Bernese Oberland. Among its more stunning views is one of the **Gries Glacier.** The so-called **Lake of the Dead** is named to honor the soldiers who lost their lives in the battle between the French and the Austrians in 1799.

If you're exploring at all in this area, you may want to see the snowy summit of the **Galenstock,** and the **Furka Pass,** which heads toward Andermatt on the way to Lucerne and the heart of Switzerland. In the vicinity of **Gletsch,** on the road to the Furka Pass, you can stop at the **Belvedere Hotel,** one of the most scenic vistas along this trail. You can also order drinks and food.

From here you can see the celebrated **Rhône Glacier,** where the Swiss have carved an ice grotto. The vista of both the Alps of the Bernese Oberland and the Valais Alps is stunning.

Back in the vicinity of the Grimsel Pass, you may want to seek out food and lodging for the night.

Hotel Grimselblick, CH-3861 Grimsel-Passhöhe, Switzerland (tel. 028/73-11-26), is set across the road from a lake in a well-maintained white building with red shutters and plenty of space for parking. The Gemmet family, your hosts, seem to take a great interest in rock crystals. They charge 28F ($19.05) to 46F ($31.30) daily for a single and 48F ($32.65) to 78F ($53.05) for a double, including breakfast. Rooms are simply but comfortably furnished. However, the cheaper accommodations don't contain private baths. The hotel is open only from June to October.

CHAPTER VIII

LAUSANNE AND LAKE GENEVA

□ □ □

In the footsteps of Lord Byron and Shelley, tourists for decades have sought the scenic wonders of Lake Geneva (Lac Léman) in the southwest corner of Switzerland. Actually, it was native son Jean-Jacques Rousseau who caused the lake to become such a pilgrimage among the "Romantics."

Lac Léman is the largest lake in central Europe, the Lacus Lemannus of classical writers. It embraces an area of about 225 square miles, of which 134 square miles belong to the Swiss and the rest to France. The French sector takes in most of the south shore, except for Geneva in the west and Valais in the east. The Swiss-held north shore is shaped like a large arc, and is lined with vineyards which were planted on the final slopes of the Jura.

The most popular way to tour the lake is by steamer, and this has been true since 1823. Nearly all the cities, hamlets, and towns we'll visit along the lake have schedules posted at the landing quays. Service is usually from Easter to October. However, in this chapter I'll assume you'll be touring by car or bus, which will allow you to stop and visit the sights along the way. Railways also run along both shores.

Lake Geneva is formed by the Rhône. It consists of both a Grand Lac to the east and a Petit Lac to the west, the latter in the Genevese portions (for a description of Geneva and its surrounding environs, turn to Chapter IX). Where the muddy Rhône enters the lake there is a turbidness, but eventually the river-born mud sinks to the bottom and Lac Léman's waters become a transparent blue.

The list of celebrated personages who have chosen to live on the lake is staggering: not only Edward Gibbon, but Balzac and Dumas, André Gide, Richard Wagner, Franz Liszt, and George Eliot.

In more modern times a host of international stars—none more celebrated than the late Charlie Chaplin—have chosen a home on the lake. Along with the little tramp, I'll cite just a few of the stars and celebrities who have been attracted to the lake: Yul Brynner, Audrey Hepburn, James Mason, Noël Coward, William Holden, David Niven, Sophia Loren, and Charles Lindbergh. Of course, many went there for tax reasons.

Our exploration will begin in the "capital" of Lac Léman, the ancient city of Lausanne.

1. LAUSANNE

Lausanne, whose 135,000 inhabitants make it the second-largest city on Lake Geneva and the fifth-largest city in Switzerland, rises in tiers from the lake. The city is built on five hills overlooking the lake. The inhabitants of Lausanne prefer to call the lake Lac Léman; they deplore hearing it called Lake Geneva. The upper and lower towns are connected by funicular.

A haunt of international celebrities who live along the lake, and celebrated for its schools, Lausanne is connected by motorway to Geneva, 38 miles away. In the opposite direction, the Great St. Bernard road tunnel is some 60 miles from Lausanne.

The locale has been inhabited since the Stone Age, and was the ancient Roman town of Lousanna. In 1803 it became the 19th canton to join the Confederation, and is today the capital of the canton of Vaud.

For centuries Lausanne has been a favorite haunt of expatriates. Figures show that in 1930 foreigners numbered 10,548 out of the city's total population of 75,915. The city has long attracted royal families (many of them deposed). It particularly flourished in the Age of Enlightenment when it was associated with such personalities as Voltaire, Napoleon, Goethe, and Rousseau.

The **Cité** or old town still evokes the Middle Ages, as a nightwatchman calls the hours from 10 p.m. to 2 a.m. from the top of the cathedral's belfry.

As for orientation, the hub of the town's traffic, the **place St-François,** is the shopping and business heart of Lausanne. The Church of St. Francis, from the 13th and 14th centuries, is all that remains of an old Franciscan friary. Today the square is filled with office blocks and the main post office. Regrettably, La Grotte, the villa with the terrace on which Gibbon completed his famous history in 1787, was torn down in 1896 to make room for the post office. From St. François Square you can walk up **rue de Bourg,** one of the most typical shopping streets of Lausanne. Or you can take the underground to **Ouchy,** which is now the lakefront of Lausanne. Once it was just a sleeping fishing hamlet, but no more. For more about Lausanne's geography, refer to "What to See."

TRANSPORTATION: Lausanne has a good public transportation network of trolleys and buses operated by the TL (Lausanne Public Transport Company). The **trolley** or **bus** fare is 1.50F ($1) regardless of the distance for a single trip completed within 60 minutes on lines 1 to 19 of the TL urban network and on the Lausanne-Ouchy métro. A book of ten tickets sells for 12.50F ($8.50). For short trips up to four stops (consult plan displayed at stops), the fare is 1F (86¢), and a book of ten tickets costs 8.50F ($5.80). You purchase or stamp your tickets at slot machines installed at most stops, or else ask the driver. (A surcharge is collected if you get your ticket from the driver at a stop with a slot machine.) A one-day season ticket is only 4.50F ($3.05) for adults, 2.50F ($1.70) for children. For three consecutive days, the season ticket costs 12F ($8.15) for adults, 6F ($4.10) for children.

An underground (or métro) offers rapid service; for example, the trip between the heart of the old town and Ouchy down by the lake takes six minutes. Departures are every 7½ minutes from 6:15 a.m. and 11:45 p.m. (from 6:30 a.m. on Saturday, Sunday, and holidays; from 8:30 to 11:45 p.m., the trains run every 15 minutes between October 1 and March 31). A ticket from the town center to Ouchy costs 1.20F (80¢), and a book of ten tickets goes for 10F ($6.80).

A bus shuttle service is operated between the railway station and the town center daily except Sunday from 6:30 a.m. to 8:30 p.m. The charge for a ticket is .60F (40¢) or 5F ($3.40) for a book of ten tickets.

If you want to take a **taxi,** some 45 taxi ranks are at your disposal, or you can telephone 141, 021/23-11-11, or 021/23-11-12. The meter starts at 4.60F ($3.15), with each increment of one kilometer (.62 miles) costing 1.80F ($1.20) in town; 2.10F ($1.45) from 10 p.m. to 6 a.m. and on Sunday and holidays; 2.80F ($1.90) outside the town limits. The first 22 pounds of luggage is free, with 1F (68¢) charged for every 66 pounds thereafter.

Persons **driving** in Lausanne should know that the wearing of seat belts is compulsory, and that children under 12 are not allowed to ride in the front seat. There are four kinds of parking zones in the town; time unlimited white zone; 15 hours maximum, with a parking disk, in a red zone; 1½ hours maximum with a parking disk in the blue zone; and the parking meter zone with varying times. Parking disks are obtainable free at police stations and offices of automobile clubs.

To rent **boats** or **pedalos,** try the ports at Ouchy and Parc Bouget pavilion at Vidy.

You can rent **bicycles** at the Lausanne Railway Station at the baggage forwarding counter (tel. 021/42-21-62) Monday to Friday from 6:30 a.m. to 8:50 p.m., Saturday and Sunday from 7 a.m. to 7:50 p.m.

Airport Service

Lausanne doesn't have an airport, so most visitors fly to Cointrin at Geneva, then take a direct train from there to Lausanne, leaving every 20 minutes. The trip takes about 45 minutes. The Lausanne office of the **Swiss Federal Railways** (CFF) is at 43 avenue de la Gare (tel. 021/42-11-11). You can check your luggage in Lausanne for a flight leaving Geneva. Inquire at the railway station.

PRACTICAL FACTS: Besides the general information pertaining to the entire country, given in "The ABCs of Switzerland" in Chapter II, a few facts about Lausanne may make your visit more enjoyable.

Drugstores: You can always find one open in Lausanne. A poster prominently displayed in all pharmacies indicates those that are on duty, and the local newspapers run lists of them.

Information: To assist visitors, the major **Lausanne Tourist Office,** 2 avenue de Rhodanie (tel. 021/27-73-21), is open from 8 a.m. to 6 p.m. Monday to Friday, from 8 a.m. to noon and 1 to 6 p.m. Saturday, and from 9 a.m. to noon and 1 to 6 p.m. Sunday. There's also a tourist office in the main hall of the railway station (tel. 021/23-19-35).

Lost property: Go to the office at 6 rue Saint-Laurent (tel. 021/20-70-64) from 7:30 to 11:45 a.m. and 1 to 5 p.m. Monday to Friday, from 7:30 to 11:30 a.m. Saturday; closed Sunday.

Medical care: For day and night medical service, including dental care, telephone the doctors' exchange at 021/32-99-32.

Post office: There are various branches of the post office throughout Lausanne, but the main office is at Avenue de la Gare and Place de la Gare (tel. 021/40-01-11). It's open Monday to Friday from 7:30 a.m. to noon and 1:30 to 6:30 p.m. (on Saturday, from 7:30 to 11 a.m. only). Telegrams and Telexes can be sent in the telegraph office in the station, Place de la Gare.

ACCOMMODATIONS: In the top hotels of the city an air of luxury and ele-

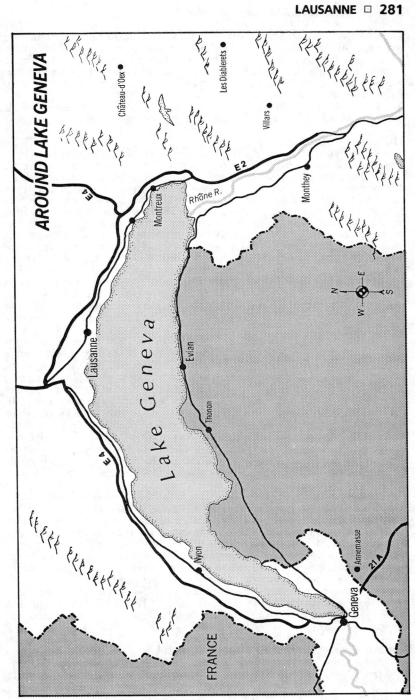

AROUND LAKE GENEVA

Château-d'Oex •

Les Diablerets •

Villars •

E2

Rhône R.

Montreux

Monthey •

E4

N
W — E
S

Lausanne

Evian

Lake Geneva

Thonon

E4

Nyon

Annemasse •

Geneva

21A

FRANCE

gance long ago made the city a favorite visiting place for the English. In summer space is tight, so try to get a reservation. Lausanne is also a city of trade fairs, conferences, and conventions, so many of its better hotels are fully booked at certain times of the year, including, for example, the International Tourism Fair in March. The tourist office will help you find a room if you're without a place to stay (or even if you aren't).

If you want to be directly on the lake, seek out an accommodation in Ouchy; otherwise, you'll find many fine hotels in Lausanne proper.

The Deluxe Choices

Beau-Rivage Palace, 18 place du Général Guisan, CH-1006 Lausanne-Ouchy, Switzerland (tel. 021/26-38-31), one of the leading hotels in the world, is set in ten acres of the most exquisitely maintained gardens in Lausanne, with cedars, many kinds of begonias, and grassy areas dotted with sculptures. It is a citadel of beauty and tradition, and in its some 120 years it has been host to scores of European aristocrats. The hotel dates from 1861, but another wing was added in 1908. The Beau-Rivage is a vastly proportioned and elaborately detailed structure with a mansard roof, tall French windows, and miles of wrought-iron balconies. The rotunda inside is a mammoth rococo room with columns, statues of heroic deities, and a series of illuminations worthy of Vienna at its peak. Artfully lit from beneath, the room serves as one of the hotel's many public salons. This is one of the last bastions of a more formal Europe, so appropriate clothing should be worn. Perhaps you'll spot an Italian contessa or two. The public rooms are vast, exquisitely decorated, and very formal. On the premises are an indoor and an outdoor pool, tennis courts, a jogging path, and a sporting club among the hotel's many amenities.

The hotel offers 204 beautifully furnished rooms, 12 of which are suites. Of these, 115 contain a private terrace or balcony. Each of the accommodations is individually decorated, with period furniture, private bath with shower (eight suites and junior suites with Jacuzzi), radio, refrigerator, and color TV, along with direct-dial phone and, in some rooms, a safety deposit box. Singles range from 190F ($129.20) to 260F ($176.80) daily, with doubles costing from 260F ($176.80) to 500F ($340). Junior suites for two range from 390F ($265.20) to 650F ($442). One of the hotel's restaurants, Terrasse-Rotonde, offers a panoramic view over the lake and mountains and serves three meals a day. The Café Beau-Rivage is a Parisian-style brasserie under the hotel arcades facing the quay. It offers regional dishes and seasonal specialties. The hotel also has several bars, including Le Bar Anglais with a piano player and Café Beau-Rivage Bar with musical entertainment.

Lausanne Palace, 7-9 Grand-Chêne, CH-1002 Lausanne, Switzerland (tel. 021/20-37-11), is as grand and elegant a hotel as you'll find anywhere in Europe. Those details that are not authentically 19th century (the columns, plaster detailing, marble floors, and richly oiled woodwork of the bar area) are attractive 20th-century additions, usually in keeping with the well-maintained tradition of "The Palace," as British visitors over the years have called it. The hotel is in the heart of Lausanne, with a good view of the mountains and the lake from many of its bedroom windows. Tapestries, crystal chandeliers, and gilded rococo furniture from a more ornate era fill many of the corners. The spacious bedrooms have private bath, renting for 195F ($132.60) to 270F ($183.60) daily in a single and 270F ($183.60) to 370F ($251.60) in a double, depending on the season and the accommodation.

Medium-Priced and Upper Bracket Hotels

Hôtel Aulac, 4 place de la Navigation, CH-1006 Lausanne-Ouchy, Switzerland (tel. 021/27-14-51). The baroque yellow façade is highlighted with white trim and a Renaissance-style porch which extends up three tiers of floors between two elaborate columns. The mansard roof is inlaid with tiles set into geometric designs. The entire endearing structure is crowned with a tall narrow clock tower that is unmistakably Victorian. All of this sits on the water's edge with dozens of sailboats bobbing in the lake nearby. The interior has been renovated several times to include a restaurant with a nautical theme, lots of conference rooms, and well-maintained, simply furnished rooms, many quite spacious. Year round, singles rent for 100F ($68) to 140F ($95.20) daily, while doubles cost 130F ($88.40) to 190F ($129.20), with breakfast included. All units contain TV, radios, phones, and mini-bars.

Le Château d'Ouchy, 2 place du Port, CH-1006 Lausanne-Ouchy, Switzerland (tel. 021/26-74-51), is a complete retrospective of pre-20th-century architectural styles. The central feature is a fortified tower with a black-and-red tile roof. This is surrounded by a marvelously crafted series of wings, dungeons, Renaissance-style gables, and Romanesque arches, all of it made of gray stones set intricately together. The management tells me that all this was pieced together in the 19th century around a 12th-century core. Today it's a comfortable hotel with an impressive series of public rooms and a nightclub that's one of the most popular in town. The renovated bedrooms are furnished, in part, with Louis XIII–style pieces, at rates ranging from 115F ($78.20) to 155F ($105.40) daily in a single and from 160F ($108.80) to 210F ($142.80) in a double. Breakfast is included in the tariffs quoted.

Hôtel la Résidence, 15 place du Port, CH-1006 Lausanne-Ouchy, Switzerland (tel. 021/27-77-11). Three separate buildings, all of them in the Regency style, make up this hotel. Separated from one another with flowered walkways, all front on the lake. The entrance to the reception area has black and white diamond-shaped slabs of stone set into the floor, a massive fireplace, and a beamed ceiling. This building was at one time an annex of the neighboring Beau-Rivage (it still maintains strong ties to it), and before that an offshoot of the town hall. Two of the three remaining buildings were once private villas, while the other is a convincing copy. Set on the shores of the lake in what is considered the best part of Ouchy, the hotel employs staff who appreciate the rigors of travel. Karine Schnyder, the director, charges 120F ($81.60) to 160F ($108.80) daily in a single and 180F ($122.40) to 230F ($156.40) in a double, including breakfast.

Royal Savoy, 40 avenue d'Ouchy, CH-1000 Lausanne, Switzerland (tel. 021/26-42-01), is set in a park with a swimming pool and towering trees. The former residence of the Spanish royal family, it has 1900s nostalgia but modern comforts. The building is designed château fashion, with many chimneys, a mansard roof, turrets capped by round pointed roofs, and gracefully arched windows with balconies. The bedrooms are spacious and filled with Oriental rugs and good reproduction antiques. Singles rent for 135F ($91.80) to 180F ($122.40) daily, while doubles cost 200F ($136) to 260F ($178.60). Half board is offered for another 40F ($27.20) per person daily. The several restaurants and the bar combine good service with elegant decor. The Savoy Restaurant is traditional, with gourmet fare, and Jardin d'Hiver offers seasonal specialties in a setting of greenery.

Hôtel de la Paix, 5 avenue Benjamin-Constant, CH-1002 Lausanne, Switzerland (tel. 021/20-71-71), is a large 19th-century hotel with row upon row of elaborate balconies and loggias, many of them with wrought-iron detailing. The summer awnings prevent too much sunlight from entering the rooms with southern exposure. Many of the bedrooms overlook the lake. Each of the rooms has a private bath or shower, and rates include a generous breakfast. Singles rent for 130F ($88.40) to 175F ($119) daily, while doubles cost 190F ($129.20) to 260F ($176.80).

Hôtel Alpha, 34 Petit-Chêne, CH-1003 Lausanne, Switzerland (tel. 021/23-01-31), is one of the Fassbind hotels, which also operate properties in Geneva and Lugano. This well-run hotel chain operates a winning hotel about 200 yards from the train station in Lausanne. Opened in 1970, it was redecorated in 1984. All its well-furnished accommodations are air-conditioned with individual controls, and windows are soundproof. The hotel has a fire-prevention system, meeting the latest standards, and each of the units is equipped with bath or shower with a hairdryer, color TV and video, along with radio and direct-dial phone, as well as a mini-bar. Singles rent for 130F ($88.40) to 180F ($122.40) daily, while doubles cost 190F ($129.20) to 260F ($176.80), with a buffet breakfast included.

Hotel Agora, 9 avenue Rond-Point, CH-1006 Lausanne, Switzerland (tel. 021/27-12-11), is a four-star hotel which opened in 1986 after a total renovation of an old hotel on this site. It lies only 300 yards from the train station. All rooms are soundproof, and a fire prevention system has been installed. Each room has a bath/shower equipped with a hairdryer, color TV and video in four languages (America Today news from the U.S. is transmitted by satellite to your TV the day it is aired), radio, direct-dial phone, mini-bar, and a personal safe on request. The modern, comfortable bedrooms rent for 130F ($88.40) to 180F ($122.40) daily in a single, and doubles go for 190F ($129.20) to 260F ($176.80), with a buffet breakfast included. The hotel's luxury restaurant is served by a French chef-de-cuisine. Free parking is provided for guests.

Continental Hotel, 2 place de la Gare, CH-1001 Lausanne, Switzerland (tel. 021/20-15-51), is very much of a downtown commercial hotel, as it's near the train station and the airport bus terminal in a glass-and-concrete rectangle. The reception area is glossily outfitted with black trim and a metallic ceiling, while the comfortable bedrooms are exactly what you'd expect from such a format. Each of the accommodations has its own bath, phone, radio, TV, and mini-bar. Singles rent for 115F ($78.20) to 130F ($88.40) daily, and doubles or twins cost 135F ($91.80) to 180F ($122.40). Some three-bedded rooms are available for 240F ($163.20). The hotel has a grill room and a formal restaurant, Le Beaujolais, a rôtisserie considered one of the finest in the city. It specializes in rack of lamb with herbs of Provence, lobster (seasonal), salmon trout with sorrel, and bouillabaisse in the style of Marseilles, along with sea bass flambé with fennel. It's open daily from 11:30 a.m. to 3 p.m. and 6:30 to midnight, with meals costing from 75F ($51). The hotel also contains the popular disco, the Birdwatcher's Club, recommended separately.

Hôtel Bellerive, 99 avenue de Cour, CH-1007 Lausanne, Switzerland (tel. 021/26-96-33), is in the center of town with a clear view from the top floors over the nearby houses and trees as far as the lake. The interior is comfortably appointed with elegantly upholstered armchairs. The bedrooms are filled with fresh colors, and comfortable furniture. Singles rent for 100F ($68) to 140F ($95.20) daily, with doubles costing 150F ($102) to 200F ($136). Half board is available for another 25F ($17) per person daily. Each bedroom contains a radio, phone, and refrigerator.

Hôtel de la Navigation, place Navigation, CH-1006 Lausanne-Ouchy (tel. 021/26-20-41), is a flat-roofed hotel with gray masonry walls and a covered terrace which serves meals and drinks to a crowd of locals who enjoy the view of the sailboat port. The interior is attractively lit from pin spots and concealed sources, and outfitted with modern furniture. The colorful bedrooms all have private bath, radio, phone, mini-bar, and TV. Singles rent for 90F ($61.20) to 130F ($88.40) daily, and doubles cost from 140F ($95.20) to 190F ($129.20), depending on the view, the season, and the plumbing.

Hôtel Jan, 8 avenue de Beaulieu, CH-1004 Lausanne, Switzerland (tel. 021/36-11-61), is slightly to the west of the center of Lausanne in a massive building made of concrete and glass. The hotel is close to the Palais de Beaulieu, where international congresses and sports events take place. If you're driving, you'll appreciate the garage facilities. The bedrooms are spacious and clean, as well as simply furnished with slightly dated pieces which are nonetheless comfortable. All accommodations contain private baths. Singles rent for 100F ($68) to 150F ($102) daily, with doubles going for 150F ($102) to 220F ($149.60).

Hôtel Carlton, 4 avenue de Cour, CH-1000 Lausanne, Switzerland (tel. 021/26-32-35), looks best in summertime when a collection of awnings decorates the arched windows of the white façade. The hotel, appropriate for its position in a green park with a view of the lake, is designed almost like a Mediterranean villa, with a gently sloping red-tile roof and emphatic horizontal lines. The garden restaurant is popular in summer. André Chollet is the manager, overseeing the 50 rooms, all of which contain private baths, TV, and direct-dial phones. Singles range from 130F ($88.40) to 160F ($108.80) daily, and doubles cost 180F ($122.40) to 220F ($149.60), including breakfast. Half board is an additional 35F ($23.80) per person daily. The hotel is noted for the cuisine in its restaurant. If you're dining light, you can order snacks in Carlton's bar, which is a cafeteria.

Budget to Medium-Priced Hotels

Hôtel d'Angleterre, 9 place du Port, CH-1006 Lausanne-Ouchy, Switzerland (tel. 021/26-41-45), is a symmetrical four-story 19th-century building with a café on the ground floor and a position directly on the water. From the windows of the comfortable bedrooms you can see across to the mountains on the other side. The pleasantly furnished accommodations are clean and neat. Singles rent for 65F ($44.20) to 105F ($71.40) daily, while doubles cost 95F ($64.60) to 145F ($98.60), including breakfast. The least expensive contain hot and cold running water but no private baths.

Hôtel Élite, 1 avenue Sainte-Luce, CH-1003 Lausanne, Switzerland (tel. 021/20-23-61), is a five-story white painted hotel with a flat roof, several balconies, and a series of reproduction neoclassical details that are lost behind the large illuminated sign on the front lawn. That doesn't detract from the welcome offered by hotelier M. Zufferey, who directs the establishment with style and élan. The comfortable rooms rent for 80F ($54.50) to 120F ($81.60) daily in a single with shower or bath, whereas similar doubles pay from 120F ($81.60) to 180F ($122.40), including breakfast.

Hôtel à la Gare, 14 rue du Simplon, CH-1006 Lausanne, Switzerland (tel. 021/27-92-52). The exterior of this three-star hotel is covered with stucco, with summer flowers in many of the windowboxes. It's about a block away from the train station, so owner Pierre Goy usually welcomes travel-weary clients even late into the night. A glance at the interior is enough to convince you you're in the Alps instead of in lakeside Lausanne. The public rooms and the bedrooms have lots of pine paneling stained in several different tones. All of the accommodations have private baths or showers, toilets, color TV, and direct-dial phones. Singles range from 80F ($54.40) to 120F ($81.60) daily, and doubles cost from 120F ($81.60) to 180F ($122.40). Children under 14 years of age can share their parents' room free. On the same premises is a rustic restaurant where many local residents go for raclette and specialties of the Vaud.

Hôtel Crystal, 5 rue Chaucrau, CH-1003 Lausanne, Switzerland (tel. 021/20-28-31), is a well-ordered establishment that is very much of a downtown city hotel. Its façade curves in a gentle arc to correspond to the shop-lined pedestrian walkway on which it stands. The Fiora family, the managers, have decorated many of the public rooms to look like sections of a comfortably conservative private home. A terrace opens onto a partial view of the Alps and the lake. If you're driving, the local police will allow your car access to the pedestrian street for purposes of loading and unloading luggage. There's covered parking at the nearby Place Riponne. All but 6 of the 38 pleasantly furnished rooms contain a private bath. Each unit also has a phone, color TV, and a radio, and there's a 24-hour bar on the premises. A Swiss buffet breakfast is included in the rates. Bathless singles range from 55F ($37.40) to 75F ($51) daily, singles with bath costing from 90F ($61.20) to 110F ($74.80). Bathless doubles are priced from 80F ($54.40) to 100F ($68) daily, climbing to 120F ($81.60) to 165F ($112.20) with bath. Half board is 25F ($17) per person per day extra.

Hôtel City, 5 rue Caroline, CH-1007 Lausanne, Switzerland (tel. 021/20-21-41), is a centrally located hotel just outside the old town, only 300 yards from a covered swimming pool and the parking lot of Mon Repos. All rooms are soundproof, and the hotel has a fire-prevention system. Each room offers a bath/shower, color TV and video in four languages, radio, direct-dial phone, and mini-bar. A comfortable hotel with few frills, the City is perfectly satisfactory if most of your time is spent sightseeing. Singles cost 80F ($54.40) to 120F ($81.60) daily, and doubles range from 120F ($81.60) to 180F ($122.40), with a buffet breakfast included.

On the Outskirts

Novotel Lausanne, 35 route de Condémines, CH-1030 Bussigny, Switzerland (tel. 021/89-28-71), might have been conceived with the commercial traveler in mind, but it has much to recommend it to tourists. First, its location west of Lausanne on the autoroute to Geneva is ideal for motorists who don't want to drive into either big city at night. Novotel is not only reasonably priced but functions somewhat like a motel. To save on tips and to keep costs low, guests are given pushcarts to wheel their luggage to their rooms. In all, there are 100 bedrooms, each comfortably up to date, with a large desk space, a private direct-dial phone, a TV, a separate toilet, and a private bath, and a sofa that converts into an extra bed at night. Prices are reasonable, costing 95F ($64.60) daily in a single, going up to 115F ($78.20) in a double. An extra person is housed for another 20F ($13.60) per person. The hotel caters to families, who delight in the swimming pool in fair weather.

It also contains a grill, open daily from 6 a.m. to midnight, with an à la carte menu. However, the chef also features two set menus every day costing from 14F ($9.50) and 19F ($12.90), served only from noon to 2 p.m. and 7 to 10 p.m. Guests can relax in comfortable chairs at the convivial bar. To reach the hotel, leave the autoroute (after departing Lausanne) at the Lausanne-Crissier exit and continue in the direction of Sullens. Novotel, part of a world-wide chain, is signposted from there.

WHERE TO DINE: The range of restaurants in Lausanne is large, from typical Swiss places in the old town to attractive little inns on the outskirts, which are always my favorite spots, especially if they open onto Lac Léman. Many Vaudois and Swiss specialties are offered, but you also get a selection of French, Greek, Italian, and Chinese eateries as well.

If you see the Geneva lake fish, omble chevalier, on the menu, please order it. Trout and perch from the lake are also popular, and in autumn many restaurants feature game dishes.

The Upper Bracket

Girardet, 1 rue d'Yverdon, Hôtel de Ville, at Crissier, near Lausanne (tel. 021/634-05-05). There are some who say that Fredy Girardet is the world's greatest chef. Certainly he's on every serious gourmet's gastronomic tour of Europe. This is a friendly, well-decorated restaurant, in the modest 1929 Crissier town hall, where daily shipments of fresh fish contribute to a menu that uses only the best possible ingredients. The restaurant, on the outskirts of Lausanne, attracts many devotees from Geneva, 38 miles away.

Chef Girardet, along with a brigade of talented assistants, prepares a delectable assortment of food that, at times, can be deceptively simple. He once told reporters that he's been known to copy some recipes from his grandmother's favorite collection. However, in the main he is greatly inspired by such famous French chefs as the Troisgros brothers, Roger Vergé, and Paul Bocuse. Monsieur Girardet, of course, is a devotee of cuisine moderne. Some of his specialties (and they change all the time) include a ragoût of fresh quail with young vegetables, crayfish in caviar butter, and many seasonally adjusted dishes. Among these are "wild" salmon steak with small turnips and a perfect chervil sauce, and desserts such as passion fruit soufflé and the most spectacular ice creams you are ever likely to devour. Reservations are essential, and they often need to be made three months in advance for dinner; for weekday lunch, two weeks are required, and for Saturday lunch, two months in advance. Fixed-price menus cost from 135F ($91.80), while à la carte dinners range from 125F ($85) to 200F ($136).

The restaurant is open from noon to 2 p.m. and 7 p.m. to midnight except Sunday and Monday and for three weeks sometime in July and August and for another three weeks sometime in December and January. Monsieur Girardet takes no credit cards, but then again, he doesn't have to.

Restaurant L'Agora, 9 avenue du Rond-Point (tel. 021/27-12-11), offers many culinary virtues in its own right, but at least some of its recipes and methods of presentation were taught by the famous French chef Georges Bardet, voted the best chef in France in 1985. Georges Fassbind, the proprietor, and his chef, Pascal Santailler, prepare excellent meals at this establishment where traditional Vaudois specialties compete with grand platters from the culinary strongholds of France. A fixed-price menu du marché includes an "amuse bouche" and four courses, all for 48F ($32.65). A six-course menu goes for 110F ($74.80). Meals are served daily from noon to 2 p.m. and 7 to 11 p.m. except Saturday at lunch and all day Sunday. Annual vacation is from mid-July to mid-August.

L'Agora has become one of the best restaurants of Lausanne. Its reputation is based on such dishes (likely to change) as a terrine of goose liver, a delicious version of halibut with curry sauce, baked lobster with a concentrated essence of vintage wine, and Bresse chicken with a cabbage and mushroom cream sauce. A dessert specialty is fresh figs with vanilla ice cream. The restaurant is contained within the Hotel Agora.

La Grappe d'Or, 3 rue Cheneau-de-Bourg (tel. 021/23-07-60), is a rôtisserie in the old city, with a luxurious decor and excellent food that attracts a well-heeled crowd of locals. The chef has an interesting menu of fish and shellfish, including scampi, red mullet, sea bass, and fennel. You can also order excellent meat dishes, and roebuck is served in season. Set lunches are offered for 49F ($33.30) and 68F ($46.25), main dishes varying according to the day of the week. Fixed-price evening meals, gourmet style, cost 87F ($59.15), 108F ($73.45), and 110F ($74.80), while à la carte dinners range from 55F ($37.40) to 110F ($74.80). Food is served from noon to 2:15 p.m. and 7 to 10 p.m. except at lunchtime Saturday and all day Sunday.

Restaurant San Marino, 20 avenue de la Gare (tel. 021/22-93-69), is reputed to be the finest Italian restaurant in the city. The decor is elegant, the prices are high, and all of the dishes are prepared by a team of chefs who are experienced and skilled. Even though the decor owes its loyalty to Venice, the cuisine is pure Tuscan. There is no stinting on quality. The ingredients that go into the dishes are fresh and handled with a certain delicacy and flair. Full of novelty and style, an unusual version of saltimbocca is prepared here with seawolf and baby zucchini instead of the usual "jump-in-your-mouth" version of veal and ham. Among the other meticulous and colorful dishes are braised quail with artichokes, quail stuffed with risotto, and saffron-laden shellfish and filet of poultry on a bed of leeks. Fixed-price meals cost from 50F ($34) to 75F ($51), and service is from

8 a.m. to midnight. The restaurant is closed on Saturday and also for Sunday lunch, and it takes an annual holiday the last two weeks of July.

Budget to Medium-Priced Dining

Café Beau-Rivage, Beau-Rivage Palace, 18 place du Général Guisan, Ouchy (tel. 021/26-38-31). Its grandeur and elegance easily help it to compete with some of the finest restaurants in the city. Prices are deliberately kept within the median range, although the kitchen uses only carefully chosen, fresh ingredients. The location in a lakeside pavilion is on the grounds of this previously recommended deluxe hotel, surrounded with a flowering terrace and graceful bay windows. It is open daily from 9 a.m. to 1 a.m., serving hot food from 11:45 a.m. to 11:45 p.m. Its decor evokes an upscale café in Paris, and is ringed with mirrors, pilasters, pillars, moldings, and brass lamps copied from lighting fixtures within the Grand Trianon at Versailles. Full meals are reasonably priced at 40F ($27.20) each, and might include champagne or vintage wine by the glass. Typical dishes are steak tartare, a marmite de pêcheur, fricassée of chicken flavored with vinegar and tarragon, and tagliatelle with seafood. Sumptuous desserts can be ordered from the trolley. Platters of the day rarely cost more than 20F ($13.60) each. The most opulent hotel in town is justifiably proud of this café, upon which it lavished millions of Swiss francs. After 7:30 p.m. the place becomes a high desirable piano bar (see my nightlife suggestions).

La Voile d'Or, avenue de Rhodanie, at Lausanne-Vidy (tel. 021/27-80-11). Driving into this lakeside park evokes a scene from the French Riviera. You'll need to park your car and follow the signs on foot for a few hundred feet over lawns and through conifers before arriving at the lakeside terrace of this popular restaurant. The place is especially full on summertime weekends, when almost everyone in town seemingly comes here for a beer or glass of wine. After 9 p.m. there's dancing on the terrace. The entire establishment overlooks a marina. You can choose to eat inside or else out on the terrace. A fixed-price menu costs 35F ($23.80) to 45F ($30.60). Specialties include entrecôte bordelaise, filets of perch from the lake, and wild game in season. The restaurant is closed from mid-December to the first week of March. Otherwise it's open daily from 9:30 a.m. to 1 a.m., although it doesn't serve warm food during all those hours. Meals are offered only from 11:30 a.m. to 2 p.m. and from 7 to 10 p.m.

Buffet de la Gare CFF, place de la Gare (tel. 021/20-78-01), is a vast and homey place, consisting of both a low-cost brasserie, offering set meals from 13F ($8.85), and a restaurant, where you can order a table d'hôte from 22F ($14.95), as well as more expensive à la carte selections. You're likely to see large groups of friends dining here. There are lots of seating platforms and cubbyholes at this main railway station terminal. The chefs prepare a large choice of dishes, including vol-au-vent toulousaine, filets of sole "Uncle Charles," poached turbot in a hollandaise sauce, and mignons of pork in a cream sauce. Both dining places are open daily throughout the year. The brasserie serves from 5 a.m. to 1 a.m., and the first-class restaurant is open from 6 a.m. to midnight.

Le Mandarin, 7 avenue du Théâtre (tel. 021/23-74-84), is one of the finest Chinese restaurants in Lausanne. The cookery is consistently enjoyable, using some of the best dishes from both the Peking and Cantonese kitchens. It caters admirably to the diners who pass through its doors in pursuit of such dishes as sautéed chicken with black mushrooms, beef Shanghai style, Mongolian shrimps, and sautéed fish with hot sauce. You might, among the noodle dishes, order "emperor's wedding." You can travel across China as you order: the Canton menu at 29F ($19.70), the Shanghai menu at 39F ($26.50), and the Peking gastronomic menu at 49F ($33.30). With a typical Oriental decor, the restaurant lies off Place St. François under a market arcade. It is closed Sunday but open otherwise from noon to 2 p.m. and from 7 to 10 p.m.

Café du Jorat, 1 place de l'Ours (tel. 021/20-22-61), is at a busy traffic corner in a building with a format of recipes such as "raclette à go-go." It's very much a local hangout in an obscure part of the city, but it's well known and respected locally for its regional cuisine. They offer six cheese and three meat fondues, each priced at about 15F ($10.20) per person. These include fondue vigneronne (with red meat and bouillon made from red wine); fondue aux bolets (with meat and flap mushrooms); and fondue valaisanne (made with three different cheeses). A fixed-price lunch (soup, salad, and a main course) is offered for 15F ($10.20). Otherwise, à la carte meals range from 22F ($14.95) to 45F ($30.60) per person. The café is open daily except Sunday from 11:30 a.m. to 2:30 p.m. and 6 to 11 p.m. This is the kind of honest, wholesome, and traditional place where the staff is correct, precise, and polite.

Il Grottino, 4 Grand-Chêne (tel. 021/22-76-58), is a pizzeria open every evening until 11. However, the adjacent bar, l'Escalier, stays open until midnight. Pizzas range from 9F ($6.10) to 12F ($8.15), while a wide assortment of pastas cost only a little more. No one will mind if you order only a pizza and a beer. However, if you're in the mood, and hungry enough, you can ask for a well-prepared meal of veal, fish, or beef, each dish costing from 22F ($14.95). The dessert menu includes divinely caloric ice cream as well as fruit dishes. Hours are 11:30 a.m. to 2 p.m. and 6 to 10:30 p.m. daily. The pizzeria closes at 3 p.m. on Saturday and remains closed on Sunday as well.

Manuel, 5 place St-François (tel. 021/23-17-64), in the heartbeat center, is set within an elaborate ornate building with garlands of stone fruit. To the side of the cathedral, the ground floor is blatantly modernized. It contains a pâtisserie, selling some of the most sumptuous, calorie-loaded items in Lausanne. A tiny elevator takes you to a series of rooms above street level for a fashionable tearoom decorated in a Louis XV style. A second-floor terrace and café overlooks the cobblestone square. Light meals include viande sechée des Grisons, tortellini with smoked salmon, cassolette de langoustes aux fines herbes, and filet mignon. Closed Sunday, the establishment is open from 7:30 a.m. to 7 p.m. daily; light meals cost from 30F ($20.40).

Pinte Besson, 4 rue d'Ale (tel. 021/22-72-27). This entire establishment measures only about 20 by 40 feet. Half of the place is covered by a smoke-stained vault of hand-chiseled masonry, which looks as if it hasn't been touched in two centuries (it's been around since 1780). A varied collection of locals (some rather tough critters) sit shoulder to shoulder on the benches, drinking wine. You can see into part of the tiny kitchen. Wine is sold by the glass or by the carafe. The establishment is celebrated in Lausanne for its fondues. It also serves croûtes au crouton champignons frois (fresh mushrooms) and sausages, as well as dried alpine beef, even occasionally offering horsesteak. The average meals begin at 18F ($12.25), going up. The establishment opens at 7:30 a.m. as a café and remains open for snacks and drinks until midnight. Hot meals are served daily from noon to 2 or 2:30 p.m. and 6:30 to 10:30 p.m. On Saturday, it closes at 7 p.m., and is closed all day Sunday. Sidewalk tables are placed out front in summer.

Churrasco, 51 rue de Bourg (tel. 021/23-14-23), is part of the Argentine steakhouse chain that has swept over all the major Swiss cities. The decor is South American and rustic, and waiters are dressed as "Saturday night gauchos." The people of Lausanne come here when they're in a festive mood, escaping their own traditions for a night on the pampas. Meals range from 50F ($34) up, and include the mandatory sangría, gazpacho, as well as beefsteak grilled on a wood fire (comes in both medium and large sizes). You can select rumpsteak, entrecôte, or filet. For dessert, it's the tequila sherbet, of course. The restaurant is open daily from 11:30 a.m. to 11:30 p.m.

WHAT TO SEE: The focal point of the Cité, the **Cathedral of Notre Dame,** stands 500 feet above the lake, one of the finest medieval churches in Switzerland. Begun in 1175 and consecrated in 1275, it's considered one of the most beautiful Gothic structures in Europe. When Pope Gregory X came to Lausanne to consecrate the cathedral, he also met Rudolph of Habsburg, Emperor of Germany and of the Holy Roman Empire.

The doors and façade of the cathedral are luxuriantly ornamented with sculptures and bas-reliefs. The interior is relatively austere except for some 13th-century choir stalls. The beautiful rose window is from the 13th century. The cathedral is surmounted by two towers. One you can visit for a 2F ($1.35) admission if you don't mind a climb up some 220 steps. Once there, you'll be rewarded with a view of the town, the lake, and the Alps in the distance.

Viollet-le-Duc began a restoration of the cathedral in the 19th century, and it's still going on. Hours are April 1 until the end of September from 7 a.m. to 7 p.m. (till 5:30 p.m. in winter). On Saturday the cathedral is open from 8 a.m. to 7 p.m. (till 5:30 p.m. in winter). The cathedral cannot be visited on Sunday morning because of services, but it is open in the afternoon from 2 to 7 p.m. (till 5:30 p.m. in winter).

The **Ancien-Evêché,** formerly the bishop's palace, at least until the beginning of the 15th century, has a 13th-century fortified tower at 2 Place de la Cathédrale (tel. 021/22-13-68), along with a historical and iconographic collection of Old Lausanne. The hours depend on the seasons. From October to March it is open daily from 2 to 5 p.m. (on Thursday, to 7 p.m.); closed Monday. April to June and in September it is open daily except Monday from 10 a.m. to noon and 2 to 6 p.m. (on Thursday, to 8 p.m.). In July and August, open daily except Monday from 10 a.m. to 6 p.m. (on Thursday, to 8 p.m.). Free admission.

From the cathedral, head north to the end of the Cité for a visit to the **Château St-Maire,** from 1397. Built of brick and stone, it was constructed in the 14th and early 15th centuries, and was also a residence of the powerful bishops, until they were replaced by the Bernese bailiffs, who turned Lausanne into a virtual colony. It's now used for administrative offices of the canton.

In the center of town is the **place de la Palud,** which lies to the south of the place de la Riponne. Completely restored in the late 1970s, the **Hôtel de Ville** (town hall), from the 17th century with a Renaissance façade, sits on this square. It's the headquarters of the Communal Council, and can be visited on a guided tour daily Monday to Friday on request. Phone 021/43-22-55. On the square is a Fountain of Justice from 1726. A clock with animated historical scenes acts out a drama every hour from 9 a.m. to 7 p.m. A traditional market is held in this square and along the side streets every Wednesday and Saturday.

From the square the **Escaliers du Marché,** a covered flight of medieval stairs, can be scaled if you care to visit the cathedral at this point.

The **Palais de Rumine,** on the place de la Riponne, houses several museums, along with the university and cantonal library (with some 700,000 volumes) and the university itself, which was originally founded as an academy in 1537. The palace was built in 1906 in an Italianate style.

Chief of the city's museums is the **Musée Cantonal des Beaux-Arts** (cantonal museum of fine arts), 6 place de la Riponne (tel. 021/22-83-32). This museum is largely devoted to the works of the 19th-century artists who painted in western Switzerland. But it also has an impressive collection of many famous artists of the French school, including Degas, Renoir, Bonnard, Matisse, and Utrillo. Temporary exhibitions are also staged here, usually costing from 3F ($2.05) to 5F ($3.40). It is open from 11 a.m. to 6 p.m. Tuesday and Wednesday, from 11 a.m. to 8 p.m. Thursday, and from 11 a.m. to 5 p.m. Friday, Saturday, and Sunday. Closed Monday. Other museums in this complex include the Geological Museum, the Museum of Paleontology, the Archaeological and Historical Museum, and the Zoological Museum.

On the east side of town, **Mon Repos Park** is filled with landscaped gardens and the Empire Villa where Voltaire performed *Zaïre* to an audience of friends. In the northern sector of the park stands the **Tribunal Fédéral,** constructed in the 1920s, which is today the supreme court of Switzerland.

The **Signal de Sauvabelin** (or *le signal,* as it's called), rises above the town to the north, a good 20-minute hike if you're fit. At 2,125 feet, it has a restaurant and a belvedere, opening onto Lake Geneva with the Fribourg Alps in the background.

On the northwest side of town, at 11 avenue des Bergières, the **Château de Beaulieu** (tel. 021/37-54-35) dates from 1756. In the west wing of this castle the **Musée de l'Art Brut** (museum of the maladjusted) has been installed. A fascinating, curious mélange of art, it was collected by the famous painter Jean Dubuffet, and presented to the city. All the art, both painting and sculpture, is the work of prisoners, the mentally ill, or the criminally insane. The museum is open daily from 2 to 6 p.m., except Monday, charging an admission of 5F ($3.40).

As mentioned, **Ouchy** is the lakeside resort and bustling port city for Lausanne. Its tree-shaded quays with flower gardens stretch for almost a mile, and its small harbor contains a marina with berths for about 700 craft. As you walk along, you'll see the Savoy Alps on the opposite shore.

In the Château d'Ouchy, now a hotel and restaurant, a peace treaty was signed in 1923 among the Allies, Greece, and Turkey. The 13th-century keep of the hotel is still standing. In the Hôtel d'Angleterre (formerly the Auberge de l'Ancre) there's a plaque commemorating the stay of Lord Byron, who wrote *The Prisoner of Chillon* there. In the Beau-Rivage, the Treaty of Lausanne was ratified in 1932, at the end of the conference to settle the final reparations disputes growing out of World War I.

At **Pully,** a Roman villa, the first vestiges of which were discovered in 1921, has been restored and opened to the public. It boasts a double apse and a fresco of 215 square feet, which is the most important first-century mural north of the Alps.

This **Pully Roman Villa Museum** is at place du Prieuré (tel. 021/28-33-04). It shows a reconstruction of the ruins and a display of objects found on the site of the excavations. Admission free, it's open from the end of October until April 1 on Saturday and Sunday from 2 to 5 p.m. However, during the rest of the year it can be visited daily (except Monday) from 2 to 5 p.m.

A short distance north of Lausanne, you can visit the elegantly furnished **Château of Lucens** (tel. 021/906-80-32), on a hill fortified by the bishops of Lausanne in the Middle Ages to protect their town of Moudon and maintain a barrier across the valley of the little Broye River. The fortress has undergone trouble and change since it was established—destroyed in 1127, rebuilt, burned in 1190, enlarged to be the summer palace of the bishops, occupied by the Bernese, made the seat of the bailiffs of Moudon, finally becoming the property of the canton of Vaud which sold it to a private owner in 1801. By the end of the 19th century it was a boys' college and had undergone vast changes. New work begun in 1921 has restored the château to its original appearance.

The present owner, Galerie Koller, an important European auction house, has decorated it with paintings, furniture, clocks, and objets d'art that are, of course, for sale. Of special interest, but with no particular link to the château that I could discover, is an old Sherlock Holmes museum in one of the vaulted cellars, billed as an exact replica of the sitting room of the famous detective. Perhaps Holmes came here on a search for Moriarty!

The château is open from 10 a.m. to 6 p.m. daily except Monday and Tuesday from mid-June to mid-September. Off-season hours are from 10 a.m. to 5 p.m. Saturday and Sunday. Admission is 5.50F ($3.75) for adults, 3.30F ($2.25) for children 6 to 16.

AN ORGANIZED TOUR: The best way to get acquainted with the city is to take the **Lausanne City Tour,** with a drive through surrounding vineyards. You'll get an overall picture and will go through the old town and later to the wine district. The tour costs 18F ($12.25) for adults and 9F ($6.10) for children. The city tour departs at 10 a.m. daily except Sunday in front of the tourist office at 2 avenue de Rhodanie (tel. 021/27-73-21). It lasts two hours. It's recommended that visitors telephone the tourist office for a reservation. All the major hotels, however, sell tickets for this tour, as does the city tourist office in the main train station in the heart of Lausanne.

A WALKING TOUR: The shopping and business center of Lausanne, the Place Saint-François, is a good place to begin a short walk through the heart of the Cité. Named for the church of Saint-François, the 13th-century house of worship of the Franciscan Friary built at that time and the only friary building still standing, the church is a sort of demarcation point. Road traffic has been assigned to the south of the church and the north side transformed into a pedestrian precinct. Here, north of Saint-François, are more than 1¼ miles of streets where only pedestrian traffic is allowed.

Just north of the church of Saint-François, turn right onto rue de Bourg, which is a typical Lausanne shopping street, worth strolling along if only to windowshop. At the end of rue de Bourg, with the little rue de la Paix on right, turn left onto the big, bustling rue Caroline. This will lead shortly to a left turn to cross over Pont Bessières, one of the three bridges that were built in the late 19th–early 20th century to connect the three hills on which Lausanne was built. Even before you get across the bridge, you will see on your right the Cité (old town), with the 13th-century Cathedral of Notre Dame.

This is a good chance to visit the Ancien-Evêché, once the bishop's palace, and the Cathedral Museum, previewed above. Walk around the cathedral square from which you get a good overview of the town. There are several little narrow streets rambling around the area, inviting you to take a look. Pick one you want to follow to the north, and at the end of it, just a couple of blocks, you'll come to the Château Saint-Maire, a 14th-century structure once lived in by bishops and now housing the offices of canton administration.

From here, head back southward. I suggest following avenue de l'Université, which will bring you to the place de la Riponne, with the Palais de Rumine on its east side. Stroll down rue Madeleine, jog left, and you come to the place de la Palud. If you prefer, when you leave place de la Riponne, follow rue Pierre Viret, which will bring you to the escaliers du Marché, a covered stairway dating back to the Middle Ages. On the side of place de la Palud stands the 17th-century Hôtel de Ville (town hall).

Going south out of the place de la Palud is rue du Pont, which soon becomes Saint-François (after crossing the rue Centrale), and you're back to the point where you started this walk. From this general area, at place du Flon, you can take the Underground (subway) to Ouchy.

SHOPPING: Lausanne is an interesting shopping adventure. Many first-class stores are found along rue St-François and rue de Bourg. In the center of town, several squares and shopping streets are for pedestrians only. Best busy are watches and jewelry, clothes, leather goods, cigarettes, and the traditional Swiss souvenirs and chocolates.

Pharmacie Bullet, 30 rue de Bourg (tel. 021/22-86-82), is a centrally located pharmacy which is happy to suggest over-the-counter Swiss substitutes for American medications.

Pavillon Christofle, 10 rue de Bourg (tel. 021/20-60-50), is the major outlet of Christofle crystal in the Lausanne region. A showroom of glass shelves is loaded with glittering objects. It is open Monday to Saturday but is closed on Monday morning.

Tabacs-Cigares Besson, 22 rue de Bourg (tel. 021/22-67-88), is one of the leading tobacco shops of Lausanne. The owner has a special climate-controlled room for the storage of his best cigars, many of which come from Cuba. Other merchandise includes Davidoff cigars, meerschaum pipes, and all sorts of tobacco. The staff will mail certain goods back to North America for a small fee.

La Vieille Fontaine Antiquités, 9-13 rue Cheneau-de-Bourg (tel. 021/23-47-87), sells French 18th-century furniture and works of art, Oriental sculpture, and Chinese and Japanese artwork in a building with beautifully hand-painted beams and Oriental rugs. The showrooms are crowded, so be very careful as you walk between these treasures.

Magasin Cardas, 10 rue de Bourg (tel. 021/312-55-60), is an unusual store with a physical plant of skylights and crosscut tree trunks set into a white gravel floor. The establishment sells goods from 15 countries, many of them Oriental, which include ceramics, sculpture, and textiles. Before or after inspecting this shop you might stop for a coffee in the courtyard in front. There a café, La Cour (10 rue de Bourg), has set up three of four outdoor tables beside a modern fountain.

Leinenweberei Langenthal, 8 rue de Bourg (tel. 021/23-44-02), is directed by Mme Lutz, who, along with her staff, sells Swiss embroideries, Langenthal table linens, napkins, and crocheted potholders, as well as satin sheets. The store also sells lace from St. Gallen.

Bucherer, 5 place Saint-François (tel. 021/20-63-54), is the biggest jeweler in Lausanne, with a well-established international reputation.

The best place for men's fashion in Lausanne is **Nelson Boutique,** Galerie Saint-François (tel. 021/22-21-24). It has both stylish clothes for men as well as conservative fashion, along with shoes, luggage, suits, and sportswear.

Koba Cuir, 12 rue de la Madeleine (tel. 021/23-89-80), is considered one of the finest leather specialists in Lausanne. They sell leather goods from France, Germany, Spain, and Switzerland. Leather is fashioned into a selection of shoes, pants, vests, coats, trinkets, and hats.

Payot, 4 place Pepinet (tel. 021/20-33-31), is considered one of the biggest —some say the best—book store in Lausanne. They sell many English language titles.

SPORTS: As the seat of the International Olympic Committee, Lausanne has many first-rate sports facilities, and the lake itself offers not only swimming, but rowing, yachting, waterskiing, and windsurfing. You can also play tennis or golf, ride a bike, go horseback riding, or hiking.

Even in summer you can ski on the glacier of Les Diablerets (9,840 feet), 38 miles from Lausanne. In winter, five covered curling rinks are active, along with two ice-skating rinks.

The Swiss Ski School of Lausanne, with **skiing** at Chalet-a-Gobet above Lausanne, has a floodlit ski track operating daily until 10 p.m. with marked courses for cross-country skiing. There is a small ski lift for children open Wednesday afternoon, Saturday, and Sunday. For inquiries about lessons, in either alpine or cross-country skiing, call 021/26-55-65. The Service des Sports of the commune of Lausanne can be reached by phoning 021/43-42-91.

Winter skating: The Montchoisi open-air skating rink, 30 avenue du Servan (tel. 021/26-10-62), and La Pontaise open-air rink, 11 Plaines-du-Loup (tel. 021/36-81-63), are both open from October to March. Intercommunal Ice-Skating Centre at Malley, 14 Chemin du Viaduc (tel. 021/24-21-22), with one indoor and two open-air rinks, is open from October to mid-March.

Winter curling: Ouchy Curling Link, La Nautique building, at Ouchy (tel.

021/27-60-31), has five playing areas active from mid-September until the end of March.

From spring on, **golf** is played at En Marin (tel. 021/91-63-16), which has an 18-hole course above Lausanne. The course, open April to November, is at an altitude of 2,800 feet.

Swimming year round: Both indoor and outdoor pools are operated. **Mon Repos** indoor pool, 4 avenue du Tribunal-Fédéral (tel. 021/23-45-66), is closed from June to September, but there's access to the lawn solarium. **Bellerive Beach and Pool,** 23 avenue de Rhodanie (tel. 021/27-81-31), is open May to September, as is the **Montchoisi** pool, 30 avenue du Servan (tel. 021/26-10-62). There's a public beach at Vidy, **La Voile d'Or Beach** (tel. 021/27-80-11), to which admission is free.

Waterskiing: There's a stretch of water at the Ouchy promenade (near the Tour Haldimand) that attracts skiers in fair weather (tel. 021/22-00-88 for information).

Horseback riding: This sport is possible at the Chalet-à-Globet Equestrian Centre (tel. 021/91-64-34), which has a jumping paddock among other facilities.

Tennis: This can be played at number of places. The **Lausanne Tennis Association** has six hard-cover indoor and 19 outdoor courts at Vidy at the Clubhouse Stade-Lausanne (tel. 021/691-99-91). **Montchoisi Tennis Club,** 15 avenue de l'Elysee (tel. 021/26-36-25), offers six hard courts and two in "greenset" synthetic surface, in operation from the first of April to mid-November.

LAUSANNE AFTER DARK: Lausanne ranks with Geneva as the focal point of intellectual life in French-speaking Switzerland. This is reflected in a rich cultural tradition. The city's cultural life is a four-season affair. Orchestras, famous soloists, theater, and ballet troupes from all over the world perform here. The tourist board will be helpful in giving you information on what's currently available.

In the spring an international festival brings together the world's musical elite in dance and opera; and in late June during the city festival and the Fête of Lausanne, the streets are jam-packed and alive with modern troubadours who entertain free.

One of the most prestigious places for concerts, operas, and ballet is the **Beaulieu Théâtre,** 10 avenue des Bergières (tel. 021/45-11-11).

The **Théâtre Municipal de Lausanne,** 12 avenue du Théâtre (tel. 021/22-64-33), has a distinguished program of opera, ballets, and concerts as part of its annual repertoire.

If you speak French, the **Les Faux-Nez** theater, 5 rue de Bourg (tel. 021/22-31-73), is a boîte de chansons, with an occasional daring production.

If you want your action a little "hotter," try one of the following establishments.

The Dancing-Bar at the **Château d'Ouchy,** place du Port, at Ouchy (tel. 021/26-74-51), is in one of the inner rooms of this famous hotel (see my hotel recommendations). You'll be able to see the lake from the stone-rimmed windows here, with a view of the people in the café below. The large wood-paneled room has an arched ceiling with festive red and blue lights. Someone has painted wall murals of the masked courtiers of Mozart's day. The establishment draws an older crowd who like to come here to drink and dance to the music. The place opens at 9:30 p.m. nightly, and drinks average 14F ($9.50) to 20F ($13.60). Closed Monday.

The opulent **Café Beau-Rivage,** Beau-Rivage Palace, 18 place du Général Guisan, Ouchy (tel. 021/26-38-31), was previously recommended as a place to dine. But it also offers live music from a piano bar, beginning nightly at

7:30. You'll pay from 12F ($8.15) for a glass of champagne or about 4F ($2.70) for a beer.

Bar du Relais, Lausanne Palace, 7-9 rue du Grand Chêne (tel. 021/20-37-11), is one of the most fashionable bars in Lausanne, rivaling that of Le Beau Rivage Palace. Open from 11:30 a.m. to 1 p.m. daily, it is luxurious in appointment, evoking certain grand bars in London hotels. If you want to be both discreet and refined while enjoying ultimate comfort, then Bar du Relais might be ideal for a rendezvous. Whiskies cost from 12F ($8.15). The large square room is lined with red velvet and some neo-Impressionistic paintings.

Birdwatcher's Club, Continental Hotel, 2 place de la Gare (tel. 021/20-15-51), is the top disco dancing spot in town. Across from the railway station, it is open daily except Monday from 9:30 p.m. to 4 a.m. When a band isn't performing, the intervals are filled with recorded disco music. Most clients, however, come to listen to the jazz groups, which are imported from as far away as America. Within a modern decor, you'll pay around 18F ($12.25) for a beer.

La Cravache, 7 rue du Grand Chêne (tel. 021/22-88-10), next to the Lausanne Palace, is one of the most reliable and most inviting drinking spots in town. It is set behind a wall of small paned bull's eye glass. Lausanne yuppies mingle with the pillars of the community, and an occasional politician strolls in, or perhaps a stripper from a club nearby. It's all very cosmopolitan. Drinks cost from 12F ($8.15). The place opens at 7 a.m. (yes, that's right) daily except Saturday when its doors fly open at 5 p.m. Closing time is 8 p.m. on Monday, 1 a.m. on Tuesday, Wednesday, and Thursday, and 2 a.m. on Friday and Saturday. Closed Sunday.

Le Paddock, Hotel Victoria, 46 avenue de la Gare (tel. 021/20-57-75), is a popular disco set in a framework of mirrors. An accessible DJ most often plays what you want. The management collects a 5F ($3.40) cover charge Friday and Saturday, and drinks begin at 13F ($8.85). The club is open daily except Monday from 9:30 p.m. to 4 a.m.

2. FROM LAUSANNE TO NYON

This trip, heading west from Lausanne along the northern arch of Lac Léman, is a distance of less than 30 miles, but there's much to see along the way. You can do it in two hours, but you'll enjoy it more if you allow at least half a day.

West from Lausanne, I suggest that you detour to St. Sulpice, four miles away.

ST. SULPICE: This exclusive suburb of summer homes is usually visited by those wishing to see its 12th-century Romanesque convent church. Within sight of the Savoy Alpine range and Lac Léman, the church retains its original transept and chancel. It's crowned by a cross on a rectangular tower. The interior is rather austere.

Food and Lodging

Hostellerie du Débarcadère, CH-1025 St. Sulpice, Switzerland (tel. 021/691-57-47), is one of the most charming places to stay along the lake, but it seems little known except by some discriminating visitors from Lausanne and Geneva, who regard it as their secret hideaway. Standing along the roadside, it evokes a visit to a private home more than a hotel. Tony and Caroline Kluvers-Jaeger are considerate hosts, and they receive visitors all year except in January when it's too cold and they need a rest. Each accommodation has an attractive individualized decor and many thoughtful amenities. Each unit is also blessed with a private bath. Daily rates in a single are 125F ($85) to 165F ($112.20), going up to 170F ($115.60) to 260F ($176.80) in a double.

The food, served in a stylized regional room with hanging draperies and a beamed ceiling, is one of the reasons for staying here. The cuisine is wisely based on the season. Service is thoughtful and efficient, but it doesn't intrude, and the cookery is excellent in the truest continental sense. In the cooler months you can enjoy a cozy bar, in summer you can head for the terrace with a fountain and garden furniture much like that you left at home. Guests can also dine outside under a canopy. The hotel is easy to spot, right near the 12th-century Romanesque church.

Back on the road again, the next stop is in—

MORGES: With the Savoy Alps as a backdrop, Morges is a small town that's a significant headquarters for vineyards in the area. Right on the shore of the lake, the port was built on a prehistoric site inhabited by lake-dwellers. A chic international yachting set gathers here.

The **Vaud Military Museum** (tel. 021/801-26-16) has been installed in the Castle of Morges, a Savoyan stronghold that was once a moated castle built by Duke Amadeus of Savoy in 1286. He wanted an imposing bastion to protect himself against the bishopric of Lausanne. It became the residence of a Bernese bailiff from 1536 to 1798, eventually passing to the canton of Vaud which used it as an arsenal. Weapons and uniforms on display go back to the end of the 18th century and forward to modern times. It's open from the end of January until mid-December, Monday to Friday from 10 a.m. to noon and 1:30 to 5 p.m., Saturday, Sunday, weekends and holidays from 1:30 to 5 p.m. only, charging an admission of 2.50F ($1.70).

Much more interesting than the military museum is the **Alexis Forel Museum,** a museum of dolls and toys, in an old patrician house that once belonged to the engraver, at 54 Grand'Rue (tel. 021/801-26-47). Visiting hours are daily except Monday from 2 to 5 p.m. Admission costs 4F ($2.70) for adults, free for children. An important collection of dolls and toys, explaining their history and illustrating the different types, is exhibited.

On the last weekend in September, a riotous wine festival is staged here annually.

Where to Dine

Fleur du Lac, 70 route de Lausanne (tel. 021/802-43-11), is housed in a pretty building on the quays at the edge of the lake, some seven miles from Lausanne. Many residents of the bigger city make weekend excursions here to taste the unusual food prepared by one of the area's most respected kitchens, famous for Lake Geneva perch and imported seafood. Among other specialties, with a cuisine moderne touch, are baby Dover sole filets with lime sauce and an assortment of fresh dishes on the seasonally adjusted menu, depending on what's available at the market. Fixed-price meals range from 40F ($27.20) to 88F ($59.85), while à la carte dinners cost from 56F ($38.10) up. More than 150 domestic and foreign wines are listed. On warm days, you'll enjoy the outdoor terrace with a view of the greenery around the lake. The restaurant is open daily from noon to 11 p.m. The smaller "bistro" offers delicious specialties of the day at 16F ($10.90).

Continuing west for eight miles will lead to—

ROLLE: This is the center of a wine-growing district between Morges and Coppet known as La Côte. Light white wines are grown here, and apparently the yield is small because nearly all of the vintage is consumed locally.

Rolle's main street is flanked by old burghers' homes and some vintners' houses. The 13th-century castle with four towers, originally constructed by a prince of Savoy, was owned at one time by Jean Baptiste Tavernier (1605–1689), the French traveler who was a pioneer of trade with India. His narratives on world travel have earned him a place in history.

From Rolle, you can head up in the hills to **Aubonne,** passing many little wine-growing villages such as Féchy. Aubonne is a 16th-century village where not much ever happens, and if you're as lucky as I was, you can sometimes purchase bottles of the local wine from a vintner.

Food and Lodging

Hôtel Rives Rolle, 42 route de Lausanne, CH-1180 Rolle, Switzerland (tel. 021/825-34-91). On a sloping hillside about a mile from the center of town, this modern and angular building contains the best rooms and the most sophisticated dining and nightlife options in the region. Erected in 1982, it offers 32 stylishly spartan rooms with warm earth tones and black accents. The units facing the lake contain TV, radios, mini-bars, phones, and balconies. Depending on the view and the season, singles range from 90F ($61.20) to 170F ($115.60) daily, and doubles cost 150F ($102) to 270F ($185.60), with breakfast, service, and taxes included.

As you register, you'll catch a glimpse of the glassed-in swimming pool. There's a chic "day bar" outfitted in shades of blue and black, also with a view of the pool, and a stylish modern restaurant, Le Magellan. A la carte meals begin at 55F ($37.40), but you can eat at lunch for 25F ($17) if you select from the list of daily specials. Full meals are served from noon to 2 p.m. and 7 to 10 p.m. every day. Specialties include rabbit terrine with crisp vegetables, lobster ravioli with vegetable pearls, and filet of lamb gros sel.

There's a health club on the premises and a bar immediately beneath the swimming pool whose watery illumination comes from circular portholes set into its ceiling. Known as the Barbe Rousse Piano Bar, it has live music from a piano, champagne cocktails for 16F ($10.90), and a small and sedate dance floor. It's open nightly except Sunday from 9:30 to 2 a.m.

Hôtel la Tête Noire, 94 Grand-Rue, CH-1180 Rolle, Switzerland (tel. 021/825-22-51). Set on the main street of town, behind a wrought-iron bracket holding a silhouette of a Moor, it was originally erected as an inn in 1628. To reach the 15 bedrooms, you climb an impressive staircase, illuminated by a skylight. The quieter rooms in back don't benefit from a lake view. The best lake view rooms are high on the third floor, opening onto balconies. The hotel charges 50F ($34) to 70F ($47.60) daily in a single, 80F ($54.40) to 110F ($74.80) in a double, with breakfast included. Each room has a private bath, phone, and radio.

The hotel has a charmingly old-fashioned restaurant, but don't confuse it with a simple working class café at the opposite end of the lobby. Beneath heavy ceiling beams, you can enjoy full meals at 40F ($27.20). Served daily from 11:30 a.m. to 2 p.m. and 6:30 to 9:45 p.m., they might include lobster bisque with cognac, foie gras from Strasbourg, provençale-style frogs' legs, two varieties of meat fondue, three different preparations of veal, and tournedos with sweetbreads on a slate, followed by lemon sorbet with vodka.

Across the street from the hotel, within a timber-filled 17th-century building which once served as a stable for both horses and carriages, is a nightclub owned and managed by the hotel. Called the **Club la Debridée,** 94 Grand-Rue (tel. 021/825-25-75), it's one of the most popular nightspots in the region, especially for the under-25 crowd. Open daily all year from 8 p.m. to 2 a.m., it charges a weekend cover of 10F ($6.80). Scotch and soda costs 10F ($6.80). Closed Monday.

NYON: This summer resort along Lac Léman has the by-now-familiar flower-bedecked quays where the little lakeside steamers arrive, letting off passengers and picking up new ones. Julius Caesar established a Roman station here for his soldiers, who left behind many artifacts. From 1781 to 1813 Nyon became known for its porcelain.

The **Castle of Nyon,** Place du Château (tel. 022/61-38-81), is an impressive stronghold dating from the 13th century, built by the Counts of Savoy. It was completely transformed in the 16th and 18th centuries. Today it houses the

Historical and Porcelain Museum, which can be visited daily from 9 to 11 a.m. and 2 to 6 p.m. It's closed from November to March. On the first floor, you'll see porcelain made in Nyon's heyday. The second floor, where the district court and town council meet, is closed to the public. From the belvedere there's a great view of the lake and the Alps, with Mont Blanc looming in the background.

The **Lake of Geneva Museum,** 8 Quai Louis-Bonnard (tel. 022/61-09-49), is the only museum devoted solely to the lake. It contains exhibits on pleasure boating, sailing, scenes of Lake Geneva, and an aquarium. It can be visited daily from 9 to 11 a.m. and 2 to 6 p.m. from March to November. From November to March, it is open only from 2 to 5 p.m. daily except Monday.

The **Roman Basilica and Museum,** rue Maupertuis (tel. 022/61-75-91), displays antiquities from the Roman colony in Nyon, including architecture, statuary, inscriptions, mosaics, crafts, amphorae, pottery, glasswork, and coins. The basilica was a public building for justice and commerce, standing at one end of the Forum of the Roman colony (Colonia Julia Equestris). It is open daily from 9 to 11 a.m. and 2 to 6 p.m. from March to November and only from 2 to 5 p.m. daily except Monday from November to March.

A ticket for 5F ($3.40) entitles you to visit all three museums.

Food and Lodging

Hôtel Beau-Rivage, 49 rue de Rive, CH-1260 Nyon, Switzerland (tel. 022/61-32-31), is a cozily old-fashioned hotel, sitting right on the quays of the old town. Its wrought-iron balconies are usually covered with flowers, have one of the best lakeside views in Nyon. A summertime ambience fills the public rooms because of their aquamarine window blinds and the placement of modern paintings in bright colors in prominent places. Each of the accommodations has color TV, radio, mini-bar, and direct-dial phone. Singles rent for 100F ($68) to 150F ($102) daily, while doubles cost from 135F ($91.80) to 200F ($136), including breakfast. Private parking is available for another 10F ($6.80) per day.

Hôtel du Clos de Sadex, CH-1260 Nyon, Switzerland (tel. 022/61-28-31), is a dignified establishment with gables and a tile roof in its own park on the shores of the lake, about one-half mile from the center of Nyon. The hotel has an elaborately crafted staircase, parquet floors, and 19th-century antiques, some of which were part of the original furnishings of this former private residence. The hotel rents 18 bedrooms, the majority of which contain private bath. The de Tscharner family, the owners, charge from 65F ($44.20) to 160F ($108.80) daily in a single and from 110F ($74.80) to 230F ($156.40) in a double, according to the season and the view. Half board is offered for an additional 40F ($27.20) per person daily.

Your best choice for dining in the area is **Le Léman,** 28 rue de Rive (tel. 022/61-22-41), beside the lake, a seafood restaurant, looking out over a jetty where the very boat that caught that day's specialty might be moored. Julio and Françoise de Ancos, the charming Spanish and Swiss owners, greet guests in their comfortable dining room, whose walls are used as a backdrop for paintings by local artists. These exhibits are changed from time to time. Specialties of the house are foie gras either in a terrine or in sautéed slices, a small but succulent portion of filet of perch served as an appetizer, lobster ragoût with endive, cream of lobster soup with herbettes (baby herbs), sweetbreads roasted with exotic mushrooms, roast guinea fowl with lentils, roast pigeon from the Haut-Anjou (High Anjou region of France), and filet mignon of lamb. Fixed-price lunches cost 32F ($21.75). Set dinners go for 56F ($38.08) and 76F ($51.70). If you prefer to dine à la carte, expect to pay 70F ($47.60) to 90F ($61.20) for a complete dinner. This is a popular place, so reservations are important. Hours are from noon to 2 p.m. and 7 to 10 p.m. daily except Sunday night and all day Monday.

Hostellerie du XVIe Siècle, place du Marché, CH-1260 Nyon, Switzerland (tel. 022/61-24-41), contains an elegant Rôtisserie with walls of exposed stone. Here, Louis XIII–style furnishings embellish a historic villa from the 16th century, built on ancient Roman foundations. Marc and Suzanna Chatelus, along with William Basset, offer a fine cuisine here. You can enjoy very fresh produce or perhaps fish from Lake Geneva. A la carte meals in the Rôtisserie cost from 17F ($11.55) to 110F ($74.80), depending on what you order. However, inexpensively priced platters of food are served for just 12F ($8.16). The restaurant is open daily from 10 a.m. to 2 p.m. and 5 p.m. to 1 a.m. The hostellerie also has a piano and cocktail bar, offering live entertainment. The owners rent 14 pleasantly furnished bedrooms, each with shower, toilet, and phone. The cost ranges from 60F ($40.80) to 80F ($54.40) daily in a single, rising to 75F ($51) to 105F ($71.40) in a double, including service and tax.

3. THE LAVAUX CORNICHE

Back in Lausanne, we now strike out for an eastward trek along the lake, in a section of hillsides and vineyards known as the "Lavaux Corniche," or Corniche Vaudoise. The first stopover, Pully, with its Roman remains, was already previewed in the section on Lausanne.

Our final goals will be world-famed Vevey, at a distance of 17 miles, and Montreux. Personally I find this section one of the loveliest in the country, and I'm not alone in that judgment. All along the way, you'll have views of the towering peaks looming at the upper end of Lake Geneva.

You'll pass the vintner's village of **Corsier,** with its 12th-century church and Romanesque tower. Charlie Chaplin, who died in 1977, is buried here.

CHEXBRES: The road to **Cully,** some five miles east of Lausanne, will give you a fine view of Lac Léman as it takes you to the heart of the wine-growing region of Lavaux which covers the mountain slopes on the northeastern side of Geneva's lake. Cully offers swimming, fishing, and boating in the little bay on which it lies and in the lake.

If you have time, I recommend that you turn right on the Corniche (the cliff road) which will take you through thriving vineyards to the little summer resort of **Chexbres.** The drive alone is worth this short detour, as it offers stunning views. Chexbres, positioned on the Corniche, has been called "the balcony of the lake." From here, you can enjoy a stroll through the nearby vineyards and forests and perhaps a stop at one of the wine cellars to taste the product of the grapevines you've passed by.

Continue along the road to **Dézaley,** which produces a light white wine favored by the Genevese.

Food and Lodging

Hôtel du Signal, Puidoux Gare, CH-1604 Chexbres, Switzerland (tel. 021/946-25-25), is set in 60 acres of parkland, much of it heavily forested and leading down to the lake. The four-star hotel is a château-like building with modern additions, including a structure for the 30-yard indoor swimming pool and a tennis court. The contemporary furniture in the public rooms is sometimes complemented with an Oriental rug or a grouping of Victorian furniture. Wide glass windows give panoramic views over Lake Léman and the gently rolling hills of the Vaud. Accommodations at this four-star hotel, run by the Gunten family, are wide ranging in size and amenities, but for the most part offer streamlined comfort. Singles rent for 68F ($46.24) to 120F ($81.60) daily, while doubles cost 126F ($85.70) to 180F ($122.40), and deluxe doubles for 190F ($129.20) to 220F ($149.60). A French restaurant and a terrace serve good food for 29F ($19.05) and up for a meal.

Hôtel Cécil, CH-1605 Chexbres, Switzerland (tel. 021/946-12-92), is a modern chalet hotel with an elaborate series of decorative stone posts and lintels that separate its gardens from the street. On the conifer-dotted lawns is a swimming pool. Bernard Cachin, the owner, charges from 45F ($30.60) to 80F ($54.40) daily in a single and 80F ($54.40) to 120F ($81.60) in a double, depending on the season and the plumbing. Rooms are pleasant and comfortable.

The best dining in the area is found at **Auberge du Raisin,** 1 place de l'Hotel de Ville (tel. 021/799-21-31), at Cully, halfway between Montreux and Lausanne. This very old house with a warmly rustic decor is an attractive stopping off point if you're going from one city to the other. The chef is a devotee of cuisine moderne with many Swiss overtones. At a location near the town hall, this is a romantic auberge de campagne. It offers such dishes as medallions of veal in citrus sauce, salmon with fresh chives, and crayfish or turbot in a tarragon sauce. Dinners cost 75F ($51) and up. Giacomo Bustodero, who has been the maître d' for a quarter of a century, sees that you get personalized service any time from noon to 2 p.m. and 7 to 9:30 p.m. Closed all day Sunday and at lunchtime Monday.

4. VEVEY

The home of Nestlé chocolate, the resort of Vevey has been popular with English visitors since the 19th century.

About every 25 years Vevey stages the riotous **Fêtes des Vignerons,** a winegrowers' carnival in honor of Bacchus, the god of wine. The last celebration was in 1977, and perhaps you'll be around for the next one if you missed it.

Vevey lies at the foot of Mt. Pèlerin, to which an excursion can be made. The town, dating from Roman times, was built at the mouth of the Veveyse River, and is the center of the Lavaux vineyards. In the Middle Ages it was known as an important trading post on the route from Piedmont in Italy to Burgundy in France. As such, it has long been accustomed to receiving and entertaining visitors.

You might begin your exploration on the **Grand-Place,** a mammoth market plaza fronting Lac Léman. The corn exchange on the north dates from the early 19th century. Jean-Jacques Rousseau lodged at the Auberge de la Clef in 1730, in the vicinity of the Théâtre. As you walk in this area and along the quay you'll have views of the Savoy Alps.

Vevey's antique curiosity is the **Church of St. Martin,** dating from the 12th century and standing on a belvedere overlooking the resort. A large rectangular tower with a quartet of turrets characterizes the church, from which there's a good view of Vevey.

The **Jenisch Museum** is an art gallery with some fine works by Courbet, plus some local modern Swiss painters. It's open daily from the first of May until the end of October from 10 a.m. to noon and 2 to 4 p.m. (to 5 p.m. on Monday). Otherwise it's open Tuesday to Saturday from 2 to 4 p.m. and on Sunday and holidays from 11 a.m. to noon and 2 to 4 p.m.; closed Monday.

Musée du Vieux-Vevey, 43 rue d'Italie (tel. 021/921-07-22), is a château with two museums: Musée Historique du Vieux-Vevey and Musée de la Confrérie des Vignerons. They are both open from Monday to Saturday from 10 a.m. to noon and 2 to 5 p.m. (on Sunday from 11 a.m. to noon and 2 to 5 p.m.). If you missed the Bacchus festival, you'll see many of the costumes displayed here. In addition, the museums exhibit 18th-century antiques and mementos of the vintners. Exhibits include a big collection of wrought-iron work, as well as arms, pewter, and tools, and paintings and other works by local artists. Displays recovered by archaeological digs in the area are also exhibited. In all, it is a rich evocation of the Vevey region.

The most important excursion in the area is to **Mt. Pèlerin,** a distance of slightly more than 15 miles. As you ascend, you'll have a panoramic sweep of

Lake Geneva, the Savoy Alps, and the valley of the Rhône. You can drive via Corsier or go by funicular via Corseaux.

WHERE TO STAY: Considered the leading hotel at Vevey, **Hôtel Les Trois Couronnes,** 49 rue d'Italie, CH-1800 Vevey, Switzerland (tel. 021/921-30-05), has a desirable location in the center of town, in a nobly detailed building of white stucco and gray stone at the edge of the lake. It is famous for being the setting for Henry James's first important work, the novella *Daisy Miller.* The Bogdanovich film was also made here. The interior lobby has an elegant gallery where visitors can peer over white balustrades to the carpeted lobby three floors below. The redecorated bedrooms still retain much of their 19th-century allure, including some attractive antiques in the more expensive rooms. Singles rent for 135F ($91.80) to 250F ($170) daily, while doubles range from 250F ($170) to 350F ($238), the latter for suite accommodations. All tariffs include breakfast. Half board is available for another 45F ($30.60) per person daily.

Hôtel du Lac, rue d'Italie, CH-1800 Vevey, Switzerland (tel. 021/921-10-41), has for years and years enthralled visitors with its lakeside view. A favorite hotel, especially with the visiting English, it has a swimming pool on its grounds and a gardenside terrace. It's affiliated with Les Trois Couronnes, but is cheaper. The English-speaking director, Monsieur Ehrensperger, has a competent staff, and the hotel is run efficiently. Many guests prefer a resort holiday here instead of going on to nearby Montreux. Rooms are pleasantly furnished and most comfortable (some, of course, are far superior to others). Singles cost 120F ($81.60) to 170F ($115.60) daily, the latter price if you have *that* view from your bedroom window. Doubles range from 170F ($115.60) to 255F ($173.40), with half board costing another 35F ($23.80) per person daily. All rooms have baths. In addition to the rooms with a lake view, the season also affects the price.

Hôtel Touring et Gare, place de la Gare, CH-1800 Vevey, Switzerland (tel. 021/921-06-47), is an old-fashioned resort hotel with red shutters, a mansard roof, semi-baroque gables, and a popular restaurant under an awning on the ground floor. The 30 bedrooms range from 40F ($27.20) to 70F ($47.60) daily in a single and from 70F ($47.60) to 120F ($81.60) in a double, depending on the season and the plumbing. The rooms are slightly dated, but reasonably comfortable. Half board goes for another 20F ($13.60) per person daily.

Hôtel de Famille, 20 rue des Communaux, CH-1800 Vevey, Switzerland (tel. 021/921-39-31), is in the very center of commercial Vevey on a busy street near the railway station. A large 19th-century building in the old resort style, the interior has been remodeled into a modern format. If you don't seek historical authenticity in decor, you'll find this a clean and comfortable hotel. Singles cost 52F ($35.35) to 65F ($44.20) per day, with doubles going for 46F ($31.30) to 65F ($44.20) per person, including a buffet breakfast. Children who stay in their parents' room receive discounts of 50% if they're under 6, 30% for ages 6 to 12. La Veranda is a snack/tea room where meals are served from 11 a.m. to 9:30 p.m. A small indoor swimming pool and a rooftop terrace with chaise longues and card tables are additional benefits.

WHERE TO DINE: The best dining spot in Vevey is **Café Restaurant du Raisin,** 3 place du Marché (tel. 021/921-10-28). Since it was purchased by a talented team of wine and food experts from France, it has garnered a gratifying number of culinary awards. It stands a few paces from the sprawling open-air market where, twice a week, farmers from throughout the region come to sell their produce. This establishment contains two floors of well-appointed comfort. On the street level is a cozy brasserie serving full meals costing from 35F ($23.80).

Upstairs the modern and stylish decor is a reflection of the cuisine prepared by Philippe Corsaletti and served by his wife, Catherine. Wine is dispensed by partner Martin Mayoly from an impressive caveau. Full meals cost from 70F ($47.60) and might include a salad of sweetbreads with an essence of eggplant, gratin of curried lobster with baby vegetables and homemade pasta, and roast monkfish with rosemary. You might also try roast lamb with olives and artichokes. Dessert might be a collection of three types of chocolate mousse served with mint sauce. A menu dégustation costs 85F ($57.80) per person. Meals are served on both levels of the restaurant daily except Sunday evening and all day Monday from noon to 2 p.m. and 7 to 9:30 p.m.

Taverne du Château, 43 rue d'Italie (tel. 021/921-12-10). This generously proportioned stucco building probably had a commercial use when it was constructed near the lake in 1681. Because of its hip roof and its size it looks almost like a grange, and even has a large carved beam extending from above one of the top-floor windows, presumably for pulleying supplies upstairs. You'll identify the place by the wrought-iron and gilt sign above the pavement, representing two men and a horse fighting with one another. The owner prepares such menu items as filet of beef in a morel sauce, roebuck with pears and red wine, and smoked salmon. Dessert might be a lemon soufflé. Specialties vary with the seasons, so the items listed might not be available when you visit, but there'll be others of similar taste value. Fixed-price meals cost 52F ($35.35) and 68F ($46.25), with full à la carte menus going for about 80F ($54.40) to 85F ($57.80). Hours are from noon to 1:45 p.m. and 7 to 9:45 p.m. except on Sunday night. In winter, it's closed on Monday also.

La Terrasse, 2 rue Chenevières (tel. 021/944-33-96), is in the center of town, across from the Hôtel du Lac, near the Church of Notre Dame. It offers a flowery terrace for dining, which is covered and heated when the weather requires it. The regular menu features dishes such as filet of fried perch, sole with almonds served with fine herbs, and filet of beef with morels. Raclette specials are offered on Friday night in summer. Full hot meals are served daily from 11 a.m. to 2 p.m. and 6 to 9:30 p.m., but the place opens as a café daily at 9 a.m., serving drinks and snacks until midnight. Fixed-price meals begin at 25F ($17). À la carte selections can, of course, go much higher.

La Pinte de l'Hôtel de Ville, rue de l'Hôtel de Ville (tel. 021/922-63-43). In case you're wondering, *pinte* is old French for "bistro." Now reduced in size, this remains a landmark café in Vevey. It overlooks the trees and cobblestones of this old square, where tables are placed outside in fair weather. The menu is simple but good. You might begin with assiette valaisanne, a plate of air-dried beef, and go on to such dishes as steak maison or steak with mushroom sauce. Yes, Virginia, they serve horsesteak here as well. They also offer three kinds of fondue and will even prepare you a sandwich. Meals cost from 35F ($23.80) and are served daily from 11:30 a.m. to 2 p.m. and 7:30 to 10 p.m. It is closed all day Sunday, and in winter it also closes for dinner Saturday.

Brasserie Feldschlösschen, 45 rue du Simplon (021/921-31-67), is a working-person's brasserie on a busy commercial street in downtown Vevey, named after a popular beer. A 35-foot glass window opens in summertime onto a geranium-filled green area with a fountain. One end of the room is filled with a large nickel-plated serving area and a large mural of medieval maps of Vevey. Fixed-price meals range from 20F ($13.60) and might include peppersteak, Indian rice, or two types of spaghetti, along with good hams, sausages, and hors d'oeuvres. The brasserie is open every day from 7 a.m. to midnight, with hot meals available from 11 a.m. until closing.

White Horse Pub, 33 rue du Simplon (tel. 021/921-02-34), is a popular tavern, with smoky paneling, comfortable Jacobean chairs, pink lampshades, and an amplified radio station playing recently released music. The clientele tends to be quite young. Whiskey begins at 6F ($4.10), and a large local beer—referred to here as "sailor's size"—costs 5F ($3.40). Cheeseburgers, french fries, steaks, soups, and ice creams are the only food items, along with a plate of hors d'oeuvres. The establishment is open daily except Sunday from 7 a.m. to midnight, on Sunday from 4 p.m. to midnight. Snacks are offered at all open hours, but a somewhat more formal meal is available at lunchtime, from noon to 2 p.m. Platters of food at this time cost around 12F ($8.15).

5. MONTREUX

Built on a curve of the great bay of Lac Léman, the queen of the Vaud Riviera, Montreux, rises like an amphitheater from the shores of Lake Geneva. It's an Edwardian town with a decided French accent. Expatriates since the 19th century have lived here—including novelist Vladimir Nabokov, who spent his last years in Montreux—reporting on its balmy climate that allows Mediterranean vegetation to grow. The mountains in the background protect the resort from the winds of winter, and along the shore grow walnut trees, fruit trees, cypresses, magnolias, bay trees, almonds, and even palm trees. Montreux's climate is considered the mildest on the north side of the Alps.

The city has grown and expanded greatly in this century, taking over former villages along the shoreline. One of these is Clarens, which was used by Rousseau as the setting for *La Nouvelle Héloïse*.

As a world-class tourist resort, Montreux, the "pearl of the Swiss Riviera," has had rough times. It began as a place for winter only. By 1860 it had 18 hotels, and by 1912 had grown to 85 hotels. Historians now call this the "golden age" of Montreux, when it hosted such distinguished visitors as Tolstoy, Flaubert, Dostoyevsky, and Ruskin. It was at its peak at the beginning of World War I when everything came tumbling down, and had started to gain ground again in the 1920s, when the Great Depression arrived. During the 1930s it searched for an identity, virtually giving up when Europe was plunged into war in 1939. In more recent times it has begun to revive, and today about three-fourths of the resort's 20,000 inhabitants are engaged in some capacity in the business of catering to tourists.

Summer is now the town's peak visiting time, and it is overrun with traffic from the Great St. Bernard Tunnel, that links Germany's autobahn with Italy's autostrada. It's also on the main Simplon railway line. Many mountain railways terminate here: The best known is the Montreux Oberland Bahn, taking visitors into the famous ski resorts of the Bernese Oberland.

The year-round resort is the setting for various festivals, when it's virtually impossible to get a hotel room without advance reservations.

The best known of these is the **Festival de Jazz** beginning the first Friday in July. Billed as an extravaganza, it lasts 2½ weeks. Everybody you can dream of is likely to show up. Tickets begin at 35F ($23.80) for some performances but could go as high as 85F ($57.80). For more information, write to **Festival de Jazz,** Case Postale 97, CH-1820 Montreux, Switzerland (tel. 021/963-12-12).

At the end of summer, there's a classical music festival. For information on this, write to **Festival de Musique,** Case Postale 162, CH-1820 Montreux, Switzerland.

Old Montreux is worth exploring with its typical vintage houses and narrow, crooked streets, and, later, a stroll along the quayside promenade by the lake is in order.

WHERE TO STAY: Many of the leading hotels of Montreux have greatly improved in recent years but the money spent in improvements has gone into the expensive palaces, not the less expensive hotels. The town, unfortunately, lacks really good budget accommodations.

The Upper Bracket

Le Montreux Palace, 100 Grand'Rue, CH-1820 Montreux, Switzerland (tel. 021/963-53-73), has opulent 19th-century detailing. The salons and bedrooms have been renovated in a style more or less conforming to the original plans. These include embellished ceilings, parquet floors, and crystal chandeliers. In one room, an art nouveau stained-glass skylight is set above an arched ceiling with statues of cupids and demigods. On the well-maintained lakefront grounds is a large, abstractly shaped swimming pool with nine angular sides, as well as a bar and refreshment facility. There are also tennis courts. Everyone in town knows "The Palace." It even has its own parking garage, which you'll be grateful for in congested Montreux, along with an 18-hole golf course in another part of town. Depending on the season, singles rent for 200F ($136) to 280F ($190.40) daily, and doubles cost 320F ($217.60) to 390F ($265.20).

Hyatt Continental, 97 Grand'Rue, CH-1820 Montreux, Switzerland (tel. 021/963-51-31), is decorated with elegant materials and unusual lighting. Vistas from inside the public rooms and the bedrooms face the lake. The decor is at the same time refined but lighthearted. A piano bar on the ground floor is plushly upholstered in subtle colors. The 163 bedrooms have all the conveniences you'd expect in a luxury hotel. Because of the parking problem in Montreux there's an underground garage. Singles rent for 160F ($108.80) to 260F ($170) daily, and doubles range from 210F ($142.80) to 310F ($210.80), depending on the season. There's an indoor pool and sauna, and the lakeside location is on one of the most beautifully maintained promenades along the water. You get superb French cuisine in the Régence Restaurant which features a fixed-price menu for 85F ($57.80). There is also a beautifully decorated coffeeshop called Romance, which serves à la carte meals based on the fresh produce of the season. In the Garden Terrace in summer you can enjoy fresh fish from Lake Geneva, along with grilled steaks and a salad buffet. Subject to weather conditions, musical entertainment is presented here once or twice a week.

Grand Hotel Excelsior, 21 rue Bon Port, CH-1820 Montreux, Switzerland (tel. 021/963-32-31), is a renowned Montreux landmark. You enter a world of quiet opulence and discreet personal service. The elegant marble foyer sets the tone, containing such accents as Venetian sedan chairs, along with marquetry and Queen Anne antiques. Oil paintings, baroque sculpture, and antiques enhance the charm of the place. The hotel opens impressively onto lakefront footage. Its spacious bedrooms, many with lakefront balconies, contain good coordinated furnishings and many amenities that befit a five-star hotel. Rates in the 80 rooms are based on the season, and include breakfast, tax, and service: 170F ($115.60) to 220F ($149.60) daily in a single, 290F ($197.20) to 390F ($265.20) in a double. Half board is another 45F ($30.60).

Dining is in the elegant grill room, Le Yaka, or else more informally on La Terrasse. Both serve a superb French cuisine. You can also enjoy light fare at Le Snack Piscine by the swimming pool. The hotel is avid for fitness, and has many health care regimes, along with its covered swimming pool stretching 82½ feet. It also has a sauna, massage parlor, gym, hairdresser, and beauty salon. In other words, you'll be well cared for here if you can pay the freight charges.

Better for the Budget

Hotel Eden au Lac, 11 rue du Théâtre, CH-1820 Montreux, Switzerland (tel. 021/963-55-51), evokes scenes from the movie *Death in Venice*. With its lingering nostalgia and its beautiful restoration, it is in many ways my favorite hotel in Montreux, and it's less expensive than the palaces, both old and new. Built in a grand 19th-century style, this 105-room hotel regally stands on the lakeside promenade, enjoying one of the best quayside positions at the resort. Its façade is like an art nouveau wedding cake. You may find that your favorite nook is the pink-and-white neobaroque Gatsby Bar, with stained-glass windows and all the luxury of the year 1900.

Others prefer the garden terrace, enjoying the magnolias and clipped chestnuts. Modern-day Victorians will also gravitate to the well-appointed and often very spacious accommodations, which are under the keen-eyed direction of Bernard and Nicole Tschopp. Depending on the season and room assignment, they charge 95F ($64.60) to 180F ($122.40) daily in a single, from 130F ($88.40) to 250F ($170) in a twin. For those who can afford the ultimate in luxury, you can rent either a junior or senior suite—and these are among the most opulent accommodations at Montreux—at prices that begin at 200F ($136) for two persons, going up all the way to 490F ($333.20).

The food is another reason for staying here, or for visiting if you're a nonresident. I'd suggest the menu dégustation at 69F ($46.90). It changes daily and is based on the use of the fresh produce that is handled carefully in the kitchen. You have a choice of the belle-époque style dining room, the "1900," or else La Terrasse, which has been called "for connoisseurs." During the day you can enjoy buffets in the Garden Restaurant right at lake level.

Grand Hotel Suisse Majestic, 43 avenue des Alps, CH-1820 Montreux, Switzerland (tel. 021/963-51-81), is a monumental landmark, in the literal heart of Montreux, set beside the lake in all its 19th-century opulence. You take an elevator past trompe l'oeil murals, to the top-floor reception area set in an art nouveau lobby. From there, you can walk out onto a panoramic terrace filled with classical statuary. Comfort and subdued elegance have for decades been the key to this hotel's continued success. You quickly may adopt the Majestic cocktail bar as your favorite watering hole in Montreux. Three elevators take you to your well-appointed bedrooms. Most rooms reflect an updated belle-époque decor combined with modern comforts and amenities. Singles rent for 95F ($65.95) to 170F ($115.60) daily, and doubles for 150F ($102) to 250F ($170).

The restaurant, Français, connected to the coffeeshop, is one of the reasons for stopping over, and the food is backed up by one of the finest wine cellars in the region. Dishes are sometimes flambéed at your table. Specialties include such delectable fare as poached fresh salmon, a chaudrée of seafood flavored with saffron, or a perfectly done entrecôte with three peppers. A set menu is 38F ($25.85), but you can spend far more ordering à la carte.

Eurotel Riviera, 81 Grand-Rue, CH-1820 Montreux, Switzerland (tel. 021/963-49-51), is a silvery high-rise hotel on the main road to Vevey, with a frontage on the lake. It has most of the facilities you'd expect from such a large hotel, including an indoor swimming pool, a piano bar, a solarium, a sauna, and lakeview balconies, along with predictably modern rooms, including a foyer in wood and leather. There's a covered garage under the building. The establishment is run with a kind of big city efficiency, and there's usually a room available (except at convention times), and it will be clean and comfortable. All the accommodations have been recently renewed. Singles cost 100F ($68) to 170F ($115.60) daily, while doubles range from 150F ($102) to 250F ($170), with a buffet breakfast included. Twice a week in summer the management provides free waterskiing and sailing for guests.

Hôtel L'Ermitage, CH-1820 Clarens-Montreux, Switzerland (tel. 021/964-44-11), is a pleasantly situated family-run hotel with a mansard roof, three floors of comfortable rooms, and a sun terrace covered with an awning. Some of the rooms inside are spacious, opening onto views of the lake. The hotel is comfortable, and children are welcome (chances are, they'll find plenty of playmates). Pleasingly furnished rooms range from 50F ($34) to 90F ($61.20) daily in a single and from 80F ($54.40) to 170F ($115.60) in a double, depending on the plumbing and the season.

DINING IN AND NEAR MONTREUX: At Brent, a small village a short distance from the center of Montreux, **Le Pont de Brent** (tel. 021/964-52-30) is in a renovated town house. Gérald Rabaey is the owner and chef, and it's rumored he can put virtually any delicacy within a delicious envelope of puff pastry. The decor is most tasteful. Menus change seasonally. The soups are exceptional, including one made with leeks and mussels, or another with lobster flavored with basil. For your main fish dish, you might try a filet de loup (sea bass) with Pinot Noir or perhaps rabbit in a mustard sauce or roast pigeon with cabbage. There is always a list of impressive desserts, highlighted by sorbets made with the fresh fruits of the season. A fixed-price menu costs 95F ($64.60), although two persons can order the "menu surprise" at 115F ($78.20) each. To dine à la carte will cost around 95F ($64.60) per person. The restaurant, open noon to 2 p.m. and 7 to 9:30 p.m., is closed Sunday evening and all day Monday.

   Le Yaka, Grand Hotel Excelsior, 21 rue Bon Port (tel. 021/963-32-31), is one of the most superb French restaurants at the resort, housed elegantly in this already recommended landmark five-star hotel. The entrance is through the marble lobby. Once grandly seated by the maître d', you'll enjoy the peaceful charms of this most agreeable dining room, which is warmly decorated, nautical, and masculine. The lake in the background adds to the charm of the dining area. Highly accomplished cookery and impeccable service make a meal here an occasion. Set meals, considering their quality, are reasonably priced at 37F ($25.15), but most à la carte orders will begin (and I mean begin) at 50F ($34). From the well-selected continental menu, you can make such selections as trout meunière, veal kidneys in a whisky sauce, or steak tartare. You might begin with a refreshing, well-seasoned soup, or else one of the subtle hot or cold hors d'oeuvres. Desserts are classic. Meals are served daily from 11 a.m. to 2 p.m. and 7 to either 9:30 or 10 p.m.

   La Vielle Ferme (tel. 021/964-65-65), at Montreux-Chailly, 2½ miles north of Montreux, is set in the country in a rustic stone house that has regional music playing almost every night of the week except Monday, when it's closed (it is also closed in July). You'll leave Montreux for the village of Chailly, a few miles away. The owner, Monsieur Mabillard, welcomes you with his specialties, which include ham, boneless quail, veal, salmon, and a superb homemade terrine. Perhaps you'll prefer a gratin of shrimp or beef grilled. Fixed-price meals begin at 38F ($25.85), and à la carte menus cost from 68F ($46.25). Meals are served from noon to 1:45 p.m. and 7 to 10 p.m. The place is closed all day Monday and for lunch on Tuesday. Be warned that your intimate dinner here might at any moment be interrupted by the arrival of a big group of tour participants.

   Restaurant Chinois Wing Wah, 42 Grand-Rue (tel. 021/963-34-47), offers hearty portions of well-prepared Chinese food that brings out the crowds, often families, to its precincts right in the heart of Montreux. The owner from Hong Kong has decorated the interior in scarlet and gold, and he offers his bill of fare daily from 11:30 a.m. to 2:30 p.m. and 6 to 10:30 p.m. Meals costing from 45F ($30.60) are likely to feature such fare as lacquered duck, twice-grilled beef, diced chicken with hot peppers, and curried shrimp.

MONTREUX AFTER DARK: In the heart of town, the **Casino** (tel. 021/963-53-31) hogs most of the action. Since the limit of any wager is 5F ($3.40) in Switzerland, this casino, like many others, has evolved into more of an entertainment complex than a gambling hall. True, there's a green baize table and rolling balls where you can tempt Lady Luck, but the main focus is on the cabaret, disco, restaurant, three bars, music hall, and the movie theater. Parking is well-near impossible in the area, so there's a garage with coin-operated meters in the basement. The cabaret is down a long red staircase with a short tunnel at the end. This club has everything from strip acts to clowns, and is open from 10 p.m. to 4 a.m. every night but Sunday. There's no cover, but drinks cost from 15F ($10.20) apiece.

   On the main floor you can enter the American-style disco, **Platinum,** which has comfortable banquettes, lots of chrome, and recently released songs. Entrance is 6F ($4.10) on Friday, going up to 8F ($5.45) on Saturday. Drinks cost from 12F ($8.15) up, and you must be at least 18. The disco opens at 9:30 p.m.

On the same floor is an exposed piano bar, a "Bar du Festival," where repeat videos are shown of the performers at the most recent Montreux Jazz Festival, and a 3,000-seat concert hall for a changing list of musical acts.

As incongruous as it may sound, the latest attraction is the **Western Saloon,** with live country music and steaks for "cowboys." It is open Tuesday through Sunday from 9 p.m. till late.

The restaurant has a panoramic view of the lake from your perch in one of its upholstered bentwood chairs. In summer, the swimming pool and the salon also draw a crowd.

Piano Bar, Hyatt Continental, 97 Grand-Rue (tel. 021/963-51-31). In a town that is not particularly noted for its nightlife, this seems to be the bar preferred by the rock musicians who come for the annual Music Festival. One floor below lobby level of the previously recommended Hyatt hotel, the bar is a stylishly modern enclave of pink granite, black lacquer, comfortable settees, and big-windowed views of the lake. If you're interested in whatever your favorite rock star likes to drink, ask the barman. All or none of these folks might be present by the time you show up. Perhaps you'll create a party of your own over one of the popular margaritas or a scotch and soda, priced from 12F ($8.15) each. The bar is open from 6 p.m. to midnight Sunday to Thursday, to 2 a.m. Friday and Saturday.

Harry's New York Bar, Le Montreux Palace, 100 Grand'Rue (tel. 021/963-53-73). Every town seemingly has to have a Harry's Bar these days, and Montreux is no exception. Modeled after no other place, this bar, a former car showroom, is a popular gathering spot at night. Paneled elegance and sophisticated brass, along with much upholstered comfort, make for an inviting ambience. The bartenders often mix cocktails the old-fashioned way, and the staff is rarely from Switzerland. Perhaps Tunisia, Portugal, maybe even East Germany. Whisky costs from 10F ($6.80), and you can also order grills, salads, sandwiches. The big spenders order the beluga caviar or the lobster thermidor. Light meals cost from 40F ($27.20) and up. It is open from 5 p.m. to 1 a.m. Monday to Friday, to 2 a.m. Saturday and Sunday.

Hazyland Disco (tel. 021/963-56-46) is on a busy street opposite the Palace at 100 Grand'Rue. The disco has big windows in an art nouveau format with fanciful wrought-iron detailing. It frequently has live acts, and when no one's playing, clients dance to disco music. You'll see a bar area to the right as you enter, and a group of lively patrons, most of whom appear to be under 25. When I was last there, a Michael Jackson look-alike sang Michael Jackson songs under a red strobe light. Beer costs from 13F ($8.85), and there is an 8F ($5.45) cover charge Friday and Saturday. It's open daily from 9:30 p.m. to 4 a.m.

EXCURSIONS IN THE ENVIRONS: Everybody seemingly heads to the **Château of Chillon** (tel. 021/963-39-11), two miles south of Montreux. The most impressive moated castle in Switzerland, Chillon was immortalized by Lord Byron in his *The Prisoner of Chillon.* Its old section is thought to be 1,000 years old; however, most of it dates from the 13th century, built under Peter II of Savoy. It's considered one of the best-preserved medieval castles of Europe, and was the scene of many trials of so-called sorcerers who were horribly tortured. Its most famous prisoner, the one given literary fame by Byron, was François Bonivard, the prior of St. Victori in Geneva who supported the Reformation. This so angered the Catholic duke of Savoy that he had him chained in the dungeon from 1532 to 1536 when he was released by the Bernese.

The château can be visited from 9 a.m. April through September, closing at 7 p.m. in July and August, at 6:30 p.m. in the other months. It opens at 10 a.m. October through March, closing at 4:45 p.m. except in March and October, when the gates close at 5:30 p.m. From November through March, it is also closed from 12:45 to 1:30 p.m. All year, last tickets are sold 45 minutes before closing. Admission is 4.50F ($3.05) for adults, 2F ($1.35) for children.

The **Rochers-de-Naye** at 6,700 feet is one of the most popular tours along Lake Geneva. From Montreux a cogwheel train takes visitors in less than an hour up to Rochers-de-Naye. The train runs about seven times a day in season, with the last departure at 4 p.m. The return is at 5 p.m., and a round-trip fare is about 32F ($21.75) per person. See Dining at Rochers-de-Naye, coming up.

The train ascends the slopes over Lac Léman, passing **Glion,** a little resort on a rocky crag almost suspended between lake and mountains. You come to **Caux** at 3,600 feet, lying on a natural balcony overhanging the blue bowl of the lake. Finally, the peak of Rochers-de-Naye rises high in the Vaudois Alps. In the distance you can see the Savoy Alps, including Mont Blanc and the Jura Alps. At the end is an alpine flower garden, the loftiest in Europe.

Skiing is possible here between December and April. There's a ski lift and a Swiss ski school, plus a hotel.

The little port town of **Villeneuve** also makes for an interesting excursion. At the end of the lake, it was here that Lord Byron wrote *The Prisoner of Chillon* in 1816. The town is used to famous visitors. Romain Rolland lived here, receiving a visit from Mahatma Gandhi. Many artists have painted the charm of the little town and countryside. The famous painter, Kokoschka, chose Villeneuve as his residence. It's within a few minutes' walk of the Château of Chillon.

Staying at Glion

Hotel Victoria, CH-1823 Glion-sur-Montreux, Switzerland (tel. 021/963-31-31), was built in 1886, in this hillside village high above Montreux, and still contains a collection of paintings and furniture that suit its grand architecture. Many of the furnishings were collected by its former owner, an antique dealer from Geneva. In 1985, the hotel was purchased by its former longstanding manager, Toni Mittermair. The dozens of charming Victorian features that make this place special include art nouveau plasterwork friezes, an array of ornate fireplaces, and an Edwardian glassed-in terrace where plants bloom amid wicker chairs in a pleasing re-creation of an antique winter garden. Each of the bedrooms has a phone, a collection of some antique furniture, and usually some kind of turn-of-the-century oil painting, large windows, and often a private terrace. Not all of the rooms have a private bath. Depending on the season, the plumbing, and the accommodation, singles rent for 80F ($54.40) to 170F ($115.60) daily. Rooms with two beds cost 130F ($88.40) to 250F ($170).

The constantly changing set menu in the dining room offers ample choice and interest. Written in an elaborate scroll, the largely French menu features such fare as grilled veal kidneys in a dijonnaise sauce with a gratin of zucchini, braised pork with Madeira, and a wide selection of grills served with creamy gratin Dauphine. A limited but well-chosen selection of fish is also offered. Meals cost from 45F ($30.60) to 65F ($44.20). You may want to order from a special seasonal menu, which presents only the freshest produce. The dining room is open daily from noon to 2 p.m. and 7 to 9 p.m.

Dining at Rochers-de-Naye

A local engineering feat that achieved great acclaim in Switzerland was the drilling of a 750-foot tunnel through solid rock for access to this panoramic restaurant, **Restaurant Plein Roc** (tel. 021/963-74-11). An excursion here is an excuse to admire mountain scenery during the 60-minute train ride from Montreux. Other than by climbing, the train ride (cog railway) is the only way to get here, and costs, from Montreux, 32F ($21.75) round trip per person. Buy a ticket to Rochers-de-Naye, and, once you descend from the train, bypass the self-service snack bar that sits near the train platform (this is the last stop for the train), and take the very long tunnel to its end, to the alpine dining room and a sweeping view of Lac Léman that stretches past Lausanne almost as far as Geneva. Of course, you'll need a good day to see this. Other than cots placed in a dormitory (used by campers and school groups) there are no hotel accommodations. So you must time your dinner to end by 8 p.m., when the last train goes down the mountain. Meals are served daily from 11:30 a.m. to 2:30 p.m. for lunch. Dinner begins at 6 p.m. A four-course meal costs 30F ($20.40). Dishes include meat fondues, veal escalope Gruyèrienne, and entrecôte with herb butter.

Snacks and drinks are served throughout the afternoon. English-born Mike Midgley is the articulate and helpful manager who rents the space from the train company.

6. CHÂTEAU-D'OEX

The unspoiled French-speaking capital of the Pays-d'Enhaut (the "upper land,"), Château-d'Oex (pronounced "shah-toh day") is popular with Europeans as a family resort. The village has lots of character and old-fashioned charm. Lying in a broad, sunny alpine valley above Lake Geneva, this area is just beginning to emerge as a winter sports center and a summer mountain resort, drawing vacationers who are interested more in a relaxed atmosphere than in the latest in chic.

In particular, Château-d'Oex is attuned to the needs of beginning and intermediate skiers, offering in winter an aerial cableway to take you to the heights and all types of skiing and other snow- and ice-associated sports, as well as ballooning, indoor horseback, riding, and—what else?—après-ski parties.

Summer attractions in this part of the "Green Highland" of Switzerland include a heated swimming pool, hard tennis courts, horseback riding along park trails, a sightseeing cable railway to take you into the mountains, hang-gliding, trout fishing, and mini-golf.

If time is on your side, take the postal bus to **Col des Mosses,** one of the most scenic rides in this part of Switzerland. You can also take the cableway from the heart of the resort to **Pra Perron** (4,020 feet) and from there go by gondola on up to **La Braye** (5,350 feet).

Château-d'Oex is halfway between Montreux and Interlaken, about 15 minutes from Gstaad.

FOOD AND LODGING: Gracefully isolated from the commercial section of the village, **Bon Acceuil,** CH-1837 Château-d'Oex, Switzerland (tel. 029/4-63-20), is the loveliest and most historic hotel in town. To reach it, you negotiate a series of winding residential streets, which lead to an alpine foothill with a panorama over the valley below. The roughly textured façade was originally built as a relais station for the postal system in 1756. What used to be a stable has been merged with the main house to create an intimate country inn. Containing only 11 rooms, it also has an excellent restaurant, a rustically chic cellar bar (see "Après Ski"), and a collection of painting and sculptures on loan from a nearby gallery. The hotel is owned by Antoine Oltramare. With breakfast included, singles rent for 65F ($44.20) to 90F ($61.20) daily, and doubles go for 120F ($81.60) to 160F ($108.80), depending on the season. Each room contains a private bath, pine paneling, the kind of fine accessories you might find in a private home, and low 18th-century ceilings.

The establishment's rustic dining room is worth a special detour. Lunch and dinner are served from noon to 2 p.m., from 7:30 to 9 p.m. every day of the week except Tuesday. In a rustically wood-trimmed room, whose beams and brick fireplace might have inspired a colonial tavern in Massachussetts, you can order well-prepared meals for 75F ($51). A menu dégustation costs 90F ($61.20), depending on the ingredients. Main dishes are likely to include filet of smoked trout with horseradish, terrine of mushrooms, cabbage stuffed with mousse of trout and crayfish, filet of rabbit with garlic and cheese, and an array of fresh fish. Reservations are very important. Both the hotel and its restaurant are closed from mid-October to Christmas.

Hôtel Résidence la Rocaille, CH-1837 Château-d'Oex, Switzerland (tel. 029/4-62-15), is a four-star hotel away from the heart of the village. This is one of the best of the small hotels, with helpful owners. Some of the accommodations have their own self-catering facilities. The bedrooms are well furnished and most comfortable, and it's a good choice for families who take their holidays together. Singles range from 75F ($51) to 160F ($108.80) daily, while doubles cost from 120F ($81.60) to 220F ($149.60), depending on the season. These tariffs include service, tax, and breakfast. The hotel has an attractive ambience, with much use made of wood paneling and beamed ceilings. It's one of the preferred stopovers among the après-ski crowd. For dining, you can select either Au Train Bleu or the Restaurant-Grill. Many guests, however, prefer the Café des Bossons, an informal fromagerie with a cozy atmosphere. Later, these same guests are likely to patronize the hotel's piano bar, Greenfizz.

Hôtel Beau-Séjour, CH-1837 Château-d'Oex, Switzerland (tel. 029/4-74-23), stands near the cableway terminal to La Braye, near the heart of the resort. This is a long-established, popular hotel in a salmon-color building. Many of the 43 accommodations have been updated with modern plumbing, and most have phones. Many of them open onto terraces. The hotel charges from 60F ($40.80) to 80F ($54.40) daily in a single and from 120F ($81.60) to 140F ($95.20) in a double, including a continental breakfast, taxes, and service. Guests enjoy the charming Old World living rooms and salons, filled with Swiss and French antiques. La Taverne in the basement is open from noon to 2 p.m. and 7 to 10 p.m. For an intimate atmosphere, head for La Salle des Chevaliers, with its vaulted ceiling and thick pinewood tables. There you can order a fondue au fromage or a fondue bourguignonne or else crêpes Gruyère, filets de truite saumonée, filets de perches au beurre blond, or three kinds of tournedos. Full meals cost from 50F ($34). The hotel is closed in November and the first week in May.

APRÈS SKI: A drink within the depths of the **Cellar Bar,** Bon Acceuil (tel. 029/4-63-20), requires a winding excursion to the top of the village. There, within the stone foundations of a chalet originally built in 1756, is an ancient-looking haven with a welcoming fire, dozens of antique artifacts (have you ever seen a 50-year-old set of snowshoes?), and wraparound sofas upholstered in soft brown leather. Don't be surprised if you discover that Tina Turner and Roger Moore have preceded you here, because despite its conscious rusticity, it attracts a glamorous crowd. There's no cover charge, but a scotch and soda costs from 11F ($7.50). In high season, the bar opens daily from 9 p.m. to 2 a.m. In low season, it's open from 10 p.m. to 2 a.m. The bar closes from mid-October to Christmas.

If you're hungry and want a gemütlich atmosphere, you might seek out **La Taverne** in the basement at the Beau-Séjour (tel. 4-74-23), serving hot food until 8:30 p.m. and remaining open until 11 p.m.

7. VILLARS

This mountain resort (4,268 feet), halfway between lake and glacier, overlooks the Rhône Valley over the vine-covered slopes around Aigle. It's considered the leading mountain resort in French-speaking Switzerland. Along with Arveyes and Chesières, Villars forms a resort area in the lower Valais (although it's still officially part of the canton of Vaud), and is far more fashionable than its companion villages.

The plateau on which the resort is situated, a true alpine belvedere, has woodland slopes of the Chamossaire to the north. To the south it has a panoramic view of the French and Swiss Alps, with Dents du Midi mountain range opposite and Mont Blanc visible in the distance.

The long-established resort, in its sheltered location, offers craft shops, nightclubs, good restaurants and hotels, and all services you may require to make your stay here pleasant.

The principal ski area is at **Bretaye** (6,050 feet), reached by mountain railroad. (You may find the cars packed at the height of the season.) From there you can take lifts in many directions. One goes to the top of **Chamossaire** (7,200 feet).

You can reach the resort by electric mountain railway from Bex, the trip taking about an hour and 20 minutes.

FOOD AND LODGING: An excellent first-class choice is the **Grand Hôtel du Parc,** CH-1884 Villars, Switzerland (tel. 025/35-21-21), on its own well-kept grounds about three minutes from the heart of Villars. The grounds are a potent lure, with two ski lifts, and three tennis courts. The hotel, which draws many repeat visitors, is pleasantly furnished, and many of the private bedrooms are generous in size (all accommodations contain private bath). The majority also have private balconies, opening onto superb views. In summer, tariffs range from 155F ($105.40) to 225F ($153) daily in a single and from 280F ($190.40) to 410F ($278.80) in a double. Even more expensive suites are available as well. The long and well-lit dining room is among the finest in town, with a traditional atmosphere. There's an "ice bar" outside for drinks before lunch, as well as an indoor swimming pool. A disco on the premises has a round area for dancing, the shape of which is repeated in the ceiling where an artist's depiction includes a galaxy of mythical beasts. The hotel is open from December to September.

Eurotel, route des Layeux, CH-1884 Villars, Switzerland (tel. 025/35-31-31), opened in 1976 in a seven-story format of a chalet, with balconies and wood detailing. The interior is filled with pleasant, easily forgettable furniture plus lots of exposed wood and metal. Some of the well-furnished rooms have kitchenettes. Singles rent for 85F ($57.80) to 139F ($94.50) daily, while doubles range from 140F ($95.20) to 228F ($155.05). Half board is another 30F ($20.40) per person daily. The difference in rates depends on the season. A sauna and swimming pool are on the premises. The hotel is closed in November.

Hôtel du Golf et Marie-Louise, CH-1884 Villars, Switzerland (tel. 025/35-24-77), is an ideal country hotel, set in the midst of a large park in the center of Villars, a quiet accommodation offering relaxation in the garden. Bedrooms are spacious, each with a lounge area, phone, and a balcony, all facing south with a magnificent view of the Rhône Valley and the Swiss Alps. The owners, the Angelini family, charge from 75F ($51) to 125F ($85) daily in a single and from 90F ($61.20) to 210F ($142.80) in a double, depending on the season. The least expensive rooms contain hot and cold running water. The tariffs include breakfast, and half board is offered for another 25F ($17) per person daily. The dining room is a combination of stucco with beams and polished paneling, and the service is attentive. Besides the dining room, you can take meals in a typical Swiss restaurant, Au Feu de Bois, offering Italian and French specialties as well as steaks, prepared in the special wood oven. The Angelinis take pride in offering guests first-class cuisine, with special barbecue dinners during the week.

APRÈS SKI: Villars has several clubs, bars, and taverns, and in the very peak season it has a lively atmosphere. Many people from Geneva like to take their holidays here.

Peppino's, at the already-recommended **Eurotel** (tel. 025/35-31-31), is about the most sought-after dining room in town. It not only has good food, but a fun-loving atmosphere and often live entertainment.

In the bar of the **Grand Hôtel Du Parc** (tel. 025/35-21-21) you can dance to a live band in season; otherwise it's disco music. The hotel's tavern grill is also a popular place for fondue and raclette.

8. LES DIABLERETS

If you turn off the main Geneva-Brig highway after passing Aigle and head into the mountains, you'll find Les Diablerets, a typical resort village of chalets set against a backdrop of towering alpine peaks. These mountains are so high that the resort gets little sun in the main part of the hamlet until about the last half of February, a fact that isn't much publicized.

This is the center of some 40 miles of ski slopes, the biggest ski area in Switzerland, with access to a mammoth lift system. It's also a good base for exploring other ski resorts.

You can visit **Glacier des Diablerets** (9,835 feet at its highest station), but unless you're a skilled skier you'll probably only want to relax at the panoramic restaurant before returning to the resort. A round-trip ticket from the hamlet to the glacier tip costs 38F ($25.85) per person. You go by gondola for some 4½ miles to Col du Pillon-Pierres Pointe, then by aerial cable on to Cabane des Diablerets (8,275 feet), and hence onward and upward to the highest station of the glacier. This route is kept in operation from February to November.

Other popular ski sites of the region are **Isenau**, where a gondola at the north of the village will take you to Palette d'Isenau (5,900 feet); and the **Les Mazonts-Meillerets** area, reached by ski tow and chair lift from the hamlet of Vers l'Eglise. You eventually reach the peak of Meillerets (6,490 feet).

Les Diablerets lies to the east of Villars and to the west of Gstaad in the Vaudoise Alps.

FOOD AND LODGING: Two hotels with the same management, **Hôtel Ermitage** and **Résidence Meurice**, CH-1865 Les Diablerets, Switzerland (tel. 025/53-15-51), stand close to one another in an alpine setting with good views. They're connected by an underground tunnel. The format for both hotels is modern, with an emphasis on gently curving balconies and big windows. There's a generous use of natural wood made on the façade of both buildings. The interiors are well upholstered and streamlined, with bedrooms that convert into living rooms thanks to a fold-away bed system. Each of the units has a private bath. The public rooms include a dancing bar, a restaurant, and an English pub, plus an indoor swimming pool. There are also tennis courts on the grounds, and horseback riding can be arranged in summer. The single rate ranges from 80F ($54.40) to 115F ($78.20) daily, depending on the season, with doubles costing from 130F ($88.40) to 180F ($122.40), plus another 32F ($21.75) per person daily for half board.

Don't expect luxury here, as the places are functional and, like the resort, a bit rowdy at times. Nevertheless, they have a kind of dormitory charm. A modern lobby downstairs at the Ermitage has a fireplace opening into two rooms. The whole establishment has a "do-as-you-please" ambience.

Hôtel Mon Abri, CH-1865 Les Diablerets, Switzerland (tel. 025/53-14-81), is an attractively dark-toned chalet with red shutters standing at the entrance to the resort, about a seven-minute stroll from the center. The hotel has a 1969 section where each well-furnished room contains a private shower or bath. However, I still prefer the older, 1920s part with lots of alpine paneling. A grill room is outfitted in the old style, and a sun terrace proves popular in summer. Rooms are simply but comfortably furnished, opening onto balconies. They cost 55F ($37.40) to 80F ($54.40) daily in a single, with doubles ranging from 88F ($59.85) to 136F ($92.50). Tariffs depend on the season. Half board is an additional 22F ($14.95) per person per day. The hotel, operated by Austrian-born Günther Nussbauer and his family, is open from May to October and December to April.

Les Lilas, CH-1865 Les Diablerets, Switzerland (tel. 025/53-11-34), is a small hotel built in 1891, one of the best in the village. You have a choice of bedrooms that are simple and clean, 16 in all, with slanted, beamed ceilings and balconies opening onto views of the mountains. The units in the old section are comfortable and cozy, the ones in the newer section also having beamed ceilings and comfort. The average price for two persons with breakfast in off-season is only 90F ($61.20) per day, rising to 150F ($102) in winter. Some bathless singles can be rented for 45F ($30.60) per person. Half board is another 30F ($20.40) per person daily.

The hotel is justly proud of its cuisine, the finest served at the resort. The owner, Jean-Pierre Matti, is the propriètaire-cuisinier. He offers a modest fixed-price lunch for 12F ($8.15), but chances are that you'll spend from 50F ($34) ordering à la carte. You might begin with a terrine maison or seafood in puff pastry, following with saltimbocca, a fricassée of snails, one of two types of fondue, or filet of beef with morels. There is also a children's menu. A gastronomique menu is good value at 54F ($36.70), as Monsieur Matti is a master chef. Lunch is served daily from 11 a.m. to 2 p.m. and dinner from 6 to 11 p.m.

Auberge de la Poste, CH-1865 Les Diablerets, Switzerland (tel. 025/53-11-24), sits behind one of the most elaborate alpine façades in town, with a wrought-iron bracket and flowerboxes filled with scarlet blooms. Built in 1789, the hotel contains only 10 rooms, each with a sink with hot and cold water, but no private bath. Don't expect a formal reception area if you decide to check in here. You'll be required to inquire at the service area of the bustling downstairs restaurant, where the brusque but kindly manager, Dolly Weymann, will help you fill out the registration forms. This is probably one of the most interesting, and probably the most colorful, budget-priced hotels in the region. Single or doubles cost 55F ($37.40) per person with breakfast.

If you're just stopping off for a complete meal, it will cost you 20F ($13) and up. Specialties include fondues, tournedos, entrecôtes, at least six vegetarian platters, children's menus, pig's foot with Madeira, and at least nine main courses concocted mainly from regional varieties of cheese. The restaurant is open for drinks and snacks throughout the afternoon, and full meals are served every day from 11:30 a.m. to 2 p.m. and 6:30 to 10 p.m.

APRÈS SKI: After dark, Les Diablerets is no Gstaad, but there is some activity if you're not too ambitious.

You might check out the action at the already-recommended **Hôtel Mon Abri** (tel. 025/53-14-81), especially in its Au Vieux Mazot, which is open daily from 10 p.m. to 3 a.m. in winter (closed in summer). Sometimes there is live music, sometimes disco, but there's no cover. You pay 5F ($3.40) for beer. The place evokes an alpine chalet, complete with stalls and rough banquettes.

Les Lilas (tel. 025/53-11-34), recommended above, has the most favored and rustic restaurant in town where you can enjoy fondue and raclette. You can drink at one end of the bar, and there's also a petit dance floor.

If you're in the mood for something authentically British, you can head for **Le Pub** (tel. 025/53-15-51), at the previously recommended Hôtel Ermitage. With its dark paneling, tufted banquettes, electronic games, and jukebox, it looks a lot like something you'd find in industrial Manchester. Someone will pull you a pint of beer from an ornate tap every day beginning at 11 a.m. to either 11 p.m. or midnight, depending on the day of the week. Management stocks more than 40 varieties of beer, challenging some visitors to attempt to try one of each of them during the course of his or her vacation. Also within the same hotel is a disco, **Refuge.** Open nightly, summer and winter, from 10:30 p.m. until very late, it's a combination of alpine beams and curved banquettes. Live music is sometimes featured. There's no cover charge, and long drinks cost from 12F ($8.15).

CHAPTER IX

GENEVA

□ □ □

The third-largest city of Switzerland, Geneva—called "proud, nobly wealthy, and sly"—stands at the lower end of Lake Geneva or, in French, Lac Léman. It's considered the most international of cities because of all the international organizations (such as the Red Cross) that have their headquarters there. The French statesman, Talleyrand, is reputed to have said that there are five continents: Europe, America, Asia, Africa, and Geneva.

Built on the Rhône, the city lies at the extreme western tip of Switzerland. In the heart of Europe—and certainly one of the crossroads of that continent—it is known as "the smallest of great capitals." Geneva is linked to the outside world by a vast network of airlines, motorways, and railways. In winter, Geneva is a ski gateway to Switzerland, France, and Italy.

A lively, cosmopolitan atmosphere prevails in Geneva, a city of parks and promenades. In summer it becomes a virtual garden. It's also considered one of the healthiest cities in the world—the north wind blows away any pollution. The situation is magnificent. It not only lies on one of the biggest alpine lakes but also within view of the glorious pinnacle of Mont Blanc.

Geneva is virtually surrounded by French territory. It's connected to Switzerland only by the lake and a narrow corridor. Geneva is definitely a Swiss city, but with a decided French accent. The cliché has it that if you've been to New York, you haven't seen America. Likewise, Geneva will not immediately bring to mind the Switzerland of legend. You see mansard roofs, iron balconies, sidewalk cafés, and shop signs with names such as *boulangerie*. There's even a *rive gauche* (left bank) and *rive droite* (right bank). But Geneva makes no pretense at being another Paris.

Geneva's history is long and action-packed, its first settlements going back to the Ice Age. Over the years it's been a Gallic town, a Roman city, a Burgundian capital, and an episcopal principality. After settlement by primitive tribes, Geneva was conquered by the Romans, who lasted some 500 years. Julius Caesar was the first of Geneva's legendary guests to arrive (he had the bridge over the

Rhône destroyed). By the end of the 11th century Geneva was ruled by bishop-princes who, more or less, engaged in battles with the House of Savoy for 200 years.

Annexed by the French in 1798 at the time of their Revolution, it was an unwilling bride to France until the collapse of Napoleon in 1814, and in 1815 was admitted to the Swiss Confederation as the capital of its own canton.

Converted by William Farel, Geneva eventually switched from Catholicism and embraced the Protestant faith in 1536. The city is inevitably linked to John Calvin, a French refugee. Puritan in all ways, he ranted against theaters and dancing and even wine and food if they were partaken for enjoyment. Stern, foreboding in character, he was known for his austerity and bigotry—he had the Spanish doctor, Miguel Serveto, who disagreed with him burned at the stake. The term *Calvinism* comes from his name.

After Calvin, Geneva became such a stronghold of the Reformation that it was known in Europe as "the Rome of the Protestants." In fairness to Calvin it should be pointed out that he helped the city regain its prosperity and made it a center of French learning, welcoming refugees from all over the continent, especially from France and Italy, but also England.

By the 18th century Geneva had become one of the intellectual centers of Europe. No name was as famous as that of Jean-Jacques Rousseau, who was born here in 1712. His rival, Voltaire, came this way, as did Byron, Goethe, Victor Hugo, Chateaubriand, and a host of other luminaries.

Henri Dunant (1828–1910) had governments sign the Geneva Convention in 1863 (regrettably some of them didn't respect it). This led to the creation of the present International Red Cross.

Woodrow Wilson in 1920 proposed that Geneva be the seat of the newly formed League of Nations, and this paved the way for the city to become polyglot. It was the seat of the League until 1946. Today diplomats from all over the world flock to Geneva, to the Palais des Nations, as the city is the host to the European headquarters of the United Nations. In some respects Geneva is the very epitome of Swiss neutrality. It has been called "the most diplomatic of cities." As one commentator put it, "superpowers come here to play trick-or-treaty." The name of the city is often flashed across the nightly news, including when it is the host for nuclear disarmament talks.

Geneva, rivaled only by Zurich, is the headquarters of those Swiss bank accounts we've heard so much about. The city, even though small, has 1,000 banks. Along the Arve and Rhône rivers are found other service-related businesses and industries, including high tech, watchmaking, and insurance.

One of the most fun times to visit Geneva is for the **Fêtes de Genève,** when the Genevese celebrate their national holiday on August 1. This is followed two weeks later by a long weekend celebration with many fireworks on the lake, street dancing, and flower-covered floats.

Another celebration on December 12 is known as **l'Escalade.** Geneva was attacked on that night in 1602 by Charles-Emmanuel, whose soldiers were unsuccessful in scaling the city ramparts. The heroine of the hour, Mère Royaume, poured a pot of boiling stew over the head of a Savoy soldier, then cracked his skull with her kettle. Citizens today stage torchlight parades through the old town, many in 17th-century costumes.

1. AN ORIENTATION

The capital of the canton of Geneva, which is the second-smallest canton in the Swiss confederation, Geneva can be explored on foot. The left bank is compact and the most colorful. The River Rhône flows through the city, and it's spanned by eight bridges. The river flows south from Lake Geneva or Lac Léman.

The founders of Geneva selected a spot in the Rhône Valley at the extreme southwestern corner of the lake, and there Geneva grew up between the Jura mountains and the Alps.

Grand-Rue is the well-preserved main street of the old town, and you may want to walk its entire length to take in the beauties of the city. It is flanked by many houses dating from the 15th and 18th centuries. Rousseau was born in a simple house at number 40. The street winds uphill from the Pont de l'Île. At place Bel-Air, it becomes the rue de la Cité, eventually Grand-Rue, and finally rue Hôtel-de-Ville before it reaches one of the most charming squares of Geneva, place du Bourg-de-Four.

South of this street is the Promenade des Bastions, a green belt area with a monument to the Reformation. It overlooks the Arve River. Directly to the west, in the northern corner of the Promenade des Bastions, is the place Neuve, which is considered the finest square in Geneva (more about this later).

From this square, you can take the rue de la Corraterie, once flanked by the city wall, to the Rhône and Pont de l'Île. On this bridge is the Tour de l'Île, or what's left of a bishops' castle from the 13th century. On the other bank of the river is found place St-Gervais, which is in the St-Gervais district. Since the 18th century, this was traditionally an area for the craftsmen engaged in the jewelry and watchmaking industries.

Along the northern shore of the river is quai du Président Wilson, named for the U.S. President who helped found the League of Nations. Its first home was here in the Hotel National.

The parks of Geneva form a green belt around the city. These include Parc de la Perle du Lac, Parc Barton, and Mon Repos. On the opposite bank is Jardin Anglais or Promenade du Lac (see the section coming up on parks, gardens, and squares for more data).

GETTING AROUND IN GENEVA: Your feet are the best means of transport in compact Geneva, and certainly the cheapest, especially considering the prices of Geneva taxis. However, most of the public transport is reasonably priced and most buses and trams keep time as well as do Swiss watches. Driving a car is definitely not recommended. Parking is too difficult.

Public Transport

For the most part, transportation originates at **place Cornavin,** fronting the main railroad station. From here, you can take bus F to the Palais des Nations. Bus 10 takes you to Geneva Airport at 1.50F ($1). In addition, **Swiss Federal Railways** runs trains to and from Cornavin main station right up to Geneva Airport. The trip takes six minutes. The one-way fare in first class is 5.40F ($3.65), in second class 3.40F ($2.30). The Lausanne-Geneva line was extended right into the center of the airport area. The station at the airport is the starting point or terminus for direct and intercity trains.

You'll often find women in the drivers' seats on the **Transports Publics Genevois (TPG)** vehicles. No tickets are sold inside buses or trams. Likewise, no tickets can be validated inside the vehicles. Every transaction must take place at one of the coin-operated vending machines placed at each stop. Types of tickets include:

1. Free circulation for one hour, with as many changes as you wish, on any vehicle. Cost of this ticket is 1.50F ($1).
2. A trip limited to three stops without changing vehicles at a cost of .90F (61¢).
3. Half-price tickets, which permit rides for one hour only, for children ages 6 to 12 as well as women over 62 and men over 65. The cost is .80F (55¢).

If you plan on using the system frequently, you can save a small amount of money by purchasing multifare tickets at the agents whose addresses are listed on the stop posts. These tickets must be validated at the vending machine before entering the vehicle. Tariffs for these tickets are 8F ($5.45), 5.50F ($3.75), and

4.50F ($3.05), respectively. Children under 6 ride free, with a limit of two children per adult.

Certain lines in the TPG system extend far into the country. These are marked "Reseau de Campagne." Tickets for long distances are sold by the conductor of each car, with the price determined by the distance the passenger wants to travel.

Most tourists will be interested in an all-day ticket good on any line, costing 6F ($4.10) for adults for one day, 3F ($2.05) for children. Two-day tickets cost adults 11F ($7.50), children 5.50F ($3.75), with adults charged 14F ($9.50) and children 7F ($4.75) for three days. These tickets may be purchased at the agents whose addresses are listed on each of the stop posts. They must be validated at the machine at the stop before you enter the vehicle. Special commuter cards, good on any line and transferable, may be purchased at the agents at a cost of 45F ($30.60) for a period of one calendar month.

Taxis

Taxis in Geneva are metered, the basic charge being 5F ($3.40). In the city, 2.50F ($1.70) is added for each kilometer (.62 miles) traveled, with the additional fee being 3.50F ($2.40) in the country. The fare from the airport is about 20F ($13.60) to 25F ($17). No tipping is required.

PRACTICAL FACTS: Your stay in Geneva may be made more enjoyable by knowing a few points of information about the city.

American Express: The office of American Express, 7 rue du Mont-Blanc (tel. 022/732-32-65-80), is open Monday to Friday from 8:30 a.m. to 5:30 p.m. and from 9 a.m. to noon on Saturday.

Banking: For financial transactions, the **Société de Banque Suisse** (Swiss Bank Corporation) is at 2 rue de la Confederation (tel. 022/22-41-11).

Consulate: If you lose your passport, go to the **U.S. Consulate,** 11 route Pregny (tel. 022/799-02-11).

Currency exchange: At Gare Cornavin, the money exchange is open from 6:30 a.m. to 10:30 p.m. Monday to Friday, from 5:30 a.m. to 8:30 p.m. Saturday and Sunday.

Emergencies: In an emergency, dial 117 for **police, an ambulance,** or **firefighters.**

Hair care: One of the best places to get your hair done—both for dames et messieurs—is **Coiffure Sofia,** 26 Boulevard Helvétique (tel. 022/735-84-40). They are open daily from 8 a.m. to 7 p.m. except Sunday and Monday afternoon.

Information: Many visitors from the continent arrive at the Gare Cornavin, where the CFF railway station is situated. The **Office du Tourisme de Genève** (main tourist office) (tel. 022/738-52-00) is open at the station for information and to make hotel reservations in Geneva and throughout Switzerland, car and motorcycle rental, excursion bookings, and an audio-guided visit of the old town. Hours are from 8:30 a.m. to 8 p.m. Monday to Friday, from 9 a.m. to 6 p.m. on Saturday, and from 4 p.m. to 8 p.m. on Sunday. In July, August, and September, the office is open daily from 8 a.m. to 10 p.m.

Laundry: If you need a Laundromat, try **Lavandière,** 8 rue Lyon (tel. 022/45-36-01), in back of the Gare Cornavin, the rail station.

Library: For reading matter, the **American Library,** 3 rue de Monthoux (tel. 022/732-80-97), has a subscription service open to those looking for a wide variety of the latest books in English. A subscription must be for at least a month.

Post Office: The post office at Gare Cornavin, 16 rue des Gares, is open Monday to Friday, from 6 a.m. to 9 p.m. on Saturday, and from 9 a.m. to 12:30 p.m. and 3 to 10 p.m. on Sunday.

Radio: For good listening, **Radio Pays de Gex** plays the American Top Ten

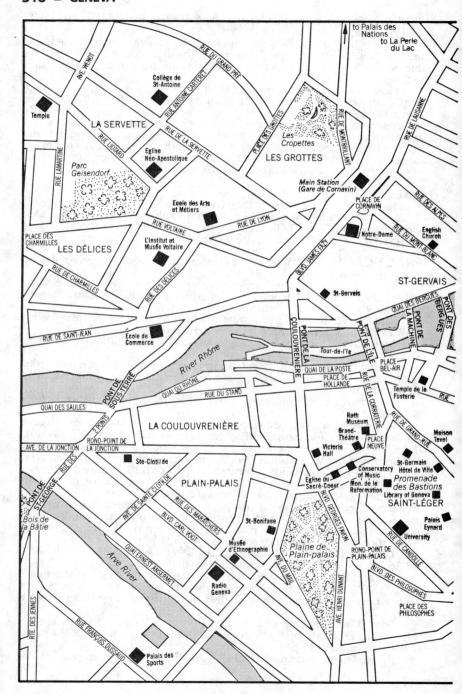

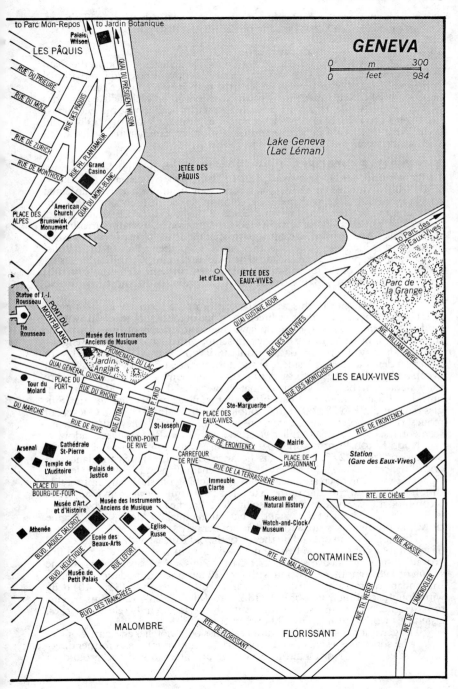

songs with comment and introduction by an American disc jockey. This program is on daily from 8 to 9 a.m. and on Saturday at 8:30 p.m.

2. WHERE TO STAY

Geneva has a lot of hotels, many of which are clustered around the main railway terminal. Because Geneva is such a city of conventions and international conferences, many of its hotels—at least the best ones in all price categories—are often booked way in advance. The ambassadors fill up such deluxe hostelries as Richemond, while the deputy assistant secretaries head for the budget hotels.

Geneva has a lot of upper-bracket hotels, in gleaming modern or Old World style. What it lacks is a sufficient number of intimate, family-run smaller hotels with atmosphere.

THE DELUXE CITADELS: Unquestionably, the greatest hotel in Geneva is **Le Richemond,** Jardin Brunswick, CH-1211 Genève, Switzerland (tel. 022/731-14-00). Founded in 1875, it is across from an immaculately maintained small park near the lake, with memorial columns, splashing fountains, and seasonally adjusted flowers. The travertine façade of the hotel is neoclassically severe, relieved only by the elaborately fashioned wrought-iron balustrades surrounding the balconies. You're likely to catch a glimpse of the actual faces of people flashed across worldwide news screens as they move from the shelter of their Rolls-Royces into the public rooms inside. The hotel restaurant, Gentilhomme, is reputed by many to be the finest dining establishment in Geneva (for more on this, see "Where to Dine"). The sidewalk café, Le Jardin, is the most fashionable in the city.

In the 19th century this was, believe it or not, a relatively unpretentious guest house, but today under the direction of one of the best hôteliers in Switzerland, Jean Armleder, whose family have owned it since it opened, its public rooms look almost like a wing of an art museum, with dozens of valuable engravings and an array of furniture dating from the days of Louis XIII. The hotel, with prices on demand, has a presidential and a royal suite, both of which have been occupied by personages with titles to justify their names. Reserve a room here early. Because of the hotel's international renown the 101 rooms and suites fill up quickly. All accommodations have private baths and a host of other luxuries. Singles rent for 270F ($183.60) while doubles cost from 450F ($306). Guests can request that the hotel arrange excursions for them, for which they will find themselves on the backseat of a Cadillac Fleetwood or a Rolls-Royce Silver Shadow.

Noga Hilton International, 19 quai du Mont-Blanc, CH-1211 Genève, Switzerland (tel. 022/731-98-11), is the largest deluxe hotel in Switzerland, and one of the best managed in the entire Hilton chain. It blends Hilton style with Genevese tradition to create a beautifully functioning physical plant impeccably run. Its location at the edge of the lake offers panoramic views from many of its accommodations. Some of these are so opulent that the Hilton, though modern, is now considered one of the "grand ladies" along quai du Mont-Blanc. Régine chose this prestigious address for a branch of her private club.

The Noga Hilton opened on the site of the old Kursaal with 316 bedrooms, of which 141 contain large beds and 124 offer twin beds. There are also five "royal" rooms, 12 alcove suites, 27 alcove rooms, and 7 apartments. In the spring of 1989, another extension with yet 120 more accommodations opened. In standard rooms, singles pay from 265F ($180.20) to 380F ($258.40) daily with doubles costing from 365F ($248.20) to 480F ($326.40). Rooms are custom designed, often furnished with beautiful woods, carefully selected textiles, tasteful art work, and an array of hi-tech amenities.

The general manager is Eric Kuhne, a Swiss-born hôtelier and native of Geneva, who supervises a staff of 450 people from many countries. A former director of sales at the Noga Hilton, he brings an international background to hotelkeeping, having worked in such diverse places as Tunisia, London, and Hong Kong.

Dining facilities at the Hilton include the gourmet restaurant, Le Cygne, and an elegant Oriental restaurant, both of which will be reviewed separately. For those with a taste for something less formal, La Grignotière offers a congenial atmosphere and good food. Its terrace has a view of the lake's waterspout. Le Bistroquai offers a selection of Swiss ice creams, sandwiches, and crisp salads, and the intimate Bar du Cygne vies with the Lobby Bar to serve you an apéritif or after-dinner liqueur. The latter spot, just a few paces from the reception area, serves drinks all day long. If you're looking for ways to keep fit, the Noga Hilton has a fitness club open to guests. Facilities include solarium cabins, saunas, and a massage area, as well as a swimming pool. Joggers can reach the lake shore through an underground tunnel. A games room, as required by Swiss law, limits the stakes to 5F ($3.40). There is an underground parking garage.

Hotel Beau-Rivage, 13 quai du Mont-Blanc, CH-1201 Genève, Switzerland (tel. 022/731-02-21), receives my highest recommendation for traditional charm, Old World hospitality, and impeccable service. This is one of the grand old hostelries of Geneva, and has witnessed many historical events. It was the headquarters for the auction of the jewels of the late Duchess of Windsor. Richard Wagner stayed here. After World War I, the treaty creating the ill-fated Republic of Czechoslovakia was signed in its glittering salons. The most tragic event in its history was the assassination of the Empress Elisabeth of Austria, who was stabbed in the autumn of 1898 by the anarchist Luigi Lucheni as she was leaving the hotel to take a trip on a lake steamer. Even today nostalgia buffs (that is, *rich* nostalgia buffs) rent the pale blue Empress Suite.

The hotel was built by Jean-Jacques Mayer, who came from Stuttgart in 1865. Its most striking feature was and is its open lobby rising five stories, an architectural innovation in its day. The hotel became the first in Europe to install elevators.

It is run today by the founder's great-grandson, with the help of a go-getting staff. There are 120 bedrooms and a half-dozen suites. As in all hotels built in the 19th century, rooms come in various sizes. Many are individualized and have much character; Some have air conditioning in summer. Depending on the room, singles range from 267F ($181.55) to 307F ($211.75) daily, while doubles cost 384F ($316.50) to 494F ($335.90). The rooms are frequently redecorated, all in good taste.

The hotel restaurant, Le Chat-Botté (Puss in Boots), will be recommended separately. It is known as one of the top five dining places of Geneva. The hotel's café terrace is also known for its good service and inspired people-watching.

Hôtel des Bergues, 33 quai des Bergues, CH-1211 Genève, Switzerland (tel. 022/731-50-50), managed by the largest hotel conglomerate in the world, Trusthouse Forte, is now well past its 150th anniversary. The aristocratic, four-story, 123-room hotel—designated as a historic monument by the Swiss—once catered to the monarchies of Europe. It is a favorite today with the international business community, along with diplomats and European society.

Jean Cocteau and Mistinguett (what a pair!) came this way, as did the duke of Edinburgh and the queen of Spain. Viziers, pashas, and the like have all stopped here, as has Edward VIII, even Emma, the Queen of Hawaii. It was host to Emperor François-Joseph and Empress Elisabeth (better known as Sissi) who was assassinated. Many of the early meetings of the newly born League of Nations took place here, and in World War II, it was known as the "hotel of the Allies," because so many free-world leaders overnighted here. The hotel today is directed by Reto Grass, one of the most capable and sophisticated big-palace hotel directors of Geneva.

The bedrooms are furnished in Directoire and Louis Philippe style, combined with numerous amenities. Each is served by an advanced phone system that assures no waiting time for internal numbers called. Singles rent for 260F ($176.80) to 290F ($197.20) daily, and doubles cost 340F ($231.20) to 390F ($265.20). Ample use is made of marble in the lobby area. The public rooms are lavish, with electronically sophisticated conference facilities, all decorated in a 19th-century grandeur. The rooms are serviced by 150 staff members, among the most efficient in Geneva. Incidentally, 50% of the hotel's visitors are repeat customers, and that says a lot. The hotel has long been ranked by *Institutional Investor* as one of the top hotels of the world. Its two restaurants, even its bar, are so inviting and superior that they are recommended separately.

Hôtel de la Paix, 11 quai du Mont-Blanc, CH-1201 Genève, Switzerland (tel. 022/732-61-50), built in the 18th century, attracted the princes and diplomats of yesterday and welcomes their descendants today. The princes of Liechtenstein and the Grimaldi family, rulers of Monaco, have been patrons of this elegant hostelry, and it has also played host to the queen of the Netherlands, guitarist Andrés Segovia, and dignitaries from all over the world. Designed by an Italian architect and built of stone from Meillerie, the building was a Sardinian possession for a long time, open to all nationalities, as it still is. Among the deluxe choices of Geneva, this is one of the smaller, more select establishments. Sitting directly on the lake, with a view of Mont Blanc, the hotel looks a lot like a city building in Paris. The main salon is a double-tiered arched extravaganza, with marble columns, elaborately carved Corinthian capitals, and a balustraded loggia overlooking a massive crystal chandelier. The 97 bedrooms and suites come in all sizes and many different decorating schemes, but they all have modern baths and all the conveniences of any deluxe hotel. Singles cost from 180F ($122.40) to 215F ($146.20) daily, and doubles range from 340F ($231.20) to 410F ($278.80). This hotel is a member of Leading Hotels of the World and of Switzerland.

Hôtel la Réserve, 301 route de Lausanne, CH-1293 Bellevue-Genève, Switzerland (tel. 022/774-17-41), is a deluxe, traditional establishment surrounded by gardens that explode into bloom every spring with thousands of tulips, dozens of Oriental trees, and Lebanese cedars. Both the private and the public rooms are testimonials to exquisite taste. Because of its beauty, its location (only 12 minutes from both the airport and from the city center), and its extravagant luxury, the hotel draws a high percentage of repeaters. La Reserve is in fact a city landmark. The hotel is set on eight acres of private grounds, focusing on an outdoor pool where summertime buffet lunches draw the svelte set, a lakeside terrace, four tennis courts, and a private pier, which offers motor launches for rent by hotel guests. In brief, this is a hotel of great style and charm. Its Chinese restaurant, Tse-Fung, has the best Oriental food in Geneva, and the French food in the main dining room costs 100F ($68) to 150F ($102) for a full meal. Handsomely furnished single rooms rent for 220F ($149.60) to 275F ($187) daily, and doubles go for 320F ($217.60) to 410F ($278.80).

Hôtel Président, 47 quai Wilson, CH-1211 Genève, Switzerland (tel. 022/731-10-00), lies on the lakeshore in a modern building that looks more like a diplomatic headquarters of some international agency than a hotel. Each of the rooms has floor-to-ceiling sliding windows to let in as much air and light as possible, and all are beautifully furnished with a rich collection of statuary, antiques, and elegant upholstery. The public rooms are nothing short of opulent, many with floors that appear to be lapis lazuli and velvet-covered walls. The Gobelin tapestries in one of the galleries will catch your attention. Service is impeccable, from the bell captain who will arrange for your luggage to be sent to your room to the waiters in the famous Grill Room. The establishment is directed by Jacques H. Farre, who works for the Swissôtel chain.

The air-conditioned rooms overlook the lake and cost 255F ($173.40) in a single (it will have two beds regardless of single occupancy), 355F ($241.40) in a double. Things do not come cheap here, but the world does indeed come to Geneva, and an elite segment of it chooses to bed down in style at the Président.

Hôtel Intercontinental, 7-9 Petit Saconnex, CH-1211 Genève, Switzerland (tel. 022/734-60-91), can be found halfway between the airport and the city center, next to the United Nations complex near the lake. The building rises high above surrounding greenery, a rectangle of steel and glass flanked by an outdoor swimming pool. The public rooms include one gourmet restaurant, Les Continents, whose Louis XV–style armchairs and polished light-grained paneling reflect the gleam of the many crystal chandeliers, and the Pergola, less formal than its companion restaurant, whose forest-green walls are covered floor to ceiling with white lattices.

The bedrooms, all air-conditioned, are decorated in a wide variety of styles, many with beautifully patterned wallpaper and matching bedspreads, while the suites experiment successfully with unusual color schemes in an opulent ambience. Singles rent for 210F ($193.80) to 285F ($142.80) per day, and doubles cost from 250F ($170) to 340F ($231.20).

Hôtel du Rhône, quai Turrettini, CH-1211 Genève, Switzerland (tel. 022/731-98-31), lies behind a row of verdant trees along a bank of the Rhône. Constructed in 1950, it has remained up-to-date and innovative. The symmetrical façade extends a long distance along the riverfront, with evenly spaced concrete ribs running vertically down the front of the building. The hotel has had enough renovations to keep it competitive with the other deluxe palaces of Geneva, and general manager Pierre Vogt and resident manager Eric Glattfelder do everything they can to ensure perfect service and personalized attention. The public rooms display tapestries by contemporary artists. There are two restaurants, one with a sun terrace, and one bar with a coffee sun terrace. The hotel has 281 rooms including eight suites, all freshly decorated with attractively patterned wall-to-wall carpeting, natural colors, and classically elegant furniture, many of them with excellent views of the city. All the units have baths, color TV, phones, and mini-bars. Singles cost from 170F ($115.60) to 225F ($153) daily, and doubles range from 350F ($238) to 550F ($374). A subterranean parking garage accommodates 120 cars. The Hotel du Rhône belongs to the Rafael Group of Hoteliers and is a member of the Leading Hotels of the World.

Hôtel Bristol, 10 rue du Mont-Blanc, CH-1201 Genève, Switzerland (tel. 022/732-38-00), is 130 years old and has been one of the most sought-after hostelries in Geneva since its establishment. It sits in a beflowered public park at the lake end of a famous street leading into the Mont Blanc Bridge. The public rooms are elegantly furnished; the bedrooms are pleasingly filled with clear colors and classically tasteful antiques; some contain the kinds of pieces you'd expect in a provincial manor house. All units have modern bath and double-glazed windows for soundproofing. Singles cost from 209F ($142.10) to 244F ($165.90) daily and doubles from 313F ($212.85) to 353F ($240.05). Some of the suites cost considerably more. The bar is popular with Geneva's business-lunch set, and so is the graceful, lighthearted, high-ceilinged restaurant, the view from which opens onto the trees in the square behind the hotel.

Hôtel de la Cigogne, 17 place Longemalle, CH-1204 Genève, Switzerland (tel. 022/21-42-42), is a deluxe hostelry totally re-created after years of post–World War II dilapidation. Combined with an adjoining building, the old hotel and its mate have the carefully renovated façades of the original 18th- and 19th-century structures. With three courtyards on the place Longemalle side, the Cigogne is one of the quietest hotels in town. The 50 double rooms are all fully air-conditioned, with direct-dial phones, TV, radios, mini-bars, wake-up systems, and safes. All have luxurious bathrooms, with marble or enameled tile, towels, and fittings in matching colors. The bedrooms are each decorated and furnished in individual styles and have handmade mattresses and bed linen with the hotel's arms embroidered on the corner. A double costs 285F ($193.80) daily, 205F ($139.40) for single occupancy. Junior suites for two go for 375F ($255), regular suites costing 560F ($380.80). An extra bed in a unit will be placed for 50F ($34) additional. Prices include breakfast, service, and taxes.

The hotel restaurant, designed in the best Harry's Bar style, has elegant leather banquettes and chairs. One side of the room is of wood, the opposite wall having a sky-blue glass screen. The cuisine is classical. Director Richard Bischoff is assisted by an attentive staff in seeing to the needs of hotel and dinner guests.

Hôtel d'Angleterre, 17 quai du Mont-Blanc, CH-1201 Genève, Switzerland (tel. 022/732-81-80). Nearly two dozen of the bedrooms of this grand old hotel of another era offer vantage points overlooking the lake. If your room has a balcony, it will usually be big enough for you and a friend to sit on for your *petit déjeuner*. Accommodations for the most part are spacious, furnished with desks, armchairs, and fine furniture, and come with high ceilings and plenty of closet space. The walls are extra thick and the windows are double-glazed for soundproofing. The uppermost rooms are the most desirable because of their view, but you'll need to reserve them at least a month in advance. R. O. Bucher is the manager, and in its category his hotel is one of the best in Geneva. A private bath comes with each of the 66 rooms, which are priced at 175F ($119) to 260F ($176.80) daily for a single, 250F ($170) to 370F ($251.60) for a double, breakfast included. The club lounge downstairs attracts visitors from the financial district, and the hotel restaurant opens onto a panoramic view of the lakeside promenade.

Hôtel l'Arbalète, 3 Tour-Maîtresse, CH-1204 Genève, Switzerland (tel. 022/28-41-55), offers the kind of rustic and elegant charm many visitors seek on trips to Europe. There are two covered parking places about a five-minute walk from the hotel. The 33 bedrooms are all different from one another, usually appointed with antiques and outfitted with heavily beamed ceilings or exposed timbers. One of the accommodations has a two-level format of light-grained wood and flowery wallpaper. Singles range from 210F ($142.80) to 250F ($170) daily, and doubles cost 275F ($189) to 320F ($217.60). All units are air-conditioned, with private bath and all the conveniences. A pub next door to the hotel is an English-style paneled room, with inviting chairs and a gently curved bar. This establishment is about a five-minute walk from the lake and the old town.

THE UPPER BRACKET: Opposite the train station is **Le Warwick,** 14 rue de Lausanne, CH-1201 Genève, Switzerland (tel. 022/731-62-50). The superstructure of this contemporary hotel rises like a network of honeycombed cells placed on top of two stories of leg-like supports that shelter restaurants, a piano bar, a gift shop, and a sauna. The lobby area is a visually striking arrangement of sweeping staircases, abstract-design loggias and balconies, hanging illuminated globes, and marble floors under a scattering of Oriental rugs. The refurbished bedrooms are sunny, boldly patterned, and comfortable, and each has soundproof windows, modern plumbing, and air conditioning, as well as TV, minibar, and direct-dial phone. Singles cost from 215F ($146.20) to 260F ($176.80) daily, and doubles range from 290F ($197.20) to 340F ($231.20), all with a buffet breakfast included.

Cristal Hôtel, 4 rue Pradier, CH-1201 Genève, Switzerland (tel. 022/731-34-00), is a four-star hotel, that opened for business in 1983. It sits on a peaceful street with lots of greenery one block south of the train station. The façade looks like a streamlined piece of poured concrete with awnings fluttering in the breeze above the entrance. Underground parking is available at the garage complex at the train station, along with most of Geneva conveniently within walking distance. The soundproof rooms are well ventilated and come with private bath, color TV, video, radio, phone, and mini-bar. They are comfortably carpeted, with vivid color schemes and tasteful furniture. A buffet breakfast is included in the daily charge of 120F ($81.60) to 150F ($102) daily in a single, 170F ($115.60) to 200F ($136) in a double.

Hôtel Ambassador, 21 quai des Bergues, CH-1201 Genève, Switzerland (tel. 022/731-72-00), is on a well-known part of Geneva's lakefront about a block away from its deluxe neighbor, the Hôtel des Bergues. The restrained façade of this establishment, with neoclassical detailings around the tall windows, faces the Place Chevelu, with its trees and its four streams of water gushing from a single fountain. If you ask for a room on one of the top two floors you'll have a view of Mont Blanc. In summer a pleasant café opens onto the pavement in front of the hotel. The smallish rooms are conservatively decorated in light colors and traditionally classic furnishings. A restaurant on the ground floor serves satisfying French-Swiss meals. The director, B. G. Zamboni, administers the 92 rooms, charging from 100F ($68) to 150F ($102) daily in a single and from 155F ($105.40) to 230F ($156.40) in a double. All rooms have bath (the hotel was built in 1966) and contain phone, radio, color TV, and refrigerator. Parking and room service are both available.

Hôtel Cornavin, Place Cornavin, 33 boulevard James-Fazy, CH-1211 Genève, Switzerland (tel. 022/732-21-00). The lobby of this renovated 125-room hotel 50 yards from the train station is laid out in gray-and-white marble in a circular pattern of random widths. The rest of the hotel is modern in styling, with a generous application of bright colors and vivid floral patterns in the carpeted bedrooms. The Cornavin is on a busy thoroughfare in the business district, but the rooms are soundproofed against the traffic noises, and 96 of them are air-conditioned. All contain showers or baths. Manager Krieger charges from 110F ($74.80) to 145F ($98.60) daily in a single and from 155F ($105.40) to 190F ($129.20) in a double, with breakfast included. There's a 30F ($20.40) charge if an extra bed is set up in any room.

Hôtel Rex, 44 avenue Wendt, CH-1203 Genève, Switzerland (tel. 022/45-71-50), is five minutes away from the airport but only a few blocks away from the train station and the lake. Its streamlined entrance is simple, with the name of the hotel written in script on a black background, surrounded by sculpted ornamental shrubs in pots serving as a framework. The rooms, tastefully furnished in restrained colors with dignified leather armchairs and containing modern baths, rent for 115F ($78.20) to 180F ($122.40) daily in a single, 215F ($146.20) to 280F ($190.40) in a double, breakfast included. Also on the premises is an English bar, a drawing room, and a beautifully appointed reading room.

Hôtel California, 1 rue Gevray, CH-1200 Genève, Switzerland (tel. 022/731-55-50). The decor, as you'd expect in a hotel of this name, is imaginatively colorful, functionally modern, and lighthearted. Only a block from the lake, behind the quai du Mont-Blanc, the hotel is housed in a six-story rectangular building of aluminum, glass, and sea-green enameled panels that looks something like an office building. Bedrooms have baths, direct-dial phones, mini-bars, cosmetic bars, color TV, hairdryers, and radios. There's one entire floor of apartments with kitchenettes available for one or two persons. In standard rooms, singles rent for 110F ($74.80) to 140F ($95.20) daily, twins for 180F ($122.40) to 210F ($142.80), and triples for 245F ($166.60). Breakfast is included in all these terms. The manager is M.L. Gaillard. There's no restaurant in the hotel, but you can get a drink in the rooftop bar until the wee hours of the morning.

Hôtel les Armures, 1 rue des Puits-St-Pierre, CH-1204 Genève, Switzerland (tel. 022/728-91-72), is a hotel discovery in the center of the old town, one of the most charming in Geneva. It's housed in a 17th-century building that until 1981 was used as a printing factory. The public rooms have been restored to reveal the original painted ceiling beams and a blue-and-gray fresco, which management thinks is from the original building. Today the lobby is covered with Oriental rugs and several pieces of well-placed modern sculpture, which complement the suit of medieval armor standing in a corner. The hotel is housed in the same building as the oldest café in Geneva (see my restaurant recommendations, coming up). It's reached through a separate entrance on the other side of the block. Parking might be a problem here as the hotel lies deep in a maze of one-way streets. Singles range from 200F ($136) to 310F ($210.80) daily, and doubles cost from 310F ($210.80) to 400F ($272). All the handsomely furnished bedrooms are air-conditioned and contain private baths, radios, phones, and color TV with video.

THE MEDIUM-PRICED RANGE: You'll recognize the **Hôtel Excelsior,** 34 rue Rousseau, CH-1201 Genève, Switzerland (tel. 022/732-09-45), in summer by the kind of sidewalk café where you'll want to stop and have coffee before returning to the onslaught of Geneva. A ground-floor restaurant, La Brocherie, serves French-Swiss food, while the rooms upstairs are comfortable and brightly decorated, with modern plumbing. They rent for 85F ($57.80) to 115F ($78.20) daily in a single and for 120F ($91.60) to 140F ($95.20) in a double, breakfast included.

Hôtel Moderne, 1 rue de Berne, CH-1211 Genève, Switzerland (tel. 022/732-81-00), is close to the train station, which, as you will find, is not far from the lake. The building is a seven-story symmetrical rectangle painted white, with a low-lying glass-walled restaurant housed in an extension of the main building. The entrance is an aperture with a glass door marked by six large decals identifying the many touring companies which have given their endorsement. The public rooms, as the name of the hotel implies, are most *moderne*, with lots of Nordic tripod tables, molded plywood chairs, and best of all, a free-form unframed mirror like a silvery protoplasm stretching eight feet across one of the walls. The bedrooms are predictably furnished, clean, comfortable, and sunny. They rent for 50F ($34) to 95F ($64.60) daily in a single, from 120F ($81.60) to 130F ($88.40) in a double, including breakfast. Not all of the rooms have private bath, so be sure to know before you commit yourself. The management speaks five languages, so communication shouldn't be a problem. The owners are the Wilhelm family.

Hôtel Suisse, 10 place Cornavin, CH-1201 Genève, Switzerland (tel. 022/732-66-30), is directly opposite the railroad station, in a modern building with pleasing proportions and oversize soundproof windows. Recent renovations include an almost complete facelift of the interior, leaving behind an inviting lobby with russet walls, lots of paintings, and a sweeping staircase. Most of the bedrooms have private baths, phones, color TV, radios, and mini-bars. Singles cost 115F ($78.20) to 130F ($88.40) daily, and doubles rent for 140F ($95.20) to 160F ($108.80), with breakfast included.

Hôtel Mon-Repos, 131 rue de Lausanne, CH-1202 Genève, Switzerland (tel. 022/732-80-10). A long expanse of green lawn is what you'll see from the lakeside windows of this hotel, on the right bank of Lake Geneva. If the day is clear you'll even see Mont Blanc in the distance. The hotel curves gently around a corner, alternating recessed balconies with elegantly detailed windows on the sandstone façade. All the comfortable bedrooms are equipped with phones, radios, and utilitarian furniture. Singles rent for 110F ($78.20) to 135F ($91.80) daily, and doubles go for 140F ($95.20) to 165F ($112.20). The hotel is owned by the Keller family, who also offer apartments with kitchenettes for guests planning to stay for longer periods.

Hôtel le Chandelier, 23 Grand-Rue, CH-1204 Genève, Switzerland (tel. 022/721-56-88), offers two dozen recently renovated bedchambers. My favorites are the ones on the top floor with sloping ceiling and gabled windows opening on views out over the rooftops of the old town. The place reeks with atmosphere and is considered one of the special hotels of Geneva, particularly since parts of the building date from the 14th century. The hotel is on a cobblestone street a few minutes' walk from the lake. In spite of the rather narrow lobby, the rooms are good-sized, with bathrooms that have been called "baronial." If you're planning an extended stay, a dozen studios come with kitchens, making this one of the special treasures of Geneva. Each room has a bath or shower, toilet, phone, radio, and color TV. Singles cost from 80F ($54.40) to 120F ($81.60) daily, while doubles range from 120F ($81.60) to 160F ($108.80). A restaurant on the ground floor is under different management. The street in front of the hotel is closed to traffic from 11 p.m. to 6 a.m., a boon to sleepers.

Hôtel du Midi, 4 place Chevelu, CH-1211 Genève, Switzerland (tel. 022/731-78-00), is on the same tree-lined square as the Hôtel Ambassador, a location ideal for sightseeing in Geneva. The building rises iike an apartment house eight stories into the air, its salmon-colored panels alternating with the big windows and the visible parts of the concrete structure. The hotel is much better than it looks from the outside. The windows are double-glazed to keep out the noise, and there's wall-to-wall carpeting in every room. The hotel is loaded with thoughtful extras, such as warming racks for towels, tiny refrigerators in the rooms, even built-in safes for your valuables. Singles cost 108F ($73.45) to 140F ($95.20) daily, and doubles rent for 145F ($98.60) to 185F ($125.80). A street-level brasserie decorated with wallpaper and hanging lamps, a tavern on the ground floor serving drinks and snacks, and a sidewalk café in front of the splashing fountain in the place Chevelu make this place a drawing card.

Hôtel la Tourelle, 26 route d'Hermance, CH-1222 Vésenaz-Genève, Switzerland (tel. 022/752-16-28), offers more than two dozen attractively styled and comfortably furnished bedrooms in what used to be a private villa in a suburb to the northeast of Geneva. Many of the rooms offer views of the lake beyond the well-maintained grounds of clipped grass and ornamental trees. Alice and Roland Klinger, the owners, charge from 90F ($61.20) to 100F ($68) daily for a single in summer, from 80F ($54.40) to 90F ($61.20) in winter. Doubles cost from 110F ($74.80) to 140F ($95.20) in summer, from 100F ($68) to 110F ($74.80) in winter. All rooms contain baths or showers, and breakfast is included in the rates. The suburb of Vésenaz is rather exclusive, so you'll get a glimpse of what the Swiss consider a wealthy residential area during your treks back and forth to the city, only 12 minutes away by car or bus.

Penta-Hôtel, 75-77 avenue Louis-Casaï, CH-1216 Cointrin-Genève, Switzerland (tel. 022/798-47-00), is close to the Geneva airport offering clean and comfortable rooms, all soundproof, with air conditioning, baths, radios, phones, color TV with in-house movies, and mini-bars. The conservatively furnished units rent for 190F ($129.20) to 285F ($193.80) daily in a single and 260F ($176.80) to 390F ($265.20) in a double. The building is sleek and modern, with lots of exposed glass, and offers two restaurants, a bar, a fitness center, a sauna, and boutiques, newsstands, and a car-rental agency. A hotel shuttle bus makes regular runs to the airport, and public buses go on frequent trips to Geneva from a bus stop in front of the hotel. Many of the conference rooms and some of the public lounges are decorated with a pattern of carpeting designed to rivet your attention to its random op-art patterns of bright green on black.

Hôtel Touring-Balance, 13 place Longemalle, CH-1204 Genève, Switzerland (tel. 022/28-71-22), about two blocks east of the lake and just off the street that runs into pont du Mont-Blanc, is a personalized hotel which represents the union of what used to be a Hotel Touring and a Hotel Balance. The team effort you can see today has proved to be a successful facility that attracts a frequently returning clientele. The interior at its best seems to represent a kind of updated Victorian, with an appealing highlighting of many of the original architectural details with different colors of paint, along with some interesting original modern paintings. The restaurant is a bright, sunny room with a high ceiling and tasteful light art nouveau chairs and serving trolleys. Singles rent for 120F ($81.60) to 140F ($95.20) daily, and doubles cost 140F ($95.20) to 180F ($122.40), with breakfast included.

Hôtel Carlton, 22 rue Amat, CH-1202 Genève, Switzerland (tel. 022/ 731-68-50), is about seven city blocks east of the railroad station, on a street some 300 yards from quai Wilson. The façade is an attractive combination of weathered vertical slats and smooth stones decoratively cemented into rectangular patterns below the modern windows. The interior is warmly decorated in browns, beiges, and wood tones, with pin lighting in the reception area. All rooms have bath and phone. Apartments and "super studios" with kitchens and terraces are available for longer stays. Rental price by the day is from 150F ($102) to 185F ($125.80) daily in a single, from 195F ($132.60) to 270F ($183.60) in a double. Prices include taxes, service, and breakfast but do not allow use of the kitchen. B. Grütter, the director, will provide monthly rates on request.

Hotel Grand-Pré, 35 rue du Grand-Pré, CH-1202 Genève (tel. 022/733-91-50), can be considered a real discovery for visitors to Geneva. The carefully selected staff will give directions to the airport or the center of Geneva, both of which are within easy reach. No restaurant is connected to the hotel. The rooms are well styled, comfortable, and attractively decorated, with maintainance on a high level. Singles in this modern hostelry go for 127F ($86.35) to 147F ($99.95) daily, from 177F ($120.35) to 197F ($133.90) in a double, breakfast included. All units contain private bath, color TV, radio, and refrigerator. Special terms are available for families and for long stays.

Hotel International & Terminus, 20 rue des Alpes, CH-1201 Genève, Switzerland (tel. 022/732-80-95), is run by the Cottier family with the assistance of the dedicated manager, A. Perucchi. It's midway between the railroad station and the lake, about a ten-minute walk to either one. A phone and radio are to be found in every room, although some are not equipped with bath. However, there's a sink in each room, and breakfast is provided free. Singles rent for 52F ($35.35) to 95F ($64.60) daily, and doubles range from 75F ($51) to 130F ($88.40). The public rooms are decorated with reproduction Louis XIII–style chairs, and Oriental rugs. *Plats du jour* in the attached restaurant start at a reasonable 9.50F ($6.45).

Hostellerie de la Vendée, 28 chemin de la Vendée, CH-1213 Geneva–Petit-Lancy, Switzerland (tel. 022/792-04-11). The terrace of this country inn three miles from the center of Geneva is covered with a bright awning beneath which guests sip drinks or coffee and listen to the birds sing. The Righetto family are your hosts, welcoming you to the semi-rural ambience of this modern hostelry which is for the most part attractively decorated in rustic Swiss fashion. The hotel has a bar, a restaurant, and sometimes a local wedding reception in one of the conference rooms. Singles rent for 110F ($74.80) to 155F ($105.40) daily, while doubles cost 180F ($122.40) to 220F ($149.60). Additional beds can be set up for 40F ($27.20) apiece. Breakfast is included in the rates. The restaurant on the premises will be previewed later.

Hôtel Eden, 135 rue de Lausanne, CH-1202 Genève, Switzerland (tel. 022/732-65-40), housed in a building close to the quai du Mont-Blanc, looks a lot like a superbly constructed seven-story stone-and-stucco fortress with many art deco influences. A generously proportioned set of steps takes you into the lobby where you register after passing below the pleasingly curved and indented two-tone façade. Bedrooms are spacious and high-ceilinged. Charges are from 110F ($74.80) to 125F ($85) daily in a single and from 150F ($102) to 170F ($115.60) in a double. Breakfast is included.

Savoy Hôtel, 8 place Cornavin, CH-1201 Genève, Switzerland (tel. 022/ 731-12-55). A quick glance at a city map will tell you that this hotel is across the square from the main railroad station. It's decorated in a tasteful, streamlined kind of way, with Directoire armchairs in a lobby inlaid with a geometric pattern of different kinds of hardwoods. Bedrooms are air-conditioned and soundproof, each with phone, radio, and color TV (usually placed out of the way on a shelf near the ceiling). Comfortably furnished singles with bath cost 107F ($72.75) to

140F ($95.20), and doubles rent for 150F ($102) to 200F ($136). The hotel has a restaurant and bar.

Hôtel Century, 24 avenue de Frontenex, CH-1207 Genève, Switzerland (tel. 022/736-80-95), is striking with its use of burnished copper and polished hardwoods in the lobby area. In the restaurant/bar, a copper chimney divided into rectangles almost like a Mondrian painting descends from the ceiling to catch the smoke from the fireplace in the center of the room. Black marble and Oriental rugs abound, creating an ambience that is warm, comfortable, and inviting. The hotel is within walking distance of both the Rhône and the lake. The 150 rooms are comfortably decorated. All units have bath. The hotel manager, Renzo Zanon, charges from 130F ($88.40) to 160F ($108.80) daily in a single and from 180F ($122.40) to 250F ($170) in a double, breakfast included.

Hôtel de Berne, 26 rue de Berne, CH-1201 Genève, Switzerland (tel. 022/731-60-00). Modern and boxy, with maroon racing stripes spanning the façade horizontally, this centrally located hotel, directed by S. DiMare, offers 88 soundproof rooms with air conditioning, bath, phone, and TV. The lobby is a high-ceilinged expanse of wood columns and patterned carpeting. Bedrooms are functionally decorated in comfortable furnishings and muted colors. Each unit has a direct-dial phone, radio, mini-bar, color TV, and a bath or shower. Singles cost from 150F ($102) daily, doubles from 190F ($129.20), and suites from 250F ($170) for two, all with breakfast included. A restaurant and bar are on the premises.

Hôtel Edelweiss, 2 place de la Navigation, CH-1201 Genève, Switzerland (tel. 022/731-36-58). My favorite rooms here are the ones furnished with naïvely provincial pine reproductions, probably from the mountain regions of Switzerland. The hotel façade rises eight stories above its neighbors near the quai Wilson. It looks something like a stack of pale-green and white building blocks piled four across and eight high, with prominent windows set in the concrete superstructure. Whoever decorated the lobby seems to have tried to recreate some alpine grange, with a reception desk fashioned something like a well. All of this aside, the rooms are comfortable, clean, and cozy, costing 89F ($60.50) to 123F ($83.65) daily in a single and 146F ($99.30) to 167F ($113.55) in a double, breakfast included. A complimentary airport shuttle service is provided from 9:30 a.m. until the last flight comes in.

Hôtel Epsom, 18 rue Richemont, CH-1202 Genève, Switzerland (tel. 022/732-08-33), offering 330 beds in two modern buildings joined by an interconnecting lobby, is within walking distance of the railroad station, the lake, and everything of note in Geneva. The management displays two flags over the entrance, one for Switzerland, one for the city of Geneva. The lobby features an elongated marble reception desk and a marble floor protected by an almost never-ending row of blue, red, and black Oriental rugs in bold geometric patterns. Singles here rent for 147F ($99.95) daily and doubles cost 215F ($146.20), breakfast included. Rooms are comfortably furnished. A restaurant and bar are on the premises.

THE BUDGET CATEGORY: Not far from the rue des Deux Ponts, the **Hôtel le Grenil,** 7 avenue de Sainte-Clothilde, CH-1205 Genève, Switzerland (tel. 022/728-30-55), rises on a plot of land between the junction of the Rhône and the Arve. Besides the many conference facilities, the hotel offers 50 rooms, many with showers and toilets. Affiliated with the YMCA, it's only a short distance from the center of town and is said to be one of the "best for value" candidates in Geneva. Everything is streamlined, modern, and warmly decorated. Although the rooms are smallish, they're sunny and clean, costing 55F ($37.40) to 80F ($54.40) daily in a single, from 75F ($51) to 100F ($68) in a double, from 96F ($65.30) to 120F ($81.60) in a triple, and from 110F ($74.80) to 130F ($88.40) in a family room, which has four beds. Breakfast is included for all registered guests in any room, and the hotel has complete facilities for handicapped patrons. The director is Harry van Dongen.

Hôtel Lido, 8 rue Chantepoulet, CH-1201 Genève, Switzerland (tel. 022/ 731-55-30), is two blocks from the train station and offers sunny, soundproof rooms with views over the city. The hotel is small enough to offer personalized service, with 32 rooms decorated in modern colors with comfortable beds. The Rossier family are your hosts. All doubles contain private baths and cost from 75F ($51) to 100F ($68) daily. However, some singles don't have private baths, and these are cheaper of course, costing from 48F ($32.65) daily, rising to 58F ($39.45) with private baths.

Hôtel Bernina, 22 place Cornavin, CH-1211 Genève, Switzerland (tel. 022/731-49-50), sits on the square opposite the train station in an old-fashioned rectangular building, with iron balustrades on the balconies and neo-classical detailing around the windows. The hotel offers 80 rooms on six floors, and windows are double-glazed to keep out street noise. Bedrooms are often spacious, all with color TV and direct-dial phones, and some of the closets are big enough to store trunks in. Paul-André à Porta, the English-speaking manager, charges from 55F ($37.40) to 85F ($57.80) daily in a single, from 85F ($57.80) to 126F ($85.70) in a double, and from 115F ($78.20) to 175F ($119) in a triple, breakfast included.

Hôtel Windsor, 31 rue de Berne, CH-1201 Genève, Switzerland (tel. 022/ 731-71-30), is four blocks from the quai Wilson and three blocks from the train station. Rooms are small and a little dated, yet for the price, you might want to make it your address in Geneva for a night. All doubles contain private baths and range in price from 100F ($68) to 130F ($88.40) daily. Singles without bath cost from 55F ($37.40) to 65F ($44.20), rising to 75F ($51) to 95F ($64.60) with private bath. A continental breakfast is included. Each unit has a phone and radio. There's a total of 100 beds. The lobby is focused around a large masonry fireplace and is decorated in shades of blue and red.

Hôtel Pâquis-Fleuri, 23 rue des Pâquis, CH-1201 Genève, Switzerland (tel. 022/731-34-53), lies only two blocks from the prestigious hotels on the quai du Mont-Blanc but is considerably cheaper. In fact it's one of the best hotel buys in town. It contains only a dozen rooms (and are they scrubbed!), which are for the most part pleasantly furnished, offer phones, and can be reached by elevator from the lobby. Some of the units face a tranquil courtyard. With showers, singles cost 70F ($47.60) daily, and doubles go for 120F ($81.60). Without showers, singles rent for 50F ($34) and doubles for 75F ($51). To cut costs, breakfast is not offered, but many cafés lie nearby. Try to get a room away from the street. Otherwise, you're likely to be bothered by traffic noises.

Hôtel du Lac, 15 rue des Eaux-Vives, CH-1207 Genève, Switzerland (tel. 022/735-45-80), is an economy oasis, the result of a Swiss-Italian alliance, both of whom are fluent in English. The Cagnoli-Spiess couple welcomes travelers who take the elevator to the sixth floor of their small hotel which lies on the left bank in the old city. The place is simple but kept spic and span. Rooms are comfortably furnished, and there are adequate showers in the hall. In a double or twin, expect to pay from 73F ($49.65) per night, the price going up to 97F ($65.95) in a triple. Singles, depending on the room, range from 47F ($31.95) to 53F ($36.05). The couple do not pretend to offer luxury service, but they make up for it with their helpfulness in providing information about their city. All their units have a radio and phone, plus a balcony opening onto city life. Take bus number 5 from the station, getting off at the place des Eaux-Vives (fifth stop).

Hôtel Jean-Jacques Rousseau, 13 rue J-J Rousseau, CH-1201 Genève, Switzerland (tel. 022/731-55-70), honors the French author and political theorist who was born in Geneva in 1712. The hotel is well located, not far from the river-fronting quai des Bergues, on a busy commercial street. The establishment is best known for its restaurant, Locanda Ticinese, but it also offers 18 bedrooms with personalized service from the family which runs it. A typical unit is well lit, carpeted, and decorated with comfortable furniture. Singles rent for 85F ($57.80) to 110F ($74.80) daily, doubles for 120F ($81.60) to 140F ($95.20), and triples for 165F ($112.20), breakfast included. Some suites are also available. You may not be able to get a room without a reservation, as the hotel is popular.

Hôtel le Clos Voltaire, 49 rue de Lyon, CH-1203 Genève, Switzerland (tel. 022/744-70-14), receives the highest recommendation in its category, especially for the history buff who'll want to know how this house was connected with Voltaire. Set in a floral park, the suburban location is tranquil. Covered with vines, the house is on the main road to Lyon, offering parking in front and an attractive garden. The hotel has 41 rooms, four of them with kitchens, 16 with showers or baths, and the rest with wash basins. Singles rent for 55F ($37.40) daily without bath, 75F ($51) with bath. Bathless doubles cost 90F ($61.20), doubles with bath going for 120F ($81.60). Breakfast is included in the rates. This hotel is ideal if you have a private car, and it is only about a five-minute walk from the train station.

Hôtel Beau-Site, 3 place du Cirque, CH-1204 Genève, Switzerland (tel. 022/728-10-08). The elevator lifts you to the reception desk of this elaborately embellished hotel near the university. It offers 55 beds in rooms that are well kept but not lavishly furnished. It's obvious that the English-speaking management has expended a lot of elbow grease here. Recent renovations have improved the public rooms too. The units offer a range of plumbing possibilities. Singles rent for 48F ($32.65) to 55F ($37.40) daily, while doubles cost from 68F ($46.25) to 75F ($51), breakfast included. Nonworking marble fireplaces are in some of the bedrooms, and oversize, heavily carved sideboards in the dining room. Take bus 1 from the train station.

3. WHERE TO DINE

Geneva is one of the gastronomic centers of Europe, with a decided French influence, as would be expected. None of the Genevese today seems to heed Calvin's warnings against "the pleasures of the table." Eating well in Geneva is practiced with consummate flair and style, and meals are frequently long, drawn-out affairs.

Despite its position as one of the international hubs of the world, there aren't as many different cuisines as you might have anticipated (although it has one of the greatest Chinese restaurants in all of Europe).

Geneva naturally serves all the typically Swiss dishes, such as filets of perch from Lake Geneva and fricassée of pork. In season, many of its restaurants offer a marvelous vegetable that has some of the taste of an artichoke. It's called *cardoon* and is usually served au gratin. By all means try the Genevese sausage, longeole. From Lac Léman emerges one of the great fishes found in any alpine lake, omble chevalier, like a grayling. Some gourmets have compared it to salmon. However, this fish has been harvested so much it is endangered.

Cheese is also important on the Genevese table, including such Swiss cheeses as tomme and Gruyère, plus, in season, vacherin from the Joux Valley. Naturally, everything will taste better with Perlan (white wine) and Gamay (red wine) from Geneva's own vineyards.

Now, the bad news. Geneva is one of the most expensive cities in Europe for dining out.

SOME DELUXE CHOICES: Increasingly acclaimed by critics as the best restaurant of Geneva, **Le Cygne,** Noga Hilton International, 19 quai du Mont-Blanc (tel. 022/731-98-11), offers a refined cuisine and impeccable service that is also warm and human. In deluxe surroundings, guests can dine with a superb view of the water fountain and Mont Blanc. This highly rated restaurant, with its elegant trappings, is a showcase for the culinary skills of a young chef, Gilles

Dupont. He worked his way up through the ranks, serving his apprenticeship in Juan-les-Pins, London, Montréal, in Sweden, where he learned the subtle techniques of marinating fish. Born in 1956, this young Frenchman has become a famous name in gastronomy in both France and Switzerland.

The menu changes, based on the seasons. A business lunch is offered for 52F ($35.35) and a set dinner for 125F ($85). You can also order from a well-chosen and well-balanced à la carte menu. One hesitates to recommend specialty dishes, because they are always changing, based on the inspired talent of Monsieur Dupont. You can select from such dishes as tartare of sea bass and oysters with olive oil, and fried duck liver with a spicy sauce and endives. You might also want to try the fried turbot with bacon and celery or the grilled red mullet with squid in a wine sauce. But, above all, try the sweetbreads, kidneys, and brains in an enriched gravy, as well as thin slices of duck breast with its own liver with a sauce made with old vinegar. Everything is prepared to perfection, and hours are daily from noon to 2 p.m. and 7 to 10:30 p.m. Guests choose from several trolleys of homemade desserts, and excellent wines may be selected from the well-stocked cellars. You can also order wine by the glass from the "California Wine Machine."

For an elegant and excellent meal, go to the **Restaurant du Parc des Eaux-Vives,** 82 quai Gustave-Ador (tel. 022/735-41-40). You'll pass through a wrought-iron gate, immaculately maintained grounds, and a winding driveway to the dining room of a pinkish-gray stone château owned by the city of Geneva. By almost everyone's vote, the restaurant lies in the most beautiful part of Geneva (a section of it reserved for the Geneva Tennis Club). The chefs adjust the menu according to the produce of the season, but tend to concentrate on the time-honored recipes of classical French cuisine. The local trout is superb, and the menu offers many game dishes in autumn. Of course everything tastes better with truffles, including lobster salad, foie gras, and suprême of sea perch with green lettuce and champagne sauce or the breast of duck with olives or cherries. The restaurant shuts down on Monday and from January until mid-February. Dinners cost around 95F ($64.60) daily, but lunchtime meals are less expensive, from 60F ($34). The restaurant serves daily from noon to 2:30 p.m. and from 7 p.m.

Restaurant L'Amphitryon, 33 quai des Bergues (tel. 022/731-50-50). At one of the most prestigious hotels of Geneva (the Hôtel des Bergues), you'll dine in the ambience of a Louis Philippe decor. The chefs, supervised by Albert Felli, produce a blend of classical and cuisine moderne that the Genevois find most alluring. Amphitryon is synonymous with "host," from the character in the Molière play. The staff provides impeccable service. It can be difficult to select from among the tempting offerings on the menu. The assortment of hot and cold appetizers is so enticing that you could make a meal just by sampling them. Pigeon of Bresse served in a mold blended with Armagnac, marinated crab claws with soya beans and pink grapefruit quarters, a terrine of fresh duck liver, and such hot appetizers as artichoke hearts with spinach leaves seasoned with shallots and a delectable shellfish ravioli in a crayfish sauce flavored with basil will tempt you. Even the soups Chef Felli prepares are unique: chicken cream soup with pieces of frogs' legs or a clear duck soup with beet juice and sour cream, among others.

Main courses vary with the season, but you might be offered such tempting choices as steamed sea bass with leeks and truffles (a dish that literally melts in your mouth), medallions of lobster with quail eggs and spinach flan, and other seafood choices. Beef lovers will enjoy the flambéed meats prepared at your table. Desserts range from rich pastries and mousses to fresh or stewed fruit or a cheese tray. At lunch, you can order a business person's menu for 48F ($32.65), but in the evening you are more likely to spend 100F ($68) if you order à la carte. The restaurant is open from noon to 3 p.m. and 7 to 11 p.m. It is closed Saturday and Sunday.

Le Chat-Botté, Hôtel Beau-Rivage, 13 quai du Mont-Blanc (tel. 022/731-65-32), serves some of the best food available in Geneva in an elegant format of tapestries and sculpture. The cuisine, although inspired by French classics, is definitely contemporary. In such surroundings in one of the most prestigious hotels in the world, you get stylish, formal service and a medley of dishes, both classic and *moderne*, designed to please both eye and palate. From a large selection, you might compose a meal of filets of fresh red mullet vinaigrette, cutlets of fresh salmon pan-fried with spices, or breast of chicken stuffed with vegetables, plus an array of other superbly prepared dishes. A wine list will open one of the finest cellars in Geneva to you. Your meal might be served on the terrace, where dining by candlelight is at its best if the weather is fine.

None of this comes inexpensively, but many satisfied diners agree that it's all worth the price. Fixed-price meals range from 48F ($32.65) for a business lunch to 100F ($68) for a gourmet repast, while à la carte dinners cost from 105F ($71.40). Reservations are important. The restaurant is open from noon to 2:15 p.m. and 7 to 10:15 p.m., which means you should get there before the closing hour set. The place is closed Saturday and Sunday and for 15 days at Christmas and Easter.

Le Gentilhomme, Hôtel Richemond, Jardin Brunswick (tel. 022/731-14-00). To have a rendezvous at the Richemond was—and *is*—one of the most chic invitations you can extend or receive in Geneva. This is the Maxim's of Geneva, and you will be served a gourmet meal in a 19th-century setting of crimson silk and glittering crystal. Specialties prepared by chef Alain Freyre include scallops and mussels salad with endives, ravioli of lobster and sliced green cabbage, champagne sauce with mosaic of fresh vegetables, and grilled lamb filet with baby marrow and zucchini mousse. The restaurant also has a unique "caviar trolley," from which five kinds of caviar are served from the original four-pound boxes, renewed daily.

Of course, the menu could well be changed at the time of your visit, because the cuisine du marché is based on only the freshest of ingredients. The wines are among the best in the city, and service is from noon to 2:30 p.m. except Saturday and 7 p.m. to midnight every day. You should arrive before 11:30 p.m. Expect to spend 110F ($74.80) and up for an à la carte meal. Set menus range from 90F ($61.20) to 125F ($85). Wear your finery to dine here, enjoying your Périgord truffles (served in a salt crust) or your lobster flown in from Brittany amid the pomp and glory of the Grand Siècle.

THE UPPER BRACKET: A well-known restaurant, **La Perle du Lac,** 128 rue de Lausanne (tel. 022/731-79-35), has been around forever and is owned and maintained by the city of Geneva under the direction of André Hauri. In fashionable Mon Repos park, not far from the United Nations complex, the restaurant has bay windows that look out over ancient trees and elaborately manicured lawns. The interior is lovely, with warm wintertime candlelight, but in summer you may want to reserve a table on the al fresco terrace. A supremely talented French chef, Christian Grenard, does a marvelous fricassée of frogs' legs. Other specialties include omble chevalier (if available), sea bass with mint sabayon, and filet mignon of veal with mushroom mousse and basil. His sorbets (ask for a mixture) are superb. This is the only restaurant in Geneva that opens directly onto the lakefront. A meal without wine will cost from 90F ($61.20). The restaurant is closed on Monday and from around Christmas until the beginning of February. Always reserve ahead. Hours are from noon to 2 p.m. and 7 to 10 p.m.

Le Béarn, 4 quai de la Poste (tel. 022/21-00-28), is a well-established culinary monument with an impressive list of clients, including the Aga Khan, the Baron de Rothschild, and a host of international celebrities. The renovated interior is filled with Empire furniture. Jean-Paul Goddard has elevated this restaurant to the best dining room in the business center of Geneva. His chefs use only the freshest ingredients, prepared to retain their natural flavors. Platters are often works of art, presented by one of the best-trained restaurant staffs in Geneva. At lunch you can order a set menu for 53F ($36.05). In the evening you can enjoy a table d'hôte menu at 85F ($57.80), a menu tradition at 100F ($68), or a menu surprise at 125F ($85). You can also order à la carte. You might begin with lobster vichyssoise with grains of Sevruga caviar or a feuillantine of crayfish with a tartare of seabass and fresh salmon, followed by pigeon suprême, wild grilled salmon, or roast lamb in the style of Provence. Reservations are important. The restaurant is open from noon to 2 p.m. and 7:15 to 10 p.m. daily. However, it is closed Saturday and Sunday from May until the end of September. During the rest of the year, it is closed for Saturday lunch and all day Sunday.

A la Mère Royaume, 9 rue des Corps-Saints (tel. 022/732-70-08), is named after the heroine of 1602 referred to in the introduction, the hearty lass who poured boiling stew over a soldier's head and cracked his skull with her kettle. After all that you'd expect robust regional fare here. What you get instead is delicately cooked French specialties. The head chef is a sophisticated artist in the kitchen, as reflected by the omble chevalier from Lake Geneva. The trout is, in the word of one diner, "divine." The food offered is very much based on the seasons. In the restaurant, fixed-price dinners go for 75F ($51) to 105F ($71.40), although a set menu at lunch is only 48F ($32.65). A la carte meals range from 85F ($57.80) to 110F ($74.80). The least expensive way to eat here is to opt for the brasserie in back of the restaurant or reachable via its own entrance on a rear street. Here set menus are priced at 34F ($23.10) and 42F ($28.55). The wood-paneled restaurant serves food from noon to 2 p.m. and 7 to 10 p.m.; closed Saturday at lunchtime and all day Sunday. Always call for a reservation. The bar is named after that epic battle of 1602.

Tse-Yang, Noga Hilton, 19 quai du Mont-Blanc (tel. 022/732-50-81), is one of the best Chinese restaurants in Switzerland, on the premises of the previously recommended hotel. *La haute gastronomie chinoise* is practiced with consummate flair here. Main dishes include a filet of beef in lobster sauce, breast of chicken in lime sauce, and prawns in black bean sauce. At lunch a set menu is offered for 38F ($25.85), whereas at night you are likely to spend from 65F ($44.20) and up, particularly if you order some of the more expensive dishes such as lacquered duck in the Peking style or a delectable Szechuan lobster. The restaurant, which is elegantly decorated, is open every day from noon to 2:30 p.m. and 7:30 to 10:45 p.m.

Le Duc, 7 quai du Mont-Blanc (tel. 022/731-73-30), is an uncompromisingly excellent restaurant that has built up a faithful clientele by serving the same superbly flavored fish dishes since it opened in 1976. Each guest is welcomed by the director with sincerity and charm, the decor is discreetly elegant, and the setting perfect for seafood prepared with finesse by the Minchelli brothers. Daily shipments of fish arrive from Rungis, the wholesale market of Paris. Standards are so high that the brothers once closed the restaurant for a day during a French strike rather than serve day-old fish. Specialties include virtually everything with gills, but some meat dishes are offered too. Try the red mullet in butter sauce or the fish and crustacean stew, perhaps the crayfish soufflé. Other recommendable main courses include John Dory in butter sauce, sea bass with lemon, or lobster in orange sauce. Count on spending from 90F ($61.20) to 130F ($88.40) for a meal here. Reservations are suggested. It's closed on Sunday and Monday, but open every other day from 12:30 to 2:30 p.m. and 7:30 to 10:30 p.m.

Hostellerie de la Vendée, 28 Chemin de la Vendée (tel. 022/792-04-11), at Petit-Lancy, has an austere, albeit expensive "Calvinist" interior, but the reformer would have been shocked at the devotion to food and service. You'll drive into a countryside district known for its outstanding restaurants. Run by the Righetto brothers, the restaurant is chic and known for its seasonal specialties and location at the edge of Geneva. Go before 10 p.m. (it opens at 7 p.m.) for dinner, or for lunch from noon to 2 p.m. It's closed on Saturday for lunch, and on Sunday, and takes a long Christmas holiday. You'll enjoy the foie gras prepared many different ways by the chef, Monsieur Bonneau. Try also his filet of sea bass or his duckling with peaches. Dessert might be a soufflé Grand Marnier. One specialty that the staff relishes is the chef's bouillabaisse, served only in January. Fixed-price menus cost from 65F ($44.20) to 100F ($68), although a set lunch goes for 45F ($30.60). À la carte meals climb from 65F ($44.20). The terrace is shaded in summertime.

Restaurant l'Arlequin, 34 quai du Général-Guisan (tel. 022/21-13-44), is part of the Hôtel Métropole. The large room is outfitted with clear colors, a classical decor, and lots of flowers. According to the day's shopping, chef Alain Jennings offers omble chevalier, trout, sea bass, and turbot, as well as mousseline of frogs' legs with a warm crayfish sauce, and côte de boeuf bourguignonne. A set business lunch costs 48F ($32.65), whereas two table d'hôte evening meals are priced from 90F ($61.20) to 110F ($74.80). The restaurant is open noon to 1 p.m. and 7 to 10 p.m. every day except Saturday and Sunday, and reservations are suggested.

Restaurant Tse-Fung, 301 route de Lausanne (tel. 022/774-17-36), qualifies as one of the best Chinese restaurants in Europe. The specialties are Pekinese, including marmite mongole, lacquered duck, steamed fish with Chinese mushrooms, and many other delectable dishes. Set meals cost 75F ($51) to 95F ($64.60). Hours are noon to 2 p.m. and 7 to 10 p.m. The restaurant is at the Hôtel La Réserve, already previewed, and has a lovely terrace by the swimming pool for use in summer. There is a bar as well as private parking.

THE MIDDLE BRACKET: An Italian restaurant, **Chez Valentino,** 63 route de Thonon (tel. 022/752-14-40), Vésenaz-Genève, has great antipasti and lots of atmosphere. Valentine Peloso, the hardworking owner, prepares many of the specialties himself. His restaurant lies in a suburb about three miles from the heart of the city. The moderately priced meals include minestrone, followed by gnocchi alla piemontese, tagliatelle with gorgonzola, or eggplant alla mozzarella. The antipasti contain a selection of everything that's wonderful in the kitchen. Main courses might feature frogs' legs provençale, pigeon, or côte de veal Valentino. À la carte meals begin at 45F ($30.60), but you'll spend far more, of course, if you order a meat dish. Food is served daily from noon to 2:30 p.m. and 7 to 10 p.m. except at lunchtime on Monday and Tuesday. The restaurant is closed from just before Christmas until during the second week in January.

A l'Olivier de Provence, 13 rue Jacques-Dalphin (tel. 022/742-04-50), at Carouge, is one of the best restaurants on the outskirts of Geneva, about three miles south of the city. It has a lovely summer garden where you dine under shade trees. Many of the most savory dishes of Provence are offered here, including loup de mer (sea bass) flambé. You can also order tournedos, entrecôtes, and fresh salmon with sorrel. Prices are 55F ($37.40) to 85F ($57.80) for a fixed-price meal and from 90F ($61.20) to 100F ($68) for an à la carte dinner. The restaurant is open daily except Sunday from noon to 2 p.m. and 7 to 9:45 p.m.

Le Chandelier, 23 Grand-Rue (tel. 022/728-11-88), nostalgically basks in its fame from the novel *Goldfinger.* This restaurant, in a hotel of the same name, was an old stamping ground of the late Ian Fleming. He always wanted to sit at the table right by the door to the kitchen. In the old town, the restaurant has a mellow glow, as it's been around for some time. It offers excellent grills and many specialties such as feuilletés de veau with three kinds of mustard in its sauce, entrecôte bordelaise, and tournedos with morels. Its main specialty, however, is fondue bourguignonne. To open your meal you might try either the lobster bisque or the real turtle soup. Bernard Zufferey is the director. Count on spending from 65F ($44.20) for an excellent meal here. Food is served daily from noon to 2 p.m. and 7 to 10:30 p.m.

Restaurant Le Pavillon, Hôtel des Bergues, 33 quai des Bergues (tel. 022/731-50-50). Sophisticated, elegant, and not overburdened with ponderously grand service, this is the less formal of the two restaurants within the previously recommended Hôtel des Bergues. It's not unlike a fashionable relais in Paris. Reservations are essential, especially at lunch. Big windows overlook the Rhône and the whizzing traffic, but inside, all is serene and well-bred comfort.

This fine restaurant, which is unpretentiously referred to as the "coffeehouse," serves breakfast, lunch, and dinner and is open from 7 a.m. to 11 p.m. Full meals or snacks are served, along with tea and pastries in the afternoon. Directed by the award-winning chef of the previously recommended L'Amphitryon, Albert Felli, Le Pavillon serves outstanding fresh French dishes, including a homemade foie gras that would rival any prepared by Switzerland's French neighbors. Both a classic and a cuisine moderne are offered. You might begin with a seafood soup and go on to a pot-au-feu of fish, grilled sole, the rosemary-flavored roast chicken, or the veal piccata with mushrooms. Desserts are lavish and tempting, and full meals cost 50F ($34) and up.

Restaurant le Curling, 9 bis Chemin du Fief-du-Chapitre (tel. 022/793-62-44), is at Petit-Lancy. You may never play curling (the rink is under the restaurant), but many of the patrons here do, and they like to eat and drink well. Pass through the brasserie to the main dining room or terrace. This is where Chef Acelsino Veiras and his charming wife, Monique, offer a delicious blend of Galician and continental cuisine. If you appreciate fish, try his renowned zarzuela. His royal paella is another Spanish specialty, or you have a choice from three varied menus priced at 25F ($17), 32F ($21.75), and 38F ($25.85). If you want a real gastronomic treat, a superb menu gives excellent value at 66F ($44.90). There is also a wide à la carte choice of fish and meat dishes with meals ranging from 22F ($14.95) to 60F ($40.80). There is an interesting wine cellar to suit most tastes and pockets. It is open daily except Sunday from 9 a.m. to midnight.

Chez Jacky, 9-11 rue Necker (tel. 022/32-86-80), is unheralded but deserves to be better known. It's the domain of Jacky Gruber, a Valais-born chef of exceptional skill. His bistro, which looks as if it belongs in some French provincial city, attracts a wide range of customers, from grandmothers to young skiers stopping off before heading by train for Verbier. There is a lightness and subtlety in Monsieur Gruber's style of cookery—he was obviously influenced by his apprenticeship under Fredy Giradet, "the world's greatest chef." From 11:15 a.m. to 3 p.m. and 7 to 10 p.m. Monday to Friday, you can sample the well-prepared viands. Be prepared to wait and sip your wine, as each order is handled individually. You might begin with Chinese cabbage and mussels, artfully arranged on a platter, and continue with filet of turbot roasted with thyme or perhaps beautifully prepared pink duck on a bed of fresh spinach with a confit of onions. A set menu costs from 42F ($28.55) with a menu dégustation going for 65F ($44.20). You can also order à la carte. The restaurant is closed on Saturday and Sunday.

La Coupole, 116 rue du Rhône (tel. 022/735-65-44), named after the famous establishment in the Montparnasse section of Paris, is a true brasserie, but it's far more elegant in decor than its namesake. The place is more popular at noon, especially with business people, than it is at night. There's a pink-and-red piano bar to the left as you enter and a green-and-black English-club-style bar to the right. Fanciful and fun, it is dotted with grandfather clocks and a bronze Venus along with Edwardian palms and banquettes. The menu is limited but sophisticated; the food surprisingly good. The French-inspired menu is very much a cuisine du marché, which is based on only the freshest ingredients available that day in the marketplace. Menus begin at 22F ($14.95), but you are more likely to spend from 50F ($34) ordering à la carte. Hours are daily from 7 a.m. to 1 a.m.

Le Francis, 8 boulevard Helvétique (tel. 022/746-32-52), is a restaurant and piano bar, currently one of the most fashionable in Geneva. *Le tout Genève* is likely to patronize the place in the evening, gathering around the grand piano in the bar till 1 or 2 a.m., where they pay from 12F ($8.15) for a Scotch. The proprietor, Francis Wehren, likes to keep a happy party going here until 1 or 2 a.m. The place also has considerable acclaim as a restaurant, which serves hot meals daily from 12:30 to 2:30 p.m. and 8 p.m. to midnight. You might begin with mussel soup with anise or a gratin of leeks with a fondue of tomatoes. For a main course, you might be tempted by a fricassée of sweetbreads, a sauté of veal and beef with a fricassée of artichokes, sea bass gros sel, or perhaps a panache of John Dory with salmon and green cabbage cooked in sauterne. A fixed-price lunch goes for 38F ($25.85), unless you'll settle for two courses at 20F ($13.60). À la carte dinners can range as high as 75F ($51).

THE BUDGET RANGE: Set against the old city wall to the side of the Eglise de la Madeleine is **Taverne de la Madeleine,** 20 rue Toutes-Âmes (tel. 022/28-40-32). If you get confused while looking for it, just circle the church until you see it on higher ground at the corner of rue des Barrières. Inside an old three-story house is a very good restaurant with brusquely efficient service, which caters to many of the local business community, especially at lunch. The establishment is operated by a philanthropic organization which forbids the consumption of alcohol. However, they do offer alcohol-free beer. A wall sign advertises eight kinds of tea. At red café chairs pulled up to small bistro tables, you can order a variety of simple and well-prepared dishes from overworked motherly waitresses who carry enormous loads of plates from one end of the restaurant to the other. Specials include four types of pasta, vegetarian sandwiches, and such hearty fare as a big plate of osso buco with pommes frites. An escalope turkey with potatoes and salad is regularly featured. One specialty the kitchen is very proud of is its filet of lake perch prepared meunière style or Vevey style, the latter with two kinds of exotic mushroome. An average à la carte meal goes for 25F ($17) and up. The full menu is offered daily except Sunday from 11:45 a.m. to 9:45 p.m. in summer and from 11:45 a.m. to 8 p.m. in winter.

    Café de la Cité, 27 rue de la Cité (tel. 21-30-60). You'll stumble upon a small art nouveau façade in beautifully grained wood with stylized violets in the corners. The handcrafted tables have been refinished to show woods more suitable for 19th-century antiques than for a café table in a working-class bistro. This is a family-operated, inexpensive hideaway on a street filled with antique stores. A menu of the day is offered, and the chef's specials are likely to include fondue with mushrooms or morels, escargots, frogs' legs provençale, and several kinds of spaghetti. At lunch, a plat du jour with salad and dessert costs only 13F ($8.85). However, in the evening, only an a la carte menu is featured, with meals ranging from 35F ($23.08) to 45F ($30.60). The café is open daily except Saturday and Sunday from 7:30 a.m. to 11 p.m., with hot meals served only from 11:30 a.m. to 2 p.m. and 7 to 10 p.m. No one will care if you drop in for a beer or some wine during nonlunch hours.

    Restaurant du Palais de Justice, 8 place du Bourg-de-Four (tel. 022/20-42-54), is a simple little place with lots of atmosphere in spite of its pretentious name. It stands in the old town on a colorful square, across from the Palais de Justice. The restaurant offers three different places at which to dine, with a separate menu for each. The more formal and most expensive restaurant is one flight up from the street level. It offers attractively served and well-prepared meals from 35F ($23.08), which might include terrine maison, and a savory array of beef dishes as well as osso buco. Adventurous souls might go down into the basement where La Taverne serves six different kinds of pizza from 10F ($6.80) to 12F ($8.15) and three kinds of fondue from 16.50F ($11.20). Finally, Restaurant du Rez-de-Chaussée serves basically the same dishes as La Taverne. It has a format of rustic wood, white stucco, and exposed masonry, along with a rattan ceiling. The upstairs restaurant serves lunch daily from noon to 1:30 p.m. and dinner from

6:30 to 11:15 p.m. (closed Sunday in June, July, and August). The Taverne keeps the same hours as the restaurant. The street-level Restaurant du Rez-de-Chaussée remains open from 9 a.m. to midnight daily, with uninterrupted service.

Restaurant les Armures, 1 rue des Puits-St-Pierre (tel. 022/28-34-42), couldn't be in a more colorful part of the old town, across a cobblestone street from a medieval arsenal. The chiseled stone façade has seen many owners, but this is still the oldest café in Geneva, with a clientele which drops in for coffee or cheese fondue whenever they're in that part of the city. The fondue is considered the best in town, and the setting is rustic enough to allow you to appreciate that recipe's mountain origins. The establishment prepares three types, along with raclette. Many Genevese make a meal out of the hash-brown potato dish, Rösti. Other specialties include eight types of pizza, along with hamburgers, french fries, five pasta courses, and good sausages with potato salad. The sauerkraut garni is a savory meal in itself. Simple meals begin at 18F ($12.25). The restaurant is open daily from 8 a.m. to 1 a.m.

Brasserie Lipp, Confédération Centre, 8 rue de la Confédération (tel. 022/29-31-22), takes its name from the famous Left Bank brasserie of Paris, haunt of celebrities of yesterday and today. In fact, when you enter this bustling place, especially at lunch, you'll think you've been transported to Paris. Waiters in black jackets and long white aprons rush about with platters of food to feed the hungry. Part of a modern shopping complex, it is reached by an elevator or escalator to the top level. Tables are placed outside in summer.

The food is that type of French fare so beloved by American expatriates who went to Paris after World War II. Like its Parisian namesake, the Geneva Lipp also specializes in sauerkraut—garnished with pork products—and platters come in several versions and sizes. You can also order three kinds of pot-au-feu and such classic dishes as a Toulousain cassoulet with confit de canard (duckling). Fresh oysters, among the best in the city, are invariably on the menu. At lunch plats du jour with garnishes range in price from 14.50F ($9.85) to 23.50F ($16). However, in the evening you are likely to spend from 40F ($27.20) for an à la carte dinner. The restaurant is open Monday to Thursday from 7:30 a.m. to midnight and Friday and Saturday from 7:30 a.m. to 1 a.m.

La Louisiane, 21 rue du Rhône (tel. 022/28-29-25), is a tea room and a coffeehouse that serves pastries, small sandwiches, and light meals to a crowd you might find in Greenwich Village. Outfitted with bamboo and wicker chairs, along with lots of plants, the establishment is open Monday to Friday from 7:30 a.m. to 7:30 p.m. from November to April and 7:30 a.m. to 11 p.m. May to October. Saturday hours are from 9 a.m. to 6 p.m. The place is closed Sunday. Caviar blinis are the most expensive item on the menu, followed by an assortment of pâtés, smoked salmon, morels, and crabmeat. An imaginative list of omelets and homemade pasta is also offered. Salads are varied, interesting, and come in generous portions. All are named after 20th-century celebrities. A James Dean omelet is made with truffles and a Laurel and Hardy omelet with smoked salmon. Meals cost from 27F ($18.35), with dessert and coffee included.

La Potinière, Jardin Anglais (tel. 022/21-71-62), could provide the kind of setting for a lovely summertime lunch where you'll probably dawdle over coffee with a friend. There's no real indoor area around here: Guests sit on a flagstone terrace, separated from the rushing traffic by an expanse of lawn and a low wall of flowers. A canopy protects against sudden cloudbursts. Black-vested waiters serve lunches to dozens of local residents, from office-workers to members of the well-heeled gentry. A weekly fixed-priced menu in English (after all, this is the Jardin Anglais) costs from 38F ($25.85) and might include both Swiss and continental dishes from cold roast beef to entrecôte. Fondue bourguignonne is a specialty. The restaurant is open daily from 11 a.m. to 10:30 p.m. in summer only (closed from October to March).

Le Lyrique, 12 boulevard du Théâtre (tel. 022/28-00-95), is carefully divided into a formal restaurant and a more interesting brasserie. With its turn-of-the-century decor, ornate plasterwork, belle-époque styling, and high ceilings, it has been attracting theater-goers for years. The brasserie is open throughout the day, but serves hot meals daily from noon to 3 p.m. and from 6:30 to either 10:30 or midnight, depending on whether there is a presentation at theater nearby. Both establishments are closed on Saturday and Sunday. In the brasserie, a plat du jour—and many make an entire meal of just that—goes for 14F ($9.52), a full meal costing from 35F ($23.80). The bill of fare is likely to include minced veal liver with leek, chicken suprême with leeks, succulent steaks, or grilled sole. It has a summertime terrace. In the restaurant with more formal service, you can order omble chevalier (the famous lake fish of Geneva) served poached or turbot stuffed with red peppers. A grilled sole with a salad of endive and Roquefort is also a popular item, as is the filet of lamb with baby onions. For dessert, try, for example, a pear gratinée with sabayon. A set menu is a good value at 35F ($23.80).

Café du Centre, 5 place du Molard (tel. 022/21-85-86). The square where this establishment, run by Philippe Schaller, is located is separated from the busy quays by a clock tower of chiseled stone. The square has very little traffic and lots of flower stalls, and in summer, many café tables. This old-fashioned brasserie has a more expensive upstairs room, when it's open, decorated with 17th-century stained glass. But most of the business takes place outdoors in summer or on the ground-floor café level which opens pleasantly onto the square, in a long narrow vista of symmetrically placed tables. A thick menu in English offers more than 120 food items. Fish is usually good here, including fera (a white lake fish), sole, dorade, or trout. The chef is known for his fine cuts of beef, including the delectable onglet. A simple menu begins at 20F ($13.60), a fisherman's menu going up to 30F ($20.40). You can also order a menu "vert" or vegetarian meal at 18F ($12.25). Upstairs, hot meals are served only from 11:30 a.m. to 2:30 p.m. and 6 p.m. to 1:30 a.m. (on Friday and Saturday until 2 a.m.). However, the street-level brasserie/café begins its morning coffee and croissants at 6 a.m. Hot meals here, however, are served from 11:30 a.m. without interruption until 1:30 or 2 a.m. The establishment is open daily. Irish coffee makes an attractive midday beverage.

Edelweiss, 2 place de la Navigation (tel. 022/731-36-58), in a hotel previously recommended, looks like an alpine fantasy of rustic wood, with geraniums, and folkloric music. Flags from all the Swiss cantons hang near the ceiling. You can go here, dine on Swiss specialties such as fondue, listen to the music, and even dance, all for a relatively moderate price of about 40F ($27.20) per person. It's economical when you consider that you get both food and entertainment, and you can make an evening of it. Go anytime between 7 p.m. and midnight daily.

Au Pied de Cochon, 4 place du Bourg-de-Four (tel. 022/20-47-97), which has a namesake in Paris at Les Halles, is the best place to go in Geneva for hearty Lyonnaise fare. The place is very popular with young people, who like to order the pigs' feet. The motto around here is practically "le cochon est roi" ("pig is king"). The setting is fin-de-siècle, and most of the meat and poultry dishes, especially the pork, are excellent, yet the cost of a meal begins at 30F ($20.40). A plat du jour is invariably featured. M. Philippe Schaller is the host-owner. Hours are daily from noon to 2:30 p.m. and 7 to 11 p.m.

Relais de l'Entrecôte, 49 rue du Rhône (tel. 022/28-05-01). The gimmick here is that the kitchen serves only entrecôte. Of course, when that's your thing, the kitchen has to make sure the cut of meat is tender and juicy and cooked to perfection. The entrecôte is served with french-fried (or steamed) potatoes, herb-flavored butter, and a crisp fresh salad flecked with walnuts. It costs only 28F ($19.05) per person. Desserts are extra, and they tend to be more elaborate, luring you into spending more money. In fact, the creativity of the kitchen really comes out in its desserts, which are likely to include a tulipe of fresh peaches and apricots or a hot apple tart with honey ice cream. The bistro is a lot like a 19th-century restaurant in Paris, with high ceilings, brass rails, and lots of paneling. Standing on the fashionable shopping street of Geneva, it is open from 11:45 a.m. to 2:15 p.m. and 7 to 11 p.m. daily.

L'Ailloli, 6 rue Adrien-Lachenal (tel. 022/736-79-71), named after the famous garlic sauce of Provence, stands opposite La Maison de Verre by Le Corbusier. It is mainly known only to the people of the neighborhood. But it's worth the search, as it offers some of the finest provençale cookery in town, served bistro style. Marius Anthoine, the owner and an opera-lover as well, was born in the Valais, but he came to Geneva to set up this popular place, which he runs along the lines of a bustling establishment on the Left Bank of Paris. A plat du jour costs only 12.50F ($8.50) at lunch. An evening meal, including an appetizer, first plate, main dish, cheese, dessert, coffee, and wine, goes for 49.50F ($33.65) per person, or you can spend more by ordering à la carte. Among featured dishes are beef Stroganoff, frogs' legs provençale, or daube provençale. He also makes a delectable pot-au-feu as well as a côte of beef with mustard. Look for the daily specials. The place is open Saturday from 10 a.m. to midnight and serves dinner nightly except Sunday from 7 to 10:30 p.m.

Le Café-Restaurant Papon, 1 rue Henri-Fazy (tel. 022/29-54-28), is one of the oldest and most venerated cafés of Geneva, lying near Tour Baudet in the vicinity of Hôtel-de-Ville in the old town. Now a restaurant, crêperie, and tea room, the café has been entertaining drinkers and diners here under vaulted ceilings since the 17th century. In summer, cold food is available throughout the afternoon, but hot meals are served daily only from noon to 2 p.m. and from 7 to 10:30 p.m. You can also come here for coffee, enjoying one of the rich pastries displayed behind a deli case. The specialty of the kitchen is called a *galette au sarrazin,* a sort of crêpe. It's served in seven different ways, often filled with Gruyère or ham and cheese, perhaps fish. You can also order more substantial fare, including fish soup with rouille, squid, a brochette of scampi, entrecôte, and, if it's your taste, pork kidneys in a Dijon mustard sauce with Rösti. A set lunch is modestly priced at 15F ($10.20), but you are likely to spend from 35F ($23.08) ordering à la carte.

4. WHAT TO SEE

If you arrive in Geneva in summer, as most tourists will, you might begin your discovery of the city by a long promenade along the **"Quays of Geneva."** As mentioned, Geneva is a city to be discovered on foot, and what follows is in essence a walking tour. It might also be called "Children's Geneva," as what will follow can be easily understood and appreciated by youngsters, providing they take delight in strolling along. In case children in tow get tired, take them to the Gare de Cornavin, where they can board *le mini-train de Genève.* This 40-minute excursion will take them along the major parks and quays of Geneva. Departures are every half hour daily from 9 a.m. to 5 p.m. April to October. Adults pay a fare of 6F ($4.10), children 5F ($3.40).

The one sight you can't miss—even if you tried!—is the **Jet d'Eau,** the famous fountain that is the trademark of the city. Visible for miles around from April to September, it throws water 460 feet into the air above the lake. The *bise* (wind) blows the spume into a feathery, fluttery fan, often wetting those below who stand too close. The Genevese call the fountain the *jeddo.* It dates from 1891, but was much improved in 1951. Many cities have sent engineers to Geneva to discover the workings of the fountain, but this remains a carefully guarded state secret. It pumps 132 gallons of water at 125 miles per hour.

Then you'll be ready to explore the quays, with their luxuriantly planted flower gardens, dotted with ancient buildings. The aquatic population consists of seagulls, ducks, and swans. A fleet of small boats, called *Mouettes genevoises,* shuttles visitors from one quay to another from spring until autumn's blasts become too chilly.

Like the water jet, the **Flower Clock** in the **Jardin Anglais** (English Garden) is another Geneva trademark. Its face is made of flowers, and it keeps perfect time (but what else in this world-famed center of watchmaking?). The Jardin Anglais is at the foot of Mont Blanc Bridge, which spans the river at the point where the Rhône leaves Lake Geneva. It was rebuilt in 1969.

After leaving the garden you can walk along quai des Bergues as far as the bridge, called pont des Bergues. If you cross this bridge you'll come to **Île Rousseau,** with a statue of Geneva's most famous son done by Pradier in 1834. This island, the former stomping ground of the philosopher, is home to any number of ducks, swans, and other aquatic fowl such as grebes. In the middle of the Rhône, it was once a bulwark of Geneva's river defenses.

You can continue crossing the bridge and can then follow the Besançon Hugues quay until you reach **Tour-de-l'Île,** farther downstream. Built in 1219, a château which once stood here was used as a prison by the counts of Savoy. A wall plaque commemorates the visit of Caesar in 58 B.C. The tower is all that remains from the 13th-century castle. It was here that freedom fighter Philibert Berthelier was decapitated in 1519. Nowadays the headquarters of the Geneva Tourist Office is located on the island. You can also explore the old markets where often there are exhibitions of the works of contemporary Genevese artists.

If you walk east along quai des Bergues you'll return to pont du Mont-Blanc. To the left, facing the lake, is the **Brunswick Monument,** the tomb of Charles II of Brunswick who died in Geneva in 1873. The duke left his fortune to the city provided it built a monument to him. Geneva accepted the fortune and modeled the tomb after the Scaglieri tombs in **Verona.**

THE SIGHTS OF VIEILLE VILLE: The old town in Geneva is one of the most remarkable in Switzerland. It stands on the left bank, where the cultural life of Geneva flourishes.

The old quarter is dominated by the **Cathedral of St. Pierre** (tel. 022/29-75-98), built in the 12th and 13th centuries and partially reconstructed in the 15th century. However, recent archaeological excavations have disclosed that as early as A.D. 400, a Christian sanctuary and important episcopal group was on the heights of what is now the old town of Geneva. The cathedral became Protestant in 1536 by the vote of the people of Geneva in the no longer existing cloister of St. Pierre's, and the interior is now austere, just the way Calvin preferred it (his seat is on the north side). The church has seen much renovation over the years, and it has a modern organ with 6,000 pipes. The northern tower was reconstructed at the end of the 19th century, with a metallic steeple erected between the two stone towers. If you don't mind 145 steps, you can climb to the north tower for a splendid vista of the city, its lake, the Alps, and the Jura mountains.

Visitors can see the St. Pierre **archaeological site** by entering at the righthand corner of the cathedral steps in the Cour St-Pierre, an underground world that extends under the present cathedral and the **Chapelle des Macchabées,** built in the early 15th century adjoining the southwest corner of the church. The chapel is in the High Gothic style, extravagantly ornate. It was restored during World War II, after having been used as a storage room following the Reformation. Underneath it all, the excavations have revealed baptisteries for immersion, a crypt, the foundations of several cathedrals built on this site plus the bishop's palace, fourth-century mosaics, and sculptures and geological strata revealing the life of the early Christians who lived on the Geneva heights.

The cathedral and the chapel are open daily from 9 a.m. to noon and 2 to

6 p.m. in March, April, May, and October; to 5 p.m. in January, February, November, and December. From June through September, hours are from 9 a.m. to 7 p.m. There is no admission charge, although donations are not discouraged. Sunday service is held in the cathedral at 10 a.m., with an hour of organ music being presented on Saturday at 6 p.m. from June through September. To visit the archaeological site, the hours are from 10 a.m. to 1 p.m. and 2 to 6 p.m. daily except Monday, and the charge is 5F ($3.40) for admission.

Next door to the cathedral is the **Temple de l'Auditoire,** or Calvin Auditorium, a Gothic church where Knox and Calvin preached. It was restored in 1959 in time for Calvin's 450th anniversary.

After leaving the cathedral, strike out across Cour St-Pierre, turning left onto rue St.-Pierre, where you'll see **Maison Tavel,** the oldest house in Geneva (see below).

The **Hôtel de Ville** (city hall), a short walk from the cathedral, dates from the 16th and 17th centuries. It has a cobbled ramp instead of a staircase. The Salle d'Alabama is the salon where arbitration between America and England in 1872 was peacefully resolved. Its Baudet Tower was constructed in 1455. Incidentally, the Red Cross originated here in 1864. Across from the city hall is the **Arsenal,** an arcaded structure dating from 1634. In the courtyard of the building is a cannon cast in 1683.

Still in this general complex, **place du Bourg-de-Four** is an irregular square dating from the Middle Ages, although long before that it was a Roman forum. The Palais de Justice here was built in 1707, and has housed courts of law since 1860. You'll find many antiquaries' shops, art galleries, and a flower-bedecked fountain.

Another pride of Geneva is the **Reformation Monument,** beneath the walls of the old town on the promenade des Bastions. One hundred yards long, it was constructed against a 16th-century rampart. In the austere style so beloved by Calvin himself, it's a bit drab, but an enduring landmark nevertheless. Erected in 1917, it depicts big statues of a quartet of Genevese reformers, including Knox, Calvin, Bèze, and Farel. On each end are memorials to Luther and Zwingli. Oliver Cromwell and even the Pilgrim Fathers get in on the act.

Also in the old town, a short walk from the cathedral is **Église St-Germain** (Church of St. Germain) which was built on the site of an early Christian church, perhaps from the fourth and fifth centuries. Restored in 1959, it has the remains of a 14th-century altar, the time of the building's construction. It saw more work in the 15th century. The stained-glass windows are contemporary.

THE HISTORY-RICH LES PÂQUIS:

One of Geneva's most animated and elegant districts, Les Pâquis, lies on the right bank of Lake Geneva facing the harbor. It is a sector of cozy bistros, night clubs, and workshops of craftsmen of various trades, as well as some discreet banks and elegant boutiques. The word *pâquis* —pâsquiers—comes from "pasturelands." The cows have long gone, but from about A.D. 1330, the district consisted of a vast expanse of fields, pastures, and wastelands. It was very far from the heart of the city and its protective ditches, and exposed to permanent danger of invasion. Nevertheless, people from the city ventured here, erecting a hut or two and some gardens.

From the 14th century, following successive transformations in the outer defenses of the city, this unincorporated territory became safer, and more and more people came here to make homes. In the 15th century, the Pâquis was the tenure of potters. Homes and small industries began to sprout up. The shores along the lake provided a living for fishermen. Geneva at the time had a flotilla of lake craft traversing the harbor.

In 1831, the district received a distinguished visitor, the French writer, Chateaubriand, who settled at the Hôtel des Etrangers, 22 rue des Pâquis. From

1851 development was fairly rapid, with the construction of quai du Mont-Blanc and of the Rotonde, the English church. An American church was also constructed, and in 1857 the Pâquis and Eaux-Vives piers were erected. The construction of the Cornavin railway station began the following year. The Mont-Blanc bridge was erected in 1862, and in the following years the lake promenade, the façade des Pâquis, the Mont-Blanc quay with its landing stages, became fashionable places for strolling.

In 1873 construction began on the Hôtel National (Palais Wilson) that in time would house the first secretariat of the League of Nations from 1925 to 1936. Another prestigious rendezvous for the smart Genevese of that time was the Kursaal, built between 1874 and 1879. One of the most infamous events in the history of the area was the assassination of Elisabeth ("Sissi"), Empress of Austria, in 1898, at the landing stage facing the Duke of Brunswick mausoleum.

Visitors today wander at leisure through the old history-rich district, and, when they get tired, they can take a lake steamer for a tour of Lake Geneva.

MORE PARKS, GARDENS, AND SQUARES: Below the old quarter, to the southwest, is **place Neuve,** with its equestrian statue of General Dufour, one of the cofounders of the Red Cross. It's considered the cultural heart of Geneva, ringed by the Grand Théâtre, the Conservatory of Music, and the Rath Museum. The Grand Théâtre (opera house) was built in 1874 and will be visited in our after-dark wanderings. The Conservatoire de Musique is from 1858. The **Rath Museum,** place Neuve (tel. 022/28-56-16), reached by tram 12 and buses 3 and 33, has temporary exhibitions of paintings and sculpture, and is open Tuesday to Sunday from 10 a.m. to noon and 2 to 6 p.m. (on Monday, only from 2 to 6 p.m.)

If you walk along the quays, heading north as if to Lausanne, you'll come to some of the most beautiful parks in Geneva. Off avenue de France lies the **Parc Mon-Repos,** and off rue de Lausanne is found **La Perle du Lac,** both stunning lakeside parks. Directly to the right is the **Jardin Botanique** (botanical garden), established in 1902. It has an alpine garden, a little zoo, greenhouses, and exhibitions, and can be visited free daily from 7 a.m. to 6:30 p.m. in summer (otherwise from 8 a.m. to 5 p.m.).

Back at the lakeside, you can take a boat to the other side, getting off at Gustave Ador quay. From there you can explore two more lakeside parks, **Parc de la Grange,** which has the most extravagant rose garden in Switzerland (at its best in June), and next to it, the equally beautiful **Parc des Eaux-Vives.**

Or alternatively, when you leave the Botanical Garden on the left bank, you can head west along avenue de la Paix to the **Palais des Nations** (tel. 022/734-60-11), the former home of the League of Nations and the present headquarters of the United Nations in Europe. A modern wing was added in 1973. The location is about a mile north from the Mont Blanc Bridge. Up to 1936 the League met at the Palais Wilson. However, in 1936 the headquarters was transferred to the Palais des Nations. The Aga Khan inaugurated the palais, but its days were numbered. After excluding Russia in 1940 it saw its influence decline, although minor operations continued through the war years until it was dissolved in 1946, as the new United Nations met in San Francisco.

Seat of several U.N. organs and also one of the busiest international conference centers in the world, it is in the Ariana Park, whose century-old trees surrounding modern monuments. The complex of buildings here is the second largest in Europe after Versailles. The palace can be visited from 9 a.m. to 5:15 p.m. in summer, and 9 a.m. to noon and 2 to 5:15 p.m. otherwise. Guided tours are given daily leaving from the visitors' entrance, 14 avenue de la Paix, opposite the Red Cross building. Admission is 6F ($4.10) for adults and 2.50F ($1.70) for school children. Children under 6 are admitted free. Inside is a philatelic museum and the League of Nations Museum, but it's the building itself that's of interest. For information, get in touch with the Visitor's Service, United Nations Office, 14 avenue de la Paix (tel. 022/734-60-11, ext. 4529).

THE LEADING MUSEUMS: Geneva's most important museum is **Musée d'Art et d'Histoire** (museum of art and history), 2 rue Charles-Galland (tel. 022/29-00-11). It lies between the boulevard Jacques-Dalcroze and the boulevard Helvétique, and is open from 10 a.m. to 5 p.m. (closed Monday). Seemingly, it has a little bit of everything, going back to relics of the prehistoric people who lived in pile dwellings and the Egyptians, of which the museum has many relics, along with Greek vases, medieval stained glass, 12th-century armory, and many paintings of the Flemish and Italian schools. The Etruscan pottery is impressive, as is the medieval furniture. See the altar piece by Konrad Witz from 1444, showing the "miraculous" draught of fishes. Swiss timepieces are duly honored, and many galleries contain works by such artists as Rodin, Renoir, Hodler, Vallotton, Le Corbusier, and Picasso.

To the west of the Palais des Nations, the **Musée Ariana,** 10 avenue de la Paix (tel. 022/734-29-50), is closed as of this writing, but check on its status at the time of your visit. The building is in the Italian Renaissance style, built in 1877 for G. Gustave Revilliod, the 19th-century Genevese writer who began the collection. Today it's one of the top three museums in Europe devoted to porcelain and pottery. Here you'll see Sèvres, along with the Delft faïence and Meissen porcelain. It's also the headquarters of the International Academy of Ceramics. The collection doesn't overlook the Orient either, with many superb pieces from Japan and China. Call for new hours and prices if it has reopened.

Musée du Petit Palais, 2 terrasse Saint-Victor (tel. 46-14-33), in a 19th-century town house, displays artwork from 1890 until the present day. It's known chiefly for its collection of impressionists and post-impressionists, although the Pointillists and Fauve artists are also represented. This private museum is like a course in art history, as you note such outstanding artists as Renoir, Cross, Picasso, Cézanne, Steinlen, Chagall, Utrillo, and Rousseau. Admission is 10F ($6.80) for adults and 3.50F ($2.40) for students. Visit from 10 a.m. to noon and 2 to 6 p.m., except on Monday morning.

Musée d'Histoire Naturelle (natural history museum), 1 route de Malagnou (tel. 022/735-91-30), is one of the most modern such museums in Europe, containing permanent exhibitions of rich and varied collections in natural science, including regional and exotic species. Among the specimens are mammals, birds, reptiles, fish, mollusks, and insects. The earth science galleries are devoted to mineralogy, fluorescent minerals, gemology, Geneva-area geology, geology of Switzerland, human history, and dinosaurs. It's open from 10 a.m. to 5 p.m.; closed Monday. Admission is free.

At place Cornavin, you can take a bus to the **Institut et Musée Voltaire,** 25 rue des Délices (tel. 022/44-71-33). Voltaire lived here during his period of exile from 1755 to 1760, and from time to time up to 1765. Part of *Candide* was written here. In this museum you get some of the feeling of this energetic man, who was a champion of intellectual liberty through his voluminous writings. The museum displays furniture, manuscripts, and letters of the great philosopher, along with portraits, plus a terracotta model of the statue by Houdon showing Voltaire seated. The museum is open Monday to Friday from 2 to 5 p.m. Admission is free.

Musée de l'Horlogerie (watch museum), 15 route de Malagnou (tel. 022/736-74-12), is in a town house on its own grounds. The history of watches and clocks from the 16th century is traced in this museum, open from 10 a.m. to noon and 2 to 6 p.m. (closed Monday morning). It displays everything from sand-timers to sundials, although most of the exhibits are concerned with the watches of Geneva, usually from the 17th and 18th centuries. The enameled watches of the 19th century are particularly outstanding (many have chimes that play when you open them).

The **Baur Collections,** 8 rue Munier-Romilly (tel. 022/746-17-29), in the 19th-century home of the original owner, with a tiny garden, is a private exhibit of Chinese (10th- to 19th-century) and Japanese (17th- to 20th-century) works of art. Ceramics, jade, lacquer, ivories, and delicate sword fittings are displayed here. It's open daily except Monday in the afternoon only, from 2 to 6 p.m., charging an admission of 3F ($2.05).

Musée des Instruments Anciens de Musique (museum of antique musical instruments), 23 rue Le Fort (tel. 022/746-95-65), displays a private collection that was purchased by the city of Geneva. The original owner is still the curator. Many of the instruments are still in working order, and are occasionally played. The museum is open Tuesday from 3 to 6 p.m.; Thursday from 10 a.m. to noon and 3 to 6 p.m., and on Friday from 8 to 10 p.m. Admission is only 1F (68¢).

Musée de l'Histoire des Sciences (museum of the history of science), at Villa Bartholoni, 128 rue de Lausanne (tel. 022/731-69-85), contains scientific instruments and other mementos of Swiss scientists showing how they've excelled in medicine, astronomy, physics, and mathematics. It's normally open April to October daily from 2 to 6 p.m. Closed for reorganization and restoration, it should be open by the time of your visit (check its status with the tourist office).

The **Library of Geneva** contains two museums. It lies on the south side of the promenade des Bastions, and has been there since 1873. Originally it was a Calvin-founded academy in 1559, and reformed theologians were trained here. The east wing of the library dates from the 15th century and has some 1.2 million volumes.

In the Salle Lullin of the library, the **Jean-Jacques Rousseau Museum,** promenade des Bastions (tel. 022/20-82-66), contains manuscripts, correspondence, prints, a bust by Houdon, and the death mask of the famous philosopher who is considered the father of the romantic movement. It is said that his attacking the divine right of kings, favoring democracy, paved the road to the French Revolution. Rousseau believed that man (or woman) was basically good, but that corruption came through social institutions. Furthermore, he advocated natural rather than revealed sectarian religion. In this museum, you can get close to the spirit of the man who wrote such world-famous works as *The Social Contract, Emile,* and the *Confessions,* the last an autobiography remarkable for its candor. Charging no admission, the museum open from 9 a.m. to noon and 2 to 5 p.m. (closed Saturday afternoon and all day Sunday).

The other museum is the **Musée Historique de la Reformation** (same phone), also in the Bibliothèque Publique (Salle Lullin) at the university on the promenade des Bastions. It will be of particular interest to those interested in Calvin and other reformers. It's open Monday to Friday from 9 a.m. to noon and 2 to 6 p.m. (on Saturday, only from 9 a.m. to noon), charging no admission.

Maison Tavel, 6 rue du Puits-St-Pierre (tel. 022/28-29-00), the oldest house in Geneva, built in 1303 and partially rebuilt after the fire of 1334, is the city's newest museum, opened in 1986. It has undergone several transformations over the centuries. Its towered front wall, decorated with medieval stone sculpted heads, is painted dark gray with white joints, typical of the 17th century. A private home until this century, the house contains a characteristic courtyard with staircase, a 13th-century cellar, and a back garden, indicating the importance of this medieval house and the status of its former inhabitants. Art objects relating to the history of the city and its daily life from the Middle Ages until the mid-19th century are displayed. One of the most outstanding attractions is the Magnin relief in the attic and a copper and zinc model of fortified Geneva in 1850, which is accompanied by a light and tape commentary. Visitors can also see numerous images of the city, and objects of daily life are displayed in the old living quarters. The house is open from 10 a.m. to 5 p.m. daily except Monday. Admission is free. Guided tours are given at 3 p.m. the second Saturday of every month. Postcards, books, slides, and small guidebooks are available at the book stand.

TOURS: A two-hour City Tour is operated daily all year by **Key Tours S.A.,** 7 rue des Alpes, square Mont-Blanc (tel. 022/731-41-40). The tour starts from gare Routière, place Dorcière, the bus station near the Key Tours office. From November through March, a tour is offered only once a day at 2 p.m. But from April through October, two tours leave daily, one at 10 a.m., another at 2 p.m. A bus will drive you through the city and you'll see famous sites, monuments, and landmarks of Geneva and the lake promenades. In the old town you can take a walk down to the Bastions Park to the Reformation Wall. After a tour through the International Center, at which, among other organizations, you'll be shown the headquarters of the International Red Cross, the bus returns to its starting place. Adults are charged 20F ($13.60); children 4 to 12 accompanied by an adult, 10F ($6.80).

Many other excursions are offered, including a 2½-hour boat trip on the Rhône aboard the *Bâteau du Rhône,* with commentary in English. The trip takes you from Geneva to the Verbois dam and back. Departure, opposite the Hôtel du Rhône, takes place at 2:30 p.m. daily from April 1 to October 30 and also at 10 a.m. on Thursday, Saturday, and Sunday. The boat trip costs 16F ($10.90) for adults, 10F ($6.80) for children 6 to 12 years of age.

Lake cruises may be taken from June to the end of September, the trips including only first-class boat transportation (no guides and no meals).

An **all-day cruise** will take you on a complete tour of the lake, leaving from Jardin Anglais pier at 8 and 10:15 a.m. daily and from Mont Blanc pier at 9:15 a.m. and returning at 6:45 p.m. The cost of the cruise, which takes you past Nyon, Lausanne, Vevey, Montreux, Evian, and Thonon, is 45F ($30.60) for adults, half price for children 6 to 16.

You can go to Montreux and Chillon on a **Castle Cruise** by boat, returning by train. The boat leaves from Mont Blanc pier daily at 9:15 a.m., arriving at Chillon at 2:15 p.m., or you can embark at Jardin Anglais pier at 10:45 a.m. and arrive at Chillon at 3:42 p.m. Trains for the one-hour round trip make the run every hour. Cost of the excursion is 53F ($36.05) for adults, half price for children 6 to 16. After Chillon, visitors must catch a bus which will take them to the railway station in Montreux, where they can board a train taking them back to Geneva.

You can also take a tour called Le Tour du Petit Lac, which will transport you around the lower part of the lake in half a day, taking you past Nyon and Yvoire. A second-class ticket on this circuit costs 20F ($13.60), rising to 26F ($17.70) in first class. The tour departs in summer every day at 9:15 a.m. from quai Mont-Blanc and from the pier at Jardin Anglais at 10:30 a.m., 2:30 p.m., and 3 p.m.

If you have time, I highly recommend a **Mont Blanc excursion,** an all-day trip to Chamonix by bus and a cable-car ride to the summit of the Aiguille du Midi (12,610 feet), for a memorable alpine panorama. The tour is offered daily from April to October; Tuesday, Thursday, Saturday, and Sunday in January, February, March, November, and December, leaving Geneva at 8:30 a.m. and returning at 5:30 p.m. from October to April and at 6:30 p.m. from May to September. Buses leave from the station, gare Routière. You must take your passport with you. You must also have a French visa, which must be obtained in advance.

Other ascents on this tour are Vallée Blanche by telecabin, an extension of the Aiguille du Midi climb, from April to October; to Mer de Glace via electric rack railway to the edge of the glacier from which you may descend to the ice grotto (not available in winter); and/or to Le Brévent, an ascent by cable car to a rocky belvedere at 7,900 feet, facing the Mont Blanc range.

Prices for a complete trip vary according to which of the options you prefer after reaching Chamonix. With lunch, adults pay 115F ($78.20), and children 4 to 12 are charged 70F ($47.60) to ascend Aiguille du Midi: adults pay 142F ($96.55) and children 84F ($57.10) for the Aiguille du Midi–Vallée trek; adults are charged 133F ($90.45) and children 79F ($53.70) to go to Aiguille du Midi and Mer de Glace or Le Brévent; adults pay 160F ($108.80) and children 93F ($63.25) to make the Aiguille du Midi–Vallée Blanche–Mere de Glace or Aiguille du Midi–Vallée Blanche–Le Brévent trip. Adults are charged 100F ($68) and children 62F ($42.15) to go from Chamonix to either Mer de Glace or Le Brévent, and it costs 118F ($80.25) for adults, 71F ($43.80) for children to go to Chamonix and then to Mer de Glace and Le Brévent.

An English-speaking guide will accompany your bus tour. Key Tours S.A., 7 rue des Alpes (square Mont-Blanc), Case Postale 490, CH-1211 Genève, Switzerland (tel. 022/731-41-40), operators of the excursions, require a minimum of eight persons per trip.

5. SHOPPING AND SPORTS

Besides the sights, Geneva has other offerings for visitors. There is a dazzling array of shops offering all the best in Swiss merchandise, as well as choice goods from other places. However, not everyone is addicted to shopping, and for those persons, a number of sports possibilities exist here, particularly aimed at keeping fit, a matter of great importance to the Swiss.

SHOPPING: From boutiques to department stores, Geneva is a shopping parade. Everybody knows that it's a world center of watchmaking and jewelry, but you can also pick up excellent items such as embroidered blouses or music boxes made by country people in the Jura during the long winter months.

A host of merchandise is sold, ranging from cuckoos from German Switzerland to cigars from Havana. Supplies of chocolate are always a temptation, and the city also is a place to buy the famous multiblade knives of the Swiss army. These knives are even favored by astronauts.

Geneva, of course, practically invented the wristwatch, not to mention the self-winding watch, the waterproof watch, etc. Watchmaking in the city dates from the 16th century. Avoid purchasing a Swiss watch in one of the souvenir stores. If a jeweler is legitimate, he or she will display a symbol of the Geneva Association of Watchmakers and Jewelers. All the fine names are sold here: Constantin, Longines, Omega, to name just a few. The city has luxury merchandise from all over the world. Sometimes there are discounts on such items as cameras. Nearly all the sales personnel I've encountered spoke English and were helpful.

Shopping might begin, as it has for centuries, at the **place du Molard.** Once this was the harbor of Geneva, but then the water receded. Before it was killed by competition from Lyon in France, merchants from all over Europe brought their merchandise to sell and display at the once-famous trade fairs of Geneva.

Or alternatively, if you're walking along **rue du Rhône** and are put off by the prices, go one block south to **rue du Marché,** which in various sections becomes rue Croix d'Or and rue de Rive. Don't be afraid to comparison-shop in Geneva. Some local residents tell me that many of the major shops on rue du Rhône price their goods so high "that only wealthy foreign buyers can afford them."

Bucherer, 26 quai du Général-Guisan (tel. 022/21-62-66), opposite Mont Blanc Bridge sells expensive watches and diamonds in a chrome-and-crystal format of great beauty. They are agents for such name watches as Rolex, Piaget, Baume & Mercier, Tissot, Rado, and Gerald Genta. Don't be intimidated by the dignified façade and elegantly futuristic ground floor. The carpeted third floor is filled with relatively inexpensive watches. Once you're on that floor, you'll also find a large selection of cuckoo clocks, music boxes, embroideries, and souvenirs, as well as charming gift items such as porcelain pill boxes.

Bruno Magli, 47 rue du Rhône (tel. 022/21-53-77), is one of the most complete shoestores in Geneva, selling an elegant variety of shoes, purses, and accessories, all made in Italy.

Hermès, 43 rue du Rhône (tel. 022/21-76-77), sells purses, leather accessories, diaries, jewelry, watches, ready-to-wear, furs, and naturally the famous Hermès scarf and tie. Everything is beautifully handcrafted in the best quality that has made Hermès such a famous name.

Gübelin Jewellers, 1 place du Molard or 60 rue du Rhône (tel. 022/28-86-55), is a family-run concern, dating from 1854, which is known mainly for watches, but you can buy a ten-carat emerald here if it suits your fancy and your pocketbook. You'll see two perpetual clocks in the windows, giving chronological as well as astrological time, with fanciful notations of the different time zones around the world in colored enamel. The watches are among the best names in Switzerland. You can also buy gift items for reasonable prices, which might include pen and pencil sets. The store is closed from noon to 2 p.m., but otherwise open every day except Sunday from 8 a.m. to 6:30 p.m., to 5 p.m. Saturday.

L. Scherrer, 29 rue du Rhône (tel. 022/21-70-96), sells a good selection of watches, diamonds, and gems from an elegant storefront on the most prestigious street in Geneva. The polite staff caters to an elite clientele who are mainly interested in the eight brands of Swiss watches sold here.

Celine, 23 rue du Rhône (tel. 022/21-14-03), sells all the clothing and accessories that any horsewoman or would-be equestrienne could use, as well as a selection of fashionably conservative skirts, blouses, and purses. Items are very expensive in a shop dedicated to preserving the allure of its name.

Davidoff et Cie, 2 rue de Rive (tel. 022/28-90-41), the most famous tobacco store in the world. It sells the best cigars you'll find in Europe. A massive climate-controlled storage room in the basement holds dozens of Cuban cigars never imported into America. Russian exile Zino Davidoff (born in 1906) set up a revolutionary system of mixing grades of tobacco from his shop in Geneva, where Lenin and other exiles gathered to ponder the fate of their mother country. Today you'll see all kinds of cigar boxes and smoking paraphernalia. The shop is open every day but Sunday.

Confiserie Rohr, 3 place du Molard (tel. 022/21-63-03) and 42 rue du Rhône (tel. 022/21-68-76), sells the kinds of chocolates you can smell from the street. They fairly pull you into the store where, displayed behind glass countertops, you'll see my personal favorite, chocolate-covered truffles, or you might try one of their "gold bars" with hazelnuts. A novelty is the poubelles au chocolat ("chocolate garbage pails"). Most candies sell for about 35F ($23.80) per pound, and the shop is open daily except Sunday until 6:45 p.m.

Art et Style, 10 Grand-Rue (tel. 022/21-45-97), is the kind of antique store that looks and feels more like a museum than a commercial enterprise. The high-ceilinged room is packed with 17th-century sculpture and enough furniture to fill a large, elegant house. The staff is eager to explain origins and prices.

Grand Passage, 50 rue du Rhône (tel. 022/20-66-11), the largest department store in Geneva, has just about everything, ranging from a travel bureau to an agency selling theater tickets, as well as a hairdresser, a newspaper kiosk, and a handful of boutiques, plus a restaurant and shop selling sandwiches to go. The latter might make an inexpensive snack or a complete lunch.

Jouets Weber (Franz Carl Weber), 12 rue de la Croix d'Or (tel. 022/28-42-55), sells children's toys of all kinds, from slide shows to cartoon characters, as well as dolls and sports equipment. Lying at the corner of rue de la Fontaine, it's the best in the city.

Pharmacie Principale, Grand Passage, 11 rue du Marché (tel. 022/21-31-30). Between the glamorous rue du Rhône and the less expensive rue du Marché is one of the world's biggest drugstores, specializing not only in medicines, but in fashions, perfumes, optical equipment, cameras, and photo supplies. If your glasses need adjusting, you can take them to the optometrist on the second floor. Hours are from 1 to 6:45 p.m. Monday, from 8:15 a.m. to 6:45 p.m. Tuesday to Friday, to 5 p.m. Saturday. It's closed Sunday.

Bon Génie, 34 rue du Marché (tel. 022/28-82-22), is a department store emporium on place du Molard that sells high-fashion items, mainly for women. Its storefront windows have cleverly assembled art objects from local museums, which are displayed alongside designer clothes. There's also a limited selection of men's clothing.

Aux Arts du Feu, 18 quai du Général-Guisan (tel. 022/21-35-21), is a waterside store with big windows and lots of brass trim, selling high-quality objects of crystal, porcelain, china, silver, and decorative objects from around the world.

Pharmacie de Saint-Gervais, 1 Tour-de-l'Île (tel. 022/21-30-05), might be the most centrally located pharmacy of all of Geneva, as it stands next door to the main tourist office. It's open Monday to Friday from 8:30 a.m. to 12:30 p.m. and 1:30 to 6:30 p.m. Closed Saturday and Sunday.

Ernest Schmitt and Co. Antiquités, 3 rue de l'Hôtel de Ville (tel. 022/28-35-40), is the kind of antique store where you'll want to know the price of everything. All of the pieces are English, and they're beautifully displayed in the ground-floor rooms of an 18th-century private house. Be sure to ask the director to take you across the cobblestone courtyard to see the other beautifully illuminated showrooms.

Ed. Sturzenegger, 3 rue du Rhône (tel. 022/28-95-34), is part of a famous chain selling fine embroidered work such as table linens, fine lingerie, blouses, nightgowns, and articles for babies.

SPORTS: In health-conscious Switzerland, this is a big item, and Geneva has many facilities to help you get and keep fit.

Tennis can be played at several clubs, among them the Geneva Tennis Club at Parc des Eaux-Vives.

Water sports include **sailing,** which is easily available along the quays, especially Mont Blanc and Wilson. Swimmers will find fine **beaches** along the lake for use in summer. The most popular is Geneva Beach (Genève Plage), where you can enjoy the water from 9 a.m. to 7 p.m. for 5F ($3.40). You can also swim in the lake at bains des Pâquis, quai du Mont-Blanc, in summer.

Fitness trails have been laid out in a number of parks of Geneva, and you can jog along the quays and the beaches. For many sports activities, the people of Geneva head for the environs. However, for sports to pursue within the city, ask at the Tourist Office for information.

6. GENEVA AFTER DARK

Geneva has more nightlife than any other city in Switzerland, and if you get bored in this former city of Calvin, you used to be able to drive in a short time across the border into France. However, because Americans and some other foreigners are now required to have a visa to enter France, that process isn't as easy as it once was. There's gambling at Divonne in France, 12½ miles away, which draws many of the Genevese since Switzerland limits bets to 5F ($3.40).

On a cultural note, the **Grand Théâtre,** place Neuve (tel. 022/21-23-18), is modeled on the Paris Opera. Opened in 1879, it burned in 1951 but has been rebuilt in the same style except for the auditorium, which is modern, with a seating capacity of 1,488. From September to July, it presents a season of eight operas and two ballet evenings, as well as recitals and chamber music concerts.

Victoria Hall, rue Général-Dufour (tel. 022/28-91-93), is the home of the celebrated Orchestre de la Suisse Romande. This is the 1,866-seat hall for symphonic or classical music.

Most Geneva nightlife centers around place du Bourg-de-Four, a former stagecoach stop during the 19th century. In the old town there are lots of outdoor cafés in summer, attracting the affluent and semi-affluent Genevese.

Maxim's Cabaret, 2 rue Thalberg (tel. 022/732-99-00), is a small Lido-style cabaret and music hall. The club is open nightly from 8:30 to dawn, with two different shows at 11 p.m. and again at 1 a.m. It's much favored by visitors and has some very good acts. Entrance is free, and most drinks cost from 22F ($14.95). A small restaurant serves a fixed-price dinner for 95F ($64.60).

Griffin's Club, 36 boulevard Helvétique (tel. 022/735-12-18), is considered the best, the most fun, and the most chic club in Geneva. But technically it's private and you may or may not get in, depending on the mood of the management at the time of your particular visit. The popularity of nightclubs comes and goes, but the collection of celebrities who have traipsed in here reads like a Who's Who from the tabloids. Jackets are required for men. The club opens at 10 p.m., closing at 4 a.m. Drinks cost from 20F ($13.60) to 26F ($17.70), and dinner goes from 110F ($74.80) per person. The owner and manager, Bernard Grobet, is a local celebrity.

Velvet, 7 rue du Jeu-de-l'Arc (tel. 022/735-00-00), is considered something of a social Olympus in Calvin's capital. Night owls of the city flock here for what the French call *le dancing à la mode.* Velvet is a combination restaurant, disco, and cabaret, usually featuring more than a dozen topless dancers. Shows begin nightly at 11. The club opens at 10 p.m. and remains open until 4 or 5 in the morning seven days a week. On Sunday night the restaurant part is closed. On Friday and Saturday nights, a 10F ($6.80) entrance is charged. Each drink, regardless of what it is, costs 18F ($12.25). A bottle of champagne costs from 120F ($81.60).

Le Gentilhomme Bar, Hotel Richemond, Jardin Brunswick (tel. 022/731-14-00). Against the backdrop of a Napoleon III decor, this is the most elegant bar in Geneva, perhaps the most elegant in Switzerland, and certainly among the top watering spots of the world. Over the years I've observed the Who's Who among the chic and/or famous who have stopped in here for a quiet libation, observing the crystal chandeliers while seated on velvet chairs. It's a place where you can even take your dog, providing the mutt is very, very elegant. Everybody from Texas ranchers to Zurich bankers to mysterious women in $20,000 furs can order hard drinks from 13F ($8.85). It's open daily from 11:30 a.m. to 2:30 p.m. and 7 p.m. to 1 a.m.

Bar des Berges, Hotel des Bergues, 33 quai des Bergues (tel. 022/731-50-50), is a fashionable place to have a rendezvous. All polished mahogany, brass, and dark-green upholstery, it is decorated with late 19th-century hand-sketched menus from an earlier all-male society—the *Cercle des Arts et des Lettres.* Patrons today sit in this comfortable lounge from 11 a.m. to midnight daily, enjoying some of the same drinks that famous visitors did more than a century ago. At lunch you can even order a meal here sent in from the top-notch kitchen. Otherwise, whisky begins at 13F ($8.85). Ask the barman for daily specials. Piano players are imported "from all over" to entertain you.

La Tour Dancing, 6 rue de la Tour de Boël (tel. 022/21-00-33), is a difficult-to-locate club on one of Geneva's most charming squares in the old town. It's in a building owned at one time by the Genevese patriot, Bezanson Hugues (1491–1532). The club has chiseled stone and stucco walls with a wrought-iron dragon sticking out over the street. Inside, three levels of balconies overlook the central dance and performance area. Musical groups play rock and dance tunes from 10 p.m. to 4 a.m. nightly. No jeans or sneakers are permitted. There's a 10F ($6.80) cover charge on Friday and Saturday only, with drinks costing from 18F ($12.25) apiece. The club is closed Monday, and it has a small restaurant.

Club 58, 15 Glacis de Rive (tel. 022/735-15-15), is a private club. Nonmembers may be allowed in, but men are required to wear jackets and to pay an entrance charge of 10F ($6.80). Women accompanying male nonmembers are admitted free. The Club 58 is mainly a disco, but it has a restaurant attached. From time to time the club presents on stage some top names of show business, such as Isaac Hayes, the Temptations, Sacha Distel, Gilbert Becaud, and others. Drinks cost from 22F ($14.95). The club opens nightly at 10, but the restaurant opens at 8 p.m. Drinks here start at 8F ($5.45).

La Garçonnière, 22 place Bémont (tel. 022/28-21-61), features transvestite acts, drawing both a straight and a gay crowd. It has a disco-cabaret format, with burlesque acts. Two nightly shows are presented at 11:30 p.m. and at 1:30 a.m. It's open every night from 10 p.m. to 4 a.m. until 5 a.m. on Friday and Saturday. The charge is 8F ($5.45) as a cover Sunday to Thursday, rising to 12F ($8.15) Friday and Saturday. Drinks cost from 18F ($12.25).

Mr. Pickwick Pub, 80 rue Lausanne (tel. 022/731-67-97), serves simple, English-style meals, but mostly the patrons come here to drink. The paneled rooms are filled in the evening with an attractive young crowd, who enjoy the dimly lit, ambience. The place gets very crowded, and can be fun. Irish coffee is a specialty, but most visitors order beer at 4.50F ($3.05) a mug. The decor is inspired by Britain, as the name would suggest, but the music on the jukebox is likely to be from the States. In Geneva, the pub is sometimes called the "Tower of Babble" because of all the polyglot tongues spoken (many employees from the United Nations hang out here). It's open from 10 a.m. to 1 a.m. Monday to Friday, from 3 p.m. to 2 a.m. Saturday. Sunday hours are 3 p.m. to 1 a.m. Naturally you can order steak-and-kidney pie. The cost is 12F ($8.15) for a good-size plate.

If it should interest you, a gay pub recommended by the tourist office is **Le Tube,** 3 rue de l'Université (tel. 022/29-82-98). Earlier in the evening it draws a mixed crowd, but every night after 9 its clientele becomes predominantly gay. A beer from the tap costs 3.50F ($2.40). Closing is at 1 a.m. except on Friday and Saturday, when it stays open until 2 a.m. The style is that of a pub, not a disco.

7. EXCURSIONS FROM GENEVA

The region around Geneva is rich in attractions. Many of the most popular places—at least around the lake—have been covered in Chapter VIII on Lausanne and Lake Geneva. Refer to that chapter for highlights around the lake itself. However, a few attractions are practically at the doorstep of the city, and we'll survey these in this section.

The limestone ridge of **Mt. Salève** ("house mountain") lies four miles south of Geneva, in France. Its peak is 4,000 feet high, but you'll need a passport and visa to reach it. If you have a car, you can take a road that goes up this mountain, which is popular with rock-climbers. Bus no. 8 will take you to **Veyrier,** on the French frontier, where there is a passport and customs control. The lower station of a cable car in six minutes will take you to a height of 3,750 feet on Mt. Salève. From the top you'll have a panoramic sweep of the Valley of the Arve, with Geneva and Mont Blanc in the background.

Carouge, a suburb of Geneva, is a bit of European nostalgia. It dates mainly from the 18th century, when it was built by the king of Sardinia as a rival of Geneva. Architects from Turin supplied the Piedmontese charm. At the 1815 Congress of Vienna, Carouge was annexed to the canton of Geneva. Once Carouge was the playground of smugglers and gold-washers who panned for the precious metal in the Arve. The Genevese themselves—at least those who wanted to escape from the puritanical city—fled here, seeking the company of prostitutes and the "low life."

Switzerland now considers Carouge a national landmark because of its architecture. Begin your exploration in the Market Square with its old fountain, plane trees, and markets. A Roman stone was imbedded in the Church of the Holy Cross. As you walk about, you'll pass the Court of the Palace of the Count of Veyrier, dating from 1783, the place du Temple with a fountain from 1857, and a Louis XVI–carved door at 18 rue St-Victor. Many bars and cafés in the town serve excellent white wine from the Genevese vineyards.

Lord Byron and Shelley both lived in the residential suburb of **Cologny,** which is reached by bus A from Geneva. It lies nine miles to the northeast. From here you'll have a panoramic view of the lake and Geneva, with its Palais des Nations. The view is especially good from the "Byron Stone" on the chemin de Ruth ("Ruth's path") leading to the Byron fields. In 1816 Byron stayed at the Villa Diodati, where he met Shelley.

The best time to go to Cologny is on a Thursday afternoon when you can visit the **Bodmeriana Library,** chemin du Guignard (tel. 022/736-23-70), a foundation established by Martin Bodmer, Zurich millionaire. At that time a private collection of first editions, rare manuscripts, and objets d'art are on display.

If you'd like to do what the Genevese themselves do on a good day, take bus C, departing from Rond-Point de Rive in Geneva, heading for **Jussy,** a charming village in a rural setting, from which you can ramble through the woods and explore the countryside around Geneva on foot.

On the lake, **Hermance,** a mellow old fishermen's village, is reached by taking bus no. 9 from Rond-Point de Rive in Geneva. The village, founded in 1245, has been restored attractively, and in summer it's in virtual bloom there are so many flowers. The town is "crowned" by a tower dating from the Middle Ages, and its Chapel of St. Catherine is from the 15th century. The Genevese come here to browse through the art galleries, later enjoying drinks and food in several café-restaurants surrounded by gardens. Before heading back, I suggest a walk along the lake.

If you'd like to see some of the vineyards of Geneva, you can visit **Russin** and **Dardagny,** taking a train from the Gare Cornavin in Geneva. In about ten minutes you'll reach Russin, in the center of a wine-growing region. Later on you can go on to Dardagny, a landmark village with a castle by the Valley of the Allondon. Take the Donzelle route through vineyards, where you'll eventually get a train to take you back to Geneva.

One of the most interesting day trips in the region is a bit farther afield at **Coppet,** a little town on the western shore of Lake Geneva, a distance of nine miles, lying in the canton of **Vaud.**

The **Château de Coppet** (tel. 022/776-10-28) attracted some of the greatest minds of the 18th and 19th centuries. Lying on the lake, this seignorial château, between Lausanne and Geneva, was purchased in 1784 by Jacques Necker, the finance minister of Louis XVI. His daughter became the legendary Madame de Staël, the great French woman of letters. Her opposition to Napoleon sent her into exile, but she continued to receive many famous visitors. Her granddaughter married the Comte d'Haussonville, and the château has remained in the possession of Necker's direct descendants. In its museum are mementos of Madame de Staël. It's open March to October daily except Monday from 10 a.m. to noon and 2 to 5:30 p.m., charging 4.50F ($3.05) for adults and 2.20F ($1.50) for children 6 to 16. Guided tours are conducted.

For the most superb food and lodging in the area, consider **Hotel du Lac,** CH-1296 Coppet, Switzerland (tel. 022/776-15-21), which many elegant people from Geneva use as their hideaway. It stands six miles from the Geneva-Cointrin airport. This lovely lakeside retreat was originally established in 1628, when it was rated a "grand logis" by sovereign decree. Guests of yesterday often used to arrive by coach or horseback (now they occasionally come by boat). Many famous guests (some incognito) have stayed here over the years, enjoying a happy combination of the old and new (the restoration was sensitive).

The bedrooms, often with stone walls and beamed ceilings, and Oriental carpets, invite you to linger in style and snugness. The innkeepers have only 18 rooms, and sometimes they're booked way ahead, so reservations are imperative. They offer regular rooms, suites, and apartments. One person pays from 110F

($74.80) to 160F ($108.80) daily, two persons are charged from 170F ($115.60) to 210F ($142.80) in a room and 300F ($204) to 800F ($544) in a suite. An apartment for two costs 400F ($272) to 800F ($544). They'll even quote your *chien* (dog) a rate.

The Rôtisserie du Lac is one of the finest dining choices on Lake Geneva. In summer, tables are placed out right along the lake. Both a classic cuisine and a cuisine moderne emerge from the kitchen here under the direction of Bertrand Hubert. You might begin with a warm salad of frogs' legs or a ravioli of snails with sweet garlic, then follow with grilled sole in a chive sauce. Omble chevalier, the famous lake fish of Geneva, is prepared here "as you like it." Full meals cost from 100F ($68) or else you can order a menu dégustation. A business person's lunch is offered on weekdays for 55F ($37.40). Hours are daily from noon to 2:15 p.m. and 7 to 10:15. The hotel also operates a night club open nightly except Monday and Tuesday from 9 p.m. to 2 a.m.

LUCERNE AND CENTRAL SWITZERLAND

□ □ □

The mountaintops of the "heartland" of Switzerland have what is called "eternal snow." The flanks are lined with glacier ice.

Paddle-steamers across the lakes in the region lead to lidos, or summer bathing beaches. You'll make much use of railways and cable cars as you climb skyward in bright alpine sun to see for yourself what the charms of Rigi or Pilatus are all about. In winter, skating and curling rinks, cross-country ski tracks, toboggan runs, indoor swimming pools, and skiing in the mountains lure the visitor.

Lucerne and its lake are part of William Tell country, where the seeds that led to the Confederation were sown. For many Americans it's all they'll ever see of Switzerland. That's a shame, as the country has so much more to offer. But if the area in and around Lucerne is all that can be seen, then it's a worthy choice, for there's much to learn of the Swiss people here.

As one local Swiss official told me, "We just call it Lake Lucerne, because that way the foreigners understand better." Actually, the lake is known in German as the Vierwaldstättersee and in French as Lac des Quatre Cantons. Either way, it's the lake of the four cantons: Lucerne, Uri, Unterwalden, and Schwyz (Switzerland gets its name from Schwyz canton). The lake lies between the steep limestone mountains, Rigi in the north and Pilatus in the southwest. Bürgenstock, a promontory that thrusts itself into the lake, is now a hotel citadel. Seelisberg, a promontory to the south, is also well known. All this irregular geography gives the lake a romantic look. The lake itself is a prehistoric terminal basin of a glacier.

It was near Brunnen that the "Everlasting league" of 1315 was made, in the meadow of Rütli, which undoubtedly will be pointed out to you as you travel along in a lake steamer. Of course many of the sights in the area have to do with

Tell and the legendary Gessler, both supposedly fictional characters.

Lucerne is the only major city in the area, and most North Americans will want to settle in there. However, if you prefer one of the secluded resorts around the lake, I've included some hotel selections for you as well.

The lake is about 24 miles long, and at its broadest point is 2 miles wide. It's the fourth largest of the lakes of Switzerland, and one of the most frequented tourist areas in all of Europe. However, your actual gateway to central Switzerland will not be Lucerne, but Zug, immediately following.

1. ZUG

The town of Zug, 18 miles from Lucerne, called the gateway to central Switzerland, stands on the northeast shore of Lake Zug, or Zugersee if you prefer the Swiss name for this second-largest lake in the region. Some 9 miles long and 2½ miles wide, the lake lies to the north of Lake Lucerne, more than a mile from that lake's Küssnacht arm.

Zug, beautifully placed in a setting of orchards and gardens, is the capital of the canton of Zug, the smallest state in the country, sometimes called "the Rhode Island of Switzerland." It joined the Confederation in 1352, with its government affairs being contained within the old walled city.

Zug is still medieval in some parts, with many fountains and old burghers' houses. Building of the **Church of St. Oswald,** of late Gothic style lavishly embellished inside, was started in 1478 and completed early in the following century. The **Rathaus** (town hall) was ready for use in 1505. Relics of the ancient fortifications that used to protect the town may still be seen. In the old town, seek out in particular the **Fischmarkt,** with its mellow old houses, some with overhanging balconies and painted gables.

Zugerberg, a flat-topped mountain (3,255 feet), overlooks Zug from the southeast. To ascend the mountain, take a steep road up for six miles or board the funicular at Schönegg. From a belvedere on the mountain you overlook the town, the canton, and the lake, as well as viewing the towering peaks of the Jungfrau, the Eiger, the Pilatus, and the Rigi. In case you don't go up the Zugerberg, you can enjoy a good view of these peaks from a lakeside promenade in the town.

While you're in Zug, sample its renowned drink, Zuger kirschwasser, made from the juice of cherries grown in the local orchards.

FOOD AND LODGING: Constructed in a series of glass-walled rectangles, the **Hotel Rosenberg,** 33 Rosenbergstrasse, CH-6301 Zug, Switzerland (tel. 042/21-43-43), is a modern building that would look appropriate on the campus of an American university. The interior, however, is far more elegant than any college dormitory. It has Oriental rugs, lots of paneling, and sunny, well-furnished bedrooms with lots of light from big windows. Singles rent for 90F ($61.20) to 120F ($81.60), while doubles cost 140F ($95.20) to 180F ($122.40), including breakfast. The hotel also offers some of the best food in town, its specialties changing with the seasons.

Hotel Löwen au Lac, Landsgemeindeplatz, CH-6300 Zug, Switzerland (tel. 042/21-77-22), is a 19th-century stone building with white walls and neoclassical detailing under its brown tile roof. The ceilings of the two restaurants inside are elaborately paneled and beamed. The rather stark bedrooms are unadorned with anything except the essential furniture, but are adequate. Bathless singles rent for 50F ($34), singles with bath going for 70F ($47.60). Doubles are priced at 70F ($47.60) bathless, 95F ($64.60) with complete facilities. Breakfast is included.

For the best food in town, book a table at **Restaurant Aklin,** Kolinplatz (tel. 042/21-18-66), run by Margrit Riegger-Aklin in a 200-year-old building in the center of town not far from the historic tower of Zytturm. You dine amid gemütlich charm in one of three different rooms, the most formal of which is the Zunftstubl. Rooms tend to be paneled and rustic with alpine allure. The food is carefully sauced and seasoned. The repertoire is likely to include such dishes as roast goose with potatoes gratinée with cheese and chives, lamb cutlets in a vinegar-based sauce, or seawolf in a fennel-flavored cream sauce. For dessert, try a medley of white chocolate mousse with sorbets made from fresh fruit. At lunch, a fixed-price menu costs from 12.50F ($8.50) to 24F ($16.30), which is amazing value considering the quality of the cuisine. At dinner, full meals range from 60F ($40.80) to 70F ($47.60), with a gourmet menu peaking at 102F ($69.35). Hours are daily except Sunday from 11:30 a.m. to 2 p.m. and 6:30 to 10 p.m. Closed for parts of July. Always call for a reservation.

You can also patronize **Restaurant Schiff,** 2 Graben (tel. 042/21-00-55), in a 200-year-old house in the old town, not far from the lake. Its color scheme is soft yellow and gray. In addition to the main dining room, there is another wood-paneled room one floor above. The paneling in this room is considered of architectural significance and can't be altered. The chef, Helmut Zubel, offers full meals from 50F ($34) per person. Some of his products include John Dory with a passion fruit sauce, salmon with champagne sauce, and zander in a zesty tomato sauce. The restaurant is open daily from 11:30 a.m. to 2 p.m. and 6 to 9 p.m. Reservations are a good idea.

2. LUCERNE

At the north end of Lake Lucerne, Lucerne (Luzern in German) always seems to be a favorite of visiting Americans, because it lives up to a cliché image of a Swiss town. That is, it has narrow, old cobblestone streets in its medieval quarter, slender spires and turrets, covered bridges, promenades, and plazas dominated by fountains, as well as frescoed houses. You have both lake and mountains here. As the people of Lucerne will tell you, "you're never very far from the snow."

Lucerne is easily reached, not only by motorway (either bus or car), but by international express trains from both north and south. The international airport at Zurich is only an hour away.

Lucerne's gate to the south is formed by two mountain giants, Rigi and Pilatus, with a backdrop of the snow-capped Alps. Its history has long been tied to the St. Gotthard Pass. In the 13th century this was a mule path, becoming a carriage route in 1820. By 1882 it had a rail tunnel.

Once a vassal city of the Habsburgs, Lucerne became the first city to join the Swiss Confederation in 1332. The Reformation didn't take over in **Lucerne,** as it did in such cities as Geneva and Zurich, and Lucerne today remains a stronghold of Catholicism.

Lucerne is at its best on Tuesday and Saturday mornings when it becomes a lively market town. The markets—sheltered under stately arcades—overflow onto both the right and left banks of the River Reuss. When you finish exploring the city, you can take literally dozens of half- or full-day excursions, so many visitors wisely allow at least five days for Lucerne on their jam-packed itineraries. Since it's a real tourist town, especially in summer, the sights and excursions are well organized. You can do everything from take a cruise in an old paddle-wheel steamer to explore an eerie petrified world of a glacier garden dating back millions of years.

It's also a city of folk festivals and culture, as well as the center of several sporting events. Richard Wagner spent several of his most productive years in Tribschen on the outskirts of Lucerne (There is a Wagner Museum there). Arturo Toscanini was a founder of the **Lucerne International Festival of Music,** which takes place in August and September and is one of the most important such events in Europe, attracting some of the world's best soloists and orchestras.

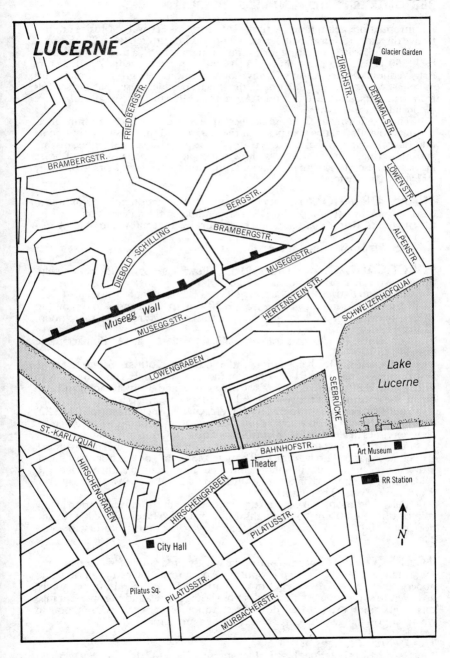

LUCERNE

FRIEDBERGSTR.

BRAMBERGSTR.

ZÜRICHSTR.

DENKMALSTR.

Glacier Garden

LÖWENSTR.

BERGSTR.

BRAMBERGSTR.

DIEBOLD -SCHILLING

ALPENSTR.

MUSEGGSTR.

HERTENSTEIN STR.

SCHWEIZERHOFQUAI

Musegg Wall

MUSEGG STR.

LÖWENGRABEN

SEEBRÜCKE

Lake
Lucerne

ST.-KARLI-QUAI

BAHNHOFSTR.

Art Museum

Theater

RR Station

HIRSCHENGRABEN

HIRSCHENGRABEN

PILATUSSTR.

N

City Hall

Pilatus Sq.

PILATUSSTR.

MURBACHERSTR.

For information, get in touch with the International Festival of Music administrative director, 13 Hirschmattstrasse, CH-6002 Luzern (tel. 041/23-35-62).

Lucerne is also the setting for a summer night festival, a tradition that dates back 250 years, with many fireworks and much entertainment. Shortly before Ash Wednesday every year it's Carnival time in Lucerne, as groups of musicians in fantastic costumes parade through the streets, producing ear-splitting sounds from trumpets, kettles, and drums. More than 400 fancy-dress balls take place before and during carnival.

The people who live here are also very sports-oriented. Every summer international rowing regattas take place on the Rotsee, and there's swimming on its lido (lake beach). On the outskirts is an 18-hole golf course, and tennis, hiking, and mountineering are also possible. The people are especially fond of horse races, and these, along with international jumping contests, are marked on many an equestrian calendar.

TRANSPORTATION: The city has a good transportation network of **buses,** costing from .80F (55¢) to 1.50F ($1), depending on the miles traversed within the city limits. Before boarding, purchase your tickets at automatic vending machines.

Bicycles can be rented at the railway station.

PRACTICAL FACTS: You may find the following items of information helpful when you are visiting Lucerne.

American Express: The Lucerne office, 4 Schweizerhofquai (tel. 041/50-11-77), is open Monday to Friday from 8:30 a.m. to noon and 2 to 6 p.m. (no checks are cashed after 5 p.m., however). Saturday hours are 8:30 a.m. to noon. Closed Sunday.

Consulate: To help Americans, the **U.S. Consulate** is at 141 Zollikerstrasse (tel. 041/55-25-66).

Information: To help visitors, the **Lucerne Tourist Office** is at 1 Frankenstrasse (tel. 041/51-71-71), near the train station. It's open Monday to Friday from 8:30 a.m. to 6 p.m. May to September and 8 a.m. to noon and 2 to 6 p.m. the remainder of the year. Saturday hours are 9 a.m. to 5 p.m.

Laundry: For a Laundromat, try **Jet-Wasch,** 28 Bruchstrasse (tel. 041/22-01-51), where you can do your washing, use an iron and ironing board, and relax between times in clean and comfortable facilities.

Post office: Next to the rail station, the main post office on Bahnhofstrasse is open Monday to Friday from 7:30 a.m. to 6:30 p.m., on Saturday to 11 a.m. However, the branch, at 2 Bahnhof behind the railway station is open Monday to Friday until 11 p.m. and on Saturday until 8 p.m. It's also open on Sunday from 9 a.m. to noon and 3 to 8 p.m.

Railway station: You can make telephone calls at the railway station at any coin box from 4:30 a.m. to midnight. Money can also be exchanged at the station from 7:30 a.m. to 9 p.m. Monday to Friday, to 6:30 p.m. Saturday and Sunday.

WHERE TO STAY: Lucerne, one of the most-visited cities of Switzerland, has a wide range of hotels, with a preponderance of those in the medium-priced and upper-bracket ranges. It suffers from a shortage of really good budget hotels, however. In summer, when the hordes from both America and Europe pour into this town, it's important to nail down a reservation. Otherwise, finding a room in whatever price range you desire should not be a problem.

The Deluxe Choices

Grand Hotel National, 4 Haldenstrasse, CH-6002 Luzern, Switzerland (tel. 041/50-11-11), is a local landmark and a Swiss hotel legend. It is a vast edifice of gray stone that was constructed, in the words of the management, "in the style of the French kings." The National looks like a wing of the Louvre at Versailles, with acres of mansard roofing and dozens of stone-flanked gables. The hotel was built in 1870 to house the flood of tourists just beginning to discover Lake Lucerne. Since then, monarchs and statesmen from all over Europe have passed through its doors, as have César Ritz and Auguste Escoffier, the latter being the head chef when the hotel first opened.

Between 1977 and 1980, Italian-born Umberto Erculiani, the owner of the property (he's also an architect) ripped apart the infrastructure of this grand palace and rebuilt it with every conceivable modern hotel convenience. Every effort was made, however, to retain the original soaring ceilings, wide hallways, and theatrical stairways which, buttressed, reinforced, and redecorated, today vie with the best of the best in Swiss hotels. The lobby has one of the thickest sculptured carpets you may ever see, tinted in abstract patterns of blues and greens.

Originally the hotel was bigger, but about half its bedrooms were converted into apartments, for which the rental market booms each year as reservations are made months in advance for these. Seventy-nine of the accommodations, however, are private bedrooms, perhaps the most comfortable in the city. Many have private balconies opening onto lake views, and each has modern amenities, although a certain old-fashioned charm has been retained. Each accommodation contains a spacious private bath entirely sheathed in slabs of colored marble. Other amenities include TV with in-house movies, mini-bars, and thick carpets. Some of the rooms have brass beds and gilded wall sconces. Singles in summer range from 180F ($122.40) to 250F ($170) daily, with doubles costing from 320F ($217.60) to 425F ($289), including a buffet breakfast. Prices are cut in winter to 140F ($95.20) to 180F ($122.40) daily in a single and 240F ($163.20) to 320F ($217.60) in a double.

An indoor swimming pool and a sauna are on the premises, along with massage facilities. The piano bar, elegantly paneled, glitters with cut crystal and reverberates with highly drinkable melodies. It is one of the town's most alluring rendezvous points. The hotel is a member of the prestigious Steigenberger Reservations System. In New York City, call 212/593-2988, or toll free in New York State 800/882-4777, or toll free nationwide dial 800/223-5652.

Palace Hotel, 10 Haldenstrasse, CH-6006 Luzern, Switzerland (tel. 041/50-22-22). The lobby of this luxurious hotel is painted in light shades of green and yellow, which are applied between the Ionic columns of the high-ceilinged room whose detailing is still a starry white. The effect is lovely, especially with the massive chandelier and the elegantly lighthearted furniture. This is one of the best hotels in Switzerland, housed in a large structure that rambles beside the lake, a monument to belle-époque style and grace. Capped with two interesting-looking towers and dominated by a mansard roof, the establishment has catered to the needs of demanding clients for years. Jürg Reinshagen, the managing director, charges from 220F ($149.60) to 320F ($217.60) daily in a single in summer and 320F ($217.60) to 500F ($340) in a twin-bedded room. Winter prices are 175F ($119) to 235F ($159.80) daily in a single, 230F ($156.40) to 390F ($265.20) in a double. All rooms have baths and other comfortable amenities. Breakfast is included in the prices.

Two restaurants are staffed with a host of waiters and chefs who prepare fine dishes. A choice dining spot is the Mignon Restaurant, one of the most elegant and formal places in town in Lucerne in the evening. While dining by candlelight and listening to piano music, you can enjoy a menu that changes with the season. The classic French dishes and cuisine moderne variations are imaginative, the elements the freshest. One of the favorite places to linger in the hotel is a Victorian-style bar with globe lights and leather-upholstered barrel chairs.

Carlton Hotel Tivoli, 57 Haldenstrasse, CH-6002 Luzern, Switzerland (tel. 041/51-30-51), is on the tree-lined promenade on the north side of the lake in a region filled with resort hotels and private homes. A five-star hotel, it has its own lakeside tennis courts and a marina built out into the lake. The ambience is one of clear open space and unobtrusive modern furniture. Because of the high ceilings, the light furniture, and the big windows, one has a feeling of being outdoors. A terrace restaurant serves good food, while a piano bar features live music every evening from 7. The 100 well-furnished accommodations, all with private bath, rent for 145F ($98.60) to 220F ($149.60) daily in a single, from 280F ($190.40) to 360F ($244.80) in a double. Arrangements can also be made for connecting a single and a double unit. A buffet breakfast is included in the tariffs.

Schweizerhof Lucerne, 3 Schweizerhofquai, CH-6002 Luzern, Switzerland (tel. 041/50-22-11), has been under the ownership of the Hauser family since 1861. It's a 19th-century palace-style hotel, with pink marble columns and pilasters in the lobby that support the plaster detailing on the cream-colored ceilings. An American bar is outfitted with rich woods, Louis XV–style armchairs, and leather bar stools. The bedrooms are the kind of spacious, well-furnished places where you could safely send your favorite nephew on his honeymoon. This hotel is a rigidly symmetrical and pleasing collection of three evenly spaced white buildings connected by arched passageways. They ramble along the lakefront for at least two full blocks, done in an architectural style whose grandeur may never be repeated. Singles rent for 190F ($129.20) to 260F ($176.80) daily and doubles for 310F ($210.80) to 410F ($278.80), depending on the location, size, and season.

The hotel's restaurant, La Rotonde, is one of the most elegant and refined dining rooms in the city. At lunch, it offers a simple businessperson's menu at 35F ($23.80), but you are likely to spend from 85F ($57.80) or more in the evening, ordering a classic continental cuisine.

The Upper Bracket

Hôtel Monopol & Métropole, 1 Pilatusstrasse, CH-6002 Luzern, Switzerland (tel. 041/23-08-66), lies behind a grand façade of carved limestone, wrought-iron balconies, and elaborately detailed windows and half-columns. Built in 1898, the hotel has individually furnished rooms, some of them modern and others in a cozily paneled format of alcove beds and chalet chairs. A tavern within the hotel looks like an inviting forest of rustic vertical beams, with a live pianist every evening from 7 to 11. A more formal French restaurant, the Arbalète, serves classic meals in a lighthearted decor of crimson walls and modern chandeliers. Each of the accommodations has a private bath, with radio, phone, and mini-bar. The charge for singles is from 105F ($71.40) to 220F ($149.60) daily, with doubles costing from 190F ($129.20) to 220F ($149.60), with breakfast included in all the tariffs.

Hotel Schiller, 15 Pilatusstrasse, CH-6002 Luzern, Switzerland (tel. 041/ 23-51-55). The entrance is indicated by a colorful awning above a busy commercial street. You'll be surrounded by other antique buildings, but this one stands out more because of its 19th-century detailing. A sidewalk café serves drinks and food. Inside, a decorator has added dramatic touches, such as dark-green walls with attractively framed prints and an occasional bronze statue. A rustic restaurant has the kind of heavy beams overhead you've come to expect in the Alps, as well as an open hearth where a staff member grills savory steaks. Guests can also patronize the American bar, Poseidon. Many of the accommodations have been modernized into a streamlined format of angular furniture and comfortable beds, with bath, phone, and in some cases, TV and mini-bar. The hotel stands only a five-minute walk from the train station. Singles range from 70F ($47.60) to 130F ($88.40) daily, and doubles cost 110F ($74.80) to 185F ($125.80), depending on the size, the plumbing, and the season.

Hotel zum Rebstock, Sankt Leodegar Platz, CH-6000 Luzern, Switzerland (tel. 041/51-35-81), run by Claudia Moser, is one of the most charming hotels in its price range in Lucerne. It's housed in a half-timbered green-shuttered house with a brown tile roof that visitors can see on their way down the hill from the nearby Hofkirche. It used to be the headquarters of the wine-growers guild (1443), and was later used as a recruitment center for the tough Swiss mercenaries who came from this region (the pope was one of the main recruiters). Bedrooms inside tend to be smaller than you may be used to, but are charmingly decorated in shades of blue and white, sometimes pink and green. If you're interested in a daytime hill-climbing expedition, the management will pack you a trail lunch. Otherwise, you might choose to eat in the thick-walled restaurant or on the garden terrace. Singles rent for 75F ($51) to 100F ($68), while doubles range from 140F ($95.20) to 190F ($129.20).

Hotel Union Luzern, 16 Löwenstrasse, CH-6002 Luzern, Switzerland (tel. 041/51-36-51), is one of the leading four-star traditional hotels of Lucerne. It still maintains high standards of comfort and service. The façade of this hotel has been renovated and is today one of the most impressive sights in Lucerne, with old medieval paintings redone by a local artist. The lobby is outfitted with conservatively modern decor which includes columns of reddish stone holding up a high ceiling. In the stairway leading to the breakfast room and the bedrooms is a massive chandelier which was skillfully designed for this space. Public rooms include an attractive bar, two restaurants, and a ballroom that you should at least have a look at. A new heating system, electrical fixtures, and plumbing have been installed. All the bedrooms have private baths. Singles cost from 80F ($54.40) to 130F ($88.40) daily, doubles from 140F ($95.20) to 230F ($156.40), and triples from 180F ($122.40) to 270F ($183.60), the price depending on the season.

Romantik-Hotel Wilden Mann, 30 Bahnhofstrasse, CH-6002 Luzern, Switzerland (tel. 041/23-16-66). If you pay for half board here, you can take your meals at two other hotels owned by the same Furler management (the Château Gütsch and the Carlton Tivoli). Chances are, however, you'll choose to eat in the Swiss paneled dining room with vaulted arches and heraldic designs. This hotel is set in the middle of the old town, in a building with flower boxes, carved stone detailing, and elegant furniture. Each of the bedrooms is different, usually more modern than the public rooms downstairs, although attractive and one-of-a-kind. Singles range from 98F ($66.65) to 132F ($89.75) daily, while doubles cost 164F ($111.50) to 288F ($195.85), with breakfast included. Prices, of course, depend on the season and the plumbing. Half board is available for an additional 34F ($23.10) per person daily.

Grand Hotel Europe, 59 Haldenstrasse, CH-6002 Luzern, Switzerland (tel. 041/30-11-11), is an elegant 19th-century hotel one block away from the north shore of the lake. It has neoclassical pediments above the windows of its white façade, and a row of red awnings sheltering the public rooms from the sunshine in the garden. Some of the sitting rooms are decorated with large tapestries, Oriental rugs, and comfortably upholstered couches and easy chairs. The bedrooms are usually spacious and well furnished. The hotel is open from the first of April until the end of October. Most rooms contain private baths, although serious economizers will seek one of the accommodations only with hot and cold running water. Depending on the plumbing and room assignment, singles rent for 86F ($58.50) to 140F ($95.20) daily, with doubles costing 144F ($97.90) to 249F ($169.30).

Hotel Astoria, 29 Pilatusstrasse, CH-6003 Luzern, Switzerland (tel. 041/24-44-66), a first-class hotel, stands in the center of Lucerne in a modern block-shaped building with prominent horizontal rows of windows. The interior is attractively subdued, with metal and stucco detailing, along with glistening accents and enameled metal. In the popular bar area the walls are upholstered in soft green, with a metallic ceiling reflecting the flames from the central tubular fireplace. Each of the 140 well-furnished rooms has a private bath, radio, color TV, and phone. Thirty new rooms were added onto the back for those desiring a tranquil location. Singles range from 90F ($61.20) to 140F ($95.20) daily and doubles from 130F ($88.40) to 200F ($136), with breakfast included. A Parisian-style restaurant, Belle Époque, serves French and Swiss specialties.

Hotel Montana, 22 Adligenswilerstrasse, CH-6002 Luzern, Switzerland (tel. 041/51-65-65), is a beautifully detailed 19th-century hotel set slightly above lake level on a quiet hillside. The hotel maintains its own private cable car so that its guests can ride in comfort down to the lakeside promenades. The interior is filled with the kind of old-fashioned grandeur that you might be looking for, including a lobby area with a contrasting series of Oriental rugs, brocaded antique chairs and settees, and polished paneling stretching up to the ornamented ceilings. A curved bar area and terrace with a panoramic view over the lake are pleasant stopping points. Singles rent for 110F ($74.80) to 149F ($101.30) daily, and doubles cost 190F ($129.20) to 256F ($174.10), with buffet breakfast included. An extra bed can be set up in any room for an additional 50F ($34). All units contain a private bath, and the hotel is closed every year from November to March.

Hotel Flora, 5 Seidenhofstrasse, CH-6002 Luzern, Switzerland (tel. 041/24-44-44), has the kind of modern decor that is warmly fashioned from wood and metal into a pleasing angularity, but which adds folkloric touches in key places to remind you that you are in Switzerland. A disco on the premises is a fantasy of comfortable banquettes and hanging pin lights, while the bars provide comfortable and up-to-date places for an intimate drink. You'll be near the railway station in a large hotel with 145 rooms and a strong dedication to good service. One of the restaurants has a folkloric musical show about every evening, with yodelers and alpine horns. If you didn't have your heart set on an old-fashioned hotel, this is a good choice. Each of the comfortable rooms has a private bath, along with TV, radio, and phone. Breakfast is included in the price, which ranges from 70F ($47.60) to 115F ($78.20) daily in a single and 120F ($81.60) to 210F ($142.80), depending on the season.

Hotel Château Gütsch, Kanonenstrasse, CH-6002 Luzern, Switzerland (tel. 041/22-02-72). If you've ever dreamed of ruling over part of your own castle, this could be your chance, although the structure never had a royal owner. It all started when a watchtower was built in 1590 on a wooded hill west of the town of Lucerne, called *gütsch,* or "peak." In 1860 a restaurant was built followed by a small inn constructed by an Englishman, who once accommodated Queen Victoria in his hostelry. After the first hotel burned in 1888, the present structure was built and the name "château" was added because of the fancy appearance and the many towers. Antiques and paintings of several periods were brought in to help justify the grand name. The outrageously ornate tower on top of this château could have been designed by Mad King Ludwig himself. The rest of the building, lying above the city, is crafted of gray stone and red tiles, sometimes with half timbering, and always surrounded by mountain paths and pleasant lawns. A swimming pool with a view of the lake is separated from the main building by a copse of trees. A rustic bar and wine cellar are outfitted with huge oval wine barrels set into the masonry walls, with wagon-wheel chandeliers illuminating the polished woodwork. Comfortably furnished singles cost from 73F ($49.65) to 132F ($89.75) daily, with doubles going for 122F ($82.95) to 238F ($161.85), with breakfast included. For half board, an extra 34F ($23.10) per person per day is added.

Hôtel Des Balances & Bellevue, Weinmarkt, CH-6002 Luzern, Switzerland (tel. 041/51-18-51), is a quiet hotel with a desirable location on the River Reuss. The riverside frontage is elaborately crafted of gray stone with lots of curlicue wrought-iron balconies. A waterside café does a thriving business on a hot day, especially since most of the town on the other side of the river will be spread out for viewing. When you exit from the front door you'll be in the most colorful square in town, opposite a building with frescoes all over the façade. Inside the hotel you'll find a pleasing blend of Oriental rugs and high ceilings. Some of the rooms have been updated in a contemporary style, but all are usually tasteful and pleasing and contain baths. Clients are authorized to drive to the hotel, even if the barricades have temporarily turned the inner city into a pedestrian zone. Accommodations on the river side are understandably more in price. The price of a room depends on the season. Singles range from 80F ($54.40) to 140F ($95.20) daily, and doubles cost 130F ($88.40) to 250F ($170), including a light breakfast.

Luzernerhof, 3 Alpenstrasse, CH-6004 Luzern, Switzerland (tel. 041/51-46-46), is a centrally located silvery rectangle of a building with brick detailing around its corners and a streetside café. Each of its spacious, well-furnished bedrooms has a private bath, modern carpeting, and classic chairs. The hotel has a restaurant, a grill room, and a bar open until late at night. Accommodations in well-maintained single or double rooms range from 85F ($57.80) to 100F ($68) daily per person, and suites cost 250F ($170), with breakfast included.

The Middle Bracket

Hotel Ambassador, 3 Zürichstrasse, CH-6004 Luzern, Switzerland (tel. 041/51-71-51), opened in 1987 near the Lion Monument and quickly established itself as one of the finest of the moderately priced hotels of the city. A four-star selection, the hotel is completely modern, its furnishings up-to-date and comfortable. Bedrooms contain a number of amenities such as radio, direct-dial phone, color TV, mini-bar, and private bathroom with hairdryer. Singles range from 90F ($61.20) to 110F ($74.80) daily, with twin-bedded rooms renting for 150F ($102) to 200F ($136), including tax and service. A breakfast buffet is served (the only meal offered, although many fine restaurants are nearby). The rear of the hotel opens onto a garden, and in the same building you'll find parking and a shopping center. The location is an eight-minute walk from the train station.

Hôtel des Alpes, 5 Rathausquai, CH-6002 Luzern, Switzerland (tel. 041/51-58-25), has an elegantly tall and narrow façade with lots of restrained detailing that leans a little toward the baroque. A riverside restaurant and café serves meals on the terrace just above the Reuss, which has a frontal view of Lucerne's famous covered bridge. Inside, the public rooms still retain some of their old-fashioned detailing. However, the bedrooms are usually streamlined, modernized, and filled with functional pieces. Parking facilities are across the river at the nearby train station. Each of the bedrooms has its own private bath, and costs 60F ($40.80) to 95F ($64.60) daily in a single and from 95F ($64.60) to 155F ($105.40) in a double, depending on the exposure and the season. Breakfast is included.

Hotel Johanniter, 18 Bundesplatz, CH-6003 Luzern (tel. 041/23-18-55), is a traditional Swiss hotel with gabled peaks lying behind the railway station about six blocks from the lake. The bedrooms are comfortable and furnished with modern pieces along with such amenities as bath or shower, toilet, phone, radio, TV, and mini-bar. Gerhard Fahrni, the host, charges from 70F ($47.60) to 93F ($63.25) daily in a single and from 124F ($84.40) to 164F ($111.50) in a double, including a breakfast buffet. This three-star hotel also has good dining facilities, serving a typically Lucerne cuisine with several continental specialties as well.

Hotel Alpina, 6 Frankenstrasse, CH-6003 Luzern, Switzerland (tel. 041/23-00-77), a one-minute walk from the train station, is a winning choice, charging reasonable prices. Its interior is attractively and comfortably furnished with plush carpeting in rich colors and painted alpine furniture. The bedrooms are spacious and often high-ceilinged, outfitted with conservative furniture. Singles range from 65F ($44.20) to 80F ($54.40) daily, and twins cost 118F ($80.25) to 142F ($96.55). An attached restaurant is rustic and wood-beamed, offering hearty fare and Swiss wines and beer.

Hotel Kolping, 8 Friedenstrasse, CH-6004 Luzern, Switzerland (tel. 041/51-23-51), has a restrained façade of gray stone and stucco. It sometimes accepts large tour groups. The interior is outfitted in modern and rustic furniture. The overall effect is pleasing and comfortable. A chalet-style restaurant is covered with blond paneling from top to bottom. The quiet, centrally located hotel is a pleasant and unpretentious establishment that tries to please. Each unit has a private bath or shower. Singles range from 51F ($34.70) to 75F ($51) daily, and doubles cost 93F ($63.25) to 134F ($91.10). You can enjoy food and drink in the hotel's dining facilities. The hotel is three minutes away from the lake shore and the Lion Monument.

Hôtel de la Paix, 2 Museggstrasse, CH-6002 Luzern, Switzerland (tel. 041/51-52-53), can be found between the Lion monument and the lake. The façade is constructed in a pastiche of styles that includes Renaissance bay windows, Italianate painted panels, and Victorian gables. All of it is incongruously capped with a baroque tower, which, considering the rest of the building, doesn't look at all out of place. The interior has two rustic restaurants, a sauna, and a small wood-ceilinged swimming pool. City parking is close to the hotel. Singles cost 56F ($38.10) to 86F ($58.50) daily and doubles from 95F ($64.60) to 155F ($105.40), depending on the season and plumbing. Breakfast is included in the price.

Hotel Hermitage, CH-6006 Luzern-Seeburg, Switzerland (tel. 041/31-37-37). Technically this hotel is in Lucerne, although you'll need to get there on a bus that leaves from the main station or on a boat that departs from the city docks. One part of the hotel is an attractive older house, painted white, with a modern extension off to one side. Guests are invited to sit on a lakeside terrace for meals or coffee, or to sun themselves on the grassy lawns. A nearby annex holds the overflow from the main hotel. Singles range from 50F ($34) to 78F ($53.05) daily and doubles cost 100F ($68) to 140F ($95.20) with breakfast included. Prices, of course, depend on the season, the plumbing, and the view.

Continental & Park, 4-13 Morgartenstrasse, CH-6002 Luzern, Switzerland (tel. 041/23-75-66), stands in the heart of Lucerne, lying behind an attractive façade of masonry and dark-gray detailing. A row of evenly spaced gables juts out from the sixth-floor roofline, while the exterior of the ground-floor restaurant is framed in burgundy. The hotel offers modern comfort in its pleasant bedrooms, 75 in all, each with private bath or shower, and toilet, TV, mini-bar, and radio. Prices, depending on the season, range from 55F ($37.40) to 108F ($73.45) daily in a single and from 100F ($68) to 180F ($122.40) in a double. The hotel has two handsomely furnished restaurants, Le Beaujolais and Locanda Ticinese, both offering a good Swiss cuisine. The location is near the railway station and the lake.

Hotel Rothaus, 4 Klosterstrasse, CH-6003 Luzern, Switzerland (tel. 041/22-45-22), stands in the center of town. The angular modern façade is relieved by the placement of red shutters near the weatherproof windows. The interior has a pleasant sitting room with upholstered chairs, contrasting Oriental rugs, and an oversize armoire in reddish carved wood dominating one wall. The other public rooms are paneled and beamed, with wood furniture and wrought-iron lighting fixtures. Comfortably furnished singles rent for 75F ($51) to 81F ($55.10) daily, while doubles cost from 130F ($88.40) to 147F ($99.95). Breakfast is included.

The Budget Range

SSR Touristenhotel, 12 St. Karliquai, CH-6004 Luzern, Switzerland (tel. 041/51-24-74), is an attractive choice for a budget hotel in Lucerne. Singles rent for 42F ($28.55) to 61F ($41.50) daily and doubles for 64F ($43.50) to 102F ($69.35). Dormitory beds are also offered, costing 25F ($17) per person nightly. Use of the showers is free. Students with the ISIC card or International Student Card are given a 10% reduction on all rates. A buffet breakfast is included. You'll recognize the hotel by its sage-green façade on the river, a few minutes from the train station.

Pension Panorama, 9 Kapuzinerweg, CH-6006 Luzern, Switzerland (tel. 041/36-67-01), is only a 10-minute walk from the center of the old town on a hillside which affords a sweeping view of the lake and the nearby mountains. Owned and operated by Kurt Matti and Barbara Roth, the building was erected along angular lines in the early 1970s. Today, its five-story design devotes three floors to this well-regarded pension. None of its 27 simple-but-comfortable bedrooms contains a private bath. However, there are adequate shared facilities (one bathroom per every quartet of rooms). Throughout the year singles rent for 38F ($25.85) and doubles for 55F ($37.40) to 75F ($51), which makes the establishment one of the better bargains of Lucerne. From the main station, take bus no. 4 or 5, getting off at the third stop (Kapuzinerweg).

Pension Villa Maria, 36 Haldenstrasse, CH-6002 Luzern, Switzerland (tel. 041/31-21-19), is a family-run pension in a three-story private home on the north shore of the lake. The public rooms are decorated like someone's comfortably cluttered living room, in shades of gold, pink, and red, while the bedrooms are spacious, clean, and comfortable. The Winkler family is happy to help guests in any way they can. Bathless singles range from 37F ($25.15) to ($31.30) daily. Doubles without bath cost 63F ($42.85) to 89F ($60.50), doubles with bath going for 96F ($65.30) to 108F ($73.45). The pension is open April to October.

WHERE TO DINE: Lucerne is blessed with some of the finest restaurants in Switzerland, in a wide range of prices. So you definitely won't be confined to your hotel dining room when it comes time to eat. Prices, in the main, are fairly reasonable.

The Upper Bracket

Chez Marianne (Restaurant zum Raben), 5 am Kornmarkt (tel. 041/51-51-35), is the personal statement of Marianne Kaltenbach, a celebrity in Switzerland because of her well-known cookbooks. In the heart of the old town, the building dates from the Middle Ages. The restaurant is divided into four elegant rooms, usually with wood panels, alpine chairs, and chandeliers of deer antlers carved into human figures, plus lots of 80-year-old photographs of a thriving Lucerne. An inner room is my personal favorite. It has exquisitely crafted Louis-Philippe chairs in a glowing hardwoods, built-in floor-to-ceiling Gothic revival cupboards, mirrors, modern paintings, and views of the river. Swiss menus are offered from 65F ($44.20) to 100F ($68). Specialties include filet of pike with a saffron cream sauce, venison pâté with nuts and bitter orange sauce, and boiled beef with horseradish. Reservations are suggested. The restaurant is open every day from noon to 2 p.m. and 6:30 to 10 p.m.

Old Swiss House, 4 Löwenplatz (tel. 041/51-61-71), is housed in such a charming half-timbered building that Anheuser-Busch built an enlarged replica of it at Busch Gardens in Tampa, Florida, in 1964. Near the Lion Monument, the house is one of the most photographed attractions of the area. Most of the interior decoration, in both the rooms for private parties upstairs and the public rooms downstairs, is 17th century. The house contains a collection of Meissen porcelain and antique glass, hand-carved oak doors with inlaid wood, wooden stairways, leaded- and stained-glass windows with heraldic panes from 1575, antique silver, and old pewter. There are also original oil paintings throughout the house. Perhaps the most outstanding item of the entire collection is a handmade porcelain stove dated 1636, in the Knight's Room. The Buholzer family has owned this place for many years.

You'll enter through an oak door with wrought-iron embellishments and be face to face with a long bar. Multilingual waitresses in regional dress hurry about, serving the tables. Your own table will probably be close to one of the leaded-glass windows in one of the heavily timbered dining rooms. On sunny days, you can have lunch on the terrace. A city parking lot is a few hundred yards away, although there are a few parking places with meters nearby. The restaurant is open daily from 9 a.m. to midnight. Specialties include homemade cheese croquettes, onion soup, a local fish caught fresh every day from Lake Lucerne, veal prepared at your table, and a deluxe Wiener schnitzel, plus veal escalope topped with ham and cheese in a velvety-smooth cream sauce. From 11 a.m. to 6 p.m. a light luncheon menu ranges in price from 18F ($12.25) to 25F ($17). A large five-course menu costs 45F ($30.60) to 65F ($44.20).

Le Manoir, 9 Bundesplatz (tel. 041/23-23-48). Roman Stübinger and his wife, Elke, achieved local fame and lots of international attention when they renovated a terraced building next to the train station a few years ago. They brought "new kitchen" cuisine in full force to Lucerne and, it's rumored, did more to change local tastes than any other restaurant. Blessed with what appears to be enormous energy, the Austrian-born owner grows many of his own herbs and personally writes out the day's menu by hand. He also prepares a constantly changing series of impeccably flavored delicacies. Everything is cuisine du marché in the freshest sense of that expression. Elke presides over the dining room with great poise, sometimes suggesting a three-course business lunch at 40F ($27.20) for clients who don't want to dawdle. More elaborate dishes include filets of turbot with sage, asparagus tips served with chive sabayon, fresh duckling, lake trout with leeks in champagne sauce, or fricassée of rabbit with prunes and old bordeaux. Fixed-price meals range from 65F ($44.20) to 100F ($68), and à la carte dinners cost from 50F ($34) to 100F ($68). Hours are daily except Monday from noon to 2 p.m. and 6:30 to 11 p.m.

Von Pfyffer Stube, Grand Hotel National, 4 Haldenstrasse (tel. 041/50-11-11). The menu and staff have changed since César Ritz and Auguste Escoffier worked here in 1870. But by anyone's standards, this is still considered one of the most prestigious restaurants of Lucerne. Named after a Swiss military hero who allied his armies with the French, it lies within one very grand wing of the previously recommended Grand Hotel National. It is paneled in matched veneers of exotic hardwoods, plushly padded with Oriental carpets, and ringed with modern drawings. Its warmth is increased in cold weather with flames from a carved limestone fireplace.

You are likely to be served such typically French-inspired dishes as ravioli stuffed with smoked salmon, roast seawolf (bass) with fresh herbs, saddle of lamb (also with fresh herbs), breast of duckling with beetroot, and grilled scampi with lobster sauce. There's even an after dinner menu for cigars and a selection of vintage port, served in the grand manner by a phalanx of white-jacketed attendants. Full meals cost from 75F ($51). However, a menu dégustation, showcasing many small portions of some of the chef's most imaginative dishes, is priced at 85F ($57.80). Reservations are important for meals served daily at dinner only, which is offered nightly from 6:30 to 11.

Arbalète, Hôtel Monopole & Métropole, 1 Pilatusstrasse (tel. 041/23-08-66), is an elegantly decorated restaurant with crimson walls and modern chandeliers in the first floor of this hotel. Typical dishes include a clear bouillon of lobster, a gratin of veal kidneys, turbot with anise sauce, and rolled filet of sole stuffed with shrimp. The restaurant, whose name means crossbow, is open from

6 a.m. to 12:30 a.m. daily. Set meals range from 24F ($16.30) for a business lunch, with à la carte dinners costing from 45F ($30.60).

The Middle Bracket

Burgerstube, at the Hotel Wilden Mann, 30 Bahnhofstrasse (tel. 041/23-16-66), has vaulted smoky ceilings and lots of paneling, the kind of well-maintained rustic ambience you normally associate with the Alps. It's been owned by the same family for the last 130 years, and today is one of the better known restaurants in the old town. A five-course fixed-price menu might offer a ragoût of fresh mushrooms and chanterelles with sage, a cutting from a side of beef with mustard sauce, or medallions of veal with leeks. Table d'hôte meals cost 30F ($20.40) to 48F ($32.65), while à la carte dinners range from 38F to 65F ($44.20). The restaurant is open every day from 10:30 a.m. to midnight.

Liedertafel, Romantik-Hotel Wilden Mann, 30 Bahnhofstrasse (tel. 041/23-16-66), is housed in this previously recommended hotel along with the just-recommended Burgerstube. Unlike the stube, the Liedertafel is the more formal restaurant, stylishly decorated with artistic scenes from old Lucerne. Long one of the most prestigious dining rooms of the city, it serves an elegant cuisine that might include salmon cutlet gratinée with herbs, filet of poached trout on a mousse of white cabbage, sautéed scallops and anglerfish with garlic, veal kidneys flambé, or Chateaubriand flambé. Full meals cost from 60F ($40.80). Hours are from noon to 2 p.m. and 6:30 to 9 p.m. daily.

Restaurant Lapin, Hôtel de la Paix, 2 Museggstrasse (tel. 041/51-52-53). This restaurant is attractively angled so that it opens like a fan from the entrance. The format is light-grained and rustic, with a separate bar area overlooking a picture window and a few comfortable banquettes. One wall is made of exposed stone. Please note that the restaurant is at the corner of the Alpenstrasse, because if you begin your search at the wrong end of the street, you'll have a very long walk up some steep hills. Specialties include international fare such as sirloin steak Café de Paris and lamb Engadine style, as well as excellent fish dishes such as sole. To honor its namesake, *lapin* (rabbit), the chef prepares a terrine made with rabbit. You can also order the classic Swiss dish, sausage and Rösti. Meals cost from 18F ($12.25) up. It is open daily from 7 a.m. to 12:30 a.m.

Schwanen Restaurants, 4 Schwanenplatz (tel. 041/51-11-77). Under the same roof are two distinctly different restaurants lying near the old bridge in the very heart of Lucerne. Le Bec Rouge upstairs is the more elegant—and expensive—of the two. The restaurant is attractively decorated and opens onto views of the lake. The lighting is intimate and the service refined. A variety of seasonal specialties, fresh from the daily market, are offered here. A special menu is offered for 35F ($23.80); this menu is adjusted seasonally. Considering the quality of the food which appears on this menu, it represents exceptionally good value. You can also order à la carte from a number of fish and meat specialties. A large selection of traditional dishes are offered, but for those whose appetites are not gargantuan, "mini" portions are also served. Count on spending from 40F ($27.20) for a fine meal here.

On the ground floor the Brasserie Steak House has a different ambience and menu. It is less formal, and is often busy for most of the day and early evening. Here you can order steaks, salads, Swiss specialties, and a wide selection of different spaghetti dishes. Count on spending from 25F ($17). Both restaurants are open daily from 11 a.m. to 2 p.m. and 6 to 9:30 p.m.

China Restaurant Li-Tai-Pe, 14 Furrengasse (tel. 041/51-10-23), is the best Chinese restaurant in Lucerne, run by Margaret Chi Tsun, now in her 80s. Her husband was once an aide to General Chiang Kai-Shek. On a narrow street in the old town, the restaurant, which is on two levels, is somberly lit and decorated with Oriental artifacts. The cuisine is Peking style, and includes crispy fried boneless chicken, "eight treasures" fried rice, beef in oyster oil, abalone with bamboo shoots, diced duck with almonds, and pork with soya noodles. The major specialty, which must be ordered a day in advance, is a whole Peking-style duck. Meals cost from 45F ($30.60), and service is from 11:30 a.m. to 2:30 p.m. and 6:30 to 11 p.m. It's closed all day Monday and Tuesday noon.

Hofstube, Hotel Rebstock, 3 Sankt-Leodegar Strasse (tel. 041/51-35-81), is the restaurant attached to the Hotel zum Rebstock (see my hotel recommendations). Next to a building used as a guildhall for Lucerne wine growers in the Middle Ages, the site is rich in history. Today a 1920s-style entrance hall is filled with valuable art deco and an extravagant bouquet of flowers. This flourishing restaurant is spread out into two gemütlich rooms, one with carved timbers. A big green courtyard is behind the hotel, and it's lit with spotlights. A table here is preferred on a warm evening. The staff serves classical specialties, including an impressive list of terrines, an elixir of morels, lake trout, tournedos 1900 style, a rack of lamb, or duckling in orange sauce. You might be more adventurous and order pigs' feet with morels or suckling veal with leafy spinach. Desserts are good as well ("cool hits for hot dates"). Fixed-price meals range from 18F ($12.25) to 45F ($30.60), while à la carte dinners cost 35F ($23.80) to 75F ($51). Hours are 11 a.m. to midnight daily.

Eichhof, 106 Obergrundstrasse (tel. 041/41-11-74), bears the name of a well-known local beer which, not surprisingly, is used in the house recipe for pigs' feet and pork shoulder. Many of the relaxed patrons will be drinking this same brew from large steins, and will usually be on the summertime terrace if weather permits. The owners often serve an extensive menu of wild game, along with other specialties such as duckling in green peppercorns with cream sauce or rack of lamb provençale. The restaurant is open from 9 a.m. to midnight except on Sunday evening, all day Monday, and for the month of February. Meals range from 25F ($17) to 45F ($30.60).

The Budget Range

Wiener Café, Grand Hotel National, 4 Haldenstrasse (tel. 041/50-11-11). Its decor and array of teas and coffees have helped to revive the 19th-century passion for a mid-afternoon respite from sightseeing. Beneath the gilded ornamentation of one of the most spectacular ceilings in Lucerne, you can order one of six kinds of special Austrian-inspired coffees or one of ten kinds of exotic teas, served the old-fashioned way with a silver strainer in a porcelain pot. Pastries, of course, are fresh and sumptuously caloric. The hours of tea blend gracefully into the end of the lunch service and the beginning of the dinner hour, roughly from 2 to 6:30 p.m. daily. Hot beverages begin at 3.50F ($2.40) apiece, and seem appropriate on briskly chilly days.

Don't overlook this place as a lunch or dinner stopover either. A daily special is a lunchtime bargain at 15F ($10.20), with full meals costing from 25F ($17) per person. Lunch is served daily from 11:30 a.m. to 2 p.m. and dinner is from 6:30 p.m. to midnight. Typical dishes include a spicy version of bouillabaisse, a chicken-based pot-au-feu, and a game terrine with goose liver. If you happen to be in Lucerne on a Sunday, and if you reserve in advance, you might want to join the locals for one of the most popular Sunday brunches in the city. It's served from 11 a.m. to 2 p.m. at a cost of 38F ($25.85) per person.

Kunst and **Kongresshaus Restaurants,** at the Bahnhof (tel. 041/23-18-16), are connected with the largest convention hall in Lucerne. Next to the train station in a modern metallic building with an equestrian statue in front, the establishments are surrounded by flowering, well-maintained parks. Three different restaurants inside (the Tell stube, the saloon, and the bistro/bar) offer well-prepared food with lunches costing from 15F ($10.20) to 26F ($17.70). In summer, a terrace area has self-serve sausages and barbecues, starting at 4F ($2.70). Hours are daily from noon to 2:30 p.m. and 6:30 to 11 p.m.

Schiffrestaurant Wilhelm Tell, 9 Landungsbrucke (tel. 041/51-23-30). When it was built in 1908 this lake cruiser sailed boatloads of happy visitors from one end of Lake Lucerne to the other. Unfortunately ships, like people, must eventually retire. Nearly 20 years ago, it was transformed into one of the most unusual restaurants in Lucerne. The bow area (they call it the "second-class section") serves drinks and snacks on café tables under the open sky or on banquettes in the area where the steering wheel used to be. In the aft section is a low-ceilinged restaurant where better-class food is served with alert attention worthy of a crew on the high seas. The engine room has been ripped off to expose the best polished boat engine in Switzerland. You can have a beer in the bow area anytime (where you'll probably want to drop bread chunks to the hungry swans). You can also dine here at prices ranging from 22F ($14.95). Meals might include fish perch filets, sole filets served seaman style, and good soups such as lobster cream. À la carte meals cost from 35F ($23.80). The restaurant sails daily from 12:30 to 2 p.m. and 5:30 to 10 p.m. April through October.

Peppino, 7 Theaterstrasse (tel. 041/23-77-71). There's nothing antique about this place, other than some painted and carved wagon wheels from the 19th century. Yet there is nonetheless an atmosphere of good taste and solidity. You might choose simply to have a drink in the stucco bar area, with its modern rustic beams and timbers and pleasantly spartan format, or you might go off to the dining room on the left. This room has a spacious, sunny format that is elegantly Italian. The menu offers simple lunches from 18F ($12.25) to 25F ($17) which might include pizza, pasta, and a list of such fish specialties as a savory kettle of mussels. The veal dishes are also very good. A pasta specialty is rigatoni all'Emiliana. À la carte meals might range as high as 50F ($34) and up. Peppino is open daily for hot meals from noon till 2 and 6 to 11:30 p.m., although pizzas are served during the afternoon and after dinner hours until 1 p.m.

Wirtshaus Galliker, 1 Schützenstrasse (tel. 041/22-10-02), is the kind of place that serves generous portions of unpretentious, well-prepared food to summertime visitors and to a loyal body of regular clients too. The decor is rustic. Many regional specialties are offered including calf's head vinaigrette with Rösti, "just like your grandmother used to make." They also serve fixed-price specials, which change according to the day of the week. On Tuesday, Thursday, and Saturday it's pot-au-feu. Farmer-style bratwurst seasoned with caraway seed is also popular, and there are good fruited desserts as well. The restaurant is closed for four weeks in summer and on Sunday. The pot-au-feu costs 27F ($18.35), and à la carte meals range from 25F ($17) to 45F ($30.60) on the average. Hours are daily from 10 a.m. to midnight.

WHAT TO SEE: The very symbol of Lucerne is the **Kappellbrücke** (Chapel Bridge), the covered wooden footbridge that crosses the River Reuss diagonally. Built in 1333 as part of the city's defenses, the bridge is about 560 feet long. One of the best preserved wooden bridges in Switzerland, the structure also has a Wasserturm (water tower), octagonal in shape, once used as a prison and torture chamber and later as a storehouse for the town's archives. The bridge has more than a hundred paintings, some done in 1599 by Heinrich Wägmann, showing the life and costumes of the people.

Farther downstream is the other famous covered wooden bridge, the **Spreuerbrücke,** also known as the "Mills Bridge." This bridge was built in 1407, spanning an arm of the Reuss, and it was restored in the 19th century. Painted gables portray a *Dance of Death.* These are from the 17th century by Kaspar Meglinger, commemorating a plague that had infected the city.

On the right bank of the Reuss, **the Altstadt** (old town) still contains many burghers' houses with oriel windows and old squares with fountains.

From **Schwanenplatz** (Swan Square), filled with many shops, you can walk to Kapellplatz, where stands **St. Peter's Chapel** from 1178, the oldest church in Lucerne. In the center of this piazza is a fountain honoring carnival.

Kappellgasse, flanked by shops, will take you to the **Kornmarkt** (grain exchange), on which stands the **Altes Rathaus** (old town hall), a Renaissance building from 1602 with impressive masonry and a tremendous roof. It's crowned by a tall rectangular tower, looking down on the market-day crowds under the arcades on Tuesday and Saturday morning.

To the east of city hall, entered on Furrengasse, is the 17th-century **Am Rhyn-Haus,** which houses a small but choice collection of the artworks of Pablo Picasso, composed of works from the last 20 years of the artist's life. The collection was a gift from Siegfried and Angela Rosengart, who presented the city of Lucerne on its 800th anniversary eight masterpieces by Picasso, one for each century. Outstanding works include *Woman and Dog Playing* (1953), *Woman Dressing Her Hair* (1954), *The Studio* (1955), *Rembrandtesque Figure and Cupid* (1969), and a sculpture, *Woman with a Hat* (1961). In the following years, the Rosengarts added a number of important drawings as well as original prints and ceramics of the same period that are now on display on two floors. You may visit April to October daily from 10 a.m. to 6 p.m. From November to March, it's open only on Friday, Saturday, and Sunday from 11 a.m. to noon and 2 to 5 p.m. Visits at other hours can be arranged by telephone: 041/51-17-73. Admission is 1F (68¢).

To the west of the Kornmarkt stands the **Weinmarkt,** a lovely old square with a splendid fountain that is a reproduction of a famous one that once stood there. Long ago, the mystery play *Confraternity of the Crown of Thorns* was performed here. Among the colorful old dwellings on the square is the Müllersche Apotheke, a "drugstore" from 1530.

At some point in your journey of discovery you'll want to see Lucerne from one of the nine lookout towers. They're part of the old fortifications built along the north side of the medieval sector between 1350 and 1408, each one in a different style. At twilight they stand in dramatic silhouette against the sky. Known as the **Museggtürme,** these ramparts are open to the public daily from 8 a.m. to 8 p.m. for a summer walk. The Schirmerturm tower is open to those who would like to climb nearly 100 steps for a view of the city and its spires.

Your eye may be drawn to the **quays of Lucerne,** along the northern rim of the lake. Planted with trees, these quays make for a satisfying promenade, and they're lined with hotels and shops. They also have beautiful views not only of Lucerne and its lake, but also of the not-so-distant Alps, which stretch from Rigi to Pilatus, which we'll view later. The quays lead to Lido beach, Lucerne's "Riviera," which is popular in the summer. Incidentally the Kursaal, with a restaurant and gaming rooms, lies at the Kurplatz on Nationalquai.

Rising above Nationalquai, the twin towers of the Catholic **Hofkirche** come into view. This is the major church of the city, known as the Collegiate Church of St. Leodegar, named after the patron saint of Lucerne. Once this was a monastery, but the present Gothic-Renaissance building dates from the 17th century. The interior has rich wrought-iron work and carvings, and a celebrated organ from 1640 which has 4,950 pipes. Concerts are given on it in summer. The church also has a beautiful courtyard with arcades, containing tombs of patrician families.

After leaving the Kurplatz, head down Löwenstrasse to the Löwenplatz, where you can view the **Panorama** (tel. 041/50-22-50), anytime mid-March to mid-November daily from 9 a.m. to noon and 12:30 to 5 p.m. (in July and August it's open all day from 9 a.m. to 6 p.m.), charging an admission of 3F ($2.05). The artist Castres, working with others, depicted the retreat of the French army into Switzerland during the 1870–1871 Franco-Prussian War. The canvas covers 11,836 square feet.

Nearby stands the landmark **Löwendenkmal,** or Lion monument. Designed by Thorwaldsen, it was dedicated in 1821. It commemorates the heroic struggle of the Swiss Guards who died at the Tuileries in 1792 trying to save the life of Marie Antoinette. One of Europe's best known monuments, it was hewn out of sandstone. When Mark Twain on his grand tour of Europe saw the *Dying Lion of Lucerne*, he called it "the saddest and most poignant piece of rock in the world."

Rising above the monument, the **Gletschergarten** (glacier garden) (tel. 041/51-43-40) dates from the Ice Age when glaciers covered Lake Lucerne. It's a series of potholes worn in a sandstone rock bed of an ancient glacier. In all, there are 32 "potholes," which were excavated in 1872. One of them is nearly 30 feet deep and 26 feet wide. A museum at the site contains a famous relief map of the Alps from the 18th century, along with prehistoric remains of plant and animal life, as well as a Swiss homeland museum. The garden is open daily from the first of March until the end of April from 9 a.m. to 5 p.m. From the first of May until mid-October, it can be visited from 8 a.m. to 6 p.m. daily. From mid-October to mid-November, the hours are from 9 a.m. to 5 p.m. and from mid-November until the end of February, 10:30 a.m. to 4:30 p.m. The garden is closed on Monday in winter. Admission is 5F ($3.40).

On the south bank of the Reuss, the Bahnhofplatz contains the railway station and the nearby docks, from which you can take tours of Lake Lucerne. At the end of the large square, near the station, is the Kunst- und Kongresshaus from 1932. It contains not only the concert hall, but the **Kunstmuseum** (fine arts museum) (tel. 041/23-92-42). Year-round hours are Tuesday, Thursday, Friday, and Saturday from 10 a.m. to noon and 2 to 5 p.m.; Wednesday from 10 a.m. to 9 p.m., and Sunday from 10 a.m. to 5 p.m. It's closed on Monday. Its regular admission is 4F ($2.70), which usually rises to 5F ($3.40) for special exhibitions. Many paintings by Swiss artists, dating from the 16th century and going up to the present, are displayed. Naturally, Ferdinand Hodler (1835–1918) gets in on the act. Many famous names decorate the walls, including Duffy and Utrillo.

West of the Hauptbahnhof on the left bank of the Reuss stands the **Jesuitenkirche,** or Jesuits' church, a baroque structure from 1666 with a 1750 rococo interior. It's quite a confection, with its pink porphyry and frescoes.

To the right of the church, Bahnhofsstrasse will lead to the **Regierungsgebäude** (government palace). Built in an opulent Renaissance style from 1556, the building was once the home of Lukas Ritter, the local bailiff. The cantonal government took it over in 1804. The original fountain that stood for years on Weinmarkt is preserved here in a covered courtyard. It dates from 1481.

To the southwest of the government building stands the **Franziskanerkirche,** or Franciscan church, which was built in the 13th century but has had so many builders over the centuries you wouldn't know it. The wooden pulpit is from 1628, the choir stalls from 1647.

Europe's number one transport museum, the **Verkehrshaus des Schweiz** (Swiss Transport Museum), is at 5 Lidostrasse (tel. 041/31-44-44), beyond the Haldenstrasse cable-car station. This is one of the top-drawing museums in the country, very popular with Americans. The old and the new in transport are combined here—everything from railway cars, airplanes, automobiles, ships, even spaceships.

The *Rigi*, the oldest ship in the country, an 1847 steamboat, has found a permanent retirement base here (it's been converted into a restaurant). The most popular exhibition is a scale model of a Swiss railway crossing the Gotthard (a dozen trains move simultaneously).

Part of the Swiss Transport Museum, the **Longines Planetarium** lies at the eastern end of the complex. It's the only planetarium in Switzerland and one of the most modern in Europe. Here you can experience the composition of the firmament and the movement of the constellations as well as view an eclipse of the sun and the moon. You'll see what the astronauts saw in space travel. Also connected with the museum, the **Hans Erni House** contains artwork by this well-known native-born son.

The museum complex is open daily from the first of March until the end of October from 9 a.m. to 6 p.m. The rest of the year, it's open Monday to Saturday from 10 a.m. to 4 p.m., on Sunday to 5 p.m. An admission of 12F ($8.15) for adults, 6F ($4.10) for children, is charged.

Another museum of note is the **Trachtenmuseum** (national costume museum) (tel. 041/36-80-58), housed in a former private villa in park-like grounds on the outskirts of Lucerne. Here are displayed folk costumes from each canton in the Confederation. Some of the costumes are from other countries in Europe as well. To reach the museum, leave Lucerne on the Dreilindenstrasse, taking the highway for about half a mile. At the junction, turn right off the road to Dietschiberg, swinging onto the Utenberg route. Visits are possible daily from 9 a.m. to 5:30 p.m. anytime from Easter Sunday until the end of October for 4F ($2.70) for admission.

The major museum in the environs is the **Richard Wagner Museum** (tel. 44-23-70) in the suburb of Tribschen, about two miles from the city. Wagner lived here from 1866 to 1872 and composed *Die Meistersinger*, among other works. The museum displays some original scores of the maestro, along with much memorabilia, including letters and pictures. In one section a collection of antique musical instruments is on view in summer. Year-round hours are 9 a.m. to noon and 2 to 6 p.m. on Tuesday, Wednesday, and Saturday. On Sunday it is open from 10:30 a.m. to noon and 2 to 5 p.m. It remains closed on other days. Admission is 4F ($2.70). To reach the museum, you can go by motorboat, which leaves every hour from in front of the railway station (rail passes are valid for this trip). You can also go by bus no. 6 or 7 to Wartegg.

TOURS: From the city, Lake Lucerne (or Vierwaldstättersee) winds along 23 miles deep into the alpine ranges of the heart of Switzerland. The **Lake Lucerne Navigation Company** (tel. 041/40-45-40) has 18 boats, of which five are paddle-steamers, to service this area. You can board the vessel and buy your ticket at the landing station opposite the Hauptbahnhof in Lucerne.

On these steamers you get waterscape with majestic mountains in the background. Many half- or full-day excursions are offered, actually an overwhelming choice if you have little time for central Switzerland. Many of these excursions can be combined with a trip to the top of a mountain by cable car or funicular. All the main steamer services have a restaurant on board.

A steamer trip from Lucerne to the farthest point, Flüelen, requires 3½ hours, affording spectacular views along the way. The boat schedule calls for a delay of about two hours at most lakeside points before it or another boat will make the return voyage to Lucerne. Therefore, a complete lake tour with stops takes about 8½ hours. First-class, round-trip fare from Lucerne to Flüelen is 47F ($31.95), and second-class passage costs 31F ($21.10). In midsummer, an early morning paddle-steamer departs from the quay at 9 a.m. Watch the return schedules carefully, as they change to avoid being caught by darkness at the far end of the lake. Most returning boats leave before 5 or 6 p.m. from Flüelen, depending on the season.

The William Tell Express links Lucerne with Lugano and Locarno during the summer. It's a combination of paddle steamer and deluxe train, including a three-course meal on the boat. Make your reservations well in advance.

WHERE TO SHOP: Lucerne is an excellent shopping center if you can wade through the junk and souvenir shops. Of course, many visitors come here to purchase a watch. Some make a day excursion from Zurich on the train to do just that.

Bucherer, Schwanenplatz (tel. 041/50-99-50), is the largest watch and jewelry retailer of Switzerland, with its head office being in Lucerne. At this major outlet, they sell more than 10,000 gift items, including not only a wide range of watches but also clocks, souvenirs, and jewelry. They specialize in Rolex, Piaget, Baume & Mercier, and Rado watches.

Juwelia, 3 Denkmalstrasse (tel. 041/51-53-29), sells more than 100 models of cuckoo clocks, as well as 400-day clocks (that's right—you don't wind them for more than a year), wristwatches, and virtually everything else that ticks. If you've always wanted to buy a music box, this place has 85 different models, from both the Black Forest and Switzerland, playing just about every kind of melody. You'll also see the flattest watch on earth. The majority of the wristwatches are relatively inexpensive. The famous Swiss army knife is also sold here with free engraving of names or initials. The staff is charming, multilingual, and helpful in every way. The location is near the Lion monument. Another Juwelia shop is at 11 Pfistergasse (tel. 041/22-64-75), near the Hotel Ilge and the second wooden bridge. Juwelia is also an agent for the Swiss Credit Bank.

Hofstetter & Berney Co. Ltd. has two outlets for watches, cuckoo and other clocks, jewelry, music boxes, crystal, and many gift items and Swiss souvenirs. Their shops are at 1 Alpenstrasse (tel. 041/51-45-40) and 6 Schweizerhofquai (tel. 041/51-31-06).

A. Hurter, 11 Löwenstrasse (tel. 041/51-24-79), sells a complete line of medium-priced and relatively moderately-priced watches and clocks. He specializes in Itraco and Hudson brands, mechanical and quartz, all made in Switzerland. One popular item is a woman's watch whose jeweled insets match the semiprecious stones of the jewelry that goes with it. He has had the same prices for a decade, and his shop is open daily, including Sunday, from 7:20 a.m. to 6 p.m.

Chalet Swiss Souvenirs, 23 Haldenstrasse (tel. 041/51-31-12), across from the Hotel National, is the biggest and most complete souvenir shop in the area. Hans Peter Hunziker and his pretty wife, Ida, sell the famous Swiss army knife, which they'll engrave for you on the spot at no extra charge. Music boxes usually have Reuge mechanisms inside, which, I'm told, are among the best in the country. They begin at 49F ($33.30). Beer steins, however, cost from 5F ($3.25), and cuckoo clocks begin at 65F ($44.20). In summer the shop is open Monday through Saturday from 8 a.m. to 10:30 p.m., on Sunday from 10 a.m. to 6 p.m.

Gift Shop Casagrande, 24 Kapellgasse (tel. 041/51-51-01), carries an extensive collection of Lladró, Hummel, and Dresden porcelain, woodcarvings (including Anri), Swiss army knives, silver, Waterford crystal, Reuge and other music boxes, tapestries, moderately priced watches, and cuckoo clocks along with others including grandfather clocks. The Casagrande family, Carlo and Kyra, and their sons, John and Robert, have expanded their business during the past four decades so that now they have three shops and a woodcarving factory turning out the world famous Casy-Boys. They're also open on Sunday from April to October; and in the evening from mid-May to the end of September. The courteous Casagrandes will ship your purchases home for you if you wish.

Bollina-Schneider, 11 Haldenstrasse (tel. 041/51-33-66), is a small, somewhat cramped shop that sells Swiss souvenir items such as cards, beer steins, Anri woodcarvings, Hummel figurines, cowbells, etchings, music boxes, Christmas cards, T-shirts, and Swiss army knives. Here, as in any shop like this, you'll see a lot of dust-gatherers, but there are nevertheless several good Swiss mementos. Piero Bollina is the articulate owner.

Sturzenneger, 7 Schwanenplatz (tel. 041/51-19-58), was established more than 100 years ago as one of the finest embroidery shops in Lucerne. It's carriage-trade clientele appreciates the high quality of virtually everything sold here, which includes women's lingerie, monogrammed handkerchiefs, petit-point embroidered purses, some folkloric items, and even a few pieces of ready-to-wear clothes.

Fritz Genhart Sport, 14 Löwenstrasse (tel. 041/51-46-41), sells everything you'd need for almost any sport you can think of, including skiing and cliff-climbing. They also have a complete line of wool coats, sneakers, and leather shorts. If you're a T-shirt devotee, you'll see 12 different models. They rent skis and ski boots too. The location is near the Hotel Union. They'll mail your purchases home if you wish.

AFTER DARK: Lucerne is not famous for its nightlife, but there is some. In summer one of the most popular nocturnal outings is to take the **Night Boat,** leaving from Pier No. 6, near the train station. For information, telephone 041/47-44-46. The cruise leaves every night, May until September, at 8:45. The trip is timed so that night falls shortly after departure. That way, riders can see the surrounding mountains from their mid-lake position in both day and night. A folkloric group puts on a show with a display of costumes, folk dances, yodeling, and alpine horn blowing, so you might want to take pictures. There's dancing afterward. Reserve tickets in advance with a travel agent or with the concierge of the larger hotels. You can ride the boat and not see the show for 27F ($18.35). But if you want the entertainment too, it will cost 35F ($23.80), including one free drink. If you want to dine as well, you'll pay from 48F ($32.65) to 75F ($51), the cuisine ranging from a bowl of cheese fondue to a typical Swiss dinner. If you're a heavy drinker (and need a few to get into the spirit of the occasion), you can end up spending considerably more. The cruise ends at 11 p.m.

After that, it's off to the **(Kursaal) Casino,** 6 Haldenstrasse (tel. 041/51-27-51). As with other casinos in Switzerland, the biggest wager allowed by law is 5F ($3.40). Therefore the entrepreneurs behind this establishment have expanded it into an entertainment complex of cabarets, discos, and floor shows. Part of your evening might be spent in the rectangular room with eerie lighting reserved strictly for gambling. But if betting doesn't flow in your veins, chances are you'll wander off to the Casino's other diversions. They're open from 6 p.m. to 2 a.m. nightly. They include the following:

Red Rose Cabaret, a strip club with nonstop shows from 10 p.m. to 2 a.m. daily. Entrance is from the sidewalk. Cover charge is from 5F ($3.40) and 11F ($7.50), with beer costing a minimum of 17F ($11.55). The wallpaper is, as you might expect, bordello red, and there's a very correct currency exchange booth in the lobby.

Black Jack Club is a disco with a red-and-gold decor, playing American and British music, for the most part. It's open from 9 p.m. to 2 a.m. daily, and there's always live music on the raised stage area. The cover charge is usually 5.50F ($2.75) Monday to Thursday, 11F ($7.50) Friday and Saturday.

Le Chalet is a vast room with a heavily timbered format of alpine rusticity, offering a program of folkloric music daily. That means all the yodeling, flag-throwing, and Swiss horns you've come to expect. It costs 30F ($20.40) without dinner and from 45F ($30.60) to 50F ($34) with dinner. When you enter after paying the cover charge, don't be surprised by the blast of music and the sight of thousands of locals swaying rhythmically to the "evergreen music."

Roulette Bar is elegantly decorated with beige-colored marble and small café tables, art nouveau style. From 7 p.m. on, meals are served from a menu specializing in grilled meats. Beer costs from 4F ($2.70); whisky, from 9F ($6.10) to 13F ($8.85). Open daily from 6 p.m. to 2:30 a.m.

Finally, the **Seegarten** serves meals with a view of the lake. On a summer afternoon the terrace is usually filled.

All these establishments are connected with a glittering series of public rooms covered with carpeting. If you want to take a breather from the activity inside, you might stroll around the gardens for a look at one of the most famous flower clocks in Switzerland.

Hazyland, 21 Haldenstrasse (tel. 041/51-19-61), is one of a chain of discos that stretches across Switzerland. Almost every weekend a different live band is presented, ranging from pop/rock to punk. Inside this one is a red-velvet ambience of strobe lights and underweight young people whose average age is 22. A medium-size dance floor is open from 9 p.m. to 2:30 a.m. seven nights a week. There's no cover charge, and beer costs from 12F ($8.15). The club is opposite the Hotel National.

Restaurant Stadtkeller, 3 Sternenplatz (tel. 041/51-47-33), offers an original Swiss folklore show at lunch and dinner from the beginning of March until the end of October. Admission is only 6F ($4.10) over and above what you eat and drink once you're in the restaurant. The music starts at 12:15 p.m. and again at 8 p.m. The show includes alpine-horn blowing, yodeling, Swiss flag-throwing, with cowbells and a variety of traditional Swiss instruments, plus plenty of audience participation and fun. The restaurant is in the old town and the original building is more than 400 years old, with a beautiful painted façade and a renovated interior. It is fully air-conditioned during the summer months.

Barstube zur Gerbern, 7 Sternenplatz (tel. 041/51-55-50), has been called by the press "a little bit of San Francisco in Lucerne." It's become a very popular bar, with a video disco in a backroom. This is about the only such establishment in town with a large gay element, which becomes more visible later in the evening. The owner estimated to the press that his club was about 70% gay, but who knows? It's open Monday through Saturday from 5 p.m. to 2 a.m. and on Sunday from 6 p.m. to 2 a.m.

3. LAKE LUCERNE, NORTH AND EAST

The scenery around Lucerne is a blend of water, sky, and mountains. It's earned the praise of poets over the years.

Your hotel room might, for example, open onto Lake Lucerne, which locals call Vierwaldstättersee (lake of the four forest cantons). If you have either the Eurail or InterRail pass, the boat cruises are "free." The lake has many Old World villages. In addition to that, mountain railways can whisk you to elevations of 10,000 or more feet in a very short time. For one of the best views of Lucerne and its lake, you can board a cable car at its bottom station in Lucerne on Haldenstrasse, which will take you to Dietschiberg at 2,065 feet. The trip takes about half an hour. You can see Pilatus and Rigi from a belvedere platform.

Another excursion will take you to the mountain plateau of **Gütsch,** at 1,715 feet. You can board a funicular on Baselstrasse for the three-minute ride. At the top is a belvedere platform at the Hotel Chateau Gütsch, which takes in the city and the lake, with the snow-capped Alps as a backdrop. Service in season is about every ten minutes. May to September this funicular operates daily from 8:30 a.m. to 12:30 p.m., 1:15 to 7:30 p.m., and 8 to 11:30 p.m. November to March it operates Monday to Friday from 10 a.m. to 12:30 p.m., 1:15 to 2 p.m., and 4 to 8 p.m. (on Saturday and Sunday from 10 a.m. to 8 p.m.). In April and October it operates from 9 a.m. to 3 p.m. and 4 to 9 p.m. Monday and Friday (on Saturday and Sunday from 9 a.m. to 9 p.m.). A round-trip fare costs only 3F ($2.05). For information about the funicular, telephone 041/22-02-72.

These excursions are only for those wanting good views from hilltop belvederes. The three-star mountain excursions from Lucerne are to Rigi and Pilatus (for data on Pilatus, refer to "Lake Lucerne, West and South").

The attractions of **Mt. Rigi** have been extolled for centuries. If you're in luck, you'll be blessed with a clear day; otherwise you're likely to be disappointed. The view from Rigi is different from that atop Mt. Pilatus, so if you see both you won't be repeating your experience exactly.

Rigi, at 5,900 feet, is in fact considered the most celebrated mountain view in the country. It's reached by two cog railways and a cableway. Of course, at Rigi you can't see such a wide-sweeping panoramic vista as you can from Pilatus, but the lookout from Rigi is, in my opinion, more beautiful.

Rigi is called the "island mountain," because it's seemingly isolated by the lake waters of not only Lucerne, but Zug and Lauerz. The most diehard and enthusiastic of the Victorians who made the "Grand Tour" at the turn of the century spent the night at Rigi-Kulm to see the sun rise over the Alps. This attraction, even today, is considered one of nature's loveliest offerings in all of Europe. For those wanting to partake of that long-ago tradition, many hotels are perched along the mountainside. Victor Hugo called it "an incredible horizon . . . that chaos of absurd exaggerations and scary diminutions." Mark Twain, as he relates in *A Tramp Abroad*, also climbed to the top to see the sun rise across the Alps. But he claimed he was so exhausted that he collapsed into sleep, from which he didn't wake until sunset. Not realizing that he had slept all day, he at first recoiled in horror believing that the sun had switched its direction and was actually rising in the west.

One way to reach the mountain is to take a lake steamer from Lucerne to Vitznau, a small resort on the northern shore of the lake. The other way to go is from Arth-Goldau, which lies on the southern part of Zug Lake. The rack railway from Vitznau to Rigi-Kulm was the first such cog railway in Europe. It dates from 1871, but the Swiss electrified it in 1937. The Arth-Goldau cog railway to Rigi-Kulm opened five years later (it lost the race to its competitor); however, it was electrified as early as 1906. Its maximum gradient is 21%, which hardly puts it in the same league as the railway to Pilatus at 48%.

The climb from either point of departure costs 36F ($24.50) in summer, 30F ($20.40) in winter for the round trip. It's possible to go up one way and come back the other if you want to see both sides of the mountain. From Vitznau to Rigi-Kulm takes about 40 minutes, from Arth-Goldau to the top, about 35 minutes. Both lines in peak season make about a dozen runs a day. Telephone 041/83-18-18 for information.

WEGGIS: Nestling at the foot of Mt. Rigi, 18½ miles from Lucerne, is the lakeside resort of Weggis, one of a trio of holiday centers sharing the sunshine and mild climate. The sunny side of the Rigi, where these resorts (Weggis, Vitznau, and Gersau) lie, has been likened to favored parts of Italy and indeed has for many years attracted visitors to its beautiful countryside. Mark Twain stayed here in 1897.

Weggis is usually the first port of call for steamers from Lucerne and is also easily accessible from the international St. Gotthard railway line, although it's not on the main traffic route. People wishing to take excursions into nearby mountains flock to the area from early spring to late autumn, many taking the aerial cableway up to Rigi-Kaltbad (4,756 feet) in back of Weggis, where a mountain health resort is maintained.

Weggis and its sister resorts are about an hour's walk (or a five-minute drive) apart. You can also make a trip from here on a Lake Lucerne steamer or on the mountain transport of the Rigi Railways.

Food and Lodging

Hotel Albana, CH-6353 Weggis, Switzerland (tel. 041/93-21-41). One of the public rooms of this *Relais & Châteaux* hotel looks almost baronial. Considered the most prestigious hotel at Weggis, it was built in the art nouveau style in 1896 and has been run by the Wolf family since 1910. However, its original architectural lines have been greatly altered over the years with many modern additions. The name *Albana* comes from the *Piz Albana* near St. Moritz, the name meaning in Romansh, "red dawn." Inside the hotel, the black sheen of the grand piano contrasts with the shiny cream color of the ten-foot ceramic stove. Heavy brass chandeliers hang from the frescoed ceiling, and very large mirrors in rococo gilt reflect the mellow patina of the wood paneling. The bedrooms are modernized, and the head- and footboards are usually crafted of knotty pine. The windows afford good views of the nearby lake. Singles cost 100F ($68) to 140F ($95.20) daily, doubles going for 174F ($118.30) to 260F ($176.80), with half board included. The Wolfs are flexible about board plans, allowing you to tell them at the beginning of each day of your stay whether you'll be on half, full, or no board for that particular day.

Designed around the panoramic windows, and a terrace that seems to command the entire lake owing to its position raised up above the water, the hotel's attractive Panorama Restaurant serves the best food at the resort. Nonresidents who make a reservation are welcome to dine here daily, from noon to 2 p.m. and 6:45 to 9:30 p.m. The cookery is international, with a wide selection of fish and meat dishes. The chef cooks with a fine light touch, using top quality produce with excellent results. Meals cost from 32F ($21.75) up. The hotel closes from November to March.

Hôtel Beau-Rivage, CH-6353 Weggis, Switzerland (tel. 041/93-14-22). There are many assets to this hotel, but one of the best is the lawn that has been extended, thanks to a masonry retaining wall, right down to the lake. The view of the mountains from here is exhilarating. The hotel is a symmetrical yellow building with a series of wrought-iron balconies, a prominent nameplate in red letters, and a Swiss flag. From your windows you'll look down onto the flagstone borders of the swimming pool. The inside is pleasantly paneled and wallpapered, with a wood-paneled restaurant and a comfortable bar. Comfortably furnished singles range from 110F ($74.80) to 140F ($95.20) daily, while twin-bedded rooms cost 180F ($122.40) to 270F ($183.60), with half board, service, and taxes included. Prices depend on the size and position of rooms. Open from April to October.

Hotel Central am See, CH-6353 Weggis, Switzerland (tel. 041/93-12-52), is an old-fashioned resort hotel with at least six gables, and many more if you count the smaller ones. It sits on a shady peninsula jutting out into the lake. The hotel swimming pool comes very close to the water's edge, and if you happen to be floating on its heated waters, you'll be in a good position to watch the steamers sailing up and down the lake. The interior is outfitted with a fancy collection of comfortable furniture. An elevator will take you to your comfortable bedroom, which will cost from 66F ($44.90) to 98F ($66.65) daily in a single, from 122F ($82.95) to 188F ($127.85) in a double, with half board included. Rooms come with and without private baths. Rates depend on the plumbing and the season.

Hotel Waldstaetten, CH-6353 Weggis, Switzerland (tel. 041/93-13-41), is a three-story hotel surrounded by a well-planned garden with lots of red leafy trees. The bedrooms all contain private bath and have low-slung beds, contrasting solid colors, and phone and radio. Some of the accommodations open onto balconies with views of the lake. With half board included, singles range from 80F ($54.40) to 120F ($81.60) daily, while doubles go for 150F ($102) to 225F ($153), depending on the room.

Hotel Rössli, CH-6353 Weggis, Switzerland (tel. 041/93-11-06), offers one of the most desirable lakefront positions at the resort. It has an elaborate shingled Victorian façade, with ornate wood cutout balustrades, russet-colored shutters, and a modern fifth-floor addition as well as an extension to one side. The inside has been renovated into a comfortable and modern format of wrought iron, wicker chairs, and hanging lamps. The Nölly family has set up a sidewalk café behind the flowers, statues, and fountain of the square on which the hotel sits. The hotel lies on the lakeside road in a tranquil position near the center of the village. Rooms are comfortable and attractively furnished. Depending on the season, the half-board rate is 74F ($50.30) to 98F ($66.65) daily in a single, 145F ($98.60) to 188F ($127.85) in a double. The hotel is open from March to November.

VITZNAU: On around Lake Lucerne in another bay at the foot of the Rigi, Vitznau (1,446 feet) enjoys the same salubrious climate as does Weggis. You can reach this spot, where an alpine panorama is mirrored in the waters of the lake, in about an hour's trip from Zurich on the motorway. A lake steamer will bring you here from Lucerne in about the same length of time, or you can drive from that city in approximately 30 minutes if you don't stop too often to drink in the scenic beauty.

From April to October Vitznau is ideal for an active holiday, offering bathing in the lake or in one of the indoor or outdoor pools, tennis, and inviting walks through meadows, woodlands, and mountains. It's at the lower terminal of the Rigi cog-wheel railway line, which causes many visitors just to pass through and therefore miss the beauty of the resort—an unfortunate oversight.

Food and Lodging

Park Hotel Vitznau, CH-6354 Vitznau, Switzerland (tel. 041/83-13-22), is a luxurious summer hotel designed like a belle-époque castle. A *Relais & Château*, it was constructed in 1903, with a new wing added in 1986. It has a central tower that you can easily imagine as part of a medieval fortification, plus a steep roof made of brown tile. A swimming pool is separated from the hotel by a sun terrace with parasols. Two tennis courts, sailing and waterskiing facilities, and miles of forested walkways give guests plenty to do. The public rooms inside are as grandly high-ceilinged as you could hope for, while each carpeted, well-furnished bedroom contains an opulent white marble private bath and an attractive assortment of furniture, often reproductions of French antiques. Each has a terrace. Singles range from 200F ($136) to 300F ($204), and doubles cost 350F ($238) to 450F ($306), depending on the accommodation and the season. Owner Rudolf-August Oetker is one of the most respected hôteliers in Europe, also operating Brenner's Park in Baden-Baden, Hotel du Cap in Cap d'Antibes, and the formidable Bristol in Paris. In all, Park Hotel Vitznau is the most idyllic retreat along what is increasingly known as the "Lucerne Riviera." It is open from mid-April to mid-October.

Hotel Schiff, CH-6554 Vitznau, Switzerland (tel. 041/83-13-57), is the best for the budget. Parts of the interior are designed like a pub in a harborside city. The hotel has plenty of brass fittings and some engine controls from an old-fashioned boat. You may get a strong dose of seaside nostalgia as you approach the house, because the Zimmermann family has landscaped a facsimile of the front of a lake cruiser into the sloping side of their garden. A pleasant terrace gives a shaded waterside view that is as good as that from many bigger establishments. There are only 16 beds in the hotel. None of the rooms has a private bath, but the facilities on each floor are perfectly adequate. Singles rent for 35F ($23.08) per night, with doubles costing 60F ($40.80), with breakfast included. It is open year round.

RIGI: On the south side of Mount Rigi, the Vitznau-Rigi railway starts from Vitznau on Lake Lucerne, and heads for Kulm peak, after passing through the mountain stations of Rigi-Kaltbad-First, Rigi Staffelhoehe, and Rigi Staffel. In summer there are also nostalgic steam trains traveling on this stretch of electric rack-and-pinion railway. Running every 30 minutes, an aerial cableway with large cabins connects Weggis, also on Lake Lucerne, with the little mountain village of Rigi Kaltbad.

I have already extolled the scenic excitement of Rigi in this section. If you'd like to do something adventurous—far removed from traffic—you might consider a mountaintop hotel in this most fascinating section of central Switzerland. Some recommendations follow:

Food and Lodging

Hostellerie Rigi, CH-6356 Rigi-Kaltbad-First, Switzerland (tel. 041/83-16-16), is a strikingly contemporary building, with wide expanses of almost unbroken glass topped with an abstract roofline that seems to fold down shelteringly above it. The inside is attractive and unusual, with ample use of natural-grain wood, stone detailing, sloped ceilings, sunny vistas, and lots of space. A desirable collection of voluptuously curved 19th-century furniture gives contrast to the angularity of some of the public rooms. An indoor swimming pool, sauna, fitness room, bowling alley, kindergarten with monitor, and a beauty salon are all part of the facilities. I especially like the darkly lit bar area, which seems to encourage a good time. Well-furnished singles rent for 55F ($37.40) to 100F ($68) daily, while doubles cost 90F ($61.20) to 180F ($122.40), depending on the season and the plumbing.

Bellevue Romantik Hotel, CH-6356 Rigi-Kaltbad, Switzerland (tel. 041/83-13-51). If you've just been married, or if you feel a little reckless, the year-round, family-run hotel has a newlywed suite with an old-fashioned bed and a double bathtub. Chances are, however, that no matter what your relationship is like, you'll eventually end up in one of the beautifully paneled public rooms or on the panoramic terrace. Almost everything about this lofty hotel is attractive and comfortable, with a view from almost every room that is magnificent. No two of the 60 bedrooms are exactly alike, but overall they're very satisfactory, with private bath, radio, and phone. Singles rent for 70F ($47.60) to 90F ($61.20) daily, while doubles cost 130F ($88.40) to 200F ($136), with breakfast included. Prices, of course, depend on the season and the accommodations.

Hotel Rigi Kulm, CH-6411 Rigi-Kulm, Switzerland (tel. 041/83-13-12), is connected by an underground tunnel to the terminus of the cog railway leading into the village. In summer, however, you might prefer to walk above ground to reach the large building with its gray stone detailing that looks as if it could withstand any winter storm. The interior is high-ceilinged and filled with tasteful furniture, which includes a good selection of antiques. From the hotel's sun terrace, where the lunch tables are covered with bright cloths, you'll see the weather patterns literally change before your eyes in the valley below. The overflow from the main house is lodged in an annex nearby, connected by underground tunnel to the main hotel. The Käppeli family are your thoughtful hosts. All their bedrooms have hot and cold running water as well as a phone and radio. Accommodations facing south also offer a private bath with a toilet. In the main building, the half-board rate ranges from 48F ($32.65) to 63F ($42.85) per person daily. But if guests stay in the Touristenhaus annex they are charged only 20F ($13.60) per person nightly for a room, with breakfast included. It's even cheaper to rent a dormitory bed at a cost of 15F ($10.20) per person nightly, including breakfast.

GERSAU: The most tranquil and least frequented of the trio of lakeside resorts along the northern rim of the eastern leg of Lake Lucerne is Gersau (1,450 feet), where laurels, chestnuts, and fig trees grow in the mild climate just as they do in Weggis and Vitznau. From April to October, Gersau makes a convenient base for exploring Rigi. You have a good view of the Alps from this bayfront resort, and I've found it an ideal stopover when I go south on the lake road to St. Gotthard.

Gersau is the oldest health resort of Lake Lucerne. From 1332 to 1798 it had the distinction of being the smallest independent republic in the world, until it joined the growing confederation of Swiss towns and cantons for safety's sake.

Food and Lodging

Hotel Müller, CH-6442 Gersau, Switzerland (tel. 041/84-19-19), rebuilt after a fire, is now the major hotel of town. Right in the center, this four-star entry stands across the street from the lakeside promenade. From a dowdy Victorian hotel, a modern and rather stylish establishment has been fashioned. Much of it has art deco overtones in shades of green, rose, and blue. Each of the accommodations opens onto a private terrace with a view of the lake, and offers thoughtful amenities such as phones and radios. Depending on the season, singles rent for 70F ($47.60) to 90F ($61.20) daily, two persons pay from 125F ($85) to 160F ($108.80). Another 25F ($17) per person is charged for half board per day. The hotel has many up-to-date facilities, including a free garage, whirlpool, sauna, and solarium. It also has the attractive Café Müller with a garden restaurant and a more formal restaurant, the Gero-Stube, serving a superb cuisine. The food here is among the finest at the resort, with meals costing from 65F ($44.20). They're served from 11 a.m. to 2 p.m. and from 5:30 to 9:30 p.m. daily.

Hôtel Beau-Rivage, CH-6442 Gersau, Switzerland (tel. 041/84-12-23), is a flat-roofed, balconied building on an attractively small scale bordering the lake. The façade is painted sea green and white, with awnings protecting the pleasant bedrooms from the waterside glare. The public rooms are outfitted with lots of plants and contemporary furniture. In summer an orchestra plays before and during dinner. There's an outdoor swimming pool, plus an elevator and table tennis available. Rates depend not only on the season but also on the plumbing, as several rooms don't have private baths. Singles range from 35F ($23.80) to 50F ($34) daily, and doubles go for 70F ($47.60) to 100F ($68), plus another 22F ($14.95) per person daily for half board. The Beau-Rivage is open from April to October.

BRUNNEN: At Brunnen, a health and holiday resort in a beautiful inlet on the southern part of Lake Lucerne, I never miss going to the lakeside quays to enjoy the fine views of the meeting of lakes and Alps. Brunnen (about 1,300 feet), at the foot of Frohnalpstock, is probably the most popular resort in the canton of Schwyz, on Lake Uri in the very heart of Switzerland. It was in this area that the Confederation was born, and you'll find many reminders of the country's historic past, including archives in Schwyz where the Confederation documents are displayed and the **Federal Chapel** in Brunnen.

This is William Tell country. Around the year 1250 several families left Raron in the Valais and crossed the Alps to establish new homes in Schächental/ Uri, until then uninhabited. Records show that among the families were the Tells. William Tell enters folk history as the hero of a decisive battle in 1315, and reportedly died in 1350, but historians have no authentication of such an individual heroic figure. The man who calmly and safely shot an apple off the head of his brave young son with a bow and arrow in a test of prowess is honored by the Swiss with the **Tell Monument.** In Sisikon, just south of Brunnen, stands the **Tell Chapel,** restored in 1881. Records of the chapel date from the dawn of the 16th century. The paintings in the chapel are by Stückelberg. Many people visit it on excursions from Brunnen.

Brunnen is the starting point of the **Axenstrasse,** the stunning panoramic road leading south toward the St. Gotthard Pass. It goes above the rim of Lake Uri (or Urnersee) in and out of subterranean passageways or galleries that were carved out of the mountain rock. The resort is a starting place for exploratory trips by ship, mountain railway, bus, or train to all points around Lake Lucerne. International express trains on the Gotthard line stop at Brunnen, and it can also be reached by road. It's about an hour's drive from Zurich's Kloten International Airport.

Food and Lodging

Seehotel Waldstätterhof, CH-6440 Brunnen, Switzerland (tel. 043/33-11-33), is one of the few five-star hotels opening onto the lake, offering grand comfort in the old style. The symmetrical white façade is capped with a modified mansard roof, while a series of well-proportioned balconies allows summer guests to enjoy the lakeside air. The year-round hotel opened in 1870, although the continuing renovations have kept it in the mainstream of modern comfort. It stands in well-kept, traffic-free grounds extending along the lake. Facilities include a tennis court, lakeside bathing area, terrace restaurant, and, close to the hotel, the landing stage for the Lake Lucerne steamer trips. The public rooms are as grand as you'd expect (be sure to notice the fanciful chandeliers in the dining room). Singles range from 105F ($71.40) to 160F ($108.80) daily, with doubles going for 170F ($115.60) to 250F ($170), depending on the accommodation and the season. Breakfast is included, and if you stay three or more nights, you can have half board for another 25F ($17) per person daily. From the hotel the famous Schiller Memorial Stone can be seen on the opposite shore of the lake.

Parkhotel Hellerbad, CH-6440 Brunnen, Switzerland (tel. 043/31-16-81), is a large château built as a villa in 1862, with gray shutters and a hipped roof that encompasses the top two floors. The interior is an attractive mixture of white walls and full-grained wood. The hotel is surrounded with pleasant lawns and old trees. On the premises are two tennis courts. The hotel has been renovated several times since its construction (the last time was in 1981). There are 80 rooms, each with a private bath or shower. Well-furnished singles range from 75F ($51) to 85F ($57.80) daily, doubles going for 140F ($95.20) to 170F ($115.60), with breakfast included. The hotel is closed in February and March.

Hotel Bellevue, CH-6440 Brunnen, Switzerland (tel. 043/31-13-18), a first-class choice, is a pleasantly renovated baroque building on the edge of the lake with a café and sun terrace that many of the locals use as their own. It has a modern extension on either side. The well-maintained bedrooms are usually carpeted, and always have private bath. Werner Achermann and his family welcome guests, charging them from 70F ($47.60) to 85F ($57.80) daily in a single and from 120F ($81.60) to 150F ($102) in a double, including breakfast. With its Tropicana Bar and Casino, the hotel is also the center of nightlife for the town. In addition to the gambling room, there's dancing to an orchestra. Other facilities include a reading and TV room, a restaurant with a view, and private parking. The hotel is open in January, March to October, and in December.

Hotel Elite-Aurora, CH-6440 Brunnen, Switzerland (tel. 043/31-10-24), is a lakeside hotel built in 1964 in a beige wood and buff-colored format and prominent balconies. Many guests spend part of the afternoon on the waterside terrace under clipped sycamores or else enjoy the panoramic sixth-floor terrace (for guests only). The public rooms are dignified and modern. The 80 bedrooms are simply and attractively decorated in earth tones, with comfortable beds. The annex, Aurora, contains mainly single units. Doubles cost from 88F ($59.85) daily, to 126F ($85.70), depending on the plumbing and the season. Singles rent for 50F ($34) to 66F ($44.90).

Hotel Alpina Brunnen, CH-6440 Brunnen, Switzerland (tel. 043/31-18-13), is housed in a large, pleasant gabled building with a second-floor veranda and wooden shutters. The Geisseler family, the English-speaking owners, do everything they can to be of help. Their bedrooms are clean and comfortable, while the dining hall has sunny windows and well-prepared food. Singles range from 40F ($27.20) to 60F ($40.80) daily, and doubles cost 70F ($47.60) to 104F ($70.70), with a large breakfast included. Half board is an additional 15F

($10.20) per person daily. Prices, of course, depend on the plumbing and the season. The hotel has a TV room, lounge, garden, and lawn with deck chairs. A short walk from the center of town, it looks toward the mountains.

After Brunnen, we continue south as far as the little port and holiday resort of Flüelen.

FLÜELEN: The resort lies on a delta at the head of the Reuss River. Many motorists prefer a stopover here before going on to the St. Gotthard Pass. Since Flüelen is the most distant point on the lake-steamer itineraries from Lucerne, many visitors prefer to take a steamer from Lucerne to Flüelen, overnight here, and continue their voyage across the lakes the following morning.

Food and Lodging

Hotel Flüelerhof, CH-6454 Flüelen, Switzerland (tel. 044/2-11-49), is a salmon-colored hotel owned by Tony Koller, built in 1981, with a modern design, between the highway and the railroad tracks. It's studded with flowered balconies, big windows, and lots of comfort. Bathrooms and bedrooms are very attractive, while the public rooms are filled with brick and wood detailing along with rustic touches. On the premises is the Grill-Rustico, a restaurant, an indoor and outdoor café, and a well-maintained garden. Singles range from 58F ($39.45) to 68F ($46.25) daily, while doubles cost 88F ($59.85) to 108F ($73.45), with breakfast included. Prices depend on the season, plumbing, and room assignment. The hotel is closed in December.

Hotel Tourist, CH-6454 Flüelen, Switzerland (tel. 044/2-15-91), is a chalet hotel with two frontal balconies, wood shutters, and darker wood clapboards. It's set high above the lake, a long walk or a short drive from the center. The ground floor is made of white stucco, with a sun terrace and café set above the road in front. The Arndt family charges 45F ($30.60) daily in a single and from 80F ($54.40) in a double, with breakfast included. Accommodations contain private showers and toilets. The hotel is open only from February to December.

Hostellerie Sternen, CH-6454 Flüelen, Switzerland (tel. 041/2-18-35), since 1870 has been a traditional stopping-off point. You'll recognize it by its gold star positioned above the curved entrance at the corner of the building, about a three-minute walk from the landing boat dock from Lucerne. The hotel rents only 19 rooms, each warm and cozy with terracottas from Italy, half-timbered walls, and wooden ceilings. Singles rent for 65F ($44.20) daily, and doubles go for 85F ($57.80) to 105F ($71.40), including breakfast. All accommodations contain private baths.

Peter and Andrea Bonetti-Christen, the owners, are known for their cuisine, considered the best in town. It's served daily from 11 a.m. to 2 p.m. and 6 to 10 p.m. Even if you're a motorist or a lake-steamer passenger, you may want to patronize their fine restaurant. You dine amid plants in a tasteful room flanked with a blue-and-white-tile grill, with big windows overlooking the town. You're tempted with such delectable fare as chicken fricassée with lemon vinegar, a chicken cocktail with curry, liver parfaits, green noodles with salmon strips, and grenadine of veal with chicory. You can order a full meal for 45F ($30.60) or else the menu gastronomique at 65F ($44.20).

4. FROM SCHWYZ TO ST. GOTTHARD

From the "birthplace" of the Confederation to the St. Gotthard Pass is one of the most historic and most frequented routes in Switzerland, taking in the William Tell country. Except for the first part of this trip, we leave the shores of Lake Lucerne, stopping off at the resorts and towns of Altdorf, Amsteg, and Andermatt before crossing the St. Gotthard Pass itself.

In the 18th and 19th centuries, roadbuilders began the long, tedious, and dangerous task of opening the pass to traffic, thus making for the shortest route from north to south.

The railway tunnel, stretching for some nine miles, goes under the towering peak of the St. Gotthard massif, which reaches a height of 3,790 feet. The toll-free St. Gotthard road tunnel opened in 1980 and was hailed at its inauguration as the longest road tunnel on earth, traversing a distance of some 10 miles. It is, of course, open all year.

The St. Gotthard Pass, at 6,920 feet, provides a link between the Grisons and the Valais Alps. It's one of the most stunning and scenic passes in Switzerland.

SCHWYZ: At the "core of Helvetia," this pleasant little town where we begin our trip—set in the midst of orchards on a mountain terrace—lent its name and flag to the whole country. Lying under the towering twin horns of Gross Mythen, it is also the repository of the country's most treasured archives. The location is between Lake Lucerne and Lake Lauerz. Its mountain "annex" is the little resort of Stoos, at 4,250 feet.

Since the 16th century, when foreign powers such as France needed mercenaries, they were often recruited here. The men of Schwyz were known for their prowess and courage. Those who lived returned to build the sturdy and often quite opulent homes you can still see today.

Schwyz was in the vanguard of the eventual Confederation when it joined with the neighboring districts of Uri and Unterwalden to create an "everlasting league" on August 1, 1291. Since then its name in a dialectical form (Schweiz) was applied by foreigners from the 14th century on to label the country.

The **Bundesbriefarchiv** (archives of the federal charters) (tel. 043/24-20-64) was erected in 1936 to house the original documents of the Swiss Confederation. It can be visited daily from 9:30 to 11:30 a.m. and 2 to 5 p.m. This rather simple concrete structure, with a frescoed façade, stands on Bahnhofstrasse, and contains the original deed of the Confederation. Many other historical documents and mementos are displayed.

The parish **Church of St. Martin,** built in 1774, is richly embellished in the flamboyant baroque style. In the nave are many frescoes. The only other building of note is the **Rathaus** (town hall), dating from 1642, its façade handsomely decorated with frescoes better than those at the national archives building. These murals recall epic moments in Swiss history. To gain entrance, apply to the concierge. In a museum tower south of the town hall is a cantonal historical museum, of interest only if you're a Swiss historian.

From Schwyz you can take the road through the Muota valley to Schlatti, a distance of only two miles. It's also possible to go by bus, a 12-minute run. There the steepest funicular in Switzerland, with a gradient up to nearly 78%, will take you in eight minutes up the treacherously steep wooded slope to **Stoos,** a hamlet clinging to a mountain plateau. Stoos is a relatively undiscovered winter ski resort. If you visit in summer, know that you'll be safe and secure in a hideaway where no one will ever find you. It has no traffic, as there are no roads. You also lose yourself among the cows in the alpine meadows, with their beautiful wildflowers, which live for such a short time if you dare pick one.

The resort has a heated high-altitude swimming pool, as well as a gym, tennis courts, and a riding school, along with bowling and boccia alleys. From an altitude of 4,300 to 6,600 feet, Stoos has good slopes for downhill skiing conditions. For cross-country skiing and skiing tours, it offers a wide variety of well-maintained tracks. A number of bars and discos take care of your après-ski needs, providing your aspirations are modest.

Back in the valley, you might consider a trip to the mammoth **Hölloch Caves,** even more intriguing. Take the Muotathal road southeast of Schwyz for about nine miles. Park in the lot of the restaurant there. It's about a 10-minute walk to the caves. The Höllochgrotte, the largest grotto in Europe, is a geological formation known all over the world. The total length of the passages is just under 60 miles, of which only about half a mile is open to visitors. Virtually unknown at the turn of the century, the grotto has been much explored in postwar years, especially in the 1950s. Of course, you'll see stalagmites and stalactites, but more than that, you'll also get to view eerie underworld formations, which reach their zenith at the "grosse Pagoda."

Visiting the caves, unfortunately, is a bit complicated. In summer, a one-hour tour is possible but only for groups composed of from five to six persons. Tours depart daily from 10 a.m. to 4 p.m. If you're an individual traveler, your best chance of joining a group is to appear at the caves in the early afternoon. At that time, the greatest number of visitors show up. A one-hour tour costs 4.40F ($3) for adults and 2.20F ($1.50) for children. Tours depart daily in summer, but only when the weather is fair and sunny. In rainy periods, the cave fills with water and is too dangerous to visit. On weekends throughout the year, an all-night exploration of the cave is offered on Friday and Saturday if enough people (from 12 to 15 explorers) telephone in advance to reserve. The price of 50F ($34) includes a pre-cave dinner in a nearby restaurant, plus breakfast the following morning.

The center for administration of the caves is in the pleasant restaurant standing near the entrance. The **Restaurant Höllgrotte,** Muotathal (tel. 043/47-12-08), is open daily from 8 a.m. to midnight, serving meals that cost from 18F ($12.25) to 35F ($23.80). The place tends to nourish cave visitors both before and after their visit underground, serving a hearty Swiss cuisine. It is closed on Tuesday in winter.

Food and Lodging in Schwyz

Hotel Wysses Rössli, Hauptplatz, CH-6430 Schwyz, Switzerland (tel. 043/21-19-22), occupies an ideal location in a five-story building across from the baroque cathedral in the center of Schwyz. A hotel has stood on this spot since 1642. When the present hostelry was restored in 1978, some of the banqueting rooms were brought in intact from an 18th-century baroque house. The part you'll see is attractively rustic, with contemporary bedrooms, 27 in all, outfitted with a leather occasional chair, private baths, phones, radios, and mini-bars. Singles range from 75F ($51) to 80F ($54.40) daily, and doubles are priced at 140F ($95.20) to 160F ($108.80). The hotel has a warmly intimate bar area.

The Turmstube is the specialty restaurant of the hotel, and it's considered one of the finest dining rooms in town. Nonresidents are welcome to stop off for a meal daily from 11:30 a.m. to 2 p.m. and from 6 to 9 p.m. Formal and charming, with tufted leather banquettes, it has a large ochre-colored ceramic stove against one wall. There's a less formal seating area to the side. If you're feeling flush and have a large appetite, you can order the menu gourmet at 75F ($51). Otherwise, à la carte orders cost from 55F ($37.40) for a full meal. The fare is elegantly continental. You might begin with such delicate and expensive items as caviar or foie gras from Strasbourg. But you can also dine more modestly. The fish dishes are prepared correctly, including sole filets with almonds or in a white wine sauce, as well as trout meunière. One large section of the menu is called *plats de resistance,* with a wide range of meat dishes. The chef considers his own specialties to be scampi flambéed with Pernod, filet of beef flambé, beef Stroganoff, beefsteak tartare, and fondue chinoise.

Outside the major hotel, the best spot for dining is the **Ratskeller,** 3 Strehlgasse (tel. 043/21-10-87). In the historical core of the town, it is a labyrinth of intimate alpine Rhenish-style rooms with leaded-glass windows and the warmth of exposed wood. The cellar is set behind wrought-iron grills in a historic building a few steps from the heartbeat Hauptplatz. It is open Tuesday to Saturday from 10 a.m. to midnight; Sunday from 3 p.m. to midnight, and closed Monday. Set menus cost 70F ($47.60) to 120F ($81.60), or else you can spend 50F ($34) or more ordering à la carte. For that, you face such well-prepared fare as beef filet with tarragon, mountain goat, venison with herbs, filet of lamb in a Roquefort sauce, homemade noodles, and veal filet in a sherry sauce. Of course, specialties change, based on the shopping of the season.

Food and Lodging at Stoos

Sporthotel Stoos, CH-6433 Stoos, Switzerland (tel. 043/23-15-15). If you'd look at this sprawling building from one angle, you'd swear it was designed around a giant hexagon. A short walk around it, however, will change that impression, particularly from the rear where it appears more like a balconied rectangle. More surprises await you inside, including enough rustically appointed niches to make any recluse happy. The four-star hotel has an intimately lit, wood-paneled bar, another bar for dancing, a children's playroom, an indoor swimming pool, and a comfortable restaurant. The 120 beds usually fold away during the day, which transforms your room into a sitting area. Many of the accommodations have kitchenettes, and all have private bath. Tennis courts are open in summer. Singles rent for 95F ($64.60) daily, while doubles range from 160F ($108.80) to 220F ($149.60), with breakfast included. Half board costs 25F ($17). The hotel is closed in November.

Before continuing our journey south to the St. Gotthard Pass, you may want to make the following detour.

A SIDE TRIP TO EINSIEDELN: Ever since the Middle Ages Einsiedeln has been known as a place of pilgrimage. The venerated statue of the "Black Madonna" in the Holy Chapel of the **Klosterkirche** (abbey church) is the lure.

The thousand-year-old Benedictine abbey, a magnificent group of monastery buildings erected from 1704 to 1770, is considered the finest example of Vorarlberg baroque architecture in Switzerland.

The town, only 18 miles from our last stopover at Schwyz, is a resort in both winter and summer, perched in a high valley of the "pre-Alps." The town is without fog for most of the year. In summer water sports are possible on Lake Sihl, and walking and mountain climbing are avidly practiced.

But it's as a pilgrimage site that the town is known, and it draws lots of the devout who come here to attend liturgical revival and ecumenical conferences. On September 14 the annual festival of the "Miracle Dedication" takes place, and there are torch-lit marches throughout the resort. Every five years (next show, 1992), the town stages performances of *The Great Theater of the World*, an ecclesiastical drama written by Don Pedro Calderón, first performed at the court of Spain in 1685.

The abbey was founded in 934, embracing a band of hermits. The monastery was erected over the grave of Meinrad, who was murdered in 861 by men thinking he was hiding gold. As the story goes, ravens followed the slayers to Zurich, where they called attention to the killers who were subsequently punished. On five different occasions the monastery was destroyed by fire, but each time it was rebuilt. French Revolutionaries at one point stormed the church, hoping to capture the 1465 "Black Madonna," but she had already been carted off to Austria.

The church has twin towers and contains, among other art and architectural curiosities, the largest fresco in the country. Its wrought-iron choir screen is from 1684. A lot of the decoration is by two brothers from Bavaria, the Asam family.

From the south side of the building complex, you can go into the Great Hall, where special exhibitions are staged, mostly coming from the monastery art collection. The stucco decoration in the hall and the fine beautifully restored frescoes date from the early 18th century. It's open daily from 1:30 to 6 p.m., and on special demand from 9 a.m. to noon. Admission is .50F (35¢). You may also see a narrated slide show in the Old Mill lecture hall, given daily at 2 p.m. (only on Sunday from November 1 to April 30). Although there is no admission charge for this show, donations for the upkeep are accepted.

After surveying the food and lodging scene here, we'll pick up the trail again and head out from Schwyz on the route south.

Food and Lodging

Hotel Drei Könige, Klosterplatz, CH-8840 Einsiedeln, Switzerland (tel. 055/53-24-41), has a modern design that features a double tier of glass-walled public rooms extending toward the baroque monastery across the square. Another two floors of cubical balconies rise above the public rooms, with a similar wing stretching toward the rear. The lobby is paved with striated brown-and-white marble beneath a timbered ceiling and leather armchairs. The comfortable bedrooms are spacious and filled with simple, dignified furniture. The 51 accommodations all have private baths and rent for 50F ($34) to 67F ($45.55) daily in a single, 100F ($68) to 135F ($91.80) in a double. Breakfast is included in all the rates. The hotel has a grill room along with a dancing bar, but its main feature is an outdoor café overlooking the mammoth parking lot and the monastery.

Hotel St. Georg, CH-8840 Einsiedeln, Switzerland (tel. 055/53-24-51), is close to the cloisters in a neoclassical town house with a modernized ground floor (they've added a picture window) and a contemporary addition to one side. The public rooms are filled with black leatherette chairs and neutral colors. Rates depend not only on the season but also on the plumbing, as many rooms don't have private baths. Comfortably furnished singles range in price from 45F ($30.60) to 65F ($44.20) daily, with doubles costing from 60F ($40.80) to 110F ($74.80). Under the same management is:

Hotel zum Storchen, 79 Hauptstrasse, CH-8840 Einsiedeln, Switzerland (tel. 055/53-37-60), which in summer has a cascade of flowers. A Renaissance-style bay window looks out from the second floor. Across the street from the Hotel St. Georg, it has a decor which is slightly more appealing than that of its neighbor, with lots of paneling and spacious bedrooms filled with simple furniture. Singles rent for 50F ($34) to 65F ($44.20) daily, and doubles cost 82F ($55.75) to 110F ($74.80). All accommodations have private bath, unlike its neighbors across the street.

Hotel Katharinahof, 6 Iigenweidstrasse, CH-8840 Einsiedeln, Switzerland (tel. 055/53-25-08), is an attractively old-fashioned building on a quiet street facing the abbey. The establishment is run by the Koch family, who have installed an elevator and added a private bath to each of the comfortable bedrooms. A sauna and a billiard room are on the premises. Singles range from 45F ($30.60) to 65F ($44.20) daily, while doubles run 82F ($55.75) to 110F ($74.80), with breakfast included.

ALTDORF: As a respite from mountain climbing, you may want to explore sights closer to the ground. Of all the folk heroes to emerge from the heartland of Switzerland, none is more famous than William Tell. The legend of William Tell's skill in shooting the apple placed on the head of his little son by order of Gessler, the tyrannical Austrian bailiff of Uri, needs no recounting here. Altdorf is the town where this incident is alleged to have happened and a statue of the legendary archer stands in the main square of town, in front of the early-19th-century town hall and a tower dating from the Middle Ages. The monument was by Richard Kissling in 1895, and it was this image, engraved on the postage stamp, that has become familiar to people all over the globe.

The Tell story, first found in a ballad, dates back to the 15th century. Over the years the tale has become closely bound up with the legendary history of the origin of the Swiss Confederation itself. The story has appeared in many versions, reaching world renown in 1804 in a play by Friedrich von Schiller who, after Goethe, was the greatest name in German literature. It really doesn't matter that William Tell probably didn't exist. The story is a fitting allegory to describe the tenacity and the independence of the Swiss people in their fight and struggle for freedom against oppression.

Altdorf is the key to the St. Gotthard Pass, lying on the north side of the Alps, and the capital of the canton of Uri, lying two miles south of the outflow of the Reuss River into Lake Uri. It's the starting point of the road over the Klausen Pass.

The road to the Klausen Pass leads to **Bürglen,** a hamlet that is one of the oldest in Uri. (Incidentally, snowdrifts block this pass from October to May.) Bürglen was the alleged birthplace of William Tell, and the village has set up the **Tell-Museum,** open from the first of June until the end of October, from 9:30 to 11:30 a.m. and 2 to 5 p.m. daily, charging an admission of 2F ($1.35). The museum contains documents and mementos relating to that period of early Swiss history in which Tell supposedly lived. The museum is in a Romanesque tower adjacent to the parish church.

The most charming way to go to Altdorf from Lucerne is by lake steamer. Take the vessel to Flüelen at the far end of the lake and allow some three hours. From Flüelen, you can make a bus connection for the short run to Altdorf.

Food and Lodging

Goldener Schlüssel, CH-6460 Altdorf, Switzerland (tel. 044/2-10-02), a three-star hotel right near the center of town, is a short walk from the William Tell statue, and is generally considered the best of an uninspired lot. At least it has the best food. A five-story historic inn, with a golden key on a wrought-iron bracket hanging out front, the hotel opens onto a tiny plaza capped by a bear. Parking is possible in the rear of the hotel under evergreen trees. Original art is used as part of the interior decoration of the hotel, and it has many other warming touches and amenities. Not all units contain private baths, so rates depend on the room assignment and plumbing. Singles cost from 45F ($30.60) to 80F ($54.40) daily, and doubles go for 65F ($44.20) to 125F ($85). A set luncheon is offered for 30F ($20.40), an à la carte dinner costing from 45F ($30.60). Plats du jour are likely to include minced veal with four types of mushrooms, scallopini florentine with saffron rice, ravioli with rosemary, and tournedos with shallots and marrow in a Pinot Noir sauce. The hotel is closed in January and shuts down every Monday in winter.

Zum Schwarzen Löwen, CH-6460 Altdorf, Switzerland (tel. 044/2-10-07), lies along the main street, the often traffic-filled Hauptstrasse, a few steps from the William Tell statue. You'll recognize this "black lion" by its gilded wrought-iron sign and its restrained baroque detailing. Goethe, in case you'd like to know, slept here in 1797. Madame de Staël, the great woman of French letters, was also a guest, as was Byron. Dating from 1509 with its original wide staircase, this hotel offers 20 simply furnished bedchambers, each with private bath and phone. Rooms are traditionally furnished, often in an old-fashioned way. Accommodations are quieter in the rear. Singles rent from 50F ($34) to 60F ($40.80) daily and doubles from 90F ($61.20) to 130F ($88.40). Five generations of the Jost family (now Dora and Heinz) have run this hotel, welcoming guests into their Beidermeier Saal. They also have a bar and restaurant, and you may want to make the black lion your dining choice, even if you're not staying over. Meals are served daily from 11:30 a.m. to 2 p.m. and from 6 to 10 p.m. Full meals in the ground-floor restaurant begin at 25F ($17).

Hotel Bahnhof, CH-6460 Altsdorf, Switzerland (tel. 044/2-10-32). The cheaper rooms are rather small but pleasantly paneled and comfortable, while the more expensive units are most spacious. This is a well-established tourist hotel, with pleasantly dated furniture, under friendly attention of Mrs. Anna

Niederberger and her family. It's located, to judge by its name, near the train station in what looks like a former private house with a modern addition in front. Singles cost 35F ($23.80) daily, while doubles range from 65F ($44.20). None of the accommodations has a private bath, but there's a sink in every room and shared facilities off the hallways.

AMSTEG: This is a traditional stop on the St. Gotthard route, and the starting point for car drivers over the passes. It's also a good center for walks and mountain excursions. The resort lies at the mouth of the Maderanertal. In the distance you can see a tall viaduct which holds the tracks of the St. Gotthard railway.

Food and Lodging

Hotel Stern und Post (Star and Post), CH-6474 Amsteg, Switzerland (tel. 044/6-44-40), is a former post house with lots of atmosphere, a steep tile roof with gently curving eaves, and long rows of small-paned windows with flower boxes. The Tresch family, owners of the hotel, has resided in Amsteg since 1474. In 1734, they took over operation of the Inn to the Golden Star, built around 1604, and the head of the family was also in charge of customs and of a private mail system. When the Swiss Federal Post started service in 1850, the Tresches became postmasters, soon adding the word Post to the name of the hotel. In the days of the famous St. Gotthard Mail Coach (1850 to 1882), the Tresches had stables for more than 400 horses, 250 of which they owned. P.A. Tresch, who is in charge of the hotel today, is also still responsible for the postal coach (mailbus) services in the area, and the post office is in a wing of the hotel.

The interior of the hotel is elegantly furnished with a combination of 19th-century parlor antiques and chalet chairs. If you decide to dine in (and the cuisine is certainly worth it), you'll be shown a table in the high-ceilinged dining room with fern-green walls and big windows. The very excellent trout comes from regional streams, and arrives in more than a half a dozen different varieties. Many of the other specialties are written tongue-in-cheek in regional dialect, so you may need a staff member to assist you. These include pork with potatoes and chestnuts, and a variety of other delicacies. Full meals begin at 35F ($23.80). Some of the bedrooms are furnished with Victorian beds and lots of gingerbread. A word of caution: If you're uncomfortable in too short a bed, these particular chambers might not be for you. Singles range from 37F ($25.15) to 80F ($54.40) daily, while doubles cost 65F ($44.20) to 160F ($108.80), with breakfast included. Prices depend on the season and plumbing.

ANDERMATT: At the crossroads of the Alps, Andermatt is known for its many days of sunshine in winter and is a major sports center. In the Urseren Valley, it's at the junction of four alpine roads. The St. Gotthard highway crosses the road to Oberalp and Furka at Andermatt.

In summer it attracts those wanting to get away from it all. Excursions and hikes across the mountain passes are possible. In winter it draws skiers to its trails, runs, and tracks down the Gemsstock, the Nätschen, the Oberalp, and the Winterhorn. There's also a 12½-mile-long cross-country ski track open from November to May, which has safety devices against snowdrifts and avalanches.

Other sporting facilities include a Swiss ski school, an ice-skating rink with curling equipment, sleigh runs, and squash tennis in winter. There's also an indoor swimming pool.

Food and Lodging

Hotel Krone, CH-6490 Andermatt, Switzerland (tel. 044/6-72-06), is perhaps the finest place to stay in Andermatt, and it enjoys a reputation for serving the best food. Set alongside the main artery of town, it is one of the oldest establishments in Andermatt, its present building dating from Victorian days. It is vaguely patterned after the chalet format. Inside richly paneled antique areas alternate with carpeted modern rooms. One floor above the reception there's a paneled and cozy Victorian parlor with sofa, chairs, and books, along with an upright piano and a big TV set. Rooms are medium-size and decorated in restrained good taste. Not all units have private bath, and these accommodations are cheaper, of course. Singles range from 53F ($36.05) to 77F ($52.35) daily, doubles 96F ($65.30) to 144F ($97.90). The Krone bar is one of the most popular stopovers on the après-ski circuit of town. A French restaurant serves excellent food. Guests can also patronize the Kronenstübl for its grills and fondues. Food is served from 11 a.m. to 10 p.m.

Hotel Drei Könige und Post, 69 Gotthardstrasse, CH-6490 Andermatt, Switzerland (tel. 044/6-72-03), is a white-walled chalet with buttressed eaves and brown shutters. A café terrace serves drinks and food in front, repeating a tradition established as early as 1234 for an inn on this site. In the old inn that stood here in 1775, Goethe spend the night before crossing the pass. This family-run hotel is a more recent construction, and was renovated in 1977 in a format of comfortably paneled bedrooms with balconies, panoramic views, and private baths. The Renner family charges 50F ($34) to 74F ($50.30) daily in a single, 100F ($68) to 148F ($100.65) in a double, with breakfast included. Prices depend on the season and your room assignment. The hotel has a sauna, whirlpool, and fitness center.

5. LAKE LUCERNE, WEST AND SOUTH

Back at Lucerne, we set out this time to the west and to the south, heading first for a major mountain excursion to **Mt. Pilatus,** a 7,000-foot summit overlooking Lucerne, and dominating the western sector of Lake Lucerne. The name probably comes from a Latin word meaning "covered with clouds," but legend ascribes it to Pontius Pilate.

A trip to Pilatus, one of the most popular excursions in Switzerland, is a three-in-one experience. First, however, you can take a lake steamer to Alpnachstad (rail passes are valid on lake steamers). At Alpnachstad, you can begin by taking a cog railway which, at a 48% gradient is considered the steepest cog-wheel railroad in the world. This famous electric Pilatus railway climbs the mountain to Pilatus-Kulm, and service is about every 45 minutes. You get off at Pilatus-Kulm (the top) to enjoy the view. At the upper platform when you get off, you'll find two mountain hotels. From the belvedere, an alpine vista will unfold for you, taking in not only the lake, but Rigi and Bürgenstock.

When you descend, you can take two different cable cars: first a large cabin-style téléphérique, then a small gondola down a different side of the mountain, eventually getting off at Kriens, which is a suburb of Lucerne. At Kriens you can catch a city trolley back into Lucerne.

Note that the undertaking I just described is available only from May to late November. Because of avalanche fears in winter, it does not operate. The cogs are always dug out by hand every spring, but the operators wait until all the snow has melted before resuming their operations.

If you want to take this excursion in winter or early spring, you are required to go to Kriens by city trolley no. 1, leaving from the Bahnhof. At Kriens, you can get a ride in a four-seater cabin of a cable car that glides over meadows and forests to Fräkmüntegg. The trip takes about half an hour, and you arrive at an elevation of 4,600 feet. At Fräkmüntegg you switch to an aerial cableway, really a stunning feat of advanced engineering, swinging alongside the cliff up to the very peak, in both summer and winter.

You can ride the two cablecars to the top of Pilatus-Kulm and back the same way for a special winter price of 27F ($18.35) round trip. If you elect this all cable-car trajectory in summer, however, when the cog railway is open, it will cost you 54F ($36.70). Eurailpass holders pay only 36.80F ($25).

Once there, you'll find that no one believes the legend about Pontius Pilate anymore. But for centuries many men in Switzerland would not climb the mountain out of fear that it was haunted by the ghost of Pilate, who would bring havoc to the weather, causing fearful storms. In fact the city fathers of Lucerne, who took this legend seriously, banned travel up the mountain until the very end of medieval times. But after that it drew a steady stream of curiosity-seekers, even, according to reports, Queen Victoria in 1868.

HERGISWIL: Five miles from Lucerne, right on the lake, this idyllic little holiday resort can be reached from the city in ten minutes by train or car. This is a peaceful vacation spot away from the motorway, offering excursions by train, boat, mountain railway, cable car, or bus as well as fine walks along the shores of the lake and hiking in the area of Mt. Pilatus.

It offers tennis courts, a lake beach, indoor swimming, and other activities if you're energetic. If you're like me, you may want to spend time just sitting on a bench and watching the steamers plying their way on Lake Lucerne or enjoying the folk entertainment offered in the evening.

Food and Lodging

Seehotel Pilatus, CH-6052 Hergiswil, Switzerland (tel. 041/95-15-55). My favorite part of this lakeside hotel is the half-timbered sitting room with red bricks filling the gaps between the beams. You'll usually see a fireplace blazing, from a traditional walled fireplace to a red-tile central chimney in the middle of the contemporary bar area. The indoor swimming pool is surrounded with plants and glass walls, while a dance bar often has live music. The bedrooms have multicolored spreads, wood slats, and panoramic balconies with alpine patterns cut into the bannisters. Part of the exterior is chalet style, with two modern extension annexes nearby in a more up-to-date style. Singles range from 85F ($57.80) to 95F ($64.60) daily, while doubles cost 150F ($102) to 170F ($115.60), with breakfast included. Prices depend on the season. The lakeside terrace is especially lovely, with lanterns hanging from closely clipped sycamore trees.

Hotel Belvédère am See, CH-6052 Hergiswil, Switzerland (tel. 041/95-01-01), is a hotel with many attractive features, among them its lakeside location near a baroque church and the marina with boats moored almost in front of the hotel restaurant. This four-star hotel is considered by many to be the finest place in town. Over the years, it has grown and grown, changing its appearance, but its best drawing card has always remained the same: a lakeside terrace with good views and tables for drinking or dining. This sunny terrace is enjoyed by guests as a spot for relaxation. The restaurant serves consistently good food in a handsome setting. Comfortably furnished bedrooms rent for 74F ($50.30) to 90F ($61.20) daily in a single, 96F ($65.30) to 150F ($102) in a double. Half board costs an additional 25F ($17) per person daily.

BÜRGENSTOCK: The choicest place along Lake Lucerne, Bürgenstock is both a six-mile limestone ridge and a hotel colony that is virtually a deluxe citadel. Many celebrities (like Audrey Hepburn and Sophia Loren) who have chosen to live here have only added to its international reputation.

Don't go here for heights: You've already had those, especially if you made the trek up Mt. Pilatus. At its highest point, Bürgenstock rises only 1,640 feet on its northern side. The southern side gently drops in slopes, often with contented cows, to the Stans Valley.

You can drive to Bürgenstock, about ten miles south of Lucerne, by going first to Stansstad. From there, a three-mile road is steep and narrow and recommended only to the most skilled of drivers.

However, I prefer to take a half-hour steamer trip from Lucerne to the landing platform at Kehrsiten. At Kehrsiten, a funicular will whisk you to

Bürgenstock in about eight minutes. The funicular has a gradient of 45%. At the upper stations of the platform you'll encounter one of the poshest spots of luxury in all Switzerland.

Once there, you can walk along the Felsenweg, a cliff path skirting the Hammetschwand. At the Hammetschwand elevator you can go to the upper station at 3,580 feet. From the summit, you'll have a vista of the lakes of the heart of Switzerland and the Bernese Alps.

Food and Lodging

Bürgenstock Hotel Estate, CH-6366 Bürgenstock, Switzerland (tel. 041/63-25-45). If you didn't bring your evening clothes, don't assume that the management will let you in to dinner. This is one of the most exclusive hotels in Europe, certainly one that will make you feel privileged to be there. It's the largest privately owned hotel estate in Switzerland. The public rooms are almost awash with priceless art treasures (especially Rubens, but also van Dyck, Tintoretto, and Brueghel) collected by the father of the present owner, Fritz Frey. Even the furniture inside is worthy of a modern-day Versailles.

The estate is actually a complex of three buildings, the Grand, the Palace, and the less exclusive residence, the Park. On the grounds you'll be surrounded by a natural greenery that has been cultivated and trained into one of the most beautiful spots in the Alps. Facilities include a free-form outdoor swimming pool, an indoor pool, a health center, a tavern, a rustically beamed nightclub, a golf course, and lots of open fireplaces, plus Le Club, a restaurant serving all three hotels. A resident of the hotel told me that everything about this place is idyllic except for the occasional lack of sunny weather (which all the money in the world can't guarantee) and the infrequent groups of curious nonresidents who want to promenade through the hotel grounds.

All bedrooms at the Grand and the Palace have complete baths and rent for 210F ($142.80) to 240F ($163.20) daily in a single, depending on the season, the size of the room, and the amenities provided. Doubles range from 360F ($244.80) to 410F ($278.80), with suites costing more. At the Park, bathless singles, some with toilets, cost from 70F ($47.60) to 90F ($61.20), with similar doubles going for 74F ($50.30) to 140F ($95.20). Prices for rooms with bath are 120F ($81.60) to 150F ($102) daily in singles, from 200F ($136) to 230F ($156.40) in doubles, depending on the season and the size of the room. Rates in all three hotels include a continental breakfast, service, and taxes. They are open from April to October.

Want something far less expensive than such a deluxe citadel? Try one of the following recommendations:

Hotel Fürigan, CH-6366 Bürgenstock, Switzerland (tel. 041/63-22-22), is a resort hotel with white walls and a red-tile roof divided into gables and an occasional tower. It's set on a wooded hillside high above the lake, although a private beach is connected to the hotel by a private funicular. The comfortable bedrooms offer good views of the lake. Guests usually relax on the terraces, in the dancing bar, or in the pleasant restaurant. Singles range from 80F ($54.40) to 105F ($71.40) daily, with doubles costing 140F ($95.20) to 180F ($122.40), depending on the season, with breakfast included in all rates. Halfboard is another 25F ($17) per person daily.

Hotel Waldheim, CH-6366 Bürgenstock, Switzerland (tel. 041/63-23-83), is a modern hotel with elegant lounges, an elevator, and a restaurant with a terrace. Most of the bedrooms have private baths, balconies, phones, radios, and TV connections. Rates for bed and breakfast are 37F ($25.15) to 67F ($45.55) per person. The surcharge for half board is 20F ($13.60), 35F ($23.80) for full board. A heated swimming pool, a solarium, and a children's play area are among the amenities of the hotel. It is reached by taking a single lane road (paved) that winds through an alpine meadow dotted with huts, pine trees, cows, and 19th-century chalets. The hotel is cantilevered over these sloping meadows, with many accommodations below the lobby level and a handful above. You can sit on a narrow terrace overlooking the view with the snowy mountains in the distance, or move into the paneled lounge, which is very alpine, very cozy. A hotel actually has stood on this spot since 1895. The present building is a reconstruction, having been rebuilt after a fire in 1958. If you want to avoid the high prices of dining at the Bürgenstock Hotel Estate, you can find meals here costing from 35F ($23.80). Food is served daily from 11 a.m. to 2 p.m. and from 6 to 9:30 p.m.

STANSSTAD: From Lucerne, it's only an eight-minute drive here by the N2 motorway. By rail or lake steamer, allow anywhere from 20 minutes to half an hour. Stansstad is a good center for exploring the chic Bürgenstock area, just recommended. However, it's much cheaper. In summer you can bathe and fish in Lake Lucerne, and there are many possibilities for sailing, waterskiing, and rowing, along with riding, hiking, and summer skiing on the **Titlis.**

Food and Lodging

Hotel Schützen, CH-6362 Stansstad, Switzerland (tel. 041/61-13-55), in the commercial outskirts, began with a 19th-century house that the owners expanded into a modern complex of flat roofs and recessed balconies. The entire hotel is painted old rose and surrounded by a flower garden, with a sun-terrace café, and there are two restaurants, Bachus and Muhlerad. The bedrooms are modern and comfortable. Singles cost 85F ($57.80) daily, and doubles rent for 150F ($102).

STANS: Stans, to the south of Bürgenstock, attracts relatively few American visitors, but it's a good center if you plan to tour yet another mountain, the **Stanserhorn.**

The town is of much more interest to the Swiss because of its connections with some of the country's major heroes: Arnold von Winkelried, a martyr of the Battle of Sempach in 1386 against the Austrians; Nikolaus von Flüe, a hermit who saved the Confederation through peaceful arbitration; and Heinrich Pestalozzi (1746–1827), the famous Swiss educator, who is revered in the country because of his tireless efforts to aid poor, orphaned, and helpless children.

The capital of the half-canton of Nidwalden, Stans is a little market town set in the midst of many orchards. Its parish church, in the baroque style, dates from the 1640s, and there's a monument to von Winkelried.

Stans has a **Historisches Museum,** on Stansstaderstrasse (tel. 041/61-17-81), containing regional dress, weapons, local paintings, and many religious items. Visitors are welcome from 9 to 11 a.m. and from 2 to 5 p.m. Wednesday to Monday but only from March to October.

To reach Stans from Lucerne, you can drive there in your own car or else go via the Engelberg railway.

At the lower station of the Stanserhorn funicular, you can board a combined funicular and cable-car ride to the top of the Stanserhorn at 6,235 feet. The ascent to the panoramic restaurant of Stanserhorn-Kulm takes about half an hour. Once at the summit, you're rewarded with a majestic view of the Bernese Alps and Lake Lucerne.

Hotel Zur Linde, CH-6370 Stans, Switzerland (tel. 041/61-28-26), is the traditional favorite, lying in the historic center of town. A substantial building, it sits on the main square of town, welcoming wayfarers. Its symmetrical façade is covered with neoclassical trompe d'oeil designs and wooden shutters. Café tables are set up on the cobblestone square, facing the cathedral. You'll spot the hotel by its golden bough in wrought iron hanging from a corner of the building. You don't get luxury at this small 18-bed hotel, but you'll receive a good, clean room, each with private bath, and a fair price. Singles cost 65F ($44.20) daily, and doubles go for 140F ($95.20). Food is served in the restaurant daily except Monday and Tuesday.

Hotel Stanserhof, CH-6370 Stans, Switzerland (tel. 041/61-41-22), is set on the main commercial street of town, near the center, in the vicinity of the museum. The brick-faced and gabled building looks like it was once a private house. Today, with its glass-fronted extension and a parking lot, it is a good bet for a clean, no-frills accommodations. In winter, the hotel is closed on Sunday and Monday. The rest of the hotel is well maintained, often paneled, and comfortable. The smallish bedrooms are predictably furnished in forgettable furniture, yet are usually sunny and clean. Singles range from 35F ($23.80) to 40F ($27.20) daily, and doubles run from 70F ($47.60) to 80F ($54.40), including breakfast. Prices depend on the season and the plumbing.

ENGELBERG: An hour by train from Lucerne will deliver you to Engelberg, a popular summer and winter resort in an alpine valley that "glistens with perpetual snow," in the words of one Swiss poet. Many international skiing tournaments take place here, but mainly the village is visited because it's an excursion center for exploring **Mt. Titlis** at 10,627 feet.

The town is well equipped to receive visitors, with ski runs in the heights where the snow can still fly from your skis even when it's springtime in the valley. It has eight mountain track and cable railways, plus 14 ski tows and chair lifts. Other attractions include cross-country ski trails, an extensive sled run, ice skating, curling, a Swiss ski school, more than 20 miles of level walking and hiking paths, indoor swimming pools, a casino, and sports activities planned especially for children.

The **Benedictine abbey** in town was founded about 1120, and the entire valley was ruled from here until the French invasion of 1798. Much of the complex, certainly the church, can be visited by the public, although parts of it are now a religious college. The church, incidentally, contains one of the largest organs in the country.

But you may not want to linger long, as Mt. Titlis is a powerful lure. Titlis is always covered by snow and ice, and it's the highest elevation in the heart of Switzerland that you can visit for a panorama of the Alps, including an "ice cave" and a glacier trail.

It will take a funicular and three cable cars to enable you to reach the highest belvedere, at 9,900 feet. But once there, it will be worth it, for you'll have a view of not only the Jungfrau and the Matterhorn, but on a clear day you can see as far as Zurich and Basel. Incidentally, the last stage of the cable-car trip is the most spectacular, because you are taken right over the glacier. Visitors with respiratory problems may want to forgo this trip because of the thinness of the air at this elevation.

Titlis has a summit terminal with an observation lounge and a large sun terrace. In summer there's also a ski run with a ski lift. Two restaurants here are the Panorama Restaurant Titlis at 10,000 feet and the Gletscher-Restaurant Stand at 8,040 feet.

Excursions from Lucerne's Bahnhof to Titlis require a normal train from Lucerne to Engelberg, where passengers change to a cable car as described above. Departures from the Lucerne train station are every 30 to 60 minutes, depending on the season. The round-trip fare, paid for in full at the Lucerne Bahnhof, is 54F ($36.70).

Food and Lodging

Ring Hotel, CH-6390 Engelberg, Switzerland (tel. 041/94-18-22), is a modern concrete four-star hostelry that sits in a pleasant green area with a good view. From one side you'll see a blank concrete wall, but from two of the others the view improves, with evenly spaced rows of wood-trimmed loggias. A sun terrace is placed for a maximum view of the valley below. Bedrooms are comfortable and modern, with brightly colored curtains to keep out the morning light. A dance band plays every night in winter, and a hotel bus provides a link to the center of the village. Each of the accommodations has a private bath, balcony, radio, and phone. Doubles rent for 120F ($81.60) to 208F ($141.45) daily, and singles cost 70F ($47.60) to 130F ($88.40), depending on the floor and the season. Half board is another 25F ($17) per person daily. Open May to October and December to April.

Hotel Bellevue, CH-6390 Engelberg, Switzerland (tel. 041/94-12-13) is a Victorian elephant of a building, with lots of different architectural features that seem to be connected only by a complicated roofline with lots of gables and curves. The overall effect is authentically 19th century. The surrounding gardens are thoughtfully planned around curved walkways and flowering shrubs. The interior has some uncluttered rustic sections and a few modern touches from the '60s (especially the bedrooms). But the lobby area is the real prize. It's supported by white marble columns and bedecked with contrasting Oriental rugs, deep leather chairs, and huge windows. Tennis courts are on the premises. The cost of the 45 rooms depends on the season and the plumbing (or lack of it). The cheaper rooms are without bath, costing from 57F ($38.75) to 78F ($53.05) daily in a single and 88F ($59.85) to 108F ($73.45) in a double. With bath, prices rise to 76F ($51.70) to 97F ($65.95) daily in a single, 126F ($85.70) to 168F ($114.25) in a double. The hotel is open from May to October and December to April.

The hotels have a monopoly on fine dining, as reflected in the **Hotel Restaurant Hess,** CH-6390 Engelberg, Switzerland (tel. 041/94-13-66), one of the most charming restaurants in the area. In a 100-year-old hotel with rustic paneling and plenty of evening candlelight, it serves local specialties, often accompanied by Rösti. You might start off with cream of broccoli soup or a terrine of wild game (in season). Another good dish is filet of goose with leeks. The house specialty is "Hesstopf" (ask the waiter to explain). An attractive bar area with a live pianist is a popular place to relax either before or after a meal, which costs from 35F ($23.80). Food is served daily from 10:30 a.m. to 2 p.m. and 6 to 9 p.m. The Hess family offers comfortably furnished rooms in their hotel for 55F ($37.40) to 123F ($83.65) daily in a single, 80F ($54.40) to 226F ($153.70) in a double, including breakfast. Prices depend on the season and the plumbing. There are tennis courts on the premises. The establishment is closed the first two weeks in May and from mid-October to mid-December.

BECKENRIED/KLEWENALP:
Some 12½ miles from Lucerne along the N2 motorway in one of the most beautiful sections of the heartland of Switzerland lies this center for both winter and summer sports. The peaceful atmosphere and mild climate of **Beckenried** invite you to forget the stresses of everyday life back home and enjoy the many recreational activities offered here: excursions on the lake and into the mountains, swimming, boating, fishing, and walking through the meadows and woods.

Klewenalp (5,200 feet), above Beckenried, is a sun terrace overlooking Lake Lucerne. Besides summer pleasures, the resort is a joy to skiers in winter, with fine slopes and runs, five ski lifts, a ski school, and lots of sunshine.

Beckenried is accessible by car via the Germany-Basel-Italy motorway, by car-ferry from Gersau, or by lake steamer, train, or bus. An aerial cableway, one of the largest in the lake area, takes you rapidly up to Klewenalp. The round-trip cost is 18F ($12.25).

Food and Lodging
Sternen Hotel am See, CH-6375 Beckenried, Switzerland (tel. 041/64-11-07), is the best known lakeside hotel, standing on its own grounds on the

main road through town. It's a few steps from the ferryboat departure landing for Gersau, next door to a gasoline station. The bowling alley inside is a Teutonic version, with a heavily timbered ceiling, four lanes, and a collection of chalet chairs and cloth-covered tables off to the side. The public rooms have elaborately carved cupboards, lots of paneling, and a mildly heraldic decor. The hotel offers balconies off every room, plus a café terrace angled for maximum exposure to the sunlight. There's a sun-flooded modern restaurant, with an adjacent lakeside terrace, but many diners prefer the warmly rustic stube on the same level as the reception. Rates in a double range from 110F ($74.80) to 144F ($97.90) daily, and singles pay 65F ($44.20) to 82F ($55.70), including breakfast. Prices depend on the season. All accommodations contain private baths, radios, and phones.

Hotel Edelweiss, CH-6375 Beckenried, Switzerland (tel. 041/64-12-52), is a roadside hotel with a Victorian octagonal tower rising above the main lobby. The sitting room has a wintertime fireplace and a slate floor. The dining room has big-windowed views of the lake. The renovated bedrooms are somewhat on the small side, but are comfortable and simply furnished with modern furniture. Singles cost 46F ($31.30) to 65F ($44.20) daily, while doubles range from 68F ($46.25) to 110F ($74.80) per person, including breakfast. Prices depend on the plumbing, the view, and the season.

SACHSELN: Heading south from Lake Lucerne, en route to Interlaken, you may want to consider a stopover at Sachseln, a tiny resort where the lake, plains, and mountains form a landscape of rare harmony. This lakeside village is particularly popular in the summer months, drawing a lively family trade, mostly Europeans. Sachseln lies in the half-canton of Obwalden, which takes in the beautiful Sarner See. Also in summer there is much tourist traffic from Lucerne to Interlaken over the Brünig Pass. This pass goes to Brienz, which is studded with lakeside resorts.

Food and Lodging

Hotel Kreuz, CH-6072 Sachseln, Switzerland (tel. 041/66-14-66). Since parts of the walls and foundations date from the Middle Ages, the management has understandably tried to blend the architectural styles of the annexes into the spirit of the main building. Most of the bedrooms are in the newer sections, and they're filled with a scattering of old furniture and wall-to-wall carpeting. The main house has wood-paneled public rooms filled with 19th-century antiques, and some stained glass from 1656. Among the many celebrities who have stayed here are Pablo Casals, Konrad Adenauer, and the future Pope Paul VI (called Cardinal Montini at the time), as well as Zita, the empress of Austria. All accommodations contain private bath, and rent for 45F ($30.60) to 65F ($44.20) daily in a single and from 80F ($54.40) to 100F ($68) in a double. Half board is another 20F ($13.60) per person daily. The Kreuz is open all year.

MELCHSEE-FRUTT: This well-known mountain holiday center, at an altitude of 6,300 feet, draws vacationers in both summer and winter. Lying in a beautiful valley on the shore of an alpine lake, the Melchsee, the resort enjoys an invigorating, high-altitude climate with strong sunshine in which visitors may participate in summer activities such as walking along signposted paths, going on excursions amid the alpine flowers and wooded areas, trout fishing, bicycling, indoor swimming, or just relaxing with excellent views of the Titlis mountain chain to look at.

Winter brings ample snow from December to the end of April, with good facilities for skiers from the ranks of beginners up to experts. You can leave the small-fry under capable supervision at a day nursery while you take ski lessons, try curling or ice skating on the rinks, or enjoy other winter activities. The road up to nearby Stöckalp is open throughout the winter, with ample free parking for your car, and a snow taxi will take you on to the resort.

Melchsee-Frutt is in the canton of Obwalden in central Switzerland.

Food and Lodging

Hotel Reinhard am See, CH-6068 Melchsee-Frutt, Switzerland (tel. 041/67-15-25), has a bright interior containing a few antiques and an attractive detailing of masonry walls and heavy timbers. There's a comfortable restaurant, and the bedrooms are streamlined with patterned carpeting and harmonious colors. Rates in doubles with half board range from 100F ($68) to 170F ($115.60) daily, depending on the season. A single on the same arrangement pays from 50F ($34) to 95F ($64.60). The cheaper rooms do not have private baths. The hotel is open in July, August, and September and from December to April.

CHAPTER XI

THE GRISONS AND THE ENGADINE

□ □ □

The Grisons by any other name is still the largest, most easterly, and least developed of all the Swiss cantons. Its German name is Graubünden; to the Romansh-speaking population it's Grischun; and the Italians call it Grigioni. We'll stick with Grisons, its French name, which is the name used by English-speaking people. Adding to this somewhat puzzling situation is the fact that French is not generally spoken in this canton.

This sparsely settled region is quite mountainous and has some 140 square miles of glaciers. Forests cover one-fifth of the canton's total area. Juf, nearly

7,000 feet above sea level, is the highest permanently inhabited village in the Alps. Even the 150 or so valleys of the Grisons are high, between 2,953 and 6,562 feet, and the highest peak, Bernina, reaches 13,285 feet. The alpine scenery here differs from that of other areas of Switzerland because of the altitude and topography, and the air is clear and invigorating, which has led to the establishment of many health centers in the Grisons. The height makes it cooler at night in summer, but it enjoys the extra daytime warmth of other southern cantons.

The Grisons contain the sources of the Rhine, which is served by many tributaries, and of the Inn (En in Romansh) Rivers, whose upper stretches form the major valleys of the canton.

The territory of the Grisons was once a part of Rhaetia, peopled by Celtic tribes in pre-Christian times. In 15 B.C. the Romans conquered the Rhaetians, began colonization, and built alpine roads, some along courses that have not till now been much changed. The Franks, a West Germanic people, entered the Roman provinces in the third century and established themselves along the Rhine. They and their fellow Germanic successors, the Ostrogoths, largely Teutonized the Roman territories they seized, gradually changing the language of the inhabitants to Germanic dialects, especially in the northern regions. German is spoken today by about half of the Grisons population, mainly around Davos and Chur, the capital of the canton. About a sixth of the people of the Grisons, those living in the southern portion, speak the language of their next-door neighbor, Italy.

The people of the upper valleys of the Rhine and the Inn were protected from Germanization by the seclusion of their habitation, and today they still cling to their ancestral tongue, called Romansh, the language of a third of the Swiss living in the Grisons. Both the dialect spoken in the Engadine, Ladin, and that of the Vorderrhein (front or upper Rhine) Valley, Surveltisch, are direct descendants of the Latin spoken in the Roman province of Rhaetia. The centuries have altered it, until to me it sounds like Spanish spoken by a person with a cleft palate and a heavy German accent. This stubborn persistence in retaining the tongue of their ancestors led to the recognition in 1938 of Romansh as the fourth Swiss national language.

From the time of the Romans through the Middle Ages you could take the High Road, the *Obere Strasse*, which used the Juli Julier and the Septimer Passes, and I could take the Low Road, the *Untere Strasse* via Splügen Pass, and we would have had lots of company. These roads gave Rhaetia a monopoly on almost all transalpine traffic through the territory then, and even today the route of the Low Road is still used. The Septimer Pass fell into disuse following the building of a more car-worthy road running through the San Bernardino Pass, which now has a tunnel, allowing use of the north-south route all year.

It seems reasonable to say that the roads in the Grisons, many of which were repaired and linked with a network in the early 19th century, owe at least part of their survival to the fact that until 1927 the citizens of this canton did not allow motor vehicles on their roads. Even today it's illegal to drive cars in Arosa after nightfall.

This ban on use of roads by motor cars made popular the Rhaetian railway, with its narrow-gauge trains running on a track along hairpin curves and through tunnels. This ride is still a pleasant and thrilling journey through the Grisons. Or you can embark on excursions via postal buses to take you to the high passes.

The peasants of this canton banded together in 1395 to form the Ligue Grise ("Gray League"), from which the name Grisons is derived. Two other such leagues were formed in the area, all joining to oppose Habsburg domination. In 1803 the three leagues formed a single canton, which joined the Swiss Confederation. The Reformation was adopted by only part of the canton.

Much of the population of the Grisons today earns its living by catering to tourists, who find this a separate world with major ski resorts and small settlements waiting to help them have happy holidays. If you always like to drink the "spirit of the land" when you travel, add to your happiness by trying the local wine, veltliner. Chances are it will be red, but you may be fortunate enough to taste the rare "green" veltliner.

While you're in the Grisons, be on the lookout for embroidery done by the women of the canton during the long winter evenings. It's exquisite. You can also purchase hand-woven linens.

1. CHUR

The capital of the Grisons, Chur is the oldest town in Switzerland, dating back, according to recent excavations, to 3000 B.C. The Romans founded a settlement here in 15 B.C., calling it Curia Rhaetorum. At an elevation of 1,955 feet, it lies in the Rhine Valley, surrounded by towering mountains. The River Plessur flows through it on its way to the Rhine.

Chur is a meeting point for routes from Italy over the alpine passes, and as such it combines both Rhaetian and Italian influences. This mountain town is a tourist favorite, but also the largest trading center between Zurich and Milan. Incidentally, Chur lies 75 miles from Zurich, which is reached in about 90 minutes.

The town is also an important rail center, the terminus of some international lines such as the standard-gauge railway from Sargans. It's also the starting point for the narrow-gauge line to St. Moritz, known as the Rhätische Bahn. The Chur-Arosa line and the *Glacier Express* also start here.

In 450 Chur became the see of a bishop, and much of its history has been tied up with that position. It still has a bishop, but he no longer has the power, of course, that his predecessors did. These bishops virtually ruled the town until 1526.

THE SIGHTS: Because of its position as a transportation network, Chur is a good center for exploring the Grisons. At the **tourist office** on Bahnhofplatz (tel. 081/22-18-18), you can get information on fascinating train trips that start here, including excursions on the *Bernina Express*, *Glacier Express*, and *Palm Express*. Other possibilities will be outlined for you as well. Ask about the trip to Splügen, which is said to have the prettiest mountain-pass village in the area.

Many possibilities for sports also exist—in both summer and winter. In summer you can hike on marked trails and go skiing at 9,000 feet (only 1¼ hours away), as well as participate in swimming and riding. In winter Chur is the starting point for 20 top ski areas.

You'll also want to spend as much time as possible in Chur, as it offers many attractions. Emperors and kings, armies and traders, have marched through Chur, and many have left their legacies. City officials have made it easy for you to go on a self-guided tour of the medieval sector (green and red footprints are painted on the sidewalks). You'll come across squares with flower-bedecked fountains and narrow streets, along with elegant houses and many towers.

The **cathedral,** erected from 1178 to 1282, has seen much rebuilding, one as recent as the 19th century. It was constructed on the site of an even older building. Inside it displays a 15th-century triptych in gilded wood at the high altar. This is the largest Gothic triptych in Switzerland. To visit the Dom Treasury, you'll have to apply to the sacristan at building no. 2 on the square. For a cost of 1.50F ($1), he'll show you many medieval reliquaries, among other treasures, including the relics of St. Lucius of the second century.

Close to the cathedral, the **Bishop's Palace,** still the residence of a bishop, was begun in 1732 in the baroque style. The palace opens onto the Hofplatz, the site of a Roman fort.

The town has at least two museums worthy of your attention, including the

Rhaetic Museum **(Rätisches Museum)**, 15 Quaderstrasse (tel. 081/22-29-88), open from 10 a.m. to noon and 2 to 5 p.m. except Monday, charging an admission of 3F ($2.05). It's installed in the Buolsches Haus, which was constructed from 1674 to 1680. The museum presents exhibits illustrating the history and folklore of the canton and has an archaeological collection as well.

Bündner Kunstmuseum (fine arts museum), Postplatz (tel. 081/22-17-63), stands in a park. It's open from 10 a.m. to noon and 2 to 5 p.m. daily except Monday, charging an admission of around 3F ($2.05). Known as the Villa Planta, it displays paintings and sculptures from many artists who earned acclaim in the Grisons. Some of its works are by such world-famed artists as Giovanni, Segantini, Angelika Kauffmann, Ferdinand Hodler, and Cuno Amiet, as well as Alberto, and Augusto Giacometti. But I always make a special pilgrimage to it to see the large collection of one of my all-time favorite artists, the incomparable Ernst Ludwig Kirchner (1880–1938), the German painter and leader of the "Bridge" school of expressionists. His figures are distorted, his pictures sharply patterned and colored. The Nazis destroyed many of his works, finding them decadent, and he subsequently committed suicide before the outbreak of World War II.

WHERE TO STAY: The only four-star hostelry in Chur, the **Duc de Rohan,** 44 Masanerstrasse, CH-7000 Chur, Switzerland (tel. 081/22-10-22), is the finest but also the most expensive. The establishment, consisting of a hotel and what is reputed to be the best restaurant in town, is five minutes from the train station. This hotel presents a dual aspect: One part is a white-walled neoclassical villa with elaborate lintels, the other a modern, flat-topped addition. The inside has a large indoor swimming pool, a sauna, massage facilities, and fitness club. Many of the public rooms have been elegantly outfitted with rococo and 19th-century antiques, grouped into pastel-colored conversation areas. Well-furnished singles cost from 80F ($54.40) to 95F ($64.60) daily, doubles from 130F ($88.40) to 160F ($108.80), breakfast included.

Hotel Chur, 2 Welschdörfli, CH-7000 Chur, Switzerland (tel. 081/22-21-61), has an imposing façade of tall windows, arched ground-floor windows, and fifth-floor gables. The interior has been renovated into an attractive format of three restaurants and comfortably updated bedrooms, each of which has a private bath, phone, mini-bar, radio, and on occasion a well-placed reproduction of a Queen Anne chair. Singles cost 63F ($42.85) to 74F ($50.32) daily, and doubles go for 108F ($73.45) to 146F ($99.30), breakfast included. The Cava Grischa is an informal cellar room with black-vested waiters, rustic paneling, and nighttime folkloric or modern music with dancing. The Bistro is an art nouveau fantasy of wrought iron and bentwood chairs, with crêpes and light snacks offered. Finally, the Welschdörfli is an elegant dining room, serving cuisine moderne and Grisons-style cookery.

Hotel Stern, 11 Reichsgasse, CH-7000 Chur, Switzerland (tel. 081/22-35-55), is one of Switzerland's Romantik hotels, which usually means a greater-than-usual level of antique authenticity and charm. The outside looks like a giant strawberry mousse, painted a vivid pink with white shutters. The management will meet you at the train station if you call ahead; however, it's only a seven-minute walk. The staff wears regional costumes, and many of the walls are covered with pine paneling, some of it dating from 1646. The ceilings often are vaulted or timbered. The bedrooms are usually more up-to-date, but with a wood-grained format that corresponds well with the antiques and wrought iron used in the public rooms. Emil Pfister, the owner, charges from 80F ($54.40) to 90F ($61.20) daily in a single and from 135F ($91.80) to 145F ($98.60) in a double, breakfast included. The hotel has one of the finest dining rooms in town, which you may want to patronize even if you aren't a hotel guest. Meals costing

40F ($27.20) are served from 11:30 a.m. to 2 p.m. and 6:30 to 9:30 p.m. daily. The chefs specialize in regional fare, including capon Oberland (poached in bouillon), calves' liver in a red wine sauce, and pan-fried trout. A special gourmet menu is offered for 58F ($39.45). You have a choice of three dining rooms. The hotel has free parking.

Hotel Freieck, 50 Reichsgasse, CH-7000 Chur, Switzerland (tel. 081/22-17-92), is a tall building with shutters, an uncomplicated roofline, and a series of black line drawings representing grape vines, a sundial, and two lions. The establishment is about five minutes on foot from the rail station. The bedrooms have been renovated into a streamlined format of simple furniture and comfortable low beds. The emphasis of the establishment, however, is on the restaurants inside, which range from a rustic stucco room with massive beams stretching just below the vaulting to a paneled contemporary room with plain tables. The Stockmann family, your hosts, charge 64F ($43.50) to 80F ($54.40) daily in a single and 102F ($69.35) to 130F ($88.40) in a double, with breakfast included.

Hotel Zunfthaus zur Rebleuten, Pfisterplatz, CH-7000 Chur, Switzerland (tel. 081/22-17-13), was built in 1483 in the middle of the old town. It sits in front of a fountain behind blue shutters and a beautiful type of ground-floor window ornamentation. The inside is paneled, with elaborate chandeliers, leaded-glass windows, and hunting trophies. The bedrooms sometimes have exposed timbers between the white stucco, along with comfortable beds with pine head- and footboards. Ralph Cottiati, the owner, charges from 45F ($30.60) to 52F ($35.35) daily in a single and from 72F ($48.95) to 100F ($68) in a double, with breakfast included. The establishment is known for its good food.

Posthotel, 11 Poststrasse, CH-7000 Chur, Switzerland (tel. 081/22-68-44), is a straightforward hotel garni (serving breakfast only) in a five-story rectangular building with a flat roof and a series of privately run shops behind the glass windows of part of the ground floor. The inside is functionally modern, with bright colors and predictable functional furnishings. The Huber family, your hosts, charge 46F ($31.30) to 75F ($57.12) daily in a single and 78F ($53.05) to 140F ($95.20) in a double, with breakfast included. Prices depend on the plumbing.

Hotel Drei Könige, 18 Reichsgasse, CH-7002 Chur, Switzerland (tel. 081/22-17-25), is a historical middle-class hotel, lying at the entrance to the old town, about five minutes by foot from the central rail station. The foundation of the building dates from at least as far back as the 14th century. Excavations in the hotel cellar unearthed a collapsed tunnel that led to the archbishop's palace at the opposite end of the old city. Since 1911 the Schällibaum family, now in its third generation of management, has run the hotel with dedication. Over the years they've welcomed royal personages, high-ranking politicians, and world-famous artists. The Drei-König Hall on the premises used to be a part of a monastery and, later, a seat of government.

There is a wide variety of well-scrubbed rooms, containing a number of accessories. Except for a handful of budget-priced units under the eaves, most have private baths, phones, TV, comfortable furniture, and views over the medieval architecture of Chur. Bathless singles under the eaves rent for 25F ($17) per night, with breakfast included—one of the ultimate values found in Chur. The frequently renovated more comfortable rooms rent for 42F ($28.55) to 65F ($44.20), and doubles go for 78F ($53.05) to 110F ($74.80). The hotel also has one of the most popular places in town for wining and dining (see below).

WHERE TO DINE: Many Swiss gastronomes consider the **Duc de Rohan,** 44 Masanerstrasse (tel. 081/22-10-22), the best dining in town. It's certainly the most elegantly decorated, regardless of what level you dine on. The restaurant is part of an already recommended four-star hotel, lying on the north side of town, a few minutes on foot from the train station. Open from 9:30 a.m. to 11:30 p.m. daily, it always hires top-notch chefs and provides not only good-tasting meals but polished service. Specialties of the chef include strips of beef grilled at your table with a homemade sauce. You can also help yourself to a buffet of crisp, freshly made salads. Beef also appears in other forms, including Stroganoff, T-bone grilled to perfection, and one savory entry known as Madagascar. You might also order the grilled trout, even goat with flap mushrooms. Meals cost from 50F ($34).

Don't overlook the possibility of a drink in the keller-level bar, with its vaulted ceiling and baronial granite fireplace jutting into the room. As you sit on a comfortable banquette, you'll know you're having a drink at the most elegant bar in town.

Drei Könige, 18 Reichsgasse (tel. 081/22-17-25), was already previewed as a hotel, with a duet of pleasant but different dining rooms. The more raucous, and probably the more interesting of the two, has a door opening directly onto the street, downstairs from the hotel's reception desk. Known as the Weinstube, it's covered with well-used paneling whose nicks and scratches only add to the character of the large room. Don't expect haute couture or haute cuisine: What you'll find is an honest and unassuming kind of warmth. Amid hunting trophies, collections of winning medals for sports events, and semi-antique framed photographs, you can enjoy hot food from 11 a.m. to 2 p.m. and 5 to 9 p.m. every day. Full meals feature Swiss specialties and cost from 25F ($17). From 2 to 5 p.m. and 9 p.m. to midnight a limited menu is offered to accompany the foaming beer, the wine, and the hubbub of dozens of citizens conversing with one another.

The more formal of the two hotel's restaurants is the Usteria, one floor above street level, a few steps from the reception desk. The genteel owners, the Schällibaum family, welcome some of Chur's most prominent citizens to this well-recommended restaurant. Full meals cost from 40F ($27.20), and are served from noon to 2 p.m. and from 6:30 to 9 p.m. every day. The cookery is savory and sometimes the chef prepares specialties, including a double entrecôte Marchand de vin or a Chateaubriand Henri IV. You can also order more standard fare such as pot-au-feu served as an appetizer, polenta with cheese, and any number of grilled veal, pork, and beef dishes.

Obelisco, 12 Vazerolgasse (tel. 081/22-58-58), named after the obelisk in the square outside, has earned for itself a reputation as one of the best dining rooms in Chur. Certainly for Italian food it is unsurpassed. Sheathed with pinewood paneling, with neobaroque touches, it has an inviting ambience. You have a choice of three different dining rooms found right in the heart of the old town. In friendly, relaxed surroundings, you can explore the menu. You can select from one of the more than a dozen offerings of pastas to begin your meal. Ingredients range from gorgonzola to many classic Italian dishes, including veal with tuna and saltimbocca, or perhaps a perfectly done sole. Your hosts are the Gennaro Garofalo family, who receive their dinner guests daily from noon to 2 p.m. and from 6 to 10 p.m. Meals cost from 45F ($30.60).

Zunfthaus zur Rebleuten, Pfisterplatz (tel. 081/22-17-13). You'll certainly get a sense of history from the walls of this second-floor restaurant, part of an already recommended hotel. It's actually better known for its food than for its accommodations. Some of the decoration was painstakingly inlaid with darker woods, making the wall coverings more like furniture than paneling. The building dates from 1483, but the recipes served are far more contemporary. You can enjoy a lunch here costing from 15F ($10.20). Dinners, however, are likely to run from 50F ($34), with a gourmet menu for two going for 96F ($65.30). Among dishes calculated to tempt you are bouillabaisse, roast breast of goose in a cabbage and kirsch sauce, pork filets with apples and hazelnuts, and calves' liver in wine with Rösti. For an appetizer, I suggest the stuffed trout in a saffron sauce. The restaurant is open daily from 7 a.m. to 2 p.m. and 4 p.m. to midnight. Reservations for dinner are suggested.

2. AROSA

One of the highest of the alpine resorts, Arosa (6,000 feet) lies in a sheltered basin at the top of the Schanfigg Valley, off the main road but reachable from Chur. The village has existed since the 14th century. Arosa is known for its pure mountain air and a certain unaffected ambience, set against a backdrop of pine-and-larch-studded hills. There are many small lakes in the area also. If St. Moritz is too ultra chic for you, Arosa may be your answer. In other words, with an exception or two, you don't have to pack a formal gown or a dinner jacket if you like to spend your vacation at a ski resort. Arosa lures family trade through such attractions as kindergartens for the smaller visitors.

To make the 19-mile drive from Chur in good weather, allow at least an hour as the road is steep, with hairpin curves. As for making the drive in icy weather, my advice is to forget it. Instead, take the narrow-gauge railway that has been in operation since the first year of World War I. Even if you make the trip by car, you'll have to make other arrangements if you want to circulate at night, because it's illegal to drive in Arosa from midnight to 6 a.m. However, this restriction does not apply to vehicles entering or leaving the town. Even so, you won't be stranded without transportation. Taxis are always available, but you should also consider the following.

In winter, a Night Express taxi service runs continually from 8 p.m. to 2 a.m., costing 2F ($1.35) for a trip. The vehicles are marked **Night Express** and can be stopped for boarding or getting off at any spot along the way.

The village consists of one main street, lined with hotels, as this is the most popular resort in the Grisons after Davos and St. Moritz.

WHERE TO STAY: Arosa hotels, for the most part, are modern or at least up-to-date. In the peak season months reservations are imperative—that is, in winter. In summer it's much easier to find accommodations. The only problem is that Arosa is generally endowed with expensive and upper-bracket hotels, whereas the pickings in the budget category are slim indeed.

The Deluxe Category
Tschuggen Grand Hotel, CH-7050 Arosa, Switzerland (tel. 081/31-02-21). The literature distributed by this hotel reads almost like an invitation to a private party. The façade is high-rise and modern, and the interior is enhanced by decorating devices seemingly from the pages of *Architectural Digest*: potted palms, distressed tortoise-shell wallpaper, and geometric brass frames surrounding lots of mirrors. In fact, the hotel is one of the most glamorous choices in the Swiss Alps, attracting a clientele appropriate to its setting.

In the basement is a ski shop that will equip you fully, in the latest winter slope fashion. At night the place is lively with a bowling center, plus a handsome, intimate Bündnerstube where everybody seems in a festive mood on a snowy night. You can dine at the Restaurant Français and have lunch at the panoramic roof-garden restaurant. There's also a dancing room with an orchestra. The penthouse indoor swimming pool is dramatic, as is the view from the open-air terrace. Many fitness facilities are contained within the premises, including a sauna, massage parlor (even an underwater massage), sun-ray treatment, a hairdressing salon, beauty parlor, and a kindergarten with a nurse.

The rooms are handsomely decorated and beautifully kept, all with color TV. The hotel's high season is in February and March 24 to March 27. At that time, singles on the half-board plan pay from 210F ($142.80) to 320F

($217.60) daily, whereas doubles rent for 160F ($108.80) to 335F ($227.80) per person on the same terms. Low season extends from January 7 to January 28 and February 25 to March 26. Rates then are much softer, with singles on half board paying from 170F ($115.60) to 255F ($173.40) daily, and doubles costing from 130F ($88.40) to 260F ($176.80) per person on the same terms. Each week, there are two *soirées élégantes* for which evening dress is compulsory. The winter season starts at the first of December with Arosa's traditional ski weeks, continuing until the end of March. The hotel is closed in summer.

Arosa Kulm Hotel, CH-7050 Arosa, Switzerland (tel. 081/31-01-31). The modern hotel with the wide glass windows that you see on this site is only the most recent reincarnation of a series of hotels, all with the same name, which have been built and rebuilt on this site since the first establishment was erected as a simple guest house in 1882. During summer you'll find outdoor tennis courts competing for your attention with the nearby rushing streams and hill walks that the region provides. A heated swimming pool with glass walls opening to the mountains is available all year round, along with a wide range of fitness, massage, and cosmetic programs. The array of public rooms includes rustically attractive restaurants, a weinstube, and nightclubs with a sophisticated clientele that should provide whatever it is you're looking for. The bedrooms frequently afford panoramic views from behind large windows. Their decor is often a combination of warmly tinted fabrics, pine paneling, and comfortable furnishings. Low season is in summer, in January, and from mid-March. High season is February and Easter, and at Christmas prices go even higher than those cited. On the half-board plan, singles range from 195F ($132.60) to 390F ($265.20) daily and doubles from 300F ($204) to 680F ($462.40) daily. The hotel is open July to September and December to April.

Alexandra Palace, CH-7050 Arosa, Switzerland (tel. 081/31-01-11), is designed in a semicircular curve of balconied rooms layered on top of one another, with oversize windows and a view over Arosa and the snow-covered mountains in the distance. Inside is a heated swimming pool, a sauna, a disco, an invitingly attractive restaurant, called Modern Art, and a tavern. The hotel offers 150 panoramic rooms for sports enthusiasts, who usually spend their days skiing or hiking through the neighboring hills. Free bus transportation is provided by the hotel to key points in the area, although most guests choose to walk the 500 yards to the nearby ski lifts. The hotel often stages an evening entertainment program to amuse guests. Examples of this might include a fondue party with folklore music, a candlelight buffet, a bowling tournament, or a sleigh ride. The hotel is open only in winter, charging 120F ($81.60) to 170F ($115.60) daily in a single, including half board. Doubles booked in here on a similar arrangement are charged 200F ($136) to 300F ($204).

Hotel Park, CH-7050 Arosa, Switzerland (tel. 081/31-01-65), a luxury five-star hotel, is housed in a modern building shaped like an elongated rectangle, which sprawls over an extended distance behind the frontyard parking lot. The interior is richly decorated, with ample use of leather, intimate lighting, velvets, and everywhere the aura of a complacent comfort coming after an invigorating day outdoors. On the premises you'll find a bowling alley, pinball machines, a disco, an intimately lit bar, and several restaurants that seem to share one thing in common—warmth. Insofar as fitness is concerned, the hotel provides one indoor tennis court, two squash courts, and a swimming pool illuminated by natural light from a panoramic window view of the Alps. In winter, with the snow outside, you'll find the juxtaposition comforting. There are also two saunas, a whirlpool, and a thorough regime of massage and cosmetic treatments.

Bedrooms, offering views of the gradually changing seasons, are richly upholstered in corduroys, velvets, and brocades. The rates per person per day are 115F ($78.20) to 225F ($153) in winter, including half board, service, taxes, use of the swimming pool, bus service to the ski lifts, and free parking. The hotel is open only from December to April.

The Upper Bracket

Golfhotel Hof Maran, CH-7050 Arosa, Switzerland (tel. 081/31-01-85), is an attractive hotel that looks like a full-scale mountain chalet, particularly since it sits high in an alpine meadow away from the congestion of downtown Arosa. In winter, you'll notice the narrow tracks made by the dozens of cross-country skiers who pass by on one of their routes through the hills. The public rooms are rustically decorated with heavy beamed ceilings, carpeting in autumnal colors, and comfortable armchairs ideal for sinking into after a day spent outdoors. Many of the bedrooms have balconies with enough sunlight to afford a tan, even in winter. All accommodations have radios and phones. In summer, a single on the half-board plan ranges from 90F ($61.20) to 150F ($102) daily, and a double costs 240F ($163.20) to 270F ($183.60). Rates in winter for rooms and half-board are 110F ($74.80) to 198F ($134.65) daily in a single, 270F ($183.60) to 400F ($272) in a double. Two tennis courts with an on-the-spot tennis pro are for the sole use of hotel guests, while many scenic and well-marked mountain trails begin and end at the hotel. There's a skating rink, which is well maintained in the winter, a hotel bus that takes guests at regular intervals to the town center and to the ski lifts, and nightly dancing with live music. There's also a nine-hole golf course nearby.

Waldhotel-National Hotel, CH-7050 Arosa, Switzerland (tel. 081/31-13-51). The reception room of this large, symmetrical hotel set into a forest has apricot-colored stencils decorating the arched ceiling and a beautifully carved and painted booth that looks almost like part of a pulpit of some regional church. This sprawling hotel was designed with two wings on either side of a central core. A wood-paneled restaurant has a Swiss tile oven at one end and a quality of craftsmanship that is outstanding. The management offers a weekly gala dinner by candlelight, a breakfast buffet that is by any comparison copious, and a heated swimming pool with a wide range of massage and stress-reduction treatments.

In the low season, singles on the half-board plan pay from 130F ($88.40) to 165F ($112.20) daily, and two persons are charged from 210F ($142.80) to 290F ($197.20) on the same arrangement. In high season, singles, also on half board, cost 175F ($119) to 210F ($142.80), while two persons pay from 260F ($176.80) to 360F ($244.80). The price difference is determined by the view from the room, the exposure, and the plumbing. Skiers will be glad to know that it's possible for them to begin and end a day of skiing from the hotel without (unless they fall) removing their skis. A chair lift and a cable car begin at a point just below the hotel. Accommodations are available from December until April and from June until September.

Hotel Excelsior, CH-7050 Arosa, Switzerland (tel. 081/31-16-61), can be found in a quiet place in the center of town. It blends attractively into the conifer-dotted lawn around it, with a series of cantilevered balconies over wall-size panoramic windows. The hotel has a swimming pool, where depictions of stylized fish seem to splash in and out of the water. A host of public rooms includes a cozily rustic weinstube and an inviting series of lounges, plus a restaurant and a bar with a dance floor and live music. Oscar Rederer, the owner, directs that Tuesday be reserved for a farmer's buffet and Thursday be held for the weekly gala dinner, which guests at this lively hostelry seem to enjoy greatly. The Bündnerstübli serves à la carte. Swiss specialties. Bedrooms are invitingly decorated with comfortable furniture, and your gaze will be drawn to the mountain vista beyond your terrace. For half board, singles pay 100F ($68) to 190F ($129.20) daily, and doubles are charged 190F ($129.20) to 360F ($244.80). The most expensive rates are charged over Christmas and New Year's, when a minimum stay of 14 days is required. All accommodations have private baths, although you'll find a wide price difference between rooms with and without southern exposure and balconies. The hotel is open only from December to April.

Hotel Eden, CH-7050 Arosa, Switzerland (tel. 081/31-02-61), is surrounded by pine trees in the center of Arosa near the cable car and ski lift. The hotel is pleasingly proportioned, with five tiers of weathered balconies and a gridwork design of sunstreaked planking over white walls. Each of the spacious bedrooms has its own private bath, radio, and phone, and all units with southern exposure open onto their own balconies. Half-board prices quoted by your hosts, the Leu family, are 110F ($74.80) to 160F ($108.80) daily in singles, 190F ($129.20) to 290F ($197.20) in doubles in low season. High-season tariffs, which are charged from December 17 to January 9 and February 4 to March 11, are 160F ($108.80) to 200F ($136) daily in singles, 280F ($190.40) to 360F ($244.80) on the half-board plan. You must write for reservations long in advance. A covered skating rink and a ski school are connected to the hotel, which also has a heated whirlpool, a fitness room, a children's playroom, and a piano bar with live music. The public rooms are accented with marble floors, Oriental rugs, hanging lamps, and wall-to-wall carpeting. Eden is open only from December to April.

Hohe Promenade, CH-7050 Arosa, Switzerland (tel. 081/31-26-51). The views from the terrace of this eight-story balconied hotel look down a hillside into a valley surrounded by jagged mountains. If you have vertigo, you'll want to keep the curtains of your bedroom closed because in any season the mountains seem to loom up into the carpeted space of your private quarters. All the pleasant bedrooms have tile bathrooms, radios, and phones. In off-season, singles pay from 65F ($44.20) to 110F ($74.80) daily, and two persons are charged from 120F ($81.60) to 230F ($156.40), with half board included. In winter on the half-board plan, a single costs 110F ($74.80) to 130F ($88.40) daily, and doubles go for 200F ($136) to 260F ($176.80). The restaurant is attractively beamed and timbered. The center of Arosa is five minutes away by foot, but some of the ski lifts are even closer. The Ackermann family are the owners. Open June to September and December to April.

Sporthotel Valsana, CH-7050 Arosa, Switzerland (tel. 081/31-02-75), was recently renovated to offer even more personalized service to the many guests who stay here. The building has five tiers of balconies above a row of high arched windows that direct sunlight into the public rooms. An intimately lit bar area is crowned with an intricate coffered ceiling that rests on top of the beveled pine walls. The hotel has four tennis courts on the premises, both an outdoor and indoor pool, sauna and massage facilities, a playground for children, an attractive restaurant, and a weinstube with roughly hewn walls. The dancing-bar area often engages live musicians. The hotel is conveniently located for cross-country skiers and downhill racers and hikers. A kindergarten provides supervised activities for children.

Each room, with much wood and Grisons *sgraffito,* has a toilet and shower or bath, as well as a phone, TV connection, radio, mini-bar, and safe-deposit box. The upper regions of the price scale are activated at Christmas and New Year's. In the low season, singles on the half-board plan cost 80F ($54.40) to 166F ($112.90) daily, while two persons are charged from 140F ($95.20) to 304F ($206.70). In high season, the single rate for half board is 140F ($95.20) to 197F ($133.95), and twin rooms rent for 262F ($178.15) to 362F ($246.15). The Valsana is open from June to October and December to April.

Hotel Panorama Raetia, CH-7050 Arosa, Switzerland (tel. 081/31-02-41), is housed in chalets on a pine-covered hillside with its own parking facilities, overlooking the main drag of Arosa. Some of its devotees find its site the best at the resort. The decor is both tasteful and rustically inviting. The main salon has a wooden ceiling, and warmly tinted carpeting leads up to the panoramic windows that look out over the Alps. Singles in winter range from 95F ($64.60) to 180F ($122.40) daily with half board, and doubles on the same plan cost 160F ($108.80) to 300F ($204). There is a dancing bar with a red-tile floor where guests can whirl away their problems. The Panorama Restaurant has a good view, as promised by its name, but it also serves excellent food, both Swiss and continental dishes. The Grill Restaurant serves a creative cuisine, presenting à la carte dining nightly. But for lovers of the rustic, there is the Bündnerstube, all in local wood, offering such regional dishes as cheese fondue. The hotel is open only from December to April.

The Middle Bracket

Hotel Belri, CH-7050 Arosa, Switzerland (tel. 081/31-12-37). A first-time visitor to Arosa might consider one end of the village to be a collection of chalets strung out along pathways carved into the alpine meadows. One of these outlying buildings in Arosa doesn't look that much different from its neighbors, except that the Belri is the domain of Fräu Ly Leonhard, who personally supervises almost everything that happens in her gemütlich hotel. From the outside the establishment looks like a well-maintained fieldstone and varnished-pine oversize cottage, with balconies and blue shutters. Inside, it's a fantasy of carved, beveled, turned, and polished knotty pine. Some of the bedrooms in the more modern annex are not as carefully handcrafted, but they nonetheless have pine paneling and cozy comfort. During the winter singles with showers (but without private toilet) rent for 85F ($57.80) to 90F ($61.20) daily with half board. Doubles with full bath and half board cost 95F ($64.60) to 110F ($74.80) per person, depending on the exposure. Children receive deductions of up to 50%. The hotel is normally closed in summer.

Hotel Central, CH-7050 Arosa, Switzerland (tel. 081/31-02-52), is housed in an unpretentious building a few minutes from the train station. The entrance is at one end of the large, modern complex, designed like a well-proportioned addition to a much larger house. Many of the units have weathered wooden balconies and baths, radios, TV outlets, phones, and mini-bars, and are attractively furnished with a collection of upholstered settees and wooden chalet chairs. A collection of antique pewter rests on a shelf near the ceiling of the wood-paneled restaurant, and in summer, guests enjoy the view from the terrace. A fitness center with exercise machines, whirlpool, and sauna offers relaxation to guests who come here to climb hills or ski. In fine weather, Andy Abplanalp, Jr., the helpful owner, often organizes mountain picnics and excursions through the region for interested guests. In summer, on half board, singles rent for 59F ($40.10) to 81F ($55.10) daily, and doubles go for 94F ($63.90) to 200F ($136). In winter, the half-board rate for singles is 70F ($47.60) to 195F ($132.60) daily, while doubles go for 140F ($95.20) to 248F ($168.75). The highest prices apply at Christmas.

Hotel Merkur, CH-7050 Arosa, Switzerland (tel. 081/31-16-66), is a family-run hotel next to a bus stop in the middle of the village. This gemütlich hotel is run by Hans Tobler and his family. In a pine-wood restaurant, regional à la carte meals are served in summer. In winter, hotel guests take meals in the rôtisserie by candlelight. The bedrooms, with soundproof doors, are sometimes covered floor to ceiling with lightly finished white pine boards, with the main color coming from the blue-green mountains you'll see through the window. All rooms have direct-dial phones and radios. Many accommodations have balconies, and there is a wide range of plumbing that will determine the cost of your room. Room tariffs are separated into high, middle, and low season in winter, and there's an even cheaper set of rates in summer. In winter, singles range from 73F ($49.65) to 104F ($70.72) daily in bathless units, the price dropping to 60F ($40.80) in summer. Doubles with baths or showers and toilets cost 176F ($119.70) to 240F ($163.20) daily in winter, 120F ($81.60) to 140F ($95.20) in summer. All rates include half board. If you take only bed and breakfast, there is a reduction of 15F ($10.20) per day per person.

Hotel Streiff, CH-7050 Arosa, Switzerland (tel. 081/31-11-17), is separated from the road by a narrow but attractive series of terraced gardens. The hotel is housed in two rectangular buildings, which open their many recessed balconies toward the mountains in the distance. Mr. and Mrs. Christen Streiff usually have a Swiss flag flying from the flattened rooftop, welcoming guests into their hotel with personal service. The hotel is away from the main street but still near the center. Many walking and hiking trails as well as the cableways and chair and ski lifts can be easily reached. All the bedrooms have direct-dial phones and radios. In low season, bathless singles cost 50F ($34) to 68F ($46.25) daily, singles with bath going for 72F ($48.95) to 103F ($70.05). During this season, doubles cost 46F ($31.30) to 64F ($43.50) per person for a bathless unit, 68F ($46.25) to 98F ($66.65) per person with bath. High-season prices are 54F ($36.70) to 85F ($57.80) daily for a bathless single, 76F ($51.70) to 130F ($88.40) for a single with bath. Doubles in high season go for 50F ($34) to 81F ($55.08) per person in an accommodation without bath, 72F ($48.95) to 120F ($81.60) per person with bath. All these tariffs include half board.

Hotel Alpensonne, CH-7050 Arosa, Switzerland (tel. 081/31-15-47). Five floors of well-proportioned, chalet comfort make this small hotel worth trying. Containing only 65 beds, the establishment is in the middle of Arosa, near the ski lifts. The dining room and many of the bedrooms afford panoramic views of the Alps. The bedrooms are clean and attractively simple, with highlights of vivid color against pure white walls. Many of the walls are paneled with the knotty pine, and the overall effect is pleasant. All units have shower or baths, and some contain mini-bars. With half board included, singles in winter range from 91F ($61.90) to 134F ($91.10) daily, and doubles go for 182F ($123.75) to 260F ($176.80) on the same terms. At other times, rates go down to 63F ($42.85) to 123F ($83.65) daily in a single, 126F ($85.70) to 238F ($161.85) for two persons, again with half board. The hotel has a dining room and a restaurant. It is operated by the Bareit family, who close it down in May.

The Budget Range

Vetter, CH-7050 Arosa, Switzerland (tel. 081/31-17-02), is a conglomeration of glassed-in verandas, open porches, and wooden balconies, looking a lot like a cube with window apertures. The interior is a cozy blending of wrought iron, heavy timbers set between stucco ceilings, half-round logs with the original bark set up vertically as partitions, and pithy bits of wisdom stenciled in German above a masonry fireplace. Everything is clean and comfortable, and in winter in Arosa after a day outdoors that means a lot. Many rooms are bathless, and these are the bargains, of course. Hallway facilities are adequate. Many of the accommodations don't contain private baths, and these are the best bargains, of course. Half board in low season ranges from 43F ($29.25) to 95F ($64.60) daily in a single, from 86F ($58.50) to 190F ($129.20) in a double. In winter, half-board rates in a single rise to 65F ($44.20) to 105F ($71.40) daily, with doubles costing 130F ($88.40) to 210F ($142.80). The Vetter is closed in May and November. It's in the middle of town, a few steps from the railroad station.

Hotel Alpina, CH-7050 Arosa, Switzerland (tel. 081/31-16-58). Finally, I found a budget hotel in Arosa that looks from the outside like the type of chalet one fantasizes about. There's a lot of handcarving around the balconies and trim of the steep-roofed hotel with the terraced garden and the ubiquitous Swiss flag on a pole by the entrance. My favorite room is up under the eaves with sloping ceilings on two of the sides and a double window on the third. The walls are covered in flowered wallpaper. The public rooms are accented with various antiques, from a Voltaire couch (just picture a Voltaire chair expanded to seat two) to a baroque clock to painted chests and cupboards. Thanks partially to the efforts of Hans Eberhard, the owner, everything gives off a contented aura of well-being. You'll be less than 600 feet from the Bahnhof here. Rates with half board are from 60F ($40.80) to 70F ($47.60) daily per person in summer. Winter half-board rates range from 70F ($47.60) to 108F ($73.85) daily per person. Since the hotel only contains 35 rooms, you'll get a sense of intimacy here, together with your views over the mountains. Closed May and November.

WHERE TO DINE: Most guests book into the Arosa resort hotels on the board basis. Nearly all the major restaurants are in hotels—hence the shortage of well-known independent dining spots. However, if you can break away for one main meal (and assuming you're not already a guest), you may want to try the cuisine at the following places.

Grill Room, Arosa Kulm Hotel (tel. 081/31-01-31), in a windowless, high-ceilinged inner room of the Kulm Hotel, is considered one of the most stylish and best-recommended dining spots in Arosa. Its strong lines, almost stark simplicity, and striking spaces look Japanese in concept and design. That feeling is strengthened by the presence of a single horizontal line painted in scarlet that encircles the perimeter of an otherwise black room. From a semiconcealed space behind a bar, a piano and violin provide live music for dancing. The establishment is open for dinner only, every night from 7 to 10 p.m. The meals are based on the theories of modern French cuisine. The menu changes frequently, according to the availability of the seasonal ingredients. You might begin with a half lobster stuffed with caviar, sweetbreads braised with flap mushrooms and served in puff pastry, medallions of roebuck with juniper berries, and finish an elaborate array of desserts. Full meals cost from 70F ($47.60) and require an advance reservation. A seven-course menu gastronomique costs from 90F ($61.20) per person.

Chez André, Hotel Central (tel. 081/31-15-13), is one of the best dining rooms in Arosa. In the center of the village, it welcomes guests to its precincts and invites them to order a drink in its warm modern bar on the lobby level before dinner. You dine in one of two pine-sheathed alpine rooms from 11:30 a.m. to 2 p.m. and from 5:30 to 10 p.m. daily. A fixed-price meal costs 25F ($17) at lunch, 38F ($25.85) at dinner. A regular à la carte dinner costs from 40F ($27.20) but could go much higher. The chef's talents are well suited for a repertoire likely to begin with either filet of smoked trout and an artichoke stuffed with goose liver and follow with brochette of scampi grilled, veal piccata with Emmenthal, beefsteak tartare, and filet of veal with raspberry vinegar. Occasional gourmet menus are also featured.

Stüva, or Tattoria Toscana, (tel. 081/31-03-31), is in a log-sided building belonging to the nearby Kulm Hotel, but it takes its true flavor from its managers, Armando Solaro and Raffaelo Limone. Mr. Solaro worked for several years as the personal chef of the Aga Khan, an experience which he draws on even today when dealing with the various demands of his international clientele. The restaurant sits within a few steps of the Inner-Arosa Tschuggen chair lift, near the top of the village. There's little emphasis on a dress code, so you might see a woman in mink dining next to a couple in ski parkas. One side of the cozy room overlooks the spectator seats and battered floorboards that ring one of the village's ice-skating rinks. In sunny weather, you can dine outside.

The daube de boeuf is a specialty, requiring up to a full day of marination before it's served with spinach and fresh vegetables. Other continental specialties are also well prepared. Meals cost from 40F ($27.20). The establishment is open from 11 a.m. to 2 p.m. and 6 p.m. to midnight daily. In the afternoon, it is open for drinks and snacks. Closed April to mid-December.

Arven Restaurant and **Chamanna Hotel Merkur** (tel. 081/31-16-66) are two restaurants in a previously recommended hotel. Both are cozy chambers loaded with alpine accents. The Hotel Merkur's more formal Chamanna Rôtisserie offers basically the same menu as the Arven but is in business only in ski season. The Chamanna has cubbyholes, large window with views, a stenciled ceiling of coffered wood, and half timbering. It serves daily from 6:30 to 9:30 p.m. The Arven keeps the same dinner hours, but is also open from 11:30 a.m. to 2 p.m., when business is usually light, because most skiers are out on the slopes. It stays open all year except in May. Most critics rank the cuisine served here as among the top five or six dining establishments at the resort. The menu tempts you with lots of good things, with full meals costing from 50F ($34). You might begin with well-flavored snails in garlic butter or else spaghetti carbonara. Lamb medallions are served in a mustard sauce, or you can order flounder meunière, and grilled scampi and trout. On a winter's night, filet goulash Stroganoff is hearty fare, or else you can order cheese fondue.

SPORTS: As a ski center, Arosa enjoys world repute, drawing an international crowd to its slopes. It does a thriving summer business, but it is mostly in winter that the skiers throng to this resort. It offers some of the best ski runs in the Grisons, some 15 miles of them, plus one of the best ski schools in Switzerland, the **Swiss Ski School Arosa,** with some 100 instructors.

Skiing is popular in the Obersee area at the eastern edge of the resort, reached by cable car to Weisshorn (8,700 feet). To the west, skiers take the Hörnli gondola, reaching Hörnligrat (8,180 feet) in about 16 minutes. Drag lifts at Hörnligat fan out, taking skiers to their destinations.

Skiing lessons for classes at the Swiss Ski School cost 21F ($14.20) for half a day, 110F ($74.80) for six half-days for adults; 19F ($12.70) for half a day to 100F ($68) for six half-days for children. Private ski instruction is possible through the **Grison Association of Private Ski Instructors Arosa** (tel. 081/31-14-07) and a group of private professional instructors (tel. 081/31-34-48).

Ice-skating rinks are busy here, one at **Inner-Arosa** and another, where ice hockey is also played, at **Obersee Sports Grounds.** The cost for skating for adults is 3.50F ($2.40). Prices for children 6 to 16 are 2F ($1.35).

Bavarian curling is popular, played at the Inner-Arosa rink. Other winter sports are tobogganing and horse-drawn sleigh rides on the famous Arlenwald road.

Pursuits to be followed in both winter and summer are tennis and squash inside hall courts at hotels, plus indoor golf. Walks can be taken over 18 miles of easy, sunny, and varied trails kept open in winter. Bowling is another winter/summer possibility with alleys found at several hotels.

It has been estimated that at least half of the guests who come to Arosa are here for sports and activities other than skiing, especially après ski.

APRÈS SKI: Since many guests nowadays come to Arosa only for the après-ski activities, the action often continues until the morning hours. As the partygoers are making their way back to their hotels or chalets for much-needed sleep, serious skiers are just getting up for an early run on the slopes.

Several of the hotels, as mentioned, stage special events, and if you call in advance you can sometimes attend if a hotel's own guests haven't taken up all the seating.

Arosa has the usual run of taverns, bars, and gemütlich restaurants. However, the most exciting event, in my opinion, is to take a sleigh ride along the famous Arlenwald Road (ask at the tourist office for current details about this ride).

The most popular place in town is the all-around **Kursaal** (tel. 081/31-21-15), which has not only a casino (you can only bet 5F, however), but the Espresso Bar open daily from 9 p.m. to 3 a.m.; the Da Giancarlo, an Italian specialty restaurant serving fresh food from 11 p.m. to 3 a.m., meals costing from 50F ($34); and the Nuts dancing bar and disco with a DJ, open from 9 p.m. to 2 a.m., with drinks averaging 12F ($8.15).

Arosa Kulm Hotel (tel. 081/31-01-31) has a variety of places for après-ski fun, feasting, and relaxation. The Taverne is the least formal of any of the restaurants in the already previewed Kulm Hotel, and as such, it's sought out by skiers after a day on the slopes. Best of all for a change of pace, there are two bowling alleys against one wall. Most clients, however, come to drink in the big-windowed, modern room lined with rustic wood trim. Open daily from 5 p.m. to 2 a.m., it serves fondue, raclette, selections from a salad bar, roast beef, and beer. Kulm Night Club, one floor below the reception desk of the hotel, has an undeniably stylish ambience, with black walls bathed in pinpointed pools of light. It's open from 9 p.m. until early the following morning. Entrance is free, but once you're inside, long drinks are expensive costing from 20F ($13.60). Beer is cheaper at 13F ($8.85). There's almost always a live band. **Espresso Bar/ Conditorei** serves among the most elaborate pastries in town, in a big-windowed modern room on the lobby level of the Kulm Hotel. Some kind of live musicians, often a Hungarian duet of violin with piano, plays from 3 to 5 p.m. daily in winter. A slice of some kind of gooey confection costs from 3F ($2.05) per slice, and might be accompanied with a steaming mug of coffee, hot chocolate, or sherry. The establishment is open daily from 8 a.m. to 6 p.m.

Hotel Park (tel. 081/31-01-65) is another lively spot in peak season. The manager here likes to keep his guests entertained, and throughout the long winter, he stages gala dinners, raclette parties, Bauern buffets, fondue parties, a festival du poisson with a splendid offering of fish, buffet Italianos, and even what is called a "spaghettata." You'll have to call to see what's happening and if there's room for you so that you can make a reservation.

Posthotel (tel. 081/31-01-21), run by Jacques Rüdisser, is another beehive center of activity, especially in winter. The après-ski fun begins here at 5 p.m. in the Fondue and Raclettekeller. You face a choice of various fondues, Vaudoise or Valaisanne, chinoise or bourguignonne. Prices begin at 20F ($13.60). You can also patronize the Pizzeria da Giacomo for Italian specialties, not only pizzas but good pastas, with meals costing from 35F ($23.80), or else go drinking in the Post Stübli, which has a rustic decor. Perhaps you'll stick around for dinner at the Restaurant Post or a specialty Chinese restaurant, Peking. Finally, you may end your night by dancing to live music in the Postbar.

You may want to check out the action at **Sporthotel Valsana** (tel. 081/31-02-75), which can be a lively spot if the night is right. A lovely bar and a dance floor are set between harlequin-painted columns supporting a series of ceiling vaults in the hotel lobby. There's a stage for live music and comfortably modern chairs. Long drinks costs from 11F ($7.50), beer from 3.50F ($2.40). Live music begins at 8 p.m. in winter or summer.

If you want something intimate and cozy, there are many quiet hotel bars in town, often with a pianist to put you and your companion in a dreamy mood.

3. KLOSTERS

Life at this 4,000-foot-high village lying in the shadow of Thomas Mann's "Magic Mountain" has changed greatly from the time a cloister was founded here in 1222. Today only the name remains to remind us of the previous life of this winter and summer resort lying in the wide Prättigau Valley. Many discriminating winter visitors tell me they prefer Klosters to Davos, finding its smaller size and more intimate ambience attractive, especially to a younger crowd. Also, many people find the Klosters' innkeepers more hospitable than those in Davos. The local residents claim that the popular sport of tobogganing originated here.

The main road to Davos runs right through Klosters, some eight miles away. Klosters has few if any unattractive structures. All of its buildings are constructed in the chalet style, providing architectural harmony, far prettier than the ugly, eyesore edifices of St. Moritz. Famous visitors of the past have included Sir Arthur Conan Doyle and Robert Louis Stevenson, who is said to have finished

Treasure Island here, writing about tropical chicanery while surrounded by alpine beauty. In the heyday of tax benefits (earned by stars living abroad) Klosters became known as "Hollywood on the rocks." It still attracts an international crowd, likely to include Gore Vidal, Gene Kelly, and Kirk Douglas. It has also been given the royal seal of approval. The king and queen of Sweden visit regularly, but generating more publicity are Prince Charles and Princess Diana, who have made it their "favorite resort."

WHERE TO STAY: The most modern and elegant hotel in Klosters is the five-star **Piz Buin Hotel,** CH-7250 Klosters, Switzerland (tel. 083/4-81-11). It is located in the heart of the village, just a stroll away from the Gotschna-lift which takes you straight to the skiing and hiking area of Parsenn. The hotel, built in 1984, is designed as a chalet. The large yet cozy rooms are all equipped with two beds, a balcony lounge, mini-bar, direct-dial phone, color TV, and private bath. In winter, half-board rates in a single range from 230F ($156.40) to 275F ($187) daily, rising to 320F ($217.60) to 420F ($285.60) in a double. In summer, half board in a single costs 170F ($115.60) to 240F ($163.20) daily, going up to 290F ($197.20) to 400F ($272) in a double.

The hotel has three restaurants, serving modern culinary dinners and vegetarian dishes, as well as typical Swiss menus. You'll also be tempted by sports and entertainment possibilities. Memorable evenings are offered at the house bar and the Funny Place dancing area, the most modern nightspot in Klosters. Guests can relax and stay (or get) in shape by taking advantage of the fitness center facilities, such as a swimming pool, whirlpool, sauna, solarium, gym room, massage, and cosmetic treatments, as well as eucalyptus, Kneipp, and Turkish baths.

Chesa Grischuna, CH-7250 Klosters, Switzerland (tel. 083/4-22-22), was rebuilt in 1938 on the foundation of a much older building. With a carefully decorated façade, it has hosted some of the most illustrious personalities of Europe. In summer, the Guler family turns the exterior of the hotel into a riot of color by hanging flowerboxes from practically every horizontal surface. Much of the hotel's fame is a result of the chic generated night after night in its restaurant (see "Where to Dine"), although its 27 cozy bedrooms are certainly worth special mention. Each is carefully sheathed with pine planking and contains a private bath and all the accessories you'd expect from a four-star hotel. Depending on the season and the plumbing, singles range from 100F ($68) to 225F ($153) daily and doubles from 190F ($129.20) to 400F ($272), with half board included. The overflow from the main house is lodged at a comfortable annex nearby. The hotel is closed every year from mid-April to early June.

Hotel Pardenn, CH-7250 Klosters, Switzerland (tel. 083/4-11-41), is a rambling modern structure with a flat roof, lots of wood trim, and a low-lying extension containing a tile indoor swimming pool, which has been used by Princess Diana and her children. A popular sun terrace overlooks the well-landscaped lawn, and in summer vivid flowerbeds bloom between the flagstone walks. Guests reach their comfortable rooms via the green-marble circular staircase. Many of the 75 accommodations are accented with pine paneling, while others contain flowery carpets and Louis XV–style armchairs. In the low season, singles on half board range from 140F ($95.20) to 200F ($136) daily, while two persons pay from 280F ($190.40) to 400F ($272). In high season, one person on the half-board plan is charged from 170F ($115.60) to 220F ($149.60) daily, and two persons pay from 340F ($231.20) to 440F ($299.20). Prices depend on the time of year and the plumbing. Within the establishment are an elevator, sauna, and massage facilities. My favorite bit of the restaurant is the central grill whose smoke is funneled through an inverted copper funnel, and Deborah Kerr, a frequent visitor, seems to like it, too. You can watch the uniformed chef as he prepares your meal. The Pardenn is closed in May and November.

Hotel Rufinis, CH-7252 Klosters-Dorf, Switzerland (tel. 083/4-13-71).

Near the entrance to the resort, this attractively decorated chalet hotel is owned by Thomas Jost (whose skilled photography has been exhibited throughout the region). The textured plaster walls of the hotel sometimes display examples of the alpine photographs that have attracted lots of publicity for both the artist and the hotel. In addition to a pleasant restaurant (see my dining recommendations), the hotel offers a stone-trimmed terrace flanked by both an outdoor swimming pool and a view of the mountains. It also has a lovely English garden. A balcony terrace is covered with a canvas awning for breakfasts with panoramic views. The bedrooms have big windows and vistas. Units are comfortable and pleasingly furnished. Depending on the season, a bathless single rents for 25F ($17) to 42F ($28.55) daily, a bathless double costing the same rate per person. However, some doubles with complete baths and balconies cost from 78F ($53.05) to 130F ($88.40) daily. Half board is another 20F ($13.60) per person daily.

Hotel Vereina, CH-7250 Klosters, Switzerland (tel. 083/4-11-61), is a favorite hotel in Klosters, thanks partly to the attentive efforts of Eva and Stephan Diethelm, the owners. The crowning feature of the exterior of this buff-color stucco palace is the baroque dome that sits close to the main entrance. Many of the second-floor windows are grandly arched and multi-paned, with at least five stories of well-maintained rooms rising above them. Much of the establishment is sheltered by a mansard roof that extends over either one or two floors, depending on which section you look at. Inside you'll find a glass-walled swimming pool and a series of public rooms. Something always seems to be happening in the pub and the piano bar. The decorator understood the romantic appeal of warmly tinted chintzes and ceiling beams. An elegant restaurant serves good wines and fine food in an intimate ambience of soft lights and aristocratic decor. There is also a popular pizzeria, open from noon to 2 p.m. and 6 to 11 p.m. daily, with a large selection of pizzas and a guitar player on weekends. The entire facility is surrounded by a two-acre park containing fountains, tennis courts, table tennis tables, and a children's playground. There is also a free kindergarten for children of hotel guests, open daily except Saturday and Sunday from 9 a.m. to 4 p.m. The Vereina is close to nearly every sports facility in town and only a few minutes' walk from the railway station. In winter, the charge for half board is 140F ($95.20) to 180F ($122.40) daily in a single, 190F ($129.20) to 360F ($244.80). Off-season, half board costs 110F ($74.80) to 140F ($95.20) daily in a single, 150F ($102) to 270F ($183.60) in a double. The hotel is open from June to September and December to the end of March.

Hotel Walserhof, CH-7250 Klosters, Switzerland (tel. 083/4-42-42), designed like an updated version of a chalet, was built in 1981, in an unlikely position beside the road, about a quarter of a mile north of the center of town. After it opened, it quickly gained a reputation for its charm, finesse, and comfort. Much of its fame rests with its excellent restaurant (see "Where to Dine"), which has attracted a famous clientele since it opened. It would be wrong, however, to overlook its 11 comfortable and stylish rooms and its one apartment. Each is outfitted with the furniture and wall coverings of pine whose grain is so light that it still looks new after a number of years. Many of the rooms have balconies, and all have marble-lined baths. Depending on the season, singles rent for 115F ($78.20) to 145F ($98.60) daily, and two persons are charged 195F ($132.60) to 305F ($207.40), all tariffs including half board.

Bad Serneus Kur- und Sporthotel, CH-7250 Klosters, Switzerland (tel. 083/4-14-44), is a beautifully located house with a solid-looking façade painted in a baroque yellow with black shutters. On the premises is a swimming pool with big glass windows and a covered loggia above one side. The public rooms are attractively beamed, with clean white walls and regional-style stenciling. A fireplace blazes in winter. The bedrooms are filled with pine furniture, including generously sized armoires and warmly tinted fabrics. With half board included, rates range from 78F ($53.05) to 98F ($66.65) daily in a single, from 150F

($102) to 232F ($157.75) in a double, the price depending on the season, the plumbing, and the exposure. Sauna and massage facilities are on the premises. Since the hotel is set behind a meadow filled with flowers, you'll have lots of opportunities for safely chosen nature walks in summer. The nearby mineral springs are popular for their reputed healing properties. The hotel is closed in November.

Hotel Rustico, CH-7250 Klosters, Switzerland (tel. 083/4-12-93), lives up to its name. Across the river, it is a budget oasis run by Marion Theus and Jurg Benkert. Its only drawback is that it's been known to fill up with tour groups from England in midwinter. Fronting a major traffic artery, it has stenciled baroque detailing above its window. Only 15 simply furnished rooms are available in this 120-year-old former private house. With half board included, bathless singles rent for 70F ($47.60) to 90F ($61.20) daily. Doubles come with and without bath, costing from 138F ($93.85) to 180F ($122.40), also including half board. No rooms are rented in May or November. The hotel has a little specialty restaurant, offering regional dishes of the Grisons, and it also has a pool lounge with an open fireplace.

Hotel-Pension Silvapina, CH-7252 Klosters-Dorf, Switzerland (tel. 083/4-14-68), is a pleasant chalet building with reddish shutters only a few color shades different from the weathered wood of the façade. The contrast is attractive, as are many of the other comfortably rustic details about the inside. The hotel is close to the railway station and the Klosters-Madrisa funicular. Tennis courts are a few steps away. The owners, the Gruober family, charge from 57F ($38.75) to 70F ($47.60) per person daily in winter for half board. From June to October, half board costs from 48F ($32.65) to 51F ($34.70) per person daily. The hotel is open from June to October and December to the end of April.

Hotel Pension Büel, CH-7252 Klosters-Dorf, Switzerland (tel. 083/4-26-69), is a family-run, L-shaped building with lots of stucco walls, brown trim, and balconies. The inside is clean and rustic. The dining room has a knotty-pine ceiling and chalet chairs, while one of the sitting rooms has a cozy fireplace rimmed with stone and a flagstone floor. Walter Hongler, your English-speaking host, rents out pleasantly furnished rooms and apartments, the latter suitable for two to four persons. All units have showers or bathrooms, phones, and toilets. With half board included, singles cost 56F ($38.10) to 90F ($61.20) daily, and doubles go for 50F ($34) to 75F ($51) per person. Prices depend on the season. The pension receives guests from June to October and from December to April.

WHERE TO DINE: A choice place to dine in Klosters is **Chesa Grischuna** (tel. 083/4-22-22). Its tables are so intensely sought after that some departing celebrities have booked seats here a year in advance. Some of the luminaries who have graced its portals include Truman Capote, Rex Harrison, Audrey Hepburn, the Aga Khan, Winston Churchill, Deborah Kerr, and Queen Juliana of the Netherlands. Despite its warmly decorated alpine walls, with its scattering of unusual portraits, it may be difficult to understand why the place is almost unreasonably popular. Part of it has to do with the genteel welcome of the Guler family, and certainly, the food is among the best at the resort. Specialties include a crêpe suedoise, stuffed with shrimp, chicken livers in puff pastry on a bed of leeks, a slice of grilled salmon with white butter and tomato sauce, and rack of lamb. À la carte meals cost from 85F ($57.80). Four-course fixed-price meals go for 35F ($23.80) at lunch from noon to 2:30 p.m. and from 50F ($34) at dinner from 7 to 9:30 p.m. The restaurant is open every day, except during the annual closings of the hotel. In summer, service moves to the raised outdoor terrace.

Walserstube, Walserhof Hotel (tel. 083/4-42-42). Béat Bolliger enjoys a reputation in Klosters for his cuisine, entertaining everybody from celebrities to regular folks like us. He offers imaginative daily specials under his menu du marché, using only the freshest of ingredients from the marketplace. These top quality ingredients combine with highly developed cookery skills to form a winning combination. You might begin with something rich and elegant such as a duckling foie gras or else something less fattening (a yogurt mousse with fruits of the season). In season, asparagus is featured and prepared in any number of elegant ways. Lobster appears under soups, this time served with profiteroles. The fish is special here, including salmon with onions, a fricasée of lobster, or trout grilled and served with ratatouille. You can also order excellent meat dishes such as Scottish lamb seasoned with thyme. Try, for example, veal kidneys in a mustard sauce.

Set menus are offered for 59F ($40.12), 82F ($55.75), and 105F ($71.40).In peak season, make reservations as far in advance as possible. Lunch is served from 11 a.m. to 2 p.m. and 6 to 11 p.m. except Monday in shoulder season. You dine beneath massive beams amid alpine carvings, while sitting on banquettes with light coming in through leaded glass windows. The ticking clocks are a perfect foil for the "on time" service.

Hotel Rufinis, at Klosters-Dorf (tel. 083/4-13-71), has a rustic restaurant in a modern chalet near the train station. Inside is a large salad buffet, French cookery, and a grill area that prepares well-presented regional specialties. A garden terrace might be your choice if you're here on a summer day, since the establishment is also billed as a tea room with excellent ice creams and pastries. The restaurant, in three different rooms, is charmingly handcrafted, with waitresses in regional costume. There's enough exposed wood and stone to make you feel safe and cozy. You might begin with a salmon terrine, a good-tasting soup, or some other hors d'oeuvres. Main dishes are likely to feature calves' liver in red wine sauce, veal saltimbocca, tournedos with tarragon sauce, trout with mushrooms and cognac, and the inevitable fondue. À la carte meals range from 45F ($30.60). Hours are daily from 11 a.m. to 2 p.m. and 6 to 10 p.m. It is closed Monday in summer.

Alte Post, Klosters-Aeuja (tel. 083/4-17-16), in a hamlet outside town, is a roadside chalet, where John M. Ehrat-Flury, a master chef de cuisine, "pampers the palate" with specialties of the Grisons. His secret lies, in part, in the use of fresh ingredients. At the right season, this chef prepares superb game dishes, and fish dishes are also outstanding. Guests dine in the restaurant or the intimate grill room in which meats are grilled over an open fire. It's a fun, informal place, and has long been a celebrity favorite. Guests enjoy such fare as smoked trout with juniper, suprême of salmon with pink peppercorns, and fresh mushrooms resting in a nest of homemade noodles. A menu dégustation costs 75F ($51), or else you can order à la carte from 50F ($34). Hours are from 11:30 a.m. to 2:30 p.m. and from 6 to 10 p.m. It is closed Monday and Tuesday.

Hotel Wynegg Restaurant (tel. 083/4-13-40) is in a small hotel, only 15 rooms, but it has a good reputation for its kitchen. That's because of the hard work of Ruth Guler, the niece of the owner of the Chesa Grischuna. Dating from 1878, this hotel came into prominence when Prince Charles arrived with four bodyguards, preferring the modest place for a discreet afternoon of drinking in the corner with one of his cousins. He was finally rescued at the saloon by his princess, who, according to the staff, had smiles for everybody. In this plain alpine stübl, you order simple but well-prepared meals, costing from 30F ($20.40). These include air-dried beef of the Grisons, hearty soups, entrecôtes, and veal steak with Rösti. Lunch is served daily from noon to 2 p.m. and from 6 to 10 p.m. If you want a room here, know they are strictly no-frills, but the price of half board is good on the wallet: from 60F ($40.80) to 90F ($61.20) per person daily. At the cheaper rate, you get no private bath. The place is closed in summer.

SPORTS: Some of the finest downhill skiing in the world is here, with slopes for beginners as well as for the most advanced skiers. A kindergarten will look after the very young while you hit the slopes. The main part of the village is called Klosters Platz, the area around the rail station; the smaller, Dorf, site of a superb ski school, is about a mile away (it's the northern end of the village).

Of the two principal areas for skiing, the most popular is the **Gotschna-Parsenn.** You board the Gotschnagrat cableway in Klosters Platz, riding in a car that will carry more than 50 skiers up to the 7,545-foot Gotschnagrat elevation. In the peak season, especially around February, expect lines of passengers awaiting transport up. A series of cableways, a chair lift, and 18 ski lifts hook up with the Davos-Parsenn skiing areas, where your highest point will be Weissfluhgipfel (9,260 feet). The Parsenn area enjoys world renown among skiers and has some of the longest runs in Europe. It offers a variety of more than 14 different cableways and ski lifts, plus more than 85 miles of well-kept runs.

The other major area, **Madrisa,** dates from the 1960s. To reach it, you go to Dorf via bus, which leaves from Klosters Platz every 30 minutes. From Dorf, the Klosters-Albeina gondola will take you to a height of 6,323 feet. Then by drag lift, known as the Schaffüggli, you rise to 7,850 feet.

Nontransferable Rega (season) tickets are priced according to the number of days you plan to ski. Horse sleighing, curling, and skating are popular sports for those who don't ski.

In summer, Klosters is in the center of fine hiking grounds. The Madrisa and Gotschna-Parsenn cable cars will carry you to starting points on both sides of the valley for hikes on well-marked trails through woods and alpine meadows. In Klosters you can enjoy tennis, squash, and swimming in a heated pool.

APRÈS SKI: It's quite customary for many guests of the hotels in Klosters to head to nearby Davos for nightlife. Others prefer the more subdued nighttime fun in Klosters itself. Klosters has a good sampling of bars, taverns, restaurants, and a few nightclubs that stir to life when the season comes and snowflakes fill the air.

One of the resort's most popular bars is called **Black Bird Bar** and is at the Hotel Vereina (tel. 083/4-13-23). It is managed by Armin Kaufmann, a local artist who also displays some of his works here. It's not a real dancing place, but that activity has been known to take place if the spirits are high. Drinks start at 7F ($4.75), and hours are daily except Sunday from 9 p.m. to 2 a.m. If you want a snack, there's an adjoining pizzeria.

Hotel Chesa Grischuna (tel. 083/2-22-22) has the popular Chesa Bar. The fact that the nightspot is immediately below one of the most chic restaurants in all of Switzerland doesn't prevent it from being a lot of fun. Under vaulted ceilings, amid walls stenciled with Engadine designs, there's a warm, cozy drinking enclave where a pianist contributes to the ambience nightly from 5 to 7 and again from 9 p.m. to whenever the bar closes. Entrance is free, and long drinks cost 12F ($8.15) to 15F ($10.20). The bar has an entrance leading directly from the sidewalk.

One of the town's most attractive and most electronically sophisticated nightspots is at the **Piz Buin Hotel** (tel. 083/4-81-11), called the Funny Place. Drinks cost from 14F ($9.50), and you should go after 10 p.m. The club is closed in November.

4. DAVOS

Davos, a premier Swiss resort along with St. Moritz and Zermatt, has some of the finest sports facilities in the world, as well as a diversified choice of après-ski life and entertainment, which make it a favorite holiday spot for the chic, the wealthy, and the famous. However, it also attracts a goodly assortment of ordinary folk out to have a good time in the mountains in both summer and winter.

Its two sections, **Davos-Dorf** (5,128 feet) and **Davos-Platz** (5,118 feet), are linked by a boulevard flanked by fashionable boutiques, shops, hotels, and cafés.

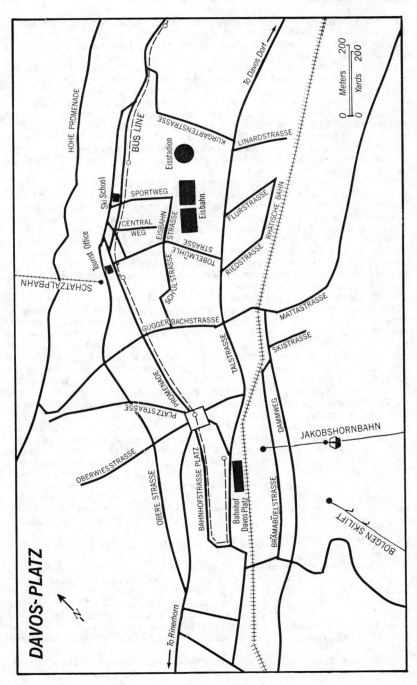

DAVOS-PLATZ

This main thoroughfare is the famous Promenade, which takes the one-way traffic flow from Dorf to Platz (however, if you're driving, beware, as buses go along this artery in both directions). The lower artery, the Talstrasse, runs along the railway tracks, linking the railway station in Platz to the one in Dorf.

The two sections, Dorf and Platz, were once separate entities, but in the last two decades or so buildings on the land between have obliterated any difference, making Davos today a small city somewhat larger than St. Moritz.

The canton of Davos, a high valley, is the second largest in Switzerland. It's surrounded by forest-covered mountains that shelter it from rough winds, giving it the bracing climate that led to its becoming a celebrated summer and winter resort. Davos first entered the world limelight as a health resort when Dr. Alexander Spengler prescribed mountain air for his tuberculosis patients. He brought the first summer visitors here in 1860 and the first winter ones in 1865. There are still several sanatoriums in the general area.

Thomas Mann used Davos, lying at the foot of the Zauberberg, as the setting for his book, *The Magic Mountain.* The German author saw it as a place where consumptives went to die, so used the resort as a background and symbol of the sickness of Europe as it approached the dawn of the first World War. Robert Louis Stevenson was another visitor. He wrote the last seven chapters of *Treasure Island* there between 1881 and 1882. Stevenson was in Davos hoping for a cure for his consumptive wife. Another writer, Sir Arthur Conan Doyle he engaged in a daring run on skis over the Furka Pass to Arosa. Unfortunately, the much celebrated villa where all three writers stayed, Am Stein, no longer takes in paying guests but contains private apartments.

The name Davos (first Tavauns, later Dafaas) entered written history in 1160 in a document in the episcopal archives of Chur, and in 1289 a group of families from the Valais established homes here. In 1649 Davos bought its freedom from Austria. Among the old buildings to be seen in Davos-Platz are the parish **Church of St. John the Baptist,** with a nave dating from 1280–1285 and the remainder, now restored, completed in 1481. A window in the choir is by Augusto Giacometti. The adjoining **Rathaus** (town hall) has been restored. Its paneled Great Chamber (Grosse Stube) dates from 1564. In Davos-Dorf, you can see the 14th-century **Church of St. Theodulus,** and at 1 Museumstrasse is the **Old Prebend House** (Altes Pfrundhaus), the only surviving example of an old burgher's house, now sheltering a local museum.

You don't come to Davos to visit museums, but there is an interesting one on the top floor of the post office, the **Kirchner Museum,** 43 Promenade (tel. 083/6-64-84), devoted to Ernst Ludwig Kirchner, who lived for a while in this part of Switzerland. This leader of the "Bridge" group of expressionists who gathered in Dresden in 1905 committed suicide in 1938. Entrance to the museum is 6F ($4.10) for adults, 2F ($1.35) for children. In winter, the museum is open daily except Monday from 2 to 6 p.m. In May, June, September, and October, it is open from 4 to 6 p.m. Wednesday, Saturday, and Sunday. In July and August, it is open from 4 to 6 p.m. Tuesday, Wednesday, Saturday, and Sunday.

PRACTICAL FACTS: Some pertinent information about this resort area may make your stay here more pleasant. **Buses:** Buses run from Davos-Dorf to Davos-Platz every 20 minutes from 7 a.m. to 11:20 p.m. all year. A single ride costs 1.20F (82¢), a book of tickets for 12 rides going for 12F ($8.15). The **postal bus** leaves from Davos-Platz railway station. Check the timetable for when to show up. Organized excursions are available via postal bus also. For information, go to the nearest post office.

Children: Children's public **playgrounds** are found in the Kurpark at Davos-Platz and opposite the lower terminal station of the Parsenn Funicular at Davos-Dorf.

Information: For information about skiing, hotels, other sports, whatever,

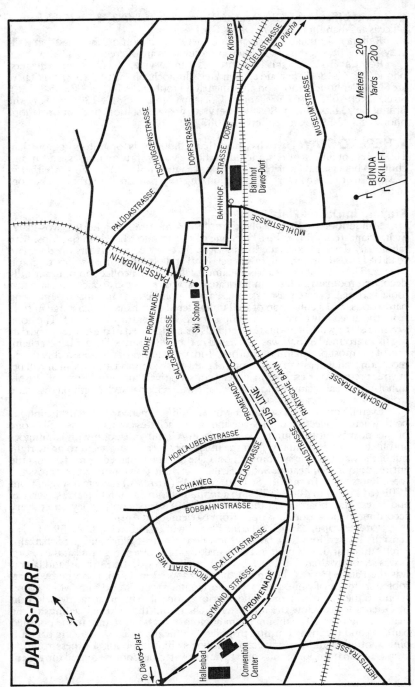

the **tourist office** is at 67 Promenade, Davos-Platz (tel. 083/3-51-35). A branch office is at 7 Bahnhofstrasse in Davos-Dorf.

Railway: To make a reservation or get information on the **Rhaetian Railway,** phone 083/3-50-50. Numerous excursions are offered.

Rescue: To reach the **Parsenn Rescue Service,** 7 Lehenweg, Klosters, phone 083/4-48-48; first-aid station Weissfluhjoch, phone 083/5-38-01. There are SOS telephone stations on all principal ski routes: Pischa (tel. 083/5-17-28), Strela (tel. 083/3-67-57), and Gotschna (tel. 083/4-13-91). For the **Bränabüel/Jakobshorn Rescue Service** first-aid station and information, phone 083/3-59-59; for Rinerhorn, 083/4-92-58.

WHERE TO STAY: Davos has more than 20,000 beds for visitors in more than 100 hotels of all categories, including holiday flats, private houses, and health clinics. My personal favorite in a wide price range follow. You can stay either in Davos-Platz or Davos-Dorf. If you're looking for a bargain, read from the bottom of the list.

Staying in Davos-Platz

Steigenberger Hotel Belvédère, 89 Promenade, CH-4270 Davos-Platz, Switzerland (tel. 083/2-12-81), is one of the grandest hotels in the Alps, with fabulously detailed construction in virtually every corner. It sits on the main road of Davos-Platz, in a light-gray classical-style building that seems to go on forever. The vast lobby area has an almost labyrinthine collection of beautifully decorated rooms. You'll see an intricately carved, pleasingly scaled fireplace that looks baronial, ornate plaster ceilings, a well-polished bar area made of glowing hardwoods, and a collection of well-upholstered armchairs, which range in style from the gracefully curving contemporary to 19th-century Victorian. The hotel was one of the world-famous resort hotels that originated in the last century, dating from around 1875. It was purchased in the 1980s by the Steigenberger chain, one of the most prestigious in Europe. Today a member of the impeccably suited reception staff will assign you to one of the 146 accommodations, which will be, at your preference, designed in either a conservatively modern format of plushly upholstered mahogany, belle-époque, or Swiss regional style, with pieces made from a local wood called *arvenholz.*

Even if you're not a swimmer, you should promenade down to the indoor pool, where a collection of massage and sauna facilities awaits you, as well as one of the most beautiful murals I've ever seen. A Tahitian lagoon with flamingoes and lifelike jungle plants sway in the imaginary breeze, and seem to grow right out of the waters of the swimming pool. The illusion is helped by the fact that the entire room is well heated. Sports facilities include clay tennis courts across the road. Rates range from 90F ($61.20) to 210F ($142.80) daily in a single, from 170F ($115.60) to 400F ($272) in a twin, including a buffet breakfast, service, and taxes. Half board is another 40F ($27.20) per person per day. Prices vary according to the season. It is open from November to April.

Hotel Europe, CH-7270 Davos-Platz, Switzerland (tel. 083/3-59-21), is a centrally located longtime favorite close to the tourist office and the Schatzalp-Strela funicular. It was built in 1868, making it the oldest big hotel at the resort. It was seriously altered in 1914, becoming a health spa, and later it was the Palace Hotel. The present name, adopted in 1956, is borne by a flat-roofed structure of white stucco with horizontal rows of wood trim, which correspond to the rustic balconies. The interior is formal, with an attractive selection of Oriental rugs below the upholstered chairs and the textured ceilings of the main sitting room. The dining room has lots of character thanks to the polished paneling and the many hunting trophies. On the premises is a dancing bar with pink spotlights and live music, an indoor swimming pool, a fitness room, a sauna, and an outdoor tennis court. The renovated bedrooms are well furnished.

All of them contain private baths and cost 100F ($68) to 210F ($142.80) daily in a single, 180F ($122.40) to 400F ($272) in a double, including half board. Prices depend on the season and the accommodation you're assigned. This is one of the few big hotels that is open all year.

Morosani Posthotel, 42 Promenade, CH-7270 Davos-Platz, Switzerland (tel. 083/2-11-61), stands at the gateway to the Promenade in Platz. For more than a century this landmark Davos property has been efficiently run by a family of Swiss hoteliers, the Morosanis. They have a series of three buildings connected with a rustic underground tunnel. They specialize in traditional hospitality, Grisons style. The hotel complex offers 160 beds in 90 comfortably furnished single and double rooms, as well as a few apartments. Units are equipped with their own private baths, toilets, radios, color TV, direct-dial phones, and mini-bars (and in some cases, a private balcony). Half-board rates are higher in winter, costing from 170F ($115.60) to 220F ($149.60) daily in a single and from 316F ($214.90) to 410F ($278.80) in a double. Off-season discounts can range from 88F ($59.84) to 185F ($124.80) daily in a single and 172F ($116.75) to 358F ($243.45) in a double, also including half board. From Christmas to New Year's, the hotel requires a stay of 12 nights. There is an indoor swimming pool, plus a children's playground, a sauna, and a specialty restaurant with a bar and resident orchestra. The lobby has an open fireplace, just right for a cozy evening when the snowflakes are flying outside. Closed May and November.

Central Sporthotel, CH-7270 Davos-Platz, Switzerland (tel. 083/3-65-22), is a rambling 19th-century hotel built in what looks like many different sections and several different styles, all painted white and gray, and all connected by a ground-floor row of widely arched windows. Many of the accommodations have wooden balconies, as well as big sunny windows and lots of space. Some of them are filled with cabriole-legged armchairs and settees, and all have TV and mini-bars. With half board included, singles rent for 90F ($61.20) to 210F ($142.80) daily, and doubles range from 180F ($122.40) to 390F ($265.20), depending on the season and the room assignment. Higher prices are charged in winter. On the premises is a wood-ceilinged room with a well-lit swimming pool, a sauna, an elegant series of public rooms with occasional live music in the piano bar, and one of the liveliest discos in town. This is in a darkish wood-covered room where many of the vertical timbers are carved into regional designs. Guests dine in the wood-paneled Bündnerstübli or in the regional restaurant.

Sunstar Park Hotel, CH-7270 Davos-Platz, Switzerland (tel. 083/2-12-41), is a modern, flat-roofed building with brown-and-white detailing and lots of individual balconies. The structure is set in the middle of a cluster of conifers, which pleasantly break some of the angular lines of the exterior. My favorite room is the bar area, which has a complicated series of overhead beams and timbers bolted into a circular pattern. There is also a rustic restaurant, plus a squash court, a sauna, a swimming pool, a solarium, a beauty parlor, a children's playroom, a dancing bar, and a pool room with video games. Each of the modern well-equipped bedrooms has a private bath. Singles rent for 80F ($54.40) to 200F ($136) daily and doubles for 140F ($95.20) to 170F ($115.60), all with half board included. Rates depend on the season. The hotel is open June to October and December to April.

Sunstar Hotel, CH-7270 Davos-Platz, Switzerland (tel. 083/2-12-41), is under the same ownership as the Sunstar Park (see above). The format is much the same, both inside and out, as its bigger sister, only it has fewer sports facilities. Rooms here are cheaper, however. Doubles range from 110F ($74.80) to 280F ($190.40) daily, with half board included. Singles are not offered except in peak seasons. Open June to October and December to April.

Kongress Hotel Davos, 94 Promenade, CH-7270 Davos-Platz, Switzerland (tel. 083/6-11-81), is a first-class hotel that made its première in 1982. Its bedrooms are fashioned of blond wood and a collection of fabrics whose colors blend with it beautifully. You'll be just a little bit removed from the center of the village, but many of its enthusiastic clients seem to prefer that, especially since the view from the public rooms includes a wide swathe of summer greenery just outside the windows. This hotel is inside the Convention Center of Davos, in the same building as the indoor swimming pool complex. Virtually all the sports facilities of Davos are close by. In addition, a public bus stops in front of the hotel for frequent rides to the ski runs. Each of the comfortably furnished bedrooms has a private bath, radio, phone, and mini-bar. A sauna is available, as well as a garage and a car park. Singles range from 83F ($56.45) to 165F ($112.20) daily, while doubles cost 150F ($102) to 310F ($210.80), with half board included. Rates depend on the season. The Frey family, the attentive managers, do everything they can to be of help. The hotel is open from June to October and December to April.

Hotel Davoserhof, CH-7270 Davos-Platz, Switzerland (tel. 083/3-68-17), is in the center of Davos-Platz, a short distance off the main road. It's a symmetrical 24-room hotel with Grisons designs on its façade, plus four floors of weatherproof windows and stone detailing on the exposed corners. The rendezvous points on the inside (that is, the dancing bar, the two restaurants, and the sun terrace) are all attractively decorated in rustically finished paneling, with lots of atmosphere and even a few antiques. My favorite bedrooms are the ones with glowing wood on the ceiling and all sides. Paul Petzold and his family, the owners, charge from 75F ($51) to 130F ($88.40) daily in singles, the least expensive of which are bathless, and 160F ($108.80) to 240F ($163.20) in doubles, all with baths. Half board is included in the rates. Prices depend on the season. Closed in May.

Hotel Ochsen, CH-7270 Davos-Platz, Switzerland (tel. 083/3-52-22), is housed in a dark salmon-colored building with recessed loggias that in summer burst into bloom with flowers. It's only a few minutes on foot from the railway station. The lobby area is tasteful, uncluttered, and filled with leather and wood tones brightened by the colors of an Oriental rug that sits on top of the wall-to-wall carpeting. The restaurant is covered with knotty pine and filled with chalet chairs. The bedrooms contain colorful draperies and upholstery, along with white walls. It's an attractive hotel whose charges run from 77F ($52.36) to 130F ($88.40) daily in a single and from 134F ($91.10) to 240F ($163.20) in a double, with half board. The rates depend on the season and the plumbing.

Zur Alte Post, CH-7272 Davos-Platz, Switzerland (tel. 083/3-54-03), is a good bargain. You'll quickly notice that someone worked hard to carve intricate designs into each of the overhead beams in the paneled dining room, which otherwise is filled with rustic chalet chairs. There are only 30 beds in the hotel, all of them with private shower although some don't have toilets. Depending on the season, doubles rent for 88F ($59.85) to 160F ($108.80) daily and singles for 50F ($34) to 80F ($54.40), with half board included. Your hosts are the Camenzind-Flühmann family, and meals are served in their restaurant, Tavaaser Schtuba. The food is good, hearty country fare, including filet goulash Stroganoff, pork cutlets, and piccata with saffron rice. The hotel is open from July to November and December to April.

Staying in Davos-Dorf

Flüela Hotel, CH-7260 Davos-Dorf, Switzerland (tel. 083/6-12-21). More than 110 years after its opening, this comfortable hotel is still in the hands of the Gredig family. The current owners are Andreas and Ruth Gredig, who oversee the maintenance of the establishment with style. Next to the train station, the hotel is a tall beige structure. In recent years many rooms have been redone and changed into either junior suites or ordinary suites. The bedrooms are attractively styled and well maintained, and guests are accepted only from November to April. Depending on the time of winter, the single half-board rate ranges from

145F ($98.60) to 255F ($173.40) daily, doubles on the same arrangement paying 290F ($197.20) to 490F ($333.20). These tariffs also include free use of the pool, sauna, and Turkish bath. This is a five-star hotel, and its drinking and dining facilities often lure many nonresidents. In the Stübli, raclettes and fondues are served until 5 p.m. After that, guests are treated to a Swiss and French cuisine, with several nouvelle variations. A restaurant, Flüela Post, is open both to guests and drop-ins, and has a large choice on its à la carte menu. The hotel also maintains a salon de coiffure for both women and men, as well as a riding school with a riding hall.

Derby Hotel, CH-7260 Davos-Dorf, Switzerland (tel. 083/6-11-66), near the Parsenn funicular, is comfortable and stylish, and has kept up-to-date since it was constructed in the closing year of the 19th century. For three generations it has been in the hands of the Walsoe family. Alexander Walsoe is currently in charge. A well-equipped hotel, it has wood-trimmed balconies facing south over eight curling rinks. You'll know you're in an elegant hotel as soon as you cross through the grandly arched wrought-iron front door. Construction details include the usual woodworking polished to a glossy luster, as well as a series of attractive antiques, such as the lyre-backed Empire chairs in one of the sitting rooms. A pianist is on duty in winter in one of the public rooms. A restaurant is intimately lit and gemütlich, and the rustic, high-ceilinged bar area often has dancing. Bedrooms are modern and balconied, often with separate sleeping alcoves apart from the main area of the accommodation (curtained off). Facilities include two restaurants, a fitness room, a sauna, an indoor swimming pool, massage facilities, a children's playroom, curling, and summer tennis on three courts. The sun terrace is set under the arcades of the second floor. The Palüda Grill is an elegant rendezvous point in winter with evening dancing.

Guests are accepted from June to October and from December to April. Peak rates are charged in winter when half board ranges from 115F ($78.20) to 195F ($132.60) daily in a single and from 230F ($156.40) to 390F ($265.20) in a double. At other times of the year, half board prices are lowered: 70F ($47.60) to 160F ($108.80) daily in a single, 170F ($115.60) to 320F ($217.60) in a double. Rates depend on the quality of the room, the most superior having private baths, mini-bars, and balconies with southern exposure.

Parsenn Sporthotel, CH-7260 Davos-Dorf, Switzerland (tel. 083/5-32-32). From the front, this is a large and substantial Engadine chalet, covered with intricate stencils. Built around the turn of the century, it sits beside a large parking lot, amid a cluster of gas stations, in Davos-Dorf, not far from the base of several ski lifts. The ceilings of the public rooms are invariably beamed or vaulted, sheltering a simplified mountain-rustic decor with few frills. The bedrooms contain solid furniture and private baths. The Parsenn accepts half-board guests for 103F ($70.05) to 130F ($88.40) daily in a single, and for 190F ($129.20) to 244F ($165.90) in a double. The hotel's most attractive aspects lie in the lobby-level stübli, where so many skiers come in on snowy days. They recongregate after the formal dinner hour, lasting from 6 to 9 p.m., to fill the pine-sheathed nooks, crannies, and cubbyholes that make this warmly decorated restaurant and beerhall so popular. Lunch is served from noon to 2 p.m. The restaurant remains open throughout the afternoon for a limited menu and drinks. Closing time is around 11 p.m. The hotel is open December to April only.

Hotel Meierhof, CH-7260 Davos-Dorf, Switzerland (tel. 083/6-12-85). The covered balconies of this family-run hotel overwhelm the 19th-century roof peeking out from above them. Much of the outside is covered with greenery, overlooking a pleasant sun terrace set into the grassy lawns. The interior has been renovated and luxuriously decorated in local style, featuring much wood paneling, warm colors, and the occasional antique. A more modern wing boasts an indoor swimming pool with a complete range of fitness facilities, as well as an underground car park. All 70 large rooms and suites are equipped with baths or showers, direct-dial phones, color TV, and mini-bars. In summer, singles rent for 100F ($68) to 120F ($81.60) daily, and doubles go for 180F ($122.40) to 220F ($149.60). In winter, singles cost 140F ($95.20) to 215F ($146.20) daily, and doubles rent for 260F ($176.80) to 400F ($272). All these tariffs include half board. The hotel is open from June to September and December to April.

Montana Sporthotel, CH-7260 Davos-Dorf, Switzerland (tel. 083/5-34-44), an Edwardian-era hotel, lies in a sunny position near the Parsennbahn. Its façade is traditional, with big-arched windows and a gabled roof. The inside has massive beams supporting the roof of one of the taverns, and an elegant lobby area with marble columns and a plaster ceiling embellished with curved ornamentation. The sun terrace attracts a winter crowd, as the hotel is open only from December through April. The bedrooms usually have lots of exposed wood, plus big sunny windows spilling light onto the wall-to-wall carpeting. The cheapest way to stay here is to ask for one of the bathless rooms, but there are only four in this category in the 80-bed hotel. Chances are you'll get a room with bath. If so, tariffs are 85F ($57.80) to 150F ($102) per person daily, including half board. The dining room has one of the most beautiful ceilings in Davos. Some guests have been coming here for 50 years, ever since the owners, the Hüsler family, took over.

Hôtel des Alpes, CH-7260 Davos-Dorf, Switzerland (tel. 083/6-12-61), is a modern, four-story building with a flat roof, a slightly recessed ground floor, and sunny windows, which usually open onto small balconies. The bedrooms are clean and cozily up-to-date. Inside are three restaurants—Italian, Swiss regional, and a raclette stube—along with two bowling alleys. Each of the 50 comfortable bedrooms has a private bath, radio, TV, and mini-bar. On the half-board plan, singles range from 85F ($57.80) to 175F ($119) daily, while doubles cost 150F ($102) to 270F ($183.60). Prices depend on the season. Guests are received year round.

Hotel Dischma, 128 Promenade, CH-7260 Davos-Dorf, Switzerland (tel. 083/5-33-23), is a modern, rustic hotel in the middle of Davos-Dorf, open year-round. The restructured, renovated rooms all have radios, direct-dial phones, and mini-bars. For half board, they rent for 78F ($53.05) to 115F ($78.20) daily in a single, 146F ($99.30) to 200F ($136) in a double, the price depending on the season and the position of the room. The hotel has two good restaurants, and there's dancing in the cellar until 3 a.m., with live bands providing all kinds of music.

Sporthotel Bellavista, CH-7260 Davos-Dorf, Switzerland (tel. 083/5-42-52), is a flat-roofed, five-story, balconied building with wood detailing and an arched entry. There's a comfortable collection of public rooms. In winter, a fire usually burns in the sitting room and bar area, which is outfitted with Windsor chairs, Oriental rugs, and a simple but cozy collection of furnishings. With half board included, singles rent for 75F ($51) to 170F ($115.60) daily, while doubles cost 120F ($81.60) to 270F ($183.60), depending on the season and the plumbing. Open June to September and December to April.

Hotel Meisser, CH-7270 Davos-Dorf, Switzerland (tel. 083/5-23-33), is a sunny hotel with a brown-and-white façade accented by stone detailing around the front door and regional designs painted onto the panels between the windows. Some of the accommodations have a private balcony. The dining room is appropriately paneled, with a scattering of regional antiques, and the hotel has a biological sauna and solarium. Ralf and Kathrin Meisser are the busy owners. The highest rates are charged in winter: from 90F ($61.20) to 100F ($68) daily in a single, from 184F ($125.10) to 204F ($138.70) for two persons, including half board. Half-board terms are reduced otherwise to 59F ($53.70) to 94F ($63.90) daily in a single and from 178F ($120.05) to 190F ($129.20) in a double. Guests are received from June to September and December to May. The hotel is only a few steps from the funicular of the famous ski mountain, Parsenn.

Hotel Anna Maria, CH-7260 Davos-Dorf, Switzerland (tel. 083/5-35-55), is a family-run boardinghouse off the main road of town. You'll go up a gently winding road until you see this tall, well-kept building with a southern exposure turned toward the mountains, affording excellent views from the redwood balconies. The Buchmann family owns this hotel. Singles range from 49F ($33.30) to 68F ($46.25) daily, and doubles cost 95F ($64.60) to 146F ($99.30), with half board included. In summer, guests can use the heated outdoor swimming pool. The hotel is open from June to September and December to May.

Gasthaus Brauerei, CH-7260 Davos-Dorf, Switzerland (tel. 083/5-14-88). Many local youth groups use this hotel's 60-bed dormitory during their sports outings, yet the chances are that you can rent one of the 20 comfortable beds placed in private accommodations with private baths. On the half-board arrangement, singles rent for 50F ($34) to 80F ($54.40) daily, while doubles cost 94F ($63.90) to 150F ($102). The hotel is a simple white structure with a flowery balcony and a parasol-covered sun terrace. Breakfast is included, and there's a pleasant restaurant on the premises. It receives year round.

Staying in Davos-Schatzalp

Berghotel Schatzalp, CH-9720 Davos-Platz, Switzerland (tel. 083/3-58-31), is the ideal choice for those who want to get away from it all. The only public access is by the Schatzalp funicular, whose departure point is in the middle of Davos-Platz. The staff of the funicular takes care of your luggage, and you will find it again in your room. The last car usually leaves at 11 p.m. in summer, 2 a.m. in winter. Aside from the unusual access to it, you'll know you're in a special hotel as soon as you see the front entrance. It's an arched wrought-iron door with Grisons gray-and-white foliage painted on the plaster around it. This is an extravaganza of a hotel, made all the more opulent by its inaccessibility. It has long colonnades where guests can sunbathe even in winter. Built in 1900 as a sanatorium, the hotel is said to receive four more hours of sunshine a day than Davos center. The sunny and well-decorated public rooms never seem to end. The belle-époque dining room has alpine scenes painted among the white paneling. The terrace-restaurant is called Snow Beach. The hotel has a heated, ten-foot-deep swimming pool, massage, sauna, and therapy facilities, a well-staffed kindergarten, and a vast wine cellar.

Many of the bedrooms have exquisitely carved Swiss beds. The charge in summer is from 48F ($32.64) to 102F ($69.25) per person daily, rising in winter to 90F ($61.20) to 250F ($170) per person daily. A reservation is necessary in the high winter season. It's not uncommon for adventurous guests to go to Davos on a toboggan. There's a run just outside the hotel. You also have direct access to the Strela cable cars 165 feet away, taking you to the Strela ski resort in ten minutes or to the Parsenn district in 20 minutes. Guests are received from July to October and December to April.

Staying at Davos-Laret

Built a century ago as a relay station for horses and their riders, **Hubli's Landhaus,** Kantonsstrasse, CH-7265 Davos-Laret, Switzerland (tel. 083/5-21-21), is one of the best overnight choices in the region. Much of the energy of its dynamic owners is focused on their excellent restaurant (see "Where to Dine"). This helps to create a feeling of a country inn with superb gastronomy and a handful of cozy bedrooms. These are connected to the sprawling white-walled restaurant by an underground tunnel lined with amusing pen and ink drawings. Most rooms contain private baths, views of a meadow, and a comfortably conservative collection of earth-tone fabrics and furniture. Highest tariffs are charged in winter when half-board rates in a single go from 72F ($48.95) to 120F ($81.60) daily, with doubles costing 144F ($97.90) to 240F ($163.20). The lowest-priced accommodations don't have private baths. Half-board rates off-season go from 58F ($39.45) to 105F ($71.40) daily in a single, 116F ($78.90) to 210F ($142.80) in a double. In the height of midwinter, the hotel provides free transportation to the ski lifts of Davos for any of its guests.

WHERE TO DINE: One outlying restaurant well worth the excursion is **Hubli's Landhaus,** Kantonsstrasse (tel. 083/5-21-21), in Laret. Within the solid white walls of what was built a century ago as a relay station for horses, the structure now contains a handful of simple dining rooms that serve superb cuisine. The creative forces behind it all are the hardworking owners, Felix and Anne-Marie Hubli. Lunch is served only in summer, noon to 2 p.m., every day except Thursday. Dinner is served daily in winter, and every day except Thursday in summer, from 6:30 to 11 p.m. A la carte meals cost from 70F ($47.60) per person. Fixed-price meals range from 75F ($51) for a four-course "menu simple" to 130F ($88.40) for a hedonistic "menu surprise."

Specialties change with the seasons and with the availability of the ingredients. Representative fare includes a salad of quail with fresh asparagus, fresh morels with noodles and sweetbreads, fricassée of lobster with asparagus, roast duckling with blackberries, and a parfait of Peruvian mangoes. The berries and the mushrooms used in many of Mr. Hubli's dishes are picked in the nearby woods, often the day they're consumed, and much of the lamb he serves is raised on the outskirts of Davos. Sorbets are made fresh every evening, and include such exotics as gooseberry, melon, lime, and rhubarb. The restaurant is closed April 15 to June 15 and October 15 to December 10. Reservations are important.

Davoserstübl, Hotel Davoserhof, Davos-Platz (tel. 083/3-68-17). Paul Petzold offers some of the finest dining in Davos. His is very much a cuisine moderne, cuisine du marché, based on using only the freshest ingredients available in any season. The fixed-priced menus are memorable, none more so than a menu du marché at 95F ($64.60). You can dine, for example, on lobster bisque, filet trout, a maigret of duckling with raspberry vinegar, and filet of beef with shallots, finishing with mangoes in puff pastry. Full à la carte meals cost from 60F ($40.80). A business lunch is offered for just 25F ($17). Hours are daily from noon to 2 p.m. and 6 to 11 p.m. Diners eat beneath a pinewood ceiling, within an intimate, not very large, paneled room laden with alpine charm, flowers.

Restaurant Pöstli, Morosani Posthotel, Davos-Platz (tel. 083/2-11-61), is an elegant room, with live music from 4:30 to 5:30 p.m. and then from 8:30 p.m. till closing. Many guests combine a refined dinner here with a later sojourn to the Pöstli Club (see "After Dark"), whose stairs lie at the far corner of this large restaurant. The restaurant combines a bar with a more formal seating area beneath a beamed ceiling with waist-high dividers of plants. Hot meals are served daily from 11 a.m. to 2 p.m. and 6 p.m. to 1 a.m. Full à la carte meals cost from 60F ($40.80), but could go higher or lower, depending on what you order. The chefs cook with real panache. Tasty platters of food are placed before you, and the choice is extensive. For example, you can order a different fresh fish daily, or you may prefer something classic, such as Tafelspitz (boiled beef in the style of old Vienna). Other selections include veal liver with polenta, venison in a hunter's sauce, filet of U.S. beef with mushrooms, and rack of lamb with braised cabbage. Also platters come in large or small portions, allowing you to tailor-make your meal. Most main dishes are for two persons. The restaurant is open only from late November to April.

Trattoria Toscana, Hotel des Alpes, Davos-Dorf (tel. 083/6-12-61), is the finest northern Italian restaurant at the resort, enjoying a tavern setting with much "south-of-the-border" local color. Clients sit on comfortable chairs or on upholstered banquettes under a ceiling of heavy beams. Dining is on two different levels. Few guests can bypass the temptations of the antipasto misto, although the carpaccio Piedmont style is a lure as well. The pastas are excellent, including tortellini, ravioli, spaghetti, and tagliatelle prepared in many different ways. Fish is also good, and grilled meats are very tasty, usually cooked to your specifications over an open fire. Lamb appears on the menu in the Tuscan style. The place is not cheap, with dinners costing from 60F ($40.80). Lunch is served only in winter from noon to 2 p.m.; however, you can order dinner all year from 6 to 11 p.m. daily.

Bündnerstübli, 8 Dischmastrasse, Davos-Dorf (tel. 083/5-33-93). Very little of the wall and ceiling area of this cozy place is not covered with local scotch pine, polished and mellowed by the presence of hundreds of local diners. The menu reads like a history book of local recipes. The staff might help you translate some of the items, including "Maluns," potatoes served with applesauce and local cheese. Other dishes include a fondue with grated potatoes, a richly flavored barley soup, and a daily farmer's menu with copious amounts of well-prepared food served at a reasonable price. Grilled specialties and a variety of cold platters are also offered. Fixed-price meals cost from 35F ($23.80) to 40F ($27.20), while à la carte dinners range from 50F ($34) to 60F ($40.80). The restaurant shuts down on Monday and in May and June. Otherwise, hours are from 3 to 11 p.m.

Restaurant Gentiana, 53 Promenade, Davos-Platz (tel. 083/3-56-49), the only authentic bistro in Davos, is housed in a gold-colored building beside the jewelry store, Bucherer, opposite the Hotel Schweizerhof. It is known for eight types of fondue (cheese and meat) and is unique in its variety of snails offered. The menu features a wide choice of air-dried beef of the Grisons and local ham. Inexpensive daily specials are posted. Try the local pears in cinnamon syrup and honey ice cream and, by all means, the best chocolate mousse in town. Fondue begins at 16F ($10.90), while à la carte meals range upward from 40F ($27.20). There is a good variety of local wines by the carafe. Don't overlook the pair of bistro-style dining rooms upstairs with a Kirchner blue painting. The restaurant serves lunch daily from 11 a.m. to 2 p.m. and dinner from 5:30 to 9:30 p.m. It is closed every Wednesday in summer.

On the Outskirts

Gasthaus Islen (tel. 083/3-58-56), in the hamlet of Islen, 1¼ miles south of Platz, is a popular summer excursion with visitors on an "outing," and also a rendezvous point in winter with cross-country skiers. Claus Wertmann, the innkeeper, will welcome you to enjoy his cuisine any time from noon to 2 p.m. and from 6 to 9 p.m. daily. You can take the train from Davos, arriving here in a rural setting, enjoying the rustic artifacts such as antique cowbells. A wide deck is available for meals in the sun, providing the sun will cooperate. Meals cost from 40F ($27.20), and the menu is wide ranging and continental, traveling as far as Provence for the inspiration for some dishes. The Cordon Bleu kitchen is also represented. The chef specializes in grills such as filet steak, veal steak, or entrecôte. You might begin with one of the good-tasting, creamy pasta dishes, including tortellini carbonara or else fish soup.

Gasthof Landhaus, Frauenkirche (tel. 083/3-63-35), is an idyllic little rural retreat, lying three miles south of Davos-Platz on the road to Tiefencastel. Now in its third century, the inn has an alpine decor of pinewood ceilings and numerous cubbyholes, with lots of mountain memorabilia such as stag horns, rifles, and wrought iron. Food is served from 11:30 a.m. to 2 p.m. and from 6 to 10 p.m. daily (closed Wednesday in summer). For such a roadside place, the menu is surprisingly elaborate, costing from 30F ($20.40) to 50F ($34) at dinner. However, at lunch you can settle for a platter of spaghetti (invariably a large helping) or else an omelet with a salad for only 14F ($9.50). At night, you may want to sample some of the more elaborate fare.

SPORTS: Skiing for fun was launched here in 1888, but Davos began to appear on the world sports stage in 1899 when a large ice rink was opened for the world figure-skating and the European speed-skating championship competitions. In the same year the Davos-Schatzalp funicular and the Schatzalp toboggan run were inaugurated. Now Davos is considered one of the best ski regions in the world.

On both sides of the valley you're faced with five large ski areas, of which the most noted is the **Parsenn-Weissfluh.** Some experts say this is the finest ski area in Europe. To reach it, you take the Parsennbahn (railway) from Davos-Dorf to Weissfluhjoch (8,740 feet), the gateway to the major ski area, with a huge number of runs in every category, especially a few descents leading back to Davos that are suitable for only the most skilled skiers.

From Weissfluhjoch, where there is a restaurant, take the cableway to Weissfluhgipfel (9,260 feet). It takes about 2½ hours to reach here from Davos-Dorf. From here you can reach the celebrated Kublis run to the north. The inauguration of the Parsenn funicular in 1931 opened up the greatest snow fields in Switzerland.

Davos shares its snow with Klosters, which can be a skiing goal for you if you wish, but cable cars and T-bar lift service may keep you happy with the ski opportunities nearer to Davos. Beginners are advised to stick to Rinerhorn, the Strela slopes, or perhaps Pischa, where, if you're graded "intermediate" by your ski school instructor, you may be directed to Jakobshorn.

A number of winter sports besides skiing are offered here.

For information on curling, call the **Davos Curling Club,** 46 Promenade, Davos-Platz (tel. 083/3-67-30), or the **Davos-Village Curling Club,** Derby Hotel, Davos-Dorf (tel. 083/6-11-66). One hour of curling costs 15F ($10.20) per person or else you can purchase a season ticket for 120F ($81.60).

If you're interested in ice skating on the **Natureisbahn,** Davos-Platz, the largest natural ice rink in Europe, phone 083/3-59-51. Admission costs 3.50F ($2.40) for adults, 2F ($1.35) for children. Davos-Platz also has a huge artificial ice rink open daily from 9:30 a.m. to 4:30 p.m. These hours could change, so call 083/3-73-54 for more information.

Many Davos sports facilities can be used both winter and summer, so Davos isn't only for winter holiday crowds. In summer, it becomes a green lure, with first-class tennis courts, sailing and windsurfing on Lake Davos, swimming, and horseback riding. The wide mountain valleys offer opportunities for walking on about 200 miles of signposted paths. There's an 18-hole golf course, and a large indoor ice rink if you want to keep your skills and your skates sharp during the summer months.

Davos has an impressive **Tennis + Squash Center** at Clavadelerstrasse (tel. 083/3-31-31) in Davos-Platz, which is open from 7 a.m. to 11 p.m. daily. Prices depend on when you play, day or night. The rental of a court costs 32F ($21.75) from 7:30 a.m. to 4:30 p.m. daily, rising to 39F ($26.50) from 4:30 to 9:30 p.m.

You can get golf course information by calling the clubhouse (tel. 083/5-56-43).

Want to go swimming? Call 083/3-64-63 for information on either indoors in winter or summer or outdoors, only in summer, of course. Adults are charged 4.50F ($3.05), and children pay 2F ($1.35), including changing room facilities. With use of the mixed sauna included, adults pay 11F ($7.50).

DAVOS AFTER DARK: This resort rivals St. Moritz for the brightest lights in the Alps, with lots of après-ski fun. Drinks cost from 9F ($6.10) but could go even higher if some special live entertainment has been booked, particularly around New Year's and the Christmas holidays.

Cabanna Club, Hotel Europe (tel. 083/3-59-21), has a disco with video, live bands, and a series of pink spotlights that make everybody look terrific. Dancing begins at 9 p.m., lasting till 3 a.m. Sometimes there are cabaret shows on a revolving schedule, which you can check at the hotel or tourist office. A 12F ($8.15) entrance fee is charged in winter.

Cava Grischa-Kellerbar-Dancing, (tel. 083/3-59-21), also in the Hotel Europe, offers the only folkloric nightclub in Davos, featuring live evergreen music. Chances are that within the hour you'll be swaying to the rhythmic melodies of the flügelhorn and alpine guitar. Order beer at 6F ($4.10) for the evening show, which begins at 9 p.m. nightly, followed by dancing until 3 a.m.

Palüda Grill, in the Derby Hotel in Davos-Dorf (tel. 083/6-11-66), has a dinner-dance every evening in winter, beginning at 7:30. The clientele tends to be a distinguished older crowd. There's a rustic ambience in the Grisons style. The bar area offers raclette, apéritifs, and snails during happy hour from 6 to 7 p.m., with beer on tap. Specialties offered in the restaurant include fondue bourguignonne, flambées, seafood, and T-bone steaks. There's a large open grill. Meals cost from 25F ($17).

Sporthotel Central (tel. 083/2-11-81) offers nightly dancing in a vaulted room with wood paneling and dozens of gaily striped chairs and banquettes. Musical groups include such local artists as the Dominoes, which might evoke some nostalgia. Music begins at 9 nightly. Most of the informally dressed dancers are under 30.

Hotel Dischma (tel. 083/5-33-23) often has live bands performing danceable music. The place attracts mostly younger people in an ambience of darkly timbered rustic walls and an occasional garland of party decorations. The restaurant serves meals for 50F ($34) until 11 p.m.

Montana-Stübli, Hotel Montana (tel. 083/5-34-44), offers a cozy, distinguished ambience to an older crowd who listen to the music from the piano bar and dance beginning at 8 p.m. It's a rustic room, lined with pine. Many cozy corners are here for intimate conversations while you enjoy an excellent dinner. Your hosts are the Hüsler family. The place is open only in winter, and the hours "depend."

Jacobshorn Club, Hotel Davoserhof (tel. 083/3-68-17), is a disco attached to this hotel, and it's indicated with an illuminated sign leading to a side entrance. It attracts a younger crowd of drinkers and dancers, who enjoy the colored spotlights and the logs burning in the massive fireplace. Action lasts from 5 p.m. to 2 a.m. daily. Happy hour is every day from 5 to 8 p.m. Dinner is served until closing. Entrance is free.

Pöstli Club, part of the Morosani Posthotel (tel. 083/2-11-61), opens only in winter. Many aficionados consider it the number one club in Davos. It's decorated in a typical Grisons style and atmosphere, and live bands from all over the world are brought in to entertain. It is open daily from 9 p.m. to 3 a.m. A cover charge of 5F ($3.40) to 8F ($5.45) is assessed on Friday and Saturday nights. Drinks cost from 10F ($6.80).

5. FLIMS AND LAAX

The following resort area, close to Chur, is actually a triumvirate of resorts consisting of not only Flims but also Falera and Laax. Of the three, Flims and Laax are the most developed.

FLIMS: Very much a European family resort not much known to North Americans, Flims (3,450 feet) is the most important holiday resort of the Grisons Oberland. Tourists have been coming to this small Swiss town, about an hour and a half from Zurich's Kloten Airport and 20 minutes from Chur, since the late 19th century, but Flims is considered a modern resort, experiencing a tourism boom during the last 20 or so years. This "sun terrace" of the Grisons lies on a scenic route leading over the Oberalp Pass and has good bus and train connections. Leave the main highway at Reichenau, six miles west of Chur, and you'll find Flims after a seven-mile drive onward.

This resort, with an exposure due south, is in two sections—Flims-Dorf, the original mountain village lying at the foot of the Flimserstein cliffs, mostly residential; and Flims-Waldhaus, a little more than half a mile south in a woodland of conifers, with many hotels. Flims lies on a sunny, protected plateau overlooking the Rhine Valley, the result of a huge landslide. This gargantuan slide blocked the river valley, forcing the Rhine to find another course. The result of this convulsion of nature is some rather bizarre topography, the resulting "debris" of the landslide being scattered over a 16-square-mile area.

The southern exposure of Flims brings mild winter temperatures, and visitors find a wealth of sports activities possible. You can go alpine skiing from 30 different locations with their 134 miles of slopes plus 35 miles of cross-country skiing trails and a special ski run for children. You can take the chair lift to **Foppa** (4,660 feet), with a second stage going to **Alp Naraus** (6,035 feet), and a final swing into heaven taking you by tiny cableway to **Cassons Grat** (8,560 feet). In case you get hungry during the ascent or on your way down, there's a restaurant at each of the three stages.

A second major area is **Startgels** and **Grauberg**. A gondola you board in the southwestern section of Dorf takes you to Startgels (5,200 feet), where there's a restaurant at which you can stoke up before you continue by cableway to Grauberg (7,300 feet).

Other winter frolics include curling, ice skating, tobogganing, horseback riding, horse-drawn sleigh riding, indoor swimming, and 30 miles of hiking trails.

Unlike most parts of Switzerland, you can swim outdoors here from May to September from the bathing beach at Lake Cauma, which is warmed by underground hot springs. You can also go boating on the lake, play tennis, or try the fitness tracks.

Don't expect to find a typical Swiss village if you go to Flims, as most of the buildings are modern.

Food and Lodging

Park Hotels Waldhaus, CH-7018 Flims-Waldhaus, Switzerland (tel. 081/39-01-81), is the finest hotel in Flims, with an elegance and a service worthy of the name "Grand Hotel." It's actually a big complex of at least five buildings, which are joined by covered walkways. The snow gets so deep here that piles on either side create a series of tunnels. In summer the complex is surrounded by lawns and conifers that come almost to the edge of the nine outdoor tennis courts, an outdoor swimming pool, and a separate curling hall. An indoor swimming pool is framed with a curved row of glass windows set into metal struts, giving a futuristic look to the 19th-century buildings near it. Two indoor tennis courts are set under a roof of laminated wood.

Throughout the park you'll find comfortable and elegant lounges, often with old-fashioned fireplaces, fieldstone detailing, and heavy beams and paneling. The restaurant, Pavilion, is one of the finest in town, decorated in a modern format of clustered lights held together in geometric brass chandeliers and lots of plants. A less formal charcoal grill and an Italian trattoria complete the dining facilities, while a live orchestra performs in the Chadafö bar. Bedrooms are a little on the small side in many cases, but are nonetheless immaculate and comfortable. I prefer the high-ceilinged older rooms. Singles range from 170F ($115.60) to 225F ($153) daily, while doubles cost 325F ($221) to 430F ($292.40), with half board included. Prices depend on the season and the accommodation. It's open from June through September and December through April.

Apart-Hotel Des Alpes, CH-7018 Flims-Waldhaus, Switzerland (tel. 081/39-01-01), has a concrete and glass façade with lots of windows that looks like an updated chalet. The garden in front of the indoor swimming pool allows sunbathing and relaxing in pleasant surroundings. The interior has been totally renovated and offers dining and wining in a distinguished way. Each of the well-furnished accommodations has a private bath and balcony. Prices are from 120F ($81.60) to 190F ($129.20) daily in a double, with half board included. Guests are received from June to October and December to April.

Hotel Adula, CH-7018 Flims-Waldhaus, Switzerland (tel. 081/39-01-61), is a modern hotel with lots of sunny balconies fashioned, chalet style, from weathered planking. The interior is filled with mellow paneling, brass candle-sticks, intimate lighting, and stucco vaulting. The popular bar area usually provides a live piano player, and the hotel organizes weekly romantic dinners with regional buffet meals. Peter Hotz, who runs the hotel, offers not only a main restaurant but a specialty à la carte dining room called La Clav. It has an original ceiling painted by the famous artist Alois Carigiet. Typical homemade Italian pastas are offered along with grilled meat and fish dishes, followed by sumptuous desserts. There is also an excellent selection of Italian wines. In summer it's possible to order light meals on the terrace. A glass-walled indoor swimming pool is part of the hotel, as well as three outdoor clay-surface tennis courts. The 121 rooms are reached via two elevators, while a nearby annex holds the hotel's overflow. The Hotz family even organizes the three-times-weekly guided nature walks lasting half or full days. Singles range from 100F ($68) to 180F ($122.40) daily, while doubles cost 180F ($122.40) to 430F ($292.40), with half board included. Prices depend on the season and room assignment. These tariffs assume a minimum stay of three days, and week-long packages can often be arranged in advance. The hotel closes in November.

Schlosshotel, CH-7018 Flims-Waldhaus, Switzerland (tel. 081/39-12-45). The Romanesque-revival façade with the steep gabled roof and the well-proportioned tower could inspire just about everyone from a reader of gothic romances to a ghost-story writer. It really is a marvel of the mason's craft, completely fashioned from rough-textured rocks into a château-like building where you should be very comfortable. The Puksic family maintains this place, where the simply furnished bedrooms look like something from a much more modern house and where the public rooms are attractively paneled and rustic. The overflow from the main building is housed in one of the two adjoining annexes, the villas Gentiana and Auricula. Tariffs depend on the plumbing and the season. On the half-board plan, singles cost from 76F ($51.70) to 105F ($71.40) daily, while two persons pay from 152F ($103.35) to 210F ($142.80). Guests are received from May through October and from December through April.

Hotel National Comfort Inn, CH-7018 Flims-Waldhaus, Switzerland (tel. 081/39-12-24), is a family-run hotel in the center of the resort. The interior is functionally and rustically furnished and has a cozy atmosphere. Besides fish specialties, the restaurant offers raclette twice a week. In winter the Eigenmann family hosts a lunchtime ski barbecue in an alpine hut near the slopes, and the ski lifts can easily be reached by the private hotel bus. Recent renovations have given each of the comfortable bedrooms a private bath. Singles rent for 88F ($59.85) to 93F ($63.24) daily, while doubles range from 165F ($112.20) to 225F ($153), with half board included.

Hotel Miraval, CH-7018 Flims-Waldhaus, Switzerland (tel. 081/39-12-50), run by the Häusel family, offers 22 handsomely furnished accommodations, each with balcony and private shower and toilet, along with a radio and direct-dial phone. The hotel, among the latest to be erected at Flims, is on a little hill in a setting of forests and meadows overlooking the village and the valley beyond. It's constructed directly by the ski slope. Nearby are outdoor tennis courts in summer, or, in winter, ice fields where you can skate and curl. The Miraval also has a comfortable lounge, a dining room, and a small restaurant. The atmosphere is cozy, and the cookery is old-fashioned "home style." Depending on the season, doubles range from 130F ($88.40) to 170F ($115.60) daily and singles from 75F ($51) to 85F ($57.80), each tariff including half board. Closed in November.

All the hotels recommended serve a good cuisine, but if one were to be singled out, it would be the **Restaurant Barga** in the Hotel Adula (tel. 081/39-01-61), a warmly rustic dining room inside the attractive chalet hotel described earlier. A pianist entertains while guests dine in front of an open fire. Its specialties include a delectable selection of appetizers, along with such dishes as rabbit terrine, lobster soup with basil, poached salmon, and many excellent veal dishes. Fixed-price meals range from 50F ($34) to 75F ($51), while à la carte dinners cost from 60F ($40.80). The restaurant is open only from 6 to 10 p.m. daily; closed from mid-October to mid-December. Also on the premises is an Italian specialty restaurant, La Clav.

LAAX: About three miles from Flims, Laax, whose ski area reaches out to take in the hamlets of **Falera** and **Murschetg,** is at the foot of the "White Arena," a vast ski lift and trail network shared by Flims. Murschetg lies nearest to the lifts, and Falera is less than two miles from Laax, the biggest of the three villages. A good ski bus connects the trio of resort hamlets.

Major ski areas include the **Murschetg–Crap Sogn Gion.** From Crap Sogn Gion (7,280 feet), which you reach by cableway from Murschetg, you can go to **Crap Mesegne** (8,120 feet), which is a connecting point with the Vorab glacier.

If you have little experience in skiing, you can take the two-stage gondola from Crap Mesegne to the Vorab glacier restaurant. From the restaurant site, a two-way ski lift goes to the loftiest citadel in the whole section, a height of 9,900 feet.

The Vorab area is a popular ski center in winter and summer. During the 1982 Christmas season, Prince Charles and Princess Diana were taken by helicopter to the glacier when Scotland was short of snow.

Food and Lodging

Rancho Sporthotels, CH-7031 Laax, Switzerland (tel. 086/3-01-31), is a sports and relaxation complex housed in an attractive large building with a shape that looks vaguely like a bird poised for flight. The hotel offers access to practically every sport you could pursue in this region, including hiking, canoeing, horseback riding, swimming, cricket, bowling, cycling, and skiing, but also a few others that you might not have thought of: frisbee, archery, crossbow shooting, cross-country running, gymnastics, and ice-stick throwing. The hotel is divided into eight separate units housed under the same roof, connected by nine elevators. The establishment has 60 doubles and 40 apartment units, some of which contain their own fireplaces. One of the trained sports instructors will videotape your performance on the slopes to help you improve it. Facilities exist for babysitting and for organizing children's activities. Under 6 years old, they get a 50% reduction; from the ages of 7 to 16, a 30% reduction. If you include the sun terrace, the hotel has seven different restaurants, many with their own bar. The public rooms are decorated with monochromatic stencils, Grisons style, and are outfitted with tile floors and a scattering of Oriental rugs. A wide selection of bedrooms is available. With half board included, the cost ranges from 109F ($74.10) to 167F ($113.55) daily in a single, 178F ($121.05) to 294F ($199.90) in a double.

Sporthotel Signina, CH-7031 Laax, Switzerland (tel. 086/39-01-51), is a large, chalet hotel with detailed craftsmanship throughout. Some of the balconies are fashioned of patterned wooden slats, while the interior has beamed and patterned ceilings of well-polished local woods. Two bar areas sometimes offer live entertainment. Sports facilities include seven tennis courts, a bowling alley, a covered swimming pool, and a tavern. The 120 bedrooms are comfortable and well furnished. Singles on half board pay 90F ($61.20) to 133F ($90.45) daily, doubles on half board being charged 164F ($111.50) to 236F ($160.50). Prices depend on the season and the room assignment. Open June to September and November to April.

Crap Sogn Gion, CH-7031 Laax, Switzerland (tel. 086/39-21-92), is a ten-minute cable-car ride from the valley below. The 40 rooms at the top are comfortably modern, often with paneled ceilings. There are plenty of diversions inside this remote place, including a covered swimming pool, a sauna, two restaurants, a cafeteria, two bowling alleys, a news kiosk, and a sun terrace with lounge chairs. From the downhill side the construction looks like one huge solar panel, with a curved metallic-and-glass area directed toward the valley below. Singles range from 62F ($42.15) to 115F ($78.20) daily, doubles costing 79F ($53.70) to 200F ($136) daily, with half board included. Prices depend on the season and the plumbing, as not all rooms contain private baths. The hotel is open from June through October and December through April.

Sporthotel Larisch, CH-7031 Laax, Switzerland (tel. 086/3-47-47), looks like a double chalet connected by a center section with balconies. It lies just outside the center of Laax, and offers a lovely view from its dining room. It has 20 double bedrooms plus five apartments suitable for families. Guests can use the swimming pool at the hotel next door, although there's a sauna on the premises. Bedrooms are simple, colorful, and very clean. They range in price from 54F ($36.70) to 112F ($76.15) daily in a single, 89F ($60.50) to 184F ($125.10) in a double, depending on the season and the plumbing. Not all rooms have private baths. Half board is included in the price. The Kern family are your helpful hosts. The hotel is closed in November.

APRÉS SKI IN THE AREA: The Chadafö dance bar at the previously recommended **Park Hotels Waldhaus** (tel. 081/39-01-81), in Flims, is a major nighttime rendezvous. There is music and dancing every night from 9 in an elegant atmosphere with an orchestra or entertainer.

Hotel Adula (tel. 081/39-01-61), in Flims, is known for its Barga dining room, one of the most popular at the resort. A pianist entertains while guests dine in front of an open fire (see above).

6. SPLÜGEN

This is a mountain village on the route to the Splügen Pass where many noted personages have visited, not so much for its own attractions but because it's on the way to somewhere else. The village lies in the Hinterrhein and controls alpine passes. From here, the highway to the San Bernardino Pass leads to Switzerland's Italian-speaking section, the Ticino. It also leads to the Zapport glacier, the source of the Rhine.

Splügen lies in a wide valley at the foot of the Kalkberg and is both a winter and a summer holiday center. You can take ski lifts to Danatzhöhe (7,080 feet). The little village has many attractive stone homes and a parish church dating from 1690.

For food and lodging, try the **Posthotel Bodenhaus,** CH-7435 Splügen, Switzerland (tel. 081/62-11-21), a large symmetrical building near the village church. It has four floors of black-shuttered windows below a gently sloping Mediterranean-style roof. It was built in 1722, and still retains many of the charming architectural features that were there originally, including flagstone floors, stone-trimmed vaultings, smallish windows, and geometrically paneled ceilings. Famous guests from the past have included Queen Victoria, Napoleon, the kings of Württemberg, and Lady Hamilton. The public rooms have small collections of Empire-style chairs, while the modernized bedrooms contain light-grained pine accents and provincial chalet furniture. There's an elevator, along with a sun terrace, restaurant, and pub. Singles range from 35F ($23.80) to 90F ($61.20) daily, while doubles cost 68F ($46.25) to 150F ($102), with breakfast included. Rates depend on the season and the plumbing. Half board is offered for another 30F ($20.40) per person daily. The hotel closes in November.

7. VALBELLA / LENZERHEIDE

Lying beside Lake Heid (the Heidsee) in a setting of alpine scenery at an altitude of 4,757 feet, these two resorts make a good center for seeing the mountains or taking part in sports. The two attractive villages, about a mile and a quarter apart separated by the lake, are on the major road to the Julier Pass.

Dozens of bus and mountain railway excursions are offered, and you can stop for a fine meal in one of the several mountain restaurants where you can dine on piquant cheese and air-dried Grisons beef. On a two-stage cableway journey up to Rothorn (9,400 feet), I found a good restaurant at the first station at 6,230 feet, and there's another dining room at the top. You can also go to the top of Schwarzhorn by chair lift, where you'll have beautiful views of the Hörnli Valley. A good lift system allows exploration of the western part of the resort area. The Tgantieni drag lift goes to 5,675 feet (there are dining facilities here), and you can then proceed, still by drag lift, to Piz Schalottas (7,635 feet).

In winter skiers can enjoy some 90 miles of ski runs of all grades, made accessible by 34 cable cars and elevators. There's a children's ski school with its own elevator and ski garden, which attracts families to these resorts. About 25 miles of cross-country ski trails, more than ten curling rinks, and a huge natural ice-skating rink draw winter sports crowds.

In summer, water sports are popular on the Heidsee, with rowing, swimming, sailing, windsurfing, and fishing taking center stage. This is good country for horseback riding, and there's an 18-hole golf course. Lenzerheide has more than 85 miles of signposted footpaths.

FOOD AND LODGING AT LENZERHEIDE: In a quiet, sunny position behind a cluster of fir trees, **Grand Hotel Kurhaus Alpina,** CH-7078 Lenzerheide, Switzerland (tel. 081/34-11-34), is built in a pastiche of styles that had its core in an alpine dairy farm a century ago. The main building was constructed at the beginning of this century, but many alterations and additions later, the hotel is a mixture of old masonry and elegantly crafted modern extensions. A restaurant, a sympathetic bar, and a disco (the Tic-Tac) often have live entertainment. There's a heated swimming pool, as well as a sauna, on the premises. Singles range from 75F ($51) to 185F ($125.80) daily, while doubles cost 130F ($88.40) to 360F ($244.80), with half board included. The hotel is open from June to October and December to April.

Hotel Guarda Val, CH-7078 Lenzerheide-Sporz, Switzerland (tel. 081/34-22-14), is in the remote hamlet of Sporz in a collection of buildings that used to be way stations for farmers on their way with their herds up to alpine summer pastures. The hamlet is a five-minute bus ride heading up the mountain from the center of Lenzerheide, on transportation which the hotel runs frequently. The hotel is spread out in eight rustic buildings and contains 80 beds in renovated rooms that have an undeniable charm. Known for its restaurant, the hotel is classified as a *Relais & Châteaux*, one of the few in the region. Each accommodation has a private bath, plus one of a variety of floor plans that include rustic beams and irregular shapes. With half board included, winter rates range from 105F ($71.40) to 165F ($112.20) daily in a double, from 135F ($91.80) to 170F ($115.60) in a single. In summer, most guests stay on a breakfast-only basis, arranging their meals in the dining room as they wish. Then, singles rent for 75F ($51) to 110F ($74.80) daily and doubles for 95F ($64.60) to 105F ($71.40).

In any season, apartments with kitchenettes and no meals begin at 220F ($149.60) per day.

A Japanese bath (Ofuro Taneo) and sand tennis courts are on the grounds. If you're a hiker, dozens of nearby foot trails will please you. In winter, you'll appreciate the several fireplaces and the masses of snow that almost engulf the village. This is not a typical hotel, and it might prove to be just what you're looking for if you want rustic peace, quiet, and calm. The hotel, ably directed by Heinz and Beatrice Wehrle, is open June to October and December to April.

Schweizerhof, CH-7078 Lenzerheide, Switzerland (tel. 081/34-01-11). Very little of what you've seen before will prepare you for the dimensions and shape of some of the rooms of this hotel. It is at the same time rustic and modern. Light-grained paneling covers many of the walls, and many of the accessories, such as hanging lamps, are made of polished brass. The full-length windows often open onto ground-level terraces or upper-level wood-trimmed balconies. The dining room is outfitted with hanging Tiffany-style lamps and knotty-pine paneling, and the other rendezvous points are universally conducive to good music and conversation. On the premises is a swimming pool, plus a sauna, indoor tennis courts, squash courts, a bowling alley, a table-tennis room, massage facilities, and a fitness room. With half board included, singles range from 100F ($68) to 230F ($156.40) daily, while doubles cost 160F ($108.80) to 310F ($210.80), depending on the season and the room assignment. The place is closed in November.

Sunstar Hotel, CH-7078 Lenzerheide, Switzerland (tel. 081/34-01-21), is a modern hotel with a flat roof, well-defined balconies, and well-furnished rooms of ample size. It's opposite the ski school and has its own garage. The rustically comfortable lobby is filled with leather chairs. Many of the bedrooms overlook the ice-skating rink. An indoor swimming pool will give you the chance to lose some of the weight you might have gained in the attractively rustic dining room, whose stucco and paneled walls are intimately lit with hanging lamps that look almost like origami sculpture fashioned from metal and glass. Each of the 95 bedrooms has its own private bath, phone, and radio. Singles range from 81F ($55.10) to 164F ($111.50) daily, and doubles go for 162F ($110.15) to 328F ($223.05), with half board included. Prices, of course, depend on the season. The Sunstar is open from May through October and December through April.

Sporthotel Lenzerhorn, CH-7078 Lenzerheide, Switzerland (tel. 081/34-11-05), in the center of town, is a symmetrical 19th-century building with ruddy-colored shutters and a modern extension stretching off to one side. The interior has a bar with a heavily timbered ceiling and short Doric columns made of granite supporting its thick stucco arches. A wide range of summer and winter sports are available nearby. The dancing bar closes in winter every night at 2 a.m. The hotel charges 48F ($32.65) to 90F ($61.20) daily in a single and 86F ($58.50) to 180F ($122.40) in a double, with half board included. Prices depend on the plumbing and the season. Not all rooms have private baths.

All the hotels serve a good, hearty mountain cuisine, with continental overtones. However, one is more distinguished than the rest. It's the **Restaurant Guarda Val** in the previously recommended Hotel Guarda Val (tel. 081/34-22-14), in the hamlet of Sporz. One flight above the lobby level, it serves a modern French cuisine in a heavily beamed two-story room with a wrap-around gallery. A grill fireplace and very formal napery in a candlelit ambience create a warm rusticity, surprisingly sophisticated in such a remote and rural setting. Food is served daily from 11:30 a.m. to 2 p.m. and from 6:30 to 9:30 p.m.

Set menus are offered for 78F ($53.05) to 98F ($66.65), or else you can order from an à la carte menu costing from 60F ($40.80), which changes seasonally. Quality produce is carefully handled to retain its full freshness and flavor here. Meats are often grilled over an open fire (called *feu du bois*). These include lamb chops from Scotland or an entrecôte double bordelaise, fish and shellfish, including scampi. Soups are imaginative, including one recently sampled with fennel and salmon. For a main course, you might decide on duckling suprême with ginger accompanied by a comfit of oranges or filet of sole with bacon. The restaurant is closed from April until some time in mid-June, and it also shuts down from mid-October to mid-December.

FOOD AND LODGING AT VALBELLA: The well-managed, comfortable **Posthotel Valbella,** CH-7077 Lenzerheide-Valbella, Switzerland (tel. 081/34-12-12), has dark balconies that contrast attractively with the light yellow of the concrete superstructure. The interior is finished with well-buffed hardwoods, skillfully set masonry, and bright colors. If you count the sun terrace, the establishment contains three different restaurants and three separate bars, all of them rustically paneled in woods. In winter, guests dance to live musical groups. In summer the bar turns into a disco. A large indoor swimming pool, a sauna, a massage room, and two outdoor tennis courts are part of the sports facilities. Rates with half board included are 115F ($78.20) to 200F ($136) daily in a single and 190F ($129.20) to 360F ($244.80) in a double, depending on the season, the plumbing, and exposure. Walter and Miriam Trösch, your hosts, are conscientious and helpful. The hotel closes in May and November.

    Valbella-Inn, CH-7077 Valbella, Switzerland (tel. 081/34-36-36), is about a hundred yards off the main street of Valbella, in a modern chalet with beautiful views, plus a restaurant guaranteed to make you feel at home. It has a beamed ceiling and chalet chairs around tables with bright napery. The indoor swimming pool has plants growing near its panoramic windows, while the main sitting room is large, and a fireplace crackles in winter. Facilities include a dancing bar, a sauna, two tennis courts, and a sun terrace, plus a cafeteria providing snacks. There's also a children's playroom staffed by a professional kindergarten teacher. All the comfortable rooms contain private bath, ranging from 145F ($98.60) to 212F ($144.15) daily in a single and from 226 F ($153.70) to 326F ($221.70) in a double, with half board included. Prices depend on the season and the exposure of the room. The inn is open from June through October and December through April.

APRÈS SKI: Check out the previously recommended **Hotel Kurhaus Alpina** (tel. 081/34-11-34), in Lenzerheide, which has a stube bar and dancing to a live band in season. You might begin your evening with an apéritif in the Steivetta Bar, later gyrating to the action in the Tic-Tac disco. Drinks cost from 9F ($5.85).

    The other "hot spot" at the resort is the just-recommended **Valbella-Inn** (tel. 081/34-36-36), whose Heini Hemmi Bar (you remember the Olympic gold medalist) provides music and dancing. It's an ideal place to meet people and relax.

8. SAVOGNIN

If you go to this small, unpretentious winter resort, your friends are likely to ask, "How's that, again?" Savognin is something of a discovery, and it's not spoiled. Yet!

    A major town in the Oberhalbstein, it lies at the mouth of the Val Nandro. Three of its churches are from the 17th century. Savognin was the home of the painter Giovanni Segantini.

    The small resort has a good system of chair lifts and ski lifts, some going as high as 8,900 feet. It advertises itself as the biggest snowmaker in Europe, producing fake snow for ski trails with a "snow cannon" when necessary. There are 50 miles of ski slopes, a ski school, and 12 miles of cross-country ski trails, plus tobogganing, a natural ice-skating rink with two curling rinks, sleigh and horse back riding, and lots of signposted walking paths. This is a good family resort, conducting ski races for children. Those too small to ski can be left at the Pinocchio Club (nursery).

Savognin has some good hotels with reasonable prices.

FOOD AND LODGING: In the center of town is **Hotel Cresta,** CH-7460 Savognin, Switzerland (tel. 081/74-17-55), a modern four-star hotel. The Taverna bar is an active disco usually filled with young dancers who boogie to live bands. A sun terrace and a swimming pool offer panoramic views, while a rustically beamed restaurant has hanging lamps. The hotel offers good sports facilities such as a sauna, a solarium, bowling, and an indoor-outdoor tennis court that is playable in winter. The bedrooms are simple and attractive, and often have spread-out views of the countryside around the hotel. Singles range from 67F ($45.55) to 113F ($76.85) daily, while doubles cost 114F ($77.50) to 206F ($140.10), breakfast included. Half board is another 20F ($13.60) per person daily. Prices depend on the season and room assignment, and each unit has a private bath. The Cresta is open from June to October and December to April.

Hotel Danilo, CH-7460 Savognin, Switzerland (tel. 081/74-14-66), is a country-style hotel in the center of the village. On the premises one dining room welcomes hotel guests only, but there are also two restaurants and two bars (one of them with dancing) for outsiders. The hotel was built in 1970, and furnished in a rustic format of heavy stained beams, modern leather armchairs, and carpeting. With breakfast included, the rate in a double ranges from 94F ($63.90) to 172F ($116.95) daily. Singles pay from 62F ($42.15) to 95F ($64.60). Each guest is charged another 20F ($13.60) per person daily for half board. The hotel is open from June to October and December to April.

Tgesa Romana, CH-7460 Savognin, Switzerland (tel. 081/74-15-44), is a rustic family-run, breakfast-only hotel with heavy beams, lots of polished wood, and a sloping staircase leading to the accommodations from the conservatively decorated reception area. A dancing nightclub gives winter diversion to guests, while three restaurants serve regional à la carte specialties. The hotel is in the center of town, on the main street, with all the sports facilities close at hand. Depending on the season and the plumbing, singles range from 50F ($34) to 70F ($47.60) daily, while doubles cost 90F ($61.20) to 130F ($88.40). The Savoldelli family keeps the hotel open year round.

THE ENGADINE

The Valley of the Inn (or the En, as the locals call it in Romansh) stretches for 60 miles, from the Maloja Plateau (5,955 feet) to Finstermünz, with all villages except Sils lying at a higher altitude than the plateau. The highest is St. Moritz, at 6,036 feet.

Lower Engadine is reached from Davos over the Fluëla Pass (7,818 feet) and by the Ofen Pass (7,050 feet). Four major passes lead into the **Upper Engadine:** Maloja (5,955 feet), Julier (7,493 feet), Albula (7,585 feet), and Bernina (7,621 feet). The upper valley contains several lakes, including the St. Moritz.

The Engadine is enclosed by great mountain ranges with alpine meadows and forests on the steep hillsides. The villages are built of stone, originally as a protection against fires that swept the narrow windy valleys. The white-washed houses in the villages, known for their *chaminades,* or larders, often have *sgraffito* decoration with mottoes and heraldic devices, and you'll see many a *balcun tort* (oriel). The population is of Rhaeto-Romanic heritage and is mostly Protestant.

From the Maloja Pass the road runs northeast through the Upper Engadine, where the clear mountain skies and dry, light breezes make the area popular both in summer and in winter, despite its somewhat stark scenery. Since the 19th century when Upper Engadine became fashionable for its "air cure," it has developed into a primarily winter sports center, highlighted by St. Moritz.

In the Lower Engadine, where the valley is narrower and more forested, two major attractions are the mineral springs of Scuol and the Swiss National Park, a wildlife sanctuary stretching for some 55 miles. Here true alpine flora and fauna abound.

Some of Engadine's ancient customs have died out, but two that are upheld throughout the area are the Chalanda Marz (the first of March) and the Schlitteda.

The **Chalanda Marz,** celebrated by the youth of Engadine, descended from the old Roman New Year festival and has been obserpthe old Roman New Year festival and has been observed since the time when the Rhaetian valleys were under Roman rule. Early on the morning of March 1 schoolboys congregate at the center meeting place of each Engadine village. With bells large and small, the boys create a hullabaloo to frighten the winter monster and lure spring from its snowy bed. The boys are divided into "herds" that go from house to house soliciting goodies such as fruit, sweets, and chestnuts. Romantic songs of spring are sung, in which the girls of the village are requested to join. Money is accepted from visitors and locals in lieu of edible goodies, with the proceeds usually being used for school trips.

An especially beautiful custom is the observance of **Schlitteda,** a romantic horse-drawn sleigh ride in January, participated in by the unmarried youth of the villages. The couples dress in the colorful traditional costume of the region, *schlittunza,* a scarlet festive garb. In a decorated sleigh, they set out for a nearby village on a ride that usually takes about two hours. When they reach their goal they're served a hot spiced wine drink and pastries to strengthen them for their trip home after music and dancing. Back home after a romantic ride through the Engadine night, each couple dines at the girl's home. Visitors enjoy the brightly dressed pairs against the background of snowy fields and mountains as well as the festivities as the sleigh rides get under way, with outriders in three-cornered hats and jabots arranging the procession. Musicians in traditional costumes accompany the young couples in another sleigh and are greeted in the villages they pass through by townspeople dancing in the square.

In summer, music lovers are drawn to the Engadine Concert Weeks during which chamber music concerts are given throughout the area, arranged by the Upper Engadine Tourist Office.

9. SCUOL/FTAN/TARASP/VULPERA

One of the easternmost extremities in this guide is represented by a string of spas that, viewed as a whole, form a fine holiday center of the Lower Engadines. These rather old-fashioned spas are where Europeans used to (and still do) go to "take the waters," as opposed to the more modern meaning of diet farms.

Bad Scuol (Schul on some maps) is the leading and most historic center. This old Engadine town, the most active part of the quartet of resorts being explored, was for many decades a famous spa, surrounded by beautiful woodland. Lying on the left bank of the River Inn, it's on the major road from St. Moritz to Landeck bypass. Scuol gets lots of sunshine, even in winter, and while many people come here for the treatment of gastrointestinal problems, others come just to relax and have a vacation.

Ftan is a little "eagle's nest" village in the Lower Engadine Valley, high on a lookout. Scuol, almost four miles away, can be seen from here. Ftan is reached via a dangerously winding road from Scuol, but its *Relais & Châteaux* (Haus Paradies, recommended below) is worth the drive. It's very close to the Swiss border with Austria. Once at Ftan, you can wander through the village with its baroque clock tower that evokes a hamlet in Austria. It's on cross-country and alpine ski trails in winter and has more than 60 miles of hiking trails for summer visitors to follow. The postal code for Ftan is 7551, its phone area code 084.

Tarasp, a hamlet in a sheltered locale in the Valley of the Inn, about four miles west of Bad Scuol, is actually the spa center. The springs here have often been compared to those at Karlsbad.

The most important man-made site in the area is the gleaming white hilltop **Castle of Tarasp** (tel. 084/9-12-29), which enjoys a majestic view of the En valley from its lofty precincts on a conically shaped hill. The castle is considered one of the most impressive of all apoine strongholds. Dating from the 11th century, it became part of the Grisons in 1803. A Dresden industrialist purchased the castle and restored it in the years before World War I. At present, it's owned by the Grand Duke Ernest Ludwig of Hesse-Darmstadt, who uses it as a private residence. It contains many antiques from the Engadines as well as the Tyrolean country.

The duke allows guided tours to be given at 2:45 p.m. Monday to Saturday in June; at 2:15 and 3:15 p.m. from July 1 to July 10; at 10:30 a.m., 2:15 p.m., 3:15 p.m., and 4:15 p.m. daily from July 11 to August 20; and at 2:45 p.m. Monday to Saturday from August 20 to October 15. Admission is 5F ($3.40) for adults, 2F ($1.35) for children. The castle can be reached by postal bus from Scuol-Tarasp.

You can also visit the **Kreuzberg belvedere** (4,846 feet), from which you have an excellent view of the castle as well as of the Lower Engadine.

Vulpera, a small resort, is little more than a cluster of first-class hotels, German and Swiss holiday-type chalets, on a terraced hillside alive with flowers in summer. This is essentially a summer resort, but it's starting to make a bid for winter business.

FOOD AND LODGING: On a sunny plateau half a mile from Ftan, **Haus Paradies,** CH-7551 Ftan, Switzerland (tel. 084/9-13-25), is a peaceful hotel skillfully operated by Roland and Brigitte Jöhri. From the handsome mountainside buildings, guests can view the Lower Engadines all the way to the Castle of Tarasp and the Swiss National Park. The original Haus Paradies sits above recent additions, all with big windows and terraces. The public rooms, including a beamed library, a spacious lounge and a writing room (both with open fireplaces), and a reception hall, are furnished with a pleasing blend of antiques and contemporary pieces and lots of wood. Rooms and suites at this 40-bed hotel are of various sizes and shapes, all with wooden ceilings, a bar, windows to the south with sweeping views of the valley, and a private balcony or terrace. Year-round prices for double occupancy with half board range from 363F ($246.85) to 480F ($326.40) daily per accommodation. The more expensive units contain apartments with fireplaces. Singles, also on the half-board plan, are charged 200F ($136).

Roland Jöhri is in charge of the kitchen, producing excellent meals with emphasis on giving half-board guests meals to remember. Orders can be from four fixed-price meals or from an à la carte menu. The food is the finest in the area, and nonresidents can visit for a meal if they reserve. Service is daily from noon to 2 p.m. and 7 to 9 p.m. Meals begin at 65F ($44.20). Mr. Jöhri makes up new menus daily, depending on fresh ingredients he brings from the markets in a wide area. Service in both the hotel and the dining room is courteous and capable, supervised by Mrs. Jöhri. If you travel by train, the Jöhris will arrange for you to be picked up in Scuol. The hotel is open from early June to mid-October and from the week before Christmas to the week after Easter.

A hotel that grew out of an Engadine farmhouse, **Romantik Hotel Guardaval,** CH-7550 Bad Scuol, Switzerland (tel. 084/9-13-21), is filled with charming touches that make it a really pleasant place at which to stay, even though it has an angular modern concrete façade. A well-placed scattering of antiques (among them an old spinning machine with a small wheel) decorate the public rooms. Most of the lower floors are tastefully accented with light-grained wood paneling that, when coupled with the painted chests, make an attractive format. The hotel is about ten minutes away from the railway station and Motta Naluns cable railway, next door to the Trü sports center. It has a panoramic terrace and a faithful clientele. Since not all rooms contain private baths, rates depend on the plumbing as well as the season. Charges range from 68F ($46.25) to 130F ($88.40) daily in a single, going up to 130F ($88.40) to 240F ($163.20) in a double. Guests are received from May to October and December to April.

Hotel Bellaval, CH-7550 Bad Scuol, Switzerland (tel. 084/9-14-81), lies outside the center of Bad Scuol in the direction of Ftan, next to the cable car stop, Scuol–Motta Naluns. The stonework of the exterior of this building could make any mason proud of the craft. It rises five red-shuttered stories, and is constructed entirely of textured rocks. It's capped by a red tile roof and has summer café tables set up outside. The hotel seemingly could withstand any storm, and that knowledge, coupled with the coziness of the renovated public rooms inside, should make you feel safe and snug. The Schoch family charges from 54F ($36.70) to 95F ($64.60) daily in a single and from 108F ($73.45) to 185F ($125.80) in a double, with half board included. Prices depend on the season and the plumbing, since the least expensive rooms don't contain private baths. The hotel is open from June to October and December to April.

Villa Silvana, CH-7552 Bad Tarasp–Vulpera, Switzerland (tel. 084/9-13-54), is a 45-bed hotel in the middle of the village of Vulpera, operated by the Kratzer family, who receive guests from May through October and from December through April. This family-run pension has an inviting atmosphere and a restaurant offering Grisons specialties. A popular bar can be found in the basement. Rooms are pleasantly furnished and comfortable. The lowest-priced accommodations don't have private baths. With half board included, singles range from 60F ($40.80) to 80F ($54.40) daily, with doubles costing 120F ($81.60) to 160F ($108.80). The Silvana is a solid buff-color Engadine house with several rambling additions, including a wrap-around sun-flooded section in front.

10. GUARDA

Under the protection of the government, which has strong landmark preservation laws, the little mountain village of Guarda is called "the museum village" of the Engadine. Once it was an important stopover for coaches on the narrow old road that ran between Milan and Munich. But in 1865 a new road was built, cutting through the valley, and Guarda was left to itself. It virtually stopped growing, and that is just the way the local populace of 140 inhabitants want to keep it. The etched ornamentation of its antique buildings, called *sgraffiti,* is under federal protection. Many structures are from the 17th century.

The name, Guarda, is derived from the Romansh word *Schau.* It stands on a sunny terrace in the Lower Engadine, above the Inn Valley at an elevation of 5,423 feet. You can set out on walking trails in many directions and from almost any position in the village views of towering mountain peaks surround you. The location is east of Davos, along the road that leads to Scuol-Tarasp-Vulpera (see above) and eventually to Innsbruck, Munich, and Vienna. And if you're in Guarda when the cows come home for milking, you will think you have wandered back in time.

For food and lodging, head for the **Hotel Meisser,** CH-7549 Guarda, Switzerland (tel. 084/9-21-32), a sister hotel of one previously recommended in Davos. This one is quite different, attracting a summer crowd. It was a farmhouse until it was restored in 1893 and turned into a charming little hotel. Ralf and Kathrin Meisser are in charge. It lies on a promontory opening onto a *How Green Was My Valley* valley below. In 25 old-fashioned bedrooms, guests are received from June to November. Some units have private baths. A few accommodations are spacious; others are those tiny under-the-eaves rooms so familiar to devotees of Swiss hostelries. Depending on the plumbing and the season, half-board rates range from 74F ($50.30) to 94F ($63.90) daily in a single and from 148F ($100.65) to 192F ($130.55) in a double. The food in the cozy restaurant is good and served by waitresses in alpine attire. The wood and gypsum ceiling of the dining room reflects the art of the 19th century. The restaurant has a lovely view over the valley. In summer guests can also dine in a garden restaurant. A few antiques and alpine chairs and chests give the relatively modern hotel its antique character. Hand-carved ceilings and wooden walls contribute even more. In the evening, guests gather around the fireplace. The hotel is for those who like hiking and relaxing.

11. S-CHANF AND ZUOZ

These two Engadine resorts can provide an attractive alternative for living in the region without having to pay the high prices of St. Moritz, directly to their southwest. Heading south from our last stopover in the resort area of Scuol/Ftan/Tarasp/Vulpera, I recommend a visit to these two villages.

S-CHANF: This village with a most unusual name is a summer and winter resort at the entrance to the Swiss National Park, about 5,100 feet above sea level. It's a choice starting point for excursions and tours in the Upper and Lower Engadine and in the park. Valley Trupchun is the park hunting ground abounding in the indigenous game of the Grisons.

S-chanf is a peaceful, relaxing village with easy access to several busy sports centers, including St. Moritz. It lies on the Engadine cross-country ski marathon trail.

After a brief visit here, head directly south to a more interesting town.

ZUOZ: This Old World village, once the chief place in the Engadine, lies near the River Inn amid alpine meadows and lush forests, its view of the Inn Valley and mountain range backdrop making it look almost like a stage setting brought to life.

This is the best-preserved village in the Upper Engadine, with the most striking collection of Engadine houses to be found anywhere in the valley. The houses appear to be decorated for some festival, but they're like that all the time. The best-known is the famed **Planta House** (two houses, actually), on the main square of the village, with an outdoor staircase and a rococo balustrade. The Planta family, historically important in the Grisons, built most of the spectacular structures in town. The slender-towered church merits a visit. Inside, look for the severed-bear's-paw theme, a heraldic symbol of the Plantas. Augusto Giacometti designed some of the church's modern stained-glass windows. The Planta family bear symbol also appears on a fountain in the main square.

For most of the 1,200 inhabitants of Zuoz, Romansh is their ancestral language.

A fledgling summer resort, Zuoz offers tennis, climbing and mountaineering, horse-drawn carriage rides, fishing, swimming, horseback riding, and summer skiing.

At 5,740 feet above sea level, this minor winter sports center has a ski school for beginners, including children, as well as for advanced pupils. Experienced skiers will gravitate to the heights of the Piz Kesch region or else journey ten miles by train to St. Moritz. Numerous cross-country tracks lead through Zuoz in all directions, and the village is the finishing point of the Engadine ski marathon. Curling, ice skating, and sledging are other winter sports pursued here.

Because of its location at the entrance to the Swiss National Park, many people use Zuoz as a base for visits to the fascinating habitat of alpine birds, animals, and plants.

FOOD AND LODGING: Both of these tiny resorts offer accommodations and dining rooms, should you decide to stay over.

In S-chanf

Parkhotel Aurora, CH-7525 S-chanf, Switzerland (tel. 082/7-12-64), a year-round hotel, the best in town, has a modern addition stretching toward the front yard, planted with seasonal flowers. The hotel was renovated into a format of paneled and vaulted ceilings, rustic niches, and Oriental rugs. Even the double-laned bowling alley has a paneled ceiling and an alpine format. Mrs. Dora Langen, your hostess, does everything she can to be hospitable. Rooms come with and without private baths. Half-board rates, depending on the season, range from 52F ($35.35) to 90F ($61.20) daily in a single, from 112F ($76.15) to 194F ($131.90) in a double. The highest tariffs are in effect in winter.

Hotel Scaletta, 52 via Maistra, CH-7525 S-chanf, Switzerland (tel. 082/7-12-71), was originally built in 1624 as a relay station for horses struggling over the Engadine passes. Today, it boasts the most baroque *sgraffito* of any building in town. Centrally located in the center of the village, it sits opposite a tiny square, a few steps from the village church. When the hospitable owner, Jörg Bauder, bought the hotel in 1984, he retained the hotel's original name, which was derived from the name of one of the mountain passes leading to Davos, and made much-needed improvements to many of the bedrooms. This is a good and atmospheric alternative to the high price of accommodations in St. Moritz. As such, many skiers and summer climbers prefer it as a budget-conscious base. A few of the pine-covered bedrooms do not have private baths, although each has a sink, phone, cabinets, cozy alpine furniture, and lots of warm and intimate comfort. Cost: 54F ($36.20) to 60F ($40.80) per person daily. The hotel contains a pleasantly rustic restaurant, the Arvenstube, serving Swiss specialties as part of full meals that are reasonably priced from 30F ($20.40) each.

In Zuoz

Posthotel Engiadina, CH-7524 Zuoz, Switzerland (tel. 082/7-10-21), has seven floors (if you count the double row of gables) and a beautifully preserved baroque façade, which is painted a pretty pink. The hotel is more than 100 years old, and is today owned and managed by the Arquint family. The public rooms remain faithful to the style of their original construction, but have been charmingly updated with original murals covering the space between paneled ceilings and half-paneled walls. They show 19th-century gentry amusing themselves on a winter landscape. The management has been careful to preserve some of the original plaster detailing of the ceilings. One floor above the lobby level is a cluster of public rooms, including a pine-sheathed solarium with high windows on three sides. There is also an old-fashioned parlor with good antiques, art deco chandeliers, and an unusual collection of slowly ticking antique clocks. Singles rent for 104F ($70.70) to 142F ($96.55) daily and doubles for 164F ($111.50) to 256F ($174.10), with half board included. On the premises are a heated swimming pool, tennis courts, a sauna, curling rinks, and a dance bar, plus two restaurants serving both Swiss and Italian specialties. Guests are received from June to October and December to April.

12. SAMEDAN AND CELERINA

These twin resorts lie virtually at the doorstep of St. Moritz. Many Swiss and German tourists know of their charms and amenities and seek them out instead of being guests of their high-priced neighbor to the north. Both have been referred to as suburbs of St. Moritz, but that's an unsuitable and somewhat demeaning label, as Samedan and Celerina have much Engadine style, and each has its own special character.

SAMEDAN: Originally a Roman settlement, Samedan survived to become a principal village of the Upper Engadine. Over the years many well-known Swiss families have made their homes here. Seek out the **Planta House** (the same family who made its mark on Zuoz), and note its large roof and impressive library of Romansh works.

The village (5,160 feet) has its own ski lift and ice-skating rink, plus a ski school. In summer it's ideal for mountain walks and climbing. Visitors can fish or play tennis and golf. When there's snow it's possible to take a horse-drawn sleigh to St. Moritz in less than an hour, and all mountain transportation can be reached in a short time.

Food and Lodging

Hotel Quadratscha, CH-7503 Samedan, Switzerland (tel. 082/6-42-57), was built around 1870 as a step-roofed private house. When it was enlarged as a hotel in the 1970s, a modern balconied extension was designed to jut over the slope of the hillside in back. The lobby retains most of the paneling, the high ceilings, and the elaborate murals of the original 19th-century construction, and one of the dining rooms, the Arvenstube, has one of the most beautifully crafted wood ceilings in town. The 40 bedrooms are tastefully streamlined, with unadorned stucco walls, balconies, bath, comfortable no-frills furniture, and a view of the mountains. Each room contains a private bath. With half board included and depending on the season, singles range from 92F ($62.55) to 136F ($92.50) daily, with doubles costing 174F ($118.30) to 262F ($178.15). On the premises of the hotel are a sauna, solarium, and massage facilities.

Hotel Bernina, CH-7503 Samedan, Switzerland (tel. 082/6-54-21), was built in 1865 and today maintains much of the grand manner associated with it then, although in a modernized format. Its symmetrical façade curves in a gentle arc, embracing a series of low-lying extensions in front. The entire edifice is painted beige and gray, with Italianate detailing over the windows. The comfortable bedrooms are outfitted in a rustic Engadine style, with patterned carpeting and big windows. On the premises, guests can use a tennis court or else enjoy a summer terrace and a private park. A vegetable garden supplies the well-staffed restaurant. All units contain private baths, and, with half board included, singles rent for 92F ($62.55) to 136F ($92.50) daily and doubles for 174F ($118.30) to 262F ($178.15), according to the season. The hotel is open from mid-June to October and mid-December to April.

Hotel Donatz, CH-7503 Samedan, Switzerland (tel. 082/6-46-66), has a simple green-shuttered façade capped by a flat roof. You'll see a sun terrace on top of the extension attached to the front, and regional designs faintly painted onto the second and third floors. Inside are a series of wood-paneled public rooms, with intricate carving on some of the horizontal posts and lots of sunlight. A restaurant, La Padella, serves regional specialties in an alpine setting. The paneling of the downstairs extends into many of the bedrooms, which are brightly carpeted and comfortable. The owner, René Donatz, charges from 145F ($98.60) daily in a double, 90F ($61.20) in a single, with half board included in all tariffs. Each unit contains a private bath or shower, toilet, radio, and TV. The hotel takes an annual holiday in May.

Hotel Hirschen, CH-7503 Samedan, Switzerland (tel. 082/6-52-74), is a small and personalized hotel that has been run by the same family for almost 40 years. The public rooms are spacious and vaulted, sometimes covered with paneling, and tastefully decorated with stone floors, a scattering of antiques, and Oriental rugs. The bedrooms are pleasing, comfortable, and warmly inviting. Each has its own bathroom. A ground-floor pizzeria offers rustic comfort and musical entertainment. An Engadine manor house, with its 16th-century vaults, is connected to the hotel. Singles range from 60F ($40.80) to 85F ($57.80) daily, while doubles cost 110F ($74.80) to 160F ($108.80), with half board included.

For dining, try **Le Pavillon** in the already-recommended Hotel Bernina (tel. 082/6-54-21), a pleasant restaurant with a garden terrace and a dancing bar. It serves such delectable items as fresh goose liver and when available, fresh mushrooms made into several delicious dishes. Fixed-price meals range from 30F ($20.40) to 45F ($30.60), with à la carte dinners averaging about the same. The restaurant serves food daily from 9 a.m. to midnight except from mid-April to mid-June and from the first of October until mid-December. The service is as good as the food. Reservations are advised.

Arvenstübli/Stuvetta, Hotel Quadratscha (tel. 082/6-42-57). Its paneling and elaborate pinewood ceiling remain intact from a villa that used to stand here in 1870. Only dinner is served every night from 7 to 10 p.m. Full meals cost from 70F ($47.80) and are served by a politely discreet service staff. Typical dishes include a darne of salmon, a "turban" of sole with shrimp, a platter containing three different filet mignons, quail with truffles, and an array of succulent grills. If for any reason, the Arvenstübli is full, or management has decided to close it, dinner will be served in an adjacent room, the Stuvetta.

CELERINA: This hamlet on the River Inn (about 5,675 feet) has long been overshadowed by its more celebrated neighbors, St. Moritz, less than two miles away, and Pontresina, about three miles distant. But for those in search of local color, Celerina is a worthy choice as a resort center for a holiday, either in winter or summer. Known for its charming Engadine houses, this little village on a sunny plain is sheltered from bitter winds. Besides the houses, Celerina also has an old Romanesque church, **St. John's** (San Gian), with a painted ceiling dating from 1478. The Romansh name of the town is Schlarigna.

The Cresta run, a mecca for bobsledders, starts from St. Moritz and terminates near Celerina. The village also has ice rinks for curling and skating, a toboggan run, and a ski school. Winter Celerinade packages for skiing, cross-country, and curling are offered, as well as Summer Celerinade guided mountain bikes tours with a picnic included.

Several interesting conducted **tours** are offered in summer through the **Tourist Information Office** (tel. 082/3-39-66). An experienced guide will take you on an exploration tour through the **Swiss National Park** for 6F ($4.10) per person, or you can join a botanical excursion to see alpine flowers in bloom, 12F ($8.15). Strenuous geological and mineralogical tours cost 19F ($12.90), and you can make an exciting journey from the Diavolezza over the glacier to Morteratsch for 15F ($10.20), with an experienced guide. The latter is offered only in spring and summer.

Celerina is known for its belvederes which give stunning panoramic vistas. One is **Piz Nair** at 10,000 feet. To reach it, you can take a cable car from St. Moritz, departing every 20 minutes daily from 8:30 a.m. to 4 p.m. You'll ride from St. Moritz to Corviglia. Round-trip passage between the two sites costs 13F ($8.84) per person. At Corviglia, you board another cable car between Corviglia and Piz Nair. The round-trip passage from Corviglia to Piz Nair is 23F ($15.65) per person. The circular panorama takes in the Bernina summits, and provides a panorama that is breathtaking by anyone's standards.

You can also visit **Muottas Muragl** (8,040 feet). From the lower station at Punt Muragl, funicular departures are about every 30 minutes. The round-trip fare is 14F ($9.10). You will have stunning views of the Upper Engadine gap, and in the distance you can see the peaks of the Bernina massif, each with "Piz" in its name. Ibex and marmots inhabit the lofty plateau. You'll probably see them as you take mountain walks.

Food and Lodging

Hotel Cresta Kulm, CH-7505 Celerina, Switzerland (tel. 082/3-33-73), is a first-class hotel, run by Jürg and Genevieve Küng. It lies in a particularly sunny and quiet position, off the main road. The famous Cresta run and the St. Moritz–Celerina bobsled run comes to an end in front of the hotel. The building is an unusually designed hotel, with a series of irregularly shaped indented windows inserted into a white concrete façade. The hotel is set on a grassy lawn, where guests in summer take chairs out for sunbathing. The interior is filled with modern curves and well-crafted stone floors, white stucco walls, and comfortable furniture. The rates for half board range from 75F ($51) to 115F ($78.20) per person daily in summer and 90F ($61.20) to 135F ($91.80) per person in winter. Each of the 45 rooms is furnished with private bath, direct-dial phone, radio, color TV, and mini-bar. Guests are received from June through September and from December through April.

Cresta Palace Hotel, CH-7505 Celerina, Switzerland (tel. 082/3-35-64), is a very large building that was constructed at the turn of the century. It has three frontal gables that you'll notice immediately, and several smaller ones that contribute to an overall effect of grandeur. The inside contains several public rooms, including a bar and an elegant restaurant, as well as a swimming pool, a sun terrace where (if the weather's right) you might have breakfast, and a skating rink. The bedrooms are brightly colored, often with rustic pine furnishings. Singles range from 85F ($57.80) to 200F ($136) daily, while doubles cost 160F ($108.80) to 410F ($278.80). Prices vary according to the season and plumbing, but they always include half board. The hotel is open from June through September and from December through April.

Hotel Misani, CH-7505 Celerina, Switzerland (tel. 082/3-33-14). From the front, the shape and detailing of this hotel look vaguely like that of an American Federal-style house, except that this one has been painted a dark pink. The building has heavy molding around the roofline and a symmetrical placement of the white-shuttered windows. The interior has some regional antiques, lots of full-grained paneling, and comfortable and sunny bedrooms. You'll be only a three-minute walk from the ski lifts and cable car. Depending on the plumbing and the season, doubles rent for 84F ($57.10) to 178F ($121.05) daily, with half board included. Singles pay 47F ($31.95) to 89F ($60.50) on the same arrangement. Part of the hotel encloses one of the finest places to dine in town. It's the intimate and cozy Stuvetta, an Engadine restaurant serving good food daily from noon to 2 p.m. and 6:30 to 9 p.m. You enter from a side door of the hotel. Emerging from the kitchen is an array of fine dishes, including savory snails, steak in the style of the patron, raclette, trout meunière, and many veal dishes. A four-course, fixed-price meal goes for 20F ($13.60), with à la carte dinners costing from 30F ($20.40). Parking is nearby. The hotel is open June to October and December to April.

13. ST. MORITZ

St. Moritz is the *ne plus ultra* of winter glamor, a haven for the aristocracy (what's left of it) from Germany and Italy and the gathering place of chic jetsetters who arrive in early February and stay until March. Elegance is the password that admits you to this prestigious resort, and money is the key to participation in the lifestyle that exists here. St. Moritz may well be the most fashionable resort in the world.

On the southern side of the Alps in the Upper Engadine, at an altitude of 6,000 feet, St. Moritz (San Murezzan in Romansh, the native language of the area) was originally known for its mineral springs, which were discovered, probably by the Celts, some 3,000 years ago. From Roman times through the Middle Ages visitors came here in summer to experience the curative powers of the spring waters. The hamlet first appears in written history in an official document referring to the sale of the Upper Engadine by a count to the bishop of Chur in 1138. It was first referred to as a spring by the Swiss-born alchemist and physician known as Paracelsus.

Use of the spring waters was a summer pursuit, and it was not until 1834 that the first winter guest stayed in the area. The first skiers appeared on the Upper Engadine scene in 1859 (the natives thought they were nutty), and in 1864 a pension owner, Johannes Badrutt, brought a group of English people to St. Moritz to spend the winter, starting what has grown into a flood of tourism.

PRACTICAL FACTS: The following tips may make your visit to St. Moritz more pleasant.

Children: Day nursery care for children costs 28F ($19.05) for a whole day with lunch. Ask at the tourist office for the nursery locations.

Information: The tourist office, **Kur- und Verkehrsverein,** in St. Moritz can be visited at St. Moritz–Dorf or telephoned at 082/3-31-47 for a wealth of information.

Post office: The St. Moritz post office is open Monday to Friday from 7:45 a.m. to noon and 1:45 to 6:15 p.m. Saturday hours are 7:45 to 11 a.m. You can arrange postal bus excursions here.

Telegrams: The St. Moritz telegraph office is open daily from 7:30 a.m. to 11 a.m.

WHERE TO STAY: St. Moritz is well equipped with accommodations, with dozens of hotels, pensions, and chalet-style apartments. But because it's expensive, you may prefer to anchor in at one of several neighboring resorts, such as Pontresina, Silvaplana, Sils Maria, Samedan, or Celerina, all of which are recommended in this chapter. For those who want to be right in the heart of the action, here goes:

In a Class By Itself

Badrutt's Palace Hotel, CH-7500 St. Moritz, Switzerland (tel. 082/2-11-01). Few hotels in Switzerland command the attention and fame of this monument to grandeur. It sits in the middle of the resort, behind a chiseled stone façade and a series of fortified towers. Despite any confusion about its architecture, the Palace is known in many circles as one of the most desirable turn-of-the-century resorts in the world. It was built by Caspar Badrutt, reportedly the first hôtelier in Europe to install private bathrooms in the more expensive suites, an unheard-of luxury at the time. Over the years the chic and famous have come through the doors of the Palace, including the Shah of Iran, Greta Garbo, Barbara Hutton, Noël Coward, and the Duke of Alba. Everyone still speaks about the visits of Onassis during his Maria Callas period. If you're rich enough, and appropriately dressed, most of the hotel's drinking and dining facilities will welcome you. Many of them are separately described in the "After Dark" and "Where to Dine" sections.

The hotel's Great Hall soars in dimensions best described as Gothic, above twin black-marble fireplaces, clusters of antique furniture, and massive bouquets of flowers. The room, entirely sheathed in intricately crafted pine paneling, has witnessed some of the grandest entrances and exits in the world.

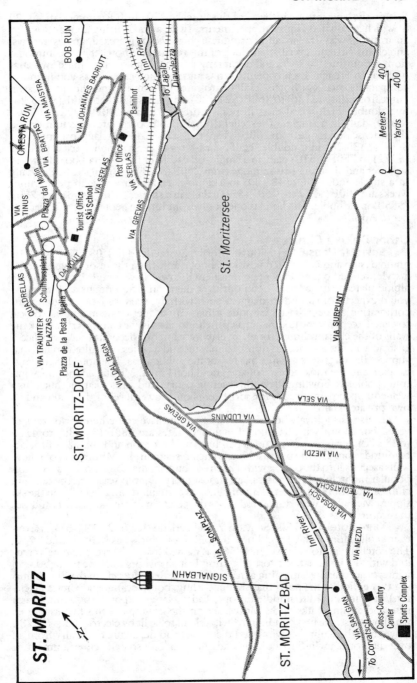

Within the labyrinthine hallways of this hotel lie 270 plush accommodations, 20 of which are owned as private apartments. Twice a year, during annual closings, an army of Swiss, Italian, and Portuguese employees replaces, upgrades, renews, and cleans virtually every square inch of this remarkable hotel. The accommodations are outfitted in styles and decor ranging from high-quality alpine Swiss traditional to French. Each contains extras and as much comfort as you'll find in comparably excellent hotels. Half-board rates in summer and shoulder season range from 200F ($136) to 360F ($244.80) daily in a single and 340F ($435.20) in a double. Half-board rates in peak winter weeks are 400F ($272) to 750F ($510) daily in a single, 60 excellent hotels. Half-board rates in summer and shoulder season range from 200F ($136) to 360F ($244.80) daily in a single and 340F ($435.20) in a double. Half-board rates in peak winter weeks are 400F ($272) to 750F ($510) daily in a single, 60 excellent hotels. Half-board rates in summer and shoulder season range from 200F ($136) to 360F ($244.80) daily in a single and 340F ($435.20) in a double. Half-board rates in peak winter weeks are 400F ($272) to 750F ($510) daily in a single, 600F ($408) to 1,250F ($850) in a double. The hotel is open only from June to September and December to April.

Other Deluxe Choices

Suvretta House, CH-7500 St. Moritz, Switzerland (tel. 082/2-11-21). Its grand design and its forested position about a mile from the resort have earned it a style, reputation, and clientele uniquely its own. It was built in 1912 on an alpine plateau that affords views out over the nearby mountains and lakes. As you'd expect from an Edwardian-era hotel with five stars, its façade is grand, incorporating an ochre-faced baroque gable with a duet of neomedieval conical towers. Except for the luxuriant oak paneling and massive columns that flank the walls of the elegant dining room, an elaborate interior decor has been sacrificed. Instead you get a clean, no-nonsense plaster and a series of vaulted arches that support the Engadine *sgraffito* of a few of the public areas. The hotel has the largest park and the most acreage of any grand hotel in St. Moritz, an indoor swimming pool, two bowling alleys, three tennis courts, and an ice-skating rink, plus a well-equipped games room for adolescents on a lower level of the hotel and its own private ski lift.

It also has a loyal clientele, some of whom have come here for dozens of years. For rooms with half board included, rates are 135F ($91.80) to 415F ($282.20) per person per day, depending on the season and the size of the accommodation. On the premises is a French restaurant, Le Miroir, one of whose walls ascends into the ceiling with a push of a button, thereby exposing a view to a popular nightclub. Live music plays almost every night in season at the dancing club La Voilière, and a duet of mountain huts contains dining facilities on the ski slopes. Men must wear dinner jackets or dark suits in winter and jackets and ties in summer.

Kulm Hotel, CH-7500 St. Moritz, Switzerland (tel. 082/2-11-51), is an elegant collection of three buildings, the oldest of which was built around 1760. The hôtelier who took it over in 1856 was named Joseph Badrutt, and he's credited with the imaginative effort of getting British visitors to come to the Alps in wintertime, thereby launching a major industry. Residents claim that it was during this period at the hotel that skiing, curling, bobsledding, and Cresta (skeleton) was introduced to middle Europe. Today a large part of the bob run, Cresta run, and curling rinks of St. Moritz are on the grounds of this historic hotel, which was also the first building in Switzerland to be lit by electric lights (1878). Since then the Kulm has witnessed the arrival and departure of royalty from all over the world, including the kings and queens of industry and entertainment. It was the center of the Olympic Games in 1928 and 1945. Today the Sunny Bar is one of the most popular rendezvous points in town (usually with live music). The public rooms are beautifully paneled, and left in their natural grain with occasionally vaulted ceilings. In the case of the high-ceilinged dining room, the ceiling was painted a light-reflecting ivory. One of the salons has pumpkin-colored walls and white detailing that emphasize the Doric columns and the molded ceilings.

On the premises are an indoor swimming pool with views of the mountains, a sauna, a gym, massage facilities, and in winter an ice rink and a curling rink, in summer tennis courts, both with resident pros. There's also a children's playground with a playroom. The rates in a double run from 135F ($91.80) to 400F ($272) per person daily, with half board. Rates depend on the period involved during the season, which is from June through September and from November through April.

Carlton Hotel, CH-7500 St. Moritz, Switzerland (tel. 082/2-11-14), sits in a position regally isolated from the rest of the resort. Now owned by Grand Hotel Tschuggen, the structure was originally built for Nicholas II, the last czar of Russia. With a view of the lake and the mountains, it's one of the loveliest hotels in St. Moritz. It has a château façade covered with ochre paint, bay windows, and balconies. An elegant set of public rooms gives off a formalized kind of warmth and well-being. Aside from the plaster and wood-paneled detailing, the best part about the sitting room is its tall, narrow fireplaces with neoclassical designs. Rooms which have been redecorated are well furnished with new bathrooms (complete with hairdryer, bidet, and make-up mirror). Half-board rates in summer in a single range from 100F ($68) to 180F ($122.40) daily, with two persons paying from 220F ($149.60) to 480F ($326.40). In winter, the single half-board rate ranges from 150F ($102) to 320F ($217.60) daily, with two persons paying from 340F ($231.20) to 740F ($503.20).

Dining is at various restaurants, including the elegantly appointed Tschiné, with its various continental and regional specialties. You can also dine in the rustically decorated Restaurant Prüveda. International musicians perform at the hotel's bar, and other amenities include a kindergarten as well as a hairdresser and cosmetician. Sporting facilities on the premises include a glass-walled swimming pool with a wood ceiling and tile floor, a sauna, solarium, and massage. Free bus service is available to the ski lifts and the center of town. The hotel is open from June to September and December to April.

Hotel Schweizerhof, CH-7500 St. Moritz, Switzerland (tel. 082/2-21-71), has been owned since it was built in 1896 by the von Gugelberg family. It's considered among the ten best hotels in town. A four-star hotel, it has attractively modernized rooms, many furnished in the soft pastel hues of today. The better units face south, opening onto views of the lake (frozen in winter). With half board included, singles rent for 175F ($119) to 270F ($183.60) daily and doubles for 290F ($197.20) to 490F ($333.20), depending on the season. Many of the accommodations also have luxuriously appointed bathrooms.

What makes this hotel exceptional, aside from its heartbeat location, is the wealth of services and facilities available, along with an array of drinking and dining choices. For example, it has an alpine hut, the Clavadatsch, where in a rustic, rural setting you can enjoy food and wine in the mountains, warmed by a fireplace in the corner. A fitness center is on the ground floor, with a massage parlor and a sauna. There's even a kindergarten in the hotel run by "childminders" daily from 9 a.m. to 6 p.m. Guest on "en pension" take not only their buffet breakfast in the Segantini Dining Room but also well-prepared meals there at night. Tables are placed under a painting by the famous Giovanni Segantini. Those seeking more celestial viands can head for La Terrine, an intimate French restaurant open nightly from 7 to midnight, lying off the main lobby. Open only in the season, it serves such fare as lobster bisque, superb hors d'oeuvres, a cassolette of veal shank, delectable sole and turbot dishes, and lamb provençale style. Meals cost from 65F ($44.20). The other specialty restaurant, Acla, is previewed separately, as is the Schwyzerhof-Stübli in the cellar and the Pianobar.

Park Hotel Kurhaus, CH-7500 St. Moritz, Switzerland (tel. 082/2-21-11), set on a flat alpine meadow in St. Moritz–Bad, is a Victorian-era hotel lying below the main congestion of the resort. Built in the grandest 19th-century tradition, it has twin baroque towers and symmetrical wings extending off to each side. Many of its rooms overlook a pine forest where concerts of classical music are presented in summer. Rather than considering its isolation from the town a drawback, many repeat visitors find it an advantage. Recognizing this, the hotel seems to try harder to create an array of activities, such as concerts and nature walks. Connected with a passageway to the spa and the mineral springs, the hotel sits near one of the cable car lifts (the Signal). A cross-country-ski school has its headquarters here and the hotel maintains four squash courts and a tennis school.

The 160 bedrooms, with modern furnishings, rent for 105F ($71.40) to 130F ($88.40) daily in bathless singles, 120F ($81.60) to 200F ($136) in singles with bath. Doubles cost 190F ($129.20) to 240F ($163.20) bathless, 220F ($149.60) to 390F ($265.20) with bath. All tariffs include half board, the prices depending on the season. The hotel is open from June to September and from December to April.

The Upper Bracket

Monopol-Grischuna, CH-7500 St. Moritz, Switzerland (tel. 082/3-44-33), has a stucco façade built within the last 20 years, with an occasional bay window extending above the busy street below. Guests patronize a nightclub and restaurant (the Grischuna) and enjoy an elegant series of public rooms furnished with French pieces, a few oil paintings, and well-polished wood detailing. The spacious bedrooms are colorfully designed around Louis XV, Louis XVI, or rustic furniture. There's a large covered pool on the top floor, along with a sunny roof terrace. Each of the accommodations has a private bath, and costs 90F ($61.20) to 200F ($136) daily in a single and 180F ($122.40) to 420F ($285.60) in a double, with half board included. Prices, of course, depend on the season and the room assignment.

Hotel Crystal, CH-7500 St. Moritz, Switzerland (tel. 082/2-11-65), is a large white building with curved corners that looks oddly futuristic when you see it next to the 19th-century buildings around it. The interior combines comfortable alpine rusticity with knotty-pine cabinets and ceiling beams, along with such up-to-date touches as wall-to-wall carpeting and cozy informal furniture. The bedrooms are outfitted with a combination of walnut and lighter grained woods, along with an occasional carved headboard. The in-house Grotto restaurant serves Italian specialties. A nearby piano bar provides midafternoon entertainment. Residents have free access to the swimming pool in the neighboring Kulm Hotel. With half board included, singles range from 115F ($78.20) to 205F ($139.40) daily, and doubles cost 200F ($136) to 400F ($272). All accommodations contain private bath, and rates depend on the season. The hotel shuts down in November.

Hotel Steffani, CH-7500 St. Moritz, Switzerland (tel. 082/2-21-01), was built in 1869 by a man named Lorenzo Steffani. It eventually ended up in the hands of the Märky family, who today welcome an elegant clientele into the rustic lobby where beams resembling railroad ties from the balconies of the two-tiered lobby. If you like soft-grained woods carved into regional designs, you'll find plenty of it here, especially in one of the restaurant areas. The management also offers a fitness room and an indoor swimming pool. Guests are accepted year round, but rates come in a wide range, depending not only on the season but on the amount of plumbing in the room. The single rate ranges from 100F ($68) to 180F ($122.40) daily in summer, from 190F ($129.20) to 220F ($149.60) in winter with private bath. Two persons pay from 160F ($108.80) to 320F ($217.60) daily in summer, from 360F ($244.80) to 420F ($285.60) in winter. All these tariffs include half board. You may have difficulty recognizing the entrance to the hotel section of this multifaceted establishment because of the many separate approaches to its restaurant and nightlife facilities. Some of these are covered separately in the "Where to Dine" and "After Dark" sections below.

Hotel Albana, CH-7500 St. Moritz, Switzerland (tel. 082/3-31-21). A hostelry was established at this site in 1644, and the building you see today has been under the same management since 1971. This is a popular hotel, painted a salmon color with white trim, and decorated inside with regional designs and an occasional hunting trophy. The ceilings are rustically beamed and painted, the bar area has stenciled primitive illustrations, and the lobby is filled with leather sofas, lots of wrought iron, and room dividers. The bedrooms are often rustically elegant, usually with ceiling beams or elaborate paneling and an occasional regional armoire. Other chambers are quite plain. On the premises are a sauna, fitness room, whirlpool, two restaurants, and a bar. Heinrich J. Weinmann and his family, your hosts, charge 85F ($57.80) to 190F ($129.20) daily in a single and 80F ($54.40) to 190F ($129.20) per person in a double, with half board included. Prices vary according to the season and the exposure of the room assigned. All rooms have baths or showers, color TV, mini-bars, and direct-dial phones.

Neues Posthotel, CH-7500 St. Moritz, Switzerland (tel. 082/2-21-21), is a year-round four-star hotel that is more inviting and comfortable than chic, even though it's placed right in the left ventricle of St. Moritz. Built in 1908, the hotel has seen many renovations and improvements since that day, but it still remains an effective period piece. The lower floor facing the lake supports a stone arch, and in the rear is a dramatic upper bridge that towers over the street. Peter and Elli Graber welcome guests into this much-used bastion, where a winter fireplace is kept blazing. The armchairs were designed for relaxed conviviality and placed there for no other reason, certainly not style. Rooms are comfortably furnished, and many are quite spacious. Accommodations with private balconies were built on the top floor. All units contain private baths, and two persons can stay here on half board terms, ranging from 180F ($122.40) to 360F ($244.80) daily, depending on the season. Singles pay from 90F ($61.20) to 180F ($122.40) on the same arrangement. A sauna and whirlpool are part of the facilities. The hotel also pleases guests with its cookery. Those who reserve get the desired seating with a view of the lake. Portions are most generous, including the almost mandatory "second helping" served on a clean plate.

The Middle Range

Hotel Languard Garni, CH-7500 St. Moritz, Switzerland (tel. 082/3-31-37), is a sunny family-run hotel a few buildings away from the main street of town. It was built a century ago as the private home of the owner, Mr. Languard, of the nearby Kulm Hotel. Today, after many alterations and expansions, it's owned by the Trivella family. A display case holding their various skiing awards hangs proudly near the reception desk. (One of the Trivella sons, Roberto, was a 1978 skiing champion.) The hotel has a thermometer with three different gauges set into the granite of the entryway, so you can check the day's temperature before leaving your room every morning. Its pine-paneled interior is clean and very charming, with a breakfast room that overlooks the valley and the lake. The staff is old-fashioned, very Swiss, and conservative, but willing to make your stay as comfortable as possible. Some of the accommodations have private balconies, private baths, radios, direct-dial phones, and safes. The Trivella family charges 60F ($40.80) to 100F ($68) daily in a single and 100F ($68) to 240F ($163.20) in a double, depending on the season. Breakfast is included in the price. The hotel is usually closed during all of May and November.

Hotel Bellevue, CH-7500 St. Moritz, Switzerland (tel. 082/2-21-61), is a white and buff-colored building with an occasional balcony to relieve the boxiness of its façade. Some of the public rooms extend along one of its sides, with panoramic views that justify the hotel's name. The inside is functionally attractive, with patterned carpeting, the obligatory paneling over some of its surface, and comfortable bedrooms with wood-grained furniture, sometimes upholstered in leather. In summer, a double begins at 165F ($112.20) daily, going up to 235F ($159.80) in winter. The lowest priced single in summer is 98F ($66.65), rising to a high of 133F ($90.45) in winter. All these tariffs include a buffet breakfast.

Sporthotel Bären, CH-7500 St. Moritz, Switzerland (tel. 082/3-36-56). My favorite part about this hotel is the 54-foot swimming pool with the fireplace set where another hotel might have placed a diving board. The other public rooms are tastefully decorated with Oriental rugs and ceiling beams, with a lot of rough-hewn stones set into decorative areas to remind you that the mountains are indeed very near. Bedrooms are simple and comfortable, usually with views out over the hillside where the hotel is planted. Each of the accommodations has a private bath. Rates depend on the season: singles range from 65F ($44.20) to 120F ($81.60) daily, and doubles cost 120F ($81.60) to 230F ($156.40). The higher rates are in effect in winter.

Hotel Eden, CH-7500 St. Moritz, Switzerland (tel. 082/3-61-61), is a pleasant garni (breakfast only) hotel off a quiet street in the center of town. It was built more than 100 years ago, and has been in the Degiacomi family for almost 40 years. It doesn't cost as much as either of its more glamorous neighbors, the Kulm a few paces uphill and the ultra-expensive Badrutt's Palace of which it has a view. The Eden opens onto a tiny plaza behind a symmetrical façade that reminds you of a Tuscan villa. Inside is a pine-sheathed parlor filled with family antiques. There's a covered skylight above the wood-trimmed lobby, illuminating the wrought-iron balustrades of the upper two stories. Each of the modernized bedrooms has a private bath and conservative furniture. Depending on the season, singles range from 65F ($44.20) to 105F ($71.40) daily, and doubles cost 120F ($81.60) to 210F ($142.80). Open July to October and December to April.

Hotel Waldhaus Am See, CH-7500 St. Moritz, Switzerland (tel. 082/3-76-76). From a position at the side of the nearby lake, this property looks a lot like a scaled-down version of a Teutonic castle. Built in 1880 as a tavern, the structure was later expanded into a private home by a Swiss industrialist. It has steeply sloping roofs, decorative crenellations, and a massively protruding stone expansion. You can dine in one of three lovely rooms, the largest of which has access to a sheltered sun terrace and big-windowed views over the lake. Halen and Claudio Bernasconi-Mettier, the hosts, offer comfortably conservative rooms, each with a private phone and radio and some with color TV, mini-bars, and private baths. Depending on the season and the plumbing, they charge from 65F ($44.20) to 125F ($85) daily in a single and from 130F ($88.40) to 300F ($204) in a double, these tariffs including half board. Closed in November.

Budget Living

Hotel Bernina, CH-7500 St. Moritz, Switzerland (tel. 082/3-60-22), is very close to the lake in St. Moritz–Bad. It has a pleasant, earth-colored lobby with warm textiles and lots of wood. Its format is low-key and unpretentious, with a reception area you'll reach after crossing through a cozy restaurant. This has been under the management of the Herrmann family for several generations. They charge 90F ($61.20) to 200F ($136) daily in a double, and 55F ($37.40) to 105F ($71.40) in a single, with half board included. Prices, of course, depend on the season. The Bernina is closed in May and October.

Hotel National, CH-7500 St. Moritz, Switzerland (tel. 082/3-32-74), is an old-fashioned, symmetrically proportioned hotel with neoclassical detailing around its windows and wrought-iron balconies. The interior has a scattering of Oriental rugs and informal furniture. Fredy Wissel is the friendly and helpful manager. The hotel is one of the better bargains in St. Moritz, with comfortably furnished rooms, some of which have private bath or shower. With half board included, singles range from 55F ($37.40) to 90F ($61.20) daily, while doubles cost 110F ($74.80) to 180F ($122.40), depending on the season. Rates depend on the plumbing and the season. The hotel is opposite a large indoor swimming pool. Open June to September and December to April.

WHERE TO DINE: Chances are, you'll be staying on some sort of boarding arrangement at your hotel, but you may want to escape occasionally for a change-of-pace meal, if only to sample the wares at another hotel. There are also some good independent eateries in St. Moritz.

Restaurant/The Grill Room, Badrutt's Palace Hotel (tel. 082/2-11-01), are two pockets of posh. The main dining room (also called The Restaurant) is presided over by the professional and polite maître d', Hugo Keusch, who has worked at the hotel in one capacity or another since 1952. Mr. Keusch can indicate the tables formerly occupied by the Shah of Iran and his Farah Diba, the Aga Khan, or Alfred Hitchcock. A staff of 70 serves the room. A fixed-price meal costs from 75F ($51) at lunch, from 80F ($54.40) at dinner. À la carte meals go from 85F ($57.80) way up. Representative menu listings include fresh oysters, smoked trout, risotto with exotic mushrooms, julienne of veal with white wine sauce, saddle of roebuck, and an array of desserts. Guests on en pension take their meals here.

Some guests prefer their meals amid the green and gold baroque decor of the high-ceilinged grill room a few steps from the entrance of the main dining room, on the lobby level of the hotel. Menus are à la carte, priced from 85F ($57.80) for a full meal. Here the cuisine and the specialties are more lavish than those in the hotel's main dining room. Menu items include hearts of artichoke with a salad of truffles, terrine of shellfish with smoked salmon and watercress sauce, lobster cocktail with aged cognac, fettuccine with foie gras and two varieties of exotic mushrooms, and poached quail with grapes. At the height of high season, meals are served in the main dining room from 12:15 to 3 p.m. and 7:30 to 10 p.m. daily. Meals in the Grill Room are 12:30 to 2:30 p.m. and 8 to 11 p.m. daily. Reservations and appropriate attire in either restaurant are strongly recommended.

Trattoria Kings, Badrutt's Palace Hotel (tel. 082/2-11-01), is the least-formal restaurant in the hotel, one of the establishment's few corners where jackets and ties are not required, and it manages to impart a wholesome feeling of well-polished alpine warmth. The place opens for drinks in the late afternoon, and meals are served only at dinner from 7:30 p.m. to midnight every day in winter only. A pianist adds to the gemütlichkeit. At first glance the place appears like a well-decorated stube, but full meals are sophisticated affairs costing from 80F ($54.40) per person. Typical dishes include trout soup with shrimp, skewered brochette of lamb with mint, and sautéed veal kidneys with flap mushrooms. If you order it in advance, the chef will prepare a succulent version of bouillabaisse or paella. Reservations are suggested. This pine-sheathed haven lies one flight below the reception desk of the hotel but has a separate entrance of its own from the street.

Chesa Veglia, 2 via Veglia, in Dorf (tel. 082/3-35-96). *Chesa* means "house" in Romansh, and that's exactly what this Engadine-style building once was. Built of stone, stucco, and carved hand-hewn wood in 1658, it still retains much of its original paneling and carving, as well as entire rooms removed piece by piece from the houses of constantly feuding local leaders who would be horrified if they knew that many of their possessions are today under the same roof. You'll enter through a massively arched door made of carved oak, and there you'll find three restaurants, each on a different floor, all of them rustically decorated. The Chadafö Grill cooks your meat over a wood fire visible from the dining room. The Patrizier-Stube serves regional specialties. The Hayloft, the least expensive place to dine, is a pizzeria, with a wood-stoked oven. Simple meals in either the stube or pizzeria begin at 36F ($23.80). Local musicians will probably be playing folkloric music while you eat, which many clients consider reason enough for coming here. Chesa Veglia is the only authentic Engadine house remaining in St. Moritz. If you're visiting for a gourmet repast, expect to spend from 90F ($61.20) up. For that, you're given a wide choice of international dishes, ranging from Italian (saltimbocca) to Hungarian (goulash) to Russian (chicken Kiev). Try the grilled scampi or trout meunière. The desserts are equally elegant, including soufflés and mousses. Hours in summer are 11 a.m. to midnight, in winter from 11 a.m. to 2 a.m. daily. The restaurant is closed from the beginning of April till the end of June and from mid-September until the beginning of December. It's owned and operated by the Palace Hotel.

Restaurant Chesa Pirani, La Punt-Chamues (tel. 082/7-25-15), is a charming Engadine house about 12 miles from the center of St. Moritz. The Hitzbergers are the attractive couple who have set up this first-class restaurant with excellent cuisine and service. You'll be shown into one of a series of dining rooms, none of them holding more than four or five tables. Mr. Hitzberger prepares his original recipes in the kitchen, and these might include an avocado salad with shrimp and a sour vinegar sauce, a hearty cabbage soup, foie gras made by himself, and a wide range of seafood. The quiet dining rooms are supervised by Mrs. Hitzberger, who spares no effort to be of service. Dessert might be a champagne sorbet. À la carte meals range from 75F ($51) to 110F ($74.80), while fixed-price dinners cost 70F ($47.60) and 90F ($61.20). The restaurant is closed on Monday in summer, open seven days a week in winter from 11 a.m. to 3 p.m. and 6 p.m. to midnight. It's also closed the last week in April until mid-June, and in November.

La Marmite, at Corviglia Bergstation (tel. 082/3-63-55), is the best high-altitude restaurant in the Grisons. You'll need to take the funicular to reach this woodsy restaurant, and once you're there you'll probably be tempted to ski home after your meal. The place is appropriately rustic, with excellent service and a sophisticated menu choice offered by the Mathis family. There's also a less expensive cafeteria on the premises that in midwinter is usually crowded with skiers. An à la carte meal in the more elegant room will range from 40F ($27.20) to 60F ($40.80). It might include hot red deer cream soup, fresh duck liver with truffles, calves' foot in a truffle sauce, or a bone-warming bouillon, perfect for a cold day, flavored with marrow, vegetables, sherry, and meat. If you're in the mood, you might ask for the six-course caviar menu or a seafood omelet. Desserts might be figs soaked in grappa, although a buffet of some 25 to 30 desserts is available if you prefer something less potent. The restaurant is open from noon to 4 p.m. and 6 to 10 p.m. daily from November 20 until April 20 and from early June until mid-October.

Restaurant Acla, Hotel Schweizerhof (tel. 082/2-21-71), means "little house on the mountain" in the local language, Romansh. This is a pretty elegant place, but in spirit it tries to live up to its namesake, serving savory Swiss specialties along with an international selection of dishes from 11 a.m. to midnight daily. The restaurant's more popular name, at least among the locals, is "Chez

Molly." The best value is the fixed-price two-course lunch, costing 15F ($10.20).
However, if you order à la carte, either at lunch or dinner, you can easily spend
from 65F ($44.20) and go nowhere near the Iranian caviar. You're given the fa-
mous tafelspitz (the boiled beef of Vienna), blinis with caviar and smoked salmon,
and the "original" Viennese fried chicken. Trout is from the Inn, and you can
also order poached fresh salmon and filets of sole bonne femme.

    Restaurant Steffani, Hotel Steffani (tel. 082/2-21-01). Half-board guests
of the hotel usually dine upstairs in the elegant grill room, but in many ways, I
prefer the warm wood-lined decor and the polite service of the street-level tavern.
Open to the public, the place is atmospheric and staffed with uniformed waiters
who seem to have been trained in Italy. A four-course fixed-price meal is a bargain
at 35F ($23.80), although no one will mind if you order just a platter of food
with a garnish for 18F ($12.25). Meals are served without interruption every day
from 11:30 a.m. to 11:30 p.m. daily. Specialties include tagliatelle Alfredo,
poulet chasseur with polenta, alpine goat with rosemary, at least six different
kinds of pasta, trout, lobster, and pepper steak. À la carte meals cost from 65F
($44.20).

    Rôtisserie des Chevaliers, Hotel Kulm, 18 via Veglia, in Dorf (tel. 082/2-
11-51), is the grill room of one of the most historic hotels in St. Moritz. In addition to the square yards of exquisite paneling, there are mementos of the Cresta
bobsled run decorating some of the walls outside the main room. The smaller of
the two menus lists changing daily specialties, which include seasonal food such
as fresh asparagus, along with terrine of goose liver, grilled sea bass flambé, and a
unique stuffed veal Hotel Kulm. Dessert might be an apple sherbet or a flambéed
fruit. Meals begin at 50F ($34) going up. The restaurant is open from noon to
3 p.m. and 7 p.m. to midnight daily except from mid-September until the end of
November and from mid-April until the end of June.

    Veltliner-Keller, 11 Via del Bagn (tel. 082/3-40-09). Evening meals are
served on the elegant first floor, where many of St. Moritz's wintertime ski bums
always seem to have a good time. The bill of fare lists mushroom salad, trout with
mushrooms, spaghetti, a wide selection of meats and fish, along with a tasty risotto. Desserts include just about every in-season fruit in Europe. À la carte dinners cost from 35F ($23.80) to 50F ($34). It is open from 9 a.m. to midnight.

    Grotto, Hotel Crystal, 1 via Traunter Piazzas (tel. 082/2-11-65), is the best
place in St. Moritz for Ticino food in a dining room that, if you didn't know you
were in the Engadine, you'd swear was in the Italian-speaking part of the country. Many of the hors d'oeuvres are laid out on a buffet. Main courses might include rabbit with thyme, an array of pasta dishes, codfish with polenta, and
fondue Piedmont style. You might begin with a steaming hot bowl of minestrone. Desserts are smooth and rich, including a classic zabaglione. Meals cost
from 40F ($27.20). Hours are daily from noon to 4 p.m. and 5 to 10 p.m.
Closed in November.

    Restaurant Cascade, 6 via Somplaz, in Dorf (tel. 082/3-15-22), also offers
Italian-inspired recipes from the Ticino. Its popular bar is visited in the "Après
Ski" section, but you can also come in here for a meal daily from 11 a.m. to
11 p.m. (on Sunday from 3 to 11 p.m.). It's inexpensively priced, at least if you
stick to the 22F ($14.95) set menu. Next door to the Hotel Steffani, it offers in-
ternational dishes, including carpaccio, saltimbocca, and gnocchi Piedmont
style, but mainly it specializes in pastas and entrecôtes. Usually a young, fun
crowd patronizes this establishment. You can eat or drink in denim or ski parkas
in a setting of etched glass mirrors and bentwood chairs.

    Al Réduit, Piazza Mauritius (tel. 082/3-66-57), is a typical trattoria and
pizzeria that offers good food in a rustic setting with red-and-white-checked tablecloths. Hours are from 11 a.m. to midnight except on Sunday when it doesn't
open until 4 p.m. That makes it a popular late-night rendezvous for enjoying
food after many dining rooms have closed. It's reached by walking down steps

into a shopping arcade near the Hotel Albana. Most diners come for one of 15 different kinds of pizza, but you can also order more substantial fare, such as rib-sticking pastas, prepared in any number of ways. Meats are grilled to perfection on an open grill. If the weather's right, you can also select a table on one of the best sun terraces in town. Meals average 35F ($23.80).

Restaurant Engiadina, 2 Piazza da Scoula (tel. 082/3-32-65), is sort of an old-fashioned family dining room, unusual for St. Moritz. Right in the center of Dorf, it's run by the Melcher family. In summer, meals are served from 10 a.m. to 2 p.m., dinner from 5 to 9:30 p.m. except Sunday. In winter, however, it remains open from 10 a.m. to 10 p.m. daily and also opens on Sunday (4 to 10 p.m.). Pleasant, comfortable, and simple, the restaurant stands across from the town hall, the most impressive public building in St. Moritz. It consists of two hunters'-style rooms filled with trophies and alpine accents such as pinewood tables and paneling. There's even an outdoor wooden deck for drinking or dining if the weather is right. You get good value for your money here, feasting on such fare as carpaccio, petite marmite, fondues (with cheese or champagne), grilled steaks, goulash, and snails in garlic butter. The average price of a meal is 40F ($27.20).

Le Mandarin, Hotel Steffani (tel. 082/2-21-01), is one of the rare Chinese restaurants in the region. Because of its novelty, and because its team of chefs comes from Hong Kong, it does a thriving business, especially later in the evening. Lunch is served only in the height of the midwinter season, between 11:30 a.m. and 2 p.m. daily. Dinner is offered throughout the year from 6:30 to 11 p.m., every day except from late April to early June. The decor is predictably Chinese, with black lacquer screens and hanging lanterns. The menu is large, beginning with a wide selection of hors d'oeuvres and soups, then following with such dishes as squid with peppers, sautéed fish in hot sauce, and butterfly prawns. Duck is prepared in any number of ways, the house specialty being Peking duck, which is made only for three or four diners. The pork and veal dishes are especially delectable. Meals cost from 40F ($27.20) up.

Landgasthof Meierei (tel. 082/3-32-42). The solid and sprawling collection of farm-related buildings that contains it was built a century ago as a relay station and stables for the Swiss Postal Service. Today, one of the paneled and spacious buildings contains a quartet of rustically alluring dining rooms, which have been frequented by some of the most glamorous winter residents of St. Moritz. They include the late Shah of Iran, Gunther Sachs, Picasso, the Aga Khan, and everybody's favorite deposed monarch, King Farouk of Egypt.

The drawback (or advantage, if you're health conscious) of this establishment is that no diner is allowed to drive a car along the difficult-to-navigate service roads that reach it. You can hire a taxi, or you can hire a horse-drawn sleigh and make getting there a part of your midwinter experience. My recommendation is that you park your car in the public parking lot near the edge of the lake, just below the Hotel Waldhaus am See, and walk the 20-minute lakeside promenade to the restaurant. The footpath has been carefully paved, and there are only a few rolling slopes to negotiate. Before you set out, it's best to phone the restaurant to confirm that they're open. Meals, costing from 50F ($34), are served daily from 11:30 a.m. to 3 p.m. and 6:30 to 9:30 p.m. Considering the glamorous clientele the place has attracted, its menu is earthy and simple.

Hanselmann, 8 via Maistra (tel. 082/3-38-64), is traditionally popular with the après-ski crowd (see below), but it is also one of the best places in town to have breakfast or lunch. Since its beginning in the middle of the last century when St. Moritz became a magnet for English tourists, the place has grown to occupy a much-embellished building decorated with *sgraffito* in red and pale brown arranged in borders and rosettes. Tea rooms are on the first two floors. For breakfast, you might choose an omelet (from a German language menu), an egg and cheese dish, bacon and eggs, or a country plate with Black Forest ham and

Valais rye rolls. Toast dishes include Welsh rarebit, smoked salmon with buttered toast, and others with scrambled egg, mushrooms, or ham. With tea, coffee, or cocoa, your morning meal will cost around 10F ($6.80) to 15F ($10.20) (salmon is more expensive). A fixed-price lunch will cost around 20F ($13.60) and you get a good, filling meal whose menu changes daily. The place is open daily from 7 a.m. to 7 p.m., with the upstairs restaurant opening at 11:30 a.m. Reservations are taken only for lunch. The grandson of the founder, Fritz Mutschler, owns the establishment.

MUSEUMS: You can get a glimpse of the history of St. Moritz and the Engadines by visiting the **Engadine Museum,** 39 via dal Bagn (tel. 082/3-43-33), open on Monday to Saturday from 9:30 a.m. to noon and 2 to 5 p.m., on Sunday from 10 a.m. to noon. It is closed on Saturday and in May and November. Admission is 4F ($2.70) for adults, 2.50F ($1.70) for children. Here you will learn about *sgraffito* (designs in plasterwork) on Engadine buildings, local styles of architecture, and see a collection of Engadine antiques and regional furniture. The elegantly decorated state room shows how noblemen in the area lived. Artifacts from the Bronze Age when Druids lived in the land are also on display, including the 3,000-year-old encasement of the spring of Mauritius. St. Moritz stands on a former "mystic place" of the Druids.

The **Segantini Museum** 30 via Somplaz (tel. 082/3-44-54), displays works by the artist Giovanni Segantini, who lived in the Engadine (Maloja) during the last years of his life. He died at the end of the 19th century. The artist's work is famous for his technique, the Divisionism, and his most important work is a triptych called *Birth, Life, Death,* which is exhibited at the museum among other important pictures. The museum is open in summer from 9 a.m. to 12:30 p.m. and 2:30 to 5 p.m. Tuesday to Saturday and from 10:30 a.m. to 12:30 p.m. and 2:30 to 4:30 p.m. Sunday. Winter hours are from 10 a.m. to 12:30 p.m. and 3 to 5 p.m. Tuesday to Saturday, from 10:30 a.m. to 12:30 p.m. and 3 to 5 p.m. in winter. It is closed Monday. Admission is 5F ($3.40).

SHOPPING: St. Moritz has a concentration of boutiques and shops rivaling those of Paris and London, with prices in line with those charged in the big cities. It has the quality found in the cities but, of course, not the quantity. Smart shoppers have long known that the best time to buy in St. Moritz is during the winter and summer clearance sales. You can stroll along the inner village streets and find all the shops easily. Some of the most important ones are on the **Via Maistra** (main shopping street) and in the **Palace-Arcades.**

In spite of its bland architecture, **Gallaria Caspar Badrutt** is a choice shopping arcade that has a number of services as well. For example, it offers a fitness center, called Caribbean Sunshine, along with a pharmacy, an elegant hairdressing salon, an art gallery, and a host of chic little boutiques that come and go. These sell everything from men's wear to perfumes, from lingerie to furs by Balenciaga or fashions by Saint Laurent.

There are dozens of fashionable bars and cafés. Relax with a cup of coffee and a piece of pastry in one of the world-renowned *Konditoreien* (coffeehouses).

SPORTS—WINTER AND SUMMER: Although snow skiing in all its forms is the premier sport engaged in in this resort area today, other winter sports activities, including curling, ice skating, tobogganing, bobsledding, and an early form of ice hockey were enjoyed by most winter visitors in the last part of the 19th century. With the introduction of competitive skiing and ski jumping, this sport forged ahead in popularity and is likely to remain in the number one spot.

Winter is now the top season in St. Moritz, with its "champagne climate" and attractions for top-flight winter sports figures drawing a cosmopolitan and very well-heeled clientele annually. Long a favorite of movie stars, St. Moritz also attracts persons prominent in the higher economic, cultural, and political echelons of the Western world. Then, too, as the author Peter Viertel once wrote, it attracts "the hangers-on of the rich . . . the jewel thieves, the professional backgammon players and general layabouts, as well as the high-class ladies of doubtful virtue (if such a thing still exists)."

The world's oldest ski school is at Moritz-Dorf, founded in 1927. A total of five ski complexes encircles St. Moritz, the nearest being Corviglia–Piz Nair, which has some challenging, mile-long runs back to the base. There's an abundance of snow in winter on 250 miles of downhill ski runs, 100 miles of cross-country ski trails, and the Olympic ski-jumping hill. For skiing here, you have a choice of five mountains, all of which can be skied on one lift pass. Corvatsch, with 5,800 feet of height, is known for the open-bowl skiing that is possible on top. Corviglia has broad runs attracting fledgling and intermediate skiers and is the staging area for skiing Piz Nair, the highest skiable mountain, 10,837 feet, with a vertical drop of 4,748 feet. Nearby, in Pontresina, a neighbor resort to be visited in the next section, are the steep Piz Lagalb and Diavolezza with skiing for all levels of experience, including a run over the Morteratsch glacier.

In all, St. Moritz has a total of 25 mountain railways and 58 ski lifts. A six-day general ski pass costs 190F ($129.20) for adults, 140F ($95.20) for children under 16. Various other ski passes are also sold.

The groomed and tracked cross-country runs in the Upper Engadine valley include a tame one-mile loop near the cross-country center, and trails are laid out between the valley resorts. A one-mile segment is lit for night skiing. The Engadine cross-country ski marathon is a major annual event. And of course, in this chic and elegant ambience, the après-ski social activities are always special.

Horse racing on the frozen lake of St. Moritz is also popular, or you can take taxi rides on the bobsled natural-ice run. There are 30 curling rinks, winter golf played on the frozen lake, and tobogganing on the Cresta run. Indoor tennis and squash can be played.

Instruction in cross-country skiing, available in groups on Monday, Wednesday, and Friday from 10 a.m. to noon, costs 19F ($12.90) for a half day and 49F ($33.30) for three half days. A day's excursion costs 25F ($17).

If you're interested in curling but don't know how, you can have a first training session free (40 minutes). Individual lessons thereafter cost 25F ($17). Rental of equipment costs 20F ($13.60) per day.

A bobsled ride costs 100F ($68), but you get your picture taken (for you to keep), a drink, and a certificate in addition to the ride.

The spa section of this resort is called **St. Moritz–Bad,** where you can take mud and carbon dioxide mineral-water baths, physical therapy, and physiotherapy while you enjoy the stimulating alpine climate in a modern Health Spa Center in Bad (tel. 082/3-31-47), next to the Parkhotel Kurhaus. The spa opened in 1976. From Roman times to now, "taking the waters" has been a popular pursuit for persons seeking natural curative treatment for relief from pain and stress. The charge for a mineral-water bath is 14F ($9.50); for a peat-mud bath, 50F ($34). For additional treatments you can get a special price list.

In summer, in this area with 25 sparkling mountain lakes, there are many pursuits for visitors, including walking on scenic panorama trails. A rich cultural program and all types of sports activities are offered.

Windsurfing at St. Moritz and on the lakes of nearby resorts has boomed in popularity, with the Engadine surf marathon in July drawing competitors from all over the world. A two-hour lesson costs from 30F ($20.40) to 40F ($27.20) per person. The lake is also a sailboat lure.

Greens fees on the 18-hole golf course are 50F ($34) per day. Rates at the 25 tennis courts vary from 23F ($15.65) to 47F ($31.95) per hour. For tennis and squash information, consult the Corviglia Tennis Center (tel. 082/3-15-00).

Fishing may be done only by persons over 16, with special permission.

There's summer skiing on Crovatsch, costing 30F ($20.40) for all day. Only half-day passes on the Diavolezza, costing 24F ($16.30) per person, are sold, because the afternoon sun turns the mountainside into slush at midday. Information, reservations, whatever, about any and all of these sports is available from the tourist office (see "Practical Facts" above).

ST. MORITZ AFTER DARK: The nightlife here in winter is the most glamorous in Switzerland, centering around the Palace, but there are dozens of other bars, restaurants, and taverns. In some chic discos you might see a man and woman at one table in formal attire, while a couple at the next table will be clad in jeans. Nightlife is chic and very expensive, and case after case of French champagne is hauled into some of these dives, especially in February. But no one looks askance if you should order a beer.

Immediately after a skier returns from the slopes, he or she heads for **Hanselmann,** 8 via Maistra (tel. 082/3-38-64), recommended separately as a place to have breakfast and lunch. Open from 7:30 a.m. to 7 p.m. daily, the tea room has its busiest hours from 4:30 to 6 p.m. The place is famous for its pastries, cakes, and chocolates. After a day in the open air, a genial crowd gathers to have hot chocolate, café espresso, tea, or even a cup of grog with rum. Expect to spend from 10F ($6.80), more if you choose a large-size Engadiner Nusstorte (a delectable pastry of walnuts, butter, and honey), the Baumkuchen, or caviar toast. Hanselmann's also has a retail counter where you can choose chocolates or other confections to take home.

After a rest and dinner, it's time for fancier action.

King's Club, Badrutt's Palace Hotel (tel. 082/2-11-01). Every grand hotel has a disco where members of the outside community can mingle with the rich and famous. The price of entrance to this basement-level club is designed to keep out the homeless, but if you want to pay it, you'll be ushered into its stone-trimmed recesses. A "membership card" costs 30F ($20.40) in low season, 50F ($34) in high season, and gives its purchaser the right to one free drink. In season, the club is open nightly from 10 p.m. to 6 a.m. Nestled on comfortable banquettes, you'll admire naïve jungle-inspired paintings illuminated with spotlights and listen to recently released and danceable music. Unlike many other corners of Badrutt's Palace, jackets and ties are not required.

Grand Bar, Badrutt's Palace Hotel (tel. 082/2-11-01). The tables are tiny, the drinks are expensive, and the stand-up bar is inconveniently set up on the wrong side of the stage, behind the sight lines of the tables. Still, this is considered a citadel of chic. Murals that might have been executed by Jean Cocteau add visual interest when the music is not playing. The quality of your evening might depend on the musical artist of the moment, but in its past, the place has seen some winners. There's no cover charge, but scotch and soda goes for 22F ($14.95) and up. You'd be well advised to reserve a table in advance. The place is open from 10 p.m. to 4 or 5 a.m. every night when the hotel is open.

Schwyzerhof-Stübli, Hotel Schweizerhof (tel. 082/2-21-71), in the basement of this previously recommended hotel, has a separate entrance favored by skiers who often head directly here after they leave the slopes. Incongruously for such a staid, conservative hotel, the Stübli often gets quite rowdy in the hearty Teutonic tradition. Some people buy wine by the bottle and serve glasses of it to their party. Many guests, in spite of the crowds, prefer to order a platter of food, their dinner, served on top of the bar. The place looks much older than it probably is, with a coffered alpine ceiling and pinewood paneling, along with trestle tables. Open from 4 p.m. to midnight daily, it offers Warsteiner beer from the keg at 6F ($4.10) and raclette at 17F ($11.55) per portion.

The **Pianobar,** Hotel Schweizerhof (tel. 082/2-21-71), offers one of the most delightful and mellow evening's entertainment in St. Moritz. The barman, Edi, who is well-known by all guests here, serves smooth cocktails in a "refined" atmosphere from 8 p.m. to 2 a.m. daily. The hotel imports a changing array of pianists to entertain you. Drinks cost from 15F ($10.20).

La Cava Steffani, Hotel Steffani (tel. 082/2-21-01). This might be the ultimate après-ski cellar bar. Contained beneath vaulted ceilings in the lowest level of the previously recommended Hotel Steffani, it's decorated with antique skis, ski poles, and Engadine chairs. You can order full meals, which begin at 30F ($20.40). There's an array of wine (including champagne) sold by the glass. Wine costs from 2F ($1.35) per glass, from 10F ($6.80) for a bottle, which you can share with your party by candlelight. Menu items include fondue chinoise, picatta with spaghetti, rumpsteak, two varieties of ravioli, and entrecôte. The place is open from 4 p.m. to midnight every day.

Cresta Bar, Hotel Steffani (tel. 082/2-21-01), is small, cramped, and nearly concealed behind a thick door a few steps from the hotel's reception desk. It isn't particularly noteworthy in any way, except that its pair of rooms are almost mobbed with skiers at the end of a midwinter's day. Beer costs from 4.50F ($3.05). The bar is open every day from 4 p.m. to midnight.

Vivai Disco, Hotel Steffani (tel. 082/2-21-01). Guests of the Hotel Steffani enter free, but everyone else pays a cover charge, which varies from 10F ($6.80) to 20F ($13.60), depending on the season and the night of the week. Once you're inside, beer costs 14F ($9.50). You'll reach it via its own separate entrance, which opens onto the square in front of the hotel. Its basement-level portal is etched in Engadine line drawings, but inside all is intimately lit and modern. The music is hot, recently released, and danceable.

Sunny Bar, Hotel Kulm (tel. 082/2-11-51), is one of the most popular rendezvous points in town, and certainly one in a hotel with a long history. Guests dance beneath the yellow representation of the signs of the zodiac. No entrance fee is charged, but drinks can cost from 9F ($6.10). It is open nightly to 3 a.m.

Cascade Bar, 6 via Somplaz, (tel. 082/3-15-22), is an art nouveau establishment with stained and etched glass. It can get quite rowdy at times, but it's a lot of fun. The posters are unabashedly explicit, at least for Paris of 1903. Music lovers will appreciate the unsolicited groups of men singing spontaneous choruses of everything from barbershop quartets to operatic trios. Cordon Rouge chills invitingly in Plexiglas buckets near the naturalistic sculpture on the zinc bartop, although drinks cost from 9F ($6.10). A restaurant is attached. It is open daily to 11 p.m.

14. PONTRESINA

It doesn't have the fame of St. Moritz, but Pontresina (5,916 feet) is nonetheless one of the leading headquarters for hiking and mountaineering in the area. It lies in the Upper Engadines on the road to the Bernina Pass, at the mouth of the Bernina Valley, surrounded by woodland made up of larches and stone pines. The towering peaks of the Alps surround and shelter it. From Pontresina you have views of the glacier amphitheater of the Roseg.

This was first a summer resort, the early tourists being attracted to the fresh mountain air, but now it's a leading ski resort, known for its huge jump. The village today is filled with hotels and shops. Unlike St. Moritz, Pontresina has much old Engadine architecture.

The long hours of sunshine in winter and the easy accessibility of all the noted ski sites in the greater St. Moritz area have shown visitors that it's not necessary to stay in crowded St. Moritz, unless they have a real yen to do so. Sites that are lures for skiers in winter are attractive for sightseeing tours in summer. Many trips are possible. The **Diavolezza** tour, which starts at 5,765 feet and passes over four glaciers on the way down, is one of the major attractions of the Engadines. You go by road toward Bernina as far as the lower station of the Diavolezza cable car, which takes you up to where you can go on to 10,000 feet by drag lift if your purpose is skiing. From the 9,765-foot height there's a celebrated ski run down to the valley or down the glacier to Morteratsch. If you go with a guide for this glacier walk, allow about three hours. In season the Diavolezza cable car is likely to be crowded, the journey up taking about half an hour. Round-trip fare is 20F ($13.60). In summer beautiful alpine tours are made from here.

Closer at hand is **Alp Languard,** rising to some 8,500 feet, directly above Pontresina with slopes for young and old. You reach it by ski lift, a round-trip costing 12F ($8.15). **Muottas Muragl,** about a 12-minute bus ride from Pontresina, has panoramic views, nursery slopes, and easy runs, and **Piz Lagalp** is steep and challenging. Hiking trails in the mountains lead to the little way stations, huts of the Swiss Alpine Club. Horse-drawn sleigh and coach rides in the Val Roseg and to Morteratsch are popular.

WHERE TO STAY: Looking like a small-scale palace for some minor royalty, **Grand Hotel Kronenhof,** CH-7540 Pontresina, Switzerland (tel. 082/6-01-11), embraces a circular driveway with its symmetrical arms. It sits in the center of town, behind iron gates, within earshot of a stream and a pair of tennis courts. Inside, Corinthian columns, vaulted and frescoed ceilings, and laughing faces of mythical courtiers gaze, in art nouveau splendor, from the coves of the ceilings. This is without competition the grandest hotel in town. Its oldest section dates from 1848, but the impressive detailing that greets you, dates (with many careful overhauls) from 1898. The Oriental carpets and the English club–style furniture gracefully complement the columns and the formally dressed reception staff. There's the high-ceilinged and grand dining room you'd expect, a winter ice-skating rink, both an indoor and an outdoor swimming pool, and organized activities that include curling contests, films, gala dinners for half-board clients, and access to local ski schools.

Each of the 104 rooms contains a phone, radio, mini-bar, and (if requested) a TV. Depending on the plumbing and the time of year, singles cost 140F ($95.20) to 220F ($149.60) daily, and doubles go for 130F ($88.40) to 210F ($142.80) per person, with half board, service, and taxes included. It's open from June to September and December to March. The hotel restaurant, the Kronenstübli, is reviewed separately.

Hotel Walther, CH-7504 Pontresina, Switzerland (tel. 082/6-64-71). The ground-floor rooms have ceilings high enough to give a baronial impression of 19th-century spaciousness. If you tear yourself away from the piano bar for a walk onto the lawns surrounding the hotel, you'll see a façade that looks like a cross between a stronghold of the Knights Templar and a Wagnerian fantasy of Disneyland. Despite the medieval aspects of the façade, the bar area inside couldn't be more 20th century, with long rows of bottles lined up behind the serving area, plus a restaurant in the castle style, with good service and food. Tennis courts, an indoor swimming pool, Jacuzzi, sauna, massage room, and children's playroom give plenty of activity. Each of the accommodations has a private bath and is priced according to the season and size. On the half-board arrangement, singles pay 135F ($91.80) to 180F ($122.40), and two persons are charged 250F ($170) to 360F ($244.80). The hotel is open from June to October and December to April.

Hotel Schweizerhof, CH-7504 Pontresina, Switzerland (tel. 082/6-64-12), was built in 1910, but it was so drastically modernized in 1975 that oldtime visitors would hardly recognize it, as much of the crowning glory of its roofline, including the towers and turrets, was removed. Nonetheless, this is a huge, comfortable, and expansive hotel, a member of the Best Western chain. The lobby of this hotel is walled with hewn stone and capped with a ceiling of weathered wood slats. Coupled with the bright carpeting, it gives an airy, comfortable impression of relaxed grandeur that is repeated throughout the rest of the hotel. The dining room has Engadine-style painting under the arches, and a beamed ceiling. The outside are long rows of white walls accented with yellow balconies. All accommodations contain private bath, and range in price from 105F ($71.40) to 150F ($102) daily in a single and 200F ($136) to 290F ($197.20) in a double, with half board included. Prices depend on the season. Guests are accepted from June through October and from December through April.

Sporthotel, CH-7504 Pontresina, Switzerland (tel. 082/6-63-31), is a tall, symmetrical Victorian building. The manager speaks English, and offers the best breakfast buffet in town. Many residents eat so much they can afford to skip lunch. The comfortable bedrooms offer good views, and are colorful, tasteful, and equipped with a private bath. The beamed dining room has alpine chairs and Engadine illustrations of animals and plants. Much of the rest of the place is cozily paneled and filled with softly upholstered armchairs. Singles cost from 86F ($58.50) to 135F ($91.80) daily, and doubles range from 164F ($111.50) to 256F ($174.10), with half board included. Prices depend on the season and the plumbing. Guests are received from June through October and from December through April.

Rosatsch Hotel, CH-7504 Pontresina, Switzerland (tel. 082/6-77-77), is an elegantly rustic, 1914 building with six floors of brown-shuttered windows, a small cupola, and a carefully crafted vertical row of bay windows rising at one corner. The Albrecht family in 1983 added a modern annex connected to the main building by a passageway leading to a swimming pool with its bar. There's a sauna as well as a squash hall and a massage cabin. The hotel is in the middle of the village, with proximity to everything. The sitting rooms are paneled and comfortable. Both an elevator and a parking garage are on the premises. In both buildings, guests are received year round except in May. Rates depend on the season and the plumbing. Only doubles are rented, costing from 210F ($142.80) to 310F ($210.80) daily, depending on the season.

Hotel Garni Chesa Mulin, CH-7504 Pontresina, Switzerland (tel. 082/6-75-75), in a central, quiet, and sunny location is a 50-bed hotel whose owners, Mr. and Mrs. Schmid, and their staff go out of their way to make guests feel welcome and comfortable. Flowers and plants used throughout the public areas add to the beauty of the spotless wooden ceilings, doors, and some walls. Bedrooms all have toilets and baths or showers, radios, phones, mini-bars, and TV. Down comforters on the beds add to the coziness. Summer rents for the large, airy units are from 75F ($51) to 95F ($64.60) daily in a single, depending on the plumbing, the location, and the specific time of year. Doubles, with the same qualifications, go for 120F ($81.60) to 150F ($102). In winter, rates are 80F ($54.40) to 100F ($68) daily in a single and 130F ($88.40) to 170F ($115.60) in a double. All tariffs include a buffet breakfast, service, and tax. The hotel has a good restaurant, a sauna, a solarium, a terrace, and a garage.

Hotel Bernina, CH-7504 Pontresina, Switzerland (tel. 082/6-62-21), is a traditional family owned-and-managed hotel. The Schmid family welcomes you with old-fashioned hospitality. You're assigned to one of their 80 beds in accommodations equipped with private bath or shower. Depending on the season, a double rents for 160F ($108.80) to 240F ($163.20) daily, and a single runs 85F ($57.80) to 126F ($85.70), each tariff including half board. A dining room is decorated with local wood, and the hotel's popular restaurant has excellent à la carte specialties. It's a place where the locals from the ski schools meet in winter. The Bernina is open from June through October and from December through April.

Hotel la Collina & Soldenella, CH-7504 Pontresina, Switzerland (tel. 082/6-01-21), is an elegant, white-walled hotel with gables and a corner turret that makes the entire construction look somewhat like a château. The inside has lots of knotty-pine paneling, a few regional antiques, and beamed ceilings stretching over a scattering of Oriental rugs. Bedrooms are conservatively modern, spacious, and decorated in attractive colors. Singles range from 80F ($54.40) to 126F ($85.70) daily, while doubles cost 120F ($81.60) to 240F

($163.20), with half board included. Prices depend on the season and the plumbing. Guests are accepted from June through October and from December through April.

WHERE TO DINE: Serving both French and Chinese food is the **Restaurant Sarazena** (tel. 082/6-63-53). Its façade is covered with designs from the Engadine Valley. You can enjoy a sunny afternoon on the outdoor terrace, but most people wait until mealtime, daily from noon to 2 p.m. and 6 to 9:30 p.m., to order food. The most unusual section of this place lies within the innermost room, where Chinese calligraphic symbols of good luck and red paper lanterns hang beneath the solid ceiling vaults of an otherwise totally Swiss room. Chinese food is served only in the evening, as part of full meals that cost from 45F ($30.60) for à la carte, and from 40F ($27.20) for fixed-price meals. A wide array of Chinese food is available, including prawns in Szechuan sauce, abalone with mushrooms and bamboo, pork with asparagus and bamboo, and sweet and sour chicken.

In the same room, there's also a continental menu for more traditional tastebuds. A fixed-price menu costing 40F ($27.20) changes weekly. À la carte meals cost 50F ($34). The menu lists dishes such as a duet of veal and pork with béarnaise sauce, scallops with spinach and mornay sauce, and flambéed veal kidneys with mustard sauce. If you're interested in light meals, pizzas, or a pasta dinner, be sure to sit in the first (outmost) dining room. There, full meals cost from 20F ($13.60) to 40F ($27.20) and include raclette, scampi with pepper, rumpsteak, and scallopini milanese. The restaurant is closed on Monday and from late April to late May and for most of October and November. In January, no lunch is served.

Hotel Schweizerhof (tel. 082/6-64-12). The dining room is full of regional charm, with primitively drawn characters painted on many of its walls. An open fireplace grills meats as you watch. Other house specialties include fresh lobsters and oysters, filet of beef, ravioli maison, lobster bisque in champagne, noodles with a salmon cream sauce, and smoked river trout, along with such game dishes as roebuck (in season). Dessert might be a satisfying portion of flambéed raspberries with cream. In summer there's dining on a garden terrace. Fixed-price meals range from 40F ($27.20) to 110F ($74.80), with à la carte dinners beginning at 30F ($20.40). Reservations are suggested. The restaurant is open from 11 a.m. to 11 p.m. except in May and November.

Kronenstübli (tel. 082/6-01-11), at the Grand Hotel Kronenhof, is one of the most popular restaurants in the heart of the resort. It's filled with valuable brass and pewter, and the wood paneling is from the mid-19th century. You might enjoy the suprême de turbot et baudroie aux fleurs de safran or mignons de veau à la mousse de foie gras. There is a weekly *carte* with the chef's specialties, inspired by nouvelle cuisine. For dessert, you might have the chance to try their fried ice cream. À la carte dinners range from 55F ($37.40) to 80F ($54.40), and a menu dégustation costs 90F ($61.20). Hours are from 10 a.m. to 10 p.m. daily.

APRÈS SKI: It is no longer necessary to head over to St. Moritz for after-dark action. Pontresina has plenty of nighttime diversions. Life here is decidedly more informal than it is in St. Mortiz. The most popular place in town, the **Sarazena, a** combined nightclub and restaurant, has already been recommended.

One of the most frequented bar and restaurant selections at the resort is the Stuev' Alva at the already-recommended **Rosatsch Hotel.** This place is warm, charming, and cozily decorated, with wood paneling and candlelight.

Sarazena DDC Club (tel. 082/6-63-53). Its initials stand for "Dancing, Disco, Cabaret," for which you'll pay a cover charge of 15F ($10.20) whenever live music is playing. You can drink in the gallery above the rustically beamed bar, or you can dance to recorded or live music. The lights are kept dim, since all of this looks a bit better in semishadow. Snacks are available, which include goulash soup, sandwiches, or a platter containing an entrecôte with french fries. Scotch and soda costs from 15F ($10.20), domestic beer 10F ($6.80). Contained within the Sarazena restaurant's building, the club is open every night except Monday from 9 to 2 a.m.

Kronenstübli, Grand Hotel Kronenhof (tel. 082/6-01-11), in an outlying wing of the most glamorous hotel in town, is in a rustic tavern style, with lots of paneling and vague hints of art nouveau styling. As in many Swiss restaurants, you can dine here for from 30F ($20.40), although the menu is so comprehensive that many visitors spend around twice that much. A fixed-price menu dégustation costs 90F ($61.20). Both classical French dishes and Teutonic and regional fare are served daily from noon to 2 p.m. and 7 to 10 p.m. The restaurant is open only from mid-June to mid-September and from mid-December to the end of March. Typical menu specialties include pork steak with mushrooms, roast filet of beef, medallions of veal forestière, and a pavé of banana with rum sauce, and a champagne-flavored sorbet.

Restaurant Locanda, Hotel Bernina (tel. 082/6-62-21), in a hotel previously recommended, has a rustic ambience with a vaulted ceiling. A terrace is angled toward the sun in both winter or summer. Inside are small intimate rooms where guests gather on snowy nights for raclette and fondues. Of course, other fare, such as pastas, fresh trout, steaks, and schnitzels, are also offered. Meals begin at 22F ($14.95), going up.

The Nordeska Bar at the well-recommended **Sporthotel Pontresina** (tel. 082/6-63-31) has a tranquil atmosphere, with a small dance floor if you're so inclined. Call to see if there's any action.

In season, some hotels also have candlelight buffet dinners accompanied by piano music.

15. SILVAPLANA

Lying on Lake Silvaplana, in sight of Lake Champfèr, the little village of Silvaplana (5,900 feet) is at the foot of Piz (mount) Corvatsch (11,338 feet) at the beginning of the Julier Pass. This village is about four miles from St. Moritz, and visitors from that more celebrated resort go windsurfing on Lake Silvaplana. The hamlet of Silvaplana is one of the most unspoiled resorts in the Engadine, with a parish church in the late Gothic style having been built one year before Columbus made his first sea voyage to America.

Whether you're a skier, a mountaineer, a nature lover, or just a traveling sightseer, you may want to visit **Corvatsch.** From Silvaplana, go across the narrow neck of water where Lake Champfèr and Lake Silvaplana join, and take an aerial cable car at Surlej. In just 15 minutes you'll reach the mountain station from which you have a view of the lakes, meadows, forests, and villages of the Upper Engadine. From the lookout terrace you take in a panorama of what appears to be an infinity of mountain peaks, with the giant glacier of the Bernina group looking close enough to touch.

From November to May skiers find nearly 50 miles of snowy runs, while in summer they can take advantage of the glacier ski lifts and a summer ski school. Swimming, sailing, riding, and fishing are lots of fun for Silvaplana's summer visitors.

FOOD AND LODGING: The best place to stay is the **Hotel Albana,** CH-7513 Silvaplana, Switzerland (tel. 082/4-92-92). Run by Peter and Gertrud Konrad, the hotel has well-insulated windows, chalet balconies with patterned wood slats, and regional monochromatic stencils running vertically up the corners of the façade. The design is charmingly repeated around many of the ground-floor archways. The hotel is picturesquely outfitted with a collection of beamed ceilings, stone fireplaces, and half-timbered walls. The bedrooms are streamlined of any rusticity, but are very appealing and each bedroom has a private bath. With half board included, singles range from 110F ($74.80) to 175F ($119) daily, while doubles cost 220F ($149.60) to 320F ($224.40), depending on the season, the room size, and the exposure. The hotel is closed in May and November.

Hotel Sonne, CH-7513 Silvaplana, Switzerland (tel. 082/4-81-52), is an elegantly detailed, four-story rectangular building. The façade has been relieved with louvered shutters, flower boxes, regional monochromatic designs, and neoclassical detailing over a few of the many windows. The interior is rustically modern, and elegant with settees in the salon and old-fashioned wallpaper and paneling in the dining rooms. The hotel also has a well-maintained garden and a dancing bar. With half board included, singles are charged from 100F ($68) to 115F ($78.20) daily, while two persons pay 200F ($136) to 230F ($156.40). Prices depend on the season and the plumbing, and the hotel stays open year round.

Hotel Julier-Chesa Arsa, CH-7513 Silvaplana, Switzerland (tel. 082/4-81-86), is a three-star, four-story building with gently curved steps and a warmly traditional interior. At the entrance to the road leading to the Julier Pass, it sits in front of an octagonal fountain. The bedrooms contain knotty-pine furniture, bright colors, and pleasant proportions. In the public rooms, you'll see lots of half-timbering and a few antiques. The less expensive rooms are bathless, costing from 63F ($42.85) to 93F ($63.25) daily in a single and 116F ($78.90) to 166F ($112.90) in a double, depending on the season. With bath, the single rate, again depending on the season, goes from 73F ($49.65) to 103F ($70.05) daily, with doubles costing 136F ($92.50) to 236F ($160.50). All tariffs include half board. Closed in May and November.

Hotel Chesa Grusaida, CH-7513 Silvaplana, Switzerland (tel. 082/4-82-92), is an Engadine house with white walls, a gently sloping roof, and a location in the middle of a grassy lawn. It's popular with skiers. The interior is rustic, with a scattering of ceiling beams and a restaurant that serves well-prepared meals. Rooms are comfortably furnished, each containing a private bath. Depending on the season, and with half board included, singles range from 75F ($51) to 95F ($64.60) daily, with doubles costing 150F ($102) to 190F ($129.20). The hotel is open from June to October and December to April.

Hotel Staila, CH-7513 Silvaplana, Switzerland (tel. 082/4-81-47), was originally built in smaller form in 1710. Today, it's a substantial and solid Engadine house, covered with monochromatic stencils and filled with pinewood and Victorian-era antiques. As if to celebrate their Romansh native tongue, the Strahle family gave their hotel a Romansh name. Translated into English, it means "star." The hotel boasts a number of pleasantly old-fashioned sitting rooms, a restaurant, and 17 well-insulated bedrooms, all but three with private baths. Each has a phone, radio, and usually, beds which can be folded one beneath the other to create either single or double units. Depending on the plumbing and the season, singles cost 60F ($40.80) to 110F ($74.80) daily, and doubles go for 140F ($95.20) to 210F ($142.80). These prices include half board, service, and taxes. The hotel is closed from Easter to early June and from October to early December.

For dining in Silvaplana, the best choice is the **Restaurant Albana,** in the Hotel Albana (tel. 082/4-92-92). It has a warmly appealing decor of wrought iron, heavy timbers, and striped fabrics stretched over chairs and comfortable banquettes. The Büsser family and their chef prepare such specialties as medallions of pork with grapes and nuts, sweetbreads in an artichoke sauce with a purée of asparagus, filet of lamb with black truffles, and filet of red mullet with saffron and fresh morels. A la carte meals cost from 75F ($51), and a menu dégustation goes for 79F ($53.72). The restaurant is open from 7 a.m. to midnight daily except from early May to mid-June and from mid-October to mid-December. The hotel also maintains a less-glamorous second floor dining room, the Spunta, offering Engadine dishes and full meals from 45F ($30.60).

16. SILS-MARIA/SILS-BASELGIA

Lying at an altitude of nearly 6,000 feet beside the lakes of the Upper Engadine are two townships at the beginning of the Inn Valley—**Sils-Baselgia,** a hamlet with some hotels, and **Sils-Maria,** which is slightly larger. A church in Sils-Baselgia dates from 1446. Many budget-minded European travelers stay here and then take the bus to all the ski facilities in the greater St. Moritz area, but this resort has its own attractions as well, and many winter and summer sports fill its crowded agenda.

There are some excellent hotels in this resort area, with reasonable prices. Nietzsche lived in Sils-Maria in the summer from 1881 to 1889. Besides the Edelweiss Hotel, there's a small house where he lived while he wrote *Thus Spake Zarathustra.* This has been turned into a little museum with some mementos of the German philosopher on display.

A modern cableway takes you to **Furtschellas** (about 7,500 feet), where skiers can use ski lifts and 25 miles of runs without having to line up and wait their turn. The Sils resort provides opportunities for hiking via footpaths in all directions, curling, sailing, windsurfing, horseback riding, and tennis. If you're here in summer, why not try a horse-drawn bus excursion trip up the Fex Valley? I found it an enjoyable experience.

If you're touring in the area, consider a visit to **Grevasalvas,** to the east of Sils-Maria, about six miles southwest of St. Moritz. When filmmakers remade *Heidi,* needed the "Dorfli" of the novel, they selected this Engadine farming village as the nearest real-life equivalent. Overlooking Lake Sils, it commands views of the Bernina and Bergell mountain chains from its lofty perch at 6,000 feet. In spring, you can just imagine the fictional Heidi gathering flowers in her apron. Grevasalvas contains nearly two dozen farmhouses today, although many are no longer used for that purpose, but are in fact vacation homes. Residents can take their cars into Grevasalvas, but visitors must park outside, then make the 30-minute trek on foot. There are no tourist facilities here, but people come anyway to see "how life used to be." The most intrepid hikers will climb to Lej Nair, an alpine lake lying some 3,300 feet above Grevasalvas, and reached along a steep, potentially dangerous pathway that is best taken only with an experienced guide.

HOTELS IN SILS-MARIA: The comfortable, extravagantly designed **Hotel Waldhaus,** CH-7514 Sils-Maria, Switzerland (tel. 082/4-53-31), built in 1908, is in a neo-Renaissance style with *sgraffito* decorations. It has provided shelter for such illustrious guests as Albert Einstein, Thomas Mann, and Richard Strauss. You'll reach it by riding or climbing to the top of a forested Laret Hill whose conifers come almost to the front door. It's designed like a residential palace, with square towers rising at either end of a long white center section. The interior has a collection of high-ceilinged rooms such as the reception area, whose wrought-iron staircase railing curves alongside a red-and-black patterned Oriental rug, and a dining room whose massive chandeliers look like art nouveau gilded steel. The food in the traditional Swiss style is among the best in the area. The oversize bedrooms are filled in part with elegant furniture, including some antiques, and usually have good views of the surrounding mountains. On the premises is a large covered swimming pool, plus facilities to amuse children while their parents are playing. A band usually plays dance music in the bar area, while a winter bus service provided by the hotel transports guests to and from the alpine ski slopes.

With half board included, singles range from 145F ($98.60) to 240F ($163.20) daily, and doubles cost 240F ($163.20) to 450F ($306), depending on the season and the room assignment. Many of the hotel's most desirable accommodations contain private balconies opening onto some of the finest views in the Engadine. The hotel is open from June to October and December to April.

Hotel Pensiun Privata, CH-7514 Sils/Segl-Maria, Switzerland (tel. 082/4-52-47), is a five-story ochre building with wood-grain shutters and a flagstone roof. Its central position is not far from the village church. The Giovanoli family, your hosts, charge from 170F ($115.60) to 195F ($132.60) daily for a double and 95F ($64.60) to 110F ($74.80) for a single, with half board included. Rooms are comfortably furnished and well maintained. The hotel is open from June to October and December to April.

HOTELS IN SILS-BASELGIA: A former private home, the **Hotel Margna,** CH-7517 Sils-Maria-Baselgia, Switzerland (tel. 082/4-53-06) was built in 1817 in the baroque style. Since then it's had many extensions and additions. It's covered in pink stucco, and still retains its wrought-iron detailing and patrician staircase in front. Inside, vaulted ceilings and well-polished paneling embellish the temporary home for the hundreds of visitors who enjoy the good food in the two restaurants and the rustically attractive cellar bar. An outdoor terrace, sauna, fitness room, and lots of trees in the summer garden are included among the facilities. Sepp and Dorly Müssgens are the owners of this pleasant establishment, charging 120F ($81.60) to 185F ($125.80) per person daily, depending on the season and the room assignment, with half board included. The Margna is open from June to October and December to April.

Chesa Randolina, CH-7515 Sils-Baselgia, Switzerland (tel. 082/4-52-24), is a rambling Engadine house with stucco that appears either orange, salmon, or pink according to the light and the time of day. The front doorway has a massively arched area covered with gray-and-white regional designs, and a herringbone-shaped pattern built into the rustic front door. The interior is filled with knotty-pine built-in furniture, as well as wall paneling and brightly colored carpeting. The building used to be a farmhouse, but now it's owned by Wally and Hans Clavadetscher. Rooms are comfortably furnished, but not all of them contain private baths. Depending on the season, and with half board included, singles range from 85F ($57.80) to 135F ($91.80) daily, with doubles costing 95F ($64.60) to 210F ($142.80). These tariffs include half board. The hotel is closed from the end of April to early June and from the end of October until a few days before Christmas.

WHERE TO DINE IN SILS-MARIA: In the Hotel Waldhaus, the **Waldhaus Restaurant** (tel. 082/4-53-31), is set in a forested area a slight distance from the center of Sils-Maria. The dining room has a very high ceiling, big-windowed views of the larchwood forest outside. Its menu is proclaimed by many as the finest in the village. You might enjoy turbot with hollandaise sauce or tournedos, perhaps a salmon ragoût or filet of sole poached in white port. A Lake Sils specialty is a sautéed pork steak prepared from an old Engadine recipe. Every other Saturday night the management serves specialties from any one of four Swiss regions, including the Ticino. Fixed-price meals range from 40F ($27.20) to 60F ($40.80), with à la carte dinners costing from 50F ($34) to 100F ($68). The restaurant is closed from mid-April until early June and from mid-October until mid-December. Otherwise, meals are served daily from noon to 2:15 p.m. and 7 to 9:30 p.m.

Chesa Marchetta (tel. 082/4-52-32) is maintained by two sisters, Christina and Maria Godly, who cook and act as hostess. Their restaurant is in the center of the village on the town square in an old building with steep eaves and a prominent stone foundation. The menu is small and select, offering only a few well-prepared specialties, such as homemade pasta, polenta, meat fondue, and other regional dishes. À la carte meals range in price from 30F ($20.40) to 60F ($40.80). Reservations are essential. Open daily from 3:30 p.m. to midnight.

MALOJA PASS: South of Sils you reach the famous Maloja Pass or crossing. This historic pass connects the Engadine with the Lake Como region in Italy. At the pass belvedere stands the old Maloja Kulm Hotel. Even if you're just passing through, every motorist stops here for a look at the Bergell Valley. This "pass" is reached by hairpin roads.

For food and lodging, try the **Hotel Maloja Kulm,** CH-7516 Maloja, Switzerland (tel. 082/4-31-05), a historic hotel at the top of the pass. It has a spectacular view of the winding road you just came up on, and a few contented cows grazing near the observation platform. The building has a Victorian hipped roof on one section and on the other the kind of flagstone roof you might have noticed on other buildings in the Grisons. Inside you'll see animal skins decorating the paneled and stucco walls, stone floors, and a panoramic restaurant and bar serving nourishing alpine meals. The management once added a more modern wing. Rooms are comfortably furnished. The least-expensive don't contain private baths. Depending on the time of year, half board costs from 60F ($40.80) to 98F ($66.65) daily in a single, rising to 72F ($48.95) to 196F ($133.30) in a double.

CHAPTER XII

LUGANO, LOCARNO, AND THE TICINO

□ □ □

If you don't normally think of palm trees in Switzerland, you haven't seen Ticino, the Italian-speaking part of Switzerland. Also called "The Tessin," it's the so-called Swiss Riviera. Although Italian is the major language, many of its people also speak German, French, and English. It's very international, owing to its diverse number of visitors.

Officially, Ticino begins at Airolo, which is the exit of the St. Gotthard Tunnel, and the St. Gotthard railway traverses the canton for about 75 miles from Airolo, at the southern mouth of the tunnel. But most vacationers head instead for the major resorts of Locarno, Lugano, and fast-rising Ascona. As Switzerland goes, they find the prices much cheaper in this canton, especially outside those three just-named resorts and in the little villages and hamlets of the canton, where the people are among the most hospitable in the country.

Both Lugano and Locarno share the magnificent lakes of Lugano and Maggiore with Italy, their neighbor to the south. Relations between the two countries weren't always as peaceful as they are today, and Ticino was the setting of many a battle between the Swiss and the Lombards. Essentially, the canton was carved out of Swiss conquests of the Duchy of Milan.

Ticino is the most southerly of the cantons, and its name is taken from the Ticino River, a left-bank tributary of the Po. Its weather is almost guaranteed between March and November. The balmy climate produces much subtropical vegetation. The rest of the year can be damp and cold.

The architecture is remarkably different in Ticino from that of the rest of Switzerland. It shows the influence of northern Italy, particularly in its buildings of natural stone. The food and wine are also different. You eat Lombard-style here, but with a definite Swiss accent. Sometimes in the same trattoria along a lakeshore, you'll have a German husband and his wife of Italian origin, and the cuisine they turn out is an amazing concession to both culinary traditions.

You could spend two weeks at least just touring through the valleys of the canton. In almost every case they offer tranquil seclusion and rustic charm. Every visitor soon adopts his or her favorite village.

If you're like most visitors you'll come to the Ticino after leaving central Switzerland, perhaps having visited Andermatt. If so, you'll cross through St. Gotthard, arriving in Ticino.

1. AIROLO

This hamlet in the heart of the Alps gets all the traffic from the St. Gotthard highway or through the tunnel, lying within easy reach of the pass and the Nufenen road. It has amenities making it pleasant in both summer and winter, including a cableway and ski lift. Airolo is a convenient spot for an overnight stopover.

FOOD AND LODGING: An attractive cube of a building, **Hotel delle Alpi,** CH-6780 Airolo, Switzerland (tel. 094/88-17-22), a two-star inn, has a gently sloping gabled roof and louvered shutters in natural-grain wood. The bedrooms have modern furnishings and private baths. Singles range from 45F ($30.60) to 55F ($37.40) daily, and doubles cost 70F ($47.60) to 90F ($61.20), breakfast included. For sojourns of more than three days, half board is an additional 22F ($14.95) per person daily. The hotel also has a restaurant with home-made food, a disco, a bar, and an elevator. Closed in November.

Outside the hotel just recommended, you can also dine at the **Forni Ristorante,** Viale Stazione (tel. 094/88-12-97), which has good, familiar food and some good rooms to rent. Try their beefsteak in a green pepper sauce or their lobster with curry. A set menu is offered for 22F ($14.95) but you are more likely to spend from 40F ($27.20) ordering à la carte. It is closed on Wednesday in winter and during the month of November but open otherwise from 7 a.m. to midnight daily.

2. FAIDO

Faido lies to the south of Airolo and might be another stopover for travelers using the St. Gotthard highway or car and rail tunnel. It's the major town in the beautiful Valle Leventina. You'll see here an architectural mix of stone houses and half-timbered buildings.

If you're driving from the north to go south through the tunnel, you'll notice in Faido the mulberry trees and other vegetation that suggest the dramatic contrast of the Ticino with the rest of Switzerland. A convenient rest stop between St. Gotthard and Bellinzona, Faido is also a good center for exploring the charming village of Giornico.

FOOD AND LODGING: Looking undeniably Italian, **Hotel Milano,** CH-6762 Faido, Switzerland (tel. 094/38-13-07), has a grandly proportioned loggia with a triple arch soaring above the rest of the building and exotic vegetation growing around it. The interior is filled with streamlined furniture in bright colors. This is one of the best bargains around, managed by the Lentini family. The location is quiet, lying a few hundred yards off the main road. The clean and simple accommodations, with private baths, rent for 46F ($31.30) to 60F ($40.80) daily in a single, while doubles cost 76F ($51.68) to 100F ($68), with breakfast included. The hotel is open from March through October.

Albergo Pedrinis, Piazza Fontana, CH-6760 Faido, Switzerland (tel. 094/ 38-12-41), has the best food in the area, and should be considered if you're only a motorist passing through. The owner, Aldo Biasca, has a fine chef, who cooks such delectable specialties as noodles Pedrini, spaghetti Scalinada, risotto with seafood, entrecôte with green peppercorns, a brochette of three kinds of well-flavored meat, and such regional dishes as braised beef with polenta. The restaurant is closed on Sunday in winter and from mid-December to mid-January. Fixed-price meals begin at 35F ($23.80). It's open in summer from 11:30 a.m. to 2:30 p.m. and 6:30 to 10 p.m. In winter they usually close about an hour earlier. This year-round establishment is also a 35-bed albergo, renting bathless rooms at 40F ($27.20) daily in a single and 64F ($43.50) in a double.

3. BELLINZONA

The political capital of the canton of Ticino, Bellinzona lies 14 miles from Locarno. Celts, Ligurians, and then Romans occupied the Ticino area, and Bellinzona may have been of Roman origin, since the best routes to Rome led through here. Mention is first made of the town in documents of 590. As the key to the St. Gotthard, San Bernardino, and Lucomagno passes, it loomed large in the history of Lombardy. In the eighth century, it was owned outright by the bishop of Como, and ownership went back and forth between Como and Milan in the 13th and 14th centuries. By 1798, it had become the capital of its own canton, Bellinzona. Five years later, however, it was united with the newly formed canton of Ticino and has remained so ever since.

With the building of the St. Gotthard railway tunnel and later the auto tunnel, this once remote town, lying on a plain on Italy's side of the Alps, has become accessible to travelers, who have come to appreciate the beauty of the old city and nearby hills, as well as the hospitality of the Swiss-Italian inhabitants.

Saturday morning is a good time to visit here to see the lively outdoor market, best between 7 and 11:30 a.m. Peddlers, vendors, country people, artisans, and townsfolk converse over the wares speaking Italian.

FOOD AND LODGING: A three-star hotel, the best in town, **Hotel Unione,** 1 via General Guisan, CH-6500 Bellinzona, Switzerland (tel. 092/25-55-77), was a fairly nondescript white rectangular building until someone added a balconied extension in pink marble. It's surrounded by gardens, some of them with fountains, and has a series of modern accommodations with flowery carpeting or beige-colored tiles. Singles range from 50F ($34) to 80F ($54.40) daily, with doubles costing 85F ($57.80) to 140F ($95.20), with breakfast included. The cheaper rooms are bathless. The hotel is known for its food, the finest served in Bellinzona. You can enjoy Italian dishes such as ravioli filled with pâté of the house, saltimbocca with saffron-flavored risotto (or else, in season, with truffles), or else selections from a cold buffet in summer. A set menu is offered for 28F ($19.05), and hours are daily except Sunday from noon to 2 p.m. and from 7 to 9 p.m. The restaurant closes from December 20 to mid-January.

SIGHTS: Between the 13th and 15th centuries Bellinzona was fortified by three castles, which form a trio of its three major sightseeing attractions today: the Schwyz, the Unterwald, and the Uri.

The **Castle of Uri** (Castello Grande or San Michele, in Italian) is the most ancient and the largest castle in town. It dates from 1280. In 1983 a generous gift from a citizen led to its restoration. It contains a restaurant, as well as a banqueting room and a congress hall. You can view it daily from 10 a.m. to noon and 2 to 6 p.m., April to September.

Schwyz Castle (Castello di Montebello, in Italian) has been turned into a museum devoted to history and archaeology. If you have time to visit only one of the trio of medieval fortifications, make it this one, as it's clearly the most outstanding. It has a 13th-century château with a courtyard, but other additions were made in the latter half of the 15th century. At the turn of this century it was totally restored after having fallen into great disrepair. You can drive to it from the Viale Stazione, following the steep ramp up to this huge citadel. It's open Easter to mid-September daily from 9 a.m. to noon and 2 to 5 p.m.

The third member of the fortification, the **Castle of Unterwald** (Castello di Sasso Corbaro, in Italian), built in 1479, can be reached on the same road that goes up to the Schwyz. The view from the terrace here is the finest in Bellinzona. You'll see not only the lower valley of the Ticino, but on a clear day (or night), a view of Lake Maggiore as well. The museum contains costumes of the canton and some arts and crafts of the region. Its hours are Easter to October daily from 9 a.m. to noon and 2 to 5 p.m. (closed Monday).

Also of note, the collegiate **Church of SS. Peter and Stephen** dates from the 16th century. It's a fine Renaissance structure, with a richly embellished baroque interior.

A GIORNICO POSTSCRIPT: For those traveling the St. Gotthard road, a worthwhile excursion is to the village of Giornico, lying on both banks of the Ticino River. This, in my judgment, is the most charming stop on the road.

The hamlet lies in a setting of vineyards. In the middle of the river is a small island with stone roofs, aged by time. It's reached by a pair of old arched bridges. On the right bank are two Romanesque churches.

The finest of these is the **Church of San Nicolao,** from the 12th century. The columns of the gateway are supported by sculptured mythical beasts, showing a marked Lombard influence. Try, if possible, to explore the crypt, with its sculptures. The other church is higher up in a vineyard setting, **Santa Maria di Castello.**

Incidentally, Giornico was the battleground on which 600 Swiss defeated more than 10,000 Milanese soldiers in 1478. A monument in the village commemorates that long-ago victory.

4. LOCARNO

This ancient Ticinese town sprawls at the north end of Lake Maggiore (which also washes up on the shores of Italy). A holiday resort, it's known for its mild climate, which produces a rich, Mediterranean vegetation even though still in Switzerland. Camellias and magnolias bloom in the spring, as do mimosa and wisteria, azaleas and oleander. Palm fronds flap in the lake wind, and you'll spot eucalyptus like the kind grown in Italy. Olives, figs, and pomegranates flourish in this climate, and myrtle blooms in August. Spring and fall are the ideal times to visit.

Locarno is 14 miles southwest of Bellinzona by rail. Since 1923 the town has been connected by electric railway with Domodossola and the Simplon via the Centovalli (the latter name derived from the hundred valleys that slope down toward the river, on whose banks lie small villages). This international railway, called the Locarno-Domodossola, serves as a link between the Gotthard and the Simplon lines. To cover this difficult terrain required audacious bridge constructions.

Beyond the Italian frontier at Carnedo, the railway climbs up to the plateau of Santa Maria Maggiore, a wide, barren, and solitary district that stretches out for about six miles at 2,800 feet above sea level. A steep descent leads down to the railway junction of Domodossola.

From there, one can continue to Brig in the Rhône Valley by railway through the Simplon tunnel. From Brig, one travels on, either to Bern through the Lötschberg tunnel, or to the Lake of Geneva. By direct trains the journey from Lausanne or Bern to Locarno is about four hours.

Locarno itself entered world history books in 1925 because of a series of agreements known as the Pact of Locarno. It was in Locarno that the former enemies of World War I committed themselves to a peaceful policy, even though it wasn't to last. Locarno was chosen over Lucerne, reportedly, because the mistress of the French minister preferred it and persuaded him to demand that the meeting be held on Lake Maggiore. Mussolini arrived and so did Chamberlain, along with the other statesmen, including Stresemann from Germany.

WHERE TO STAY: Locarno has a number of good accommodations that can be most desirable if you're coming to or from Italy. Many are pleasant if you want to spend a lakeside holiday in the Italian-speaking part of Switzerland. During the International Film Festival in August, you'll need a reservation way in advance.

The Upper Bracket

Hotel la Palma au Lac, 29 viale Verbano, CH-6600 Locarno-Muralto, Switzerland (tel. 093/33-01-71), sits beside the lake in a sparklingly white building with vivid green awnings covering the long modern balconies. The lawns leading down to the water are dotted with sun chairs and chaise longues, while indoors guests can use the sauna, the swimming pool, a private lido with a barbecue snackbar, and all water sports facilities. The public rooms are furnished in an updated fashion that retains an air of 19th-century grace, thanks in part to the oil paintings and tapestries. There's also a dancing bar, along with eating places, both indoors and outdoors (the Coq d'Or is the premier restaurant in town). The elegantly furnished bedrooms reveal an unmistakable Italian flair. Rates range from 130F ($88.40) to 210F ($142.80) daily per person, depending on the season, the accommodation, and the plumbing. Half board is another 35F ($23.80) per person daily.

Hotel Muralto, 8 Piazza Stazione, CH-6600 Locarno, Switzerland (tel. 093/33-01-81), is a white-walled rectangular block pierced by long horizontal rows of silvery windows. From the promenade along the lake you'll see dozens of summertime parasols tilted at angles above the sun chairs on the modern balconies. The bedrooms are clean and gracefully furnished with desirable reproductions of older pieces. They're invariably sunny, and outfitted with clear and pleasant colors. Each of the accommodations has a private bath, TV, phone, and radio. One of my favorite parts of this hotel is the tile sun terrace, raised above ground level on a concrete platform and surrounded by semitropical plants. Singles range from 63F ($42.85) to 165F ($112.20) daily, while doubles cost 116F ($78.90) to 270F ($183.60), with a buffet breakfast included. Rates depend on the season. Half board is available for an additional 30F ($20.40) per person daily.

Hotel Orselina, CH-6600 Locarno, Switzerland (tel. 093/33-02-32), at the top of the funicular at Orselina, offers the most dramatic views of any hotel at Locarno, and is in fact like a Spanish parador. Spread out on a hillside-clinging site, it opens onto a swimming pool. Guests are accepted here from March through November, and housed in comfortable, well-furnished bedrooms. Singles, depending on the season, range from 115F ($78.20) to 145F ($98.60) daily and doubles from 190F ($129.20) to 290F ($197.20), plus another 20F ($13.60) per person per day charged for half board. The most desirable, and the most expensive units, have a southern exposure with balcony, with distant views of the lake. A serene and peaceful oasis, the hotel is also known for its good food, prepared by master chefs. Guests often dine in the loggia, enjoying not only specialties of the Ticino but the fresh breezes from the lake. In chilly weather, they retreat for quiet relaxation in the lounge, with its wood-burning fireplace and massive overhead beams.

Hotel Arcadia al Lago, Lungolago G. Motta, CH-6600 Locarno, Switzerland (tel. 093/31-02-82), is completely modern. It's separated from the water only by an expanse of greenery and a whimsically fashioned wrought-iron fence, dividing the grounds from the lakeside promenade. The dozens of balconies give residents a chance to improve their suntans. The bedrooms are filled with full-grained angular modern furniture, wall-to-wall carpeting, and lots of sunlight. The hotel is open year round except in January, and rates depend on the season. Each unit has a private bath, and costs from 84F ($57.10) to 160F ($108.80) daily in a single, from 132F ($89.75) to 240F ($163.20) in a double, with a copious breakfast buffet.

Hotel Reber au Lac, 55 viale Verbano, CH-6600 Locarno-Muralto, Switzerland (tel. 093/33-02-02), a first-class hotel, has been owned by a family with the same name since 1886. It has a Spanish bar and grill room outfitted in shades of scarlet, with a French restaurant with Corinthian columns and high ceilings. You'll enjoy the lakeside sun terrace, the outdoor heated pool, the private pier, and the large semitropical garden, along with a private tennis court. The piano bar, Contenotte, has sophisticated colors and a psychedelic dance floor. The rest of the hotel is attractive and comfortable. The entire complex is set in a garden with flowers that bloom in every season. Singles range from 100F ($68) to 180F ($122.40) daily, while doubles cost 180F ($122.40) to 320F ($217.60), according to the season and the exposure. These tariffs include breakfast. Half board is available for another 40F ($27.20) per person daily.

Hotel Quisisana, 17 viale del Sole, CH-6600 Locarno, Switzerland (tel. 093/33-01-41), is a rambling white-walled hotel with blue trim, a top floor of big-windowed sliding doors surrounded by balconies, and gracefully curved balustrades outside the windows of the lower floors. The entire building is surrounded with exotic vegetation that always seems to be flowering and looks like something you'd find much farther south. Oriental rugs cover many of the floors of the interior. The public rooms have a comfortable collection of conservatively upholstered armchairs and lots of light. The bedrooms are simple, modern, and attractive. Other facilities include an indoor swimming pool, a solarium, and a fitness room. You'll be only a few minutes away from the railway station. Singles range from 80F ($54.40) to 130F ($88.40) daily, while doubles cost 140F ($95.20) to 250F ($170), with breakfast included. Prices depend on the season.

Hotel Esplanade, via Esplanade in Minusio, CH-6600 Locarno-Minusio (tel. 093/33-21-21), is a very large ochre-colored building in an Italian Renaissance format of double towers connected by long rows of covered loggias. The interior is as high-ceilinged and elegant as its outside would imply. A grand piano in one of the salons plays evening music. There's also a sun terrace, along with a large outdoor swimming pool, as well as three outdoor tennis courts with an instructor. The establishment is set in the middle of a large park filled with flowers. Some rooms do not have private baths, and these are always cheaper, of course. Singles range from 50F ($34) to 135F ($91.80) daily, with doubles costing from 80F ($54.40) to 240F ($163.20).

The Middle Bracket

Hôtel Beau-Rivage, 31 viale Verbano, CH-6600 Locarno, Switzerland (tel. 093/33-13-55). A Doric colonnade supports the sun terrace just above the main entrance, with masses of shrubbery growing between the pillars. Above that, the white façade is usually festooned with masses of flowers, which thrive in the lakeside sunshine. Each of the balconies is crafted of white wrought iron. The interior is furnished in an elegant simplicity that includes vaulted ceilings, floors set with salmon-colored marble, and a few touches of neoclassical gilt-edged mirrors. A terrace restaurant is popular in summer. Singles range from 65F ($44.20) to 85F ($57.80) daily, and doubles cost 130F ($88.40) to 170F ($115.60), breakfast included. Half board is another 25F ($17) per person daily. Prices depend on the plumbing and the season. The hotel is closed from November to March.

Hôtel du Lac, Livio Piazza Grande, CH-6600 Locarno, Switzerland (tel. 093/31-29-21), is a rambling white-painted building with a gently sloping Mediterranean-style roof and a functionally updated interior. The dining room is divided almost in two by a grandly arched stucco wall. It has immaculate white napery and a big row of windows. The bedrooms are comfortably modern, with bright colors and big windows, which usually face south. The hotel not only has an elevator, but a good cuisine. Singles range from 55F ($37.40) to 65F ($44.20) daily, and doubles cost from 105F ($71.40) to 120F ($81.60), with breakfast included. Rates depend on the season.

Remorino Hotel-Garni, 29 via Verbano, CH-6648 Minusio-Locarno, Switzerland (tel. 093/33-10-33), lies in an area which is full of residential houses surrounded by flowers. In this secluded location, only a short walking distance from the center of town, the Remorino is about two minutes from the lakeside promenade. Offering much modern comfort, it has rooms with bath and balcony, overlooking the lake and the Alps. Each accommodation has a mini-bar and a private bath, along with a strongbox, direct-dial phone, and radio. Singles cost 65F ($44.20) to 90F ($61.20) daily, and doubles go for 130F ($88.40) to 180F ($122.40), including a breakfast buffet, service, and taxes. Rates depend on the season. An outdoor swimming pool is set into well-maintained gardens, with a large patio and solarium. Guests are accepted from March through October.

The Budget Range

Hotel Atlantico, 6 via Cattori, CH-6600 Locarno, Switzerland (tel. 093/31-18-64), is a hotel garni, meaning it serves breakfast only. In its classification, it is one of the bargains of the resort. This balconied hotel, constructed about a quarter of a century ago, is one of the safe bets for those desiring a fairly priced, clean, and attractive lodging. It has a green neon sign over the top floor, which you can see from the center of the old town a few blocks away. The bedrooms are sunny and very spacious, often with pleasingly irregular shapes, and usually with a balcony offering a view of the lake. The owner is a charming Italian, Merizzi Tullio, who personally greets his guests each morning at breakfast. You'll usually find parking on one of the side streets nearby, or near a beautiful fountain a block away. The lake is only three minutes from the hotel, and the surrounding neighborhood is filled with old houses. Rooms come with and without private baths. Singles in a bathless room range from 49F ($33.30) to 70F ($47.60) daily, with doubles costing from 56F ($38.08) to 85F ($57.80). With bath, singles are priced from 80F ($54.40) to 90F ($61.20) daily, with doubles costing 85F ($57.80) to 130F ($88.40). The building has an elevator, and there are satisfactory communal baths for those in bathless rooms. The hotel is open from April through November.

Rosa Seegarten, 25 viale Verbano, CH-6600 Locarno, Switzerland (tel. 093/33-87-31), is a cream-colored, old-fashioned hotel that sits right on the lake. It represents a bargain for expensive Locarno. Half board is encouraged by the helpful management. Meals are taken on a lakeside terrace under a grape arbor. Many of the older clients prefer to eat inside, which is outfitted with white walls and wood tones. The hotel lies only three minutes from the train station. An elevator will take you to your comfortable bedroom. Rates in a single room range from 62F ($42.15) to 90F ($61.20) daily, from 116F ($78.90) to 172F

($116.90) in a double, with breakfast included. Each unit has a shower, toilet, radio, and phone. Prices depend on the season and the plumbing. Closed November to March.

Hotel dell'Angelo, 1 Piazza Grande, CH-6601 Locarno, Switzerland (tel. 093/31-81-75), is a clean, attractive hotel with a central location and bedrooms that represent a good bargain. It has lots of atmosphere and simply furnished accommodations, renting for 55F ($37.40) to 90F ($61.20) daily in a single and 100F ($68) to 150F ($102) in a double, with breakfast included. The more expensive accommodations contain showers or private baths, as well as toilets, radios, and phones. The cheaper rooms are bathless.

WHERE TO DINE: For many visitors, Locarno will be their introduction to an unfamiliar type of cookery: Swiss-Italian. It's best represented at the establishments recommended below.

La Centenario, 15 Lungolago (tel. 093/33-82-22), in Muralto. This restaurant bases its menu on the availability in the market of fish, meats, and vegetables. The creations that emerge from the kitchen of Gérard Perriard, served in this simple dining room with austere white walls, are as colorful as they are delectable. You'll be seated in a straight-backed chair by the Catalán-born co-owner, Jordi Giner, who will hand you a menu, listing such specialties as sea bass with fennel (like that served on the French Riviera), foie gras of duck with salad, filet of roebuck (in season) with mushrooms, roast guinea fowl with sauerkraut and truffles, and shrimp St. Jacques. But for a really unusual first course, ask for a cold consommé of quail eggs swirled into patterns of various natural colors caused by the vegetables contained within, garnished with caviar. Fixed-price meals range from 40F ($27.20) to 85F ($57.80), while à la carte dinners cost 90F ($61.20) to 125F ($85). The restaurant is open noon to 2 p.m. and 7 to 10 p.m. except Sunday and Monday and for a month every year sometime in midwinter.

Pierre de Lusi, Le Petit Champignon, 96 Via Simen (tel. 093/33-11-66), at Minusio, lies right outside of Locarno in a stone-built building on a busy traffic artery. Discounting for the moment the already recommended La Centenario, it serves the finest food in the area. The owner, Pierre de Lusi, is also the chef, and an outstanding one he is. A meal here at one of the most elegant dining choices in the Ticino is special indeed. Service is polished and unobtrusive, and fresh seasonal ingredients are used with quiet artistry. You can take the easy way out—that is, order a menu de dégustation at 98F ($66.65)—or else you can plunge into the decision-making à la carte, costing from 75F ($51). You're faced with such selections as a gratin de fruits of the season with champagne, le pigeon escalope, sea bass in sauterne, or a côte de boeuf with a confit of shallots. Desserts are equally enticing. Meals are served from noon to 2 p.m. and from 7 p.m. to midnight, except on Tuesday. The annual closing is for three weeks in November.

Le Coq d'Or, Hotel la Palma au Lac, 29 viale Verbano (tel. 093/33-01-71), at Muralto. You might choose to have a drink in the huge bar area before going in to dinner. The bar is marble-floored, with a pianist tinkling melodies in the corner. Almost everything here is in Valentine red, including the textured ceiling, the leather armchairs, and the accessories. The restaurant opens spaciously off the bar and is highlighted by paintings and accents of well-polished paneling. Even the candles are red. This place is not done in the best of classical tastes, but it's attractive and comfortable, and best of all, it has an exposed kitchen area with an elegant layout where you can see the uniformed chefs preparing your dinner. The head chef is Artino de Marchi, who delighted gourmets at the Ritz and Prunier in London before bringing his talents to the Ticino. The prices are steep, but for many gourmets it's worth it. An à la carte meal could cost as much as 140F ($95.20), while the fixed-price menu gastronomique is 90F ($61.20). Menus change seasonally, but you are likely to enjoy le potage aux citrons verts or a suprême of pigeon in gelatin to get you started, followed by filets of sole with tomatoes and fresh mushrooms, roebuck with fresh morels in season and medallions of sautéed beef with flap mushrooms. Desserts are luscious, including soufflés and various kinds of mousse. The restaurant is open from 7 to 11 p.m. except Monday and Tuesday.

Restaurant Cittàdella, 18 via Cittàdella (tel. 093/31-58-85), lies in the center of the old town on a cobblestone street behind an arcade concealed from traffic by vines and granite columns. A pizzeria is downstairs, with timbered ceilings and stucco walls, giving a rustic quality to the informal atmosphere. Pizzas begin at 12F ($8.15). Upstairs, however, is a chic enclave of cuisine moderne. Specialties include a goose-liver terrine and a salad of large shrimp with nuts and mango. One dish is a mixed grill with both salt- and freshwater fish. Another favorite is risotto with "fruits of the sea." A special gourmet menu with a choice of seven courses is presented for 77F ($48.95) per person, or you might order à la carte at an average price of 65F ($44.20). The restaurant is open from 8:30 a.m. to 2 p.m. and 5 p.m. to midnight. It's closed Monday and Tuesday for lunch and for three weeks in June.

Ristorante Zurigo, Viale Verbano, CH-6600 Locarno, Switzerland (tel. 093/33-16-17), serves savory Italian food to a loyal clientele every day from 7 a.m. to midnight. It's right on the lakefront, in a Mediterranean-style building with flowered balconies and shuttered windows. The establishment was built at the beginning of the 20th century, and has a gregarious staff who work in an art nouveau framework. The flagstone terrace is dotted with chestnut trees and festive lights, which make it one of the finest dining choices in Locarno on a summer night. There's also a green-and-white interior, with lots of its own kind of turn-of-the-century appeal. One specialty is three types of pasta served on one platter. Many Italian specialties such as risotto verde and saltimbocca appear on the menu, or you may prefer the grilled beefsteak, a regular feature. For dessert, the chef prepares a superb zabaglione. A children's menu is offered for 9.50F ($6.45). Food is served daily from 11:30 a.m. to 2:30 p.m. and 6 to 9 p.m. The Zurigo is also a hotel, offering comfortably furnished and reasonably priced rooms for 47F ($31.96) to 95F ($64.60) daily in a single and from 84F ($57.12) to 178F ($120.05) in a double.

Restaurant Carbonara, Piazza Stazione (tel. 093/33-67-14). You're greeted by the sight of a plentifully stocked bar area, with one side opening onto the outdoors. Behind a glass wall is a heavily beamed ceiling, with hanging ornate lamps, white stucco walls, and lots of visual distraction from the many art objects, such as copper pots, hanging from the walls. Specialties include veal kidney with grappa and mushrooms, saltimbocca, and a large pasta menu, featuring macaroni with four different types of cheese. You'll also be served braciola alla pizzaiola, as well as grilled shrimp. Fixed-price menus cost from 19F ($12.90), with à la carte meals starting at 25F ($17). About 15 different types of pizza are also offered, pizza and pasta menus costing from 9F ($6.10). The restaurant is open daily from 11:30 a.m. to 2 p.m. and 6:30 to 10 p.m. Downstairs, with an entrance from the street, you'll find a cellar bar in stark moderno.

Mövenpick Oldrati, Lungolago (tel. 093/33-85-44), is one of the best and most elegant members of this popular chain. Its two floors open right onto the lake. A stairwell inside is carpeted with an Oriental runner and covered in fabric woven like an American needlepoint sampler. It leads to a room slightly more formal than the restaurant downstairs. There's also sidewalk dining. Many daily specials cost from 35F ($23.80). The chef specializes in curry dishes, and the Italian kitchen predominates, as reflected by the good pasta courses and the saltimbocca (literally, "jump in your mouth"). The kitchen also does very good terrines if you haven't already settled for an appetizer of the air-dried beef of the Grisons. The sole meunière is among the more favored dishes. The place is open daily from 11 a.m. to 11 p.m.

Restaurant Cervo, 11 via Toretta (tel. 093/31-41-31). You'll recognize it by the pink stucco façade with a wrought-iron bracket holding a replica of a deer head. The sign advertises, medieval style, the brown-shuttered hotel with the summertime flower boxes. This is a well-kept, smallish hotel with a separate restaurant. Everything is rustically decorated. The kitchen, in the main, turns south to Italy for its inspiration. Specialties include gnocchi in the style of the chef, minestrone Ticinese, saltimbocca, risotto with mushrooms, and a special dessert "del padrone." Expect to spend 40F ($27.20) or more for an excellent, typical meal here. It's open from noon to 2 p.m. and 6:30 to 9 p.m. except Sunday for dinner and all day Monday.

AFTER DARK: You'd better turn in with a good book and get an early start on sightseeing the following day. Nightlife in Locarno doesn't impress me. Drag out dinner, have a nightcap in a bar at your hotel, and save your money. After checking out several clubs, and getting ripped off for a beer in each of them ("The Ticino is very expensive, sir"), I decided to tear up my notes and head back to my room. However, for that nightcap, I'd recommend either of the following two establishments where you can spend a relaxing hour or two:

Arcadia Bar and Café, Hotel Arcadia, Lungolago G. Motta (tel. 093/31-02-82), is one of the most attractive rendezvous points in Locarno. Built in 1983, it's decorated with black and pink marble flooring, palm trees, and rattan chairs that evoke the Caribbean. Every evening from 8 p.m. to midnight, they offer piano music and dancing. The big windows open onto panoramic views of the gardens, and you can sit around the curved bar if you prefer. Mixed drinks cost from 15F ($10.20). Closed Monday.

Café Debarcadero (tel. 093/31-52-52) is a bar/café/restaurant right on the lakeside at Lungolago G. Motta. It stands next to the embarkation point where you can purchase tickets for those cruises on Lake Maggiore. You'll see café tables under an awning. Inside the unpretentious room you'll find comfortable wood chairs. The big sunny windows let in lots of light and open onto a side view of the lake. A gin and tonic goes for 10F ($6.80), and beer begins at 3.50F ($2.40). Open 7 a.m. to midnight daily.

SIGHTS: Today a host of international celebrities come to Locarno to attend the **International Film Festival,** which takes place every summer against the backdrop of the **Piazza Grande,** the main square of the town. From here you can walk under the arcades, sheltering you from the hot August sun, to explore the shops on the piazza's north side. Here you're likely to find high fashion (often from Milan), antiques, art galleries, and both Swiss and Italian handcrafts.

From the Piazza Grande, follow the curvy **Via Francesco Rusca** (note all the Italian street names), to the old town. Along the way, you can visit the **Castello Visconti,** 1 via Francesco Rusa (tel. 093/31-59-72), a late medieval castle, the sole survivor of a former extensive stronghold where the dukes of Milan lived before it was largely destroyed in 1518. It's now a Museum Civico, which displays many Roman artifacts excavated in the area. It's open from the first of April until the end of October from 10 a.m. to noon and 2 to 5 p.m. (closed on Monday).

On a tree-studded crag above Locarno, the **Church of the Madonna del Sasso** is the resort's most important site. If you're a devout pilgrim, you can climb up to it (the church stands at an elevation of 1,165 feet). However, I'd recommend the funicular, which leaves about every 15 minutes between 7 a.m. and 11 p.m., a round-trip fare costing 4.60F ($3.15) for adults, 2.30F ($1.55) for children. Founded in 1480, the church was reconstructed in 1616. The basilica has been filled with much artwork, the most enticing being Bramantino's *Flight into Egypt* of 1536. The views from the terrace certainly compete with the ecclesiastical treasures inside. The glory of Lake Maggiore lies before you. The church was built after a friar, Bartolomeo da Ivrea, reportedly saw a vision of the Virgin in 1480.

EXCURSIONS: After visiting this pilgrimage site, you can continue by cable car to **Alpe Cardada,** at 4,430 feet. The one-mile trip takes ten minutes, but the view, once you get there, is worth it. From Cardada, a chair lift goes to the summit of **Cimetta** at 5,480 feet, from which a magnificent sweep of Lake Maggiore and the Alps unfolds. There's good skiing here, with several ski lifts. The total round-trip fare from Orselina—reached by cable railway—to Cardada to Cimetta is 22F ($14.95). Service is daily from 7:30 a.m. to 8 p.m. in season. For information, call 093/31-26-79.

The other popular excursion is the **Ronco Tour,** which can also be done easily from the competitive resort of Ascona, as can a trip to the island of **Brissago** (see later in this chapter for a description).

The tourist office in Locarno will outline a number of full- or half-day trips possible from the resort, especially through valleys and up steep, hairpin mountain roads that only very skilled drivers should explore on their own.

One of these, and some say the most fascinating, is to the **Val Verzasca,** a distance of about 20 miles. This Ticinese valley, with its tile-roofed houses and old churches with campaniles, could easily be in some valley in northern Italy. The valley itself (get a good map before striking out) is relatively uninhabited, except for some very wise people who retreat here in summer to enjoy their vacation homes in a most tranquil atmosphere.

To reach it, leave Locarno on the road to Bellinzona. At Gordola, a village at the entrance to the valley, continue on to Sonogno. Along the way you'll see the Verzasca Dam, which was built in the 1960s to prevent flooding in the area. The dam made a lake, called the Lago di Vogorno.

Skirting the lake, you'll pass through seven tunnels. Eventually you'll arrive at Brione, at the head of the Valle d'Osola. The hamlet has a four-towered castle but is known mainly for its church, with its frescoes dating from the 14th century. The post road—so called because postal coaches make this run—terminates at Sonogno, a mountain hamlet at an elevation of 3,020 feet.

5. VIRA-GAMBAROGNO

For seekers of tranquility, this secluded spot on Lake Maggiore is ideal. Gambarogno and Vira are twin resorts on the opposite side of the lake from Locarno. The whole area is filled with small lakefront villages built of stone, with red roofs. You can go sightseeing in the small hamlets or hike through the protected Bolle di Magadino area to see its rare plants and waterbirds.

FOOD AND LODGING: Above the shores of Lake Maggiore, **Touring Mot-Hotel Bellavista,** CH-6574 Vira-Gambarogno, Switzerland (tel. 093/61-11-16), is a collection of villas set in a subtropical garden with a swimming pool. With its vistas of the mountains, its masonry detailing, and its rustic decor of paneled ceilings and modern rattan furniture, you could as easily imagine yourself in the Caribbean as in Europe. The Berger family, the owners, supervise the grounds and the well-planned cuisine served in the sunny dining room. Doubles range from 130F ($88.40) to 170F ($115.60) daily, and singles cost 72F ($48.95) to 83F ($56.45). These tariffs include a buffet breakfast. Prices depend on the accommodation and the season, and all units contain private bath. The hotel is open from March through November.

Hotel Viralago, CH-6574 Vira-Gambarogno, Switzerland (tel. 093/61-15-91), is a balconied, salmon-colored building many of whose rooms look over the lake shore. The interior is uncluttered and streamlined, with light neutral colors picked up by the accents of the Oriental rugs and the leather furniture. An indoor pool and a sauna are on the premises, along with rustically stuccoed walls in the snack restaurant. A more formal restaurant serves grilled specialties. Musical entertainment is frequently provided. Singles range from 65F ($40.80) to 95F ($64.60) daily, while doubles cost 115F ($78.20) to 180F ($122.40). Half board is another 22F ($14.95) per person daily, and the hotel is open only from March to November.

6. ASCONA

Only 2½ miles from Locarno, and a rival resort, Ascona lies snugly on Lake Maggiore. Once it was a tiny and sleepy fishing port, but it has grown into one of the most popular destinations in the Ticino. The town has long been a popular rendezvous point for painters, writers, and other celebrities. Lenin found the place ideal, as did Isadora Duncan and Carl Jung. Rudolf Steiner likewise was attracted to Ascona, and so were Hermann Hesse and Paul Klee. Erich Maria Remarque, the German novelist who wrote *All Quiet on the Western Front*, also lived here.

Much of the old town that these famous people knew has now been swallowed up by new developments that seemed to devour the place like a Minotaur. But the heart of Ascona is still worth exploring, with its colorful little shops, art galleries (some good but some tawdry), and antique stores.

Because of its mild climate, Ascona has subtropical vegetation. All year round, even in the middle of winter, some flowers are in bloom. The resort is well equipped with sports facilities, including a "lido" and its Kursaal (casino). There's also a golf course in the interior. September is a month that music lovers circle on their calendars, for that's the time of the annual Ascona Music Weeks.

The **Collegio Pontificio Papio,** dating from 1584, has one of the most beautiful Renaissance courtyards in the country, with two-story loggias in the Italianate style. The **Church of Santa Maria della Misericordia,** on which construction began in the closing year of the 14th century, belongs to a Dominican monastery. Its chief treasure is one of the most mammoth late Gothic frescoes in Switzerland.

The 1620 **Casa Serodine** (also called Casa Borrani) has one of the most richly embellished façades of any secular structure in the country.

If you're in Ascona in the right season, the **Isole di Brissago,** reached by a boat trip, contains a botanical garden of Mediterranean and subtropical flora. Palm fronds rustle in the lake breezes, and there's also a small Roman bath. Including the round-trip boat fare and the admission, the cost is 6F ($4.10) per person. Ask at the tourist office in Ascona if the gardens are open, and also about what boats are likely to go there on any given day.

You can also journey to the little village of **Ronco,** reached by following the road to Verbania. Built on the flank of a slope, this very Italian-style village has one of the most charming settings in all of the Ticino. From the belvedere of the church, you'll have a good view.

WHERE TO STAY: If you like colorful, regional-style inns, you may prefer Ascona to most of the accommodations in Locarno or Lugano. It's the third most popular base for exploring the lake, from one of the hotels recommended below.

The Upper Bracket

Castello del Sole, 142 viale Muraccio, CH-6612 Ascona, Switzerland (tel. 093/35-02-02), about 1½ miles from the center, is the grandest place to stay. In the last few years it has been completely rebuilt. Surrounded by its large park and green meadows, it stands quite near the spot where the Maggia River falls into Lake Maggiore. As such, it offers perfect tranquility and peace. Lodging here evokes life on a private estate, with a good beachfront and an 18-hole golf course a mile away. The hotel, with its many courtyards, was constructed around an antique palazzo. Spacious vaulted public rooms are set off by granite columns, marble-covered terraces, and charming accents ranging from 19th-century wrought iron to modern and tasteful decorative accessories. The hotel operates from March 30 until the end of October. A farm belonging to the hotel provides much of the produce served in the dining room (the hotel even produces its own wine). The Barbarossa restaurant serves many savory specialties. In summer, buffets are often served (the chefs specialize in grilled meats). There are also five outdoor tennis courts, plus two courts in a tennis hall. The hotel also has an indoor and outdoor swimming pool, as well as a sauna and massage facilities. All accommodations contain private balconies, and are beautifully furnished and well equipped. The cost ranges from 200F ($136) to 300F ($204) daily in a single, from 300F ($204) to 450F ($306) in a double.

Hotel Ascolago, Via Albarelle, CH-6612 Ascona (tel. 093/35-20-55), enjoys an ideal position, in a flower-and-sculpture-filled city park at the edge of the lake, near the center of town. It has an unusual angular façade, capped with a roof that looks like the top of a Chinese pagoda. Near the entrance, a pair of porticos that might have been designed by Le Corbusier protect entrants from the rain. The interior is not as stylish or avant-garde as the exterior might have promised. Much of its ground floor is devoted to a warmly paneled, large restaurant, whose tables extend out onto a lakeside terrace in summer. Upstairs, 45 beds are contained within modern rooms, each of which has a lake view, private bath, thick carpeting, mini-bar, radio, phone, safe, and TV. Single rooms cost 115F ($78.20) to 170F ($115.60) daily, doubles from 210F ($142.80) to 310F ($210.80), depending on the season and the accommodation. The hotel contains a big-windowed indoor pool, a sauna, a bar, and a parking garage.

Hotel Losone, CH-6616 Ascona-Losone, Switzerland (tel. 093/35-01-31), on the outskirts of Ascona, is an intelligently designed, one-story building that sprawls across a landscaped garden dotted with trees and flowerbeds. The various wings of the establishment curve at right angles around a free-form swimming pool which, with its nearby terrace, serves as the social center of the hotel. Inside, the decor is filled with massively paneled ceilings that look far older than they are, thanks to the regional designs painted between the beams. You'll also find masonry detailing, flagstone floors, Oriental rugs, and open bedrooms, each with a private bath and an access directly onto the lawns outside. The hotel lies midway between Locarno and Ascona, and is maintained by the Glaus family. With breakfast included, singles rent for 130F ($88.40) to 200F ($136) daily, and doubles run 230F ($156.40) to 330F ($224.40). Half board is an extra 25F ($17) per person daily, and the hotel receives guests from March through November.

Hotel Eden Roc, via Albarelle, CH-6612 Ascona, Switzerland (tel. 093/35-01-71), was designed around its location at the entrance to an indentation in the shoreline of the lake. The grounds around the hotel have been disciplined into terraces and flowerbeds, all of them leading gently down to the water. A swimming pool is surrounded by palm trees and a short expanse of well-maintained lawn. The interior is lightheartedly modern, decorated with a sense of style that is more Italian than Teutonic. Bedrooms are sunny and fairly spacious, some of them frilly and romantic, others more modern. Each of the accommodations contains a private bath, balcony, TV, radio, phone, and mini-bar. Doubles range from 300F ($204) to 420F ($285.60) daily, depending on the season, the exposure, and the size of the unit. It's open from March to November.

Albergo Casa Berno, CH-6612 Ascona, Switzerland (tel. 093/35-32-32), lies between Monte Verita and Ronco-sur-Ascona. It is a large hotel with several outcroppings of different balconied wings rising up from the steep hillside into which it's been built. The setting is dramatically forested, with the lake dominating the view from most of the bedrooms. An outdoor swimming pool is cantilevered behind a stone embankment which, because of the steepness of the hill, places it close to the flower-covered roof terrace of the main building. The comfortable bedrooms are filled with elegant furniture, including some painted Louis XVI–style chairs, and flowery curtains. Facilities include a sauna, a massage room, a hairdresser, two restaurants, and a bar. Each of the accommodations contains a private bath, balcony, southern exposure, and a mini-bar. Singles range from 170F ($115.60) to 200F ($136) daily, while doubles cost 142F ($96.55) to 135F ($132.60) per person, with half board included. The hotel is open from March through October.

Hotel Sasso Boretto, Via Locarno, CH-6612 Ascona, Switzerland (tel. 093/35-71-15). The entire balconied structure of this establishment seems to be set on top of cement columns. Glass windows frame the ground floor, which is surrounded by red brick terraces and Mediterranean trees. The hotel has a swimming pool decorated with abstract wall murals and a sauna, along with restaurants and garden cafés, as well as a modern bar. The bedrooms, for the most part, are in brown and beige. The larger accommodations are decorated with Italian flair, while the more nondescript smaller ones are cozy and comfortable. You can park in the underground garage. Bruno Nötzli, the director, organizes once-a-week sightseeing tours in the environs. Singles range from 105F ($71.40) to 135F ($91.80) daily, while twin-bedded units cost 140F ($95.20) to 200F ($136), with breakfast included. Half board is an extra 25F ($17) per person daily. From November 1 to March 20, the hotel and restaurant are closed, but the apartments remain open.

Hotel Acapulco au Lac, Porto Ronco, CH-6612 Ascona, Switzerland (tel. 093/35-45-21). From almost everywhere in this elegant hotel you'll have a sense of being on the water. It's set between the road and the lake, on a hill that's so steep you'll park your car on the roof before heading down to the reception desk. A terrace has been built out over the lake, as well as a marina for waterskiing. The lake might tempt you for a swim, but the heated indoor pool might suit you better. The gaily decorated rustic restaurant overlooks the water, and the cozy Fiesta Bar has outdoor terraces. Each of the pleasant bedrooms has its own balcony (or else a terrace facing south), as well as a private bath, color TV, phone, mini-bar, and radio. The lounge area is filled with rattan furniture and summer colors. Singles range from 95F ($64.60) to 147F ($99.95) daily while doubles cost from 74F ($50.30) to 128F ($87.05) per person, including breakfast. Half board is another 32F ($21.75) per person daily, and guests are received from March through November.

Budget to Medium-Priced Accommodations

Seeschloss-Castello, Piazza G. Motta, CH-6612 Ascona, Switzerland (tel. 093/35-01-61). The tower you see today was constructed in 1250 by a countess of Milan from the Ghiriglioni family. It was the fortified dwelling of the clan who eventually controlled most of the navigation on the lake. For the past 50 years this building has been a hotel. Today palms and palmettos surround the flagstone terrace, and the stone entrance curves gracefully up to an antique-filled lobby. You'll pull a wrought-iron bell handle to call the receptionist, who will assign you one of the smallish rooms, which open onto the backyard pool or the lake in front. All the clean and comfortable rooms have private baths or showers and toilets. Singles range from 100F ($68) to 150F ($102) daily, while doubles cost 172F ($116.95) to 260F ($176.80), with breakfast included. Half board is another 25F ($17) per person daily. Tariffs depend on the season and the type of unit. The hotel is open from March to November. Across the street in front of the hotel is a private park bordering the lake.

Hotel la Perla, 14 via Collina, CH-6612 Ascona, Switzerland (tel. 093/35-35-77), is a white-walled balconied hotel with stone retaining walls built around it to hold the terraced gardens in place. It isn't located on the water, but still has a good view of the mountains and there's a swimming pool on the grounds. The homes around it usually date from the 19th century, with lots of deciduous trees set nearby. Each of the attractive units has a balcony, phone, radio, and private bath. There's also an elevator, plus a parking garage on the premises. Singles range from 60F ($40.80) to 90F ($61.20) daily, and doubles cost 120F ($81.60) to 180F ($122.40), with breakfast included. Accommodations in the nearby annex are slightly cheaper.

Tamaro au Lac, Piazza G. Motta, CH-6612 Ascona, Switzerland (tel. 093/ 35-02-82), has a welcoming greeting painted in Latin above the huge arch leading into the flagstone hall of the lounge and reception area. If you go a few steps farther you'll be in a skylit central courtyard with vines growing over the massive vaults of its surrounding arcade. Tables have been set up inside this area, which makes the already charming layout even better. This is a former hospice and abbey. Today the furnishings are far more secular, but still include some antiques and some romantically seasoned artifacts. Complicated ceiling structures in themselves identify the building as a very old one. From the street the establishment with its café looks like many of the other Mediterranean-style, pastel-colored buildings along the quays. Some of the bedrooms in the rear open from under a covered arcade onto a pleasant garden. Annette and Paolo Witzig, the owners, charge from 80F ($54.40) to 120F ($81.60) daily in a single, from 140F ($95.20) to 210F ($142.80) in a double. Half board is an extra 19F ($12.90) per person daily. Prices depend on the plumbing and the season. The hotel closes from November to March.

Albergo Elvezia, Piazza G. Motta, CH-6612 Ascona, Switzerland (tel. 093/35-15-14), has a terrace on the cobblestones facing the lake, with an indoor restaurant just behind it. The upper-story terrace is surrounded by vines, which even grow above the flower boxes set onto the balustrade. The ground-floor restaurant looks typically rustic, with Oriental rugs, wooden tables, and hanging chandeliers. Meals begin at 30F ($20.40) and include many Italian specialties, such as good pasta (especially one made with four different kinds of cheese), fritto misto (fried mixed fish), scampi prepared in several different ways, osso buco, and veal piccata. The Crociani family rents out twin-bedded rooms with bath for 120F ($81.60) to 200F ($136) daily, including breakfast, service, taxes, phone, TV, and a small refrigerator. Singles, also with bath, range from 70F ($47.60) to 110F ($74.80).

WHERE TO DINE: Ascona has many fine restaurants—in fact the harborfront is lined with them. Most guests dine al fresco on a summer's night, looking at the lake. However, you shouldn't overlook the many excellent establishments found on the cobblestone streets of the old town either. My favorites follow:

Giardino, Via Segnale (tel. 093/35-01-01), in the elegant Hotel Giardino, is considered one of the finest dining rooms in Switzerland, certainly in the Ticino. Many gourmets drive all the way from Milan to enjoy the excellent cuisine served here. For a long time, the albergo was in Brissago, with some of its furnishings coming from a nearby cloister. This original furniture was moved to the present location in Ascona, so that customers feel at home here. You'll be warmly welcomed by Fernanda Mazzi-Conti Rossini, who will hand you a menu listing dishes prepared by chef Bruno Keist. Meals cost from 90F ($61.20) to 120F ($81.60), according to the number of courses you choose. Restaurant hours are from 7 p.m. to 10 p.m. daily except Monday and Tuesday. Reservations are essential. The place is closed in winter.

Ristorante da Ivo, 141 via Collegio (tel. 093/35-10-31). A trip through the winding streets of the old town might be an adventure in itself, even if it didn't eventually lead to the sophisticated cuisine of Ivo Balestra. If you're looking for nouvelle cuisine, you've come to the right place. It's graced with a large fireplace in a rustically pretty house, with light-grained paneling and dozens of folkloric artifacts covering the cream-colored walls. The menu changes every month, according to the availability of the ingredients at the market on any particular day. But specialties include such delicacies as suckling lamb with local cabbage, turbot à l'orange with pink peppercorns, baby veal with white truffles in puff pastry, and salmon flan with leaf lettuce. The tagliatelle alla panna is an excellent pasta selection. At lunch, a business menu is offered for only 30F ($20.40), and a menu gastronomique is offered for 80F ($54.40). The restaurant is closed Monday and Tuesday, and during all of January and February. Otherwise its hours are noon to 2 p.m. and 6:30 to 10 p.m.

Al Pontile, 31 Piazza G. Motta (tel. 093/35-46-04). Many restaurants along the quays look alike and have almost the same menu choices, but the decor at this one seems a little warmer and more intimate than that of its neighbors. The darkly rustic interior has hanging straw lamps. But most guests in fair weather prefer to dine outside on the terrace, opening onto the lake. Meals here cost from 35F ($23.80) and could include quail with risotto, osso buco, saltimbocca, and good pasta dishes such as lasagne, ravioli, or spaghetti. Fish dishes include scampi, sole, and salmon. For dessert, I suggest one of the homemade pies that are made fresh daily. Hours are daily from noon to 2 p.m. and 6:30 to 9:30 p.m.

Ristorante Borromeo, 16 via Collegio (tel. 093/35-12-98), is one of the most crowded restaurants in the old town, and with good reason. The tables are filled with local people who seem to know each other. It has three rooms of rustic, high-ceilinged charm, and many more if you count the garden terraces. The rooms are joined by a central entryway where the maître d' stands guard over the flock, much the way the Catholic priests stood guard at the door when this was a monastery and one of the biggest church schools in the region. Meals, costing from 30F ($20.40), might include risotto milanese with saffron, a mixed grill, piccata marsala, trout, scampi, or osso buco. Always look for the daily specials that are posted. Open daily from noon to 2 p.m. and 6 to 9 p.m.

Osteria Nostrana, Via Albarelle (tel. 093/35-51-58), is one of the most active harborfront restaurants. It has an invitingly rustic interior, and its sidewalk tables overlook the lake and the fashionable promenade. The well-prepared food items that come out of the kitchen might include 11 different types of spaghetti (try the carbonara), although you can also order lasagne verdi, cannelloni, tortelloni, and tagliatelle. The chef also does veal and beefsteak well. In the enlarged part of the Osteria Nostrana, you will find a typical Italian pizzeria. You can choose from 12 different kinds of homemade crisp pizza baked in a white-oak-burning stove (try the calzone). The restaurant is open all year round from 9 a.m. to midnight daily. Meals from 15F ($10.20) up.

Al Torchio, Contrada Maggiore (tel. 093/35-71-26). Many guests choose to eat in the first room they see, which has a warm rustic decor, red candles, and imaginative designs painted onto the plaster walls. However, if it's a warm night, you might continue past the American-style salad bar in the back of the restaurant and turn left into the vine-covered courtyard. There, stone pillars support a grape arbor in a Mediterranean ambience. An average meal here will cost about 40F ($27.20), and could include calves' liver Venetian style, osso buco, a winter fondue, spaghetti with clams, and a host of other typical Italian specialties. Dessert might be a gelato misto (a mixed selection of ice cream) or a sorbet with vodka. Hours are daily from noon to 2 p.m. and 5:30 to 10 p.m. However, throughout the day and after 10 p.m. you can still order lasagne, cannelloni, or a salad and sandwich. Every Friday evening jazz is performed in the cellar.

AFTER DARK: A popular disco with a good DJ is the **Dancing Club Cincilla,** Via Brissago (tel. 093/35-51-71). The club is painted in dark colors. Everything is carpeted, and the owners seem to have gone out of their way to create an urban ambience. There's no cover charge, and drinks cost from 15F ($10.20) apiece. The club opens nightly at 9 p.m., closing at 3:30 a.m. A sign warns: "Proper dress is required."

Happyville Night Club, Via Borgo (tel. 093/35-11-58), is a disco and cabaret with a band and seven artists performing a mixture of striptease with song and
dance. A tiny dance floor accommodates disco lovers between shows, which are
put on every night at 11:30 and again at 1:30 a.m. The ambience is one of comfortable banquettes with red carpeting covering the walls and most of the floor.
The cover charge is 5F ($3.40), and most drinks cost from 15F ($10.20). Closing time is 4 a.m. The club takes a vacation in midwinter.

7. BRISSAGO

This little town opening onto Lake Maggiore near the Italian border might
be considered if you prefer not to lodge in either Ascona or Locarno. It's on the
mainland (and not to be confused with the Island of Brissago), and is reached by
heading southwest from Ascona, bypassing Ronco on the way.

Lying at the foot of Monte Limidario (7,180 feet), Brissago is the lowest
spot in Switzerland, 679 feet above sea level. Only a mile from the border, it's
popular with summer vacationers from Italy. Much of the village's activity centers on the lake, where waterskiing, swimming, and sailing prevail. A long, thin
Virginia-type cigar, known as the "Brissago," is manufactured here.

FOOD AND LODGING: Set between the lake and the winding road that
stretches from Ascona to the Italian border, **Hotel Villa Cäsar,** CH-6614
Brissago, Switzerland (tel. 093/65-27-66), is a modern re-creation of an ancient
Roman villa. It's capped with a miniature version of a Roman temple, ringed
with interpretations of classical urns, and flanked on two sides with mature rows
of Italian cypresses. One of the truly lovely touches is the Roman-inspired pool
flanked with copies of classical statuary. The bedrooms have baths covered with
handpainted tiles, views of the lake, Iberian headboards of frilly tendrils of
wrought iron, and patterned carpeting. Singles cost 180F ($122.40) to 260F
($176.80) daily, and doubles go for 260F ($176.80) to 390F ($265.20). The
hotel is open only between March and October.

If you elect to have a meal here, your path down to the restaurant will be
edged with Roman portrait busts and murals showing cupbearers and musicians
entertaining someone who might be Caesar. The in-house restaurant serves the
best food in the area. Specialties include spaghetti with "fruits of the sea" en papillote, sole and lobster bordelaise, and a timbale of eggplant. Menus cost 55F
($37.40), 75F ($51), and 100F ($68).

8. LUGANO

Because of its geographical configuration, Lugano is called the "Rio de
Janeiro of Europe." But that could be a very misleading comparison. It is a Swiss
town with a decided Italian flavor, as reflected by its al fresco cafés, sun-filled piaz-
zas, arcaded cobblestone streets, and terracotta roofs.

The cultural center of Ticino—also the major town—Lugano has long
been a haven for artists. However, as a resort it's patronized almost solely by Germans, and seems relatively undiscovered by the Americans who visit Switzerland.

On Lake Lugano, which the Italians call Lake Ceresio, Lugano is spread out
between the peaks of San Salvatore and Monte Brè. Its low mountains protect it
from cold alpine winds, and it enjoys an ideal climate from March to November.

PRACTICAL FACTS: To make your visit to Lugano more pleasant, here are
some facts that might help.

Emergencies: Some important phone numbers are: **police,** 117; **fire department,** 118; **ambulance,** 091/22-91-91; **doctor or dentist,** 111; **first aid,**
091/58-61-11; **road service,** 140; **taxi** 091/51-21-21 or 091/54-44-66.

Information: For information about hotels, sights, excursions, or whatever,
go to the **Lugano Tourist Office,** 5 Riva Albertolli (tel. 091/21-46-64).

Transportation: To use the Lugano city transport facilities, get an information leaflet at the Public Transport Board, Azienda Comunale dei Trasporti, via Carducci (tel. 091/21-22-22), or at the tourist office. It tells you all about fares and the use of ticket machines. As in other Swiss cities, you must get a valid ticket *before* boarding a transport vehicle, or you'll have to pay a 20F ($13.60) penalty. You can purchase a one-day ticket from each automatic ticket machine at a rate of 5F ($3.40). This ticket is valid for 24 hours from the moment you purchase it on all public transport of the Lugano Transport Company, including the Funicular Lugano–Main Street SBB. It is not valid, however, on the line 12 Lugano-Bré.

WHERE TO STAY:
Lugano is better equipped with hotels than any other resort in Ticino, and they come in all price ranges. Many are located in the outskirts in the districts of Paradiso, Cassarate, and Castagnola, but wherever you're located, know that you're only a few minutes from the heart of town.

Grand Hotel Villa Castagnola au Lac, 31 viale Castagnola, CH-6900 Lugano, Switzerland (tel. 091/51-22-13), is styled like a Mediterranean villa, with flagstone terraces, exotic trees and plants, and carefully groomed lawns. The façade is ochre-color, with shutters that make the whole setting look vaguely Neapolitan. An indoor swimming pool is in a separate ground-floor extension, with sliding panoramic windows overlooking banana plants, palms, evergreens, cactus, and severely pruned topiaries. Two tennis courts are shielded from view by a row of hedges. The public rooms have polished marble floors in gray, pink, and beige. Other rooms have parquet floors, big fireplaces, a baronial decor, with lots of elegant nooks and crannies for having tea or before-dinner drinks. The clientele is mainly an older crowd. All of this physical plant sits across the street from the lake, where the hotel maintains a private beach. With breakfast included, singles range from 120F ($81.60) to 190F ($129.20) daily, and doubles run 190F ($129.20) to 280F ($190.40). Half board is another 30F ($20.40) per person daily. Guests are received from March through January.

Hotel Admiral, 15 via Geretta, CH-6902 Lugano-Paradiso, Switzerland (tel. 091/54-23-24), a superior first-class hotel, was built in 1975, and it's one of the finest hotels in this little satellite resort of Lugano. A year-round hotel, it rises seven concrete-and-glass floors above an area near the Lugano-Sud exit from the main highway. Many of the public rooms are outfitted with red leather accents and wood trim, while a showplace salon has French-style armchairs, Oriental rugs, and big windows with a view of the garden. An indoor and a rooftop outdoor swimming pool are the most dramatic of the hotel's facilities, which also include a sauna, a private garage, a bar, two restaurants, and a cafeteria. The comfortable accommodations, 92 in all, have private baths, radios, refrigerators, cosmetic bars, and direct-dial phones. The rates range from 120F ($81.60) to 175F ($119) daily in a single and from 180F ($122.40) to 270F ($183.60) in a double, with breakfast included. Half board is available for another 40F ($27.20) per person daily. The hotel is a member of the Steigenberger Reservation Service. For reservation and information, call 212/593-2988 in New York City or toll free 800/882-4777 in New York State. The toll-free number for the United States is 800/223-5652.

The Upper Bracket
Villa Principe Leopoldo, 5 via Montalbano, CH-6900 Lugano, Switzerland (tel. 091/55-88-55), was built in the early 1900s as the elegantly proportioned villa of Prince Leopold of Austria's von Hohenzollern monarchs. After World War I, it was sold to a Swiss industrialist, who made it his family seat for many years. In 1986, discreetly expanded and filled with sumptuous examples of understated Italian style, it embarked on a new life-cycle as the most chic and desirable hotel in Lugano. From the circular driveway in front, a visitor might think the place a villa in the meadows of Tuscany. Inside, however, 24 junior suites

contain many yards of beige-colored travertine trim. The entrance to the modern addition that contains the rooms leads past a two-story atrium, which is introduced with a cascade of illuminated water. Each room has a terrace overlooking the lake and the suburb of Paradaiso through a screen of trees. With breakfast, service, and taxes included, singles cost 220F ($149.60) to 350F ($238) daily, and doubles go for 290F ($197.20) to 400F ($272), depending on the season.

The staff here is polite and will show you the way to the in-house restaurant and the elegant bar area. Contained within a trio of garden rooms, the restaurant accepts dining guests who phone ahead. Meals cost from 55F ($37.40) and are served daily from noon to 3:30 p.m. and from 7 to 11 p.m. Menu items include an Italian-inspired array of pastas, such as tagliolini with squid or tagliatelle with pesto, grilled lobster, and rack of lamb pre-salé. A pianist provides music every evening in the bar from 8 to 11. Rene Signorini is the capable and charming manager.

To reach this hotel, you'll have to negotiate a winding road to the upper heights of Lugano, to a flower and shrub-filled suburb of wealthy private homes. The neighborhood is called Collina d'Oro.

Grand Hotel Eden, 7 Riva Paradiso, CH-6900 Lugano-Paradiso, Switzerland (tel. 091/55-01-21), at Lugano-Paradiso, is a large contemporary five-star hotel with an unbroken façade of lakeside balconies angling toward the sunlight. A deluxe establishment, it's considered the finest hotel in the area of Lugano. A low-lying, flat-roofed extension rests on the sun terrace built out over the lake. Inside, a large swimming pool has panoramic views of the café tables and chaise longues. The entire complex is air-conditioned, while each of the handsomely furnished accommodations has color TV, radio, TV-video, mini-bar, phone, and safe. Singles range from 130F ($88.40) to 200F ($136) daily, while doubles cost 220F ($149.60) to 370F ($251.60), with breakfast included. Half board is another 45F ($30.60) per person per day.

Hotel Splendide Royal, 7 Riva A. Caccia, CH-6900 Lugano, Switzerland (tel. 091/54-20-01). Parts of this hotel are indeed splendid, as its name implies. It was opened in 1888, and over the years the famous and the infamous of the world have visited its precincts, everybody from Maria, Queen of Romania, to Vittorio Emanuele di Savoia. The balconied lake side with a mansard roof is elegantly 19th century, but my favorite part of the outside is the side entrance with the wrought-iron and glass canopy hanging over the door. A covered swimming pool is shaped like an oyster, with grandly arched modern walls opening onto the rock garden. The public rooms are appropriately filled with columns, crystal and gilt chandeliers, Venetian furniture, and Oriental rugs. The most magnificent bedrooms even have ceiling frescoes in some cases. There's a restaurant and bar on the premises. With breakfast included, singles range from 130F ($88.40) to 220F ($136) daily, while doubles cost 220F ($149.60) to 390F ($265.20). Half board is offered for another 45F ($30.60) per person daily. Some people come here just to dine in its lovely restaurant, La Veranda, overlooking the Riva Caccia with views of the lake.

Hotel Montalbano, Via Montalbano, CH-6900 Lugano, Switzerland (tel. 091/55-88-11), owned and operated by the same investors who developed the previously recommended Villa Principe Leopoldo (which sits across the street), occupies a tree-shaded plot of land surrounded by expensive residential houses. It lies within the hills above Lugano, in a gilt-edged neighborhood appropriately named La Collina d'Oro. Modern in its concept and decor, it opened in 1987 and was awarded five stars by the Swiss government. It's built in two sienna-sided wings, in a design that, if the sea were nearby, might pass for a resort hotel in the Caribbean. Each accommodation has curved walls, sophisticated lighting fixtures, surfaces of polished granite, and the kind of furniture you'd expect to find in an urban art gallery. With breakfast, service, and taxes included, singles rent for 130F ($88.40) to 230F ($156.40) daily, doubles for 180F ($122.40) to

290F ($197.20), depending on the season. On the premises are a pair of outdoor swimming pools, a fine restaurant, and many beds of carefully tended flowers.

Hotel Bellevue au Lac, 10 Riva Caccia, CH-6902 Lugano, Switzerland (tel. 091/54-33-33), is a large white-walled, four-star hotel turned sideways to the lake so that only a limited number of bedrooms have frontal views of the water. As it turns out, the other accommodations contain balconies with lots of sunshine and a pleasant view of the garden with a big swimming pool and sun terrace. Each of the accommodations has a balcony, private bath, phone, radio, and refrigerator. On the half board plan, the Foery family includes a sangría party followed by a candlelight dinner, plus weekly barbecue parties. With a generous breakfast included, overnight rates in a single range from 110F ($74.80) to 140F ($95.20) daily, and in a double, from 170F ($115.60) to 250F ($170). Half board is an additional 35F ($23.80) per person daily. The hotel is open from April to October.

Europa Grand Hotel au Lac, 1 via Cattori, CH-6902 Lugano, Switzerland (tel. 091/54-36-21), is a well-organized hotel presenting a handsomely proportioned façade of almost pure white to its flowered garden. An indoor swimming pool opens its glass doors during warm weather to a terraced view of the lake. The interior is functional, modern, and informal, with touches of streamlined elegance amid the contemporary furnishings. A cabaret and nightclub offers an international ambience. Well-furnished singles range from 130F ($88.40) to 175F ($119) daily, while doubles rent for 200F ($136) to 270F ($183.60), with a buffet breakfast included. Half board is an extra 40F ($26) per person daily. All the accommodations have private baths, phones, air conditioning, radios, color TV, mini-bars, and cosmetic bars, as well as balconies or terraces overlooking the lake. The hotel has private parking, a shopping center, and a café boulevard with a hot and cold kitchen open all day.

Hotel Meister, 11 via San Salvatore, CH-6902 Lugano-Paradiso, Switzerland (tel. 091/54-14-12), is a grand building with five floors of white walls and shutters, and a white wrought-iron balcony in front of almost every window. Many of the bedrooms look down over the grassy lawns and swimming pool, and all of them contain private baths, phones, and radios. Singles rent for 90F ($61.20) to 135F ($91.80) daily, and doubles cost 140F ($95.20) to 210F ($142.80). Half board is an extra 25F ($17) per person daily. The public rooms have ornate plaster ceilings, marble or parquet floors, and conservative furniture. The dining room is 19th century, with gilt-framed antique mirrors and crystal chandeliers. The hotel is in the suburb of Paradiso, a two-minute walk from the lakeshore. If you're driving, get off at the exit marked "Lugano-Sud." There's parking behind the hotel, as well as covered parking at the nearby Hotel Admiral where guests at the Meister are allowed free use of the indoor swimming pool. The hotel receives guests from April to October.

Hotel Pullman Commodore, 6 Riva Caccia, CH-6900 Lugano, Switzerland (tel. 091/54-39-21), is a well-designed modern four-star hotel, a Pullman chain member with two very large wings extending toward the lake. Their balconies are usually covered with flowers, and a series of sun terraces has been built into the central area between the different sections. The hotel sits on the lakeshore promenade in the center of town. The Neptune restaurant inside offers an airy and sunny atmosphere, with burgeoning terrace shrubs just outside its windows and a decor of blue and green with glossy white Chinese Chippendale–style chairs. The lounges are filled with plush armchairs and light colors. The comfortable bedrooms are well furnished in summertime colors and accents of wood and brass. Singles range from 130F ($88.40) to 150F ($102) daily, while doubles cost 180F ($122.40) to 210F ($142.80). Half board is an additional 45F ($30.60) per person daily.

Hotel Belmonte, 29 via Serenella, CH-6976 Lugano, Switzerland (tel. 091/51-40-33), at Lugano-Castagnola, is in a suburb of Lugano about a two-minute ride from the center by trolleybus. The façade is a typically balconied structure, a grand format of big-windowed comfort, with palm trees growing from the front lawn and a view of the nearby lake. The outdoor swimming pool is designed in a narrow angled format that stretches a long distance along the accommodating chaise longues of the flagstone borders around it. Singles cost 100F ($68) to 140F ($95.20) daily, and doubles are priced at 160F ($108.80) to 230F ($156.40), with breakfast included. Half board is another 30F ($20.40) per person daily, and guests are received from March to November.

The Middle Bracket

Romantik Hotel Ticino, 1 Piazza Cioccaro, CH-6901 Lugano, Switzerland (tel. 091/22-77-72), presents a narrow façade to one of the most charming squares in the old town of Lugano. It was a former convent whose present owners have carefully maintained the arcaded central courtyard, which today burgeons with plants. They've covered the small area that used to be open to the sky, and now a glass ceiling allows year-round comfort. Antique cupboards and chests are in the stairwell area. Each of the small bedrooms is uniquely furnished, usually with 19th-century provincial pieces. There's a private bath with each chamber, along with a phone, radio, and mini-bar. With breakfast included, singles range from 130F ($88.40) to 160F ($108.80) daily, while doubles cost 230F ($156.40) to 280F ($190.40). Triples are available from 300F ($204). From the kitchen comes specialties of the various regions of Switzerland and Italy. The hotel closes in January.

Strandhotel Seegarten, 24 viale Castagnola, CH-6900 Lugano-Cassarate, Switzerland (tel. 091/54-23-21), is a symmetrical white hotel that sprawls over an elongated section of lake-front property near the Lido. The management has built a swimming pool out over the water, planting it with the subtropical vegetation that grows so well in Lugano. There's a private parking lot and garage, for which you'll be grateful. The location is about a five-minute walk from the center of town. The Huber family charges from 40F ($27.20) to 95F ($64.40) daily in a single, 80F ($54.40) to 160F ($108.80) in a double, with breakfast included. Rooms are comfortably furnished, but for the cheaper prices quoted, you don't get a private bath. Half board is another 22F ($14.95) per person daily. The hotel is open from March to October.

Hotel Delfino, 6 via Casserinetta, CH-6900 Lugano, Switzerland (tel. 091/54-53-33), is a well-designed hotel built in 1972. It looks especially attractive at night, when it's illuminated from the outside. It has a swimming pool below the angled corners of its façade, and modern balconies decorated with clusters of cascading plants. The interior has certain elegant touches, including an elaborate carving and antique pewter that decorate the hardwoods of the reception desk. An ornate baroque chest and Oriental rugs make the place even more appealing. The hotel lies on a side street a few blocks from the lake, and has a bar as well as a dining room with chandeliers. Bed and breakfast costs 80F ($54.40) to 90F ($61.20) daily in a single, 150F ($102) to 170F ($115.60) in a double. The place is open from April to November.

Hotel Colorado, 19 via Maraini, CH-6901 Lugano, Switzerland (tel. 091/54-16-31). The name of the hotel might inspire nostalgia for Americans traveling abroad, and the balconied eight-story building might remind you of those you've seen back home. The hotel has a TV, radio, mini-bar, phone, and private bath in each of its comfortable bedrooms. Singles range from 75F ($51) to 110F ($74.80) daily, while doubles cost from 120F ($81.60) to 170F ($115.60), with breakfast included. Facilities include a lounge, bar, terrace, dining room, and a typical restaurant, Tavernetta Grill, offering nouvelle cuisine, regional, and international specialties. An à la carte meal costs from 30F ($20.40).

La Residenza, 16 Piazza della Riscossa, CH-6900 Lugano-Cassarate, Switzerland (tel. 091/52-18-31). If you're fond of modern architecture and shades of beige and brown, you'll gravitate to this hotel. Its façade looks like a monochromatic op-art by Warhol. The dun color of the textured concrete is repeated in dozens of places throughout the interior. Furniture is comfortable, providing color accents of flame orange and deep red. The dining room has wicker chairs, white tablecloths, and hanging lamps shaped like inverted tulips. The bar area has two-dimensional cutouts hanging erratically from the ceiling. Each of the bedrooms, also dun colored, has a private bath, phone, radio, and TV. Singles range from 75F ($51) to 95F ($64.60) daily, while doubles cost 120F ($81.60) to 150F ($102) with breakfast included.

Hotel Arizona, 20 via Massagno, CH-6900 Lugano, Switzerland (tel. 091/22-93-43), is an attractive modern hotel at the north end of the city, its façade composed of alternating areas of reddish brick and white concrete. A sun terrace with an above-ground swimming pool is built into the roof stretching above the attractive ground-floor lobby. A totally renovated and tastefully furnished restaurant and bar offer guests a quiet place to get away from it all. Many of the bedrooms, thanks to the angled façade, have irregular shapes, big windows facing south, and unusually large sizes. The Brunner family, your hosts, charge 90F ($61.20) to 120F ($81.60) daily in a single, 140F ($95.20) to 170F ($115.60) in a double. A generous buffet breakfast is included in the rates. To get there, get off the autobahn at the Lugano-Nord exit and turn left at the first traffic light in the direction of Massagno. Then follow the signs to Lugano, which will turn you right at the via San Gottardo, which leads you to signs indicating the hotel.

Holiday Hotel Select, 4 via G. Zoppi, Salita dei Frati, CH-6900 Lugano, Switzerland (tel. 091/23-61-72). The concrete balconies of this white-walled hotel rise from a quiet position near the business center of Lugano, only a few minutes from the lake. The lobby is filled with light-hearted furniture, sometimes of upholstered plastic, and most of the functional bedrooms have views of the lake. All units have private baths or showers. Singles rent for 80F ($54.40) to 120F ($81.60) daily, while doubles cost 130F ($88.40) to 195F ($132.60), with a continental breakfast, taxes, and service included. The hotel is closed from November to March.

Carlton Hotel Villa Moritz, 9 via Cortiva, CH-6976 Lugano-Castagnola, Switzerland (tel. 091/51-38-12), is housed in at least two 19th-century buildings. A free-form swimming pool is set into gray flagstones, receiving a maximum amount of sunlight because of its location on the sunny side of Mount Brè. The hotel is in a park some distance from a main road, so peace and quiet are assured. The public rooms are attractively up-to-date, with well-designed stone accents in the fireplaces and around the bar area. Public buses can carry guests to the center of Lugano in ten minutes. The Wernli family are your hosts. Their least-expensive rooms don't contain private baths. Depending on the season, singles range from 45F ($30.60) to 76F ($51.70) daily, with doubles costing 90F ($61.20) to 144F ($97.90). There is underground parking nearby. The hotel is open from March to October.

The Budget Range

Albergo Domus, 24a Riva Paradiso, CH-6900 Lugano-Paradiso (tel. 091/54-34-21), lies on the main road to Paradiso from Lugano. It's a balconied building with red brick walls and an imposing modern format. The attractive and airy interior is decorated with a light touch of neutral-colored furniture, potted palms, and Oriental rugs. The uncluttered bedrooms are outfitted with a light-hearted southern touch of clear colors and big windows. Singles range from 40F ($27.20) to 80F ($54.40) daily, while doubles cost 80F ($54.40) to 130F ($88.40) daily, with breakfast included. The albergo is open from March to November.

Hotel Marina, Via della Scuole, CH-6900 Lugano-Cassarete, Switzerland (tel. 091/51-45-14), is a flat-topped, solid-looking three-star with symmetrical rows of concrete balconies. The entrance hall is attractively austere, with a marble floor and marble facing over part of it. The rest of the public rooms are outfitted in pastel colors, tile floors, and flowered curtains. The bedrooms are spacious and sunny, with wood-grained furniture, homey knickknacks, and clean sheets. Singles range from 60F ($40.80) to 90F ($61.20) daily and doubles run from 100F ($68) to 135F ($91.80), depending on the season, the plumbing, and the exposure. Breakfast is included. All rooms have a toilet and shower or bath. The Schreiber family are your congenial hosts.

Hotel Zurigo, 13 Corso Pestalozzi, CH-6900 Lugano, Switzerland (tel. 091/23-43-43), is an unpretentious hotel, lying near the center of town. Relatively nondescript but pleasant, it is one of the better bargains around. It contains room for 50 guests in accommodations which don't always have a private bath. Bathless singles, depending on the plumbing, range from 30F ($20.40) to 35F ($23.80), whereas similar doubles rent for 60F ($40.80) to 68F ($46.25) per day. Rooms with bath cost 38F ($25.85) to 55F ($37.40) in a single, the cost going up to 68F ($46.25) to 96F ($65.30) in a double, with breakfast included.

Post Hotel Simplon, 12 Via General Guisan, CH-6900 Lugano-Paradiso, Switzerland (tel. 091/54-44-41), open only from March to December, is another reasonably priced hotel. It is slightly older than the Zurigo, lying in Lugano Paradiso, yet its rooms are comfortable and the welcome is polite. It charges year-round prices of 60F ($40.80) to 75F ($51) daily in a single, with doubles costing 110F ($74.80) to 140F ($95.20), with breakfast included.

Hotel Monte Ceneri, 44 via Nassa, CH-6900 Lugano, Switzerland (tel. 091/23-33-40), is the one-star hotel attached to one of the best of the inexpensive restaurants in Lugano (see my dining recommendations). You'll walk up a big skylit staircase to the reception area, as there is no elevator (expect some stains on the carpet). The location is only a block from the lake, and your room is likely to be slightly shabby and a little run-down, but fairly clean, sunny, and safe. The place is a real bargain in an expensive city, charging 35F ($23.80) daily in a single and 65F ($44.20) in a double. No room has a private bath, however.

WHERE TO DINE: Lugano is well equipped with independent restaurants, ranging from cuisine moderne to Italian dishes. Many of its restaurants are expensive, but others are real bargains.

Ristorante Al Portone, 3 viale Cassarate (tel. 091/23-59-95). If you have a passion for nouvelle cuisine Italian style, or even if you don't know what that means, you can head toward this elegantly sophisticated restaurant, the domain of Roberto and Doris Galizzi. He cooks and she supervises the service, a winning combination of talents. A fixed-price menu—"according to the wishes of Roberto"—is served for 95F ($64.60), and you might be better off ordering it, although you can also venture into the uncharted waters of the à la carte listings. Like all cuisine moderne restaurants, many of the combinations sound bizarre, but the taste is usually sensational. The sole in the style of Roberto is a palate-pleaser, as is the veal liver with champagne. The desserts are also exceptional. The restaurant is open from noon to 2 p.m. and 7 to 9:30 p.m. It's closed on Sunday, until dinner on Monday, and also for the month of August.

Da Bianchi, 3 via Pessina (tel. 091/22-84-79), has a forest-green turn-of-the-century façade set symmetrically between red carved-stone pillars. It's on a narrow street in the old town, and has a decor that includes paneled and gold brocade walls, red carpeting, and red upholstered chairs, rounded belle-époque ironwork, and a single carriage lamp hanging over the door. The service is courteous and attentive. Your meal might include Italian dishes such as scampi with curry, filet of sole in white wine, veal cutlet milanese, and risotto with fresh mushrooms. A specialty in this restaurant, one of the oldest and most venerated in Lugano, is a selection of three pastas on one platter. Some dishes are accompanied by deep-fried potatoes with pine nuts, another dish of which the chef is justly proud. Fixed-price meals begin at 39F ($23.08), and à la carte dinners cost about 65F ($44.20). The restaurant is open from noon to 2:30 p.m. and 6:30 to 10 p.m. daily except Sunday and during August.

Ristorante Orologio, 2 via Nizzola (tel. 091/23-23-38), is a high-quality restaurant on the ground floor of a buff-colored building with a restrained exterior. A view of the inside reveals leaded-glass windows and French-provincial 19th-century chairs. You'll also see lots of copperware on the window ledges above the banquettes, plus an exposed ice chest for the display of salads and condiments. Amusing illustrations advertise the menu items, including such things as a bare-breasted mermaid "discreetly" suggesting the fish courses. Vincenzo Campanile and his family are the owners, and they charge from 50F ($34) for a well-prepared meal, which might include five kinds of spaghetti, four kinds of scampi, osso buco, smoked fish, the inevitable minestrone alla Ticinese, and a springtime celebration of seasonal vegetables such as asparagus and melon. The restaurant is open from noon to 2 p.m. and 6:30 to 10 p.m. except on Saturday and for three weeks in August.

Albergo Restaurant Ticino, 1 Piazza Cioccaro (tel. 091/22-77-72), part of a previously recommended Romantik hotel, not only opens onto one of the most charming squares of the old town but serves some of the best food. You dine beneath vaulted ceilings, with art deco lighting sconces, in a long and narrow room with a uniformed staff. Food is served daily from 11:30 a.m. to 3 p.m. and 6:30 to 11 p.m. The menu contains an array of familiar dishes prepared well, and fresh ingredients, whenever possible, are used. Set menus begin at 45F ($30.60). You are likely to be served scampi curry, Chateaubriand, Ticino minestrone, and osso buco. For a strictly local dish, order a serving of porcini mushrooms with risotto and polenta. If you're feeling festive and flushed, try the grilled rock lobster.

Gambrinus, Piazza Riforma (tel. 091/23-19-55), is housed in an 18th-century building in a recessed corner of the Piazza Riforma, opening onto Via Giacomo Luvini. It's usually laden with masses of flowers, and has two carved cherubs holding up a fluted column above the main doorway, which is set at an angle to the façade. If you're not careful you might crash into a waiter scurrying out the door laden with food for customers waiting at the outdoor café. Most of the interior curves around the windowed section of this place, with a central bar forming a big rectangle inside. Specialties include saltimbocca, trout meunière, risotto marinara, air-cured beef from Davos, and pasta dishes. Meals start at around 35F ($23.80). The restaurant is open daily from 9 a.m. till midnight in summer and 11:30 a.m. to 11 p.m. during the rest of the year. It's closed for three weeks in February.

Ristorante Galleria, 4 via Vegezzi (tel. 091/23-62-88). The entrance to this elegant place is under an old-fashioned covered passageway that you could easily imagine as being in Naples. The façade of the restaurant is painted a memorable fire-engine red with gilt trim and big windows. You'll see an informal bar area on your left as you enter, and on your right a well-furnished room with white stucco arches, a beautifully textured wood ceiling with heavy beams, and original prints and lithographs by well-known artists, usually Italian. The owner welcomes many local bankers and business people at lunch, a clientele that gives way to a more fun-loving crowd at night. You can have coffee or a drink at any time outside at the café table set on a mosaic floor under the arcade. Meals, however, are served from noon to 2 p.m. and 7 to 10:30 p.m. The restaurant is closed on Sunday and during all of August. Specialties include brochette Galleria, kebabs, fondue bourguignonne (or else chinoise), risotto with salmon, and five kinds of scampi. Fixed-price meals begin at 30F ($20.40), and à la carte dinners are likely to cost from 50F ($34).

Mövenpick Ristorante Parco Ciani, Piazza Indipendenza, at the Palazzo dei Congressi (tel. 091/23-86-56), is decorated to look like a village restaurant filled with an abundant Italian harvest. Guests select from two distinct dining areas here, only with modern bentwood armchairs and another with reproduction Empire-style rush-bottom antiques. Vines cover the rafters of one room, and bunches of ripened corn in another. The complex is housed in a modern concrete building with irregular balconies and big windows at the edge of a city park. You can have drinks or coffee on the terrace while overlooking the shrubs and flowers. The staff serves wild game in season, very good veal-and-rice dishes, tortellini, three kinds of risotto, well-prepared curry dishes, and a mixed medley of broiled fresh fish and meats. Meals cost 40F ($27.20) and up. Service is daily from 9 a.m. to midnight.

Locanda del Boschetto, 8 via Boschetto (tel. 091/54-24-93). Many of the clients at this well-known grill restaurant make the trip up from Milan, claiming it's cheaper to cross into Switzerland than it is to dine at home. Part of the entertainment is to watch the owner and chef, Vincenzo De-Martino, grilling his daily arrays of beef and fish over the glowing coals of the dining room's focal point. He produces a simple but flavorful cuisine, which includes a mixed fish grill (each of the catch coming from a nearby lake), spaghetti with clam sauce, grilled calves' liver, and a wide array of succulent beef dishes. This establishment lies in a wooded area near the highway. It contains a covered porch for fair weather, as well as two indoor dining areas. Full meals, which are served daily from noon to 2 p.m. and 7 to 10 p.m. except Monday and during January, represent good value at 45F ($30.60) to 60F ($40.80).

Ristorante Monte Ceneri, 44 via Nassa (tel. 091/23-33-40), has an ornate plastic ceiling, red-checked tablecloths, big windows, and a setting that quickly lets you know that this is very much a local eatery. It's a family-run and a family-style establishment where people bring their friends, their lovers (often their wives or husbands), and most definitely their pet dogs. The Campanile family offers one of the best bargains in town: 27F ($18.35) for a fixed-price meal, which might include an array of typically Italian local specialties, such as fresh mushrooms, polenta, or risotto. Try one of their four different kinds of fondue or a penciled-in special of the day that's usually very good. My favorite, when featured, is a delectable platter of fresh mushrooms with polenta. Service is daily from 11:30 a.m. to 2 p.m. and 6:30 to 10 p.m.

La Tinera, 2 Via dei Gorino (tel. 091/23-52-19), is an inexpensive restaurant serving good food. It offers a familiar array of Italian specialties, including fresh pasta and risotto, along with some good meat dishes. This typical Ticinese restaurant lies in the center of town, off the Piazza Riforma. Meals begin at 30F ($20.40), and are served daily except Sunday from 11:30 a.m. to 2 p.m. and 6:30 to 9:30 p.m.

On the Outskirts

Motto del Gallo, CH-6807 Taverne, Switzerland (93-28-71). Many visitors come here just for a view of the 15th-century hamlet in which the restaurant is located. The setting is a baroque house whose interior practically bursts with atmosphere. It contains a collection of antiques, both decorative and functional, that might grace a private home. Diners reserve ahead and consider a meal a festive occasion. After being seated at a lace-covered table, you'll be able to enjoy such delicacies as one of the homemade pastas, risotto with champagne, a succulent choice of fresh fish, and a salad of fresh foie gras. Main courses include a baked beef heart with levisticum (wild celery), and rabbit with truffles and zucchini, as well as an alpine-inspired variety of lamb and fish dishes, many laced with mountain cheese. A business lunch is offered for 45F ($30.60), but a gastronomique menu goes for 86F ($58.50). Full dinners on the à la carte menu cost from 95F ($64.60) to 120F ($81.60) per person. The chefs, Nico and José de la Iglesias, sometimes make their appearance in the dining room. The restaurant is open for lunch and dinner daily except Sunday from noon to 2 p.m. and 7:30 to 10:30 p.m. It's closed for the first two weeks in January. There are also three romantic suites available, costing two persons 150F ($102) to 180F ($122.40) daily.

WHAT TO SEE: The city park, **Parco Civico,** lies by Lake Lugano. Within this park sit the Palazzo dei Congressi (the convention center) and the Casino of Lugano. In good weather, open-air concerts are staged here.

In the municipally run park, you can visit **Villa Ciani,** Parco Civico (tel. 091/23-61-62), which is open all year, Tuesday to Sunday from 10 a.m. to noon and 2 to 6 p.m., charging an admission of 2F ($1.35). Both Swiss and Quattrocento artists are displayed, along with some European masters (see works by Lucas Cranach the Elder, Vela, Serodine, Mola, Piazzetta, Monet, Pissarro, Rousseau, and Derain). Works by Hodler are displayed, as is art by both Augusto and Alberto Giacometti. The sculpture gallery exhibits pieces by Marini, Martini, and Messina. The museum was founded in 1903, and it became the property of the city of Lugano in 1912.

The **Cattedrale di San Lorenzo** (cathedral of St. Lawrence), in the old town, was built as a Romanesque church but was mainly reconstructed in the 13th and 14th centuries, then massively renovated again in the 17th and 18th centuries. It has an outstanding trio of Renaissance doorways, and inside the decoration is baroque. Look for the 16th-century tabernacle at the end of the south aisle, designed by the Rodari brothers of Maroggia.

The other important church of Lugano is the **Chiesa di Santa Maria deglo Angioli** (Church of St. Mary of the Angels), on the south side of the resort. This convent church was built in the closing year of the 15th century and is celebrated throughout the Ticino for its frescoes by Bernardino Luini, the Lombard painter. His huge fresco, *The Crucifixion*, is from 1529. Many critics have compared the beauty of his work to that of Leonardo da Vinci. Latter-day admirers, including John Ruskin, found an "unstudied sweetness" in Luini's work. Until 1848 the church was occupied by Franciscans.

In Castagnola, to the east of Lugano, the 17th-century **Villa Favorita** contains one of the great private art collections of the world. The collection belongs to Baron Hans Heinrich Thyssen-Bornemisza, who shares it with the public in his luxuriously furnished villa. It can be seen daily except Monday from 10 a.m. to 5 p.m. from April 20 to October 29. Admission is 12F ($8.15). Special exhibitions are also staged annually. The collection covers the period from the Middle Ages to the 19th century, including many Flemish and German works. You'll be able to view paintings by Cranach the Elder, Dürer, Holbein the Younger, Memling, and Van Eyck (see his masterpiece, *The Annunciation*). The Italian school is well represented by Titian, Raphael, Fra Angelico, Caravaggio, and Correggio.

The home of noted architect Wilhelm Schmid is maintained as the **Schmid Museum** at the Lugano suburb of Brè, where many of his works and documents are displayed. The city of Lugano received the house as a legacy on the death of Schmid's widow. The architect was deeply involved in the "new objectivity" of the '20s and '30s, and a significant selection of his paintings from that period are on display, together with ceramics, work tools, furniture decorated by Schmid, and books and other papers that reveal his artistic interests and his awareness of the political events that saw him driven out of Nazi Germany in 1936, back to his native Switzerland. The museum is open Easter to mid-October, Tuesday to Sunday, from 10 a.m. to noon and 3 to 5 p.m. Brè is about 5½ miles from Lugano and can easily be reached by car, by bus costing 2.40F ($1.65), or by the funicular, which costs 6F ($4.10). There is no charge for admission. For more information, phone 091/52-63-13.

On a different note, especially if you have a child in tow, you may want to visit the **Swiss Miniature Village** at Melide-Lugano (tel. 091/68-79-51). Artisans have created small copies of the major buildings in all the Swiss cantons, including the twin castles at Sion. All of them are set into a labyrinth of asphalt paths, and you'll have to buy the official guidebook if you want detailed explanations. Entrance fee is 8F ($5.45) for adults, 3.50F ($2.40) for children under 14. The village is open from 8:30 a.m. to 10 p.m. seven days a week from mid-July to August 20, and to 6 p.m. from March until the end of October. It's closed in winter.

Villa Heleneum, 24 Via Cortivo, Lugano-Cassarate (tel. 091/52-63-12), houses the **Museum of Extra-European Cultures.** This Lugano landmark building lies on the famous walk linking this spot with Gandria. The objects exhibited originated in various regions of Oceania (New Guinea, New Britain, New Ireland, the Solomon Islands, Vanuatu, New Caledonia, Polynesia), Indonesia (Sumatra, Kalimantan, Nias, Timor), and Africa (Dan, Senufo, Ibo, Yoruba). They were donated to the city of Lugano by Serge Brignoni, an authoritative exponent of the surrealistic movement. This collection, also well known in the United States, is presented at this museum for the first time in its entirety. There is also a center of ethnographic studies with a relevant library annexed to the museum. The museum opened in 1989, but call for hours and admission prices as they weren't set at presstime.

EXCURSIONS: Lugano is not only ideal for excursions on its own lake, but on Lake Como and Lake Maggiore as well. The **Societa Navigazione del Lago di Lugano** (tel. 091/51-52-23) operates morning, midday, afternoon, and even evening cruises. Gandria and Marcote are among the favored destinations.

If you plan to vacation in Ticino, you may want to purchase a 35F ($23.80) ticket, allowing you unlimited free boat trips on the lake for three days.

If you like belvederes with viewing platforms, you'll find Lugano rich in mountain scenery. The most exciting is generally conceded to be the funicular to **Monte San Salvatore,** a round-trip ticket costing about 12F ($8.15). From the top of the mountain you'll have a great view of all three lakes, as well as both the Swiss and French Alps (Matterhorn, Monte Rosa). The funicular operates daily from mid-March to mid-November, and leaves from **Paradiso.**

The funicular to **Monte Brè** is almost as impressive, leaving from Cassarate, a round-trip ticket costing 15F ($10.20). Monte Brè is called the sunniest mountain in Switzerland. From its peak you'll have a view of the Valaisan and Bernese Alps, including Monte Rosa and the Matterhorn. From Lugano you can take a trolleybus to Cassarate where you board the funicular for the ascent.

You can also take a cog-wheel train to **Monte Generoso.** From Lugano you go by boat or train to Capolago, and from there by cog-wheel train to Monte Generoso. At 5,590 feet, the summit offers a peerless panoramic view of the lakes of Ticino and into northern Italy. A round-trip ticket is 32F ($21.75).

A PHARMACY AND SHOPS: Need a drugstore? **Farmacia San Luca,** 9 via Pioda (tel. 091/23-84-55), is a friendly pharmacy right in the center of Lugano. It can take care of most minor ailments, and allows you to stock up on much-needed supplies. English is spoken.

Frankly, you don't come to Lugano to shop. However, there is one store that's exceptional if you're seeking not only souvenirs, but good handcrafts. It's **Bottega dell'Artigiano,** 18 via Canova (tel. 091/22-81-40), selling such Ticino-made goods as textiles, woodcarvings, pottery, and metalware. You get cordial service in a small area filled with displays. The shop is run by the Cooperativa per l'Artigianato Ticinese.

A true dreamland for children, **Dreamland Franz Carl Weber,** 5 via Nassa (tel. 091/23-53-21), is considered the best toy store in the Ticino. It's part of a nationwide chain.

SPORTS: Sports activities in Lugano are largely water oriented, and there are also facilities for golf, tennis, cycling, and many fitness pursuits.

You can **swim** at sandy Lido Beach (tel. 091/51-40-41), a bathing resort surrounded by green lawns, with a self-service restaurant on an outside terrace. The charge, with use of a changing cabin is 4F ($2.70) for adults, 2F ($1.35) for children from 2 to 14. The beach is open from 9 a.m. to 7 p.m. in summer. Many hotels have heated pools, some with saltwater. Swimming in the lake is also possible at the public bath, Riva Caccia (tel. 091/54-20-35), and at Lido San Domenico, Castagnola (tel. 091/51-65-66), both charging 2F ($1.35) for adults, 1F (68¢) for children. At Lido Piscina Comunale, Paradiso (tel. 091/54-75-62), the charge is 4F ($2.70) for adults, 1.50F ($1) for children.

Waterski at Club Nautico–Lugano, 9 via Calloni, between Lugano and Melide (tel. 091/68-61-39), for an hour at a cost of 120F ($81.60), including instruction. Club Sci Nautico Ceresio (tel. 091/54-19-21), which also gives instruction in the sport, charges 150F ($102) for an hour's skiing. Saladin, Piazza B. Luini (tel. 091/23-57-97), offers a half-hour's skiing for 60F ($40.80), an hour of the sport for 120F ($81.60).

Windsurfing on the lake can also be arranged at Club Nautico–Lugano, at the address and phone given above; Albergo Lago di Lugano, Paradiso (tel. 091/54-19-21); and Circolo Velico, Lago di Lugano, Foce Cassarate (tel. 091/51-09-75). The charge is 15F ($10.20) to 25F ($17) per hour.

Sailing is available at the Circolo Velico, at the above address. The cost ranges from 25F ($17) to 35F ($23.80) per hour.

Rowboats and motorboats are available for rental at many spots along the lakefront.

Underwater swimming is a possibility at Lugano-Sub, G. Bucher, 3 Corso Elvezia (tel. 091/22-96-29).

NIGHTLIFE: Everybody heads to Italy! Not really—but the major gambling casino for Lugano is on Italian soil, a bit of Italian geography completely surrounded by Switzerland. Long ago the imperial fiefdom of Campione was presented to a Milanese monastery. It has remained Italian ever since, in spite of incredible political turmoil in the area. The men of Campione were famous for their stonework, and many buildings in Milan are a testament to their skill. However, very few people go there to admire their handiwork—they go to gamble. The Italians, wanting to pick up some badly needed Swiss francs and other currencies have installed a gambling casino in Campione.

Casino Municipale (tel. 091/68-79-21), offers such games as blackjack and chemin de fer, along with the inevitable slot machines. The casino lies across the lake from Lugano, and is reached by frequent ferry service, only 20 minutes away. The casino is a glittering, glamorous establishment where Swiss citizens and seemingly all foreign visitors go to take their chance with baccarat and roulette, among other games. Here, unlike Switzerland, the stakes are unlimited. However, the currency is Swiss.

Back in Lugano, you can also try your luck at the **Casino Kursaal** (tel. 091/23-32-81), where the betting ceiling is limited to 5F ($3.40). This establishment is mainly a place of entertainment, offering all kinds of cabaret, from striptease to magic. Drinks cost from 15F ($10.20). It's best to go after 10 p.m.

Your nighttime stroll might begin at the famous **Piazza Riforma** of Lugano, a flagstone square, a huge one at that, where practically everyone in town shows up at one time or another. You'll be surrounded by arcaded buildings with masses of flowers.

Many cafés surround this square, but the favorite is the **Café Olimpia,** Piazza

Riforma (tel. 091/22-74-88), housed in an elegant stone building with hundreds of chairs set out front. It sometimes has live music (on occasion Mexican). The café remains open from 7 a.m. to midnight daily, but hot meals are served only from noon to 2 p.m. and 6:30 to 11 p.m. Full meals, costing from 30F ($20.40), feature daily specials, along with pastas, curries, and meat dishes. Especially popular at night are the pizzas at 11F ($7.50). Inside (if anyone ever goes inside) is a charming, old-fashioned decor with a wood bar along with a more formal dining room and immaculate napery.

Recommending nightclubs and discos in Lugano is risky business. Their life span is often short. Drinks usually cost from 10F ($6.80), and you shouldn't show up at any of these places before 10 p.m. However, here goes—**Dancing Cecil,** in Paradiso (tel. 091/54-21-21), attracts an under-30 crowd for dancing or whatever.

Europa 1001 Notte, also in Paradiso (tel. 091/54-21-21), attracts an older, more sophisticated and well-dressed crowd for its cabaret shows.

Capo San Martino, Pazzallo-Lugano (tel. 091/54-15-31), lies on a promontory facing the Casino of Campione d'Italia. From each corner can be admired a good view toward the center of Lugano as well as the northern basin of the Ceresio. You can come here for food or drink, ordering a good Italian meal costing from 40F ($27.20). If you want to dance the night away, the entrance fee, including your first drink, costs 15F ($10.20).

Dancing La Romantica, at Melide (tel. 091/68-75-21), is an elegant establishment, with both a restaurant and an orchestra, catering to an over-35 crowd of well-dressed night owls.

Pegasus/Morandi, 56 via Trevano (tel. 091/51-22-91), is a modern place that plays lots of recently released discs. It's one of the most popular discos in Lugano, with attractively dressed youngish dancers and drinkers.

La Piccionaia, Via Pioda (tel. 091/23-45-46), is an elegant and modern establishment drawing a young crowd.

La Rustica, at Cassarate (tel. 091/51-30-66), is one of the better and more popular discos in Lugano. Its decor is rustic and woodsy, and the disco music is up-to-date. When a live group appears you can expect a cover charge.

9. GANDRIA

Hundreds of steps, intricate lanes and courtyards, a southern sun shining on lush vegetation, playing on the waves of the lake of Lugano. This is definitely travel brochure cliché time, and that is what Gandria is. A short drive from Lugano, it is a small romantic oasis built at the foot of Monte Bré. It's so popular that it's likely to be overrun in warm weather with hordes of tourists.

Those visitors should be in good physical condition, however. An afternoon spent climbing up and down the steep, narrow streets of Gandria can exhaust an athlete. The terraced Ticinese village was miraculously built on this steep slope in such a way that it virtually seems to rise from the lake. Artists have long been drawn to its arcades and narrow lanes, set against a backdrop of vineyards.

FOOD AND LODGING: Most people come here to shop for souvenirs, and to dine, and then they're on their way. However, Gandria does have a hotel. It's the **Hotel Moosmann,** CH-6978 Gandria, Switzerland (tel. 091/51-72-61), and it opens directly onto the water. A family-run place, it has an inviting atmosphere and comfortable (but far from luxurious) rooms. However, the setting compensates, particularly if you get a room with a view opening directly onto the lake. From March to November, guests are received here and housed in rooms with private bath, costing 50F ($34) to 80F ($54.40) daily in a single, 90F ($61.20) to 130F ($88.40) in a double. The hotel offers a beautiful terrace looking onto the lake, and it also serves well-prepared Ticinese specialties in case you'd like to stop in for a meal.

Alternatively, you can find any number of independent places operating in Gandria. These include **Locanda Gandriese** (tel. 091/51-41-81), a place so Italian you'll think you crossed over the border. Its lakeside terrace is so popular that it's hard to get a table in fair weather. However, I prefer a cold day when the fireplace is going in the old-fashioned dining room, and a cast-iron pot of polenta is cooking. From noon to 2 p.m. and 6 to 10 p.m. daily, you can order full meals for 35F ($23.80). These are likely to include carpaccio, spaghetti bolognese, lasagne, and several veal dishes. There is also an elaborate dessert menu.

Antico (tel. 091/51-48-71) is one of the most acclaimed restaurants in Gandria, and it has three rooms to rent. Many visitors stop off here in the afternoon to order one of their more elaborate desserts. You're welcomed by Luciano Bartolini, the owner. On a cobblestone street, the restaurant is known for its elaborate lakeside terrace, which is glassed in from the wind on chilly days. Meals cost from 45F ($30.60) and are likely to include grilled crayfish, Ticinese minestrone, arrosto misto (mixed boiled meats) served with polenta, fondue bourguignonne, or steak tartare. Hours are daily from noon to 2 p.m. and from 6 to 10 p.m.

10. MORCOTE

Morcote, reached either by boat or car, is considered one of the most idyllic and charming villages of Switzerland. Its arcaded houses and old streets are built on the southern slopes of Monte Arbostora at 2,755 feet. Cypresses stud the vine-clad slopes. The pilgrimage **Church of the Madonna del Sasso** dates from the 13th century, although it was reconstructed much later and given a baroque overlay. It has some beautiful 16th-century frescoes. At the church you can take more than 400 steps down to the village on the shores of the lake. Many famous persons were buried in the Morcote cemetery.

Of special interest is **Scherrer Park,** with its typical Ticino trees and vegetation, along with artistic and architectural objects of interest, including sculpture from the Far East. It's open from 9 a.m. to 5 p.m. except on Tuesday and Thursday. The entrance fee is 2.50F ($1.70). On Tuesday and Thursday there are conducted tours with a guide who explains everything. This, of course, is the best time to visit. He conducts tours at 10 a.m., 1:30 p.m., and again at 3:30 p.m., charging an entrance fee then of 5F ($3.40).

FOOD AND LODGING: From the lakeside road as you pass, **Olivella au Lac,** CH-6922 Morcote, Switzerland (tel. 091/69-10-01), won't look very impressive. Once you park, however, and look over the edge of the road, you'll see a lovely oasis of green lawns, flowers, and terraced elegance. Going down several flights, you'll reach the spacious and intimate ambience of what is acknowledged as one of the top restaurants of Switzerland. Service here is impeccable, and chef Dario Ranza, has elevated Ticino cookery to a fine art. You might begin your meal with foie gras or a lobster cocktail, perhaps turtle soup, either selection a proper introduction to this outstanding restaurant, La Voile d'Or. The chef might recommend a filet of sole Caruso or game dishes such as roebuck, featured in season. Specialties of the house include duck à l'orange and beef Wellington, blue trout meunière is also outstanding. A menu gastronomique is offered for 95F ($64.60).

If you want to spend the night, or else make this place a headquarters for your Ticino holiday, it would be an excellent choice. The hotel has two swimming pools, along with waterskiing and windsurfing facilities. There's plenty of atmosphere, and at the piano bar in the evening you're likely to meet your fellow guests. A resident nurse will care for your children as part of your accommodation fee. Singles range from 110F ($74.80) to 170F ($115.60) daily, while doubles cost 190F ($129.20) to 310F ($217.60), with breakfast included. Half board is an extra 45F ($30.60) per person daily. All rooms have private bath, and most of them have a balcony as well, along with a radio, phone, and mini-bar. The hotel is closed in January and February.

Albergo Carina, CH-6922 Morcote, Switzerland (tel. 091/69-11-31). The hotel lobby has many contrasting colors and patterns woven into the Oriental rugs and upholstery. Even the façade repeats the lighthearted theme, with its Italianate design and pink-and cream-colored trim and its lime-green shutters. The many terraces are filled with potted plants and small tables, where local residents often stop in for coffee. The former owner of this charming place was the Morcote-born architect Gaspare Fossati, who died in 1883. He helped direct the renovations on the mosaics and superstructure of Saint Sophia in Istanbul. Some of the awards he received from the Ottoman sultan are displayed in the lobby. Heidi and Horst Echsle have directed this place for several years. Their elegant bedrooms, filled with provincial furniture, some of it antique, rent for 90F ($61.20) to 130F ($88.40) daily in a single and 160F ($108.80) to 220F ($149.60) in a double, with breakfast included. Half board costs an additional 35F ($23.80) per person daily. There's a swimming pool as well as a waterside restaurant on the premises. The albergo is open from March to November.

Hotel Rivabella, CH-6922 Morcote, Switzerland (tel. 091/69-13-14), is housed in an old Italian-style country house some distance down the lakefront from the most congested part of Morcote. It has a terrace built out over the water, beneath which sailboats and motorboats are moored. The Tamborini family have planted flower boxes filled with begonias and geraniums that thrive in the sunshine of the rustically covered porches. Rooms are comfortably and pleasantly furnished. They come with and without bath. Depending on the season and the plumbing, the single rate ranges from 40F ($27.20) to 60F ($40.80) daily, with doubles costing 80F ($54.40) to 120F ($81.60). Half board is an additional 15F ($10.20) per person per day. It's open from April through October.

For dining outside the hotels recommended, try **Ristorante della Posta** (tel. 091/69-11-27). This unusual restaurant is housed on a terrace built out over the lake. Waiters scurry with food-laden trays from the kitchens across the street. The setting is charming, but because of the traffic, a little hectic. Specialties include risotto with mushrooms, osso buco with polenta, lake fish, and real Italian pizza. Meals cost from 35F ($23.80). The restaurant serves from 11:30 a.m. to 2:30 p.m. and 5 to 11 p.m. daily except Wednesday and from the first of November to mid-March.

LIECHTENSTEIN

□ □ □

If you want to come back from Europe and let your friends think you've toured a remote and obscure place in that much-traveled continent, pay a visit to Liechtenstein. This tiny principality, nestled snugly between a small portion of Austria with a short stretch of the Rhine River dividing it from Switzerland, is one of the smallest independent sovereign states of Europe, ranking along with San Marino in Italy and Andorra in the Pyrenees between Spain and France. The whole country encompasses only about 60 square miles. It's separated on its western border from the Swiss canton of St. Gallen by the Rhine River, its eastern frontier borders the Austrian province of Vorarlberg, and its southern boundary is a strip less than ten miles long dividing it from the Grisons of Switzerland. The country is cradled in the Three Sisters (Dreï Schwestern) mountains.

Actually, Liechtenstein is not as isolated as it's often made out to be. In fact, if you're touring through eastern Switzerland, it's easily reached by good roads. It lives up to its cliché image of fairytale castles (one inhabited by a real prince), Rhine meadows, and geranium-bedecked chalets in small villages high up in the Alps. It was once on the Grand Tour, at least in Queen Victoria's day, but in spite of its accessibility it still tends to be thought of as remote, so that a visit there almost constitutes an offbeat adventure. Since border guards rarely stamp passports of travelers coming nowadays from Austria, and since there's no customs to clear if you're motoring in from Switzerland, if you want to prove you've been there, you'll have to get someone at the tourist office to stamp the Liechtenstein seal on your passport.

If you're based in Switzerland you can make Liechtenstein in an easy morning's drive, and unless you choose to stay in one or the other of the towns or villages, it doesn't take long to motor through this 16-mile-long, 4-mile-wide country.

1. GETTING ACQUAINTED

Low taxes and low unemployment linked with carefully planned industrial development and a high standard of living make the Principality of Liechtenstein almost a phenomenon in today's world, but this is a development dating from the end of World War II, as a look at the past will show.

HISTORY: The region that today is Liechtenstein was in a part of Europe that for centuries was inextricably connected with Switzerland and Austria, and its history follows the same paths for long eras. Tribal settlements, particularly those of the Celts, left traces showing habitation of the section from about 4000 B.C., with the Romans occupying the Rhine Valley in 15 B.C. and holding control until the middle of the fifth century A.D. What is today Liechtenstein was part of the Roman province of Rhaetia, and establishment of a military and trade route by the Emperor Augustus preceded the coming of the Alemanni, Germanic tribes, who settled here over the centuries from A.D. 300 to 700.

When Charlemagne made all the alpine region a part of the Holy Roman Empire, the area now comprising Liechtenstein became portions of royal estates, as shown in a document drawn up in about A.D. 850, called the *Rhaetican Register*. Descendants of family connections of Charlemagne owned rich estates in the region of Lake Constance and the Lower Alps, which were continually broken up through hereditary claims, resulting in the formation of the County of Vaduz on the east side of the Rhine. Vaduz, the name of the present capital of Liechtenstein, was under the immediate rule of the Roman Empire and not of any territorial lord.

Since 1437 both parts of the country, the old County of Vaduz (called Oberland, or the Upper Country) and the Lordship of Schellenberg (Unterland, or Lower Country) have been united, with the same boundaries of the principality that exist today. The many wars in which the little state became involved during the Middle Ages saw dependency changing from Switzerland to Austria and the country beset with religious strife and the plague. Many of the rulers were tyrants who imposed devastating taxes or by other means brought misery to the land. This sometimes-peaceful, sometimes-war-torn country passed from count to count and lord to lord through inheritance and outright sale of the Schellenberg and Vaduz estates. Finally, Prince John Adam Andrew of Liechtenstein was able to purchase first the estates of Schellenberg and then the County of Vaduz, and in 1719 the two territories were given the title "Imperial Principality of Liechtenstein," becoming thus a member of the Holy Roman Empire and not just a possession of some other ruler. As a result, if you're crossing from Switzerland into Liechtenstein, it's commonly pointed out to tourists that they are leaving one of the world's oldest democracies and entering the last remaining outpost of the Holy Roman Empire.

Under the old German Empire, Liechtenstein was under obligation to provide 5 men for the Imperial Army, a figure finally raised to 80 under the German Confederation. After a tour of duty in 1866 lasting six weeks on the Tyrol-Italian frontier, during which time the soldiers never set eyes on the enemy, the Liechtenstein contingent was never again called up, and in 1869 the principality's army was disbanded permanently by Prince John II.

Until the end of World War I the country had a close alliance with Austria, but in 1921 it signed a postal treaty with Switzerland, followed in 1924 by adoption of Swiss currency and inclusion in the Swiss Customs Union. Since 1959 Switzerland has been Liechtenstein's diplomatic representative abroad. This political marriage with Switzerland was a smart move by the principality. It did not have to suffer Austria's fate when World War II came, and because of its close ties with Switzerland and the same neutrality stance, Liechtenstein escaped occupation by Nazi troops.

Prince John II had the longest reign of any Liechtenstein ruler, 71 years, ending with his death in 1929. He lavished part of his vast fortune on improving life in the principality.

The present titular head of state is the first to make his permanent home in the country, after becoming ruling prince in 1938. He and his wife, Princess Gina, are the parents of five children, four of them sons. The present prince is

Franz Joseph II, Prince of Liechtenstein, Duke of Troppau and Jaegerndorf, Knight of the Golden Fleece, and Count of Reitberg. He was the world's longest reigning monarch after the late Emperor Hirohito of Japan until he decided at the age of 78 in 1984 to turn over actual power to his son, Crown Prince Hans Adam, who assumed control at the age of 39. Franz Joseph II is still a much-loved ruler and keeps his position as titular head of Liechtenstein.

Although his family has lost vast tracts of its lands in eastern Europe, the prince is still one of the wealthiest men in Europe, though he doesn't believe in flaunting his wealth.

The Principality of Liechtenstein celebrated its 250th anniversary in 1969.

THE PEOPLE: Most of the population of this tiny country is of German origin and therefore, of course, German speaking. However, English is understood all over Liechtenstein. It's a predominantly Roman Catholic principality. You'll search hard to find anyone who is unemployed in the country. In fact a citizen of Liechtenstein today enjoys one of the highest standards of living in the world, although many oldtimers remember World War I, when the little principality was virtually cut off from food supplies because of blockades and suffered much hunger and hardship.

Since the end of World War II Liechtenstein has had a social and economic growth period exceeding that of any other Western country. Citizens pay relatively little in taxes, and they have an export revenue of some $14,000 annually per citizen.

The people of Liechtenstein enjoy a flourishing cultural ambience, benefiting from royal patronage and the cooperation of neighboring countries. Sports, trades and crafts, and agriculture also are actively promoted among the citizenry.

Considered today to be one of the most industrialized countries in the world, Liechtenstein, with some 26,000 citizens scattered throughout 11 communities, has been careful to keep the country attractive. The industrial development is hardly noticeable if you're touring the principality, as factories and workshops are hidden among orchards, meadows, and woodlands in order to have them blend with the environment. There are no factory smokestacks or fumes to pollute the atmosphere. Agriculture and industry are the two top economic resources of the country (one of its commercial specialties is the manufacture of false teeth).

When you hear about all this good life, you may want to become a citizen of Liechtenstein immediately. Forget it! Citizenship is almost impossible to obtain, and unless you're a woman who marries a man of the country, it would require an act of the state's parliament.

GOVERNMENT: The Principality of Liechtenstein is a constitutional hereditary monarchy with a democratic and parliamentary basis. The state power is vested in the prince and the people. The prince's state prerogatives derive from hereditary succession to the throne and are independent of the will of the people. The people, on the other hand, are invested with a right to participate in the guidance of state affairs independently of the prince. Therefore both parties must work together in accordance with the constitution.

The parliament, called the Diet, is elected by the people in national general elections, with the right to vote being constitutionally universal, equal, secret, and direct. Referendum is a vital part of the Liechtenstein people's right. Any law passed by the Diet that is not declared as urgent may be put to referendum. Besides the universal and equal right to vote, the constitution assures Liechtenstein citizens freedom of expression of opinion, freedom of the press, and freedom of assembly, among other privileges.

Liechtenstein has a prime minister and four government councillors. They act as a connecting link between the prince and the Diet.

STAMPS: Liechtenstein is known all over the world for its postage stamps, finely engraved issues that are an important source of revenue (about 25%) for the country. The design and quality of these stamps are appreciated by philatelists and by other collectors with artistic interests. The stamps depict the special features of the principality, taking subjects from the religion, monarchy, art, history, landscape, nature, work, and leisure of the country. The Postal Museum at Vaduz, the capital, displays both the issues of Liechtenstein from the first ones in 1912 and those received from other members of the Universal Postal Union, formed in 1921, plus many other items of interest to stamp collectors. The post office frequently issues new stamp series.

PRACTICAL FACTS: The cost of a holiday in Liechtenstein is about the same as one in Switzerland. Perhaps prices are a little lower in the principality, but in general they're not as low as the tariffs charged in Austria.

    Currency: The Swiss franc is legal tender. The same rates of exchange prevail (see "The ABCs of Switzerland" in Chapter II).

    Documents: All travel documents recognized by Swiss authorities are valid in Liechtenstein. However, you'll encounter the formalities of any western European border crossing if you enter through Austria.

    Holidays: Public holidays observed in Liechtenstein are New Year's Day, Epiphany (January 6), Candlemas (February 2), Shrove Tuesday, Feast of St. Joseph (March 19), Holy Friday, Easter Monday, Labor Day (May 1), Ascension Day, Whit Monday, Corpus Christi, Feast of the Assumption-National Day (August 15), the Nativity of Our Lady (September 8), Immaculate Conception (December 8), Christmas, and St. Stephen's Day (December 26).

    Information: For information about the principality, consult the **Liechtenstein National Tourist Office,** Städtle, P.O. Box 139, FL-9490 Vaduz, Fürstentum Liechtenstein (tel. 075/2-14-43).

    Mail and phone: The country's mail and phone rates are the same as those of Switzerland. You can telephone any number you want in Liechtenstein from Switzerland by dialing 075, followed by the number you want.

    Railway: Express trains don't actually stop in Liechtenstein, although many such trains cross its borders. The railway plays a subsidiary role in the principality. There is a station at Nendeln as well as a halt at Schaan and Schaanwald. However, there are good bus connections from the stations at Sargans (10½ miles from Vaduz), Buchs/SG (less than 4½ miles from Vaduz), and Feldkirch/Austria (about 9 miles from Vaduz) to all communities in Liechtenstein.

2. VADUZ

Vaduz (pronounced Va-dootz), capital of the Principality of Liechtenstein, is a little town at the foot of the castle where the royal family makes its home. Surrounded by sunlit vineyards, Vaduz was once a rural community known mainly for its good wines. Today it's a hospitable, sociable town with attractions for tourists. There are many entertainment and sports facilities, including a miniature golf course, tennis courts, and a large swimming pool.

    The main street of the town is **Städtle,** which has one-way traffic flow. The **Rathaus** (town hall) stands in the center of the capital.

    Schloss Vaduz, the prince's castle, has origins dating back to the 12th century, the keep and buildings on the east side being the oldest surviving parts. The castle was burned down by Swiss troops in 1499 and rebuilt at the beginning of the 16th century with round bastions at the northeast and southwest. Once a bleak and gloomy fortress, the castle is now much improved, and visitors report on its lavish furnishings and antiques, as well as near-priceless artworks.

    You can't visit the castle of the prince, but you can climb up to it (allow about 20 minutes). A wooded footpath or trail begins between the Burg Café and the Hotel Engel. Some locals visit the terraces and meadows around the castle with a picnic lunch. Once up there, you'll have a sweeping vista that will make the trip worthwhile.

Before you begin exploring, you might visit the **National Tourist Office,** 37 Städtle (tel. 075/2-14-43), where you'll be given free brochures and information about the country.

In the same building as the tourist office is the National Art Gallery and the Postal Museum. The post office is across the street.

Princes of the House of Liechtenstein have been art collectors since the 17th century, and their treasures were in a palace in Vienna until 1940. Prince Franz Joseph II decided to display his collections to the world, and it has become the highlight of many a visitor's trip to Liechtenstein. The prince's collection occupies two floors of a gallery above the tourist office. It's formally called the **Art Collection of the Principality of Liechtenstein,** 37 Städtle (tel. 075/2-23-41). It's well lit and handsomely exhibited, showing to advantage the Rubens collection, considered to be among the greatest on earth, including a cycle of nine large paintings illustrating the history of a Roman consul. See also his *Toilet of Venus.* In my opinion, this is the country's most outstanding attraction. Many of the pictures shown here are reproduced on the famous stamps of Liechtenstein.

The art gallery is open daily from 10 a.m. to noon and 1:30 to 5:30 p.m. In winter the hours are 10 a.m. to noon and 2 to 5:30 p.m. Admission for adults is 3F ($2.05); for children over 6 and students, 1.50F ($1).

The **Postage Stamp Museum,** 37 Städtle (tel. 075/6-62-59), is one of the country's biggest attractions, drawing philatelists from all over the world. Founded in 1930 to display the popular Liechtenstein stamps, which have grown to be of great value, and stamps of member states of the Universal Postal Union, the museum has a wealth of other philatelic objects. Lack of space at present prevents exhibition of all the printing plates, postal and philatelic documents, and other collected items, but special exhibitions are staged from time to time in addition to the 300 permanent showcases. Museum hours are daily from 10 a.m. to noon and 2 to 6 p.m. Admission is free.

The **Liechtenstein National Museum,** 43 Städtle (tel. 075/2-23-10), called Landesmuseum, was founded in 1954 and today has as its contents items from the collections of the prince, that state, and the Liechtenstein Historical Society. Since 1972 the museum has been housed in a completely renovated building that is also of historic interest. Originally it was the Stag Inn on the stagecoach route, later becoming the princely tavern and customshouse. In the early 19th century it was named the Eagle Inn, and then until 1905 it was the seat of government, its basement housing the state prison.

The museum displays artifacts from the prehistoric times of the region, as well as from the Roman period, Alemannic burial articles, records of the early Christian era, medieval coinage and weapons, rare stamps and some antique Rhineland jewelry. Hours are daily from 10 a.m. to noon and 1:30 to 5:30 p.m. from May 1 to October 31; only from 2 to 5:30 p.m. daily except Monday from November 1 to April 20. Admission is 3F ($1.35) for adults, 1F (68¢) for children. The museum is closed December 24, December 25, December 31, and January 1.

In the upper village, on the road to the castle, is the **Red House,** the seat of the Vaistlis, vassals of the counts of Werdenberg, during the Middle Ages. The house, probably in its present form with the exception of the tower, was acquired along with the vineyard by the Monastery of St. Johann in the Toggenburg.

WHERE TO STAY: Most of the hotels, quite naturally, are in the capital.

Park Hotel Sonnenhof, FL-9490 Vaduz, Fürstentum Liechtenstein (tel. 075/2-11-92), is the finest hotel in the principality and among the finest in Europe. It has only 29 rooms, beautiful gardens, and the best clientele in Vaduz.

Diplomatic receptions are held here frequently, and the princess of Liechtenstein comes over about once a week to use the swimming pool. The establishment was built in the late 19th century, but has been modernized into a streamlined chalet format with balconies and awnings. It has entertained everyone from J. Paul Getty to the crowned heads of virtually everything.

Only hotel guests, regrettably, are allowed in the dining room. Emil Real is the chef and he's celebrated. (He's the brother of another distinguished chef, Felix Real, who owns the Hotel Real.) Emil Real is at home entertaining royalty or Mr. and Mrs. Smith from Kansas. A native of Italy, he was once a chef at Maxim's in Paris. He and his brother were flown by the Shah of Iran in 1972 to cook at that great bash he tossed at Persepolis. His English-speaking wife, Jutta, is the charming hostess. Rooms are handsomely decorated and furnished. Singles range from 140F ($95.20) to 190F ($129.20) daily, while doubles cost 220F ($149.60) to 290F ($197.20). Half board is another 45F ($30.60) per person daily.

Hotel Real, 21 Städtle, FL-9490 Vaduz, Fürstentum Liechtenstein (tel. 075/2-22-22), is a well-maintained hotel on the main street of Vaduz. It sits at the bottom of a forested bluff, on top of which is the fortress-like palace of the prince. The hotel is modern, its boxy façade decorated with summer flower boxes. The rooms are clean and comfortable and have been renovated in an elegant modern style. Singles range from 120F ($81.60) to 160F ($108.80) daily, while doubles cost from 130F ($88.40) to 190F ($129.20). The restaurant inside is covered in the dining recommendations.

Hotel Schlössle, 68 Schloss-Strasse, FL-9490 Vaduz, Fürstentum Liechtenstein (tel. 075/2-56-21), is an ochre-colored hotel with medieval-style Teutonic turrets designed into the roofline. It sits on the main route from Vaduz to the prince's castle. The façade has a clock tower with gingerbread trim, and a small carillon of bells hanging above the statue of a Liechtenstein couple in regional garb. The bedrooms are charmingly outfitted with painted furniture. Singles cost 90F ($61.20) to 98F ($66.65) daily, and doubles rent for 130F ($88.40) to 170F ($115.60), with breakfast included.

Hotel Engel, 13 Städtle, FL-9490 Vaduz, Fürstentum Liechtenstein (tel. 075/2-10-57), is a small hotel with a convincing decor of rustic artifacts, such as an antique winescrew in the grill room. The well-maintained public rooms include a covered terrace and an intimate French restaurant. The hotel rises three modern stories, with summertime flowers filling many of its balconies. The 17 bedrooms are priced at 60F ($40.80) to 90F ($61.20) daily in a single and from 82F ($55.75) to 98F ($66.65) in a double. Roland Huber (who is not the same Roland Huber as the well-known jeweler who has a shop next door) and his charming wife are among the most gracious hôteliers in Vaduz.

Hotel Vaduzerhof, 3 Städtle, FL-9490 Vaduz, Fürstentum Liechtenstein (tel. 075/2-84-84), is a large hotel with shutters and an array of drinking and dining facilities. It sits in the center of town, with a canopy above the front door crowned by masses of flowers. The rooms are filled with wood-grained, pleasantly designed furniture. Singles cost 42F ($28.55) to 67F ($45.55) daily, and doubles range from 66F ($44.90) to 94F ($63.90). The cheaper accommodations do not have private baths. The hotel's Trattoria Toscana is recommended separately, but you can also dine at the Zum Güggel, enjoying fine food. You might have poached salmon with hollandaise, trout meunière, chicken curry, or veal steak with morels. Interesting and unusual on a hotel menu are the special dishes native to Liechtenstein, a nice touch that other hotels might well emulate. A modest lunch begins at 12F ($8.15), with dinners going for 25F ($17) and up. Go from 11 a.m. to 2 p.m. and 6 to 11 p.m. daily. The hotel also runs one of the most popular bars in town and has a cozy wine stube. The metal tables of a sidewalk cage ring the trunk of an old tree planted in the hotel's center.

Hotel Landhaus Prasch, 16 Zollstrasse, FL-9490 Vaduz, Fürstentum

Liechtenstein (tel. 075/2-46-64), is a modern hotel about 800 yards from the center of town. It's outfitted like a large country house, with heavy timbers in the lobby area. It also has an elevator and a rustic dining room with Windsor chairs and a big fireplace, plus an on-site swimming pool, whirlpool, and sauna. The bedrooms are simple and clean, with private baths, TV, and balconies. The hotel charges from 65F ($44.20) to 75F ($51) daily in a single and from 89F ($60.50) to 119F ($80.90) in a double, with breakfast.

WHERE TO DINE: As you approach the **Restaurant Real,** 21 Städtle (tel. 075/2-22-22), on the main street of Vaduz, you'll see the prince's castle looming on top of a cliff almost directly above it. The outside has café tables and chairs in plastic rattan, while inside, the wood-paneled rooms are usually filled with contented diners. The lighting fixtures are shaped like grape garlands, while the entire place gives the impression of well-polished and understated prosperity. The room upstairs offers the same menu as below, in a slightly more formal setting. This establishment is operated by the second famous Real brother, Felix. (His older brother, Emil, owns the already-recommended Sonnenhof.) Felix is a celebrated chef, a native of Italy. Even the royal family drops in for dinner here from time to time. The food is very capably cooked, and might include coquilles St. Jacques with Noilly Prat and leeks, or duck liver salad followed by any one of six lobster dishes, wild game specialties, filet of wild trout with Riesling, salmon with champagne, or a good range of meat and chicken dishes. The management offers a fixed-price "menu of the month" with five courses for 95F ($64.60). However, an à la carte dinner will likely cost you from 75F ($51) and up. Hours are daily from 11:30 a.m. to 2 p.m. and 6:30 to 10 p.m.

    Restaurant Torkel, 9 Hintergasse (tel. 075/2-44-10), is a country inn owned by the prince. It's on the site of an old wine press, with a location right outside of town in the midst of the royal vineyards. You park your car in a lot designated, then follow the signs a short distance to a low-lying building, which is today one of the most charming restaurants in Vaduz. The chefs prepare good veal dishes, filet goulash Stroganoff, and a specialty called Torkelsteak, along with noodle and Rösti dishes. À la carte meals cost from 40F ($27.20). You can sample the wine from the royal cellars. It is open from noon to 2 p.m. and 7 to 9 p.m. except on Sunday and Monday.

    Restaurant Français, Hotel Engel (tel. 075/2-10-57), on the second floor of this previously recommended hotel, is one of the finest dining places in Vaduz. In fair weather, tables are placed out on the terrace. Special menus are based on the seasons, but grilled specialties are always available, and they're served daily from noon to 2 p.m. and from 6 to 10 p.m. House specialties include tender filet of chicken breast Indonesian style (marinated in soya sauce and sake and served with vegetables and noodles), pork steak gratinée with pepper butter, filet of lamb served on a bed of leeks, medallions of rabbit with saffron rice and peppers, and sirloin steak with herb butter. Salmon trout with slices of lime and buttery potatoes is also served. A number of grill specialties, including veal steak, are offered. You can begin your repast with a wide selection of both hot and cold appetizers, such as ravioli stuffed with salmon, or one of the delectable soups, perhaps a bowl of consommé made with sweetbreads, vegetables, and mushrooms. Meals cost from 50F ($34).

    Alternatively, you can also dine at the **Ratskeller** downstairs, ordering the same dinner menu in the evening. It's open from 11 a.m. to 10 p.m. daily. You can also visit for a good-tasting and inexpensively priced lunch, costing from 12.50F ($8.50). For drinks or refreshments in the afternoon, you can patronize its outdoor café, opening onto the main street of Vaduz with a view of the prince's fairy-tale castle.

    Trattoria Toscana, Hotel Vaduzerhof, 3 Städtle (tel. 075/2-84-84), serves the finest Italian food in Vaduz. In the rear of a previously recommended hotel, it is a wood-paneled room often decorated with the bright colors of Italy itself. It prepares a classic cuisine, including, for starters, either straciatella or minestrone, followed by such dishes as Tuscan-style lamb cutlets or scallopini marsala. You might want to begin with either the hot or cold antipasti, perhaps a combination of both. The pasta dishes are excellent, especially the tagliatelle with seafood. Lunch is daily from 11 a.m. to 2 p.m., dinner from 6 to 11 p.m., with meals costing from 35F ($23.80).

Old Castle Inn, 22 Aeulestrasse (tel. 075/2-10-65), in downtown Vaduz opening onto a view of the castle, is a popular place for locals, who usually sit around the long, half-timbered bar on stools to drink and gossip. Italian and German folk/rock music plays on the sound system. The place is brightly lit to the point where you can see across the bar, yet it's dim to the point you can feel intimate with whomever you happen to be with. Black-skirted waitresses and black-vested waiters will take your order, which you'll eat on green leatherette banquettes at wood tables. Outside, you'll discover a geranium-bordered terrace with a striped canopy. Hot food is served daily from 11 a.m. to 1 a.m. The special Italian menu might include some antipasti, risotto with mushrooms, or other good-tasting dishes, a meal costing from 20F ($13.60). There's also a good selection of würst and steak dishes, or you might drop in for just a sandwich. One good bargain is the paprika schnitzel with pommes frites and a salad. Your meal might also include minestrone, spaghetti, lasagne, and veal liver Venice style. Try for an outside table when the weather is fair.

Café Wolff, 29 Städtle (tel. 075/2-23-21), has two floors to tempt you. Upstairs is a tea room, with an inviting display of open-faced sandwiches and pastries. It caters to a gentle older crowd as well as to a constantly changing array of stamp-collecting visitors. Downstairs is the Apero Bar, where champagne and fine wine are sold by the glass. This is a stylish U-shaped bar. Light meals at this establishment cost from 20F ($13.60) and are served daily except Monday from 7 a.m. to 11 p.m.

A SHOPPING NOTE: Most visitors stop off here just to purchase stamps. But if the bus isn't pulling out, you may have time to drop into at least one shop. The best is **L'Atelier,** 36 Städtle (tel. 075/3-21-64). Even the script of the orange neon sign announcing this shop is chic and in good taste. The place specializes in handcrafts such as lamps, dolls, stoneware, pewter, sculpture, and virtually anything else that's labored over by hand. You'll also find famous European glass for collectors, jewelry in sterling silver and precious stones, and hand-painted silks. It has a beautifully polished stone floor and a cork ceiling dotted with pin lights. The store is run by Hélène de Marchi, who opens it from 9:30 a.m. to noon and 2 to 6:30 p.m. Monday to Friday, from 9 a.m. to noon and 1 to 4 p.m. on Saturday.

3. THE UNTERLAND

Formed by the Rhine Valley, Liechtenstein's Unterland (lowland) contains eight villages on or around the slopes of the Eschnerberg at the foot of the Three Sisters (Drei Schwestern) mountains. The little hamlets comprise five parishes: Ruggell, Schellenberg, Eschen-Nendeln, Gamprin-Bendern, and Mauren-Schaanwald. The rugged country of the Unterland is unspoiled, still having tracts of virgin landscape with flora and fauna that are not common elsewhere. Even the pockets of agricultural and industrial development have not been allowed to damage the environment. You'll find wooded hills sheltering wildlife, broad expanses of fields and meadows with wildflowers, clean brooks, and attractive villages.

An extensive footpath network, the **Eschnerberg Historical Trail,** a joint project of the Unterland localities, and a nature trail offer pleasant and informative exercise. The Eschnerberg hills were a secure refuge for prehistoric settlers, offering an island-like setting in the then-marshy Rhine Valley some 5,000 years ago. Hiking the mountain track, you'll learn the history of the people who have lived in this region through the centuries.

RUGGELL: This village was first recorded in A.D. 933 in documents conveying a farm, or a *run* (cleared land) in the Rhaeto-Romanic terminology. The locality has been known for efficient farms, although the number has dropped with the springing up of various small industries. The landscape of the parish is mostly water meadows. Some 225 acres of this meadowland is designated as a protected area to prevent the extinction of the plant and animal life peculiar to the area. Ruggell is the northernmost village of Liechtenstein and the lowest geographical spot.

SCHELLENBERG: This second-smallest parish in the principality (population 577), with the smallest surface area, is the only place in Liechtenstein to bear a wholly German name. It was already settled when the New Stone Age arrived. Some of the Iron Age artifacts displayed in the National Museum in Vaduz were unearthed here. The Herren von Schellenberg built two castles here in the Middle Ages, the ruins of one of which, the **Obere Burg Schellenberg,** have been restored and are a popular excursion spot with views attracting visitors. Schellenberg is a starting point for Eschenerberg Historical Trail.

MAUREN-SCHAANWALD: In the midst of more rolling meadows, these two villages lie about a mile apart, in a parish covering only three square miles. Mauren, known as the "village of the seven hillocks" because of its location and topography, is in one of the loveliest settings in Liechtenstein. It was first mentioned in recorded history in 1178 under the name of Muron, but the remains of Roman baths and a second-century farmhouse or outbuilding have been excavated here. The village is also known for its fine parish church, dating from 1787. Between Mauren and Schaanwald, which lies on the Schaan-Feldkirch road leading into Austria, the meadows and woodlands have been designated a bird sanctuary. This contains a pond biotope under conservation and a nature trail.

GAMPRIN-BENDERN: This small parish, almost a cliché of picture-postcard charm with the Rhine flowing by, embraces two hamlets on the west spur of Eschnerberg. Being rich in archaeological discoveries, it's one of the best documented localities in Liechtenstein. Excavations have shown that the area was inhabited continuously from about 2500 B.C. to the Roman era. Discoveries around Gamprin have yielded a wealth of information on the culture of the New Stone Age, and remains of a farm and a small church dating from A.D. 55 have been found on the hill on which the Bendern church stands today. This church belonged to the convent of Schänis (St. Gallen) from 809 to 1177 and to the monastery of St. Luzi (Chur) from 1200 to 1816. After the Reformation, the St. Luzi monks built a larger structure, which included the abbot's quarters. Recently restored, this building now serves as a vicarage for the Bendern church.

Bendern's **Kirchhügel** is a favorite local scenic place. It was on this site in 1699 that the men of the lowlands swore loyalty to the Prince of Liechtenstein. You'll find an intersport keep-fit track and a camping site here, as well as a path following a trail of local history. The **Mariengrotte** (Mary's Grotto) at Bendern is the only shrine of its kind in the country.

ESCHEN-NENDELN: The existence of Eschen in the Liechtenstein Unterland was first noted in the Carolingian land registry about A.D. 850 under the name of Essane, which is believed to be derived from the Celtic word *esca,* meaning "by the water" and referring to the nearby brook, the Esche. The parish incorporates Nendeln, a village of equal economic importance. Flint artifacts from the Middle Stone Age, about 5000 B.C., have been found, and excavations at the sites of the prehistoric settlements at Malanser and Schneller have provided evidence of New Stone Age culture. At Nendeln the foundation of a Roman villa and a prehistoric settlement have been discovered. In medieval times the area was owned by monasteries and counts.

Buildings of interest are the Pfrundhaus (prebend structure), Holy Cross Chapel on the Rofenberg (formerly a place of public assembly), the restored church at Eschen with the original walls of the old church laid bare, and the St. Sebastian and Rochus Chapels at Nendeln. Liechtenstein's first industrial enterprise was a tile factory founded at Nendeln in 1836, which for a century was the only industrial plant in the Unterland.

The upper part of Eschen, Schönbühl, is one of the country's most attractive residential sections. You can enjoy swimming in a pool open to the public at Eschen and a nature health-cure trail at Nendeln, as well as the peaceful mountain footpaths on the Eschnerberg trail.

Food and Lodging

Hotel Landhaus, 263 Churer Strasse, FL-9485 Nendeln, Fürstentum Liechtenstein (tel. 075/3-20-11), is on the road from Vaduz to the Austrian border. It has a large antique wine press in the yard and a dark modern façade. Inside, the large ground floor contains two rooms furnished in a modern and pleasant style and decorated corresponding to the seasons. If you happen to get there on a Sunday morning, you'll see friendly groups of older men reminiscing together. The international menu has foods such as beef goulash with spätzli, spaghetti carbonara, sole meunière, Wiener schnitzel, and steak au poivre, with fixed-price meals beginning at 25F ($17). You can drop in at night for a drink in the exotically painted bar. Bedrooms at the hotel cost 58F ($39.45) daily in a single and from 95F ($64.60) in a double, with breakfast included.

4. THE OBERLAND

Besides the capital, Vaduz, the Oberland or Upper Country of Liechtenstein, formerly the region owned by the count of Vaduz, is made up of five parishes or communes: Planken, Schaan, Treisen, Triesenberg, and Balzers. Looking at the map, you may have difficulty placing this southern part of the country as "upper" and the Unterland (Lower Country) as being really that. But the explanation is to be found in the topography. The major portion of the Unterland is mainly meadows and hills gently rising from the Rhine Valley, whereas the Oberland, from Planken south, consists of higher country, reaching up to the Liechtenstein Alps.

Towered over by the Three Sisters, the Oberland is rich in woodlands and mountain trails, and most of its parishes provide numerous sports activities for visitors as well as for the locals. Domestic traditions and indigenous customs are followed, especially in the settlements founded by Swiss immigrants some 700 years ago.

Throughout this part of the principality you can find alpine flowers and protected animal species. A wealth of nature trails vary from easy walking to more rugged hiking. The winter sports attractions of Liechtenstein are centered in the alpine portion of the Oberland.

PLANKEN: Three miles from Nendeln lies Planken, the smallest parish in Liechtenstein (population 285), on a natural terrace in a woodland setting. The name of this little hamlet is from the Rhaeto-Romanic word *planca* or *plaunca,* meaning a pasture or meadow upland. Planken was settled by immigrants from the Valais in Switzerland in the latter part of the 13th century, and the inhabitants still speak a dialect quite different from that of the valley people. The village is the starting point for excursions to the Three Sisters (Drei Schwestern) area. From here you have an outstanding panorama of the Rhine Valley and the Swiss mountains, having a view from the Pizol section to Lake Constance. A chapel dedicated to St. Joseph contains copies of old masters and a bronze cross by Georg Malin in the chancel.

SCHAAN: The Carolingian land registry (circa A.D. 831) contains mention of Liechtenstein's second-largest parish under the name Scana. Archaeological finds, however, reveal that this was the site of a Roman fort, and digs have yielded two Roman legionnaires' helmets from the first century of the Christian era as well as an Alemannic decorative shield from the sixth or seventh century A.D. See also the 12th-century Romanesque church.

Schaan, just two miles from Vaduz, is the country's main communications center, with its railroad station on the Arlberg line. It lies at the foot of the Three Sisters massif and is the site of much of Liechtenstein's industry. Besides hikes into the mountains, Schaan also has a sports center by a forest, with tennis courts, a health center, an indoor swimming pool, public baths, and a children's playground. Schaan's **Theater am Kirchplatz** is one of the important cultural centers of the region, with performances by international artists. The town is also the center of the Liechtenstein carnival.

Food and Lodging

Hotel Sylva, FL-9494 Schaan, Fürstentum Liechtenstein (tel. 075/2-39-42), is such a desirable little place you may want to anchor here for the night and make the easy commute to Vaduz. A chalet hotel, it is sheltered and ringed with a forest, lying about a block above the main road. It offers well-furnished rooms, a pool, a garden, and a sauna. Doubles rent for 140F ($95.20) to 160F ($108.80) daily. In fact, all the rooms are doubles but can be rented to a single party for 95F ($64.60) to 110F ($74.80).

A mother and daughter, Friederecke and Sylva Eberle, offer also some of the best food in the area, served daily from 7 a.m. to 11 p.m. Meals are served in a warmly decorated room with big windows, Oriental rugs, and a garden terrace. A fixed-price gourmet menu costs 75F ($51), but you can also settle for a three-course regular meal for 40F ($27.20). Specialties of the chef include duck liver (sliced and fried), cream of salmon duck, a lobster salad with tarragon vinegar, a panache of fish cooked with champagne, medallions of pork with calvados, and filet of lamb with shallots. For dessert, try the apple crêpe with ice cream.

Schaanerhof, 3 In der Ballota, FL-3494 Schaan, Fürstentum Liechtenstein (tel. 075/2-18-77), is a modern hotel with balconies facing different exposures and a valentine-colored façade of pink and white. A swimming pool is inside, along with a sleek bar near the reception area. The inside is uncommittedly modern, comfortable, and warm. Rates depend on the plumbing (or lack of it). In the least expensive units, singles cost 42F ($28.55) daily, with doubles going for 74F ($50.30) to 94F ($63.90). However, with private bath, singles cost from 72F ($48.95) to 92F ($62.55) daily, with doubles going for 124F ($84.40) to 144F ($97.90).

Dux Hotel, FL-9494 Schaan, Fürstentum Lichtenstein (tel. 075/2-17-27), is a superior tourist-class country house hotel built in 1924 with a backdrop of rugged mountains. It is a white stucco building with a large sun terrace, a flat roof, and an uninterrupted length of wrought-iron balconies that give it a vaguely Iberian look. Its lawns are dotted with old oak trees. Rooms are comfortable with wood ceilings, and such modern amenities as bath or shower, radio, and phone. There is also wheelchair accessibility. Renovated in 1987, the hotel charges from 50F ($34) to 60F ($40.80) daily in a single and from 70F ($47.60) to 90F ($61.20) in a double. In the restaurants, three in all, the chef specializes in regional cookery as well as continental dishes. Fondue is a particular favorite. Facilities include a solarium and sauna, and guests are within walking distance of a fitness center and tennis courts.

Hotel Linde, FL-9494 Schaan, Fürstentum Liechtenstein (tel. 075/2-17-04), has a semibaroque façade with a single ornate gable. A pumpkin-colored extension stretches off to one side, with well-pruned hedges guarding the sun terrace from the street traffic on the other side. Bedrooms inside are outfitted with big-patterned wallpaper in colors you might find overwhelming, but which are nonetheless comfortable and clean. All have baths or showers. Singles range from 45F ($30.60) to 48F ($32.65) daily, while doubles cost 76F ($51.70) to 82F ($55.75), with breakfast and taxes included.

TRIESEN: Already a settlement in Roman times, Triesen was first recorded in 1155 and can be called the oldest compact community in the principality. It lies at the foot of the Falknis cliffs in beautiful country between the Rhine and the Liechtenstein alpine areas, a pleasant setting which caused noble families from the Roman days on to make their homes here until fairly recent times. It's within easy walking distance of Vaduz, to the north.

Of special interest are the old quarter of the Upper Village, the St. Mamerten and Maria Chapel, and the large Kosthaus, built more than a century ago. Health enthusiasts will enjoy tennis courts, a swimming pool, bicycle paths, and attractive footpaths. There's also a children's playground, a nature reserve with a small lake, and two large camping sites. Hikes and mountain tours are offered along a wild gorge to the high alp of Lawena.

Food and Lodging

Hotel Restaurant Meierhof, FL-9495 Triesen, Fürstentum Liechtenstein (tel. 075/2-18-36), lies on the main Triesenberg road about a mile south of Vaduz. It is laid out in a format of a conservatively designed modern building with an annex. Roland Kindle and his family operate one of the best hotels in the principality, known not only for its rooms if you'd like to stop over but for its excellent cuisine. Bedrooms are cozy and comfortable, equipped with private baths or showers. Some spacious apartments suitable for four guests are also rented. Many have balconies. Doubles range from 82F ($55.75) to 90F ($61.20) daily, with singles costing from 55F ($37.40) to 65F ($44.20) with breakfast included. Behind the hotel is a swimming pool for the use of guests. In summer, when the geraniums are in bloom, guests dine outside on a terrace. In any weather conditions, they can enjoy the wood-paneled, tavern-like setting for the dining room. The hotel has both a good kitchen and a fine wine cellar. There is also a Stübli.

Hotel/Restaurant Sonne, FL-9495 Triesen, Fürstentum Liechtenstein (tel. 075/2-15-05), has only four bedrooms, which almost ensures a close relationship with your hosts, the Stadler family. A granite arch leads from the outside into the main hallway, which is full of deer heads and rustically decorated paneling. Singles average 35F ($23.80) daily, and doubles cost 65F ($44.20), with breakfast included. Accommodations are bathless. The rustic restaurant serves such savory dishes as filet Stroganoff and entrecôte, and such Italian dishes as spaghetti al pesto and piccata milanese. Meals cost from 35F ($23.80), although less expensive snacks are also available. Dessert might be an apple strudel.

For food outside the hotels recommended, try the **Restaurant Adler** (tel. 075/2-13-57), which is popular with locals in the area. Along the main road, this restaurant is also a pizzeria and has an often busy bar. Service is daily from 11 a.m. to 2:30 p.m. and 6 to 11 p.m. Full meals cost from 35F ($23.80) and include fettuccine, ravioli, gnocchi with gorgonzola, filet of beef Stromboli (that is, with pepperoni, artichokes, and olives), and osso buco. Veal is also prepared Valdostan style with cheese.

TRIESENBERG: This largest and highest parish of Liechtenstein has big sections of woodland and scrub, arable land and pasture, a small portion of unproductive land, and a village of just over 2,000 inhabitants high above the Rhine Valley at an altitude of 2,600 feet, making it the starting point for the principality's alpine world. Triesenberg was settled in the late 13th century by the same immigration wave from the Swiss Valais as was Planken, and the dialect of the two parishes is similar. Many Triesenberg residents wear colorful regional garb, and the style of some of the houses, although of modern construction, dates from the early 14th century and shows the Valaisian influence.

Within recent decades Triesenberg has changed from a predominantly farming community to a rapidly growing light industry center. A restored and elegant town hall and a community center with a local museum and exhibition of wood engravings may interest you, but perhaps its increasing popularity as a tourist resort within easy reach of the Liechtenstein Alps will be more of a drawing card.

Fine highways and well-tended hiking trails lead from Triesenberg to the alpine resorts: Masescha (4,100 feet), Silum (5,000 feet), Gaflei (5,000 feet), Malbun (5,250 feet), and Steg (4,600 feet). Steg is on the way to Malbun and features the Valüna-Lopp cross-country skiing center and a ski lift. The half-mile-long Gnalp-Steg tunnel connects the valley with the alpine area.

Food and Lodging

Hotel Martha Bühler, FL-9497 Triesenberg, Fürstentum Liechtenstein (tel. 075/2-57-77), is one of my favorite hotels in the upper reaches of Liechtenstein. It was founded in 1976 by the beautiful and charming Martha Bühler, who was the first Liechtenstein woman to participate in the Winter Olympic Games, in Grenoble (1968) and Sapporo (1972). In winter she offers free weekly ski lessons to the guests of her hotel. Her cozy establishment is set close to a baroque tower, and has a sweeping view of the valley below from many of the tastefully paneled rooms. The public rooms are cozy and filled with elaborate wood detailing and warmly inviting colors and textures. Today with her children and her world-traveled husband, Gerald Tschikof, she welcomes guests, especially foreigners, with all of the sophistication that Olympic competition has taught her.

Her rooms are cozy and comfortable and well furnished. She offers 13 double rooms and three suites, each with private shower, toilet, TV, phone, and balcony. Doubles rooms, including breakfast, are rented year round for the price of 77F ($52.35) to 90F ($61.20) daily. Singles pay 51F ($34.70). A suite for two persons costs 130F ($88.40) daily. The restaurant served a limited menu of well-prepared meals, with snacks costing from 12F ($8.15) and a full dinner starting at 35F ($23.80).

Hotel Kulm, FL-9497 Triesenberg, Fürstentum Liechtenstein (tel. 075/2-87-77), is in the center of the village with a wide view of the valley. It was built in 1980, with a pink and light-grained wood façade with blossoms cascading down the front balconies in spring. A sidewalk café has been set up in front, while the interior alternates between rustically modern and rough-hewn regional. Comfortably furnished singles range from 50F ($34) to 60F ($40.80) daily, while doubles cost from 80F ($54.40) to 90F ($61.20), with breakfast included. Half board is another 15F ($10.20) per person daily.

Hotel Steg, FL-9497 Steg/Triesenberg, Fürstentum, Liechtenstein (tel. 075/2-21-46), is a well-kept and family-run hotel. The Lamberts do everything they can to provide a good cuisine and comfortably lodgings for their loyal guests. The hotel lies on the road to Steg, in a chalet with lots of paneling and unpretentious comfort. Doubles cost 34F ($22.10) to 60F ($40.80) daily. None of the accommodations has a private bath. The restaurant serves traditional alpine food, including savory specialties such as veal, steak, and pork, along with two kinds of spaghetti and lots of different cheese and meat salads. Full dinners range from 22F ($14.95).

MASESCHA: This small resort hamlet lies about two miles to the north of

Triesenberg and is a favorite goal for hikers and mountaineers who want to enjoy the beauties of the alpine world high above the Rhine Valley. Sheer cliffs, spreading woods, lush meadows, and clear mountain brooks provide the hiking nature lover with a memorable experience. Of special interest in the village is the restored medieval Theodul's Chapel.

MALBUN: Fast rising as a winter ski area, Malbun is the center of winter sports in Liechtenstein, with ski lifts, chair lifts, a ski school, and hotels with indoor swimming pools. You can take the chair lift up to the Bettlerjoch Peak, at 6,900 feet. The Prince of Wales and Princess Anne learned to ski here many years ago. In summer this is an ideal starting point for mountain walks.

Food and Lodging
Hotel Malbunerhof, Malbun, FL-9497 Triesenberg, Fürstentum Liechtenstein (tel. 075/2-29-44), is a four-star, chalet hotel near the ski lifts. It has a swimming pool, a sauna, a bowling alley, a disco, and a comfortable bar with padded armrests. A wintertime fire is usually blazing in the timbered lounge area where rustic farm implements decorate the stucco walls. The comfortable bedrooms all have private bath, and rent for 75F ($51) to 110F ($74.80) daily in a single, 130F ($88.40) to 200F ($136) in a double, with a generous breakfast included. Excellent meals are served in the dining room, and the place has a homey atmosphere.

Hotel Montana, Malbun, FL-9497 Triesenberg, Fürstentum Liechtenstein (tel. 075/2-73-33), is a 15-room family hotel in a well-maintained building with wood balconies and a white stucco façade. A sun terrace and restaurant extend to one side of the low building. The interior is paneled and filled with bright upholstered chairs along with functional wooden furniture. The bedrooms, each with a bath and toilet, plus a mini-bar, rent for 50F ($34) to 75F ($51) daily in a single, depending on the season. In a double, again depending on the season, rates range from 40F ($27.20) to 65F ($44.20) per person per day. Tariffs include breakfast, and half board is offered for another 20F ($13) per person daily. The hotel is owned and managed by Peter and Renate von Seemann.

Alpenhotel, Malbun, FL-9497 Triesenberg, Fürstentum Liechtenstein (tel. 075/2-11-81), is one of the oldest hotels in Malbun. It's been in the same family for more than 75 years, and is filled with such charming details as chandeliers made from deer antlers. The wooden ceilings are painted with alpine floral designs, and the heavy timbers are carved with regional reliefs. The owners are among the loveliest people I've met in Liechtenstein: Jacob and Elsa Vögeli-Schroth. Eager to contribute to the well-being of their guests, they maintain 30 bathless rooms in the main hotel and 15 accommodations with bath in a nearby modern annex. On the premises is a covered swimming pool. Singles rent for 25F ($17) to 50F ($34) daily, and doubles cost 50F ($34) to 100F ($68). An attractive restaurant on the premises serves savory food in a panoramic setting. The hotel is closed from the end of October until mid-December and from Easter until mid-May.

BALZERS: If you've looked all over the high country in Switzerland and Liechtenstein for Heidi tending her flock and picking edelweiss, maybe in your mind's eye you'll see her here, as Balzers could have been her home in the storybook. The parish comprises the communities of Balzers and Mäls, both first listed in the Carolingian land registry sometime after A.D. 850. Artifacts from various eras indicate that people have lived here since about 3000 B.C. Archaeologists have identified a Rössener jug, figurines from the Celto-Etruscan era, and early Roman coins, graves, and buildings.

This southernmost parish in the principality was once a staging post on the old Lindau-Milan post road, and a tablet on the tower of the old cemetery honors a Milanese emissary who died making the trek. Balzers was the first official philatelic center in Liechtenstein, established in 1817.

The Gutenberg Castle, privately owned, dominates the town. Built above a prehistoric mound during the Middle Ages, it belonged to the Habsburgs until 1824. Other places of interest are the Mariahilf and St. Peter chapels with belfries, the restored Old Vicarage, and the old schoolhouse with a local museum and library.

There are good sports facilities and a public indoor swimming pool. Nature reserves contain unusual plant species.

Food and Lodging

Hotel Post, FL-9476 Balzers, Fürstentum Liechtenstein (tel. 075/4-12-08), represents a good bargain, even though Balzers is somewhat out of the way from what you might want to see in Vaduz. For a one-night stopover, it's clean and attractive. The management speaks English, and charges from 85F ($57.80) daily in a double and from 60F ($40.80) in a single with private bath. The hotel was built in the 18th century, but it has frequently been modernized since then. It offers a restaurant and bar, along with a sycamore-shaded garden suitable for a summer stop.

5. NIGHTLIFE IN LIECHTENSTEIN

You won't go broke in the nightclubs of Liechtenstein. All are inexpensively priced. Hours in general are daily from 8:30 p.m. to 1 a.m. (until 2 a.m. on Friday and Saturday). There's rarely a cover charge, and when there is it's small. Drinks cost from 10F ($6.80), beer 3.50F ($2.40).

Here's a brief run-down of after-dark diversions:

Hotel Engel (tel. 075/2-10-57) in Vaduz has a musician playing at night in winter.

Maschlina Bar (tel. 075/2-26-90) in Triesen offers disco music in summer in the rustic ambience of the provinces. In winter it often has live music.

Restaurant Palazoles (tel. 075/4-10-10) in Balzers is a youth-oriented disco. But you'll have to travel from Vaduz south to Balzers toward the Swiss border to see this one.

Hotel Gorfion (tel. 075/2-43-07) in Malbun caters to an older crowd, often featuring regional music in a rustic country ambience.

Roxy Bar (tel. 075/4-12-82), back in Balzers, is outfitted in strident shades of red, with lots of mirrors, leather chairs, and a big bar counter. The music is disco, and the crowd tends to be under 30.

Hotel Turna (tel. 075/2-34-21) in Malbun has a very small dance floor, very small tables near banquettes, and lots of candlelight. The music is disco. This place is mainly visited in the winter.

Tiffany Bar (tel. 075/3-13-43) in Eschen is a disco with a wood-paneled rustic ambience of lots of couches and dim lights.

INDEX

LIECHTENSTEIN

NOW, SAVE MONEY ON ALL YOUR TRAVELS!
Join Frommer's™ Dollarwise® Travel Club

Saving money while traveling is never a simple matter, which is why, over 28 years ago, the **Dollarwise Travel Club** was formed. Actually, the idea came from readers of the Frommer publications who felt that such an organization could bring financial benefits, continuing travel information, and a sense of community to economy-minded travelers all over the world.

In keeping with the money-saving concept, the annual membership fee is low—$18 (U.S. residents) or $20 U.S. (Canadian, Mexican, and foreign residents)—and is immediately exceeded by the value of your benefits which include:

1. The latest edition of any TWO of the books listed on the following pages.
2. A copy of any Frommer City Guide.
3. An annual subscription to an 8-page quarterly newspaper *The Dollarwise Traveler* which keeps you up-to-date on fastbreaking developments in good-value travel in all parts of the world—bringing you the kind of information you'd have to pay over $35 a year to obtain elsewhere. This consumer-conscious publication also includes the following columns:
   Hospitality Exchange—members all over the world who are willing to provide hospitality to other members as they pass through their home cities.
   Share-a-Trip—requests from members for travel companions who can share costs and help avoid the burdensome single supplement.
   Readers Ask . . . Readers Reply—travel questions from members to which other members reply with authentic firsthand information.
4. Your personal membership card which entitles you to purchase through the club all Frommer publications for a third to a half off their regular retail prices during the term of your membership.

So why not join this hardy band of international Dollarwise travelers now and participate in its exchange of information and hospitality? Simply send $18 (U.S. residents) or $20 U.S. (Canadian, Mexican, and other foreign residents) along with your name and address to: Frommer's Dollarwise Travel Club, Inc., 15 Columbus Circle, New York, NY 10023. Remember to specify which *two* of the books in section (1) and which *one* in section (2) above you wish to receive in your initial package of member's benefits. Or tear out the next page, check off your choices, and send the page to us with your membership fee.

FROMMER BOOKS
PRENTICE HALL TRAVEL
15 COLUMBUS CIRCLE
NEW YORK, NY 10023

Date_____

Friends:
Please send me the books checked below:

FROMMER™ GUIDES

(Guides to sightseeing and tourist accommodations and facilities from budget to deluxe, with emphasis on the medium-priced.)

☐ Alaska $13.95	☐ Japan & Hong Kong $13.95
☐ Australia.........................$14.95	☐ Mid-Atlantic States................$13.95
☐ Austria & Hungary $14.95	☐ New England.....................$14.95
☐ Belgium, Holland & Luxembourg........$13.95	☐ New York State $13.95
☐ Bermuda & The Bahamas.............$14.95	☐ Northwest $14.95
☐ Brazil $14.95	☐ Portugal, Madeira & the Azores $13.95
☐ Canada.........................$14.95	☐ Skiing Europe....................$14.95
☐ Caribbean.......................$14.95	☐ Skiing USA—East..................$13.95
☐ Cruises (incl. Alask, Carib, Mex, Hawaii,	☐ Skiing USA—West.................$13.95
Panama, Canada & US) $14.95	☐ South Pacific $13.95
☐ California & Las Vegas...............$14.95	☐ Southeast & New Orleans $14.95
☐ England & Scotland.................$14.95	☐ Southeast Asia....................$14.95
☐ Egypt...........................$13.95	☐ Southwest.......................$14.95
☐ Florida..........................$14.95	☐ Switzerland & Liechtenstein $13.95
☐ France $14.95	☐ Texas $13.95
☐ Germany.........................$14.95	☐ USA $15.95
☐ Italy $14.95	

FROMMER $-A-DAY® GUIDES

(In-depth guides to sightseeing and low-cost tourist accommodations and facilities.)

☐ Europe on $40 a Day.................$15.95	☐ New Zealand on $40 a Day $12.95
☐ Australia on $30 a Day $12.95	☐ New York on $50 a Day...............$13.95
☐ Eastern Europe on $25 a Day $13.95	☐ Scandinavia on $60 a Day $13.95
☐ England on $50 a Day................$13.95	☐ Scotland & Wales on $40 a Day..........$12.95
☐ Greece on $30 a Day................$12.95	☐ South America on $35 a Day $13.95
☐ Hawaii on $60 a Day................$13.95	☐ Spain & Morocco on $40 a Day..........$13.95
☐ India on $25 a Day $12.95	☐ Turkey on $30 a Day $12.95
☐ Ireland on $35 a Day................$13.95	☐ Washington, D.C., & Historic Va. on
☐ Israel on $35 a Day.................$13.95	$40 a Day $13.95
☐ Mexico on $25 a Day $13.95	

FROMMER TOURING GUIDES

(Color illustrated guides that include walking tours, cultural & historic sites, and other vital travel information.)

☐ Australia.........................$9.95	☐ Paris............................$8.95
☐ Egypt...........................$8.95	☐ Scotland.........................$9.95
☐ Florence.........................$8.95	☐ Thailand.........................$9.95
☐ London..........................$8.95	☐ Venice $8.95

TURN PAGE FOR ADDITONAL BOOKS AND ORDER FORM.

FROMMER CITY GUIDES
(Pocket-size guides to sightseeing and tourist accommodations and facilities in all price ranges.)

☐ Amsterdam/Holland $5.95
☐ Athens. $5.95
☐ Atlantic City/Cape May $5.95
☐ Belgium $5.95
☐ Boston. $5.95
☐ Cancún/Cozumel/Yucatán. $5.95
☐ Chicago. $5.95
☐ Dublin/Ireland $5.95
☐ Hawaii. $5.95
☐ Las Vegas. $5.95
☐ Lisbon/Madrid/Costa del Sol $5.95
☐ London $5.95
☐ Los Angeles $5.95
☐ Mexico City/Acapulco. $5.95
☐ Minneapolis/St. Paul $5.95
☐ Montréal/Québec City. $5.95
☐ New Orleans. $5.95
☐ New York $5.95
☐ Orlando/Disney World/EPCOT $5.95
☐ Paris $5.95
☐ Philadelphia $5.95
☐ Rio $5.95
☐ Rome. $5.95
☐ San Francisco $5.95
☐ Santa Fe/Taos/Albuquerque. $5.95
☐ Sydney. $5.95
☐ Washington, D.C. $5.95

SPECIAL EDITIONS

☐ A Shopper's Guide to the Caribbean. .$12.95
☐ Beat the High Cost of Travel $6.95
☐ Bed & Breakfast—N. America $11.95
☐ California with Kids $14.95
☐ Guide to Honeymoon Destinations
  (US, Canada, Mexico & Carib) $12.95
☐ Manhattan's Outdoor Sculpture $15.95
☐ Motorist's Phrase Book (Fr/Ger/Sp) . . .$4.95
☐ Paris Rendez-Vous $10.95
☐ Swap and Go (Home Exchanging). . . .$10.95
☐ The Candy Apple (NY for Kids). $11.95
☐ Travel Diary and Record Book $5.95
☐ Where to Stay USA (Lodging from $3
  to $30 a night) $10.95
☐ Marilyn Wood's Wonderful Weekends (NY, Conn, Mass, RI, Vt, NH, NJ, Del, Pa) $11.95
☐ The New World of Travel (Annual sourcebook by Arthur Frommer previewing: new travel trends, new modes of travel, and the latest cost-cutting strategies for savvy travelers). $14.95

SERIOUS SHOPPER'S GUIDES
(Illustrated guides listing hundreds of stores, conveniently organized alphabetically by category)

☐ Italy. $15.95
☐ London $15.95
☐ Los Angeles $14.95
☐ Paris $15.95

GAULT MILLAU
(The only guides that distinguish the truly superlative from the merely overrated.)

☐ The Best of Chicago $15.95
☐ The Best of France $16.95
☐ The Best of Italy $16.95
☐ The Best of Los Angeles $14.95
☐ The Best of New England $15.95
☐ The Best of New York $14.95
☐ The Best of San Francisco $14.95
☐ The Best of Washington, D.C. $14.95

ORDER NOW!

In U.S. include $2 shipping UPS for 1st book; $1 ea. add'l book. Outside U.S. $3 and $1, respectively. Allow four to six weeks for delivery in U.S., longer outside U.S.

Enclosed is my check or money order for $_____

NAME _____

ADDRESS _____

CITY _____ STATE _____ ZIP _____